MICHIE'S™
ANNOTATED CODE
OF THE PUBLIC GENERAL LAWS
OF MARYLAND

Maryland Rules

Prepared by the Editorial Staff of the Publishers

Consultants

State Department of Legislative Services

Volume 2

1999 Replacement Volume

*(Including amendments through December 1, 1998, and
annotations taken from Atlantic Reports
through 712 A.2d 1)*

LEXIS Law Publishing
CHARLOTTESVILLE, VIRGINIA
1998

ISBN 0-327-06593-1

4400616

Summary Table of Contents

Volume 1

Volume 2

SUMMARY TABLE OF CONTENTS

SUMMARY TABLE OF CONTENTS

MARYLAND RULES

TITLE 9. FAMILY LAW ACTIONS

Editor's note. — The Court of Appeals, by Order dated June 5, 1996, effective January 1, 1997, rescinded Subtitles A, D, E, J, P, Q, R, T, U, V, W, Y, Z, BB, BD, BE, BG, BH, BJ, BL, BP, BQ, BR, BS, BW, and BY of Chapter 1100 of the Maryland Rules of Procedure, rescinded Subtitles P, BB, BQ, and BW of the Maryland District Rules, and rescinded Forms 22a, 23, 24, 25, and 26. The Order substituted for certain of the rules and forms rescinded new Title 9, Chapter 100, Title 10, Title 12, Title 13, Title 14, and Title 15 of the Maryland Rules of Procedure. Furthermore, the Order transferred, without readoption, Chapter 900, Chapter 1200, and Subtitles S, BU, and BV of Chapter 1100 of the Maryland Rules of Procedure and Chapter 1200 of the Maryland District Rules to be Title 9, Chapter 200, Title 11, and Title 16 of the Maryland Rules of Procedure. The Order provides that the new rules shall "apply to all actions commenced on or after January 1, 1997, and insofar as practicable, to all actions then pending."

Many of the cases in the notes to the various rules were decided prior to the 1996 revision. These cases have been retained under pertinent rules of this title where it is thought that such cases will be of value in interpreting the present rules.

A table of comparable rules, relating those rules rescinded effective January 1, 1997, to the revised rules in Title 9 through Title 16 is to be found in Volume 2 following the end of the Maryland Rules.

CHAPTER 100. ADOPTION; GUARDIANSHIP TERMINATING PARENTAL RIGHTS.

Rule 9-101. Definitions.

The words "child placement agency," "disability," "father," and "guardianship" as used in Rules 9-101 through 9-113 have the meanings stated in Code, Family Law Article, § 5-301. In addition, the word "parent" includes the biological mother, a "natural father" as defined in Code, Family Law Article, § 5-310, the biological father or one claiming to be the biological father who does not meet the criteria of § 5-310, and a person who is a child's parent by reason of a previous adoption.

Committee note. — This Rule does not apply to the guardianship of persons and property of minors and disabled persons governed by Code, Estates and Trusts Article, § 13-101 *et seq.*

Source. — This Rule is in part derived from former Rule D71 and is in part new.

Rule 9-102. Consents; requests for attorney or counseling.

(a) *Generally.* Except when otherwise permitted by Code, Family Law Article, § 5-312, § 5-313, or § 5-313.1, a judgment of adoption or guardianship may not be entered without the consents prescribed by Code, Family Law Article, § 5-311 or § 5-317 (c) (2).

Cross references. — *See* Code, Family Law Article, § 5-314 for provisions governing the validity of consents.

(b) *Revocation of consent.* (1) Time for revoking consent. An individual to be adopted may revoke his or her consent at any time before entry of a judgment of adoption. Any other person or agency executing a required consent to an adoption or guardianship may revoke the consent within 30 days after the consent is signed.

(2) Procedure for revoking. An individual may revoke a consent to an adoption or guardianship only by a signed writing actually delivered by mail or in person to the clerk of the circuit court designated in the consent to receive the revocation. An agency entitled to revoke a consent to an adoption may do so (A) by counsel on the record at the hearing required by Rule 9-109 or (B) in a writing signed by the executive head of the agency and filed with the court.

Cross references. — Rule 9-112.

(3) Action by court upon revocation. If a consent is revoked pursuant to this Rule, the court shall (A) schedule a hearing within three days to determine the status of the petition and temporary custody of the child, (B) determine the immediate custody of the child pending that hearing, and (C) send to all parties and all persons who previously consented to the adoption or guardianship, including the person who revoked the consent, a copy of the revocation, notice of the immediate custody determination, and notice of the scheduled hearing.

This subsection does not apply to actions governed by Code, Family Law Article, § 5-312, § 5-313, or § 5-313.1.

Cross references. — Code, Family Law Article, §§ 5-311 and 5-317.

(c) *Form of consent of parent to adoption.* The consent of a parent to an adoption shall be in substantially the following form:

CONSENT TO ADOPTION/GUARDIANSHIP
OR
REQUEST FOR ATTORNEY OR COUNSELING

1. Name.
   My name is _____.
2. Age and Competence.
   My date of birth is _____ and I am capable of understanding what this consent means.
3. Status as Parent. **Check all that apply.**
   (a) I am [ ] the mother [ ] the father (or) [ ] alleged to be the father of
_____, born on _____ , _____
at _____ ,
          (name of hospital or address of birthplace)
in _____ .
          (city, state, and county of birth)
   (b) I was married to the mother of the child [ ] at the time of conception [ ] at the time the child was born.
4. Right to Attorney.
   I understand that:
   (a) The court will appoint an attorney for me if I am under 18 years of age or if, because of a disability, I am incapable of consenting to the adoption/ guardianship or of effectively participating in the adoption/guardianship proceeding.
   (b) Even if I am not entitled to a court-appointed attorney, I am entitled to consult an attorney chosen by me. If this is a consent to an adoption, the adoptive parents may agree to pay all or part of the attorney's fees on my behalf and, if this is an independent adoption (that is, where an agency is not involved), the court may order the adoptive parents to do so.
   (c) If I choose to seek the appointment or advice of an attorney, I cannot now consent to the adoption/guardianship and this Consent Form will be ineffective as a consent.
   Check one of the following statements:
   [ ] I do not want an attorney.
   [ ] I already have an attorney whose name, address, and telephone number
       are _____

_____ .
     (Name)   (Address)   (Telephone Number)
   [ ] I want an attorney.

3

5. Option of Adoption Counseling.

I understand that, if this is an independent adoption, I have the option of receiving adoption counseling and guidance for which a court may require the adoptive parents to pay. I also understand that if I choose to seek such counseling or guidance, I cannot now consent to the adoption and this Consent Form will be ineffective as a consent to adoption.

Check one of the following statements:

[   ] I do not want adoption counseling and guidance.

[   ] I am already receiving or have received adoption counseling and guidance.

[   ] I want adoption counseling and guidance.

[IF A REQUEST IS MADE FOR AN ATTORNEY OR FOR ADOPTION COUNSELING AND GUIDANCE, SIGN HERE AND DO NOT COMPLETE THE REST OF THIS FORM]

_____   _____
(Date)   (Signature)

                                    _____
                                    (Address)

                                    _____
                                    (Telephone Number)

6. Compensation.

I understand that by Maryland law I am not allowed to receive compensation of any kind for the placement of my child, except that reasonable and customary charges or fees for hospital or medical or legal services may be paid on my behalf.

7. Effect of Consent.

I UNDERSTAND THAT, BY SIGNING THIS CONSENT, I AGREE TO THE CONTENTS OF IT, AND THAT, UNLESS THIS IS A STEPPARENT ADOPTION IN WHICH MY (HUSBAND)(WIFE) IS PROPOSING TO ADOPT MY CHILD, I AM GIVING UP ALL RIGHTS, DUTIES, AND OBLIGATIONS WITH RESPECT TO MY CHILD AND ALL RIGHTS TO PARTICIPATE IN ANY PROCEEDING FOR ADOPTION OR GUARDIANSHIP OF MY CHILD.

8. Right to Revoke Consent — Limitations.

I understand that the only way in which I can revoke this consent is by delivering my revocation to the following person:

Clerk of the Circuit Court for _____
                                      (Name of County)

Attention: Adoption Clerk

_____
            (Address and Telephone Number of Court)

in writing no later than _____ ,
which is 30 days from the date I sign this consent, that my consent is revoked. The revocation must be signed by me and should contain my printed name and address and, to the extent known, the name, sex, and date of birth of my child.

I understand that revocation by telephone or other oral conversation or by writing to anyone other than the person named above will not constitute a valid revocation. I understand that I may deliver my written revocation by mail or in person, but if it is not *received* by the clerk by the date stated above, it will not constitute a valid revocation.

9. Consent.

Having read carefully all of the above statements **(check one of the following statements)**:

[　] I freely, voluntarily, and unequivocally consent to the adoption of my child by _____ and _____ or the person or persons whose name(s) is/are unknown to me, but known to the court. I further consent that the prospective adoptive parents may have immediate and temporary custody of my child.

[　] I freely, voluntarily, and unequivocally consent to a judgment appointing _____ as the guardian of my child, with the right of the guardian to consent to adoption or long-term care short of adoption.

10. Waiver of Notice of Adoption or Guardianship Proceeding.

I understand that, based on this consent, a petition for adoption or guardianship will be filed in court and that I have the right to be notified when the petition is filed and of further proceedings concerning the guardianship or adoption. I also understand that I may waive my right to notice.

Check one of the following statements:

[　] I waive notice of all proceedings concerning the adoption or guardianship, including entry of judgment. I understand that a court representative may nonetheless contact me in connection with these proceedings.

[　] I want to receive notice of the filing of the petition but waive notice of all further proceedings concerning the adoption or guardianship. I understand that notice will be sent to the address given by me on this form unless I advise the clerk of the court stated in Paragraph 8 of this consent, in writing, of a change in my address.

[　] I want to receive notice of the filing of the petition and of further proceedings concerning the adoption or guardianship until my parental rights have been terminated. I understand that notice will be sent to the address given by me on this form unless I advise the clerk of the court stated in Paragraph 8 of this consent, in writing, of a change in my address.

11. I acknowledge that I have read this consent or have had it read to me, that I understand it, and that I have received a copy of the signed consent to keep. I further acknowledge that no one has persuaded me to sign this consent or any other form or paper regarding this adoption or guardianship against my will.

I solemnly affirm under the penalties of perjury that the contents of the foregoing consent form are true to the best of my knowledge, information, and belief.

_____   _____
(Date)   (Signature)

                                 _____
                                 (Address)

                                 _____
                                 (Telephone Number)

5

(d) *Form of consent of person to be adopted.* The consent of a person to be adopted shall be in substantially the following form:

CONSENT TO ADOPTION
OR
REQUEST FOR ATTORNEY

1. Name.
   My name is _____ .
2. Age and Place of Birth.
   (a) I am at least 10 years old. My date of birth is _____ .
   (b) I was born at _____
   _____ ,
   (name of hospital or address of birthplace)
   in _____ .
   (city, state, and county of birth)
3. Right to Attorney.
   I understand that:
   (a) The court will appoint an attorney for me if (i) because of a disability, I am incapable of consenting to the adoption or of effectively participating in the adoption proceeding or (ii) my adoption or guardianship would involuntarily terminate the parental rights of at least one of my parents.
   (b) Even if the court is not required to appoint an attorney for me, if I am under 18 years of age the court may nevertheless appoint an attorney for me.
   (c) If I choose to seek the appointment or advice of an attorney, I cannot now consent to the adoption and this Consent Form will be ineffective as a consent.
   Check one of the following statements:
   [ ] I do not want an attorney.
   [ ] I already have an attorney whose name, address, and telephone number are _____
   _____ .
   (Name)   (Address)   (Telephone Number)
   [ ] I want an attorney.
   [IF A REQUEST IS MADE FOR AN ATTORNEY, SIGN HERE AND DO NOT COMPLETE THE REST OF THIS FORM]

_____   _____
(Date)   (Signature)

                       _____
                       (Address)

                       _____
                       (Telephone Number)
4. Effect of Consent and Adoption
   I understand that, by signing this Consent, I agree to the contents of it. I also understand that, if a court enters a judgment of adoption, I will become the child of the persons who adopt me and I will no longer be the legal child of any parent whose parental relationship to me is terminated by the judgment.

6

5. Right to Revoke Consent — Limitations

I understand that the only way in which I can revoke this Consent is by delivering my revocation to the following person:

Clerk of the Circuit Court for _____

(Name of County)

Attention: Adoption Clerk

_____

(Address and Telephone Number of Court)

_____

in writing, prior to entry of a judgment of adoption by a court, that my consent is revoked. The revocation must be signed by me and should contain my printed name, address, sex, date of birth, and the names of my parents or guardian.

I understand that revocation by telephone or other oral conversation or by writing to anyone other than the person named above will not constitute a valid revocation. I understand that I may deliver my written revocation by mail or in person, but if it is not *received* by the clerk prior to entry of a judgment of adoption by a court, it will not constitute a valid revocation.

6. Consent

Having read carefully all of the above statements, I freely, voluntarily, and unequivocally consent to being adopted by _____ and _____ and (if applicable) I consent to the change of my name to _____.

7. Waiver of Notice of Adoption Proceeding

I understand that, based on this consent, a petition for adoption will be filed in court and that I have the right to be notified when the petition is filed and of further proceedings concerning the adoption. I also understand that I may waive my right to notice.

Check one of the following statements:

[ ] I waive notice of all proceedings concerning the adoption, including entry of judgment. I understand that a court representative may nonetheless contact me in connection with these proceedings.

[ ] I want to receive notice of the filing of the petition but waive notice of all further proceedings concerning the adoption. I understand that notice will be sent to the address given by me on this form unless I advise the clerk of the court stated in Paragraph 8 of this consent, in writing, of a change in my address.

[ ] I want to receive notice of the filing of the petition and of further proceedings concerning the adoption. I understand that notice will be sent to the address given by me on this form unless I advise the clerk of the court stated in Paragraph 8 of this consent, in writing, of a change in my address.

8. I acknowledge that I have read this consent or have had it read to me, that I understand it, and that I have received a copy of the signed consent to keep. I further acknowledge that no one has persuaded me to sign this consent or any other form or paper regarding this adoption against my will.

I solemnly affirm under the penalties of perjury that the contents of the foregoing consent form are true to the best of my knowledge, information, and belief.

_____

(Date)

_____

(Signature)

_____

(Address)

_____

(Telephone Number)

Source. — This Rule is derived in part from former Rule D73 and is in part new.

Interests of child are paramount. — In both custody and adoption cases the interests of the child are paramount. Goodyear v. Cecil County Dep't of Social Servs., 11 Md. App. 280, 273 A.2d 644, rev'd on other grounds, 263 Md. 611, 284 A.2d 426 (1971); Nutwell v. Prince George's County Dep't of Social Servs., 21 Md. App. 100, 318 A.2d 563 (1974); Brendoff v. Titus, 22 Md. App. 412, 323 A.2d 612 (1974).

But adoption is not decreed over parental objection unless clearly justified. — But since the consequential loss to a natural parent in an adoption case is much more drastic than in a custody case, adoption will never be decreed over the objection of a natural parent or parents unless that course is clearly justified. Goodyear v. Cecil County Dep't of Social Servs., 11 Md. App. 280, 273 A.2d 644, rev'd on other grounds, 263 Md. 611, 284 A.2d 426 (1971); Nutwell v. Prince George's County Dep't of Social Servs., 21 Md. App. 100, 318 A.2d 563 (1974).

The Court of Appeals has indicated that it will not permit trial courts to decree adoptions over the expressed objection of the natural parent or parents, save in very strong cases. Goodyear v. Cecil County Dep't of Social Servs., 11 Md. App. 280, 273 A.2d 644, rev'd on other grounds, 263 Md. 611, 284 A.2d 426 (1971); Nutwell v. Prince George's County Dep't of Social Servs., 21 Md. App. 100, 318 A.2d 563 (1974).

And welfare of child must be weighed against parental objection. — The welfare and best interests of the child must be weighed with great care against every just claim of an objecting parent. Goodyear v. Cecil County Dep't of Social Servs., 11 Md. App. 280, 273 A.2d 644, rev'd on other grounds, 263 Md. 611, 284 A.2d 426 (1971); Nutwell v. Prince George's County Dep't of Social Servs., 21 Md. App. 100, 318 A.2d 563 (1974).

The test as to what is to the best interests of the child necessarily depends on the facts and circumstances in each case. Schwartz v. Hudgins, 12 Md. App. 419, 278 A.2d 652 (1971).

No parental right to absolute, arbitrary veto. — Although the rights of the natural parent, or parents, must be closely considered, and although without a natural parent's consent the case for adoption must be strong, there is no right to an absolute, arbitrary veto on the part of the parent. Lloyd v. Schutes, 24 Md. App. 515, 332 A.2d 338, cert. denied, 275 Md. 752 (1975).

Determination whether parental consent is being withheld contrary to best interests of child necessarily depends on the facts of each particular case, but it is evident that willful abandonment, failure to contribute to support, neglect to see or visit, and unfitness of a natural parent are some of the more important factors to be considered by a court in reaching its conclusion. Goodyear v. Cecil County Dep't of Social Servs., 11 Md. App. 280, 273 A.2d 644, rev'd on other grounds, 263 Md. 611, 284 A.2d 426 (1971).

Factors to be considered in determining whether consent has been unjustifiably withheld are failure to contribute to support, neglect to see or visit the offspring and unfitness. Brendoff v. Titus, 22 Md. App. 412, 323 A.2d 612 (1974).

All of the facts and circumstances of the particular case must be considered in determining whether consent has been unjustifiably withheld and the natural rights of a natural parent, which have not been lost or forfeited, must be carefully weighed in deciding the question. Brendoff v. Titus, 22 Md. App. 412, 323 A.2d 612 (1974).

Where the evidence tends to show that mother's determination not to consent to the adoption of her baby daughter was born of a genuine concern that by consenting she would sever permanently the natural and legal rights and obligations binding parent and child, she did not lose or forfeit her parental rights, and did not unjustifiably withhold her consent contrary to the child's best interests. Brendoff v. Titus, 22 Md. App. 412, 323 A.2d 612 (1974).

Chancellor's finding that natural mother withheld her consent contrary to the best interest of her children was not supported where there was no evidence of wilful or intentional conduct on mother's part manifesting an intent to relinquish, renounce or forsake her parental right to her children. Nutwell v. Prince George's County Dep't of Social Servs., 21 Md. App. 100, 318 A.2d 563 (1974).

Agency's consent not withheld contrary to best interests of child. — In a case of a contested petition for adoption by an unmarried individual with whom contractual placement of a child had been made, which placement and adoption were contested by the placement agency, where the evidence re-vealed that the petitioner and her husband had jointly applied for placement, but they had been separated at time of placement, that neither the out-of-state nor the local agency was apprised of their marital difficulties which culminated in divorce, but rather this information appeared to be suppressed, that petitioner represented she had not previously been married, when in fact she had been twice married and twice divorced, and that sharp discrepancies existed with respect to her finances, the chancellor did not abuse his discretion in deciding that the agency's consent was not withheld contrary to the best interests of the child. Bernhardt v. Lutheran Social Servs. of Nat'l Capital Area, Inc., 39 Md. App. 334, 385 A.2d 1197 (1978).

Applied in Attorney Grievance Comm'n v. Sabghir, 350 Md. 67, 710 A.2d 926 (1998).

Cited in In re Adoption No. 93321055, 344 Md. 458, 687 A.2d 681 (1997).

Rule 9-103. Petition.

(a) *Titling of case.* Except as otherwise provided in Rule 9-105, a proceeding shall be titled, "In the matter of the Petition of _____

_____

(name of petitioner(s))

for the Adoption of [a Minor] [an Adult]," or "In the matter of the Petition of

_____ for

(name of petitioner(s))

Guardianship with Right to Consent to Adoption or Long-Term Care Short of Adoption," as the case may be.

(b) *Petition for adoption.* (1) Contents. A petition for adoption shall be signed and verified by each petitioner and shall contain the following information:

(A) The name, address, age, business or employment, and employer of each petitioner;

(B) The name, sex, and date and place of birth of the person to be adopted;

(C) The name, address, and age of each parent of the person to be adopted;

(D) Any relationship of the person to be adopted to each petitioner;

(E) The name, address, and age of each child of each petitioner;

(F) A statement of how the person to be adopted was located (including names and addresses of all intermediaries or surrogates), attaching a copy of all advertisements used to locate the person, and a copy of any surrogacy contract;

Committee note. — If the text of an advertisement was used verbatim more than once, the requirement that a copy of all advertisements be attached to the petition may be satisfied by attaching a single copy of the advertisement, together with a list of the publications in which the advertisement appeared and the dates on which it appeared.

(G) If the person to be adopted is a minor, the names and addresses of all persons who have had legal or physical care, custody, or control of the minor since the minor's birth and the period of time during which each of those persons has had care, custody, or control, but it is not necessary to identify the names and addresses of foster parents, other than a petitioner, who have taken care of the minor only while the minor has been committed to the custody of a child placement agency;

(H) If the person to be adopted is a minor who has been transported from another state to this State for purposes of placement for adoption, a statement of whether there has been compliance with the Interstate Compact on the Placement of Children (ICPC);

(I) If applicable, the reason why the spouse of the petitioner is not joining in the petition;

(J) If there is a guardian with the right to consent to adoption for the person to be adopted, the name and address of the guardian and a reference to the proceeding in which the guardian was appointed;

(K) Facts known to each petitioner that may entitle the person to be adopted or a parent of that person to the appointment of an attorney by the court;

(L) If a petitioner desires to change the name of the person to be adopted, the name that is desired;

(M) As to each petitioner, a statement whether the petitioner has ever been convicted of a crime other than a minor traffic violation and, if so, the offense and the date and place of the conviction;

(N) That the petitioner is not aware that any required consent has been revoked; and

(O) If placement pending final action on the petition is sought in accordance with Code, Family Law Article, § 5-507 (c), a request that the court approve the proposed placement.

(2) Exhibits. (A) The following documents shall accompany the petition as exhibits:

(i) A certified copy of the birth certificate or "proof of live birth" of the person to be adopted;

(ii) A certified copy of the marriage certificate of each married petitioner;

(iii) A certified copy of all judgments of divorce of each petitioner;

(iv) A certified copy of any death certificate of a person whose consent would be required if that person were living;

(v) A certified copy of all orders concerning temporary custody or guardianship of the person to be adopted;

(vi) A copy of any pre-placement report concerning a petitioner;

(vii) A document evidencing the annual income of each petitioner;

(viii) The original of all consents to the adoption and, if available, a copy of any written statement by the consenting person indicating a desire to revoke the consent, whether or not that statement constitutes a valid revocation;

Cross references. — Code, Family Law Article, § 5-311.

(ix) If a parent of the person to be adopted cannot be identified or located, an affidavit of each petitioner and the other parent describing the attempts to identify and locate the unknown or missing parent;

(x) A copy of any agreement between a parent of the person to be adopted and a petitioner relating to the proposed adoption;

(xi) If the adoption is subject to the Interstate Compact on the Placement of Children, the appropriate ICPC approval forms; and

Cross references. — Code, Family Law Article, § 5-601.

(xii) A brief statement of the health of each petitioner signed by a physician or other health care provider.

(B) The following documents shall be filed before a judgment of adoption is entered:

(i) Any post-placement report relating to the adoption;

(ii) A brief statement of the health of the child by a physician or other health care provider;

(iii) If required by law, an accounting of all payments and disbursements of any money or item of value made by or on behalf of each petitioner in connection with the adoption;

Cross references. — Code, Family Law Article, § 5-327 (c).

(iv) An affidavit of counsel, if any, for a minor parent or parent under a disability attesting to the voluntariness of the parent's consent;

Cross references. — Code, Family Law Article, § 5-314 (b).

(v) If the adoption is subject to the Interstate Compact on the Placement of Children, the required post-placement form;

(vi) A proposed judgment of adoption; and

(vii) A Department of Health and Mental Hygiene Certificate of Adoption Form.

Cross references. — Code, Health-General Article, § 4-211 (f).

(c) *Petition for guardianship.* A petition for guardianship shall state all facts required by subsection (b) (1) of this Rule, to the extent that the requirements are applicable and known to the petitioner. It shall be accompanied by all documents required to be filed as exhibits by subsection (b)(2) of this Rule, to the extent the documents are applicable. The petition shall also state the license number of the child placement agency.

Cross references. — Code, Family Law Article, § 5-317 (b).

(d) *If facts unknown or documents unavailable.* If a fact required by subsection (b) (1) or section (c) of this Rule is unknown to a petitioner or if a document required by subsection (b) (2) or section (c) is unavailable, the petitioner shall so state and give the reason in the petition or in a subsequent affidavit. If a document required to be submitted with the petition becomes available after the petition is filed, the petitioner shall file it as soon as it becomes available.

(e) *Judgment from foreign country.* When a judgment of adoption or guardianship is sought pursuant to Code, Family Law Article, § 5-313.1, an exemplified copy of the judgment granted by the foreign jurisdiction shall be filed with the petition.

Committee note. — For exemplification procedure, *see* Federal Rule of Civil Procedure 44 (a) (2).

(f) *Disclosure of facts known to child placement agency.* If any fact required by subsection (b) (1) of this Rule to be stated is known to a child placement agency and the agency declines to disclose it to a petitioner, the agency shall disclose the fact to the court in writing at the time the petition is filed.

Source. — This Rule is derived in part from former Rule D72, in part from former Rule D80, and is in part new.

Rule 9-104. Notice to consenting persons.

(a) Upon the filing of a petition for adoption or guardianship, the court shall send a notice of the filing to each person whose parental rights have not previously been terminated and who, pursuant to Rule 9-102, has consented to the adoption or guardianship but has requested notice of the filing of the petition. If the person has also requested notice of further proceedings concerning the adoption or guardianship, the court shall send notice of any hearing to be held prior to the entry of a judgment terminating that person's parental rights and of the entry of any judgment terminating those parental rights.

(b) Notice under this Rule shall be sent by first class mail to the address given on the consent form unless the person has, in writing, provided a new address.

(c) The sending of notice pursuant to this Rule does not affect the consent signed by the person or give the person any standing to participate in the action.

Source. — This Rule is new.

Rule 9-105. Show cause order; other notice.

(a) *Requirement.* Upon the filing of a petition for adoption or guardianship, the court shall enter a show cause order in the form set forth in section (h) of this Rule unless all parties entitled to service of the show cause order under section (b) of this Rule have consented to the adoption or guardianship. If the petition seeks adoption of a minor, the show cause order shall not divulge the name of the petitioner. If the petition seeks appointment of a guardian, the show cause order shall state the name of the child placement agency seeking guardianship.

(b) *Persons to be served.* (1) In adoption proceeding. (A) Subject to paragraphs (1) (B), (1) (C), and (1) (D) of this section, if the petition seeks adoption, the show cause order shall be served on (i) the person to be adopted, if the person is 10 years old or older; (ii) the parents of the person to be adopted; and (iii) any other person the court directs to be served.

(B) If the parental rights of the parents of the person to be adopted have been terminated by a judgment of guardianship with the right to consent to adoption, service shall be on the guardian instead of the parents.

(C) If an attorney has been appointed to represent a parent or the person to be adopted, service shall be on the attorney instead of the parent or person to be adopted.

Cross references. — *See* Rule 9-106 (a) concerning appointment of attorney.

(D) The show cause order need not be served on: (i) a parent of a person to be adopted if the person to be adopted has been adjudicated to be a child in need of assistance in a prior juvenile proceeding, the petition for adoption is filed by a child placement agency, and the court is satisfied by affidavit or testimony that the petitioner has made reasonable good faith efforts to serve the show cause order on the parent by both certified mail and private process at the addresses specified in Code, Family Law Article, § 5-322 (b) and at any other address actually known to the petitioner as one where the parent may be found; or (ii) a person who has executed a written consent pursuant to Rule 9-102.

(2) In a guardianship proceeding. (A) Subject to paragraphs (2) (B) and (2) (C) of this section, if the petition seeks guardianship, the show cause order shall be served on (i) the parents of the person for whom a guardian is to be appointed and (ii) any other person that the court directs to be served.

(B) If an attorney has been appointed to represent a parent or the person for whom a guardian is to be appointed, service shall be on the attorney instead of the parent or person for whom a guardian is to be appointed.

(C) The show cause order need not be served on: (i) a parent of a person for whom a guardian is to be appointed if the person for whom a guardian is to be appointed has been adjudicated to be a child in need of assistance in a prior juvenile proceeding and the court is satisfied by affidavit or testimony that the petitioner has made reasonable good faith efforts to serve the show cause order on the parent by both certified mail and private process at the addresses specified in Code, Family Law Article, § 5-322 (b) and at any other address actually known to the petitioner as one where the parent may be found; or (ii) a person who has executed a written consent pursuant to Rule 9-102.

(c) *Method of service.* Except as otherwise provided in this Rule, the show cause order shall be served in the manner provided by Rule 2-121. If the court is satisfied by affidavit or testimony that the petitioner or a parent, after reasonable efforts made in good faith, has been unable to ascertain the identity or whereabouts of a parent entitled to service under section (b) of this Rule, the court may order, as to that parent, that the show cause order be published one time. Publication shall be in the county of that parent's last known residence. When a show cause order is published, unless the court orders otherwise, the show cause order shall identify the individual who is the subject of the proceeding only as "a child born to" followed by the name of any known parent of the child and shall set forth the month, year, county, and state of the child's birth, to the extent known.

Cross references. — *See* Code, Family Law Article, § 5-322 (c) (2) (ii), which provides that an indigent petitioner may serve notice by posting. *See* Code, Family Law Article, § 5-322 (e), setting forth the efforts necessary to support a finding that a reasonable, good faith effort has been made by a local department of social services to locate a parent.

(d) *Time for service.* Unless the court orders otherwise, a show cause order that is served in the manner provided by Rule 2-121 shall be served within 90 days after the date it is issued. If service is not made within that period, a new show cause order shall be issued at the request of the petitioner.

(e) *Notice of objection.* When the show cause order is served pursuant to Rule 2-121, it shall be accompanied by a pre-captioned notice of objection in substantially the form set forth in section (i) of this Rule.

(f) *Additional notice in a guardianship.* The petitioner in an action for guardianship of a child who has been adjudicated a child in need of assistance in a prior juvenile proceeding shall also send a copy of the petition and show cause order by first class mail to each attorney who represented a parent and to the attorney who represented the child in the juvenile proceeding.

(g) *Notice of change of name.* If the person to be adopted is an adult and the petitioner desires to change the name of the person to be adopted to a surname other than that of the petitioner, notice of a proposed change of name shall also be given in the manner provided in Rule 15-901.

(h) *Form of show cause order.* The show cause order shall be in substantially the following form:

THIS IS A COURT ORDER. IF YOU DO NOT UNDERSTAND WHAT THE ORDER SAYS, HAVE SOMEONE EXPLAIN IT TO YOU.

IN THE MATTER OF A PETITION
FOR _____
    (adoption/guardianship)
OF _____
    (Name of individual who is
    the subject of the proceeding)

IN THE
CIRCUIT COURT
FOR
_____
    (county)

_____
    (docket reference)

SHOW CAUSE ORDER

TO:
_____
(name of person to be served)
_____

_____
(address, including county)
_____

(relationship of person served to individual who is the subject of the proceeding)

You are hereby notified that:

1. Filing of petition.

A petition has been filed for _____
                                    (adoption/guardianship)

of _____ who
        (name of individual who is the subject of the proceeding)

was born at _____ on _____.
                (birthplace)   (date of birth)

(If the petition is for guardianship, include the following sentence: The petition
was filed by _____).
                (name of child placement agency seeking guardianship)

2. Right to object; time for objecting.

(A. This portion should be included when the show cause order is to be served
pursuant to Rule 2-121.)

If you wish to object to the _____ ,
                                      (adoption/guardianship)

you must file a notice of objection with the clerk of the court at
_____
                        (address of courthouse)

within _____ days after this Order is served on you. For your convenience,
a form notice of objection is attached to this Order.

(B. This portion should be included when the show cause order is to be
published or posted.)

If you wish to object to the _____
                                      (adoption/guardianship)

you must file a notice of objection with the clerk of the court on or
before _____ at _____.
        (date)   (address of courthouse)

WHETHER THE PETITION REQUESTS ADOPTION OR GUARDIAN-
SHIP, IF YOU DO NOT FILE A NOTICE OF OBJECTION OR A REQUEST
FOR AN ATTORNEY BY THE DEADLINE STATED ABOVE, A JUDGMENT
TERMINATING PARENTAL RIGHTS MAY BE ENTERED WITHOUT YOUR
CONSENT.

3. Right to an attorney. (a) You have the right to consult an attorney and
obtain independent legal advice.

(b) An attorney may already have been appointed for you based on statements in the petition. If an attorney has been appointed and has already
contacted you, you should consult with that attorney.

(c) If an attorney has not already contacted you, you may be entitled to have
the court appoint an attorney for you if:

(1) you are the person to be adopted and:

(A) you are at least ten years old but are not yet 18; or

15

(B) you are at least ten years old and have a disability that makes you incapable of consenting to the adoption or of participating effectively in the proceeding.

(2) you are the person to be adopted or the person for whom a guardian is sought and the proceeding involves the involuntary termination of the parental rights of your parents.

(3) you are a parent of the person to be adopted or for whom a guardian is sought and:

(A) you are under 18 years of age; or

(B) because of a disability, you are incapable of consenting to the adoption or guardianship or of participating effectively in the proceeding; or

(C) you object to the adoption and cannot afford to hire an attorney because you are indigent.

IF YOU BELIEVE YOU ARE ENTITLED TO HAVE THE COURT APPOINT AN ATTORNEY FOR YOU AND YOU WANT AN ATTORNEY, YOU MUST NOTIFY THE COURT BEFORE THE TIME YOUR NOTICE OF OBJECTION MUST BE FILED. YOU MAY FILE A REQUEST FOR AN ATTORNEY WITHOUT FILING A NOTICE OF OBJECTION.

For your convenience, a request for appointment of an attorney is printed on the notice of objection form attached to this Order. (Omit the last sentence from a published or posted show cause order.)

(d) If you are a parent of the person to be adopted, you are entitled to consult an attorney chosen by you, even if you are not entitled to an attorney appointed by the court. If you employ an attorney, you may be responsible for any fees and costs charged by that attorney unless this is an adoption proceeding and the adoptive parents agree to pay, or the court orders them to pay all or part of those fees or expenses.

(e) If you wish further information concerning appointment of an attorney by the court or concerning adoption counseling and guidance, you may contact

_____

(name of court official)

_____

(address)

_____

(telephone number)

4. Option to receive adoption counseling. If this is an adoption proceeding, you also may have the option to receive adoption counseling and guidance. You may have to pay for that service unless the adoptive parents agree to pay or the court orders them to pay all or part of those charges.

Date of issue: _____

_____

(Judge)

(i) *Form of notice of objection.* The notice of objection shall be in substantially the following form:

IN THE MATTER OF A PETITION   IN THE
FOR _____   CIRCUIT COURT FOR
    (adoption/guardianship)

OF _____   _____
         (Name of individual who is   (county)
         the subject of the proceeding) _____
                                                 (docket reference)

NOTICE OF OBJECTION

(Instructions to the person served with the show cause order:
IF YOU WISH TO OBJECT, YOU MUST FILE YOUR NOTICE OF OBJEC-
TION WITH THE COURT ON OR BEFORE THE DEADLINE STATED IN
THE SHOW CAUSE ORDER. You may use this form to do so. You need only
sign this form, print or type your name, address, and telephone number
underneath your signature, and mail or deliver it to the court at the address
shown in paragraph 2 of the show cause order. If you wish to state your
reasons, you may state them on this sheet.)

I object to the _____ of the
                        (adoption/guardianship)
above-named individual. My reasons for objecting are as follows:

_____
_____
_____
_____

                              _____
                              (Signature)

                              _____
                              (Name, printed or typed)

                              _____
                              (Address)

                              _____
                              (Telephone number)

(j) *Form of request for attorney.* A request for attorney shall be in substantially the following form:

REQUEST FOR APPOINTMENT OF AN ATTORNEY

I want the Court to appoint an attorney to represent me. **(Check appro-
priate box or boxes)**
  [ ] I am the person to be adopted *and*:
  [ ] I am at least ten years old but am not yet 18; or
  [ ] I am at least ten years old and I have a disability that makes me
       incapable of consenting to the adoption or of participating effectively in
       the proceeding; or
  [ ] the proceeding involves the involuntary termination of the parental
       rights of my parents.
  [ ] I am a parent of the person to be adopted or for whom a guardian is
       sought *and*:

[   ] I am under 18 years of age; or

[   ] because of a disability, I am incapable of consenting to the adoption or guardianship or of participating effectively in the proceeding; or

[   ] I object to the adoption or guardianship and cannot afford to hire an attorney because I am indigent.

_____

(Signature)

_____

(Name, printed or typed)

_____

(Address)

_____

(Telephone Number)

Committee note. — *See* Rule 9-103 (a). The caption of the petition designated in the show cause order is different from the caption of the case record referred to in Rule 9-103, which is kept by the clerk. The caption in the show cause order preserves the anonymity of the prospective adoptive parents. The caption in the case record preserves the anonymity of the adoptee.

Source. — This Rule is in part derived from former Rule D74 and is in part new.

Purpose of former Rule D74. — See Palmisano v. Baltimore County Welfare Bd., 249 Md. 94, 238 A.2d 251, cert. denied, 393 U.S. 853, 89 S. Ct. 93, 21 L. Ed. 2d 123 (1968). **Scope of Rule.** — This Rule extends § 5-322 (a) of the Family Law Article and requires more detailed information. In re Adoption No. 93321055, 344 Md. 458, 687 A.2d 681 (1997). **Application of notice provisions.** — The notice provisions of former Rule D74 applied to a proceeding for guardianship with the right to consent to long-term care short of adoption. 57 Op. Att'y Gen. 18 (1972).

The consent of the father of a child born out of wedlock and never legitimated is not necessary in a proceeding for guardianship preceding adoption nor is the father entitled to notice of the filing of a petition for such guardianship. 57 Op. Att'y Gen. 18 (1972).

Court-appointed counsel for child was entitled to a notice and hearing on a petition for guardianship. In re Adoption/Guardianship No. 3155, 103 Md. App. 300, 653 A.2d 521 (1995).

Rule 9-106. Appointment of attorney — Investigation.

(a) *Appointment of attorney.* The court shall appoint an attorney for any person entitled to the appointment pursuant to Code, Family Law Article, § 5-323. The court may appoint an attorney for a minor who is not otherwise entitled by statute to a court-appointed attorney. If the petition shows that a person is entitled to a court-appointed attorney, the court shall appoint an attorney for that person promptly after the filing of the petition.

Cross references. — *See In Re Adoption No. A91-71A,* 334 Md. 538 (1994).

(b) *Investigation by court.* If the proceeding is contested, the court shall order an investigation of the facts of the case and if the proceeding is uncontested, the court may order an investigation. The court may designate any person or agency to conduct the investigation. That person or agency shall report the findings of the investigation to the court in writing and, also, if requested by the court, the recommendation of the person or agency.

(c) *Reports.* The reports of any investigation shall be filed among the records of the proceeding.

Source. — This Rule is derived from former Rule D75.

Disclosure. — The court may order disclosure of information reported to it by its investigators to other government authorities; to the extent that disclosure is not connected with the State's administration of its foster care and adoption programs, however, the court should weigh its interest in disclosure against the privacy interests of the parties. In all cases, the court should limit disclosure to that information necessary to serve its interest. 79 Op. Att'y Gen. (March 9, 1994).

Court may consider facts learned in proceedings to adopt another child of same father. — The chancellor did not err when she considered facts she had learned in an earlier case relating to the adoption of another of the objecting father's children, since the court may act without investigation in cases where it has personal knowledge of the facts. Walker v. Gardner, 221 Md. 280, 157 A.2d 273 (1960).

Investigation by court of county where former statute inapplicable. — There was nothing in repealed § 76 of Article 16 similar to this Rule, to prevent the court in any county in which the section did not apply from having proper investigation made as to the home, etc., of adoptive parents. Anderson v. Barkman, 195 Md. 94, 72 A.2d 709 (1950).

It was appropriate, and within the court's discretion to order an investigation, although this Rule mandates an investigation only in contested cases. In re Adoption No. 90072022/CAD, 87 Md. App. 630, 590 A.2d 1094 (1991).

Rule 9-107. Objection.

(a) *In general.* Any person having a right to participate in a proceeding for adoption or guardianship may file a notice of objection to the adoption or guardianship. The notice may include a statement of the reasons for the objection and a request for the appointment of an attorney.

Cross references. — *See* Rule 9-105 for Form of Notice of Objection.

(b) *Time for filing objection.* (1) In general. Except as provided by subsections (b) (2) and (b) (3) of this Rule, any notice of objection to an adoption or guardianship shall be filed within 30 days after the show cause order is served.

(2) Service outside of the State. If the show cause order is served outside the State but within the United States, the time for filing a notice of objection shall be within 60 days after service.

(3) Service outside of the United States. If the show cause order is served outside the United States, the time for filing a notice of objection shall be within 90 days after service.

(4) Service by publication or posting. If the show cause order is served by publication or posting, the time for filing a notice of objection shall be the date stated in the show cause order, which shall be not earlier than 30 days after the posting or first publication of the show cause order.

(c) *Service.* The clerk shall serve a copy of any notice of objection on the petitioner in the manner provided by Rule 1-321.

(d) *Response.* Within ten days after being served with a notice of objection, the petitioner may file a response challenging the standing of the person to file the notice or the timeliness of the filing of notice of objection.

19

(e) *Hearing.* If the petitioner files a response, the court shall hold a hearing promptly on the issues raised in the response.

(f) *Access to records.* If the court determines that the person filing the notice of objection has standing to do so and that the notice is timely filed, it shall enter an order permitting the person to inspect the papers filed in the proceeding subject to reasonable conditions imposed in the order.

Source. — This Rule is derived in part from former Rule D76 and is in part new.

Stated in In re Adoption No. 93321055, 344 Md. 458, 687 A.2d 681 (1997).

Rule 9-108. Temporary custody.

The court may make an award of temporary custody of a minor prior to a hearing.

Source. — This Rule is derived from former Rule D78 (d).

The court may make a temporary award of custody prior to a hearing if it deems such actions in the child's best interests. Thumma v. Hartsook, 239 Md. 38, 210 A.2d 151 (1965).

Rule 9-109. Hearing on merits.

(a) *Requirement.* The court shall hold a hearing on the merits in a contested guardianship action and in every adoption action prior to entering a judgment of adoption or guardianship. The court may hold a hearing on the merits in any guardianship action. The hearing shall be on the record.

(b) *Guardianship.* When the court holds a hearing in a guardianship action, it shall make the findings required by Code, Family Law Article, § 5-313 on the record.

(c) *Adoption.* (1) Persons present at hearing. Unless excused for good cause shown, each petitioner and the person to be adopted shall be present at the hearing on the merits in an adoption action. The hearing shall be conducted out of the presence of all persons other than the petitioners, the person to be adopted, and those persons whose presence the court deems necessary or desirable.

Committee note. — Social policy against public disclosure of adoption proceedings compels all hearings to be as private as possible. This Rule leaves to the discretion of the trial court the extent to which this consideration must be relaxed in the interest of fair trial.

(2) Findings by the court. In an adoption action, the court shall determine on the record whether:

(A) Necessary consents have been filed;

(B) Any required consents have been revoked;

Cross references. — Rules 9-111 (b) and
9-112 (a).

(C) Appropriate notices have been served;

(D) Investigative reports are in order;

(E) All questioned or disputed issues have been resolved;

(F) In a contested case where adoption will terminate a parent's rights, the parents are unfit or extraordinary circumstances exist;

(G) The adoptive parents are fit and proper to be the parents of the person to be adopted;

(H) The best interests of the person to be adopted will be served by the adoption; and

(I) Other appropriate matters have been resolved.

Source. — This Rule is in part derived from former Rule D77 and is in part new.

No hearing was required on petition for visitation rights by natural mother. Weinschel v. Strople, 56 Md. App. 252, 466 A.2d 1301 (1983).

Rule 9-110. Accounting report.

(a) *Duty to file.* In an independent adoption other than an adoption by a stepparent or relative of the person to be adopted, each petitioner shall file an accounting report before the entry of a final judgment of adoption.

(b) *Contents.* The accounting report shall include:

(1) a statement of all payments and disbursements of money or any item of value, including benefits in kind, made by or on behalf of any petitioner in connection with the adoption;

(2) the approximate date the payment or disbursement was made or the benefit was provided;

(3) the name of the payee and the beneficiary; and

(4) the amount of the payment or disbursement or the reasonable value of the benefit provided.

The court may require the production of documentation to substantiate the accounting report.

Cross references. — Code, Family Law Article, §§ 5-321 and 5-327 (c).
Source. — This Rule is new.

Rule 9-111. Judgment of adoption or guardianship.

(a) *Time.* The court may not enter a judgment of adoption or guardianship before the later of (1) 30 days after the birth of the child or (2) expiration of the time for revoking all required consents.

(b) *Information from other court.* If a required consent indicates that any revocation of the consent must be filed in a court other than the trial court, the trial court may not enter a judgment of adoption or guardianship until it has obtained from the other court a copy of all papers filed in connection with the consent or an affidavit of the clerk of the other court that no papers were filed in connection with the consent.

(c) *Supplemental report.* Before entering a judgment of adoption or guardianship, the court may require a supplemental written report from the investigating officer or agency.

(d) *Change of name.* If the name of the person adopted is changed, the judgment of adoption shall state the new name of the person adopted and the names of the adopting parents.

(e) *Spouse of parent.* If the adopting parent is the spouse of a natural or biological parent of the person to be adopted, the judgment shall specifically state whether and to what extent the parental rights of the natural or biological parent are affected.

Committee note. — Any attempt to set aside a judgment of adoption by reason of a procedural defect shall be filed with the court within one year following entry of the judgment. Code, Family Law Article, § 5-325.

An adoptive relationship created by a judgment of adoption in another jurisdiction shall be given full faith and credit by the courts of this State. Code, Family Law Article, § 5-326. For the legal effect of adoption of an adult, *see* Code, Family Law Article, § 5-308.

Source. — This Rule is derived from former Rule D79.

Stated in In re Adoption No. 93321055, 344 Md. 458, 687 A.2d 681 (1997).

Rule 9-112. Court records.

(a) *Dockets.* The clerk shall keep separate dockets for (1) adoption and guardianship proceedings and (2) revocations of consent to adoption or guardianship for which there are no pending adoption or guardianship proceedings in that county. These dockets are not open to inspection by any person, including the parents, except upon order of court. If the index to a docket is kept apart from the docket itself, the index is open to inspection.

(b) *Sealing of records.* All pleadings and other papers in adoption and guardianship proceedings shall be sealed when they are filed and are not open to inspection by any person, including the parents, except upon an order of court. If a final decree of adoption was entered before June 1, 1947 and the record is not already sealed, the record may be sealed only on motion of a party.

Cross references. — *See* Code, Health-General Article, § 4-211, concerning the amendment and replacement of birth certificates following adoption and the requirement that the clerk transmit to the Department of Health and Mental Hygiene a report of adoption or revocation of adoption.

Source. — This Rule is derived from former Rule D80 a and c.

University of Baltimore Law Review. — For article, "The Adoption Trilemma: The Adult Adoptee's Emerging Search for his Ancestral Identity," see 8 U. Balt. L. Rev. 496 (1979).

Rule 9-113. Medical history.

(a) *Duty to provide.* Except in an adoption by a stepparent or relative, the person authorized to place a minor child for adoption shall compile a medical history of the child, file it with the court, and make it available to a prospective adoptive parent and to the adoptive parent.

(b) *Contents.* The medical history shall contain to the extent obtainable:

(1) current physical and mental health status of the child;

(2) the prenatal history of the child;

(3) the birth history of the child;

(4) the health history of both biological parents; and

(5) the family health history of both biological parents.

Cross references. — Code, Family Law Article, § 5-328.
Source. — This Rule is new.

CHAPTER 200. DIVORCE, ANNULMENT AND ALIMONY.

Rule 9-201. Venue — General.

a. *Divorce.* A bill of divorce shall be filed in a county where the plaintiff resides, or where the defendant resides, is regularly employed or has a place of business. (Art. 16, § 22.)

Cross references. — See Code, Family Law Article, § 7-101 (a), providing that where cause for divorce has occurred out of the State, no application for divorce may be made in Maryland unless at least one of the parties has resided in Maryland for at least one year last preceding the application.

b. *Annulment.* A bill for annulment shall be filed in a county where the plaintiff resides, or where the defendant resides, is regularly employed or has a place of business, or in the county where the marriage ceremony was performed. (Art. 16, § 22.)

c. *Alimony.* A bill for alimony alone shall be filed in the county where the defendant resides, is regularly employed or has a place of business. (Amended June 5, 1996, effective Jan. 1, 1997.)

Cross references. — See Code, Family Law Article, Title 11, relating to powers of court in regard to alimony.
Source. — This Rule is former Rule S70.

Editor's note. — An Order dated June 5, 1996, effective Jan. 1, 1997, renumbered this Rule, which was formerly Rule S70.

Article 16, § 22, which is referred to in sections (a) and (b), has been repealed. For present provisions regarding venue for annulment actions, see § 6-202 of the Courts and Judicial Proceedings Article.

Jurisdiction in divorce action. — For jurisdiction in a divorce action to exist in a Maryland court, at least one of the parties must have been a "bona fide" resident of Maryland when the complaint was filed. Fletcher v. Fletcher, 95 Md. App. 114, 619 A.2d 561 (1993).

This Rule adds to the places specified in former Article 16, § 22 (now CJ § 6-202), the county wherein a defendant is regularly employed or has a place of business. Fisher v. Demarr, 226 Md. 509, 174 A.2d 345 (1961).

It does not extend jurisdiction of equity court. — Section a of this Rule would not have been recommended and adopted if the Rules Committee or the Court of Appeals had thought it extended the jurisdiction of courts of equity in divorce cases. Fisher v. Demarr, 226 Md. 509, 174 A.2d 345 (1961).

Waiver of provisions respecting venue. — Where defendant in a divorce suit was summoned personally and failed to answer, she waived the provisions of this Rule respecting venue. Shaw v. Shaw (Cir. Ct. No. 2, of Balt. City, Niles, C.J.), Daily Record, Sept. 9, 1959.

Rule 9-202. Process.

The same process as is had in other actions shall be had in an action for divorce, annulment or alimony. (Art. 16, § 22; amended Apr. 6, 1984, effective July 1, 1984; June 5, 1996, effective Jan. 1, 1997.)

Cross references. — See Title 2, Chapter 100. See also Rule 2-122 (a) which provides for mailing to the defendant's last known address and posting or publication where an action is based on in rem or quasi in rem jurisdiction and it is shown to the Court's satisfaction that the whereabouts of the defendant are unknown and that reasonable efforts to locate him have been made in good faith.

Source. — This Rule is former Rule S71.

Editor's note. — An Order dated June 5, 1996, effective Jan. 1, 1997, renumbered this Rule, which was formerly Rule S71.

Rule 9-203. Pleading.

a. *Signing.* 1. Bill of complaint. A bill for divorce, annulment, or alimony shall be signed by the plaintiff in person.

2. Answer. An answer to a bill for divorce, annulment or alimony shall be signed by the defendant in person.

b. *Mentally incompetent defendant — Answer.* 1. Guardian or attorney. Where the defendant is mentally incompetent, then upon the return of process duly served, or upon proof of due publication or mailing and posting, the court shall require the guardian, if there be one appointed by a court of this State, to appear and answer. If there be no such guardian, or if the court shall deem it proper for the protection of the defendant, the court shall appoint an attorney to appear and answer for said defendant. (Art. 16, § 26; amended Feb. 2, 1970; amended June 30, 1973, effective July 1, 1973.)

Cross references. — See Rule 2-202 (c).

2. Appointment of attorney for guardian. Before such guardian shall answer said complaint, the court shall appoint an attorney of its own independent selection to appear for and represent the guardian. (Art. 16, § 26; amended Feb. 2, 1970.)

3. Attorney fee. The compensation of the attorney so appointed shall be fixed by the court, and paid as the court shall direct. (Art. 16, § 26.)

c. *Supplemental bill.* 1. In general. A supplemental bill alleging grounds for divorce occurring subsequent to the filing of the original bill shall be permitted.

2. For divorce *a vinculo* following *a mensa.* A party who has obtained a decree of divorce a mensa et thoro may, without leave of court, file a supplemental bill for a divorce a vinculo not later than eighteen months after the entry of the a mensa decree, where the sole ground for the a vinculo decree

is that by reason of the lapse of sufficient time the basis of the a mensa decree has ripened into a ground for divorce a vinculo. A copy of the supplemental bill shall be served in accordance with Rule 1-321. No in personam relief shall be granted on such supplemental bill except to the extent jurisdiction to grant the same is validly reserved in the a mensa decree, or unless the party against whom such relief is sought is served so as to give the court personal jurisdiction over him. (Amended March 28, 1966; June 16, 1975, effective July 1, 1975; Apr. 6, 1984, effective July 1, 1984.)

Committee note. — Subsection 1 is intended to change the law set forth in the two Schwab cases, 93 Md. 382 and 96 Md. 592. See Smith v. Smith, 216 Md. 141, 140 A.2d 58 (1958).

d. *Ne exeat — Affidavit required.* In an action involving alimony or support of children the writ of *ne exeat* may issue upon petition verified by or on behalf of the person applying for the writ, stating that the person against whom the writ is to be directed intends to leave the State and place himself beyond the jurisdiction of the court.

e. *Child custody.* In any case wherein the custody of a minor child is involved, the information required by Code, Family Law Article, § 9-209 (Uniform Child Custody Jurisdiction Act) need not be furnished unless and until it shall come to the attention of the court upon the suggestion of a party or otherwise that a court of another state or foreign country has or might have jurisdiction over or an interest in the issue of custody, in which case, the court shall order the parties to file a verified amended or supplemental pleading or a separate affidavit which fully complies with the requirements of Code, Family Law Article, § 9-209. (Added Dec. 17, 1975, effective Jan. 1, 1976.)

f. *Financial statements to be filed.* 1. Generally. Except as otherwise provided in subsection f.2. of this Rule, current financial statements under affidavit, itemizing assets and liabilities and showing income (after taxes) and expenses, shall be filed by the litigants in all actions in which alimony, maintenance, or support, including child support, is claimed, unless an agreement thereon is alleged to exist. The statements shall be attached to all pleadings that make such claims and to responsive pleadings thereon and shall be considered a part of the formal pleadings.

2. Child support. If the establishment or modification of child support in accordance with the guidelines set forth in Code, Family Law Article, §§ 12-201 — 12-204 is the only support issue in the action and no party seeks an amount of support outside of the guidelines, the required financial statement need contain only the information relevant to the computation of child support in accordance with the guidelines. (Added Oct. 1, 1980, effective Jan. 1, 1981; amended Jan. 10, 1995, effective Feb. 1, 1995; June 5, 1996, effective Jan. 1, 1997.)

Source. — This Rule is former Rule S72.

Editor's note. — An Order dated June 5, 1996, effective Jan. 1, 1997, renumbered this Rule, which was formerly Rule S72.

For present provisions regarding mentally incompetent defendants in an action for absolute divorce, see § 7-103 (a) (6) of the Family Law Article.

Construction of section c 2. — The Court of Special Appeals reads nothing into section c 2 of this Rule beyond its expressly stated limitations. Furman v. Glading, 36 Md. App. 574, 374 A.2d 414 (1977), aff'd, 282 Md. 200, 383 A.2d 398 (1978).

Essential facts occurring after suit was filed may not be brought in by amendment. Lukat v. Lukat, 21 Md. App. 354, 319 A.2d 818 (1974).

Judicial admissions. — The facts and averments as to the properties made in the statements required by this Rule and Rule 9-206 constitute judicial admissions and may be considered as evidence without the necessity for the formal introduction at trial of these documents. Beck v. Beck, 112 Md. App. 197, 684 A.2d 878 (1996).

Right to request writ of ne exeat. — Under article 5 of the Declaration of Rights, the inhabitants of this State are entitled to the common law as it existed in England on July 4, 1776, assuming of course, Maryland has made no change in the intervening period of time.

One of the rights to which the inhabitants of Maryland are entitled is, in an appropriate case, to request a court of chancery to issue a writ of ne exeat. Jackson v. Jackson, 15 Md. App. 615, 292 A.2d 145 (1972).

In Maryland there is no statute nor constitutional provision expressly modifying the common law with respect to the writ of ne exeat. Jackson v. Jackson, 15 Md. App. 615, 292 A.2d 145 (1972).

Writ of ne exeat in nature of injunction. — Although a writ of ne exeat has somewhat different qualities from an injunction, a part of it ordering that the defendant not leave the State of Maryland without permission of the court appears to be in the nature of an injunction and therefore, immediately appealable prior to the passage of a final decree. Jackson v. Jackson, 15 Md. App. 615, 292 A.2d 145 (1972).

A writ of ne exeat cannot be issued prior to the time there has been a default under a decree for alimony or support. Jackson v. Jackson, 15 Md. App. 615, 292 A.2d 145 (1972).

Alimony and support for children are not debts within the constitutional provisions prohibiting imprisonment for debt. Jackson v. Jackson, 15 Md. App. 615, 292 A.2d 145 (1972).

Rule 9-204. Default of defendant — Order of default — Testimony.

Where a defendant is in default in proceedings for divorce, annulment, or alimony an order of default may be entered pursuant to Rule 2-613. A judgment may be entered pursuant to Rule 2-613 (e) only upon testimony. (Art. 16, § 22, G.E.R. 10A; amended June 30, 1973, effective July 1, 1973; Apr. 6, 1984, effective July 1, 1984; June 5, 1996, effective Jan. 1, 1997.)

Cross references. — See Rule 2-122.

Committee note. — A default judgment cannot be entered against a defendant under

disability. See Rule 2-202 (c).

Source. — This Rule is former Rule S73.

Editor's note. — An Order dated June 5, 1996, effective Jan. 1, 1997, renumbered this Rule, which was formerly Rule S73.

Rule 9-204.1. Educational seminar.

(a) *Applicability.* This Rule applies in actions in which child support, custody, or visitation are involved and the court determines to send the parties to an educational seminar designed to minimize disruptive effects of separation and divorce on the lives of children.

Cross references. — Code, Family Law Article, § 7-103.2.

(b) *Order to attend seminar.* (1) Subject to subsection (b) (2) of this Rule and as allowed or required by the case management plan required by Rule 16-202 b., the court may order the parties to attend an educational seminar within the time set forth in the plan. The content of the seminar shall be as prescribed in section (c) of this Rule. If a party who has been ordered to attend a seminar fails to do so, the court may not use its contempt powers to compel attendance or to punish the party for failure to attend, but may consider the failure as a factor in determining custody and visitation.

(2) A party who (A) is incarcerated, (B) lives outside the State in a jurisdiction where a comparable seminar or course is not available, or (C) establishes good cause for exemption may not be ordered to attend the seminar.

Committee note. — Code, Family Law Article, § 7-103.2 (c) (2) (v) prohibits exemption based on evidence of domestic violence, child abuse, or neglect.

(c) *Content.* The seminar shall consist of one or two sessions, totaling six hours. Topics shall include:

(1) the emotional impact of divorce on children and parents;

(2) developmental stages of children and the effects of divorce on children at different stages;

(3) changes in the parent-child relationship;

(4) discipline;

(5) transitions between households;

(6) skill-building in

(A) parental communication with children and with each other,

(B) explaining divorce to children,

(C) problem-solving and decision-making techniques,

(D) conflict resolution,

(E) coping strategies,

(F) helping children adjust to family change,

(G) avoiding inappropriate interactions with the children, and

(H) developing constructive parenting arrangements; and

(7) resources available in cases of domestic violence, child abuse, and neglect.

(d) *Scheduling.* The provider of the seminar shall establish scheduling procedures so that parties in actions where domestic violence, child abuse, or neglect is alleged do not attend the seminar at the same time and so that any party who does not wish to attend a seminar at the same time as the opposing party does not have to do so.

(e) *Costs.* The fee for the seminar shall be set in accordance with Code, Courts Article, § 7-202. Payment may be compelled by order of court and assessed among the parties as the court may direct. For good cause, the court may waive payment of the fee. (Added Jan. 13, 1998, effective July 1, 1998.)

Source. — This Rule is new.

Rule 9-205. Mediation of child custody and visitation disputes.

a. *Scope of rule.* This Rule applies to any case under this Chapter in which the custody of or visitation with a minor child is in issue, including an initial action to determine custody or visitation, an action to modify an existing order or judgment as to custody or visitation, and a petition for contempt by reason of non-compliance with an order or judgment governing custody or visitation.

b. *Duty of court.* (1) Promptly after an action subject to this Rule is at issue, the court shall determine whether:

(A) both parties are represented by counsel;

(B) mediation of the dispute as to custody or visitation is appropriate and would likely be beneficial to the parties or the child; and

(C) a properly qualified mediator is available to mediate that dispute.

(2) If counsel for a party or a child represents to the Court in good faith that there is a genuine issue of physical or sexual abuse of the party or child, and that, as a result, mediation would be inappropriate, the court shall not order mediation.

(3) If the court concludes that mediation is appropriate and feasible, it shall enter an order requiring the parties to mediate the custody or visitation dispute. The order may stay some or all further proceedings in the action pending the mediation on terms and conditions set forth in the order.

Cross references. — With respect to qualifications and selection of mediators, see Rule 17-104. With respect to subsection b (2) of this Rule, see Rule 1-341 and Rules 3.1 and 3.3 of the Maryland Rules of Professional Conduct.

c. *Scope of mediation.* (1) The court may not in its initial order require the parties to attend more than two mediation sessions; however, for good cause shown and upon the recommendation of the mediator, the court may order up to two additional mediation sessions. The parties may voluntarily continue with further mediation.

(2) Mediation under this Rule shall be limited to the issues of custody and visitation unless the parties and their counsel agree otherwise in writing.

d. *Agreement.* If the parties reach a proposed agreement on some or all of the disputed issues, the mediator shall prepare a written draft of the agreement and send copies of it to the parties and their attorneys. If the agreement is approved as submitted or as modified by the parties, the mediator shall submit it to the court for approval and entry as an order. If no agreement is reached or the mediator determines that mediation is inappropriate, the mediator shall so advise the court but shall not state the reasons.

e. *Pendente lite relief.* If the court does not order mediation or the case is returned to the court after mediation without an agreement as to all issues in the case, the court shall promptly schedule the case for hearing on any requested pendente lite relief not covered by a mediation agreement.

f. *Confidentiality.* Except for an agreement submitted to the court pursuant to section d of this Rule, no statement or writing made in the course of mediation is subject to discovery or admissible in evidence in any proceeding under this Chapter unless the parties and their counsel agree otherwise in writing. Neither the mediator nor an attorney may be called as a witness in such a proceeding to give evidence regarding the mediation or custody or visitation.

Committee note. — See Code, Family Law Article, § 5-701 et seq. for provisions that require the reporting of suspected child abuse.

g. *Costs.* Payment of the compensation, fees, and costs of a mediator may be compelled by order of court and assessed among the parties as the court may direct. In the order for mediation, the court may waive payment of the compensation, fees, and costs.

h. *Court approval of mediator.* The court shall develop and maintain a list of qualified mediators approved by it. The court shall appoint a mediator from that list unless the parties agree upon another mediator approved by the court. (Amended June 28, 1990, effective July 1, 1990; June 5, 1996, effective Jan. 1, 1997; Oct. 5, 1998, effective Jan. 1, 1999.)

Source. — This Rule is former Rule S73A.

Effect of amendments. — The 1996 amendment substituted "Chapter" for "Subtitle" in a. and f.; and rewrote the Source note. The 1998 amendment added the present first sentence in the cross references note in b.

Editor's note. — An Order dated June 5, 1996, effective Jan. 1, 1997, renumbered this Rule, which was formerly Rule S73A.

Rule 9-206. Joint statements of marital and non-marital property.

a. *When required.* When a monetary award or other relief pursuant to Code, Family Law Article, § 8-205 is at issue, the parties shall file a joint statement listing all property owned by one or both of them. The statement shall be filed at least ten days before the scheduled trial date or by any earlier date fixed by the court.

b. *Contents.* The joint statement shall be in the form set forth in section c of this Rule and shall contain:

1. a listing of each item of property that the parties agree is "marital property" as defined by Code, Family Law Article, § 8-201;

2. a listing of each item of property that the parties agree is not "marital property" because the property was acquired before the marriage, the property was acquired by inheritance or gift from a third person, the property is excluded by valid agreement of the parties, or the property is directly traceable to any of these sources;

3. a listing of each item of property that the parties cannot agree to classify as marital or non-marital property; and

4. as to each item of property:

(a) an agreed statement of how the property is titled or a statement that the title is in dispute,

(b) the agreed fair market value of the property or a statement that the fair market value is in dispute,

(c) if title or fair market value is in dispute, each party's assertion concerning title or fair market value of the property; and

(d) the nature and amounts of any liens or encumbrances on the property or debt directly attributable to the property.

c. *Form of property statement.* The joint statement shall be substantially in the following form:

JOINT STATEMENT OF PARTIES CONCERNING MARITAL AND NON-MARITAL PROPERTY

1. The parties agree that the following property is "marital property" as defined by Code, Family Law Article, § 8-201:

Description of Property	How Titled	Fair Market Value	Liens, Encumbrances, or Debt Directly Attributable

2. The parties agree that the following property is not marital property because the property (a) was acquired by one party before marriage, (b) was acquired by one party by inheritance or gift from a third person, (c) has been excluded by valid agreement, or (d) is directly traceable to any of these sources:

Description of Property	Reason Why Non-marital	How Titled	Fair Market Value	Liens, Encumbrances, or Debt Directly Attributable

3. The parties are not in agreement as to whether the following property is marital or non-marital:

Description of Property	How Titled	Fair Market Value	Liens, Encumbrances, or Debt Directly Attributable

Date ....
                                      Plaintiff or Attorney
Date ....
                                      Defendant or Attorney

INSTRUCTIONS:

1. If the parties do not agree concerning the title or value of any property, the parties shall set forth in the appropriate column a statement that the title or value is in dispute and each party's assertion relative to how the property is titled or the fair market value.

2. In listing property that the parties agree is non-marital because the property is directly traceable to any of the listed sources of non-marital property, the parties shall specify the source to which the property is traceable.

d. *Procedure.* At least 30 days before the joint statement is due to be filed, each party shall prepare and serve on the other party a proposed statement in the form set forth in section c of this Rule. At least 15 days before the joint statement is due, the plaintiff shall sign and serve on the defendant for approval and signature a proposed joint statement that fairly reflects the positions of the parties. Within the time prescribed in section a of this Rule the defendant shall file the joint statement, which shall be either signed by the defendant or accompanied by a written explanation of the specific reasons why it is not signed by the defendant.

e. *Sanctions.* If a party fails to comply with this Rule, the court, on motion or on its own initiative, may enter any orders in regard to the noncompliance that are just, including:

(1) an order that the classification of property as marital or non-marital shall be taken to be established for the purpose of the action in accordance with the statement filed by the complying party;

(2) an order refusing to allow the noncomplying party to oppose designated allegations on the other party's statement filed pursuant to this Rule, or prohibiting the noncomplying party from introducing designated matters in evidence.

Instead of any order or in addition thereto, the court, after opportunity for hearing, shall require the noncomplying party or the attorney advising the

31

noncompliance or both of them to pay the reasonable expenses, including attorney's fees, caused by the noncompliance, unless the court finds that the noncompliance was substantially justified or that other circumstances make an award of expense unjust. (Amended June 5, 1996, effective Jan. 1, 1997.)

Committee note. — The Joint Statement of Marital and Non-marital Property is not intended as a substitute for discovery in domestic relations cases.

Source. — This Rule is former Rule S74.

Effect of amendments. — The 1996 amendment rewrote the Source note.

Editor's note. — An Order dated June 5, 1996, effective Jan. 1, 1997, renumbered this Rule, which was formerly Rule S74.

Judicial admissions. — The facts and averments as to the properties made in the statements required by this Rule and Rule 9-203 constitute judicial admissions and may be considered as evidence without the necessity for the formal introduction at trial of these documents. Beck v. Beck, 112 Md. App. 197, 684 A.2d 878 (1996).

Rule 9-207. Referral of matters to masters.

a. *Referral.* (1) As of course. In a court having a master appointed for the purpose, unless the court directs otherwise in a specific case, the clerk shall refer the following matters arising under this Chapter to the master as of course when a hearing has been requested or is required by law:

(A) Uncontested divorce, annulment, or alimony actions;

(B) Alimony pendente lite;

(C) Support of child pendente lite;

(D) Support of dependents;

(E) Preliminary or pendente lite possession or use of the family home or family-use personal property;

(F) Subject to Rule 9-205, custody of or visitation with children, including pendente lite relief, modification of an existing order or judgment, or contempt by reason of noncompliance with an order or judgment, following service of a show cause order upon the person alleged to be in contempt;

(G) Contempt by reason of noncompliance with an order or judgment relating to the payment of alimony or support or the possession or use of the family home or family-use personal property, following service of a show cause order upon the person alleged to be in contempt;

(H) Modification of an existing order or judgment as to the payment of alimony or support or the possession or use of the family home or family-use personal property;

(I) Counsel fees and assessment of court costs in any action or proceeding referred to a master under this Rule;

(J) Stay of an earnings withholding order; and

(K) In the seventh Judicial Circuit, all other domestic relations matters.

(2) By order. On motion of any party or on its own initiative, the court, by order, may refer to a master any other matter or issue arising under this Chapter that is not triable of right before a jury.

b. *Proceedings before master.* The master shall have the powers provided in Rule 2-541 (c) and shall conduct the hearing as provided in Rule 2-541 (d).

c. *Findings and recommendations.* The master shall prepare written recommendations, which shall include a brief statement of the master's findings and shall be accompanied by a proposed order. The master shall notify each party of the master's recommendations, either on the record at the conclusion of the hearing or by written notice served pursuant to Rule 1-321. In any matter referred or referrable as of course pursuant to subsection a (1) of this Rule, the written notice shall be given within three days after the conclusion of the hearing. In any other matter referred by order pursuant to subsection a (2) of this Rule, the written notice shall be given within 30 days after the conclusion of the hearing. Promptly upon notification to the parties, the master shall file the recommendations and proposed order with the court.

d. *Exceptions.* Within five days after recommendations are placed on the record or served pursuant to section c of this Rule, a party may file exceptions with the clerk. Within that period or within three days after service of the first exceptions, whichever is later, any other party may file exceptions. Exceptions shall be in writing and shall set forth the asserted error with particularity. Any matter not specifically set forth in the exceptions is waived unless the court finds that justice requires otherwise.

e. *Transcript.* A transcript shall be ordered and filed as required by Rule 2-541 (h) (2).

f. *Entry of orders.* (1) In general. Except as provided in subsections (2) and (3) of this section,

(A) the court shall not direct the entry of an order or judgment based upon the master's recommendations until the expiration of the time for filing exceptions, and, if exceptions are timely filed, until the court rules on the exceptions; and

(B) if exceptions are not timely filed, the court may direct the entry of the order or judgment as recommended by the master.

(2) Immediate orders as to pendente lite relief. Upon a finding by a master that extraordinary circumstances exist and a recommendation by the master that an order concerning pendente lite relief be entered immediately, the court may direct the entry of an immediate order after reviewing the file and any exhibits, reviewing the master's findings and recommendations, and affording the parties an opportunity for oral argument. The court may accept, reject, or modify the master's recommendations. An order entered under this subsection remains subject to a later determination by the court on exceptions.

(3) Contempt orders. On the recommendation by the master that an individual be found in contempt, the court may hold a hearing and direct the entry of an order at any time.

g. *Hearing on exceptions.* (1) Generally. The court shall hear and decide exceptions in accordance with Rule 2-541 (i).

(2) When hearing to be held. A hearing on exceptions, if timely requested, shall be held within 60 days after the filing of the exceptions unless the parties otherwise agree in writing. If a transcript cannot be completed in time for the scheduled hearing and the parties cannot agree to an extension of time, each party shall file, at least five days before the hearing, a written proffer of the evidence on which the party intends to rely. The court may then use either the proffers or the electronic recording in lieu of the transcript at the hearing.

h. *Costs.* The assessment and payment of costs shall be in accordance with Rule 2-541 (j). (Added June 4, 1991, effective July 1, 1991; amended June 5, 1996, effective Jan. 1, 1997.)

Cross references. — See, Code, Family Law Article, § 10-131, prescribing certain time limits when a stay of an earnings withholding order is requested.

Source. — This Rule is former Rule S74A.

Effect of amendments. — The 1996 amendment substituted "Chapter" for "Subtitle" in the introductory language of a. (1) and in a. (2); substituted "Rule 9-205" for "Rule S73A" in a. (1) (F); and rewrote the Source note.

Editor's note. — An Order dated June 5, 1996, effective Jan. 1, 1997, renumbered this Rule, which was formerly Rule S74A.

Construction with other Rules. — Additional three days granted under Rule 1-203(d) are not to be aggregated with the five days provided under section (d) of this Rule to determine whether weekends and holidays are to be included in determining whether exceptions were timely filed. Kosinski v. Evans, 102 Md. App. 595, 650 A.2d 1374 (1994).

Purpose. — Former Rule S74A (see now this Rule) was adopted in 1991 for the purpose of streamlining and expediting the procedures for filing exceptions in domestic relations cases in an effort to address certain issues regarding Rule 2-541 raised in Stach v. Stach, 83 Md. App. 36, 573 A.2d 409 (1990). Morales v. Morales, 111 Md. App. 628, 683 A.2d 1124 (1996).

This Rule incorporates the use of masters in domestic relations matters. Under this Rule and Rule 2-541, masters have the power to issue subpoenas, administer oaths to witnesses, rule on admissibility of evidence, examine witnesses, conduct a hearing, recommend sanctions to the court, and make findings of fact and conclusions of law. Miller v. Bosley, 113 Md. App. 381, 688 A.2d 45 (1997).

Immediate order awarding custody of children. — The court may direct the entry of an immediate order awarding custody of children based upon a master's recommendations, even when exceptions to the master's recommendations have been timely filed and a hearing on those exceptions requested. Wise-Jones v. Jones, 117 Md. App. 489, 700 A.2d 852 (1997).

Trial court erred in entering an immediate order modifying custody of the parties' children based on master's recommendations, where the master did not make any findings of fact, but merely provided that custody should be granted to appellee. Wise-Jones v. Jones, 117 Md. App. 489, 700 A.2d 852 (1997).

A judge may not issue a child custody order based on a master's recommendations until after the judge reviews the file, exhibits and master's findings, and affords an opportunity for oral argument; and the judge must affix his signature to the order. Wise-Jones v. Jones, 117 Md. App. 489, 700 A.2d 852 (1997).

Oral delivery of recommendations constitutes notice. — Once the master orally delivers his recommendations on the record, the parties are on notice of the recommendations, and the time for filing begins to run; the issuance of subsequent written notice does not act to cancel the fact that the parties already are on notice (interpreting former Rule S74A). Morales v. Morales, 111 Md. App. 628, 683 A.2d 1124 (1996).

Notification and the filing and service of the written recommendations are distinct items, and this Rule contemplates that the written recommendations shall be filed after notification to the parties (interpreting former Rule S74A). Morales v. Morales, 111 Md. App. 628, 683 A.2d 1124 (1996).

Standard of review. — After an exceptions review, the court must subject the master's first-level fact finding to a clearly erroneous standard. The chancellor is then charged with exercising independent judgment concerning the proper conclusion to be reached from those well found facts. Simply put, the trial judge may not blindly accept the master's recommendations. Miller v. Bosley, 113 Md. App. 381, 688 A.2d 45 (1997).

In all cases lacking timely exceptions, any claim that the master's findings of fact were clearly erroneous is waived. Because no exceptions were filed and to the extent that the master made first-level findings of fact, the court, the chancellor, and the parties must accept those facts as established for purposes of the pertinent proceedings leading to the appeal. Miller v. Bosley, 113 Md. App. 381, 688 A.2d 45 (1997).

Effect of failure to predicate recommendations on finding of "extraordinary circumstances." — Where the master did not make the requisite finding that extraordinary circumstances existed, although he did recommend an immediate change of custody, the court concluded that the master's failure to predicate his recommendation on a finding of "extraordinary circumstances" prevented disposition under section (f) (2). Miller v. Bosley, 113 Md. App. 381, 688 A.2d 45 (1997).

Judge may not abdicate responsibilities. — Once the judge is called into the fray, he or she may not abdicate his or her responsibility to review the order and insure that a sufficient basis for the recommended order exists. Miller v. Bosley, 113 Md. App. 381, 688 A.2d 45 (1997).

For the purposes of a section (f) (2) hearing, a trial judge, without benefit of a transcript, must accept the sufficiency of the master's first-level factual findings. This, however, does not unburden the chancellor of his or her obligation to exercise independent judgment to insure that the proper conclusion is reached based on those necessarily accepted facts. Miller v. Bosley, 113 Md. App. 381, 688 A.2d 45 (1997).

Power to detain. — The phrase "regulate all proceedings," as used in Rule 2-541 (c), does not confer upon the master the power to hold someone in custody pending judicial review of a master's recommendation for immediate incarceration; to hold that the Rule implicitly includes the power to detain, because such power is inherent in the authority conferred upon a master to "regulate all proceedings" at a hearing, would engraft upon the Rule a meaning not evident from the plain text and would be wholly inconsistent with the advisory, clerical, and ministerial functions that masters have traditionally performed. Wiegmann v. State, 118 Md. App. 317, 702 A.2d 928 (1997), aff'd, 350 Md. 585, 714 A.2d 841 (1998).

This Rule and Rule 2-541 do not grant express or implied power to a domestic master to hold a litigant against his will after a non-support hearing, although masters are authorized to conduct evidentiary hearings and to make findings of fact and recommendations to the circuit court. Wiegmann v. State, 118 Md. App. 317, 702 A.2d 928 (1997), aff'd, 350 Md. 585, 714 A.2d 841 (1998).

Section (f) (2) hearings. — A section (f) (2) hearing requires that the judge intervene and determine the correctness of the entire master's recommendation. Miller v. Bosley, 113 Md. App. 381, 688 A.2d 45 (1997).

The plain meaning of section (f) (2) places the entire propriety of the pendente lite award before the court at the hearing. In other words, the scope of the section (f) (2) hearing is not limited to a determination of the propriety of immediate relief. Miller v. Bosley, 113 Md. App. 381, 688 A.2d 45 (1997).

Section (f) (2) requires that the judge conduct a hearing before granting the order based on the master's recommendations. Miller v. Bosley, 113 Md. App. 381, 688 A.2d 45 (1997).

Transcript of master's hearing. — A transcript of the master's hearing will usually not be available at a section (f) (2) hearing due to the immediacy of the chancellor's hearing necessitated by the recommended relief. The exceptions hearing procedures, like section (f) (2), contemplate review of the file and exhibits before the master, but ordinarily also require that the excepting party provide a transcript of the master's hearing. Miller v. Bosley, 113 Md. App. 381, 688 A.2d 45 (1997).

Despite the lack of transcript, the standard of review at section (f) (2) hearings is the same as that governing an exceptions hearing in many ways. When exceptions to the report and recommendations of a master are filed, the chancellor must exercise independent judgment to determine the proper result. Miller v. Bosley, 113 Md. App. 381, 688 A.2d 45 (1997).

Rule 9-208. Testimony.

a. *Generally.* In an action for divorce, annulment or alimony, no final decree shall be entered except upon testimony. In an uncontested case, testimony shall be taken before an examiner or master unless the court directs otherwise. Testimony not taken before an examiner or master or in open court may not be used as evidence in such an action unless otherwise ordered by the court for good cause. (Amended Sept. 15, 1961; Oct. 1, 1980, effective Jan. 1, 1981; Oct. 6, 1981, effective Jan. 1, 1982; June 4, 1982, effective July 1, 1982; Mar. 3, 1987, effective July 1, 1987; June 10, 1996, effective Jan. 1, 1997.)

Cross references. — See Rules 2-541 and 2-542. See also Rule 2-414 and MYERBERG, THE PRACTICAL ASPECTS OF DIVORCE PRACTICE, Second Edition, (1961) pp. 132-133.

Committee note. — Under this section, where a witness will not be available for testimony before an examiner, an order of court should be obtained to authorize the taking of such testimony before some other person for use as evidence in the action.

b. *Default cases — Over thirty days old.* Where testimony before an examiner or master in an action for divorce, annulment, or alimony has been taken more than 30 days prior to the time the decree is presented for signature, an affidavit of non-military service shall be filed by the plaintiff. (Amended Oct. 1, 1980, effective Jan. 1, 1981; Oct. 6, 1981, effective Jan. 1, 1982; June 4, 1982, effective July 1, 1982; Mar. 3, 1987, effective July 1, 1987; June 10, 1996, effective Jan. 1, 1997.)

Cross references. — For requirements of corroboration in divorce actions, see Code, FL § 7-101 (b).

Committee note. — In considering a suggestion from the Bar that the necessity for military affidavits should be eliminated in every sort of proceeding, the Committee concluded that aside from the question of whether it is legally possible to eliminate the military affidavit, the continued existence of the draft, and the various programs of temporary active duty military service would seem to make desirable the retention of the military affidavit requirement. The 1957 Maryland Code does not contain the content of the Soldiers' and Sailors' Civil Relief Act (Laws 1941, ch. 710) but merely notes that it expired October, 1952. For affidavits of military service, see 50 U.S.C. § 520. Article 87A, § 5 (1951 Code), contained a similar provision. See also Opinions of the Attorney General (Md.), The Daily Record, December 17, 1958.

c. *Stale testimony.* In an action for divorce, annulment, or alimony in which the testimony has been concluded for more than 90 days without entry of a final decree, a final decree may not be entered until supported by additional testimony justifying the conclusion that there has been no substantial change since the prior testimony was concluded. (Added Oct. 1, 1980, effective Jan. 1, 1981; amended Oct. 6, 1981, effective Jan. 1, 1982; June 4, 1982, effective July 1, 1982; Mar. 3, 1987, effective July 1, 1987; June 5, 1996, effective Jan. 1, 1997.)

Source. — This Rule is former Rule S75.

Effect of amendments. — The 1996 amendment added the Source note.

Editor's note. — An Order dated June 5, 1996, effective Jan. 1, 1997, renumbered this Rule, which was formerly Rule S75.

Intent of Rule. — This Rule is intended to ensure that nothing in the nature of reconciliation, resumption of cohabitation, or other event that would render the granting of a divorce inappropriate has occurred since testimony was taken. Noffsinger v. Noffsinger, 95 Md. App. 265, 620 A.2d 415, cert. denied, 331 Md. 197, 627 A.2d 539 (1993).

Applicability. — Section c of this Rule clearly applies only to actions for "divorce, annulment, or alimony," and does not apply to hearings on marital property issues. Davis v. Davis, 97 Md. App. 1, 627 A.2d 17 (1993), aff'd, 335 Md. 699, 646 A.2d 365 (1994).

This Rule has no applicability to and no effect upon the validity of a marital property determination. Davis v. Davis, 335 Md. 699, 646 A.2d 365 (1994).

Neither § 8-203(a) of the Family Law Article nor section c of this Rule is jurisdictional in nature and a trial court's failure to comply with either provision has no effect upon the power of the court to render a valid and binding judgment. Davis v. Davis, 335 Md. 699, 646 A.2d 365 (1994).

A divorce decree sub judice was a final appealable judgment, where the remaining property issue had no effect on the finality of the decree; therefore, because husband did not file a notice of appeal until over 19 months after the court entered the divorce decree, he was precluded from challenging the validity of that decree under section c. of this Rule. Davis v. Davis, 97 Md. App. 1, 627 A.2d 17 (1993), aff'd, 335 Md. 699, 646 A.2d 365 (1994).

Error held waived. — Error was waived where neither party raised the issue of stale evidence or brought it to the attention of the court, where neither party requested that additional evidence be taken, and where neither party moved to vacate, alter, or amend the judgment. Noffsinger v. Noffsinger, 95 Md.

App. 265, 620 A.2d 415, cert. denied, 331 Md.
197, 627 A.2d 539 (1993).

Rule 9-209. Annulment — Criminal conviction.

When a court shall convict one or both of the spouses of bigamy or of marrying within any prohibited degree, the judgment of conviction shall serve as an annulment of the unlawful marriage, provided that there shall be recorded at the instance of any interested person on the records of the circuit court of the same county, a complete transcript of the docket entries in the criminal proceedings leading to said judgment of conviction. (Art. 62, § 16; amended July 1, 1974; Apr. 6, 1984, effective July 1, 1984; June 5, 1996, effective Jan. 1, 1997.)

Cross references. — For within what degrees of kindred or affinity marriages to be void, see Family Law Article, §§ 2-201 and 2-202. For crime of bigamy, see Article 27, § 18. For crime of unlawful marriage, see Family Law Article, § 2-202.

Source. — This Rule is former Rule S76.

Effect of amendments. — The 1996 amendment added the Source note.

Editor's note. — An Order dated June 5, 1996, effective Jan. 1, 1997, renumbered this Rule, which was formerly Rule S76.

Maryland Law Review. — For article discussing void and voidable marriages in Maryland and their annulment, see 2 Md. L. Rev. 211 (1938).

For article discussing fifteen years of change in Maryland marriage and annulment law and domestic relations procedures, see 13 Md. L. Rev. 128 (1953).

History of statutory source. — See Townsend v. Morgan, 192 Md. 168, 63 A.2d 743 (1949).

Rule 9-210. Decree.

a. *Revocation of a mensa divorce — Joint application.* A divorce *a mensa et thoro* may be revoked at any time by the court granting it, upon the joint application of the parties to be discharged from the operation of the decree. (Art. 16, § 25.)

b. *Incorporation of agreement.* A deed, agreement or settlement between husband and wife as described in Art. 16, Sec. 28 of the Annotated Code of Maryland may be received in evidence and made a part of the record in an action for divorce, annulment or alimony and may be incorporated, insofar as the court may deem proper, into the decree. (Amended June 5, 1996, effective Jan. 1, 1997.)

Cross references. — See Article III, § 38, Maryland Constitution. See also Koger v. Koger, 217 Md. 372, 142 A.2d 599 (1958); Weiss v. Meinicove, 218 Md. 571, 147 A.2d 763 (1959). For other powers of court as to such decrees, see Code, Family Law Article, §§ 1-201 and 1-203.

Source. — This Rule is former Rule S77.

Effect of amendments. — The 1996 amendment added the Source note.

Editor's note. — An Order dated June 5, 1996, effective Jan. 1, 1997, renumbered this Rule, which was formerly Rule S77.

Former Article 16, § 28, referred to in section b of this Rule was repealed by Acts 1984, ch. 296, § 1, effective October 1, 1984. For present provisions derived from former Article 16, § 28, see FL §§ 8-101 through 8-103.

For present provisions regarding the revocation of a limited divorce, see § 7-102 of the Family Law Article.

Incorporation of separation agreement. — Where a separation agreement was incorporated into a divorce decree, the provisions with respect to child support became as much a part of the decree as if set forth therein in haec verba. Luhmann v. Luhmann, 37 Md. App. 185, 376 A.2d 1141 (1977); Hamilos v. Hamilos, 52 Md. App. 488, 450 A.2d 1316 (1982), aff'd sub nom. Johnston v. Johnston, 297 Md. 48, 465 A.2d 436, aff'd, 297 Md. 99, 465 A.2d 445 (1983).

When incorporation accomplished. — Incorporation of a settlement agreement is accomplished when, and to the extent that, the court refers to or identifies the agreement, or the parts of it to be incorporated, and either expressly states that it is to be incorporated into the judgment or otherwise makes clear that its provisions are to be regarded not merely as covenants of the parties but also as court directives. Ruppert v. Fish, 84 Md. App. 665, 581 A.2d 828 (1990).

Partial incorporation. — Where there is only a partial incorporation, those parts of the agreement not incorporated retain their status as contractual provisions, and while they may, in some instances, necessarily be affected or limited by the judgment and they may, in turn, affect or explain parts of the judgment, absent any clear inconsistency with the judgment, they are not abrogated by the judgment. Ruppert v. Fish, 84 Md. App. 665, 581 A.2d 828 (1990).

Effect of incorporation of property settlement. — Where the property settlement agreement is presented to the court for approval and is approved by the court and incorporated in the divorce decree, the validity of the agreement is conclusively established and the doctrine of res judicata operates so as to preclude a collateral attack on the agreement. Johnston v. Johnston, 297 Md. 48, 465 A.2d 436 (1983).

Separation agreement, incorporated but not merged, remains separate, enforceable contract. — Where the parties intend a separation agreement to be incorporated but not merged in the divorce decree, the agreement remains a separate, enforceable contract and is not superseded by the decree. Johnston v. Johnston, 297 Md. 48, 465 A.2d 436 (1983).

Court to examine whole incorporated agreement. — In interpreting a decree that incorporates an agreement, a court should examine the whole agreement and not just those provisions specifically incorporated by reference. Goldberg v. Goldberg, 290 Md. 204, 428 A.2d 469 (1981).

Incorporation does not transform contractual payments into alimony. — Where the parties do not intend an award of technical (and thus modifiable) alimony, but rather provide for contractual spousal support in the separation compact, the fact that the agreement, or that provision of it, is incorporated into a decree does not operate to transform the contractual payments into technical alimony. Goldberg v. Goldberg, 290 Md. 204, 428 A.2d 469 (1981).

Incorporated contractual obligations subject to court's enforcement powers. — Once made a part of the decree, contractual obligations become subject to the enforcement powers of the court of equity, not the least of which of course is the contempt power. Goldberg v. Goldberg, 290 Md. 204, 428 A.2d 469 (1981).

Once incorporated, the contractual provisions become part of the decree, modifiable by the court where appropriate and enforceable through contempt proceedings. Johnston v. Johnston, 297 Md. 48, 465 A.2d 436 (1983).

TITLE 10. GUARDIANS AND OTHER FIDUCIARIES

Editor's note. — The Court of Appeals, by Order dated June 5, 1996, effective January 1, 1997, rescinded Subtitles A, D, E, J, P, Q, R, T, U, V, W, Y, Z, BB, BD, BE, BG, BH, BJ, BL, BP, BQ, BR, BS, BW, and BY of Chapter 1100 of the Maryland Rules of Procedure, rescinded Subtitles P, BB, BQ, and BW of the Maryland District Rules, and rescinded Forms 22a, 23, 24, 25, and 26. The Order substituted for certain of the rules and forms rescinded new Title 9, Chapter 100, Title 10, Title 12, Title 13, Title 14, and Title 15 of the Maryland Rules of Procedure. Furthermore, the Order transferred, without readoption, Chapter 900, Chapter 1200, and Subtitles S, BU, and BV of Chapter 1100 of the Maryland Rules of Procedure and Chapter 1200 of the Maryland District Rules to be Title 9, Chapter 200, Title 11, and Title 16 of the Maryland Rules of Procedure. The Order provides that the new rules shall "apply to all actions commenced on or after January 1, 1997, and insofar as practicable, to all actions then pending."

Many of the cases in the notes to the various rules were decided prior to the 1996 revision. These cases have been retained under pertinent rules of this title where it is thought that such cases will be of value in interpreting the present rules.

A table of comparable rules, relating those rules rescinded effective January 1, 1997, to the revised rules in Title 9 through Title 16 is to be found in Volume 2 following the end of the Maryland Rules.

CHAPTER 100. GENERAL PROVISIONS.

Rule 10-101. Applicability of title; jurisdiction.

(a) *Applicability.* Except as otherwise provided by law, the rules in this Title apply to proceedings concerning: (1) the guardianship of minors and disabled persons or their property; (2) a fiduciary estate; and (3) the distribution of property to an absent or unknown person.

(b) *Scope of jurisdiction.* In proceedings under this Title, the court may exercise its jurisdiction generally or for a limited purpose. An investment in a common trust fund by a fiduciary administering an estate subject to the jurisdiction of a court does not bring the administration of the common trust fund under the jurisdiction of the court.

Cross references. — For the definition of "common trust fund," *see* Code, Financial Institutions Article, § 3-501 (b).

Committee note. — The rules in this Title do not apply to a guardian with the right to consent to adoption (Code, Family Law Article, § 5-301 *et seq.* and Title 9, Chapter 100 of these rules); a trustee appointed to foreclose a mortgage or deed of trust or to make a judicial sale (Title 14, Chapters 200 and 300 of these rules); a trustee of a recovery by a minor in tort (Code, Estates and Trusts Article, § 13-401 *et seq.*); a custodian of property under the Maryland Uniform Transfers to Minors Act (Code, Estates and Trusts Article, § 13-301 *et seq.*); or a receiver or assignee for the benefit of creditors (Title 13 of these Rules).

Source. — This Rule is derived in part from former Rule V71 and is in part new.

Rule 10-102. Applicability of Titles 1 and 2.

(a) *Applicability of Title 1.* Except as otherwise provided in this Title, the rules in Title 1 apply to this Title.

(b) *Applicability of Title 2.* Any interested person may obtain discovery in a contested matter pursuant to Title 2, Chapter 400 of these Rules, unless otherwise ordered by the court. Except as otherwise provided in this Title, a court may apply any of the rules in Title 2 as appropriate.

Source. — This Rule is new.

Rule 10-103. Definitions.

In this Title the following definitions apply except as expressly otherwise provided or as necessary implication requires:

(a) *Court.* "Court" means the circuit court for any county and, where it has jurisdiction, the Orphans' Court.

Cross references. — *See* Code, Estates and Trusts Article, § 13-105 for the jurisdiction of the Orphans' Court over guardians of the person of a minor and protective proceedings for minors. *See also* 92 Op. Atty. Gen. 009 (March 20, 1992).

(b) *Disabled person.* (1) In connection with a guardianship of the person, "disabled person" means a person, other than a minor, who, because of mental disability, disease, habitual drunkenness, or addiction to drugs, has been adjudged by a court to lack sufficient understanding or capacity to make or communicate responsible decisions concerning himself or herself, such as provisions for health care, food, clothing, or shelter, and who, as a result of this inability, requires a guardian of the person.

(2) In connection with a guardianship of property, "disabled person" means a person, other than a minor, (A) who has been adjudged by a court to be unable to manage his or her property and affairs effectively because of physical or mental disability, disease, habitual drunkenness, addiction to drugs, imprisonment, compulsory hospitalization, confinement, detention by a foreign power, or disappearance, (B) who has or may be entitled to property or benefits that require proper management, and (C) who, as a result of this inability, requires a guardian of the property.

Cross references. — Code, Estates and Trusts Article, §§ 13-101, 13-705 (b) and 13-201 (c).

(c) *Fiduciary.* "Fiduciary" means (1) a guardian of the property of a minor or disabled person, (2) a guardian of the person of a minor or disabled person to the extent that the guardian exercises control over any property of the minor or disabled person, (3) a trustee acting under any inter vivos or testamentary trust over which the court has been asked to assume or has assumed jurisdiction, (4) a person administering an estate under appointment by a court as a "committee," "conservator," or the like, and (5) a personal representative of a decedent to the extent provided in Rules 10-703 and 10-711.

(d) *Fiduciary estate.* "Fiduciary estate" means real or personal property administered by a fiduciary.

(e) *Heir.* "Heir" means a person who would be entitled under the law of this State to inherit property if, at the applicable time, the owner of the property had died intestate.

(f) *Interested person.* (1) In connection with a guardianship of the person or the authorization of emergency protective services, "interested person" means the minor or the disabled person; the guardian and heirs of that person; a governmental agency paying benefits to that person or a person or agency eligible to serve as guardian of the person under Code, Estates and Trusts Article, § 13-707; the Department of Veterans Affairs as directed by Code,

Estates and Trusts Article, § 13-801; and any other person designated by the court.

(2) In connection with a guardianship of the property or other fiduciary proceedings, "interested person" means a person who would be an interested person under subsection (f) (1) of this Rule and a current income beneficiary of the fiduciary estate; a fiduciary and co-fiduciary of the fiduciary estate; and the creator of the fiduciary estate.

(3) If an interested person is a minor or disabled person, "interested person" includes a fiduciary appointed for that person, or, if none, the parent or other person who has assumed responsibility for the interested person.

Cross references. — Code, Estates and Trusts Article, § 13-101 (j) and § 13-801.

(g) *Minor.* "Minor" means a person who is under the age of eighteen.

(h) *Public guardian.* "Public guardian" means a guardian who is the director of a local department of social services, the State Office on Aging, or an area agency on aging.

(i) *Temporary guardian.* "Temporary guardian" means (1) a person appointed under Rule 10-210 in a proceeding for emergency protective services, (2) a person who has been authorized to preserve and apply the property of a minor or alleged disabled person pending a hearing on a petition for guardianship, and (3) a guardian of the person or property appointed by the court pending the appointment of a substituted or successor guardian.

Cross references. — Code, Estates and Trusts Article, §§ 13-203 and 13-709 (c) (4).
Source. — This Rule is derived as follows:
Section (a) is derived from former Rule R70 a.
Section (b) is derived from former Rule R70 b, and Code, Estates and Trusts Article, §§ 13-201 (c) (1) and 13-705 (b).
Section (c) is derived in part from former Rule V70 b and is in part new.
Section (d) is new.
Section (e) is derived from former Rule R70 c.

Section (f). Subsection (1) is derived in part from former Rule R70 d and in part from Code, Estates and Trusts Article, § 13-707.
Subsection (2) is derived from former Rule V70 c.
Section (g) is derived from former Rule R70 e.
Section (h) is derived from Code, Estates and Trusts Article, § 13-707 (a) (10).
Section (i) is derived in part from Code, Estates and Trusts Article, §§ 13-203 and 13-709 and is in part new.

Rule 10-104. Show cause orders.

Except as provided in Rules 10-209 (b), 10-213, and 10-705, upon the filing of a petition, the court shall issue a show cause order directing a person to show cause in writing on or before a specified date why the court should not take the action described in the order. Unless the court orders otherwise, the specified date shall be 20 days after the date prescribed for service in the order. The order shall also specify who is to be served and the method of service and, if a hearing is scheduled when the order is issued, the date, time, and place of the hearing. A copy of any related petition or document shall be served with a copy of the order. If required, the Advice of Rights form and the Notice to Interested Persons form shall also be served with the copy of the order. (Amended Feb. 10, 1998, effective July 1, 1998.)

Source. — This Rule is new.

Effect of amendments. — The 1998 amendment substituted "Notice" for "Advice" in the last sentence.

Rule 10-105. Waiver of notice.

(a) *Method of waiver.* An interested person other than a minor or disabled person may waive the right to any or all notices other than original notice by filing a signed waiver. A minor or disabled person may waive the right to any or all notices other than original notice by a waiver signed and filed by his or her attorney, which shall not be effective until approved by the court.

(b) *Revocation.* A waiver of notice may be revoked at any time by the filing of a revocation, which shall be effective from the date filed.

Source. — This Rule is derived from former Rule R70 f and Rule 6-126.

Rule 10-106. Appointment of attorney or investigator.

(a) *Appointment of attorney by the court.* Upon the filing of a petition for guardianship of the person or property of a disabled person or minor who is not represented by an attorney, the court shall promptly appoint an attorney for the disabled person and may appoint an attorney for the minor. The fee of an appointed attorney shall be fixed by the court and shall be paid out of the fiduciary estate or as the court shall direct. To the extent the estate is insufficient, the fee of an attorney appointed for a disabled person shall be paid by the State.

Cross references. — Code, Estates and Trusts Article, §§ 13-211 (b) and 13-705 (d). *See also* Rule 1.14 of the Maryland Lawyers' Rules of Professional Conduct with respect to the attorney's role and obligations.

(b) *Automatic termination of appointment; continuation of representation if public guardian appointed.* If no appeal is taken from a judgment dismissing the petition or appointing a guardian other than a public guardian, the attorney's appointment shall terminate automatically upon expiration of the time for filing an appeal unless the court orders otherwise. If a public guardian has been appointed for the disabled person, the court shall either continue the attorney's appointment or appoint another attorney to represent the disabled person before the Adult Public Guardianship Review Board.

Cross references. — Code, Family Law Article, § 14-404 (c) (2).

(c) *Investigator.* The court may appoint an independent investigator to investigate the facts of the case and report written findings to the court. The fee of an appointed investigator shall be fixed by the court and shall be paid out of the fiduciary estate or as the court shall direct. To the extent the estate is insufficient, the fee of an independent investigator appointed by the court shall be paid by the State.

Source. — This Rule is derived in part from former Rules R76 and V71 and is in part new.

Payment of costs and counsel fees in proceeding for construction of will. — The costs of the proceeding for construction of the will, including the fee of the trustee's counsel, may be paid from the assets of the trust estate, but not the fees of counsel for other parties, unless they were appointed by the court to represent infants or persons under some disability. Sollers v. Mercantile-Safe Deposit & Trust Co., 262 Md. 606, 278 A.2d 581 (1971).

Rule 10-107. Assessment and waiver of fees and costs — Guardianships.

(a) *Assessment.* Upon a determination on the merits of a petition to appoint a guardian, the court may assess the filing fee and other court costs against the assets of the fiduciary estate or against the petitioner.

(b) *Waiver.* The court shall waive final costs and fees if the court finds that the person against whom the costs are assessed is unable to pay them by reason of poverty. The person may seek the waiver at the conclusion of the case in accordance with Rule 1-325 (a). If the person was granted a waiver pursuant to that Rule and remains unable to pay the costs, the affidavit required by Rule 1-325 (a) need only recite the existence of the prior waiver and the person's continued inability to pay.

Source. — This Rule is in part new and in part derived from Rule 2-603 (e).

Rule 10-108. Orders.

(a) *Order appointing guardian.* An order appointing a guardian shall state:

(1) Whether the guardianship is of the property or person or both;

(2) The name of the minor or disabled person;

(3) The name, address, and telephone number of the guardian;

(4) The reason for the guardianship;

(5) The amount of the guardian's bond, or that the bond is waived;

(6) The date upon which any annual report of the guardian shall be filed; and

(7) The specific powers and duties of the guardian and any limitations on those powers or duties. The order shall recite the powers and duties of the guardian either expressly or by referring to the specific paragraphs of an applicable statute containing those powers and duties.

Cross references. — Code, Estates and Trusts Article, §§ 13-201 (b) and (c), 13-213, 13-214, 15-102, 13-705 (b), and 13-708.

(b) *Letters of guardianship.* A court may issue letters of guardianship of the property which shall contain a list of any restrictions on the powers of the guardian.

Cross references. — Code, Estates and Trusts Article, §§ 13-215 and 13-217.

(c) *Orders assuming jurisdiction over a fiduciary estate other than a guardianship.* An order assuming jurisdiction over a fiduciary estate other than a guardianship shall state whether the court has assumed full jurisdiction over the estate. If it has not assumed full jurisdiction over the estate or if jurisdiction is contrary to the provisions in the instrument, the order shall state the extent of the jurisdiction assumed. The order shall state the amount of the fiduciary's bond or that the bond is waived.

(d) *Modifications.* The court may modify any order of a continuing nature in a guardianship or fiduciary estate upon the petition of an interested person or on its own initiative, and after notice and opportunity for hearing.

Source. — This Rule is derived as follows: Section (a) is derived in part from Code, Estates and Trusts Article, §§ 13-208 and 13-708 and is in part new.

Section (b) is derived from former Rule V77 c 3.

Section (c) is derived from former Rules V71 f 1 and f 2.

Section (d) is derived in part from former Rule R78 b and is in part new.

Court of equity assumes jurisdiction in guardianship matters to protect those who, because of illness or other disability, are unable to care for themselves. Kicherer v. Kicherer, 285 Md. 114, 400 A.2d 1097 (1979).

In reality court is guardian; an individual who is given that title is merely an agent or arm of that tribunal in carrying out its sacred responsibility. Kicherer v. Kicherer, 285 Md. 114, 400 A.2d 1097 (1979).

Stipulation not deemed decree. — A stipulation by the parties as to disability is not a specific finding by the court, so as to comply with this Rule. Kicherer v. Kicherer, 285 Md. 114, 400 A.2d 1097 (1979).

Rule 10-109. Transfer of action.

(a) *Proceedings initiated in the Orphans' Court.* Upon the petition of an interested person, the Orphans' Court may transfer a guardianship or protective proceeding for a minor to the circuit court.

Cross references. — Code, Estates and Trusts Article, § 13-105 (a); 92 Op. Atty. Gen. 009 (March 20, 1992).

(b) *Other proceedings.* During the course of an action, the court, on its own initiative or on the petition of an interested person, may transfer the action to any other circuit court if the transfer (1) is in the best interest of the minor or alleged disabled person; or (2) serves the convenience of the guardian, fiduciary, and other interested persons and witnesses, is not inconsistent with the best interest of the minor or alleged disabled person, and serves the interest of justice.

Source. — This Rule is derived from former Rule R72 d and Code, Estates and Trusts Article, § 13-105 (a).

Rule 10-110. Combination of guardianship petitions.

A petition for the appointment of a guardian of the person of a minor or alleged disabled person may also include a request for the appointment of a guardian of the person's property, and vice versa.

Source. — This Rule is derived from former Rule R71 a.

CHAPTER 200. GUARDIAN OF PERSON.

Rule 10-201. Petition for appointment of a guardian of person.

(a) *Who may file.* An interested person may file a petition requesting a court to appoint a guardian of a minor or alleged disabled person.

(b) *Venue.* (1) Resident. If the minor or alleged disabled person is a resident of Maryland, the petition shall be filed in the county where (A) the minor or alleged disabled person resides or (B) the person has been admitted for the purpose of medical care or treatment to either a general or a special hospital which is not a State facility as defined in Code, Health-General Article, § 10-406 or a licensed private facility as defined in Code, Health-General Article, §§ 10-501 to 10-511.

(2) Nonresident. If the minor or alleged disabled person does not reside in this State, a petition for guardianship of the person may be filed in any county in which the person is physically present.

(c) *Contents.* The petition shall be captioned, "In the Matter of ..." [stating the name of the minor or alleged disabled person]. It shall be signed and verified by the petitioner, may contain a request for the guardianship of property, and shall contain at least the following information:

(1) The petitioner's name, address, age, and telephone number.

(2) The petitioner's familial or other relationship to the minor or alleged disabled person.

(3) Whether the person who is the subject of the petition is a minor or alleged disabled person, and, if an alleged disabled person, a brief description of the alleged disability and how it affects the alleged disabled person's ability to function.

(4) The reasons why the court should appoint a guardian of the person and, if the subject of the petition is a disabled person, allegations demonstrating an inability of that person to make or communicate responsible decisions concerning the person, including provisions for health care, food, clothing, or shelter, because of mental disability, disease, habitual drunkenness or addiction to drugs, and a description of less restrictive alternatives that have been attempted and have failed.

Cross references. — Code, Estates and Trusts Article, § 13-705 (b).

(5) An identification of any instrument nominating a guardian or constituting a durable power of attorney, with a copy attached to the petition, if possible, and, if not, an explanation of its absence.

Cross references. — Code, Estates and
Trusts Article, § 13-701.

(6) If a guardian or conservator has been appointed for the alleged disabled person in another proceeding, the name and address of the guardian or conservator and the court that appointed the guardian or conservator. If a guardianship or conservatorship proceeding was previously filed in any other court, the name and address of the court, the case number, if known, and whether the proceeding is still pending in that court.

(7) A list of (A) the name, age, sex, and address of the minor or alleged disabled person, (B) the name and address of the persons with whom the minor or disabled person resides, and (C) if the minor or alleged disabled person resides with the petitioner, the name and address of another person on whom service can be made.

(8) The name, address, telephone number, and nature of interest of all other interested persons and all other persons exercising control of the minor or alleged disabled person, to the extent known or reasonably ascertainable.

(9) If the minor or alleged disabled person is represented by an attorney, the name and address of the attorney.

(10) A statement that the certificates required by Rule 10-202 are attached, or, if not, an explanation of their absence.

(11) If the petition also seeks a guardianship of the property, the additional information required by Rule 10-301.

(12) A statement of the relief sought.

Source. — This Rule is derived as follows: *Section (a)* is derived from former Rule R71 a.
Section (b) is derived from former Rule R72 a and b.
Section (c) is derived in part from former Rule R73 a and in part from former Rule V71 c.

Rule 10-202. Physicians' certificates — Requirement and content.

(a) *To be attached to petition.* (1) Generally. If guardianship of the person of a disabled person is sought, the petitioner shall file with the petition signed and verified certificates of two physicians licensed to practice medicine in the United States, one of whom shall have examined the disabled person within 21 days before the filing of the petition. Each certificate shall state the name, address, and qualifications of the physician, a brief history of the physician's involvement with the disabled person, the date of the physician's last examination of the disabled person, and the physician's opinion as to: (1) the cause, nature, extent, and probable duration of the disability, (2) whether the person requires institutional care, and (3) whether the person has sufficient mental capacity to understand the nature of and consent to the appointment of a guardian.

(2) Beneficiary of the Department of Veterans Affairs. If guardianship of the person of a disabled person who is a beneficiary of the United States Department of Veterans Affairs is being sought, the petitioner shall file with the petition, in lieu of the certificates of two physicians required by subsection (1) of this section, a certificate of the Administrator of the Department of

Veterans Affairs or a duly authorized representative setting forth the fact that the person has been rated as disabled by the Department in accordance with the laws and regulations governing the Department of Veterans Affairs. The certificate shall be prima facie evidence of the necessity for the appointment.

Cross references. — Code, Estates and Trusts Article, § 13-705.

(b) *Delayed filing of certificates.* (1) After refusal to permit examination. If the petition is not accompanied by the required certificate and the petition alleges that the disabled person is residing with or under the control of a person who has refused to permit examination by a physician, and that the disabled person may be at risk unless a guardian is appointed, the court shall defer issuance of a show cause order. The court shall instead issue an order requiring that the person who has refused to permit the disabled person to be examined appear personally on a date specified in the order and show cause why the disabled person should not be examined. The order shall be personally served on that person and on the disabled person.

(2) Appointment of physicians by court. If the court finds after a hearing that examinations are necessary, it shall appoint two physicians to conduct the examinations and file their reports with the court. If both physicians find the person to be disabled, the court shall issue a show cause order requiring the alleged disabled person to answer the petition for guardianship and shall require the petitioner to give notice pursuant to Rule 10-203. Otherwise, the petition shall be dismissed. (Amended Feb. 10, 1998, effective July 1, 1998.)

Cross references. — Rule 1-341.
Source. — This Rule is in part derived from former Rule R73 b 1 and b 2 and is in part new.

Effect of amendments. — The 1998 amendment added the (a) (1) designation and subsection heading; added (a) (2); and rewrote the source note.

Rule 10-203. Service; notice.

(a) *Service on minor or alleged disabled person.* The petitioner shall serve a show cause order issued pursuant to Rule 10-104 on the minor or alleged disabled person and on the parent, guardian, or other person having care or custody of the minor or alleged disabled person. Service shall be in accordance with Rule 2-121 (a). If the minor or alleged disabled person resides with the petitioner, service shall be made upon the minor or disabled person and on such other person as the court may direct. Service upon a minor under the age of ten years may be waived provided that the other service requirements of this section are met. The show cause order served on a disabled person shall be accompanied by an "Advice of Rights" in the form set forth in Rule 10-204.

(b) *Notice to other persons.* (1) To attorney. Unless the court orders otherwise, the petitioner shall mail a copy of the petition and show cause order by ordinary mail to the attorney for the minor or alleged disabled person.

(2) To interested persons. Unless the court orders otherwise, the petitioner shall mail by ordinary mail and by certified mail to all other interested persons a copy of the petition and show cause order and a "Notice to Interested Persons."

(c) *Notice to interested persons.* The Notice to Interested Persons shall be in the following form:

In the Matter of

_____

(Name of minor or alleged
   disabled person)

In the Circuit Court for

_____

(County)

_____

(docket reference)

NOTICE TO INTERESTED PERSONS

A petition has been filed seeking appointment of a guardian of the person of _____, who is alleged to be a minor or disabled person.

You are an "interested person," that is, someone who should receive notice of this proceeding because you are related to or otherwise concerned with the welfare of this person.

If the court appoints a guardian for the person, that person will lose certain valuable rights to make individual decisions.

Please examine the attached papers carefully. If you object to the appointment of a guardian, please file a response in accordance with the attached show cause order. (Be sure to include the case number). If you wish otherwise to participate in this proceeding, notify the court and be prepared to attend any hearing.

A physician's certificate attached to the petition will be admissible as substantive evidence without the presence or testimony of the physician unless you file a request that the physician appear. The request must be filed at least 10 days before the trial date, except that, if the trial date is less than 10 days from the date your response is due, the request may be filed at any time before trial.

If you believe you need further legal advice about this matter, you should consult your attorney.

Source. — This Rule is in part derived from former Rule R74 and Code, Estates and Trusts Article, § 1-103 (b) and is in part new.

Rule 10-204. Advice of rights.

The Advice of Rights required to be served on an alleged disabled person shall be in the the following form:

TO _____ (Name).

A petition has been filed seeking appointment of a guardian of your person.

IF THE COURT APPOINTS A GUARDIAN OF YOUR PERSON, YOU WILL LOSE CERTAIN VALUABLE RIGHTS, WHICH MAY INCLUDE THE RIGHT

TO MAKE DECISIONS FOR YOURSELF ABOUT WHERE YOU LIVE, HOW YOU LIVE, AND WHAT MEDICAL CARE YOU RECEIVE.

YOU HAVE CERTAIN RIGHTS IN THIS CASE:

1. [ ] The petition alleges that _____

(Name of Attorney)

is your attorney. If that is not correct, notify the clerk immediately.

[ ] The court has appointed _____

(Name of Attorney)

as your attorney, but you may hire another attorney if you wish.

2. You will have a trial if you or your attorney object to the appointment of a guardian of your person. It will be a jury trial unless you give up the right to a jury trial.

3. You have the right to be present at the trial.

4. You have the right to present evidence on your own behalf and to cross-examine witnesses against you.

5. You have the right to suggest restrictions or limitations of the guardian's powers if a guardian is appointed.

6. The trial may be closed to the public if you so request.

The above statements cannot cover all possible situations. Please read the attached papers carefully. You should consult with your attorney to determine what is in your best interest. Your or your attorney should file a response on or before the deadline stated in the attached order.

Source. — This Rule is new.

Rule 10-205. Hearing.

(a) *Guardianship of the person of a minor.* (1) No response to show cause order. If no response to the show cause order is filed and the court is satisfied that the petitioner has complied with the provisions of Rule 10-203, the court may rule on the petition summarily.

(2) Response to show cause order. If a response to the show cause order objects to the relief requested, the court shall set the matter for trial, and shall give notice of the time and place of trial to all persons who have responded.

Cross references. — Code, Estates and Trusts Article, § 13-702.

(b) *Guardianship of alleged disabled person.* (1) Generally. When the petition is for guardianship of the person of an alleged disabled person, the court shall set the matter for jury trial. The alleged disabled person or the attorney representing the person may waive a jury trial at any time before trial. If a jury trial is held, the jury shall return a special verdict pursuant to Rule 2-522 (c) as to any alleged disability. A physician's certificate is admissible as substantive evidence without the presence or testimony of the physician unless, not later than 10 days before trial, an interested person who is not an individual under a disability, or the attorney for the alleged disabled person, files a request that the physician appear.

(2) *Beneficiary of the Department of Veterans Affairs.* If guardianship of the person of a disabled person who is a beneficiary of the United States Department of Veterans Affairs is being sought and no objection to the guardianship is made, a hearing shall not be held unless the Court finds that extraordinary circumstances require a hearing. (Amended Feb. 10, 1998, effective July 1, 1998.)

Source. — This Rule is in part derived from former Rule R77 and is in part new.

Effect of amendments. — The 1998 amendment added the (b) (1) designation and subsection heading; and added (b) (2).
There is a rational basis for different treatment of the two classes of individuals who are subject to guardianship proceedings and individuals found not guilty by reason of insanity in that a guardianship proceeding, which strips the individual of voting and property rights, may be based on various disabling conditions, while the insanity acquittee has had the fact of his disablement at the time of the offense already determined by a jury when he comes before the court for a determination on the question of confinement. Dorsey v. Solomon, 435 F. Supp. 725 (D. Md. 1977), aff'd in part and rev'd in part, 604 F.2d 271 (4th Cir. 1979).

Rule 10-206. Annual report — Guardianship of a disabled person.

(a) *Report required.* A guardian, other than a temporary guardian, of a disabled person shall file an annual report in the action. The reporting year shall end on (1) the anniversary of the date the court assumed jurisdiction over the person or (2) any other date approved by the trust clerk or the court.

Cross references. — Code, Estates and Trusts Article, § 13-708 (b) (7).

(b) *Time for filing.* The report shall be filed not later than 60 days after the end of the reporting year, unless the court for good cause shown shall extend the time.

(c) *Copies to interested persons.* The guardian shall furnish a copy of the report to any interested person requesting it, unless the court orders otherwise.

(d) *Court approval.* The court shall review the report and either enter an order accepting the report and continuing the guardianship or take other appropriate action.

(e) *Form of annual report.* The guardian's report shall be in substantially the following form:

[CAPTION]

ANNUAL REPORT OF _____, GUARDIAN
        OF _____
1. The name and permanent residence of the disabled person are: _____
_____

2. The disabled person currently resides or is physically present in:
____ own home   ____ guardian's home
____ nursing home   ____ hospital or medical facility

____ foster or boarding   ____ relative's home: _____
    home   relationship
                          ____ other

(If other than disabled person's permanent home, state the name and address of the place where the disabled person lives _____
_____ .)

3. The disabled person has been in the current location since _____. If the person has moved within the past year, the
          (date)
reasons for the change are: _____
_____ .

4. The physical and mental condition of the disabled person is as follows:
_____
_____ .

5. During the past year, the disabled person's physical or mental condition has changed in the following respects: _____
_____
_____ .

6. The disabled person is presently receiving the following care: _____
_____ .

7. I have applied funds as follows from the estate of the disabled person for the purpose of support, care, or education: _____
_____
_____ .

8. The plan for the disabled person's future care and well being, including any plan to change the person's location, is: _____
_____ .

9. [ ] I have no serious health problems that affect my ability to serve as guardian.
   [ ] I have the following serious health problems that may affect my ability to serve as guardian: _____
_____ .

10. This guardianship
   [ ] should be continued.
   [ ] should not be continued, for the following reasons: _____
_____ .

11. My powers as guardian should be changed in the following respects and for the following reasons: _____
_____
_____ .

12. The court should be aware of the following other matters relating to this guardianship: _____
_____
_____ .

I solemnly affirm under the penalties of perjury that the contents of this report are true to the best of my knowledge, information, and belief.

Date _____   Guardian's Signature _____

                                     Guardian's Name (typed or printed) _____

                                     Street Address or Box Number _____

                                     City and State _____

                                     Telephone Number _____

ORDER

The foregoing Annual Report of a Guardian having been filed and reviewed, it is by the Court, this ____ day of _____, 19___,

ORDERED, that the report is accepted, and the guardianship is continued.

(or)

ORDERED, that a hearing shall be held in this matter on
_____.

(date)

_____
JUDGE

Source. — This Rule is new and is derived as follows:

Section (a) is derived from Code, Estates and Trusts Article, § 13-708 (b) (7) and former Rule V74 c 2 (b).

Section (b) is derived from former Rule V74 c 2 (b).

Section (c) is patterned after Rule 6-417 (d). *Sections (d) and (e)* are new.

Rule 10-207. Resignation of guardian of the person and appointment of substituted or successor guardian.

(a) *Commencement of action.* A petition to resign may be filed in accordance with this Rule by a guardian of the person who has exercised no control over any property of the minor or disabled person or by a public guardian. The petition shall state the reasons for the resignation and may request the appointment of a substitute or successor guardian. When a guardian of the person resigns, dies, is removed, or becomes otherwise incapable of filling the position, and there is no substituted or successor guardian of the person already named, the court may, on its own initiative or on the petition filed by any interested person, appoint a substituted or successor guardian of the person.

Committee note. — If the original guardian, other than a public guardian, has exercised control over any property of the minor or disabled person, resignation and appointment of a successor shall be in accordance with Rule 10-711.

(b) *Venue.* The petition to resign or to appoint a substituted or successor guardian shall be filed in the court that has assumed jurisdiction over the guardianship. If jurisdiction has not been assumed, the petition shall be filed pursuant to Rule 10-201 (b).

(c) *Notice.* The petitioner shall give notice to those interested persons designated by the court by mailing to them by ordinary mail a copy of the petition and a show cause order issued pursuant to Rule 10-104.

(d) *Termination of guardian's appointment.* Resignation of a guardian does not terminate the appointment of the guardian until the court enters an order accepting the resignation.

(e) *Proceedings.* The court may, and upon request shall, hold a hearing and shall grant or deny the relief sought in the petition. Pending the appointment of the successor guardian, the court may appoint a temporary guardian.

(f) *Other procedures.* This Rule is in addition to, and not in lieu of, any other procedure for the resignation or discharge of a guardian provided by law or by the instrument appointing the guardian.

Source. — This Rule is derived as follows:
Section (a) is derived from former Rule V81 a and former Rule V82 a.
Section (b) is derived from former Rule R72 a and b.
Section (c) is derived from former Rule V81 c 1.

Section (d) is new.
Section (e) is in part derived from former Rule V78 b 5 and is in part new.
Section (f) is derived from former Rule V81 e.

Rule 10-208. Removal for cause or other sanctions.

(a) *On court's initiative.* The court that has already assumed jurisdiction over the guardianship of the person may order a guardian to show cause why the guardian should not be removed or be subject to other sanctions for failure to perform the duties of that office.

(b) *On petition of interested persons.* An interested person may file a petition to remove a guardian of the person. The petition shall be filed in the court that has assumed jurisdiction or, if jurisdiction has not been assumed, pursuant to Rule 10-201 (b). The petition shall state the reasons why the guardian should be removed.

(c) *Notice and hearing.* The court shall issue a show cause order pursuant to Rule 10-104 which shall set a hearing date. If no petition for removal has been filed, the show cause order shall state the grounds asserted by the court for the removal. The order and a copy of any petition shall be served on the guardian, all interested persons, and any other persons as directed by the court. The court shall conduct a hearing for the purpose of determining whether the guardian should be removed.

(d) *Action by court.* If the court finds grounds for removal, it may remove the guardian and appoint a substituted or successor guardian as provided in Rule 10-207. Pending the appointment of the guardian, the court may appoint a temporary guardian.

Cross references. — As to the grounds for the removal of a fiduciary, *see* Code, Estates and Trusts Article, § 15-112.

(e) *Other sanctions.* In addition to or in lieu of removal, the Court may require the guardian to perform any neglected duties and may impose any other appropriate sanctions.

Source. — This Rule is derived as follows: *Section (a)* is in part derived from former Rules V84 d and V74 e 1 (a) and is in part new.

Section (b) is in part derived from former Rule V84 d 1 and d 2 and in part from former Rule R72 a and b.

Section (c) is in part derived from former Rules V74 e 1 (a) and V84 e, and is in part new.

Section (d) is new.

Section (e) is in part derived from former Rule V74 e 2 and is in part new.

Conventional trustee has broad discretionary powers which may be exercised absent evidence of bad faith, misconduct or a want of ordinary skill or judgment. Shipley v. Crouse, 279 Md. 613, 370 A.2d 97 (1977).

First obligation of the trustees is to safeguard the trust estate, and in doing so they are called upon many times to exercise a judgment; hence the judgment exercised by the trustees that they would share the final contract and let the beneficiaries know when it was submitted to the court for ratification, but would not share the step-by-step negotiations with the beneficiaries, was not a breach of their duty, but, quite to the contrary, was in furtherance of their duty to try to do what, in their judgment, was in the best interests of the trust estate. Shipley v. Crouse, 279 Md. 613, 370 A.2d 97 (1977).

Receipt of information by beneficiaries not absolute. — While beneficiaries are entitled to receive complete and accurate information as to the administration of the trust and to know what the trust property is and how the trustee has dealt with it, this is not absolute, if the trustee renders periodic reports showing collection of income and disbursements, assuming the trustee is acting in good faith and is not abusing his discretionary powers. Shipley v. Crouse, 279 Md. 613, 370 A.2d 97 (1977).

Disclosure by trustees mandated. — When there is a confidential relationship between buyer and seller, or there is an element of self-dealing, the duty of loyalty mandates a full and frank disclosure by the trustees to the beneficiaries. Shipley v. Crouse, 279 Md. 613, 370 A.2d 97 (1977).

Where removal likely required. — Where because of a disagreement between coguardians a ward has not been permitted to leave the grounds of a nursing home in which she resides, receive new eyeglasses, have any change in the medication or medical care she requires or the like, it may well be that removal of one or both of the guardians will be required. Kicherer v. Kicherer, 285 Md. 114, 400 A.2d 1097 (1979).

Rule 10-209. Termination of a guardianship of the person.

(a) *Applicability.* When a guardian of the person has exercised no control over any property of the person or if the guardian of the person is a public guardian, the termination of the guardianship shall be according to this Rule.

Committee note. — If a guardian of the person, other than a public guardian, has exercised control over any property of the minor or disabled person, termination of the guardianship shall be in accordance with Rule 10-710.

(b) *Termination not requiring prior notice.* (1) Petition; grounds. Upon a petition filed in conformity with this section, the court shall terminate a guardianship of the person without prior notice upon a finding that either (A) a minor not otherwise disabled has attained the age of majority or (B) the minor or disabled person has died, and that (C) the guardian has exercised no control over any property of the disabled person. The petition may be filed by a minor not otherwise disabled or by the guardian of a minor or disabled person. It shall contain or be accompanied by the guardian's verified statement that the guardian has exercised no control over any property of the minor or disabled person, and shall also be accompanied by either a copy of the minor person's birth certificate or other satisfactory proof of age or a certified copy of the minor or disabled person's death certificate.

(2) Time for filing. A minor who is not disabled may file a petition at any time after attaining the age of majority. A guardian shall file a petition within 45 days after discovery that grounds for termination exists.

(3) Venue. The petition shall be filed in the court that appointed the guardian or that has assumed jurisdiction over the fiduciary estate.

(4) Copy of order. The court shall send a copy of the order terminating the guardianship to the guardian, the person whose minority has ended, and any other person whom the court designates.

(c) *Termination requiring notice.* (1) Cause for termination. A guardianship of the person may be terminated upon the filing of a petition in accordance with this section if the court, after notice and hearing, finds that any of the following grounds exist:

(A) the cessation of the disability;

(B) the emancipation of a minor who has not attained the age of majority; or

(C) any other good cause for termination.

(2) Time for filing — Who may file. Within 45 days after the guardian discovers that grounds for termination may exist, the guardian shall file a petition requesting the court to terminate the guardianship. At any time after discovery of the grounds for termination the minor or disabled person or any other interested person may file a petition requesting the court to terminate the guardianship.

(3) Venue. The petition shall be filed in the court that appointed the guardian or that has assumed jurisdiction over the fiduciary estate.

(4) Contents. The petition shall be signed and verified by the petitioner and shall contain the following information:

(A) the petitioner's relationship to the minor or disabled person;

(B) the name and address of each interested person;

(C) a statement of facts establishing the grounds for termination; and

(D) a statement that the guardian has exercised no control over any property of the minor or disabled person.

(5) Documentation. (A) Medical certificate. If the cause for the termination of the guardianship is the cessation of the disability, the petitioner shall file with the petition a certificate, signed by a physician who has examined the person within 21 days of the filing of the petition, attesting to the cessation of the disability.

(B) Marriage certificate. If the cause for the termination of the guardianship is emancipation because of the marriage of the minor person, the petitioner shall file with the petition a copy of the marriage certificate.

(6) Notice. The petitioner shall give notice by mailing by ordinary mail to those persons designated by the court a copy of the petition and the show cause order issued pursuant to Rule 10-104.

(7) Proceedings and order. After the time for filing a response has expired, the court may, and upon request shall, hold a hearing and shall issue an order granting or denying the termination of the guardianship and the release of the guardian.

Source. — This Rule is in part derived from former Rule V78 and is in part new.

Rule 10-210. Petition for assumption of jurisdiction — Emergency protective services.

(a) *Who may file.* Any interested person may file a petition requesting a court to authorize emergency protective services.

Cross references. — For the statute providing for emergency protective services, *see* Code, Estates and Trusts Article, § 13-709.

(b) *Venue.* The petition shall be filed either in the county where the person alleged to need emergency services resides or where the person is physically present.

(c) *Contents.* The petition shall be captioned, "In the Matter of ..." [stating the name of the person alleged to need emergency protective services]. It shall be signed and verified by the petitioner and shall contain at least the following information:

(1) The name and address of the petitioner and the petitioner's relationship to the person alleged to be in need of emergency protective services.

(2) The name, address, and age of the person alleged to be in need of emergency protective services, and the name, address, and age of the proposed temporary guardian.

(3) A brief description of the disability.

(4) The proposed protective services.

(5) The reason for seeking the assumption of jurisdiction by the court and for the relief sought.

(6) A statement of reasons why the petitioner believes that:

(A) the person alleged to be in need of emergency protective services is living in conditions presenting a substantial risk of death or immediate and serious physical harm to that person or others;

(B) the person alleged to be in need of emergency protective services lacks the capacity to make or communicate responsible decisions; and

(C) no person authorized by law or court order to give consent is available to consent to emergency services.

(7) An explanation of steps taken by the petitioner to obtain the consent of the person alleged to be in need of emergency protective services to the proposed services and the response of the person.

(8) If the person alleged to be in need of emergency protective services is represented by an attorney, the name and address of the attorney. If the person is not represented by an attorney, a request that one be appointed.

Source. — This Rule is derived from Code, Estates and Trusts Article, § 13-709 and former Rule R72 a and b.

Rule 10-211. Notice of petition for emergency protective services.

(a) *To whom given.* Notice that a petition for emergency protective services has been filed or will be filed and the time and place of the court hearing shall be given by the petitioner to: (1) the person alleged to be in need of emergency protective services; (2) the person with whom the person is residing; (3) the attorney for the person; (4) the director of the local department of social services; and (5) those other interested persons as the court may direct.

(b) *Manner of notice.* The notice shall be in writing, unless the nature of the emergency makes written notice impracticable.

(c) *Timing of notice.* The notice shall be given at least 24 hours before the hearing unless the court shortens the time upon a finding that (1) immediate and reasonably foreseeable physical harm to the person or others will result from a 24-hour delay, and (2) reasonable attempts have been made to give notice.

Source. — This Rule is in part derived from Code, Estates and Trusts Article, § 13-709 (e) and in part new.

Rule 10-212. Hearing.

(a) *Hearing required.* The necessity for emergency protective services shall be determined by the court after a hearing.

(b) *Conduct of hearing.* The person alleged to be in need of emergency protective services is entitled to be present at the hearing unless the person has knowingly and voluntarily waived the right to be present. Waiver may not be presumed from nonappearance but shall be determined on the basis of factual information supplied by the person's attorney or a representative appointed by the court. Upon motion by or on behalf of the person alleged to be in need of emergency protective services that, because of his or her disability, the person cannot attend a hearing at the courthouse, the court may hold the hearing at a place to which the person has reasonable access. The person has a right to counsel and to present evidence and cross-examine witnesses.

Source. — This Rule is derived from Code, Estates and Trusts Article, § 13-709 (f).

Rule 10-213. Order.

(a) *Generally.* The court may issue an order authorizing the provision of protective services on an emergency basis after a finding on the record that the allegations required by Rule 10-210 (c) (6) are established by clear and convincing evidence. An order shall either be in writing or, if dictated into the record, transcribed by the court reporter immediately and placed into the record.

(b) *Appointment of temporary guardian.* In its order the court shall appoint a temporary guardian who can give consent on behalf of the disabled person for the approved protective services until the expiration of the order.

(c) *Duration of order.* The order shall expire 144 hours after it is issued, unless extended pursuant to section (d) of this Rule.

(d) *Extension of order.* The court may further extend the emergency order and the appointment of the temporary guardian until appointment of a guardian of the person upon (1) a petition of the temporary guardian filed before the expiration of the emergency order, accompanied by a petition for the appointment of a guardian of the person, and (2) a showing that the situation described in Rule 10-210 (c) (6) will probably continue or recur if the emergency order is not further extended. The petition for appointment of a guardian shall be heard on an expedited basis not later than 60 days after it is filed.

(e) *Report of temporary guardian.* When protective services are rendered on the basis of an emergency order, the temporary guardian shall submit a report to the court describing the services and outcome and any forcible entry used to obtain custody of the person. The report shall become a part of the court record. The temporary guardian shall also send a copy of the report to

(1) the disabled person and the attorney for the disabled person, and

(2) the director of the local department of social services if the disabled person is under 65, or

(3) the director of the local office on aging if the disabled person is 65 or older, and

(4) any other person or entity as required by the court or by law.

Cross references. — Code, Article 70B.
Source. — This Rule is derived from Code, Estates and Trusts Article, § 13-709.

CHAPTER 300. GUARDIAN OF PROPERTY.

Rule 10-301. Petition for appointment of a guardian of property.

(a) *Who may file.* Any interested person may file a petition requesting a court to appoint a guardian of the property of a minor or an alleged disabled person.

(b) *Venue.* (1) Resident. If the minor or alleged disabled person is a resident of Maryland, the petition shall be filed in the county where the minor or alleged disabled person resides, even if the person is temporarily absent.

(2) Nonresident. If the minor or disabled person does not reside in this State, the petition shall be filed in the county in which a petition for guardianship of the person may be filed, or in the county where any part of the property is located. For purposes of determining the situs of property, the situs of tangible personal property is its location; the situs of intangible personal property is the location of the instrument, if any, evidencing a debt, obligation, stock or chose in action, or the residence of the debtor if there is no instrument evidencing a debt, obligation, stock, or chose in action; and the situs of an interest in property held in trust is located where the trustee may be sued.

(c) *Contents.* The petition shall be captioned "In the Matter of ..." [stating the name of the minor or alleged disabled person]. It shall be signed and verified by the petitioner and shall contain at least the following information:

(1) The petitioner's name, address, age, and telephone number;

(2) The petitioner's familial or other relationship to the alleged disabled person;

(3) Whether the person who is the subject of the petition is a minor or an alleged disabled person and, if an alleged disabled person, a brief description of the alleged disability;

(4) The reasons why the court should appoint a guardian of the property and, if the subject of the petition is an alleged disabled person, allegations demonstrating an inability of the alleged disabled person to manage the person's property and affairs effectively because of physical or mental disability, disease, habitual drunkenness, addiction to drugs, imprisonment, compulsory hospitalization, confinement, detention by a foreign power, or disappearance;

Cross references. — Code, Estates and Trusts Article, § 13-201 (b) and (c).

(5) An identification of any instrument nominating a guardian for the minor or alleged disabled person or constituting a durable power of attorney;

Cross references. — Code, Estates and Trusts Article, § 13-207 (a) (2) and (5).

(6) If a guardian or conservator has been appointed for the alleged disabled person in another proceeding, the name and address of the guardian or conservator and the court that appointed the guardian or conservator. If a guardianship or conservatorship proceeding was previously filed in any other court, the name and address of the court, the case number, if known, and whether the proceeding is still pending in that court.

(7) The name, age, sex, and address of the minor or alleged disabled person, the name and address of the persons with whom the minor or alleged disabled person resides, and if the minor or alleged disabled person resides with the petitioner, the name and address of another person on whom service can be made;

(8) To the extent known or reasonably ascertainable, the name, address, telephone number, and nature of interest of all interested persons and all others exercising any control over the property of the estate;

(9) If the minor or alleged disabled person is represented by an attorney, the name, address, and telephone number of the attorney.

(10) The nature, value, and location of the property of the minor or alleged disabled person;

(11) A brief description of all other property in which the minor or alleged disabled person has a concurrent interest with one or more individuals;

(12) A statement that the exhibits required by section (d) of this Rule are attached or, if not attached, the reason that they are absent; and

(13) A statement of the relief sought.

(d) *Required exhibits.* The petitioner shall attach to the petition as exhibits (1) a copy of any instrument nominating a guardian; (2) any physician's certificates required by Rule 10-202; and (3) if the petition is for the appointment of a guardian for a minor who is a beneficiary of the Department of Veterans Affairs, a certificate of the Secretary of that Department or any authorized representative of the Secretary, in accordance with Code, Estates and Trusts Article, § 13-802.

Source. — This Rule is derived as follows: Section (a) is derived from former Rule R71 a.

Section (b) is derived from former Rule R72 a and b.

Section (c) is in part derived from former Rule R73 a and is in part new.

Section (d) is new.

Rule 10-302. Service; notice.

(a) *Service on minor or alleged disabled person.* The petitioner shall serve a show cause order issued pursuant to Rule 10-104 on the minor or alleged disabled person and on the parent, guardian, or other person having care or custody of the minor or alleged disabled person or of the estate belonging to the minor or alleged disabled person. Service shall be in accordance with Rule 2-121 (a). If the minor or alleged disabled person resides with the petitioner, service shall be made upon the minor or alleged disabled person and on such other person as the court may direct. Service upon a minor under the age of ten years may be waived provided that the other service requirements of this section are met. The show cause order served on an alleged disabled person shall be accompanied by an "Advice of Rights" in the form set forth in Rule 10-303.

(b) *Notice to other persons.* (1) To attorney. Unless the court orders otherwise, the petitioner shall mail a copy of the petition and show cause order by ordinary mail to the attorney for the minor or alleged disabled person.

(2) To interested persons. Unless the court orders otherwise, the petitioner shall mail by ordinary mail and by certified mail to all other interested persons a copy of the petition and show cause order and a "Notice to Interested Persons."

(c) *Notice to interested persons.* The Notice to Interested Persons shall be in the following form:

In the Matter of   In the Circuit Court for

_____   _____
(Name of minor or alleged   (County)
disabled person)   _____
                                 (docket reference)

NOTICE TO INTERESTED PERSONS

A petition has been filed seeking appointment of a guardian of the property of _____, who is alleged to be a minor or alleged disabled person.

You are an "interested person", that is, someone who should receive notice of this proceeding because you are related to or otherwise concerned with the welfare of this person.

If the court appoints a guardian of the property for _____, that person will lose the right to manage his or her property.

Please examine the attached papers carefully. If you object to the appointment of a guardian, please file a response in accordance with the attached show cause order. (Be sure to include the case number). If you wish otherwise to participate in this proceeding, notify the court and be prepared to attend any hearing.

A physician's certificate attached to the petition will be admissible as substantive evidence without the presence or testimony of the physician unless you file a request that the physician appear. The request must be filed at least 10 days before the trial date, except that, if the trial date is less than 10 days from the date your response is due, the request may be filed at any time before trial.

If you believe you need further legal advice about this matter, you should consult your attorney.

Source. — This Rule is in part derived from former Rule R74 and Code, Estates and Trusts Article, § 1-103 (b) and is in part new.

Rule 10-303. Advice of rights.

The Advice of Rights required to be served on an alleged disabled person shall be in the following form:

TO _____ (Name):

A petition has been filed seeking appointment of a guardian of your property.

IF THE COURT APPOINTS A GUARDIAN OF YOUR PROPERTY, YOU WILL LOSE CERTAIN VALUABLE RIGHTS, INCLUDING YOUR RIGHT TO MANAGE YOUR PROPERTY AND TO DECIDE WHETHER AND HOW TO SPEND YOUR MONEY.

YOU HAVE CERTAIN RIGHTS IN THIS CASE:

1. [ ] The petition alleges that _____

(Name of Attorney)

is your attorney. If that is not correct, notify the clerk immediately.

[ ] The court has appointed _____

(Name of Attorney)

as your attorney, but you may hire another attorney if you wish.

2. You will have a trial if you or your attorney object to the appointment of a guardian of your property.

3. You have the right to be present at the trial.

4. You have the right to present evidence on your own behalf and to cross-examine witnesses against you.

5. You have the right to suggest restrictions or limitations of the guardian's power if a guardian is appointed.

6. The trial may be closed to the public if you so request.

The above statements cannot cover all possible situations. Please read the attached papers carefully. You should consult with your attorney to determine what is in your best interest. You or your attorney should file a response on or before the deadline stated in the attached order.

Source. — This Rule is new.

Rule 10-304. Hearing.

(a) *No response to show cause order.* If no response to the show cause order is filed and the court is satisfied that the petitioner has complied with the provisions of Rule 10-302, the court may rule on the petition summarily.

(b) *Response to show cause order; place of trial.* If a response to the show cause order objects to the relief requested, the court shall set the matter for trial, and shall give notice of the time and place of trial to all persons who have responded. Upon motion by the alleged disabled person asserting that, because of his or her disability, the alleged disabled person cannot attend a trial at the courthouse, the court may hold the trial at a place to which the alleged disabled person has reasonable access.

Cross references. — Code, Estates and Trusts Article, § 13-211.

(c) *Request for attendance of physician.* When the petition is for guardianship of the property of a disabled person, a physician's certificate that complies with Rule 10-202 is admissible as substantive evidence without the presence or testimony of the physician unless, not later than 10 days before trial, an interested person who is not an individual under a disability, or the attorney for the disabled person, files a request that the physician appear. If the trial date is less than 10 days from the date the response is due, a request that the physician appear may be filed at any time before trial.

Source. — This Rule is in part derived from former Rule R77 and is in part new.

There is a rational basis for different treatment of the two classes of individuals who are subject to guardianship proceedings and individuals found not guilty by reason of insanity in that a guardianship proceeding, which strips the individual of voting and property rights, may be based on various disabling conditions, while the insanity acquittee has had the fact of his disablement at the time of the offense already determined by a jury when he comes before the court for a determination on the question of confinement. Dorsey v. Solomon, 435 F. Supp. 725 (D. Md. 1977), aff'd in part and rev'd in part, 604 F.2d 271 (4th Cir. 1979).

Rule 10-305. Administration of guardianship of the property.

A guardianship of the property shall be administered pursuant to Rules 10-702 through 10-712.

Source. — This Rule is new.

CHAPTER 400. STANDBY GUARDIAN.

Rule 10-401. Definitions.

(a) *Statutory definitions.* The definitions stated in Code, Estates and Trusts Article, § 13-901 are applicable to this Chapter.

(b) *Additional definition.* In this Chapter, "interested person" means the minor, the guardian of the minor, a person having parental rights over the minor pursuant to Code, Estates and Trusts Article, §§ 1-205 through 1-208, and includes any other person designated by the court. (Added Feb. 10, 1998, effective July 1, 1998.)

Source. — This Rule is new.

Rule 10-402. Petition by a parent for judicial appointment of a standby guardian.

(a) *Filing of petition.* Except for a petition filed by a standby guardian in accordance with Rule 10-403, a petition for the judicial appointment of a standby guardian of the person or property of a minor shall be filed by a parent of the minor. The petition shall contain the consent of each person having parental rights over the minor, unless a statement pursuant to subsection (c) (14) of this Rule is included in the petition.

(b) *Venue.* The petition shall be filed in the county where the minor resides or is physically present.

(c) *Contents.* The petition shall be captioned "In the Matter of ..." [stating the name of the minor]. It shall be signed and verified by the petitioner and shall include the following information:

(1) The petitioner's name, address, age, and telephone number;

(2) The petitioner's familial relationship to the minor;

(3) The name, address, and date of birth of the minor;

(4) Whether the minor has any siblings and, if so, their names and ages;

(5) The proposed standby guardian's name, address, age, and telephone number;

(6) The proposed standby guardian's relationship to the minor;

(7) A statement explaining why the appointment of the proposed standby guardian is in the best interests of the minor;

(8) Whether and under what circumstances the standby guardianship is to be of the minor's person, property, or both;

(9) If the standby guardian is to be a guardian of the property of the minor, the nature, value, and location of the property;

(10) A description of the duties and powers of the standby guardian, including whether the standby guardian is to have the authority to apply for, receive, and use public benefits and child support payable on behalf of the minor;

Cross references. — For a listing of the powers of a guardian of the person, see Code, Estates and Trusts Article, § 13-708 and for a guardian of the property, see Code, Estates and Trusts Article, § 15-102.

(11) Whether the authority of the standby guardian is to become effective on the petitioner's incapacity, death, or on the first of those circumstances to occur;

Cross references. — Code, Estates and Trust Article, § 13-906.

(12) A statement that there is a significant risk that the petitioner will become incapacitated or die within two years of the filing of the petition and the basis for the statement;

Cross references. — Code, Estates and Trusts Article, § 13-903 (a).

(13) If the petitioner is medically unable to appear in court for a hearing pursuant to Rule 10-404, a statement explaining why;

(14) If a person having parental rights does not join in the petition, (A) a statement that the identity or whereabouts of the person are unknown and a description of the reasonable efforts made in good faith to identify and locate the person or (B) a statement that the person is not willing to join in the petition or has not responded to a request to join in the petition and a description of the reasonable efforts made in good faith to inform the person about the petition; and

(15) If the petitioner believes that notice to the minor would be unnecessary or would not be in the best interests of the minor, a statement explaining why.

(d) *Notice.* Unless the court orders otherwise, the petitioner shall send by ordinary mail and by certified mail to all interested persons whose whereabouts are known a copy of the petition and a "Notice to Interested Persons" pursuant to section (e) of this Rule. Service upon a minor under the age of ten years may be waived provided that the other service requirements of this section are met. If the court is satisfied that the petitioner, after reasonable efforts made in good faith, has been unable to ascertain the whereabouts of a person having parental rights, the court may order, as to that individual, that the "Notice to Interested Persons Whose Whereabouts are Unknown," which is set out in section (f) of this Rule, be published one time in the county of that individual's last known residence or be posted at that county's courthouse door or on a bulletin board within its immediate vicinity.

(e) *Notice to Interested Persons.* The Notice to Interested Persons shall be in the following form:

In the Matter of   In the Circuit Court for

_____   _____

(Name of minor)   (County)

_____   _____

(Date of notice)   (docket reference)

NOTICE TO INTERESTED PERSONS

A petition has been filed seeking the appointment of a standby guardian of the   [person]   [property]   [person   and   property]   of
_____ , a minor.

You are receiving this because you are related to or otherwise concerned with the welfare of the minor.

Please examine the attached papers carefully. If you object to the appointment of a standby guardian, please file a response with the court at

_____

(address of courthouse)

no later than 30 days after the date of issue of this Notice. (Be sure to include the case number.) **If a response is not received by the court, the court may rule on the petition without a hearing. If you wish to participate in this proceeding in any way, notify the court and be prepared to attend any hearing.**

CERTIFICATE OF SERVICE

I certify that a copy of the petition and the "Notice to Interested Persons" was mailed, by ordinary mail, postage prepaid, and by certified mail, postage prepaid and return receipt requested, this _____ day of _____, to _____

_____

at _____ .

_____
Petitioner

_____
Name (printed)

_____

_____
Address

_____
Telephone Number

(f) *Notice to Interested Persons Whose Whereabouts are Unknown.* The Notice to Interested Persons Whose Whereabouts are Unknown shall be in the following form:

In the Matter of   In the Circuit Court for

_____   _____
(Name of minor)   (County)

_____   _____
(Date of notice)   (docket reference)

NOTICE TO INTERESTED PERSONS WHOSE WHEREABOUTS ARE UNKNOWN

A petition has been filed seeking the appointment of a standby guardian of the   [person]   [property]   [person   and   property]   of _____, who is alleged to be a minor.

If you are related to or otherwise concerned with the welfare of the minor, you may obtain further information from the court at _____

_____

_____ .

(address of courthouse)

Any response must be received by the court no later than 30 days after the date of issue of this Notice. (Added Feb. 10, 1998, effective July 1, 1998.)

Source. — This Rule is new.

Rule 10-403. Petition by standby guardian for judicial appointment after parental designation.

(a) *Filing of petition.* If a parent designates a standby guardian by a written designation pursuant to Code, Estates and Trusts Article, § 13-904 and the standby guardian wishes to retain authority for a period of more than 180 days, the standby guardian shall file a petition for judicial appointment within 180 days after the effective date of the standby guardianship.

(b) *Venue.* The petition shall be filed in the county where the minor resides or is physically present.

(c) *Contents.* The petition shall be captioned "In the Matter of ..." [stating the name of the minor]. It shall be signed and verified by the petitioner and shall contain the following information:

(1) The petitioner's name, address, age, telephone number, and relationship to the minor;

(2) The name, address, and date of birth of the minor;

(3) Whether the minor has any siblings and, if so, their names and ages;

(4) A statement explaining why the appointment of the proposed standby guardian is in the best interests of the minor.

(5) Whether and under what circumstances the standby guardianship is to be of the minor's person, property, or of both;

(6) If the standby guardian is to be a guardian of the property of the minor, the nature, value, and location of the property;

(7) A description of the duties and powers of the standby guardian, including whether the standby guardian is to have the authority to apply for, receive, and use public benefits and child support payable on behalf of the minor; and

(8) If the petition is filed by a person designated by a parent as alternate standby guardian pursuant to Code, Estates and Trusts Article, § 13-904 (b)(2), a statement that the person designated as standby guardian is unwilling or unable to act as standby guardian and the basis for the statement.

(d) *Documentation.* The petitioner shall file with the petition:

(1) The written parental designation of the standby guardian signed, or consented to, by each person having parental rights over the child, if available, and, if not, the documentation required by Code, Estates and Trusts Article, § 13-904 (f) (4);

(2) A copy of a physician's determination of incapacity or debilitation of the parent pursuant to Code, Estates and Trusts Article, § 13-906; and

(3) If a determination of debilitation is filed pursuant to subsection (d) (2) of this Rule, a copy of the parental consent to the beginning of the standby guardianship pursuant to Code, Estates, and Trusts Article, § 13-904 (f).

(e) *Notice.* Unless the court orders otherwise, the petitioner shall send by ordinary mail and by certified mail to all interested persons a copy of the petition and a "Notice to Interested Persons" pursuant to section (f) of this Rule. Service upon a minor under the age of ten years may be waived provided that the other service requirements of this section are met. If the court is satisfied that the petitioner, after reasonable efforts made in good faith, has been unable to ascertain the whereabouts of a person having parental rights, the court may order, as to that individual, that the "Notice to Interested

Persons Whose Whereabouts are Unknown," which is set out in section (g) of this Rule, be published one time in the county of that individual's last known residence or be posted at that county's courthouse door or on a bulletin board within its immediate vicinity.

(f) *Notice to Interested Persons.* The Notice to Interested Persons shall be in the following form:

In the Matter of	In the Circuit Court for
_____	_____
(Name of minor)	(County)
_____	_____
(Date of notice)	(docket reference)

NOTICE TO INTERESTED PERSONS

A petition has been filed seeking appointment of a standby guardian of the [person]   [property]   [person   and   property]   of
_____, a minor.

You are receiving this notice of this proceeding because you are related to or otherwise concerned with the welfare of the minor.

Please examine the attached papers carefully. If you object to the appointment of a standby guardian, please file a response with the court at

_____
(address of courthouse)

no later than 30 days after the date of issue of this Notice. (Be sure to include the case number.) **If a response is not received by the court, the court may rule on the petition without a hearing. If you wish to participate in this proceeding in any way, notify the court and be prepared to attend any hearing.**

CERTIFICATE OF SERVICE

I certify that a copy of the petition and the "Notice to Interested Persons" was mailed, by ordinary mail, postage prepaid, and by certified mail, postage prepaid and return receipt requested, this _____ day of _____, to _____

_____

at _____

_____.

_____
Petitioner

_____
Name (printed)

_____
Address

_____
Telephone Number

(g) *Notice to Interested Persons Whose Whereabouts are Unknown.* The Notice to Interested Persons Whose Whereabouts are Unknown shall be in the following form:

In the Matter of   In the Circuit Court for

_____   _____
(Name of minor)   (County)

_____   _____
(Date of notice)   (docket reference)

<u>NOTICE TO INTERESTED PERSONS WHOSE
WHEREABOUTS ARE UNKNOWN</u>

A petition has been filed seeking the appointment of a standby guardian of the   [person]   [property]   [person   and   property]   of _____, who is alleged to be a minor.

If you are related to or otherwise concerned with the welfare of the minor, you may obtain further information from the court at _____

_____

_____.

(address of courthouse)

Any response must be received by the court no later than 30 days after the date of issue of this Notice.

Cross references. — Code, Estates and Trusts Article, § 13-904(e) and (f).

(Added Feb. 10, 1998, effective July 1, 1998.)

Source. — This Rule is new.

Rule 10-404. Hearing.

(a) *No response to notice.* If no response to the notice is filed and the court is satisfied that the petitioner has complied with the provisions of Rules 10-402 or 10-403, the court may rule on the petition without a hearing.

(b) *Response to notice.* If a response is filed to the notice objecting to the appointment of the standby guardian, the court shall hold a hearing and shall give notice of the time and place of the hearing to all interested persons. Unless excused for good cause shown, the petitioner, the proposed standby guardian, and the minor named in the petition shall be present at the hearing. (Added Feb. 10, 1998, effective July 1, 1998.)

Source. — This Rule is new.

Rule 10-405. Order.

(a) *Judicial appointment of standby guardian.* After the filing of a petition for judicial appointment of a standby guardian pursuant to Code, Estates and Trusts Article, § 13-903 (a), the court shall enter an order appointing the person as a standby guardian if the court finds that the requirements of these Rules and Code, Estates and Trusts Article, § 13-903 (d) have been met.

(b) *Judicial appointment of standby guardian after parental designation.* After the filing of a petition for judicial appointment of a standby guardian who was previously designated as standby guardian or alternate standby guardian by a parent pursuant to Code, Estates and Trusts Article, § 13-904 (a), the court shall enter an order appointing the person as a standby guardian if the court finds that the requirements of these Rules and Code, Estates and Trusts Article, § 13-904 (g) have been met.

(c) *Order appointing a standby guardian.* (1) An order appointing a standby guardian shall state whether the standby guardianship is of the minor's person, property, or both, whether the guardian shall have the authority to apply for, receive, and use public benefits and child support payable on behalf of the minor, and any other duties and powers of the standby guardian; and

(2) When the order is entered pursuant to section (a) of this Rule, the order shall also

(A) Specify whether the authority of the standby guardian is effective on the receipt of a determination of the petitioner's incapacity pursuant to Code, Estates and Trusts Article, § 13-906, on the receipt of the certificate of the petitioner's death, or on whichever occurs first; and

(B) Provide that the authority of the standby guardian may become effective earlier on written consent of the petitioner in accordance with Code, Estates and Trusts Article, § 13-903 (e) (3).

(d) *Duty to file documentation.* A copy of the appropriate document referred to in subsection (c) (2) of this Rule shall be filed by the standby guardian with the court within 90 days after the standby guardian receives the document.

Cross references. — See Code, Estates and Trusts Article, § 13-906 concerning a written determination of incapacity.

(e) *Revocation of standby guardian's authority.* The court may revoke the standby guardian's authority for failure to file any of the required documentation. (Added Feb. 10, 1998, effective July 1, 1998.)

Source. — This Rule is new.

Rule 10-406. Accounting.

(a) *Records.* A court-appointed standby guardian of the property shall keep records of the fiduciary estate and, upon request of any interested person or of the court that has assumed jurisdiction over the standby guardianship of the property, shall make the records available for inspection.

(b) *Annual fiduciary accounts.* When the court has assumed jurisdiction over a standby guardianship of the property, the standby guardian shall file each year an account in substantially the form set forth in rule 10-708. The provisions of Rule 10-706 shall apply to the account, except that the end of the accounting year shall be the anniversary of the date upon which the court assumed jurisdiction over the standby guardianship. (Added Feb. 10, 1998, effective July 1, 1998.)

Source. — This Rule is new.

Rule 10-407. Removal for cause or other sanctions.

(a) *On court's initiative.* The court that has assumed jurisdiction over a standby guardianship may order the standby guardian to show cause why the guardian should not be removed or be subject to other sanctions for failure to perform the duties of that office.

(b) *On petition of interested persons.* An interested person may file a petition to remove a standby guardian. The petition shall be filed in the court that appointed the standby guardian or, if there is a written parental designation pursuant to Code, Estates and Trusts Article, § 13-904 (a) and the court has not yet assumed jurisdiction over the standby guardianship, in the county where the minor resides or is physically present. The petition shall state the reasons why the guardian should be removed.

(c) *Action by court.* The provisions of Rule 10-208 (c) and (e) shall apply to proceedings for removal of a standby guardian. If the court finds grounds for removal, it may remove the standby guardian and may appoint an alternate standby guardian pursuant to Code, Estates and Trusts Article, § 13-904 (b) (2). (Added Feb. 10, 1998, effective July 1, 1998.)

Source. — This Rule is new.

Rule 10-408. Revocation, renunciation, and resignation.

(a) *Revocation by parent.* A parent may file a petition to revoke a standby guardianship in the court that appointed the standby guardian. The petition shall state the reasons for the revocation and shall be served on the standby guardian and all interested persons. If an objection to the revocation is filed, the court shall hold a hearing prior to ruling on the petition.

(b) *Renunciation by standby guardian.* A person who is judicially appointed as a standby guardian may renounce the appointment at any time before the effective date of the person's authority by executing a written renunciation, filing the renunciation with the court that issued the order, and promptly notifying the parent in writing of the renunciation.

(c) *Resignation by standby guardian.* A person who has been judicially appointed as a standby guardian and whose authority has become effective may file a petition to resign in the court that appointed the standby guardian. The petition shall state the reasons for the resignation and shall be served on all interested persons. If an objection to the resignation is filed, the court shall hold a hearing prior to ruling on the petition. (Added Feb. 10, 1998, effective July 1, 1998.)

Source. — This Rule is new.

Rule 10-409. Bond.

The furnishing of a bond by a standby guardian shall be governed by the provisions of Code, Estates and Trusts Article, § 13-208. (Added Feb. 10, 1998, effective July 1, 1998.)

Source. — This Rule is new.

CHAPTER 500. FIDUCIARY ESTATES OTHER THAN GUARDIANSHIPS.

Rule 10-501. Petition for assumption of jurisdiction over a fiduciary estate other than a guardianship.

(a) *Who may file.* A fiduciary or other interested person may file a petition requesting a court to assume jurisdiction over a fiduciary estate other than a guardianship of the property of a minor or disabled person.

(b) *Venue.* The petition shall be filed in the county in which all or any part of the property of the estate is located or where the fiduciary, if any, resides, is regularly employed, or maintains a place of business.

(c) *Contents.* The petition shall be captioned "In the Matter of ..." [stating the name of the fiduciary estate]. It shall be signed and verified by the petitioner, and shall contain at least the following information:

(1) The petitioner's name, address, age, and telephone number.

(2) The reason for seeking the assumption of jurisdiction by the court and a statement of the relief sought, specifying the extent to which court jurisdiction over the fiduciary estate is desired.

(3) An identification of any instrument creating the estate, with a copy attached to the petition, if possible, and, if not, an explanation of its absence.

(4) The name, address, telephone number, and nature of interest of all interested persons and all others exercising control of any of the fiduciary estate, to the extent known or reasonably ascertainable.

(5) The nature of the interest of the petitioner.

(6) The nature, value, and location of the property comprising the fiduciary estate.

Source. — This Rule is derived from former Rule V71 a, b 1, and c.

Payment of costs and counsel fees in proceeding for construction of will. — The costs of the proceeding for construction of the will, including the fee of the trustee's counsel, may be paid from the assets of the trust estate, but not the fees of counsel for other parties, unless they were appointed by the court to represent infants or persons under some disability. Sollers v. Mercantile-Safe Deposit & Trust Co., 262 Md. 606, 278 A.2d 581 (1971).

Rule 10-502. Notice.

The petitioner shall serve all interested persons and all others exercising control of any or all of the fiduciary estate by mailing to them by ordinary mail and by certified mail, unless the court directs otherwise, a copy of the petition and a show cause order issued pursuant to Rule 10-104.

Source. — This Rule is in part derived from former Rule V71 d and Code, Estates and Trusts Article, § 1-103 (b), and is in part new.

Rule 10-503. Hearing.

(a) *No response to show cause order.* If no response to the show cause order is filed, and the court is satisfied that the petitioner has complied with the provisions of Rule 10-502, the court may rule on the petition summarily.

(b) *Response to show cause order.* If a response to the show cause order objects to the relief requested, the court shall hold a hearing as in any contested matter, and shall give notice of the time and place of the hearing to all interested persons and to all others exercising control over any or all of the fiduciary estate.

Source. — This Rule is derived from former Rule R77 b 2.

There is a rational basis for different treatment of the two classes of individuals who are subject to guardianship proceedings and individuals found not guilty by reason of insanity in that a guardianship proceeding, which strips the individual of voting and property rights, may be based on various disabling conditions, while the insanity acquittee has had the fact of his disablement at the time of the offense already determined by a jury when he comes before the court for a determination on the question of confinement. Dorsey v. Solomon, 435 F. Supp. 725 (D. Md. 1977), aff'd in part and rev'd in part, 604 F.2d 271 (4th Cir. 1979).

Rule 10-504. Administration of fiduciary estates other than guardianships of the property.

A fiduciary estate other than a guardianship of property shall be administered pursuant to Rules 10-702 through 10-712.

Source. — This Rule is new.

Rule 10-505. Termination of jurisdiction.

(a) *Who may file.* Upon petition filed by any interested person, a court which has assumed jurisdiction over the administration of a fiduciary estate may relinquish jurisdiction.

(b) *Notice.* Unless the court orders otherwise, the petitioner shall serve all interested persons and all others exercising control over any of the fiduciary estate by mailing to them, by ordinary mail, a copy of the petition and a show cause order issued pursuant to Rule 10-104.

(c) *Proceedings.* (1) No response to show cause order. If no response to the show cause order is filed and the court is satisfied that the petitioner has complied with the provisions of section (b) of this Rule, the court may rule on the petition summarily.

(2) *Response to show cause order.* If a response to the show cause order objects to the relief requested, the court shall hold a hearing and shall give notice of the time and place of the hearing to all persons who have responded.

Source. — This Rule is derived from former Rule V72.

CHAPTER 600. ABSENT OR UNKNOWN PERSONS.

Rule 10-601. Petition for assumption of jurisdiction — Person whose identity or whereabouts is unknown.

(a) *Who may file.* A fiduciary or interested person may file a petition requesting a court to assume jurisdiction over the fiduciary estate for the purpose of determining its distribution if the petitioner believes that there may be a person whose identity or present whereabouts is unknown who is entitled to share in the estate.

(b) *Venue.* The petition shall be filed in the court which has assumed jurisdiction over the fiduciary estate, or if jurisdiction has not been assumed, then in the county where any part of the property to be distributed is located or where the fiduciary, if any, resides, is regularly employed, or maintains a place of business.

(c) *Contents of petition.* In addition to any other material allegations, the petition shall contain at least the following information:

(1) The petitioner's name, address, and telephone number.

(2) The nature, value, and location of any property comprising the fiduciary estate.

(3) The reasons for seeking the assumption of jurisdiction by the court and the proposed distribution.

(4) An identification of any instrument creating the fiduciary estate, with a copy attached to the petition, if possible, and, if not, an explanation of its absence.

(5) The reason it is believed that there may be a person whose identity or whereabouts is unknown.

(6) Facts showing that the petitioner has searched diligently for the person whose identity or whereabouts is unknown.

Committee note. — For substantive law on absent persons, *see* Uniform Absent Persons Act, Code, Courts Article, §§ 3-101 to 3-110. For substantive law on abandoned property, *see* Uniform Disposition of Abandoned Property Act, Code, Commercial Law Article, §§ 17-301 to 17-324.

Source. — This Rule is in part derived from former Rules V71, V79, and R77 and is in part new.

Rule 10-602. Notice.

(a) *Known persons.* Unless the court orders otherwise, the petitioner shall give notice to those persons whose identity and interest in the property are known and to any others designated by the court by mailing to them by ordinary mail and by certified mail a copy of the petition and a show cause order issued pursuant to Rule 10-104.

(b) *Unknown persons.* If the court is satisfied that reasonable efforts have been made to ascertain the identity or whereabouts of a person, the court shall order that notice to those persons whose identity or whereabouts are unknown shall be made in the manner provided by Rule 2-122.

Source. — This Rule is derived from former Rule V79 b and c and from Code, Estates and Trusts Article, § 1-103 (b).

Rule 10-603. Hearing.

(a) *No response to show cause order.* If no response to the show cause order is filed, and if the court is satisfied that the petitioner has complied with the provisions of Rule 10-602, the court may rule on the petition summarily.

(b) *Response to show cause order.* If a response to the show cause order objects to the relief requested, the court shall set the matter for hearing and shall give notice of the time and place of the hearing to all persons who have responded.

Source. — This Rule is derived from former Rule R77 b 2.

There is a rational basis for different treatment of the two classes of individuals who are subject to guardianship proceedings and individuals found not guilty by reason of insanity in that a guardianship proceeding, which strips the individual of voting and property rights, may be based on various disabling conditions, while the insanity acquittee has had the fact of his disablement at the time of the offense already determined by a jury when he comes before the court for a determination on the question of confinement. Dorsey v. Solomon, 435 F. Supp. 725 (D. Md. 1977), aff'd in part and rev'd in part, 604 F.2d 271 (4th Cir. 1979).

Rule 10-604. Attorney for person whose identity or whereabouts is unknown.

The court may appoint an attorney to protect the interest of a person whose identity or whereabouts is unknown. The fee of the attorney shall be fixed by the court and paid out of the property or portion thereof to be distributed pursuant to court order.

Source. — This Rule is derived from former Rule V79 d.

Rule 10-605. Distribution.

(a) *Generally.* After the expiration of the time fixed in the order of publication for pleading by a person whose identity or whereabouts is unknown, the court may enter an appropriate order distributing the property.

(b) *To abandoned property fund.* If the court finds that all reasonable efforts have been made to locate a person whose identity or whereabouts is unknown and that person has not appeared, the court shall order the property distributable to that person, after allowing costs, to be distributed to the abandoned property fund pursuant to Code, Commercial Law Article, § 17-317.

(c) *Retention by fiduciary or distribution to trustee.* (1) Order. The court may order the fiduciary to retain or transfer to a trustee appointed by the court or to deposit with the clerk the share to which the person whose identity or whereabouts is unknown is entitled, and order any income to be accumulated for the time the court directs.

(2) Bond. The court may order a trustee to whom the property is transferred to furnish a bond to the State in an amount and for a time period prescribed by the court.

Source. — This Rule is derived from former Rule V79 e.

CHAPTER 700. FIDUCIARY ESTATES INCLUDING GUARDIANSHIPS OF THE PROPERTY.

Rule 10-701. Scope.

The rules in this Chapter apply to proceedings under the rules in Chapters 300, 500, and 600 of this Title. They do not apply to proceedings under the rules in Chapters 200 and 400 of this Title, except as otherwise provided in those rules. (Amended Feb. 10, 1998, effective July 1, 1998.)

Source. — This Rule is new.

Effect of amendments. — The 1998 amendment substituted "Chapters 200 and 400 of this Title, except as otherwise provided in those rules" for "Chapter 200 of this Title" in the second sentence.

Rule 10-702. Bond — Fiduciary estate.

(a) *When required or excused.* (1) Required by instrument. If the instrument nominating the fiduciary or creating the estate requires the fiduciary to give bond, the fiduciary, whether corporate or non-corporate, shall file a bond before commencing the performance of any fiduciary duties unless excused pursuant to subsection (5) of this section.

(2) Excused by instrument. If the instrument nominating the fiduciary or creating the estate excuses a noncorporate fiduciary from furnishing bond, the court shall not require a bond unless the court finds that, notwithstanding the provisions of the instrument, exceptional circumstances make a bond necessary for the protection of interested persons.

(3) Corporate fiduciary. Except as provided in subsection (1) of this section, a corporate fiduciary shall not be required to furnish a bond.

(4) Noncorporate fiduciary — Bond not mentioned in instrument — Court appointment. The court may require a non-corporate fiduciary, appointed by the court or nominated under an instrument that is silent as to bond, to file a bond if the court finds that exceptional circumstances make a bond necessary for the protection of interested persons.

(5) *Fiduciary estate not exceeding $10,000.* Unless the court finds that exceptional circumstances make a bond necessary for the protection of interested persons, the court shall not require a fiduciary to furnish or continue in effect a bond if the assets of the estate (A) do not exceed $10,000 in value, (B) cannot be transferred by the fiduciary without approval of the court, and (C) consist only of cash deposited in a restricted account pursuant to Rule 10-705, securities, or real property.

(b) *Petition to require or change amount of bond.* (1) Who may file. Subject to the provisions of section (a), any interested person may file a petition to require the fiduciary to file a bond if a bond has not previously been filed or to reduce any bond that has been filed.

(2) Where filed. If a court has assumed jurisdiction over the estate, the petition shall be filed in that court. Otherwise, it shall be filed in the county in which the fiduciary resides, is regularly employed, or maintains a place of business.

(3) Notice. Unless the court orders otherwise, the fiduciary shall mail by ordinary mail to all interested persons and all others exercising control of any of the fiduciary estate a copy of the petition and a show cause order issued pursuant to Rule 10-104.

(c) *Where bond to be filed.* (1) Required by court. If a court requires a bond, the bond shall be filed in that court, unless the court directs otherwise.

(2) Required by instrument. If a bond is required by the instrument that creates the fiduciary estate or nominates a fiduciary, the bond shall be filed in the following place:

(A) If the instrument specifies the county where the bond is to be filed, the bond shall be filed in the circuit court specified in the instrument;

(B) If the instrument does not specify a place or provide for a place to be selected, the bond shall be filed in the circuit court for the county where the instrument is recorded. If the instrument is not recorded, the bond shall be filed in the circuit court for the county where the estate will be administered.

(d) *Amount of bond — Other security.* (1) Generally. The amount of a fiduciary bond shall not be greater than the aggregate value of the property of the estate in the fiduciary's control, less the value of (A) securities, (B) money deposited in a financial institution as defined in Code, Estates and Trusts Article, § 13-301 (h) under arrangements requiring an order of court for their removal, and (C) real property which the fiduciary, by express limitation of power, lacks power to sell or convey without court authorization. In lieu of sureties on a bond, the court may accept other security for the performance of the bond, including a pledge of securities or a mortgage of real property. The court may at any time, subject to the maximum amount provided by this section, require the amount of the bond, or the type or value of security, to be changed. The approval of a new bond shall not discharge any liability that may have accrued under the existing bond before such approval.

(2) Specified by instrument. If the instrument creating the estate requires that the fiduciary file a bond in a specific amount, the bond shall be in the lesser of that amount or the maximum amount provided in subsection (1).

(e) *Terms of bond.* A fiduciary bond shall be to the State of Maryland and shall be conditioned upon the faithful discharge of the duties of the fiduciary as follows:

The condition of the above obligation is such, that if _____ shall well and truly perform the office of fiduciary as designated by the _____ and shall discharge the duties required by law as fiduciary without any injury or damage to any person interested in the faithful performance of the office, then the above obligation shall be void; it shall otherwise remain in full force and effect.

(f) *Payment of bond premium from income.* A fiduciary who is required to file a bond shall be entitled to pay and be allowed the cost of the premium out of the income of the estate, unless the court otherwise directs.

Cross references. — Code, Estates and Trusts Article, § 13-208.
Source. — This Rule is derived from former Rule V73, except for subsection (b) (3) which is in part derived from former Rule V71 d and is in part new.

Payment of costs and counsel fees in proceeding for construction of will. — The costs of the proceeding for construction of the will, including the fee of the trustee's counsel, may be paid from the assets of the trust estate, but not the fees of counsel for other parties, unless they were appointed by the court to represent infants or persons under some disability. Sollers v. Mercantile-Safe Deposit & Trust Co., 262 Md. 606, 278 A.2d 581 (1971).

Rule 10-703. Compromise of claim or dispute.

(a) *Petition.* A fiduciary may petition a court to authorize or ratify a compromise or settlement of any claim or matter relating to a fiduciary estate.

(b) *Venue.* The petition shall be filed in the court that has already assumed jurisdiction over the administration of the fiduciary estate or, if jurisdiction has not been assumed (A) if the petitioner is a personal representative, in the court of the county where letters of administration were issued or (B) if the petitioner is not a personal representative, by petition in the court in the county in which the fiduciary resides, is regularly employed, or maintains a place of business.

(c) *Notice.* The petitioner shall mail by ordinary mail to those interested persons designated by the court a copy of the petition and a show cause order issued pursuant to Rule 10-104.

(d) *Ratification.* The court may authorize or ratify the proposed compromise or settlement, imposing any appropriate terms and conditions, if satisfied that the action is in the best interest of the estate.

Cross references. — For the authority of the Orphans' court to authorize the compromise of any claim by a personal representative or guardian against or in favor of the estate, *see* Code, Estates and Trusts Article, § 2-102; *but see* Code, Estates and Trusts Article, § 7-401 (h), eliminating the necessity for court approval. *See* Code, Estates and Trusts Article, § 15-102 (o), which allows a fiduciary to employ an attorney, but requires court approval for attorney's fees exceeding $50 in a fiduciary estate administered under court jurisdiction. *See also* Rule 2-202 (c), authorizing the court to appoint an attorney to represent a person under disability.

Source. — This Rule is in part derived from former Rule V77 b 1, and is in part new.

Powers included in former Rule V77 applied applied to all trustees, whether or not such powers were included in the will or trust agreement. Mercantile-Safe Deposit & Trust Co. v. United States, 311 F. Supp. 670 (D. Md. 1970).

Trustee has no power to sell something he does not have. — The expansion of fiduciary powers which former Rule V77 accomplished did not confer upon a trustee a power to sell something he does not have. Jones v. Endslow, 23 Md. App. 578, 328 A.2d 339 (1974).

And therefore could not sell real property in which he held title to a life estate without prior approval. — A trustee could not sell real property placed in a trust by the testator without the approval of any beneficiary or of the court where, with respect to that property, the trustee held legal title to a life estate only. Jones v. Endslow, 23 Md. App. 578, 328 A.2d 339 (1974).

Rule 10-704. Titling of assets.

(a) *Form.* Unless otherwise ordered by the court, assets of a fiduciary estate shall be held in substantially the following form:

(1) Any account in any bank, savings and loan association, or other financial institution shall be held: A.B., (fiduciary) for _____ (or under the Will of _____).

(2) Any security held by a fiduciary shall be titled in accordance with subsection (a) (1) of this Rule or in the name of a nominee or in other form without disclosure of the interest of the fiduciary estate, but the fiduciary shall be liable for a wrongful act of the nominee in connection with the security so held.

Cross references. — Code, Estates and Trusts Article, § 15-102 (x).

(3) All other intangible assets and all tangible personal assets required to be titled shall be titled in a form similar to subsection (a) (1) of this Rule, unless it is impractical to do so.

(b) *Securities in name of disabled person.* Unless otherwise ordered by the court, nothing in section (a) of this Rule shall prohibit the fiduciary who has physical possession of securities from retaining them in the name of a disabled person.

(c) *Real estate.* Real estate need not be titled in the name of the fiduciary if (1) the real property lies in the county in which the court has assumed jurisdiction or (2) a copy of the court order or instrument naming the fiduciary has been filed in the land records in the Maryland county where the property is located (other than the county in which the court has assumed jurisdiction), or in the land records of another state where the property is located.

Cross references. — For authority of fiduciaries to deposit securities with a securities clearing corporation, *see* Code, Estates and Trusts Article, § 15-104.

Source. — This Rule is derived as follows: *Section (a)* is derived from former Rule V76 a.

Subsection (1) is derived from former Rule V76 a.

Subsection (2) is in part derived from former Rule V76 c, Code, Estates and Trusts Article, § 15-102 (x) and is in part new.

Section (b) is new.

Section (c) is new.

Rule 10-705. Restricted accounts.

(a) *Petition for restricted accounts.* When a fiduciary estate consists entirely of cash in an amount not exceeding $75,000, a fiduciary may petition the court for an order authorizing the deposit of cash in a federally insured financial institution in a single restricted account titled substantially in the following form: "A.B., (fiduciary), withdrawals subject to the order of the Circuit Court for _____ County."

(b) *Orders authorizing withdrawals.* The court may require a separate order prior to each withdrawal. The court may enter a continuing order authorizing withdrawals up to a specified amount. The continuing order may be for a definite period of time, not to exceed one year, and may on petition be renewed annually.

(c) *Proof of restricted account.* The fiduciary shall promptly provide proof of the opening of a restricted account to the trust clerk, who shall make note of it in the file.

(d) *When accounting not required.* If all of the assets of a fiduciary estate are deposited in a single restricted account in an amount not exceeding $10,000, no annual accounting is required unless the court orders otherwise.

Cross references. — For accounting requirements, *see* Rule 10-706.

Source. — This Rule is derived as follows:
Section (a) is derived from former Rule V75 a and b.
Section (b) is derived from former Rule V75 c.

Section (c) is derived from former Rule V75 d.

Section (d) is derived from former Rule V74 c 2 (e).

Rule 10-706. Accounting.

(a) *Records.* A fiduciary shall keep records of the fiduciary estate and upon request of the court that has assumed jurisdiction over the fiduciary estate or any interested person, shall make the records available for inspection.

(b) *Annual fiduciary accounts.* (1) Generally. When the court has appointed a guardian of the property or has assumed jurisdiction over a fiduciary estate, the fiduciary shall file each year an account in substantially the form set forth in Rule 10-708. The end of the accounting year shall be (A) the anniversary of the date upon which the court assumed jurisdiction over the estate or appointed the fiduciary, or (B) any other anniversary date fixed with the consent of the trust clerk or the court. The account shall be filed not later than 60 days after the end of the accounting year, unless the court or trust clerk extends the time for good cause shown. The fiduciary shall furnish a copy of the account to any interested person who requests it.

(2) Beneficiary of the Department of Veterans Affairs. In the case of a beneficiary of the Department of Veterans Affairs, the fiduciary shall send a certified copy of the account to the Office of the Department of Veterans Affairs having jurisdiction over the area in which the court is located.

Cross references. — Code, Estates and Trusts Article, § 13-804 (c).

(3) When not required. Unless the court orders otherwise, the fiduciary of a fiduciary estate consisting entirely of cash in a restricted account under Rule 10-705 (d) need not file an annual account.

(4) Trust clerk — Report and recommendation. (A) Generally. The trust clerk shall examine each annual account, report to the court any irregularity in it, raise any other matters deemed appropriate, and make recommendations. The trust clerk may require the fiduciary to furnish proof of any transactions shown in the account.

(B) Beneficiary of the Department of Veterans Affairs. In the case of a beneficiary of the Department of Veterans Affairs, the trust clerk shall endorse on the account a certificate that any securities or investments shown on the account were exhibited to the trust clerk.

Cross references. — Code, Estates and Trusts Article, § 13-804 (b).

(5) Court approval. The court shall review every annual account and either enter an order approving the account or take other appropriate action.

(c) Audit. When the court has appointed a guardian of the property or has assumed jurisdiction over a fiduciary estate, the fiduciary account need not be audited by a private auditor unless specifically required by the court. Upon a petition filed by the fiduciary or upon the court's own initiative, the court may order an audit pursuant to Rule 2-543. A fiduciary may have a private audit conducted for any period but, unless the court orders otherwise, the cost of that audit shall be borne by the fiduciary and not the fiduciary estate.

Source. — This Rule is derived in part from former Rule V74 and is in part new.

Rule 10-707. Inventory and information report.

(a) Duty to file. Within 60 days after jurisdiction has been assumed or a fiduciary has been appointed, the fiduciary shall file an inventory and information report in substantially the following form:

Part I.

[CAPTION]

INVENTORY

The FIDUCIARY ESTATE now consists of the following assets:
(attach additional sheets, if necessary; each item listed shall be valued by the fiduciary at its fair market value, as of the date of the appointment of the fiduciary or the assumption of jurisdiction by the court; unless the court otherwise directs, it shall not be necessary to employ an appraiser to make any valuation; state amount of any mortgages, liens, or other indebtedness, but do not deduct when determining estimated fair market value)

81

A. REAL ESTATE
(State location, liber/folio, balance of mortgage, and name of lender, if any)

ESTIMATED FAIR
MARKET VALUE

$ _____

TOTAL $ _____

B. CASH AND CASH EQUIVALENTS
(State name of financial institution, account number, and type of account)

PRESENT FAIR
MARKET VALUE

$ _____

TOTAL $ _____

C. PERSONAL PROPERTY
(Itemize motor vehicles, regardless of value; describe all other property
  generally if total value is under $1500; state amount of any lien; itemize, if
  total value is over $1500)

ESTIMATED FAIR
MARKET VALUE

$ _____

TOTAL $ _____

D. STOCKS
(State number and class of shares, name of corporation)

PRESENT FAIR
MARKET VALUE

$ _____

TOTAL $ _____

E. BONDS
(State face value, name of issuer, interest rate, maturity date)

PRESENT FAIR
MARKET VALUE

$ _____

TOTAL $ _____

F. OTHER
(Describe generally, e.g., debts owed to estate, partnerships, cash value of life insurance policies, etc.)

ESTIMATED FAIR
MARKET VALUE

_____ $ _____
_____   _____
_____
                                  TOTAL $ _____

Part II.

INFORMATION REPORT

(1) Are there any assets in which the minor or disabled person holds a present interest of any kind together with another person in any real or personal property, including accounts in a credit union, bank, or other financial institution?

[ ] No   [ ] Yes   If yes, give the following information as to all such property:

Name, Address, and Relationship of Co-Owner	Nature of Property	Description of Interest	Total Value of Property
_____	_____	_____	_____
_____	_____	_____	_____
_____	_____	_____	_____

(2) Does the minor or disabled person hold an interest less than absolute in any other property which has not been disclosed in question (1) and has not been included in the inventory (e.g., interest in a trust, a term for years, a life estate)?

[ ] No [ ] Yes   If yes, give the following information as to each such interest:

Description of Interest and Amount or Value	Date and Type of Instrument Establishing Interest
_____	_____
_____	_____
_____	_____

VERIFICATION:
I solemnly affirm under the penalties of perjury that the contents of this inventory and information report are true and complete to the best of my knowledge, information, and belief.

_____   _____
          Date   Date

_____   _____
Signature of Fiduciary   Signature of Fiduciary

_____   _____
Address   Address

_____   _____
Telephone Number   Telephone Number

_____
Name of Fiduciary's Attorney

_____
Address

_____
Telephone Number

(b) *Examination not required.* Unless the court otherwise directs, it shall not be necessary that the assets listed in the report be exhibited to or examined by the court, the trust clerk, or auditor.

(c) *Notice.* Unless the court orders otherwise, the trust clerk or fiduciary shall furnish a copy of the report to any interested person who has made a request for it.

Source. — This Rule is derived as follows: *Section (a)* is in part derived from former Rule V74 b 1 and 2 and is in part new. *Section (b)* is derived from former Rule V74 b 3. *Section (c)* is new.

Rule 10-708. Fiduciary's Account and report of trust clerk.

(a) *Form of account.* The Fiduciary's Account shall be filed in substantially the following form:

[CAPTION]

FIDUCIARY'S ACCOUNT

I, _____, make this [ ] periodic [ ] final Fiduciary's Account for the period from _____ to _____ .

Part I.   The FIDUCIARY ESTATE now consists of the following assets: (attach additional sheets, if necessary; state amount of any mortgages, liens, or other indebtedness, but do not deduct when determining estimated fair market value)

A.   REAL ESTATE
(State location, liber/folio, balance of mortgage, and name of lender, if any)

ESTIMATED FAIR
MARKET VALUE

_____ $ _____

_____   _____

_____   _____

                      TOTAL $ _____

B. CASH AND CASH EQUIVALENTS
(State name of financial institution, account number, and type of account)

PRESENT FAIR
MARKET VALUE

$ _____

_____

                                    TOTAL $ _____

C. PERSONAL PROPERTY
(Itemize motor vehicles, regardless of value; describe all other property
generally if total value is under $1500; state amount of any lien; itemize, if
total value is over $1500)

ESTIMATED FAIR
MARKET VALUE

$ _____

_____

                                    TOTAL $ _____

D. STOCKS
(State number and class of shares, name of corporation)

PRESENT FAIR
MARKET VALUE

$ _____

_____

                                    TOTAL $ _____

E. BONDS
(State face value, name of issuer, interest rate, maturity date)

PRESENT FAIR
MARKET VALUE

$ _____

_____

                                    TOTAL $ _____

F. OTHER
(Describe generally, e.g., debts owed to estate, partnerships, cash value of life
insurance policies, etc.)

ESTIMATED FAIR
MARKET VALUE

$ _____

_____

                                    TOTAL $ _____

Part II. The following income was collected and disbursements were made: (attach additional sheets, if necessary)

A. INCOME
(State type, e.g. pensions, social security, rent, annuities, dividends, interest, refunds)

	AMOUNT
_____	$ _____
_____	_____
_____	_____
_____	_____
_____	_____
_____	_____
_____	_____
TOTAL	$ _____

B. DISBURSEMENTS
(State to whom paid and purpose of payment)

	AMOUNT
_____	$ _____
_____	_____
_____	_____
_____	_____
_____	_____
_____	_____
TOTAL	$ _____

C. SUMMARY

Total Income .... $ _____
Total Disbursements .... $ (_____)
Net Income/(Loss) .... $ _____

Part III. The following changes in the assets of the Fiduciary Estate have occurred since the last account: (attach additional sheets, if necessary)

A. ASSETS ADDED

Date	Description of Transaction	Gross Purchase Price	Value at date of acquisition if other than by purchase

B.   ASSETS DELETED

Date	Description of Transaction	Gross Sale Proceeds	Selling Costs	Carrying Value	Gain (Loss)

A Summary of the Fiduciary Estate is as follows:

Type of Property	Value reported on last Fiduciary Account	Value reported on this Fiduciary Account
A. Real Estate	$ _____	$ _____
B. Cash and Cash Equivalents	$ _____	$ _____
C. Personal Property	$ _____	$ _____
D. Stocks	$ _____	$ _____
E. Bonds	$ _____	$ _____
F. Other	$ _____	$ _____
Total	$ _____	$ _____

The Fiduciary bond, if any, has been filed in this action in the amount of $ _____.

VERIFICATION:

I solemnly affirm under the penalties of perjury that the contents of this account are true and complete to the best of my knowledge, information, and belief.

_____   _____
          Date   Date

_____   _____
  Signature of Fiduciary   Signature of Fiduciary

_____   _____
        Address   Address

_____   _____
   Telephone Number   Telephone Number

            _____
            Name of Fiduciary's Attorney

            _____
                    Address

            _____
               Telephone Number

(b) *Report of the trust clerk and order of court.* The Report of the Trust Clerk and Order of Court shall be filed in substantially the following form:

REPORT OF TRUST CLERK AND ORDER OF COURT

I, the undersigned Trust Clerk, certify that I have examined the attached Fiduciary's Account in accordance with the Maryland Rules.

Matters to be called to the attention of the Court are as follows:

_____

_____

_____

_____

_____

_____

_____

_____

_____

| _____ | _____ |
| Date | Signature of Trust Clerk |

| _____ | _____ |
| Address of Trust Clerk | Telephone No. of Trust Clerk |

ORDER

The foregoing Fiduciary's Account having been filed and reviewed, it is by the Court, this _____ day of _____, 19__,

ORDERED, that the attached Fiduciary's Account is accepted.

(or)

ORDERED, that a hearing shall be held in this matter on _____.

(date)

_____

JUDGE

Source. — This Rule is new.

Rule 10-709. Transfer of fiduciary estate to a foreign fiduciary.

(a) *Who may file.* A fiduciary or any interested person may file a petition requesting a court to transfer a fiduciary estate to a foreign fiduciary.

(b) *Venue.* The petition shall be filed in the court that has assumed jurisdiction over the fiduciary estate, or if jurisdiction has not been assumed, in the county in which any part of the property is located, or where the transferor resides, is regularly employed, or maintains a place of business.

(c) *Contents.* The petition shall contain at least the following information:

(1) The name, address, telephone number, and interest of the petitioner.

(2) The name, address, telephone number, and interest of the foreign fiduciary.

(3) The place and date of the foreign fiduciary's appointment.

(4) The reasons why the transfer should be made.

(d) *Certificates.* A petition shall be accompanied by a certified copy of the instrument or court order appointing the foreign fiduciary, and proof that the appointment is still in effect.

(e) *Notice.* The petitioner shall give notice to all interested persons by mailing to them by ordinary mail a copy of the petition and a show cause order issued pursuant to Rule 10-104.

(f) *Final accounting.* No final accounting need be filed unless required by the court.

Source. — This Rule is in part derived from former Rule V80 and in part new.

Rule 10-710. Termination of a fiduciary estate — Final distribution.

(a) *Cause for termination.* Grounds for the termination of a fiduciary estate shall include:

(1) the occurrence of the event specified in the instrument creating the estate;

(2) the distribution by the fiduciary of all remaining assets of the estate in a manner authorized by the instrument creating the estate;

(3) the attainment by a minor of the age of majority;

(4) the emancipation of a minor who has not attained the age of majority;

(5) the cessation of a disability;

(6) the death of the minor or disabled person; or

(7) any other good cause for termination.

(b) *Time for filing — Who may file.* Within 45 days after the fiduciary discovers that the grounds for termination exist, the fiduciary shall file a petition requesting the court to terminate the estate. Thereafter, if the fiduciary has not timely filed the petition, an interested person may file a petition requesting the court to terminate the estate.

(c) *Venue.* The petition shall be filed in the court that has assumed jurisdiction over the fiduciary estate or if jurisdiction has not been assumed, in the county in which any part of the property is located, or where the fiduciary resides, is regularly employed, or maintains a place of business.

(d) *Contents.* The petition shall be signed and verified by the petitioner and shall contain the following information:

(1) the petitioner's interest in the estate;

(2) the name and address of each interested person entitled to notice of the petition;

(3) a statement of facts establishing the grounds for termination; and

(4) documentation as set forth in this Rule.

(e) *Documentation.* (1) Proof of age. If the cause for the termination of the guardianship of the property of a minor is the attainment of the age of majority, the petitioner shall file with the petition a copy of the minor person's birth certificate or other satisfactory proof of age.

(2) *Marriage certificate.* If the cause for the termination of the guardianship of the property of a minor is emancipation because of the marriage of the minor person, the petitioner shall file with the petition a copy of the marriage certificate.

(3) *Medical certificate.* If the cause for the termination of the guardianship of the property of a disabled person is the cessation of the disability, the petitioner shall file with the petition a certificate, signed by a physician who has examined the person within 21 days of the filing of the petition, attesting to the cessation of the disability.

(4) *Death certificate.* If the cause for the termination of the guardianship of the property is the death of the minor or disabled person, the petitioner shall file with the petition a copy of the death certificate.

(f) *Final accounting.* If the petitioner is the fiduciary, the petitioner shall file with the petition a final accounting containing the same information required in annual accountings by Rule 10-708, together with the proposed final distribution of any remaining assets of the estate. The accounting shall cover any period of the fiduciary's administration of the estate which has not been covered by annual accountings previously filed in the proceedings. If the petitioner is not the fiduciary, the fiduciary shall file an accounting as directed by the court.

(g) *Notice.* The petitioner shall give notice of the filing of the petition to the persons named as distributees in the proposed final distribution, to the other persons entitled to notice of annual accounts, and to all other persons designated by the court. The notice shall consist of mailing by ordinary mail a copy of the petition and a show cause order issued pursuant to Rule 10-104.

Source. — This Rule is in part derived from former Rule V78 and in part new.

Rule 10-711. Resignation of fiduciary and appointment of substituted or successor fiduciary.

(a) *Commencement of action.* A fiduciary may file a petition to resign. The petition shall state the reasons for the resignation and may request the appointment of a substituted or successor fiduciary. When a fiduciary resigns, dies, is removed, or becomes otherwise incapable of filling the position, and there is no substituted or successor fiduciary already named, the court may, on its own initiative or on petition filed by any interested person, appoint a substituted or successor fiduciary.

(b) *Venue.* (1) Guardianships of the property. The petition to resign or to appoint a substituted or successor fiduciary shall be filed in the court that has assumed jurisdiction over the guardianship. If jurisdiction has not been assumed, the petition shall be filed pursuant to Rule 10-301 (b).

(2) Other fiduciary proceedings. The petition shall be filed in the court that has assumed jurisdiction over the fiduciary estate, or if jurisdiction has not been assumed, in the county in which the property is situated, or where the fiduciary resides, is regularly employed, or maintains a place of business.

(c) *Account of resigning fiduciary.* The resigning fiduciary shall file with the petition an accounting pursuant to Rule 10-706 for any period not covered in any annual accountings previously filed, or, if none, from the date the fiduciary assumed the office.

In the case of an estate not previously subject to court jurisdiction, where all beneficiaries have filed a waiver or where the court does not require an accounting, an accounting need not be filed.

(d) *Notice.* The petitioner shall give notice to those interested persons designated by the court by mailing to them by ordinary mail a copy of the petition and a show cause order issued pursuant to Rule 10-104.

(e) *Termination of fiduciary's appointment.* Resignation of a fiduciary does not terminate the appointment of the fiduciary until the court enters an order accepting the resignation.

(f) *Proceedings.* The court may, and upon request shall, hold a hearing and shall grant or deny the relief sought in the petition. Pending the appointment of the successor fiduciary, the court may appoint a temporary fiduciary.

(g) *Resignation of co-fiduciary.* Unless otherwise ordered by the court, a co-fiduciary may resign the office pursuant to this Rule. The resigning co-fiduciary shall turn over all property belonging to the estate to the remaining co-fiduciary.

(h) *Duty of personal representative of the estate of deceased fiduciary or guardian of disabled fiduciary.* Upon the death or disability of a fiduciary, the personal representative or the guardian of the fiduciary, if any, shall, subject to order of court:

(1) Have the duty to protect all property belonging to the estate;

(2) Have the power to perform acts necessary for the protection of the estate;

(3) Immediately apply to the court for the appointment of a substituted or successor fiduciary;

(4) Upon appointment of a substituted or successor fiduciary have the duty to file an accounting pursuant to Rule 10-708 and deliver any property of the estate to the substituted or successor fiduciary.

Committee note. — Code, Estates and Trusts Article, § 13-220 (c) applies to deceased or disabled guardians of the property; section (i) of this Rule applies to all deceased or disabled fiduciaries.

(i) *Additional means of resignation.* This Rule is in addition to, and not in lieu of, any other procedure for the resignation or discharge of a fiduciary provided by law or by the instrument creating the estate or appointing the fiduciary.

Cross references. — See Code, Estates and Trusts Article, § 15-111.

Source. — This Rule is derived as follows:
Section (a) is derived from former Rule V81 a and former Rule V82 a.
Section (b)
Subsection (1) is derived from former Rule R72 a and b.
Subsection (2) is derived from former Rule V81 a.
Section (c) is in part derived from former Rule V81 b 1 and is in part new.
Section (d) is derived from former Rule V81 c 1.
Section (e) is new.
Section (f) is in part derived from former Rule V78 b 5 and is in part new.
Section (g) is new.
Section (h) is derived from former Rule V82 e.
Section (i) is derived from former Rule V81 e.

Rule 10-712. Removal for cause or other sanctions.

(a) *On court's initiative.* The court that has already assumed jurisdiction over the guardianship or estate may order a fiduciary to show cause why the fiduciary should not be removed or be subject to other sanctions for failure to perform the duties of that office.

(b) *On petition of interested persons.* An interested person may file a petition to remove a fiduciary. The petition shall state the reasons why the fiduciary should be removed.

(c) *Venue.* (1) Guardianships of the property. The petition shall be filed in the court that has already assumed jurisdiction or, if jurisdiction has not been assumed, pursuant to Rule 10-301 (b).

(2) Other fiduciary proceedings. The petition shall be filed in the court that has already assumed jurisdiction or, if jurisdiction has not been assumed, in the county in which the property is situated, or where the fiduciary resides, is regularly employed, or maintains a place of business.

(d) *Notice and hearing.* The court shall issue a show cause order pursuant to Rule 10-104 which shall set a hearing date. If no petition for removal has been filed, the show cause order shall state the grounds asserted by the court for the removal. The order and a copy of any petition shall be served on the fiduciary, the surety on any bond of the fiduciary, all interested persons, and any other persons as directed by the court. The court shall conduct a hearing for the purpose of determining whether the fiduciary should be removed.

(e) *Action by court.* If the court finds grounds for removal, it may remove the fiduciary and appoint a substituted or successor fiduciary as provided in Rule 10-711. Pending the appointment of the fiduciary, the court may appoint a temporary fiduciary.

Cross references. — As to the grounds for removal of a fiduciary, *see* Code, Estates and Trusts Article, § 15-112.

(f) *Final accounting and delivery of property.* Upon the appointment of a substituted or successor fiduciary, the removed fiduciary shall, within the time period specified by the Court,

(1) file an accounting, pursuant to section (f) of Rule 10-710; and

(2) deliver any property of the fiduciary estate to the substituted or successor fiduciary.

(g) *Other sanctions.* In addition to or in lieu of removal, the court may disallow any commissions from the time the court finds that the default began, require the fiduciary to perform the neglected duties, and impose any other appropriate sanctions.

Source. — This Rule is derived as follows:

Section (a) is in part derived from former Rules V84 d and V74 e 1 (a) and is in part new.

Section (b) is in part derived from former Rule V84 d 1 and d 2 and is in part new.

Section (c)

Subsection (1) is derived from former Rule R72 a and b.

Subsection (2) is derived from former Rule V84 c.

Section (d) is in part derived from former Rules V74 e 1 (a) and V84 e, and is in part new.

Section (e) is new.

Section (f) is derived from former Rule V84 f.

Section (g) is in part derived from former Rule V74 e 2 and is in part new.

Conventional trustee has broad discretionary powers which may be exercised absent evidence of bad faith, misconduct or a want of ordinary skill or judgment. Shipley v. Crouse, 279 Md. 613, 370 A.2d 97 (1977).

First obligation of the trustees is to safeguard the trust estate, and in doing so they are called upon many times to exercise a judgment; hence the judgment exercised by the trustees that they would share the final contract and let the beneficiaries know when it was submitted to the court for ratification, but would not share the step-by-step negotiations with the beneficiaries, was not a breach of their duty, but, quite to the contrary, was in furtherance of their duty to try to do what, in their judgment, was in the best interests of the trust estate. Shipley v. Crouse, 279 Md. 613, 370 A.2d 97 (1977).

Receipt of information by beneficiaries not absolute. — While beneficiaries are entitled to receive complete and accurate information as to the administration of the trust and to know what the trust property is and how the trustee has dealt with it, this is not absolute, if the trustee renders periodic reports showing collection of income and disbursements, assuming the trustee is acting in good faith and is not abusing his discretionary powers. Shipley v. Crouse, 279 Md. 613, 370 A.2d 97 (1977).

Disclosure by trustees mandated. — When there is a confidential relationship between buyer and seller, or there is an element of self-dealing, the duty of loyalty mandates a full and frank disclosure by the trustees to the beneficiaries. Shipley v. Crouse, 279 Md. 613, 370 A.2d 97 (1977).

Where removal likely required. — Where because of a disagreement between coguardians a ward has not been permitted to leave the grounds of a nursing home in which she resides, receive new eyeglasses, have any change in the medication or medical care she requires or the like, it may well be that removal of one or both of the guardians will be required. Kicherer v. Kicherer, 285 Md. 114, 400 A.2d 1097 (1979).

TITLE 11. JUVENILE CAUSES

Editor's note. — The Court of Appeals, by Order dated June 5, 1996, effective January 1, 1997, rescinded Subtitles A, D, E, J, P, Q, R, T, U, V, W, Y, Z, BB, BD, BE, BG, BH, BJ, BL, BP, BQ, BR, BS, BW, and BY of Chapter 1100 of the Maryland Rules of Procedure, rescinded Subtitles P, BB, BQ, and BW of the Maryland District Rules, and rescinded Forms 22a, 23, 24, 25, and 26. The Order substituted for certain of the rules and forms rescinded new Title 9, Chapter 100, Title 10, Title 12, Title 13, Title 14, and Title 15 of the Maryland Rules of Procedure. Furthermore, the Order transferred, without readoption, Chapter 900, Chapter 1200, and Subtitles S, BU, and BV of Chapter 1100 of the Maryland Rules of Procedure and Chapter 1200 of the Maryland District Rules to be Title 9, Chapter 200, Title 11, and Title 16 of the Maryland Rules of Procedure. The Order provides that the new rules shall "apply to all actions commenced on or after January 1, 1997, and insofar as practicable, to all actions then pending."

Many of the cases in the notes to the various rules were decided prior to the 1996 revision. These cases have been retained under pertinent rules of this title where it is thought that such cases will be of value in interpreting the present rules.

A table of comparable rules, relating those rules rescinded effective January 1, 1997, to the revised rules in Title 9 through Title 16 is to be found in Volume 2 following the end of the Maryland Rules.

Rule 11-101. Definitions.

a. *Statutory definitions.* The definitions stated in Section 3-801 of the Courts Article are applicable to this Title.

Cross references. — See § 3-801 of the Courts Article for definitions of "adjudicatory hearing," "adult," "child," "child in need of assistance," "child in need of supervision," "citation," "commit," "court," "custodian," "delinquent act," "delinquent child," "detention," "disposition hearing," "intake officer," "mentally handicapped child," "party," "shelter care," and "violation."

b. *Additional definitions.* The following words and phrases used in this Title are defined as follows:

1. Complaint. "Complaint" means a written statement made by any person or agency to an intake officer which, if true, would support the allegations of a juvenile petition.

2. Emergency detention or shelter care. "Emergency detention or shelter care" means detention or shelter care that is required at a time other than when a judge of the court having jurisdiction is available.

3. Juvenile petition. "Juvenile petition" means a petition filed pursuant to Section 3-810 of the Courts Article.

4. Parent. "Parent" includes a child's parent, guardian and custodian.

5. Probation. "Probation" means a status created by a court order under which a child adjudicated to be delinquent, or an adult convicted under Section 3-831 of the Courts Article, is to remain subject to supervision of the Court under conditions the Court or the agency designated by it deems proper, but is not removed from his home.

6. Respondent. "Respondent" means the person against whom a petition is filed.

7. Waiver petition. "Waiver petition" means a petition filed pursuant to Rule 11-113 (Waiver of Jurisdiction). (Amended Nov. 5, 1976, effective Jan. 1, 1977; June 5, 1996, effective Jan. 1, 1997.)

Source. — This Rule is former Rule 901.

Effect of amendments. — The 1996 amendment substituted "Title" for "Chapter" in a. and in the introductory language of b.; substituted "Rule 11-113" for "Rule 913" in b. 7.; and added the Source note.

Editor's note. — An Order dated June 5, 1996, effective Jan. 1, 1997, renumbered this Rule, which was formerly Rule 901.

University of Baltimore Law Forum. — For discussion of police investigative procedures and juveniles, see 16, No. 1 U. Balt. Law Forum 6 (1986).

Former Chapter 900 [see now this title] is exclusive rule relative to juvenile courts of this State; it does not provide for the right of intervention in a juvenile proceeding. In re Damien D., 50 Md. App. 411, 438 A.2d 932 (1982).

The Criminal Rules of Procedure under Title 4 of the Maryland Rules do not apply to an adjudicatory proceeding in a juvenile cause; juvenile delinquency proceedings are governed exclusively by this title. In re Victor B., 336 Md. 85, 646 A.2d 1012 (1994).

Preserving objection to admissibility of evidence. — In a juvenile proceeding, a pre-adjudicatory motion is not required to preserve an objection to the admissibility of evidence at an adjudicatory hearing. In re Victor B., 336 Md. 85, 646 A.2d 1012 (1994).

Rule 11-102. Complaint — Intake procedures.

a. *Complaint.* Any person or agency having knowledge of facts which may cause a person to be subject to the jurisdiction of the court may file a complaint with the Juvenile Services Agency intake officer assigned to the court having proper venue.

b. *Intake procedures.* The procedures for intake shall comply with provisions of Section 3-810 of the Courts Article. (Amended Nov. 5, 1976, effective Jan. 1, 1977; July 27, 1987, effective Aug. 17, 1987; June 5, 1996, effective Jan. 1, 1997.)

Source. — This Rule is former Rule 902.

Effect of amendments. — The 1996 amendment added the Source note.

Editor's note. — An Order dated June 5, 1996, effective Jan. 1, 1997, renumbered this Rule, which was formerly Rule 902.

Rule 11-102A. Transfer of jurisdiction from court exercising criminal jurisdiction.

a. *Applicability.* This Rule applies to actions for which a court exercising criminal jurisdiction has entered an order transferring jurisdiction pursuant to Rule 4-251 (c) (2) or 4-252 (h) (3).

Cross references. — Code, Article 27, § 594A.

b. *Juvenile petition.* Within 10 days after a court exercising criminal jurisdiction enters an order transferring jurisdiction over a defendant to the juvenile court, the State's Attorney shall file a juvenile petition pursuant to Rule 11-103 and shall attach to the petition a copy of (1) the charging document that was filed in the court exercising criminal jurisdiction and (2) the order of the court transferring jurisdiction. If the petition is not so filed, the respondent shall be released from detention, shelter care, or all conditions of pretrial release, without prejudice to the right of the State's Attorney to file a petition thereafter.

c. *Effect of provisions in order transferring jurisdiction.* Except as provided in section b of this Rule and subject to Rules 11-112 and 11-114, any conditions of release of the respondent or any placement of the respondent in detention or shelter care set forth in the order transferring jurisdiction shall remain in effect and be enforceable by the juvenile court pending the adjudicatory hearing unless modified or abrogated by the juvenile court. (Added Sept. 11, 1995, effective Jan. 1, 1996; amended June 5, 1996, effective Jan. 1, 1997.)

Source. — This Rule is former Rule 902A.

Effect of amendments. — The 1996 amendment substituted "Rule 11-103" for "Rule 903" in b.; substituted "Rules 11-112 and 11-114" for "Rules 912 and 914" in c.; and added the Source note.

Editor's note. — An Order dated June 5, 1996, effective Jan. 1, 1997, renumbered this Rule, which was formerly Rule 902A.

Rule 11-103. Juvenile petition.

a. *Form — Contents.* The juvenile petition shall be by the State of Maryland. It shall be in writing and shall comply with the requirements of this Rule.

1. Caption. The petition shall be captioned "Matter of ...."

2. Contents. The petition shall state:

(a) The respondent's name, address and date of birth. If the respondent is a child, it shall also state the name and address of his parent.

(b) Allegations providing a basis for the court's assuming jurisdiction over the respondent (e.g., that the respondent child is delinquent, in need of supervision, or in need of assistance; that the respondent adult violated Section 3-831 of the Courts Article; that the action arises under the Interstate Compact on Juveniles; or that the action arises under the compulsory public school attendance laws of this State).

(c) The facts, in clear and simple language, on which the allegations are based. If the commission of one or more delinquent acts or crimes is alleged, the petition shall specify the laws allegedly violated by the respondent.

(d) The name of each witness to be subpoenaed in support of the petition.

(e) Whether the respondent is in detention or shelter care; and if so, whether his parent has been notified and the date such detention or shelter care commenced. (Amended Mar. 3, 1987, effective July 1, 1987.)

3. Signature. Except in the case of a petition filed under the Interstate Compact on Juveniles, the petition shall be signed by the State's Attorney if delinquency or a violation of Section 3-831 of the Courts Article is alleged, or by the intake officer in other cases.

4. Interstate compact petitions. Juvenile petitions filed under Article IV of the Interstate Compact on Juveniles (Code, Health-General Article, § 6-303) shall comply with the requirements of the Interstate Compact and must be verified by affidavit.

b. *Filing.* The petition shall be filed with the clerk of the court, in a sufficient number of copies to provide for service upon the parties. (Amended Nov. 5, 1976, effective Jan. 1, 1977; June 5, 1996, effective Jan. 1, 1997.)

Committee note. — Juvenile petitions filed under Article IV of the Interstate Compact on Juveniles Code, Health-General Article, § 6-303) must be verified by affidavit.

Source. — This Rule is former Rule 903.

Effect of amendments. — The 1996 amendment added the Source note.

Editor's note. — Former Health-General Article, § 6-303, referred to in this Rule, was transferred by ch. 290, Acts 1987, effective July 1, 1987, to be Article 41C, § 3-103. Section 8, ch. 6, Acts 1988, approved Feb. 18, 1988, and effective from date of passage, transferred former Article 41C to be present Article 83C.

An Order dated June 5, 1996, effective Jan. 1, 1997, renumbered this Rule, which was formerly Rule 903.

Juvenile court proceeding is initiated by filing of petition. — A proceeding before the juvenile court is not instituted at the time of arrest but thereafter by the filing of a petition by the State's Attorney or some other person having knowledge of the facts. Bean v. State, 234 Md. 432, 199 A.2d 773 (1964).

Although "any person or agency" may originate a delinquency proceeding, such proceedings are initiated by petition and such petitions must be prepared, signed and filed by the State's Attorney. United States v. Ramapuram, 432 F. Supp. 140 (D. Md. 1977), aff'd, 577 F.2d 738 (4th Cir.), cert. denied, 439 U.S. 926, 99 S. Ct. 309, 58 L. Ed. 2d 318 (1978).

And prior to filing of petition, State has right to conduct a normal investigation, including an interrogation of the defendant, in order to determine whether a petition would be appropriate, or whether the case was one for the grand jury. Bean v. State, 234 Md. 432, 199 A.2d 773 (1964).

This Rule indicates that reasons relied on should be fully assigned, if only to prevent surprise. In re Cromwell, 232 Md. 409, 194 A.2d 88 (1963).

Victim's petition for restitution. — The juvenile court does not have jurisdiction to hear a victim's petition for adjudication and restitution pursuant to CJ § 3-829. There is no jurisdiction in a juvenile delinquency case until a petition is filed by the State. Hart v. Bull, 69 Md. App. 229, 516 A.2d 1043 (1986).

Rule 11-104. Duties of clerk.

a. *Separate Docket.* The clerk shall maintain a separate docket for Juvenile Causes. Upon the filing of a juvenile petition, or a petition for continued detention or shelter care the name of each respondent shall be entered on the docket and indexed.

b. *Scheduling of Hearing.* Upon the filing of a juvenile petition, or a petition for continued detention or shelter care the clerk shall promptly schedule a hearing.

c. *Process — Issuance — Service.* Unless the court otherwise directs, upon the filing of a juvenile petition, the clerk shall promptly issue a summons substantially in the form set forth in Form 904-S of the Appendix of Forms and returnable as provided by Rule 2-126 for each party except the petitioner and a respondent child alleged to be in need of assistance. Any summons addressed to a parent of a respondent child shall require the parent to produce the respondent child on the date and time named in the summons.

The summons, together with a copy of the juvenile petition, shall be served in the manner provided by Chapter 100 of Title 2 for service of process to obtain personal jurisdiction over a person within this State.

If the parent of the child is a nonresident, or for any reason cannot be served, notice of the pendency and nature of the proceeding shall be given as directed by the court, and proof of the steps taken to give notice that justice shall require.

d. *Subpoena.* The clerk shall issue a subpoena for each witness requested by any party, pursuant to Rule 2-510.

e. *The summons, together with a copy of the juvenile petition, shall be served in the manner provided by Chapter 100 of Title 2 for service of process to obtain personal jurisdiction over a person within this State.* The clerk shall accept for deposit security for the appearance of any person subject to the court's original jurisdiction, in the form and amount that the court determines.

f. *List of Open Hearings.* Prior to the convening of court on each day that the juvenile court is in session, the clerk shall prepare and make available to the public a list of the hearings scheduled for that day that are required by Code, Courts Article, § 3-812 to be conducted in open court. The list shall include the full name of each respondent and the time and location of the hearing. (Amended Nov. 5, 1976, effective Jan. 1, 1977; Apr. 6, 1984, effective July 1, 1984; June 5, 1996, effective Jan. 1, 1997; June 8, 1998, effective Oct. 1, 1998.)

Source. — This Rule is former Rule 904, except that section f. is new.

Effect of amendments. — The 1996 amendment added the Source note.

The 1998 amendment substituted "the parent" for "him" in the second sentence in c.; added f.; and added "except that section f. is new" in the Source note.

Editor's note. — An Order dated June 5, 1996, effective Jan. 1, 1997, renumbered this Rule, which was formerly Rule 904.

A master himself is empowered to conduct an adjudicatory hearing. In re Brown, 13 Md. App. 625, 284 A.2d 441 (1971).

Rule 11-105. Physical and mental examination.

a. *Examination procedure.* 1. Order for examination. Any order for a physical or mental examination pursuant to Section 3-818 of the Courts Article shall specify the time, place, manner, conditions and scope of the examination and the person or persons by whom it is to be made. The court shall order that the examination be conducted on an outpatient basis if, considering the child's condition, that is feasible and appropriate. The order may regulate the filing of a report of findings and conclusions and the testimony at a hearing by the examining physician, psychiatrist, psychologist or other professionally qualified person, the payment of the expenses of the examination and any other relevant matters. (Amended Nov. 5, 1976, effective Jan. 1, 1977; Apr. 18, 1980, effective July 1, 1980.)

2. Service of copies of report. Copies of all studies and reports of examinations made to the court under this Rule shall be furnished by the court to counsel for the parties when received by the court, but not later than two days before any hearing at which the results of the examinations will be offered in evidence.

b. *Use of report.* The report of examination is admissible in evidence as set forth in Section 3-818 of the Courts Article.

c. *Admissibility of testimony.* 1. In delinquency and contributing cases. In delinquency cases and in cases in which an adult is charged with a violation of Section 3-831 of the Courts Article, testimony concerning a study or examination ordered under Section 3-818 of the Courts Article by persons who conducted the study or examination is admissible

(i) at waiver and disposition hearings, and

(ii) at an adjudicatory hearing on the issues of a respondent's competence to participate in the proceedings and his legal responsibility for his acts.

2. In all other cases. In all other cases, testimony concerning a study or examination ordered under Section 3-818 of the Courts Article by persons who conducted the study or examination is admissible at any hearing. (Amended Nov. 5, 1976, effective Jan. 1, 1977; June 5, 1996, effective Jan. 1, 1997.)

Source. — This Rule is former Rule 905.

Effect of amendments. — The 1996 amendment added the Source note.

Editor's note. — An Order dated June 5, 1996, effective Jan. 1, 1997, renumbered this Rule, which was formerly Rule 905.

University of Baltimore Law Forum. — For discussion of police investigative procedures and juveniles, see 16, No. 1 U. Balt. Law Forum 6 (1986).

Disposition hearing. — Section 3-818 (c) of the Courts and Judicial Proceedings Article and section c of this Rule create a hearsay exception for admission of evaluative reports at disposition hearings in Children in Need of

Assistance cases. In re Wanda B., 69 Md. App. 105, 516 A.2d 615 (1986).

Consideration of agency study which accused's counsel has never received. — It is apparent that CJ § 3-818 and this Rule have been violated where, prior to any formal adjudication of delinquency, the court acknowledged that it had considered, and was still considering, the contents of an agency study, and where it was clear from the record that the accused's counsel had never received a copy of the report although the judge was considering disposition of the case. In re Jeffrey L., 50 Md. App. 268, 437 A.2d 255 (1981).

Rule 11-106. Right to counsel.

a. *In all proceedings — Appearance of out-of-state attorney.* The respondent is entitled to be represented in all proceedings under this Title by counsel retained by him, his parent, or appointed pursuant to the provisions of subsection b 2 and 3 of this Rule. An out-of-state attorney may enter his appearance and participate in a cause only after having been admitted in accordance with Rule 14 of the Rules Governing Admission to the Bar of

Maryland (Special Admission of Out-of-State Attorneys). Once so admitted, his appearance and participation is limited by the restrictions of that Rule.

Cross references. — See Rule 14 of the Rules Governing Admission to the Bar of Maryland.

b. *Waiver of representation — Indigent cases — Non-indigent cases.* 1. Waiver procedure. If, after the filing of a juvenile petition, a respondent or his parent indicates a desire or inclination to waive representation for himself, before permitting the waiver the court shall determine, after appropriate questioning in open court and on the record, that the party fully comprehends:

(i) the nature of the allegations and the proceedings, and the range of allowable dispositions;

(ii) that counsel may be of assistance in determining and presenting any defenses to the allegations of the juvenile petition, or other mitigating circumstances;

(iii) that the right to counsel in a delinquency case, a child in need of supervision case, or a case in which an adult is charged with a violation of Section 3-831 of the Courts Article includes the right to the prompt assignment of an attorney, without charge to the party if he is financially unable to obtain private counsel;

(iv) that even if the party intends not to contest the charge or proceeding, counsel may be of substantial assistance in developing and presenting material which could affect the disposition; and

(v) that among the party's rights at any hearing are the right to call witnesses in his behalf, the right to confront and cross-examine witnesses, the right to obtain witnesses by compulsory process, and the right to require proof of any charges.

2. Representation of indigents in delinquency, child in need of supervision, and contributing cases. (a) Unless knowingly and intelligently waived, and unless counsel is otherwise provided, an indigent party, or an indigent child whose parents are either indigent or unwilling to employ counsel, shall be entitled to be represented by the Office of the Public Defender in a delinquency case, a child in need of supervision case, or a case in which an adult is charged with a violation of Section 3-831 of the Courts Article, at any stage in a waiver, adjudicatory or disposition hearing, or hearing under Rule 11-116 (Modification or Vacation of Order).

(b) Upon request or upon the court's own motion, the Office of the Public Defender shall appoint, in a delinquency case, a child in need of supervision case, or a case in which an adult is charged with a violation of Section 3-831 of the Courts Article, separate counsel to represent any indigent party other than the child if the interests of the child and those of the party appear to conflict, and if such counsel is necessary to meet the requirements of a fair hearing.

3. Child in need of assistance cases. A party in a child in need of assistance proceeding is entitled to the assistance of counsel as provided in Section 3-821 of the Courts Article.

4. Non-indigent cases. Upon motion of any party or upon the court's motion, the court may appoint an attorney to represent a child. Compensation for the

services of the attorney may be assessed against any party. (Amended Nov. 5, 1976, effective Jan. 1, 1977; Nov. 4, 1977, effective Jan. 1, 1978; July 16, 1992; June 5, 1996, effective Jan. 1, 1997.)

Source. — This Rule is former Rule 906.

Effect of amendments. — The 1996 amendment substituted "Title" for "Chapter" in the first sentence of a.; substituted "Rule 11-116" for "Rule 916" in b. 2. (a); and added the Source note.

Editor's note. — An Order dated June 5, 1996, effective Jan. 1, 1997, renumbered this Rule, which was formerly Rule 906.

University of Baltimore Law Forum. — For discussion of police investigative procedures and juveniles, see 16, No. 1 U. Balt. Law Forum 6 (1986).

Section b must be satisfied for effective waiver. — Before the court may accept a juvenile's waiver of counsel, it must satisfy each mandate in section b of this Rule. Anything less will render the waiver void as unknowingly and unintelligently given. In re Appeal No. 101, 34 Md. App. 1, 366 A.2d 392 (1976).

Juvenile must comprehend rights and consequences. — The court must determine that the juvenile fully comprehends each of the rights and consequences delineated in this Rule. In re Appeal No. 101, 34 Md. App. 1, 366 A.2d 392 (1976).

Compliance with this Rule does not require that the court recite the full litany in the words of the Rule. Explanation, to assure full comprehension, is more important than recital. In re Appeal No. 101, 34 Md. App. 1, 366 A.2d 392 (1976).

A juvenile facing possible waiver of juvenile jurisdiction is entitled to advice of counsel. Kemplen v. Maryland, 428 F.2d 169 (4th Cir. 1970).

Review of commitment considered "proceedings" for counsel purposes. — Hearings before the juvenile court judge for "Review of Commitment for Placement" of a juvenile were "proceedings," and, therefore, there was a requirement that the juvenile be offered counsel. In re Glenn H., 43 Md. App. 510, 406 A.2d 444 (1979).

Order for psychiatric examination. — Since there is no requirement for a hearing prior to ordering a psychiatric examination of a child under § 3-818 of the Courts and Judicial Proceedings Article, the parent's entitlement to appointed counsel under section b 2 of this Rule is not implicated. In re Wanda B., 69 Md. App. 105, 516 A.2d 615 (1986).

Parents' responsibility for child's legal services deemed "necessaries." — Legal services provided to a minor may, in some circumstances, be deemed "necessaries" for which a parent may be required to pay, e.g., where they are reasonable and necessary for the protection or enforcement of the property rights of the minor or for his personal protection, liberty or relief. Serabian v. Alpern, 284 Md. 680, 399 A.2d 267 (1979).

Recoverable at law. — Recovery against the parent for "necessary" legal services provided to a minor must ordinarily be sought in an action at law. Serabian v. Alpern, 284 Md. 680, 399 A.2d 267 (1979).

Rule 11-107. Responsive pleading or motion.

a. *Denial — Admission — Preliminary objection.* A respondent may file a pleading denying or admitting all or any facts alleged in the juvenile petition, or he may file a motion raising preliminary objection. Any allegation not admitted is deemed denied. If a respondent fails to file a pleading, his failure will be taken as a denial of the allegations in the petition.

b. *Uncontested responsive pleading.* If a respondent child has filed a pleading admitting the allegations of the juvenile petition or indicates to the court his intention not to deny those allegations, the court, before proceeding with an adjudicatory hearing, shall advise the child of the nature and possible consequence of his action or intended action. The court shall neither encourage or discourage the child with respect to his action or intended action, but shall ascertain to its satisfaction that the child understands the nature and possible consequences of failing to deny the allegations of the juvenile petition, and that he takes that action knowingly and voluntarily. These proceedings shall take place in open court and shall be on the record. If the respondent is an adult, the provisions of Title 4 shall apply. (Amended Nov. 5, 1976, effective Jan. 1, 1977; Apr. 6, 1984, effective July 1, 1984; June 5, 1996, effective Jan. 1, 1997.)

Source. — This Rule is former Rule 907.

Effect of amendments. — The 1996 amendment added the Source note.

Editor's note. — An Order dated June 5, 1996, effective Jan. 1, 1997, renumbered this Rule, which was formerly Rule 907.

Applicability. — This Rule is applicable whether or not the juvenile is represented by counsel. In re Montrail, 87 Md. App. 420, 589 A.2d 1318 (1991), aff'd, 325 Md. 527, 601 A.2d 1102 (1992).

This Rule makes no distinction between delinquency cases and other juvenile cases. In re Appeal No. 544, 25 Md. App. 26, 332 A.2d 680 (1975).

Failure to file pleading deemed denial. — Although by this Rule a party may file a pleading denying or admitting all or a part of the facts alleged, if no pleading is filed, the parties are deemed to have denied the allegations. In re Appeal No. 769, 25 Md. App. 565, 335 A.2d 204 (1975).

Failure to inform defendant of consequences of failing to deny allegation. — The court accepted defense counsel's word that defendant admitted that the allegation against him was true, without inquiring of defendant whether he understood the nature and possible consequences of failing to deny the allegation, and whether his admission was knowing and voluntary, in violation of this Rule. In re Montrail, 87 Md. App. 420, 589 A.2d 1318 (1991), aff'd, 325 Md. 527, 601 A.2d 1102 (1992).

Rule 11-108. Amendment — Continuance.

a. *Juvenile petition.* A juvenile petition may be amended by or with the approval of the court at any time prior to the conclusion of the adjudicatory hearing.

b. *Other pleading.* A pleading other than a juvenile petition may be amended with the approval of the court at any time prior to the final disposition of that pleading.

c. *Continuance.* If a juvenile petition or other pleading is amended, the court shall grant the parties such continuance as justice may require in light of the amendment. (Amended Nov. 5, 1976, effective Jan. 1, 1977; June 5, 1996, effective Jan. 1, 1997.)

Source. — This Rule is former Rule 908.

Effect of amendments. — The 1996 amendment added the Source note.

Editor's note. — An Order dated June 5, 1996, effective Jan. 1, 1997, renumbered this Rule, which was formerly Rule 908.

Maryland Law Review. — For note, "Does a Juvenile Court Rehearing on the Record After a Master Has Made Proposed Findings Violate Double Jeopardy or Due Process?" see 39 Md. L. Rev. 395 (1979).

Rule 11-109. Discovery and inspection.

a. *Delinquency and contributing cases.* 1. Definition of "State" and "Respondent." In this section, "State" means the State's Attorney, and "Respondent" includes his counsel where appropriate.

2. Scope of section. This section applies to proceedings in which by petition, a child is alleged to be delinquent, or an adult is alleged to have violated Section 3-831 of the Courts Article.

3. Discovery by the respondent. The State shall without the necessity of a request by the respondent, furnish to the Respondent:

(a) any material or information within the knowledge, possession or control of the State which tends to negate the involvement of the respondent as to the offense charged;

(b) any relevant material or information regarding

(1) specific searches and seizures;

(2) wiretaps and eavesdropping.

(3) the acquisition of statements made by the respondent; and

(4) prehearing identification of the respondent by a witness for the State;

(c) the name and address of each person whom the State intends to call as a witness at any hearing to prove its case in chief or to rebut alibi testimony to the extent then known;

(d) as to all statements made by the respondent to a State agent which the State intends to use at a hearing:

(1) a copy of each written or recorded statement; and

(2) the substance of each oral statement and a copy of all reports of each oral statement;

(e) as to all statements made by a co-respondent to a State agent which the State intends to use at a hearing, unless a severance has been ordered by the court:

(1) a copy of each written or recorded statement; and

(2) the substance of each oral statement and a copy of all reports of each oral statement;

(f) any written report or statement made in connection with the particular case by each expert consulted by the State, if the State intends to offer the testimony of the expert or the report at any hearing, including the written substance of any oral report and conclusion made in connection with the particular case by each expert consulted by the State and the results of any physical or mental examination, scientific test, experiment or comparison;

(g) any book, paper, document, recording, photograph and any tangible object which the State intends to use at any hearing, in order to permit the respondent to inspect, copy and photograph them; and

(h) any item obtained from or belonging to the respondent which the State intends to use at any hearing, in order to permit the respondent to inspect, copy and photograph it.

(i) The State's Attorney's obligations under this section extend to material and information in the possession or control of members of his staff and of any others who have participated in the investigation or evaluation of the case and who either regularly report or with reference to the particular case have reported to his office.

4. Compliance by the State. Subject to the provisions of subsections 8 and 9 of this section, the State may comply with subsection 3 of this section by advising the respondent in writing or on the record, that the respondent may

inspect the entire file of the State and by allowing such inspection to occur at any time during normal business hours. However, if the State has any exculpatory information specified in subsection 3 (a) of this Rule, the State shall promptly furnish such information to the respondent, whether or not the respondent has made the inspection provided for by that subsection.

5. Matters not subject to discovery by respondent. This section does not require the State to disclose:

(a) any documents to the extent that they contain the opinions, theories, conclusions, or other work product of the State,

(b) the identity of a confidential informant, so long as the failure to disclose the informant's identity does not infringe on a constitutional right of the respondent, and the State does not intend to call the informant as a witness; and

(c) any matter which the court, under subsection 9 of this section, orders need not be disclosed.

6. Discovery by the State. Upon the request of the State, the respondent shall:

(a) appear in a lineup for identification;

(b) speak for identification;

(c) be fingerprinted;

(d) pose for photographs not involving reenactment of a scene;

(e) try on articles of clothing;

(f) permit the taking of specimens of material under his fingernails;

(g) permit the taking from his body of samples of blood, hair, and other material involving no unreasonable intrusion upon his person;

(h) provide specimens of his handwriting;

(i) submit to reasonable physical inspection of his body or mental examination;

(j) produce and permit the State to inspect and copy all written reports made in connection with the particular case by each expert who the respondent intends to call as a witness at the hearing, including the substance of any oral report and conclusion made in connection with the particular case by an expert which the respondent intends to use at the hearing and the results of any physical or mental examination, scientific test, experiment, or comparison;

(k) furnish, upon designation by the State of the time, place and date of the alleged occurrence, the name and address of each witness other than the respondent whom the respondent intends to call as a witness to show he was not present at the time, place and date designated by the State in its request.

7. Procedure for discovery — Time — Hearing on motion to compel. The State shall make the disclosure required under subsection 3 of this section, and shall request the discovery required under subsection 6 of this section, within five days after the earlier of the appearance of counsel, or the waiver of counsel under Rule 11-106. The respondent shall furnish the discovery required under this section within ten days after a request is made. The court, for good cause shown, may extend the time for discovery.

If discovery is not furnished as required, a motion to compel discovery may be filed which shall specify the items which have not been furnished. A hearing shall be held no later than three days after the motion is filed.

8. Continuing duty to disclose. If, subsequent to compliance with a request made under this Rule or with any order compelling discovery, a party learns of additional information previously requested and required to be furnished, he shall promptly furnish the information to the other party or his counsel. If the additional information is learned during a hearing, he shall, in addition to furnishing the information promptly to the other party or his counsel, notify the court that such matter is being furnished.

9. Protective orders. Upon motion and a showing of good cause, the court may order that specified disclosures be restricted. If, at any time during the proceedings, it is brought to the attention of the court that a party has failed to comply with this section or an order issued under this section, the court may:

(a) order such party to permit the discovery of the matters not previously disclosed;

(b) strike the testimony to which the undisclosed matter relates;

(c) grant a reasonable continuance;

(d) prohibit the party from introducing in evidence the matter not disclosed;

(e) grant a mistrial; or

(f) enter such other order as may be appropriate under the circumstances.

b. *All other cases.* In any proceeding in which a child is alleged to be in need of supervision or assistance, the court may, upon good cause shown, pass such orders in aid of discovery, and inspection of evidence as justice may require.

c. *Timely disclosure required.* All matters and information to which a party is entitled must be disclosed in time to permit its beneficial use. (Added Nov. 5, 1976, effective Jan. 1, 1977; amended June 5, 1996, effective Jan. 1, 1997.)

Source. — This Rule is former Rule 909.

Effect of amendments. — The 1996 amendment substituted "Rule 11-106" for "Rule 906" in the first sentence of a. 7.; and added the Source note.

Editor's note. — An Order dated June 5, 1996, effective Jan. 1, 1997, renumbered this Rule, which was formerly Rule 909.

University of Baltimore Law Forum. — For discussion of police investigative procedures and juveniles, see 16, No. 1 U. Balt. Law Forum 6 (1986).

Rule 11-110. Hearings — Generally.

a. *Before master or judge — Proceedings recorded.* Hearings shall be conducted before a master or a judge without a jury. Proceedings shall be recorded by stenographic notes or by electronic, mechanical or other appropriate means.

b. *Place of hearing.* A hearing may be conducted in open court, in chambers, or elsewhere where appropriate facilities are available. The hearing may be adjourned from time to time and, except as otherwise required by Code, Courts Article, § 3-812, may be conducted out of the presence of all persons except those whose presence is necessary or desirable. If the court finds that it is in the best interest of a child who is the subject of the proceeding, the presence of the child may be temporarily excluded except when the child is alleged to have committed a delinquent act.

c. *Minimum five-day notice of hearing — Service — Exception.* Except in the case of a hearing on a petition for continued detention or shelter care pursuant to Rule 11-112 (Detention or Shelter Care), the clerk shall issue a notice of the time, place and purpose of any hearing scheduled pursuant to the provisions of this Title. This notice shall be served on all parties together with a copy of the petition or other pleading if any, in the manner provided by section c of Rule 11-104 (Duties of Clerk) at least five days prior to the hearing.

d. *Multiple petitions.* 1. Individual hearings. If two or more juvenile petitions are filed against a respondent, hearings on the juvenile petitions may be consolidated or severed as justice may require.

2. Consolidation. Hearings on juvenile petitions filed against more than one respondent arising out of the same incident or conditions, may be consolidated or severed as justice may require. However, (i) if prejudice may result to any respondent from a consolidation, the hearing on the juvenile petition against the respondent shall be severed and conducted separately; and (ii) if juvenile petitions are filed against a child and an adult, the hearing on the juvenile petition filed against the child shall be severed and conducted separately from the adult proceeding.

e. *Controlling conduct of person before the court.* 1. *Sua sponte* or on application. The court, upon its own motion or on application of any person, institution, or agency having supervision or custody of, or other interest in a respondent child, may direct, restrain or otherwise control the conduct of any person properly before the court in accordance with the provisions of Section 3-827 of the Courts Article.

2. Other remedies. Title 15, Chapter 200 of these Rules is applicable to juvenile causes, and the remedies provided therein are in addition to the procedures and remedies provided by subsection 1 of this section. (Amended Nov. 5, 1976, effective Jan. 1, 1977; June 5, 1996, effective Jan. 1, 1997; June 8, 1998, effective Oct. 1, 1998.)

Source. — This Rule is former Rule 910.

Effect of amendments. — The 1996 amendment, in c., substituted "Rule 11-112" for "Rule 912" and substituted "Title" for "Chapter" in the first sentence and substituted "Rule 11-104" for "Rule 904" in the second sentence; substituted "Title 15, Chapter 200" for "Subtitle P (Contempt) of Chapter 1100" at the beginning of e. 2.; and added the Source note.

The 1998 amendment, in b., inserted "except as otherwise required by Code, Courts Article, § 3-812" in the second sentence and substituted "best interest of a child who is the subject of the proceeding, the presence of the child may be temporarily excluded except when the child" for "best interest and welfare of the child, his presence may be temporarily excluded except when he" in the third sentence; and substituted "the respondent" for "him" in the second sentence in d.2.

Editor's note. — An Order dated June 5, 1996, effective Jan. 1, 1997, renumbered this Rule, which was formerly Rule 910.

Maryland Law Review. — For note, "Does a Juvenile Court Rehearing on the Record After a Master Has Made Proposed Findings Violate Double Jeopardy or Due Process?" see 39 Md. L. Rev. 395 (1979).

"Hearings." — Private meetings between judge and children were hearings requiring compliance with the notice requirement of the rule where the Department of Social Services social worker was also present at the sessions and the foster mother was present at one, and they both made comments that were evidentiary in nature, although neither was under oath or subject to cross-examination and where the children's statements also were given considerable weight by the court. In re Barry E., 107 Md. App. 206, 667 A.2d 931 (1995).

Juvenile is placed in jeopardy when the State begins to offer evidence in an adjudicatory hearing before a master. Aldridge v. Dean, 395 F. Supp. 1161 (D. Md. 1975).

A judge exercising jurisdiction under CJ § 3-829 may act only after a hearing under this Rule, wherein evidence, beyond a mere finding of delinquency of the juvenile, is produced which is legally sufficient to support a conclusion that damages authorized by it were wilfully or maliciously caused by or committed by a child under 18 years of age. In re Sorrell, 20 Md. App. 179, 315 A.2d 110, cert. denied, 271 Md. 740, 744 (1974).

Record of proceedings. — Where a juvenile court conducts proceedings under this section it must use a reliable recording system or conduct the session in such a manner to assure that the entire proceeding is properly and accurately recorded. In re Barry E., 107 Md. App. 206, 667 A.2d 931 (1995).

Access by press. — Although a juvenile court has the discretion to exclude the press from a juvenile proceeding, its discretion is not unlimited and must be exercised in accord with the purposes for which it was given and within applicable constitutional limitations. Baltimore Sun Co. v. State, 340 Md. 437, 667 A.2d 166 (1995).

While a court can place reasonable restrictions on the media's use of information obtained in a confidential juvenile proceeding, it cannot limit the media's publication of information which it legitimately collected from other sources, and cannot condition access to the juvenile proceeding upon the media's publication of material specified by the court.

Baltimore Sun Co. v. State, 340 Md. 437, 667 A.2d 166 (1995).

Court records confidential. — Court records pertaining to juveniles are held in confidence, and can only be divulged by court order, or for limited educational purposes. Baltimore Sun Co. v. State, 340 Md. 437, 667 A.2d 166 (1995).

Closed proceedings. — Courts may close juvenile proceedings to the public in instances where closure would be impermissible in other court proceedings. Baltimore Sun Co. v. State, 340 Md. 437, 667 A.2d 166 (1995).

Ex parte proceedings. — In a children in need of assistance proceeding conducting a secret session with the children and social worker was error because of the lack of notice and proper recording equipment, not because it amounted to an improper ex parte proceeding. If a rule of court allows such a proceeding, as this section does, it is not per se improper. In re Barry E., 107 Md. App. 206, 667 A.2d 931 (1995).

Jury trial. — Where adults demanded and received a jury trial in Juvenile Court they acquiesced in and recognized the validity of that form of trial. Any error in granting a jury trial was waived by the appellants' being the movants in that seemingly procedural aberration. In re Jeannette L., 71 Md. App. 70, 523 A.2d 1048, cert. denied, 310 Md. 491, 530 A.2d 273 (1987).

Family counseling. — Even absent a "contributing" conviction, juvenile courts have the authority to require parents of children adjudicated "delinquent," "in need of supervision," or "in need of assistance," to participate in family counseling and to cite recalcitrant parents for contempt of court. 62 Op. Att'y Gen. 516 (1977).

Rule 11-111. Masters.

a. *Authority.* 1. Detention or shelter care. A master is authorized to order detention or shelter care in accordance with Rule 11-112 (Detention or Shelter Care) subject to an immediate review by a judge if requested by any party.

2. Other matters. A master is authorized to hear any cases and matters assigned to him by the court, except a hearing on a waiver petition. The findings, conclusions and recommendations of a master do not constitute orders or final action of the court.

b. *Report to the court.* Within ten days following the conclusion of a disposition hearing by a master, he shall transmit to the judge the entire file in the case, together with a written report of his proposed findings of fact, conclusions of law, recommendations and proposed orders with respect to adjudication and disposition. A copy of his report and proposed order shall be served upon each party as provided by Rule 1-321.

c. *Review by court if exceptions filed.* Any party may file exceptions to the master's proposed findings, conclusions, recommendations or proposed orders.

Exceptions shall be in writing, filed with the clerk within five days after the master's report is served upon the party, and shall specify those items to which the party excepts, and whether the hearing is to be de novo or on the record.

Upon the filing of exceptions, a prompt hearing shall be scheduled on the exceptions. An excepting party other than the State may elect a hearing de novo or a hearing on the record. If the State is the excepting party, the hearing shall be on the record, supplemented by such additional evidence as the judge considers relevant and to which the parties raise no objection. In either case the hearing shall be limited to those matters to which exceptions have been taken.

d. *Review by court in absence of exceptions.* In the absence of timely and proper exceptions, the master's proposed findings of fact, conclusions of law and recommendations may be adopted by the court and the proposed or other appropriate orders may be entered based on them. The court may remand the case to the master for further hearing, or may, on its own motion, schedule and conduct a further hearing supplemented by such additional evidence as the court considers relevant and to which the parties raise no objection. Action by the court under this section shall be taken within two days after the expiration of the time for filing exceptions. (Amended Nov. 5, 1976, effective Jan. 1, 1977; Apr. 6, 1984, effective July 1, 1984; June 5, 1996, effective Jan. 1, 1997.)

Source. — This Rule is former Rule 911.

Effect of amendments. — The 1996 amendment substituted "Rule 11-112" for "Rule 912" in a. 1.; and added the Source note.

Editor's note. — An Order dated June 5, 1996, effective Jan. 1, 1997, renumbered this Rule, which was formerly Rule 911.

Maryland Law Review. — For note, "Does a Juvenile Court Rehearing on the Record After a Master Has Made Proposed Findings Violate Double Jeopardy or Due Process?" see 39 Md. L. Rev. 395 (1979).

This Rule does not violate Fifth Amendment. — A proceeding under this Rule does not impinge on the purposes of the double jeopardy clause. Swisher v. Brady, 438 U.S. 204, 98 S. Ct. 2699, 57 L. Ed. 2d 705 (1978).

Purpose of Rule. — This Rule is a direct product of the desire of the State to continue using masters to meet the heavy burden of juvenile court caseloads while at the same time assuring that their use not violate the constitutional guarantee against double jeopardy. Swisher v. Brady, 438 U.S. 204, 98 S. Ct. 2699, 57 L. Ed. 2d 705 (1978).

Juvenile is placed in jeopardy when the State begins to offer evidence in an adjudicatory hearing before a master. Aldridge v. Dean, 395 F. Supp. 1161 (D. Md. 1975).

Court may hear testimony of victim. — This Rule permits the court to hear testimony of a victim if it chooses. Hazell v. State, 12 Md.

App. 144, 277 A.2d 639, cert. denied, 263 Md. 715 (1971).

A juvenile master may be assigned by the court to hear cases involving waivers of juvenile jurisdiction. Hazell v. State, 12 Md. App. 144, 277 A.2d 639, cert. denied, 263 Md. 715 (1971).

Master may conduct adjudicatory hearing. — A master himself is empowered to conduct an adjudicatory hearing. In re Brown, 13 Md. App. 625, 284 A.2d 441 (1971).

Exceptions to master's proposed findings. — The double jeopardy clause of the federal Constitution does not prohibit State officials, acting in accordance with this Rule, from taking exceptions to a master's proposed findings. Swisher v. Brady, 438 U.S. 204, 98 S. Ct. 2699, 57 L. Ed. 2d 705 (1978).

Time for filing exceptions. — In section c, phrase "within five days" of the service of the master's report means that the motion must be filed within a discrete five day period beginning with the date of that service. In re Danielle B., 78 Md. App. 41, 552 A.2d 570 (1989).

Double jeopardy clause precludes subsequent adjudicatory hearing where mistrial had been declared in a previous juvenile adjudicatory hearing, without manifest necessity and without the juvenile's consent.

In re Mark R., 294 Md. 244, 449 A.2d 393 (1982).

Scope of review. — The report of a juvenile master is reviewed by the trial court on the same basis as that of any other master authorized by the court, except for the added burden placed on a juvenile judge by the special nature of his role. In re Danielle B., 78 Md. App. 41, 552 A.2d 570 (1989).

Where it was clear from the master's opinion that the conclusion that the state has failed to prove a prima facie case is premised upon not believing the testimony, the circuit court is bound to review the facts as they were presented before making it's own independent disposition of them. This review involves a two-step process: 1) the court must look to the fact and the conclusions reached by the master; 2) the court must make its own judgment of what those facts mean. In re Danielle B., 78 Md. App. 41, 552 A.2d 570 (1989).

Power of judge regarding master's proposals. — Regardless of which party is initially favored by the master's proposals, and regardless of the presence or absence of exceptions, the judge is empowered to accept, modify, or reject those proposals. Swisher v. Brady, 438 U.S. 204, 98 S. Ct. 2699, 57 L. Ed. 2d 705 (1978).

Findings of fact do not result in final judgment. — Findings of fact and rulings of law made by a master in juvenile proceedings do not result in a final judgment on the merits. Caldor, Inc. v. Bowden, 330 Md. 632, 625 A.2d 959 (1993).

Findings of fact and rulings of law do not result in final judgment. — In juvenile proceedings, although the master must make written findings of fact, conclusions of law, and

recommendations with respect to adjudication and disposition, the master's findings and recommendations are not final orders of the court; it is the chancellor's role, and not the master's, to determine the ultimate rights of the parties. In re Michael G., 107 Md. App. 257, 667 A.2d 956 (1995).

Supplemental findings. — To the extent the juvenile court judge makes supplemental findings in a manner permitted by this Rule — either sua sponte, in response to the State's exceptions, or in response to the juvenile's exceptions, and either on the record or on a record supplemented by evidence to which the parties raise no objection — he does so without violating the constraints of the double jeopardy clause. Swisher v. Brady, 438 U.S. 204, 98 S. Ct. 2699, 57 L. Ed. 2d 705 (1978).

Additional evidence in de novo hearing. — It is not error to receive additional evidence as to a child in need of assistance (CINA) determination in a de novo hearing. In re Michael W., 89 Md. App. 612, 599 A.2d 458 (1991).

Authority to reject determination. — Juvenile court had authority to reject child in need of assistance (CINA) determination made by master, even though exception had been taken to proposed disposition and not to recommended adjudication, as the CINA determination was element of disposition hearing. In re Michael W., 89 Md. App. 612, 599 A.2d 458 (1991).

Rule governs over CJ § 3-813. — Although this Rule differs from CJ § 3-813, in significant aspects, under Maryland decisional law, the Rule governs. Swisher v. Brady, 438 U.S. 204, 98 S. Ct. 2699, 57 L. Ed. 2d 705 (1978).

Rule 11-112. Detention or shelter care.

a. *Emergency detention or shelter care.* 1. Authority. The court or an intake officer may authorize emergency detention or shelter care of a child taken into custody in accordance with Section 3-815 (b) of the Courts Article.

2. Report to court — Petition for continued detention or shelter care. If a child is placed in emergency detention or shelter care, the intake officer shall, on the next day the court is sitting:

(i) report that fact to the court, together with the circumstances that led to the child being placed in emergency detention or shelter care; and

(ii) if continued detention or shelter care is sought, file a petition for continued detention or shelter care showing cause why continued detention or shelter care is warranted.

3. Hearing. If a petition for continued detention or shelter care is filed pursuant to this Rule, a hearing shall be held on the day the petition is filed and the respondent shall be brought to court for the hearing. The hearing may be postponed or continued by the court for good cause shown, but it may not be postponed for more than eight days following the commencement of respon-

dent's emergency detention or shelter care. Reasonable notice of the date and time of the hearing shall be given to the respondent, and if possible to his parent and his counsel, if known.

b. *Continued detention or shelter care pending adjudication or waiver.*

1. Finding. Detention or shelter care may not be continued beyond emergency detention or shelter care unless after a hearing the court finds that one or more of the circumstances stated in Section 3-815 (b) of the Courts Article exists.

2. Maximum period of detention or shelter care. Continued detention or shelter care pending the adjudicatory or waiver hearing may not be ordered for a period of more than thirty days.

c. *Continued detention or shelter care after waiver or adjudicatory hearing.* The court may, on petition or of its own motion, continue detention or shelter care for a period not longer than thirty days after a denial of a petition for waiver or an adjudicatory hearing.

d. *Title 5 not applicable.* Title 5 of these rules does not apply to detention or shelter care hearings. (Amended Nov. 5, 1976, effective Jan. 1, 1977; Dec. 15, 1993, effective July 1, 1994; June 5, 1996, effective Jan. 1, 1997.)

Cross references. — See Rule 11-113 (Waiver of Jurisdiction) for procedures following waiver.

Source. — This Rule is former Rule 912.

Effect of amendments. — The 1996 amendment substituted "Rule 11-113" for "Rule 913" in the Cross reference note; and added the Source note.

Editor's note. — An Order dated June 5, 1996, effective Jan. 1, 1997, renumbered this Rule, which was formerly Rule 912.

University of Baltimore Law Forum. — For discussion of police investigative procedures and juveniles, see 16, No. 1 U. Balt. Law Forum 6 (1986).

Rule 11-113. Waiver of jurisdiction.

a. *Initiating waiver.* 1. On the court's own motion. Upon the filing of a juvenile petition alleging delinquency the court may on its own motion waive its exclusive original jurisdiction so that the respondent may be tried in the criminal court.

2. Petition by State's Attorney — Requirements. The State's Attorney may file a petition requesting the court to waive its exclusive jurisdiction over a juvenile respondent alleged to be delinquent. The petition shall:

(i) be filed with or after the filing of a juvenile petition, but before the commencement of an adjudicatory hearing;

(ii) comply with the provisions of Section 3-817 (a) of the Courts Article; and

(iii) state in clear, concise and specific language the reasons why the State's Attorney requests the waiver, taking into account the factors required to be considered by the court under Section 3-817 (c) and (d) of the Courts Article.

b. *Investigation.* Upon the filing of a waiver petition, the court shall order that a waiver investigation be made. The report of the waiver investigation shall include all social records that are to be made available to the court at the waiver hearing, and a copy of the report shall be served upon counsel for the parties at least two days before the hearing.

c. *Hearing.* 1. Hearing required — Exceptions. Except as provided by sections e and f of this Rule, the court may not waive its jurisdiction without first conducting a waiver hearing.

2. Time of hearing. The hearing shall take place

(i) after notice has been given pursuant to Rule 11-110 (Hearings — Generally).

(ii) prior to the commencement of an adjudicatory hearing.

3. Purpose of hearing. A waiver hearing is for the sole purpose of determining whether the court should waive its jurisdiction. The court shall assume, for purposes of that determination, that the respondent committed the delinquent act or crime alleged in the juvenile petition.

d. *Consideration in determining waiver.* In determining whether to waive its jurisdiction, the court shall comply with the provisions of Section 3-817 (c) and (d) of the Courts Article. In the interest of justice, the court may decline to require strict application of the rules in Title 5, except those relating to the competency of witnesses.

e. *Summary review.* If the court has once waived its jurisdiction with respect to a respondent who again comes before the court on a juvenile petition alleging delinquency, the court, on its motion or on a waiver petition filed by the State's Attorney, may waive its jurisdiction in the subsequent proceeding after summary review and without a hearing.

f. *Adult respondent.* Jurisdiction over an adult respondent charged under Section 3-831 of the Courts Article shall be waived by the court upon the motion of the State's Attorney or the adult respondent. Jurisdiction may be waived by the court upon its own initiative or after a hearing upon the motion of any party, if charges against the adult respondent arising out of the same incident are pending in the criminal court.

g. *Order.* 1. Jurisdiction waived. If the court concludes that its jurisdiction should be waived, it shall:

(a) state the grounds for its decision on the record or in a written memorandum filed with the clerk.

(b) enter an order:

(i) waiving its jurisdiction and ordering the respondent held for trial under the appropriate criminal procedure;

(ii) placing the respondent in the custody of the sheriff or other appropriate officer in an adult detention facility pending a pretrial release hearing pursuant to Rule 4-222.

2. Juvenile petition a charging document pending bail hearing. The juvenile petition shall be considered a charging document for the purpose of detaining the respondent pending a bail hearing.

3. True copies to be furnished appropriate officer. A true copy of the juvenile petition and of the court's signed order shall be furnished forthwith by the clerk to the appropriate officer pending a bail hearing.

h. *Effect of appeal.* Deleted Mar. 3, 1987, effective July 1, 1987. (Amended Nov. 5, 1976, effective Jan. 1, 1977; Apr. 6, 1984, effective July 1, 1984; Mar. 3,

1987, effective July 1, 1987; Dec. 15, 1993, effective July 1, 1994; June 5, 1996, effective Jan. 1, 1997.)

Source. — This Rule is former Rule 913.

Effect of amendments. — The 1996 amendment substituted "Rule 11-110" for "Rule 910" in c. 2. (i); and added the Source note.

Editor's note. — An Order dated June 5, 1996, effective Jan. 1, 1997, renumbered this Rule, which was formerly Rule 913.

This Rule establishes procedural requirements for a waiver of jurisdiction. Thomas v. State, 10 Md. App. 458, 271 A.2d 197 (1970), cert. denied, 261 Md. 729 (1971).

Right to jury trial recognized. — Because the penalty prescribed for violation of CJ § 3-831 is substantial, a trial by jury is required, if demanded. CJ § 3-804 (c) and section f of this Rule are but recognition of that right. In re Jeannette L., 71 Md. App. 70, 523 A.2d 1048, cert. denied, 310 Md. 491, 530 A.2d 273 (1987).

Summary review to be conducted in proceeding meeting due process requirements. — Although a "full blown" hearing is not required to waive jurisdiction, the due process clause requires that summary review may only be conducted in a proceeding in which the juvenile is provided at least with adequate notice, the right to counsel and the right to be present. In re Michael W., 53 Md. App. 271, 452 A.2d 1278 (1982).

Discretion of juvenile judge. — Waiver in a juvenile case is committed to the sound discretion of the juvenile judge, to be disturbed on appeal only upon a finding that such discretion has been abused. In re Appeal No. 646, 35 Md. App. 94, 369 A.2d 150 (1977).

Waiver hearing was improper. — A waiver hearing was patently improper at the stage where there had already been an adjudicatory hearing. In re Nawrocki, 15 Md. App. 252, 289 A.2d 846, cert. denied, 266 Md. 741 (1972).

Degree of proof. — Waiver is justified where a preponderance of the legally sufficient evidence shows that such a determination is proper in light of the factors to be considered under CJ § 3-817. Hazell v. State, 12 Md. App. 144, 277 A.2d 639 (1971).

Nothing in the Constitution, State or federal, requires the State to satisfy the court beyond a reasonable doubt that waiver is proper; the inquiry at the waiver hearing does not require a finding of guilt or innocence, or proof of the elements of any criminal offense. Hazell v. State, 12 Md. App. 144, 277 A.2d 639, cert. denied, 263 Md. 715 (1971).

Statement of grounds for decision, separate from order of transfer, required when case is transferred to criminal court. — If a case is transferred to criminal court the statement by the court of the grounds for the decision, separate from the order of transfer, shall be made as required by this Rule. In re Toporzycki, 14 Md. App. 298, 287 A.2d 66 (1972).

Purpose of the statement required by section g 1 (a) of this Rule is to provide the parties and the reviewing court with the benefit of the trial court's reasons for its determination that the juvenile is an unfit subject for juvenile rehabilitative measures. In re Appeal No. 646, 35 Md. App. 94, 369 A.2d 150 (1977).

Contents of statement. — The statement required by section g 1 (a) of this Rule need not contain a point by point exposition of the trial court's consideration of each of the five enumerated criteria in CJ § 3-817. At a minimum, however, the statement should contain such factual findings as would permit the conclusion that the trial court has considered the criteria individually and in relation to each other and the basis on which it has reached its conclusion. In re Appeal No. 646, 35 Md. App. 94, 369 A.2d 150 (1977).

Suspension of lower court's jurisdiction pending appeal. — If an appeal is noted from an order of waiver in accordance with the Maryland Rules, the criminal court, pending the determination of the appeal has no jurisdiction over the case. The Court of Special Appeals is then vested with the exclusive power and jurisdiction over the subject matter of the proceedings, and the authority and control of the lower court with reference thereto are suspended. Aye v. State, 17 Md. App. 32, 299 A.2d 513 (1973).

When criminal court may proceed to try case. — Unless the authority over and control of a criminal case are suspended by an appeal to the Court of Special Appeals from an order of waiver, the criminal court may, upon termination of the period within which such appeal may be filed, then proceed to hear, try and determine the case against a child. Aye v. State, 17 Md. App. 32, 299 A.2d 513 (1973).

Bad faith not shown. — There was nothing in the record to show bad faith on the part of the State's Attorney in offering into evidence a waiver of jurisdiction by the juvenile court. Halstead v. State, 4 Md. App. 121, 241 A.2d 439 (1968).

No stenographic transcript. — See
Jefferson v. State, 218 Md. 397, 147 A.2d 204
(1958).

Rule 11-114. Adjudicatory hearing.

a. *Requirement.* After a juvenile petition has been filed, and unless jurisdiction has been waived, the court shall hold an adjudicatory hearing.

b. *Scheduling of hearing.* 1. Adjudicatory hearing. An adjudicatory hearing shall be held within sixty days after the juvenile petition is served on the respondent unless a waiver petition is filed, in which case an adjudicatory hearing shall be held within thirty days after the court's decision to retain jurisdiction at the conclusion of the waiver hearing. However, upon motion made on the record within these time limits by the petitioner or the respondent, the administrative judge of the county or a judge designated by him, for extraordinary cause shown, may extend the time within which the adjudicatory hearing may be held. The judge shall state on the record the cause which requires an extension and specify the number of days of the extension.

2. Prehearing detention or shelter care. If the respondent is in detention or shelter care, the adjudicatory hearing shall be held within thirty days from the date on which the court ordered continued detention or shelter care. If an adjudicatory hearing is not held within thirty days, the respondent shall be released on the conditions imposed by the court pending an adjudicatory hearing, which hearing shall be held within the time limits set forth in subsection 1 of this section.

c. *Presentation of evidence.* If the juvenile petition alleges delinquency, the State's Attorney shall present the evidence in support of it unless excused by the court. In all other cases the appropriate governmental or social agency or other persons authorized by the court shall present the evidence.

d. *Respondent's right to remain silent.* A respondent may remain silent as of right during an adjudicatory hearing on an allegation of delinquency and in all other cases where permitted on constitutional grounds; and the respondent shall be advised of this right by the court.

e. *Evidence — Proof of allegations of petition.* 1. Petition alleging delinquency. The allegations of a juvenile petition that the respondent has committed a delinquent act must be proved beyond a reasonable doubt. An uncorroborated extra judicial confession is not sufficient to establish that the respondent committed the delinquent act.

2. Petition alleging contributing. The allegations of a juvenile petition that an adult respondent violated Section 3-831 of the Courts Article must be proved beyond a reasonable doubt.

3. Other cases. All other allegations of a juvenile petition must be proved by a preponderance of the evidence.

f. *Adjudication — Finding — Adjudicatory order.* If the hearing is conducted by a judge, at its conclusion, he shall announce and dictate to the court stenographer or reporter, or prepare and file with the clerk, an adjudicatory order stating the grounds upon which he bases his adjudication. If the hearing is conducted by a master, the procedures set forth in Rule 11-111 (Masters) shall be followed. (Amended Nov. 5, 1976, effective Jan. 1, 1977; Nov. 13, 1981, effective Jan. 1, 1982; June 5, 1996, effective Jan. 1, 1997.)

Source. — This Rule is former Rule 914.

Effect of amendments. — The 1996 amendment substituted "Rule 11-111" for "Rule 911" in the second sentence of f.; and added the Source note.

Editor's note. — An Order dated June 5, 1996, effective Jan. 1, 1997, renumbered this Rule, which was formerly Rule 914.

Legislative intent. — The General Assembly intended to maintain the distinct functions of the adjudicatory hearing and the dispositional hearing by eliminating all inquiry into the child's need for guidance or treatment from the former, thereby preventing irrelevant and potentially prejudicial facts from being taken into consideration in the adjudication of pending charges. In re Ernest J., 52 Md. App. 56, 447 A.2d 97 (1982).

"Adjudicatory hearing." — The "adjudicatory hearing" is not that phase of the proceeding, frequently conducted ex parte and frequently conducted in camera, whereat the supervising judge ratifies, modifies or rejects the findings and recommendations of the master. In re Brown, 13 Md. App. 625, 284 A.2d 441 (1971).

The clear contemplation of the Maryland law is that the "adjudicatory hearing" is that phase of the total proceeding whereto witnesses are summoned; whereat they are sworn, confronted with the alleged delinquent, examined and cross-examined; whereat their demeanor is observed, their credibility assessed and their testimony weighed; whereat the testimony is subject to the rules of evidence and is transcribed by a court reporter; whereat the alleged delinquent is represented by counsel and where he enjoys the right to remain silent; whereat the State's Attorney marshals and presents the evidence for the petitioner; and whereat the presiding judge or master makes and announces his finding including "a brief statement of the grounds upon which . . . [he] bases . . . [his] determination." In re Brown, 13 Md. App. 625, 284 A.2d 441 (1971).

"Held." — As used in this Rule, "held" does not mean completed, but means that the hearing should be initiated within thirty days and completed with a reasonable degree of continuity; by a reasonable degree of continuity, it is meant that a hearing once begun must continue, insofar as possible, on a day to day basis until completed. In re Vanessa C., 104 Md. App. 452, 656 A.2d 795 (1995).

Primary purpose of adjudicatory hearing is to determine the merits of the allegation in the petition. In re Ernest J., 52 Md. App. 56, 447 A.2d 97 (1982).

A juvenile proceeding is not a criminal proceeding. Pennsylvania ex rel. Warren v. Warren, 204 Md. 467, 105 A.2d 488 (1954); Moquin v. State, 216 Md. 524, 140 A.2d 914 (1958).

The adjudicatory hearing is not a criminal proceeding. In re Appeal No. 544, 25 Md. App. 26, 332 A.2d 680 (1975).

This Rule anticipates breach of its provisions in one part of its mandate, but imposes a sanction substantially less severe than dismissal of the petition. In re Howard L., 50 Md. App. 498, 438 A.2d 939 (1982).

Master is empowered to conduct an adjudicatory hearing. — A master himself is empowered to conduct an adjudicatory hearing. In re Brown, 13 Md. App. 625, 284 A.2d 441 (1971).

Time interval between waiver and adjudicatory hearings. — While setting forth no minimum time interval between a waiver hearing and an adjudicatory hearing, section b 1 of this Rule sets forth a maximum period of 30 days from the conclusion of the waiver hearing. Parojinog v. State, 282 Md. 256, 384 A.2d 86 (1978).

Thirty-day requirement in this Rule must be read in conjunction with method for time computation set forth in Maryland Rules. In re Stephen J., 48 Md. App. 736, 429 A.2d 307 (1981).

Degree of proof. — Only in a determination that a child is delinquent and in cases in which an adult is charged under the subtitle "Juvenile Causes" in the Courts Article must the allegations be proved beyond a reasonable doubt. Woods v. Department of Social Servs., 11 Md. App. 10, 272 A.2d 92, cert. denied, 261 Md. 724, 730, 404 U.S. 965, 92 S. Ct. 340, 30 L. Ed. 2d 285 (1971).

A disposition hearing separate and distinct from a delinquency adjudication hearing is required. — That a disposition hearing separate and distinct from the delinquency adjudication hearing is required subsequent to the finding of delinquency is plainly mandated by CJ §§ 3-819 and 3-820, and by the provisions of this Rule and Rule 915 (now Rule 11-115). In re Wooten, 13 Md. App. 521, 284 A.2d 32 (1971).

A disposition hearing separate and distinct from the delinquency adjudication hearing is required subsequent to the finding of delinquency and is plainly mandated by CJ §§ 3-819 and 3-820, and by the provisions of this Rule and Rule 915 (now Rule 11-115). The reason for such a bifurcated process is equally clear. The adjudicatory hearing is solely to determine the merits of the allegations of delinquency. In re Roberts, 13 Md. App. 644, 284 A.2d 621 (1971).

Interwoven adjudicatory and disposition hearing violated rules. — Where the adjudicatory hearing and disposition hearing were interwoven and the juveniles were actually ordered committed to the Maryland Training School before they were adjudged "delinquent," the hearing before the juvenile judge was violative of the rules. In re Arnold, 12 Md. App. 384, 278 A.2d 658 (1971).

Sanction for violation of Rule. — In determining whether dismissal is an appropriate sanction for violation of this Rule, such as a violation of the time limitations in this Rule, a judge presiding over a juvenile cause should examine the totality of the circumstances as required by Rule 1-201. In doing so, the judge must keep in mind the overriding purpose of the juvenile statute along with the fact that this purpose will ordinarily not be served by dismissal of the juvenile proceeding. Neither the juvenile nor society should be denied the benefits of the juvenile's rehabilitation because of a technical violation of scheduling requirements. In re Keith W., 310 Md. 99, 527 A.2d 35 (1987).

Findings not res judicata in restitution proceeding. — Findings of adjudicatory proceeding against child were not res judicata as to parent in restitution proceeding. In re Appeal No. 769, 25 Md. App. 565, 335 A.2d 204 (1975).

Rule 11-115. Disposition hearing.

a. *Hearing — Scheduling.* If after an adjudicatory hearing the court determines that the allegations of the petition at issue in the adjudicatory hearing have been sustained, it shall promptly schedule a separate disposition hearing. The disposition hearing shall be held no later than thirty days after the conclusion of the adjudicatory hearing.

b. *Disposition — Judge or master.* The disposition made by the court shall be in accordance with Section 3-820 (b) of the Courts Article. If the disposition hearing is conducted by a judge, and his order includes placement of the child outside the home, the judge shall announce in open court and shall prepare and file with the clerk, a statement of the reasons for the placement. If the hearing is conducted by a master, the procedures of Rule 11-111 shall be followed. In the interest of justice, the judge or master may decline to require strict application of the rules in Title 5, except those relating to the competency of witnesses. A commitment recommended by a master is subject to approval by the court in accordance with Rule 11-111, but may be implemented in advance of court approval.

c. *Placement in a State mental hospital.* 1. Standard for commitment. A court may not commit a child to the Department of Health and Mental Hygiene for inpatient care and treatment at a State mental hospital unless the court finds that

(a) the child has a mental disorder, and

(b) the child needs inpatient care and treatment for the protection of himself or others, and

(c) the child is unable or unwilling to be voluntarily admitted to such hospital, and

(d) there is no less restrictive form of intervention available which is consistent with the child's condition and welfare.

2. Order for evaluation. If the court has reason to believe that a child should be committed to the Department of Health and Mental Hygiene for inpatient care and treatment at a State mental hospital, it shall order that the child be evaluated, pursuant to Section 3-818 of the Courts Article and Rule 11-105. The order shall require the agency conducting the evaluation to submit a written report setting forth its findings regarding

(a) the extent to which the standard for commitment set forth in subsection c 1 of this Rule is met,

(b) the bases for these findings,

(c) its recommended disposition, and

(d) the reasons for its recommended disposition.

The evaluation shall be conducted on an outpatient basis if, considering the child's condition, that is feasible and appropriate. Where an inpatient evaluation is necessary, the court may authorize the admission of the child to a State mental hospital for a period not to exceed 30 days for the purpose of the evaluation.

3. Modification or vacation of commitment order. (a) Periodic review. A commitment order issued under section b of this Rule shall require the Department or the hospital to file progress reports with the court at six-month intervals throughout the commitment. The report shall comply with the requirements of an evaluation report under subsection c 2 of this Rule. A copy of each report shall be given to the child's attorney of record. The court shall review each report promptly and consider whether the commitment order should be modified or vacated. Upon the request of any party, the Department, or the hospital, or upon its own motion, the court shall grant a hearing for the purpose of hearing testimony pertinent to its review.

(b) Other review. In addition to the periodic review provided for in subsection c 3 (a) of this Rule, the court may at any time upon the petition of any party, the Department, or the hospital, or upon its own motion, modify or vacate its order, provided that the court may not modify or vacate its order without notice and opportunity for hearing.

d. *Commitment to Department of Social Services.* In cases in which a child is committed to a local department of social services for placement outside the child's home, the court, within 18 months after the original placement and periodically thereafter at intervals not greater than 18 months, shall conduct a review hearing to determine whether and under what circumstances the child's commitment to the local department of social services should continue. Considerations pertinent to the determination include whether the child should (1) be returned home, (2) be continued in foster care for a specified period, (3) be placed for adoption, or (4) because of the child's special needs or circumstances, be continued in foster care on a permanent or long-term basis. The hearing shall be conducted as prescribed in Rule 11-110 or, if conducted by a master, as prescribed in Rule 11-111, except that the child's presence shall not be required if presence at the hearing is likely to cause serious physical, mental, or emotional harm to the child. (Amended Nov. 5, 1976, effective Jan. 1, 1977; Apr. 18, 1980, effective July 1, 1980; June 23, 1983, effective July 1, 1983; Dec. 15, 1993, effective July 1, 1994; June 5, 1996, effective Jan. 1, 1997.)

Source. — This Rule is former Rule 915.

Effect of amendments. — The 1996 amendment substituted "Rule 11-111" for "Rule 911" twice in b.; substituted "Rule 11-105" for "Rule 905" in the introductory language of c. 2.; in d., substituted "Rule 11-110" for "Rule 910" and substituted "Rule 11-111" for "Rule 911"; and added the Source note.

Editor's note. — An Order dated June 5, 1996, effective Jan. 1, 1997, renumbered this Rule, which was formerly Rule 915.

Applicability of section b. — Section b applies to placement of a child outside of the home following a determination on allegations contained in a petition. In re Jessica M., 72 Md. App. 7, 527 A.2d 766 (1987), aff'd, 312 Md. 93, 538 A.2d 305 (1988).

Direction of dispositional process. — The dispositional process is directed toward the termination of a committal or other disposition when the juvenile court finds the child to be rehabilitated, and directed away from setting mandatory periods of commitment, which would be more in the nature of punishment. In re No. 1140, S.T. 1977, 39 Md. App. 609, 387 A.2d 315 (1978).

A disposition hearing separate and distinct from a delinquency adjudication hearing is required. — That a disposition hearing separate and distinct from the delinquency adjudication hearing is required subsequent to the finding of delinquency is plainly mandated by CJ §§ 3-819 and 3-820, and by the provisions of former Rule 914 (now Rule 11-114) and this Rule. In re Wooten, 13 Md. App. 521, 284 A.2d 32 (1971).

A disposition hearing separate and distinct from the delinquency adjudication hearing is required subsequent to the finding of delinquency and is plainly mandated by CJ §§ 3-819 and 3-820, and by the provisions of former Rule 914 (now Rule 11-114) and this Rule. The reason for such a bifurcated process is equally clear. The adjudicatory hearing is solely to determine the merits of the allegations of delinquency. In re Roberts, 13 Md. App. 644, 284 A.2d 621 (1971).

Interwoven adjudicatory and disposition hearing violated rules. — Where the adjudicatory hearing and disposition hearing were interwoven and the juveniles were actually ordered committed to the Maryland Training School before they were adjudged "delinquent," the hearing before the juvenile judge was violative of the rules. In re Arnold, 12 Md. App. 384, 278 A.2d 658 (1971).

No requirement that disposition hearing be completed within 30 days. — No useful purpose is served by interpreting this Rule to require that the disposition hearing must be completed within 30 days of the adjudicatory hearing; all that this Rule necessitates is that the disposition hearing be commenced within that time frame, provided exigent circumstances do not foreclose that possibility. In re Phillip P., 50 Md. App. 235, 437 A.2d 892 (1981).

Unlike section b, section d does not require the court to announce its reasons in open court and to prepare a statement thereof. In re Jessica M., 72 Md. App. 7, 527 A.2d 766 (1987), aff'd, 312 Md. 93, 538 A.2d 305 (1988).

Dismissal of proceeding concerning juvenile is not proper sanction for violation of 30-day requirement of this Rule. In re Dewayne H., 290 Md. 401, 430 A.2d 76 (1981).

Section b is mandatory. In re Virgil M., 46 Md. App. 654, 421 A.2d 105 (1980).

Reasons upon which disposition made. — Section b refers to CJ § 3-820 and indicates that among the reasons upon which the judge must base his determination as to the placement of a child are the best interests of the child and the feasibility of programs which allow the child to remain at home. In re Virgil M., 46 Md. App. 654, 421 A.2d 105 (1980).

Statement of reasons for placement outside home. — When the Court of Appeals adopted this Rule, it expected, desired and required by way of reasons under section b for placement of a child outside his home something more than perfunctory statements in the court's summary. In re Appeal No. 1327, 32 Md. App. 478, 361 A.2d 156 (1976).

When child is placed in custody of Department of Health and Mental Hygiene for inpatient care at a State mental hospital, section b of this Rule as well as CJ § 3-820 (h) (duplicated on April 18, 1980 as Md. Rule 915 c) spell out the prerequisites of such commitment, based upon clear and convincing evidence. In re Jeffrey L., 50 Md. App. 268, 437 A.2d 255 (1981).

Rule 11-116. Modification or vacation of order.

a. *Revisory power.* An order of the court may be modified or vacated if the court finds that action to be in the best interest of the child or the public, except in cases involving commitment of a child to the Department of Health and Mental Hygiene for placement in a State mental hospital. In cases involving such commitment the court shall proceed as provided in Rule 11-115. (Amended Nov. 7, 1976, effective Jan. 1, 1997; Apr. 18, 1980, effective July 1, 1980.)

b. *Sua sponte or on petition.* The court may proceed under section a of this Rule on its own motion, or on the petition of any party or other person, institution or agency having supervision or custody of the respondent, setting forth in concise terms the grounds upon which the relief is requested. If the court proceeds on its own motion, the order shall set forth the grounds on which it is based.

c. *Hearing — When required.* If the relief sought under section a of this Rule is for revocation of probation and for the commitment of a respondent, the court shall pass an order to show cause why the relief should not be granted and setting a date and time for a hearing. The clerk shall cause a copy of the petition and Show Cause Order to be served upon the parties. In all other cases, the court may grant or deny the relief, in whole or in part, without a hearing.

d. *Conduct of hearing.* In the interest of justice, at any hearing held pursuant to this Rule the court may decline to require strict application of the rules in Title 5, except those relating to the competency of witnesses. (Amended Nov. 5, 1976, effective Jan. 1, 1977; Dec. 15, 1993, effective July 1, 1994; June 5, 1996, effective Jan. 1, 1997.)

Source. — This Rule is former Rule 916.

Effect of amendments. — The 1996 amendment substituted "Rule 11-115" for "Rule 915" in the second sentence of a.; and added the Source note.

Editor's note. — An Order dated June 5, 1996, effective Jan. 1, 1997, renumbered this Rule, which was formerly Rule 916.

Maryland Law Review. — For article, "Maryland's Exchangeable Children: A Critique of Maryland's System of Providing Services to Mentally Handicapped Children," see 42 Md. L. Rev. 823 (1983).

Constitutional considerations may preclude availability of relief. — Constitutional considerations other than the double jeopardy prohibition may preclude the availability of relief under this Rule; for example, due process principles would limit the time period within which reconsideration may be granted and would preclude the State from repeatedly seeking reconsiderations of the same petition. In re John P., 311 Md. 700, 537 A.2d 263 (1988).

Operation of this Rule is unlimited with respect to the time running from the original order. In re No. 1140, S.T. 1977, 39 Md. App. 609, 387 A.2d 315 (1978).

But not guarantee of limited commitment. — Reliance on this Rule alone will not guarantee that children committed under CJ § 3-820 or the general involuntary admission provisions will remain committed only so long as is medically necessary. Johnson v. Solomon, 484 F. Supp. 278 (D. Md. 1979).

Granting motion for reconsideration did not violate Fifth Amendment or Maryland common law. — Granting motion for reconsideration of order dismissing "child in need of assistance" petitions on the merits did not violate the Double Jeopardy Clause of the Fifth Amendment or the Maryland common-law double jeopardy prohibition. In re John P., 311 Md. 700, 537 A.2d 263 (1988).

Reinstatement of restitution claim against juvenile. — The Juvenile Court has authority to vacate an order dismissing a restitution claim against a juvenile and to reinstate the claim. In re Darnell F., 71 Md. App. 584, 526 A.2d 971, aff'd, 311 Md. 144, 532 A.2d 1371 (1987).

Rule 11-117. Custody — Appointment of guardian — Pending support proceedings.

a. *Custody — Appointment of guardian of the person.* The court shall determine the custody or appoint a guardian of the person of a child only if the question arises in connection with a matter which is within its exclusive jurisdiction under Sections 3-804 and 3-805 (a) of the Courts Article, and the determination of the question is necessary to make an appropriate disposition.

b. *Pending support proceedings.* The court shall give due consideration to orders or proceedings pertaining to custody or support issued by or pending in other courts. However, this shall not affect the court's authority to detain, commit, or place in shelter care a child under its jurisdiction, or to exercise its authority in accordance with Sections 3-827 and 3-830 of the Courts Article. (Amended Nov. 5, 1976, effective Jan. 1, 1977; June 5, 1996, effective Jan. 1, 1997.)

Cross references. — For authority of a judge in juvenile proceedings to determine the custody or appoint a guardian "of a juvenile subject to the jurisdiction of equity courts," see § 3-820 (b) and (c) of the Courts Article. For procedure for exercise of appointment of a guardian, see Title 10, Chapter 100. For requirement of notice in the original summons with respect to custody and support payments, see subsection c of Rule 11-104 (Duties of Clerk). The notice, when given in accordance with that Rule, shall be sufficient to permit the consideration and determination of these questions at hearings held after service of the summons.

Source. — This Rule is former Rule 917.

Effect of amendments. — The 1996 amendment, in the Cross reference note, substituted "Title 10, Chapter 100" for "Subtitle R (Minors and Persons Under Disability)" in the second sentence and substituted "Rule 11-104" for "Rule 904" in the third sentence; and added the Source note.

Editor's note. — An Order dated June 5, 1996, effective Jan. 1, 1997, renumbered this Rule, which was formerly Rule 917.

Rule 11-118. Parents' liability — Hearing — Recording and effect.

a. *Hearing.* If, at any stage of a proceeding, the court believes a respondent has committed acts for which the respondent's parent or parents may be liable under Code, Article 27, § 807, the court shall summon the parent or parents in the manner provided by Chapter 100 of Title 2 for service of process to obtain personal jurisdiction over a person to appear at a hearing to determine liability. This hearing may be conducted contemporaneously with a disposition hearing, if appropriate.

b. *Recording.* Recordation of a judgment of restitution shall be governed by Code, Article 27, § 807. (Amended Nov. 5, 1976, effective Jan. 1, 1977; Apr. 6, 1984, effective July 1, 1984; June 5, 1996, effective Jan. 1, 1997; June 8, 1998, effective Oct. 1, 1998.)

Source. — This Rule is derived in part from former Rule 918 and is in part new.

Effect of amendments. — The 1996 amendment added the Source note.

The 1998 amendment rewrote the Rule.

Editor's note. — An Order dated June 5, 1996, effective Jan. 1, 1997, renumbered this Rule, which was formerly Rule 918.

Matter of restitution should be considered and resolved no later than at a juvenile's disposition hearing. In re Yoldande L., 49 Md. App. 310, 431 A.2d 743 (1981).

Relief where parent not afforded proper notice of claim or fair opportunity to defend. — Where appellant's mother was not afforded proper notice of the claim for restitution to be asserted against her and a fair opportunity to defend the claim, judgment as to the mother must be vacated. On remand, she should be served with a copy of the delinquency petition, receive notice of the hearing, and be afforded a reasonable opportunity to be heard and to present evidence in her behalf. In re James B., 54 Md. App. 270, 458 A.2d 847 (1983).

Rule 11-119. Disposition of property brought into court.

Property brought into court shall be returned to the owner, or otherwise disposed of as the court may direct. (Amended Nov. 5, 1976, effective Jan. 1, 1977; June 5, 1996, effective Jan. 1, 1997.)

Source. — This Rule is former Rule 919.

Effect of amendments. — The 1996 amendment added the Source note.

Editor's note. — An Order dated June 5, 1996, effective Jan. 1, 1997, renumbered this Rule, which was formerly Rule 919.

Rule 11-120. Final order of termination.

A final order of termination of the proceedings may, in the court's discretion, be entered on the court's own motion at any time after the court's jurisdiction over the respondent is terminated, or upon the recommendation of the appropriate governmental or social agency exercising supervision over the respondent. (Amended Nov. 5, 1976, effective Jan. 1, 1977; June 5, 1996, effective Jan. 1, 1997.)

Source. — This Rule is former Rule 920.

Effect of amendments. — The 1996 amendment added the Source note.

Editor's note. — An Order dated June 5, 1996, effective Jan. 1, 1997, renumbered this Rule, which was formerly Rule 920.

Rule 11-121. Court records — Confidentiality.

a. *Sealing of records.* Files and records of the court in juvenile proceedings, including the docket entries and indices, are confidential and shall not be open to inspection except by order of the court or as otherwise expressly provided by law. On termination of the court's juvenile jurisdiction, the files and records shall be sealed pursuant to Section 3-828 (c) of the Courts Article, and all index references shall be marked "sealed." If a hearing is open to the public pursuant to Code, Courts Article, § 3-812, the name of the respondent and the date, time, and location of the hearing are not confidential.

b. *Unsealing of records.* Sealed files and records of the court in juvenile proceedings may be unsealed and inspected only by order of the court. (Amended Nov. 5, 1976, effective Jan. 1, 1977; June 5, 1996, effective Jan. 1, 1997; June 8, 1998, effective October 1, 1998.)

Cross references. — For confidentiality in appellate proceedings, see Rule 8-121 (Appeals from Courts Exercising Juvenile Jurisdiction — Confidentiality).

Source. — This Rule is former Rule 921.

Effect of amendments. — The 1996 amendment added the Source note.

The 1998 amendment, in a., added "or as otherwise expressly provided by law" in the first sentence and added the last sentence.

Editor's note. — An Order dated June 5,

1996, effective Jan. 1, 1997, renumbered this Rule, which was formerly Rule 921.

Closed proceedings. — Courts may close juvenile proceedings to the public in instances where closure would be impermissible in other court proceedings. Baltimore Sun Co. v. State, 340 Md. 437, 667 A.2d 166 (1995).

Access to proceedings by press. — Although a juvenile court has the discretion to exclude the press from a juvenile proceeding, its discretion is not unlimited and must be exercised in accord with the purposes for which it was given and within applicable constitutional limitations. Baltimore Sun Co. v. State, 340 Md. 437, 667 A.2d 166 (1995).

While a court can place reasonable restrictions on the media's use of information obtained in a confidential juvenile proceeding, it cannot limit the media's publication of information which it legitimately collected from other sources, and cannot condition access to the juvenile proceeding upon the media's publication of material specified by the court. Baltimore Sun Co. v. State, 340 Md. 437, 667 A.2d 166 (1995).

Access by agents of Division of Parole and Probation. — Although court records pertaining to juveniles are to be maintained in a confidential manner as a general rule, agents of the Division of Parole and Probation may have access to such records when they are carrying out, at the direction of a court of competent jurisdiction, any of the Division's statutory duties. 63 Op. Att'y Gen. 502 (1978).

Opening or divulging court records. — Court records pertaining to juveniles are held in confidence, and can only be divulged by court order, or for limited educational purposes. Baltimore Sun Co. v. State, 340 Md. 437, 667 A.2d 166 (1995).

Rule 11-122. Intervention.

a. *Of right.* Upon timely application, any parent not served with original process shall be permitted to intervene for any purpose.

Cross references. — Rule 11-101 b 4.

b. *Permissive.* Upon timely application, any person, other than a parent, seeking custody or guardianship of the respondent child may be permitted to intervene for dispositional purposes only, including the filing of a petition to review, modify or vacate a disposition order. Any person permitted to intervene pursuant to this section shall not be deemed a "party" for the purposes of Rule 11-106, and for the purposes of Rule 11-105, counsel for the intervenor, upon request, shall only be entitled to be furnished copies of such studies and reports as directly relate to the intervenor's petition for custody or guardianship of the respondent child.

c. *Procedure.* 1. Motion. An application to intervene shall be made by motion. If the applicant claims a right of intervention under section a of this Rule, the motion shall be accompanied by an affidavit showing that the applicant is a parent of the respondent child.

2. Leave of court. Leave to intervene shall be granted only by court order. When intervention is pursuant to section b of this Rule .the order shall designate the intervenor as a defendant for dispositional purposes only.

3. Service. A copy of the motion, the affidavit, any order thereon, and any pleading filed by the intervenor shall be served as provided by Rule 1-321. (Added Nov. 8, 1982, effective Jan. 1, 1983; amended Apr. 6, 1984, effective July 1, 1984; June 5, 1996, effective Jan. 1, 1997.)

Source. — This Rule is former Rule 922.

Effect of amendments. — The 1996 amendment substituted "Rule 11-101" for "Rule 901" in the Cross reference note in a.; in b., substituted "Rule 11-106" for "Rule 906" and substituted "Rule 11-105" for "Rule 905"; and added the Source note.

Editor's note. — An Order dated June 5, 1996, effective Jan. 1, 1997, renumbered this Rule, which was formerly Rule 922.

Rule 11-501. Termination of parental rights and related adoption proceedings in the juvenile court.

(a) *Applicability of Rule.* This Rule applies to actions in which the juvenile court is exercising jurisdiction pursuant to Code, Courts Article, § 3-804 (a) (2).

(b) *Definition.* The word "guardianship" as used in this Rule has the meaning stated in Code, Family Law Article, § 5-301.

(c) *Applicability of Titles 1, 2, 5, and 9.* The Rules in Titles 1, 2, and 5 and Chapter 100 of Title 9 apply to actions under this Rule, except as otherwise provided by law or ordered by the court.

(d) *Petition.* A proceeding for adoption or guardianship shall be initiated by the filing of a petition in a new action, separate from any other proceedings involving the child who is the subject of the adoption or guardianship proceeding. In addition to complying with the requirements of Rule 9-103, the petition shall state the basis for the juvenile court's jurisdiction and the name of the court and case number of the proceeding in which the child was adjudicated a child in need of assistance.

(e) *Consolidation.* A proceeding for adoption or guardianship may be consolidated with, or severed from, any other case pending in the juvenile court involving the child who is the subject of the proceeding, as justice may require.

(f) *Hearing — Before whom held.* All hearings conducted pursuant to this Rule shall be held before a judge.

(g) *Judgments of adoption — Recording and indexing.* The clerk shall record and index each judgment of adoption entered by the juvenile court on or after October 1, 1996 in the adoption records of the circuit court for the county where the judgment was entered. (Amended June 10, 1997, effective July 1, 1997.)

Committee note. — Judgments of adoption under this section include judgments entered under former Rule 923.

Source. — This Rule is new.

Effect of amendments. — The 1997 amendment added (g) and the Committee note.

Editor's note. — The 1997 amendment takes effect July 1, 1997, and applies to all judgments entered by the juvenile court on or after October 1, 1996.

Former similar provisions embodied in Rule 923 were rescinded effective January 1, 1997.

Rule 11-601. Expungement of criminal charges transferred to the juvenile court.

(a) *Procedure.* A petition for expungement of records may be filed by a respondent who is eligible under Code, Article 27, § 737 (b) to request expungement. Proceedings for expungement shall be in accordance with Title 4, Chapter 500 of these Rules, except that the petition shall be filed in the juvenile court and shall be substantially in the form set forth in section (b) of this Rule.

(b) *Form of petition.* A petition for expungement of records under this Rule shall be substantially in the following form:

(Caption)

PETITION FOR EXPUNGEMENT OF RECORDS

(Code*, Article 27, § 737 (b))

1. On or about _____ , I was arrested by an officer of the _____
(Law Enforcement Agency)
at _____ , Maryland, as a result of the following incident _____
_____ .

2. I was charged with the offense of _____
_____ .

3. The charge was transferred to the juvenile court under Code*, Article 27, § 594A and (check one of the following boxes):
☐ No petition under Code*, Courts Article, § 3-810 was filed;
☐ The decision on the juvenile petition was a finding of facts-not-sustained; or
☐ I was adjudicated delinquent and I am now at least 21 years of age.
WHEREFORE, I request the Court to enter an Order for Expungement of all police and court records pertaining to the above arrest, detention, confinement, and charges.

I solemnly affirm under the penalties of perjury that the contents of this Petition are true to the best of my knowledge, information and belief, and that the charge to which this Petition relates was not made for any violation of the Vehicle Laws of the State of Maryland, or any traffic law, ordinance, or regulation, nor is it part of a unit the expungement of which is precluded under Code*, Article 27, § 738.

_____   _____
(Date)   Signature

                                 _____
                                    (Address)

                                 _____
                                  (Telephone No.)

* References to "Code" in this Petition are to the Annotated Code of Maryland. (Added June 8, 1998, effective Oct. 1, 1998.)

Source. — This Rule is new.

TITLE 12. PROPERTY ACTIONS

Editor's note. — The Court of Appeals, by Order dated June 5, 1996, effective January 1, 1997, rescinded Subtitles A, D, E, J, P, Q, R, T, U, V, W, Y, Z, BB, BD, BE, BG, BH, BJ, BL, BP, BQ, BR, BS, BW, and BY of Chapter 1100 of the Maryland Rules of Procedure, rescinded Subtitles P, BB, BQ, and BW of the Maryland District Rules, and rescinded Forms 22a, 23, 24, 25, and 26. The Order substituted for certain of the rules and forms rescinded new Title 9, Chapter 100, Title 10, Title 12, Title 13, Title 14, and Title 15 of the Maryland Rules of Procedure. Furthermore, the Order transferred, without readoption, Chapter 900, Chapter 1200, and Subtitles S, BU, and BV of Chapter 1100 of the Maryland Rules of Procedure and Chapter 1200 of the Maryland District Rules to be Title 9, Chapter 200, Title 11, and Title 16 of the Maryland Rules of Procedure. The Order provides that the new rules shall "apply to all actions commenced on or after January 1, 1997, and insofar as practicable, to all actions then pending."

Many of the cases in the notes to the various rules were decided prior to the 1996 revision. These cases have been retained under pertinent rules of this title where it is thought that such cases will be of value in interpreting the present rules.

A table of comparable rules, relating those rules rescinded effective January 1, 1997, to the revised rules in Title 9 through Title 16 is to be found in Volume 2 following the end of the Maryland Rules.

CHAPTER 100. GENERAL PROVISIONS.

Rule 12-101. Writ of survey.

(a) *Availability.* On motion of a party in an action involving real property, the court may issue a writ of survey if it finds that a plat is necessary for illustration or that one of the following matters is in dispute: (1) the location of the property in dispute; (2) the location or extent of any property claimed to be damaged; or (3) the location of a dividing line if the parties are claiming under the same title. The motion shall contain a description sufficient to locate the property that is the subject of the claim. The court may condition issuance of the writ on the deposit by the moving party of the estimated cost of executing the writ.

(b) *Survey.* A writ of survey shall be issued to a surveyor designated by the court. The surveyor shall survey the property in accordance with the writ.

(c) *Plat.* The surveyor shall file the original and three copies of each plat with the clerk. Upon receiving payment of reasonable charges, the surveyor shall furnish a copy to any party.

Source. — This Rule is derived from former Rule T44.

The statutory source made radical changes in the practice. The court may, when it is satisfied that there is a dispute about boundaries, order a warrant of resurvey to be issued although defendant has not taken defense on warrant; when a warrant is so issued, the practice applicable to surveys made after defense on warrant is taken applies. The defendant may no longer take defense on warrant as a matter of right, and have a resurvey of the disputed land. Application must be made to court and warrant can only issue on its order or by agreement of parties. The warrant may be taken out at the instance of either party. The foregoing statements apply in an action of trespass q.c.f. Andrews v. Pitts, 126 Md. 328, 95 A. 203 (1915).

Application in action of trespass q.c.f. — An action of trespass q.c.f. is often resorted to in trying titles to land, and in actions involving locations it is much more satisfactory to have a warrant of resurvey. B & O R.R. v. Silbereisen, 121 Md. 407, 121 Md. 420, 88 A. 252, 89 A. 102 (1913).

Same — Lis pendens. — There was some indication in former §§ 34, 35 and 36 of Article 75 that the doctrine of lis pendens applied in a case of trespass quare clausum fregit, where a warrant of resurvey was issued. The point was not, however, decided in the case. Corey v. Carback, 201 Md. 389, 94 A.2d 629 (1953).

Bona fide dispute about location of property. — It is incumbent upon party applying for warrant of resurvey to furnish satisfactory evidence that there is a bona fide dispute about location of property or division line thereof. Where description of land sued for is identical with that claimed by defendant, and where both parties claim title from a common source, there is no necessity for issue of such warrant. Kelso v. Stigar, 75 Md. 376, 24 A. 18 (1892).

Mode of proof of land embraced within described boundaries not changed. — Former § 34 of Article 75 did not change laws and practice regulating surveys and locations, as to mode of proof of land actually embraced within boundaries described in patents, deeds, etc. Clary v. Kimmell, 18 Md. 246 (1862); Newman v. Young, 30 Md. 417 (1869).

Plats held to be authorized for illustration only. — See New York, P. & N.R.R. v. Jones, 94 Md. 24, 50 A. 423 (1901).

Plaintiff must locate every title paper in strict conformity with calls. — Since Acts 1852, ch. 177, gives defendant right to take defense on warrant, plaintiff must locate every title paper in strict conformity with the calls, etc., and if plats and explanations do not show them to be so located, they must be rejected at trial. Clary v. Kimmell, 18 Md. 246 (1862).

Rule 12-102. Lis pendens.

(a) *Scope.* This Rule applies to an action filed in a circuit court or in the United States District Court for the District of Maryland that affects title to or a leasehold interest in real property located in this State.

(b) *Creation — Constructive notice.* In an action to which the doctrine of lis pendens applies, the filing of the complaint is constructive notice of the lis pendens as to real property in the county in which the complaint is filed. In any other county, there is constructive notice only after the party seeking the lis pendens files either a certified copy of the complaint or a notice giving rise to the lis pendens, with the clerk in the other county.

(c) *Termination.* (1) While action is pending. On motion of a person in interest and for good cause, the court in the county in which the action is pending may enter an order terminating the lis pendens in that county or any other county in which the lis pendens has been created.

(2) Upon conclusion of action. If (A) the action is dismissed, or (B) judgment is entered in favor of the defendant and a timely appeal is not taken or the judgment is affirmed on appeal, or (C) judgment in favor of the plaintiff is reversed on appeal, vacated, or satisfied, the plaintiff shall file a certified copy of the appropriate docket entry with the clerk in each county in which a certified copy of the complaint or notice was filed pursuant to section (b) of this Rule. If the plaintiff fails to comply with this subsection, the court with jurisdiction over the action, on motion of any person in interest and upon such notice as the court deems appropriate in the circumstances, may enter an order terminating the lis pendens. In the order terminating the lis pendens, the court shall direct the plaintiff to pay the costs and expenses incurred by the person obtaining the order, including reasonable attorney's fees, unless the court finds that the plaintiff had a reason justifying the failure to comply.

(3) Duty of clerk. Upon entry of an order terminating a lis pendens, the clerk of the court of entry shall transmit a certified copy of the order to the clerk in any other county specified in the order.

Source. — This Rule is derived as follows: *Section (a)* is new.
Section (b) is derived from former Rule BD1 and BD2.

Section (c) is derived from former Rule BD3.

Maryland Law Review. — For comment, "Lis Pendens and Procedural Due Process: A Closer Look after Connecticut v. Doehr", see 51 Md. L. Rev. 1054 (1992).

University of Baltimore Law Review. — For discussion, "Property Disposition Upon Divorce in Maryland: An Analysis of the New Statute," see 8 U. Balt. L. Rev. 377 (1979).

Rule 12-103. Action for release of lien instrument.

When a mortgage or deed of trust remains unreleased of record, the mortgagor, grantor, or a successor in interest entitled by law to a release may file a complaint for release of the lien instrument in any county where the lien instrument is recorded. The person bringing the action shall include as defendants all other parties to the instrument unless their interest has been assigned or transferred of record, and in that case their successors in interest. If the court orders the lien instrument released of record, the clerk shall record the release in the manner prescribed by law.

Cross references. — Code, Real Property Article, § 7-106 (e) and § 3-105 (d).
Source. — This Rule is new.

CHAPTER 200. CONDEMNATION.

Rule 12-201. Applicability.

The rules in this Chapter govern actions for acquisition of property by condemnation under the power of eminent domain.

Cross references. — Code, Real Property Article, §§ 12-101 and 12-102; Maryland Constitution, Article III, §§ 40 and 40A.

Committee note. — These rules are not intended to cover "condemnation" of property as hazardous to health, etc., or to repeal or supersede statutory or constitutional authority for "quick take" procedures.

Source. — This Rule is derived from former Rule U1.

University of Baltimore Law Review. — For article, "State Constitutional Law for Maryland Lawyers: Individual Civil Rights," see 7 U. Balt. L. Rev. 299 (1978).

Maryland statute controls in proceedings by federal government to condemn. — In proceedings by federal government to condemn land, the procedure is controlled by Maryland statute, except as modified by federal statute. United States v. Certain Parcels of Land, 40 F. Supp. 436 (D. Md. 1941).

Proceeding is one at law. — A condemnation proceeding for the acquisition of private property for public use has always been held to be a proceeding at law, and Article 33A (now RP, Title 12) of the Code does not change the proceeding into an equitable one. Ridgeley v. Mayor of Baltimore, 119 Md. 567, 87 A. 909 (1913).

Proceedings initiated by property owner. — Neither Title 12 of the Real Property Article, nor former Subtitle U of the Maryland Rules provides that proceedings may be initiated by a property owner who believes that his property has been taken, either by condemnation or by virtue of proceedings or governmental action short of condemnation. Millison v. Wilzack, 77 Md. App. 676, 551 A.2d 899, cert. denied, 315 Md. 307, 554 A.2d 393 (1989).

Order condemning property for railroad crossing. — When property is being condemned for a railroad crossing, the order of court should limit the condemnation to such purpose, and the condemnation should be subject to the rights of the public. Mayor of Hyattsville v. Washington, W. & G.R.R., 120 Md. 128, 87 A. 828 (1913).

When sanitary commission exercised power of eminent domain and paid jury's award to clerk of the court, all as authorized and directed by statute, it conducted the condemnation in conformity with former Subtitle U, and the award paid into court was for the use of the defendant. This being so, it was "paid or tendered" to the defendant, the person entitled thereto, before her private property was taken for public use, thus, gratifying Md. Const., article III, § 40. Payment to the clerk is payment to the court of which he is an agent, and payment to a court has been held to be payment to the litigant entitled thereto. Fitzgerald v. Somerset County San. Comm'n, 231 Md. 242, 189 A.2d 601 (1963).

Rule 12-202. Venue.

An action for condemnation shall be brought in the county where the property sought to be condemned is located. If the property lies in more than one county, the action for condemnation may be brought in any county where a part of the property lies. The court in which proceedings are first brought shall have jurisdiction over the entire property.

Cross references. — Code, Courts Article, § 6-203. For constructive notice of a proceeding in another county, see Rule 12-102. For limitations on the constitutional right of removal in condemnation cases, see Mayor and City Council of Baltimore v. Kane, 125 Md. 135 (1915) and Mayor and City Council of Baltimore v. Libowitz, 159 Md. 27 (1937).

Source. — This Rule is derived from former Rule U2.

Petition should be filed where land is situated. — A petition for condemnation should be filed in the county or the City of Baltimore, where property is situated. Park Land Corp. v. Mayor of Baltimore, 128 Md. 611, 98 A. 153 (1916).

Proceedings initiated by property owner. — Neither Title 12 of the Real Property Article, nor former Subtitle U of the Maryland Rules provides that proceedings may be initiated by a property owner who believes that his property has been taken, either by condemnation or by virtue of proceedings or governmental action short of condemnation. Millison v. Wilzack, 77 Md. App. 676, 551 A.2d 899, cert. denied, 315 Md. 307, 554 A.2d 393 (1989).

Removal. — The right of removal has no application to condemnation proceedings under Acts 1912, ch. 117. Mayor of Baltimore v. Kane, 125 Md. 135, 93 A. 393 (1915).

Rule 12-203. Required parties defendant.

An action for condemnation shall be brought against all persons, known or unknown, whose interest in the property is sought to be condemned.

Committee note. — *See Department of Natural Resources v. Welsh*, 308 Md. 54 (1986) relating to the consequences of failure to join required parties defendant.

Source. — This Rule is derived from former Rule U4 b.

Persons bound by proceeding. — A condemnation proceeding is a proceeding in rem and is binding upon all persons who are interested in the res even though they may not be, technically, parties to the suit. Bugg v. Maryland Transp. Auth., 31 Md. App. 622, 358 A.2d 562, cert. denied, 278 Md. 717 (1976), appeal dismissed, 429 U.S. 1082, 97 S. Ct. 1088, 51 L. Ed. 2d 529 (1977).

Right to proceed and to close in condemnation cases rests with condemnor. Harford Bldg. Corp. v. Mayor of Baltimore, 58 Md. App. 85, 472 A.2d 479, cert. denied, 300 Md. 153, 476 A.2d 722 (1984).

No statutory authority gives a property owner the status of a plaintiff with the corresponding right to open and close a case. Harford Bldg. Corp. v. Mayor of Baltimore, 58 Md. App. 85, 472 A.2d 479, cert. denied, 300 Md. 153, 476 A.2d 722 (1984).

Interest of owner not a party. — When the condemnation of land is effected by judicial decree, failure to designate in the petition (and to make a party respondent) the owner of any interest in the land taken whose title appears of record or is otherwise ascertainable on reasonable inquiry renders the proceedings ineffectual to transfer such interest to the condemnor. Department of Natural Resources v. Welsh, 308 Md. 54, 521 A.2d 313 (1986).

Suit to condemn common elements of condominium. — While a trial judge is correct in directing that condominium unit owners and any mortgagees be added as parties to a suit to condemn a portion of the general common elements of the condominium, he subsequently errs when he fails to include their names on the inquisition form submitted to the jury. Andrews v. City of Greenbelt, 293 Md. 69, 441 A.2d 1064 (1982).

It is not enough that the inquisition form submitted to the jury in a suit to condemn a portion of the general common elements of the condominium named the council of unit owners of the condominium as the defendant because, even though the council is a legal entity comprised of all unit owners, it does not have legal title to the collectively held property and nothing in § 11-109 of the Real Property Article allows the association, acting in a representative capacity for the unit owners, to transfer title to regime property. Andrews v. City of Greenbelt, 293 Md. 69, 441 A.2d 1064 (1982).

Quoted in Conrad v. Department of Natural Resources, 30 Md. App. 479, 352 A.2d 904, cert. denied, 278 Md. 719 (1976).

Cited in Department of Natural Resources v. Welsh, 308 Md. 54, 521 A.2d 313 (1986).

Rule 12-204. Acquisition of cemetery.

(a) *Notice by publication before filing complaint.* Before filing a complaint for condemnation of property used as a cemetery, the plaintiff shall give notice by publication in a newspaper of general circulation in each county where any part of the property is located.

(b) *Contents of notice.* The notice shall contain the following information:

(1) the name of the plaintiff,

(2) an identification of the cemetery and a description of the part that is sought to be condemned,

(3) the purpose for which the property is sought to be condemned, and

(4) the name of the court in which the complaint is to be filed.

(c) *Time of publication.* The notice shall be published at least once a week for three successive weeks, and the last publication shall be made at least seven days before the filing of a complaint.

(d) *Proof of publication.* The plaintiff shall file a certificate of publication as an exhibit to the original complaint.

(e) *Effect of failure to publish.* If it appears to the court at any time before entry of judgment that there has been a failure to comply with the provisions of this Rule, the court shall suspend further proceedings in the action until publication is made and may order any other means of notice that it deems appropriate in the circumstances. No objection based on failure to comply with this Rule shall be made after final judgment.

Committee note. — The notice required by this Rule is not a substitute for process pursuant to Chapter 100 of Title 2 of these Rules.

Source. — This Rule is in part derived from former Rule U5 and in part new.

Rule 12-205. Complaint.

An action for condemnation shall be commenced by filing a complaint complying with Rules 2-303 through 2-305 and containing:

(a) The names of all persons whose interest in the property is sought to be condemned. If any person is a nonresident or not known, that fact shall be stated. If any person is the unknown heir of a decedent, that person shall be described as the unknown heir of _____, deceased.

(b) A description of the property sought to be condemned. If the subject matter of the action is real property, the description shall be:

(1) by lot and block or square when an entire lot, block, or square shown on a subdivision map, plat, or record is sought to be condemned, or

(2) by metes and bounds when an entire tract is sought to be condemned, or

(3) by metes and bounds clearly and legibly set forth on a plat showing the area and stating the amount of land sought to be condemned. The plat shall set forth the beginning point for the description, referenced to an existing marker, call, monument, or point outside the area sought to be condemned, in a recorded deed or plat identified by liber and folio. The deed or plat shall be in the chain of title of the property sought to be condemned, but if no marker, call, monument, or point can be found in the chain of title, reference may be made to the chain of title of adjoining property.

(c) A statement of the nature of the interest that the plaintiff seeks to acquire by the proposed condemnation.

(d) A statement of the purpose for which the property is sought to be condemned.

(e) A statement that there is a public necessity for the proposed condemnation.

(f) A statement that the parties are unable to agree or that a defendant is unable to agree because that defendant is unknown or under legal disability.

(g) A statement of the amount of any money paid into court and the date of the payment.

(h) A statement of the date of taking if a taking has occurred.

(i) A request that the property be condemned.

Source. — This Rule is derived from former Rule U6.

Statement of purposes required. — The reason for the requirement that there be in the petition for condemnation a "statement of the purposes for which the property is sought to be condemned" is that without such a statement courts and litigants would not be able to determine whether a condemnation was proposed for a public purpose. Prince George's County v. Beard, 266 Md. 83, 291 A.2d 636 (1972).

A mere recital that a proposed property is needed for a particular public use is insufficient when dealing with the deprivation of private property rights. High Ridge Ass'n v. County Comm'rs, 105 Md. App. 423, 660 A.2d 951 (1995).

Corporation need not allege public necessity for construction for which land is petitioned to be condemned. Realty Imp. Co. v. Consolidated Gas Elec. Light & Power Co., 156 Md. 581, 144 A. 710 (1929).

Validity of ordinance relied on. — No rule of pleading requires that a city acting in reliance on an ordinance justify the validity of the ordinance in its petition for condemnation, nor need it allege the chain of legislative or constitutional authority of which the ordinance was the last link. Herzinger v. Mayor of Baltimore, 203 Md. 49, 98 A.2d 87 (1953).

Where authority to condemn is based on an ordinance, reliance thereon will make a prima facie case and shift the burden to the person attacking it to show that it is arbitrary and unreasonable. Herzinger v. Mayor of Baltimore, 203 Md. 49, 98 A.2d 87 (1953).

Amendment. — See Brack v. Mayor of Baltimore, 125 Md. 378, 93 A. 994 (1915).

Amendment to include parties necessary to obtain fee simple title. — There was no abuse of discretion on the part of the trial judge when he permitted the condemnor to file an amended petition for the purpose of including as parties defendant such parties as were claimed necessary to obtain a valid, fee simple title to the land sought to be condemned, which parties were not included in the original petition. D.C. Transit Sys. v. State Rds. Comm'n, 259 Md. 675, 270 A.2d 793 (1970).

Rule 12-206. Discovery.

(a) *Generally.* Except as otherwise provided in this Rule, discovery in actions for condemnation shall be conducted pursuant to Chapter 400 of Title 2 of these Rules.

(b) *Experts not expected to be called at trial; fees and expenses.* A party may obtain discovery of the identity, findings, and opinions of an expert, even though the expert is not expected to be called as a witness at trial, if the expert (1) was retained by another party in anticipation of litigation or preparation for trial and (2) has examined or appraised all or part of the property sought to be condemned for the purpose of determining its value or has prepared a report pertaining to its value. The court shall require the party seeking discovery to reimburse the other party for a fair portion of the fees and expenses reasonably incurred in obtaining findings and opinions from the expert.

Source. — This Rule is derived from former Rule U12 b and from Fed. R. Civ. P. 26 (b) (4).

Rule 12-207. Trial.

(a) *Trial by jury unless otherwise elected.* An action for condemnation shall be tried by a jury unless all parties file a written election submitting the case to the court for determination. All parties may file a written election submitting an issue of fact to the court for determination without submitting the whole action.

Committee note. — The issue of the plaintiff's right to condemn is a question of law for the court. *Bouton v. Potomac Edison Co.*, 288 Md. 305 (1980).

(b) *Opening statement.* Each party to the action may make an opening statement to the trier of fact before the trier of fact views the property sought to be condemned. A plaintiff may reserve the opening statement until after the view. A defendant may reserve the opening statement until after the view or until the conclusion of the evidence offered by the plaintiff.

(c) *View.* Before the production of other evidence, the trier of fact shall view the property sought to be condemned unless the court accepts a written waiver filed by all parties. In a jury trial, each party shall inform the court, before the jury leaves for the view, of the name of the person to speak for that party at the view. Only one person shall represent all of the plaintiffs and only one person shall represent all of the defendants, unless the court orders otherwise for good cause. Only those persons shall be permitted to make any statement to the jury during the view, and the court shall so instruct the jury. These persons shall point out to the jury the property sought to be condemned, its boundaries, and any adjacent property of the owner claimed to be affected by the taking. They may also point out the physical features, before and after the taking, of the property taken and of any adjacent property of the owner claimed to be affected by the taking. The judge shall be present at and shall supervise the view unless the court accepts a written waiver filed by all parties.

The parties, their attorneys, and other representatives may be present during a view. A jury shall be transported to and attend a view as a body under the charge of an officer of the court, and the expense of transporting the jury shall be assessed as costs.

Source. — This Rule is derived from former Rules U15, U17, and U18.

Editor's note. — See Mayor of Baltimore v. Kane, 125 Md. 135, 93 A. 393 (1915), regarding removal in condemnation proceedings.

Rule is valid regulation of court administration. — Former Rule U15 was a reasonable regulation in the matter of court administration, and is valid. Maryland Community Developers, Inc. v. State Rds. Comm'n, 261 Md. 205, 274 A.2d 641, appeal dismissed, 404 U.S. 803, 92 S. Ct. 62, 30 L. Ed. 2d 35 (1971).

Constitutional right to jury trial on damage issue. — Maryland Constitution, Article III, § 40, mandates that the issue of damages be tried by a jury, but the issue of the right to condemn remains for the court's determination. Bouton v. Potomac Edison Co., 288 Md. 305, 418 A.2d 1168 (1980).

Former Rule U15 was intended to implement Maryland Constitution, Article III, § 40, which provides for a jury on the issue of the quantum of compensation due. Bouton v. Potomac Edison Co., 288 Md. 305, 418 A.2d 1168 (1980).

Common law right to jury trial in civil proceedings does not include condemnation cases which are special proceedings.

Bouton v. Potomac Edison Co., 288 Md. 305, 418 A.2d 1168 (1980).

The right to a jury trial may be subjected to reasonable regulation; indeed, it is generally acknowledged that it can, for all practical purposes, become meaningless to the individual and burdensome to the State unless the exercise of it is regulated to some extent. Maryland Community Developers, Inc. v. State Rds. Comm'n, 261 Md. 205, 274 A.2d 641, appeal dismissed, 404 U.S. 803, 92 S. Ct. 62, 30 L. Ed. 2d 35 (1971).

No guarantee of right to trial by court. — It is the right of trial by jury which is guaranteed by the Constitution, not the right of trial by court. Maryland Community Developers, Inc. v. State Rds. Comm'n, 261 Md. 205, 274 A.2d 641, appeal dismissed, 404 U.S. 803,

92 S. Ct. 62, 30 L. Ed. 2d 35 (1971).

But certain questions should not be submitted to jury. — The question of whether a modified line route for an overhead electric transmission line complies with a Public Service Commission order should not be submitted to a jury for it is a question for the court to decide. Bouton v. Potomac Edison Co., 288 Md. 305, 418 A.2d 1168 (1980).

Obligation of contract in charter not impaired. — The method of condemnation provided under former § 6 of Article 33A did not impair obligation of contract in Baltimore & O. R.R. charter, the section merely changing the remedy to enforce the right of condemnation. B & OR.R. v. Maughlin, 153 Md. 367, 138 A. 334 (1927).

Rule 12-208. Inquisition — Form and contents.

(a) *Form and signature.* The trier of fact shall render a special verdict in the form of an inquisition signed by each member of the jury or, if the action is tried without a jury, by the judge hearing the action.

(b) *Description of property.* The inquisition shall contain a description of the property condemned. If the property is real property, the description shall be in the form required by Rule 12-205 (b).

(c) *Nature of plaintiff's estate.* The inquisition shall state the nature of the interest in the property acquired by the plaintiff.

(d) *Award of damages.* The inquisition shall set forth the amount of any damages to which each defendant or class of defendants is entitled or, if the court so orders, the total amount of damages awarded, or both.

(e) *Other matters.* The inquisition shall contain findings on any other issues submitted by the court to the trier of fact for special findings.

Cross references. — Code, Real Property Article, §§ 12-103, 12-108, 12-110, and 12-112.

Source. — This Rule is derived from former Rule U19.

Rule 12-209. Judgment.

(a) *Upon finding of right to condemn.* If the court decides that the plaintiff is entitled to condemn, the court, upon the return of the inquisition, shall enter judgment for the plaintiff for the property condemned and for each defendant or class of defendants against the plaintiff for the amount of damages and costs awarded to each defendant or class of defendants.

(b) *Upon finding of no right to condemn.* (1) After trial. If the court decides that the plaintiff is not entitled to condemn, the court shall enter judgment against the plaintiff and for each defendant or class of defendants for costs as provided in Code, Real Property Article, § 12-106.

(2) After appeal. If the final decision on appeal is that the plaintiff is not entitled to condemn, the trial court shall award a reasonable attorney's fee to the defendant and assess the fee against the plaintiff together with the other costs of the action.

Cross references. — Code, Real Property Article, § 12-107.

Source. — This Rule is derived from former Rules U21 and U25.

Procedure governing entry of judgment absolute under former Rule U21 appears identical with that governing other civil cases. State Rds. Comm'n v. Adams, 238 Md. 371, 209 A.2d 247 (1965).

Determination of damages. — While in conventional condemnation proceedings, an owner is entitled to interest from the date of the entry of judgment nisi until the time of payment, damages should not be determined by applying the State's rate of return on its investments during that period to the amount of the payment withheld, but rather by applying the legal rate of interest. Acting Dir., Dep't of Forests & Parks v. Walker, 39 Md. App. 298, 385 A.2d 806 (1978), aff'd, 284 Md. 357, 396 A.2d 262 (1979).

Rule 12-210. Acquisition of title and possession.

At any time after entry of a judgment for the plaintiff for the property condemned and awarding compensation to the defendant, the plaintiff may obtain possession of the condemned property by (1) paying to the defendant or to the clerk of the court for the use of the defendant the amount awarded the defendant and the costs as determined by the judgment and (2) if the defendant files a timely appeal and the plaintiff is a person other than the State or any of its subdivisions or instrumentalities, filing a bond in an amount and with a surety approved by the court. The bond shall be conditioned on the plaintiff paying the defendant, if the judgment is reversed on appeal, all damages the plaintiff causes the defendant by taking possession of and using the property before final determination of the appeal.

Cross references. — *See* Maryland Constitution, Art. III, § 40 and Code, Real Property Article, §§ 12-102, 12-106, 12-108, 12-110, and 12-112.

Source. — This Rule is derived from former Rule U23.

Having recognized that an owner suffers additional damage when payment of a condemnation award is delayed, the General Assembly has authorized compensation for the loss of the use of money to the extent of the payment of interest from the date of the judgment nisi. Acting Dir., Dep't of Forests & Parks v. Walker, 39 Md. App. 298, 385 A.2d 806 (1978), aff'd, 284 Md. 357, 396 A.2d 262 (1979).

Liability to adverse claimant for compensation paid pursuant to award. — When a condemnor voluntarily pays to the wrong person, he does so at his peril, but when the compensation is paid pursuant to an award of court, the condemnor is not liable to an adverse claimant even though the court award may be erroneous. Bugg v. Maryland Transp. Auth., 31 Md. App. 622, 358 A.2d 562, cert. denied, 278 Md. 717 (1976), appeal dismissed, 429 U.S. 1082, 97 S. Ct. 1088, 51 L. Ed. 2d 529 (1977).

Rule 12-211. Abandonment.

(a) *Method.* A plaintiff may abandon an action for condemnation only by filing a written election to abandon it. A copy of the election shall be served as provided in Rule 1-321 upon each defendant over whom the court has obtained personal jurisdiction, and as the court may direct upon each other defendant.

(b) *When not allowed.* An action for condemnation may not be abandoned:

(1) after taking has occurred; or

(2) more than 120 days after the entry of judgment unless an appeal is taken; or

(3) if an appeal was taken, more than 120 days after the receipt by the clerk of the lower court of a mandate of the Court of Special Appeals or, if the Court of Appeals assumes jurisdiction, of the Court of Appeals evidencing (A) the dismissal of the appeal by the Court, (B) the affirmance of the judgment, (C) the entry of judgment pursuant to Rule 8-604 (e), or (D) the modification of the judgment without the award of a new trial. For purposes of this subsection, an appeal taken by the plaintiff that is stricken pursuant to Rule 8-203 or voluntarily dismissed shall be treated as if not taken, and the time allowed for abandonment shall be determined in accordance with subsections (1) and (2) of this section.

(c) *Effect.* The filing of the election shall reduce any money judgment entered in the civil action to a judgment for costs only, and the clerk shall make entries on the docket and judgment record necessary to reflect this effect. The filing of the election shall also annul any inquisition returned and any judgment entered in the action, to the extent that the inquisition or judgment affects the title of any defendant to the property that was sought to be condemned, and the clerk of any court where the inquisition has been recorded among the land records shall make a notation in the land records, in the same manner in which a release of a lien instrument is recorded, that the action has been abandoned.

(d) *Recovery of expenses.* Upon the abandonment of an action for condemnation, the defendant is entitled to recover from the plaintiff the reasonable legal, appraisal, and engineering fees actually incurred by the defendant because of the condemnation proceeding. If the parties agree on an amount, they shall file with the clerk statement of their agreement. If the parties cannot agree, the court shall determine the amount on motion of either party. The clerk shall enter the amount agreed upon or determined by the court as a part of the costs.

Cross references. — *See* Code, Real Property Article, § 12-109 relating to abandonment generally. *See also* Code, Real Property Article, § 12-102 as to when a "taking" occurs.

Source. — This Rule is derived from former Rule U26.

For circumstances under which amendment or abandonment in condemnation cases is permitted, see Concannon v. State Rds. Comm'n, 231 Md. 87, 188 A.2d 700 (1963).

Former Rule U26 d (see now section (d) of this Rule) is nearly identical to § 12-109 (e) of the Real Property Article. Southern Md. Elec. Coop. v. Albrittain, 256 Md. 39, 259 A.2d 311 (1969).

Any liability of condemning authority for extraordinary costs, such as are set forth in section (d) of this Rule and in § 12-109 (e) of the Real Property Article, is not automatic and must be supportable for reasons independent of the operation of former Rule 530 (now see Rule 2-507). 61 Op. Att'y Gen. 105 (1976).

A taking of property may occur without actual physical appropriation, entry or seizure. Hardesty v. State Rds. Comm'n, 276 Md. 25, 343 A.2d 884 (1975).

And without formally divesting owner of title. — There can be a taking of property giving rise to a vested right of compensation without formally divesting the owner of his title. Hardesty v. State Rds. Comm'n, 276 Md. 25, 343 A.2d 884 (1975).

Amending extent of taking to scenic easement. — See Hardesty v. State Rds. Comm'n, 276 Md. 25, 343 A.2d 884 (1975).

Rule 12-212. Recording.

(a) *Generally.* Upon the entry of judgment for the plaintiff for the property condemned and the filing of a certification by the plaintiff that the award has been paid to the defendant or into court, the clerk shall record the inquisition among the land records of the county in the same manner in which deeds are recorded. If the judgment is reversed on appeal or otherwise vacated or modified, the clerk shall make a notation to that effect in the land records in the same manner in which a release of a lien instrument is recorded, and if the judgment and inquisition have been recorded in any other county, the clerk shall give notice in the manner provided by Rule 2-622 (b).

(b) *Recording inquisition in other county.* Upon the entry of judgment in an action for condemnation of real or leasehold property located in more than one county, the plaintiff shall file with the clerk of the circuit court of each other county in which any part of the property is located a certified copy of the judgment, the docket entries, the complaint, and the inquisition. The clerk shall promptly record and index these documents in accordance with Rule 2-623.

Source. — This Rule is derived from former Rules U22 and U24b.

Condemning authority has no right to possession until condemnation judgment paid in full. — In conventional condemnation cases, no right to possession of the property is obtained by the condemning authority until it pays the full amount of the condemnation judgment, plus costs. King v. State Rds. Comm'n, 298 Md. 80, 467 A.2d 1032 (1983).

Rule 12-213. Board of property review procedure.

(a) *Scope.* This Rule applies to all actions under Code, Transportation Article, Title 8, Subtitle 3 that are certified to a board of property review.

Cross references. — The property review board procedure applies to acquisitions by condemnation by the State Roads Commission under Code, Transportation Article, Title 8, Subtitle 3.

(b) *Plats and maps.* In addition to any other requirements, plats and maps that are to be filed with the clerk of the court in proceedings subject to this Rule shall (1) state the amount of land sought to be taken, (2) refer to an existing permanent marker or monument outside the land sought to be taken from each owner, and (3) define and show the land sought to be taken from each owner so that its area may be computed with substantial accuracy from the plat or map.

Cross references. — *See* Code, Transportation Article, § 8-321.

(c) *Certificate to board.* (1) Filing. No later than six calendar months after the plats or maps referred to in section (b) of this Rule have been filed with the clerk of court as provided by law, a party may have the action referred to the board by filing a written notice to that effect with the clerk of the court.

(2) Duty of clerk. Upon the filing of the notice, the clerk shall certify the action promptly to the board by sending all pleadings and exhibits and a certified copy of the docket entries to the chairman of the board.

(d) *Hearing.* (1) Date. The board shall hear the action promptly but in no event later than three months after the filing of the notice of referral. Priority shall be given to an action involving a residence or commercial building.

(2) Notice. The board shall give each party at least ten days written notice of the date, time, and place of the hearing.

(3) Conduct — In general. The hearing may be conducted in an informal manner, and the board is not bound by the rules of evidence or procedure, except as provided in this Rule.

(4) Rights of parties. Each party has the right to be represented by counsel, to introduce evidence, to cross-examine, and to make oral argument upon the evidence.

(5) View. Unless waived in writing by all parties, the board shall view the property in question before taking testimony.

(6) Witnesses to be sworn. Witnesses shall be sworn by a member of the board or by some other person authorized to administer oaths.

(e) *Award.* As soon as practicable but in no event more than 30 days after the conclusion of the hearing, the board shall file with the clerk of the court a written award that explains the basis of its decision. The board shall serve the award pursuant to Rule 1-321 and file proof of service pursuant to Rule 1-323.

(f) *Case unheard or undetermined.* If the board has not heard the action within three months after the filing of the notice of referral or if the board has not filed a copy of its award with the clerk of the court within 30 days after the conclusion of the hearing, any party may serve upon the chairman of the board a written request that the board relinquish jurisdiction of the action. Upon service of the request, the board shall return to the clerk of the court the pleadings and exhibits in the action, and the case shall proceed as if notice of dissatisfaction with an award of the board was given.

(g) *Dissatisfaction with award.* (1) Notice — Time. Within 30 days after the filing of the award of the board with the clerk of the court, any dissatisfied party may file written notice of dissatisfaction with the clerk of the court.

(2) Plaintiff's duty to file complaint. Unless it has already done so, the condemning party shall file a complaint for condemnation within 30 days after the filing of notice of dissatisfaction. Except as provided in subsection (3) of this section, the action shall proceed thereafter as if the matter had never been certified to the board.

(3) Extension of time to file description. For good cause, the court may extend the time for filing the description required to be filed with the complaint for a period, not to exceed 90 days from the date of the filing of the complaint for condemnation, as may be just.

Cross references. — Code, Real Property Article, § 12-101 and Transportation Article, §§ 8-318 through 8-331.

Source. — This Rule is derived from former Rule U27.

Former Rule U27 was mandatory. State Rds. Comm'n v. Laurel Pines Country Club, 256 Md. 605, 261 A.2d 480 (1970).

Purpose of Rule. — The evident purpose of § 8-330 of the Transportation Article, and former Rule U27 was to give the Commission a defined and restricted limit within which to proceed to condemn. The owner cannot institute a condemnation suit so the law gave him the right to require the Commission, who can, to do so promptly, that is, within thirty days. First Nat'l Realty Corp. v. State Rds. Comm'n, 247 Md. 709, 234 A.2d 577 (1967).

The purpose of former Rule U27 could not be frustrated by filing a revised notice of the award, the avowed and single purpose of which was to extend the thirty-day period. State Rds. Comm'n v. Laurel Pines Country Club, 256 Md. 605, 261 A.2d 480 (1970).

The board of property review has only three months for a hearing. State Rds. Comm'n v. Orleans, 239 Md. 368, 211 A.2d 715 (1965).

And it has only an additional month to make an award. State Rds. Comm'n v. Orleans, 239 Md. 368, 211 A.2d 715 (1965).

The thirty-day provision under section (g) (2) is mandatory once the owner's notice of dissatisfaction is filed. First Nat'l Realty Corp. v. State Rds. Comm'n, 247 Md. 709, 234 A.2d 577 (1967).

Section (g) (2) requiring the condemning party to institute condemnation proceedings within thirty days after a notice of dissatisfaction is filed is mandatory, not directory. State Rds. Comm'n v. O'Boyle, 250 Md. 512, 243 A.2d 530 (1968).

Once the owner files a notice of dissatisfaction the Commission's duty to condemn within thirty days thereof is mandatory and ineluctable. State Rds. Comm'n v. O'Boyle, 250 Md. 512, 243 A.2d 530 (1968).

Discrepancy between section (g) and

§ 8-323 (a) (1) of the Transportation Article. — Under §§ 8-325 and 8-326 of the Transportation Article, referral to the board occurs after the petition for condemnation is filed but section (g) suggests that the petition is not filed until after the board has rendered its award or the case has been removed from its jurisdiction; it appears that the Commission has resolved this apparent inconsistency by referring to the first petition, that filed pursuant to § 8-323 of the Transportation Article, as an "informal" petition and regarding as the "formal" petition that actually commences the litigation that which is filed pursuant to the Rule. State Roads Comm'n v. G.L. Cornell Co., 85 Md. App. 765, 584 A.2d 1331 (1991), cert. denied, 325 Md. 248, 600 A.2d 418 (1992).

"Right of appeal." — The "right of appeal" given to a party dissatisfied with the award of a review board is the right of the owner to compel the filing of a condemnation case within thirty days of a demand therefor and the right of the condemnor to file a condemnation suit within thirty days of the review board's award. State Rds. Comm'n v. O'Boyle, 250 Md. 512, 243 A.2d 530 (1968).

Failure to file petition for condemnation. — Where the State files a notice of dissatisfaction and then fails to file its petition for condemnation within thirty days, under section (g) (2) it loses its right to have the Court of Appeals hear the petition. State Rds. Comm'n v. O'Boyle, 250 Md. 512, 243 A.2d 530 (1968).

Failure to hear case or make award within time provided by Rule. — If the case is not heard by the Board within three months or if an award is not made within thirty days after the hearing, either side may order the matter sent to court for the filing of a condemnation petition. State Rds. Comm'n v. Orleans, 239 Md. 368, 211 A.2d 715 (1965).

CHAPTER 300. MECHANICS' LIENS.

Rule 12-301. Applicability — Definitions.

(a) *Applicability.* The rules in this Chapter govern actions in which establishment and enforcement of a mechanics' lien are sought.

(b) *Definitions.* In this Chapter, the following definitions apply:

(1) Building. "Building" includes any unit of a nonresidential building that is leased or sold separately as a unit.

(2) Contract. "Contract" means an agreement of any kind or nature, express or implied, for doing work or furnishing material, for or about a building that may give rise to a mechanics' lien.

(3) Contractor. "Contractor" means a person who has a contract with an owner.

(4) Land. "Land" means the interest in land to which a mechanics' lien extends or the interest in land within the boundaries established by proceed-

ings in accordance with Rule 12-308. "Land" includes the improvements to the land.

(5) Mechanics' lien or lien. "Mechanics' lien" or "lien" means a lien established pursuant to Code, Real Property Article, §§ 9-101 through 9-112.

(6) Owner. "Owner" means the owner of record of the land except that, when the contractor executes the contract with a tenant for life or for years, "owner" means the tenant.

(7) Subcontractor. "Subcontractor" means a person who has a contract with anyone except the owner or the owner's agent.

Cross references. — Code, Real Property Article, § 9-101.

Source. — This Rule is derived from former Rule BG70.

University of Baltimore Law Review. — For analysis of the new mechanics' lien law, see 6 U. Balt. L. Rev. 181 (1976).

For article, "The Maryland Rules — A Time for Overhaul," see 9 U. Balt. L. Rev. 1 (1979).

Notice to owner of property. — Notice is required under § 9-104 of the Real Property Article for the protection of the owner of the property; on receipt of notice, the owner is afforded an opportunity to withhold, from the sums due the contractor, the amount the owner ascertains to be due the subcontractor. National Glass, Inc. v. J.C. Penney Properties, Inc., 329 Md. 300, 619 A.2d 528 (1993).

Quoted in Wolf Org., Inc. v. Oles, 119 Md. App. 357, 705 A.2d 40 (1998).

Rule 12-302. Commencement of action.

(a) *How commenced.* An action to establish a mechanics' lien shall be commenced by filing a complaint in the county where all or any part of the land to be subject to the lien is located.

(b) *Complaint.* The complaint shall be under oath by the plaintiff or a person making oath on the plaintiff's behalf. It shall be accompanied by the original or sworn, certified, or photostatic copies of material papers that constitute the basis of the lien unless their absence is explained in the complaint. In addition to complying with Rules 2-303 through 2-305, the complaint shall set forth facts upon which the plaintiff claims entitlement to the lien in the amount specified and shall contain at least the following:

(1) the name and address of the plaintiff;

(2) the name and address of the owner;

(3) the kind of work done or the kind and amount of materials furnished, the time when the work was done or the materials furnished, the name of the person for whom the work was done or to whom the materials were furnished, and the amount claimed to be due, less any credit recognized by the plaintiff, and if the lien is sought to be established against two or more buildings on separate lots or parcels of land owned by the same person, a designation of the amount claimed to be due on each building;

Cross references. — *See* Code, Real Property Article, § 9-105 (a) (1) for the consequence of failing to make the designation required when multiple buildings on separate lots are involved.

(4) a description of the land, including, if part of the land is located in another county, a statement to that effect, and a description adequate to identify the building;

(5) if a building is not newly erected, a statement that it has been repaired, rebuilt, or improved to the extent of 15 percent of its value; and

(6) if the plaintiff is a subcontractor, facts showing that the notice required under Code, Real Property Article, § 9-104 was properly mailed or served upon the owner or, if so authorized, posted on the building.

(c) *Defendants.* The plaintiff shall bring an action to establish a mechanics' lien against the owner of the land against which the lien is sought to be established. The plaintiff may join, but is not required to join, any other person who has or may have an interest in the land and who may be entitled to share in the proceeds of a sale of the land.

Source. — This Rule is derived from former Rule BG71.

Maryland Law Review. — For article discussing mechanics' liens in Maryland after *Barry Properties*, see 36 Md. L. Rev. 733 (1977).

University of Baltimore Law Review. — For analysis of the new mechanics' lien law, see 6 U. Balt. L. Rev. 181 (1976).

For article, "The Maryland Rules — A Time for Overhaul," see 9 U. Balt. L. Rev. 1 (1979).

Proceeding in rem. — All proceedings for the enforcement of mechanics' liens are exclusively in rem. The subject matter adjudicated is the lien in favor of the claimant upon a specific piece of property. Gaybis v. Palm, 201 Md. 78, 93 A.2d 269 (1952).

Setoff. — In a mechanics' lien action, the owner was allowed a setoff for failure to perform certain work properly, but not on account of an unusual water condition which made the specified construction inadequate, there being no warranty that the plans and specifications were sufficient. Gaybis v. Palm, 201 Md. 78, 93 A.2d 269 (1952).

Stated in Wolf Org., Inc. v. Oles, 119 Md. App. 357, 705 A.2d 40 (1998).

Rule 12-303. Amendment.

Pleadings in an action to establish a mechanics' lien may be amended pursuant to Rule 2-341, except that after the expiration of the period within which notice of the lien claim must be given, or the complaint to establish the lien must be filed if notice is not required, no amendment shall be permitted that will increase the amount of the claim or materially alter the description of the land.

Cross references. — Code, Real Property Article, § 9-112.

Source. — This Rule is derived from former Rule BG72.

Maryland Law Review. — For article discussing mechanics' liens in Maryland after *Barry Properties*, see 36 Md. L. Rev. 733 (1977).

University of Baltimore Law Review. — For analysis of the new mechanics' lien law, see 6 U. Balt. L. Rev. 181 (1976).

For article, "The Maryland Rules — A Time for Overhaul," see 9 U. Balt. L. Rev. 1 (1979).

Rights to amend are stated in § 9-112 of the Real Property Article and in this Rule. Mervin L. Blades & Son v. Lighthouse Sound Marina & Country Club, 37 Md. App. 265, 377 A.2d 523 (1977).

Rule prevails in conflict. — To the extent that there was a conflict between § 9-112 of the Real Property Article and former Rule BG72, the Rule prevailed until it was repealed or modified by a subsequent statute or rule. Scott & Wimbrow, Inc. v. Wisterco Invs., Inc., 36 Md. App. 274, 373 A.2d 965 (1977).

It is difficult to imagine any more extensive power of amendment than that allowed in proceedings concerning mechanics' liens. Baltimore Contractors v. Valley Mall Assocs., 27 Md. App. 695, 341 A.2d 845 (1975).

Amendment held to materially alter de- **scription of property.** — An amendment of the lien claim which would set forth the locality of the building, or buildings, and a description adequate to identify them, would materially alter the description of the property against which the lien claim was recorded. Mervin L. Blades & Son v. Lighthouse Sound Marina & Country Club, 37 Md. App. 265, 377 A.2d 523 (1977).

Rule 12-304. Proceedings.

(a) *Court review.* The court shall review the complaint and any exhibits and may require the plaintiff to supplement or explain any of the matters set forth in the complaint and exhibits.

(b) *Order.* (1) Entry; contents. If the court determines that there is a reasonable ground for the lien to attach, it shall enter an order directing the defendant to file an answer under oath on or before a date indicated in the order, showing cause why a lien for the amount claimed should not attach to the land described in the complaint, provided that a copy of the order together with copies of the pleadings and exhibits filed shall have been served on the defendant by the deadline for service specified in the order. The order also shall (A) set a date for hearing no later than 45 days from the date of the order, (B) advise the defendant of the defendant's right to appear and present evidence at the hearing, and (C) warn the defendant that if the defendant fails to file a timely answer, the facts set forth in the plaintiff's complaint shall be deemed admitted and the hearing waived, and the court may enter an order establishing the lien.

(2) Service. The order, together with copies of the pleadings and exhibits filed, shall be served on the defendant in the manner provided by Rule 2-121.

(c) *Answer; failure to file deemed admission.* A defendant may controvert any statement of fact in the plaintiff's complaint by filing an answer under oath. The failure to file an answer within the time allowed by the order shall constitute an admission for the purpose of the action of all statements of fact in the plaintiff's complaint, but shall not constitute an admission that the complaint is legally sufficient.

(d) *Hearing.* If the defendant fails to answer within the time allowed by the order, the court may at any time thereafter, without hearing and without further notice to the defendant, enter an order in conformity with section (e) of this Rule. If the defendant files an answer in compliance with the order, a hearing shall be held as scheduled.

(e) *Relief granted.* (1) Judgment if no genuine dispute. (A) If the pleadings and admissions on file and any evidence show that there is no genuine dispute as to any material fact and that the lien should attach as a matter of law, the court shall enter a judgment establishing the lien. If it appears that there is no genuine dispute as to a portion of the lien claim, the court shall enter an order establishing the validity of the lien as to that portion and the action shall proceed only on the disputed amount of the lien claim.

(B) If the pleadings and admissions on file and any evidence show that there is no genuine dispute as to any material fact and that the plaintiff, as a matter of law, has failed to establish a right to a lien, a judgment shall be entered denying the lien.

(2) Interlocutory order if probable cause. If the court determines from the pleadings and admissions on file and any evidence that a judgment under subsection (e)(1)(A) should not be entered, but that there is probable cause to believe the plaintiff is entitled to a lien, the court shall enter an interlocutory order that:

(A) establishes a lien;

(B) describes the land to which the lien attaches;

(C) states the amount of the claim for which probable cause is found;

(D) specifies the amount of a bond which may be filed by the defendant to have the land released from the lien; and

(E) assigns a date within six months for a trial of all matters that may be necessary to adjudicate the establishment of the lien.

The owner or any other person interested in the land may move at any time for modification or dissolution of the lien established by the interlocutory order.

(3) Probable cause not found. If no judgment or interlocutory order is entered under subsections (1) and (2), the court shall enter an order that the portion of the complaint seeking to establish the lien be dismissed unless the plaintiff, within 30 days thereafter, files a written request that the portion of the complaint seeking to establish the lien be assigned for trial.

(4) Bond by plaintiff. In an interlocutory order entered under subsection (2) of this section, the court may require the plaintiff to file a bond in an amount that the court determines to be sufficient for damages, including reasonable attorney's fees. The lien shall not attach until any required bond is filed.

(5) Trial. At the conclusion of the action a judgment shall be entered either continuing or terminating a lien established by an interlocutory order, or establishing or denying the lien.

Committee note. — This Rule renders impermissible an oral response to a show cause order previously permitted by Code, Real Property Article, § 9-106.

Source. — This Rule is derived from former Rule BG73.

Maryland Law Review. — For article discussing mechanics' liens in Maryland after *Barry Properties*, see 36 Md. L. Rev. 733 (1977).

University of Baltimore Law Review. — For analysis of the new mechanics' lien law, see 6 U. Balt. L. Rev. 181 (1976).

For article, "The Maryland Rules — A Time for Overhaul," see 9 U. Balt. L. Rev. 1 (1979).

Probable cause. — The probable cause determination is similar to a criminal case: whether, based on the pleadings and evidence before the trial judge, and weighing the facts, the trial judge believes that the petitioner is more or less likely to prevail at the trial on the merits. Reisterstown Lumber Co. v. Royer, 91 Md. App. 746, 605 A.2d 980, cert. denied, 327

Md. 626, 612 A.2d 257 (1992).

Benefit of doubt. — In truly close cases, the benefit of the doubt at a show cause hearing should go to the materialman seeking the mechanics' lien, for two reasons. First, an owner burdened with a mechanics' lien may post a bond to have the lien removed, under former Rule BG76 a 1, while the materialman denied an interlocutory lien has no alternative means by which to protect himself. Second, to restrict a materialman's right to a mechanics' lien too severely would likely have a negative economic impact on the housing market, as materialmen would be less likely to extend credit to either general contractors or property owners. Reisterstown Lumber Co. v. Royer, 91 Md. App. 746, 605 A.2d 980, cert. denied, 327

Md. 626, 612 A.2d 257 (1992).

In determining whether there is genuine dispute of material fact and, if not, whether the claimant is, or is not, entitled to a lien as a matter of law, the court is in the same position as a judge passing upon a motion for summary judgment and it is not justified in weighing the evidence and adjudicating the case. E.L. Gardner, Inc. v. Bowie Joint Venture, 64 Md. App. 302, 494 A.2d 988, cert. denied, 304 Md. 296, 498 A.2d 1183 (1985).

Rule 12-305. Enforcement of lien.

(a) *Time for filing motion to enforce.* A plaintiff may not enforce a lien or execute on a bond given to obtain a release of the lien until the lien has been established by a judgment. To enforce a lien or to execute on any bond given to obtain a release of the lien, the plaintiff shall file a motion in the original action within one year after the date on which the complaint to establish the lien was filed. The motion to enforce may be included in the original complaint to establish the lien.

(b) *Order.* An order granted pursuant to a motion to enforce shall direct that the land be sold unless the amount found to be due is paid on or before a date specified in the order, which shall be not more than 30 days after the date of the order.

(c) *Sale.* The sale shall be conducted pursuant to Title 14, Chapter 300 of these rules.

Source. — This Rule is derived from former Rule BG74.

Maryland Law Review. — For article discussing mechanics' liens in Maryland after *Barry Properties*, see 36 Md. L. Rev. 733 (1977).

University of Baltimore Law Review. — For analysis of the new mechanics' lien law, see 6 U. Balt. L. Rev. 181 (1976).

For article, "The Maryland Rules — A Time for Overhaul," see 9 U. Balt. L. Rev. 1 (1979).

A decree for enforcement of a mechanics' lien has the standing of any other decree in equity. Weinberg v. Fanning, 208 Md. 567, 119 A.2d 383 (1956).

Rule 12-306. Referral to auditor.

After a sale under Rule 12-305, the court shall refer the proceedings to an auditor pursuant to Rule 2-543 to state an account.

Source. — This Rule is derived from former Rule BG75.

Maryland Law Review. — For article discussing mechanics' liens in Maryland after *Barry Properties*, see 36 Md. L. Rev. 733 (1977).

University of Baltimore Law Review. —

For analysis of the new mechanics' lien law, see 6 U. Balt. L. Rev. 181 (1976).

For article, "The Maryland Rules — A Time for Overhaul," see 9 U. Balt. L. Rev. 1 (1979).

Rule 12-307. Release of lien.

(a) *Motion.* At any time after a complaint to establish a mechanics' lien is filed, the owner of the land or any other person interested in the land may move to have the land released from any lien that has been established by court order or that may thereafter be established.

(b) *Bond; order.* Unless a bond has previously been set pursuant to Rule 12-304, the court, after an opportunity for a hearing, shall determine the amount of bond sufficient to protect the plaintiff. Upon the filing of the bond in the amount set by the court, the court shall enter an order releasing the land from the lien.

(c) *Entry of satisfaction.* (1) By plaintiff. If the amount of a mechanics' lien is paid or otherwise satisfied, the plaintiff or plaintiff's successor in interest, upon payment of costs, shall file promptly an order of satisfaction of the lien in every court where the lien is a matter of record.

(2) Entry upon motion. If the plaintiff or plaintiff's successor in interest fails to file an order of satisfaction, the owner of the land or any other person interested therein may move for entry of an order of satisfaction pursuant to Rule 2-626.

Source. — This Rule is derived from former Rule BG76.

Maryland Law Review. — For article discussing mechanics' liens in Maryland after *Barry Properties*, see 36 Md. L. Rev. 733 (1977).

University of Baltimore Law Review. — For analysis of the new mechanics' lien law, see 6 U. Balt. L. Rev. 181 (1976).

For article, "The Maryland Rules — A Time for Overhaul," see 9 U. Balt. L. Rev. 1 (1979).

Order releasing lien is interlocutory **and not expressly included as appealable.** — An order granting a petition under section a of former Rule BG76, releasing a mechanics' lien upon the filing of a bond, is an interlocutory order not expressly included among the interlocutory orders of a court of equity which can be appealed before final judgment by virtue of former Article 5, § 7 (see now § 12-303 of the Courts Article). Maietta v. Greenfield, 267 Md. 287, 297 A.2d 244 (1972).

Rule 12-308. Designation of boundaries.

(a) *Before commencement of construction.* An owner of land who, before commencement of construction, desires to define the boundaries of the land in accordance with Code, Real Property Article, § 9-103 (b) shall file a notice to establish boundaries in an ex parte proceeding in the county in which the property is located. The notice shall be captioned, filed, and indexed as any other civil action under the name of the owner of the land and shall contain:

(1) a reference to the conveyance or other means by which the owner acquired title to the land;

(2) a description of the newly established boundaries sufficient to identify the land with reasonable certainty; and

(3) a brief description of the construction for which the boundaries are established.

(b) *After commencement of construction.* (1) Motion. After the commencement of construction of any improvement upon land that might be subject to a claim for a mechanics' lien, the owner of the land or any other person interested in the land, including anyone who has or might assert a mechanics' lien against the land by reason of the construction, may file a motion in the circuit court for the county where the land is located requesting the court to designate the boundaries pursuant to this Rule and to issue a writ of survey for that purpose. If the person filing the motion is a party to a proceeding to establish or enforce the lien, the motion shall be filed in the first proceeding to which the person became a party.

(2) Parties. A motion filed under this section shall be served on the owner of the land, each person who has moved for or established a mechanics' lien against the land, and any other person designated by the court in accordance with Rule 2-121, except that if the motion is filed in a pending proceeding, it shall be served in accordance with Rule 1-321.

(3) Surveyor. The court shall issue a writ to a surveyor directing the surveyor to make a report to the court in which the surveyor shall determine and describe the boundaries of the land, including within the boundaries as much of the land as is necessary for the use of the improvement thereon for the purpose for which it is designated or reasonably adaptable.

(4) Action on report. A copy of the surveyor's report shall be furnished to the moving party and to each person required to be served under section (b)(2) of this Rule. Within 15 days thereafter any person to whom the surveyor's report is required to be furnished may file a motion requesting the court to determine boundaries other than those that the surveyor has reported. After a hearing on the motion or upon expiration of the 15 day period for filing a motion if no motion is filed, the court shall determine the boundaries or approve the surveyor's report for filing in the proceedings.

Source. — This Rule is derived from former Rule BG77.

Maryland Law Review. — For article discussing mechanics' liens in Maryland after *Barry Properties*, see 36 Md. L. Rev. 733 (1977).

University of Baltimore Law Review. — For analysis of the new mechanics' lien law, see 6 U. Balt. L. Rev. 181 (1976).

CHAPTER 400. PARTITION.

Rule 12-401. Partition or sale in lieu of partition.

(a) *Scope.* This Rule applies in any action where the relief sought is the partition of real or personal property or the sale of real or personal property in lieu of partition.

Cross references. — *See* Code, Real Property Article, § 14-107.

(b) *Judgment for sale.* (1) When permitted. When the relief sought is a sale in lieu of partition, the court shall order a sale only if it determines that the property cannot be divided without loss or injury to the parties interested.

(2) *Conduct of sale.* The sale shall be conducted in the manner provided by Title 14, Chapter 300 of these rules.

(c) *Judgment for partition.* (1) Appointment of commissioners. When the court orders a partition, unless all the parties expressly waive the appointment of commissioners, the court shall appoint not less than three nor more than five disinterested persons to serve as commissioners for the purpose of valuing and dividing the property. On request of the court, each party shall suggest disinterested persons willing to serve as commissioners. The order appointing the commissioners shall set the date on or before which the commissioners' report shall be filed. The commissioners shall make oath before a person authorized to administer an oath that they will faithfully perform the duties of their commission. If the appointment of commissioners is waived by the parties, the court shall value and divide the property.

(2) Report of commissioners. Within the time prescribed by the order of appointment, the commissioners shall file a written report. At the time the report is filed the commissioners shall serve on each party pursuant to Rule 1-321 a copy of the report together with a notice of the times within which exceptions to the report may be filed.

(3) Exceptions to report. Within ten days after the filing of the report, a party may file exceptions with the clerk. Within that period or within three days after service of the first exceptions, whichever is later, any other party may file exceptions. Exceptions shall be in writing and shall set forth the asserted error with particularity. Any matter not specifically set forth in the exceptions is waived unless the court finds that justice requires otherwise. The court may decide the exceptions without a hearing, unless a request for a hearing is filed with the exceptions or by an opposing party within five days after service of the exceptions.

(d) *Costs.* Payment of the compensation, fees, and costs of the commissioners may be included in the costs of the action and allocated among the parties as the court may direct.

Source. — This Rule is derived as follows:
Section (a) is new.
Section (b) is derived from former Rule BJ71.

Section (c) is derived from former Rule BJ72 and BJ73.
Section (d) is new.

Court determines whether property shall be partitioned in kind or be sold in lieu of partition. Boyd v. Boyd, 32 Md. App. 411, 361 A.2d 146 (1976).

And chancellor's determination is reversed only if clearly erroneous. — Because the determination of the propriety of partition is exclusively in the province of the chancellor, an appellate court can reverse his determination only if it were clearly erroneous. Boyd v. Boyd, 32 Md. App. 411, 361 A.2d 146 (1976).

Court must first conclude that partition in kind is proper. — The appointment of commissioners (unless waived by the parties) becomes a factor only after the court itself has concluded that partition in kind is proper. Boyd v. Boyd, 32 Md. App. 411, 361 A.2d 146 (1976).

The sole responsibility of the commissioners is to "value and divide" the property in question. Boyd v. Boyd, 32 Md. App. 411, 361 A.2d 146 (1976).

CHAPTER 500. REDEMPTION OF GROUND RENT.

Rule 12-501. Redemption of ground rent vested in trustee without power of sale.

(a) *Scope.* This Rule applies to the redemption of a ground rent, whether reserved by lease or sublease, that is vested in a trustee without a power of sale. As used in this Rule, "trustee" includes a trustee under a will, deed, or other instrument, a life tenant, and the holder of a defeasible estate.

(b) *When action may be brought — Venue — Parties.* When a ground rent that is or becomes redeemable is vested in a trustee without a power of sale, the owner of the leasehold or the trustee may file an action for redemption in the county where the land subject to the ground rent is located. The owner of the leasehold interest and the trustee are necessary parties. The plaintiff may join, but is not required to join, a remainderman or any other person who has or may have a beneficial interest in the land and who may be entitled to share in the redemption money.

(c) *Complaint — Content.* In addition to complying with Rules 2-303 through 2-305, the complaint shall be under oath and shall set forth:

(1) the location and description of the land;

(2) the date and place of record of the lease or sublease by which the reversion and rent were created;

(3) the amount of the annual rent and the redemption price of the leasehold interest;

(4) a statement that the owner of the leasehold desires to redeem the ground rent; and

(5) a statement that the notice required by law or by the lease has been given by the owner of the leasehold interest.

(d) *Bond.* Unless the trustee has previously given a bond that protects the redemption money or has been excused from filing a bond by the instrument creating the trust, the trustee shall file a bond as prescribed by Rule 10-702. Upon deposit of the redemption money by the trustee in the manner provided by Rule 10-705, the bond shall be released regardless of the amount of the entire estate or the amount of the redemption money.

(e) *Order of conveyance — Appointment of substitute trustee.* The court may order the trustee to convey the reversion in the land to the owner of the leasehold interest upon payment of the sum of money for which the ground rent is redeemable together with the amount of annual rent accrued to the date of payment. If the trustee is the owner of the leasehold interest, the court may appoint a substitute trustee to receive the redemption money and execute the deed.

(f) *Accounting and investment by trustee.* The trustee shall account promptly to the court for the redemption money received by the trustee. The court may order the redemption money invested for the purpose of holding it in place of the redeemed ground rent for the benefit of the persons entitled to the redeemed ground rent.

(g) *Costs.* If the relief sought in the complaint is granted, the court costs of the action, including the expenses of obtaining a bond, shall be paid out of the money received for the redemption. Otherwise, the court shall allocate costs pursuant to Rule 2-603.

Source. — This Rule is derived as follows:

Section (a) is derived from former Rules Y70 and Y71.

Section (b) is derived from former Rules Y71, Y72, and Y73.

Section (c) is derived from former Rule Y74.
Section (d) is derived from former Rule Y76.
Section (e) is derived from former Rule Y77.
Section (f) is derived from former Rule Y78.
Section (g) is derived from former Rule Y79.

Maryland Law Review. — For article, "The Law/Equity Dichotomy in Maryland," see 39 Md. L. Rev. 427 (1980).

CHAPTER 600. REPLEVIN AND DETINUE.

Rule 12-601. Possession of personal property before judgment — Replevin.

(a) *Action in District Court.* A person claiming the right to immediate possession of personal property may file an action under this Rule for possession before judgment. The action shall be filed in the District Court.

(b) *Defendant.* The action shall be brought against the person who has possession of the property at the time the complaint is filed. A person who obtains possession after the complaint is filed shall be joined as a defendant.

Cross references. — Rule 3-211.

(c) *Complaint.* In addition to complying with Rules 3-303 through 3-305, the complaint shall contain (1) a description of the property claimed and an allegation of its value, (2) an allegation that the defendant unjustly detains the property, (3) a claim for return of the property, and (4) any claim for damages to the property or for its detention.

(d) *Summons and notice.* (1) Upon the filing of the complaint, the clerk shall issue a summons as in other civil actions and a notice to the defendant.

(2) The notice shall:

(A) indicate the time within which the notice must be served;

(B) advise the defendant that before trial on the complaint a hearing will be held to determine the right to possession before judgment, if the notice, the complaint, and any exhibits are served within the time prescribed in the notice;

(C) indicate the date of the hearing on the right to possession before judgment, which may not be less than seven days after service of the notice on the defendant unless the court orders otherwise;

(D) advise the defendant of the right to appear and present evidence at the hearing; and

(E) warn the defendant that the court may grant the plaintiff's request for possession before judgment and direct the sheriff to place the plaintiff in possession of the property unless the defendant appears personally and shows cause why the property described in the complaint should not be immediately returned to the plaintiff.

(e) *Service.* The notice shall be served with the summons and complaint and any exhibits.

(f) *Hearing.* The hearing shall be held as scheduled and shall proceed ex parte if the defendant fails to appear in response to the notice.

Cross references. — *See* Code, Courts Article, § 4-402 (e) (2) regarding the jurisdiction of the District Court to conduct the show cause hearing, to enforce any ancillary injunction, and to issue, renew, and receive returns on the writ of possession even if a jury trial is demanded.

(g) *Decision.* If the court determines that the plaintiff is entitled to possession before judgment, the court shall order issuance of a writ directing the sheriff to place the plaintiff in possession of the property, provided that the plaintiff files a bond for the satisfaction of all costs and damages that may be awarded to the defendant or a claimant of the property by reason of the possession. The order shall prescribe the amount of and security for the bond. If the claimed property cannot be found and the writ is returned unexecuted, the plaintiff may request reissuance of the writ or may proceed pursuant to section (h) of this Rule.

(h) *Further proceedings pursuant to Rule 12-602.* After the issue of the right to possession before judgment is determined, the action shall proceed as an action for recovery of property after judgment under Rule 12-602. If the value of the property remains at issue and that value and any damages claimed exceed the monetary jurisdiction of the District Court or a timely demand for jury trial has been filed, the clerk shall transmit the record to the circuit court in accordance with the procedures set forth in Rule 3-325.

Committee note. — For a thorough history and explanation of the action of replevin and its relationship to actions of detinue and trover, *see Wallander v. Barnes*, 341 Md. 553 (1996).

Source. — This Rule is derived from former M.D.R. BQ41 through BQ45 and BQ49.

In a replevin suit damages are limited to the damage for detention of the property. Koch v. Mack Int'l Motor Truck Corp., 201 Md. 562, 95 A.2d 105 (1953).

Judgment against certain defendants for damages only. — In action against four defendants to recover shares of stock, or their value, or damages for detention, declaration was in form one of detinue, while only one of defendants (bank commissioner, as receiver) was in possession of stock, hence judgment against others could be for damages only; action for detinue cannot be joined with one for damages, but point was not raised in lower court. Mylander v. Page, 162 Md. 255, 159 A. 770 (1932).

When judgment final. — The requirements of former § 59 of Article 75 were not so fundamental in their nature as to prevent a judgment, if not entered strictly in accordance with its terms from being a valid final judgment subject to be appealed. Harford Accident & Indem. Co. v. State ex rel. Ritter, 201 Md. 433, 94 A.2d 639 (1953).

Verdict held erroneous. — A verdict "in favor of the defendant for the return of the property replevied and one cent damages and costs" is erroneous. Standard Horseshoe Co. v. O'Brien, 88 Md. 335, 41 A. 898 (1898).

Correction of erroneous verdict. — Although the verdict as originally rendered is erroneous, if it is properly corrected by jury before its record, error is cured. Farmers' Packing Co. v. Alexander Brown & Sons, 87 Md. 1, 39 A. 625 (1898).

How irregularity in verdict should be

raised. — See Standard Horseshoe Co. v. O'Brien, 88 Md. 335, 41 A. 898 (1898).

Case remanded in order that property might be valued, and judgment entered in accordance with former § 59 of Article 75. B & O R.R. v. Rueter, 114 Md. 687, 80 A. 220 (1911).

Rule 12-602. Recovery of property or value after judgment — Detinue.

(a) *Action.* (1) A person claiming the right to possession of personal property may file an action under this Rule.

(2) The action:

(A) shall be brought in the District Court if the value of the property and any damages claimed are within the exclusive jurisdiction of that court;

(B) may be brought in either the District Court or a circuit court if the value of the property and any damages claimed are within the concurrent jurisdiction of those courts; and

(C) shall be brought in the circuit court if the value of the property and any damages claimed exceed the monetary jurisdiction of the District Court.

(3) If the plaintiff has brought an action under Rule 12-601, a separate action under this Rule shall not be brought. If required by Rule 2-326, a new complaint shall be filed in accordance with that Rule.

(b) *Defendant.* The action shall be brought against the person who has possession of the property at the time the complaint is filed. A person who obtains possession after the complaint is filed shall be joined as a defendant.

Cross references. — Rules 2-211 and 3-211.

(c) *Complaint.* In addition to complying with Rules 2-303 through 2-305 or 3-303 through 3-305, the complaint shall contain (1) a description of the property claimed and an allegation of its value, (2) an allegation that the defendant unjustly detains the property, (3) a claim for return of the property or payment of its value, and (4) any claim for damages to the property or for its detention.

(d) *Judgment.* (1) For plaintiff. A judgment for the plaintiff shall award possession of the property or, in the alternative, payment of its value. The judgment shall separately set forth the value of the property and any amount awarded for damage to or detention of the property. Unless the court orders otherwise for good cause or the plaintiff agrees on the record to accept the value of the property as fixed by the judgment instead of return of the property, the plaintiff may enforce return of the property pursuant to Rules 2-647 or 3-647. The plaintiff may also seek enforcement of any damages awarded pursuant to the rules contained in Chapter 600 of Title 2 or Title 3, as appropriate.

(2) For defendant. If a judgment is entered for the defendant after the plaintiff has obtained immediate possession of the property pursuant to Rule 12-601, the court shall order return of the property to the defendant. On motion filed within 15 days after entry of the judgment, the court shall enter judgment for any damages sustained by the defendant by reason of the plaintiff's possession.

Source. — This Rule is derived from former M.D.R. BQ51 and former Maryland Rule BQ 53.

Objection to defect in amount of bond. — A defect in the amount of a bond must be immediately objected to or such defect will be deemed waived. See Burrier v. Cunningham Piano Co., 135 Md. 135, 108 A. 492 (1919).

Bond forfeited on breach of conditions. — See Doogan v. Tyson, 6 G. & J. 453 (1834); Crabbs v. Koontz, 69 Md. 59, 13 A. 591 (1888).

TITLE 13. RECEIVERS AND ASSIGNEES

Editor's note. — The Court of Appeals, by Order dated June 5, 1996, effective January 1, 1997, rescinded Subtitles A, D, E, J, P, Q, R, T, U, V, W, Y, Z, BB, BD, BE, BG, BH, BJ, BL, BP, BQ, BR, BS, BW, and BY of Chapter 1100 of the Maryland Rules of Procedure, rescinded Subtitles P, BB, BQ, and BW of the Maryland District Rules, and rescinded Forms 22a, 23, 24, 25 and 26. The Order substituted for certain of the rules and forms rescinded new Title 9, Chapter 100, Title 10, Title 12, Title 13, Title 14, and Title 15 of the Maryland Rules of Procedure. Furthermore, the Order transferred, without readoption, Chapter 900, Chapter 1200, and Subtitles S, BU, and BV of Chapter 1100 of the Maryland Rules of Procedure and Chapter 1200 of the Maryland District Rules to be Title 9, Chapter 200, Title 11, and Title 16 of the Maryland Rules of Procedure. The Order provides that the new rules shall "apply to all actions commenced on or after January 1, 1997, and insofar as practicable, to all actions then pending."

Many of the cases in the notes to the various rules were decided prior to the 1996 revision. These cases have been retained under pertinent rules of this title where it is thought that such cases will be of value in interpreting the present rules.

A table of comparable rules, relating those rules rescinded effective January 1, 1997, to the revised rules in Title 9 through Title 16 is to be found in Volume 2 following the end of the Maryland Rules.

CHAPTER 100. GENERAL PROVISIONS.

Rule 13-101. Definitions.

In this Title the following definitions apply except as expressly otherwise provided or as necessary implication requires:

(a) *Assignee.* "Assignee" means a person to whom a debtor has made a general assignment of property in trust for the benefit of creditors.

(b) *Court.* "Court" means the court that has appointed a receiver or that has assumed jurisdiction over the estate of an assignee.

(c) *Debtor.* "Debtor" means a person who has made a general assignment to an assignee or for whom a receiver has been appointed.

(d) *Estate.* "Estate" means property assigned to an assignee or administered by a receiver.

(e) *Receiver.* "Receiver" means a person, other than an assignee, appointed by a court to take charge of an estate that is within the scope of the rules in this Title.

Committee note. — "General assignment" is a term of art used to describe an assignment of all or substantially all of a debtor's property for the benefit of creditors. The validity of a general assignment in a particular case is a matter of substantive law.

Source. — This Rule is derived from former Rule BP1 a.

Rule 13-102. Scope.

(a) *Generally.* Except as provided in section (b), the rules in this Title apply in the circuit court to the estate of:

(1) an assignee;

(2) a receiver appointed under the general equitable power of a court to take charge of an estate;

(3) a receiver appointed under any statutory provision that specifically provides that these rules apply to the proceeding; and

(4) any other statutory receiver to the extent that (A) the rules in this Chapter are not inconsistent with the statutory provisions authorizing the appointment of the receiver, and (B) the court orders that the rules apply.

(b) *No application.* The rules in this Title do not apply to the estate of:

(1) a receiver appointed pursuant to the terms of a mortgage or deed of trust pending foreclosure who takes charge of only the property subject to that mortgage or deed of trust; or

(2) a person appointed for purposes of enforcement of health, housing, fire, building, electric, licenses and permits, plumbing, animal control, or zoning codes or for the purpose of abating a public nuisance.

Cross references. — For an example of a statute specifically providing that these rules apply, *see* Code, Financial Institutions Article, § 9-708. For examples of statutes authorizing the appointment of a receiver, *see* Code, Corporations and Associations Article, §§ 3-411, 3-414, 3-415, and 3-514; Financial Institutions Article, §§ 5-605 and 6-307; Commercial Law Article, §§ 6-106 and 15-210; and Health-General Article, § 19-334. This list is illustrative only.

Source. — This Rule is derived in part from former Rule BP1 b.

Rule 13-103. Applicability of other rules.

(a) *Discovery.* A receiver, an assignee, or any person in a contested matter may obtain discovery pursuant to Title 2, Chapter 400 of these Rules. Any other person having an interest in the estate may obtain discovery only upon order of court.

(b) *Title 2 rules.* The Title 2 rules apply to proceedings under this Title except to the extent that a rule in this Title is inconsistent with a particular rule in Title 2 or the court determines that the application of a rule in Title 2 would be inappropriate.

(c) *Other rules.* Except as otherwise specifically provided in this Title, the procedures for making a sale of property of the estate shall be governed by Title 14, Chapter 300 of these Rules.

Source. — This Rule is in part derived from former Rule BP5 and is in part new.

Rule 13-104. Service.

Unless otherwise specifically provided by the rules in this Title or ordered by the court, no paper required or permitted to be filed by a rule in this Title need be served on any person.

Source. — This Rule is new.

Rule 13-105. Eligibility to serve as receiver, assignee, or professional.

(a) *Generally.* Except as otherwise provided by law or by section (b) of this Rule, a person may not serve as a receiver or assignee, or as an attorney, accountant, appraiser, auctioneer, or other professional representing or assisting the receiver or assignee, if the person:

(1) is a creditor or a holder of an equity security of the debtor;

(2) is or was an investment banker for any outstanding security of the debtor;

(3) has been, within three years before the date of the appointment of a receiver or the assumption of jurisdiction over the estate of an assignee, an investment banker for a security of the debtor, or an attorney for such an investment banker, in connection with the offer, sale, or issuance of a security of the debtor;

(4) is or was, within two years before the date of the appointment of a receiver or the assumption of jurisdiction over the estate of an assignee, a director, an officer, or an employee of the debtor or of an investment banker specified in subsection (2) or (3) of this section, except that an employee of the debtor may serve as an assignee if the court finds that this is in the best interest of the estate and that there is no actual conflict of interest by reason of the employment;

(5) has an interest materially adverse to the interest of any class of creditors or equity security holders by reason of any direct or indirect relationship to, connection with, or interest in the debtor or an investment banker specified in subsection (2) or (3) of this section, or for any other reason;

(6) otherwise has or represents an interest adverse to the estate;

(7) has, at any time within five years before the date of the appointment of a receiver or the assumption of jurisdiction over the estate of an assignee, represented or been employed by the debtor or any secured creditor as an attorney, accountant, appraiser, or other professional, if the court finds an actual conflict of interest by reason of the representation or employment;

(8) is an "insider" as defined by 11 U.S.C. § 101; or

(9) represents or is employed by an unsecured creditor of the debtor and, on objection of a person in interest, the court finds an actual conflict of interest by reason of the representation or employment.

(b) *Special counsel or accountant.* An attorney or accountant who has represented or has been employed by the debtor is eligible to serve for a specified limited purpose if the employment is in the best interest of the estate and if the attorney or accountant does not represent or hold any interest materially adverse to the debtor or to the estate with respect to the purpose for which the attorney or accountant is to be employed.

(c) *Ineligibility no bar to assumption of jurisdiction.* The court shall not refuse to assume jurisdiction over the estate of a debtor solely because it finds that the assignee is ineligible to serve under this Rule. After assuming jurisdiction, the court shall remove the ineligible assignee pursuant to Rule 13-701 and may take any action permitted or required by Rule 13-703.

Source. — This Rule is derived in part from former Rule BP3 a and c and is in part derived from 11 U.S.C. § 101 and § 327.

Rule 13-106. Petition for assumption of jurisdiction over estate of an assignee.

(a) *Venue.* A petition requesting the court to assume jurisdiction over the estate of an assignee shall be filed in the county where the debtor resides, is employed, or maintains a place of business, or in any county where some part of the estate is located.

(b) *Contents of petition.* A petition for the assumption of jurisdiction over the estate of an assignee shall be signed by the petitioner and shall contain at least the following information:

(1) the name and address of the assignee;

(2) a statement that an assignment for the benefit of creditors has been executed;

(3) in the case of a corporation, a statement indicating that articles of transfer transferring assets to the assignee have been executed;

(4) in the case of a corporation, a statement indicating that required corporate resolutions have been executed; and

(5) the nature, approximate value, and location of the property comprising the estate, to the best of the petitioner's knowledge, information, and belief.

(c) *Exhibits to petition.* The petitioner shall attach to the petition a copy of the following documents or shall explain in the petition their absence:

(1) the executed assignment for the benefit of creditors;

(2) in the case of a corporation, the executed articles of transfer and the executed corporate resolutions of the corporation; and

(3) the affidavit of an assignee, as required by Rule 13-302.

Source. — This Rule is new.

Rule 13-107. Bond.

(a) *Duty to file.* Before taking charge of an estate, a receiver shall file a bond in the court in which the receiver has been appointed and an assignee shall file a bond in the court in which a petition to assume jurisdiction of the estate has been filed.

(b) *Amount of bond.* Notwithstanding any contrary provision in Rule 1-402, the amount of the bond shall be no greater than the net value of the property of the estate. In the event of a later sale of property by the receiver or assignee, the court shall evaluate the bond previously filed and may permit a decrease in the amount of the bond.

(c) *Motion to modify amount of bond; notice.* If a motion to modify the amount of a bond is filed pursuant to Rule 1-402, notice shall be given to such persons as the court may direct.

(d) *Terms of bond.* The bond shall be to the State of Maryland and shall be conditioned upon the faithful discharge of the duties of the receiver or assignee.

(e) *Payment of bond premium from estate.* Unless the court orders otherwise, a receiver or assignee is entitled to pay and be allowed the cost of the premium out of the estate.

Cross references. — Code, Commercial Law Article, § 15-103; Title 1, Chapter 400.

Source. — This Rule is derived in part from former Rule V73.

CHAPTER 200. NOTICE AND SCHEDULES.

Rule 13-201. Publication of notice to creditors.

(a) *Notice by receiver or assignee.* Promptly but in no event later than 5 days after the court appoints a receiver or assumes jurisdiction over the estate of an assignee, the receiver or assignee shall file a form of Notice to Creditors with the clerk, who shall issue the Notice. The receiver or assignee shall cause the Notice to be published.

(b) *Form of notice.* The Notice to Creditors shall be substantially in one of the following three forms, as applicable:

[CAPTION]

NOTICE TO CREDITORS
BY RECEIVER

TO ALL PERSONS INTERESTED IN THE ESTATE OF _____,
DEBTOR

Notice is given with respect to _____,
(Name in bold type)

whose business address is _____

_____

and whose business is _____,
that this Court has appointed _____,
(Name in bold type)

whose address is _____,
as Receiver.

All persons having claims against the Debtor should file them, under oath, with the Clerk of the Circuit Court at the address below not later than 120 days from the date this Notice was issued.

Date Notice Issued	Clerk of the Circuit Court for
Receiver	Attorney for Receiver
Address	Address
Telephone Number	Telephone Number

[CAPTION]

NOTICE TO CREDITORS
BY ASSIGNEE

TO ALL PERSONS INTERESTED IN THE ESTATE OF _____,
DEBTOR

Notice is given with respect to _____,
(Name in bold type)

whose business address is _____
_____

and whose business is _____,
that the Debtor has executed an Assignment for the Benefit of Creditors and
that _____,
(Name in bold type)

whose address is _____
has been designated as Assignee.

The deed of assignment [ ] does [ ] does not contain a provision requiring
creditors to release their claims against the debtor as a condition to (1) sharing
in the distribution under the deed or (2) being accorded a preferred status over
other creditors.

All persons having claims against the Debtor should file them, under oath,
with the Clerk of the Circuit Court at the address below not later than 120
days from the date this Notice was issued.

Date Notice Issued	Clerk of the Circuit Court for
Assignee	Attorney for Assignee
Address	Address
Telephone Number	Telephone Number

[CAPTION]

NOTICE TO CREDITORS
OF BULK TRANSFER

TO ALL PERSONS INTERESTED IN THE ESTATE OF _____,
BULK TRANSFEROR

    Notice is given with respect to _____,

                        (Name in bold type)

whose business address is _____

_____

and whose business is _____,
that the Transferor has effected a bulk transfer of property to
_____, transferee, whose

              (Name in bold type)

address is _____

_____

and that _____ whose address is

              (Name in bold type)

has been appointed as Receiver pursuant to Code, Commercial Law Article,
§ 6-106.

    All persons having claims against the Transferor should file them, under
oath, with the Clerk of the Circuit Court at the address below not later than
120 days from the date this Notice was issued.

Date Notice Issued	Clerk of the Circuit Court for
Receiver	Attorney for Receiver
Address	Address
Telephone Number	Telephone Number

    (c) *Where published; frequency.* A copy of the Notice to Creditors shall be
published in a newspaper of general circulation in the county where the court
is located. The Notice shall be published at least once a week in each of three
successive weeks, and the last publication shall occur not less than ninety days
before the date specified in the Notice as the last day for filing claims.

    (d) *Certificate of publication.* On or before the last day for filing claims, the
receiver or assignee shall file a certificate that publication has been made
pursuant to this Rule.

    Source. — This Rule is derived from former
Rule BP4 a 1.

Late filing. — The present rules reflect the earlier case law that, absent laches amounting to prejudice to others, late filing is permitted as a matter of course as to undistributed funds in the hands of the court. Eastern Air Lines v. Phoenix Sav. & Loan Ass'n, 239 Md. 195, 210 A.2d 515 (1965).

A creditor who files late has an absolute right which does not, except to the extent that prejudice to others results from the late filing, depend on good cause shown to participate in funds in the hands of the court available for distribution. Eastern Air Lines v. Phoenix Sav. & Loan Ass'n, 239 Md. 195, 210 A.2d 515 (1965).

A creditor may come in and file his claim at any time before a distribution of the proceeds of sale has been actually made under a finally ratified auditor's account. Coppage v. Maryland Thrift Sav. & Loan Co., 253 Md. 238, 252 A.2d 869 (1969).

Where creditor's claim was timely filed, receiver could not object to claim on ground that he had been misled to believe claim had been paid. Coppage v. Maryland Thrift Sav. & Loan Co., 253 Md. 238, 252 A.2d 869 (1969).

Equitable principles will not bar creditor's claim where receiver's failure to follow procedures in the Maryland Rules allowed claim to be timely filed. Coppage v. Maryland Thrift Sav. & Loan Co., 253 Md. 238, 252 A.2d 869 (1969).

Rule 13-202. Mailing of notice to creditors.

(a) *After appointment of receiver or assumption of jurisdiction.* Within five days after the clerk issues the Notice to Creditors, the receiver or assignee shall send a copy of the Notice by first class mail, postage prepaid, to all known creditors of the debtor. The receiver or assignee shall file a certificate of mailing of the Notice within five days after the initial mailing.

(b) *After filing of schedule.* Within five days after the expiration of the time for the debtor to file the schedule required by Rule 13-203, the receiver or assignee shall send a copy of the Notice by first class mail, postage prepaid, to all creditors shown on the schedule to whom the Notice was not sent pursuant to section (a) of this Rule. Not later than the last day for filing claims, the receiver or assignee shall file a certificate of mailing.

(c) *Later-discovered creditors.* The receiver or assignee shall promptly send a copy of the Notice by first class mail, postage prepaid, to all creditors whose identity is discovered at any time after the schedule is filed or the expiration of the time for filing it. Not later than the last day for filing the final report and account, the receiver or assignee shall file a certificate of mailing.

Source. — This Rule is in part derived from former Rule BP4 a 2 and is in part new.

Late filing. — The present rules reflect the earlier case law that, absent laches amounting to prejudice to others, late filing is permitted as a matter of course as to undistributed funds in the hands of the court. Eastern Air Lines v. Phoenix Sav. & Loan Ass'n, 239 Md. 195, 210 A.2d 515 (1965).

A creditor who files late has an absolute right which does not, except to the extent that prejudice to others results from the late filing, depend on good cause shown to participate in funds in the hands of the court available for distribution. Eastern Air Lines v. Phoenix Sav. & Loan Ass'n, 239 Md. 195, 210 A.2d 515 (1965).

A creditor may come in and file his claim at any time before a distribution of the proceeds of sale has been actually made under a finally ratified auditor's account. Coppage v. Maryland Thrift Sav. & Loan Co., 253 Md. 238, 252 A.2d 869 (1969).

Where creditor's claim was timely filed, receiver could not object to claim on ground that he had been misled to believe claim had been paid. Coppage v. Maryland Thrift Sav. & Loan Co., 253 Md. 238, 252 A.2d 869 (1969).

Equitable principles will not bar creditor's claim where receiver's failure to follow procedures in the Maryland Rules allowed claim to be timely filed. Coppage v. Maryland Thrift Sav. & Loan Co., 253 Md. 238, 252 A.2d 869 (1969).

Rule 13-203. Schedule.

(a) *Preparation and filing by debtor.* Within fifteen days after the court appoints a receiver or assumes jurisdiction over the estate of an assignee, the debtor shall prepare and file with the clerk a schedule of property and debts under oath.

(b) *Form of schedule.* The debtor's schedule shall be in substantially the following form:

[CAPTION]

SCHEDULE OF PROPERTY AND DEBTS

Name of Debtor _____

Residence Address _____

_____

Occupation/Nature of Business _____

Business Address _____

_____

I solemnly affirm under the penalties of perjury that the contents of the attached schedule are true to the best of my knowledge, information, and belief.

_____   _____

Date   Signature of Debtor

A. Property of debtor.

Nature and description	Location	Estimated Market Value	Amount of Lien or Encumbrance
_____	_____	_____	_____
_____	_____	_____	_____
_____	_____	_____	_____
_____	_____	_____	_____

B. Debts and taxes owed by debtor.

	Name and address of creditor including taxing authority	Security held by creditor, if any	Whether claim is contingent, unliquidated, or disputed	Nature of and consideration for the debt	Amount due or claimed
1. Priority Claims	_____	_____	_____	_____	_____
A. Taxes	_____	_____	_____	_____	_____
B. Wages	_____	_____	_____	_____	_____
C. Other	_____	_____	_____	_____	_____
2. Secured Creditors	_____	_____	_____	_____	_____
3. General Unsecured Creditors	_____	_____	_____	_____	_____

C. Recent transfers.

1. Did the Debtor transfer or dispose of any property, other than in the ordinary course of business, to a spouse during the three years immediately

preceding the making of the assignment for the benefit of creditors or the appointment of the receiver?

                                                    Yes   No

2. Did the Debtor transfer or dispose of any property, other than in the ordinary course of business, to anyone other than a spouse during a period of one year immediately preceding the making of the assignment for the benefit of creditors or the appointment of the receiver?

                                                    Yes   No

3. If the answer to either of the above questions is "Yes," give the following information as to each transfer or disposition:

Date of transfer or disposition	Transferee and relation to debtor, if any	Description of property	Consideration and disposition thereof

D. Property claimed as exempt (applies only to individuals).

Nature and description	Location	Basis for exemption	Estimated market value

(c) *Preparation and filing by assignee or receiver.* If the debtor fails to file the schedule within the required time, the receiver or assignee to the extent able to supply the information shall prepare and file a schedule containing the information required by section (b) of this Rule. The schedule shall be filed within thirty days after the debtor's required filing date.

(d) *Failure of receiver or assignee to file schedule.* If a receiver or assignee who is required to file a schedule fails to do so within the required time, any person having an interest may file a report of the delinquency with the court. Upon the filing of a report or on its own initiative, the court may issue an order to the receiver or assignee to show cause in writing on or before a specified date why the receiver or assignee should not be compelled to file the schedule or be removed. Unless the court orders otherwise, the specified date shall be 20 days after the date prescribed for service in the order. The order shall also specify the persons to be served with the order, the method of service, and, if a hearing is scheduled when the order is issued, the date, time, and place of the hearing. Unless cause is shown or the schedule is filed, the court shall remove the receiver or assignee pursuant to Rule 13-701 and may take any action permitted or required by Rule 13-703.

(e) *Order compelling disclosure; sanction.* The court at any time may order the debtor, an officer or director of the debtor, or any other person who may have information that is necessary for the completion of the schedule to appear before the court or before an examiner pursuant to Rule 2-542 and to disclose the information. The debtor, an officer or director of a debtor, or other person who refuses to comply with an order compelling disclosure may be held in contempt pursuant to Title 15, Chapter 200 of these Rules.

Source. — This Rule is derived in part from former Rule BP2 a and b and is in part new.

Chancellor erred in issuing orders compelling president and sole shareholder of insolvent company to file schedules under former section a, by (1) ignoring the alternative provided by former section b in the event that the debtor fails to file a schedule; (2) issuing a contempt order for failure to comply with the Rule without any finding that such failure was wrongful as required by former subsection b 3; and (3) attempting to "pierce the corporate veil" of the debtor by ordering the director and shareholder to do that which was required of the corporate "debtor" under the provisions of former Rule BP 2. Rosenbloom v. Electric Motor Repair Co., 31 Md. App. 711, 358 A.2d 617 (1976).

Although officers of debtor corporation may be required to disclose information. — The officers of a corporation for which a receiver has been appointed may be compelled to disclose information to the receiver which is necessary for the preparation of the schedule under former section a, or to produce corporate records in their custody for that purpose. Rosenbloom v. Electric Motor Repair Co., 31 Md. App. 711, 358 A.2d 617 (1976).

And they are charged with knowledge of information required in schedules. — Both the president and the board chairman of a corporate insolvent are charged with the knowledge of all of the facts and information required in the schedule called for by former

section a. Rosenbloom v. Electric Motor Repair Co., 31 Md. App. 711, 358 A.2d 617 (1976).

Former subsection b 2 contemplates a debtor who may fail to file for reasons that are not wrongful, i.e., delinquent but not wrongfully so. When read in conjunction with the next subsection, it brings into play the alternative provision for the receiver to assume the filing responsibility with the necessary information being compulsorily provided by the delinquent debtor. Rosenbloom v. Electric Motor Repair Co., 31 Md. App. 711, 358 A.2d 617 (1976).

Presumably, the penalty for contempt in former subsection b 3 is not available for mere delinquency in filing or simple refusal to disclose. Rather, to be punishable, the conduct must be wrongful. Before a judgment of wrongdoing may be rendered, the reasons for the failure to file (or the failure to disclose) must be ascertained by the court. Rosenbloom v. Electric Motor Repair Co., 31 Md. App. 711, 358 A.2d 617 (1976).

Court must be satisfied that failure was wrongful. — Before contempt is available as a punishment for failure to disclose under former subsection b 3, the court must first be satisfied by evidentiary offerings that the failure to disclose was wrongful. Rosenbloom v. Electric Motor Repair Co., 31 Md. App. 711, 358 A.2d 617 (1976).

CHAPTER 300. EMPLOYMENT OF PROFESSIONALS.

Rule 13-301. Employment of attorney, accountant, appraiser, auctioneer, or other professional.

(a) *Court approval required.* A receiver or assignee shall not employ an attorney, accountant, appraiser, auctioneer, or other professional without prior approval of the court. With the court's prior approval, a receiver or assignee may serve as attorney or accountant for the estate.

(b) *Application; contents.* An application requesting authority to employ an attorney, accountant, appraiser, auctioneer, or other professional shall be accompanied by the affidavit required by Rule 13-302 and shall set forth:

(1) the necessity for the employment; and

(2) in the event the schedule required by Rule 13-203 has not been filed, the nature and approximate amount of the debtor's property and debts.

(c) *Prior approval of compensation in certain instances.* If the application requesting authority to employ an attorney, accountant, appraiser, auctioneer, or other professional sets forth in reasonable detail the basis for the proposed compensation of the person to be employed, the court, by order, may authorize compensation to be paid without further order of court for work completed within stated limits. This section does not apply to a receiver or assignee who serves as attorney or accountant for the estate.

Source. — This Rule is derived in part from former Rule BP6 a and b and is in part new.

———————

Cited in Ferguson v. Cramer, 349 Md. 760, 709 A.2d 1279 (1998).

Rule 13-302. Disclosures by receiver, assignee, and professionals.

(a) *Required disclosure by affidavit.* A receiver or assignee and each attorney, accountant, appraiser, auctioneer, or other professional to be employed by the assignee or receiver shall file an affidavit that states the following:

(1) whether the person has, within five years before the date of the appointment of a receiver or the assumption of jurisdiction over the estate of an assignee, represented or been employed by the debtor, an insider of the debtor as defined by 11 U.S.C. § 101, any secured or unsecured creditor of the debtor, or an investment banker of the debtor, and the nature of the representation or employment;

(2) if the debtor, insider, secured or unsecured creditor, or investment banker is a corporation, association, or partnership, whether the assignee, receiver, accountant, appraiser, auctioneer, or other professional had, within five years before the date of the appointment of a receiver or the assumption of jurisdiction over the estate of an assignee, any financial interest in the corporation, association, or partnership and the extent of the financial interest; and

(3) that the person is not disqualified for any of the reasons set forth in Rule 13-105.

(b) *When filed.* The affidavit shall be filed:

(1) by an assignee, with the petition;

(2) by a receiver, prior to assuming the duties of office;

(3) by an attorney, accountant, appraiser, auctioneer, or other professional, with the application requesting authority to employ the person.

(c) *Supplemental disclosure.* A person who has filed an affidavit under this Rule and who learns that the information in the affidavit is inaccurate or incomplete shall promptly file a supplemental affidavit.

(d) *Penalty for failure to disclose required information.* In addition to any other remedies provided by law, the court, pursuant to Rule 13-701, may remove any person who fails to disclose any information required to be disclosed by this Rule and may take any action permitted or required by Rule 13-703.

Source. — This Rule is derived from former
Rule BP3 a, b, and d.

Rule 13-303. Compensation and expenses for receiver, assignee, or professional.

(a) *Application for allowance of compensation and expenses.* Before a receiver, assignee, or any person performing services for the estate pursuant to Rule 13-301 is paid compensation or reimbursed for expenses not previously approved by the court, the receiver or assignee shall file with the court an application for the allowance of compensation and expenses. The application shall include:

(1) the estimated gross amount of the estate;

(2) the estimated total of the sums to be paid for liens, preferences, and costs of administration;

(3) the estimated approximate sum for distribution among secured, priority, and unsecured creditors;

(4) a detailed description of the services rendered, time expended, and expenses incurred;

(5) the amount of compensation and expenses requested;

(6) the amount of any compensation or expenses previously allowed by the court;

(7) the amount of any compensation and expenses received from or to be paid by any source other than the estate; and

(8) a detailed description of any agreement or understanding for a division of the compensation between the person rendering services and any other person except those specifically permitted to share in compensation by section (c) of this Rule.

(b) *Allowance.* The court shall review the application and any evidence presented and shall determine the appropriate amount of compensation and expenses to be paid to the receiver, assignee, or person performing services for the receiver or assignee. In determining the amount, the court is not bound by any compensation or commission fixed in an assignment for the benefit of creditors or in any other agreement.

(c) *Sharing of compensation.* Without the express written approval of the court, a receiver, assignee, or person performing services for a receiver or assignee shall not, in any form or manner, share or agree to share compensation for services rendered with any person other than a partner, employer, or regular employee of the person rendering services.

Source. — This Rule is derived from former
Rule BP7.

CHAPTER 400. CLAIMS.

Rule 13-401. Proof of claim.

(a) *Filing.* Any person who wishes to make a claim against the estate of a debtor shall file a verified proof of claim with the clerk. The proof of claim shall be filed within 120 days after the date the Notice to Creditors is issued by the clerk.

(b) *Form.* A proof of claim shall be in substantially the following form with supporting documentation attached as indicated:

[CAPTION]

CLAIM AGAINST DEBTOR

BY _____
                    Name of Claimant

The claimant certifies that the debtor owes the claimant the sum of $_____.

The consideration or basis for the debt is _____ .

The debt is:

[   ] an unsecured claim in the amount of $_____ (attach statement of account, invoices, promissory notes, or other evidence of claim); or

[   ] a secured claim in the amount of $_____ (attach evidence of perfection of security interest).

The undersigned certifies, in accordance with the verification below, that the debtor is indebted to the claimant in the amount shown, that there is no security for the debt other than that stated above or in an attachment to this claim form, that no unmatured interest is included, and that the undersigned is authorized to make this claim.

[   ] I solemnly affirm under the penalties of perjury and upon personal knowledge that the contents of the foregoing claim are true; or

[   ] I solemnly affirm under the penalties of perjury that I am employed by the claimant firm as _____ ;
                                                    (insert title)

that the claimant keeps regular books of account; that the keeping of these books is in my charge or under my supervision; that the entries in these books were made in the regular course of business; and that the entries show the facts set forth in this claim.

_____	_____
Name of Claimant	Signature of claimant or person authorized to make verifications on behalf of claimant
_____	
Name and Title of Person Signing Claim	Address
	_____
_____	_____
Date	Telephone Number

Instructions:

If the claim is based upon an obligation owed jointly to two or more persons, any one of the joint creditors may verify the claim. If the claimant is a corporation, association, or partnership, any officer, partner, or authorized agent may verify the claim. If the original and all copies of a written instrument securing a claim are lost or destroyed, the claimant must attach a statement explaining the circumstances of the loss or destruction.

(c) *Late filed claims.* (1) Before reference to auditor. A proof of claim that is filed late but before any reference to an auditor for the stating of an account is entitled to the same consideration for distribution as a timely filed proof of claim.

(2) After reference to auditor. A person who files a proof of claim after reference to an auditor is not entitled to participate in the next distribution unless the court on application of the claimant and for good cause shown orders otherwise. If the court permits participation, it may order the claimant to pay the cost of restating the account if the auditor must do so in whole or in part to include the claim. A proof of claim filed too late to be included in one or more auditor's accounts, if allowed, shall be included in any subsequent account, and the claimant is entitled to receive a distribution on the same basis as those already received by other creditors on prior accounts. The distribution shall be made before those creditors receive any further distribution. Thereafter, the claimant shall share with them in any future distributions.

Source. — This Rule is derived from former Rule BP4 b and c.

Late filing. — The present rules reflect the earlier case law that, absent laches amounting to prejudice to others, late filing is permitted as a matter of course as to undistributed funds in the hands of the court. Eastern Air Lines v. Phoenix Sav. & Loan Ass'n, 239 Md. 195, 210 A.2d 515 (1965).

A creditor who files late has an absolute right which does not, except to the extent that prejudice to others results from the late filing, depend on good cause shown to participate in funds in the hands of the court available for distribution. Eastern Air Lines v. Phoenix Sav. & Loan Ass'n, 239 Md. 195, 210 A.2d 515 (1965).

A creditor may come in and file his claim at any time before a distribution of the proceeds of sale has been actually made under a finally ratified auditor's account. Coppage v. Maryland Thrift Sav. & Loan Co., 253 Md. 238, 252 A.2d 869 (1969).

Where creditor's claim was timely filed, receiver could not object to claim on ground that he had been misled to believe claim had been paid. Coppage v. Maryland Thrift Sav. & Loan Co., 253 Md. 238, 252 A.2d 869 (1969).

Equitable principles will not bar creditor's claim where receiver's failure to follow procedures in the Maryland Rules allowed claim to be timely filed. Coppage v. Maryland Thrift Sav. & Loan Co., 253 Md. 238, 252 A.2d 869 (1969).

Rule 13-402. Objections to claims.

An objection to a proof of claim may be filed at any time before final ratification of the auditor's account in which the claim is allowed. The grounds for the objection shall be stated with particularity. The objection shall be served pursuant to Rule 1-321 on the claimant and, unless the receiver or assignee is the objecting party, on the receiver or assignee. On request, the claimant or the objecting party is entitled to a hearing.

Source. — This Rule is derived from former Rule BP4 d.

Late filing. — The present rules reflect the earlier case law that, absent laches amounting to prejudice to others, late filing is permitted as a matter of course as to undistributed funds in the hands of the court. Eastern Air Lines v. Phoenix Sav. & Loan Ass'n, 239 Md. 195, 210 A.2d 515 (1965).

A creditor who files late has an absolute right which does not, except to the extent that prejudice to others results from the late filing, depend on good cause shown to participate in funds in the hands of the court available for distribution. Eastern Air Lines v. Phoenix Sav. & Loan Ass'n, 239 Md. 195, 210 A.2d 515 (1965).

A creditor may come in and file his claim at any time before a distribution of the proceeds of sale has been actually made under a finally ratified auditor's account. Coppage v. Maryland Thrift Sav. & Loan Co., 253 Md. 238, 252 A.2d 869 (1969).

Where creditor's claim was timely filed, receiver could not object to claim on ground that he had been misled to believe claim had been paid. Coppage v. Maryland Thrift Sav. & Loan Co., 253 Md. 238, 252 A.2d 869 (1969).

Equitable principles will not bar creditor's claim where receiver's failure to follow procedures in the Maryland Rules allowed claim to be timely filed. Coppage v. Maryland Thrift Sav. & Loan Co., 253 Md. 238, 252 A.2d 869 (1969).

Rule 13-403. Compromise of claim or dispute.

(a) *Application.* A receiver or assignee may file an application requesting the court to authorize or ratify a compromise or settlement of any claim or matter relating to an estate.

(b) *Ratification.* If satisfied that the action is in the best interest of the estate, the court may authorize or ratify the proposed compromise or settlement and may impose any appropriate terms and conditions.

Source. — This Rule is in part derived from former Rule V77 b 1 and is in part new.

Powers included in former Rule V77 applied to all trustees, whether or not such powers are included in the will or trust agreement. Mercantile-Safe Deposit & Trust Co. v. United States, 311 F. Supp. 670 (D. Md. 1970).

Trustee has no power to sell something he does not have. — The expansion of fiduciary powers which former Rule V77 accomplished did not confer upon a trustee a power to sell something he does not have. Jones v. Endslow, 23 Md. App. 578, 328 A.2d 339 (1974).

And therefore could not sell real property in which he held title to a life estate without prior approval. — A trustee could not sell real property placed in a trust by the testator without the approval of any beneficiary or of the court where, with respect to that property, the trustee held legal title to a life estate only. Jones v. Endslow, 23 Md. App. 578, 328 A.2d 339 (1974).

CHAPTER 500. REPORTS AND DISTRIBUTIONS.

Rule 13-501. Reports.

(a) *Annual and final report; filing.* A receiver or assignee shall file an annual report under oath within 60 days after the end of the reporting period. The reporting period shall be (1) the year ending on the anniversary of the date upon which the court appointed the receiver or assumed jurisdiction over the estate; (2) upon notice to the trust clerk, any other one-year period chosen by the receiver or assignee, provided that the interval between the last report (or appointment or assumption of jurisdiction) and the report submitted shall not exceed one year; or (3) any other period ordered by the court. Before any interim or final distribution of the estate may be made, the receiver or assignee shall file a report for the period from the closing date of the last annual report until the proposed date on which the estate will be partially or fully distributed.

(b) *Form of report.* A report shall be in substantially the following form:

[CAPTION]

REPORT OF RECEIVER OR ASSIGNEE

_____   _____
Name of Debtor   Name of Receiver or Assignee
Reporting Period _____ 19___ to _____ 19___.

1. Summary of property held in fiduciary capacity at beginning of reporting period:

Nature and Description of Property	Estimated Market Value

2. Changes during the period covered by this report:

A. Collections and Receipts, including interest and dividends received:

Date	Description	Amount Received

Total Receipts $_____

B. Expenditures and distributions:

Date	Description	Amount Paid

Total Payments $_____

C. Property sold or otherwise transferred:

Date	Description	Court Order Reference	Transferee	Consideration Received

167

D. Property acquired:

Date	Description	Court Order Reference	Transferor	Consideration Paid

3. Summary of property held in fiduciary capacity at end of reporting period:

Nature and Description of Property	Estimated Market Value

4. Proposed distribution (distribution reports only):
Previous distributions were:

Date Authorized by Court	Amount of Distribution

Total distributions to date: _____

The amount available for [ ] partial [ ] final distribution is $_____.

If the proposed distribution is partial, the amount proposed to be retained in estate is $_____.

(Include in final reports only) All property of the estate has been accounted for and the undersigned knows of no debts incurred during the administration of the estate other than those which have been paid or which are reflected in this Report.

(Include in all reports) I solemnly affirm under the penalties of perjury that the contents of this Report are true to the best of my knowledge, information, and belief.

Date: _____   _____
                                   Receiver/Assignee

                                   _____
                                   Address

                                   _____

(c) *Weekly report if conducting a business.* For each calendar week during which the receiver or assignee conducts the business of the debtor, the receiver or assignee shall also file a report listing the receipts and disbursements in reasonable detail. The report shall be filed not later than the third day after the end of the weekly reporting period.

(d) *Further accountability.* Nothing in this Rule shall be construed to abridge the power of the court to require a receiver or assignee to submit reports covering periods greater or lesser, or at times earlier or later, than those prescribed in this Rule or to require the submission of more detailed information than that which is prescribed in this Rule.

(e) *Failure to file reports; penalties.* (1) Order. If a receiver or assignee fails to file a timely annual report, the trust clerk shall inform the court in writing, and the court shall issue an order to the receiver or assignee to show cause within 15 days why the receiver or assignee should not be removed. The order shall be served on the receiver or assignee and a copy sent to the surety on the bond of the receiver or assignee in accordance with Rule 13-701 (b).

(2) Sanctions. If the receiver or assignee does not comply with the order by filing an answer and all overdue reports, the court may remove the receiver or assignee pursuant to Rule 13-701 and may take any action permitted or required by Rule 13-703.

(f) *Examination by trust clerk.* (1) Examination of reports. The trust clerk shall examine all reports submitted pursuant to this Rule, except those referred to an auditor pursuant to Rule 13-502. The trust clerk shall determine whether all of the required information has been submitted and whether the amount of and surety on the bond of the receiver or assignee are sufficient to protect the estate.

(2) Examination of property not required. Unless the court orders otherwise, the trust clerk need not examine the property of the estate.

(3) Report and recommendation. The trust clerk shall (A) report any irregularities in the report to the court, (B) bring to the court's attention any other matter that the trust clerk considers appropriate, and (C) make any appropriate recommendation.

Source. — This Rule is derived from former Rule BP9 a, b, d, e, f, and g.

When reference to auditor unnecessary. — If an account consists of very few items it may not be necessary to refer the case to the auditor for adjustment, but the court in its discretion may perform this duty and ascertain the proper amounts without the aid of an audit; and so, if there is but a single item to be determined, which the court may ascertain, a reference to an auditor is unnecessary. And where a sum for distribution was so small that it would be wholly consumed in the expense of stating an account, the court considered it proper to distribute it as interest among those entitled, without the expense of another audit. Coppage v. Maryland Thrift Sav. & Loan Co., 253 Md. 238, 252 A.2d 869 (1969).

Rule 13-502. Referral to auditor.

(a) *When required.* The court shall refer to an auditor pursuant to Rule 2-543 all papers filed for the purpose of making a partial or final distribution of the estate.

(b) *Action by auditor.* The auditor shall audit a final or interim distribution report filed pursuant to Rule 13-501 and shall state an account setting forth the distribution of the estate.

(c) *Notice by auditor.* (1) To whom given. The auditor shall give notice by first class mail, postage prepaid, to the debtor, the receiver or assignee, and each creditor who has filed a claim in the proceedings that an auditor's account has been stated.

(2) Contents. In addition to the requirements of Rule 2-543, the notice by the auditor shall contain the following information:

(A) the total amount of property stated in the account;

(B) the total amount of approved liens and priorities;

(C) the total costs of administration, including as separate items the court costs and the compensation of the receiver, assignee, or person employed as a professional;

(D) the amount available for distribution to general creditors;

(E) the percentage of the creditor's claim to be paid; and

(F) whether the distribution is final or partial.

(d) *Interim distribution.* On application of the receiver, assignee, or other person in interest, the court may direct such partial distribution as may be safely made from the money in the hands of the receiver or assignee to those creditors whose claims are not in dispute, reserving sufficient assets to secure, after final settlement of all claims, a proportionate distribution among all creditors whose claims are finally allowed.

Source. — This Rule is derived from former Rule BP9 b and c and BP10 b.

When reference to auditor unnecessary. — If an account consists of very few items it may not be necessary to refer the case to the auditor for adjustment, but the court in its discretion may perform this duty and ascertain the proper amounts without the aid of an audit; and so, if there is but a single item to be determined, which the court may ascertain, a reference to an auditor is unnecessary. And where a sum for distribution was so small that it would be wholly consumed in the expense of stating an account, the court considered it proper to distribute it as interest among those entitled, without the expense of another audit. Coppage v. Maryland Thrift Sav. & Loan Co., 253 Md. 238, 252 A.2d 869 (1969).

Rule 13-503. Distribution.

(a) *Final ratification required.* Until the final account has been audited pursuant to Rule 13-502 and finally ratified by the court, a final distribution shall not be made to creditors, the estate shall not be closed, and any bond of the receiver or assignee shall not be released.

(b) *Payment.* Promptly after final ratification of an auditor's account in which a distribution to creditors has been stated, the receiver or assignee shall make distribution as stated in the account.

(c) *Disposition of unclaimed distributions.* The receiver or assignee shall pay into court any distributions that remain unclaimed for ninety days after final ratification of the auditor's final distribution account. The receiver or assignee shall file a list of the names and last known addresses of persons who have not claimed distributions, showing the amount of each person's distribution. The clerk shall issue a receipt for the payment, and the receipt shall release and discharge the receiver or assignee making the payment. Thereafter, the unclaimed distributions shall be subject to escheat as provided by law.

Source. — This Rule is derived from former Rules BP9 b 2 and BP10.

When reference to auditor unnecessary. — If an account consists of very few items it may not be necessary to refer the case to the auditor for adjustment, but the court in its discretion may perform this duty and ascertain the proper amounts without the aid of an audit; and so, if there is but a single item to be determined, which the court may ascertain, a reference to an auditor is unnecessary. And where a sum for distribution was so small that it would be wholly consumed in the expense of stating an account, the court considered it proper to distribute it as interest among those entitled, without the expense of another audit. Coppage v. Maryland Thrift Sav. & Loan Co., 253 Md. 238, 252 A.2d 869 (1969).

CHAPTER 600. ABANDONMENT OF PROPERTY AND RECORDS.

Rule 13-601. Abandonment of property and records.

(a) *Abandonment of property.* On application of a receiver, an assignee, or a creditor, the court may order the abandonment of any property of the debtor that is worthless, overburdened, or otherwise of inconsequential value and benefit to the estate.

(b) *Abandonment or destruction of books and records.* (1) Application. After the final ratification of an auditor's account that provides for the final distribution of the estate, the receiver or assignee may apply to the court for permission to destroy, return to the debtor, or otherwise dispose of all or part of the books and records of the debtor or of the estate.

(2) Notice to debtor and tax authorities. Notice of the application shall be given by first class mail, postage prepaid, to the Commissioner of Internal Revenue of the United States, the Comptroller of the Treasury of the State of Maryland, and the debtor at the debtor's last known address. If an objection is filed within 30 days after notice is given, the court shall hold a hearing.

Committee note. — This Rule does not address the consequences of destruction of books and records under state and federal revenue laws.

(3) Order. For good cause shown, the court may authorize the receiver or assignee to destroy, return to the debtor, or otherwise dispose of all or part of the books and records of the debtor or of the estate by or after a date fixed in the order.

Source. — This Rule is derived from former Rule BP8.

CHAPTER 700. REMOVAL AND RESIGNATION.

Rule 13-701. Removal of assignee, receiver, or professional.

(a) *On court's own initiative; by petition.* The court or any person having an interest in the estate may initiate proceedings to remove a receiver, assignee, or any person employed as a professional by the receiver or assignee. The court may initiate removal proceedings by filing an order pursuant to section (b) of this Rule and shall state in the order the reasons for the proposed removal. An interested person may initiate removal proceedings by filing a petition that shall state the reasons for the requested removal and may include a request for the appointment of a successor receiver, assignee, or professional.

(b) *Show cause order; service.* If removal proceedings are initiated, the court shall order the receiver, assignee, or professional to show cause why the receiver, assignee, or professional should not be removed or be subject to other sanctions. The order, together with a copy of any petition, shall be served pursuant to Rule 2-121 on the person sought to be removed or, if it is shown by affidavit that the whereabouts of the person sought to be removed are unknown and that reasonable efforts have been made in good faith to locate the person, the court may order service pursuant to Rule 2-122. Copies of the show cause order and any petition shall also be sent by first class mail, postage prepaid, to the surety on the bond of the receiver or assignee and to any other persons directed by the court.

(c) *Disposition.* After a hearing and for cause, including ineligibility, the court may remove a receiver, assignee, or professional.

Cross references. — As to the statutory grounds for the removal of a fiduciary, including a receiver or assignee, *see* Code, Estates and Trusts Article, § 15-112.

Source. — This Rule is in part derived from former Rule V84 and is in part new.

Conventional trustee has broad discretionary powers which may be exercised absent evidence of bad faith, misconduct or a want of ordinary skill or judgment. Shipley v. Crouse, 279 Md. 613, 370 A.2d 97 (1977).

First obligation of the trustees is to safeguard the trust estate, and in doing so they are called upon many times to exercise a judgment; hence the judgment exercised by the trustees that they would share the final contract and let the beneficiaries know when it was submitted to the court for ratification, but would not share the step-by-step negotiations with the beneficiaries, was not a breach of their duty, but, quite to the contrary, was in furtherance of their duty to try to do what, in their judgment, was in the best interests of the trust estate. Shipley v. Crouse, 279 Md. 613, 370 A.2d 97 (1977).

Receipt of information by beneficiaries not absolute. — While beneficiaries are entitled to receive complete and accurate information as to the administration of the trust and to know what the trust property is and how the

trustee has dealt with it, this is not absolute, if the trustee renders periodic reports showing collection of income and disbursements, assuming the trustee is acting in good faith and is not abusing his discretionary powers. Shipley v. Crouse, 279 Md. 613, 370 A.2d 97 (1977).

Disclosure by trustees mandated. — When there is a confidential relationship between buyer and seller, or there is an element of self-dealing, the duty of loyalty mandates a full and frank disclosure by the trustees to the beneficiaries. Shipley v. Crouse, 279 Md. 613, 370 A.2d 97 (1977).

Where removal likely required. — Where because of a disagreement between coguardians a ward has not been permitted to leave the grounds of a nursing home in which she resides, receive new eyeglasses, have any change in the medication or medical care she requires or the like, it may well be that removal of one or both of the guardians will be required. Kicherer v. Kicherer, 285 Md. 114, 400 A.2d 1097 (1979).

Rule 13-702. Resignation of receiver or assignee.

(a) *Petition.* A receiver may file a petition for permission to resign in the court in which the receiver was appointed. An assignee may file a petition to resign in the court in which a petition to assume jurisdiction of the estate has been filed. The petition shall state the reasons for the proposed resignation and may include a request for the appointment of a successor receiver or assignee.

(b) *Report to be filed.* The receiver or assignee shall file with the petition a report pursuant to Rule 13-601 for any period not covered in an annual report previously filed or, if no annual report has been filed, from the date the receiver or assignee took charge of the estate.

(c) *Notice.* The receiver or assignee shall mail a copy of the petition by first class mail, postage prepaid, to those interested persons designated by the court.

(d) *Termination of appointment.* The resignation of a receiver or assignee does not terminate the appointment until the resignation has been approved by the court.

(e) *Proceedings.* The court may grant or deny the requested relief with or without a hearing. In an order granting the petition, the court may specify any conditions for the acceptance of the resignation that the nature of the case may require.

Source. — This Rule is in part derived from former Rule V81 and is in part new.

Rule 13-703. Appointment of successors; forfeiture of compensation.

When a receiver, assignee, or professional dies, resigns, or is removed, the court may appoint a successor on its own initiative or on the petition of any person having an interest. The court shall order that all appropriate papers, records, and property be turned over to the successor and may order that a removed or resigning receiver or assignee file any report required by Rule 13-501. The court may order the person removed to forfeit any future compensation and return any compensation for services previously rendered.

Source. — This Rule is derived from former Rule V82 a.

TITLE 14. SALES OF PROPERTY

Editor's note. — The Court of Appeals, by Order dated June 5, 1996, effective January 1, 1997, rescinded Subtitles A, D, E, J, P, Q, R, T, U, V, W, Y, Z, BB, BD, BE, BG, BH, BJ, BL, BP, BQ, BR, BS, BW, and BY of Chapter 1100 of the Maryland Rules of Procedure, rescinded Subtitles P, BB, BQ, and BW of the Maryland District Rules, and rescinded Forms 22a, 23, 24, 25, and 26. The Order substituted for certain of the rules and forms rescinded new Title 9, Chapter 100, Title 10, Title 12, Title 13, Title 14, and Title 15 of the Maryland Rules of Procedure. Furthermore, the Order transferred, without readoption, Chapter 900, Chapter 1200, and Subtitles S, BU, and BV of Chapter 1100 of the Maryland Rules of Procedure and Chapter 1200 of the Maryland District Rules to be Title 9, Chapter 200, Title 11, and Title 16 of the Maryland Rules of Procedure. The Order provides that the new rules shall "apply to all actions commenced on or after January 1, 1997, and insofar as practicable, to all actions then pending."

Many of the cases in the notes to the various rules were decided prior to the 1996 revision. These cases have been retained under pertinent rules of this title where it is thought that such cases will be of value in interpreting the present rules.

A table of comparable rules, relating those rules rescinded effective January 1, 1997, to the revised rules in Title 9 through Title 16 is to be found in Volume 2 following the end of the Maryland Rules.

CHAPTER 100. GENERAL PROVISIONS.

Rule 14-101. Location of public sale of interest in real property.

A public sale of an interest in real property conducted pursuant to these Rules shall take place immediately outside the courthouse entrance, on the property being sold, or elsewhere as ordered by the court, or as specified in the advertisement placed pursuant to Rule 14-206.

Source. — This Rule is new.

Rule 14-102. Judgment awarding possession.

(a) *Generally.* Whenever the purchaser of an interest in real property at a sale conducted pursuant to these Rules is entitled to possession, and the person in actual possession fails or refuses to deliver possession, the purchaser may file a motion requesting the court to enter a judgment awarding possession of the property. Except as otherwise provided in this Rule, the procedure shall be governed by Rule 2-311.

(b) *Service.* The motion shall be served on the person in actual possession and on any other person affected by the motion. If the person was a party to the action that resulted in the sale or to the instrument that authorized the sale, the motion may be served in accordance with Rule 1-321. Otherwise, the motion shall be served in accordance with Rule 2-121, and shall be accompanied by a notice advising the person to file a response to the motion within the time prescribed by sections (a) and (b) of Rule 2-321 for answering a complaint.

Cross references. — Rule 2-647.
Source. — This Rule is derived from former Rule 637.

CHAPTER 200. FORECLOSURE OF LIEN INSTRUMENTS.

Rule 14-201. Scope and definitions.

(a) *Scope.* The rules in this Chapter apply to foreclosure of liens upon property that are created or authorized to be created by a lien instrument or are created by a statute providing for foreclosure in the manner specified for foreclosure of mortgages. The procedure set forth in these Rules shall provide the sole remedy for the vendor for repossession of property sold under a land installment contract executed pursuant to Code, Real Property Article, Title 10, Subtitle 1 or its statutory predecessor. Otherwise, the foreclosure procedure provided in these Rules does not preclude other remedies, including but not limited to self-help, that may be available under Code, Commercial Law Article; Code, Real Property Article; or other law.

(b) *Definitions.* The following definitions apply in the rules in this Chapter:

(1) Assent to a decree. "Assent to a decree" means a provision in a lien instrument declaring an assent to the entry of an order for the sale of the property subject to the lien upon a specified default.

(2) Debt. "Debt" means a monetary obligation secured by a lien.

(3) Debtor. "Debtor" means the record owner of the property at the time the lien was created and the purchaser under a land installment contract.

(4) Lien. "Lien" means a statutory lien or a lien upon property created or authorized to be created by a lien instrument.

(5) Lien instrument. "Lien instrument" means a mortgage, a deed of trust, a land installment contract, including those defined in Code, Real Property Article § 10-101 (b), a contract creating a lien pursuant to Code, Real Property Article, §§ 14-201 through 14-205, a deed or other instrument reserving a vendor's lien, an instrument creating or authorizing the creation of a lien in favor of a homeowners' association, a condominium council of unit owners, a

property owners' association or a community association, a security agreement, and any other instrument creating or authorizing the creation of a lien upon the property.

(6) Power of sale. "Power of sale" means a provision in a lien instrument authorizing a person to sell the property upon a specified default.

(7) Property. "Property" means real and personal property of any kind situated within this State.

(8) Record owner of property. "Record owner of property" includes the record holder of the rights of a purchaser under a land installment contract.

(9) Sale. "Sale" means foreclosure sale.

(10) Secured party. "Secured party" means a mortgagee, the holder of a note secured by a deed of trust, a vendor holding a vendor's lien, a condominium council of unit owners, a homeowners' association, a property owners' or community association, and any other party secured by a lien. "Secured party" includes any assignee or successor in interest of a secured party.

(11) Statutory lien. "Statutory lien" means a lien on property created by a statute providing for foreclosure in the manner specified for the foreclosure of mortgages.

Source. — This Rule is derived as follows: *Section (a)* is derived from former Rules W70 b and W79 c.

Section (b) is in part derived from former Rule W70 a and in part new.

Former Subtitle W Rules met due process requirements of the Fourteenth Amendment to the United States Constitution and article 24 of the Maryland Declaration of Rights. Billingsley v. Lawson, 43 Md. App. 713, 406 A.2d 946 (1979), cert. denied, 446 U.S. 919, 100 S. Ct. 1853, 64 L. Ed. 2d 273 (1980).

Counterclaim by mortgagor. — Prior to 1984, when the distinctions between law and equity for purposes of pleadings, parties, court sittings, and dockets were eliminated, the foreclosure of a deed of trust pursuant to a power of sale contained therein was an exclusively equitable remedy; today, however, nothing in the Maryland Rules of Procedure prohibits a mortgagor who voluntarily appears in a mortgage foreclosure proceeding from filing a counterclaim. Fairfax Sav. v. Kris Jen Ltd. Partnership, 338 Md. 1, 655 A.2d 1265 (1995).

Notice may be given by attorney. — A notification given by an attorney, who is an agent with authority to act in the premises, is the act of the client. Bob Holding Corp. v. Normal Realty Corp., 223 Md. 260, 164 A.2d 457 (1960).

Where the plaintiff's attorney signed the notice required by former Article 21, § 113, instead of "the vendor," the notice was properly given. Bob Holding Corp. v. Normal Realty Corp., 223 Md. 260, 164 A.2d 457 (1960).

The fact that the letter of notification was signed by the attorney was not material. In so doing, he was acting as the attorney for and agent of the plaintiff. His act was the act of the plaintiff. The notice was by the "vendor" within the meaning of the statute. Bob Holding Corp. v. Normal Realty Corp., 223 Md. 260, 164 A.2d 457 (1960).

Form of notice is not prescribed. — The ingredients only, not the form of the notice, are prescribed by the statute. Bob Holding Corp. v. Normal Realty Corp., 223 Md. 260, 164 A.2d 457 (1960).

And "foreclosure" may be used instead of "terminate." — Where notice used the word "foreclosure" instead of the word "terminate," the notice was not defective, since there is no substantial difference between the meanings of the two words; foreclosure of mortgage meaning termination of all rights of mortgagor. Bob Holding Corp. v. Normal Realty Corp., 223 Md. 260, 164 A.2d 457 (1960).

It is sufficient if data are furnished from which the time may be computed with certainty. Bob Holding Corp. v. Normal Realty Corp., 223 Md. 260, 164 A.2d 457 (1960).

Ejectment is not a permissible remedy under the Land Installment Contracts Law. Hudson v. Maryland State Hous. Co., 207 Md. 320, 114 A.2d 421 (1955).

But ejectment proceedings do not in-

validate contract. — The fact that vendor used ejectment proceedings against purchaser, which are not a permissible remedy under the statute, did not invalidate a land installment contract. Hudson v. Maryland State Hous. Co., 207 Md. 320, 114 A.2d 421 (1955).

Quoted in May Dep't Stores v. Montgomery County, 118 Md. App. 441, 702 A.2d 988 (1997).

Rule 14-202. Parties.

(a) *Who may institute action.* (1) Under power of sale. When the lien instrument contains a power of sale or when a statute provides that a lien may be foreclosed as if it contained a power of sale, an action to foreclose the lien may be instituted by any natural person authorized to exercise the power of sale, except that an action to foreclose a deed of trust shall be instituted by any trustee appointed in the deed or any successor trustee.

(2) Under assent to decree. When the lien instrument contains an assent to a decree or when a statute provides that a lien shall be foreclosed as if it contained an assent to a decree, an action to foreclose the lien may be instituted by the secured party, except that an action to foreclose a deed of trust shall be instituted by the beneficiary of the deed of trust, any trustee appointed in the deed, or any successor trustee.

(b) *Action by fractional owners of debt secured by a lien.* (1) Minimum of 25% must be represented. A power of sale shall not be exercised, and the court shall not enter an order for a sale under an assent to a decree, unless the power is exercised or application for an order is made or consented to by the holders of not less than 25% of the entire debt due under the lien instrument.

(2) Exclusive right to foreclose. Subject to the provisions of section (b) of Rule 14-207, the first party instituting an action to foreclose a lien instrument containing either a power of sale or an assent to a decree, thereby acquires the exclusive right to foreclose the lien.

(c) *Exceptions — Deed of trust.* The provisions of subsection (b) (1) of this Rule shall not apply in an action to foreclose a deed of trust.

Source. — This Rule is derived from former Rule W71 with the exception of section (c) which is derived from former Rule W77 b.

General creditor having no lien upon the property is not a proper party, initially or by intervention, to a foreclosure suit. Balance Ltd. v. Short, 35 Md. App. 10, 368 A.2d 1116 (1977).

For most purposes a deed of trust is a mortgage and is subject to some (but not all) statutory provisions relating to mortgages. Burroughs v. Garner, 43 Md. App. 302, 405 A.2d 301 (1979).

Obligor's interest after full payment. — Neither default nor institution of foreclosure in any way negates the fact that where full payment has been made, the obligor has, at the least, complete equitable ownership of the property, and the trustee has, at most, only bare legal title to it. Burroughs v. Garner, 43 Md. App. 302, 405 A.2d 301 (1979).

Bond of trustee under former statute. — See Union Trust Co. v. Ward, 100 Md. 98, 59 A. 192 (1904); Real Estate Trust Co. v. Union Trust Co., 102 Md. 41, 61 A. 228 (1905); Cummings v. Wildman, 116 Md. 307, 81 A. 610 (1911); Richardson v. Malthan, 133 Md. 542, 105 A. 766 (1919); Briley v. Pinkston, 215 Md. 417, 136 A.2d 563 (1958).

Rule 14-203. Conditions precedent; venue.

(a) *Conditions precedent.* (1) Generally. An action to foreclose a lien may be filed after (A) the instrument creating or giving notice of the existence of the lien has been filed for record, and (B) there has been a default in a condition upon which the lien instrument provides that a sale may be made or there is a default in the payment of the debt secured by a statutory lien.

Cross references. — Code, Real Property Article, §§ 14-201 through 14-206.

(2) Land installment contract. An action to foreclose a land installment contract as defined in Code, Real Property Article, § 10-101 (b) shall be instituted only after the secured party: (A) serves on the debtor and the current record owner of the property, either by delivery to the person to be served or by certified mail to the last known address of the person to be served, a written notice stating the amount of payment in default and the nature of any claimed default in any other condition or requirement of the contract, and advising the person served that foreclosure proceedings will be instituted on or after a designated day, not less than 30 days after service of the notice, unless the debtor or the current record owner before that time cures the default, and (B) files proof by affidavit that the required notice has been given.

(b) *Venue.* An action to foreclose a lien shall be filed in the county in which all or any part of the property subject to the lien is located.

(c) *Jurisdiction — Attaches upon commencement of action.* The jurisdiction of the court over property subject to a lien shall attach upon the commencement of an action filed pursuant to Rule 14-204, with or without the bond described in Rule 14-206 (a).

Source. — This Rule is derived from former Rule W72 and W79.

Purpose of foreclosure statutes. — One of the main objects of § 5 (now § 7-105 (a)) of the Real Property Article and repealed §§ 6 and 7 of Article 66, from which former Rules W72 and W74 were derived, was to bring sales made by their authority and the resulting equity proceedings under the cognizance and guidance of the court, and such proceedings are to be conducted and the validity of the sales tested as ordinary sales made by a trustee appointed by a decree of the court. Ex parte Aurora Fed. Sav. & Loan Ass'n, 223 Md. 135, 162 A.2d 739 (1960).

An order to docket is not a pleading. This is so in spite of the fact that it is the delivery of the order to the clerk which gives the equity court jurisdiction over the mortgaged property when a power of sale is being exercised. Saunders v. Stradley, 25 Md. App. 85, 333 A.2d 604 (1975).

And need not make factual allegations

sufficient to show a right to proceed. — See Saunders v. Stradley, 25 Md. App. 85, 333 A.2d 604 (1975).

It is not designed to be answered, denied or traversed so as to arrive at issues. Saunders v. Stradley, 25 Md. App. 85, 333 A.2d 604 (1975).

No process is issued or served upon the filing of an order to docket. Saunders v. Stradley, 25 Md. App. 85, 333 A.2d 604 (1975).

Scope of court's function not affected by order to docket. — An order to docket neither broadens nor narrows the scope of the court's function in a case. Saunders v. Stradley, 25 Md. App. 85, 333 A.2d 604 (1975).

A foreclosure-triggering default is a condition precedent to a Maryland mortgage foreclosure: ordinarily the existence of that essential will be demonstrated by the statement of mortgage debt that is required to accompany the order to docket the summary

رcribed

proceeding. Fairfax Sav. v. Kris Jen Ltd. Partnership, 338 Md. 1, 655 A.2d 1265 (1995).

No sale under decree until default. — Before the passage of former Rule W72, a decree might properly be entered at any time after the execution of a mortgage containing an assent to a decree, whether there was or not at the time a default on the part of the mortgagor in respect to the covenants of the mortgage, but there could be no sale under the decree until default. United States v. Eastern Woodworks, Inc., 151 F. Supp. 95 (D. Md. 1957); Better v. Williams, 203 Md. 613, 102 A.2d 750 (1954).

Time for sale. — Foreclosure pursuant to a power of sale is intended to be a summary, in rem proceeding. In that type of proceeding, a sale of the mortgaged property can be held in approximately twenty-one days after docketing. G.E. Capital Mtg. Servs., Inc. v. Levenson, 338 Md. 227, 657 A.2d 1170 (1995).

Where a party interested in mortgaged property tenders mortgagee full amount due, for purpose of redeeming mortgage, as he has a right to do, mortgagee has no right to institute foreclosure proceedings thereafter, and may be enjoined from doing so. Kent Bldg. & Loan Co. v. Middleton, 112 Md. 10, 75 A. 967 (1910).

When jurisdiction attaches — Former law. — Formerly in Maryland jurisdiction of the equity court in a case of foreclosure under a power of sale was not complete until the property was sold and the trustee under the mortgage had filed his report of the sale. In Warehime v. Carroll County Bldg. Ass'n, 44 Md. 512 (1876), it was said that, in the case of a sale under a power in a mortgage, the trust commenced with the filing of the trustee's bond; his report of sales was his first official intercourse with the court, and its supervisory power then commenced. In re Hurlock, 23 F.2d 500 (D. Md. 1928).

Sale will not be set aside because mortgage notes were not filed, no application having been made for that purpose and indebtedness and ownership of notes not being denied. Heider v. Bladen, 83 Md. 242, 34 A. 836 (1896).

Bankruptcy of mortgagor. — Where suit is entered in State court, to foreclose mortgage before petition in bankruptcy against mortgagor is filed foreclosure case may be prosecuted without interference of bankruptcy court; otherwise, however, where (as formerly the case where a mortgage was foreclosed under a power of sale) State court does not acquire jurisdiction until property sold and report of sale filed. In re Hurlock, 23 F.2d 500 (D. Md. 1928).

Notice may be given by attorney. — A notification given by an attorney, who is an agent with authority to act in the premises, is the act of the client. Bob Holding Corp. v. Normal Realty Corp., 223 Md. 260, 164 A.2d 457 (1960).

Where the plaintiff's attorney signed the notice required by former Article 21, § 113, instead of "the vendor," the notice was properly given. Bob Holding Corp. v. Normal Realty Corp., 223 Md. 260, 164 A.2d 457 (1960).

The fact that the letter of notification was signed by the attorney was not material. In so doing, he was acting as the attorney for and agent of the plaintiff. His act was the act of the plaintiff. The notice was by the "vendor" within the meaning of the statute. Bob Holding Corp. v. Normal Realty Corp., 223 Md. 260, 164 A.2d 457 (1960).

Form of notice is not prescribed. — The ingredients only, not the form of the notice, are prescribed by the statute. Bob Holding Corp. v. Normal Realty Corp., 223 Md. 260, 164 A.2d 457 (1960).

And "foreclosure" may be used instead of "terminate." — Where notice used the word "foreclosure" instead of the word "terminate," the notice was not defective, since there is no substantial difference between the meanings of the two words; foreclosure of mortgage meaning termination of all rights of mortgagor. Bob Holding Corp. v. Normal Realty Corp., 223 Md. 260, 164 A.2d 457 (1960).

It is sufficient if data are furnished from which the time may be computed with certainty. Bob Holding Corp. v. Normal Realty Corp., 223 Md. 260, 164 A.2d 457 (1960).

Ejectment is not a permissible remedy under the Land Installment Contracts Law. Hudson v. Maryland State Hous. Co., 207 Md. 320, 114 A.2d 421 (1955).

But ejectment proceedings do not invalidate contract. — The fact that vendor used ejectment proceedings against purchaser, which are not a permissible remedy under the statute, did not invalidate a land installment contract. Hudson v. Maryland State Hous. Co., 207 Md. 320, 114 A.2d 421 (1955).

Quoted in Schaller v. Castle Dev. Corp., 111 Md. App. 40, 680 A.2d 528 (1996).

Rule 14-204. Commencement of action and process.

(a) *Methods of commencing action.* An action to foreclose a lien pursuant to a power of sale shall be commenced by filing an order to docket. An action to foreclose a lien pursuant to an assent to a decree or where the lien instrument contains neither a power of sale nor an assent to a decree shall be commenced by filing a complaint to foreclose. When a lien instrument contains both a power of sale and an assent to a decree, the lien may be foreclosed pursuant to either the power of sale or the assent to a decree. The complaint or order to docket shall be accompanied by:

(1) the original or a certified copy of the lien instrument or, in an action to foreclose a statutory lien, an original or a certified copy of a notice of the existence of the lien,

(2) a statement of the debt remaining due and payable supported by an affidavit of the plaintiff or the secured party or the agent or attorney of the plaintiff or the secured party,

(3) in the case of a deed of trust, a copy of the debt instrument certified by the attorney or the trustee conducting the sale, and

(4) if any defendant is a natural person, an affidavit that either the person is not in the military service of the United States as defined in Section 511 of the Soldiers' and Sailors' Civil Relief Act of 1940, as amended, 50 U.S.C. Appendix, 520, or that the action is authorized by the Act.

(b) *Process and hearing not required.* In an action to foreclose a lien pursuant to a power of sale or pursuant to an order for sale under an assent to a decree, it is not necessary that process issue or that a hearing be held prior to sale.

Cross references. — Sections 511 and 532 of the Soldiers' and Sailors' Civil Relief Act of 1940, 50 U.S.C. Appendix.

Source. — This Rule is derived from former Rule W72 c, d, and e.

Editor's note. — Section 511 of the Soldiers' and Sailors' Civil Relief Act of 1940, referred to in section (a) (4), is codified as 50 U.S.C. App. § 571.

Purpose of foreclosure statutes. — One of the main objects of § 5 (now § 7-105 (a)) of the Real Property Article and repealed §§ 6 and 7 of Article 66, from which former Rules W72 and W74 were derived, was to bring sales made by their authority and the resulting equity proceedings under the cognizance and guidance of the court, and such proceedings are to be conducted and the validity of the sales tested as ordinary sales made by a trustee appointed by a decree of the court. Ex parte Aurora Fed. Sav. & Loan Ass'n, 223 Md. 135, 162 A.2d 739 (1960).

An order to docket is not a pleading. This is so in spite of the fact that it is the delivery of the order to the clerk which gives the equity court jurisdiction over the mortgaged property when a power of sale is being exercised. Saunders v. Stradley, 25 Md. App. 85, 333 A.2d 604 (1975).

And need not make factual allegations sufficient to show a right to proceed. — See Saunders v. Stradley, 25 Md. App. 85, 333 A.2d 604 (1975).

It is not designed to be answered, denied or traversed so as to arrive at issues. Saunders v. Stradley, 25 Md. App. 85, 333 A.2d 604 (1975).

No process is issued or served upon the filing of an order to docket. Saunders v. Stradley, 25 Md. App. 85, 333 A.2d 604 (1975).

Scope of court's function not affected by order to docket. — An order to docket neither broadens nor narrows the scope of the court's function in a case. Saunders v. Stradley, 25 Md. App. 85, 333 A.2d 604 (1975).

A foreclosure-triggering default is a condition precedent to a Maryland mortgage foreclosure: ordinarily the existence of that essential will be demonstrated by the statement of mortgage debt that is required to accompany the order to docket the summary proceeding. Fairfax Sav. v. Kris Jen Ltd. Partnership, 338 Md. 1, 655 A.2d 1265 (1995).

No sale under decree until default. — Before the passage of former Rule W72, a decree might properly be entered at any time after the execution of a mortgage containing an assent to a decree, whether there was or not at the time a default on the part of the mortgagor in respect to the covenants of the mortgage, but there could be no sale under the decree until default. Better v. Williams, 203 Md. 613, 102 A.2d 750 (1954); United States v. Eastern Woodworks, Inc., 151 F. Supp. 95 (D. Md. 1957).

Amendment of statement of mortgage debt after foreclosure. — Where a first mortgage lender amended the statement of mortgage debt after a foreclosure sale had been conducted and ratified, where the judgment of ratification had become final and unappealable, and where the amendment obliterated a surplus that would have been distributed to junior lienors, the first mortgage lender had the burden of proving that there was no prejudice in fact to junior lienors. Schaller v. Castle Dev. Corp., 347 Md. 90, 698 A.2d 1106 (1997).

Time for sale. — Foreclosure pursuant to a power of sale is intended to be a summary, in rem proceeding. In that type of proceeding, a sale of the mortgaged property can be held in approximately twenty-one days after docketing. G.E. Capital Mtg. Servs., Inc. v. Levenson, 338 Md. 227, 657 A.2d 1170 (1995).

Where a party interested in mortgaged property tenders mortgagee full amount due, for purpose of redeeming mortgage, as he has a right to do, mortgagee has no right to institute foreclosure proceedings thereafter, and may be enjoined from doing so. Kent Bldg. & Loan Co. v. Middleton, 112 Md. 10, 75 A. 967 (1910).

When jurisdiction attaches — Former law. — Formerly in Maryland jurisdiction of the equity court in a case of foreclosure under a power of sale was not complete until the property was sold and the trustee under the mortgage had filed his report of the sale. In Warehime v. Carroll County Bldg. Ass'n, 44 Md. 512 (1876), it was said that, in the case of a sale under a power in a mortgage, the trust commenced with the filing of the trustee's bond; his report of sales was his first official intercourse with the court, and its supervisory power then commenced. In re Hurlock, 23 F.2d 500 (D. Md. 1928).

Sale will not be set aside because mortgage notes were not filed, no application having been made for that purpose and indebtedness and ownership of notes not being denied. Heider v. Bladen, 83 Md. 242, 34 A. 836 (1896).

Bankruptcy of mortgagor. — Where suit is entered in State court, to foreclose mortgage before petition in bankruptcy against mortgagor is filed foreclosure case may be prosecuted without interference of bankruptcy court; otherwise, however, where (as formerly the case where a mortgage was foreclosed under a power of sale) State court does not acquire jurisdiction until property sold and report of sale filed. In re Hurlock, 23 F.2d 500 (D. Md. 1928).

Rule 14-205. Lien instruments or statutory liens — Containing neither power of sale nor assent to decree.

(a) *Commencement of action and process.* When a complaint to foreclose a lien instrument or statutory lien containing neither a power of sale nor an assent to a decree is filed, process shall issue and be served, and the action shall proceed as in any other civil action.

(b) *Order of court directing sale — Conditions.* (1) Generally. In an action to foreclose a lien instrument or statutory lien containing neither a power of sale nor an assent to a decree, the court shall first determine whether a default has occurred. If the court finds that a default has occurred it shall (A) fix the amount of the debt, interest, and costs then due and (B) provide a reasonable time within which payment may be made. The court may order that if payment is not made within the time fixed in the order, so much of the property as may be necessary to satisfy the amount due shall be sold.

(2) Order directing sale before judgment in exceptional case. If after a hearing the court is satisfied that the interests of justice require an immediate sale of the property that is subject to the lien, and that a sale would be ordered as a result of the final hearing of the action, the court may order a sale of the

property before judgment and shall appoint a person to make the sale pursuant to Rule 14-207. The court shall order the proceeds of any sale before judgment to be deposited or invested pending distribution pursuant to judgment.

Source. — This Rule is derived from former Rule W73.

Rule 14-206. Procedure prior to sale.

(a) *Bond.* Before making a sale of property to foreclose a lien, the person authorized to make the sale shall file a bond to the State of Maryland conditioned upon compliance with any court order that may be entered in relation to the sale of the property or distribution of the proceeds of the sale. Unless the court orders otherwise, the amount of the bond shall be the amount of the debt plus the estimated expenses of the proceeding. On application by a person having an interest in the property or by the person authorized to make the sale, the court may increase or decrease the amount of the bond pursuant to Rule 1-402 (d).

(b) *Notice.* (1) By publication. After commencement of an action to foreclose a lien and before making a sale of the property subject to the lien, the person authorized to make the sale shall publish notice of the time, place, and terms of sale in a newspaper of general circulation in the county in which the action is pending. "Newspaper of general circulation" means a newspaper satisfying the criteria set forth in Code, Article 1, Section 28. A newspaper circulating to a substantial number of subscribers in a county and customarily containing legal notices with respect to property in the county shall be regarded as a newspaper of general circulation in the county, notwithstanding that (1) its readership is not uniform throughout the county, or (2) its content is not directed at all segments of the population. For the sale of an interest in real property, the notice shall be given at least once a week for three successive weeks, the first publication to be not less than 15 days prior to sale and the last publication to be not more than one week prior to sale. For the sale of personal property, the notice shall be given not less than five days nor more than 12 days before the sale.

(2) By certified and first class mail. (A) Before making a sale of the property, the person authorized to make the sale shall send notice of the time, place, and terms of sale by certified mail and by first class mail to the last known address of (i) the debtor, (ii) the record owner of the property, and (iii) the holder of any subordinate interest in the property subject to the lien.

(B) The notice of the sale shall be sent not more than 30 days and not less than ten days before the date of the sale to all such persons whose identity and address are actually known to the person authorized to make the sale or are reasonably ascertainable from a document recorded, indexed, and available for public inspection 30 days before the date of the sale.

(3) Other notice. If the person authorized to make the sale receives actual notice at any time before the sale is held that there is a person holding a subordinate interest in the property and if the interest holder's identity and address are reasonably ascertainable, the person authorized to make the sale

shall give notice of the time, place, and terms of sale to the interest holder as promptly as reasonably practicable in any manner, including by telephone or electronic transmission, that is reasonably calculated to apprise the interest holder of the sale. This notice need not be given to anyone to whom notice was sent pursuant to subsection (b) (2) of this Rule.

(4) *Return receipt or affidavit.* The person giving notice pursuant to subsections (b) (2) and (b) (3) of this Rule shall file in the proceedings an affidavit (A) that the person has complied with the provisions of those subsections or (B) that the identity or address of the debtor, record owner, or holder of a subordinate interest is not reasonably ascertainable. If the affidavit states that an identity or address is not reasonably ascertainable, the affidavit shall state in detail the reasonable, good faith efforts that were made to ascertain the identity or address. If notice was given pursuant to subsection (b) (3), the affidavit shall state the date, manner, and content of the notice given.

(c) *Postponement.* If the sale is postponed, notice of the new date of sale shall be published in accordance with subsection (b) (1) of this Rule. No new or additional notice under subsection (b) (2) of this Rule need be given to any person to whom notice of the earlier date of sale was sent, but notice shall be sent to persons entitled to notice under subsections (b) (2) (B) and (3) of this Rule to whom notice of the earlier date of sale was not sent.

Source. — This Rule is derived in part from former Rule W74 and is in part new.

I. GENERAL CONSIDERATION.

Nature of proceedings. — It is possible for a mortgage foreclosure proceeding in Maryland in which no deficiency decree is sought to be purely in rem: it is also possible, if the mortgagor voluntarily appears, for the proceeding to include judgments, in the form of rulings on exceptions to the sale and to the auditor's report, respectively, that have in personam collateral estoppel effect. Fairfax Sav. v. Kris Jen Ltd. Partnership, 338 Md. 1, 655 A.2d 1265 (1995).

Sales governed by same rules as other sales in equity. — Foreclosure sales under power of sale when brought within control of a court of equity are governed by same rules as other sales in equity. Warfield v. Dorsey, 39 Md. 299 (1874); Gaither v. Tolson, 84 Md. 637, 36 A. 449 (1897).

Foreclosure sales, when the proceedings are brought under the cognizance and guidance of the court, are to be conducted and determined in all respects as ordinary sales by a trustee appointed by decree of the court. Ivrey v. Karr, 182 Md. 463, 34 A.2d 847 (1943).

Proceedings are same for sale under power as for sale under decree. — The object of former § 7 of Article 66 was to confer upon courts the same jurisdiction, and to direct that the same proceedings should be had in sales made under a power in a mortgage, as if such sales had been made under a decree of the court. Patapsco Guano Co. v. Elder, 53 Md. 463 (1880); Beetem v. Garrison, 129 Md. 664, 99 A. 897 (1917); United States v. Eastern Woodworks, Inc., 151 F. Supp. 95 (D. Md. 1957); Walsh v. Jefferson Fed. Sav. & Loan Ass'n, 216 Md. 131, 139 A.2d 847 (1958).

Courts apply the rules more strictly to sales made under power of sale than to sales made under a decree in equity. Chilton v. Brooks, 69 Md. 584, 16 A. 273 (1888).

The court has the power not to hold the trustee to strict compliance when it would be unjust and inequitable to do so. United States v. Eastern Woodworks, Inc., 151 F. Supp. 95 (D. Md. 1957).

No decree prior to the sale is necessary to effectuate a valid sale under a power of sale. United States v. Eastern Woodworks, Inc., 151 F. Supp. 95 (D. Md. 1957).

Only the terms of the mortgage and the statute need be met in a foreclosure under a power of sale. Blanch v. Collison, 174 Md. 427, 199 A. 466 (1938); United States v. Eastern Woodworks, Inc., 151 F. Supp. 95 (D. Md. 1957).

Court order directing sale held not to change nature of proceedings. — The fact that the court entered an order directing the "trustees," not appointed by the court under a decree but so designated by, and acting pursuant to, the terms of the deed of trust, containing a power of sale, to sell the chattels described in the deed of trust did not change the proceedings from a foreclosure under power of sale pursuant to Article 66, former § 5 (see now § 7-105 of the Real Property Article), to a foreclosure under former § 6 of that article. United States v. Eastern Woodworks, Inc., 151 F. Supp. 95 (D. Md. 1957).

"Mortgagor." — The word mortgagor, as customarily used, specifically refers to the maker or creator of a mortgage and not to one who is the grantee of or holds title under that person. Gaspin v. Browning, 265 Md. 552, 290 A.2d 507 (1972).

All rights of mortgagors cease to exist on date of sale. — See Butler v. Daum, 245 Md. 447, 226 A.2d 261 (1967).

Unless satisfactory proof is shown before final ratification that sale should be set aside. — See Butler v. Daum, 245 Md. 447, 226 A.2d 261 (1967).

Hence, the right of redemption is divested by a valid foreclosure sale. Butler v. Daum, 245 Md. 447, 226 A.2d 261 (1967).

Although the jurisdiction of equity does not become complete until the filing of the report of sale, nevertheless the sale in effect forecloses the mortgage and divests the mortgagors of all right of redemption. Butler v. Daum, 245 Md. 447, 226 A.2d 261 (1967).

Power to call off sale upon payment of past-due instalments, etc. — An assignee, even though acting under the power of sale in a mortgage, has the right, when the past-due instalments and costs are paid, to call off a sale, thereby staying the sale of the property, and leave the equity proceedings open as a further security to enforce future payments.

And, after a further default and he decides again to advertise the property for sale, he is not starting a new and independent proceeding, nor does he need an order of court to make the sale. Walsh v. Jefferson Fed. Sav. & Loan Ass'n, 216 Md. 131, 139 A.2d 847 (1958).

A foreclosure sale under a second mortgage must be subject to the first mortgage, unless the first mortgagee is a party to the proceedings or intervenes therein, or unless he releases his mortgage or assents to a sale free and clear of it. Baltimore Fed. Sav. & Loan Ass'n v. Eareckson, 221 Md. 527, 158 A.2d 121 (1960).

Assignee of mortgage. — When an attorney is acting as the assignee of the mortgage and not as its agent, he need not be specially named in the power of sale in order to have the authority to act. Whitworth v. Algonquin Assocs., 75 Md. App. 479, 541 A.2d 1328 (1988).

There is no requirement that an assignee of a mortgage be specifically named in the mortgaged instrument to have the power to conduct a sale and that the assignee is an attorney is of no consequence under the applicable statute or rules and it is likewise of no consequence under the relevant case law. Whitworth v. Algonquin Assocs., 75 Md. App. 479, 541 A.2d 1328 (1988).

Statute of frauds. — A foreclosure sale under a power of sale in a mortgage is not within the fourth section of the statute of frauds. Warfield v. Dorsey, 39 Md. 299 (1874).

Writ of fieri facias does not constitute license to sell property of debtors without regard to its value in relation to the bids offered. McCartney v. Frost, 282 Md. 631, 386 A.2d 784 (1978).

Setting aside sale. — A sheriff's sale will not be set aside for mere inadequateness of price, but if the sale is so grossly inadequate as to shock the conscience of the court, or if there be but slight circumstances of unfairness in addition to great inadequateness of price, a sale will be set aside. McCartney v. Frost, 282 Md. 631, 386 A.2d 784 (1978).

Terms of sale held reasonable. White v. Malcolm, 15 Md. 529 (1860).

As to change in terms of sale, see Hubbard v. Jarrell, 23 Md. 66 (1865).

Invalidity of sale not presumed. — The invalidity of a mortgage sale, like other judicial sales, is not presumed, and the burden of proving the contrary is on the one attacking the sale. Butler v. Daum, 245 Md. 447, 226 A.2d 261 (1967).

Inadequacy of price must imply constructive fraud. — To justify a court of equity in setting aside an adequately advertised sale of property upon the ground of inadequacy of price, facts must be shown from which the conclusion arises that the price is so insignificant as to shock the conscience of the court. The facts must be such as to compel the conclusion that because of the inadequacy of the price, constructive fraud is implied. Butler v. Daum, 245 Md. 447, 226 A.2d 261 (1967).

The burden of proving inadequacy of price is on the exceptants. Butler v. Daum, 245 Md. 447, 226 A.2d 261 (1967).

Spread between fair market value and sale price indicates unfair sale. — While one does not expect a price produced at a forced sale to be commensurate with fair market value, the spread between a fair market value of $18,000 ($24,000 appraisal less mortgage of $6,000) and a $2,000 sale price is indicative of an unfair sheriff's sale, such as shocks the conscience of the court. McCartney v. Frost, 282 Md. 631, 386 A.2d 784 (1978).

Commissions. — See Johnson v. Glenn, 80 Md. 369, 30 A. 993 (1895); Goldberg v. Price, 218 Md. 602, 147 A.2d 745 (1959).

Stated in Schaller v. Castle Dev. Corp., 111 Md. App. 40, 680 A.2d 528 (1996).

II. BOND.

The bond must be given by the party making the sale and not by mortgagee. White v. Malcolm, 15 Md. 529 (1860).

Time of filing. — Where a bond is filed on the day of sale, the law presumes that it was filed before the sale. Hubbard v. Jarrell, 23 Md. 66 (1865); Hebb v. Mason, 143 Md. 345, 122 A. 318 (1923).

Second bond required where first inadequate. — Trustee appointed to sell at foreclosure proceedings may be required to give second bond on account of inadequacy of first bond. Employers' Liab. Assurance Corp. v. State ex rel. Hudgins, 163 Md. 119, 161 A. 249 (1932).

Defect raised by exception. — If a bond is defective, the defect must be raised by exceptions to ratification of sale, and cannot be inquired into collaterally. Cockey v. Cole, 28 Md. 276 (1868); Hebb v. Mason, 143 Md. 345, 122 A. 318 (1923).

Bond filed in Circuit Court for Baltimore City conditioned to fulfill any order or decree of Baltimore County court is a nullity, and sale will be set aside. McCabe v. Ward, 18 Md. 505 (1862).

Who may bring suit. — Substituted trustee held to be among persons interested and entitled to institute suit on bond. Employers' Liab. Assurance Corp. v. State ex rel. Hudgins, 161 Md. 103, 155 A. 324 (1931).

III. NOTICE.

Rule sets forth only notice required. — The only notice of a mortgage foreclosure proceeding which is required is that set forth in former Rule W74. Butler v. Daum, 245 Md.

447, 226 A.2d 261 (1967).

Objective underlying notice requirement. — In recommending the adoption of section a 2 (b) of former Rule W74 to the Court of Appeals, the Rules Committee stated that it did not intend to create a burdensome requirement. Instead it indicated that its objective was to give notice to the original maker of the mortgage of both the sale and the fact that he can be called upon to pay any deficiency caused by the failure of the mortgaged property to produce sufficient funds necessary to extinguish the debt. Gaspin v. Browning, 265 Md. 552, 290 A.2d 507 (1972).

Strict compliance. — Former Rule W74, which replaced an earlier statute, makes more stringent and more precise the minimal requirements as to notice and must be strictly complied with. Fleisher Co. v. Grice, 245 Md. 248, 226 A.2d 153 (1967).

Hence, although the parties to a mortgage are free to contract in respect to the notice given, whatever else the terms agreed upon in the mortgage require the agent of the mortgagor to do in respect of the publication of the advertisement of sale, he must publish "at least once in each of three successive weeks" before the sale. The first of these three publications must be "not less than fifteen days" before the sale and the last of the same three publications must be "not more than one week" before the sale. Fleisher Co. v. Grice, 245 Md. 248, 226 A.2d 153 (1967).

Compliance with terms of decree. — Under former § 6 of Article 66 the terms of the decree were, by force of the statute, made a part of the statute and were to be as fully and strictly complied with as if they had been in terms embraced in the statute. United States v. Eastern Woodworks, Inc., 151 F. Supp. 95 (D. Md. 1957).

Rules controlling adequacy of advertisement. — In addition to the "time, place and terms" of sale, the cases state that the rules generally controlling the adequacy of an advertisement of a judicial sale are: (1) That the advertisement is sufficient if it describes the property so that it can be located by the exercise of ordinary intelligence and so that more detailed information concerning it can be obtained if desired; (2) the failure to mention or fully describe the nature and extent of the improvements will not vitiate a sale unless the exceptant meets the burden of overcoming the presumption of the validity of the sale by showing that the omission was prejudicial to the sale of the property at a fair and adequate sum and that a resale would be likely to produce a greater amount. Butler v. Daum, 245 Md. 447, 226 A.2d 261 (1967); Waring v. Guy, 248 Md. 544, 237 A.2d 763 (1968).

. **Notice in excess of requirements.** — Notice of sale given by the trustees was suffi-

cient and resulted in no injustice being done
the defendant where notice in excess of that
required by the statute and by the terms of the
deed of trust was given. United States v. Eastern Woodworks, Inc., 151 F. Supp. 95 (D. Md.
1957).

**Failure to describe improvements in
advertisement.** — In an advertisement of a
foreclosure sale a failure to describe fully the
nature and extent of improvements will not
vitiate the sale, unless it is shown that the
omission was prejudicial to the sale of the
property at a fair and adequate sum, and that
a resale would be likely to produce a greater
amount. Hardy v. Gibson, 213 Md. 493, 133
A.2d 401 (1957); Waring v. Guy, 248 Md. 544,
237 A.2d 763 (1968).

**Personal notice not required prior to
1969.** — No one (prior to 1969) was entitled to
personal notice that foreclosure of a mortgage
or deed of trust was pending. The only warning
required to be given those affected by the
proceedings, including the buying public, was
through the published advertisements of sale
mandated by section a 2 (b) of former Rule
W74. Gaspin v. Browning, 265 Md. 552, 290
A.2d 507 (1972).

Personal notice of a mortgage foreclosure
proceeding formerly was not necessary. Butler
v. Daum, 245 Md. 447, 226 A.2d 261 (1967);
Scott & Wimbrow, Inc. v. Calwell, 31 Md. App.
1, 354 A.2d 463, cert. denied, 278 Md. 733
(1976).

**But attempt to give personal notice to
mortgagor is now required.** — The only
requirement in section a 2 (c) of former Rule
W74 is that an attempt be made to give personal notice to the original maker of the mortgage. Gaspin v. Browning, 265 Md. 552, 290
A.2d 507 (1972).

**Although not to prior or subsequent
lienholder.** — Although the mortgagee, under
paragraph (c) in subsection 2 of section a of
former Rule W74, must endeavor to personally
notify the mortgagor of the impending sale, no
similar provision is contained in this Rule with
respect to prior or subsequent lienholders.
Scott & Wimbrow, Inc. v. Calwell, 31 Md. App.
1, 354 A.2d 463, cert. denied, 278 Md. 733
(1976).

Advertising of sale held sufficient to
meet the requirements of former subsection (c)
of Article 66, § 5. deTamble v. Adkins, 210 Md.
414, 124 A.2d 276 (1956).

Time for sale. — Foreclosure pursuant to a
power of sale is intended to be a summary, in
rem proceeding. In that type of proceeding, a
sale of the mortgaged property can be held in
approximately twenty-one days after docketing. G.E. Capital Mtg. Servs., Inc. v. Levenson,
338 Md. 227, 657 A.2d 1170 (1995).

Procedure in Baltimore. — Compliance
with the statutory provisions of former subsection (c) of Article 66, § 5, relative to notice, was
held to be a compliance with the court's order
that notice be given in the manner usually
prescribed for advertising chattel foreclosure
sales in Baltimore City. United States v. Eastern Woodworks, Inc., 151 F. Supp. 95 (D. Md.
1957).

Other cases under former statutes. —
For other cases relating to notice and adver-
tisement under former statutes, see White v.
Malcolm, 15 Md. 529 (1860); Eichelberger v.
Hardesty, 15 Md. 548 (1860); Warehime v.
Carroll County Bldg. Ass'n, 44 Md. 512 (1876);
Bank of Commerce v. Lanahan, 45 Md. 396
(1876); Roberts v. Loyola Perpetual Bldg.
Ass'n, 74 Md. 1, 21 A. 684 (1891); Chilton v.
Brooks, 71 Md. 445, 18 A. 868 (1889); Knapp v.
Anderson, 89 Md. 189, 42 A. 933 (1899); Lewis
v. Beale, 162 Md. 18, 158 A. 354 (1932); Preske
v. Carroll, 178 Md. 543, 16 A.2d 291 (1940).

IV. PLACE OF SALE.

Statute mandatory. — Former § 11 of
Article 66, from which section b of former Rule
W74 was derived, was mandatory, and if sale
was not made in the county where the property lay, it would be set aside. Webb v. Haeffer,
53 Md. 187 (1880).

And applied to technical mortgages. —
Former § 11 of Article 66 applied to technical
mortgages. When an instrument was held not
to be a technical mortgage, the application of
the section was denied. Harrison v. Annapolis
& E.R.R., 50 Md. 490 (1879).

**Where multiple mortgages are secured
by multiple parcels of property** constituting one integrated business operation, the
foreclosure sale of all of the property in one
jurisdiction is proper. Federal Land Bank of
Baltimore, Inc. v. Esham, 43 Md. App. 446, 406
A.2d 928 (1979).

**Express waiver in regard to one sale
applicable to other similar sales.** — Since
the two Worcester County properties were
simultaneously sold at the Wicomico County
sale, the express waiver of the objection to the
place of sale of one of the properties operated
to waive any similar objection to the sale of the
other property. Federal Land Bank of Baltimore, Inc. v. Esham, 43 Md. App. 446, 406 A.2d
928 (1979).

**Where location changed by annexation
act.** — Where a mortgage when executed covered property in Baltimore County, and subsequently annexation act changed geographical
location of the property to Baltimore City, the
sale thereafter should take place in the city.

Chilton v. Brooks, 71 Md. 445, 18 A. 868 (1889).

V. PROCEDURE FOLLOWING SALE; REPORT; RATIFICATION.

A. In General.

Report of sale is merely an offer. — The sale is not a complete contract, and when reported is merely an offer not accepted until ratified by court. Hanover Fire Ins. Co. v. Brown, 77 Md. 64, 25 A. 989, reh'g overruled, 77 Md. 64, 27 A. 314 (1893).

Sale must be ratified to pass title. — Sale under a foreclosure decree did not pass the title to the property sold until the sale was ratified and confirmed. Before ratification, the transaction was merely an offer to purchase which had not been accepted. Plaza Corp. v. Alban Tractor Co., 219 Md. 570, 151 A.2d 170 (1958).

Since Maryland law provides that a mortgage foreclosure sale is subject to the approval of the court, such a sale does not pass title to the property until ratified by the court. Fisher v. Federal Nat'l Mtg. Ass'n, 360 F. Supp. 207 (D. Md. 1973).

Report may be amended. — A case will not be reversed because report of sale does not state terms, nor compliance with them by purchasers — the report should be seasonably amended. White v. Malcolm, 15 Md. 529 (1860).

Report held correct. — Report held to be substantially correct. Hubbard v. Jarrell, 23 Md. 66 (1865).

Effect of filing report under former law. — Under the former statutes providing for foreclosure pursuant to a power of sale, the jurisdiction of the court became complete on the filing of the report of sale; until then the proceedings were ex parte. Warehime v. Carroll County Bldg. Ass'n, 44 Md. 512 (1876); Beetem v. Garrison, 129 Md. 664, 99 A. 897 (1917).

Final ratification of mortgage foreclosure sale is res adjudicata as to validity of sale, except in case of fraud or illegality, and may not be attacked in collateral proceedings. Bachrach v. Washington United Coop., 181 Md. 315, 29 A.2d 822 (1943).

Order ratifying sale under deed of trust established the validity of the deed of trust and the title of the purchaser at the sale thereunder free of lien asserted by contract purchasers who had given down payment to mortgagor. Gerber v. Karr, 231 Md. 180, 189 A.2d 353 (1963).

Motion to consolidate prior suit with foreclosure proceedings. — Appellees foreclosed a mortgage upon appellants' property, and appellants moved to consolidate with that proceeding a prior suit in which they had sought to have declared void the deed of trust upon which the foreclosure suit was based. The Court of Appeals affirmed the foreclosure sale, without prejudice to any proceedings remaining open in the prior suit to have the deed of trust declared void. Witt v. Zions, 194 Md. 186, 70 A.2d 594 (1949).

In absence of fraud or irregularity, court has no power to question sale sua sponte. — Where a mortgage foreclosure sale is ratified by the court without objection and the court authorizes the conveyance to be made to substituted purchasers, it is error for the court sua sponte to question the validity of such sale in the absence of fraud or illegality. Walker v. Ward, 65 Md. App. 443, 501 A.2d 83 (1985).

B. Exceptions and Objections.

Objections to the sale may be filed by any person interested in the property. Warfield v. Ross, 38 Md. 85 (1873); Albert v. Hamilton, 76 Md. 304, 25 A. 341 (1892).

The sale, when made, may be accepted to by the party authorized to redeem the mortgage and who made the tender. Kent Bldg. & Loan Co. v. Middleton, 112 Md. 10, 75 A. 967 (1910).

Exceptions cannot be filed by one who has no legal interest in, or record title to, property, but alleges a secret trust, person against whom the trust is sought to be enforced not being a party to proceedings. Bentley v. Beacham, 91 Md. 677, 47 A. 1024 (1900).

Holder of vendor's interest, under conditional sales contract, in hot water heating system, could not object to mortgage foreclosure sale of house, for if system was personalty, he had no interest in mortgaged property, and only persons interested in property can object to sale. Heating & Plumbing Fin. Corp. v. Glyndon Permanent Bldg. Ass'n, 167 Md. 222, 173 A. 198 (1934).

A person whose interest is not affected by the sale cannot intervene. Warfield v. Ross, 38 Md. 85 (1873).

Ordinarily, the holder of a prior mortgage has no standing in court to file exceptions to the ratification of a sale made under a junior mortgage; because, generally, such a sale is made subject to the prior mortgage and does not affect the rights of the prior mortgagee. Plaza Corp. v. Alban Tractor Co., 219 Md. 570, 151 A.2d 170 (1958).

General creditor cannot object to sale of property under mortgage. Hannan v. Lyddane, 164 Md. 357, 165 A. 308 (1933).

Ordinarily, a general creditor has no standing to interpose objections to the ratification of a sale under a mortgage. Scott & Wimbrow, Inc. v. Calwell, 31 Md. App. 1, 354 A.2d 463, cert. denied, 278 Md. 733 (1976).

An exceptant who consented and stipu-

lated that the court ratify and confirm a sale and that the claims of all the parties to the chattels be transferred to the proceeds of the sale thereof, was in no position to challenge the power of the court below to make the sale. Plaza Corp. v. Alban Tractor Co., 219 Md. 570, 151 A.2d 170 (1958).

When exceptions may be filed. — Exceptions may be filed at any time before the ratification of the sale. Aukam v. Zantzinger, 94 Md. 421, 51 A. 93 (1902).

Objections are not limited to matters of irregularity in conduct of the sale, but extend to questions concerning validity of mortgage. Albert v. Hamilton, 76 Md. 304, 25 A. 341 (1892).

The mortgagors have a right in objecting to the ratification of the sale, to show that their title ought not to pass. Albert v. Hamilton, 76 Md. 304, 25 A. 341 (1892).

Where a party interested tenders mortgagee full amount due for purpose of redeeming mortgage as he has a right to do, the mortgagee has no right thereafter to foreclose mortgage, and party making tender may except to mortgage sale. Kent Bldg. & Loan Co. v. Middleton, 112 Md. 10, 75 A. 967 (1910).

Failure to file mortgage notes. — Where no exception is taken on ground that mortgage notes were not filed, and where there is no dispute about their ownership, or amount due on them, sale will not be set aside because notes were not filed. Heider v. Bladen, 83 Md. 242, 34 A. 836 (1896).

Objection that there was no decree authorizing sale is unavailing. Walker v. Cockey, 38 Md. 75 (1873).

Equity court has full power to hear and determine all objections which may be filed against the sale. Fisher v. Federal Nat'l Mtg. Ass'n, 360 F. Supp. 207 (D. Md. 1973).

Supersedeas bond on appeal from overruling of exceptions. — See Scott & Wimbrow, Inc. v. Calwell, 31 Md. App. 1, 354 A.2d 463, cert. denied, 278 Md. 733 (1976).

VI. RESALE.

It is not absolutely necessary that court should order a resale, and a sale made without such order will not be set aside. Reeside v. Peter, 35 Md. 220 (1872).

Selling at private sale. — Where a trustee or attorney offers property at public sale in accordance with mortgage and withdraws it because he does not receive a satisfactory bid,

he is authorized to sell property at private sale subject to ratification of court, and court has jurisdiction to set aside or ratify sale. Beetem v. Garrison, 129 Md. 664, 99 A. 897 (1917).

Resale at risk of defaulting purchaser. — In case of resale ordered by court at defaulting purchaser's risk under former § 163 of Article 16, previous sale being under the foreclosure statutes and reported to court for ratification, etc., court becomes vendor and assignee of mortgage is agent or trustee of court. Bilbrey v. Strahorn, 153 Md. 491, 138 A. 343 (1927).

VII. PAYMENT OF DEBT; INTEREST.

A mortgagee is not actually paid his claim upon the date of the sale of the mortgaged premises. The sale must be reported to, and ratified by, the court; and the auditor must prepare his account, which must, likewise, be ratified before the proceeds of sale may be safely distributed. Ex parte Aurora Fed. Sav. & Loan Ass'n, 223 Md. 135, 162 A.2d 739 (1960).

Agreement of parties controls interest on mortgage debt. — The time during which interest on a mortgage runs is sometimes regulated by statute; but in the absence of statute the agreement of the parties controls. Ex parte Aurora Fed. Sav. & Loan Ass'n, 223 Md. 135, 162 A.2d 739 (1960).

And statute did not prohibit agreement to continue such interest after date of foreclosure sale. — The requirement in former § 6 of Article 66 that the proceeds of a sale should be distributed in the manner usual in cases of sales under decree did not prohibit the parties to a mortgage from agreeing that lawful interest on the mortgagor's indebtedness should continue after the date of foreclosure sale; and such requirement did not vary, by implication, such an agreement, so as to cut off interest on a mortgage after the date of the sale. Ex parte Aurora Fed. Sav. & Loan Ass'n, 223 Md. 135, 162 A.2d 739 (1960).

Thus, where mortgage stated that interest was payable from date of mortgage until principal and interest "shall be paid," the court held that, in the absence of statute, interest was payable beyond foreclosure sale until the auditor's report could be ratified. Ex parte Aurora Fed. Sav. & Loan Ass'n, 223 Md. 135, 162 A.2d 739 (1960).

Rule 14-207. Sale.

(a) *Place of sale.* Unless the court, for good cause, orders otherwise (1) a sale shall be made in the county in which the property subject to the lien is located; and (2) when property is located in more than one county, the sale shall be made in the county in which the action is pending.

Cross references. — Rule 14-101.

(b) *Person authorized to sell.* (1) Under power of sale. A sale of property pursuant to a power of sale shall be made by a natural person who is either the secured party, if the secured party is granted that authority by the lien instrument, or any other natural person designated by name in the lien instrument to exercise the power of sale, except that a sale of property subject to a deed of trust shall be made by the trustee appointed in the deed or a successor trustee. The trustee shall be a natural person.

(2) Under assent to a decree. A sale of property pursuant to an assent to a decree shall be made by a trustee or by a substituted trustee appointed by the court to make the sale. The trustee shall be a natural person.

(c) *Terms of payment.* (1) Under power of sale. A sale of property under a power of sale shall be made upon the terms as to payment provided in the lien instrument. If no terms as to payment are provided in the lien instrument or the sale is made pursuant to a statutory lien, the sale shall be made upon terms that are reasonable under the circumstances.

(2) Under assent to a decree. A sale of property under an order of court entered pursuant to an assent to a decree shall be made upon the terms as to payment provided in the order.

(d) *Procedure following sale.* The procedure following a sale made pursuant to this Rule shall be as provided in Rules 14-305 and 14-306, except that an audit is mandatory.

(e) *Resale — Who may conduct.* If a sale is set aside by the court, the court may order that the property be resold by the person who made the previous sale, or by a special trustee appointed by the court.

(f) *Conveyance to purchaser.* (1) When made. After a sale has been finally ratified by the court and the purchase money paid, the person making the sale shall convey the property to the purchaser or the purchaser's assignee. If conveyance is to the purchaser's assignee, the purchaser shall join in the deed.

(2) Under power of sale — Where vendor and purchaser are the same. If the vendor and purchaser at a sale made pursuant to a power of sale are the same person, in the order of ratification the court shall appoint a trustee to convey the property to the purchaser on the payment of the purchase money. The trustee need not furnish bond unless the court so provides in its order.

(3) To substituted purchaser. At any time after sale and before conveyance, the court, upon ex parte application and consent of the purchaser, substituted purchaser, and person making the sale, may authorize the conveyance to be made to a substituted purchaser.

Source. — This Rule is derived from former Rule W74 b through g.

I. GENERAL CONSIDERATION.

Nature of proceedings. — It is possible for a mortgage foreclosure proceeding in Maryland in which no deficiency decree is sought to be purely in rem: it is also possible, if the mortgagor voluntarily appears, for the proceeding to include judgments, in the form of rulings on exceptions to the sale and to the auditor's report, respectively, that have in personam collateral estoppel effect. Fairfax Sav. v. Kris Jen Ltd. Partnership, 338 Md. 1, 655 A.2d 1265 (1995).

Sales governed by same rules as other sales in equity. — Foreclosure sales under power of sale when brought within control of a court of equity are governed by same rules as other sales in equity. Warfield v. Dorsey, 39 Md. 299 (1874); Gaither v. Tolson, 84 Md. 637, 36 A. 449 (1897).

Foreclosure sales, when the proceedings are brought under the cognizance and guidance of the court, are to be conducted and determined in all respects as ordinary sales by a trustee appointed by decree of the court. Ivrey v. Karr, 182 Md. 463, 34 A.2d 847 (1943).

Proceedings are same for sale under power as for sale under decree. — The object of former § 7 of Article 66 was to confer upon courts the same jurisdiction, and to direct that the same proceedings should be had in sales made under a power in a mortgage, as if such sales had been made under a decree of the court. Patapsco Guano Co. v. Elder, 53 Md. 463 (1880); Beetem v. Garrison, 129 Md. 664, 99 A. 897 (1917); United States v. Eastern Woodworks, Inc., 151 F. Supp. 95 (D. Md. 1957); Walsh v. Jefferson Fed. Sav. & Loan Ass'n, 216 Md. 131, 139 A.2d 847 (1958).

Courts apply the rules more strictly to sales made under power of sale than to sales made under a decree in equity. Chilton v. Brooks, 69 Md. 584, 16 A. 273 (1888).

The court has the power not to hold the trustee to strict compliance when it would be unjust and inequitable to do so. United States v. Eastern Woodworks, Inc., 151 F. Supp. 95 (D. Md. 1957).

No decree prior to the sale is necessary to effectuate a valid sale under a power of sale. United States v. Eastern Woodworks, Inc., 151 F. Supp. 95 (D. Md. 1957).

Only the terms of the mortgage and the statute need be met in a foreclosure under a power of sale. Blanch v. Collison, 174 Md. 427, 199 A. 466 (1938); United States v. Eastern Woodworks, Inc., 151 F. Supp. 95 (D. Md. 1957).

Court order directing sale held not to change nature of proceedings. — The fact that the court entered an order directing the "trustees," not appointed by the court under a decree but so designated by, and acting pursuant to, the terms of the deed of trust, containing a power of sale, to sell the chattels described in the deed of trust did not change the proceedings from a foreclosure under power of sale pursuant to Article 66, former § 5 (see now § 7-105 of the Real Property Article), to a foreclosure under former § 6 of that article. United States v. Eastern Woodworks, Inc., 151 F. Supp. 95 (D. Md. 1957).

"Mortgagor." — The word mortgagor, as customarily used, specifically refers to the maker or creator of a mortgage and not to one who is the grantee of or holds title under that person. Gaspin v. Browning, 265 Md. 552, 290 A.2d 507 (1972).

All rights of mortgagors cease to exist on date of sale. — See Butler v. Daum, 245 Md. 447, 226 A.2d 261 (1967).

Unless satisfactory proof is shown before final ratification that sale should be set aside. — See Butler v. Daum, 245 Md. 447, 226 A.2d 261 (1967).

Hence, the right of redemption is divested by a valid foreclosure sale. Butler v. Daum, 245 Md. 447, 226 A.2d 261 (1967).

Although the jurisdiction of equity does not become complete until the filing of the report of sale, nevertheless the sale in effect forecloses the mortgage and divests the mortgagors of all right of redemption. Butler v. Daum, 245 Md. 447, 226 A.2d 261 (1967).

Power to call off sale upon payment of past-due instalments, etc. — An assignee, even though acting under the power of sale in a mortgage, has the right, when the past-due instalments and costs are paid, to call off a sale, thereby staying the sale of the property, and leave the equity proceedings open as a further security to enforce future payments. And, after a further default and he decides again to advertise the property for sale, he is not starting a new and independent proceeding, nor does he need an order of court to make the sale. Walsh v. Jefferson Fed. Sav. & Loan Ass'n, 216 Md. 131, 139 A.2d 847 (1958).

A foreclosure sale under a second mortgage must be subject to the first mortgage, unless the first mortgagee is a party to the proceedings or intervenes therein, or unless he releases his mortgage or assents to a sale free and clear of it. Baltimore Fed. Sav. & Loan Ass'n v. Eareckson, 221 Md. 527, 158 A.2d 121 (1960).

Assignee of mortgage. — When an attorney is acting as the assignee of the mortgage and not as its agent, he need not be specially named in the power of sale in order to have the authority to act. Whitworth v. Algonquin Assocs., 75 Md. App. 479, 541 A.2d 1328 (1988).

There is no requirement that an assignee of a mortgage be specifically named in the mortgaged instrument to have the power to conduct a sale and that the assignee is an attorney is of no consequence under the applicable statute or rules and it is likewise of no consequence under the relevant case law. Whitworth v. Algonquin Assocs., 75 Md. App. 479, 541 A.2d 1328 (1988).

Statute of frauds. — A foreclosure sale under a power of sale in a mortgage is not within the fourth section of the statute of frauds. Warfield v. Dorsey, 39 Md. 299 (1874).

Writ of fieri facias does not constitute license to sell property of debtors without regard to its value in relation to the bids offered. McCartney v. Frost, 282 Md. 631, 386 A.2d 784 (1978).

Setting aside sale. — A sheriff's sale will not be set aside for mere inadequateness of price, but if the sale is so grossly inadequate as to shock the conscience of the court, or if there be but slight circumstances of unfairness in addition to great inadequateness of price, a sale will be set aside. McCartney v. Frost, 282 Md. 631, 386 A.2d 784 (1978).

Terms of sale held reasonable. White v. Malcolm, 15 Md. 529 (1860).

As to change in terms of sale, see Hubbard v. Jarrell, 23 Md. 66 (1865).

Invalidity of sale not presumed. — The invalidity of a mortgage sale, like other judicial sales, is not presumed, and the burden of proving the contrary is on the one attacking the sale. Butler v. Daum, 245 Md. 447, 226 A.2d 261 (1967).

Inadequacy of price must imply constructive fraud. — To justify a court of equity in setting aside an adequately advertised sale of property upon the ground of inadequacy of price, facts must be shown from which the conclusion arises that the price is so insignificant as to shock the conscience of the court. The facts must be such as to compel the conclusion that because of the inadequacy of

the price, constructive fraud is implied. Butler v. Daum, 245 Md. 447, 226 A.2d 261 (1967).

The burden of proving inadequacy of price is on the exceptants. Butler v. Daum, 245 Md. 447, 226 A.2d 261 (1967).

Spread between fair market value and sale price indicates unfair sale. — While one does not expect a price produced at a forced sale to be commensurate with fair market value, the spread between a fair market value of $18,000 ($24,000 appraisal less mortgage of $6,000) and a $2,000 sale price is indicative of an unfair sheriff's sale, such as shocks the conscience of the court. McCartney v. Frost, 282 Md. 631, 386 A.2d 784 (1978).

Commissions. — See Johnson v. Glenn, 80 Md. 369, 30 A. 993 (1895); Goldberg v. Price, 218 Md. 602, 147 A.2d 745 (1959).

II. BOND.

The bond must be given by the party making the sale and not by mortgagee. White v. Malcolm, 15 Md. 529 (1860).

Time of filing. — Where a bond is filed on the day of sale, the law presumes that it was filed before the sale. Hubbard v. Jarrell, 23 Md. 66 (1865); Hebb v. Mason, 143 Md. 345, 122 A. 318 (1923).

Second bond required where first inadequate. — Trustee appointed to sell at foreclosure proceedings may be required to give second bond on account of inadequacy of first bond. Employers' Liab. Assurance Corp. v. State ex rel. Hudgins, 163 Md. 119, 161 A. 249 (1932).

Defect raised by exception. — If a bond is defective, the defect must be raised by exceptions to ratification of sale, and cannot be inquired into collaterally. Cockey v. Cole, 28 Md. 276 (1868); Hebb v. Mason, 143 Md. 345, 122 A. 318 (1923).

Bond filed in Circuit Court for Baltimore City conditioned to fulfill any order or decree of Baltimore County court is a nullity, and sale will be set aside. McCabe v. Ward, 18 Md. 505 (1862).

Who may bring suit. — Substituted trustee held to be among persons interested and entitled to institute suit on bond. Employers' Liab. Assurance Corp. v. State ex rel. Hudgins, 161 Md. 103, 155 A. 324 (1931).

III. NOTICE.

Rule sets forth only notice required. — The only notice of a mortgage foreclosure proceeding which is required is that set forth in former Rule W74. Butler v. Daum, 245 Md. 447, 226 A.2d 261 (1967).

Objective underlying notice requirement. — In recommending the adoption of section a 2 (b) of former Rule W74, to the Court of Appeals, the Rules Committee stated that it did not intend to create a burdensome requirement. Instead it indicated that its objective was to give notice to the original maker of the mortgage of both the sale and the fact that he can be called upon to pay any deficiency caused by the failure of the mortgaged property to produce sufficient funds necessary to extinguish the debt. Gaspin v. Browning, 265 Md. 552, 290 A.2d 507 (1972).

Strict compliance. — Former Rule W74, which replaced an earlier statute, makes more stringent and more precise the minimal requirements as to notice and must be strictly complied with. Fleisher Co. v. Grice, 245 Md. 248, 226 A.2d 153 (1967).

Hence, although the parties to a mortgage are free to contract in respect to the notice given, whatever else the terms agreed upon in the mortgage require the agent of the mortgagor to do in respect of the publication of the advertisement of sale, he must publish "at least once in each of three successive weeks" before the sale. The first of these three publications must be "not less than fifteen days" before the sale and the last of the same three publications must be "not more than one week" before the sale. Fleisher Co. v. Grice, 245 Md. 248, 226 A.2d 153 (1967).

Compliance with terms of decree. — Under former § 6 of Article 66 the terms of the decree were, by force of the statute, made a part of the statute and were to be as fully and strictly complied with as if they had been in terms embraced in the statute. United States v. Eastern Woodworks, Inc., 151 F. Supp. 95 (D. Md. 1957).

Rules controlling adequacy of advertisement. — In addition to the "time, place and terms" of sale, the cases state that the rules generally controlling the adequacy of an advertisement of a judicial sale are: (1) That the advertisement is sufficient if it describes the property so that it can be located by the exercise of ordinary intelligence and so that more detailed information concerning it can be obtained if desired; (2) the failure to mention or fully describe the nature and extent of the improvements will not vitiate a sale unless the exceptant meets the burden of overcoming the presumption of the validity of the sale by showing that the omission was prejudicial to the sale of the property at a fair and adequate sum and that a resale would be likely to produce a greater amount. Butler v. Daum, 245 Md. 447, 226 A.2d 261 (1967); Waring v. Guy, 248 Md. 544, 237 A.2d 763 (1968).

Notice in excess of requirements. — Notice of sale given by the trustees was sufficient and resulted in no injustice being done the defendant where notice in excess of that required by the statute and by the terms of the deed of trust was given. United States v. Eastern Woodworks, Inc., 151 F. Supp. 95 (D. Md. 1957).

Failure to describe improvements in advertisement. — In an advertisement of a foreclosure sale a failure to describe fully the nature and extent of improvements will not vitiate the sale, unless it is shown that the omission was prejudicial to the sale of the property at a fair and adequate sum, and that a resale would be likely to produce a greater amount. Hardy v. Gibson, 213 Md. 493, 133 A.2d 401 (1957); Waring v. Guy, 248 Md. 544, 237 A.2d 763 (1968).

Personal notice not required prior to 1969. — No one (prior to 1969) was entitled to personal notice that foreclosure of a mortgage or deed of trust was pending. The only warning required to be given those affected by the proceedings, including the buying public, was through the published advertisements of sale mandated by section a 2 (b) of former Rule W74. Gaspin v. Browning, 265 Md. 552, 290 A.2d 507 (1972).

Personal notice of a mortgage foreclosure proceeding formerly was not necessary. Butler v. Daum, 245 Md. 447, 226 A.2d 261 (1967); Scott & Wimbrow, Inc. v. Calwell, 31 Md. App. 1, 354 A.2d 463, cert. denied, 278 Md. 733 (1976).

But attempt to give personal notice to mortgagor is now required. — The only requirement in section a 2 (c) of former Rule W74 is that an attempt be made to give personal notice to the original maker of the mortgage. Gaspin v. Browning, 265 Md. 552, 290 A.2d 507 (1972).

Although not to prior or subsequent lienholder. — Although the mortgagee, under paragraph (c) in subsection 2 of section a of Former Rule W74, must endeavor to personally notify the mortgagor of the impending sale, no similar provision is contained in this Rule with respect to prior or subsequent lienholders. Scott & Wimbrow, Inc. v. Calwell, 31 Md. App. 1, 354 A.2d 463, cert. denied, 278 Md. 733 (1976).

Advertising of sale held sufficient to meet the requirements of former subsection (c) of Article 66, § 5. deTamble v. Adkins, 210 Md. 414, 124 A.2d 276 (1956).

Time for sale. — Foreclosure pursuant to a power of sale is intended to be a summary, in rem proceeding. In that type of proceeding, a sale of the mortgaged property can be held in approximately twenty-one days after docketing. G.E. Capital Mtg. Servs., Inc. v. Levenson, 338 Md. 227, 657 A.2d 1170 (1995).

Procedure in Baltimore. — Compliance with the statutory provisions of former subsection (c) of Article 66, § 5, relative to notice, was held to be a compliance with the court's order that notice be given in the manner usually prescribed for advertising chattel foreclosure sales in Baltimore City. United States v. Eastern Woodworks, Inc., 151 F. Supp. 95 (D. Md. 1957).

Other cases under former statutes. — For other cases relating to notice and advertisement under former statutes, see White v. Malcolm, 15 Md. 529 (1860); Eichelberger v. Hardesty, 15 Md. 548 (1860); Warehime v. Carroll County Bldg. Ass'n, 44 Md. 512 (1876); Bank of Commerce v. Lanahan, 45 Md. 396 (1876); Chilton v. Brooks, 71 Md. 445, 18 A. 868 (1889); Roberts v. Loyola Perpetual Bldg. Ass'n, 74 Md. 1, 21 A. 684 (1891); Knapp v. Anderson, 89 Md. 189, 42 A. 933 (1899); Lewis v. Beale, 162 Md. 18, 158 A. 354 (1932); Preske v. Carroll, 178 Md. 543, 16 A.2d 291 (1940).

IV. PLACE OF SALE.

Statute mandatory. — Former § 11 of Article 66, from which section b of former Rule W74 was derived, was mandatory, and if sale was not made in the county where the property lay, it would be set aside. Webb v. Haeffer, 53 Md. 187 (1880).

And applied to technical mortgages. — Former § 11 of Article 66 applied to technical mortgages. When an instrument was held not to be a technical mortgage, the application of the section was denied. Harrison v. Annapolis & E.R.R., 50 Md. 490 (1879).

Where multiple mortgages are secured by multiple parcels of property constituting one integrated business operation, the foreclosure sale of all of the property in one jurisdiction is proper. Federal Land Bank of Baltimore, Inc. v. Esham, 43 Md. App. 446, 406 A.2d 928 (1979).

Express waiver in regard to one sale applicable to other similar sales. — Since the two Worcester County properties were simultaneously sold at the Wicomico County sale, the express waiver of the objection to the place of sale of one of the properties operated to waive any similar objection to the sale of the other property. Federal Land Bank of Baltimore, Inc. v. Esham, 43 Md. App. 446, 406 A.2d 928 (1979).

Where location changed by annexation act. — Where a mortgage when executed covered property in Baltimore County, and subsequently annexation act changed geographical location of the property to Baltimore City, the sale thereafter should take place in the city. Chilton v. Brooks, 71 Md. 445, 18 A. 868 (1889).

V. PROCEDURE FOLLOWING SALE; REPORT; RATIFICATION.

A. In General.

Report of sale is merely an offer. — The sale is not a complete contract, and when reported is merely an offer not accepted until ratified by court. Hanover Fire Ins. Co. v. Brown, 77 Md. 64, 25 A. 989, reh'g overruled, 77 Md. 64, 27 A. 314 (1893).

Sale must be ratified to pass title. — Sale under a foreclosure decree did not pass the title to the property sold until the sale was ratified and confirmed. Before ratification, the transaction was merely an offer to purchase which had not been accepted. Plaza Corp. v. Alban Tractor Co., 219 Md. 570, 151 A.2d 170 (1958).

Since Maryland law provides that a mortgage foreclosure sale is subject to the approval of the court, such a sale does not pass title to the property until ratified by the court. Fisher v. Federal Nat'l Mtg. Ass'n, 360 F. Supp. 207 (D. Md. 1973).

Report may be amended. — A case will not be reversed because report of sale does not state terms, nor compliance with them by purchasers — the report should be seasonably amended. White v. Malcolm, 15 Md. 529 (1860).

Report held correct. — Report held to be substantially correct. Hubbard v. Jarrell, 23 Md. 66 (1865).

Effect of filing report under former law. — Under the former statutes providing for foreclosure pursuant to a power of sale, the jurisdiction of the court became complete on the filing of the report of sale; until then the proceedings were ex parte. Warehime v. Carroll County Bldg. Ass'n, 44 Md. 512 (1876); Beetem v. Garrison, 129 Md. 664, 99 A. 897 (1917).

Final ratification of mortgage foreclosure sale is res adjudicata as to validity of sale, except in case of fraud or illegality, and may not be attacked in collateral proceedings. Bachrach v. Washington United Coop., 181 Md. 315, 29 A.2d 822 (1943).

Order ratifying sale under deed of trust established the validity of the deed of trust and the title of the purchaser at the sale thereunder free of lien asserted by contract purchasers who had given down payment to mortgagor. Gerber v. Karr, 231 Md. 180, 189 A.2d 353 (1963).

Motion to consolidate prior suit with foreclosure proceedings. — Appellees foreclosed a mortgage upon appellants' property, and appellants moved to consolidate with that proceeding a prior suit in which they had sought to have declared void the deed of trust upon which the foreclosure suit was based. The Court of Appeals affirmed the foreclosure sale, without prejudice to any proceedings remaining open in the prior suit to have the deed of trust declared void. Witt v. Zions, 194 Md. 186, 70 A.2d 594 (1949).

In absence of fraud or irregularity, court has no power to question sale sua

sponte. — Where a mortgage foreclosure sale is ratified by the court without objection and the court authorizes the conveyance to be made to substituted purchasers, it is error for the court sua sponte to question the validity of such sale in the absence of fraud or illegality. Walker v. Ward, 65 Md. App. 443, 501 A.2d 83 (1985).

B. Exceptions and Objections.

Objections to the sale may be filed by any person interested in the property. Warfield v. Ross, 38 Md. 85 (1873); Albert v. Hamilton, 76 Md. 304, 25 A. 341 (1892).

The sale, when made, may be accepted to by the party authorized to redeem the mortgage and who made the tender. Kent Bldg. & Loan Co. v. Middleton, 112 Md. 10, 75 A. 967 (1910).

Exceptions cannot be filed by one who has no legal interest in, or record title to, property, but alleges a secret trust, person against whom the trust is sought to be enforced not being a party to proceedings. Bentley v. Beacham, 91 Md. 677, 47 A. 1024 (1900).

Holder of vendor's interest, under conditional sales contract, in hot water heating system, could not object to mortgage foreclosure sale of house, for if system was personalty, he had no interest in mortgaged property, and only persons interested in property can object to sale. Heating & Plumbing Fin. Corp. v. Glyndon Permanent Bldg. Ass'n, 167 Md. 222, 173 A. 198 (1934).

A person whose interest is not affected by the sale cannot intervene. Warfield v. Ross, 38 Md. 85 (1873).

Ordinarily, the holder of a prior mortgage has no standing in court to file exceptions to the ratification of a sale made under a junior mortgage; because, generally, such a sale is made subject to the prior mortgage and does not affect the rights of the prior mortgagee. Plaza Corp. v. Alban Tractor Co., 219 Md. 570, 151 A.2d 170 (1958).

General creditor cannot object to sale of property under mortgage. Hannan v. Lyddane, 164 Md. 357, 165 A. 308 (1933).

Ordinarily, a general creditor has no standing to interpose objections to the ratification of a sale under a mortgage. Scott & Wimbrow, Inc. v. Calwell, 31 Md. App. 1, 354 A.2d 463, cert. denied, 278 Md. 733 (1976).

An exceptant who consented and stipulated that the court ratify and confirm a sale and that the claims of all the parties to the chattels be transferred to the proceeds of the sale thereof, was in no position to challenge the power of the court below to make the sale. Plaza Corp. v. Alban Tractor Co., 219 Md. 570, 151 A.2d 170 (1958).

When exceptions may be filed. — Exceptions may be filed at any time before the ratification of the sale. Aukam v. Zantzinger, 94 Md. 421, 51 A. 93 (1902).

Objections are not limited to matters of irregularity in conduct of the sale, but extend to questions concerning validity of mortgage. Albert v. Hamilton, 76 Md. 304, 25 A. 341 (1892).

The mortgagors have a right in objecting to the ratification of the sale, to show that their title ought not to pass. Albert v. Hamilton, 76 Md. 304, 25 A. 341 (1892).

Where a party interested tenders mortgagee full amount due for purpose of redeeming mortgage as he has a right to do, the mortgagee has no right thereafter to foreclose mortgage, and party making tender may except to mortgage sale. Kent Bldg. & Loan Co. v. Middleton, 112 Md. 10, 75 A. 967 (1910).

Failure to file mortgage notes. — Where no exception is taken on ground that mortgage notes were not filed, and where there is no dispute about their ownership, or amount due on them, sale will not be set aside because notes were not filed. Heider v. Bladen, 83 Md. 242, 34 A. 836 (1896).

Objection that there was no decree authorizing sale is unavailing. Walker v. Cockey, 38 Md. 75 (1873).

Equity court has full power to hear and determine all objections which may be filed against the sale. Fisher v. Federal Nat'l Mtg. Ass'n, 360 F. Supp. 207 (D. Md. 1973).

Supersedeas bond on appeal from overruling of exceptions. — See Scott & Wimbrow, Inc. v. Calwell, 31 Md. App. 1, 354 A.2d 463, cert. denied, 278 Md. 733 (1976).

VI. RESALE.

It is not absolutely necessary that court should order a resale, and a sale made without such order will not be set aside. Reeside v. Peter, 35 Md. 220 (1872).

Selling at private sale. — Where a trustee or attorney offers property at public sale in accordance with mortgage and withdraws it because he does not receive a satisfactory bid, he is authorized to sell property at private sale subject to ratification of court, and court has jurisdiction to set aside or ratify sale. Beetem v. Garrison, 129 Md. 664, 99 A. 897 (1917).

Resale at risk of defaulting purchaser. — In case of resale ordered by court at defaulting purchaser's risk under former § 163 of Article 16, previous sale being under the foreclosure statutes and reported to court for ratification, etc., court becomes vendor and assignee of mortgage is agent or trustee of court. Bilbrey v. Strahorn, 153 Md. 491, 138 A. 343 (1927).

VII. PAYMENT OF DEBT; INTEREST.

A mortgagee is not actually paid his claim upon the date of the sale of the mortgaged premises. The sale must be reported to, and ratified by, the court; and the auditor must prepare his account, which must, likewise, be ratified before the proceeds of sale may be safely distributed. Ex parte Aurora Fed. Sav. & Loan Ass'n, 223 Md. 135, 162 A.2d 739 (1960).

Agreement of parties controls interest on mortgage debt. — The time during which interest on a mortgage runs is sometimes regulated by statute; but in the absence of statute the agreement of the parties controls. Ex parte Aurora Fed. Sav. & Loan Ass'n, 223 Md. 135, 162 A.2d 739 (1960).

And statute did not prohibit agreement to continue such interest after date of foreclosure sale. — The requirement in former § 6 of Article 66 that the proceeds of a sale should be distributed in the manner usual in cases of sales under decree did not prohibit the parties to a mortgage from agreeing that lawful interest on the mortgagor's indebtedness should continue after the date of foreclosure sale; and such requirement did not vary, by implication, such an agreement, so as to cut off interest on a mortgage after the date of the sale. Ex parte Aurora Fed. Sav. & Loan Ass'n, 223 Md. 135, 162 A.2d 739 (1960).

Thus, where mortgage stated that interest was payable from date of mortgage until principal and interest "shall be paid," the court held that, in the absence of statute, interest was payable beyond foreclosure sale until the auditor's report could be ratified. Ex parte Aurora Fed. Sav. & Loan Ass'n, 223 Md. 135, 162 A.2d 739 (1960).

Rule 14-208. Proceeds of sale.

(a) *Distribution of surplus.* At any time after a sale of property pursuant to Rule 14-207 and before the final ratification of the auditor's account, any person claiming an interest in the property or in the proceeds of the sale of the property may file with the court an application for the payment of that person's claim from the surplus proceeds of the sale. The court shall order distribution of the surplus equitably among the claimants.

(b) *Insufficiency of proceeds — Deficiency judgment.* At any time within three years after the final ratification of the auditor's report, a secured party or any party in interest entitled under the covenants of the lien instrument to maintain an action for a deficiency judgment may file a motion for a deficiency judgment if the net proceeds (after deducting the costs and expenses allowed by the court) of sale of the entire property subject to the lien are insufficient to satisfy the debt and accrued interest. After notice of the motion has been given in the manner provided by Rule 2-121, the court may enter a judgment in personam for the amount of the deficiency against the party to the action who is liable for payment.

Source. — This Rule is derived from former Rule W75.

Maryland Law Review. — For article discussing mortgagee's rights in the event of deficiency, see 1 Md. L. Rev. 128 (1937).

Distribution of surplus generally. — Former § 10 of Article 66, from which section a of former Rule W75 is derived, was analogous to right existing on part of subsequent holders of liens in regard to sales under usual modes of proceeding in equity. Leonard v. Groome, 47 Md. 499 (1878).

The purpose of former Rule W75 was to require a sale of all ("all" in the sense used in this Rule being synonymous with or the equivalent of "whole") the mortgaged property that remains within reach of the mortgagee at the time of sale as a condition precedent to the right to move for a deficiency decree. Brown v. Fraley, 229 Md. 445, 184 A.2d 710 (1962).

Nature of proceedings. — It is possible for a mortgage foreclosure proceeding in Maryland in which no deficiency decree is sought to be purely in rem; it is also possible, if the mortgagor voluntarily appears, for the proceeding to include judgments, in the form of rulings on exceptions to the sale and to the auditor's report, respectively, that have in personam collateral estoppel effect. Fairfax Sav. v. Kris Jen Ltd. Partnership, 338 Md. 1, 655 A.2d 1265 (1995).

The term "whole mortgaged property"

means only that property which has not been released from the lien of the mortgage. Brown v. Fraley, 229 Md. 445, 184 A.2d 710 (1962).

Hence, decree in personam not barred by release of part of mortgaged property. — This Rule does state that "if, after a sale of the whole mortgaged property, the net proceeds of sale ... are insufficient to pay the mortgage debt and accrued interest, ... a motion for a deficiency decree may be made," but that does not mean that if some of the mortgaged property has been released, the mortgagee is barred from obtaining a decree in personam against the mortgagor. Brown v. Fraley, 229 Md. 445, 184 A.2d 710 (1962).

Claim which has not become an absolute lien upon the property cannot be considered in the disposition of any surplus, however equitable the claim may be. Balance Ltd. v. Short, 35 Md. App. 10, 368 A.2d 1116 (1977).

The liability of a defaulting purchaser under former Rule W75 was beyond the amount of the first lien on the real property sold. Funds in excess of the first lien accrue to secondary lienholders and then to owners of land. McCann v. McGinnis, 257 Md. 499, 263 A.2d 536 (1970).

Any money remaining after the satisfaction of the expenses of sale and the first lien would accrue to the underlying lienholders in order of priority and, if an excess still remained, to the owners of the land. Balance Ltd. v. Short, 35 Md. App. 10, 368 A.2d 1116 (1977).

Liability of guarantor not party to deed of trust can only be determined in an action at law on the note and guaranty agreement. Walde v. Capital Mtg. Invs., 286 Md. 343, 407 A.2d 1143 (1979).

Where the first mortgagee was not a party to the proceedings and filed no claim therein, it was improper for the auditor to state an account distributing the net proceeds of a sale under the second mortgage, first to the payment of the first mortgage and the balance toward the second mortgage claim, leaving nothing for a judgment creditor who had filed a claim in the proceedings. Baltimore Fed. Sav. & Loan Ass'n v. Eareckson, 221 Md. 527, 158 A.2d 121 (1960).

Stipulation may transfer claims from chattels to proceeds of sale. — Where a stipulation of the parties was made before a sale was ratified, it transferred the claims of all of the parties to the chattels sold from the chattels to the proceeds of their sale. The stipulation effectively placed before the court the respective claims to the proceeds of the sale. Plaza Corp. v. Alban Tractor Co., 219 Md. 570, 151 A.2d 170 (1959).

Purpose of provisions for personal decree; it does not affect right of action on covenants. — The portion of former § 156 of Article 16 relative to a personal decree was enacted to avoid the delay and expense of a separate suit, and such remedy is cumulative and does not affect the right of action on the covenants to pay the mortgage debt. Commercial Bldg. & Loan Ass'n v. Robinson, 90 Md. 615, 45 A. 449 (1900).

Or question whether covenants run with land. — Former § 156 of Article 16, authorizing a deficiency decree provided the mortgagee would be entitled to maintain an action on the covenants in the mortgage, did not affect the question whether covenants ran with the land. Commercial Bldg. & Loan Ass'n v. Robinson, 90 Md. 615, 45 A. 449 (1900).

Construction. — The provision for the entry of a deficiency decree should be strictly construed because it is in derogation of the common law, but as it is remedial it should be construed to accomplish the object for which it was designed whenever possible. Austraw v. Dietz, 185 Md. 245, 44 A.2d 437 (1945).

As former § 15 of Article 66 was remedial in nature, it should be interpreted so as to accomplish the object for which it was designed when possible. Boyd v. Goldstein, 223 Md. 255, 164 A.2d 336 (1960).

Mortgagee may proceed as common creditor unless estopped. — If sale of mortgaged property fails to satisfy mortgage debt, interest and costs, the mortgagee may proceed as common creditor against mortgagor for the balance unless he is estopped by his deed or acts in pais. Mizen v. Thomas, 156 Md. 313, 144 A. 479 (1929).

If a sale of mortgaged property does not produce enough to pay the mortgage debt, interest and costs, the mortgagee may proceed as any other creditor against the mortgagor for the balance of the indebtedness unless some element of estoppel is present. Brown v. Fraley, 229 Md. 445, 184 A.2d 710 (1962).

Former section b did not prevent separate action at law. — Section b of former Rule W75 provides that where there has been a sale at a mortgage foreclosure and the net proceeds of the sale are insufficient to pay the mortgage debt and the accrued interest, as found by the court upon the report of the auditor, a motion for a decree in personam for the deficiency may be made. This is really done as an accommodation to the mortgagee so that he may obtain a deficiency judgment in the same suit without having to institute a separate action. However, there is nothing in former Rule W75 to prevent the mortgagee from proceeding by a separate action at law. Ketz v. Simcha Co., 251 Md. 227, 246 A.2d 555 (1968).

General creditor not entitled to attach distribution. — If a general creditor has no standing to intervene in the mortgage foreclosure, and if he has no standing to demand payment from any surplus, he is certainly not entitled to attack a distribution of funds from a sale after foreclosure. Balance Ltd. v. Short, 35 Md. App. 10, 368 A.2d 1116 (1977).

Junior lienholder of portion of property. — Where a foreclosure sale of property encumbered by a first mortgage produces a surplus, a junior lienholder of only a portion of that property should, in equity, receive only those proceeds derived from the sale of property encumbered to it. William H. Metcalfe & Sons v. Canyon Defined Benefit Trust, 318 Md. 565, 569 A.2d 669 (1990).

In personam judgment. — A deficiency judgment is an in personam judgment. Fairfax Sav. v. Kris Jen Ltd. Partnership, 338 Md. 1, 655 A.2d 1265 (1995).

Attorney named in mortgage to foreclose may obtain deficiency decree. — An attorney named in a mortgage to foreclose in default has the same functions as a person who is subsequently named as assignee of a mortgage for the purpose of foreclosure after default has occurred and consequently has the same rights as an assignee to obtain a deficiency decree in personam. Austraw v. Dietz, 185 Md. 245, 44 A.2d 437 (1945).

Deficiency decree may be entered only against party who might be sued on covenants in mortgage, not against guarantor. Kushnick v. Lake Drive Bldg. & Loan Ass'n, 153 Md. 638, 139 A. 446 (1927).

When the General Assembly provided that the right to a deficiency decree should exist only where the mortgagee could have maintained an action at law upon the covenants contained in the mortgage, it meant that the right should exist only against the proper parties to the proceeding and such parties as were bound by the covenants and could have been sued at law thereon. Hence, as stated in Kushnick v. Lake Drive Bldg. & Loan Ass'n, 153 Md. 638, 139 A. 446 (1927), the right would not exist where the foreclosure suit was against an heir of the mortgagor, or was brought to foreclose a mortgage not under seal, because in such a case the person sought to be charged would not be liable on covenants in the mortgage and could not be sued thereon. Austraw v. Dietz, 185 Md. 245, 44 A.2d 437 (1945).

Deficiency decree against wife was properly entered, though she might not have been fully aware of contents of note and mortgages. Bletzer v. Cooksey, 154 Md. 568, 141 A. 380 (1928).

The mortgagor may raise any defense that could be made in an action at law on the covenants in the mortgage, when pressed for a deficiency decree; that is, any defense such as payment or release, or any other defense to the claim which has arisen since confirmation of the sale. McKenna v. Sachse, 225 Md. 595, 171 A.2d 732 (1961).

A deficiency decree is permitted where recovery could be had on the covenants of the mortgage in a suit at law and the same defenses that might be urged there may be set up. Kirsner v. Cohen, 171 Md. 687, 190 A. 520 (1937).

Thus if mortgage is not under seal no decree in personam may be entered. — If the mortgage is not under the seal of the mortgagor, no decree in personam can be entered because no action of covenant could be maintained. McDonald v. Workingmen's Bldg. Ass'n, 60 Md. 589 (1883).

Assertion of fraud does not extend right to intervene in the distribution of proceeds in an equity court. Balance Ltd. v. Short, 35 Md. App. 10, 368 A.2d 1116 (1977).

Cause of action is based upon covenants in mortgage. — When a deficiency decree is requested, the parties are in the same relative position as litigants at law, and for the party who requests the deficiency decree to prevail, he must show all of the requirements of a successful plaintiff at law, with his cause of action based upon the covenants in the mortgage. Boyd v. Goldstein, 223 Md. 255, 164 A.2d 336 (1960); Kirsner v. Cohen, 171 Md. 687, 190 A. 520 (1937).

A deficiency decree cannot be rendered against a debtor unless the party seeking the decree has a right to maintain an action at law on a covenant contained in the mortgage. Brown v. Fraley, 229 Md. 445, 184 A.2d 710 (1962).

And under the common law no implied covenant arises where deed of trust contains none. — Under the common law of Maryland, if a deed of trust is given as security for an indebtedness, but contains no covenant to pay the indebtedness, no implied covenant to do so arises. Boyd v. Goldstein, 223 Md. 255, 164 A.2d 336 (1960).

Obligation of mortgagor where mortgagee is purchaser at sale. — The Maryland Rule in regard to ameliorating the obligations of a mortgagor to pay a deficiency when the mortgagee buys in the property at foreclosure sale is clear and fixed: In the absence of fraud or breach of actual trust, it is well established that since the confirmation of a foreclosure sale is the final determination by the court that the mortgaged property was sold at a fair price, the defense of inadequacy of price cannot be raised in subsequent proceedings, and for the purpose of a deficiency decree the price obtained at the sale is conclusive on the question of the market value of the property. McKenna v. Sachse, 225 Md. 595, 171 A.2d 732 (1961).

Rights of mortgagee are not lessened because he is purchaser at foreclosure sale.

McKenna v. Sachse, 225 Md. 595, 171 A.2d 732 (1961).

He is not required to account for rents or profits. — Mortgagee who purchased at sale not required to account to mortgagor for rents or profits on property purchased by him after ratification of sale. Moss v. Annapolis Sav. Inst., 177 Md. 135, 8 A.2d 881 (1939).

The mortgagee is not required to account to the mortgagor for profit made upon resale. McKenna v. Sachse, 225 Md. 595, 171 A.2d 732 (1961).

Equitable chattel mortgage or implied covenant not excluded. — There is nothing in the provisions of former Rule W75 (as to who may make a motion for a deficiency decree) excluding an equitable chattel mortgage or an implied covenant. Brown v. Fraley, 229 Md. 445, 184 A.2d 710 (1962).

Even if there was no express covenant to pay the mortgage debt and interest, there was still a covenant sufficient to maintain an action of law under former Rule W75, since the bill of sale of a trucking business and its equipment was in substance a chattel mortgage and could be deemed to contain an implied covenant to pay the debt and interest specified therein pursuant to former Article 21, § 47, of the Code. Brown v. Fraley, 229 Md. 445, 184 A.2d 710 (1962).

Bill of sale and contract of sale, read as one instrument, contained sufficient covenant. — Where an express covenant to pay the mortgage debt and interest, though not included in the bill of sale of a trucking business and its equipment, was embodied in the contract of sale, which, as the Court of Appeals had already said, constituted one instrument, the Court of Appeals held that, when both instruments are read as one, the bill of sale — which was in substance a chattel mortgage — contained a covenant sufficient to maintain an action at law under former Rule W75. Brown v. Fraley, 229 Md. 445, 184 A.2d 710 (1962).

Statute of limitations. — Petition for a deficiency judgment was not available where barred by § 5-102 of the Courts Article, relating to limitations on specialties. County Trust Co. v. Harrington, 168 Md. 101, 176 A. 639 (1935).

Former § 156 of Article 16, as amended by ch. 507, Acts 1939, did not repeal § 853 of the Baltimore City Charter (1938 Ed.), which provided for a deficiency decree within twelve years. Loeffler v. Carey, 181 Md. 648, 31 A.2d 619 (1943).

Rule 14-209. Release and assignment — Stay — Insolvency.

(a) *Release or assignment of claim.* A person entitled to release or assign a claim under a lien may file in the pending action to foreclose the lien a written release or assignment of the claim and of any order for the sale of the property entered in the action. The release or assignment shall be signed and acknowledged before a person authorized to take acknowledgments of deeds. The release or assignment shall take effect at the time of entry upon the docket and shall thereupon be effective to discharge the property from the lien or to assign the claim.

(b) *Injunction to stay foreclosure.* (1) Motion. The debtor, any party to the lien instrument, or any person who claims under the debtor a right to or interest in the property that is subordinate to the lien being foreclosed, may file a motion for an injunction to stay any sale or any proceedings after a sale under these rules. The motion shall not be granted unless the motion is supported by affidavit as to all facts asserted and contains: (1) a statement as to whether the moving party admits any amount of the debt to be due and payable as of the date the motion is filed, (2) if an amount is admitted, a statement that the moving party has paid the amount into court with the filing of the motion, and (3) a detailed statement of facts, showing that: (A) the debt and all interest due thereon have been fully paid, or (B) there is no default, or (C) fraud was used by the secured party, or with the secured party's knowledge, in obtaining the lien.

(2) Injunction based on misrepresentation. If the court finds that an injunction to stay an action to foreclose a lien was obtained through misrepresentation, it shall order the person who obtained the injunction to pay to the

secured party interest on the amount of the debt at the rate of five percentage points over the rate otherwise payable in connection with the debt from the time of the grant of the injunction until its dissolution. This remedy is in addition to any other remedy that may be available.

(c) *Insolvency proceeding — Effect on foreclosure.* When property of an insolvent is subject to a lien, the institution of or pendency of insolvency proceedings by or against the insolvent under the laws of this State, shall not stay a sale of property pursuant to a foreclosure action instituted prior to the insolvency proceeding.

Source. — This Rule is derived from former Rule W76.

The Maryland insolvency law has been suspended by the federal bankruptcy law, except as to certain classes of persons not provided for by the federal law such as farmers, who may be proceeded against involuntarily under the State law. Old Town Bank v. McCormick, 96 Md. 341, 53 A. 934 (1903).

Two opportunities to challenge legality of foreclosure. — Under Maryland foreclosure procedures, plaintiff homeowners were afforded two separate opportunities in which they may challenge in a state court the legality of the foreclosure. First, under section b of former Rule W76, they may move prior to sale to enjoin the foreclosure. Secondly, after the sale but before ratification, they have the opportunity to file objections to the sale. Fisher v. Federal Nat'l Mtg. Ass'n, 360 F. Supp. 207 (D. Md. 1973).

Former Rule W76 placed certain limitations on who may obtain an injunction. Saunders v. Stradley, 25 Md. App. 85, 333 A.2d 604 (1975).

Injunction may be sought in either of two proceedings. — Former Rule W76 does not specify whether an injunction may be sought by a petition in the same proceeding, or by a separate equity proceeding, and it appears that it may be done either way. Saunders v. Stradley, 25 Md. App. 85, 333 A.2d 604 (1975).

Purpose of former statute authorizing injunction. — See Powell v. Hopkins, 38 Md. 1 (1873); Talbott v. Laurel Bldg. Ass'n, 140 Md. 565, 118 A. 63 (1922).

Statutory requirements must be complied with before an injunction can issue. Goldsborough v. County Trust Co., 180 Md. 59, 22 A.2d 920 (1941).

Conditions precedent to granting of injunction under section b 2 of former Rule W76 presume the existence of a valid mortgage on the subject property. Frank v. Storer, 66 Md. App. 459, 504 A.2d 1163, rev'd on other grounds, 308 Md. 194, 517 A.2d 1098 (1986).

Proof of default. — Upon any pre-sale challenge to the mortgage foreclosure by petition for injunctive relief, the mortgagee is permitted to offer proof of default of any of the default provisions of the mortgage, and generally the sale may not be enjoined unless it is determined that none of the pertinent provisions of the mortgage are in default. Pacific Mtg. & Inv. Group, Ltd. v. LaGuerre, 81 Md. App. 28, 566 A.2d 780 (1989).

When a petition to foreclose a mortgage pursuant to an assent to a decree is filed, stating simply that the mortgage is in default, such petition is sufficient to sustain the foreclosure proceeding so long as any one of the provisions of the mortgage, the violation of which can constitute a default under the terms of the mortgage, is in default. Pacific Mtg. & Inv. Group, Ltd. v. LaGuerre, 81 Md. App. 28, 566 A.2d 780 (1989).

The breach of a covenant to insure contained within a mortgage constitutes a default which allows acceleration under an acceleration clause. Pacific Mtg. & Inv. Group, Ltd. v. LaGuerre, 81 Md. App. 28, 566 A.2d 780 (1989).

Objections overruled. — Where a petition for an injunction alleged that the mortgage debt and interest were fully satisfied under the terms of an agreement, and appeal was from a final decree for a permanent injunction on that ground, the objection that the petition did not allege that the mortgage and all interest due thereon had been paid, and the contention that the bond filed as a prerequisite to issue of a preliminary injunction was not in the form prescribed by law, were properly overruled. Green v. Redmond, 132 Md. 166, 103 A. 431 (1918).

Bill held insufficient. Fowler v. Pendleton, 121 Md. 297, 88 A. 124 (1913).

Allegations in bill determine jurisdiction of court. Barrick v. Horner, 78 Md. 253, 27 A. 1111 (1893).

Amount due must be paid or brought into court. — Where the mortgagor admits in his bill that a balance is due mortgagee, that amount must be paid mortgagee or brought into court before mortgagor is entitled to an injunction. Talbott v. Laurel Bldg. Ass'n, 140 Md. 565, 118 A. 63 (1922).

Before court will grant an injunction to restrain a sale upon default in a mortgage, the mortgagor must pay into court amount admitted to be due. Buckner v. Cronhardt, 132 Md. 612, 104 A. 169 (1918).

An allegation of payment in cash is not required, and it is sufficient that a contract to cancel the mortgage debt in consideration of a transfer of the land to the mortgagee is alleged. Johnson v. Wheeler, 174 Md. 531, 199 A. 502 (1938).

Mere payment of usury will not entitle mortgagor to an injunction; otherwise, if payments on principal and interest are equal to or greater than indebtedness. Gantt v. Grindall, 49 Md. 310 (1878); Walker v. Cockey, 38 Md. 75 (1873); Powell v. Hopkins, 38 Md. 1

(1873); Talbott v. Laurel Bldg. Ass'n, 140 Md. 565, 118 A. 63 (1922).

A sale will not be stayed because a stranger has instituted ejectment, there being no allegation that his claim is valid. Gayle v. Fattle, 14 Md. 69 (1859).

One who has a valid contract to purchase property by reason of exercise of an option, may secure an injunction to stay foreclosure proceedings and is entitled to redeem property when it is being sold under foreclosure of mortgage proceedings. Tender held sufficient to entitle plaintiff to injunction. Wingert v. Brewer, 116 Md. 518, 82 A. 157 (1911).

Bond. — See Thrift v. Bannon, 111 Md. 303, 73 A. 660 (1909); Wingert v. Brewer, 116 Md. 518, 82 A. 157 (1911); American Bonding Co. v. State ex rel. Com. & Farmers' Nat'l Bank, 120 Md. 305, 87 A. 922 (1913); Wolf v. Oldenburg, 154 Md. 353, 140 A. 494 (1928).

Injunction improperly granted. — See Buckner v. Cronhardt, 132 Md. 612, 104 A. 169 (1918).

Rule 14-210. Deed of trust — Removal of trustee.

(a) *Inapplicable where procedure set forth in lien instrument.* The procedure for removal of a trustee under a deed of trust set forth in this Rule shall not supersede or nullify any procedure for the removal or substitution of a trustee that may be provided for in the deed of trust.

(b) *Motion to remove trustee.* When a trustee who has the right to institute a foreclosure action fails or refuses to do so, or if there exists any other good and sufficient reason for the removal of the trustee under a deed of trust, secured parties holding not less than 25%, or any lesser percentage provided in the deed of trust, of the beneficial interest under the deed of trust may file a motion for the removal of the trustee and appointment of a new trustee. The motion shall be supported by affidavit and shall contain facts showing the failure or refusal to foreclose or any other reason for removal alleged to exist. The motion may be filed in any court in which the action to foreclose may be instituted.

(c) *Notice to trustee.* Notice of the filing of the motion shall be given to the trustee by mailing a copy of the motion by certified mail to the last known address of the trustee, unless the court orders otherwise.

Source. — This Rule is derived from former Rule W77 d.

For most purposes a deed of trust is a mortgage and is subject to some (but not all) statutory provisions relating to mortgages. Burroughs v. Garner, 43 Md. App. 302, 405 A.2d 301 (1979).

Obligor's interest after full payment. —

Neither default nor institution of foreclosure in any way negates the fact that where full payment has been made, the obligor has, at the least, complete equitable ownership of the property, and the trustee has, at most, only bare legal title to it. Burroughs v. Garner, 43

Md. App. 302, 405 A.2d 301 (1979).

Bond of trustee under former statute. — See Union Trust Co. v. Ward, 100 Md. 98, 59 A. 192 (1904); Real Estate Trust Co. v. Union Trust Co., 102 Md. 41, 61 A. 228 (1905);

Cummings v. Wildman, 116 Md. 307, 81 A. 610 (1911); Richardson v. Malthan, 133 Md. 542, 105 A. 766 (1919); Briley v. Pinkston, 215 Md. 417, 136 A.2d 563 (1958).

CHAPTER 300. JUDICIAL SALES.

Rule 14-301. Applicability.

Except as otherwise specifically provided in Rules 2-644 and 3-644 and Chapter 200 of this Title, the rules in this Chapter govern all sales of property that are subject to ratification by a court.

Source. — This Rule is derived from former Rule BR1.

University of Baltimore Law Review. — For article, "New Balance in the Rights of Creditors and Debtors: The Effect on Maryland Law," see 2 U. Balt. L. Rev. 236 (1973).

Rule 14-302. Sales — Generally.

(a) *When court may order.* At any stage of an action, the court may order a sale if satisfied that the jurisdictional requisites have been met and that the sale is appropriate.

Cross references. — *See* Code, Family Law Article, § 11-104 and *Keen v. Keen*, 191 Md. 31 (1948) for sale of nonresidents' property to satisfy alimony decree; Code, Family Law Article, § 8-202 for sale of real or personal property incident to a divorce decree; Code, Business Regulations Article, § 5-501 for sale of burial grounds; Code, Real Property Article, § 14-107 for sale in lieu of partition; Code, Article 16, § 159 for sale of personal property jointly owned; Code, Real Property Article, § 14-110 for sale of consecutive interests in land by agreement of parties; Code, Tax Property Article, §§ 14-808 through 14-854 for tax sales; and Code, Tax General Article, § 13-810 for sale to enforce income tax lien.

(b) *Appointment of trustee.* When the court orders a sale it may appoint a trustee to make the sale. The trustee shall be a natural person.

Cross references. — *See* Code, Article 16, § 107 for the appointment of a trustee to execute a deed; Code, Real Property Article, § 4-202 (e) for a form of a trustee's deed under a decree; Code, Estates and Trusts Article, § 14-101, for general jurisdiction of equity concerning trusts; and Code, Article 16, § 114 for the appointment of a trustee to complete the collections of a sheriff or tax collector. Regarding fiduciaries generally, *see* Code, Estates and Trusts Article, § 15-101 *et seq.*

Source. — This Rule is derived from former Rule BR2.

Editor's note. — Article 16, which is referred to in the Cross Reference notes to sections (a) and (b), has been repealed. Former §§ 114 and 159 of Article 16 were repealed by § 7, ch. 31, Acts 1997, as obsolete or duplicative of the Maryland Rules; former § 107 of Article 16 was revised as § 11-111 of the Courts Article.

Object of statute providing for sale before final decree and effect of order of sale thereunder. — See Kelly v. Gilbert, 78 Md. 431, 28 A. 274 (1894).

Sale of decedent's real estate to pay debts. — It was the habit of the court to apply former § 161 of Article 16, authorizing a sale of property before final decree, in applications for sales of real estate to pay debts under former Article 16, § 157. Hammond v. Hammond, 2 Bland Ch. 306 (1830).

Sale of trust property where court has assumed jurisdiction of trust. — Where court has assumed jurisdiction of trust, it may order sale of trust property before final decree. Elkton Elec. Co. v. Perkins, 145 Md. 224, 125 A. 851 (1922), cert. denied, 266 U.S. 602, 45 S. Ct. 90, 69 L. Ed. 462, appeal dismissed, 266 U.S. 585, 45 S. Ct. 124, 69 L. Ed. 454 (1924).

Statute should be applied only in plain and unquestionable cases. — Former § 161 of Article 16 should never be applied except in very plain and unquestionable cases, and even then only after a full hearing. Kelly v. Gilbert, 78 Md. 431, 28 A. 274 (1894).

Where sale must inevitably be decreed at final hearing. — To justify a sale before final decree, it should appear beyond a reasonable doubt that a sale must be inevitably decreed at the final hearing. Donohue v. Daniel, 58 Md. 595 (1882).

Order of sale may be passed without waiting for defendant's appearance or answer. — Upon satisfactory proof as prescribed in the statute, the court may pass an order of sale at any time after bill filed, without waiting for the defendant's appearance or answer. Dorsey v. Dorsey, 30 Md. 522 (1869).

Bill of complaint may be amended after decree of sale. Kelly v. Gilbert, 78 Md. 431, 28 A. 274 (1894).

Order of sale is reviewable on appeal. —

The discretion of the court in ordering a sale before final decree is reviewable on appeal. Dorsey v. Dorsey, 30 Md. 522 (1869).

But decree of sale cannot be inquired into collaterally. — A decree of sale under former § 161 of Article 16 could not be inquired into collaterally, provided the court had jurisdiction. Dorsey v. Garey, 30 Md. 489 (1869).

And no appeal lies from refusal or rescission of order of sale. — No appeal lay from the refusal to order a sale under former § 161 of Article 16, nor from the rescission of an order of sale. An appeal would lie, however, under former Article 5, § 7 (see now § 12-303 of the Courts Article), from an order directing a sale. Washington City & Point Lookout R.R. v. Southern Md. R.R., 55 Md. 153 (1880).

A sale held not to have been ordered under former § 161 of Article 16, and the proof did not justify a sale thereunder. Cornell v. McCann, 37 Md. 89 (1872).

Proof held insufficient to justify sale. — See Kelly v. Gilbert, 78 Md. 431, 28 A. 274 (1894).

The trustee is the mere attorney of the court acting under specially delegated authority. Andrews v. Scotton, 2 Bland Ch. 629 (1830).

A trustee may be appointed to execute an assignment of a patent, if the patentee fails to execute such assignment, as directed by a decree. Ager v. Murray, 105 U.S. 126, 26 L. Ed. 942 (1881).

Rule 14-303. Procedure prior to sale.

(a) *Bond.* (1) Trustee appointed by court. Unless excused by the court, a trustee appointed by the court to make a sale shall file a bond with the clerk. The bond shall be to the State of Maryland in an amount determined by the court and conditioned on faithful performance and execution of the trust.

(2) Trustee appointed under certain instruments. Unless otherwise ordered by the court, the trustee need not file a bond if the sale is for the benefit of either the grantor of the trust instrument or a person who paid a valuable consideration for the deed of trust and who is entitled to the proceeds of sale.

Cross references. — For payment of the premium of the bond out of the estate being administered, *see* Rule 10-702 (f). *See also* Code, Commercial Law Article, § 15-103 (a) concerning bond requirements before passage of title to an assignee for the benefit of creditors.

(b) *Public sale — Advertisement.* Unless otherwise ordered by the court, a trustee proposing to make a public sale shall give notice by advertisement of the time, place, and terms of sale in a newspaper of general circulation in each county where any portion of the property is located. The notice shall describe the property to be sold sufficiently to identify it and shall be given as follows:

(1) for the sale of an interest in real property, at least once a week for three successive weeks, the first publication to be not less than 15 days before the sale and the last publication to be not more than one week before the sale; or

(2) for the sale of personal property, not less than five days nor more than 12 days before the sale.

(c) *Private sale; appraisal.* Before making a private sale, the person proposing to make it shall file in the proceedings an appraisal made by a competent appraiser within six months before the date of sale. An appraisal need not be filed if the filing is excused by order of the court or if the sale is made by a personal representative of an estate administered in the circuit court under a will that grants a power of sale without expressly requiring an appraisal.

Source. — This Rule is derived from former Rule BR3.

Complete accuracy in an advertisement is not required and a judicial sale will not be set aside without a clear showing that an omission misled anyone or had a prejudicial effect. Woelfel v. Tyng, 221 Md. 539, 158 A.2d 311 (1960).

Sufficient description of real property. — A description in an advertisement of a judicial sale of real property which describes the property so that it could be located by the exercise of ordinary intelligence and so that more detailed information concerning it could be obtained, if desired, is sufficient. Woelfel v. Tyng, 221 Md. 539, 158 A.2d 311 (1960).

Cited in 91st St. Joint Venture v. Goldstein, 114 Md. App. 561, 691 A.2d 272 (1997).

Rule 14-304. Place of sale.

Unless otherwise ordered by the court, a sale shall be made in a county where all or a part of the property is located.

Source. — This Rule is derived from former Rule BR4.

Rule 14-305. Procedure following sale.

(a) *Report of sale.* As soon as practicable, but not more than 30 days after a sale, the person authorized to make the sale shall file with the court a complete report of the sale and an affidavit of the fairness of the sale and the truth of the report.

(b) *Affidavit of purchaser.* Before a sale is ratified, unless otherwise ordered by the court for good cause, the purchaser shall file an affidavit setting forth:

(1) whether the purchaser is acting as an agent and, if so, the name of the principal;

(2) whether others are interested as principals and, if so, the names of the other principals; and

(3) that the purchaser has not directly or indirectly discouraged anyone from bidding for the property.

(c) *Sale of interest in real property; notice.* Upon the filing of a report of sale of real property or chattels real pursuant to section (a) of this Rule, the clerk shall issue a notice containing a brief description sufficient to identify the property and stating that the sale will be ratified unless cause to the contrary is shown within 30 days after the date of the notice. A copy of the notice shall be published at least once a week in each of three successive weeks before the expiration of the 30-day period in one or more newspapers of general circulation in the county in which the report of sale was filed.

(d) *Exceptions to sale.* (1) How taken. A party, and, in an action to foreclose a lien, the holder of a subordinate interest in the property subject to the lien, may file exceptions to the sale. Exceptions shall be in writing, shall set forth the alleged irregularity with particularity, and shall be filed within 30 days after the date of a notice issued pursuant to section (c) of this Rule or the filing of the report of sale if no notice is issued. Any matter not specifically set forth in the exceptions is waived unless the court finds that justice requires otherwise.

(2) Ruling on exceptions; hearing. The court shall determine whether to hold a hearing on the exceptions but it may not set aside a sale without a hearing. The court shall hold a hearing if a hearing is requested and the exceptions or any response clearly show a need to take evidence. The clerk shall send a notice of the hearing to all parties and, in an action to foreclose a lien, to all persons to whom notice of the sale was given pursuant to Rule 14-206 (b).

(e) *Ratification.* The court shall ratify the sale if (1) the time for filing exceptions pursuant to section (d) of this Rule has expired and exceptions to the report either were not filed or were filed but overruled, and (2) the court is satisfied that the sale was fairly and properly made. If the court is not satisfied that the sale was fairly and properly made, it may enter any order that it deems appropriate.

(f) *Referral to auditor.* Upon ratification of a sale, the court, pursuant to Rule 2-543, may refer the matter to an auditor to state an account.

(g) *Resale.* If the purchaser defaults, the court, on application and after notice to the purchaser, may order a resale at the risk and expense of the purchaser or may take any other appropriate action.

Source. — This Rule is derived from former Rule BR6.

Former Rule BR6 was a restatement or recodification of preexisting practice in this State as was its statutory predecessor which came into being in 1841. McCann v. McGinnis, 257 Md. 499, 263 A.2d 536 (1970).

Scope of court's authority. — Section b 4 of former Rule BR6 gave the trial court the specific authority to ratify a foreclosure sale if the trial court finds that the sale was fairly and properly made and no exceptions are filed or exceptions are filed and overruled. If the trial judge finds that the sale was not fairly and properly held, then denial of ratification is appropriate. Former Rule BR6 provided no discretion or authority to do otherwise. Smith v. Lawler, 93 Md. App. 540, 613 A.2d 459 (1992), cert. denied, 329 Md. 110, 617 A.2d 1055 (1993).

Time for filing purchaser's affidavit. — There is no requirement that the purchaser's affidavit be filed 30 days after the sale although such an affidavit must obviously be filed before final ratification, unless otherwise ordered by the court for good cause shown. Southern Md. Oil, Inc. v. Kaminetz, 260 Md. 443, 272 A.2d 641 (1971).

The best obtainable offer accepted and reported by a trustee should be ratified in the absence of fraud, improper dealing or inadequacy of price as of the time the sale was made. Gilden v. Harris, 197 Md. 32, 78 A.2d 167 (1951); Standish Corp. v. Keane, 220 Md. 1, 150 A.2d 728 (1959).

Even though someone else is willing to give more. — The general rule is that if a trustee, acting diligently and without fraud, accepts an offer at private sale for the most that he is able to obtain for the property at the time, and reports that offer to the court, it will not be set aside merely because someone else is later willing to give more for the property. Standish Corp. v. Keane, 220 Md. 1, 150 A.2d 728 (1959).

Unless inadequate price is due to trustee's lack of diligence. — A sale should not be ratified if the inadequate price reported is attributable to a lack of diligence on the part of the person making the sale or to the failure of such person to make a thorough investigation of local conditions before fixing a price at which the property would be sold. Knight v. Nottingham Farms, Inc., 207 Md. 65, 113 A.2d 382 (1955); Webb & Knapp, Inc. v. Hanover Bank, 214 Md. 230, 133 A.2d 450 (1957); Standish Corp. v. Keane, 220 Md. 1, 150 A.2d 728 (1959).

Sale reported by trustee named in deed or will. — The court is invested with the same powers with respect to a sale reported by a trustee named in a deed or will, as it would have had if the sale had been made by a trustee appointed by the court. Berry v. Foley, 92 Md. 311, 48 A. 146 (1901).

Sale does not pass title until ratified. — Since Maryland law provides that a mortgage foreclosure sale is subject to the approval of the court, such a sale does not pass title to the property until ratified by the court. Fisher v. Federal Nat'l Mtg. Ass'n, 360 F. Supp. 207 (D. Md. 1973).

A rescission of the order of ratification of the sale does not automatically relieve the purchaser of responsibility for any loss in the event of resale. McCann v. McGinnis, 257 Md. 499, 263 A.2d 536 (1970).

It is necessary for good cause to exist for relieving the original purchaser from further liability. McCann v. McGinnis, 257 Md. 499, 263 A.2d 536 (1970).

Res judicata. — The final ratification of the sale of property in foreclosure proceedings is res judicata as to the validity of such sale, except in case of fraud or illegality, and hence its regularity cannot be attacked in collateral proceedings. Ed Jacobsen, Jr., Inc. v. Barrick, 252 Md. 507, 250 A.2d 646 (1969).

Substantial compliance. — The purchaser's affidavit substantially complied with the provisions of former Rule BR6, where it stated that the purchaser bought the property as "principal and not as agent for anyone else," and that "neither he nor anyone connected with him directly or indirectly discouraged anyone from bidding on said property." Southern Md. Oil, Inc. v. Kaminetz, 260 Md. 443, 272 A.2d 641 (1971).

Former statute providing for resale was constitutional. Capron v. Devries, 83 Md. 220, 34 A. 251 (1896).

Object of statute; law prior to its adoption. — See Warfield v. Dorsey, 39 Md. 299 (1874).

It applied to sales under powers. — Former § 163 of Article 16, applied to sales under powers as well as to sales by trustees appointed by the court. The court is the vendor in a resale. Bilbrey v. Strahorn, 153 Md. 491, 138 A. 343 (1927).

Former § 163 of Article 16 applied to sales made under powers in mortgages. Middendorf v. Baltimore Refrigerating & Heating Co., 117 Md. 17, 82 A. 1047 (1911).

Sale to defaulting purchaser may be abandoned and rescinded. — Where a purchaser is insolvent a sale to him although finally ratified may be abandoned and rescinded, the property sold again and a clear title conveyed to the second purchaser. Sloan v. Safe Deposit & Trust Co., 73 Md. 239, 20 A. 922 (1890).

Bond given for balance of purchase money may be enforced. — Where a purchaser paid part of the purchase money in cash, and gave a bond for the balance, payment of the latter could be enforced by petition under former § 163 of Article 16. Stephens v. Magruder, 31 Md. 168 (1869).

Necessity for order nisi and service thereof on defaulting purchaser. — Judgment in personam entered before order *nisi* is passed and served on defaulting purchaser in case foreclosure sale is void, and may be collaterally attacked by creditor of defaulting purchaser. Mercantile Bank v. Maryland Title Guar. Co., 153 Md. 320, 138 A. 251 (1927).

Court may order resale at purchaser's risk. — Where purchaser has failed to comply with terms of sale, the court may, on application of trustee appointed to make the sale, order resale at purchaser's risk. Miller v. Mitnick, 163 Md. 113, 161 A. 157 (1932).

Setting aside sheriff's sale. — A sheriff's sale will not be set aside for mere inadequateness of price, but if the sale is so grossly inadequate as to shock the conscience of the court, or if there be but slight circumstances of unfairness in addition to great inadequateness of price, a sale will be set aside. McCartney v. Frost, 282 Md. 631, 386 A.2d 784 (1978).

Property is not regarded as belonging to defaulting purchaser. — Upon a resale the property is not to be regarded as belonging to the defaulting purchaser. Dalrymple v. Taneyhill, 4 Md. Ch. 171 (1853); Werner v. Clark, 108 Md. 627, 71 A. 305 (1908).

Order of resale not providing notice to purchaser. — The fact that an order for resale did not provide for notice to the purchaser and afford him an opportunity to show cause, although it might have been better practice for it to have done so, was held to be of no consequence where he received notice and had adequate opportunity to protest. Stofberg v. Levland, Inc., 213 Md. 477, 132 A.2d 122 (1957).

Mortgagor may except to ratification of resale. — Where a mortgage is being foreclosed, the mortgagor is entitled to except to the ratification of the resale. Dalrymple v. Taneyhill, 4 Md. Ch. 171 (1853); Werner v. Clark, 108 Md. 627, 71 A. 305 (1908).

There was no reversible error in order directing resale of property. Middendorf v. Baltimore Refrigerating & Heating Co., 117 Md. 17, 82 A. 1047 (1911).

Trustee's fees and commissions. — The trustee making the sale will be allowed his legal fee for filing the petition, and commissions on the proceeds of the resale, but no other compensation for the collection of the money. Farmers & Planters Bank v. Martin, 7 Md. 342 (1855).

Dismissal of claims for allowances from proceeds of anticipated sale. — During a partition suit, dismissal of claims for allowances from the proceeds of an anticipated sale is without prejudice with regard to subsequent presentation to an auditor since a dismissal with prejudice would operate as an adjudication on the merits. Wooddy v. Wooddy, 270 Md. 23, 309 A.2d 754 (1973).

Quoted in Schaller v. Castle Dev. Corp., 111 Md. App. 40, 680 A.2d 528 (1996).

Cited in 91st St. Joint Venture v. Goldstein, 114 Md. App. 561, 691 A.2d 272 (1997).

Rule 14-306. Real property — Recording.

Upon the entry of a final order of ratification, the person making a sale of an interest in real property in a county other than one in which all of the property is located shall cause to be recorded among the land records of each county where any part of the property is located a certified copy of the docket entries, any complaint, the report of sale, the final order of ratification, and any other orders affecting the property.

Source. — This Rule is derived from former Rule BR5.

University of Baltimore Law Review. — For discussion, "Property Disposition Upon Divorce in Maryland: An Analysis of the New Statute," see 8 U. Balt. L. Rev. 377 (1979).

CHAPTER 400. BURIAL GROUND.

Rule 14-401. Sale for other use.

(a) *Venue.* An action for sale of a burial ground for a use other than burial purposes shall be brought in the county in which the burial ground is located. When the burial ground is located in more than one county, the action may be brought in any county in which all or any part of the burial ground is located.

(b) *Complaint.* The action for sale of a burial ground shall be commenced by filing a complaint that, in addition to complying with Rules 2-303 through 2-305, shall contain:

(1) a description of the burial ground sufficient to enable it to be located,

(2) a statement that the ground has been dedicated and used for burial purposes,

(3) a statement that the burial ground has ceased to be used for burial purposes,

(4) a list of names and last known addresses of all known lot owners, or their assignees, if any, and

(5) a statement of the reasons why it is desirable to sell the burial ground for other uses.

(c) *Notice — Publication and posting.* Upon the filing of the complaint, the clerk shall issue a notice instead of a summons. The notice shall be signed by the clerk and shall (1) include the caption of the action, (2) describe the substance of the complaint and the relief sought, and (3) inform all lot owners or other persons in interest of the latest date by which a response may be filed. The notice shall be published as provided in Rule 2-122, and a copy of the notice shall be posted in a conspicuous place on the property and at all principal gates or entrances to the burial ground. Additionally, a copy of the notice shall be sent by ordinary mail to each person whose name and last known address are listed in the complaint pursuant to subsection (b)(4) of this Rule.

(d) *Proceedings when no response filed.* If no party in interest appears in response to the notice, the action shall proceed ex parte. The court may order testimony to be taken and enter judgment as it deems proper.

CHAPTER 500. TAX SALES.

Rule 14-501. Applicability.

The rules in this Chapter govern actions to foreclose the right of redemption in property sold at a tax sale.

Rule 14-502. Foreclosure of right of redemption — Complaint.

(a) *Contents.* In an action to foreclose the right of redemption in property sold at a tax sale, the complaint, in addition to complying with Rules 2-303 through 2-305, shall set forth:

(1) the fact of the issuance of the certificate of sale;

(2) a description of the property in substantially the same form as the description appearing on the certificate of tax sale;

(3) the fact that the property has not been redeemed by any party in interest; and

(4) a statement of the amount necessary for redemption.

(b) *Documents.* The complaint shall be accompanied by:

(1) the original certificate of sale, or a photocopy of the certificate;

(2) a copy of a title report supported by an affidavit by the person making the search that a complete search of the records has been performed in accordance with generally accepted standards of title examination for the period of at least 40 years immediately before the filing of the complaint; and

(3) a notice setting forth (A) the substance of the complaint and the relief sought, (B) a description of the property in substantially the same form as the description appearing on the collector's tax records, (C) the time within which a defendant must file an answer to the complaint or redeem the property, and (D) a statement that failure to answer or redeem the property within the time allowed may result in a judgment foreclosing the right of redemption.

Cross references. — *See* Code, Tax-Property Article, § 14-833 for provisions governing limitations on the time for bringing an action to foreclose the right of redemption and Code, Tax-Property Article, § 14-841 for the limitation on the number of certificates that may be joined in one action. *See also* Code, Tax-Property Article, §§ 14-836 and 14-837 governing parties to the action. For purchaser's obligations once a complaint has been filed, *see Scheve v. Shudder, Inc.*, 328 Md. 363 (1992).

Source. — This Rule is new but is consistent with Code, Tax-Property Article, §§ 14-835 and 14-838 and is derived in part from Code, Tax-Property Article, §§ 14-840 and 14-836.

Rule 14-503. Process.

(a) *Notice to defendants whose whereabouts are known.* Upon the filing of the complaint, the clerk shall issue a summons as in any other civil action. The summons, complaint, and exhibits, including the notice prescribed by Rule 14-502 (b) (3), shall be served in accordance with Rule 2-121 on each defendant named in the complaint whose whereabouts are known.

(b) *Notice to defendants whose whereabouts are unknown, unknown owners, and unnamed interested persons.* When the complaint includes named defendants whose whereabouts are unknown, unknown owners, or unnamed persons having or claiming to have an interest in the property, the notice filed in accordance with Rule 14-502 (b) (3), after being issued and signed by the clerk, shall be served in accordance with Rule 2-122.

(c) *Posting of property.* Upon the filing of the complaint, the plaintiff shall cause the sheriff to post a notice in a conspicuous place on the property. The content of the notice shall be as prescribed in Rule 14-502 (b) (3).

(d) *Notice to collector.* Upon the filing of the complaint, the plaintiff shall mail a copy of the complaint and exhibits to the collector of taxes in the county in which the property is located.

Cross references. — For due process requirements, *see St. George Church v. Aggarwal*, 326 Md. 90 (1992).

Source. — This Rule is new. Section (a) is derived in part from Code, Tax-Property Article, § 14-839 (a). Section (b) is derived in part

from Code, Tax-Property Article, § 14-840.
Section (c) is new. Section (d) is derived from
Code, Tax-Property Article, § 14-839 (c).

Rule 14-504. Notice to persons not named as defendants.

The plaintiff shall send the notice prescribed by Rule 14-502 (b) (3) to each person having a recorded interest, claim or judgment, or other lien who has not been made a defendant in the proceeding. If all or part of the property is a common area owned by or legally dedicated to a homeowners' association, the plaintiff shall also send the notice to the homeowners' association governing the property. The notice shall be sent to the person's last reasonably ascertainable address by certified mail, postage prepaid, return receipt requested, bearing a postmark from the United States Postal Service, and shall be accompanied by a copy of the complaint. The plaintiff shall file the return receipt from the notice or an affidavit that the provisions of this section have been complied with or that the address of the holder of the subordinate interest is not reasonably ascertainable. If the filing is made before final ratification of the sale, failure of a holder of a subordinate interest to receive the notice does not invalidate the sale.

Source. — This Rule is new but is derived from Code, Tax-Property Article, § 14-836.

Rule 14-505. Defense of invalidity.

Any issue as to the validity of the taxes, the proceedings to sell the property, or the sale, shall be raised by separate affirmative defense.

Cross references. — Rule 2-323.
Source. — This Rule is new but is consis-tent with Code, Tax-Property Article, § 14-842.

TITLE 15. OTHER SPECIAL PROCEEDINGS

Editor's note. — The Court of Appeals, by Order dated June 5, 1996, effective January 1, 1997, rescinded Subtitles A, D, E, J, P, Q, R, T, U, V, W, Y, Z, BB, BD, BE, BG, BH, BJ, BL, BP, BQ, BR, BS, BW, and BY of Chapter 1100 of the Maryland Rules of Procedure, rescinded Subtitles P, BB, BQ, and BW of the Maryland District Rules, and rescinded Forms 22a, 23, 24, 25, and 26. The Order substituted for certain of the rules and forms rescinded new Title 9, Chapter 100, Title 10, Title 12, Title 13, Title 14, and Title 15 of the Maryland Rules of Procedure. Furthermore, the Order transferred, without readoption, Chapter 900, Chapter 1200, and Subtitles S, BU, and BV of Chapter 1100 of the Maryland Rules of Procedure and Chapter 1200 of the Maryland District Rules to be Title 9, Chapter 200, Title 11, and Title 16 of the Maryland Rules of Procedure. This Order provides that the new rules shall "apply to all actions commenced on or after January 1, 1997, and insofar as practicable, to all actions then pending."

Many of the cases in the notes to the various rules were decided prior to the 1996 revision. These cases have been retained under pertinent rules of this title where it is thought that such cases will be of value in interpreting the present rules.

A table of comparable rules, relating those rules rescinded effective January 1, 1997, to the revised rules in Title 9 through Title 16 is to be found in Volume 2 following the end of the Maryland Rules.

CHAPTER 100. ARBITRATION.

Rule 15-101. Application of Uniform Arbitration Act to certain proceedings.

(a) *Binding arbitration while court action pending.* (1) Not applicable to certain actions. This Rule does not apply to actions for judicial review of an order or action of an administrative agency.

(2) Consent; order of referral. If before trial all parties agree on the record or file a written stipulation agreeing to binding arbitration of the action or any issue, the court shall enter an order of referral to arbitration.

(3) Maryland Uniform Arbitration Act. Except to the extent provided otherwise in the order of referral, the Maryland Uniform Arbitration Act applies to the arbitration.

(b) *Court proceedings regarding binding arbitration not governed by Uniform Arbitration Act.* In connection with a binding arbitration conducted or sought to be conducted under common law or under a statute other than the Maryland Uniform Arbitration Act, unless otherwise required by applicable law, (1) court proceedings to confirm, vacate, modify, or enter judgment on a final written award are governed by the provisions of the Maryland Uniform Arbitration Act and (2) to the extent practicable, the procedure for obtaining other judicial relief shall be the same as the procedure in connection with an arbitration under the Maryland Uniform Arbitration Act.

Cross references. — Code, Courts Article, Title 3, Subtitles 2 and 2B.

Source. — This Rule is in part new and is derived in part from former Rules E2, E3, and E4.

University of Baltimore Law Review. — For article, "Confirmation of Out-of-State Arbitration Awards Under Maryland's Uniform Arbitration Act," see 9 U. Balt. L. Rev. 37 (1979).

Relationship between former Rule E2 and cases arising under § 301 of Labor Management Relations Act, 29 U.S.C. § 185. — See Brophy v. McLean Trucking Co., 552 F. Supp. 680 (D. Md. 1982).

Suit to recover the amount awarded, based on the award, was properly brought in the District Court. State of Md. Cent. Collection Unit v. Gettes, 321 Md. 671, 584 A.2d 689 (1991).

Authority of court. — Former Rule E3 gave the trial court authority to order litigants to submit to an arbitration that does not conform to the requirements of the Maryland Uniform Arbitration Act. Kovacs v. Kovacs, 98 Md. App. 289, 633 A.2d 425 (1993), cert. denied, 334 Md. 211, 638 A.2d 753 (1994).

Waiver. — Litigants may waive their rights under the Maryland Uniform Arbitration Act and submit to arbitration proceeding that do not meet all of the requirements of the Act. Kovacs v. Kovacs, 98 Md. App. 289, 633 A.2d 425 (1993), cert. denied, 334 Md. 211, 638 A.2d 753 (1994).

CHAPTER 200. CONTEMPT.

Rule 15-201. Applicability.

This Chapter applies to both civil and criminal contempts. It does not supersede or modify Code, Labor and Employment Article, § 4-322. (Amended Dec. 10, 1996, effective Jan. 1, 1997.)

Cross references. — As to the distinctions between civil and criminal contempt, see *State v. Roll and Scholl*, 267 Md. 714 (1973) and *Lynch v. Lynch*, 342 Md. 509 (1996).

Source. — This Rule is derived from former Rule P2 a and c.

Effect of amendments. — The 1996 amendment rewrote the cross reference.

University of Baltimore Law Review. — For comment, "A Pragmatic Look at Criminal Contempt and the Trial Attorney," see 12 U. Balt. L. Rev. 100 (1982).

The line of distinction between civil and criminal contempt is often indistinct. Often the same acts or omissions may constitute both or at least embrace aspects of each. State v. Roll, 267 Md. 714, 298 A.2d 867 (1973).

In this State, the distinction between the two types of contempt has been preserved and is important. State v. Roll, 267 Md. 714, 298 A.2d 867 (1973).

The form of punishment does not determine the nature of the contempt proceedings, but rather, from the nature of the proceedings flows the manner of punishment. Hare v. Hare, 21 Md. App. 71, 318 A.2d 234 (1974).

When contempt is civil or criminal. — If the punishment is coercive and the contemnors carry "the keys of their prison in their own pockets," it is civil, but if the sanction is to punish, it is criminal. State v. Roll, 267 Md. 714, 298 A.2d 867 (1973).

In this State, the nature of the contempt proceeding is determined before the time for imposing punishment is reached. State v. Roll, 267 Md. 714, 298 A.2d 867 (1973).

If any part of the contempt sentence is punishment, the contempt must be classified as a criminal one. Roll v. State, 15 Md. App. 31, 288 A.2d 605 (1972), modified and aff'd, 267 Md. 714, 298 A.2d 867 (1973).

Sentences in criminal and civil contempt distinguished. — The sentence in a criminal contempt is a determinate one while in a civil contempt the contemnor carries the keys to the prison in his pocket, that is, compliance with the courts' command effects his release. Roll v. State, 15 Md. App. 31, 288 A.2d 605 (1972), modified and aff'd, 267 Md. 714, 298 A.2d 867 (1973).

If it is a civil contempt the sanction is coercive and must allow for purging, but if it is criminal, it is punitive and must be determinate. State v. Roll, 267 Md. 714, 298 A.2d 867 (1973); Hare v. Hare, 21 Md. App. 71, 318 A.2d 234 (1974).

The penalty imposed in a criminal contempt is punishment for past misconduct which may not necessarily be capable of remedy. Therefore, such a penalty does not require a purging provision but may be purely punitive. State v. Roll, 267 Md. 714, 298 A.2d 867 (1973); Jones v. Wright, 35 Md. App. 313, 370 A.2d 1144 (1977).

A penalty in a civil contempt must provide for purging. State v. Roll, 267 Md. 714, 298 A.2d 867 (1973); Jones v. Wright, 35 Md. App. 313, 370 A.2d 1144 (1977).

When civil contempt indicated. — The five factors which generally point to a civil contempt are: (1) the complainant is usually a private person as opposed to the State; (2) the contempt proceeding is entitled in the original action and filed as a continuation thereof as opposed to a separate and independent action; (3) holding the defendant in contempt affords relief to a private party; (4) the relief requested is primarily for the benefit of the complainant; (5) the acts complained of do not of themselves constitute crimes or conduct by the defendant so willful or contumelious that the court is impelled to act on its own motion. State v. Roll, 267 Md. 714, 298 A.2d 867 (1973); Hare v. Hare, 21 Md. App. 71, 318 A.2d 234 (1974).

A civil contempt proceeding is intended to preserve and enforce the rights of private parties to a suit and to compel obedience to orders and decrees primarily made to benefit such parties. These proceedings are generally remedial in nature and are intended to coerce future compliance. State v. Roll, 267 Md. 714, 298 A.2d 867 (1973).

Proof required. — The degree of proof required to establish a civil contempt need be only by a preponderance of the evidence. State v. Roll, 267 Md. 714, 298 A.2d 867 (1973).

A criminal contempt must be shown beyond a reasonable doubt. State v. Roll, 267 Md. 714, 298 A.2d 867 (1973).

Maryland Rule 4-215 applies to civil contempt proceedings. Jones v. Johnson, 73 Md. App. 663, 536 A.2d 116 (1988).

If grand jury witnesses with immunity refused to testify and their refusals were contemptuous, their acts would be criminal contempts. State v. Roll, 267 Md. 714, 298 A.2d 867 (1973).

Criminal contemnor not entitled to grand jury indictment or jury trial. — A contemnor in a criminal contempt proceeding in Maryland is not entitled to indictment by a grand jury and may not have a right to a jury trial. State v. Roll, 267 Md. 714, 298 A.2d 867 (1973).

When civil contempt proceeding can terminate as criminal contempt. — Situations may arise where at a hearing held pursuant to an order to show cause in what properly began as a civil contempt, facts are presented which indicate that the alleged contemnor cannot comply with the order of the court that directed him to perform an act for the benefit and advantage of another party to the suit. If this inability to comply was caused by a deliberate effort or a wilful act of commission or omission by the alleged contemnor committed with the knowledge that it would frustrate the order of the court, the civil contempt proceeding should be terminated, and new proceedings may be instituted which can result in a finding of criminal contempt. State v. Roll, 267 Md. 714, 298 A.2d 867 (1973).

Cited in Aronson v. Aronson, 115 Md. App. 78, 691 A.2d 785 (1997), cert. denied, 346 Md. 371, 697 A.2d 111 (1997).

Rule 15-202. Definitions.

(a) *Constructive contempt.* "Constructive contempt" means any contempt other than a direct contempt.

(b) *Direct contempt.* "Direct contempt" means a contempt committed in the presence of the judge presiding in court or so near to the judge as to interrupt the court's proceedings.

Source. — This Rule is derived from former Rule P1.

University of Baltimore Law Review. — For article "New Balance in the Rights of Creditors and Debtors: The Effect on Maryland Law," see 2 U. Balt. L. Rev. 236 (1973).

For discussion of child abduction by a relative and Maryland's misdemeanor offense to deter parental child stealing, see 8 U. Balt. L. Rev. 609 (1979).

For comment, "A Pragmatic Look at Criminal Contempt and the Trial Attorney," see 12 U. Balt. L. Rev. 100 (1982).

The purpose of the contempt power is to provide a means for a judge to uphold the dignity of the judicial process. This dignity is upheld in two related but distinct ways: first, by imposing punishment a judge makes a statement that what was done was improper and discourages others from engaging in similar acts; and second, the act of imposing punishment serves the purpose of maintaining control of the proceedings in the person of the judge. Johnson v. State, 100 Md. App. 553, 642 A.2d 259 (1994).

Classifications of contempts. — A contempt may be direct and civil, or direct and criminal, or constructive and civil, or constructive and criminal. Pearson v. State, 28 Md. App. 464, 347 A.2d 239 (1975).

Under what classification a contempt falls may be of the utmost importance, and the proper classification is often hard to come by. Pearson v. State, 28 Md. App. 464, 347 A.2d 239 (1975).

The two types of contempts, direct contempt and constructive contempt, may be further classified as civil or criminal; a civil contempt serves a remedial purpose, while a criminal contempt serves a punitive purpose. Johnson v. State, 100 Md. App. 553, 642 A.2d 259 (1994).

Contumacious intent. — In order to find someone guilty of a direct, criminal contempt, the behavior must be contemptuous on its face or it must be shown that the person possessed contumacious intent. Cameron v. State, 102 Md. App. 600, 650 A.2d 1376 (1994).

Direct contempts may be summarily punished. State v. Roll, 267 Md. 714, 298 A.2d 867 (1973).

Conduct need not halt proceedings to constitute direct contempt. — In order to constitute direct contempt, it is not necessary that the conduct bring the proceedings in progress to a halt. Mitchell v. State, 320 Md. 756, 580 A.2d 196 (1990).

Occurrence of conduct in the course of judicial proceedings. — Where defendant directed gesture with middle finger at judge following sentencing and as he was being led out of the courtroom, conduct occurred in the course of judicial proceedings as judge was still on the bench and court remained in session. Mitchell v. State, 320 Md. 756, 580 A.2d 196 (1990).

Party cannot be held in criminal contempt, absent contemptuous behavior or a contumacious intent, merely for appearing in court in an intoxicated condition. Cameron v. State, 102 Md. App. 600, 650 A.2d 1376 (1994).

Before a party may be held in contempt of a court order, the order must be sufficiently definite, certain, and specific in its terms so that the party may understand precisely what conduct the order requires. Droney v. Droney, 102 Md. App. 672, 651 A.2d 415 (1995).

Failure of attorney to make appearance not direct criminal contempt. — Defendant's nonappearance in the circuit court when her case was called was not direct criminal contempt. Jones v. State, 61 Md. App. 94, 484 A.2d 1050 (1984).

Procedure explicit. — Once the initial decision is made as to whether to proceed as a direct or constructive contempt, the procedures to be followed are explicit. State v. Roll, 267 Md. 714, 298 A.2d 867 (1973).

Power not to be abused. — The power to immediately and summarily hold a person in contempt is awesome and abuses of it must be guarded against. State v. Roll, 267 Md. 714, 298 A.2d 867 (1973).

A summary contempt proceeding is only proper in cases where the action of the alleged contemnor poses an open, serious threat to orderly procedure that instant, and summary punishment, as distinguished from due and deliberate procedures, is necessary. State v. Roll, 267 Md. 714, 298 A.2d 867 (1973).

Summary punishment for direct contempt only. — Only a direct contempt may be punished summarily; if the contempt is constructive, the court must give the accused an opportunity to challenge the alleged basis for the contempt and show cause why a contempt order should not be entered. Betz v. State, 99 Md. App. 60, 635 A.2d 77 (1994).

Direct contempt procedures are designed to fill the need for immediate vindication of the dignity of the court. State v. Roll, 267 Md. 714, 298 A.2d 867 (1973).

Witness' refusal to answer in course of trial is direct contempt. — A witness commits a direct contempt when he refuses to answer a question when ordered to do so in the course of a trial. Roll v. State, 15 Md. App. 31, 288 A.2d 605 (1972), modified and aff'd, 267

Md. 714, 298 A.2d 867 (1973).

Reaction to sentence of incarceration. — When imposing a sentence, a sentencing judge must be sensitive to the fact that a sentence of incarceration is a ruling that may visit a most dramatic impact upon the emotions of a person who has just been deprived of his or her freedom; in certain situations, if a person believes the sentence to be unfair, it is quite possible that a flash of displeasure could be communicated in a manner that is contemptuous, and while such an outburst cannot be condoned, a judge needs to be sensitive to the reality that the language of the street is not the language of the courtroom. Johnson v. State, 100 Md. App. 553, 642 A.2d 259 (1994).

A refusal to testify before the grand jury is not in the "presence" of the lower court within the contemplation of the definition in former Rule P1, nor may it be deemed in any way as interrupting the lower court's proceedings. Roll v. State, 15 Md. App. 31, 288 A.2d 605 (1972), modified and aff'd, 267 Md. 714, 298 A.2d 867 (1973).

Procedure where witness refuses to testify before grand jury. — It is a customary procedure in Maryland that upon refusal of a witness to testify before the grand jury, the entire grand jury and the witness appear before the court. The court orders the witness to testify. The grand jury, to observe the requirements of secrecy, then retire with the witness. If he is adamant in his refusal to testify the entire grand jury and the witness again go before the court and the jury inform the court what occurred. The court may then cite the witness for contempt. Roll v. State, 15 Md. App. 31, 288 A.2d 605 (1972), modified and aff'd, 267 Md. 714, 298 A.2d 867 (1973).

Contemnor is entitled to trial by jury where sentence is six months or more. — In criminal contempts, both direct and constructive, where the sentence imposed is not petty, that is, the sentence imposed is six months or more, the alleged contemnor is entitled to a trial by jury, thus restricting, in the case of direct criminal contempts, the power of the court to inflict punishment summarily. Roll v. State, 15 Md. App. 31, 288 A.2d 605 (1972), modified and aff'd, 267 Md. 714, 298 A.2d 867 (1973).

Judicial review. — Decision of whether to hold a party in contempt is vested in the trial court; the reviewing court will only reverse such a decision upon a showing that a finding of fact upon which the contempt was imposed was clearly erroneous or that the court abused its discretion in finding particular behavior to be contemptuous. Droney v. Droney, 102 Md. App. 672, 651 A.2d 415 (1995).

Rule 15-203. Direct civil and criminal contempt.

(a) *Summary imposition of sanctions.* The court against which a direct civil or criminal contempt has been committed may impose sanctions on the person who committed it summarily if (1) the presiding judge has personally seen, heard, or otherwise directly perceived the conduct constituting the contempt and has personal knowledge of the identity of the person committing it, and (2) the contempt has interrupted the order of the court and interfered with the dignified conduct of the court's business. The court shall afford the alleged contemnor an opportunity, consistent with the circumstances then existing, to present exculpatory or mitigating information. If the court summarily finds and announces on the record that direct contempt has been committed, the court may defer imposition of sanctions until the conclusion of the proceeding during which the contempt was committed.

Cross references. — As to possible constitutional limitations on summary imposition of sanctions, including the right to jury trial and the right to counsel, see *Codispoti v. Pennsylvania*, 418 U.S. 506 (1974); *Bloom v. Illinois*, 391 U.S. 194, 202 (1968); *Cheff v. Schnackenberg*, 384 U.S. 373 (1966); *Kawamura v. State*, 299 Md. 276, 292 (1984); *Wilkins v. State*, 293 Md. 335 (1982); *Dorsey v. State*, 56 Md. App. 54 (1983).

Committee note. — Sanctions may be imposed immediately upon the finding of the contempt, or, in the court's discretion, may be deferred to a later time in the proceeding. Deferral of a sanction does not affect its summary nature. The sanction remains summary in nature in that no hearing is required; the court simply announces and imposes the sanction.

(b) *Order of contempt.* Either before sanctions are imposed or promptly thereafter, the court shall issue a written order stating that a direct contempt has been committed and specifying:

(1) whether the contempt is civil or criminal,

(2) the evidentiary facts known to the court from the judge's own personal knowledge as to the conduct constituting the contempt, and as to any relevant evidentiary facts not so known, the basis of the court's findings,

(3) the sanction imposed for the contempt,

(4) in the case of civil contempt, how the contempt may be purged, and

(5) in the case of criminal contempt, (A) if the sanction is incarceration, a determinate term, and (B) any condition under which the sanction may be suspended, modified, revoked, or terminated.

(c) *Affidavits.* In a summary proceeding, affidavits may be offered for the record by the contemnor before or after sanctions have been imposed.

(d) *Record.* The record in cases of direct contempt in which sanctions have been summarily imposed shall consist of (1) the order of contempt; (2) if the proceeding during which the contempt occurred was recorded, a transcript of that part of the proceeding; and (3) any affidavits offered or evidence admitted in the proceeding. (Amended Dec. 10, 1996, effective Jan. 1, 1997.)

Source. — This Rule is derived from former Rule P3.

Effect of amendments. — The 1996 amendment, in (a), substituted "impose sanctions on" for "punish" near the beginning of the first sentence and substituted "sanctions" for "punishment" in the last sentence; substituted "sanction" for "penalty" and "punishment" throughout (b); substituted "contemnor before or after sanctions have" for "defendant before or after punishment has" in (c); substituted "in which sanctions have been summarily imposed" for "summarily punished" in (d); and made related changes in the cross reference and Committee note in (a).

University of Baltimore Law Review. — For comment, "A Pragmatic Look at Criminal Contempt and the Trial Attorney," see 12 U. Balt. L. Rev. 100 (1982).

The purpose of former Rule P3 was to enable the appellate court to determine, by an inspection of the record, whether a contempt has in fact been committed or whether the court had jurisdiction to punish it. Kandel v. State, 252 Md. 668, 250 A.2d 853 (1969); Jones v. State, 32 Md. App. 490, 362 A.2d 660 (1976).

Classification of contempt determines punishment. — Whether the defendant is subject to summary punishment or is entitled to an adversary hearing hinges on whether the contempt is classified as direct or constructive. Murphy v. State, 46 Md. App. 138, 416 A.2d 748 (1980).

By holding a party in direct contempt the court vindicates its authority and punishes the offender. A.V. Laurins & Co. v. Prince George's County, 46 Md. App. 548, 420 A.2d 982 (1980).

Accused's intent. — A criminal contempt, and thus the accused's intent, must be shown beyond a reasonable doubt; this becomes an important factor in examining when it is permissible for a court to treat a criminal contempt as a direct contempt that may be punished summarily. Betz v. State, 99 Md. App. 60, 635 A.2d 77 (1994).

One must look to the nature of the alleged contemptuous acts to determine whether they occurred in the presence of the court. Murphy v. State, 46 Md. App. 138, 416 A.2d 748 (1980).

A direct contempt occurs when the actions of the contemnor interrupt the order of the courtroom and interfere with the conduct of business. When such disruption occurs within the sensory perception of a presiding judge he will have a sufficient knowledge of the contemptuous act which tends to interrupt the proceedings and will not have to rely on other evidence to establish all the details, though some of them can be supplied by additional testimony. State v. Roll, 267 Md. 714, 298 A.2d 867 (1973); Murphy v. State, 46 Md. App. 138, 416 A.2d 748 (1980); Dorsey v. State, 295 Md. 217, 454 A.2d 353 (1983).

Individual retorts during single episode. — A trial judge could not order contempt convictions for each venomous retort hurled at him by the defendant during a single heated exchange. Johnson v. State, 100 Md. App. 553, 642 A.2d 259 (1994).

Determination whether refusal to testify is privileged required. — Because of the critical role which the right against compulsory self-incrimination plays in the legal system, a trial judge, before finding a witness in contempt, must ascertain, by inquiry when necessary, whether a refusal to testify is privileged. Kober v. State, 41 Md. App. 174, 395 A.2d 1228 (1979).

Where there had been no inquiry by the trial judge as to whether appellant's refusal to testify was privileged under his constitutional right against compulsory self-incrimination, there was no basis for a finding of contempt. Kober v. State, 41 Md. App. 174, 395 A.2d 1228 (1979).

Direct contempt not authorized where judge does not have personal knowledge of facts. — When the judge does not have personal knowledge of the facts and must learn of them totally from others, direct contempt proceedings are not authorized. State v. Roll, 267 Md. 714, 298 A.2d 867 (1973); Dorsey v. State, 295 Md. 217, 454 A.2d 353 (1983).

Proper to proceed under former Rule P4 where proof of contemptuous act not within knowledge of trial judge. — Although defendants were cited for direct contempt in violation of former Rule P3, where the proof was not within the knowledge of the trial judge, it was proper to proceed under the procedural requirements of former Rule P4. Dorsey v. State, 295 Md. 217, 454 A.2d 353 (1983).

An attorney's failure to attend court at the time appointed when he has a duty or obligation to be present may amount to, and be punishable as, contempt. Kandel v. State, 252 Md. 668, 250 A.2d 853 (1969).

Failure to appear in court in violation of an oral order is contemptuous on its face. Kandel v. State, 252 Md. 668, 250 A.2d 853 (1969).

Unjustified failure of an attorney to appear in court on time is at least misbehavior on the part of an officer of the court. Kandel v. State, 252 Md. 668, 250 A.2d 853 (1969); Murphy v. State, 46 Md. App. 138, 416 A.2d 748 (1980).

An attorney's unjustified failure to appear or to give reasonable notice thereof is a contempt committed in the presence of the court and, therefore, punishable summarily under this Rule. Murphy v. State, 46 Md. App. 138, 416 A.2d 748 (1980).

Lateness of attorney. — Since lateness of an attorney is misbehavior of an officer of the court, the guilty one may be punished summarily. Kandel v. State, 252 Md. 668, 250 A.2d 853 (1969).

Contempt procedures may be initiated because of a party's absence from court and must reveal sufficient evidence showing the party's requisite willful disobedience or deliberate disruption. A.V. Laurins & Co. v. Prince George's County, 46 Md. App. 548, 420 A.2d 982 (1980).

Direct contempt by juvenile. — Courts Article, § 3-804 (a), conferring exclusive original jurisdiction over a juvenile, is inapplicable to a case of direct contempt committed in another court and the court in which the contempt occurs possesses full power to deal with the contemptuous juvenile in the same manner as it would any adult person who had committed a similar offense. Thomas v. State, 21 Md. App. 572, 320 A.2d 538, cert. denied, 272 Md. 749 (1974).

Appeal from denial of motion to quash subpoena did not preclude issuance of contempt order against the custodian of certain dental records. In re Special Investigation No. 281, 299 Md. 181, 473 A.2d 1 (1984).

Written findings and court order are mandatory. — The requirements in former Rule P3, of written findings by the court, were mandatory. Thomas v. State, 99 Md. App. 47, 635 A.2d 71 (1994).

Where there were neither findings setting forth the basis for the contempt judgement nor a written order signed by the judge and entered in the record, judgment of contempt had to be reversed. Thomas v. State, 99 Md. App. 47, 635 A.2d 71 (1994).

Requirement of section b of former Rule P3 is more than mere formality. — The requirement that a summary order of contempt shall recite the facts is more than a formality. It is essential to disclosure of the basis of decision with sufficient particularity to permit an informed appellate review. Robinson v. State, 19 Md. App. 20, 308 A.2d 712 (1973).

The requirement of former section b is as much directed toward providing meaningful appellate review of a contempt conviction as it is aimed at assuring procedural protection for the defendant. Jones v. State, 32 Md. App. 490, 362 A.2d 660 (1976).

Summary contempt procedures where conduct directed at judge. — Trial judge was not precluded from using summary contempt procedures when the nature of the contempt was conduct directed toward him. Mitchell v. State, 320 Md. 756, 580 A.2d 196 (1990).

The purpose of the recitation of facts under section b of former Rule P3 is not to provide the reviewing court an opportunity to reevaluate and weigh the evidence, but to provide a basis for an assessment of its legal

sufficiency. Jones v. State, 32 Md. App. 490, 362 A.2d 660 (1976).

The purpose of the rule's requirement of written findings is to enable the appellate court to determine whether a direct, criminal contempt has been committed and whether the court had jurisdiction to punish it. Thomas v. State, 99 Md. App. 47, 635 A.2d 71 (1994).

No man should be deprived of his liberty on the basis of judicial ipse dixits alone. To hold otherwise would be to ignore the language and clear purpose of former Rule P3 and flaunt due process. Robinson v. State, 19 Md. App. 20, 308 A.2d 712 (1973); Jones v. State, 32 Md. App. 490, 362 A.2d 660 (1976).

The specific facts constituting the contempt must be set out in the order; conclusionary language and general citations to the record will not suffice. Robinson v. State, 19 Md. App. 20, 308 A.2d 712 (1973).

Otherwise appellate review will be pro tanto circumscribed. — The trial courts should remember that to the extent a contempt order does not specify those facts, appellate review of a conviction for summary contempt will be pro tanto circumscribed. Robinson v. State, 19 Md. App. 20, 308 A.2d 712 (1973); Jones v. State, 32 Md. App. 490, 362 A.2d 660 (1976).

It is contempt of court for a person to disregard an order, made by a court having authority to make it, of which he has knowledge. Weaver v. State, 244 Md. 640, 224 A.2d 684 (1966).

And the subtle defeat of an order of court is a contempt. Weaver v. State, 244 Md. 640, 224 A.2d 684 (1966).

That failure to comply with a judicial command was based on advice of counsel is generally held to be no justification. Weaver v. State, 244 Md. 640, 224 A.2d 684 (1966).

Contempt based on motion for disqualification of judge. — Where appellant made a good faith motion for disqualification, the manner of delivery was not improper, and the language was not sufficient to constitute an "imminent threat to the administration of justice," contempt conviction could not withstand constitutional scrutiny. Cohen v. State, 19 Md. App. 85, 309 A.2d 294 (1973).

Person who voluntarily absents himself after his trial has commenced commits a constructive contempt. Pearson v. State, 28 Md. App. 464, 347 A.2d 239 (1975).

Proof in a direct contempt case must be shown beyond a reasonable doubt. Robinson v. State, 19 Md. App. 20, 308 A.2d 712 (1973); A.V. Laurins & Co. v. Prince George's County, 46 Md. App. 548, 420 A.2d 982 (1980).

Where a chancellor has stated conclusions as proof of a direct contempt but has not specified the facts which allegedly gave rise to

217

contempt within the presence of the court, the reasonable doubt standard has not been met. A.V. Laurins & Co. v. Prince George's County, 46 Md. App. 548, 420 A.2d 982 (1980).

Opportunity for allocution before sentencing. — Where defendant was held in direct contempt for gesture directed at judge following sentencing and was immediately recalled to be sentenced for contempt, trial judge should have afforded defendant at least a brief opportunity for allocution before imposing sentence. Mitchell v. State, 320 Md. 756, 580 A.2d 196 (1990).

Due process does not require that an alleged contemnor must, in every instance, be given an opportunity to respond before an adjudication of direct criminal contempt is made in a summary proceeding. In some cases, affording a defendant an opportunity to speak in explanation of his conduct may only invite additional invective. Furthermore, where the conduct or speech is direct or unequivocal, there may be little or no room for helpful explanation. Mitchell v. State, 320 Md. 756, 580 A.2d 196 (1990).

Where the record clearly indicated that the case was one in which affording the defendant an opportunity to speak only invited additional invective, leaving little room for helpful explanation, this was not the sort of case in which the alleged contemnor had to be given an opportunity for allocution before imposition of sentence. Thomas v. State, 99 Md. App. 47, 635 A.2d 71 (1994).

Applied in Solomon v. Solomon, 118 Md. App. 96, 701 A.2d 1199 (1997).

Rule 15-204. Direct contempt if no summary imposition of sanctions.

In any proceeding involving a direct contempt for which the court determines not to impose sanctions summarily, the judge, reasonably promptly after the conduct, shall issue a written order specifying the evidentiary facts within the personal knowledge of the judge as to the conduct constituting the contempt and the identity of the contemnor. Thereafter, the proceeding shall be conducted pursuant to Rule 15-205 or Rule 15-206, whichever is applicable, and Rule 15-207 in the same manner as a constructive contempt. (Amended Dec. 10, 1996, effective Jan. 1, 1997.)

Source. — This Rule is new.

Effect of amendments. — The 1996 amendment, in the first sentence, substituted "for which" for "which" and substituted "impose sanctions" for "punish."

Rule 15-205. Constructive criminal contempt; commencement; prosecution.

(a) *Separate action.* A proceeding for constructive criminal contempt shall be docketed as a separate criminal action. It shall not be included in any action in which the alleged contempt occurred.

(b) *Who may institute.* (1) The court may initiate a proceeding for constructive criminal contempt by filing an order directing the issuance of a summons or warrant pursuant to Rule 4-212.

(2) The State's Attorney may initiate a proceeding for constructive criminal contempt committed against a trial court sitting within the county in which the State's Attorney holds office by filing a petition with that court.

(3) The Attorney General may initiate a proceeding for constructive criminal contempt committed (A) against the Court of Appeals or the Court of Special Appeals, or (B) against a trial court when the Attorney General is exercising the authority vested in the Attorney General by Maryland Constitution, Art. V, § 3, by filing a petition with the court against which the contempt was allegedly committed.

(4) The State Prosecutor may initiate a proceeding for constructive criminal contempt committed against a court when the State Prosecutor is exercising the authority vested in the State Prosecutor by Code, Article 10, § 33B, by filing a petition with the court against which the contempt was allegedly committed.

(5) The court or any person with actual knowledge of the facts constituting a constructive criminal contempt may request the State's Attorney, the Attorney General, or the State Prosecutor, as appropriate, to file a petition.

(c) *Appointment of prosecutor.* If the proceeding is commenced by a court on its own initiative, the court may appoint the State's Attorney of the county in which the court sits, the Attorney General, or the State Prosecutor to prosecute the charge.

(d) *Contents; service.* An order filed by the court pursuant to section (b)(1) of this Rule and a petition filed by the State's Attorney, the Attorney General, or the State Prosecutor shall contain the information required by Rule 4-202 (a). The order or petition shall be served, along with a summons or warrant, in the manner specified in Rule 4-212 or, if the proceeding is in the Court of Appeals or Court of Special Appeals, in the manner directed by that court.

(e) *Waiver of counsel.* The provisions of Rule 4-215 apply to constructive criminal contempt proceedings.

(f) *Jury trial.* The provisions of Rule 4-246 apply to constructive criminal contempt proceedings.

Source. — This Rule is new.

Editor's note. — Artticle 10, § 33B, referred to in section (b) (4), has been revised as §§ 9-1202 through 9-1210 of the State Government Article.

Rule 15-206. Constructive civil contempt.

(a) *Where filed.* A proceeding for constructive civil contempt shall be included in the action in which the alleged contempt occurred.

(b) *Who may initiate.* (1) The court may initiate a proceeding for constructive civil contempt by filing an order complying with the requirements of section (c) of this Rule.

(2) Any party to an action in which an alleged contempt occurred and, upon request by the court, the Attorney General, may initiate a proceeding for constructive civil contempt by filing a petition with the court against which the contempt was allegedly committed.

(3) In a support enforcement action where the alleged contempt is based on failure to pay spousal or child support, any agency authorized by law may bring the proceeding.

(c) *Content of order or petition.* (1) An order filed by the court pursuant to section (b) (1) of this Rule and a petition filed pursuant to section (b) (2) shall comply with Rule 2-303 and, if incarceration to compel compliance with the court's order is sought, shall so state.

(2) Unless the court finds that a petition for contempt is frivolous on its face, the court shall enter an order. That order, and any order entered by the court on its own initiative, shall state:

(A) the time within which any answer by the alleged contemnor shall be filed, which, absent good cause, may not be less than ten days after service of the order;

(B) the time and place at which the alleged contemnor shall appear in person for a hearing, allowing a reasonable time for the preparation of a defense; and

(C) if incarceration to compel compliance with the court's order is sought, a notice to the alleged contemnor in the following form:

TO THE PERSON ALLEGED TO BE IN CONTEMPT OF COURT:

1. It is alleged that you have disobeyed a court order, are in contempt of court, and should go to jail until you obey the court's order.

2. You have the right to have a lawyer. If you already have a lawyer, you should consult the lawyer at once. If you do not now have a lawyer, please note:

(a) A lawyer can be helpful to you by:

(1) explaining the allegations against you;

(2) helping you determine and present any defense to those allegations;

(3) explaining to you the possible outcomes; and

(4) helping you at the hearing.

(b) Even if you do not plan to contest that you are in contempt of court, a lawyer can be helpful.

(c) If you want a lawyer but do not have the money to hire one, the Public Defender may provide a lawyer for you. You must contact the Public Defender at least 10 business days before the date of the hearing. The court clerk will tell you how to contact the Public Defender.

(d) If you want a lawyer but you cannot get one and the Public Defender will not provide one for you, contact the court clerk as soon as possible.

(e) DO NOT WAIT UNTIL THE DATE OF YOUR HEARING TO GET A LAWYER. If you do not have a lawyer before the hearing date, the court may find that you have waived your right to a lawyer, and the hearing may be held with you unrepresented by a lawyer.

3. IF YOU DO NOT APPEAR FOR THE HEARING, YOU MAY BE SUBJECT TO ARREST.

(d) *Service of order.* The order, together with a copy of any petition and other document filed in support of the allegation of contempt, shall be served on the alleged contemnor pursuant to Rule 2-121 or 3-121 or, if the alleged contemnor has appeared as a party in the action in which the contempt is charged, in the manner prescribed by the court.

(e) *Waiver of counsel if incarceration is sought.* (1) Applicability. This section applies if incarceration to compel compliance is sought.

(2) Appearance in court without counsel. (A) If the alleged contemnor appears in court pursuant to the order without counsel, the court shall make certain that the alleged contemnor has received a copy of the order containing notice of the right to counsel;

(B) If the alleged contemnor indicates a desire to waive counsel, the court shall determine, after an examination of the alleged contemnor on the record, that the waiver is knowing and voluntary;

(C) If the alleged contemnor indicates a desire to have counsel and the court finds that the alleged contemnor received a copy of the order containing notice of the right to counsel, the court shall permit the alleged contemnor to explain the appearance without counsel. If the court finds that there is a meritorious reason for the alleged contemnor's appearance without counsel, the court shall continue the action to a later time and advise the alleged contemnor that if counsel does not enter an appearance by that time, the action will proceed with the alleged contemnor unrepresented by counsel. If the court finds that there is no meritorious reason for the alleged contemnor's appearance without counsel, the court may determine that the alleged contemnor has waived counsel by failing or refusing to obtain counsel and may proceed with the hearing.

(3) Discharge of counsel. If an alleged contemnor requests permission to discharge an attorney whose appearance has been entered, the court shall permit the alleged contemnor to explain the reasons for the request. If the court finds that there is a meritorious reason for the alleged contemnor's request, the court shall permit the discharge of counsel, continue the action if necessary, and advise the alleged contemnor that if new counsel does not enter an appearance by the next scheduled hearing date, the action will be heard with the alleged contemnor unrepresented by counsel. If the court finds that the alleged contemnor received a copy of the order containing notice of the right to counsel and that there is no meritorious reason for the alleged contemnor's request, the court may permit the discharge of counsel but shall first inform the alleged contemnor that the hearing will proceed as scheduled with the alleged contemnor unrepresented by counsel. (Amended Dec. 10, 1996, effective Jan. 1, 1997.)

Source. — This Rule is new.

Effect of amendments. — The 1996 amendment substituted "alleged contemnor" for "defendant" and substituted "alleged contemnor's" for "defendant's" throughout the Rule; in (b) (3), substituted "may bring" for "to bring"; and substituted "an alleged contemnor" for "a defendant" in (e) (3).

Applied in Solomon v. Solomon, 118 Md. App. 96, 701 A.2d 1199 (1997).

Rule 15-207. Constructive contempt; further proceedings.

(a) *Consolidation of criminal and civil contempts.* If a person has been charged with both constructive criminal contempt pursuant to Rule 15-205 and constructive civil contempt pursuant to Rule 15-206, the court may consolidate the proceedings for hearing and disposition.

(b) *When judge disqualified.* A judge who enters an order pursuant to Rule 15-204 or who institutes a constructive contempt proceeding on the court's own initiative pursuant to Rule 15-205 (b) (1) or Rule 15-206 (b) (1) and who reasonably expects to be called as a witness at any hearing on the matter is disqualified from sitting at the hearing unless (1) the alleged contemnor consents, or (2) the alleged contempt consists of a failure to obey a prior order or judgment in a civil action or an "order of restitution" as defined in Code, Article 27, § 640 (a) (9).

(c) *Hearing.* (1) Contempt of appellate court. Where the alleged contemnor is charged with contempt of an appellate court, that court, in lieu of conducting the hearing itself, may designate a trial judge as a special master to take evidence and make recommended findings of fact and conclusions of law, subject to exception by any party and approval of the appellate court.

(2) Failure of alleged contemnor to appear. If the alleged contemnor fails to appear personally at the time and place set by the court, the court may enter an order directing a sheriff or other peace officer to take custody of and bring the alleged contemnor before the court or judge designated in the order. If the alleged contemnor in a civil contempt proceeding fails to appear in person or by counsel at the time and place set by the court, the court may proceed ex parte.

(d) *Disposition — Generally.* (1) Applicability. This section applies to all proceedings for contempt other than proceedings for constructive civil contempt based on an alleged failure to pay spousal or child support.

(2) Order. When a court or jury makes a finding of contempt, the court shall issue a written order that specifies the sanction imposed for the contempt. In the case of a civil contempt, the order shall specify how the contempt may be purged. In the case of a criminal contempt, if the sanction is incarceration, the order shall specify a determinate term and any condition under which the sanction may be suspended, modified, revoked, or terminated.

(e) *Constructive civil contempt — Support enforcement action.* (1) Applicability. This section applies to proceedings for constructive civil contempt based on an alleged failure to pay spousal or child support, including an award of emergency family maintenance under Code, Family Law Article, Title 4, Subtitle 5.

(2) Petitioner's burden of proof. Subject to subsection (3) of this section, the court may make a finding of contempt if the petitioner proves by clear and convincing evidence that the alleged contemnor has not paid the amount owed, accounting from the effective date of the support order through the date of the contempt hearing.

(3) When a finding of contempt may not be made. The court may not make a finding of contempt if the alleged contemnor proves by a preponderance of the evidence that (A) from the date of the support order through the date of the contempt hearing the alleged contemnor (i) never had the ability to pay more than the amount actually paid and (ii) made reasonable efforts to become or remain employed or otherwise lawfully obtain the funds necessary to make payment, or (B) enforcement by contempt is barred by limitations as to each unpaid spousal or child support payment for which the alleged contemnor does not make the proof set forth in subsection (3)(A) of this section.

Cross references. — Code, Family Law Article, § 10-102.

(4) Order. Upon a finding of constructive civil contempt for failure to pay spousal or child support, the court shall issue a written order that specifies (A) the amount of the arrearage for which enforcement by contempt is not barred by limitations, (B) any sanction imposed for the contempt, and (C) how the contempt may be purged. If the contemnor does not have the present ability to purge the contempt, the order may include directions that the contemnor make specified payments on the arrearage at future times and perform specified acts to enable the contemnor to comply with the direction to make payments. (Amended Dec. 10, 1996, effective Jan. 1, 1997.)

Committee note. — Section (e) modifies the holding in *Lynch v. Lynch*, 342 Md. 509 (1996), by allowing a court to make a finding of constructive civil contempt in a support enforcement action even if the alleged contemnor does not have the present ability to purge. In support enforcement cases, as in other civil contempt cases, after making a finding of contempt, the court may specify imprisonment as the sanction if the contemnor has the present ability to purge the contempt.

If the contemnor does not have the present ability to purge the contempt, an example of a direction to perform specified acts that a court may include in an order under subsection (e) (4) is a provision that an unemployed, able-bodied contemnor look for work and periodically provide evidence of the efforts made. If the contemnor fails, without just cause, to comply with any provision of the order, a criminal contempt proceeding may be brought based on a violation of that provision.

Source. — This Rule is derived in part from former Rule P4 c and d 2 and is in part new.

Effect of amendments. — The 1996 amendment rewrote the Rule.

Editor's note. — Article 27, § 640, which is referred to in section (b), has been transferred to be Article 27, § 887.

University of Baltimore Law Review. — For discussion of child abduction by a relative and Maryland's misdemeanor offense to deter parental child stealing, see 8 U. Balt. L. Rev. 609 (1979).

For comment, "A Pragmatic Look at Criminal Contempt and the Trial Attorney," see 12 U. Balt. L. Rev. 100 (1982).

Basic requirements of "due process" declared by former Rule P4. — Former Rule P4 is declaratory of the basic requirements of due process of law in the prosecution of constructive contempts. Reamer v. Reamer, 246 Md. 532, 229 A.2d 74 (1967).

The provisions of former Rule P4 are declaratory of the basic requirements of due process of law in the prosecution of constructive contempts. Savage v. State, 19 Md. App. 1, 308 A.2d 701 (1973).

Classification of contempt determines punishment. — Whether the defendant is subject to summary punishment or is entitled to an adversary hearing hinges on whether the contempt is classified as direct or constructive. Murphy v. State, 46 Md. App. 138, 416 A.2d 748 (1980).

It is the act itself which determines whether a contempt is constructive. Murphy v. State, 46 Md. App. 138, 416 A.2d 748 (1980).

Summary punishment for direct contempt only. — Only a direct contempt may be punished summarily; if the contempt is constructive, the court must give the accused an opportunity to challenge the alleged basis for the contempt and show cause why a contempt order should not be entered. Betz v. State, 99 Md. App. 60, 635 A.2d 77 (1994).

Constructive contempts may not be summarily punished by the court. As they are contempts which are not committed in the presence of the court, or so near as to interrupt its proceedings, the court would not be a personal observer of the facts. Roll v. State, 15 Md. App. 31, 288 A.2d 605 (1972), modified and aff'd, 267 Md. 714, 298 A.2d 867 (1973).

There is no need for summarily disposing of an alleged contempt when the behavior of the accused is not personally known to the judge or does not occur so near to the court as to interrupt proceedings then being conducted by the judge. State v. Roll, 267 Md. 714, 298 A.2d 867 (1973).

Attachment of defendant. — Former Rule P4, setting forth the steps to be followed in constructive contempt proceedings, is silent on the question of whether the defendant may be subject to attachment to answer the alleged contempt. The Court of Appeals assumed without deciding that attachment was permissible where the court had reason to believe the defendant might conceal himself or flee the State to avoid personal service in the contempt proceeding. Reamer v. Reamer, 246 Md. 532, 229 A.2d 74 (1967).

Person who has allegedly violated an order of court is entitled to: (1) formal notice of the precise violation alleged, (2) an opportunity to be heard on the merits of that issue, and (3) the right to counsel if confinement is the sanction to be imposed for the violation. Reed v. Foley, 105 Md. App. 184, 659 A.2d 325 (1995).

Person who voluntarily absents himself after his trial has commenced commits a constructive contempt. Pearson v. State, 28 Md. App. 464, 347 A.2d 239 (1975).

Proper to proceed under former Rule P4 where proof of contemptuous act not within knowledge of trial judge. — Although defendants were cited for direct contempt in violation of former Rule P3, where the proof was not within the knowledge of the trial judge it was proper to proceed under the procedural requirements of former Rule P4. Dorsey v. State, 295 Md. 217, 454 A.2d 353 (1983).

Unexplained absence is not a contempt committed in the actual presence of the court. A.V. Laurins & Co. v. Prince George's County, 46 Md. App. 548, 420 A.2d 982 (1980).

Show cause order delivered in court complied with former Rule P4. — Delivery of unsigned copy of show cause order to defendant in open court as directed by judge complied with former Rule P4. Dorsey v. State, 56 Md. App. 54, 466 A.2d 546 (1983).

Contemnor failed to establish her inability to purge her contempt for failure to pay child support, where she presented a bare affidavit which did not indicate her income from her present employment or how long she had been working, and where counter evidence was presented and the trial court found she voluntarily impoverished herself. Schwartz v. Wagner, 116 Md. App. 720, 698 A.2d 1222 (1997).

Juveniles. — It was abuse of discretion to find juvenile guilty of criminal contempt for violation of court order to attend school without considering available alternatives which would have afforded the guidance, treatment or rehabilitation contemplated by CJ § 3-801 et seq. In re Ann M., 309 Md. 564, 525 A.2d 1054 (1987).

Quoted in Ott v. Frederick County Dep't of Social Servs., 345 Md. 682, 694 A.2d 101 (1997).

Rule 15-208. Bail.

A contemnor committed for contempt is entitled to the same consideration with respect to bail pending appeal as a defendant convicted in a criminal proceeding. (Amended Dec. 10, 1996, effective Jan. 1, 1997.)

Cross references. — Rule 4-348.

Source. — This Rule is derived from former Rule P5.

Effect of amendments. — The 1996 amendment substituted "contemnor" for "defendant."

University of Baltimore Law Review. —

For comment, "A Pragmatic Look at Criminal Contempt and the Trial Attorney," see 12 U. Balt. L. Rev. 100 (1982).

CHAPTER 300. HABEAS CORPUS.

Rule 15-301. Habeas corpus — Applicability.

The rules in this Chapter apply to all habeas corpus proceedings challenging the legality of the confinement or restraint of an individual.

Source. — This Rule is new.

Rule 15-302. Petition.

(a) *Generally.* A petition for a writ of habeas corpus shall be supported by affidavit of the petitioner and shall include:

(1) a statement that the individual by or on behalf of whom the writ is sought is unlawfully confined or restrained;

(2) the place where the individual is confined or restrained, if known;

(3) the name and any official capacity of the person by whom the individual is confined or restrained or, if not known, a description sufficient to enable that person to be identified;

(4) the circumstances and the cause of the confinement; and

(5) if the confinement is pursuant to a judgment or order of a court, the name of the court, the date of the judgment or order, and the case number, if known.

(b) *Certain confinements.* If a petition is filed by or on behalf of an individual confined as a result of a sentence for a criminal offense, of an order in a juvenile proceeding, or of a judgment of contempt of court, the petition, in addition to complying with the provisions of section (a) of this Rule, shall state, to the best of the petitioner's knowledge, information, and belief:

(1) whether any previous petition for habeas corpus or other post conviction relief has been filed with respect to the confinement;

(2) with respect to each previous petition for habeas corpus or other post conviction relief: (A) the court or judge to whom the petition was directed, (B) all grounds of the petition, (C) the determination made on the petition, (D) whether any appeal or application for leave to appeal was filed from any order on the petition, and (E) any determination made on the appeal or application for leave to appeal; and

(3) all grounds for the issuance of the writ that were not asserted in any previous petition for habeas corpus or other post conviction relief.

Cross references. — Code, Courts Art., § 3-702 (a).

Source. — This Rule is derived from former Rule Z42.

Writ should issue where application conforms with former Rule Z42. — Where an application for the issuance of a writ was in conformance with former Rule Z42, the judge should have issued the writ, and, upon production of the applicant inquired into the legality and propriety of the confinement. Washburn v. Sheriff, Cecil County, 16 Md. App. 611, 298 A.2d 462 (1973).

Only custodian need be named in petition. — There is no provision in the Maryland Rules explicitly requiring the habeas corpus petitioner to name the person by whom he or she is confined as the respondent; the rules only require that the petitioner's custodian be named in the petition. Nnoli v. Nnoli, 101 Md. App. 243, 646 A.2d 1021 (1994).

Rule 15-303. Procedure on petition.

(a) *Generally.* Upon receiving a petition for a writ of habeas corpus, the judge immediately shall refer it as provided in section (c) of this Rule or act on the petition as provided in section (d) or (e) of this Rule, except that if the petition seeks a writ of habeas corpus for the purpose of determining admission to bail or the appropriateness of any bail set, the judge may proceed in accordance with section (b) of this Rule.

(b) *Bail.* (1) Pretrial. If a petition by or on behalf of an individual who is confined prior to or during trial seeks a writ of habeas corpus for the purpose of determining admission to bail or the appropriateness of any bail set, the judge to whom the petition is directed may deny the petition without a hearing if a judge has previously determined the individual's eligibility for pretrial release or the conditions for such release pursuant to Rule 4-216 and the petition raises no grounds sufficient to warrant issuance of the writ other than grounds that were or could have been raised when the earlier pretrial release determination was made.

Cross references. — Rule 4-213 (c).

(2) After conviction. (A) Except as otherwise provided in subsection (2)(B) of this section, if a petition by or on behalf of an individual confined as a result of a conviction pending sentencing or exhaustion of appellate review seeks a writ of habeas corpus for the purpose of determining admission to bail or the appropriateness of any bail set, the judge to whom the petition is directed may deny the writ and order that the petition be treated as a motion for release or for amendment of an order of release pursuant to Rule 4-349. Upon entry of the order, the judge shall transmit the petition, a certified copy of the order, and any other pertinent papers to the trial judge who presided at the proceeding as a result of which the individual was confined. Upon receiving of the transmittal, the trial judge shall proceed in accordance with Rule 4-349.

(B) A circuit court judge to whom a petition for a writ of habeas corpus is directed shall not enter an order under subsection (2) (A) of this section if the petition is by or on behalf of an individual confined as a result of a conviction in the District Court that has been appealed to a circuit court.

(c) *Referral.* If the petition is made by or on behalf of an individual confined or restrained as the result of a prior judicial proceeding, a judge to whom the petition has been made may refer the petition, without taking other action, to the administrative judge of the court in which the prior proceeding was held. In exercising the discretion to refer the petition, the judge to whom the petition has been directed shall consider the interests and convenience of the parties and the State. Upon receiving the referral, the administrative judge shall assign the petition to a judge in accordance with the assignment procedures of that court, except that, without the written consent of the individual confined or restrained, the petition shall not be assigned to any judge who sat at the proceeding as a result of which the individual was confined or restrained. The judge to whom the petition has been assigned may not further refer the petition and shall act on it immediately pursuant to section (d) or (e) of this Rule.

(d) *Show cause order.* (1) Entry; contents. If the individual is confined as a result of a sentence in a criminal case, including a proceeding for criminal contempt other than a direct criminal contempt summarily punished, or as a result of a disposition or post-dispositional order following an adjudication of delinquency in a juvenile proceeding, the judge, prior to taking any further action, may enter an order directed to the person having custody of the individual to show cause why the writ should not issue. The show cause order may be entered regardless of whether the petition complies with Rule 15-302. The show cause order shall:

(A) state a date by which the order must be served upon the person having custody of the individual;

(B) state a date by which the person having custody may file a response and a date by which a copy of any response must be served on the petitioner in accordance with subsection (4) of this section;

(C) state that the petitioner may file a reply to the response within 30 days after service of the response; and

(D) require the petitioner to serve a copy of any reply on the person having custody by first class mail, postage prepaid.

(2) Service of show cause order. The show cause order, together with a copy of the petition, shall be served by certified mail on the person having custody of the individual confined. The show cause order shall be served by first class mail, postage prepaid, on the petitioner.

(3) Notice in response. A response to the show cause order shall include notice to the petitioner in substantially the following form:

NOTICE TO _____, PETITIONER
                (Name of Petitioner)

This response alleges your petition for a writ of habeas corpus should be denied because (check all that apply):

☐ There is no good reason why new grounds now raised by the petition were not raised in previous proceedings.

☐ There has been unjustified delay in filing the petition and that delay has prejudiced the ability of _____ (Name of person having custody of the individual confined) to respond to the petition.

☐ Other reasons for denial (specify):

_____

_____

_____

_____

You may file a reply to this response. Any reply must be filed with the court by _____ [Calendar Date] and you must mail a copy of your reply to _____.
                (Name of person having custody)

If you do not file a reply by that date or if your reply does not show the court a good reason why the allegations in this response are wrong, the court may deny your petition.

Committee note. — The calendar date for a reply shall be 30 days after personal service is made or 33 days after service by mail is mailed.

(4) Service of response. The person having custody shall serve a copy of the response on the petitioner or the petitioner's attorney by first class mail, postage prepaid, or by hand-delivery. The response shall be accompanied by a

certificate of service showing the date and manner of making service and, if service is by hand-delivery, the name of the individual making service.

(5) *If show cause order or response not timely served.* If (A) the show cause order was not timely served upon the person having custody and the person having custody has not filed a response or (B) the response was not timely served upon the petitioner and the petitioner has not filed a reply, the judge shall either reissue the show cause order or set the matter in for a hearing.

(e) *Action on petition.* (1) Preliminary determination. Unless the judge refers the petition pursuant to section (c) of this Rule, the judge shall first determine whether the petition complies with the provisions of Rule 15-302, except that if a show cause order was entered in accordance with section (d) of this Rule, the judge may defer making this determination until the time for a reply has expired. In determining whether the writ should be granted or denied, a judge shall consider any response or reply filed pursuant to a show cause order entered under section (d) of this Rule and may examine public records.

(2) *Noncompliance with Rule 15-302.* If the petition fails to comply with the provisions of Rule 15-302, the judge may (A) deny the petition; (B) permit the petition to be amended or supplemented; or (C) grant the writ if there is a sufficient showing of probable illegal confinement or restraint.

(3) *Compliance with Rule 15-302.* If the petition complies with the provisions of Rule 15-302, the judge shall grant the writ unless:

(A) the judge finds from the petition, any response, reply, document filed with the petition or with a response or reply, or public record that the individual confined or restrained is not entitled to any relief;

(B) the petition is made by or on behalf of an individual confined as a result of a sentence for a criminal offense, of an order in a juvenile proceeding, or of a judgment of contempt of court, the legality of the confinement was determined in a prior habeas corpus or other post conviction proceeding, and no new ground is shown sufficient to warrant issuance of the writ;

(C) there is no good reason why new grounds now raised by the petitioner were not raised in previous proceedings; or

(D) there has been an unjustified delay in filing the petition that has prejudiced the ability of the person having custody of the individual confined or restrained to respond to the petition.

(4) *Exception; notice, reply.* The judge may not deny the writ on a ground set forth in subsection (e)(3)(C) or (e)(3)(D) of this Rule unless the petitioner has been given notice of that ground and has had an opportunity to reply, either in accordance with section (d) of this Rule or as otherwise directed by the court.

Source. — This Rule is derived in part from former Rules Z54, Z43, Z44, and Z52 and is in part new.

Insufficient allegation of facts. — Order refusing petition for habeas corpus affirmed on appeal on ground that petitioner did not allege facts entitling him to relief. Nance v. Warden of Md. House of Cor., 189 Md. 112, 53 A.2d 554 (1947).

Prisoner's application for a writ of habeas corpus held not to make out a prima facie case for relief. Bernard v. Warden of Md. House of Cor., 187 Md. 273, 49 A.2d 737 (1946).

Dismissal of petition without hearing testimony. — In absence of evidence tending to show that trial was a sham, dismissal of petition without hearing testimony was within court's discretion. Reeder v. Warden of Md. Penitentiary, 196 Md. 683, 77 A.2d 1 (1950).

The fact that petitioner did not receive copy of indictment, as required by law, did not entitle him to release on habeas corpus. Ballam v. Warden of Md. House of Cor., 196 Md. 644, 75 A.2d 95 (1950).

Appeal from denial of relief from excessive bail. — From a denial of relief from excessive bail by the judge before whom the writ is returnable, petitioner has the right to file an application to the Court of Special Appeals under Code, § 3-707 of the Courts Article, for leave to appeal. Lewis v. Warden of Md. House of Cor., 16 Md. App. 339, 296 A.2d 428 (1972).

An examination of public records is authorized in habeas corpus petitions. White v. Warden of Md. Penitentiary, 211 Md. 623, 126 A.2d 294 (1956).

What are public records. — In passing upon a petition for a writ of habeas corpus, the trial judge properly had before him, and took into consideration, a certified copy of the docket entries in the court where petitioner

was convicted, a transcript of the proceedings at the time of petitioner's arraignment and a copy of a medical report relating to him. These documents were public records. However, a letter from the judge before whom petitioner was tried was not a public record, and hence was not properly before the judge to whom application was made for the writ. Walker v. Warden of Md. House of Cor., 209 Md. 654, 121 A.2d 714 (1956).

Original commitment order. — Examination of the original commitment order in determining whether or not to grant the application is proper in habeas corpus. Roberts v. Warden of Md. House of Cor., 211 Md. 639, 126 A.2d 857 (1956), cert. denied, 355 U.S. 966, 78 S. Ct. 556, 2 L. Ed. 2d 540 (1958).

Hearing, etc., to determine complaints not refuted by docket entries. — Where petitioner made certain complaints on habeas corpus relating to his counsel and to the conduct of his criminal trial, which were not refuted by the docket entries in that trial, the only records of the trial before the judge who considered and denied the habeas corpus petition, there should have been a hearing or some further investigation of the records to determine whether or not petitioner had been deprived of any constitutional right, the denial of which would render his judgment of conviction a nullity. Bell v. Warden of Md. Penitentiary, 218 Md. 666, 146 A.2d 56 (1959).

Rule 15-304. Alternate remedy — Post Conviction Procedure Act.

When a petition for a writ of habeas corpus is filed by or on behalf of an individual confined as a result of a sentence for a criminal offense, including a criminal contempt, or a commitment order in a juvenile delinquency proceeding, the judge may order that the petition be treated as a petition under the Post Conviction Procedure Act if the individual confined consents in writing or on the record and the judge is satisfied that the post conviction proceeding is adequate to test the legality of the confinement. Upon entry of the order, the judge shall transmit the petition, a certified copy of the order, and any other pertinent papers to the court in which the sentence or judgment was entered. Subsequent procedure shall be as in a post conviction proceeding.

Cross references. — See Rules 4-401 through 4-408 and Code, Article 27, § 645A, et seq.

Source. — This Rule is derived from former Rule Z55.

Continued incarceration after expiration of sentence. — Applicant's continued incarceration after the expiration of his sentence was a proper subject for inquiry on a petition for a writ of habeas corpus; but since it was not attacked for any alleged infirmity in

the judgment under which he was sentenced, or in the sentence itself, nor even in the order by which he was transferred to the Patuxent Institution for examination, it did not present any question cognizable under the Post Conviction Procedure Act. Roberts v. Director of

Patuxent Inst., 226 Md. 643, 172 A.2d 880
(1961).

Rule 15-305. To whom writ directed — Before whom returnable.

A writ of habeas corpus shall be directed to the person having custody of the individual confined or restrained. The writ shall be returnable before the judge granting it or, in the discretion of that judge, before some other judge designated in the writ except that without the written consent of the individual confined or restrained, the judge designated in the writ shall not be a judge who sat at the proceeding as a result of which the individual was confined or restrained. In exercising the discretion granted by this Rule, the judge granting the writ shall consider the interests and convenience of the parties and the State.

Source. — This Rule is derived from former Rule Z45.

Conclusion that defendant lacked ability to comply held erroneous. — Habeas corpus judge erred in concluding upon the evidence heard by trial judge, but not heard by habeas corpus judge, that defendant charged with contempt lacked the present ability to comply with the court's order, a decision directly contrary to that reached by the trial judge who heard the evidence and had the opportunity to observe the demeanor of the witnesses. Nnoli v. Nnoli, 101 Md. App. 243, 646 A.2d 1021 (1994).

Quoted in Maryland House of Cor. v. Fields, 348 Md. 245, 703 A.2d 167 (1997).

Rule 15-306. Service of writ; appearance by individual; affidavit.

(a) *Service.* Except as provided in section (c) of this Rule, a writ of habeas corpus and a copy of the petition shall be served by delivering them to the person to whom the writ is directed or by mailing them by first class mail, postage prepaid, as ordered by the court.

Cross references. — *See* Rules 2-121 and 3-121.

(b) *Production of individual.* At the time stated in the writ, which, unless the court orders otherwise, shall not be later than three days after service of the writ, the person to whom the writ is directed shall cause the individual confined or restrained to be taken before the judge designated in the writ.

(c) *Immediate appearance.* If the judge finds probable cause to believe that the person having custody of the individual by or on whose behalf the petition was filed is about to remove the individual or would evade or disobey the writ, the judge shall include in the writ an order directing the person immediately to appear, together with the individual confined or restrained, before the judge designated in the writ. The sheriff to whom the writ is delivered shall serve the writ immediately, together with a copy of the petition, on the person having custody of the individual confined or restrained and shall bring that person, together with the individual confined or restrained, before the judge designated in the writ.

Cross references. — *See* Code, Courts Article, § 2-305 for the penalty on a sheriff for failure to act as provided in section (b) of this Rule; *see* Code, Article 27, § 617 for the penalty on an officer or other person failing to furnish a copy of a warrant of commitment when demanded.

Source. — This Rule is derived from former Rules Z46 and Z47.

Rule 15-307. Absence of judge — Return to another court or judge.

If the judge designated in the writ is unavailable when the individual confined or restrained is produced, the individual shall be taken before another judge of the same judicial circuit. If the individual is confined or restrained as a result of a sentence for a criminal offense, including a criminal contempt, or as a result of an order in a juvenile proceeding, the individual shall not be taken before a judge who sat at any proceeding as a result of which the individual was confined or restrained unless the individual consents in writing.

Source. — This Rule is derived from former Rule Z49.

Rule 15-308. Notice to State's Attorney and Attorney General.

If a judge grants a writ with respect to an individual confined as a result of a sentence for a criminal offense, including a criminal contempt, or as a result of an order in a juvenile proceeding, the judge shall instruct the clerk to give notice of the time and place of the hearing to the State's Attorney for the county in which the sentence or order was entered. If the petition presents an issue of illegal confinement in the Division of Correction unrelated to the underlying conviction or order, notice shall also be directed to the Attorney General.

Cross references. — For the entry of judgment in a removed case, *see* Rule 4-254 (b) (3).

Source. — This Rule is derived from Rule Z50.

Rule 15-309. Hearing.

Upon the production of the individual confined or restrained, the judge shall conduct a hearing immediately to inquire into the legality and propriety of the individual's confinement or restraint. The individual confined or restrained for whom the writ is issued may offer evidence to prove the lack of legal justification for the confinement or restraint, and evidence may be offered on behalf of the person having custody to refute the claim.

Source. — This Rule is derived from former Rules Z46 b and Z48.

Generally. — The facts stated in the return may be controverted, and it may be shown that no judgment or execution in fact exists, or that the court had no jurisdiction. But if there is a judgment by a competent court, then there can be no inquiry as to whether judgment is erroneous. Habeas corpus is not a writ of error. Ex parte Maulsby, 13 Md. 625 (1859), appendix. See also In re Glenn, 54 Md. 572 (1880).

Rule 15-310. Disposition.

(a) *Appropriate remedy.* If the judge determines that the individual is confined or restrained without legal warrant or authority, the judge shall order that the individual be released or discharged immediately, or shall enter such other order as justice may require. If the judge determines that the confinement or restraint is lawful and proper, the individual shall be remanded to custody or admitted to bail pending trial or retrial.

(b) *Errors on face of commitment — Correction.* The judge to whom the writ is returned shall not discharge the individual confined or restrained merely because of errors, omissions, or irregularities on the face of the warrant or other written authority for commitment. The judge may direct that the warrant or other written authority be sent for correction to the court or judicial officer who issued it and that, after correction, it be redelivered to the person having custody of the individual.

Cross references. — *See* Rule 4-102 (f) for the definition of "judicial officer."

Source. — This Rule is derived from former Rules Z46 b and Z51.

Rule 15-311. Memorandum by judge.

The judge to whom the petition is made or referred shall dictate into the record or prepare and file a memorandum setting forth the grounds of the petition, the questions involved, and the reasons for the action taken. A copy of the memorandum or a transcription of the dictation shall be sent to the petitioner and the person having custody of the individual confined or restrained.

Source. — This Rule is derived from former Rule Z53.

In habeas corpus proceedings concerning bail conducted prior to sentence, whether before or after conviction, it is equally essential that the hearing judge file a memorandum which shall include his reasons for the action taken by him. Hunter v. Warden, Baltimore City Jail, 17 Md. App. 86, 299 A.2d 846 (1973).

Where the record does not contain a statement by the judge, "setting forth the grounds of the application, the questions involved, and the reasons of the court for the action taken," ordinarily it might be necessary to remand the case so that such a statement might be supplied. However, where the record before the Court of Appeals shows that petitioner is lawfully imprisoned the reason for the court's action is apparent and it is unnecessary to remand the case. State v. Warden of Md. House of Cor., 190 Md. 765, 59 A.2d 791 (1948); State v. Warden of Md. House of Cor., 190 Md. 759, 59 A.2d 790 (1948).

Where petitioner in habeas corpus proceeding was discharged, and Superintendent of State Reformatory for Males appealed, but where papers were not transmitted until nearly 4 months thereafter, without any statement by judge of trial court and no brief, application for leave to appeal was denied. Raymond v. Reed, 195 Md. 716, 73 A.2d 885 (1950).

Prior memorandum sufficient. — When the trial court denying a writ of habeas corpus failed to state any reason for doing so, but on a former application to a different judge on the same grounds an opinion had been filed and it appeared that the petitioner was lawfully imprisoned, it was not necessary to remand the case for that purpose. Agner v. Warden of Md. House of Cor., 203 Md. 665, 99 A.2d 735 (1953).

The dictation to a stenographer by a judge of a statement of his reasons for denying a writ, which statement the petitioners could have obtained from the stenographer, was sufficient. Mason v. Warden of Baltimore City Jail, 203 Md. 659, 99 A.2d 739 (1953).

Statement of judge held not to comply with statute. — Where the petition in a habeas corpus proceeding properly raised on its face constitutional questions that should have been resolved, but the judge to whom the petition was referred, in denying the writ, stated in an opinion filed only that the contention that the weight of the evidence was against the verdict was no ground for relief,

this was not a compliance with former § 5 of Article 42. Webster v. Warden of Md. House of Cor., 211 Md. 632, 126 A.2d 613 (1956).

Applied in Lomax v. Warden, Md. Cor. Training Ctr., 120 Md. App. 314, 707 A.2d 395 (1998).

Rule 15-312. Discharge on ground of unconstitutionality — Review.

When an individual is released or discharged under a writ of habeas corpus on the ground that all or part of the statute or law under which the individual was convicted is unconstitutional, the memorandum or the transcription required by Rule 15-311 shall be filed by the judge within five days after the judge orders the release or discharge. The clerk shall promptly transmit the record to the Clerk of the Court of Special Appeals for further proceedings.

Cross references. — *See* Code, Courts Article, § 3-706 and Rule 8-413.

Committee note. — The provisions of Title 8 are applicable to proceedings under this Rule

except to the extent otherwise provided.

Source. — This Rule is derived from former Rule Z56.

Review. — Judge's order in a habeas corpus matter is not reviewable by the Court of Appeals, except in the event he declared a public law of the State to be unconstitutional. Simon v. Warden of Md. House of Cor., 238 Md. 27, 207 A.2d 484 (1965), overruled on other grounds, McMannis v. State, 311 Md. 534, 536 A.2d 652 (1988).

Order granting habeas corpus and releasing patient from Patuxent Institution was held not

appealable in State v. Musgrove, 241 Md. 521, 217 A.2d 247 (1966)

Court of Special Appeals has no jurisdiction to review grant of writ of habeas corpus based on unconstitutionality of defective delinquent provisions as opposed to writ granted on basis of the unconstitutionality of statute under which petitioner was convicted. State v. Layman, 28 Md. App. 332, 345 A.2d 444 (1975).

CHAPTER 400. HEALTH CLAIMS ARBITRATION.

Rule 15-401. Judicial review — Health claims arbitration.

The rules in this Chapter apply to judicial review of an award determining a health care malpractice claim under Code, Courts Article, Title 3, Subtitle 2A and to an assessment of costs under an award.

Cross references. — *See* generally Code, Courts Article, §§ 3-2A-01 through 3-2A-09 (Health Care Malpractice Claims), relating to arbitration of certain claims against health

care providers for medical injury.

Source. — This Rule is derived from former Rule BY1.

University of Baltimore Law Review. — For article, "The Health Care Malpractice Claims Statute: Maryland's Response to the Medical Malpractice Crisis," see 10 U. Balt. L. Rev. 74 (1980).

For article, "Health Claims Arbitration in Maryland: The Experiment Has Failed," see 14 U. Balt. L. Rev. 481 (1985).

For article, "Judicial Review of Health

Claims Arbitration Awards: Practice and Pitfalls," see 17 U. Balt. L. Rev. 433 (1989).

Notice of action to nullify Health Claims Arbitration award is element of action itself and is governed by the Maryland Rules. Cherry v. Seymour Bros., 306 Md. 84, 507 A.2d 613 (1986).

Discretion of court. — The court abused its discretion when it dismissed the action because of an insubstantial noncompliance with this Subtitle — a noncompliance which in no way subverted the policy served by this Subtitle, and which amounted to little more than the filing of a complaint which would be subject to dismissal for failure to state a claim, but with leave to amend. Ott v. Kaiser-Georgetown Community Health Plan, Inc., 309 Md. 641, 526 A.2d 46 (1987).

Rule 15-402. Definitions.

In these Rules the following definitions apply except as expressly otherwise provided or as necessary implication requires:

(a) *Arbitration panel.* "Arbitration panel" means the arbitrators selected to determine a health care malpractice claim in accordance with Code, Courts Article, Title 3, Subtitle 2A.

(b) *Award.* "Award" means a final determination of a health care malpractice claim by an arbitration panel or by the panel chair.

Cross references. — For the authority of the panel chair to rule on issues of law, *see* Code, Courts Article, § 3-2A-05 (a).

(c) *Defendant.* "Defendant" means the health care provider.

(d) *Director.* "Director" means the Director of the Health Claims Arbitration Office.

(e) *Plaintiff.* "Plaintiff" means the party making a claim against a health care provider.

Source. — This Rule is new.

Rule 15-403. Action to reject health claims award or assessment of costs.

(a) *Rejection of award or costs.* A party may reject for any reason an award, the assessment of costs under an award, or both. An action to reject filed pursuant to this Rule constitutes the notice of rejection required by Code, Courts Article, § 3-2A-06 (a). An action to reject shall not impair the award or the assessment of costs as to any party before the arbitration panel who has not rejected the award or the assessment of costs and is not named as a defendant in the action.

(b) *Plaintiff's action to reject.* (1) How commenced. The plaintiff shall commence an action to reject by filing a complaint with a circuit court or with any other court of competent jurisdiction. The complaint shall (A) identify the award and state whether the award, the assessment of costs, or both are being rejected, (B) state that the plaintiff is the rejecting party, and (C) identify all defendants as to whom the plaintiff rejects the award, the assessment of the costs, or both. If the complaint is filed in a circuit court, it shall comply with Rules 2-303 through 2-305. The complaint may state that the amount of damages sought is more than the required jurisdictional amount, but the amount sought shall not be stated.

Committee note. — *See Ott v. Kaiser Georgetown Health Plan*, 309 Md. 641 (1987), recognizing that an action to reject an award may be filed in a United States District Court.

(2) Time for filing. The complaint shall be filed within the later of (A) 30 days after the Director serves the award or the assessment of costs or (B) ten days after service by the chair of the panel or the Director, whichever first occurs, of the disposition of a timely-filed application for modification or correction. A complaint filed before the disposition of an application does not deprive the panel of jurisdiction to dispose of the application. The action in the circuit court shall not proceed until the date a copy of the disposition is filed in that court. All time periods provided for in this Rule shall begin to run from that date.

(c) *Defendant's action to reject.* (1) How commenced. The defendant shall commence an action to reject an award, the assessment of costs, or both by filing a notice of action to reject with the Director. The notice shall (A) identify the award, state whether the award, the assessment of costs, or both are being rejected, (B) state that the defendant is the rejecting party, (C) identify all plaintiffs as to whom the defendant rejects the award, the assessment of costs, or both, and (D) allege that the monetary amount being rejected is more than the required jurisdictional amount.

(2) Time for filing. The notice shall be filed within the later of (A) 30 days after the Director serves the award or the assessment of costs or (B) ten days after service by the chair of the panel or the Director, whichever first occurs, of the disposition of a timely-filed application for modification or correction. A notice filed before the disposition of an application does not deprive the panel of jurisdiction to consider the application.

(3) Plaintiff to file complaint. When a defendant files a notice of action to reject, a plaintiff who desires to contest the action or reject the award or the assessment of costs shall file a complaint against any rejecting defendants and any defendants as to whom the plaintiff rejects the award or the assessment of costs. The complaint shall be filed within the later of (A) 30 days after service of the notice or (B) ten days after service by the chair of the panel or the Director, whichever first occurs, of the disposition of a timely-filed application for modification or correction. The complaint shall (A) identify the award and whether the award, the assessment of costs, or both are being rejected, (B) state who rejects the award, the assessment of costs, or both, and (C) identify all parties against whom the award, the assessment of costs, or both are rejected. If the complaint is filed in a circuit court, it shall comply with Rules 2-303 through 2-305. The complaint may state that the amount of damages sought is more than the required jurisdictional amount, but the amount sought shall not be stated.

(d) *Service.* (1) Of complaint. The plaintiff shall serve the complaint upon each defendant named in the complaint, the Director, and all other parties to the arbitration proceeding. Service upon the defendant shall be either in the manner prescribed by Rule 2-121 or, if the defendant was represented by counsel in the arbitration proceeding, on counsel by certified mail, return receipt requested. Service upon all other parties to the arbitration proceeding and upon the Director shall be in the manner prescribed by Rule 1-321.

(2) Of notice of action to reject. The defendant shall serve a copy of the notice to reject upon the plaintiff and all other parties to the arbitration proceeding.

Service upon the plaintiff shall be either in the manner prescribed by Rule 2-121 or, if the plaintiff was represented by counsel in the arbitration proceeding, on counsel by certified mail, return receipt requested. Service upon all other parties to the arbitration proceeding shall be in the manner prescribed by Rule 1-321.

(e) *Modification, correction, or vacation of award or assessment of costs by court.* (1) Motion; when filed. In an action to reject, an allegation that an award or the assessment of costs is improper because of any ground stated in Code, Courts Article, § 3-223 (b), § 3-224 (b) (1), (2), (3), or (4), or § 3-2A-05 (h) shall be made by motion filed at least 30 days before trial, or the ground is waived. The court shall decide the motion before trial.

(2) Modification of award. If the court finds that a condition stated in Code, Courts Article, § 3-223 (b) exists, or that the award or assessment of costs was not appropriately modified in accordance with Code, Courts Article, § 3-2A-05 (h), it shall modify or correct the award or the assessment of costs. If the rejecting party still desires to proceed with judicial review, the modified or corrected award or the assessment of costs shall be substituted for the original award.

(3) Vacation of award. If the court finds that a condition stated in Code, Courts Article, § 3-224 (b) (1), (2), (3), or (4) exists, it shall vacate the award or the assessment of costs, and trial of the case shall proceed as if there had been no award or assessment of costs.

Cross references. — *See* Code, Courts Article, § 3-2A-06 (c).

Source. — This Rule is in part derived from Rules BY2 through BY4 and in part new.

University of Baltimore Law Review. — For article, "The Health Care Malpractice Claims Statute: Maryland's Response to the Medical Malpractice Crisis," see 10 U. Balt. L. Rev. 74 (1980).

For article, "Health Claims Arbitration in Maryland: The Experiment Has Failed," see 14 U. Balt. L. Rev. 481 (1985).

· For article, "Judicial Review of Health Claims Arbitration Awards: Practice and Pitfalls," see 17 U. Balt. L. Rev. 433 (1989).

Notice requirements mandatory. — Section 3-2A-06 of the Courts Article and former Rule BY2 require that the notice of rejection "must" be filed and the notice of action "shall" be filed within the prescribed time period. These sections imply that the notice requirements are mandatory, and that some sanction may be imposed for noncompliance therewith. Tranen v. Aziz, 59 Md. App. 528, 476 A.2d 1170 (1984), aff'd, 304 Md. 605, 500 A.2d 636 (1985).

Action to nullify arbitration award is two-step process: first, a notice of the action must be filed with the clerk of the court within 30 days after the award is served on the rejecting party; and second, a declaration must be filed setting forth the allegations to be proved entitling the aggrieved party to relief. Tranen v. Aziz, 304 Md. 605, 500 A.2d 636 (1985).

Action to nullify not notice. — Where an action to nullify is concerned only with the panel's allocation of costs, the action to nullify is not the notice of the action created by section (a) of former Rule BY2. State of Md. Cent. Collection Unit v. Gettes, 321 Md. 671, 584 A.2d 689 (1991).

When defendant files notice of action to nullify award in jurisdiction different from that in which plaintiff files declaration, the filing of the declaration with a certified copy of the defendant's notice of action amounts to an automatic consolidation of the two cases which, once the venue question is settled, divests the court in which defendants' notice of action was filed of venue; nothing in the statute or the rules required the defendants to move to consolidate their filing with the plaintiff's case in another jurisdiction. Teimourian v. Spence, 59 Md. App. 74, 474 A.2d 919, cert. denied, 301 Md. 43 481 A.2d 802 (1984).

Action to nullify and complaint in a single document. — The requirement that judicial proceedings be commenced by filing an action to nullify, under § 3-2A-06 (b) of the Courts Article, may be met, by a single document which includes both the notice of action to nullify and the complaint required by this Subtitle, if it complies with the time, information, and service requirements of former Rule BY2 and former Rule BY4. Ott v. Kaiser-Georgetown Community Health Plan, Inc., 309 Md. 641, 526 A.2d 46 (1987).

Realignment of parties. — Former Maryland Rules of Procedure, BY2, BY3 and BY4, in conjunction with the Maryland Health Care Malpractice Claims Act (§ 3-2A-01 et seq. of the Courts Article), force a realignment of the parties to the adversarial positions in a traditional malpractice court action in those arbitrated cases in which the health care provider is aggrieved by the award on the merits, files a notice of rejection, and is required by § 3-2A-06 (b) (1) of the Courts Article to file an action in court to nullify the award. State of Md. Cent. Collection Unit v. Gettes, 321 Md. 671, 584 A.2d 689 (1991).

Miscaption on notice of action to nullify Health Claims Arbitration award held not misleading. — See Cherry v. Seymour Bros., 306 Md. 84, 507 A.2d 613 (1986).

Use of photocopy permissible. — In the absence of any provision in either Subtitle 2A of Title 3 of the Courts Article or the Maryland Rules prohibiting the use of a photocopy to institute a court action, the use of such a photocopy did not warrant dismissal. Cherry v. Seymour Bros., 306 Md. 84, 507 A.2d 613 (1986).

Failure to file declaration within 30-day period prescribed by subsection 1 of section a of former Rule BY4 does not require dismissal of the court action and automatic nullification of the arbitration award regardless of the circumstances. Golub v. Spivey, 70 Md. App. 147, 520 A.2d 394, cert. denied, 310 Md. 2, 526 A.2d 954 (1987).

Mere misappellation of a pleading should not ordinarily provide the predicate for a dismissal without leave to amend. Osheroff v. Chestnut Lodge, Inc., 62 Md. App. 519, 490 A.2d 720, cert. denied, 304 Md. 163, 497 A.2d 1163 (1985).

Failure to caption properly "Notice of Action to Nullify" so as to indicate that it was being filed in circuit court instead of with the Health Claims Arbitration Office was not fatal to the plaintiffs in a medical malpractice suit, where the notice to nullify, the notice of rejection, and the declaration were all filed at the same time and the declaration stated that the proceeding was in the circuit court. Brothers v. Sinai Hosp., 63 Md. App. 235, 492 A.2d 656 (1985), aff'd, 306 Md. 84, 507 A.2d 613 (1986).

CHAPTER 500. INJUNCTIONS.

Rule 15-501. Injunctions — Definitions.

The following definitions apply in the rules in this Chapter:

(a) *Injunction.* "Injunction" means an order mandating or prohibiting a specified act.

(b) *Preliminary injunction.* "Preliminary injunction" means an injunction granted after opportunity for a full adversary hearing on the propriety of its issuance but before a final determination of the merits of the action.

(c) *Temporary restraining order.* "Temporary restraining order" means an injunction granted without opportunity for a full adversary hearing on the propriety of its issuance.

Source. — This Rule is derived from former Rule BB70.

Maryland Law Review. — For article, "Survey of Developments in Maryland Law, 1983-84," see 44 Md. L. Rev. 323 (1985).

Jurisdiction. — Court acquired jurisdiction to issue a prejudgment attachment-type interlocutory injunction based on the substantial evidence offered at the hearing which showed a substantial likelihood that: (1) the defendant had committed fraud, (2) he would dispose of assets before judgment and (3) the assets were fraudulently obtained; notwithstanding the defendant's opposition, as opposed to consent, to the injunction. Teferi v. Dupont Plaza Assocs., 77 Md. App. 566, 551 A.2d 477 (1989).

Considerations in entry of interlocu-

tory injunction. — Trial court should consider four factors in determining whether entry of an interlocutory injunction is proper: 1) The likelihood that the plaintiff will succeed on the merits; 2) the "balance of convenience" determined by whether greater injury would be done to the defendant by granting the injunction than would result from its refusal; 3) whether plaintiff will suffer irreparable injury unless the injunction is granted; and 4) the public interest. Teferi v. Dupont Plaza Assocs., 77 Md. App. 566, 551 A.2d 477 (1989).

Prisoners' grievances not subject of Rules. — In the light of the passage of the Inmate Grievance Commission Act, the Court of Appeals finds it to have been the legislative intent that prisoners' grievances, even when involving constitutional rights, are not to be the subject of § 3-401 et seq. of the Courts Article, or former Rules BB70-BB80. State v. McCray, 267 Md. 111, 297 A.2d 265 (1972).

Order denying motion to stay Human Relations Commission decision. — Order of the circuit court denying motion to stay a decision of the Commission on Human Relations was not an "injunction" which could be appealed, and no party could be held in contempt for violating the order. LOOC, Inc. v. Kohli, 347 Md. 258, 701 A.2d 92 (1997).

Existence of some right which will be irreparably injured is prerequisite. — The mere existence of an injury, even if irreparable, is no guarantee that injunctive relief will issue. The existence of some right, which will be irreparably injured, is a prerequisite to the extraordinary relief of an injunction. Anne Arundel County v. Whitehall Venture, 39 Md. App. 197, 384 A.2d 780 (1978).

Mandatory or affirmative injunction should be issued with caution. — Although a mandatory or affirmative injunction should be issued with caution, and is ordinarily restricted to cases where adequate redress at law is not afforded, or where the injury is not compensable in damages, and in weighing the propriety of issuing it, a court should consider the relative convenience and inconvenience which will result to the parties from granting or refusing this form of injunctive relief, the issuance of a mandatory injunction may be peculiarly appropriate, as in this instance, for the erection of a fence. Maryland Trust Co. v. Tulip Realty Co., 220 Md. 399, 153 A.2d 275 (1959).

Under balance of convenience test, the benefits to plaintiff must be equal to or outweigh potential harm which defendant may incur if injunction is granted. Rowe v. C & P Tel. Co., 56 Md. App. 23, 466 A.2d 538 (1983).

Injunction restraining county from implementing charter section permitted. — Granting preliminary injunction to restrain county from implementing or enforcing charter section prohibiting county governments from purchasing and contracting for telephone services from certain company unless certain subscribers included was not clearly erroneous, arbitrary or capricious. Rowe v. C & P Tel. Co., 56 Md. App. 23, 466 A.2d 538 (1983).

Interlocutory injunction to prevent franchisor from terminating agreement expired, by operation of law, when judgment absolute was entered so that there was no valid restraining order in effect against franchisor, and franchisor could not be found in contempt. GMC v. Miller Buick, Inc., 56 Md. App. 374, 467 A.2d 1064 (1983), cert. denied, 299 Md. 136, 472 A.2d 999 (1984).

Appeal from interlocutory injunction not moot. — Although the appeal from an ex parte injunction is moot, the appeal from an interlocutory injunction is not. State Comm'n on Human Relations v. Suburban Hosp., 113 Md. App. 62, 686 A.2d 706 (1996).

Rule 15-502. Injunctions — General provisions.

(a) *Exception to applicability — Labor disputes.* Rules 15-501 through 15-505 do not modify or supersede Code, Labor and Employment Article, Title 4, Subtitle 3 or affect the prerequisites for obtaining, or the jurisdiction to grant, injunctions under those Code sections.

(b) *Issuance at any stage.* Subject to the rules in this Chapter, the court, at any stage of an action and at the instance of any party or on its own initiative, may grant an injunction upon the terms and conditions justice may require.

(c) *Adequate remedy at law.* The court may not deny an injunction solely because the party seeking it has an adequate remedy in damages unless the adverse party has filed a bond with security that the court finds adequate to provide for the payment of all damages and costs that the adverse party might be adjudged to pay by reason of the alleged wrong.

(d) *Not binding without notice.* An injunction is not binding on a person until that person has been personally served with it or has received actual notice of it by any means.

(e) *Form and scope.* An order granting an injunction shall (1) be in writing or on the record, (2) set forth the reasons for issuance; (3) be specific in terms; and (4) describe in reasonable detail, and not by reference to the complaint or other document, the act sought to be mandated or prohibited.

(f) *Modification or dissolution.* A party or any person affected by a preliminary or a final injunction may move for modification or dissolution of an injunction.

Cross references. — For enforcement of an injunction, *see* Rule 2-648.

Source. — This Rule is derived from former Rules BB71, 76, 77, 78, and 79.

Rule does not interfere with court's power to issue injunctions. — While former Rule BB71 did not govern injunctions issued in divorce, alimony, support of wife or child, custody of child or annulment of marriage actions, it in no way purports to interfere with the right of a court to issue such injunctions if otherwise authorized. Winston v. Winston, 290 Md. 641, 431 A.2d 1330 (1981).

Legal remedy must be fully adequate. — To justify refusal of equitable relief on the ground that the appellant has a remedy at law, the legal remedy must be fully adequate and complete. The remedy at law which precludes relief in equity must be as practical and efficient to the ends of justice and its prompt administration as the remedy in equity. State v. Ficker, 266 Md. 500, 295 A.2d 231 (1972).

An "adequate remedy at law" must be adequate; for if at law it falls short of what the party is entitled to, that founds a jurisdiction in equity. And it must be complete, obtaining the full end and justice of the case. It must reach the whole mischief, and secure the whole right of the party in a perfect manner, at the present time and in the future; otherwise, equity will interfere and give such relief and aid as the exigency of the particular case may require. The jurisdiction of a court of equity is, therefore, sometimes concurrent with the jurisdiction of a court of law, it is sometimes exclusive of it; and it is sometimes auxiliary to it. State v. Ficker, 266 Md. 500, 295 A.2d 231 (1972).

Adequate remedy at law in the form of damages is not an absolute bar to injunctive relief. Anne Arundel County v. Whitehall Venture, 39 Md. App. 197, 384 A.2d 780 (1978).

Injunctive relief against commission of criminal acts. — Equity will enjoin criminal acts if such operate to the injury of complainant's property rights or cause him pecuniary harm for which there is no adequate legal remedy. State v. Ficker, 266 Md. 500, 295 A.2d 231 (1972).

Where acts complained of are violations of the criminal law, courts of equity will not on that ground alone interfere by injunction to prevent their commission. Former Rule BB76, however, does not preclude injunctive relief against the commission of criminal acts which, unless enjoined, would operate to cause an irreparable injury to property or rights of a pecuniary nature. If criminal offenses are primarily and essentially an injury to property, preventive relief may be granted within the same limits as where the element of criminality is entirely absent. In such a case the court does not interfere to prevent the commission of crime, although that may incidentally result, but it exerts its force to protect individual property from destruction. State v. Ficker, 266 Md. 500, 295 A.2d 231 (1972).

Former § 98, Article 16, held not to justify the continuing of an injunction, since the evidence showed that the defendant had property in this State ample to meet any damages recovered. Bartlett v. Moyers, 88 Md. 715, 42 A. 204 (1898).

General contract creditor held not entitled to injunction. — Creditor, before judgment, who became such under a general contract, was not entitled to injunction or to have receiver appointed. Perlmutter v. Minskoff, 196 Md. 99, 75 A.2d 129 (1950).

Exclusive distribution contracts enforceable by injunction. — Exclusive distribution contracts are a recognized subject for enforcement by injunction. Plaintiff in the instant case was entitled to relief by injunction and to accounting for damages for sales made in violation of the contract. Foster-Porter Enters., Inc. v. De Mare, 198 Md. 20, 81 A.2d 325 (1951).

Jurisdiction to grant injunction on account of fraud. — Even if appellee could have sued appellant at law for fraud in view of former § 98, Article 16, the jurisdiction of equity to grant an injunction on account of such fraud was not affected. Michael v. Rigler, 142 Md. 125, 120 A. 382 (1923).

Intent. — See Conner v. Groh, 90 Md. 674, 45 A. 1024 (1900).

Former § 98, Article 16, was intended to reach the class of cases in which injunction or mandamus had been refused because the plaintiff could be compensated in damages in suits at law. Universal Realty Corp. v. Felser, 179 Md. 635, 22 A.2d 448 (1941); Frederick County Nat'l Bank v. Shafer, 87 Md. 54, 39 A. 320 (1898).

Applicable to cases where damages, not debt, are involved. — Former § 98, Article 16, related to cases where damages, as contradistinguished from debt, were involved. Frederick County Nat'l Bank v. Shafer, 87 Md. 54, 39 A. 320 (1898); Conner v. Groh, 90 Md. 674, 45 A. 1024 (1900).

Hearing and burden of proof. — Former § 98, Article 16, was not intended to be applicable on demurrer, but only after such hearing as might make it appear to the court that the defendants, in a given case, could respond to damages, or could give a bond, and that such relief would be adequate. The burden is on the defendants in this respect. Universal Realty Corp. v. Felser, 179 Md. 635, 22 A.2d 448 (1941).

Remedy at law held clearly inadequate. — Where illegal posting of political campaign signs in inordinate numbers in direct violation of a county ordinance caused irreparable injury to the county's rights of a pecuniary nature for which loss the criminal sanction was plainly inadequate, and where relief sought by the county — removal of the remaining illegal signs at the posting party's own expense, reimbursement for expenses previously incurred in removing the signs, and damages for injury to its property — would not have accrued to the county from successful criminal prosecution, the remedy at law was plainly inadequate. State v. Ficker, 266 Md. 500, 295 A.2d 231 (1972).

Injunction not embraced in prayer. — Former § 89 of Article 16, from which former Rule BB77 was derived, cured any defect arising out of an injunction not being embraced in the prayer for that writ. Board of County Sch. Comm'rs v. Board of County Sch. Comm'rs, 77 Md. 283, 26 A. 115 (1893); Supreme Lodge v. Simering, 88 Md. 276, 40 A. 723 (1898); B & O R.R. v. Silbereisen, 121 Md. 407, 88 A. 252, 89 A. 102 (1913).

Issue and continuance of injunction upheld. — See Horner v. Nitsch, 103 Md. 498, 63 A. 1052 (1906).

Requiring injunction bond of county. — An appeal involving the right of the chancellor to require an injunction bond of a county was dismissed on other grounds, and the matter not decided in Montgomery County v. Maryland-Washington Metro. Dist., 200 Md. 525, 92 A.2d 350 (1952).

Role of court in granting injunctive relief. — It is not the role of the court in issuing an order granting injunctive relief to clarify hypothetical shades of meaning which the drafters of a regulation did not see fit to address. Chesapeake Outdoor Enters., Inc. v. Mayor of Baltimore, 89 Md. App. 54, 597 A.2d 503 (1991).

Injunctive decree must not be broader than issue raised by pleadings. Rocks v. Brosius, 241 Md. 612, 217 A.2d 531 (1966).

Order which lacks specific terms and reasonable detail is too vague, too broad and failed to conform with the mandatory requirements of section a of former Rule BB78. Franzen v. Dubinok, 45 Md. App. 728, 415 A.2d 621 (1980), aff'd, 290 Md. 65, 427 A.2d 1002 (1981).

Order to restore land to original topography held too vague and overbroad. — An order requiring a party to restore land to its original topography, when there was no evidence in the record as to what that topography was and how the party is to comply, was too vague and overbroad to comply with former Rule BB78. Joy v. Anne Arundel County, 52 Md. App. 653, 451 A.2d 1237 (1982).

Scope of injunction in trade secret cases. — For a discussion of the two different American views as to the scope of an injunction in trade secret cases, see Space Aero Prods. Co. v. R.E. Darling Co., 238 Md. 93, 208 A.2d 74, cert. denied, 382 U.S. 843, 86 S. Ct. 77, 15 L. Ed. 2d 83 (1965).

Punishment for contempt where terms of injunction not specific and definite. — See Rocks v. Brosius, 241 Md. 612, 217 A.2d 531 (1966).

There may be remand for revision of a decree to comply with former Rule BB78 without upsetting effect of decree. — A matter may be remanded for revision of a decree to comply with the requirements of section a of former Rule BB78 without upsetting the effect of the decree. Arundel Supply Corp. v. Cason, 265 Md. 371, 289 A.2d 585 (1972).

Injunction held improper. — Trial court erred in enjoining automobile manufacturer from establishing a new dealership in proximity of existing dealer, where, although the existing dealer could lose a portion of its business without the injunction, the new dealership was certain to lose all of its business with the injunction in place, and the balance of hardships favored the new dealership. Antwerpen Dodge, Ltd. v. Herb Gordon Auto

World, Inc., 117 Md. App. 290, 699 A.2d 1209 (1997).

Trial court erred in granting interlocutory injunction enjoining automobile manufacturer from establishing a new dealership in proximity of existing dealer, where existing dealer failed to demonstrate a strong likelihood it would be entitled to a permanent injunction based on § 15-207(d)(2) of the Transportation Code. Antwerpen Dodge, Ltd. v. Herb Gordon Auto World, Inc., 117 Md. App. 290, 699 A.2d 1209 (1997).

Temporary injunction properly dis-

solved. — Where, even accepting petitioner's allegations that the actions of the respondents in terminating his employment were arbitrary, capricious and without cause as true, his bill, nevertheless, failed to show that he would suffer irreparable injury, and the grievance procedure available under the Maryland Department of Personnel provided an adequate remedy, the temporary injunction was properly dissolved. Coster v. Department of Personnel, 36 Md. App. 523, 373 A.2d 1287, cert. denied, 281 Md. 735 (1977).

Rule 15-503. Bond — Temporary restraining order and preliminary injunction.

(a) *Generally.* Except as otherwise provided in this Rule, a court may not issue a temporary restraining order or preliminary injunction unless a bond has been filed. The bond shall be in an amount approved by the court for the payment of any damages to which a party enjoined may be entitled as a result of the injunction.

(b) *State of Maryland.* If the injunction is sought by the State of Maryland, a political subdivision of the State of Maryland, or an officer or agency of the State or subdivision, the court may dispense with the requirement of a bond and shall do so when required by law.

(c) *Waiver.* On request, the court may dispense with the requirement of surety or other security for a bond if it is satisfied that (1) the person is unable to provide surety or other security for the bond, (2) substantial injustice would result if an injunction did not issue, and (3) the case is one of extraordinary hardship. The request shall be supported by an affidavit or testimony under oath stating the grounds for entitlement to the waiver.

Cross references. — Title 1, Chapter 400.
Source. — This Rule is derived from former Rule BB75.

Compliance with Rules required. — Equity courts should be especially alert to see that the parties comply with the applicable Rules before an ex parte injunction is ordered. Saunders v. Stradley, 25 Md. App. 85, 333 A.2d 604 (1975).

Rule 15-504. Temporary restraining order.

(a) *Standard for granting.* A temporary restraining order may be granted only if it clearly appears from specific facts shown by affidavit or other statement under oath that immediate, substantial, and irreparable harm will result to the person seeking the order before a full adversary hearing can be held on the propriety of a preliminary or final injunction.

(b) *Without notice.* A temporary restraining order may be granted without written or oral notice only if the applicant or the applicant's attorney certifies to the court in writing, and the court finds, that specified efforts commensurate with the circumstances have been made to give notice. Before ruling, the judge may communicate informally with other parties and any other person against whom the order is sought or their attorneys.

(c) *Contents and duration.* In addition to complying with Rule 15-502 (e), the order shall (1) contain the date and hour of issuance; (2) define the harm that the court finds will result if the temporary restraining order does not issue; (3) state the basis for the court's finding that the harm will be irreparable; (4) state that a party or any person affected by the order may apply for a modification or dissolution of the order on two days' notice, or such shorter notice as the court may prescribe, to the party who obtained the order; and (5) set forth an expiration date, which shall be not later than ten days after issuance for a resident and not later than 35 days after issuance for a nonresident. The order shall be promptly filed with the clerk. On motion filed pursuant to Rule 1-204, the court by order may extend the expiration date for no more than one additional like period, unless the person against whom the order is directed consents to an extension for a longer period. The order shall state the reasons for the extension.

(d) *Service; binding effect.* A temporary restraining order shall be served promptly on the person to whom it is directed, but it shall be binding on that person upon receipt of actual notice of it by any means.

(e) *Denial.* If the court denies a temporary restraining order, the clerk shall note the denial by docket entry in accordance with Rule 2-601 (b).

(f) *Modification or dissolution.* A party or person affected by the order may apply for modification or dissolution of the order on two days' notice to the party who obtained the temporary restraining order, or on such shorter notice as the court may prescribe. The court shall proceed to hear and determine the application at the earliest possible time. The party who obtained the temporary restraining order has the burden of showing that it should be continued.

Source. — This Rule is derived from former Rules BB72, 73, and 79, and Fed.R.Civ.P. 65 (b).

University of Baltimore Law Review. — For article, "New Balance in the Rights of Creditors and Debtors: The Effect on Maryland Law," see 2 U. Balt. L. Rev. 236 (1973).

Compliance with Rules required. — Equity courts should be especially alert to see that the parties comply with the applicable Rules before an ex parte injunction is ordered. Saunders v. Stradley, 25 Md. App. 85, 333 A.2d 604 (1975).

Orders issued under former Rule BB72 are intended to suspend action until an opportunity is afforded the defendants to answer and defend. Harford County Educ. Ass'n v. Board of Educ., 281 Md. 574, 380 A.2d 1041 (1977).

Restrictions on injunctions in labor disputes. — Former Article 100, §§ 63 to 75 (now see § 4-301 et seq. of the Labor and Employment Article), places restrictions on the power

of equity courts to grant injunctions in labor disputes. District 1199E, Nat'l Union of Hosp. & Health Care Employees v. Johns Hopkins Hosp., 293 Md. 343, 444 A.2d 448 (1982).

Since the Maryland Anti-Injunction Act only covers "labor disputes," ex parte injunctions still may be obtained in proceedings not covered by the Act; unlike an injunction obtained pursuant to the Act, ex parte injunctions can be obtained virtually immediately, and without extensive procedural prerequisites. District 1199E, Nat'l Union of Hosp. & Health Care Employees v. Johns Hopkins Hosp., 293 Md. 343, 444 A.2d 448 (1982).

Evidence. — In granting an injunction against a contemplated use of property which is not unlawful per se, the chancellor should require the plaintiff to present to the court strong prima facie evidence of the facts upon which his equity rests, and he must prove every material allegation by a preponderance of the evidence. Air Lift, Ltd. v. Board of County Comm'rs, 262 Md. 368, 278 A.2d 244 (1971).

Where terms of injunction are not specific and definite, a defendant will not be punished for contempt for noncompliance. Harford County Educ. Ass'n v. Board of Educ., 281 Md. 574, 380 A.2d 1041 (1977).

Collateral attack on violated injunction not permitted. — A party enjoined may not violate the terms of an injunction and then attack the injunction collaterally in a contempt proceeding, civil or criminal. Harford County Educ. Ass'n v. Board of Educ., 281 Md. 574, 380 A.2d 1041 (1977).

Temporary restraining order improperly issued. — Temporary restraining order of circuit court requiring compliance with administrative agency decision was not issued in accordance with the rules where the appellant was not given an opportunity for a hearing, and where the order did not contain an expiration date. LOOC, Inc. v. Kohli, 347 Md. 258, 701 A.2d 92 (1997).

Temporary injunction properly dissolved. — Where, even accepting petitioner's allegations that the actions of the respondents in terminating his employment were arbitrary, capricious and without cause as true, his bill, nevertheless, failed to show that he would suffer irreparable injury, and the grievance procedure available under the Maryland Department of Personnel provided an adequate remedy, the temporary injunction was properly dissolved. Coster v. Department of Personnel, 36 Md. App. 523, 373 A.2d 1287, cert. denied, 281 Md. 735 (1977).

Rule 15-505. Preliminary injunction.

(a) *Notice.* A court may not issue a preliminary injunction without notice to all parties and an opportunity for a full adversary hearing on the propriety of its issuance.

(b) *Consolidation with trial on merits.* Before or after commencement of the hearing on the preliminary injunction, the court may order that a trial on the merits be advanced and consolidated with the preliminary injunction hearing, so long as any right to trial by jury is preserved.

Cross references. — Rule 2-511 (a).
Source. — This Rule is derived from former Rule BB74 and Fed.R.Civ.P. 65 (a).

Permanent injunction is invalid without determination on merits. National Collegiate Athletic Ass'n v. John Hopkins Univ., 301 Md. 574, 483 A.2d 1272 (1984).

Temporary restraining order improperly issued. — Temporary restraining order of circuit court requiring compliance with administrative agency decision was not issued in accordance with the rules where the appellant was not given an opportunity for a hearing, and where the order did not contain an expiration date. LOOC, Inc. v. Kohli, 347 Md. 258, 701 A.2d 92 (1997).

Mootness. — Although the appeal from an ex parte injunction is moot, the appeal from an interlocutory injunction is not. State Comm'n on Human Relations v. Suburban Hosp., 113 Md. App. 62, 686 A.2d 706 (1996).

CHAPTER 600. JUDICIAL RELEASE.

Rule 15-601. Judicial release of individuals confined for mental disorders.

(a) *Statutory definitions.* The definitions stated in Code, Health-General Article, § 10-101 are applicable to this Rule except that in this Rule, the term "facility" includes hospitals operated by the Department of Veterans Affairs.

(b) *Applicability.* This Rule applies to petitions filed pursuant to Code, Health-General Article, § 10-805 for release from a facility.

(c) *Contents of petition.* A petition for judicial release of a patient from a facility treating or caring for patients with mental disorders shall be titled "In the Matter of _____ for the Judicial Release From _____". The petition shall comply with Rules 2-303 through 2-305 and shall set forth:

(1) the name and address of the petitioner;

(2) the name of the patient and the facility at which the patient is confined;

(3) if the petition is filed by a person other than the patient, the petitioner's relationship to the patient and a description of the interest of the petitioner in the welfare of the patient;

(4) petitioner's best information as to the date of admission of the patient to the facility;

(5) whether the admission was voluntary or involuntary;

(6) the ground upon which the release is requested, which shall be that at the time the petition is filed one of the following is true: (A) the patient has no mental disorder; or (B) if the patient has a mental disorder, the disorder does not require inpatient medical care or treatment for the protection of the patient or others;

(7) a statement to the best of the petitioner's knowledge as to whether there were previous proceedings for the judicial release of the patient and, if so, a description of the proceedings, including a docket reference and any outcome; and

(8) if a jury trial is desired, a request for jury trial in the form prescribed in Rule 2-325.

Source. — This Rule is derived from former Rule R80 c 1.

CHAPTER 700. MANDAMUS.

Rule 15-701. Mandamus.

(a) *Commencement of action.* An action for a writ of mandamus shall be commenced by the filing of a verified complaint, the form and contents of which shall comply with Rules 2-303 through 2-305. The plaintiff shall have the right to claim and prove damages, but a demand for general relief shall not be permitted.

(b) *Defendant's response.* The defendant may respond to the complaint as provided in Rule 2-322 or Rule 2-323. An answer shall be verified and shall fully and specifically set forth all defenses upon which the defendant intends to rely, but the defendant shall not assert any defense that the defendant might have relied upon in an answer to a previous complaint for mandamus by the same plaintiff for the same relief.

(c) *Amendment.* Amendment of pleadings shall be in accordance with Rule 2-341.

(d) *Ex parte action on complaint.* (1) Upon default by defendant. If the defendant is in default for failure to appear, the court, on motion of the plaintiff, shall hear the complaint ex parte. The plaintiff shall be required to introduce evidence in support of the complaint. If the court finds that the facts and law authorize the granting of the writ, it shall order the writ to issue without delay. Otherwise, the court shall dismiss the complaint.

(2) Upon striking of defendant's answer. If the court grants a motion to strike an answer filed pursuant to Rule 2-322 (e) and the court does not permit the filing of an amended answer, the court may enter an order authorizing the writ to issue without requiring the plaintiff to introduce evidence in support of the complaint.

(e) *Writ of mandamus.* (1) Contents and time for compliance. The writ shall be peremptory in form and shall require the defendant to perform immediately the duty sought to be enforced. For good cause shown, however, the court may extend the time for compliance. It shall not be necessary for the writ to recite the reasons for its issuance.

(2) Certificate of compliance. Immediately after compliance, the defendant shall file a certificate stating that all the acts commanded by the writ have been fully performed.

(3) Enforcement. Upon application by the plaintiff, the court may proceed under Rule 2-648 against a party who disobeys the writ.

(f) *Adequate remedy at law.* The existence of an adequate remedy in damages does not preclude the issuance of the writ unless the defendant establishes that property exists from which damages can be recovered or files a sufficient bond to cover all damages and costs.

Source. — This Rule is derived from former Rules BE40, BE41, BE43, BE44, BE45, and BE46.

I. In General.
II. When Mandamus Will Issue.
III. Procedure.

I. IN GENERAL.

Editor's note. — For definition of "affidavit," see Rule 1-202 (b). As to restrictions on writ of mandamus against State or officer thereof to prevent collection of tax, see TG § 13-505.

The following sections of the Code specifically authorize application for a writ of mandamus to be made for the purposes indicated:

Article 25, § 117 — To compel county drainage district or board of drainage commissioners to levy tax or special assessment in order to remedy default in payment of bond.

Article 33, § 17-7 — To compel board of election canvassers to correct errors.

State Government, § 17-103 — To officeholder when there has been an inadvertent issuance of a commission.

University of Baltimore Law Review. — For article, "State Constitutional Law for Maryland Lawyers: Judicial Relief for Violations of Rights," see 10 U. Balt. L. Rev. 102 (1980).

Nature of writ. — Mandamus, while resembling in some respects a decree in equity

for specific performance, is a common law process issued for the special purpose indicated in the writ, and the relief prayed cannot be modified according to circumstances, such as under a prayer for general relief in a bill in equity. The writ of mandamus depends upon the facts, circumstances, and conditions existing at the time the petition for mandamus is filed. Town of District Heights v. County Comm'rs, 210 Md. 142, 122 A.2d 489 (1956).

Mandamus is a remedy that is based upon reasons of justice and public policy to preserve peace, order and good government, and although the writ is issued by the law courts, it may be compared to a bill in equity for specific performance. Ipes v. Board of Fire Comm'rs, 224 Md. 180, 167 A.2d 337 (1961).

Mandamus is a writ in the nature of a prerogative writ, and is an extraordinary remedy. The writ is issued by the law courts. Ipes v. Board of Fire Comm'rs, 224 Md. 180, 167 A.2d 337 (1961).

The writ of mandamus, as generally used, is to compel inferior tribunals, public officials or administrative agencies to perform their function, or perform some particular duty imposed upon them which in its nature is imperative and to the performance of which duty the party applying for the writ has a clear legal right. Criminal Injuries Comp. Bd. v. Gould, 273 Md. 486, 331 A.2d 55 (1975); Rodgers v. Washington Sub. San. Comm'n, 32 Md. App. 664, 363 A.2d 633, cert. denied, 278 Md. 738 (1976).

Alternative writs and returns abolished. — The old alternative writs and returns are abolished, the respondent answers the petition, the petitioner is permitted to traverse the answer, and the case proceeds in much the same manner as do other actions. Ipes v. Board of Fire Comm'rs, 224 Md. 180, 167 A.2d 337 (1961).

II. WHEN MANDAMUS WILL ISSUE.

Generally. — Although mandamus is not a writ ex debito justitiae but rests in the sound discretion of the court, such discretion may not be exercised arbitrarily. The discretion must be exercised under the established rules of law and if under those rules a party is entitled to the writ, it must be issued. Weber v. Zimmerman, 23 Md. 45 (1865); Hardcastle v. Maryland & D.R.R., 32 Md. 32 (1870); Brooke v. Widdicombe, 39 Md. 386 (1874); Kinlein v. Mayor of Baltimore, 118 Md. 576, 85 A. 679 (1912).

Mandamus is not a writ of right, nor is it granted as of course, but only in the sound legal discretion of the judge who directs the issuance thereof, and, in approaching the question concerning the issuance, vel non, of the writ, the courts invoke equitable principles to reach the real merits of the controversy between the parties. Ipes v. Board of Fire Comm'rs, 224 Md. 180, 167 A.2d 337 (1961).

The writ will never be granted where it is unnecessary or would work injustice or be nugatory or introduce confusion into municipal administration. Kinlein v. Mayor of Baltimore, 118 Md. 576, 85 A. 679 (1912).

The writ will not be granted if it would be nugatory, or where it would demand an abstract right but not subserve any just or useful purpose. Town of District Heights v. County Comm'rs, 210 Md. 142, 122 A.2d 489 (1956).

Where the urgency of establishing a rule of future conduct in matters of important public concern is imperative and manifest, a departure from the general rule and practice of not deciding academic questions may be justified. Board of Educ. v. Montgomery County, 237 Md. 191, 205 A.2d 202 (1964).

Mandamus will lie to remedy arbitrary abuses of discretion. State Dep't of Health v. Walker, 238 Md. 512, 209 A.2d 555 (1965).

In absence of statutory provision for hearing or review. — Judicial review can properly be sought by a petition for writ of mandamus where there is no statutory provision for hearing or review. State Dep't of Health v. Walker, 238 Md. 512, 209 A.2d 555 (1965).

But mandamus is not proper to review nonministerial acts of public officials or agencies. State Dep't of Health v. Walker, 238 Md. 512, 209 A.2d 555 (1965).

Nor to circumvent administrative remedies. — A person cannot circumvent possible administrative remedies by simply bringing an action for mandamus. Myers v. Chief of Baltimore County Fire Bureau, 237 Md. 583, 207 A.2d 467 (1965).

A ministerial duty may be enforced by mandamus. Sudler v. Lankford, 82 Md. 142, 33 A. 455 (1895).

But a discretionary duty may not be enforced by mandamus. Devin v. Belt, 70 Md. 352, 17 A. 375 (1889).

Where acts and duties necessarily call for the exercise of judgment and discretion on the part of officials, mandamus will not lie to direct the manner in which such discretion shall be exercised. Criminal Injuries Comp. Bd. v. Gould, 273 Md. 486, 331 A.2d 55 (1975).

Appropriate where law has established no specific remedy. — Mandamus is appropriate in all cases where the law has established no specific remedy, and where in justice there ought to be one. Harwood v. Marshall, 9 Md. 83 (1856); Legg v. Mayor of Annapolis, 42 Md. 203 (1875).

Mandamus will not lie when there is an adequate remedy at law. Brown v. Bragunier, 79 Md. 234, 29 A. 7 (1894).

Petitioner must show clear legal right and imperative duty on part of defendant. — Mandamus will not issue unless petitioner shows a clear legal right in himself and a corresponding imperative duty on part of defendant. Upshur v. Mayor of Baltimore, 94 Md. 743, 51 A. 953 (1902); County Comm'rs v. Fout, 110 Md. 165, 72 A. 765 (1909); Whittle v. Munshower, 221 Md. 258, 155 A.2d 670, cert. denied, 362 U.S. 981, 80 S. Ct. 1069, 4 L. Ed. 2d (1960); Myers v. Chief of Baltimore County Fire Bureau, 237 Md. 583, 207 A.2d 467 (1965).

To be entitled to the issuance of the writ of mandamus, the relator must have a real interest in the subject matter of the suit whether it be his alone or shared by a great number of people, and the respondent must owe him, or the group of which he is a member, an imperative duty. Rodgers v. Washington Sub. San. Comm'n, 32 Md. App. 664, 363 A.2d 633, cert. denied, 278 Md. 738 (1976).

Laches is a proper ground for refusing to issue a writ of mandamus. Ipes v. Board of Fire Comm'rs, 224 Md. 180, 167 A.2d 337 (1961).

Medical malpractice actions. — An order denying a motion for change in venue in a medical malpractice arbitration proceeding is not immediately reviewable in circuit court through an action for writ of mandamus or certiorari. Dorchester Gen. Hosp. v. Sober, 79 Md. App. 110, 555 A.2d 1074 (1989).

III. PROCEDURE.

Facts must be stated and proved or admitted. — In an application for mandamus all the facts necessary for the writ must be stated and proved or admitted on the record. McCurdy v. Jessup, 126 Md. 318, 95 A. 37 (1915); Potee v. County Comm'rs, 138 Md. 381, 113 A. 884 (1921); Brack v. Wells, 184 Md. 86, 40 A.2d 319 (1944).

Affidavit required. — Petition for writ of mandamus without affidavit of applicant was held to be insufficient. Brack v. Wells, 184 Md. 86, 40 A.2d 319 (1944).

The failure of petitioner to file exhibits is waived by answer not objecting on that score. Brooke v. Widdicombe, 39 Md. 386 (1874).

Former Rule BE41 replaces alternative writ of mandamus. — The answer required by former Rule BE41 stands in the place of the return to the alternative writ of mandamus under former practice, and seems to have been primarily directed to the degree of certainty and precision with which the defendant is required to set forth the facts relied upon by him in his answer. Ipes v. Board of Fire Comm'rs, 224 Md. 180, 167 A.2d 337 (1961).

Sufficiency of answer generally. — The exact degree of definiteness and certainty required in an answer in a mandamus case is difficult to determine. While undoubtedly the passage of former § 3 of Article 60 and similar statutes in other jurisdictions simplifying the procedure has caused a general relaxation of the old common-law rule, such action has not obviated the necessity for precision, nor has it entirely removed the strictness with which the courts have always dealt with the pleadings in such cases. Pennington v. Gilbert, 148 Md. 649, 129 A. 905 (1925).

If the answer sets up any good defense, it should not be quashed because it is in other respects evasive or irresponsive. Legg v. Mayor of Baltimore, 42 Md. 203 (1875).

Answer must state positive and definite facts. — If answer is indefinite and uncertain, relief will be granted. Pennington v. Gilbert, 148 Md. 649, 129 A. 905 (1925).

Answer held insufficient. — See Creager v. Hooper, 83 Md. 490, 35 A. 159 (1855).

The answer stands in the place of the return to the alternative writ under former

practice, and seems to have been primarily directed to the degree of certainty and precision with which the defendant is required to set forth the facts relied upon by him in his answer. Ipes v. Board of Fire Comm'rs, 224 Md. 180, 167 A.2d 337 (1961).

Defense which could not have been relied on in previous case. — Former § 4 of Article 60, similar to section c of former Rule BE41, had no application where the defense could not have been relied upon in previous case. County Comm'rs v. Fout, 110 Md. 165, 72 A. 765 (1909).

Prerequisites to issuance of writ where defendant fails to answer. — When defendant fails to answer, the writ cannot issue without due proof of facts and judge's being satisfied on law. Legg v. Mayor of Annapolis, 42 Md. 203 (1875); Sudler v. Lankford, 82 Md. 142, 33 A. 455 (1895); Upshur v. Mayor of Baltimore, 94 Md. 743, 51 A. 953 (1902); Beasley v. Ridout, 94 Md. 641, 52 A. 61 (1902).

A statement in opinion of lower court that "at the hearing the questions at issue were waived or admitted" is equivalent to full proof. Beasley v. Ridout, 94 Md. 641, 52 A. 61 (1902).

Discretion of court to refuse writ. — Former § 9 of Article 60 did not take away the discretion of the court to refuse the writ of mandamus. Webber v. Zimmerman, 23 Md. 45 (1865).

A claim for costs and damages is inchoate, and cannot be considered as personal assets until judgment is entered. Booze v. Humbird, 27 Md. 1 (1867).

Attorney's fees incurred by successful party. — Provisions of former Rule BE44 do not authorize the assessment of attorney's fees incurred by a successful party in a mandamus action as damages or costs in such an action merely on the basis that the party against whom the attorney's fees are sought is the unsuccessful litigant. Hess Constr. Co. v. Board of Educ., 102 Md. App. 736, 651 A.2d 446 (1995).

Mandamus will not issue where a plain, adequate remedy exists in an ordinary course of law. Walter v. Board of County Comm'rs, 179 Md. 665, 22 A.2d 472 (1941).

Mandamus will not lie to compel county commissioners to repair roads, as the legal remedy for damages in such cases is adequate. Walter v. Board of County Comm'rs, 179 Md. 665, 22 A.2d 472 (1941).

Intent. — See Conner v. Groh, 90 Md. 674, 45 A. 1024 (1900).

Former § 98, Article 16, was intended to reach the class of cases in which injunction or mandamus had been refused because the plaintiff could be compensated in damages in suits at law. Frederick County Nat'l Bank v. Shafer, 87 Md. 54, 39 A. 320 (1898); Universal

Realty Corp. v. Felser, 179 Md. 635, 22 A.2d 448 (1941).

Applicable to cases where damages, not debt, are involved. — Former § 98, Article 16, related to cases where damages, as contradistinguished from debt, were involved. Frederick County Nat'l Bank v. Shafer, 87 Md. 54, 39 A. 320 (1898); Conner v. Groh, 90 Md. 674, 45 A. 1024 (1900).

Hearing and burden of proof. — Former § 98, Article 16, was not intended to be applicable on demurrer, but only after such hearing as might make it appear to the court that the defendants, in a given case, could respond to damages, or could give a bond, and that such relief would be adequate. The burden is on the defendants in this respect. Universal Realty Corp. v. Felser, 179 Md. 635, 22 A.2d 448 (1941).

CHAPTER 800. MARYLAND AUTOMOBILE INSURANCE FUND.

Rule 15-801. Actions involving the Maryland Automobile Insurance Fund.

The rules in this Chapter apply to actions involving the Maryland Automobile Insurance Fund that are authorized by Code, Article 48A, § 243H.

Cross references. — For procedure governing claims against the Fund not rising to the level of a civil action, *see* C.O.M.A.R. 14.07.04.01 — .06, Uninsured Persons' Claims for Compensation from the Maryland Automobile Insurance Fund.

Source. — This Rule is derived from former Rule BW1 b.

Editor's note. — Article 48A, § 243H, which is referred to in this Rule, has been revised as §§ 20-601 and 20-603 through 20-608 of the Insurance Article.

Rule 15-802. Definitions.

In Rules 15-803 through 15-805 the following definitions apply:

(a) *Claimant.* "Claimant" means a person who claims damages resulting from an act or omission of a disappearing motorist, an unidentified motorist, or an uninsured motorist.

Cross references. — Code, Article 48A, § 243H (a).

(b) *Disappearing motorist.* "Disappearing motorist" means a motor vehicle owner or operator (1) whose identity is known but whose whereabouts cannot be ascertained for the purpose of serving process and (2) who was uninsured at the time of the act or omission or whose status as insured or uninsured cannot be ascertained, after all reasonable efforts have been made.

(c) *Executive Director.* "Executive Director" means the Executive Director of the Maryland Automobile Insurance Fund or a designee of the Executive Director.

(d) *Fund.* "Fund" means the Maryland Automobile Insurance Fund.

(e) *Unidentified motorist.* "Unidentified motorist" means a motor vehicle owner or operator whose identity and whereabouts are not known.

(f) *Uninsured motorist.* "Uninsured motorist" means a motor vehicle owner or operator whose whereabouts are ascertainable for the purpose of serving process, but who was uninsured at the time of the act or omission.

Source. — This Rule is derived from former Rule BW1 a.

Editor's note. — Article 48A, § 243H (a), which is referred to in the Cross Reference note to section (a), has been revised as § 20-601 of the Insurance Article.

Rule 15-803. Uninsured motorist — Action against motorist.

(a) *Against whom brought.* An action on a claim against an uninsured motorist shall be brought against the uninsured motorist. The Fund shall not be named as a defendant.

(b) *Notice to Executive Director.* Within 15 days after the filing of the complaint, the claimant shall mail a copy of the complaint and summons to the Executive Director. Failure to give notice pursuant to this section shall not defeat the claim against the Fund if the Fund has reasonable notice of the pendency of the action and a reasonable opportunity to defend.

(c) *Order for payment.* (1) By consent. After entry of a money judgment against the uninsured motorist, the claimant may file with the court a stipulation, signed by the Executive Director, setting forth the deductions required by law and consenting to entry of an order directing payment of a specified amount by the Fund.

(2) On motion. After entry of a money judgment against the uninsured motorist, the claimant may file a motion for payment of a specified amount by the Fund. The motion shall be supported by affidavit, shall set forth the grounds for entitlement to payment by the Fund and all the deductions required by law, and shall be served on the Executive Director.

Cross references. — *See* Code, Article 48A, § 243-I, for required deductions from payment by the Fund.

Source. — This Rule is derived from former Rules BW4 and BW6.

Editor's note. — Article 48A, § 243-I, which is referred to in the Cross Reference note to this Rule, has been been revised as § 20-602 of the Insurance Article.

Rule 15-804. Unidentified or disappearing motorist — Action against Fund.

(a) *Against whom brought.* An action on a claim against an unidentified or disappearing motorist shall be brought against the Fund.

(b) *Condition precedent to action against Fund.* Prior to bringing an action against the Fund for damages resulting from an act or omission of an unidentified motorist or a disappearing motorist, the claimant shall first present a request to the Executive Director, in the manner and form prescribed by the Executive Director, for a stipulation by the Fund that the claimant has met the procedural requirements for bringing an action against the Fund.

(c) *Venue.* The venue of an action against the Fund shall be either the county in which the claimant resides or the county in which the alleged act or omission by the unidentified motorist or disappearing motorist occurred.

(d) *Complaint.* In addition to complying with Rules 2-303 through 2-305, the complaint shall contain a statement as to whether the stipulation requested pursuant to section (b) of this Rule was granted or refused. If the stipulation was granted, a copy of the stipulation shall be filed with the complaint.

(e) *Motion to dismiss.* If the stipulation requested pursuant to section (b) of this Rule was refused, the Fund, within the time for filing an answer to the complaint, may file a motion to dismiss the complaint for failure of the claimant to meet the procedural requirements for bringing an action against the Fund. This defense may be joined with any other defense raised by motion pursuant to Rule 2-322 and is waived if not raised by motion before an answer is filed. When a motion is filed pursuant to this section, the time for filing an answer is extended without special order of the court to 15 days after entry of an order denying the motion.

(f) *Order for payment.* (1) By consent. After determination of the claimant's gross damages, the claimant may file a stipulation, signed by the Executive Director, setting forth the deductions required by law and consenting to entry of an order directing payment of a specified amount by the Fund.

(2) On motion. After determination of the claimant's gross damages, either party may file a motion for an order directing payment by the Fund of a specified amount. The motion shall set forth the deductions required by law.

Cross references. — Code, Article 48A, § 243-I.

Source. — This Rule is derived from former Rules BW2, BW3, and BW5.

Editor's note. — Article 48A, § 243-I, which is referred to in the Cross Reference note to this Rule, has been been revised as § 20-602 of the Insurance Article.

Rule 15-805. Consent judgment.

If the claimant and the Fund enter into a settlement agreement, in an action involving a claim for payment by the Fund, the court may enter a judgment by consent of the parties upon the filing of a motion setting forth the grounds for the claimant's entitlement to payment by the Fund, all the deductions required by law, and the amount of the agreed settlement. The motion shall be accompanied by a stipulation signed by the Executive Director consenting to entry of an order directing payment of a specified amount by the Fund.

Source. — This Rule is derived from former Rule BW7.

CHAPTER 900. NAME — CHANGE OF.

Rule 15-901. Action for change of name.

(a) *Applicability.* This Rule applies to actions for change of name other than in connection with an adoption or divorce.

(b) *Venue.* An action for change of name shall be brought in the county where the person whose name is sought to be changed resides.

(c) *Petition.* (1) Contents. The action for change of name shall be commenced by filing a petition captioned "In the Matter of ..." [stating the name of the person whose name is sought to be changed] "for change of name to ..." [stating the change of name desired]. The petition shall be under oath and shall contain at least the following information:

(A) the name, address, and date and place of birth of the person whose name is sought to be changed;

(B) whether the person whose name is sought to be changed has ever been known by any other name and, if so, the name or names and the circumstances under which they were used;

(C) the change of name desired;

(D) all reasons for the requested change;

(E) a certification that the petitioner is not requesting the name change for any illegal or fraudulent purpose; and

(F) if the person whose name is sought to be changed is a minor, the names and addresses of that person's parents and any guardian or custodian.

(2) Documents to be attached to petition. The petitioner shall attach to the petition a copy of a birth certificate or other documentary evidence from which the court can find that the current name of the person whose name is sought to be changed is as alleged.

(d) *Service of petition — When required.* If the person whose name is sought to be changed is a minor, a copy of the petition, any attachments, and the notice issued pursuant to section (e) of this Rule shall be served upon that person's parents and any guardian or custodian in the manner provided by Rule 2-121. When proof is made by affidavit that good faith efforts to serve a parent, guardian, or custodian pursuant to Rule 2-121 (a) have not succeeded and that Rule 2-121 (b) is inapplicable or that service pursuant to that Rule is impracticable, the court may order that service may be made by (1) the publication required by subsection (e)(2) of this Rule and (2) mailing a copy of the petition, any attachments, and notice by first class mail to the last known address of the parent, guardian, or custodian to be served.

(e) *Notice.* (1) Issued by clerk. Upon the filing of the petition, the clerk shall sign and issue a notice that (A) includes the caption of the action, (B) describes the substance of the petition and the relief sought, and (C) states the latest date by which an objection to the petition may be filed.

(2) Publication. Unless the court on motion of the petitioner orders otherwise, the notice shall be published one time in a newspaper of general circulation in the county at least fifteen days before the date specified in the notice for filing an objection to the petition. The petitioner shall thereafter file a certificate of publication.

(f) *Objection to petition.* Any person may file an objection to the petition. The objection shall be filed within the time specified in the notice and shall be supported by an affidavit which sets forth the reasons for the objection. The affidavit shall be made on personal knowledge, shall set forth facts that would be admissible in evidence, and shall show affirmatively that the affiant is competent to testify to the matters stated in the affidavit. The objection and affidavit shall be served upon the petitioner in accordance with Rule 1-321. The petitioner may file a response within 15 days after being served with the objection and affidavit. A person desiring a hearing shall so request in the objection or response under the heading "Request for Hearing."

(g) *Action by court.* After the time for filing objections and responses has expired, the court may hold a hearing or may rule on the petition without a hearing and shall enter an appropriate order, except that the court shall not deny the petition without a hearing if one was requested by the petitioner.

Source. — This Rule is derived in part from former Rules BH70 through BH75 and is in part new.

Common law right to adopt name. — The common law recognizes the right of any person, absent a statute to the contrary, to adopt any name by which he may become known, and by which he may transact business and execute contracts and sue or be sued. Stuart v. Board of Supvrs. of Elections, 266 Md. 440, 295 A.2d 223 (1972).

In the absence of a statute to the contrary, a person may adopt any name by which he wishes to become known, as long as he does so consistently and nonfraudulently. Hardy v. Hardy, 269 Md. 412, 306 A.2d 244 (1973).

Right of married woman to retain birth-given name. — Maryland law permits a married woman to retain her birth-given name by the procedure of consistent, nonfraudulent use following her marriage. Stuart v. Board of Supvrs. of Elections, 266 Md. 440, 295 A.2d 223 (1972).

A married woman's surname does not become that of her husband where she evidences a clear intent to consistently and nonfraudulently use her birth-given name subsequent to her marriage. Stuart v. Board of Supvrs. of Elections, 266 Md. 440, 295 A.2d 223 (1972).

The mere fact of marriage does not, as a matter of law, operate to establish the custom and tradition of married women adopting their husbands' surname as their own. Stuart v. Board of Supvrs. of Elections, 266 Md. 440, 295 A.2d 223 (1972).

Woman not required to register to vote in surname of husband. — The provisions of Article 33, § 3-18 (a) (3) and (c), do not require that a married woman register to vote in the surname of her husband unless her name has been changed by legal proceedings under former Maryland Rules BH70-BH75, and Article 16, § 123, of the Annotated Code of Maryland. That section, even with the aid of a long-standing and uniform administrative practice, does not effect such a derogation of the common law. Stuart v. Board of Supvrs. of Elections, 266 Md. 440, 295 A.2d 223 (1972).

Child taking name of foster parents. — Where a court set aside a co-guardianship order, any advantage to the subject child in having the same last name as his foster parents no longer existed, and his name was not changed. In re Adoption/Guardianship No. 3155, 103 Md. App. 300, 653 A.2d 521 (1995).

The purpose of requiring publication is to apprise as many people as possible of the pendency of the petition so anyone who reasonably wishes to offer relevant information to aid the court in performing its functions can do so. Hardy v. Hardy, 269 Md. 412, 306 A.2d 244 (1973).

Waiver of publication in case involving infant. — It is difficult to imagine a case which has as its purpose the change of an infant's name under former Subtitle BH, as distinguished from other types of name change proceedings, where it would be proper to waive publication. Hardy v. Hardy, 269 Md. 412, 306 A.2d 244 (1973).

Where a motion seeking waiver of publication was based solely on the fact that a young child had no assets or liabilities, nor had he ever used his name for any instrument, while these grounds might form an appropriate basis for waiver of publication in a name change case involving an adult, they do not create a sufficient foundation for waiver on such a petition filed on behalf of an infant by another person under this subtitle. Hardy v. Hardy, 269 Md. 412, 306 A.2d 244 (1973).

Waiver or publication on motion of petitioner. — A court may waive publication under section (e) (2) of this Rule on motion of the petitioner, but not on its own initiative; in light of the disfavored status of waivers of publication, motions for waiver should be viewed by the court cautiously. 82 Op. Att'y Gen. (August 21, 1997).

CHAPTER 1000. WRONGFUL DEATH.

Rule 15-1001. Wrongful death.

(a) *Applicability.* This Rule applies to an action involving a claim for damages for wrongful death.

Cross references. — *See* Code, Courts Article, §§ 3-901 through 3-904, relating to wrongful death claims generally. *See also* Article 101, § 58 relating to wrongful death claims when worker's compensation may also be available, and Code, Article 48A, § 243H, relating to certain wrongful death claims against the Maryland Automobile Insurance Fund. *See also* Code, Estates and Trusts Article, § 8-103, relating to the limitation on presentation of claims against a decedent's estate.

(b) *Plaintiff.* If the wrongful act occurred in this State, all persons who are or may be entitled by law to damages by reason of the wrongful death shall be named as plaintiffs whether or not they join in the action. The words "to the use of" shall precede the name of any person named as a plaintiff who does not join in the action.

(c) *Notice to use plaintiff.* The party bringing the action shall mail a copy of the complaint by certified mail to any use plaintiff at the use plaintiff's last known address. Proof of mailing shall be filed as provided in Rule 2-126.

(d) *Complaint.* In addition to complying with Rules 2-303 through 2-305, the complaint shall state the relationship of each plaintiff to the decedent whose death is alleged to have been caused by the wrongful act.

Source. — This Rule is derived as follows: *Section (a)* is derived from former Rule Q40. *Section (b)* is derived from former Rule Q41 a.

Section (c) is new.
Section (d) is derived from former Rule Q42.

Editor's note. — Article 101, § 58, which is referred to in the Cross Reference note to section (a), has been been revised as § 9-901 et seq. of the Labor and Employment Article.

Article 48A, § 243H, which is referred to in the Cross Reference note to section (a), has been been revised as §§ 20-601 and 20-603 through 20-608 of the Insurance Article.

Maryland Law Review. — For note concerning person entitled to sue for wrongful death caused and occurring outside state of forum, see 2 Md. L. Rev. 168 (1938).

History and purpose of former Article 67, § 3. — See Kaufmann v. Service Trucking Co., 139 F. Supp. 1 (D. Md. 1956); Olewiler v. Fullerton Supply Co., 162 F. Supp. 563 (D. Md. 1958).

CJ § 3-903 must be read in conjunction with this Rule. Huber v. B & O R.R., 241 F. Supp. 646 (D. Md. 1965).

Suits must be filed in name of real parties in interest. — Since the adoption of former Rule Q41, suits under causes of action arising within this State must now be filed in the name of the real parties in interest, rather than in the name of the State. Robinson v. Lewis, 20 Md. App. 710, 317 A.2d 854 (1974).

Illinois administrator may sue in Maryland under Virginia statute. — A domiciliary administrator appointed in Illinois can maintain an action in a Maryland federal district court or any other court under the Virginia statute without qualifying in Virginia. Kaufmann v. Service Trucking Co., 139 F. Supp. 1 (D. Md. 1956).

Determination of status of compensation insurer. — In a wrongful death case arising under the Maryland law where workmen's compensation benefits have been paid, the compensation insurer would be required to be a party plaintiff. Maryland, however, does not apply such a rule in a conflict of laws situation, but, rather, would look to the law of the jurisdiction in which the insurer's rights arose to determine its status as a party plaintiff. Maryland ex rel. Geils v. Baltimore Transit Co., 37 F.R.D. 34 (D. Md. 1965).

Consent to settlement. — The settlement

by one wrongful death beneficiary requires the consent of the other joined beneficiaries or the approval of the court; the Wrongful Death Statute, § 3-901 et seq. of the Courts Article, and the rules relating to it implicitly require mutual consent or court approval. Walker v. Essex, 318 Md. 516, 569 A.2d 645 (1990).

TITLE 16. COURTS, JUDGES, AND ATTORNEYS

Editor's note. — The Court of Appeals, by Order dated June 5, 1996, effective January 1, 1997, rescinded Subtitles A, D, E, J, P, Q, R, T, U, V, W, Y, Z, BB, BD, BE, BG, BH, BJ, BL, BP, BQ, BR, BS, BW, and BY of Chapter 1100 of the Maryland Rules of Procedure, rescinded Subtitles P, BB, BQ, and BW of the Maryland District Rules, and rescinded Forms 22a, 23, 24, 25, and 26. The Order substituted for certain of the rules and forms rescinded new Title 9, Chapter 100, Title 10, Title 12, Title 13, Title 14, and Title 15 of the Maryland Rules of Procedure. Furthermore, the Order transferred, without readoption, Chapter 900, Chapter 1200, and Subtitles S, BU, and BV of Chapter 1100 of the Maryland Rules of Procedure and Chapter 1200 of the Maryland Dis-

trict Rules to be Title 9, Chapter 200, Title 11, and Title 16 of the Maryland Rules of Procedure. The Order provides that the new rules shall "apply to all actions commenced on or after January 1, 1997, and insofar as practicable, to all actions then pending."

Many of the cases in the notes to the various rules were decided prior to the 1996 revision. These cases have been retained under pertinent rules of this title where it is thought that such cases will be of value in interpreting the present rules.

A table of comparable rules, relating those rules rescinded effective January 1, 1997, to the revised rules in Title 9 through Title 16 is to be found in Volume 2 following the end of the Maryland Rules.

CHAPTER 100. COURT ADMINISTRATIVE STRUCTURE, JUDICIAL DUTIES, ETC.

Rule 16-101. Administrative responsibility.

a. *Chief Judge of the Court of Appeals.* 1. Generally. The Chief Judge of the Court of Appeals is responsible for the administration of the courts of the State. Pursuant to this responsibility he shall appoint, to serve at his pleasure, a State Court Administrator. In order to promote the efficient utilization of judicial manpower, the equalization of judicial workloads, and the expeditious disposition of cases, he may assign a judge of any court to sit temporarily in any other court within the judicial system. He may delegate administrative duties within the judicial system.

2. Pretrial proceeding in certain criminal cases. The Chief Judge of the Court of Appeals may, by Administrative Order, require in any county a pretrial proceeding in the District Court for an offense within the jurisdiction of the District Court punishable by imprisonment for a period in excess of 90 days. (Amended June 16, 1975, effective July 1, 1975.)

Committee note. — Article IV, § 18, of the Constitution designates the Chief Judge of the Court of Appeals as administrative head of the judicial system. His authority to name the State Court Administrator appears in § 13-101 of the Courts Article of the Annotated

Code. These provisions are repeated here so that the basic administrative authority of the Chief Judge will be outlined in one place, as part of a rule which generally establishes the administrative responsibility for various parts of the judicial system.

b. *Chief Judge of the Court of Special Appeals.* The Chief Judge of the Court of Special Appeals shall, subject to the direction of the Chief Judge of the Court of Appeals, and pursuant to the provisions of this Title, be responsible for the administration of the Court of Special Appeals. With respect to the administration of the Court of Special Appeals, and to the extent applicable, he shall possess the authority granted to a County Administrative Judge in section d of this Rule.

c. *Circuit Administrative Judge.* 1. Designation. In each judicial circuit there shall be a Circuit Administrative Judge. He shall be appointed by order, and serve at the pleasure of the Chief Judge of the Court of Appeals, provided that in the absence of any such appointment, the Chief Judge of the judicial circuit shall be the Circuit Administrative Judge.

2. Duties. (a) Generally. Each Circuit Administrative Judge shall be generally responsible for the administration of the several courts within his judicial circuit, pursuant to these Rules and subject to the direction of the Chief Judge of the Court of Appeals. Each Circuit Administrative Judge shall also be responsible for the supervision of the County Administrative Judges within his judicial circuit and may perform any of the duties of a County Administrative Judge. He shall also call a meeting of all judges of his judicial circuit at least once every six months.

(b) Removed cases — Approval authority. In the interest of expediting the trial of a removed action, criminal cause, or issue, and of equalizing judicial work loads to the extent feasible, it shall be the duty of a judge, before exercising removal authority designating a Court within his judicial circuit to which such action, criminal cause, or issue shall be removed, to obtain the approval of the Circuit Administrative Judge for such designation. It shall also be the duty of a judge, before exercising removal authority to a jurisdiction without the judicial circuit, to make inquiry of the Circuit Administrative Judge of the Circuit to which it is proposed to make the removal concerning the trial calendar and judicial work loads of any Court to which it is contemplated the action, criminal cause, or issue may be removed and to give consideration to the recommendations of such Circuit Administrative Judge. The Circuit Administrative Judge, in the interest of expediting the removal process, may at any time or from time to time delegate his approval authority under this Rule to any judge or judges within his judicial circuit. (Amended Oct. 13, 1970.)

Cross references. — For more detailed provisions pertaining to duties of Circuit Administrative Judges, see Rule 4-344 (d); Rule 16-103 (Assignment of Judges); Rule 16-104 (Judicial Leave); Rule 16-105 (Reports to Be Filed); Rule 16-106 (Court Sessions — Holidays — Time for Convening); Rule 16-201 a (Motion Day). For removal in civil actions and criminal causes, see Rules 2-505 and 4-254.

Committee note. — Section c of this Rule is based on portions of the Court of Appeals Administrative and Procedural Regulation of July 17, 1967. Under the Rule, and particularly the portions thereof, dealing with the Circuit Administrative Judge, the Chief Judge of the Court of Appeals is free to appoint any judge of a circuit, including but not necessarily limited to the Chief Judge of that circuit, to be Circuit Administrative Judge. The judge so appointed, even if he is not the Chief Judge of the Circuit, exercises the administrative powers granted in this and other rules, such as Rule 16-103, dealing with assignment of judges. The intent of this Rule is to vest administrative power, at the judicial circuit level, in the Circuit Administrative Judge. In this regard, it should be noted that a Chief Judge has no inherent administrative power or authority, with the exception of the right to preside at sessions of his court, when more than one judge is present. *See Bean v. Loryea*, 81 Cal. 151, 22 Pac. 513 (1889); *In re Opinion of the Justices*, 271 Mass. 575, 171 N.E. 237, 240 (1930), and 48 C.J.S. "Judges," § 2. Under this and other rules, the duty of selecting a panel for review of criminal sentences, as set forth in Article 27, § 645JA, of the Code, would be vested in the Circuit Administrative Judge and not the Chief Judge. So would the duty of arranging for a sitting of the court en banc under article IV, § 22, of the Constitu- tion. However, this Rule is not intended to interfere with the present practice of issuing process in the name of the Chief Judge of a Circuit.

d. *County Administrative Judge.* 1. Designation. In the first seven judicial circuits, the Circuit Administrative Judge of a judicial circuit may, from time to time, and with the approval of the Chief Judge of the Court of Appeals, by order appoint a judge of the Circuit Court for any county within his judicial circuit to be County Administrative Judge of the Circuit Court for such county. A County Administrative Judge may be replaced by the Circuit Administrative Judge of his circuit with the approval of the Chief Judge of the Court of Appeals or by the Chief Judge of the Court of Appeals on his own motion. In the Eighth Judicial Circuit the Circuit Administrative Judge shall have all the powers and duties of a County Administrative Judge.

Committee note. — This is essentially the language of Paragraph 3 of the July 17, 1967 Administrative and Procedural Regulation of the Court of Appeals, except that the Circuit Administrative Judge is made the basic ap- pointing and replacing authority to emphasize and reinforce his position in the administra- tive hierarchy. No express provision is made for a "County Administrative Judge" in any of the Supreme Bench courts, since the peculiar organization of these courts and their present method of functioning seems to make such unnecessary. The Circuit Administrative Judge in the Eighth Judicial Circuit is given the powers of a County Administrative Judge and pursuant to subsection 3 of this section may delegate portions of his authority to other judges of the Supreme Bench.

2. Duties. Subject to the general supervision of the Chief Judge of the Court of Appeals and to the direct supervision of his Circuit Administrative Judge, particularly with reference to assignment of judges and of cases, a County Administrative Judge shall be responsible for the administration of justice and for the administration of the court for which he is County Administrative Judge. His duties shall include:

(i) Supervision of all judges of his court, and of officers and employees of such court, including the authority to assign judges within his court pursuant to Rule 16-103 (Assignment of Judges).

(ii) Supervision and expeditious disposition of cases filed in his court, and the control of the trial and other calendars therein, including the authority to assign cases for trial and hearing pursuant to Rule 16-102 (Chambers Judge) and Rule 16-202 (Assignment of Actions for Trial).

(iii) Preparation of the budget of his court.

(iv) Ordering of the purchase of all equipment and supplies for his court and its ancillary services, such as master, auditor, examiner, court administrator, court stenographer, jury commissioner, staff of the medical and probation offices, and all additional court personnel other than personnel comprising the Clerk of Court's office.

(v) Subject to the approval of a majority of the judges of his court, supervision of, and responsibility for, the employment, discharge and classifi- cation of court personnel and personnel of its ancillary services and the maintenance of personnel files. However, each judge (subject to budget limitations) shall have the exclusive right to employ and discharge his personal secretary and law clerk.

Committee note. — Article IV, § 9, of the Constitution gives the judges of any court the power to appoint officers, and thus requires joint exercise of the personnel power. A similar provision was included in the July 17, 1967 Administrative and Procedure Regulation.

(vi) In general, the implementation and enforcement of all policies, rules and directives of the Court of Appeals, its Chief Judge, the Director of the Administrative Office of the Courts, and his Circuit Administrative Judge, and the performance of such other duties as may be necessary for the effective administration of the judicial business of his court and the prompt disposition of litigation therein.

Cross references. — For specific duties of a County Administrative Judge, see Rule 16-102 (Chambers Judge); Rule 16-103 (Assignment of Judges); Rule 16-201 (Motion Day — Calendar); Rule 16-202 (Assignment of Actions for Trial).

3. Power to delegate. (i) A County Administrative Judge, with the approval of his Circuit Administrative Judge, may delegate to any judge or to any committee of judges of his court, or to any officer or employee of such court, such of the responsibilities, duties and functions imposed upon him as he, in his discretion, shall deem necessary or desirable.

(ii) In the implementation of Code, Article 27, § 591 and Rule 4-271 (a), a County Administrative Judge may (A) with the approval of the Chief Judge of the Court of Appeals, authorize one or more judges to postpone criminal cases on appeal from the District Court or transferred from the District Court because of a demand for jury trial, and (B) authorize not more than one judge at a time to postpone all other criminal cases.

4. Single judge counties. In any county in which there is but one resident judge of the Circuit Court, such judge shall exercise, as appropriate, the power and authority of a County Administrative Judge. (Amended Mar. 23, 1989, effective July 1, 1989; June 5, 1996, effective Jan. 1, 1997.)

COMMENT

In general, section d (County Administrative Judge) is based upon the Court of Appeals Administrative and Procedural Regulation of July 17, 1967. Authority for the Rule is derived from article IV, § 18, of the Constitution, designating the Chief Judge of the Court of Appeals as administrative head of the judicial system and granting general rule-making and assignment power; the grant of administrative rule-making authority contained in chapter 444, Acts of 1966, the provisions of chapter 468, Acts of 1968, dealing with the distribution of judicial work loads and vacations; the provisions of CJ § 1-201, of the Code dealing with rule-making power of the judges of the several courts of the State; and the inherent power of courts to prescribe rules to effectuate the administration of justice, including the inherent power of superior courts to regulate inferior courts; see, e.g., Petite v. Estate of Papachrist, 219 Md. 173, 148 A.2d 377 (1959); Annots., "Power of Court to Prescribe Rules of Pleadings, Practice and Procedure," 110 A.L.R. 22 (1937); 158 A.L.R. 705 (1945); Dowling, *The Inherent Power of the Judiciary*, 21 A.B.A.J. 835 (1935); Pound, *Procedure Under Rules of Court in New Jersey*, 66 Harv. L. Rev. 28 (1952).

Source. — This Rule is former Rule 1200.

Effect of amendments. — The 1996 amendment substituted "Title" for "Chapter" in b.; in c., rewrote the Cross reference note and substituted "Rule 16-103" for "Rule 1202" in the third sentence of the Committee note; substituted "Rule 16-103" for "Rule 1202" in d. 2. (i); in d.2.(ii), substituted "Rule 16-202; for "Rule 1211"; and added the Source note.

Editor's note. — An Order dated June 5, 1996, effective Jan. 1, 1997, renumbered this Rule, which was formerly Rule 1200.

Courthouse security procedures. — A county administrative judge has authority to institute reasonable courthouse security procedures, and the State's Attorney and his staff may be required to adhere to those procedures. 78 Op. Att'y Gen. (March 15, 1993).

Rule 16-102. Chambers judge.

a. *Designation.* 1. Eighth Judicial Circuit. In the Eighth Judicial Circuit, the Circuit Administrative Judge shall from time to time designate one or more of the judges sitting in the courts of the Supreme Bench of Baltimore City to sit therein as chambers judge.

2. Other judicial circuits. In a county with more than four resident judges, the County Administrative Judge shall, and in any other county, he may, from time to time designate one or more of the judges sitting in his court to sit therein as chambers judge.

3. Responsibility of County Administrative Judge. In the Eighth Judicial Circuit, and in any county where designation of a chambers judge is mandatory pursuant to subsection 2 of this section, it shall be the responsibility of the County Administrative Judge to insure that a chambers judge is on duty in the courthouse whenever the courthouse is open for the transaction of judicial business therein.

Cross references. — In the Eighth Judicial Circuit the Circuit Administrative Judge has all the powers and duties of a County Administrative Judge. See section d 1 of Rule 16-101 (Administrative Responsibility).

b. *Duties.* A chambers judge shall have primary responsibility for:

(i) Prompt disposition of motions and other preliminary matters which may be disposed of without hearing, except for motions made or filed during the course of a trial or on the day a case is set for trial, which motions shall be disposed of by the trial judge.

(ii) Consideration of and, when appropriate, signing show cause orders.

(iii) Conduct of pre-trial conferences and control of the pre-trial calendar, if one has been established.

(iv) Unless a different procedure is prescribed by the County Administrative Judge, consideration of and, when appropriate, signing orders and decrees in uncontested or ex parte cases, and the disposition of motions for continuances or postponements, except such motions made on the day of or during trial, which shall be disposed of by the trial judge. (Amended Apr. 6, 1984, effective July 1, 1984; June 5, 1996, effective Jan. 1, 1997.)

Committee note. — While a chambers judge, where one has been designated, will have primary responsibility for performing the duties set forth in this Rule, the Rule is not intended to affect the power of other judges to perform these duties should a chambers judge not be available. The Rule does contemplate that in those jurisdictions in which a chambers judge must be designated, some judge will be available to perform the duties of a chambers judge at all times during the normal 9:00 a.m. — 5:00 p.m. working day, Monday through Friday.

Source. — This Rule is former Rule 1201.

Effect of amendments. — The 1996 amendment substituted "Rule 16-101" for "Rule 1200" in the Cross reference note in a.; and added the Source note.

Editor's note. — An Order dated June 5, 1996, effective Jan. 1, 1997, renumbered this Rule, which was formerly Rule 1201.

Rule 16-103. Assignment of judges.

a. *Chief Judge of the Court of Appeals.* 1. Assignment between courts. The Chief Judge of the Court of Appeals may by order assign any judge to sit temporarily in any court other than the one to which he was appointed or elected. The order of assignment shall specify the court in which the judge is to sit and the duration of the assignment. During the period of his assignment, the assigned judge shall possess all the power and authority of a judge of the court to which he is assigned.

COMMENT

This section, like the constitutional provision (article IV, § 18) on which it is based, gives the Chief Judge of the Court of Appeals full vertical and horizontal assignment power.

2. Assignment to National College of State Trial Judges. The Chief Judge of the Court of Appeals may from time to time assign, by order, one or more judges to attend the National College of State Trial Judges. Such assignment shall be made with the consent of the judge or judges concerned. Nothing in this Rule shall prevent a judge not so assigned from attending the National College of State Trial Judges during his annual vacation.

b. *Circuit Administrative Judge.* 1. Assignment within first seven judicial circuits. Except for assignments made pursuant to section a of this Rule, the Circuit Administrative Judge of each of the first seven judicial circuits may assign any judge of his judicial circuit to sit as a judge of the Circuit Court of any county in the judicial circuit, in any specific case or cases or for any specified time. Such assignments may be made orally or in writing.

2. Assignment within Supreme Bench of Baltimore City. Except for assignments made pursuant to section a of this Rule, assignment of judges within the Supreme Bench of Baltimore City shall be pursuant to Article IV, Section 32 of the Constitution.

Cross references. — For rotation of judges, see Supreme Bench Rule 31 (Rotation of Judges).

c. *County Administrative Judge.* Except for assignments made pursuant to section a or subsection 1 of section b of this Rule, assignment of judges within the Circuit Court for a county in which there is more than one resident judge shall be made by the County Administrative Judge. Such assignments may be made orally or in writing.

d. *Use of assignment power.* The assignment power herein established shall be exercised to insure full use of judicial manpower throughout the judicial system, to equalize, to the extent feasible, judicial work loads and to expedite the disposition of pending cases. (Amended June 5, 1996, effective Jan. 1, 1997.)

Cross references. — See ch. 468, Acts 1968, for declaration that the judicial work load shall be distributed as uniformly as possible by exercise of the authority of assignment by the Chief Judge of the Court of Appeals.

Source. — This Rule is former Rule 1202.

Effect of amendments. — The 1996 amendment added the Source note.

Editor's note. — An Order dated June 5, 1996, effective Jan. 1, 1997, renumbered this Rule, which was formerly Rule 1202.

Article IV, § 32 of the Maryland Constitution, referred to in section b 2, was repealed by Acts 1980, ch. 523, ratified November 4, 1980.

Constitutionality. — Former Rule 1202, which grants a circuit administrative judge broad powers of assignment of judges, which power and authority encompass all facts of the internal management of the courts, does not violate Md. Const., art. IV, § 18. Whitaker v. Prince George's County, 307 Md. 368, 514 A.2d 4 (1986).

No new designation required. — No new designation under former Rule 1202 would be required for a District Court judge who sentenced the defendant to probation, while temporarily assigned to the circuit court, to preside over the hearing to revoke that probation; thus it would not be impractical to have the original sentencing judge preside at the revocation hearing. Peterson v. State, 73 Md. App. 459, 534 A.2d 1353 (1988), vacated on other grounds, 315 Md. 73, 553 A.2d 672 (1989).

Rule 16-104. Judicial leave.

a. *Definition of "judge."* In this Rule, "judge" means a judge of the Court of Appeals of Maryland, the Court of Special Appeals, a circuit court or the District Court of Maryland.

b. *Annual leave.* 1. In general. Subject to the provisions of section f of this Rule, a judge is entitled to annual leave of not more than 27 working days. The leave accrues as of the first day of the calendar year except that (1) during the first year of a judge's initial term of office, annual leave accrues at the rate of 2.25 days per month accounting from the date the judge qualifies for office, and (2) during the calendar year in which the judge retires, annual leave accrues at the rate of 2.25 days per month to the date the judge retires.

2. Accumulation. If in any year a judge takes less than the full amount of annual leave the judge has accrued in that year, the judge may accumulate within any consecutive three year period, the difference between the leave accrued and the annual leave actually taken by the judge in any year during the period. However, no more than ten working days annual leave may be accumulated in any one year, and no judge may accumulate more than 20 working days annual leave in the aggregate.

3. Consecutive appointment — Leave status. A judge who is appointed or elected as a judge of another court, and whose term on the second court begins immediately following service on the first court has the same leave status as though the judge had remained on the first court.

c. *Personal leave.* 1. In general. In addition to annual leave as provided above and except as otherwise provided in subsection 2 of this section, a judge is entitled to six days of personal leave in each calendar year and personal leave accrues on the first day of each calendar year. Any personal leave unused at the end of the calendar year is forfeited.

2. First calendar year of initial term. During the first calendar year of a judge's initial term of office, the judge is entitled to:

A. six days of personal leave if the judge qualified for office in January or February,

B. five days of personal leave if the judge qualified for office in March or April,

C. four days of personal leave if the judge qualified for office in May or June, or

D. three days of personal leave if the judge qualified for office on or after July 1.

d. *Sick leave.* In addition to the annual leave and personal leave as provided for above, a judge is entitled to sick leave with respect to any period of illness necessitating absence from judicial duties of the judge. Sick leave may not be charged against annual or personal leave.

e. *Termination of judicial service.* A judge whose judicial service is terminated for any reason, and who is not elected or appointed to another court without break in service, loses any annual or personal leave unused as of the date of termination of service.

f. *Discretion of chief judge or administrative judge.* A judge's annual leave and personal leave shall be taken at the time or times prescribed or permitted by the chief judge of the judge's appellate court, if the judge is a judge of an appellate court; the Circuit Administrative Judge of the judge's judicial circuit, if the judge is a judge of a circuit court; or the Chief Judge of the District Court, if the judge is a judge of that court. In determining when a judge may take annual leave and for what period of time, the judge exercising supervisory authority under this Rule shall be mindful of the necessity of retention of sufficient judicial staffing in the court or courts under the judge's supervision to permit at all times the prompt and effective disposition of the business of that court or those courts. A request for leave at a certain time or for a certain period of time may be rejected by the judge exercising supervision under this Rule if the granting of the requested leave would prevent the prompt and effective disposition of business of that court or those courts, except that personal leave requested for observance of a religious holiday may not be denied.

g. *Supervision by Chief Judge of the Court of Appeals.* The operation of this Rule is at all times subject to the supervision and control of the Chief Judge of the Court of Appeals. (Amended Apr. 11, 1977, effective July 1, 1977; Nov. 13, 1981, effective Jan. 1, 1982; June 28, 1988, effective July 1, 1988; Dec. 31, 1991, effective Jan. 1, 1992; June 5, 1996, effective Jan. 1, 1997; Dec. 10, 1996, effective Jan. 1, 1997.)

Source. — This Rule is former Rule 1203.

Effect of amendments. — The first 1996 amendment added the Source note.

The second 1996 amendment rewrote the Rule.

Editor's note. — An Order dated June 5, 1996, effective Jan. 1, 1997, renumbered this Rule, which was formerly Rule 1203.

Rule 16-105. Reports to be filed.

a. *Report by judge.* Every judge of the Circuit Court shall submit to the Circuit Administrative Judge of his judicial circuit, reports as may from time to time be required by the Chief Judge of the Court of Appeals on forms prescribed and supplied by the State Court Administrator, and approved by the Chief Judge of the Court of Appeals. Each judge shall forward a copy of such reports to the State Court Administrator and to the County Administrative Judge, if any.

b. *Report by County Administrative Judge.* Each Circuit or County Administrative Judge shall furnish such other reports as may from time to time be required by the Chief Judge of the Court of Appeals. (Amended June 16, 1975, effective July 1, 1975; Nov. 8, 1982, effective Jan. 1, 1983; June 5, 1996, effective Jan. 1, 1997.)

Committee note. — The reports contemplated by section a of this Rule are those dealing with day-to-day operations of the trial courts, and should provide information as to current case loads, backlogs, etc., so as to permit the Circuit and County Administrative Judges to make prompt and sensible decisions as to the assignment of judges, cases and the like; see proposed New Jersey Rule 1:32.

Since other types of reports may be required to obtain a proper view of the overall operations of the judicial system, section b of the Rule makes provision for the same. However, it is hoped that the weekly reports will in general be framed in such a way as to permit the compilation of overall data by the State Court Administrator from them, keeping to a minimum any additional reporting requirements.

Source. — This Rule is former Rule 1204.

Effect of amendments. — The 1996 amendment added the Source note.

Editor's note. — An Order dated June 5, 1996, effective Jan. 1, 1997, renumbered this Rule, which was formerly Rule 1204.

Rule 16-106. Court sessions — Holidays — Time for convening.

a. *Court sessions — Holidays.* A court shall be in session each day from Monday through Friday except on holidays. On holidays, no trials or other court proceedings shall be conducted except in emergency matters or when ordered by the Chief Judge of the Court of Appeals or a judge of the particular court as the judicial business and public welfare may require. In an emergency and in the interest of the public welfare, the Chief Judge of the Court of Appeals may order a court to be closed on any day.

Cross references. — For the definition of "holiday," see Rule 1-202.

b. *Time for convening.* All scheduled proceedings will stand for hearing at 10:00 A.M. unless otherwise ordered by the court. (Amended Sept. 9, 1969; Oct. 13, 1970; Dec. 13, 1973; Nov. 5, 1976, effective Jan. 1, 1977; June 28, 1988, effective July 1, 1988; July 16, 1992; June 5, 1996, effective Jan. 1, 1997; Dec. 10, 1996, effective Jan. 1, 1997.)

Committee note. — This Rule is not intended to prevent the convening of court earlier than 10:00 o'clock A.M. when circumstances so require or when such a procedure is established under rules like Seventh Circuit Rules 507 and 707. However, if court is to convene at an earlier hour, reasonable notice should be furnished counsel. It is intended that conferences or other work in chambers shall not conflict with or postpone the regular time for convening court. It is contemplated that a court will remain in session for as long as is necessary for the effective disposition of the business before it.

Source. — This Rule is former Rule 1205.

Effect of amendments. — The first 1996 amendment added the Source note.

The second 1996 amendment rewrote the Rule.

Editor's note. — An Order dated June 5, 1996, effective Jan. 1, 1997, renumbered this Rule, which was formerly Rule 1205.

Pending before the Court of Appeals at press time is the One-Hundred Thirty-Third Report of the Court's Standing Committee on Rules of Practice and Procedure, which includes an amendment to this Rule to conform the holiday schedule of the Court to other divisions of State government in light of the General Assembly's passage of Chapter 347, Acts 1996, effective October 1, 1996.

Rule 16-107. Court and jury terms.

a. *Term of court.* For accounting and statistical reporting purposes, each circuit court shall hold a single term each year beginning on July 1 and ending on the following June 30.

b. *Term of jury.* The County Administrative Judge shall set the terms of the petit and grand juries for that county in the juror selection plan authorized by Code, Courts Article, § 8-201. (Rescinded and new, Jan. 18, 1996, effective July 1, 1996; amended June 5, 1996, effective Jan. 1, 1997.)

Source. — This Rule is former Rule 1206.

Effect of amendments. — The 1996 amendment added the Source note.

Editor's note. — An Order dated June 5, 1996, effective Jan. 1, 1997, renumbered this Rule, which was formerly Rule 1206.

Rule 16-108. Conference of Circuit Judges.

a. *Purpose.* There shall be a Conference of Circuit Judges that represents the interests of the circuit courts and is a policy advisory body to the Chief Judge of the Court of Appeals, the Court of Appeals, and other judicial branch agencies in all circuit court matters.

b. *Powers.* 1. Administration Policies. To fulfill its purpose, the Conference shall work collaboratively and in consultation with the Chief Judge of the Court of Appeals in developing policies affecting the administration of the circuit courts, including but not limited to:

(A) programs and practices that will enhance the administration of justice;

(B) the level of operational and judicial resources to be included in the Judiciary Budget;

(C) legislation that may affect the circuit courts; and

(D) the compensation and benefits of circuit court judges.

2. Consultants. With the approval of the Chief Judge, the Conference may retain consultants in matters relating to the circuit courts.

3. Consultation with Chief Judge of the Court of Appeals. The Conference shall consult with the Chief Judge of the Court of Appeals:

(A) on the appointment of circuit judges to committees of the Judicial Conference in accordance with Rule 16-802 f.2.; and

(B) to recommend circuit judges for membership on other committees and bodies of interest to the circuit courts.

4. Majority Vote. The Conference and the Executive Committee of the Conference each shall exercise its powers and carry out its duties pursuant to a majority vote of its authorized membership.

c. *Membership and operation.* 1. Composition. The Conference shall comprise 16 members including the circuit administrative judge from each judicial circuit and one circuit judge from each judicial circuit who shall be elected every two years by majority vote of the circuit judges then authorized in the circuit.

2. Chair and Vice-Chair. The Conference shall elect from its members every two years a Chair and Vice-chair.

3. Quorum. A majority of the authorized membership of the Conference shall constitute a quorum.

4. Meetings. The Conference shall meet at least four times a year.

d. *Executive Committee.* 1. Power and Composition. There shall be an Executive Committee of the Conference. It shall consist of the Conference Chair and Vice-Chair and such other members as may be designated by the Conference and shall be empowered to act with the full authority of the Conference when the Conference is not in session. The actions of the Executive Committee will be reported fully to the Conference at its next meeting.

2. Quorum. A majority of the authorized membership of the Executive Committee shall constitute a quorum.

3. Convening the Executive Committee. The Executive Committee shall convene at the call of the Conference Chair. In the absence of the Chair, the Vice-Chair is authorized to convene the Executive Committee.

e. *Conference staff.* The Administrative Office of the Courts shall serve as staff to the Conference and its Executive Committee. (Added Mar. 14, 1972; amended Nov. 28, 1978; June 5, 1996, effective Jan. 1, 1997; amended June 8, 1998, effective Oct. 1, 1998.)

Source. — This Rule is new.
This Rule is former Rule 1207.

Effect of amendments. — The 1996 amendment added the Source note.
The 1998 amendment rewrote the Rule.

Editor's note. — An Order dated June 5, 1996, effective Jan. 1, 1997, renumbered this Rule, which was formerly Rule 1207.

Rule 16-109. Photographing, recording, broadcasting or televising in courthouses.

a. *Definitions.* 1. "Extended coverage" means any recording or broadcasting of proceedings by the use of television, radio, photographic, or recording equipment by:

(i) the news media, or

(ii) by persons engaged in the preparation of educational films or recordings with the written approval of the presiding judge.

2. "Local administrative judge" means the county administrative judge in the Circuit Court and the district administrative judge in the District Court.

3. "Party" means a named litigant of record who has appeared in the proceeding.

4. "Proceeding" means any trial, hearing, motion, argument on appeal or other matter held in open court which the public is entitled to attend.

5. "Presiding judge" means a trial judge designated to preside over a proceeding which is, or is intended to be the subject of extended coverage. Where action of a presiding judge is required by this rule, and no trial judge has been designated to preside over the proceeding, presiding judge means the local administrative judge. Presiding judge in an appellate court means the Chief Judge of that Court, or the senior judge of a panel of which the Chief Judge is not a member.

b. *General provisions.* 1. Extended coverage of proceedings in the trial and appellate courts of this State is permitted unless prohibited or limited in accordance with this rule.

2. Outside a courtroom but within a courthouse or other facility extended coverage is prohibited of persons present for a judicial or grand jury proceeding, or where extended coverage is so close to a judicial or grand jury proceeding that it is likely to interfere with the proceeding or its dignity and decorum.

3. Possession of cameras and recordings or transmitting equipment is prohibited in all courtrooms and adjacent hallways except when required for extended coverage permitted by this rule or for media coverage not prohibited by this rule.

4. Nothing in this rule is intended to restrict in any way the present rights of the media to report proceedings.

5. Extended coverage shall be conducted so as not to interfere with the right of any person to a fair and impartial trial, and so as not to interfere with the dignity and decorum which must attend the proceedings.

6. No proceeding shall be delayed or continued to allow for extended coverage, nor shall the requirements of extended coverage in any way affect legitimate motions for continuance or challenges to the judge.

7. This rule does not apply to:

(i) The use of electronic or photographic equipment approved by the court for the perpetuation of a court record;

(ii) Investiture or ceremonial proceedings, provided, however, that the local administrative judge of a trial court and the Chief Judge of an appellate court shall have complete discretion to regulate the presence and use of cameras, recorders, and broadcasting equipment at the proceedings.

c. *Request for extended coverage.* 1. All requests for extended coverage shall be made in writing to the clerk of the court at which the proceeding is to be held at least five days before the proceeding is scheduled to begin and shall specifically identify the proceeding to be covered. For good cause a court may honor a request which does not comply with the requirements of this subsection. The clerk shall promptly give notice of a request to all parties to the proceeding.

2. Where proceedings are continued other than for normal or routine recesses, weekends, or holidays, it is the responsibility of the media to make a separate request for later extended coverage.

Cross references. — For the definition of "holiday," see Rule 1-202.

d. *Consent to extended coverage.* 1. Extended coverage shall not be permitted in any proceeding in a trial court unless all parties to the proceeding have filed their written consent in the record, except that consent need not be obtained from a party which is a federal, state, or local government, or an agency or subdivision thereof or an individual sued or suing in his official governmental capacity.

2. Consent once given may not be withdrawn, but any party may at any time move for termination or limitation of extended coverage in accordance with this rule.

3. Consent of the parties is not required for extended coverage in appellate courts, but any party may at any time move for termination or limitation of extended coverage in accordance with this rule.

e. *Restrictions on extended coverage.* 1. Extended coverage of the testimony of a witness who is a victim in a criminal case shall be terminated or limited in accordance with the request or objection of the witness.

2. Extended coverage of all or any portion of a proceeding may be prohibited, terminated or limited, on the presiding judge's own motion or on the request of a party, witness, or juror in the proceedings, where the judge finds a reasonable probability of unfairness, danger to a person, undue embarrassment, or hinderance of proper law enforcement would result if such action were not taken. In cases involving police informants, undercover agents, relocated witnesses, and minors, and in evidentiary suppression hearings, divorce and custody proceedings, and cases involving trade secrets, a presumption of validity attends the request. This list of requests which enjoy the presumption is not exclusive, and the judge may in the exercise of his discretion find cause in comparable situations. Within the guidelines set forth in this subsection, the judge is granted broad discretion in determining whether there is cause for termination, prohibition or limitation.

3. Extended coverage is not permitted of any proceeding which is by law closed to the public, or which may be closed to the public and has been closed by the judge.

4. Extended coverage in the judicial area of a courthouse or other facility is limited to proceedings in the courtroom in the presence of the presiding judge.

5. There shall be no audio coverage of private conferences, bench conferences, and conferences at counsel tables.

f. *Standards of conduct and technology.* 1. Not more than one portable television camera (film camera — 16 mm sound on film (self-blimped) or video tape electronic camera), operated by not more than one camera person, shall be permitted in any trial court proceeding. Not more than two television cameras, operated by not more than one camera person each, shall be permitted in any appellate court proceeding.

2. Not more than one still photographer, utilizing not more than two still cameras with not more than two lenses for each camera and related equipment approved by the presiding judge shall be permitted in any proceeding in a trial or appellate court.

3. Not more than one audio system for broadcast purposes shall be permitted in any proceeding in a trial or appellate court. Audio pickup shall be accomplished from existing audio systems, except that if no technically suitable audio system exists unobtrusive microphones and related wiring shall be located in places designated in advance by the presiding judge. Microphones located at the judge's bench and at counsel tables shall be equipped with temporary cutoff switches. A directional microphone may be mounted on the television or film camera, but no parabolic or similar microphones shall be used.

4. Any "pooling" arrangements among the media required by these limitations on equipment and personnel shall be the sole responsibility of the media without calling upon the presiding judge to mediate any dispute as to the appropriate media representative or equipment authorized to cover a particular proceeding. In the absence of advance media agreement on disputed equipment or personnel issues, the presiding judge shall exclude all contesting media personnel from extended coverage.

5. Only television, movie, and audio equipment which does not produce light or distracting sound shall be employed. Specifically, such photographic and audio equipment shall produce no greater sound than the equipment designated in Schedule A annexed hereto, when the same is in good working order. No artificial lighting device of any kind shall be employed in connection with the television and movie cameras.

6. Only still camera equipment which does not produce distracting sound shall be employed to cover judicial proceedings. Specifically, such still camera equipment shall produce no greater sound than a 35 mm Leica "M" series Rangefinder camera with manual film advance. No artificial lighting device of any kind shall be employed in connection with a still camera.

7. It shall be the affirmative duty of media personnel to demonstrate to the presiding judge adequately in advance of any proceeding that the equipment sought to be utilized meets the sound and light criteria enunciated herein. A failure to obtain advance judicial approval for equipment shall preclude its use in any proceedings.

8. Television or movie camera equipment shall be positioned outside the rail of the courtroom, or if there is no rail, in the area reserved for spectators, at a location approved in advance by the presiding judge. Wherever possible, recording and broadcasting equipment which is not a component part of a television camera shall be located outside the courtroom in an area approved in advance by the presiding judge.

9. A still camera photographer shall be positioned outside the rail of the courtroom or if there is no rail, in the area reserved for spectators, at a location approved in advance by the presiding judge. The still camera photographer shall not photograph from any other place, and shall not engage in any movement or assume any body position which would be likely to call attention

to himself, or be distracting. Unless positioned in or beyond the last row of spectators' seats, or in an aisle to the outside of the spectators' seating area, the still photographer shall remain seated while photographing.

10. Broadcast media representatives shall not move about the courtroom while proceedings are in session, and microphones and recording equipment once positioned shall not be moved during the pendency of the proceeding.

11. Photographic or audio equipment shall not be placed in or removed from the courtroom except prior to commencement or after adjournment of proceedings each day, or during a recess. Neither film magazines nor still camera film or lenses shall be changed within a courtroom except during a recess in the proceeding.

12. With the concurrence of the local administrative judge, and before the commencement of a proceeding or during a recess, modifications and additions may be made in light sources existing in the courtroom provided such modifications or additions are installed and maintained without public expense.

SCHEDULE A

FILM CAMERAS .... 16mm Sound on Film (self-blimped)

1.	CINEMA PRODUCTS	CP-16A-R	Sound Camera
2.	ARRIFLEX	16mm-16BL Model	Sound Camera
3.	FREZZOLINI	16mm (LW16)	Sound on Film Camera
4.	AURICON	"Cini-Voice"	Sound Camera
5.	AURICON	"Pro-600"	Sound Camera
6.	GENERAL CAMERA	SS III	Sound Camera
7.	ECLAIR	Model ACL	Sound Camera
8.	GENERAL CAMERA	DGX	Sound Camera
9.	WILCAM REFLEX	16mm	Sound Camera

VIDEO TAPE ELECTRONIC CAMERAS

1.	Ikegami	HL-77 HL-33 HL-35 HL-34 HL-51 HL-52 HL-53 HL-79
2.	RCA	TK 76
3.	Sony	DXC-1600 Trinicon
4.	ASACA	ACC-2006
5.	Hitachi	SK 80 SK 90
6.	Hitachi	FP-3030
7.	Philips	LDK-25
8.	Sony BVP-200	ENG Camera
9.	Fernseh	KCN-92
10.	JVC-8800 u	ENG Camera
11.	AKAI	CVC-150 VTS-150
12.	Panasonic	WV-3085 NV-3085
13.	JVC	GC-4800u
14.	Sony	BVP 300

15. NEC   MN-71
16. Ampex   BCC-14

Video Tape Recorders/used with Video Cameras

1. Ikegami   3800
2. Sony   3800
3. Sony   BVU-100
4. Ampex   VPR-20
5. Panasonic   NV-9400
6. JVC   4400
7. Sony   3800H
8. Sony   BVU-50
9. Sony/RCA   BVH-500/TH 50
10 Fernseh   BCN-20

(Added Nov. 10, 1980, effective Jan. 1, 1981; amended June 5, 1996, effective Jan. 1, 1997; Dec. 10, 1996, effective Jan. 1, 1997.)

Source. — This Rule is former Rule 1209.

Effect of amendments. — The first 1996 amendment added the Source note.

The second 1996 amendment added the cross reference in c.

Editor's note. — Extended coverage of criminal proceedings in the trial courts of Maryland is prohibited by Article 27, § 467B of the Maryland Code.

An Order dated June 5, 1996, effective Jan. 1, 1997, renumbered this Rule, which was formerly Rule 1209.

Rule stems from powers granted in article IV, § 18 (a) of Maryland Constitution. — This rule — regulating the recording of court proceedings by the new media — is a rule of administration or procedure that falls within the concurrent rulemaking powers granted by article IV, § 18 (a) of the Maryland Constitution. 66 Op. Att'y Gen. 80 (1981).

CHAPTER 200. THE CALENDAR — ASSIGNMENT AND DISPOSITION OF MOTIONS AND CASES.

Rule 16-201. Motion day — Calendar.

a. *Motion day.* Each Circuit Administrative Judge shall prescribe for each court in his judicial circuit motion days on which all motions and other preliminary matters pending in that court and scheduled for hearing shall be heard.

b. *Motions calendar.* The clerk in each county shall maintain a motions calendar in such form as may be prescribed by the County Administrative Judge. Upon the filing of a response pursuant to Rule 2-311 (b), or upon the date on which such response should have been filed, the clerk will list the case on the motions calendar.

c. *Assignment when hearing required.* The County Administrative Judge in each county and the Circuit Administrative Judge of the Eighth Judicial Circuit shall provide for review of the motions calendar at appropriate intervals and the determination of what matters thereon require hearings. He shall provide for assignment of hearing dates for such matters and notices thereof shall be given to all parties.

d. *Notice of lengthy hearing.* If it is anticipated that the hearing on a motion will exceed a total of 30 minutes, the parties shall inform the assignment clerk, in which event the motion may be calendared specially. (Amended June 30, 1973, effective July 1, 1973; Dec. 17, 1975, effective Jan. 1, 1976; Oct. 1, 1980, effective Jan. 1, 1981; Apr. 6, 1984, effective July 1, 1984; June 5, 1996, effective Jan. 1, 1997.)

Committee note. — It is intended that the Circuit Administrative Judge will prescribe a different motion day for each court in his judicial circuit. Thus, attorneys with motions pending in a number of courts within the judicial circuit will not be called upon to argue several of them in different courts on the same day.

Source. — This Rule is former Rule 1210.

Effect of amendments. — The 1996 amendment added the Source note.

Editor's note. — An Order dated June 5, 1996, effective Jan. 1, 1997, renumbered this Rule, which was formerly Rule 1210.

Rule 16-202. Assignment of actions for trial.

a. *Generally.* The County Administrative Judge in each county shall supervise the assignment of actions for trial to achieve the efficient use of available judicial personnel and to bring pending actions to trial and dispose of them as expeditiously as feasible. Procedures instituted in this regard shall be designed to:

(1) eliminate docket calls in open court;

(2) insure the prompt disposition of motions and other preliminary matters;

(3) provide for the use of scheduling and pretrial conferences, and the establishment of a calendar for that purpose, when appropriate;

(4) provide for the prompt disposition of uncontested and ex parte matters, including references to an examiner-master, when appropriate;

(5) provide for the disposition of actions under Rule 2-507;

(6) establish trial and motion calendars and other appropriate systems under which actions ready for trial will be assigned for trial and tried, after proper notice to parties, without necessity of a request for assignment from any party; and

Cross references. — *See* Rule 16-201 (Motion Day — Calendar).

(7) establish systems of regular reports which will indicate the status of all pending actions with respect to their readiness for trial, the disposition of actions, and the availability of judges for trial work.

b. *Case management plan; information report.* (1) The County Administrative Judge shall develop and, upon approval by the Chief Judge of the Court of Appeals, implement and monitor a case management plan for the prompt and efficient scheduling and disposition of actions in the circuit court. The plan shall include a system of differentiated case management in which actions are classified according to complexity and priority and are assigned to a scheduling category based on that classification. In courts that have a family division, the plan shall provide criteria for (A) requiring parties in an action assigned to the family division to attend a scheduling conference in accordance with Rule 2-504.1 (a) (1) and (B) identifying actions in the family division that are appropriate for assignment to a specific judge who shall be responsible for the entire case unless the County Administrative Judge subsequently decides to reassign it.

Cross references. — See Rule 9-204.1 for provisions that may be included in the case management plan concerning an educational seminar for parties in actions in which child support, custody, or visitation are involved.

(2) In developing and implementing the case management plan, the County Administrative Judge shall (i) consult with the Administrative Office of the Courts and with other county administrative judges who have developed or are in the process of developing such plans in an effort to achieve as much consistency and uniformity among the plans as is reasonably practicable, and (ii) seek the assistance of the county bar association and such other interested groups and persons as the judge deems advisable.

(3) As part of the plan, the clerk shall make available to the parties, without charge, a form approved by the County Administrative Judge that will provide the information necessary to implement the case management plan. The information contained in the information report shall not be used for any purpose other than case management.

(4) The clerk of each circuit court shall make available for public inspection a copy of the current administrative order of the Chief Judge of the Court of Appeals exempting categories of actions from the information report requirement of Rule 2-111 (a). (Amended Apr. 6, 1984, effective July 1, 1984; June 7, 1994, effective July 1, 1994; Jan. 10, 1995, effective Feb. 1, 1995; June 5, 1996, effective Jan. 1, 1997; Jan. 13, 1998, effective July 1, 1998.)

Source. — This Rule is former Rule 1211.

Effect of amendments. — The 1996 amendment substituted "Rule 16-201" for "Rule 1210" in the Cross reference note to a. (6); and added the Source note.

The 1998 amendment, in b. (1), added the third sentence and the Cross reference.

Editor's note. — An Order dated June 5, 1996, effective Jan. 1, 1997, renumbered this Rule, which was formerly Rule 1211.

Effect of assignment clerk's failure to set trial date and send notification thereof. — Even if an assignment clerk was responsible for setting a trial date and sending notification thereof under this Rule, and failed to do so, the plaintiff is not relieved of prosecuting his case and providing proof of proceedings therein on the record. Fact that the clerk has failed in his responsibility under one rule does not relieve appellants from their responsibility under another. Driver v. Parke-Davis & Co., 29 Md. App. 354, 348 A.2d 38, cert. denied, 277 Md. 736 (1975).

Rule 16-203. Special docket for asbestos cases.

(a) *Definition.* In this Rule, "asbestos case" means an action seeking money damages for personal injury or death allegedly caused by exposure to asbestos or products containing asbestos. It does not include an action seeking principally equitable relief or seeking principally damages for injury to property or for removal of asbestos or products containing asbestos from property.

(b) *Special docket.* The Circuit Court for Baltimore City, by order entered by the Administrative Judge for the Eighth Judicial Circuit, may establish a special inactive docket for asbestos cases filed in or transferred to that court. The order:

(1) shall specify the criteria and procedures for placement of an asbestos case on the inactive docket and for removal of a case from the docket;

(2) may permit an asbestos case meeting the criteria for placement on the inactive docket to be placed on that docket at any time prior to trial; and

(3) with respect to any case placed on the inactive docket, may stay the time for filing responses to the complaint, discovery, and other proceedings until the case is removed from the docket.

(c) *Transfer of cases from other circuits.* (1) The circuit administrative judge for any other judicial circuit, by order, may

(A) adopt the criteria established in an order entered by the Administrative Judge for the Eighth Judicial Circuit pursuant to section (b) of this Rule for placement of an asbestos case on the inactive docket for asbestos cases;

(B) provide for the transfer to the Circuit Court for Baltimore City, for placement on the inactive docket, of any asbestos case filed in a circuit court in that other circuit for which venue would lie in Baltimore City; and

(C) establish procedures for the prompt disposition in the circuit court where the action was filed of any dispute as to whether venue would lie in Baltimore City.

(2) If an action is transferred pursuant to this Rule, the clerk of the circuit court where the action was filed shall deliver the file or a copy of it to the clerk of the Circuit Court for Baltimore City, and, except as provided in subsection (c) (3) of this Rule, the action shall thereafter proceed as if initially filed in the Circuit Court for Baltimore City.

(3) Unless the parties agree otherwise, any action transferred pursuant to this section, upon removal from the inactive docket, shall be retransferred to the circuit court in which it was originally filed and all further proceedings shall take place in that court.

(d) *Exemption from Rule 2-507.* Any action placed on an inactive docket pursuant to this Rule shall not be subject to Rule 2-507 until the action is removed from that docket.

(e) *Effect on Rule 2-327 (d).* To the extent of any inconsistency with Rule 2-327 (d), this Rule shall prevail.

Committee note. — This section (e) does not preclude a transfer under Rule 2-327 upon retransfer of an action under subsection (c) (3) of this Rule.

(f) *Applicability of Rule.* This Rule shall apply only to actions filed on or after December 8, 1992. (Added Dec. 8, 1992; amended June 5, 1996, effective Jan. 1, 1997.)

Source. — This Rule is former Rule 1211A.

Effect of amendments. — The 1996 amendment added the Source note.

Editor's note. — An Order dated June 5, 1996, effective Jan. 1, 1997, renumbered this Rule, which was formerly Rule 1211A.

Rule 16-204. Family division and support services.

(a) *Family division.* (1) Established. In each county having more than seven resident judges of the circuit court authorized by law, there shall be a family division in the circuit court.

(2) Actions assigned. In a court that has a family division, the following categories of actions and matters shall be assigned to that division:

(A) dissolution of marriage, including divorce, annulment, and property distribution;

(B) child custody and visitation, including proceedings governed by the Maryland Uniform Child Custody Jurisdiction Act, Code, Family Law Article, Title 9, Subtitle 2, and the Parental Kidnapping Prevention Act, 28 U.S.C. § 1738A;

(C) alimony, spousal support, and child support, including proceedings under the Maryland Uniform Interstate Family Support Act;

(D) establishment and termination of the parent-child relationship, including paternity, adoption, guardianship that terminates parental rights, and emancipation;

(E) criminal nonsupport and desertion, including proceedings under Code, Family Law Article, Title 10, Subtitle 2 and Code, Family Law Article, Title 13;

(F) name changes;

(G) guardianship of minors and disabled persons under Code, Estates and Trusts Article, Title 13;

(H) involuntary admission to state facilities and emergency evaluations under Code, Health General Article, Title 10, Subtitle 6;

(I) family legal-medical issues, including decisions on the withholding or withdrawal of life-sustaining medical procedures;

(J) actions involving domestic violence under Code, Family Law Article, Title 4, Subtitle 5;

(K) juvenile causes under Code, Courts Article, Title 3, Subtitle 8;

(L) matters assigned to the family division by the County Administrative Judge that are related to actions in the family division and appropriate for assignment to the family division; and

(M) civil and criminal contempt arising out of any of the categories of actions and matters set forth in subsection (a) (2) (A) through (a) (2) (L) of this Rule.

(3) *Family support services.* Subject to the availability of funds, the following family support services shall be available through the family division for use when appropriate in a particular action:

(A) mediation in custody and visitation matters;

(B) custody investigations;

(C) trained personnel to respond to emergencies;

(D) mental health evaluations and evaluations for alcohol and drug abuse;

(E) information services, including procedural assistance to pro se litigants;

(F) information regarding lawyer referral services;

(G) parenting seminars; and

(H) any additional family support services for which funding is provided.

(4) *Responsibilities of the County Administrative Judge.* The County Administrative Judge of the Circuit Court for each county having a family division shall:

(A) allocate sufficient available judicial resources to the family division so that actions are heard expeditiously in accordance with applicable law and the case management plan required by Rule 16-202 b;

(B) provide in the case management plan required by Rule 16-202 b criteria for:

(i) requiring parties in an action assigned to the family division to attend a scheduling conference in accordance with Rule 2-504.1 (a) (1) and

(ii) identifying those actions in the family division that are appropriate for assignment to a specific judge who shall be responsible for the entire case unless the County Administrative Judge subsequently decides to reassign it;

Cross references. — For rules concerning
the referral of matters to masters as of course,
see Rules 2-541 and 9-207.

(C) appoint a family support services coordinator whose responsibilities include:

(i) compiling, maintaining, and providing lists of available public and private family support services,

(ii) coordinating and monitoring referrals in actions assigned to the family division, and

(iii) reporting to the County Administrative Judge concerning the need for additional family support services or the modification of existing services; and

(D) prepare and submit to the Chief Judge of the Court of Appeals, no later than October 15 of each year, a written report that includes a description of family support services needed by the court's family division, a fiscal note that estimates the cost of those services for the following fiscal year, and, whenever practicable, an estimate of the fiscal needs of the Clerk of the Circuit Court for the county pertaining to the family division.

(b) *Circuit courts without a family division.* (1) Applicability. This section applies to circuit courts for counties having less than eight resident judges of the circuit court authorized by law.

(2) Family support services. Subject to availability of funds, the family support services listed in subsection (a) (3) of this Rule shall be available through the court for use when appropriate in cases in the categories listed in subsection (a) (2) of this Rule.

(3) Family support services coordinator. The County Administrative Judge shall appoint a full-time or part-time family support services coordinator whose responsibilities shall be substantially as set forth in subsection (a) (4) (C) of this Rule.

(4) Report to the Chief Judge of the Court of Appeals. The County Administrative Judge shall prepare and submit to the Chief Judge of the Court of Appeals, no later than October 15 of each year, a written report that includes a description of the family support services needed by the court, a fiscal note that estimates the cost of those services for the following fiscal year, and, whenever practicable, an estimate of the fiscal needs of the Clerk of the Circuit Court for the county pertaining to family support services. (Added Jan. 13, 1998, effective July 1, 1998.)

Source. — This Rule is new.

CHAPTER 300. CIRCUIT COURT CLERKS' OFFICES.

Rule 16-301. Personnel in clerks' offices.

a. *Chief deputy clerk.* (1) The clerk may appoint a chief deputy clerk. The appointment is not subject to subsection (d) (3) of this Rule.

(2) Subject to paragraph (3) of this section, a chief deputy clerk serves at the pleasure of the clerk.

(3) The appointment, retention and removal of a chief deputy clerk shall be subject to the authority and approval of the Chief Judge of the Court of Appeals, after consultation with the County Administrative Judge.

b. *Other employees.* All other employees in the clerk's office shall be subject to a personnel system to be established by the State Court Administrator and approved by the Court of Appeals. The personnel system shall provide for equal opportunity, shall be based on merit principles, and shall include appropriate job classifications and compensation scales.

c. *Certain deputy clerks.* Persons serving as deputy clerks on July 1, 1991 who qualify for pension rights under Code, Article 73B, § 117 shall hold over as deputy clerks but shall have no fixed term and shall in all respects be subject to the personnel system established pursuant to section (b) of this Rule.

d. *Personnel procedures.* (1) The State Court Administrator shall develop standards and procedures for the selection and appointment of new employees and the promotion, reclassification, transfer, demotion, suspension, discharge or other discipline of employees in the clerks' offices. These standards and procedures shall be subject to the approval of the Court of Appeals.

(2) If a vacancy occurs in a clerk's office, the clerk shall seek authorization from the State Court Administrator to fill the vacancy.

(3) The selection and appointment of new employees and the promotion, reclassification, transfer, demotion, suspension, discharge or other discipline of employees shall be in accordance with the standards and procedures established by the State Court Administrator.

(4) The State Court Administrator may review the selection or promotion of an employee to ensure compliance with the standards and procedures established pursuant to this Rule.

(5) An employee grievance shall be resolved in accordance with procedures established by the State Court Administrator. The clerk shall resolve a grievance within the clerk's office, but appeals of the grievance to the State Court Administrator or a designee of the State Court Administrator shall be allowed and shall constitute the final step in the grievance procedure.

(6) The Administrative Office of the Courts shall prepare the payroll and time and attendance reports for the clerks' offices. The clerks shall submit the information and other documentation that the Administrative Office requires for this purpose. (Added May 9, 1991, effective July 1, 1991; amended June 5, 1996, effective Jan. 1, 1997.)

Source. — This Rule is former Rule 1212.

Effect of amendments. — The 1996 amendment rewrote the Source note.

Editor's note. — An Order dated June 5, 1996, effective Jan. 1, 1997, renumbered this Rule, which was formerly Rule 1212.

Disclosure of personnel records. — Both the Clerk of the Circuit Court, as custodian of personnel records of employees of the Clerk's office, and Administrative Office of the Courts, as official custodian of personnel records relating to employees of the Clerk's offices, are prohibited from disclosing those records to a complainant or to a third person, such as a representative of the media. 78 Op. Att'y Gen. (November 18, 1993).

Rule 16-302. Operations in clerks' offices.

a. *Procurement.* A clerk may not purchase, lease, or otherwise procure any service or property, including equipment, except in accordance with procedures established by the State Court Administrator. Unless otherwise provided by those procedures, the clerk shall submit all procurement requests to the State Court Administrator in the form and with the documentation that the Administrator requires.

b. *General operations.* The State Court Administrator shall develop policies, procedures, and standards for all judicial and non-judicial operations of the clerks' offices, including case processing, records management, forms control, accounting, budgeting, inventory, and data processing. The current data processing systems in Baltimore City, Prince George's County, and Montgomery County shall not be replaced except by order of the Chief Judge of the Court of Appeals.

c. *Audits.* The Administrative Office of the Courts may audit the operations and accounts of the clerks' offices.

d. *Submission of budget.* Each clerk shall submit an annual budget to the State Court Administrator for the review and approval of the Chief Judge of the Court of Appeals. The budget shall be submitted at the time specified by the State Court Administrator and shall be in the form prescribed by the Secretary of Budget and Fiscal Planning.

e. *County Administrative Judge to supervise certain functions.* The case assignment function and the jury selection process, whether or not located in the clerk's office, shall be subject to the overall supervision of the County Administrative Judge or a judge designated by the County Administrative Judge. (Added May 9, 1991, effective July 1, 1991; amended June 5, 1996, effective Jan. 1, 1997.)

Source. — This Rule is former Rule 1213.

Effect of amendments. — The 1996 amendment rewrote the Source note.

Editor's note. — An Order dated June 5, 1996, effective Jan. 1, 1997, renumbered this Rule, which was formerly Rule 1213.

Disclosure of personnel records. — Both the Clerk of the Circuit Court, as custodian of personnel records of employees of the Clerk's office, and Administrative Office of the Courts, as official custodian of personnel records relating to employees of the Clerks' offices, are prohibited from disclosing those records to a complainant or to a third person, such as a representative of the media. 78 Op. Att'y Gen. (November 18, 1993).

Rule 16-303. Payment of money into court.

All money paid into court under an order or on account of a pending action shall be deposited by the clerk in a bank and noted in an appropriate record. The clerk shall disburse the money only upon order of the court and, unless the court otherwise directs, only by check payable to the order of the party entitled and the party's counsel of record. (Added Oct. 1, 1980, effective Jan. 1, 1981; amended June 5, 1996, effective Jan. 1, 1997.)

Source. — This Rule is former Rule 1214.

Effect of amendments. — The 1996 amendment added the Source note.

Editor's note. — An Order dated June 5, 1996, effective Jan. 1, 1997, renumbered this Rule, which was formerly Rule 1214.

Rule 16-304. Clerks' offices — Hours.

The office of each clerk of court shall be open to the public for the transaction of all business of the court from at least 8:30 a.m. to 4:30 p.m. Monday through Friday of each week. Each clerk's office shall be open during the additional hours and on the additional days the judge or judges of the court shall prescribe. The office shall not be open on the holidays set forth in Rule 16-106 (Court Sessions — Holidays — Time for Convening) unless otherwise ordered by the County Administrative Judge. In the event of an emergency and in the interest of the public welfare, the Chief Judge of the Court of Appeals may order a clerk's office to be closed for the transaction of all business of the court on any day. (Amended Sept. 9, 1969; Dec. 13, 1973; July 1, 1974; May 19, 1978, effective July 1, 1978; June 5, 1996, effective Jan. 1, 1997; Dec. 10, 1996, effective Jan. 1, 1997.)

Source. — This Rule is former Rule 1215.

Effect of amendments. — The first 1996 amendment substituted "Rule 16-106" for "Rule 1205" in the third sentence; and added the Source note.

The second 1996 amendment substituted "each clerk" for "every clerk" in the first sentence; and deleted "legal" preceding "holidays" in the third sentence.

Editor's note. — An Order dated June 5, 1996, effective Jan. 1, 1997, renumbered this Rule, which was formerly Rule 1215.

Rule 16-305. Dockets.

The clerks of the courts shall maintain such dockets in such form and containing such information as shall be prescribed by the Chief Judge of the Court of Appeals. (Amended June 5, 1996, effective Jan. 1. 1997.)

COMMENT

This will permit a uniform system of dockets in accordance with forms which are to be prescribed by the Chief Judge acting as administrative head of the judicial system. To permit maximum flexibility, the Rule does not specify what dockets shall be maintained. The general source of the Rule is proposed New Jersey Rule 1:32-2.

Source. — This Rule is former Rule 1216.

Effect of amendments. — The 1996 amendment added the Source note.

Editor's note. — An Order dated June 5, 1996, effective Jan. 1, 1997, renumbered this Rule, which was formerly Rule 1216.

Form for maintaining dockets in Seventh Judicial Circuit. — The following is an order of Chief Judge Murphy of the Court of Appeals.

"At the request and on the recommendation of the Judges of the Seventh Judicial Circuit of Maryland, it is, pursuant to Maryland Rule 1216, this 7th day of October, 1985.

"ORDERED, that the Clerks of the Circuit Courts in the Seventh Judicial Circuit may, at their option, discontinue the maintenance of docket books in equity, law and criminal cases, substituting therefor as the original docket, the entries made on the cover of the original Court file, or an equivalent electronic recordation. There will also be maintained a microfilm jacket known as a 'microfiche' which shall contain microphotographic images of every pleading, document and paper within each case."

Rule 16-306. Filing and removal of papers.

a. *Flat filing.* Any paper received by the clerk shall be filed flat in an appropriate folder. (Amended Apr. 6, 1984, effective July 1, 1984.)

b. *Docket entries.* Each case file shall include a copy of the docket entries pertaining to that case. (Amended Apr. 6, 1984, effective July 1, 1984.)

c. *Exhibits filed with pleadings.* The clerk shall, when practicable, file exhibits with the papers which they accompany. In other cases, the clerk shall file exhibits by such method as may be most convenient and practicable. (Amended Apr. 6, 1984, effective July 1, 1984.)

d. *Removal of papers and exhibits.* 1. Court papers and exhibits filed with pleadings. No paper or exhibit filed with a pleading in any case pending in or decided by the court shall be removed from the clerk's office, except by direction of a judge of the court, and except as authorized by rule or law; provided, however, that an attorney of record, upon signing a receipt, may withdraw any such paper or exhibit for presentation to the court, an auditor, or examiner-master, and an auditor or examiner-master, upon signing a receipt, may withdraw such paper or exhibit in connection with the performance of his official duties.

2. Exhibits filed during trial. All exhibits introduced in evidence or marked for identification during the trial of a case, and not filed as a part of or with the pleadings, shall be retained by the clerk of court or such other person as may be designated by the court. After either (i) the time for appeal has expired, or (ii) in the event of an appeal, the mandate has been received by the clerk, the clerk shall send written notice to all counsel of record advising them that if no request to withdraw the exhibits is received within 30 days from the date of the notice, the exhibits will be disposed of. Unless a request is received by the clerk within 30 days from the date of notice, or unless the court within that period shall order otherwise, the clerk shall dispose of the exhibits in any manner, including destruction, as may be appropriate. (Amended Oct. 1, 1980, effective Jan. 1, 1981; Apr. 6, 1984, effective July 1, 1984.)

Committee note. — This subsection is intended to provide for the safeguarding of trial exhibits. In the absence of a request to withdraw such exhibits, the clerk is given discretion as to their disposition. It is assumed that exhibits such as hospital records, bank records, police records, etc., would normally be returned by the clerk to the proper custodian. Other exhibits might be destroyed, although parties interested in preserving any exhibits could ask for appropriate action by the court. It should be noted that exhibits filed with the pleadings, even though admitted in evidence or marked for identification do not fall under the "disposition" provision of this subsection, but instead under subsection 1.

e. *Record of removed papers.* Whenever a court file or any paper contained therein is removed from the clerk's office pursuant to this Rule, the clerk shall maintain an appropriate record of its location while out of his hands, including a notation on the docket, if such file or papers are removed from the courthouse. (Amended Apr. 6, 1984, effective July 1, 1984; June 5, 1996, effective Jan. 1, 1997.)

COMMENT

The word "court" means the court of a circuit as defined in Rule 1-202 (e). The sources of this Rule are Supreme Bench Rule 331 and Montgomery County Rule 300. With respect to removal of exhibits introduced during trial, Baltimore County Rule 1.7 has been followed; see also Baltimore County Rule 1.12 and Seventh Circuit Rule 7.

In general, the Rule prohibits the withdrawal of exhibits filed with the pleadings without court order (compare Second Circuit Rule 9). However, exhibits introduced into evidence or marked for identification during a trial could be disposed of by the clerk of court or other person designated by the court after expiration of the time for appeal or after return of the mandate in the event of an appeal. The practice, now used in some areas, especially Baltimore City, of counsel removing exhibits after a trial would be prohibited.

Source. — This Rule is former Rule 1217.

Effect of amendments. — The 1996 amendment added the Source note.

Editor's note. — An Order dated June 5, 1996, effective Jan. 1, 1997, renumbered this Rule, which was formerly Rule 1217.

Parties permitted recovery of evidence. — This Rule does not permit a party to a case to recover the exhibit unless that party is the one who placed it in evidence, absent a showing of ownership. State v. Strickland, 42 Md. App. 357, 400 A.2d 451 (1979).

Nature of petition for return of money. — A petition for the return of money introduced into evidence, filed in the circuit court, is in the nature of trespass or trover for the determination of title and not replevin. State v. Strickland, 42 Md. App. 357, 400 A.2d 451 (1979).

And deemed civil proceeding. — A proceeding in the circuit court to recover money that was introduced into evidence in a bribery trial is civil in nature, and the State has the right to appeal an order of court directing that the money be paid over to the briber. State v. Strickland, 42 Md. App. 357, 400 A.2d 451 (1979).

Meaning of section d 2. — Section d 2 of this Rule means that the clerk of the court is required to notify all counsel in the case that the evidence will be disposed of in such manner as may be appropriate unless a motion for its return is filed within 30 days after the notice to counsel. State v. Strickland, 42 Md. App. 357, 400 A.2d 451 (1979).

Rule 16-307. Electronic filing of pleadings and papers.

a. *Applicability; conflicts with other rules.* This Rule applies to the electronic filing of pleadings and papers. A pleading or paper may not be filed by direct electronic transmission to the court except in accordance with this Rule. To the extent of any inconsistency with any other Rule, this Rule and any administrative order entered pursuant to it shall prevail.

b. *Submission of plan.* A County Administrative Judge may submit to the State Court Administrator a detailed plan for a pilot project for the electronic filing of pleadings and papers. After consulting with the County Administrative Judge, the Clerk of the Circuit Court, the vendor identified in the plan, and such other judges, court clerks, members of the bar, vendors of electronic filing systems, and other interested persons as the State Court Administrator shall choose, the State Court Administrator shall review the plan, considering among other things: (1) whether the proposed electronic filing system will be compatible with (A) the data processing and operational systems used or anticipated for use by the Administrative Office of the Courts and by the Circuit Court, and (B) electronic filing systems that may be installed by other circuit courts; (2) whether the installation and use of the proposed system will create any undue financial or operational burdens on the court; (3) whether the proposed system is reasonably available for use by litigants and attorneys at a reasonable cost or whether an efficient and compatible system of manual filing will be maintained; (4) whether the proposed system will be effective, not likely to break down, and secure; (5) whether the proposed system makes appropriate provision for the protection of privacy; and (6) whether the court can discard or replace the system during or at the conclusion of a trial period without undue financial or operational burden. The State Court Administrator shall make a recommendation to the Court of Appeals with respect to the plan.

c. *Approval; duration.* A plan may not be implemented unless approved by administrative order of the Court of Appeals. The plan shall terminate two years after the date of the administrative order approving it unless terminated earlier or extended by a subsequent administrative order.

d. *Evaluation.* The Chief Judge of the Court of Appeals shall appoint a committee consisting of one or more judges, court clerks, lawyers, legal educators, bar association representatives, and other interested and knowledgeable persons to monitor and evaluate the plan. Prior to the expiration of the two-year period set forth in section c of this Rule, the Court of Appeals, after considering the recommendations of the committee, shall evaluate the operation of the plan.

e. *Extension, modification, or termination.* By administrative order, the Court of Appeals may extend, modify, or terminate a plan at any time.

f. *Public availability of plan.* The State Court Administrator and the Clerk of the Circuit Court shall make available for public inspection a copy of any current plan. (Added June 5, 1995, effective July 1, 1995; amended June 5, 1996, effective Jan. 1, 1997.)

Source. — This Rule is former Rule 1217A.

Effect of amendments. — The 1996 amendment rewrote the Source note.
Editor's note. — An Order dated June 5, 1996, effective Jan. 1, 1997, renumbered this Rule, which was formerly Rule 1217A.

Rule 16-308. Court information system.

a. *Report of docketing and disposition of cases.* The clerk shall promptly transmit to the Administrative Office of the Courts in a manner prescribed by the State Court Administrator the data elements concerning the docketing and disposition of criminal, juvenile and civil cases as may be designated by the State Court Administrator.

b. *Reporting and transmittal of criminal history record information.* 1. The Administrative Office of the Courts shall transmit to the Central Repository of Criminal History Record Information of the Department of Public Safety and Correctional Services the data elements of criminal history record information on offenses agreed to by the Secretary of the Department of Public Safety and Correctional Services and the Chief Judge of the Court of Appeals or his designee for purposes of completing a criminal history record maintained by the Central Repository of Criminal History Record Information.

2. Transmittal of reports of dispositions. (a) Within 15 days after the conviction, forfeiture of bail, dismissal of an appeal or an acquittal in any case

involving a violation of the Maryland Vehicle Law or other traffic law or ordinance, or any conviction for manslaughter or assault committed by means of an automobile, or of any felony involving the use of an automobile, the clerk of the court shall forward to the State Motor Vehicle Administration a certified abstract of the record on a form furnished by the State Motor Vehicle Administration.

(b) When a defendant has been charged by citation and a conviction is entered by reason of his payment of a fine or forfeiture of collateral or bond before trial, the conviction is not a reportable event under Article 27, Section 747 (a) (10), Annotated Code of Maryland.

c. *Inspection of criminal history record information contained in court records of public judicial proceedings.* Unless expunged, sealed, marked confidential or otherwise prohibited by statute, court rule or order, criminal history record information contained in court records of public judicial proceedings is subject to inspection by any person at the times and under conditions as the clerk of a court reasonably determines necessary for the protection of the records and the prevention of unnecessary interference with the regular discharge of the duties of his office. (Added June 30, 1973, effective July 1, 1973; amended Nov. 4, 1977, effective Jan. 1, 1978; Dec. 21, 1977, effective Jan. 1, 1978; June 5, 1996, effective Jan. 1, 1997.)

Cross references. — See Code, Courts Article, §§ 2-203 and 13-101 (d) and (f), Article 27, §§ 743, 747, 748, and State Government Article, §§ 10-612 through 10-619.
For definition of court records see Rule 4-502 (d).

Committee note. — This Rule does not contemplate the reporting of parking violations.

Source. — This Rule is former Rule 1218.

Effect of amendments. — The 1996 amendment added the Source note.
Editor's note. — An Order dated June 5,

1996, effective Jan. 1, 1997, renumbered this Rule, which was formerly Rule 1218.

Rule 16-309. Notice to Court of Special Appeals.

By the third working day of each month, the clerk shall send to the Clerk of the Court of Special Appeals a list of all cases in which, during the preceding calendar month, (1) an order of appeal to the Court of Special Appeals has been filed, or (2) an appeal to the Court of Special Appeals has been dismissed. The list shall include the title and docket number of the case, the name and address of counsel for appellant(s), and the date on which the order of appeal or the dismissal was filed. (Added May 5, 1976, effective July 1, 1976; amended May 7, 1982, effective July 1, 1982; Apr. 6, 1984, effective July 1, 1984; June 5, 1996, effective Jan. 1, 1997.)

Source. — This Rule is former Rule 1219.

Effect of amendments. — The 1996 amendment added the Source note.

Editor's note. — An Order dated June 5, 1996, effective Jan. 1, 1997, renumbered this

Rule, which was formerly Rule 1219.
University of Baltimore Law Review. —

For article, "The Maryland Rules — A Time for Overhaul," see 9 U. Balt. L. Rev. 1 (1979).

CHAPTER 400. ATTORNEYS, OFFICERS OF COURT AND OTHER PERSONS.

Rule 16-401. Proscribed activities — Gratuities, etc.

a. *Giving prohibited.* No attorney shall give, either directly or indirectly, to an officer or employee of a court, or of an office serving a court, a gratuity, gift or any compensation related to his official duties and not expressly authorized by rule or law.

b. *Receiving prohibited.* No officer or employee of any court, or of any office serving a court, shall accept a gratuity or gift, either directly or indirectly, from a litigant, an attorney or any person regularly doing business with the court, or any compensation related to such officer's or employee's official duties and not expressly authorized by rule or law. (Amended, June 5, 1996, effective Jan. 1, 1997.)

Cross references. — For definition of "person," see Rule 1-202 (q).

Committee note. — This Rule is based in part on New Jersey Rule 1:34. It is intended as a broad prohibition against the exchange of gratuities, gifts or any compensation not expressly authorized by rule or law as between attorneys and court officials and employees, in connection with the official functions of such persons. The Rule covers sheriffs and deputy sheriffs, as well as regular court officers, employees and other persons. Among other things, it will prevent the practice, now existing in the courts of the Supreme Bench of Baltimore City, whereby certain portions of appearance fees are retained by the clerks by way of extra compensation or gratuities for the performance of their official duties. This Rule is not intended to preclude contributions to or for elected public officials as authorized by and in conformance with the provisions of article 33, §§ 26-1 through 26-20, Annotated Code of Maryland (1968 Cum. Supp.).

Source. — This Rule is former Rule 1220.

Effect of amendments. — The 1996 amendment added the Source note.

Editor's note. — An Order dated June 5, 1996, effective Jan. 1, 1997, renumbered this Rule, which was formerly Rule 1220.

The definition of "person" currently appears in Rule 1-202 (r).

University of Baltimore Law Review. — For article, "The Maryland Rules — A Time for Overhaul," see 9 U. Balt. L. Rev. 1 (1979).

Rule 16-402. Attorneys and other officers not to become sureties.

No attorney or other officer or employee of a court, or of any office serving a court, shall be accepted as security for costs or surety on any bond, or be received as bail in any case. (Amended, June 5, 1996, effective Jan. 1, 1997.)

Source. — This Rule is former Rule 1221.

Effect of amendments. — The 1996 amendment added the Source note.

Editor's note. — An Order dated June 5, 1996, effective Jan. 1, 1997, renumbered this Rule, which was formerly Rule 1221.

University of Baltimore Law Review. — For article, "The Maryland Rules — A Time for Overhaul," see 9 U. Balt. L. Rev. 1 (1979).

Rule 16-403. Trust clerk.

The circuit court for each county and the Supreme Bench of Baltimore City shall designate a trust clerk and shall determine the trust clerk's compensation. (Added Feb. 2, 1970; amended Oct. 1, 1980, effective Jan. 1, 1981; June 5, 1996, effective Jan. 1, 1997.)

Source. — This Rule is former Rule 1223.

Effect of amendments. — The 1996 amendment added the Source note.

Editor's note. — An Order dated June 5, 1996, effective Jan. 1, 1997, renumbered this Rule, which was formerly Rule 1223.

Practice of law. — An individual who is appointed a trust clerk pursuant to this rule is not, by that fact alone, prohibited from practicing law; only if the individual designated as trust clerk also is the Clerk of the Court or a member of one of the other classes expressly enumerated in BOP § 10-603 (b) (4) (e.g., an employee or appointee of the Clerk of the Court) is he or she prohibited from practicing law. 75 Op. Att'y Gen. (May 4, 1990).

Rule 16-404. Administration of circuit court reporters.

a. *Establishment of regulations and standards.* The Chief Judge of the Court of Appeals shall from time to time prescribe regulations and standards regarding circuit court reporters and the system of reporting in the courts of the State. The regulations and standards may include provisions relative to:

(1) The selection, qualifications and responsibilities of court reporters;

(2) Procedures and regulations for court reporting;

(3) Preparation, typing and format of transcripts;

(4) Charges for transcripts and copies;

(5) Preservation and maintenance of reporting notes, however recorded;

(6) Equipment and supplies utilized in reporting.

b. *Number of court reporters — Supervisory court reporter.* Each court shall have the number of court reporters recommended by the County Administrative Judge and approved by the Chief Judge of the Court of Appeals. In a county with more than one court reporter the County Administrative Judge shall designate one as supervisory court reporter, to serve at his pleasure. The Chief Judge of the Court of Appeals shall prescribe the duties of the supervisory court reporter.

c. *Supervision of court reporters.* Subject to the general supervision of the Chief Judge of the Court of Appeals and to the direct supervision of his Circuit Administrative Judge, the County Administrative Judge shall have the supervisory responsibility for the court reporters in his county. The County Administrative Judge may delegate supervisory responsibility to the supervisory court reporter, including the assignment of court reporters to attend and record at each session of the court and every other proceeding as provided in this Rule or by order of the court.

d. *Methods of reporting — Proceedings to be recorded.* Each court reporter assigned to record a proceeding shall record verbatim by shorthand, stenotype, mechanical or electronic sound recording methods, or any combination of these methods, subject to regulations and standards prescribed by the Chief Judge of the Court of Appeals.

1. Criminal cases. (a) Trial on merits other than District Court appeals. In criminal cases, other than appeals from the District Court, the entire trial on the merits held in open court, including opening statements and closing arguments of counsel;

(b) Appeals from District Court. In appeals from the District Court, upon specific request of the judge or a party, the entire trial on the merits held in open court, including opening statements and closing arguments of counsel;

(c) Motions and other proceedings. Upon specific request of the judge or a party the entire or any designated part of the hearing on all motions or other proceedings before the court.

2. Civil cases. (a) Trial on merits other than District Court appeals. In civil cases, other than appeals *de novo* from the District Court, the entire trial on the merits held in open court, excluding opening statements and closing arguments of counsel unless requested by the judge or a party;

(b) *De novo* appeals from District Court. In appeals *de novo* from the District Court, upon specific request of the judge or a party, the entire trial on the merits held in open court, including, if requested opening statements and closing arguments of counsel;

(c) Motions and other proceedings. Upon specific request of the judge or a party, the entire or any designated part of the hearing on all motions or other proceedings before the court.

e. *Maintenance and filing of administrative records.* The Chief Judge of the Court of Appeals may prescribe procedures for the maintenance and filing of administrative records and reports with the Administrative Office of the Courts and the Circuit Administrative Judge. (Amended, June 5, 1996, effective Jan. 1, 1997.)

Source. — This Rule is former Rule 1224.

Effect of amendments. — The 1996 amendment added the Source note.

Editor's note. — An Order dated June 5, 1996, effective Jan. 1, 1997, renumbered this Rule, which was formerly Rule 1224.

Purpose of section d of this Rule is to preserve a correct and precise account of the evidence and rulings at trial, and to assure the ability of courts and of counsel to perform their duties efficiently and completely. Smith v. State, 291 Md. 125, 433 A.2d 1143 (1981).

Responsibility of counsel under section d 1. — Since section d 1 of this Rule requires that opening statements and closing arguments be recorded, it is incumbent upon counsel, where all or part of the opening statements or closing arguments is challenged, to see that it is transcribed and made a part of the record for review. Blizzard v. State, 30 Md. App. 156, 351 A.2d 443, rev'd on other grounds, 278 Md. 556, 366 A.2d 1026 (1976).

Inability to prepare complete transcript not sufficient ground for reversal. — The inability to prepare a complete verbatim transcript of a criminal case, in and of itself, does not necessarily present a sufficient ground for reversal. Smith v. State, 291 Md. 125, 433 A.2d 1143 (1981).

Defective transcript imposes heavy burden on appeal. — Where there is some defect in the transcript of a trial not attributable to discrimination or inherent unfairness by the prosecution, an appellant carries a heavy burden on appeal. Smith v. State, 291 Md. 125, 433 A.2d 1143 (1981).

Effect of lack of adequate substitute for complete trial record. — Only when an adequate substitute for a complete record of a criminal trial cannot be made will a court consider an appellant's contention that he has been deprived of meaningful appellate review. Smith v. State, 291 Md. 125, 433 A.2d 1143 (1981).

Appellant's responsibility to perfect incomplete record. — Where the transcript of a criminal trial is incomplete an appellant has the responsibility to make a sincere effort to perfect the record. Smith v. State, 291 Md. 125, 433 A.2d 1143 (1981).

Rule 16-405. Videotape recording of circuit court proceedings.

a. *Authorization.* The Circuit Administrative Judge for a judicial circuit, after consultation with the County Administrative Judge for a county, may authorize the recording by videotape of proceedings required or permitted to be recorded by Rule 16-404 d in courtrooms or hearing rooms in that county.

b. *Identification.* The clerk shall affix to the videotape a label containing the following information:

1. the name of the court;
2. the date on which the videotape was recorded;
3. the docket reference of each proceeding included on the tape; and
4. any other identifying letters, marks, or numbers.

c. *Trial log; exhibit list.* The clerk or other designee of the court shall keep a written log identifying each proceeding recorded on a videotape and, for each proceeding recorded on the tape, a log listing the tape references for the beginning and end of each witness's testimony and an exhibit list. The original logs and exhibit list shall remain with the original papers in the circuit court. A copy of the logs and the exhibit list shall be kept with the videotape.

d. *Presence of court reporter not necessary; conflicts with other rules.* 1. If circuit court proceedings are recorded by videotape, it is not necessary for a court reporter to be present in the courtroom.

2. In the event of a conflict between this Rule and another Rule, this Rule shall prevail. (Added Nov. 22, 1989, effective Jan. 1, 1990; amended July 16, 1992; June 5, 1996, effective Jan. 1, 1997.)

Source. — This Rule is former Rule 1224A.

Effect of amendments. — The 1996 amendment substituted "Rule 16-404 d" for "Rule 1224 d." in a.; and rewrote the Source note.

Editor's note. — An Order dated June 5, 1996, effective Jan. 1, 1997, renumbered this Rule, which was formerly Rule 1224A.

Rule 16-406. Access to videotape recordings of proceedings in the circuit court.

a. *Control — In general.* Videotape recordings made pursuant to Rule 16-405 are under the control of the court having custody of them. Access to and copying of those recordings are subject to the provisions of this Rule.

Cross references. — Code, State Government Article, § 10-615.

b. *Direct access.* No person other than a duly authorized court official or employee shall have direct access to or possession of an official videotape recording.

c. *Right to copy; restrictions.* 1. Upon written request and the payment of reasonable costs, the authorized custodian of an official videotape recording shall make a copy of the recording, or any part requested, available to:

(A) a party to the action or the party's attorney; and

(B) a stenographer or transcription service designated by the court for the purpose of preparing an official transcript from the recording.

2. Unless authorized by an order of court, a person who receives a copy of a videotape recording pursuant to this section shall not (A) make or cause to be made any additional copy of the recording or (B) except for a non-sequestered witness or an agent, employee, or consultant of the attorney, make the recording available to any person not entitled to it pursuant to this section.

d. *Other persons.* 1. This section does not apply to the videotape of (A) a criminal proceeding, (B) a revocation of probation proceeding, or (C) any proceeding that is confidential by law. The right to obtain a copy of a videotape in those proceedings is governed solely by section c of this Rule.

2. A person not entitled to a copy of a videotape recording pursuant to section c of this Rule may file a request to obtain a copy pursuant to this section. The person shall file the request with the clerk of the circuit court in which the proceeding was conducted and shall serve a copy of the request pursuant to Rule 1-321 on each party to the action.

3. A party may file a written response to the request within five days after being served with the request. Any other interested person may file a response within 5 days after service of the request on the last party to be served.

4. The clerk shall refer the request and all responses to the judge who conducted the proceeding.

5. If the action is still pending in the court, the court shall deny the request unless (A) all parties have affirmatively consented and no interested person has filed a timely objection or (B) the court finds good cause to grant the request. If the action has been transferred to another circuit court, the court shall transfer the matter to that court. If judgment has been entered in the action, the court shall grant the request unless it finds good cause to the contrary, but the court may delay permission to obtain the copy until either all appellate proceedings are completed or the right to further appellate review has lapsed. (Added Nov. 22, 1989, effective Jan. 1, 1990; amended June 5, 1996, effective Jan. 1, 1997.)

Source. — This Rule is former Rule 1224B.

Effect of amendments. — The 1996 amendment substituted "Rule 16-405" for "Rule 1224A" in a.; and rewrote the Source note.

Editor's note. — An Order dated June 5, 1996, effective Jan. 1, 1997, renumbered this Rule, which was formerly Rule 1224B.

CHAPTER 500. COURT ADMINISTRATION — DISTRICT COURT.

Rule 16-501. Applicability.
The rules in this Chapter apply to the District Court.

Source. — This Rule is new.

Rule 16-502. Payment of money into court.
All money paid into court on account of a pending action shall be deposited by the clerk in a bank and noted in an appropriate record. The clerk shall disburse the money only upon order of the court and, unless the court otherwise directs, only by check payable to the order of the party entitled and the party's counsel of record. (Added May 14, 1992, effective July 1, 1992; amended June 5, 1996, effective Jan. 1, 1997.)

Source. — This Rule is former M.D.R. 1214.

Effect of amendments. — The 1996 amendment rewrote the Source note.
Editor's note. — An Order dated June 5, 1996, effective Jan. 1, 1997, renumbered this Rule, which was formerly Maryland District Rule 1214.

Rule 16-503. Court information system.
a. *Reporting and transmittal of criminal history record information.* 1. The District Court of Maryland shall transmit to the Central Repository of Criminal History Record Information of the Department of Public Safety and Correctional Services the data elements of criminal history record information on offenses agreed to by the Secretary of the Department of Public Safety and Correctional Services the data elements of criminal history record information on offenses agreed to by the Secretary of the Department of Public Safety and Correctional Services and the Chief Judge of the Court of Appeals or his designee for purposes of completing a criminal history record maintained by the Central Repository of Criminal History Record Information.

2. Transmittal of reports of dispositions. When a defendant has been charged by citation and a conviction is entered by reason of his payment of a fine or forfeiture of collateral before trial, the conviction is not a reportable event under Article 27, Section 747 (a) (10), Annotated Code of Maryland.

b. *Inspection of criminal history record information contained in court records of public judicial proceedings.* Unless expunged, sealed, marked confidential or otherwise prohibited by statute, court rule or order, criminal history record information contained in court records of public judicial proceedings is subject to inspection by any person at the times and under conditions as the clerk of a court reasonably determines necessary for the protection of the records and the prevention of unnecessary interference with the regular discharge of the duties of his office. (Added Dec. 21, 1977, effective Jan. 1, 1978; amended June 5, 1996, effective Jan. 1, 1997.)

Cross references. — See Code, Courts Article, §§ 2-203 and 13-101(d) and (f), Article 27, §§ 743, 747, 748, and State Government Article, §§ 10-612 through 10-619.

For definition of court records see Rule 4-502 (d).

Source. — This Rule is former M.D.R. 1218.

Effect of amendments. — The 1996 amendment added the Source note.

Editor's note. — An Order dated June 5, 1996, effective Jan. 1, 1997, renumbered this Rule, which was formerly Maryland District Rule 1218.

Rule 16-504. Recording of proceedings.

a. *Recording.* All trials and hearings before a judge or examiner shall be recorded verbatim either stenographically or by an electronic recording device provided by the court, and the recording shall be filed among the court records.

b. *Access to recording.* If a proceeding is recorded by sound recording device, a party to the proceeding shall have access to the sound recording for the purpose of having the recording replayed or transcribed, subject to such procedures and regulations as the Chief Judge of the District Court of Maryland may prescribe. (Added Apr. 6, 1984, effective July 1, 1984; amended June 5, 1996, effective Jan. 1, 1997.)

Source. — This Rule is former M.D.R. 1224.

Effect of amendments. — The 1996 amendment added the Source note.

Editor's note. — An Order dated June 5, 1996, effective Jan. 1, 1997, renumbered this Rule, which was formerly Maryland District Rule 1224.

Rule 16-505. Disposition of records.

a. *Definitions.* In this Rule, unless the context or subject matter otherwise requires:

1. Dispose. "Dispose" means to either destroy or remove records.

2. Records. "Records" mean any original papers, official books, documents, and files, including but not limited to dockets, electronic recordings of testimony and exhibits within the custody of the clerk of the court.

Cross references. — See Code, §§ 9-1009 and 10-639 through 10-642 of the State Government Article.

3. Schedule. "Schedule" means the form known as the "Records Retention and Disposal Schedule" used by the Records Management Division of the Hall of Records Commission.

b. *Authority.* Subject to the provisions of this Rule, the clerk of the court, with the written approval of the Chief Judge of the District Court and in cooperation with the Hall of Records Commission, may dispose of records within his custody.

Cross references. — See § 2-206 of the Courts Article.

c. *Procedure.* 1. Schedule preparation — Hall of Records recommendation. The clerk of the court shall prepare a schedule for the disposition of court records and submit it to the Hall of Records Commission for its recommendation.

2. Chief Judge — Approval. The schedule, together with the recommendation of the Hall of Records Commission, shall be submitted for the written approval of the Chief Judge who may approve it in whole or in part, amend it or disapprove it.

3. Court order. Approval of the schedule by the Chief Judge shall be deemed on order of court providing for disposal of the records.

4. Contents of schedule. The schedule, as approved, shall set forth:

(i) The identification of the records.

(ii) The length of time the records are to be retained by the clerk of the court before disposition.

(iii) Whether the Hall of Records Commission declines to accept the records for preservation.

(iv) Whether the records are to be destroyed or removed.

(v) The place to which the records would be removed.

(vi) Whether the schedule shall be "standing" viz., operative until changed by further order of court.

5. Removal procedures — Hall of records. In those cases where the Hall of Records Commission accepts records, they shall be removed according to the Hall of Records Commission procedures.

6. Disposal if hall of records declines custody. In those cases where the Hall of Records Commission declines records, disposition shall be according to the terms set forth in the schedule as approved. If the records are to be destroyed the clerk shall obtain the approval of the Board of Public Works and upon destruction shall file a certificate of destruction with the Hall of Records Commission.

Cross references. — See Code, § 10-642 of the State Government Article.

Committee note. — This Rule is meant to allow periodic destruction of records without the necessity of obtaining Board of Public Works approval each time if such destruction of records or classes of records had been clearly approved by the Board of Public Works in a standing schedule.

d. *Limitations upon disposal of records.* 1. Indices, dockets, and books of account. The clerk shall retain permanently all indices, dockets, and books of account.

2. Emergency evaluation and domestic violence cases. The clerk shall retain for a period of 12 years after the case is closed all original papers and exhibits in any case containing a petition for emergency evaluation or a petition for protection from domestic violence.

3. Cases involving judgment for a sum certain. In any case in which a judgment for a sum certain is entered, the clerk shall retain all original papers, exhibits, and electronic recordings of testimony for a period of three years after entry of the judgment and shall continue to retain all original papers and exhibits in the file after that three year period until the judgment expires or is satisfied.

4. Criminal cases. (i) In any criminal case which is dismissed or in which a *nolle prosequi* or stet is entered, the clerk shall retain all original papers, exhibits, and electronic recordings of testimony for a period of three years after the case is so concluded.

(ii) In any criminal case in which judgment is entered or probation before judgment is granted, the clerk shall retain all original papers, exhibits, and electronic recordings of testimony for a period of three years after the case is so concluded, and if within that three year period the defendant fails to comply with the order of court, the clerk shall continue to retain the original papers and exhibits in the file until the failure is cured or an arrest warrant issued as a result of the failure is invalidated as permitted by law.

(iii) In any criminal case for a misdemeanor in which an arrest warrant issued on the charging document or as a result of the defendant's failure to appear for trial remains unserved three years after its issuance, the clerk shall retain all the original papers and exhibits in the file until the warrant is invalidated as permitted by law.

5. Other cases. Except as provided in subsection 1, 2, 3, or 4 of this section the clerk shall retain all original papers, exhibits, and electronic recordings of testimony in a case for a period of three years after the case is concluded by dismissal, settlement, or entry of judgment.

6. Disposal if photographed, photocopied, or microphotographed — Traffic and criminal dockets. (i) Any of the records, except dockets, set forth in subsections 1 through 5 of this section may be disposed of at any time provided that the records have been photographed, photocopied or microphotographed in accordance with the Hall of Records Commission procedures and copies have been substituted therefor, including a master security negative which shall be retained permanently.

(ii) Traffic and criminal dockets may be disposed of after a period of five years if copies are retained in accordance with subsection 6 (i) above.

7. Retention by Hall of Records. Whenever this section requires the clerk to retain records, the requirement may be satisfied by retention of the records by the Hall of Records Commission. When records retained by the clerk are twenty-five years of age, if not previously transferred to the Hall of Records Commission, they shall be transferred to that Commission, or disposed of according to schedule. (Added June 16, 1975, effective July 1, 1975; amended Dec. 17, 1975, effective Jan. 1, 1976; May 6, 1977, effective July 1, 1977; June 23, 1983, effective Jan. 1, 1984; Nov. 19, 1987, effective July 1, 1988; Mar. 22, 1991, effective July 1, 1991; June 5, 1996, effective Jan. 1, 1997.)

Source. — This Rule is former M.D.R. 1299.

Effect of amendments. — The 1996 amendment added the Source note.

Editor's note. — An Order dated June 5, 1996, effective Jan. 1, 1997, renumbered this Rule, which was formerly Maryland District Rule 1299.

Section 2-206 of the Courts Article, which is referred to in the Cross Reference note to section b, has been transferred to be § 2-205 of the Courts Article.

CHAPTER 600. ATTORNEY TRUST ACCOUNTS.

Rule 16-601. Applicability.

The Rules in this Chapter apply to all trust accounts required by law to be maintained by attorneys for the deposit of funds that belong to others, except that these Rules do not apply to a fiduciary account maintained by an attorney as personal representative, trustee, guardian, custodian, receiver, or committee, or as a fiduciary under a written instrument or order of court. (Amended June 5, 1996, effective Jan. 1, 1997.)

Cross references. — BOP § 10-301 et seq. and Rule 1.15 of the Maryland Rules of Professional Conduct.

Source. — This Rule is former Rule BU1.

Effect of amendments. — The 1996 amendment substituted "Chapter" for "Subtitle"; and added the Source note.

Editor's note. — An Order dated June 5, 1996, effective Jan. 1, 1997, renumbered this Rule, which was formerly Rule BU1.

Rule 16-602. Definitions.

In these rules, the following definitions apply, except as expressly otherwise provided or as necessary implication requires:

a. *Approved financial institution.* "Approved financial institution" means a financial institution approved by the Commission in accordance with these Rules.

b. *Attorney.* "Attorney" means any person admitted by the Court of Appeals to practice law.

c. *Attorney trust account.* "Attorney trust account" means an account, including an escrow account, maintained in a financial institution for the deposit of funds received or held by an attorney or law firm on behalf of a client or third person.

d. *Bar Counsel.* "Bar Counsel" means the person appointed by the Commission as the principal executive officer of the disciplinary system affecting attorneys. All duties of Bar Counsel prescribed by these Rules shall be subject to the supervision and procedural guidelines of the Commission.

e. *Client.* "Client" includes any individual, firm, or entity for which an attorney performs any legal service, including acting as an escrow agent or as a legal representative of a fiduciary. The term does not include a public or private entity of which an attorney is a full-time employee.

f. *Commission.* "Commission" means the Attorney Grievance Commission of Maryland, as authorized and created by Rule 16-702 (Attorney Grievance Commission).

g. *Financial institution.* "Financial institution" means a bank, trust company, savings bank, or savings and loan association authorized by law to do business in this State, in the District of Columbia, or in a state contiguous to this State, the accounts of which are insured by an agency or instrumentality of the United States.

h. *Law firm.* "Law firm" includes a partnership of attorneys, a professional or nonprofit corporation of attorneys, and a combination thereof engaged in the practice of law. In the case of a law firm with offices in this State and in other jurisdictions, these Rules apply only to the offices in this State. (Amended June 28, 1989, effective July 1, 1989; June 5, 1996, effective Jan. 1, 1997.)

Source. — This Rule is former Rule BU2.

Effect of amendments. — The 1996 amendment substituted "Rule 16-702" for "Rule BV2" in f.; and added the Source note.

Editor's note. — An Order dated June 5, 1996, effective Jan. 1, 1997, renumbered this Rule, which was formerly Rule BU2.

Rule 16-603. Duty to maintain account.

An attorney or the attorney's law firm shall maintain one or more attorney trust accounts for the deposit of funds received from any source for the intended benefit of clients or third persons. The account or accounts shall be maintained in this State, in the District of Columbia, or in a state contiguous to this State, and shall be with an approved financial institution. Unless an attorney maintains such an account, or is a member of or employed by a law firm that maintains such an account, an attorney may not receive and accept funds as an attorney from any source intended in whole or in part for the benefit of a client or third person. (Amended, June 5, 1996, effective Jan. 1, 1997.)

Source. — This Rule is former Rule BU3.

Effect of amendments. — The 1996 amendment added the Source note.

Editor's note. — An Order dated June 5, 1996, effective Jan. 1, 1997, renumbered this Rule, which was formerly Rule BU3.

Disciplinary proceedings. — Lawyer was indefinitely suspended from the practice of law where he failed to maintain a trust account, commingled client funds and his own, and failed to keep proper records regarding such funds; but, the violations were unintentional, resulting from lawyer's ignorance of his obligation to refrain from commingling, and he was not motivated to use client funds for his

own benefit. Attorney Grievance Comm'n v. Awuah, 346 Md. 420, 697 A.2d 446 (1997).

Claimed ignorance of ethical duties and bookkeeping requirements is not a defense in disciplinary proceedings, but a finding with respect to the intent with which a violation was committed is relevant on the issue of the appropriate sanction. Attorney Grievance Comm'n v. Awuah, 346 Md. 420, 697 A.2d 446 (1997).

Stated in Unnamed Att'y v. Attorney Grievance Comm'n, 349 Md. 391, 708 A.2d 667 (1998).

Rule 16-604. Trust account — Required deposits.

Except as otherwise permitted by rule or other law, all funds, including cash, received and accepted by an attorney or law firm in this State from a client or third person to be delivered in whole or in part to a client or third person, unless received as payment of fees owed the attorney by the client or in reimbursement for expenses properly advanced on behalf of the client, shall be deposited in an attorney trust account in an approved financial institution. This Rule does not apply to an instrument received by an attorney or law firm that is made payable solely to a client or third person and is transmitted directly to the client or third person. (Amended, June 5, 1996, effective Jan. 1, 1997.)

Source. — This Rule is former Rule BU4.

Effect of amendments. — The 1996 amendment added the Source note.

Editor's note. — An Order dated June 5, 1996, effective Jan. 1, 1997, renumbered this Rule, which was formerly Rule BU4.

Applied in Attorney Grievance Comm'n v. Hollis, 347 Md. 547, 702 A.2d 223 (1997).

Quoted in Attorney Grievance Comm'n v. Adams, 349 Md. 86, 706 A.2d 1080 (1998).

Rule 16-605. Duty of attorney to notify institution.

An attorney may not exercise any authority to sign checks or disburse or withdraw funds from an attorney trust account until the attorney in writing:

a. Requests the financial institution to designate the account on its records as an attorney trust account, and

b. Authorizes the financial institution to report to Bar Counsel any dishonored instruments or overdrafts in the account as required by the agreement under Rule 16-610 between the institution and the Commission. (Amended, June 5, 1996, effective Jan. 1, 1997.)

Source. — This Rule is former Rule BU5.

Effect of amendments. — The 1996 amendment substituted "Rule 16-610" for "Rule BU10" in b; and added the Source note.

Editor's note. — An Order dated June 5, 1996, effective Jan. 1, 1997, renumbered this

Rule, which was formerly Rule BU5.

Stated in Unnamed Att'y v. Attorney Grievance Comm'n, 349 Md. 391, 708 A.2d 667 (1998).

Rule 16-606. Name and designation of account.

An attorney or law firm shall maintain each attorney trust account with a title that includes the name of the attorney or law firm and that clearly designates the account as "Attorney Trust Account", "Attorney Escrow Account", or "Clients' Funds Account" on all checks and deposit slips. The title shall distinguish the account from any other fiduciary account that the attorney or law firm may maintain and from any personal or business account of the attorney or law firm. (Amended, June 5, 1996, effective Jan. 1, 1997.)

Source. — This Rule is former Rule BU6.

Effect of amendments. — The 1996 amendment added the Source note.

Editor's note. — An Order dated June 5, 1996, effective Jan. 1, 1997, renumbered this Rule, which was formerly Rule BU6.

Applied in Attorney Grievance Comm'n v. Awuah, 346 Md. 420, 697 A.2d 446 (1997).

Stated in Unnamed Att'y v. Attorney Grievance Comm'n, 349 Md. 391, 708 A.2d 667 (1998).

Rule 16-607. Commingling of funds.

a. *General prohibition.* An attorney or law firm may deposit in an attorney trust account only those funds required to be deposited in that account by Rule 16-604 or permitted to be so deposited by section b. of this Rule.

b. *Exceptions.* 1. An attorney or law firm shall either (A) deposit into an attorney trust account funds to pay any fees, service charges, or minimum balance required by the financial institution to open or maintain the account, including those fees that cannot be charged against interest due to the Maryland Legal Services Corporation pursuant to Rule 16-610 b 1 (D), or (B) enter into an agreement with the financial institution to have any fees or charges deducted from an operating account maintained by the attorney or law firm. The attorney or law firm may deposit into an attorney trust account any funds expected to be advanced on behalf of a client and expected to be reimbursed to the attorney by the client.

2. An attorney or law firm may deposit into an attorney trust account funds belonging in part to a client and in part presently or potentially to the attorney or law firm. The portion belonging to the attorney or law firm shall be withdrawn promptly when the attorney or law firm becomes entitled to the funds, but any portion disputed by the client shall remain in the account until the dispute is resolved.

3. Funds of a client or beneficial owner may be pooled and commingled in an attorney trust account with the funds held for other clients or beneficial owners. (Amended Sept. 11, 1995, effective Jan. 1, 1996; June 5, 1996, effective Jan. 1, 1997; June 10, 1997, effective July 1, 1997.)

Cross references. — See Code, BOP §§ 10-301 et seq.

Source. — This Rule is former Rule BU7.

Effect of amendments. — The 1996 amendment substituted "Rule 16-604" for "Rule BU4" in a.; and added the Source note.

The 1997 amendment substituted "Rule 16-610" for "Rule BU10" in b.1.

Editor's note. — An Order dated June 5, 1996, effective Jan. 1, 1997, renumbered this Rule, which was formerly Rule BU7.

Applicability. — Subdivision b 3, which permits commingling of the funds of several clients in a single attorney trust account, does not apply to a fiduciary account maintained by an attorney as personal representative, trustee, guardian, custodian, receiver, or committee, or as a fiduciary under a written instrument or order of court. Attorney Grievance Comm'n v. Owrutsky, 322 Md. 334, 587 A.2d 511 (1991).

Source of funds in designated account. — When an account is designated an attorney trust account, inquiry into the source of the funds within the account is irrelevant. Attorney Grievance Comm'n v. Webster, 348 Md. 662, 705 A.2d 1135 (1998).

Use of designated account. — Use of the attorney trust account for personal purposes while still designated a trust account, even if it was no longer intended that the account be used for trust purposes, is prohibited regardless of whether or not client funds are deposited in the account. Attorney Grievance Comm'n v. Webster, 348 Md. 662, 705 A.2d 1135 (1998).

Unintentional violations are relevant to appropriate sanction. — Lawyer was indefinitely suspended from the practice of law where he failed to maintain a trust account, commingled client funds and his own, and failed to keep proper records regarding such funds; but, the violations were unintentional, resulting from lawyer's ignorance of his obligation to refrain from commingling, and he was not motivated to use client funds for his own benefit. Attorney Grievance Comm'n v. Awuah, 346 Md. 420, 697 A.2d 446 (1997).

Claimed ignorance of ethical duties and bookkeeping requirements is not a defense in disciplinary proceedings, but a finding with respect to the intent with which a violation was committed is relevant on the issue of the

appropriate sanction. Attorney Grievance
Comm'n v. Awuah, 346 Md. 420, 697 A.2d 446
(1997).

Rule 16-608. Interest on funds in attorney trust accounts.

Any interest paid on funds deposited in an attorney trust account, after
deducting service charges and fees of the financial institution, shall be credited
and belong to the client or third person whose funds are on deposit during the
period the interest is earned, except to the extent that interest is paid to the
Maryland Legal Services Corporation as authorized by law. The attorney or
law firm shall have no right or claim to the interest. (Amended Sept. 11, 1995,
effective Jan. 1, 1996; June 5, 1996, effective Jan. 1, 1997.)

Cross references. — See Rule BU10 b 1
(D) providing that certain fees may not be
deducted from interest that otherwise would
be payable to the Maryland Legal Services
Corporation.

Source. — This Rule is former Rule BU8.

Effect of amendments. — The 1995
amendment added the cross reference.

Editor's note. — An Order dated June 5,
1996, effective Jan. 1, 1997, renumbered this
Rule, which was formerly Rule BU8.

Rule BU10 b 1 (D), which is referred to in
the Cross Reference note to this Rule, has been
renumbered to be Rule 16-610 b 1 (D).

Applied in Attorney Grievance Comm'n v.
Hollis, 347 Md. 547, 702 A.2d 223 (1997).

Rule 16-609. Prohibited transactions.

An attorney or law firm may not borrow or pledge any funds required by
these Rules to be deposited in an attorney trust account, obtain any remuneration from the financial institution for depositing any funds in the account, or
use any funds for any unauthorized purpose. An instrument drawn on an
attorney trust account may not be drawn payable to cash or to bearer.
(Amended, June 5, 1996, effective Jan. 1, 1997.)

Source. — This Rule is former Rule BU9.

Effect of amendments. — The 1996
amendment added the Source note.

Editor's note. — An Order dated June 5,
1996, effective Jan. 1, 1997, renumbered this
Rule, which was formerly Rule BU9.

**Unintentional violations are relevant
to appropriate sanction.** — Lawyer was
indefinitely suspended from the practice of law
where he failed to maintain a trust account,
commingled client funds and his own, and
failed to keep proper records regarding such
funds; but, the violations were unintentional,
resulting from lawyer's ignorance of his obligation to refrain from commingling, and he
was not motivated to use client funds for his
own benefit. Attorney Grievance Comm'n v.
Awuah, 346 Md. 420, 697 A.2d 446 (1997).

Claimed ignorance of ethical duties and
bookkeeping requirements is not a defense in
disciplinary proceedings, but a finding with
respect to the intent with which a violation
was committed is relevant on the issue of the
appropriate sanction. Attorney Grievance
Comm'n v. Awuah, 346 Md. 420, 697 A.2d 446
(1997).

Attorney disbarred for violating Rules.
— Attorney was disbarred for violating Maryland Rules of Professional Conduct 1.1, 1.3,
1.4(a) and (b), 1.15(a), 3.3(a)(1), and 8.4(b) and
(c), § 10-306 of the Business Occupations and
Professions Article, and this Rule. Attorney
Grievance Comm'n v. Williams, 335 Md. 458,
644 A.2d 490 (1994).

Use of funds. — Use of the attorney trust
account for personal purposes while still designated a trust account, even if it was no
longer intended that the account be used for
trust purposes, is prohibited, regardless of
whether or not client funds are deposited in
the account. Attorney Grievance Comm'n v.

Rule 16-610. Approval of financial institutions.

a. *Written agreement to be filed with Commission.* The Commission shall approve a financial institution upon the filing with the Commission of a written agreement, complying with this Rule and in a form provided by the Commission, applicable to all branches of the institution located in this State.

b. *Contents of agreement.* 1. Duties to be performed. The agreement shall provide that the financial institution, as a condition of accepting the deposit of any funds into an attorney trust account, shall:

(A) Notify the attorney or law firm promptly of any overdraft in the account or the dishonor for insufficient funds of any instrument drawn on the account.

(B) Report the overdraft or dishonor to Bar Counsel as set forth in subsection b 1 (C) of this Rule.

(C) Use the following procedure for reports to Bar Counsel required under subsection b 1 (B) of this Rule:

(i) In the case of a dishonored instrument, the report shall be identical to the overdraft notice customarily forwarded to the institution's other regular account holders. The report shall be mailed to Bar Counsel within the time provided by law for notice of dishonor to the depositor and simultaneously with the sending of that notice.

(ii) If an instrument is honored but at the time of presentation the total funds in the account, both collected and uncollected, do not equal or exceed the amount of the instrument, the report shall identify the financial institution, the attorney or law firm maintaining the account, the account name, the account number, the date of presentation for payment, and the payment date of the instrument, as well as the amount of the overdraft created. The report shall be mailed to Bar Counsel within five banking days after the date of presentation, notwithstanding any overdraft privileges that may attach to the account.

(D) Not deduct from interest on the account that otherwise would be payable to the Maryland Legal Services Corporation any fees for wire transfers, presentations against insufficient funds, certified checks, overdrafts, deposits of dishonored items, and account reconciliation services.

Cross references. — Rule 16-607 b 1.

(E) Allow reasonable access to all records of an attorney trust account if an audit of the account is ordered pursuant to Rule 16-718 (Audit of Attorney's Accounts and Records).

2. Service charges for performing duties under agreement. Nothing in the agreement shall preclude an approved financial institution from charging the attorney or law firm maintaining an attorney trust account (1) a reasonable fee for providing any notice or record pursuant to the agreement or (2) the fees listed in subsection b 1 (D) of this Rule.

c. *Termination of agreement.* The agreement shall terminate only if:

1. The financial institution files a petition under any applicable insolvency law or makes an assignment for the benefit of creditors; or

2. The financial institution gives thirty days' notice in writing to Bar Counsel that the institution intends to terminate the agreement on a stated date and that copies of the termination notice have been mailed to all attorneys and law firms that maintain trust accounts with any branch of that institution; or

3. The Commission finds, after prior written notice to the institution and adequate opportunity to be heard, that the institution has failed or refused without justification to perform a duty required by the agreement. (Amended Sept. 11, 1995, effective Jan. 1, 1996; June 5, 1996, effective Jan. 1, 1997; June 10, 1997, effective July 1, 1997.)

Source. — This Rule is former Rule BU10.

Effect of amendments. — The 1996 amendment substituted "Rule 16-718" for "Rule BV18" in b 1(E); and added the Source note.

The 1997 amendment substituted "Rule 16-607" for "Rule BU7" in the Cross references.

Editor's note. — An Order dated June 5, 1996, effective Jan. 1, 1997, renumbered this Rule, which was formerly Rule BU10.

Rule 16-611. Notice of approved institutions.

The Commission shall cause to be published in the Maryland Register, at six-month intervals, a list that identifies:

1. All currently approved financial institutions; and

2. Any financial institution whose agreement has terminated since the previous list was published. (Amended June 5, 1996, effective Jan. 1, 1997; Dec. 10, 1996, effective Jan. 1, 1997.)

Source. — This Rule is former Rule BU11.

Effect of amendments. — The first 1996 amendment added the Source note.

The second 1996 amendment deleted former b. and the "a." designation.

Editor's note. — An Order dated June 5, 1996, effective Jan. 1, 1997, renumbered this Rule, which was formerly Rule BU11.

Rule 16-612. Enforcement.

Upon receipt of a report of overdraft on or dishonored instrument drawn on an attorney trust account, Bar Counsel shall contact the attorney or law firm maintaining the account and request an informal explanation for the overdraft or dishonored instrument. The attorney or law firm shall provide any records of the account necessary to support the explanation. If Bar Counsel has requested but has failed to receive a satisfactory explanation for any overdraft or dishonored check, or if good cause exists to believe that an attorney or law firm has failed to perform any duty under these Rules, Bar Counsel may secure compliance with these Rules by appropriate means approved by the Commission, including application for an audit pursuant to Rule 16-718 (Audit of

Attorney's Accounts and Records). (Amended June 5, 1996, effective Jan. 1, 1997.)

Source. — This Rule is former Rule BU12.

Effect of amendments. — The 1996 amendment substituted "Rule 16-718" for "Rule BV18" in the last sentence; and added the Source note.

Editor's note. — An Order dated June 5, 1996, effective Jan. 1, 1997, renumbered this Rule, which was formerly Rule BU12.

CHAPTER 700. DISCIPLINE AND INACTIVE STATUS OF ATTORNEYS.

Rule 16-701. Definitions.

In this Chapter, the following terms have the following meanings, except as expressly otherwise provided, or as may result from necessary implication:

a. *Attorney.* "Attorney" means any person admitted by the Court of Appeals to practice law. For purposes of discipline or inactive status, the term also includes a member of the bar of any other state, district, or territory of the United States who engages in the practice of law in this State, or who holds himself or herself out as practicing law in this State, or who has the obligation of supervision or control over another attorney who engages in the practice of law in this State.

Cross references. — See Rule 16-811 (Clients' Security Fund).

b. *Bar Association.* "Bar Association" means:

(i) In Baltimore City, The Bar Association of Baltimore City; or

(ii) In each county, the bar association with the greatest number of members who are residents of the county and who maintain their principal office for the practice of law in that county.

c. *Bar Counsel.* "Bar Counsel" means the person appointed by the Commission as the principal executive officer of the disciplinary system affecting attorneys.

d. *Charges.* "Charges" mean the initial pleading filed in the Court of Appeals against an attorney alleging that he is guilty of misconduct or that he is incompetent or both.

Cross references. — See Rule 16-812.

e. *Commission.* "Commission" means the Attorney Grievance Commission of Maryland.

f. *Court.* "Court" means the location where the judge or judges will conduct the hearing.

g. *Disbarment.* "Disbarment" when applied to an attorney not admitted by the Court of Appeals to practice law means permanent exclusion from exercising in any manner the privilege of practicing law in this State.

h. *District.* "District" means one of the Districts set forth in section 1-602 of the Courts Article.

i. *Incompetent.* "Incompetent" means unable to render adequate legal service by reason of mental or physical illness or infirmity, or addiction to or dependence upon an intoxicant or drug.

j. *Judicial Tribunal.* "Judicial Tribunal" means a court, the District Court of Maryland, the Court of Appeals, the Court of Special Appeals, any United States Court and a court of another state having general or appellate jurisdiction.

k. *Misconduct.* "Misconduct" means an act or omission by an attorney, individually or in concert with any other person or persons which violates the Maryland Rules of Professional Conduct, as adopted by Rule 16-812, whether or not the act or omission occurred in the course of an attorney-client relationship.

l. *Office for the Practice of Law.* "Office for the Practice of Law" means an office maintained for the practice of law in which an attorney usually devotes a substantial part of his time to the practice of law during ordinary business hours in the traditional work week; or if there is no such office, the last known address of the attorney.

m. *Reinstatement.* "Reinstatement" when applied to an attorney not admitted by the Court of Appeals to practice law means discontinuation of a permanent exclusion from exercising the privilege of practicing law in this State.

n. *Suspension.* "Suspension" when applied to an attorney not admitted by the Court of Appeals to practice law means temporary exclusion from exercising in any manner the privilege of practicing law in this State.' aw means temporary exclusion from exercising in any manner the privilege of practicing law in this State. (Amended Sept. 22, 1978; Apr. 6, 1984, effective July 1, 1984; Apr. 7, 1986, effective Jan. 1, 1987; June 5, 1996, effective Jan. 1, 1997; Dec. 10, 1996, effective Jan. 1, 1997.)

Source. — This Rule is former Rule BV1.

Effect of amendments. — The first 1996 amendment substituted "Chapter" for "Subtitle" in the introductory language; substituted "Rule 16-811" for "Rule 1228" in the Cross reference note in a.; substituted "Rule 16-812" for "Rule 1230" in the Cross reference note in d.; substituted "Rule 16-812" for "Rule 1230" in k.; and added the Source note.

The second 1996 amendment substituted "Maryland Rules of Professional Conduct" for "Disciplinary Rules of the Code of Professional Responsibility" in k.

Editor's note. — An Order dated June 5, 1996, effective Jan. 1, 1997, renumbered this Rule, which was formerly Rule BV1.

Maryland Law Review. — For comment, "Discipline of Attorneys in Maryland," see 35 Md. L. Rev. 236 (1975).

For survey of Court of Appeals decisions on attorney discipline for the year 1974-1975, see 36 Md. L. Rev. 351 (1976).

University of Baltimore Law Review. — For article, "The Maryland Rules — A Time for Overhaul," see 9 U. Balt. L. Rev. 1 (1979).

For article, "State Constitutional Law for Maryland Lawyers: Judicial Relief for Violations of Rights," see 10 U. Balt. L. Rev. 102 (1980).

Continuing jurisdiction. — Attorney who resigned only when notified that a disciplinary investigation was pending against him in Maryland remained, at all times pertinent to different proceedings, a member of the bar of the State of Maryland and the court therefore had jurisdiction over him for purposes of disciplinary action under these Rules. Attorney

Grievance Comm'n v. Hopp, 330 Md. 177, 623 A.2d 193 (1993).

An inquiry as to whether a person should continue in the practice of law after misconduct is exclusively regulated by this subtitle. Balliet v. Baltimore County Bar Ass'n, 259 Md. 474, 270 A.2d 465 (1970); Kerpelman v. Bricker, 23 Md. App. 628, 329 A.2d 423 (1974).

Reciprocal discipline. — The Court of Appeals was not required to apply the same sanction that Virginia applied in a disciplinary proceeding; although the Court will look to the sanction imposed by other jurisdictions, the outcome will depend on the unique facts and circumstances of each case, with a view toward consistent dispositions for similar conduct. Attorney Grievance Comm'n v. Saul, 337 Md. 258, 653 A.2d 430 (1995).

Attorney's suspension would be continued indefinitely where he had been suspended by the District of Columbia Court of Appeals since there was no basis for supposing that the District treats such matters less seriously or inconsistently with the Maryland appellate courts. Attorney Grievance Comm'n v. Gittens, 346 Md. 316, 697 A.2d 83 (1997).

Misconduct distinguished from incompetence. — Trial judge properly concluded that an attorney's action constituted misconduct, rather than incompetence, since the at-

torney could control his actions; he was unable to render adequate legal services not because of mental illness but because he was untrustworthy due to his personality and character. Attorney Grievance Comm'n v. Nothstein, 300 Md. 667, 480 A.2d 807 (1984).

Effect of non-practice on bar status. — The fact that an attorney moved from Maryland and had not practiced law there since 1962, practicing only in California to the bar of which he was also admitted, did not affect his bar status in Maryland. Attorney Grievance Comm'n v. Hopp, 330 Md. 177, 623 A.2d 193 (1993).

Suspension was appropriate sanction. — Where attorney did not profit from his misconduct, and where the bank which was the subject of his prosecution did not suffer any losses from the misconduct, suspension, rather than disbarment, was the appropriate sanction. Attorney Grievance Comm'n v. Saul, 337 Md. 258, 653 A.2d 430 (1995).

Stated in Attorney Grievance Comm'n v. Alison, 349 Md. 623, 709 A.2d 1212 (1998).

Cited in Attorney Grievance Comm'n v. Garland, 345 Md. 383, 692 A.2d 465 (1997); Attorney Grievance Comm'n v. Sachse, 345 Md. 578, 693 A.2d 806 (1997); Frederick Rd. Ltd. Partnership v. Brown & Sturm, 121 Md. App. 384, 710 A.2d 298 (1998).

Rule 16-702. Attorney Grievance Commission.

a. *Creation and purpose.* The Attorney Grievance Commission of Maryland is authorized and created. The Commission shall supervise and administer the discipline and inactive status of attorneys in accordance with this Chapter.

b. *Composition.* The Commission consists of ten members, two of whom shall not be attorneys, appointed by the Court of Appeals. One member shall be designated by the Court of Appeals as chairman of the Commission. The term of each member is four years, except that the initial terms of four of those first appointed to the Commission shall be one year, two years, three years and three years, respectively, the initial term of the eighth and ninth members shall be two years, and the initial term of the tenth member shall be three years. No member is eligible for reappointment for a term immediately following the expiration of the member's service for one full term of four years. A member of the Commission may be removed by the Court of Appeals at any time.

c. *Compensation.* A member of the Commission may not receive compensation for serving in that capacity, but is entitled to reimbursement for his expenses reasonably incurred in the performance of his duties, including but not limited to transportation costs.

d. *Disciplinary Fund.* 1. Payments by attorneys. The Disciplinary Fund is established. In addition to, and on the same date as, other sums required to be paid pursuant to Rule 16-811 (Clients' Security Fund) each attorney, including attorneys granted a certificate of special authorization under Rule 15 of the

Rules Governing Admission to the Bar, shall, as a condition precedent to the practice of law, pay annually to the Disciplinary Fund the sum, including any late charges, the Court of Appeals prescribes for any year.

2. Collection and disbursement of Disciplinary Fund. The treasurer of the Clients' Security Trust Fund of the Maryland Bar shall collect the sums paid by attorneys to the Disciplinary Fund and shall pay over such sums as the Commission from time to time directs.

3. Enforcement. Enforcement of payment of annual assessments of attorneys pursuant to this Rule is governed by the provisions of section g of Rule 16-811 (Clients' Security Fund). (Amended June 16, 1978, effective July 1, 1978; June 4, 1979, effective July 1, 1979; June 22, 1990; June 5, 1996, effective Jan. 1, 1997.)

Source. — This Rule is former Rule BV2.

Effect of amendments. — The 1996 amendment substituted "Chapter" for "subtitle" in a.; substituted "Rule 16-811" for "Rule 1228" in d.1. and d.3.; and added the Source note.

Editor's note. — An Order dated June 5, 1996, effective Jan. 1, 1997, renumbered this Rule, which was formerly Rule BV2.

Maryland Law Review. — For comment, "Discipline of Attorneys in Maryland," see 35 Md. L. Rev. 236 (1975).

For article, "The Law of Disbarment and Reinstatement in Maryland," see 36 Md. L. Rev. 703 (1977).

For article, "Survey of Developments in Maryland Law, 1985-86," see 46 Md. L. Rev. 533 (1987).

University of Baltimore Law Review. — For article, "The Maryland Rules — A Time for Overhaul," see 9 U. Balt. L. Rev. 1 (1979).

Claim that this Rule and Rule 1228 are impermissible taxes may or may not be correct, but even if the point is well taken, it would not be an excuse for unethical conduct on the part of a member of the bar, nor would it be a defense to charges relative to such conduct. Attorney Grievance Comm'n v. Kerpelman, 288 Md. 341, 420 A.2d 940 (1980), cert. denied, 450 U.S. 970, 101 S. Ct. 1492, 67 L. Ed. 2d 621 (1981).

Cited in Frederick Rd. Ltd. Partnership v. Brown & Sturm, 121 Md. App. 384, 710 A.2d 298 (1998).

Rule 16-703. Commission procedures and powers.

a. *Quorum.* A majority of the full authorized membership of the Commission constitutes a quorum for the transaction of business and the concurrence of at least that many members is required for all action taken by the Commission.

b. *Powers and duties.* The Commission has powers and duties to:

(i) Recommend to the Court of Appeals for its adoption procedural and administrative rules relating to the disciplinary system affecting attorneys;

(ii) Appoint and supervise the activities of the Bar Counsel;

(iii) Authorize the Bar Counsel to employ attorneys, investigators and clerical personnel and to prescribe their compensation;

(iv) Appoint those persons as provided in Rule 16-705 c 1 (Inquiry Committee and Review Board — Inquiry Committee — Composition) to serve as members of the Inquiry Committee and remove any members for cause; failure to assume regularly the responsibilities of a member shall be cause for removal;

(v) Appoint those persons as provided in Rule 16-705 d (Inquiry Committee and Review Board — Review Board) to serve as members of the Review Board and remove any members for cause; failure to assume regularly the responsibilities of a member shall be cause for removal;

(vi) Appoint counsel from time to time to assist the Bar Counsel in the performance of his duties;

(vii) Administer the Disciplinary Fund and file annually with the Court of Appeals, not later than September 1, an accounting thereof and a report of disciplinary activities for the previous fiscal year. The accounting and report shall be published by the Commission. There shall be an independent annual audit of the fund administered by it as directed by the Court of Appeals, the expenses of which audit shall be paid out of the fund;

(viii) Submit an annual report to the Court of Appeals, not later than September 1, evaluating the effectiveness of the disciplinary system and recommending any desirable changes. The report may include statistical data and opinions of the Review Board. The report shall be published at least annually by the Commission, subject to the provisions of Rule 16-708 (Confidentiality); and

(ix) Submit annually to the State Court Administrator a proposed budget for the disciplinary system. The budget is subject to review and approval by the Court of Appeals. (Amended June 16, 1978, effective July 1, 1978; Apr. 18, 1980, effective July 1, 1980; June 5, 1996, effective Jan. 1, 1997.)

Source. — This Rule is former Rule BV3.

Effect of amendments. — The 1996 amendment substituted "Rule 16-705 c.1." for "Rule BV5c.1." in b.(iv); substituted "Rule 16-705d." for "Rule BV5d." in b.(v); substituted "Rule 16-708" for "Rule BV8" in b.(viii); and added the Source note.

Editor's note. — An Order dated June 5, 1996, effective Jan. 1, 1997, renumbered this Rule, which was formerly Rule BV3.

Maryland Law Review. — For comment, "Discipline of Attorneys in Maryland," see 35 Md. L. Rev. 236 (1975).

For article, "The Law of Disbarment and Reinstatement in Maryland," see 36 Md. L. Rev. 703 (1977).

University of Baltimore Law Review. —

For article, "The Maryland Rules — A Time for Overhaul," see 9 U. Balt. L. Rev. 1 (1979).

Self-incrimination. — Attorney Grievance Commission's procedural guideline, warning attorney that Inquiry Panel may believe evidence which attorney does not contest, does not violate attorney's constitutional right against compelled self-incrimination. Attorney Grievance Comm'n v. Unnamed Att'y, 298 Md. 36, 467 A.2d 517 (1983).

Applied in Attorney Grievance Comm'n v. McNeill, 344 Md. 49, 684 A.2d 861 (1996).

Cited in Frederick Rd. Ltd. Partnership v. Brown & Sturm, 121 Md. App. 384, 710 A.2d 298 (1998).

Rule 16-704. Bar Counsel.

a. *Appointment.* The Commission shall appoint, subject to approval of the Court of Appeals, an attorney to serve, at the pleasure of the Commission, as Bar Counsel of the disciplinary system. The Bar Counsel is the principal executive officer of the disciplinary system, and shall receive compensation as authorized from time to time in the budget of the Commission.

b. *Powers and duties.* Subject to the supervision of the Commission, the Bar Counsel shall:

(i) Investigate all matters involving possible misconduct called to his attention whether by complaint or otherwise;

(ii) Prosecute disciplinary and inactive status cases and enforce compliance with all disciplinary orders of the Court of Appeals;

(iii) Investigate petitions for reinstatement and for termination of suspension and inactive status and applications for resignation from the practice of law, and represent the public interest in those proceedings;

(iv) Employ, at the compensation authorized by the Commission, investigative, clerical and legal personnel necessary for the efficient conduct of his office;

(v) Discharge any person whose performance is unsatisfactory to him; and

(vi) Maintain records, make reports and perform other duties prescribed by the Commission from time to time or required by these Rules.

c. *Subpoenas.* 1. Issuance and notice. After a complaint has been filed, and with the prior written approval of the Chair or Acting Chair of the Commission, Bar Counsel may issue a subpoena to compel the production of designated documents or other tangible things at a time and place specified in the subpoena. In addition to giving any notice required by law, Bar Counsel shall provide prompt notice of the issuance of the subpoena to the attorney against whom the complaint has been filed. The notice shall be personally delivered or sent by regular mail to the attorney's last known address and to the attorney's address contained in the records of the Clients' Security Trust Fund, if different.

2. Objection; enforcement. On motion of the attorney or the person served with the subpoena filed promptly and, whenever practicable, at or before the time specified in the subpoena for compliance, the circuit court for the county in which the subpoena was served may enter any order permitted by Rule 2-510 (e). Upon a failure to comply with a subpoena issued pursuant to this Rule, the court, on the motion of Bar Counsel, may compel compliance with the subpoena.

3. Confidentiality. To the extent practicable, a subpoena shall not divulge the name of the attorney against whom the complaint has been filed. Files and records of a court pertaining to any motion filed with respect to a subpoena shall be sealed and shall be open to inspection only by order of the court. Hearings before the court on any motion shall be on the record and shall be conducted out of the presence of all persons except those whose presence is necessary. (Amended Nov. 1, 1991, effective Jan. 1, 1992; June 5, 1996, effective Jan. 1, 1997.)

Cross references. — See Code, Financial Institutions Article, § 1-304, concerning notice to depositors of subpoenas for financial records, and Code, Health General Article, § 4-307, concerning notice of a request for issuance of compulsory process seeking medical records related to mental health services.

Source. — This Rule is former Rule BV4.

Effect of amendments. — The 1996 amendment added the Source note.

Editor's note. — An Order dated June 5, 1996, effective Jan. 1, 1997, renumbered this Rule, which was formerly Rule BV4.

Maryland Law Review. — For article, "The Law of Disbarment and Reinstatement in Maryland," see 36 Md. L. Rev. 703 (1977).

University of Baltimore Law Review. — For article, "The Maryland Rules — A Time for Overhaul," see 9 U. Balt. L. Rev. 1 (1979).

Quoted in Unnamed Att'y v. Attorney Grievance Comm'n, 349 Md. 391, 708 A.2d 667 (1998).

Rule 16-705. Inquiry Committee and Review Board.

a. *Creation.* An Inquiry Committee and Review Board is each authorized and created.

b. *Compensation.* Committee or of the Review Board may not receive compensation for serving in that capacity, but is entitled to reimbursement for his expenses reasonably incurred in the performance of his duties, including but not limited to transportation costs.

c. *Inquiry Committee.* 1. Composition. The Inquiry Committee consists of that number of persons, none of whom shall be judges, which the Commission from time to time determines is reasonably necessary to conduct the volume of inquiry panel proceedings. Of the number of members of the Inquiry Committee determined for each county or Baltimore City, two-thirds shall be attorneys whose principal office for the practice of law is located in that county or Baltimore City and one-third shall be non-attorneys whose residence is located in that county or Baltimore City. The attorney members of the Inquiry Committee shall be selected by the Bar Association of the appropriate county or Baltimore City, in the manner determined by it, and each attorney so selected shall be appointed by the Commission unless such attorney would be subject to removal for cause. The Commission shall establish by notice to such Bar Association the time within which that Association is to make its selections. Upon the failure of a Bar Association timely to select any Committee member, the Commission may appoint any attorney of this State who is not a judge to such membership on the Inquiry Committee. The non-attorney members shall be selected and appointed by the Commission on the basis of merit and demonstrated competence, ability and good judgment, after the solicitation of recommendations from the Bar Association of the appropriate county or Baltimore City and from the general public, in such manner as the Commission may deem appropriate. (Amended May 5, 1976, effective July 1, 1976; May 5, 1978, effective July 1, 1978; Apr. 18, 1980, effective July 1, 1980; May 7, 1982, effective July 1, 1982.)

2. Terms. The Commission shall set the term membership of each member of the Inquiry Committee. Terms of the initial appointees need not be uniform. Terms may not exceed three years except that the Commission may extend the term of any member who is assigned to a panel until the completion of a pending inquiry. Any member of the Inquiry Committee is eligible for successive terms. (Amended Apr. 18, 1980, effective July 1, 1980.)

3. Chairman. The Commission shall select from among the members of the Inquiry Committee, a chairman and one or more vice-chairmen, each to serve for a term of one year. (Amended Apr. 18, 1980, effective July 1, 1980.)

d. *Review Board.* The Review Board shall consist of eighteen persons, none of whom shall be judges. There shall be fifteen attorney members to be selected by the Board of Governors of the Maryland State Bar Association, Inc. The Commission shall appoint each attorney selected unless he would be subject to removal for cause. In each of the Appellate Judicial Circuits there are the following number of attorney members of the Review Board, each of whom has his principal office for the practice of law in that Appellate Judicial Circuit:

Appellate Judicial Circuit	Number of Members
First	1
Second	3
Third	1
Fourth	1
Fifth	1
Sixth	4
Seventh	4

The Commission shall establish by notice to such Bar Association the time within which it is to make its selections. Upon failure of the Association timely to select any Board member, the Commission may appoint any attorney whose principal office for the practice of law shall be located in the appropriate Appellate Judicial Circuit to such membership on the Review Board. There shall be three non-attorney members from the State at large who shall be selected and appointed by the Commission on the basis of merit and demonstrated competence, ability and good judgment, after the solicitation of recommendations from the Maryland State Bar Association, Inc., and from the general public, in such manner as the Commission may deem appropriate. The term of each member is three years. No member is eligible for reappointment for a term immediately following the expiration of the member's service for one full term of three years. The Commission shall designate one member as Chairman of the Review Board and one or more members as Vice-Chairman. (Amended May 5, 1976, effective July 1, 1976; Apr. 18, 1980, effective July 1, 1980; June 5, 1995, effective July 1, 1995; June 5, 1996, effective Jan. 1, 1997.)

Source. — This Rule is former Rule BV5.

Effect of amendments. — The 1996 amendment added the Source note.

Editor's note. — An Order dated June 5, 1996, effective Jan. 1, 1997, renumbered this Rule, which was formerly Rule BV5.

Maryland Law Review. — For comment, "Discipline of Attorneys in Maryland," see 35 Md. L. Rev. 236 (1975).

For article, "The Law of Disbarment and Reinstatement in Maryland," see 36 Md. L. Rev. 703 (1977).

University of Baltimore Law Review. — For article, "The Maryland Rules — A Time for Overhaul," see 9 U. Balt. L. Rev. 1 (1979).

Rule 16-706. Complaints and investigations.

a. *Bar Counsel.* 1. Filing and investigation. Every complaint that an attorney has committed an act of misconduct or that he is incompetent shall be filed with and recorded by the Bar Counsel. The Bar Counsel shall investigate each complaint.

2. Dismissals. If in the opinion of the Bar Counsel the complaint is without merit or the attorney has engaged in misconduct which does not warrant discipline, he may dismiss the complaint, subject to approval by the Chairman of the Inquiry Committee or a Vice Chairman designated by the Chairman. The Bar Counsel shall send the attorney and the person who made the complaint written notice that the complaint has been dismissed. He shall send to the complainant with a copy to the attorney any additional information

which the Chairman or a Vice Chairman directs. If in the opinion of Bar Counsel the attorney has engaged in misconduct, he may, with the approval of the Chairman or a Vice Chairman designated by the Chairman accompany the dismissal with a separate warning against future misconduct.

Committee note. — A warning by the Bar Counsel whether under this section, or at the direction of an Inquiry Panel pursuant to Rule 16-706 d 4 (b), or at the direction of the Review Board pursuant to Rule 16-707 b, is not a reprimand or discipline of any kind.

3. Reprimand. If in the opinion of Bar Counsel the attorney is guilty of misconduct for which a reprimand should be administered, if an inquiry panel proceeding has been dispensed with pursuant to Rule 16-706 b and if there is approval by the Chairman of the Inquiry Committee or a Vice Chairman designated by the Chairman and the Review Board Bar Counsel may administer a reprimand. Unless otherwise directed by the Review Board, the reprimand shall be in writing and served upon the attorney by the Bar Counsel at the attorney's Office for the Practice of Law. Upon the written request of the attorney that charges be filed against him, made within 15 days of the date of service of the reprimand, the review board shall (i) direct the Bar Counsel to file charges against the attorney pursuant to Rule 16-709 (Charges) (ii) remand for further proceedings or (iii) withdraw the reprimand and dismiss the complaint against the attorney. A court may waive the 15 day period if satisfied that the attorney has had no notice of the complaint against him.

4. Reference to Inquiry Panel. Unless a complaint is dismissed or an Inquiry Panel proceeding has been dispensed with pursuant to Rule 16-706, the Bar Counsel shall refer the complaint to an Inquiry Panel and give notice of the complaint to the attorney against whom the complaint has been made. The notice shall inform the attorney of the nature of the complaint made. In unusual or extraordinary circumstances, the Bar Counsel, in his discretion, may defer giving notice to the attorney for a reasonable time.

b. *Inquiry Panel proceeding not required.* 1. When not required. An Inquiry Panel proceeding is not required in a case where either:

(a) Both the attorney complained against and the Bar Counsel waive an Inquiry Panel proceeding in writing; or

(b) The complaint is either (i) that there has been a final judgment of conviction as defined by Rule 16-710 e 1 of a crime punishable by imprisonment for more than one year; or (ii) that the attorney has been adjudged guilty of misconduct by a judicial tribunal in a disciplinary proceeding as defined by Rule 16-710 e 1 and that the adjudication of misconduct has become final.

2. Withdrawal of waiver. A written waiver of an Inquiry Panel proceeding may not be withdrawn except upon approval of the Review Board for good cause shown.

3. Procedure. The Bar Counsel shall file any written waiver of the Inquiry Panel proceeding as part of the file in the case. If in the opinion of the Bar Counsel discipline is warranted, he shall forward his recommendation and the file relating to the complaint to the Review Board for consideration pursuant to Rule 16-707. The Review Board shall permit oral argument upon the request of either the attorney or Bar Counsel.

c. *Selection of Inquiry Panel.* The Chairman of the Inquiry Committee or a Vice Chairman designated by the Chairman shall appoint at least three members of the Inquiry Committee to serve on each Inquiry Panel and shall designate one Panel member to serve as Panel Chairman. A majority of the Panel to which a complaint is assigned shall consist of attorneys, and at least one member of each Panel shall be a non-attorney. At least one-half of the Panel to which a complaint is assigned shall consist of members from the District in which the attorney against whom the complaint has been made has an office for the practice of law, unless the Chairman of the Inquiry Committee finds this requirement to be impracticable.

d. *Inquiry Panel proceedings.* 1. Generally. Except as provided by these Rules, no action except dismissal of the complaint may be taken unless the attorney against whom the complaint has been made has been afforded an opportunity to examine and controvert the complaint and be represented by counsel. The rules of evidence need not apply at any proceeding before the Inquiry Panel. If the attorney cannot be found after the Inquiry Panel has made reasonable efforts to notify him, the Inquiry Panel may proceed pursuant to this Chapter without complying with the requirements of this section.

2. Quorum. Three members of the Inquiry Panel shall constitute a quorum, provided that a majority of the Panel members present shall be attorneys. The presence of a non-attorney member shall not be required to constitute a quorum.

3. Witnesses — Testimony — Depositions. (a) Oaths; testimony. An Inquiry Panel may administer oaths to and take the testimony of witnesses.

(b) Depositions. (1) When may be taken. Where a witness is either:

(i) unable to attend because of illness or other disability, or

(ii) unwilling to attend and is not subject to summons as provided in paragraph (c) of this subsection,

Either the Bar Counsel or the attorney against whom the complaint has been made may take the deposition of the witness and offer it as evidence before the Inquiry Panel.

(2) Procedure. Chapter 400 of Title 2 governs the taking of depositions in proceedings before an Inquiry Panel except:

(i) the notice required by Rule 2-412 shall be given to the attorney if the deposition is taken by the Bar Counsel and to the Bar Counsel if the deposition is taken by the attorney. All notices shall be filed with the Inquiry Panel and the Bar Counsel;

(ii) the filing requirements of Rules 2-404 (a) (3) and 2-415 (e) are not applicable;

(iii) the deposition shall be filed with the Panel together with the papers referred to in paragraph (c) of this subsection; and

(iv) the Panel Chairman may make rules pertaining to any deposition as justice might require.

(c) Subpoena. If in a proceeding before an Inquiry Panel the attendance and testimony of a witness or the production of books, documents or other tangible things is required, the Panel on its own motion, or on motion of the Bar Counsel or the attorney against whom the complaint has been made, shall cause a subpoena to be issued by a clerk pursuant to Rule 2-510. The subpoena may not divulge the name of the attorney against whom the complaint has been made, except to the extent that this requirement is impracticable. The sheriff's return shall be made as directed in the subpoena and the proceedings may not be docketed in court. The Bar Counsel shall maintain dockets and files of all papers filed in the proceedings.

(d) Certified letter in lieu of subpoena. If in a proceeding before an Inquiry Panel the attendance and testimony of or the production of books, documents, or other records by any attorney is required, the Panel may command the attendance and testimony of or production by that attorney by sending a letter by certified mail to the attorney. If the attorney is admitted to practice law in this State or the letter is delivered to the attorney within this State, the letter shall be as effective against the attorney as if a subpoena had been issued pursuant to paragraph (c) of this subsection.

(e) Sanction — Attachment — Contempt. Whenever any person subpoenaed to appear and give testimony or to produce books, documents or other tangible things, fails or refuses to appear or to answer any proper question or to produce the items requested, the party requesting the subpoena may, by motion which may not divulge the name of the attorney against whom the complaint has been made (except to the extent that this requirement is impracticable), request a court to issue an attachment pursuant to Rule 2-510 (h), or to cite the person for contempt pursuant to Title 15, Chapter 200 of these Rules, or both.

4. Disposition. (a) Action by inquiry panel. The Inquiry Panel may dismiss the complaint without a hearing. Otherwise, the Panel shall conduct a hearing and shall recommend that:

(i) the complaint be dismissed;

(ii) the attorney be reprimanded; or

(iii) charges be filed against the attorney.

(b) Recommendation of reprimand or charges. If the Panel finds that the attorney against whom the complaint has been filed either has committed an act of misconduct or is incompetent, the Panel shall state the basis therefor in writing. The Panel shall file with the Bar Counsel its recommendations, the reasons therefor and any evidence taken in the proceedings. A member of the Panel who disagrees with the recommendation of the majority may file a written minority report with the Bar Counsel. The Bar Counsel shall transmit to the Review Board and to the attorney, copies of the recommendations, reports and, wherever practical, copies of any evidence.

(c) Unanimous recommendation of dismissal. (i) If, with or without a hearing, the Panel determines unanimously that the complaint shall be dismissed, the Panel shall state the reasons for the dismissal in writing and shall file the statement and any evidence with the Bar Counsel. A transcript of any testimony of which a record may have been made need not be prepared if it is not requested by Bar Counsel. Unless within the time required by subparagraph (ii), the Bar Counsel requests a review pursuant to subparagraph (ii), the Bar Counsel shall send the attorney and the person who made the complaint written notice that the complaint has been dismissed. If, in the opinion of the Panel, the attorney is guilty of misconduct which does not

311

warrant discipline, Bar Counsel shall send the attorney a warning against future misconduct if the Panel so directs, in which case he may also advise the complainant that the conduct, in the opinion of the Panel, does not warrant discipline.

(ii) If, after review of the statement of reasons for dismissal, and of the evidence, including a transcript of all testimony of which a record has been made, the Bar Counsel believes that dismissal is not warranted, he may, subject to approval by the Attorney Grievance Commission, transmit to the Review Board and to the attorney, without cost to him:

(1) Copies of the Panel's reason for dismissal;

(2) A statement of the reasons why Bar Counsel is causing review to be made by the Review Board, and

(3) Copies of any evidence, including a transcript of testimony.

The transmittal shall be made within 90 days of receipt by Bar Counsel of the Panel's reasons for dismissal.

(d) Non-unanimous recommendation of dismissal. If, with or without a hearing, the Panel determines by less than a unanimous vote of all members of the Panel that the complaint should be dismissed, the Panel shall state the reasons therefor in writing. The Panel shall file its recommendations and report with the Bar Counsel, together with any evidence taken in the proceedings. Any member of the Panel opposing dismissal shall file a written minority report with the Bar Counsel. The Bar Counsel shall transmit to the Review Board and to the attorney, copies of the recommendations, reports and, wherever practical, copies of any evidence. (Amended May 5, 1976, effective July 1, 1976; Nov. 5, 1976, effective Jan. 1, 1977; Nov. 4, 1977, effective Jan. 1, 1978; Apr. 18, 1980, effective July 1, 1980; Apr. 6, 1984, effective July 1, 1984; Apr. 7, 1986, effective Jan. 1, 1987; June 5, 1996, effective Jan. 1, 1997.)

Source. — This Rule is former Rule BV6.

Effect of amendments. — The 1996 amendment, in the Committee note to a.2., substituted "Rule 16-706 d 4 b" for "Rule BV6 d 4 b" and substituted "Rule 16-707 b" for "Rule BV7 b"; in a.3., substituted "Rule 16-706 b" for "Rule BV6 b" and substituted "Rule 16-709" for "Rule BV9"; substituted "Rule 16-706" for "Rule BV6" in a.4.; in b.1.(b), substituted "Rule 16-710 e 1" for "Rule BV10 e 1" twice; in b.3., substituted "Rule 16-707" for "Rule BV7"; in d. 1., substituted "Chapter" for "subtitle" in the last sentence; in d. 3. (e), substituted "Title 15, Chapter 200" for "Subtitle P"; and added the Source note.

Editor's note. — An Order dated June 5, 1996, effective Jan. 1, 1997, renumbered this Rule, which was formerly Rule BV6.

Maryland Law Review. — For comment, "Discipline of Attorneys in Maryland," see 35 Md. L. Rev. 236 (1975).

For survey of Court of Appeals decisions on attorney discipline for the year 1974-1975, see 36 Md. L. Rev. 351 (1976).

University of Baltimore Law Review. — For article, "The Maryland Rules — A Time for Overhaul," see 9 U. Balt. L. Rev. 1 (1979).

Notification of attorney is not due process requirement. — Although subsection a 4 of this Rule generally requires Bar Counsel to notify the attorney when a complaint is first referred to an inquiry panel, this is not a due process requirement. Attorney Grievance Comm'n v. Goldsborough, 330 Md. 342, 624 A.2d 503 (1993).

Disciplinary proceedings for professional misconduct are not criminal proceedings. Their purpose is to protect the public by determining a lawyer's fitness to practice law and whether to institute disciplinary action against him. Attorney Grievance Comm'n v. Stewart, 285 Md. 251, 401 A.2d 1026, cert. denied, 444 U.S. 845, 100 S. Ct. 89, 62 L. Ed. 2d 58, reh'g denied, 444 U.S. 975, 100 S. Ct. 472, 62 L. Ed. 2d 58 (1979).

An attorney may be disciplined for acts which are criminal but do not result in a criminal conviction if Bar Counsel proves the underlying conduct at the disciplinary hearing. Attorney Grievance Comm'n v. Garland, 345 Md. 383, 692 A.2d 465 (1997).

Duty of courts and profession as a whole. — In the last analysis the duty rests upon the courts and the profession as a whole to uphold the highest standards of professional conduct and to protect the public from imposition by the unfit or unscrupulous practitioner. Maryland State Bar Ass'n v. Boone, 255 Md. 420, 258 A.2d 438 (1969).

Proceedings likened to grand jury proceedings. — Because the proceedings conducted under this Rule are investigatory in nature and are designed to aid in the determination as to whether disciplinary action should be instituted, the matter at this stage may be likened to proceedings conducted by a grand jury in criminal cases. Maryland State Bar Ass'n v. Frank, 272 Md. 528, 325 A.2d 718 (1974).

Attorney disciplinary proceedings before an inquiry panel upon a complaint that an attorney has committed an act of misconduct are similar in purpose to the accusatory proceedings conducted by a grand jury. Attorney Grievance Comm'n v. Strathen, 287 Md. 111, 411 A.2d 102 (1980).

Nature and conduct of investigative proceedings. — The proceedings conducted by the Inquiry Panel and the Review Board are investigatory in nature and informal to the extent that the rules of evidence need not apply. At these stages of the proceedings, many of the constitutional safeguards accorded an accused in criminal cases are not available. Attorney Grievance Comm'n v. Stewart, 285 Md. 251, 401 A.2d 1026, cert. denied, 444 U.S. 845, 100 S. Ct. 89, 62 L. Ed. 2d 58 (1979); Attorney Grievance Comm'n v. Harris, 310 Md. 197, 528 A.2d 895 (1987), cert. denied, 484 U.S. 1062, 108 S. Ct. 1020, 98 L. Ed. 2d 985 (1988).

As long as an attorney is given notice and opportunity to defend in a full and fair hearing following the institution of disciplinary proceedings, an irregularity in the proceedings before the Inquiry Panel and the Review Board ordinarily will not amount to a denial of due process. Attorney Grievance Comm'n v. Garland, 345 Md. 383, 692 A.2d 465 (1997).

Subpoena power. — In defining the appropriate boundaries of the Attorney Grievance Committee's subpoena power, the court is guided by the requirement of reasonableness which circumscribes an administrative agency's investigatory powers. In order to meet the test of reasonableness, an investigation of an individual by an administrative agency may not be based upon mere conjecture or supposition that a violation of law exists. Rather, it is incumbent upon an agency to demonstrate some factual basis to support its concern. In any event, the subpoenaed testimony or documents must appear relevant to the investigation. Unnamed Att'y v. Attorney Grievance Comm'n, 313 Md. 357, 545 A.2d 685 (1988).

Unemployment compensation claims. — Former Article 101, § 91, in its entirety (now see Titles 9 and 10 of the Labor and Employment Article), applies to, and may be enforced against, attorneys, and the notification required by that section should be sent to the Bar Counsel, pursuant to section a 1 of this Rule. 75 Op. Att'y Gen. (July 18, 1990).

Whether findings are supported by clear and convincing evidence is the proper test to be applied in disciplinary proceedings under this Rule. Bar Ass'n v. Marshall, 269 Md. 510, 307 A.2d 677 (1973).

Effect of full and fair hearing before judge. — If a lawyer is given notice and the opportunity to defend in a full and fair hearing, before a judge or judges, the question whether he was accorded due process of law by the Inquiry Panel and the Review Board is ordinarily immaterial. Attorney Grievance Comm'n v. Stewart, 285 Md. 251, 401 A.2d 1026, cert. denied, 444 U.S. 845, 100 S. Ct. 89, 62 L. Ed. 2d 58 (1979); Attorney Grievance Comm'n v. Harris, 310 Md. 197, 528 A.2d 895 (1987), cert. denied, 484 U.S. 1062, 108 S. Ct. 1020, 98 L. Ed. 2d 985 (1988).

Self-incrimination. — Attorney Grievance Commission's procedural guideline, warning attorney that Inquiry Panel may believe evidence which attorney does not contest, does not violate attorney's constitutional right against compelled self-incrimination. Attorney Grievance Comm'n v. Unnamed Att'y, 298 Md. 36, 467 A.2d 517 (1983).

Public reprimand, pursuant to section a 3, imposed where attorney incompetently handled the client's affairs. Attorney Grievance Comm'n v. Murray, 301 Md. 506, 483 A.2d 772 (1984).

Section d 4 makes no provision for recommendation by inquiry panel as to sanction. Attorney Grievance Comm'n v. Deutsch, 294 Md. 353, 450 A.2d 1265 (1982).

Order denying motion to quash certified letter appealable when entered. — A court order denying an attorney's motion to quash the Attorney Grievance Commission's certified letter in lieu of subpoena (section d. 3. (d)) was appealable at the time it was entered, regardless of whether a motion to hold the attorney in contempt was still pending. Unnamed Att'y v. Attorney Grievance Comm'n, 303 Md. 473, 494 A.2d 940 (1985).

Cited in Frederick Rd. Ltd. Partnership v. Brown & Sturm, 121 Md. App. 384, 710 A.2d 298 (1998).

Rule 16-707. Review procedure.

a. *Quorum.* A majority of the Review Board shall constitute a quorum, and the presence of a non-attorney member shall not be required to constitute the quorum. The concurrence of not less than a majority of the members present is necessary to a decision.

b. *Proceedings of Review Board.* The Review Board shall review each case transmitted to the Board by the Bar Counsel pursuant to sections a, b or d of Rule 16-706. The Board may request oral argument in any proceedings before it. In cases where a hearing has been conducted by an Inquiry Panel or the hearing has been dispensed with pursuant to Rule 16-706 b, the Board may approve, reject or modify the recommendation, may remand for further proceedings, or may dismiss the complaint. In a case in which the Bar Counsel has recommended a reprimand pursuant to Rule 16-706 a 3, the Board may approve the recommendation, may remand for further proceedings, may direct the filing of charges if the inquiry panel proceedings were dispensed with pursuant to Rule 16-706 b, or may dismiss the complaint. In all other cases the Review Board shall either remand the case for a hearing before a Panel, or dismiss the complaint. The Board shall state in writing the reasons for its decisions. The Bar Counsel shall send the attorney and the person who made the complaint written notice of the decision of the Board. If in the opinion of the Review Board, the attorney is guilty of misconduct which does not warrant discipline, Bar Counsel shall send the attorney a warning against future misconduct if the Review Board so directs, in which case he may also advise the complainant that the conduct in the opinion of the Review Board does not warrant discipline.

c. *Reprimand.* The Review Board may reprimand an attorney after reviewing the findings of the Inquiry Panel. Upon the written request of the attorney that charges be filed against him, made within 15 days of the date of service of the reprimand, the Review Board shall either (i) direct the Bar Counsel to file charges against the attorney pursuant to Rule 16-709 (Charges), or (ii) withdraw the reprimand and dismiss the complaint against the attorney. A court may waive the 15 day period if satisfied that the attorney has had no notice of the complaint against him. Unless otherwise directed by the Review Board, the reprimand shall be served upon the attorney by the Bar Counsel at the attorney's Office for the Practice of Law. (Amended May 5, 1976, effective July 1, 1976; Nov. 5, 1976, effective Jan. 1, 1977; Nov. 4, 1977, effective Jan. 1, 1978; May 5, 1978, effective July 1, 1978; Apr. 18, 1980, effective July 1, 1980; June 5, 1996, effective Jan. 1, 1997.)

Source. — This Rule is former Rule BV7.

Effect of amendments. — The 1996 amendment, in b., substituted "sections a, b, or d of Rule 16-706" for "Rules BV6 a, BV6 b or BV6 d" in the first sentence, substituted "Rule 16-706 b" for "Rule BV6 b" in the third and fourth sentences, and substituted "Rule 16-706 a 3" for "Rule BV6 a 3" in the fourth sentence; substituted "Rule 16-709" for "Rule BV9" in c.; and added the Source note.

Editor's note. — An Order dated June 5, 1996, effective Jan. 1, 1997, renumbered this Rule, which was formerly Rule BV7.

Maryland Law Review. — For comment, "Discipline of Attorneys in Maryland," see 35

Md. L. Rev. 236 (1975).

University of Baltimore Law Review. — For article, "The Maryland Rules — A Time for Overhaul," see 9 U. Balt. L. Rev. 1 (1979).

Disciplinary proceedings for professional misconduct are not criminal proceedings. Their purpose is to protect the public by determining a lawyer's fitness to practice law and whether to institute disciplinary action against him. Attorney Grievance Comm'n v. Stewart, 285 Md. 251, 401 A.2d 1026, cert. denied, 444 U.S. 845, 100 S. Ct. 89, 62 L. Ed. 2d 58 (1979).

Nature and conduct of investigative proceedings. — The proceedings conducted by the Inquiry Panel and the Review Board are investigatory in nature and informal to the extent that the rules of evidence need not apply. At these stages of the proceedings, many of the constitutional safeguards accorded an accused in criminal cases are not available. Attorney Grievance Comm'n v. Stewart, 285 Md. 251, 401 A.2d 1026, cert. denied, 444 U.S. 845, 100 S. Ct. 89, 62 L. Ed. 2d 58 (1979).

Effect of full and fair hearing before judge. — If a lawyer is given notice and the opportunity to defend in a full and fair hearing, before a judge or judges, the question whether he was accorded due process of law by the Inquiry Panel and the Review Board is ordinarily immaterial. Attorney Grievance Comm'n v. Stewart, 285 Md. 251, 401 A.2d 1026, cert. denied, 444 U.S. 845, 100 S. Ct. 89, 62 L. Ed. 2d 58 (1979).

Vote to reprimand which was never implemented nor made final by the procedures intended to achieve that purpose was not a final determination. Attorney Grievance Comm'n v. Brown, 308 Md. 219, 517 A.2d 1111 (1986).

Rule 16-708. Confidentiality.

a. *General rule.* There may be no public proceedings by the Inquiry Committee or the Review Board. Unless otherwise ordered by the Commission, the record of any complaint, investigation, proceeding of the Inquiry Committee or the Review Board and of any reprimand shall be private and confidential, unless and until charges arising out of the proceeding shall be filed in the Court of Appeals, except as provided in this Rule.

b. *Exceptions.* The following exceptions to privacy and confidentiality are hereby established:

(1) With the approval of the Chairman or in his absence the Vice-Chairman of the Commission the Bar Counsel may provide information involving criminal activity to law enforcement and prosecuting officials.

(2) The notification to a complainant by the Bar Counsel of the disposition of the complaint of that complainant is not private and confidential.

(3) A judicial tribunal may request and receive any information that is relevant to the business of the tribunal.

(4) If an attorney is seeking admission to the practice of law before the bar of any judicial tribunal, or is under consideration for judicial office or for employment in legal work by federal, state or local government, a judicial tribunal, the appropriate committee of a Bar Association, the National Conference of Bar Examiners, a judicial nominating commission acting through its chairman or the appointing or hiring authority acting through its duly appointed representatives may receive information concerning reprimands and charges not having resulted in dismissal.

(5) The fact that a complaint is pending may be revealed to a person authorized under subsection (4). However, the nature of the pending complaint, the facts surrounding it, and the results of any investigation completed to the date of the inquiry, may be revealed only pursuant to a waiver by the attorney involved.

(6) The Bar Counsel may from time to time prepare and publish summaries of complaints without revealing identities of complainants, attorneys or

witnesses where in his judgment the publication would tend to improve the administration of justice.

(7) If an attorney is accused of misconduct, the Commission may issue a short written statement of clarification, correction, or exoneration, or it may announce that a reprimand has been administered, if the attorney requests that the statement be issued. (Amended May 5, 1976, effective July 1, 1976; Nov. 5, 1976, effective Jan. 1, 1977; June 5, 1996, effective Jan. 1, 1997.)

Source. — This Rule is former Rule BV8.

Effect of amendments. — The 1996 amendment added the Source note.

Editor's note. — An Order dated June 5, 1996, effective Jan. 1, 1997, renumbered this Rule, which was formerly Rule BV8.

University of Baltimore Law Review. — For article, "The Maryland Rules — A Time for Overhaul," see 9 U. Balt. L. Rev. 1 (1979).

This Rule is primarily aimed at the protection of an accused attorney, against whom no charges have been filed, rather than to benefit the complainant or to protect the integrity of the inquiry panel proceeding itself. Attorney Grievance Comm'n v. Strathen, 287 Md. 111, 411 A.2d 102 (1980).

Circuit Court for Howard County qualifies as a "judicial tribunal" under this Rule and is authorized to request and receive from the Attorney Grievance Commission any information that is relevant to the business of the tribunal. Attorney Grievance Comm'n v. Strathen, 287 Md. 111, 411 A.2d 102 (1980).

Court must balance policies of secrecy and disclosure. — The court is given the delicate task of balancing the policy which requires secrecy for the proceedings of the Attorney Grievance Commission with the policy which requires that there be full disclosure of all available evidence in order that the ends of justice may be served. Attorney Grievance

Comm'n v. Strathen, 287 Md. 111, 411 A.2d 102 (1980).

"Particularized need" test not measure of relevance. — The more stringent "particularized need" test applied in grand jury cases is not the measure of relevance under section b (3) of this Rule. Attorney Grievance Comm'n v. Strathen, 287 Md. 111, 411 A.2d 102 (1980).

Records of Maryland Attorney Grievance Commission not subject to public disclosure. — Records of the Maryland Attorney Grievance Commission, consisting of notifications to complainants regarding the disposition of formal complaints filed against attorneys, are not subject to public disclosure under the Maryland Public Information Act (generally, § 10-611 et seq. of the State Government Article). Attorney Grievance Comm'n v. A.S. Abell Co., 294 Md. 680, 452 A.2d 656 (1982).

Commission permitted to notify complainant as to disposition of his complaint. — Section b (2) of this Rule permits the Commission to divulge to a complainant the disposition of his complaint, but commission records of such correspondence are otherwise confidential under section a. Attorney Grievance Comm'n v. A.S. Abell Co., 294 Md. 680, 452 A.2d 656 (1982).

Rule 16-709. Charges.

a. *Who may file.* Charges against an attorney shall be filed by the Bar Counsel acting at the direction of the Review Board.

Cross references. — For definition of "charges," see Rule 16-701 d.

b. *Where filed and heard.* Charges against an attorney shall be filed on behalf of the Commission in the Court of Appeals. The Court of Appeals by order may direct that the charges be transmitted to and heard in any court and shall designate the judge or judges to hear the charges and the clerk responsible for maintaining the record in the proceeding.

Cross references. — For the definition of court, *see* Rule 16-701 f.

c. *Form.* The charges shall be in writing and shall be sufficiently clear and specific reasonably to inform the attorney proceeded against of any misconduct charged and of the basis of any allegation that he is incompetent.

d. *Service.* The Court of Appeals shall direct in each case the manner of service of a copy of the charges which shall be served together with the order of the Court of Appeals designating the court and judge or judges to hear the charges.

Cross references. — For definition of process, see Rule 1-202 (t). For the power of the Court of Appeals to issue process, see [former] Rule 857.

e. *Pleadings.* 1. Motion for transfer. Within fifteen days following the service of the order designating a court in which the charges shall be heard, the attorney charged may move in the Court of Appeals for a transfer of the hearing to another court. Action on the motion is in the discretion of the Court of Appeals. Filing the motion shall not stay the time for answer to the charges. Procedure on the motion is governed by the applicable provisions of Rule 8-431 (Motions).

2. Time for initial pleading. The attorney responding to the charges shall file his initial pleading in the court designated to hear the charges within fifteen days after the date of service of the charges upon him, unless a different time is fixed by the order of the Court of Appeals.

3. Subsequent pleadings. Subsequent pleadings shall be governed by and filed in the court designated to hear the charges within the times set forth in the applicable provisions of Chapter 300 of Title 2. (Amended May 5, 1976, effective July 1, 1976; Sept. 22, 1978; Apr. 6, 1984, effective July 1, 1984; June 5, 1996, effective Jan. 1, 1997.)

Source. — This Rule is former Rule BV9.

Effect of amendments. — The 1996 amendment substituted "Rule 16-701 d" for "Rule BV1 d" in the Cross reference note in a.; substituted "Rule 16-701 f" for "Rule BV1 f" in the Cross reference note in b.; substituted "Rule 8-431 (Motions)" for "Rule 855 (Application for Order —Motion—Answer)" in the last sentence of e.1.; and added the Source note.

Editor's note. — An Order dated June 5, 1996, effective Jan. 1, 1997, renumbered this Rule, which was formerly Rule BV9.

The definition of process, which is referred to in the Cross Reference note to section d, is currently set out at Rule 1-202 (u).

Maryland Law Review. — For survey of Court of Appeals decisions on attorney discipline for the year 1974-1975, see 36 Md. L. Rev. 351 (1976).

For article, "The Law of Disbarment and Reinstatement in Maryland," see 36 Md. L. Rev. 703 (1977).

University of Baltimore Law Review. — For article, "The Maryland Rules — A Time for Overhaul," see 9 U. Balt. L. Rev. 1 (1979).

University of Baltimore Law Forum. — For note, *"Attorney Grievance Commission v. Gilbert:* Attorney Disbarred for Failure to Disclose Material Information on His Bar Application", see 17, No. 3 U. Balt. Law Forum 27 (1987).

Purpose of disciplinary proceedings is not to punish the offending attorney but "is to protect the public from one who has demonstrated his unworthiness to continue the practice of law." Attorney Grievance Comm'n v. Howard, 282 Md. 515, 385 A.2d 1191 (1978).

Disciplinary proceedings for professional misconduct are not criminal pro-

ceedings. Their purpose is to protect the public by determining a lawyer's fitness to practice law and whether to institute disciplinary action against him. Attorney Grievance Comm'n v. Stewart, 285 Md. 251, 401 A.2d 1026, cert. denied, 444 U.S. 845, 100 S. Ct. 89, 62 L. Ed. 2d 58 (1979).

Purpose of written form. — Section c. of this Rule is designed to insure that the attorney is afforded notice and the opportunity to defend him or herself against the charges; the notice to which the attorney is entitled is of the factual allegations against which the attorney must defend. Attorney Grievance Comm'n v. Myers, 333 Md. 440, 635 A.2d 1315 (1994).

Statute of limitations. — Disciplinary proceedings against attorneys are not barred by a general statute of limitations. Anne Arundel County Bar Ass'n v. Collins, 272 Md. 578, 325 A.2d 724 (1974).

Lawyer charged with misconduct is entitled to basic elements of due process. — Notice and opportunity to defend in a full and fair hearing. Attorney Grievance Comm'n v. Stewart, 285 Md. 251, 401 A.2d 1026, cert. denied, 444 U.S. 845, 100 S. Ct. 89, 62 L. Ed. 2d 58 (1979).

Effect of full and fair hearing before judge. — If a lawyer is given notice and the opportunity to defend in a full and fair hearing, before a judge or judges, the question whether he was accorded due process of law by the Inquiry Panel and the Review Board is ordinarily immaterial. Attorney Grievance Comm'n v. Stewart, 285 Md. 251, 401 A.2d 1026, cert. denied, 444 U.S. 845, 100 S. Ct. 89, 62 L. Ed. 2d 58 (1979).

The Court of Appeals has original and complete jurisdiction over disciplinary proceedings and renders the ultimate decision as to whether an attorney has engaged in misconduct. Attorney Grievance Comm'n v. Kent, 337 Md. 361, 653 A.2d 909 (1995).

Delay in instituting disciplinary proceedings. — Where disciplinary proceedings against an attorney, which led to the three-judge panel's recommendation that the attorney in question be reprimanded, had not been instituted more closely on the heels of the events giving rise to them, it would not serve the underlying purpose of the proceedings to disbar or suspend the attorney. Attorney Grievance Comm'n v. Howard, 282 Md. 515, 385 A.2d 1191 (1978).

When formal charges exist. — Formal charges of misconduct do not exist against an attorney until a complaint is docketed in the Court of Appeals. Attorney Grievance Comm'n v. Bailey, 285 Md. 631, 403 A.2d 1261 (1979).

Charges must be sufficiently clear and specific. — While this Rule does not require that the charges be set forth in any certain form or in extensive detail, it does establish a requirement that the charges be "sufficiently clear and specific" so as to make the attorney aware of what he is compelled to answer for and defend against. Bar Ass'n v. Cockrell, 270 Md. 686, 313 A.2d 816 (1974).

And any rule without such requirement would violate due process. — Any rule which did not require the degree of specificity of the charges prescribed in this Rule would violate the minimum requirements of constitutional due process mandated by the Maryland Declaration of Rights. Bar Ass'n v. Cockrell, 270 Md. 686, 313 A.2d 816 (1974).

Indication that alleged conduct is violation of a specific rule not required. — The command of section c of this Rule does not require Bar Counsel when he petitions the Court of Appeals for disciplinary action against an attorney to say that the alleged conduct is a violation of a specific rule, but it is the factual allegation against which the individual must defend himself. Attorney Grievance Comm'n v. McBurney, 282 Md. 116, 383 A.2d 58 (1978).

Charges filed must embody disciplinary rule most probably violated. — See Attorney Grievance Comm'n v. Wright, 306 Md. 93, 507 A.2d 618 (1986).

Authority of Bar Counsel. — The fact that the Review Board did not specify that Bar Counsel should file charges against defendant under Rules 8.4 (b) and (d) of the Rules of Professional Conduct, did not violate this Rule; the charges were plainly related and within the authority vested in Bar Counsel. Attorney Grievance Comm'n v. Hamby, 322 Md. 606, 589 A.2d 53 (1991).

It was not improper for Bar Counsel to charge in a disciplinary petition a number of rule violations not specifically found by the Review Board. Attorney Grievance Comm'n v. Goldsborough, 330 Md. 342, 624 A.2d 503 (1993).

Section a. of this Rule requires the Bar Counsel, "acting at the direction of the Review Board," to file charges against an attorney. Attorney Grievance Comm'n v. Myers, 333 Md. 440, 635 A.2d 1315 (1994).

If Bar Counsel wishes to specify a violation of certain disciplinary rules in the petition to the Court of Appeals, then he should select all rules which conceivably might have application to the facts of the particular case, because he becomes limited in the disciplinary action by such rules as he selects. Attorney Grievance Comm'n v. McBurney, 282 Md. 116, 383 A.2d 58 (1978).

Failure to file State income tax returns not considered in determining sanction for failure to file federal returns. — Attorney's failure to file Maryland income tax returns since 1965, not mentioned in the disciplinary charge brought against respondent and disclosed for the first time at a remand hearing, was properly not considered in determining the sanction to be imposed for failure to file federal returns since the requirement of procedural due process, which is applicable in disciplinary proceedings, mandates sufficiently clear and specific notice of the charges being brought before disciplinary sanctions can be imposed against an attorney. Attorney Grievance Comm'n v. Walman, 280 Md. 453, 374 A.2d 354 (1977).

Conviction for accepting illegal gratuity under federal statute was not crime involving moral turpitude. — Where an individual who was both a member of the State bar and a former United States Senator from Maryland stood convicted of accepting an illegal gratuity under 18 U.S.C. § 201 (g) (now § 201 (c) (1) (B)), this was not a crime involving moral turpitude and a petition for disciplinary action filed under this Rule charging him only with conviction of a crime involving moral turpitude must be dismissed. Attorney Grievance Comm'n v. Brewster, 280 Md. 473, 374 A.2d 602 (1977).

Order disciplining lawyer violative of Rule. — Any order disciplining a lawyer based on a finding by the hearing court of a particular form of professional misconduct would be clearly violative of this Rule where the lawyer had not been charged in the Bar Association's petition with that particular misconduct, since

it cannot be validly contended that the failure to allege that charge in any form is a charge in writing "sufficiently clear and specific reasonably to inform the attorney proceeded against" of the misconduct alleged. Bar Ass'n v. Cockrell, 270 Md. 686, 313 A.2d 816 (1974).

Amendment of pleading to make additional charge. — Where the petition as filed did not contain the requisite allegations to support disciplinary sanctions based on a finding made by the hearing court that the respondent misappropriated his client's funds, the interest of justice required that the Bar Association be granted leave to amend its pleading so as to make the additional charge, without prejudice to the respondent's prerogative to raise an objection, first in the hearing court and then in the Court of Appeals, unless he elected to waive this right. Bar Ass'n v. Cockrell, 270 Md. 686, 313 A.2d 816 (1974).

Applied in Attorney Grievance Comm'n v. Webster, 348 Md. 662, 705 A.2d 1135 (1998); Attorney Grievance Comm'n v. Alison, 349 Md. 623, 709 A.2d 1212 (1998).

Cited in Attorney Grievance Comm'n v. Awuah, 346 Md. 420, 697 A.2d 446 (1997); Attorney Grievance Comm'n v. Williams, 348 Md. 196, 702 A.2d 1271 (1997); Frederick Rd. Ltd. Partnership v. Brown & Sturm, 121 Md. App. 384, 710 A.2d 298 (1998); Attorney Grievance Comm'n v. Gavin, 350 Md. 176, 711 A.2d 193 (1998).

Rule 16-710. Hearings.

a. *Discovery — Same as in civil case.* Chapter 400 of Title 2 governs the taking of depositions and discovery in the hearing of charges.

b. *Procedural defects.* The hearing of charges shall not be stayed or challenged by reason of any procedural defects alleged to have occurred prior to the filing of charges.

c. *Number of judges.* The charges shall be heard by one judge; however, upon petition filed by the attorney charged or the Attorney Grievance Commission and for good cause shown or on its own motion the Court of Appeals may designate two additional judges to consider the charges.

d. *Hearings — Conducted as civil case.* The hearing of charges is governed by the same rules of law, evidence and procedure as are applicable to the trial of civil proceedings in equity. Factual findings shall be supported by clear and convincing evidence.

Cross references. — For burden of proof where an attorney petitions for reinstatement or for modification of suspension, see Rule 16-714 d 4.

e. *Conviction of crime — Adjudication of misconduct.* 1. Proof of guilt. In a hearing of charges pursuant to this Rule, a final judgment by a judicial tribunal in another proceeding convicting an attorney of a crime shall be conclusive proof of the guilt of the attorney of that crime. A plea or verdict of guilty, or a plea of *nolo contendere* followed by a fine or sentence, is a conviction within the meaning of this Rule. A final adjudication in a disciplinary proceeding by a judicial tribunal or a disciplinary agency appointed by or acting at the direction of a judicial tribunal that an attorney has been guilty of misconduct is conclusive proof of the misconduct in the hearing of charges pursuant to this Rule.

2. Additional evidence. The introduction of evidence in a proceeding pursuant to this Rule of an attorney's conviction of a crime in a judicial tribunal or adjudication of misconduct by a judicial tribunal, does not preclude the Commission from introducing additional evidence nor does it preclude the attorney from introducing evidence or otherwise showing cause why he should not be disciplined. (Amended May 5, 1978, effective July 1, 1978; Sept. 22, 1978; Apr. 6, 1984, effective July 1, 1984; June 5, 1996, effective Jan. 1, 1997.)

Source. — This Rule is former Rule BV10.

Effect of amendments. — The 1996 amendment substituted "Rule 16-714 d 4" for "Rule BV14 d 4" in the Cross reference note in d.; and added the Source note.

Editor's note. — An Order dated June 5, 1996, effective Jan. 1, 1997, renumbered this Rule, which was formerly Rule BV10.

Maryland Law Review. — For survey of Court of Appeals decisions on attorney discipline for the year 1974-1975, see 36 Md. L. Rev. 351 (1976).

For article, "The Law of Disbarment and Reinstatement in Maryland," see 36 Md. L. Rev. 703 (1977).

University of Baltimore Law Review. — For article, "The Maryland Rules — A Time for Overhaul," see 9 U. Balt. L. Rev. 1 (1979).

The purpose of the proceeding under this Rule is to protect the public by determining a lawyer's fitness to practice law. Attorney Grievance Comm'n v. Green, 278 Md. 412, 365 A.2d 39 (1976).

The purpose of a disciplinary action is not to punish the offending attorney, but is to protect the public from one who has demonstrated his unworthiness to continue the practice of law. Attorney Grievance Comm'n v. Pollack, 279 Md. 225, 369 A.2d 61 (1977).

The purpose of a disciplinary proceeding is to protect the public, rather than to punish the erring attorney. Attorney Grievance Comm'n v. Kahn, 290 Md. 654, 431 A.2d 1336 (1981).

Under section d of this Rule burden of proof is on Commission as the petitioning party. Attorney Grievance Comm'n v. Bailey, 285 Md. 631, 403 A.2d 1261 (1979).

Measure of proof. — The "clear and convincing" standard of section d applies to the measure of proof imposed upon the Attorney Grievance Commission in factual determinations essential to establishing its case against the attorney. It does not apply to factual matters sought to be established by the attorney in defense of the attorney's position, including whether mitigating circumstances have been shown; as to this, the preponderance of evidence standard is the applicable measure of proof. Attorney Grievance Comm'n v. Bakas, 322 Md. 603, 589 A.2d 52, modified, 323 Md. 395, 593 A.2d 1087 (1991).

Attorney can be found to have erred by "clear and convincing evidence" when the only evidence in the case is the testimonial evidence of the complaining witnesses. Attorney Grievance Comm'n v. Kerpelman, 288 Md. 341, 420 A.2d 940 (1980), cert. denied, 450 U.S. 970, 101 S. Ct. 1492, 67 L. Ed. 2d 621 (1981).

Standard of proof in defense. — An attorney in a disciplinary proceeding need only establish factual matters in defense of the attorney's position by the preponderance of evidence, including whether mitigating circumstances existed at the time of the alleged misconduct. Attorney Grievance Comm'n v. Powell, 328 Md. 276, 614 A.2d 102 (1992).

The action of a court in exercising its power to disbar is characterized as judicial in character and is essentially an inquiry in the nature of an investigation by the court into the conduct of one of its own officers. The order which is entered is only an exercise of the disciplinary jurisdiction which a court has over its officers. It is recognized in this State and generally in America that in such an investigation mere forms not affecting the merits should not stand in the way of protecting the court and the public by appropriate action after a full hearing. Maryland State Bar Ass'n v. Boone, 255 Md. 420, 258 A.2d 438 (1969).

Power of local courts. — Statutes and rules have consistently confided to the local courts the power to act in both disciplinary proceedings and reinstatement proceedings. Maryland State Bar Ass'n v. Boone, 255 Md. 420, 258 A.2d 438 (1969).

Duty of Court of Appeals. — The Court of Appeals has the right and the duty ultimately to supervise the exercise of disciplinary and reinstatement powers of the local courts. Maryland State Bar Ass'n v. Boone, 255 Md. 420, 258 A.2d 438 (1969).

Claim that Rules BV2 and 1228 (see now Rules 16-702 and 16-811) are impermissible taxes may or may not be correct, but even if the point is well taken, it would not be an excuse for unethical conduct on the part of a member of the bar, nor would it be a defense to charges relative to such conduct. Attorney Grievance Comm'n v. Kerpelman, 288 Md. 341, 420 A.2d 940 (1980), cert. denied, 450 U.S. 970, 101 S. Ct. 1492, 67 L. Ed. 2d 621 (1981).

Acts not resulting in criminal conviction. — An attorney may be disciplined for acts which are criminal but do not result in a criminal conviction if Bar Counsel proves the underlying conduct at the disciplinary hearing. Attorney Grievance Comm'n v. Garland, 345 Md. 383, 692 A.2d 465 (1997).

A disciplinary proceeding is neither an action at law, nor a criminal prosecution. Anne Arundel County Bar Ass'n v. Collins, 272 Md. 578, 325 A.2d 724 (1974).

A disciplinary proceeding for professional misconduct is not the trial of an action at law. Maryland State Bar Ass'n v. Boone, 255 Md. 420, 258 A.2d 438 (1969); Kerpelman v. Bricker, 23 Md. App. 628, 329 A.2d 423 (1974).

A disciplinary proceeding for professional misconduct is not a proceeding of a criminal character. Kerpelman v. Bricker, 23 Md. App. 628, 329 A.2d 423 (1974).

Constitutional guarantee of jury trial inapplicable. — Disciplinary proceedings against attorneys, in the absence of a rule or statute providing to the contrary, are not encompassed within the constitutional guarantees of trial by a jury, be that guarantee state or federal. Attorney Grievance Comm'n v. Kerpelman, 288 Md. 341, 420 A.2d 940 (1980), cert. denied, 450 U.S. 970, 101 S. Ct. 1492, 67 L. Ed. 2d 621 (1981).

Double jeopardy provisions of the Fifth Amendment of the Constitution of the United States are not applicable to disciplinary proceedings against lawyers since these proceedings are not criminal in nature. Attorney Grievance Comm'n v. Andresen, 281 Md. 152, 379 A.2d 159 (1977).

Notice and opportunity to defend. — As long as an attorney is given notice and opportunity to defend in a full and fair hearing following the institution of disciplinary proceedings, an irregularity in the proceedings before the Inquiry Panel and the Review Board ordinarily will not amount to a denial of due process. Attorney Grievance Comm'n v. Garland, 345 Md. 383, 692 A.2d 465 (1997).

Equity rules applicable. — Under section d of this Rule the same rules of law, evidence and procedure as used in civil proceedings in equity are applicable in disciplinary hearings. Bar Ass'n v. Cockrell, 270 Md. 686, 313 A.2d 816 (1974).

Self-incrimination. — A disciplinary action against an attorney does not involve a potential criminal or quasi-criminal sanction for the purpose of the privilege against self-incrimination provided by the Fifth Amendment to the federal Constitution. Maryland State Bar Ass'n v. Sugarman, 273 Md. 306, 329 A.2d 1 (1974), cert. denied, 420 U.S. 974, 95 S. Ct. 1397, 43 L. Ed. 2d 654 (1975).

Attorney Grievance Commission's procedural guideline, warning attorney that Inquiry Panel may believe evidence which attorney does not contest, does not violate attorney's constitutional right against compelled self-incrimination. Attorney Grievance Comm'n v. Unnamed Att'y, 298 Md. 36, 467 A.2d 517 (1983).

Signing petition for expungement of arrest records of unmet person. — It was not dishonest, fraudulent or deceitful for an attorney to sign a petition for expungement of the arrest records of a person he had never met, when asked to do so as a favor for a deputy State's attorney. Attorney Grievance Comm'n v. Miles, 280 Md. 681, 374 A.2d 1159 (1977).

Final judgment of which this Rule speaks is one that exists when all avenues of direct appeal from the judgment of conviction and sentence are no longer open to the defendant. Maryland State Bar Ass'n v. Kerr, 272 Md. 687, 326 A.2d 180 (1974).

Conviction in a criminal case, State or federal, is final for purposes of this Rule where a pending new trial motion was filed after the conviction had been affirmed on appeal and certiorari denied by the Supreme Court of the United States. Maryland State Bar Ass'n v. Rosenberg, 273 Md. 351, 329 A.2d 106 (1974).

And integrity of criminal conviction cannot be attacked in disciplinary proceeding by invoking the Court of Appeals to reweigh or to reevaluate the respondent's guilt or innocence. Attorney Grievance Comm'n v. Barnes, 286 Md. 474, 408 A.2d 719 (1979).

Nolo contendere plea is admissible in disciplinary proceedings affecting attorneys. Agnew v. State, 51 Md. App. 614, 446 A.2d 425 (1982).

Plea of nolo contendere tantamount to conviction. — Section e of this Rule provides that a plea of nolo contendere is tantamount to conviction for the purposes of disciplinary proceedings. Attorney Grievance Comm'n v. Brewster, 280 Md. 473, 374 A.2d 602 (1977).

When attorney is convicted of crime of moral turpitude, disbarment follows automatically unless compelling extenuating circumstances are established. Attorney Grievance Comm'n v. Barnes, 286 Md. 474, 408 A.2d 719 (1979); Attorney Grievance Comm'n v. Kahn, 290 Md. 654, 431 A.2d 1336 (1981).

Attorney conduct which involves moral turpitude and is infected with fraud, deceit, or dishonesty shall require disbarment unless the attorney can demonstrate by clear and convincing evidence that there are compelling extenuating circumstances that merit a less onerous sanction. Attorney Grievance Comm'n v. Burka, 292 Md. 221, 438 A.2d 514 (1981).

"Moral turpitude" is an act of baseness, vileness, or depravity in the private and social duties which a man owes to his fellow men, or to society in general, contrary to the accepted and customary rule of right and duty between man and man. Attorney Grievance Comm'n v. Barnes, 286 Md. 474, 408 A.2d 719 (1979).

Bribery may be deemed conduct involving moral turpitude. — Where circumstances clearly permit an inference of corrupt intent, bribery may be deemed to be conduct involving moral turpitude so as to justify disbarment of an attorney in the absence of compelling circumstances justifying a lesser sanction. Attorney Grievance Comm'n v. Spector, 293 Md. 324, 443 A.2d 965 (1982).

Convictions involving moral turpitude. — An attorney's convictions of obtaining money under false pretenses with intent to defraud and of fraudulent and willful appropriation of trust assets necessarily meant establishment of a fraudulent intent, and hence involves moral turpitude. Attorney Grievance Comm'n v. Andresen, 281 Md. 152, 379 A.2d 159 (1977).

Certain factors may influence sanction to be imposed. — Factors such as the age and inexperience of an attorney and the lack of personal gain involved in an act of misconduct may in some circumstances influence the sanction to be imposed. Attorney Grievance Comm'n v. Kahn, 290 Md. 654, 431 A.2d 1336 (1981).

In determining whether an attorney has exhibited the requisite foundation for a sanction less than disbarment, the Court of Appeals considers whether the proffered circumstances diminish the degree of culpability inherent in his guilt. Attorney Grievance Comm'n v. Kahn, 290 Md. 654, 431 A.2d 1336 (1981).

Attorney's mental condition was compelling extenuating circumstance where a disabling condition impeded the attorney from conducting his practice and which required treatment. Attorney Grievance Comm'n v. Burka, 292 Md. 221, 438 A.2d 514 (1981).

Right of appeal. — There is no right of appeal in cases of admission to the Bar, refusal to disbar or reinstatement to the Bar after disbarment to anyone other than the lawyer involved. Maryland State Bar Ass'n v. Boone, 255 Md. 420, 258 A.2d 438 (1969).

Factual findings of hearing judge in attorney disciplinary proceeding are prima facie correct and will not be disturbed on review unless clearly erroneous. Attorney Grievance Comm'n v. Kahn, 290 Md. 654, 431 A.2d 1336 (1981); Attorney Grievance Comm'n v. Collins, 295 Md. 532, 457 A.2d 1134 (1983).

Discretion of judge not disturbed on appeal unless arbitrarily administered. — See Bar Ass'n v. Cockrell, 270 Md. 686, 313 A.2d 816 (1974).

Affirmance of attorney's conviction by equally divided panel of appellate court is final judgment for purposes of this Rule. Attorney Grievance Comm'n v. Mandel, 294 Md. 560, 451 A.2d 910 (1982).

Dismissal of disciplinary petition for Commission's failure to proceed. — Because the purpose of disciplinary action against an attorney is to protect the public, dismissal of the disciplinary petition for the sole reason that the Attorney Grievance Commission failed to proceed with the proper dispatch is manifestly unwarranted. Attorney Grievance Comm'n v. Kahn, 290 Md. 654, 431 A.2d 1336 (1981).

Final adjudication of attorney's misconduct by foreign court is conclusive proof of the misconduct in the hearing of charges pursuant to this Rule. Attorney Grievance Comm'n v. Hines, 304 Md. 625, 500 A.2d 646 (1985).

Though New York applies a lower standard of proof in attorney discipline cases, there is no reason to believe that New York courts treat such matters less seriously or wholly inconsistently with the manner exercised by the Maryland Court of Appeals; accordingly, there is no problem in accepting a New York court's findings in attorney discipline cases based on the different standard of proof. Attorney Grievance Comm'n v. Sabghir, 350 Md. 67, 710 A.2d 926 (1998).

Final judgment in D.C. Court of Appeals conclusive in this State. — Under section e 1, the final adjudication of an attorney's misconduct by the District of Columbia Court of Appeals is conclusive proof of that misconduct in a Maryland hearing. Attorney Grievance Comm'n v. Moore, 301 Md. 169, 482 A.2d 497 (1984); Attorney Grievance Comm'n v. Gittens, 346 Md. 316, 697 A.2d 83 (1997).

Affirmation of an administrative agency finding by the U.S. Court of Appeals is not tantamount to a finding by a judicial tribunal. Attorney Grievance

Comm'n v. Miller, 310 Md. 163, 528 A.2d 481 (1987).

    Cited in Frederick Rd. Ltd. Partnership v.

Brown & Sturm, 121 Md. App. 384, 710 A.2d 298 (1998).

Rule 16-711. Disposition of charges.

    a. *Findings.* A written statement of the findings of facts and conclusions of law shall be filed in the record of the proceedings and copies sent to all parties. (Amended Sept. 22, 1978.)

    b. *Subsequent proceedings.* 1. Record. Within 15 days after the findings and conclusions are filed, unless a different time is fixed by order of the Court of Appeals, the clerk of the court shall transmit the record to the Court of Appeals. (Amended June 16, 1975, effective July 1, 1975; Sept. 22, 1978.)

    2. Exceptions. Within 15 days after the filing of the record in the Court of Appeals, the attorney or the Bar Counsel may file in the Court of Appeals exceptions to the findings and conclusions and may make recommendations respecting the disciplinary sanction to be imposed, if any, under b 4 of this Rule. An answer to the exceptions and recommendations shall be filed within 15 days from the filing of the exceptions and recommendations. Copies of exceptions, recommendations and answers shall be served upon all other parties in the manner prescribed by Rule 1-321, and proof of such service shall be made in the manner prescribed by Rule 1-323. Exceptions, recommendations and answers thereto shall be filed in eight legible typewritten copies. Cases under this Rule shall be disposed of as soon as practicable and may not be placed on the regular appeals docket. (Amended Sept. 22, 1978; June 6, 1979, effective July 1, 1979; Apr. 6, 1984, effective July 1, 1984.)

    3. Oral argument. Oral argument shall be had on any exceptions and shall be governed by Rule 8-522 (Oral argument).

    4. Review by Court of Appeals. The Court of Appeals may order (i) disbarment, (ii) suspension, (iii) reprimand, (iv) placing attorney on an inactive status, (v) dismissal of charges, or may remand the case for further proceedings. The provisions of subsections 1, 2 and 3 of this section govern proceedings after the order or remand has been complied with by the court. The Court of Appeals shall review the findings and conclusions after remand as provided in this subsection. (Amended Sept. 22, 1978.)

    5. Decision of Court of Appeals. The decision of the Court of Appeals is final. The decision is evidenced by the order of the Court of Appeals, which shall be certified under the seal of that Court by the Clerk and may be accompanied by an opinion. The record in the case shall be retained by the Clerk of the Court of Appeals. (Amended June 5, 1996, effective Jan. 1, 1997.)

    Source. — This Rule is former Rule BV11.

    Effect of amendments. — The 1996 amendment substituted "Rule 8-522" for "Rule 846" in b 3; and added the Source note.

    Editor's note. — An Order dated June 5, 1996, effective Jan. 1, 1997, renumbered this Rule, which was formerly Rule BV11.

Maryland Law Review. — For survey of Court of Appeals decisions on attorney discipline for the year 1974-1975, see 36 Md. L. Rev. 351 (1976).

For article, "The Law of Disbarment and Reinstatement in Maryland," see 36 Md. L. Rev. 703 (1977).

For article, "The Court of Appeals of Maryland: Roles, Work and Performance," see 37 Md. L. Rev. 1 (1977).

University of Baltimore Law Review. — For article, "The Maryland Rules — A Time for Overhaul," see 9 U. Balt. L. Rev. 1 (1979).

Duty rests upon the courts and the profession as a whole to uphold the highest standards of professional conduct and to protect the public from imposition by the unfit or unscrupulous practitioner. Attorney Grievance Comm'n v. Andresen, 281 Md. 152, 379 A.2d 159 (1977).

Purpose of disciplinary proceedings is not to punish the offending attorney but "is to protect the public from one who has demonstrated his unworthiness to continue the practice of law." Attorney Grievance Comm'n v. Howard, 282 Md. 515, 385 A.2d 1191 (1978).

Exercise of power to disbar. — The power to disbar an attorney should be exercised with extreme caution, but there should be no pause in exercising that power when it is apparent that such action is required for the protection of the public. Bar Ass'n v. Marshall, 269 Md. 510, 307 A.2d 677 (1973).

Severity of the sanction to be imposed is dependent on the facts and circumstances of each case. Attorney Grievance Comm'n v. Pollack, 279 Md. 225, 369 A.2d 61 (1977).

And mitigating circumstances may be considered in determining the punishment to be imposed. Attorney Grievance Comm'n v. Pollack, 279 Md. 225, 369 A.2d 61 (1977).

Disbarment follows from conviction of crime involving moral turpitude. — Absent compelling extenuating circumstances, disbarment of an attorney follows from conviction of a crime that involves moral turpitude and is characterized by dishonesty, fraud or deceit. Attorney Grievance Comm'n v. Walman, 280 Md. 453, 374 A.2d 354 (1977).

Conviction for accepting illegal gratuity under federal statute was not crime involving moral turpitude. — Where an individual who was both a member of the State bar and a former United States Senator from Maryland stood convicted of accepting an illegal gratuity under former 18 U.S.C. § 201 (g) (now § 201 (c) (1) (B)), this was not a crime involving moral turpitude and a petition for disciplinary action filed under Rule BV9 charging him only with conviction of a crime

involving moral turpitude must be dismissed. Attorney Grievance Comm'n v. Brewster, 280 Md. 473, 374 A.2d 602 (1977).

Failure to file a federal tax return may result in the imposition of any one of the sanctions prescribed by this Rule, but disbarment does not automatically follow from every such conviction. Attorney Grievance Comm'n v. Walman, 280 Md. 453, 374 A.2d 354 (1977).

Failure to file State income tax returns not considered in determining sanction for failure to file federal returns. — Attorney's failure to file Maryland income tax returns since 1965, not mentioned in the disciplinary charge brought against respondent and disclosed for the first time at a remand hearing, was properly not considered in determining the sanction to be imposed for failure to file federal returns since the requirement of procedural due process, which is applicable in disciplinary proceedings, mandates sufficiently clear and specific notice of the charges being brought before disciplinary sanctions can be imposed against an attorney. Attorney Grievance Comm'n v. Walman, 280 Md. 453, 374 A.2d 354 (1977).

Misappropriation of funds. — When a member of the bar of the Court of Appeals is found to have betrayed the high trust imposed in him by appropriating to his own use funds of others entrusted to him, then, absent the most compelling extenuating circumstances, disbarment should follow as a matter of course. Bar Ass'n v. Marshall, 269 Md. 510, 307 A.2d 677 (1973); Bar Ass'n v. Carruth, 271 Md. 720, 319 A.2d 532 (1974).

Regarding the question whether more lenient sanctions should be imposed on a lawyer who has misappropriated funds which have come into his hands in a fiduciary but not professional capacity, as distinguished from a lawyer who, in his professional capacity, has misappropriated the funds of a client, there appears to be no sound reason for regarding misappropriations committed in a nonprofessional capacity more leniently than those committed in a professional capacity. Each involves a breach of trust or of a fiduciary relationship and bear equally on the fitness of a lawyer to practice his profession so that disbarment will be recommended. Attorney Grievance Comm'n v. Silk, 279 Md. 345, 369 A.2d 70 (1977).

Sanctions when misconduct adjudicated by a foreign court. — There is no requirement that Maryland court impose the same sanction as a foreign court in attorney discipline cases. Attorney Grievance Comm'n v. Sabghir, 350 Md. 67, 710 A.2d 926 (1998).

Cited in Attorney Grievance Comm'n v. Awuah, 346 Md. 420, 697 A.2d 446 (1997).

Rule 16-712. Resignation; disbarment by consent.

a. *Where filed.* An application to resign from the practice of law in this State shall be submitted only to the Court of Appeals and must be in writing and state the reasons therefor. The submission of an application to resign does not prevent or stay disciplinary proceedings against the attorney, except as otherwise provided in Rule 16-712 d.

b. *Procedure.* The Court of Appeals shall notify the Bar Counsel of the submission of an application to resign and may cause an investigation to be made by the Bar Counsel and hearings to be held in any court it deems appropriate. The Bar Counsel shall advise the Court of Appeals and forward to the Clerk of the Court of Appeals the record of any investigation or hearing, which shall be maintained as a permanent record of that Court.

c. *Effect.* A resignation is effective only upon acceptance thereof by order of the Court of Appeals. Upon entry of an order accepting the resignation of an attorney, the provisions of Rule 16-713 (Effect of Discipline, Resignation and Inactive Status) shall be complied with.

d. *Disbarment by consent of attorney under investigation.* 1. Attorney may not resign. An attorney may not resign while he is the subject of an investigation into, or pending proceedings involving allegations of his misconduct.

2. Requirements for disbarment by consent. Upon the written recommendation of the Bar Counsel to the Court of Appeals, an attorney who is the subject of an investigation into, or pending proceedings involving allegations of his misconduct, may consent to disbarment, but only by delivering to the Bar Counsel and to the Court of Appeals an affidavit stating that he desires to consent to disbarment and that:

(i) His consent is freely and voluntarily rendered; he is not being subjected to coercion or duress; he is fully aware of the implications of submitting his consent;

(ii) He is aware that there is a pending investigation into or proceeding involving allegations of his misconduct, the nature of which he shall specifically set forth; and

(iii) He submits his consent because he knows that if charges were predicated upon the matters under investigation or if the proceedings were prosecuted, he could not successfully defend himself.

3. Effect. After completion of the requirements set forth in paragraph 2 of this subsection, the Court of Appeals may enter an order, signed by the Chief Judge or in his absence by an Associate Judge, disbarring the attorney by consent. Upon entry of an order disbarring an attorney by consent, the provisions of Rule 16-713 (Effect of Discipline, Resignation and Inactive Status) shall apply. (Amended Apr. 18, 1980, effective July 1, 1980; June 5, 1996, effective Jan. 1, 1997.)

Source. — This Rule is former Rule BV12.

Effect of amendments. — The 1996 amendment substituted "Rule 16-712 d" for "Rule BV12 d" in a; substituted "Rule 16-713" for "Rule BV13" in c; substituted "Rule 16-713" for "Rule BV13" in d 3; and added the Source note.

Editor's note. — An Order dated June 5, 1996, effective Jan. 1, 1997, renumbered this Rule, which was formerly Rule BV12.

University of Baltimore Law Review. — For article, "The Maryland Rules — A Time for Overhaul," see 9 U. Balt. L. Rev. 1 (1979).

Issuance of subpoenas. — The Court of Appeals by rule may allow for the issuance of subpoenas by Bar Counsel and the Chair of the Inquiry Panel. 82 Op. Att'y Gen. (January 6, 1997).

Continuing jurisdiction. — Attorney who resigned only when notified that a disciplinary investigation was pending against him in Maryland remained, at all times pertinent to different proceedings, a member of the bar of the State of Maryland and the court therefore had jurisdiction over him for purposes of disciplinary action under these Rules. Attorney Grievance Comm'n v. Hopp, 330 Md. 177, 623 A.2d 193 (1993).

Consent. — Attorney was disbarred upon his consent, filed pursuant to section d 2 of this Rule. Attorney Grievance Comm'n v. Beckman, 346 Md. 370, 697 A.2d 110 (1997).

Applied in Attorney Grievance Comm'n v. Martin, 343 Md. 255, 680 A.2d 1102 (1996); Attorney Grievance Comm'n v. Sine, 345 Md. 662, 693 A.2d 1156 (1997).

Stated in Attorney Grievance Comm'n v. Marquat, 345 Md. 453, 693 A.2d 352 (1997).

Cited in Attorney Grievance Comm'n v. Appler, 343 Md. 331, 681 A.2d 67 (1996); Attorney Grievance Comm'n v. Rybczynski, 344 Md. 564, 688 A.2d 443 (1997); Attorney Grievance Comm'n v. Porter, 344 Md. 639, 689 A.2d 609 (1997); Attorney Grievance Comm'n v. Vetri, 344 Md. 640, 689 A.2d 609 (1997); Attorney Grievance Comm'n v. Baker, 344 Md. 641, 689 A.2d 609 (1997); Attorney Grievance Comm'n v. Finney, 345 Md. 595, 693 A.2d 814 (1997); Attorney Grievance Comm'n v. Newell, 346 Md. 121, 695 A.2d 152 (1997); Attorney Grievance v. Wilson, 348 Md. 177, 702 A.2d 776 (1997); Attorney Grievance Comm'n v. Williams, 348 Md. 362, 704 A.2d 420 (1998).

Rule 16-713. Effect of discipline, inactive status, and resignation.

a. *Attorney admitted by the Court of Appeals.* 1. Duty of Clerk. With regard to an attorney admitted by the Court of Appeals to practice law, when an order suspending or disbarring the attorney from the practice of law, placing the attorney on inactive status, or accepting the attorney's resignation from the practice of law in this State becomes effective, the Clerk of the Court of Appeals forthwith shall strike the name of the attorney from the register of attorneys in that Court.

2. Effect. The attorney may not practice law after entry of an order disbarring the attorney, placing the attorney on inactive status, or accepting the attorney's resignation or during the period the attorney, by order, is suspended. Upon expiration of the period of suspension specified in the order, the Clerk of the Court of Appeals shall replace the name of the attorney upon the register of attorneys in that Court, and the attorney may practice law, only after (a) the attorney files with the Bar Counsel a verified statement that the attorney has complied in all respects with the terms of the suspension and (b) Bar Counsel notifies the Clerk that the statement has been filed and Bar Counsel is satisfied that the attorney has complied with the terms of the suspension.

3. Certification by Clerk. Whenever the Clerk of the Court of Appeals strikes a name from or replaces a name on the register of attorneys pursuant to this section, the Clerk shall certify that fact to the Trustees of the Clients' Security Trust Fund and the clerks of all judicial tribunals in this State.

b. *Attorney not admitted by Court of Appeals.* 1. Duty of Clerk. With regard to an attorney not admitted by the Court of Appeals to practice law, upon entry of an order disbarring or suspending the attorney in this State, the Clerk of the

Court of Appeals forthwith shall place the name of the attorney on a list maintained in that Court of non-admitted attorneys who are excluded from exercising in any manner the privilege of practicing law in this State.

2. Effect. The attorney may not practice law in this State and is disqualified from admission to practice law in this State after entry of an order disbarring the attorney or during the period the attorney, by order, is suspended. Upon expiration of the period of suspension specified in the order, the Clerk of the Court of Appeals shall strike the attorney's name from the list of non-admitted attorneys excluded from exercising the privilege of practicing law in this State only after (a) the attorney files with the Bar Counsel a verified statement that the attorney has complied in all respects with the terms of the suspension and (b) Bar Counsel notifies the Clerk that the statement has been filed and Bar Counsel is satisfied that the attorney has complied with the terms of the suspension.

3. Certification by Clerk. Whenever the Clerk pursuant to this section places a name on or strikes a name from the list of non-admitted attorneys excluded from exercising the privilege of practicing law in this State, the Clerk shall certify that fact to the Board of Law Examiners and the clerks of all judicial tribunals in this State. (Amended Apr. 7, 1986, effective Jan. 1, 1987; June 5, 1996, effective Jan. 1, 1997.)

Source. — This Rule is former Rule BV13.

Effect of amendments. — The 1996 amendment added the Source note.

Editor's note. — An Order dated June 5, 1996, effective Jan. 1, 1997, renumbered this Rule, which was formerly Rule BV13.

University of Baltimore Law Review. — For article, "The Maryland Rules — A Time for Overhaul," see 9 U. Balt. L. Rev. 1 (1979).

Reciprocal discipline. — The Court of Appeals was not required to apply the same sanction that Virginia applied in a disciplinary proceeding; although the Court will look to the sanction imposed by other jurisdictions, the outcome will depend on the unique facts and circumstances of each case, with a view toward consistent dispositions for similar conduct. Attorney Grievance Comm'n v. Saul, 337 Md. 258, 653 A.2d 430 (1995).

Suspension was appropriate sanction. — Where attorney did not profit from his misconduct, and where the bank which was the subject of his prosecution did not suffer any losses from the misconduct, suspension, rather than disbarment, was the appropriate sanction. Attorney Grievance Comm'n v. Saul, 337 Md. 258, 653 A.2d 430 (1995).

Applied in Attorney Grievance Comm'n v. Gadhia, 343 Md. 215, 680 A.2d 1082 (1996); Attorney Grievance Comm'n v. Ray, 343 Md. 254, 680 A.2d 1101 (1996); Attorney Grievance Comm'n v. Button, 345 Md. 40, 690 A.2d 1009 (1997); Attorney Grievance Comm'n v. Leishman, 345 Md. 41, 690 A.2d 1009 (1997); Attorney Grievance Comm'n v. Wright, 345 Md. 425, 692 A.2d 948 (1997); Attorney Grievance Comm'n v. Shank, 345 Md. 426, 692 A.2d 948 (1997); Attorney Grievance Comm'n v. Mattie, 345 Md. 427, 692 A.2d 948 (1997); Attorney Grievance Comm'n v. Sine, 345 Md. 662, 693 A.2d 1156 (1997).

Stated in Attorney Grievance Comm'n v. Marquat, 345 Md. 453, 693 A.2d 352 (1997).

Cited in Attorney Grievance Comm'n v. Essrick, 343 Md. 1, 680 A.2d 464 (1996); Attorney Grievance Comm'n v. Marshall, 343 Md. 110, 680 A.2d 518 (1996); Attorney Grievance Comm'n v. Appler, 343 Md. 331, 681 A.2d 67 (1996); Attorney Grievance Comm'n v. Rybczynski, 344 Md. 564, 688 A.2d 443 (1997); Attorney Grievance Comm'n v. Porter, 344 Md. 639, 689 A.2d 609 (1997); Attorney Grievance Comm'n v. Vetri, 344 Md. 640, 689 A.2d 609 (1997); Attorney Grievance Comm'n v. Baker, 344 Md. 641, 689 A.2d 609 (1997); Attorney Grievance Comm'n v. Stanback, 345 Md. 120, 691 A.2d 692 (1997); Attorney Grievance Comm'n v. Chisholm, 345 Md. 347, 691 A.2d 1367 (1997); Attorney Grievance Comm'n v. Holzman, 345 Md. 348, 691 A.2d 1368 (1997); Attorney Grievance Comm'n v. Finney, 345 Md. 595, 693 A.2d 814 (1997); Attorney Grievance Comm'n v. Kornblit, 345 Md. 693, 694

A.2d 462 (1997); Attorney Grievance Comm'n v. Marshall, 346 Md. 120, 695 A.2d 152 (1997); Attorney Grievance Comm'n v. Newell, 346 Md. 121, 695 A.2d 152 (1997); Attorney Grievance Comm'n v. Chang, 346 Md. 215, 695 A.2d 198 (1997); Attorney Grievance Comm'n v. Gordon, 346 Md. 237, 695 A.2d 1226 (1997); Attorney Grievance Comm'n v. Dean, 346 Md. 243, 696 A.2d 439 (1997); Attorney Grievance Comm'n v. Brown, 346 Md. 252, 696 A.2d 443 (1997); Attorney Grievance Comm'n v. Beckman, 346 Md. 370, 697 A.2d 110 (1997);

Attorney Grievance v. Wilson, 348 Md. 177, 702 A.2d 776 (1997); Attorney Grievance Comm'n of Md. v. Clubb, 348 Md. 178, 702 A.2d 928 (1997); Attorney Grievance Comm'n v. Goerl, 348 Md. 335, 703 A.2d 1267 (1998); Attorney Grievance Comm'n v. Gross, 348 Md. 336, 703 A.2d 1267 (1998); Attorney Grievance Comm'n v. Atkins, 348 Md. 361, 704 A.2d 420 (1998); Attorney Grievance Comm'n v. Williams, 348 Md. 362, 704 A.2d 420 (1998); Attorney Grievance Comm'n v. George, 348 Md. 721, 705 A.2d 1164 (1998).

Rule 16-714. Termination — Modification — Reinstatement.

a. *Petition — Where filed.* A petition to modify or terminate a suspension or for termination of inactive status or for reinstatement shall be filed in the Court of Appeals.

b. *Content.* The petition shall set forth facts showing that the petitioner is rehabilitated and is otherwise entitled to the relief sought. The petition shall be verified. It shall also include a docket reference to all prior proceedings with respect to the charges.

c. *Service of petition.* The petition shall be served on the Bar Counsel. The petition also shall be served in the manner the Court of Appeals directs upon the party who filed the charges and upon any other person designated by the Court of Appeals.

d. *Procedure.* 1. Dismissal without hearing. Upon receipt of a petition for reinstatement or for modification or termination of suspension or inactive status, the Court of Appeals may consider any written evidence submitted with the petition and the prior proceedings with respect to the charges and may dismiss the petition without a hearing or reserve judgment until after a hearing. The remaining provisions of this section do not apply if the petition is dismissed without a hearing.

2. Reservation of judgment pending hearing. If the Court of Appeals reserves judgment until after a hearing, the Bar Counsel shall conduct an appropriate investigation and shall refer the petition to an Inquiry Panel selected by the Chairman of the Inquiry Committee. Thereafter the petition shall be heard and determined by the Inquiry Panel in accordance with section d of Rule 16-706 (Complaints and Investigations—Inquiry Panel Proceedings) and shall be reviewed by the Review Board in accordance with Rule 16-707 (Review Procedure). The Bar Counsel shall transmit to the Court of Appeals the recommendations of the Review Board and any evidence.

3. Subsequent pleadings — Hearings — Disposition. The provisions of section e of Rule 16-709 (Charges — Pleadings), Rule 16-710 (Hearing), and section b of Rule 16-711 (Disposition of Charges—Subsequent Proceedings) are applicable to proceedings instituted pursuant to this Rule.

4. Burden of proof. The burden is upon the petitioner to establish the averments of the petition by clear and convincing proof.

5. Conviction of crime — Adjudication of misconduct. The provisions of section e of Rule 16-710 (Hearing — Conviction of Crime — Adjudication of Misconduct), are applicable to proceedings instituted pursuant to this Rule.

e. Duty of Clerk. 1. Regarding an attorney admitted by the Court of Appeals. With regard to an attorney admitted by the Court of Appeals to practice law, upon entry of an order reinstating the attorney after disbarment, resignation, or inactive status, or reducing the period of the attorney's suspension, the Clerk of the Court of Appeals shall replace the name of the attorney upon the register of attorneys in that Court.

2. Regarding an attorney not admitted by the Court of Appeals. With regard to an attorney not admitted by the Court of Appeals to practice law, upon entry of an order reinstating the attorney after disbarment or reducing the period of the attorney's suspension, the Clerk of the Court of Appeals shall strike the name of the attorney from the list maintained in that Court of non-admitted attorneys who are excluded from exercising the privilege of practicing law in this State.

3. Certification by Clerk. Whenever the Clerk of the Court of Appeals replaces a name on the register pursuant to subsection 1 of this section, the Clerk shall certify that fact to the Trustees of the Clients' Security Trust Fund and the clerks of all judicial tribunals in this State. Whenever the Clerk strikes a name from the list pursuant to subsection 2 of this section, the Clerk shall certify that fact to the Board of Law Examiners and the clerks of all judicial tribunals in this State. (Amended Apr. 7, 1986, effective Jan. 1, 1987; June 5, 1996, effective Jan. 1, 1997.)

Source. — This Rule is former Rule BV14.

Effect of amendments. — The 1996 amendment, in the second sentence of d 2, substituted "Rule 16-706" for "Rule BV6" and substituted "Rule 16-707" for "Rule BV7"; in the first sentence of d 3, substituted "Rule 16-709" for "Rule BV9," substituted "Rule 16-710" for "Rule BV10," and substituted "Rule 16-711" for "Rule BV11"; in d 5, substituted "Rule 16-710" for "Rule BV10"; and added the Source note.

Editor's note. — An Order dated June 5, 1996, effective Jan. 1, 1997, renumbered this Rule, which was formerly Rule BV14.

Maryland Law Review. — For comment, "Discipline of Attorneys in Maryland," see 35 Md. L. Rev. 236 (1975).

University of Baltimore Law Review. — For article, "The Maryland Rules — A Time for Overhaul," see 9 U. Balt. L. Rev. 1 (1979).

Purpose of disbarment is not to punish attorney, but to protect public. In re Barton, 291 Md. 61, 432 A.2d 1335 (1981).

Disbarment of an attorney does not operate as a permanent disability. In re Petition for Reinstatement to Practice Law of Braverman, 271 Md. 196, 316 A.2d 246 (1974).

Application for reinstatement involves new inquiry as to whether in the interval following the rendering of the judgment of disbarment the petitioner has become a proper person to be admitted as an attorney. In re Loker, 285 Md. 645, 403 A.2d 1269 (1979).

Burden of establishing the averments of a petition under this Rule is a heavy one. In re Petition for Reinstatement to Practice Law of Braverman, 271 Md. 196, 316 A.2d 246 (1974).

The more serious the original misconduct, the heavier is the burden to prove present fitness for readmission to the bar. In re Raimondi, 285 Md. 607, 403 A.2d 1234 (1979), cert. denied, 444 U.S. 1033, 100 S. Ct. 705, 62 L. Ed. 2d 669 (1980).

Essential factors to be evaluated in considering petition for reinstatement include: the nature and circumstances of petitioner's original misconduct, his subsequent conduct and reformation, and his present character. In re Braverman, 269 Md. 661, 309 A.2d 468 (1973).

The four principal factors to be considered in evaluating a petition for reinstatement to the bar are: (1) the nature and circumstances of the original misconduct; (2) petitioner's subsequent conduct and reformation; (3) his present character and (4) his present qualifications and competence to practice law. In re Raimondi, 285 Md. 607, 403 A.2d 1234 (1979),

329

cert. denied, 444 U.S. 1033, 100 S. Ct. 705, 62 L. Ed. 2d 669 (1980); In re Barton, 291 Md. 61, 432 A.2d 1335 (1981).

Whether petitioner is presently qualified and competent to practice law in light of long absence from the Maryland Bar is another essential factor to be evaluated in assessing the matter of his rehabilitation and determining whether he is a proper person to be readmitted to the practice of law. In re Braverman, 269 Md. 661, 309 A.2d 468 (1973).

When a petition for readmission to the Bar is considered, the concern is whether the court can be assured that the public can rely on the competence and integrity of the previously disbarred attorney. In re Barton, 273 Md. 377, 329 A.2d 102 (1974).

While disbarment does not necessarily operate as a permanent disability, it may only be overcome by a clear and convincing showing of rehabilitation and of legal competence, borne out by an applicant's conduct over a long period of time. In re Barton, 291 Md. 61, 432 A.2d 1335 (1981).

Where an applicant for readmission has not satisfied any of the required fourfold criteria set forth in In re Braverman, 271 Md. 196, 316 A.2d 246 (1974) and In re Barton, 273 Md. 377, 329 A.2d 102 (1974), his petition for reinstatement is properly denied. In re Posner, 291 Md. 686, 436 A.2d 464 (1981).

To be reinstated, one need not express "contrition" which is inconsistent with a position to which he honestly and sincerely adheres. In re Barton, 273 Md. 377, 329 A.2d 102 (1974).

Petition denied. — Misappropriation by an attorney of funds of others entrusted to his care, be the amount small or large, is of great concern and represents the gravest form of professional misconduct where such activity was spread over a number of years and involved a substantial sum of money, so any petition for reinstatement will be denied. In re Loker, 285 Md. 645, 403 A.2d 1269 (1979).

Where petitioner was convicted of an attempt to bribe in connection with a highly unusual situation in which the General Assembly was obliged to elect a Governor to serve a little more than two years of the remaining term of the Governor previously elected by the people, such conduct strikes at the very fundamentals of the state government (the more so when it is perpetrated by a member of the bar sworn to support the Constitution and laws of this State), and his petition for reinstatement to the bar will be denied. In re Raimondi, 285 Md. 607, 403 A.2d 1234 (1979), cert. denied, 444 U.S. 1033, 100 S. Ct. 705, 62 L. Ed. 2d 669 (1980).

Where greed alone would seem to have been the only reason behind petitioner's previous crime, his petition for reinstatement will be denied. In re Raimondi, 285 Md. 607, 403 A.2d 1234 (1979), cert. denied, 444 U.S. 1033, 100 S. Ct. 705, 62 L. Ed. 2d 669 (1980).

Rule 16-715. Costs.

a. *General.* Except as provided in section b of this Rule, all court costs in proceedings under this Chapter shall be paid by the State unless the Court of Appeals shall direct otherwise.

b. *Proceedings under Rule 16-714.* In proceedings under Rule 16-714 (Termination — Modification — Reinstatement), all court costs shall be paid by the attorney filing the petition, except to the extent that the Court of Appeals directs otherwise.

c. *Judgment.* Costs of proceedings under this Chapter shall be taxed by the Clerk of the Court of Appeals and included in the order as a judgment. The action of the Clerk may be reviewed by the Court of Appeals on motion.

d. *Bad faith.* The provisions of Rule 1-341 apply to proceedings under this Chapter. (Amended Apr. 6, 1984, effective July 1, 1984; June 5, 1996, effective Jan. 1, 1997.)

Source. — This Rule is former Rule BV15.

Effect of amendments. — The 1996 amendment substituted "Chapter" for "Subtitle" in a, c and d; substituted "Rule 16-714" for "Rule BV14" in b; and added the Source note.

Editor's note. — An Order dated June 5, 1996, effective Jan. 1, 1997, renumbered this Rule, which was formerly Rule BV15.

University of Baltimore Law Review. —

For article, "The Maryland Rules — A Time for
Overhaul," see 9 U. Balt. L. Rev. 1 (1979).

Rule 16-716. Suspension upon conviction of certain crimes.

a. *Filing charges.* 1. Application. This Rule shall apply to convictions in any one or more of the following categories: (i) in any Maryland court of a felony, (ii) in any federal court of a felony, unless the same crime also is a crime under Maryland law and is not a felony, (iii) in any other judicial tribunal of a crime which would have been a felony under Maryland law had the crime been committed in Maryland, and (iv) in any judicial tribunal of any other crime punishable by imprisonment for three years or more.

2. Duty of Bar Counsel — Evidence. If an attorney is convicted of a crime to which this Rule is made applicable pursuant to Rule 16-716 a 1, whether the conviction results from a plea of guilty or of *nolo contendere* or from a verdict after trial, and regardless of the pendency of an appeal or any other post-conviction proceeding, the Bar Counsel shall file charges with the Court of Appeals alleging the fact of the conviction and requesting that the attorney be suspended from the practice of law. A certified copy of the judgment of conviction shall be attached to the charges and shall be *prima facie* evidence of the fact that the attorney was convicted of the crime charged.

b. *Order.* The Court of Appeals shall issue an order to show cause why the attorney should not be suspended from the practice of law until the further order of the Court of Appeals. Upon consideration of the charges and the answer to the order to show cause the Court of Appeals may enter an order, effective immediately, suspending the attorney from the practice of law until its further order. The provisions of Rule 16-713 apply to the suspension.

c. *Further proceedings.* In any case in which the Court of Appeals has entered an order suspending an attorney until its further order, pursuant to this Rule, further proceedings on the charges shall be conducted pursuant to Rules 16-709 (Charges), 16-710 (Hearings) and 16-711 (Disposition of Charges), to determine whether the crime warrants discipline and if so, the extent thereof. If the attorney has appealed from his conviction, the hearing shall be delayed until completion of the appellate process. If the conviction is reversed at any stage of the appellate process, the suspension shall be terminated. If after the completion of the appellate process, the conviction has not been reversed, or if the attorney does not seek appellate review of the conviction, the hearing shall be held within a reasonable time after the mandate is issued, or, if no appellate review is sought, within a reasonable time after the expiration of the time for appeal from the conviction. However, if the attorney is incarcerated following termination of the appellate process or expiration of the time for an appeal (if no appeal has been taken), the hearing shall be set within a reasonable time following termination of incarceration unless the attorney.

(i) requests an earlier hearing; and

(ii) makes all arrangements, including financial arrangements, for his presence at the earlier hearing on the date set by the Court. (Amended Sept. 10, 1975, effective Feb. 20, 1975; May 5, 1976, effective July 1, 1976; May 5, 1978, effective July 1, 1978; June 5, 1996, effective Jan. 1, 1997.)

Source. — This Rule is former Rule BV16.

Effect of amendments. — The 1996 amendment substituted "Rule 16-716 a 1" for "Rule BV16" in the first sentence of a 2; substituted "Rule 16-713" for "Rule BV13" in the last sentence of b; in the first sentence of c, substituted "Rules 16-709 (Charges), 16-710 (Hearings) and 16-711" for "Rules BV9 (Charges), BV10 (Hearings) and BV11"; and added the Source note.

Editor's note. — An Order dated June 5, 1996, effective Jan. 1, 1997, renumbered this Rule, which was formerly Rule BV16.

Maryland Law Review. — For comment, "Discipline of Attorneys in Maryland," see 35 Md. L. Rev. 236 (1975).

For article, "The Law of Disbarment and Reinstatement in Maryland," see 36 Md. L. Rev. 703 (1977).

University of Baltimore Law Review. — For article, "The Maryland Rules — A Time for Overhaul," see 9 U. Balt. L. Rev. 1 (1979).

Constitutionality of Rule. — This Rule does not run afoul of the right or privilege of an attorney to practice law within the protection of the Fourteenth Amendment to the federal Constitution or the Maryland Declaration of Rights. Attorney Grievance Comm'n v. Reamer, 281 Md. 323, 379 A.2d 171 (1977).

Rule does not make suspension mandatory, but makes it discretionary in the Court of Appeals pending resolution of an appeal. Attorney Grievance Comm'n v. Klauber, 283 Md. 597, 391 A.2d 849 (1978).

Interim suspension provisions not violative of due process. — It is not a deprivation of due process that the interim suspension provisions of this Rule operate prior to the exhaustion of the appellate process because due process neither requires nor guarantees appellate review of a criminal conviction. Attorney Grievance Comm'n v. Reamer, 281 Md. 323, 379 A.2d 171 (1977).

Reason for the adoption of this Rule is to protect the public from acts of that attorney pending a determination of the propriety of his conviction and, in the event of an affirmance of that conviction involving a crime of moral turpitude, the ultimate determination by this Court of whether the attorney should be disciplined and, if so, the form of the discipline to be imposed. Attorney Grievance Comm'n v. Andresen, 279 Md. 250, 367 A.2d 1251 (1977).

Purpose of 1978 amendment. — Because the Court of Appeals came to recognize the difficulties inherent in this Rule regarding suspension for a crime involving moral turpitude, it was for that reason that in 1978 the Court amended this Rule to permit suspension of an attorney upon conviction of certain crimes. Attorney Grievance Comm'n v. Klauber, 283 Md. 597, 391 A.2d 849 (1978).

1978 amendment not to be applied retrospectively. — In adopting the 1978 amendment to this Rule, nothing was said by the Court of Appeals to indicate that it was to be applied retrospectively to acts occurring prior to its effective date (July 1, 1978). Attorney Grievance Comm'n v. Klauber, 284 Md. 306, 396 A.2d 253 (1979).

Revised Rule prospective in application. — This revised Rule is not to be applied to convictions taking place prior to its effective date (July 1, 1978). Attorney Grievance Comm'n v. Bailey, 285 Md. 631, 403 A.2d 1261 (1979).

Mail fraud. — Jury's finding of guilt of mail fraud and aiding and abetting in a mail fraud, in light of the allegations of the indictment that the attorney procured false and fraudulent medical reports and bills, clearly indicates that the attorney's convictions were within the contemplation of this Rule. Attorney Grievance Comm'n v. Reamer, 281 Md. 323, 379 A.2d 171 (1977).

Breaking and entering in combination with other crimes. — Pleading guilty to the crimes of breaking and entering the dwelling house of another and to cruelly killing an animal, warranted an immediate suspension. Attorney Grievance Comm'n v. Protokowicz, 326 Md. 714, 607 A.2d 33 (1992).

Quoted in Attorney Grievance Comm'n v. Gittens, 346 Md. 316, 697 A.2d 83 (1997).

Cited in Attorney Grievance Comm'n v. Brown, 347 Md. 152, 699 A.2d 1167 (1997).

Rule 16-717. Conservator of clients' affairs.

a. *Where applicable.* Whenever an attorney has been disbarred, suspended or placed on an inactive status or has disappeared, and no responsible party capable of conducting the affairs of the attorney is known to exist, the Bar Counsel may seek the appointment of a conservator.

b. *Petition and order.* Any petition by the Bar Counsel for the appointment of a conservator under this Rule shall be filed in the county of the last office for the practice of law of the attorney whose affairs are the subject of the petition. Upon such proof of the facts as the court may require, the court may issue an order appointing the Bar Counsel or some other attorney as conservator to inventory the files of the disbarred, suspended, inactive or disappeared attorney and to take such action as seems indicated to protect the interests of his clients until the clients have had an opportunity to obtain substitute counsel.

c. *Confidentiality.* Any attorney so appointed shall not be permitted to disclose any information contained in the files so inventoried without the consent of the client to whom the file relates, except as required to carry out the order of the court. (Added Feb. 10, 1975, effective Feb. 20, 1975; amended Apr. 6, 1984, effective July 1, 1984; June 5, 1996, effective Jan. 1, 1997.)

Source. — This Rule is former Rule BV17.

Effect of amendments. — The 1996 amendment added the Source note.

Editor's note. — An Order dated June 5, 1996, effective Jan. 1, 1997, renumbered this Rule, which was formerly Rule BV17.

University of Baltimore Law Review. —

For article, "The Maryland Rules — A Time for Overhaul," see 9 U. Balt. L. Rev. 1 (1979).

Cited in Frederick Rd. Ltd. Partnership v. Brown & Sturm, 121 Md. App. 384, 710 A.2d 298 (1998).

Rule 16-718. Audit of attorney's accounts and records.

a. *Application for audit.* Upon petition filed by (i) the Clients' Security Trust Fund of the Bar of Maryland or (ii) the Bar Counsel, an equity court in the county where an attorney resides or has his principal office, may, after reasonable notice and upon a showing of good cause, order any of the accounts and records of an attorney required to be kept by law or Rule to be audited by a Certified Public Accountant designated by the court.

b. *Form of application and notice.* 1. Titling of case. The proceeding shall be titled "In Re: Application for Audit of an Attorney's Accounts and Records."

2. Nondisclosure of name. The petition shall not divulge the name of the attorney against whom the petition is filed.

3. Show cause order. Notice to the attorney shall be given by a show cause order which shall be served in such manner as the court may direct so as to preserve the confidentiality of the proceeding.

c. *Records — Clerk.* 1. Dockets. The clerk shall keep a separate docket with an index for proceedings under this Rule, which shall not be open to inspection by any person, including the parties, except upon an order of court for good cause shown.

2. Sealing of records. The pleadings and other papers in the proceeding shall be sealed at the time they are filed, and shall not be open to inspection by any person, including the parties, except upon an order of court for good cause shown.

d. *Method of audit — Confidentiality.* The order directing the audit shall expressly require that the audit be conducted and a report be made in such manner as to preserve the confidential relation between the attorney and his clients.

e. *Cost of audit.* The court, in its discretion, may order the cost of the audit and of the proceeding to be paid in whole or in part by any party to the proceeding; provided, that the cost of the audit or of the proceeding or any part thereof shall not be assessed against the attorney in any case where the audit fails to disclose any irregularity.

f. *Finality.* An order granting or denying the application is a final order.

g. *Other proceedings.* Nothing contained in this Rule nor the pendency of a proceeding hereunder shall preclude any person having an interest in a fund held by an attorney from pursuing any legal or equitable remedy or cause of action he may have with respect thereto. (Added July 1, 1974; amended Feb. 10, 1975, effective July 1, 1975; June 5, 1996, effective Jan. 1, 1997; Dec. 10, 1996, effective Jan. 1, 1997.)

Committee note. — See Md. Rule 16-812 (Maryland Rules of Professional Conduct, Rule 1.15); Md. Code, Article 10, § 44; § 7-106, Real Property Article; and *Andresen v. Bar Ass'n,* 269 Md. 313, 305 A.2d 845 (1973).

Source. — This Rule is former Rule BV18.

Effect of amendments. — The 1975 amendment renumbered this Rule, which was formerly Rule BV11, and substituted "the Bar Counsel" for "a Bar Association, as defined in Rule BV1 b," in section a.

The first 1996 amendment substituted "Rule 16-812" for "Rule 1230" in the Committee note; and added the Source note.

The second 1996 amendment substituted "(Maryland Rules of Professional Conduct, Rule 1.15)" for "(Code of Professional Responsibility, DR 9-102)" in the Committee note.

Editor's note. — An Order dated June 5, 1996, effective Jan. 1, 1997, renumbered this Rule, which was formerly Rule BV18.

University of Baltimore Law Review. — For article, "The Maryland Rules — A Time for Overhaul," see 9 U. Balt. L. Rev. 1 (1979).

Issuance of subpoenas. — The Court of Appeals by rule may allow for the issuance of subpoenas by Bar Counsel and the Chair of the Inquiry Panel. 82 Op. Att'y Gen. (January 6, 1997).

CHAPTER 800. MISCELLANEOUS.

Rule 16-801. Promulgation of rules.

a. *Promulgation by Rules Order.* Rules of the Court of Appeals shall be promulgated by a Rules Order approved by a majority of the members of the Court of Appeals.

b. *Rules committee.* To assist the Court of Appeals in developing rules in the exercise of its rule-making power, the Court has appointed a standing committee on rules of practice and procedure, usually and herein referred to as the "Rules Committee," composed of judges, lawyers and persons familiar with judicial administration appointed for a three year term or at the Court's pleasure. The Court has also appointed a member of the bar to serve as Reporter to the Rules Committee, and from time to time, such assistant or special reporters as may be required to assist the Rules Committee in discharging its assigned responsibilities. Unless otherwise determined by the Court of Appeals, every suggestion for the adoption, amendment, or rescission of a rule shall be referred to the Rules Committee for consideration. The Rules Committee may also consider rules changes on its own initiative, and shall make its recommendations with respect to rules changes to the Court of Appeals by two or more written reports each year, submitted on or before

March 31 and September 30. A copy of each report shall be transmitted to the Maryland Register for publication under a thirty day notice of proposed rules changes soliciting public comment.

Cross references. — See §§ 13-301 to 13-303 of the Courts Article of the Annotated Code of Maryland.

Committee note. — The Rules Committee was originally appointed by order of the Court of Appeals dated January 22, 1946, to succeed an *ad hoc* predecessor Committee on Rules of Practice and Procedure appointed by order of the Court dated March 5, 1940.

c. *Publication of rules changes.* Unless the Court of Appeals determines that some emergency requires the promulgation of a rules change to take effect prior to either of the dates specified in section d of this Rule, a copy of every Rules Order adopting, amending, or rescinding a rule shall be published in the Maryland Register at least thirty days before its effective date under a notice of rules changes, and may also be published in such other publication as the Court of Appeals may direct. A Rules Order adopting or amending a rule in the form previously published in the Maryland Register as a proposed rule change shall cite the number and page of the Maryland Register on which the proposed rules change appears, and in that case the text of the rule adopted or amended need not be re-published with the order of adoption or amendment. If, however, the Court of Appeals should further amend a rule proposed for adoption or amendment during the course of the rule-making process, either in response to comment received, or of its own motion, the full text of the rule or amendment as adopted and showing such further amendment shall be republished with the Rules Order.

If the Court of Appeals determines that an emergency exists and that a rules change is required to take effect prior to either of the dates specified in section d of this Rule, it shall direct such special publication as it considers appropriate to notify the judiciary, the clerks and members of the bar.

d. *Effective date of rules changes.* Unless the Court of Appeals determines that an emergency exists, and otherwise directs, rules changes shall become effective not earlier than the first day of January or the first day of July, whichever first occurs after the entry and appropriate publication of the order promulgating the rules changes.

e. *Record of rules.* The Clerk of the Court of Appeals shall maintain a separate record designated as the "Maryland Rules of Procedure," which shall contain all rules and amendments adopted by the Court. (Added May 5, 1976, effective July 1, 1976; amended Nov. 5, 1976, effective Jan. 1, 1977; Apr. 6, 1984, effective July 1, 1984; Nov. 19, 1987, effective July 1, 1988; June 5, 1996, effective Jan. 1, 1997.)

Source. — This Rule is former Rule 1225.

Effect of amendments. — The 1996 amendment added the Source note.

Editor's note. — An Order dated June 5, 1996, effective Jan. 1, 1997, renumbered this Rule, which was formerly Rule 1225.

Section c of this Rule does not apply to local or circuit rules; this Rule, like its predecessor, former Rule 4, by its very terms applies only to the Court of Appeals. Walker v. Haywood, 65 Md. App. 1, 498 A.2d 1198 (1985).

Rule 16-802. Maryland Judicial Conference.

a. *Conference established — Objectives.* There is a Judicial Conference, known as "The Maryland Judicial Conference," to consider the status of judicial business in the various courts, to devise means for relieving congestion of dockets where it may be necessary, to consider improvements of practice and procedure in the courts, to consider and recommend legislation, and to exchange ideas with respect to the improvement of the administration of justice in Maryland and the judicial system in Maryland.

COMMENT

This is former Rule 1226 a 1, without substantive change.

b. *Membership.* The members of the Judicial Conference are the judges of the:
1. Court of Appeals of Maryland;
2. Court of Special Appeals;
3. Circuit courts of the counties and the Supreme Bench of Baltimore City;
4. The District Court of Maryland.

COMMENT

This is former Rule 1226 a 2 without substantive change.

c. *Chairman and vice-chairman.* 1. The Chief Judge of the Court of Appeals of Maryland is the chairman of the Judicial Conference.

2. At its annual session, the Judicial Conference shall elect a vice-chairman, who shall have all the powers and duties of the chairman, but who shall serve only at the direction of the chairman, or in his absence.

COMMENT

This combines former Rule 1226 a 4 and 5 as to the chairman and vice-chairman, but deletes the provisions of a 4 with respect to committees of the Conference. New provisions as to committees appear in section f of the proposed rule. See also section d 1 (b) (2). The last sentence of former Rule 1226 a 4 is omitted as unnecessary, in light of Maryland Rule 16-801.

d. *Executive Committee of Maryland Judicial Conference.* 1. Establishment — Duties. (a) There is an Executive Committee of the Judicial Conference. The Executive Committee consists of 18 members.

(b) Between plenary sessions of the Maryland Judicial Conference, the Executive Committee shall perform the functions of the Conference and shall:

(1) Submit recommendations for the improvement of the administration of justice in Maryland to the Chief Judge, the Court of Appeals, and the full Conference, as appropriate. The Executive Committee may also submit recommendations to the Governor, the General Assembly, or both of them, but

these recommendations shall be transmitted through the Chief Judge and the Court of Appeals, and shall be forwarded to the Governor or General Assembly, or both, with any comments or additional recommendations deemed appropriate by the Chief Judge or the Court.

(2) Establish committees of the Judicial Conference pursuant to Section f of this Rule, and approve and coordinate the work of those committees.

(3) Plan educational programs to improve the administration of justice in Maryland.

(4) Plan sessions of the Conference in conjunction with the Conference Chairman.

2. Members. (a) The 17 elected members of the Executive Committee are a circuit court and a District Court judge from each of the first seven judicial circuits; a judge of the Supreme Bench of Baltimore City and a judge of the District Court from the Eighth Judicial Circuit; and a judge of the Court of Special Appeals. For purposes of this Rule, the Chief Judge of the District Court is considered to be a judge of the District Court from the judicial circuit in which he resides.

(b) The Chief Judge of the Court of Appeals is a member of the Executive Committee *ex officio* without vote.

3. Terms. Subject to the provisions of paragraph 5 of this section, an elected member of the Executive Committee serves a two-year term and until his successor is elected. The term begins on July 1 and ends on June 30. An elected member may not serve more than two consecutive two-year terms in any six-year period.

4. Elections. (a) Not later than May 1 of each year, the executive secretary of the Conference shall advise the Chief Judge of the Court of Special Appeals, each circuit administrative judge, and the Chief Judge of the District Court of the number of members of the Executive Committee from each court and in each judicial circuit to be elected in that year.

(b) Not later than June 1 of each year, the Court of Special Appeals shall elect the Executive Committee member to which it is entitled in that year. The method of election shall be as determined by that court.

(c) Not later than June 1 of each year, the judges of the circuit courts in each judicial circuit (and of the Supreme Bench of Baltimore City in the Eighth Judicial Circuit) and of the District Court in each judicial circuit shall elect the members of the Executive Committee to which they, respectively, are entitled in that year. The methods of election for circuit court/Supreme Bench judges shall be as determined by the judges of those courts within each judicial circuit. The methods of election of District Court judges shall be as determined by the judges of that court within each judicial circuit.

(d) Promptly after the elections, the Court of Special Appeals, the circuit administrative judge of each judicial circuit, and the Chief Judge of the District Court shall advise the executive secretary of the individuals selected from his court level.

5. Vacancies. (a) If a vacancy occurs on the Executive Committee because an elected member resigns from the Committee, leaves judicial office, or is appointed or elected to a judicial office other than the office he held when

elected to the Committee, the executive secretary shall promptly notify the Chief Judge of the Court of Special Appeals, if the vacated position was held by a judge of that court; the circuit administrative judge of the appropriate judicial circuit, if the vacated position was held by a judge of a circuit court or of the Supreme Bench of Baltimore City; or the Chief Judge of the District Court if the vacated position was held by a judge of that court.

(b) Within 30 days after the notification, the individual notified shall cause an election to be held by the judges of the Court of Special Appeals, the judges of the circuit court or of the Supreme Bench within the appropriate judicial circuit, or the judges of the District Court within the appropriate circuit, so that the vacancy shall be filled by election of a judge from the same court or court level as that from which his predecessor had been elected. The executive secretary shall be notified promptly of the individual elected. The individual elected serves for the unexpired balance of his predecessor's term, and until his successor is elected.

6. Chairman and vice-chairman. (a) The elected members of the Executive Committee shall elect annually, from among their members, a chairman and vice-chairman, to serve until the June 30 following their election, and until their successors are elected.

(b) A vacancy in the chairmanship or vice-chairmanship shall be filled by election by the Executive Committee members from among its elected members. The individual elected to fill the vacancy serves for the unexpired balance of his predecessors' term, and until his successor is elected.

COMMENT

These provisions replace former Rule 1226 a 6. They establish the basic duties and responsibilities of the proposed Executive Committee, and provide for the members, their terms, and elections, the filling of vacancies, and for a chairman and vice-chairman elected by Committee members.

e. *Secretariat.* The Administrative Office of the Courts is the secretariat for the Conference and for all of its committees, including the Executive Committee. The State Court Administrator is the Executive Secretary of the Conference.

COMMENT

This is former Rule 1226 a 3, without substantive change.

f. *Committees.* 1. Establishment. In consultation with the chairman of the Judicial Conference, the Executive Committee shall establish the committees of the Conference it considers necessary or desirable from time to time.

2. Appointment. In consultation with the Chairman of the Judicial Conference, the Chairman of the Executive Committee shall appoint the chairman and members of each committee.

3. Duties. Each committee shall meet at the time or times its chairman designates to receive, discuss and consider suggestions pertaining to its area of responsibility. Each committee shall make reports to the Executive Committee

as required by the Committee, and shall submit an annual report to the Judicial Conference through the Executive Committee.

COMMENT

This provides for establishment and appointment of committees by the Executive Committee and its chairman, in consultation with the chairman of the Conference, and for committee reports. It replaces and enlarges upon portions of former Rule 1226 a 4, and also embodies certain existing practices.

g. *Sessions of the conference.* The Conference shall meet in general session at least once a year at the time and place designated by the Executive Committee, unless otherwise ordered by the Court of Appeals. Each session of the Conference shall be for the number of days the work of the Conference may require.

COMMENT

This is in substance former Rule 1226 a 7. (Amended June 28, 1971, effective Sept. 1, 1971; June 1, 1981; Nov. 7, 1990; June 5, 1996, effective Jan. 1, 1997.)

Source. — This Rule is former Rule 1226.

Effect of amendments. — The 1996 amendment substituted "Rule 16-801" for "Rule 1225" in the last sentence of the Comment in c.; and added the Source note.

Editor's note. — An Order dated June 5, 1996, effective Jan. 1, 1997, renumbered this Rule, which was formerly Rule 1226.

Maryland Law Review. — For note, "Discipline of Judges in Maryland," see 34 Md. L. Rev. 612 (1974).

Rule 16-803. Commission on judicial disabilities — Definitions.

The following definitions apply in Rules 16-804 through 16-810 except as expressly otherwise provided or as necessary implication requires:

(a) *Charges.* "Charges" means the charges filed with the commission by Investigative Counsel pursuant to Rule 16-808.

(b) *Commission.* "Commission" means the Commission on Judicial Disabilities.

(c) *Complainant.* "Complainant" means a person who has filed a complaint.

(d) *Complaint.* "Complaint" means a written communication under affidavit signed by the complainant, alleging facts indicating that a judge has a disability or has committed sanctionable conduct.

Committee note. — The complainant may comply with the affidavit requirement of this section by signing a statement in the following form: "I solemnly affirm under the penalties of perjury that the contents of the foregoing paper are true to the best of my knowledge, information, and belief." It is not required that the complainant appear before a notary public.

(e) *Disability.* "Disability" means a mental or physical disability that seriously interferes with the performance of a judge's duties and is, or is likely to become, permanent.

(f) *Judge.* "Judge" means a judge of the Court of Appeals, the Court of Special Appeals, a circuit court, the District Court, or an orphans' court.

339

(g) *Sanctionable conduct.* "Sanctionable conduct" means misconduct while in office, the persistent failure by a judge to perform the duties of the judge's office, or conduct prejudicial to the proper administration of justice. It includes any conduct constituting a violation of the Maryland Code of Judicial Conduct promulgated by Rule 16-813. An erroneous ruling, finding, or decision in a particular case does not alone constitute sanctionable conduct. (Added May 9, 1995, effective July 1, 1995; amended June 5, 1996, effective Jan. 1, 1997.)

Cross references. — For powers of the Commission in regard to any investigation or proceeding under § 4B of article IV of the Constitution, see Code, CJ §§ 13-401 to 13-403.

Canon 6 B. of the Maryland Code of Judicial Conduct provides that "[v]iolation of any of the provisions of this Code of Judicial Conduct by a judge may be regarded as conduct prejudicial to the proper administration of justice within the meaning of Maryland Rule 16-803 g of the Rules concerning the Commission on Judicial Disabilities."

Committee note. — The phrase "misconduct while in office" includes misconduct committed by a judge while in active service who then resigns or retires and misconduct by a retired judge during any period that the retired judge has been recalled to temporary active service pursuant to Code, Courts Article, § 1-302.

Source. — This Rule is former Rule 1227 (adopted 1995).

Effect of amendments. — The 1996 amendment rewrote the Rule heading; substituted "Rules 16-804 through 16-810" for "Rules 1227A through 1227G" in the introductory language; substituted "Rule 16-808" for "Rule 1227E" in (a); substituted "Rule 16-813" for "Rule 1231" in the second sentence of (g); substituted "Rule 16-803 g" for "Rule 1227 g" in the Cross reference note; and rewrote the Source note.

Editor's note. — An Order dated June 5, 1996, effective Jan. 1, 1997, renumbered this Rule, which was formerly Rule 1227.

Maryland Law Review. — For note, "Discipline of Judges in Maryland," see 34 Md. L. Rev. 612 (1974).

Rule was adopted pursuant to direction contained in former § 45 of Article 40. In re Formal Inquiry Concerning Diener, 268 Md. 659, 304 A.2d 587 (1973), cert. denied, 415 U.S. 989, 94 S. Ct. 1586, 39 L. Ed. 2d 885 (1974).

Power to conduct preliminary investigation on own motion. — Commission on Judicial Disabilities has the power, on its own motion, to conduct a preliminary investigation concerning a complaint against a judge which has been brought to its attention. In re Formal Inquiry Concerning Diener, 268 Md. 659, 304 A.2d 587 (1973), cert. denied, 415 U.S. 989, 94 S. Ct. 1586, 39 L. Ed. 2d 885 (1974).

Power to recommend censure. — The grant to the Commission on Judicial Disabili-

ties of the greater power to recommend retirement or removal impliedly includes the lesser power to recommend censure. In re Formal Inquiry Concerning Diener, 268 Md. 659, 304 A.2d 587 (1973), cert. denied, 415 U.S. 989, 94 S. Ct. 1586, 39 L. Ed. 2d 885 (1974).

Notice held sufficient. — See In re Formal Inquiry Concerning Diener, 268 Md. 659, 304 A.2d 587 (1973), cert. denied, 415 U.S. 989, 94 S. Ct. 1586, 39 L. Ed. 2d 885 (1974).

Judge's failure to disclose loan from bail bondsman. — Where a judge borrowed money from a bail bondsman and failed to include information relative to this loan in his financial disclosure statements for the two years during which the loan was outstanding, Rule 8 of the former Rules of Judicial Ethics was violated and the judge was subject to censure. In re Hormes, 291 Md. 673, 436 A.2d 457 (1981).

Rules of evidence inapplicable in Commission proceedings. — The ordinary rules of evidence do not apply in a proceeding before the Judicial Disabilities Commission. In re Bennett, 301 Md. 517, 483 A.2d 1242 (1984).

Indictment by grand jury not required for Commission to bring charges against judge. — Failure of the grand jury to indict a judge does not prevent the bringing of charges by the Judicial Disabilities Commission. In re Bennett, 301 Md. 517, 483 A.2d 1242 (1984).

Rule 16-804. Commission.

(a) *Chair and acting chair.* The Commission shall select one of its members to serve as Chair. If the Chair is disqualified or otherwise unable to act, the commission shall select one of its members to serve as acting chair.

(b) *Interested member.* A member of the Commission shall not participate as a member in any proceeding in which that member is a complainant or in which that member's sanctionable conduct or disability is in issue.

Cross references. — See Md. Const., Article IV, § 4B (a), providing that the Governor shall appoint a substitute member of the Commission for the purpose of a proceeding against a member of the Commission.

(c) *Executive Secretary.* The Commission may select an attorney as Executive Secretary. The Executive Secretary shall serve at the pleasure of the Commission, have the administrative powers and duties assigned by the Commission, and receive the compensation set forth in the budget of the Commission.

(d) *Investigative Counsel; assistants.* The Commission shall appoint an attorney to serve as Investigative Counsel. Investigative Counsel shall serve at the pleasure of the Commission, have the powers and duties set forth in these rules, report to the Commission as directed by the Commission, and receive the compensation set forth in the budget of the Commission. As the need arises and to the extent funds are available in the Commission's budget, the Commission may appoint additional attorneys or other persons to assist Investigative Counsel. Investigative Counsel shall keep an accurate record of the time and expenses of additional persons employed and ensure that the cost does not exceed the amount allocated by the Commission.

(e) *Quorum.* The presence of a majority of the members of the Commission constitutes a quorum for the transaction of business. The concurrence of a majority of the members is required for all action taken by the Commission other than adjournment of a meeting for lack of a quorum.

(f) *Record.* The Commission shall keep a record of all proceedings concerning a judge.

(g) *Annual report.* The Commission shall submit an annual report to the Court of Appeals, not later than September 1, regarding its operations and including statistical data with respect to complaints received and processed, subject to the provisions of Rule 16-810.

(h) *Home address of judges.* Upon request by the Commission or the Chair of the Commission, the Administrative Office of the Courts shall supply to the Commission the current home address of each judge. (Added May 9, 1995, effective July 1, 1995; amended June 5, 1996, effective Jan. 1, 1997; Dec. 10, 1996, effective Jan. 1, 1997.)

Source. — This Rule is former Rule 1227A.

Effect of amendments. — The first 1996 amendment substituted "Rule 16-810" for "Rule 1227G" in (g); and rewrote the Source note.

The second 1996 amendment substituted "a majority of the" for "four" twice in (e).

Editor's note. — An Order dated June 5, 1996, effective Jan. 1, 1997, renumbered this Rule, which was formerly Rule 1227A.

Section (e) of this Rule provides that four members of the Commission on Judicial Disabilities constitute a quorum for the transaction of business. Pending before the Court of Appeals at press-time is the One-Hundred Thirty-Fifth Report of the Court's Standing Committee on Rules of Practice and Procedure which recommends an amendment to this Rule in light of Art. IV, §§ 4A and 4B of the Maryland Constitution as amended by Chapter 113, Acts 1995, which was approved by the voters on November 5, 1996.

Rule 16-805. Complaints; preliminary investigations.

(a) *Complaints.* All complaints against a judge shall be sent to Investigative Counsel. Investigative Counsel shall number and open a file on each complaint received and promptly in writing shall (1) acknowledge receipt of the complaint and (2) explain to the complainant the procedure for investigating and processing the complaint. Upon receiving from a person information that does not qualify as a complaint but indicates that a judge may have a disability or have committed sanctionable conduct, Investigative Counsel shall, if possible, (1) inform the person providing the information of his or her right to file a complaint and (2) if the information received does not comply with the verification requirement of Rule 16-803 (d), (A) inform the person providing the information that the complaint must be verified and (B) provide to the person the appropriate form of affidavit.

(b) *Preliminary investigation.* (1) If Investigative Counsel concludes that the complaint is frivolous on its face, Investigative Counsel shall dismiss the complaint and notify the complainant, the Commission, and, upon request, the judge of the action. Otherwise, Investigative Counsel shall conduct a preliminary investigation to determine whether reasonable grounds exist to believe the allegations of the complaint.

(2) Upon receipt of information from any source indicating that a judge has a disability or has committed sanctionable conduct, Investigative Counsel, without a complaint, may make an inquiry and, following the inquiry, may undertake a preliminary investigation. Investigative Counsel shall number and open a file on each preliminary investigation undertaken under this subsection and shall promptly inform the Commission that the investigation is being undertaken.

(3) Upon application by Investigative Counsel and for good cause, the Commission may authorize Investigative Counsel to issue a subpoena to obtain evidence during a preliminary investigation.

(4) Unless directed otherwise by the Commission for good cause, Investigative Counsel, before the conclusion of the preliminary investigation, shall notify the judge who is the subject of the investigation (A) that Investigative Counsel has undertaken a preliminary investigation into whether the judge has a disability or has committed sanctionable conduct; (B) whether the preliminary investigation was undertaken on Investigative Counsel's initiative or on a complaint; (C) if the investigation was undertaken on a complaint, of the name of the person who filed the complaint; (D) of the nature of the disability or sanctionable conduct under investigation; and (E) that before the preliminary investigation is concluded, the judge may present to Investigative

Counsel, in person or in writing, any information the judge may wish to present. The notice shall be given by first class mail and by certified mail requesting "Restricted Delivery — show to whom, date, address of delivery" addressed to the judge at the judge's last known home address.

(5) Before the conclusion of the preliminary investigation and in accordance with the notice, Investigative Counsel shall afford the judge a reasonable opportunity to present, in person or in writing, such information as the judge chooses to present.

(6) Unless the time is extended by the Commission for good cause, Investigative Counsel shall complete a preliminary investigation (A) undertaken as the result of a complaint within 60 days after receiving the complaint and (B) undertaken on the initiative of Investigative Counsel within 60 days after the investigation is commenced.

(c) *Recommendation by investigative counsel.* Upon the conclusion of a preliminary investigation, Investigative Counsel shall report the results of the investigation to the Commission in such form as the Commission requires. Investigative Counsel shall recommend that (1) any complaint be dismissed and the investigation terminated, (2) the judge be offered a private reprimand by the Commission or a deferred discipline agreement, (3) the Commission authorize a further investigation, or (4) charges be filed against the judge and the Commission conduct a formal proceeding on the charges. (Added May 9, 1995, effective July 1, 1995; amended June 5, 1996, effective Jan. 1, 1997.)

Source. — This Rule is former Rule 1227B.

Effect of amendments. — The 1996 amendment substituted "Rule 16-803(d)" for "Rule 1227(d)" in (a); and rewrote the Source note.

Editor's note. — An Order dated June 5, 1996, effective Jan. 1, 1997, renumbered this Rule, which was formerly Rule 1227B.

Rule 16-806. Further investigation.

(a) *Notice to judge.* Upon approval of a further investigation by the Commission, Investigative Counsel shall notify the judge who is the subject of the investigation (1) that the Commission has authorized the further investigation, (2) of the nature of the disability or sanctionable conduct under investigation, including each Canon of Judicial Conduct allegedly violated by the judge, and (3) that the judge may file a written response. The notice shall be given (1) by first class mail and by certified mail addressed to the judge at the judge's last known home address, or (2) if previously authorized by the judge, by first class mail to an attorney designated by the judge. If authorized by the Commission for good cause, Investigative Counsel may defer the giving of notice, but if notice is deferred, notice must be given a reasonable time before Investigative Counsel makes a recommendation as to disposition.

(b) *Subpoenas.* (1) In a further investigation, upon application by Investigative Counsel, the Commission may authorize Investigative Counsel to issue a subpoena to compel the attendance of witnesses and the production of documents or other tangible things at a time and place specified in the subpoena. In addition to giving any other notice required by law, promptly after service of the subpoena Investigative Counsel shall provide notice of its service to the judge under investigation. The notice to the judge shall be sent by first class mail to the judge's last known home address or, if previously authorized by the judge, by first class mail to an attorney designated by the judge.

(2) On motion of the judge or the person served with the subpoena filed promptly and, whenever practicable, at or before the time specified in the subpoena for compliance, the circuit court for the county in which the subpoena was served or, if the judge under investigation is a judge serving on that circuit court, another circuit court designated by the Commission may enter any order permitted by Rule 2-510 (e). Upon a failure to comply with a subpoena issued pursuant to this Rule, the court, on motion of Investigative Counsel, may compel compliance with the subpoena.

(3) To the extent practicable, a subpoena shall not divulge the name of the judge under investigation. Files and records of the court pertaining to any motion filed with respect to a subpoena shall be sealed and shall be open to inspection only upon order of the Court of Appeals. Hearings before the circuit court on any motion shall be on the record and shall be conducted out of the presence of all persons except those whose presence is necessary.

(4) The Commission, in accordance with Md. Constitution, Art. IV, § 4B (a), may grant immunity from prosecution or from penalty or forfeiture to any person compelled to testify and produce evidence.

(c) *Completion and recommendation.* Unless the time is extended by the Commission for good cause, Investigative Counsel shall complete a further investigation within 60 days after it is authorized by the Commission. Upon completion, Investigative Counsel shall report the results of the investigation to the Commission in the form that the Commission requires. Investigative Counsel shall recommend that (1) any complaint be dismissed and the investigation terminated, (2) the judge be offered a private reprimand or a deferred discipline agreement, or (3) charges be filed and the Commission conduct a formal proceeding. (Added May 9, 1995, effective July 1, 1995; amended June 5, 1996, effective Jan. 1, 1997.)

Source. — This Rule is former Rule 1227C.

Effect of amendments. — The 1996 amendment rewrote the Source note.

Editor's note. — An Order dated June 5, 1996, effective Jan. 1, 1997, renumbered this Rule, which was formerly Rule 1227C.

Rule 16-807. Disposition without proceedings on charges.

(a) *Dismissal.* The Commission shall dismiss a complaint and terminate the proceeding if, after an investigation, it concludes that (1) the evidence fails to show that the judge has a disability or has committed sanctionable conduct, or (2) any sanctionable conduct that may have been committed by the judge is not likely to be repeated and was not sufficiently serious to warrant discipline. The Commission shall notify the judge and any complainant of the dismissal. The

Commission may accompany a dismissal under subsection (a) (2) of this Rule with a warning against further sanctionable conduct.

Committee note. — A warning by the Commission under this section is not a reprimand and does not constitute discipline.

(b) *Private reprimand.* (1) The Commission may issue a private reprimand to the judge if, after an investigation:

(A) the Commission concludes that the judge has committed sanctionable conduct that warrants some form of discipline;

(B) the Commission further concludes that the sanctionable conduct was not so serious, offensive, or repeated to warrant formal proceedings and that a private reprimand is the appropriate disposition under the circumstances; and

(C) the judge, in writing on a copy of the reprimand retained by the Commission, (i) waives the right to a hearing before the Commission and subsequent proceedings before the Court of Appeals and the right to challenge the findings that serve as the basis for the private reprimand, and (ii) agrees that the reprimand shall not be protected by confidentiality in any subsequent disciplinary proceeding against the judge.

(2) Upon the issuance of a private reprimand, the Commission shall notify the complainant of that disposition.

(c) *Deferred discipline agreement.* (1) The Commission and the judge may enter into a deferred discipline agreement if, after a preliminary or further investigation:

(A) The Commission concludes that the alleged sanctionable conduct was not so serious, offensive, or repeated to warrant formal proceedings and that the appropriate disposition is for the judge to undergo specific treatment, participate in one or more specified educational programs, issue an apology to the complainant, or take other specific corrective action; and

(B) The judge, in the agreement, (i) agrees to the specified conditions, (ii) waives the right to a hearing before the Commission and subsequent proceedings before the Court of Appeals, and (iii) agrees that the deferred discipline agreement shall not be protected by confidentiality in any subsequent disciplinary proceeding against the judge.

(2) The Commission shall direct Investigative Counsel to monitor compliance with the conditions of the agreement and may direct the judge to document compliance. If, after written notice to the judge of the nature of any alleged failure to satisfy and, after affording the judge a minimum 15 day opportunity to present any information or explanation that the judge chooses, the Commission finds that the judge has failed to satisfy a material condition of the agreement, the Commission may revoke the agreement and proceed with any other disposition authorized by these rules. The agreement shall specifically authorize the Commission to proceed in accordance with this paragraph.

(3) The Commission shall notify the complainant that the complaint has resulted in an agreement with the judge for corrective action, but, unless the judge consents in writing, shall not inform the complainant of the terms of the agreement. (Added May 5, 1995, effective July 1, 1995; amended June 5, 1996, effective Jan. 1, 1997.)

Source. — This Rule is former Rule 1227D.

Effect of amendments. — The 1996 amendment rewrote the Source note.
Editor's note. — An Order dated June 5, 1996, effective Jan. 1, 1997, renumbered this Rule, which was formerly Rule 1227D.

Rule 16-808. Proceedings before commission.

(a) *How commenced; caption.* After considering any recommendation of Investigative Counsel and upon a finding by the Commission of probable cause to believe that a judge has a disability or has committed sanctionable conduct, the Commission may direct Investigative Counsel to initiate proceedings against the judge by filing with the Commission charges that the judge has a disability or has committed sanctionable conduct. The charges shall (1) state the nature of the alleged disability or sanctionable conduct, including each Canon of Judicial Conduct allegedly violated by the judge, (2) specify the alleged facts upon which the charges are based, and (3) state that the judge has the right to file a written response to the charges within 30 days after service of the charges.

(b) *Service; notice.* A copy of the charges shall be delivered to the judge by a competent private person as defined in Rule 2-123 (a) or by certified mail. If it appears to the Commission that, after reasonable effort for a period of ten days, personal delivery cannot be made, service may be made upon the judge by any other means of service the Commission deems appropriate in the circumstances and reasonably calculated to give actual notice. A return of service of the charges shall be filed with the Commission pursuant to Rule 2-126. Upon service, the Commission shall send notice to any complainant that charges have been filed against the judge.

Cross references. — See Md. Const., Article IV, § 4B (a).

(c) *Response.* Within 30 days after service of the charges, the judge may file with the Commission an original and seven copies of a response.

(d) *Exchange of information.* Unless ordered otherwise by the Commission for good cause:

(1) Upon request of the judge at any time after service of charges upon the judge, Investigative Counsel shall promptly (A) allow the judge to inspect and copy all evidence accumulated during the investigation and all statements as defined in Rule 2-402 (d) and (B) provide to the judge summaries or reports of all oral statements for which contemporaneously-recorded substantially-verbatim recitals do not exist, and

(2) Not later than 10 days before the hearing, Investigative Counsel and the judge shall each provide to the other a list of the names, addresses, and telephone numbers of the witnesses that each intends to call and copies of the documents that each intends to introduce in evidence at the hearing.

(e) *Hearing.* (1) Upon the filing of a response or upon expiration of the time for filing it, the Commission shall notify the judge of the time and place of a hearing. If the hearing is on a charge of sanctionable conduct, the Commission shall also notify the complainant. The notices shall be mailed at least 30 days before the date set for the hearing.

(2) At the hearing, Investigative Counsel shall present evidence in support of the charges.

(3) The Commission may proceed with the hearing whether or not the judge has filed a response or appears at the hearing.

(4) The hearing shall be conducted in accordance with the rules of evidence in Code, State Govt. Art., § 10-213.

(5) The proceedings at the hearing shall be stenographically or electronically recorded. Except as provided in Section (j) of this Rule, the Commission is not required to have a transcript prepared. The judge may, at the judge's expense, have the recording of the proceedings transcribed.

(f) *Procedural rights of judge.* The judge has the right to be represented by an attorney, to the issuance of a subpoena for the attendance of witnesses and for the production of designated documents and other tangible things, to present evidence and argument, and to examine and cross-examine witnesses.

Cross references. — For the right of the Commission to issue subpoenas, see Code, Courts Article, § 13-401.

(g) *Amendments.* At any time before its decision, the Commission on motion of Investigative Counsel or the judge or on its own initiative may allow amendments to the charges or the response. The charges or the response may be amended to conform to proof or to set forth additional facts, whether occurring before or after the commencement of the hearing, except that, if the amendment changes the character of the disability or sanctionable conduct alleged, the consent of the judge and Investigative Counsel is required. If an amendment to the charges is made, the judge shall be given a reasonable time to respond to the amendment and to prepare and present any defense.

(h) *Extension of time.* The Commission may extend the time for filing a response and for the commencement of a hearing.

(i) *Commission findings and action.* If the Commission finds by clear and convincing evidence that the judge has a disability or has committed sanctionable conduct, it shall either issue a public reprimand for the sanctionable conduct or refer the matter to the Court of Appeals pursuant to section (j) of this Rule. Otherwise, it shall dismiss the charges filed by the Investigative Counsel and terminate the proceeding.

(j) *Record.* If the Commission refers the case to the Court of Appeals, it shall:

(1) make written findings of fact and conclusions of law with respect to the issues of fact and law in the proceeding, state its recommendations as to retirement or as to censure, removal, or other appropriate discipline, and enter those findings and recommendations in the record;

(2) cause a transcript of all proceedings at the hearing conducted by the Commission to be prepared and included in the record;

(3) make the transcript of testimony available for review by the judge and the judge's attorney in connection with the proceedings or, at the judge's request, provide a copy to the judge at the judge's expense;

(4) file with the Court of Appeals the entire record in the proceedings including any dissenting or concurring statement by a Commission member, certified by the Chair of the Commission; and

(5) promptly serve upon the judge notice of the filing of the record and a copy of the Commission's findings, conclusions, and recommendations and any dissenting or concurring statement by a Commission member. Service shall be made by certified mail addressed to the judge's last known home address or, if previously authorized by the judge, to an attorney designated by the judge. (Added May 9, 1995, effective July 1, 1995; amended June 5, 1996, effective Jan. 1, 1997.)

Source. — This Rule is former Rule 1227E.

Effect of amendments. — The 1996 amendment rewrote the Source note.

Editor's note. — An Order dated June 5, 1996, effective Jan. 1, 1997, renumbered this Rule, which was formerly Rule 1227E.

Rule 16-809. Proceedings in Court of Appeals.

(a) *Exceptions.* The judge may except to the findings, conclusions, or recommendation of the Commission by filing with the Court of Appeals eight copies of exceptions within 30 days after service of the notice of filing of the record. The exceptions shall set forth with particularity all errors allegedly committed by the Commission and the disposition sought. A copy of the exceptions shall be served on the Commission in accordance with Rules 1-321 and 1-323.

(b) *Response.* The Commission shall file eight copies of a response within 15 days after service of the exceptions. Unless the Commission appoints another counsel for the purpose, it shall be represented in the Court of Appeals by its Executive Secretary. A copy of the response shall be served on the judge in accordance with Rules 1-321 and 1-323.

(c) *Hearing.* If exceptions are filed, upon the filing of a response or the expiration of the time for filing it, the Court shall set a schedule for filing memoranda in support of the exceptions and response and a date for a hearing. The hearing on exceptions shall be conducted in accordance with Rule 8-522. If no exceptions are filed or if the judge files with the Court a written waiver of the judge's right to a hearing, the Court may decide the matter without a hearing.

(d) *Disposition.* The Court of Appeals may (1) impose the sanction recommended by the Commission or any other sanction permitted by law; (2) dismiss the proceeding; or (3) remand for further proceedings as specified in the order of remand.

(e) *Decision.* The decision shall be evidenced by the order of the Court of
Appeals, which shall be certified under the seal of the Court by the Clerk and
shall be accompanied by an opinion. Unless the case is remanded to the
Commission, the record shall be retained by the Clerk of the Court of Appeals.

(f) *Interested member of the Court of Appeals.* A judge who is a member of the
Court of Appeals shall not participate in any proceeding in that court in which
the disability or sanctionable conduct of that judge is in issue. (Added May 9,
1995, effective July 1, 1995; amended June 5, 1996, effective Jan. 1, 1997.)

Source. — This Rule is former Rule 1227F.

Effect of amendments. — The 1996
amendment rewrote the Source note.
Editor's note. — An Order dated June 5,
1996, effective Jan. 1, 1997, renumbered this
Rule, which was formerly Rule 1227F.

Rule 16-810. Confidentiality.

(a) *Generally.* Except as otherwise expressly provided by these rules, proceedings and information relating to a complaint or charges shall be confidential or public, as follows:

(1) Before service of charges. Before service of charges upon the judge, all
proceedings by and before the Commission shall be confidential, including all
information relating to a complaint.

(2) Upon service charges. Upon service of charges alleging sanctionable
conduct, whether or not joined with charges of disability, the charges and all
subsequent proceedings before the Commission on them shall be public. If the
charges allege only that the judge has a disability, the charges and all
proceedings before the Commission on them shall be confidential.

(3) Work product and deliberations. Investigative counsel's work product
and records not admitted into evidence before the Commission, the Commission's deliberations, and records of the Commission's deliberations shall be
confidential.

(4) Proceedings in the Court of Appeals. Unless otherwise ordered by the
Court of Appeals, the record of Commission proceedings filed with that Court
and any proceedings before that Court shall be public.

(b) *Permitted release of information by Commission.* (1) Written waiver. The
Commission may release confidential information upon a written waiver by
the judge.

(2) Explanatory statement. The Commission may issue a brief explanatory
statement necessary to correct any unfairness to a judge or any public
misperception about the Commission or about actual or possible proceedings
before it.

(3) Nominations; appointments; approvals. (A) Permitted disclosures.
Upon a written application made by a judicial nominating commission, a Bar
Admission authority, the President of the United States, the Governor of a

state, territory, district, or possession of the United States, or a committee of the General Assembly of Maryland or of the United States Senate which asserts that the applicant is considering the nomination, appointment, confirmation, or approval of a judge or former judge, the Commission shall disclose to the applicant:

(i) Information about any complaints or charges that did not result in dismissal, including reprimands and deferred discipline agreements; and

(ii) The mere fact that a complaint is pending.

(B) Restrictions. When the Commission furnishes information to an applicant under this section, the Commission shall furnish only one copy of the material and it shall be furnished under seal. As a condition to receiving the material, the applicant shall agree (i) not to copy the material or permit it to be copied; (ii) that when inspection of the material has been completed, the applicant shall seal and return the material to the Commission; and (iii) not to disclose the contents of the material or any information contained in it to anyone other than another member of the applicant.

(C) Copy to judge. The Commission shall send the judge a copy of all documents disclosed under this subsection. (Added May 9, 1995, effective July 1, 1995; amended June 5, 1996, effective Jan. 1, 1997.)

Cross references. — For the powers of the Commission in an investigation or proceeding under Md. Const., Article IV, § 4B, see Code, Courts Article, §§ 13-401, 402, and 403.

Source. — This Rule is former Rule 1227G.

Effect of amendments. — The 1996 amendment rewrote the Source note.

Editor's note. — An Order dated June 5, 1996, effective Jan. 1, 1997, renumbered this Rule, which was formerly Rule 1227G.

Rule 16-811. Clients' Security Fund.

a. *Promulgation of Rule.* This Rule, to be known as the "Clients' Security Fund Rule of the Court of Appeals of Maryland," is promulgated pursuant to Chapter 779, Laws of Maryland (1965).

Cross references. — See Code, BOP §§ 10-310 et seq.

b. *Creation, operation, and purpose of trust fund.* 1. Creation. A trust fund, to be known as the "Clients' Security Trust Fund of the Bar of Maryland" (hereinafter referred to as "the trust fund"), is hereby authorized and created.

2. Operation. The trust fund shall be operated and administered in accordance with this Rule by nine trustees, appointed as hereinafter provided. The trustees shall be known as the "Trustees of the Clients' Security Trust Fund of the Bar of Maryland."

3. Purpose. The purpose of the trust fund shall be to maintain the integrity and protect the good name of the legal profession by reimbursing, to the extent authorized by this Rule and deemed proper and reasonable by the trustees, losses caused by defalcations of members of the Bar of the State of Maryland or out-of-state attorneys authorized to practice in this State under Rule 15 of

the Rules Governing Admission to the Bar, acting either as attorneys or as fiduciaries (except to the extent to which they are bonded). (Amended July 3, 1980; June 22, 1990.)

c. *Appointment and compensation of trustees and officers.* 1. Number. There shall be nine trustees appointed by this Court, eight to be members of the Bar of this State, and one who shall not be a member of the Bar.

2. Appointment. One trustee who is a member of the Bar of this State shall be appointed from each of the seven appellate judicial circuits. The eighth trustee who is a member of the Bar and the trustee who is not a member of the Bar shall be appointed at large. Each appointment shall be for a term of seven years. (Amended June 4, 1979, effective July 1, 1979; June 5, 1995, effective July 1, 1995.)

3. Officers. The trustees shall from time to time elect from their membership a chairman, a treasurer and such other officers as they deem necessary or appropriate.

4. Removal. A trustee may be removed by the Court at any time in its discretion.

5. Vacancies. Vacancies shall be filled by appointment by the Court for the unexpired term.

6. Compensation. The trustees shall serve without compensation, but shall be entitled to reimbursement from the trust fund, if no other source of funds is available, for their expenses reasonably incurred in performance of their duties as trustees, including transportation costs.

d. *Powers and duties of trustees.* 1. Additional powers and duties. In addition to the powers granted elsewhere in this Rule, the trustees shall have the following powers and duties:

(i) To receive, hold, manage, and distribute, pursuant to this Rule, the funds raised hereunder, and any other monies that may be received by the trust fund through voluntary contributions or otherwise.

(ii) To authorize payment of claims in accordance with this Rule.

(iii) To adopt regulations for the administration of the trust fund and the procedures for the presentation, consideration, recognition, rejection and payment of claims, and to adopt bylaws for conducting business. A copy of such regulations shall be filed with the clerk of this Court, who shall mail a copy of them to the clerk of the circuit court for each county and to all Registers of Wills.

(iv) To enforce claims for restitution, arising by subrogation or assignment or otherwise.

(v) To invest the trust fund, or any portion thereof, in such investments as they may deem appropriate, and to cause funds to be deposited in any bank, banking institution or federally insured savings and loan association in this State, provided however, that the trustees shall have no obligation to cause the trust fund or any portion thereof to be invested.

(vi) To employ and compensate consultants, agents, legal counsel and employees.

(vii) To delegate the power to perform routine acts which may be necessary or desirable for the operation of the trust fund, including the power to authorize disbursements for routine operating expenses of the trust fund, but authorization for payments of claims shall be made only as provided in section i (Claims) of this Rule.

(viii) To sue or be sued in the name of the trust without joining any or all individual trustees.

(ix) To perform all other acts necessary or proper for fulfillment of the purposes of the trust fund and its efficient administration.

2. Report and audit — Filing. At least once each year, and at such additional times as the Court may order, the trustees shall file with this Court a written report, which shall include the audit made pursuant to subsection 3 of section j (Powers of Court of Appeals — Audits) of this Rule of the management and operation of the trust fund. (Amended June 5, 1995, effective July 1, 1995.)

e. *Meetings and quorum.* 1. Time. Meetings of the trustees shall be held at the call of the chairman or a majority of the trustees, and shall be held at least once each year, upon reasonable notice.

2. Number. Five trustees shall constitute a quorum. A majority of the trustees present at a duly constituted meeting may exercise any powers held by the trustees, except to the extent that this Rule provides otherwise. (Amended June 4, 1979, effective July 1, 1979.)

f. *Payments to fund.* 1. Payment required as condition of practice; exception. Except as otherwise provided in this section, each lawyer admitted to practice before this Court or issued a certificate of special authorization under Rule 15 of Rules Governing Admission to Bar, shall, as a condition precedent to the practice of law (as from time to time defined in Code, Business and Professsions Article) in this State, pay annually to the treasurer of the trust fund the sum, including any late charges, this Court may fix. The trustees may provide in their regulations reasonable and uniform deadline dates for receipt of payments of assessments or applications for change to inactive/retired status. A lawyer on inactive/retired status may engage in the practice of law without payment to the trust fund if (A) the lawyer is on inactive/retired status solely as a result of having been approved for that status by the trustees and not as a result of any action against the attorney pursuant to Title 16, Chapter 700 of these Rules and (B) the lawyer's practice is limited to representing clients without compensation, other than reimbursement of reasonable and necessary expenses, as part of the lawyer's participation in a legal services or pro bono publico program sponsored or supported by a local Bar Association as defined by Rule 16-701 b., the Maryland State Bar Association, an affiliated bar foundation, or the Maryland Legal Services Corporation. (Amended Dec. 8, 1992; Sept. 11, 1995, effective Jan. 1, 1996.)

2. Change of address. It is the obligation of each lawyer to give written notice to the trustees of every change in the lawyer's residence address, business address, or telephone numbers within 30 days of the change. The trustees shall have the right to rely on the latest information received by them for all billing and other correspondence. (Added Sept. 11, 1995, effective Jan. 1, 1996.)

3. Due date. Payments for any fiscal year shall be due on July 1st of each such year. (Amended June 22, 1990; Dec. 8, 1992; Sept 11, 1995, effective Jan. 1, 1996.)

4. Dishonor. If any check to the trust fund in payment of an annual assessment is dishonored, the treasurer of the trust fund shall promptly notify the attorney of the dishonor. The attorney shall be responsible for all additional charges assessed by the trustees. (Amended Aug. 30, 1989; Dec. 8, 1992; Sept. 11, 1995, effective Jan. 1, 1996.)

g. *Enforcement.* 1. List by trustees of unpaid assessments. As soon as practical after January 1, but no later than February 15 of each calendar year, the trustees shall prepare, certify, and file with the Court of Appeals a list showing:

(i) the name and account number, as it appears on their records, of each lawyer who, to the best of their information, is engaged in the practice of law and without valid reason or justification has failed or refused to pay (a) one or more annual assessments, (b) penalties for late payment, (c) any charge for a dishonored check, or (d) reimbursement of publication charges; and

(ii) the amount due from that lawyer to the trust fund.

2. Notice of default by trustees. (i) The trustees shall give notice of delinquency promptly to each lawyer on the list by first class mail addressed to the lawyer at the lawyer's last address appearing on the records of the trustees. The notice shall state the amount of the obligation to the trust fund, that payment is overdue, and that failure to pay the amount to the trust fund within 30 days following the date of the notice will result in the entry of an order by the Court of Appeals prohibiting the lawyer from practicing law in the State.

(ii) The mailing by the trustees of the notice of default shall constitute service.

3. Additional discretionary notice. In addition to the mailed notice, the trustees may give any additional notice to the lawyers on the delinquency list as the trustees in their discretion deem desirable. Additional notice may include publication in one or more newspapers selected by the trustees; telephone, facsimile, or other transmission to the named lawyers; dissemination to local bar associations or other professional associations; posting in State court houses; or any other means deemed appropriate by the trustees. Additional notice may be statewide, regional, local, or personal to a named lawyer as the trustees may direct.

4. Certification of default by trustees; order of decertification by the Court of Appeals. (i) Promptly after expiration of the deadline date stated in the mailed notice, the trustees shall submit to the Court of Appeals a proposed Decertification Order stating the names and account numbers of those lawyers whose accounts remain unpaid. The trustee also shall furnish additional information from their records or give further notice as the Court of Appeals may direct. The Court of Appeals, on being satisfied that the trustees have given the required notice to the lawyers remaining in default, shall enter a Decertification Order prohibiting each of them from practicing law in the State. The trustees shall mail by first class mail a copy of the Decertification Order to each lawyer named in the order at the lawyer's last address as it appears on the records of the trustees. The mailing of the copy shall constitute service of the order.

(ii) A lawyer who practices law after having been served with a copy of the Decertification Order may be proceeded against for contempt of court in accordance with the provisions of Title 15, Chapter 200 (Contempt) and any other applicable provision of law or as the Court of Appeals shall direct.

(iii) Upon written request from any Maryland lawyer, judge, or litigant to confirm whether a Maryland lawyer named in the request has been decertified and has not been reinstated, the trustees shall furnish confirmation promptly by informal means and, if requested, by written confirmation. On receiving confirmation by the trustees that a Maryland lawyer attempting to practice law has been and remains decertified, a Maryland judge shall not permit the lawyer to practice law in the State until the lawyer's default has been cured.

5. Payment. Upon payment in cash or by certified or bank official's check to the trust fund by a lawyer of all amounts due by the lawyer, including all related costs that the Court of Appeals or the trustees may prescribe from time to time, the trustees shall remove the lawyer's name from their list of delinquent lawyers and, if a Decertification Order has been entered, request the Court of Appeals to rescind its Decertification Order as to that lawyer. If requested by a lawyer affected by the action, the trustees shall furnish confirmation promptly.

6. Bad check; interim decertification order. (i) If a check payable to the trust fund is dishonored, the treasurer of the trust fund shall notify the lawyer immediately by the quickest available means. Within 7 business days following the date of the notice, the lawyer shall pay to the treasurer of the trust fund, in cash or by certified or bank official's check, the full amount of the dishonored check plus any additional charge that the trustees in their discretion shall prescribe from time to time.

(ii) The treasurer of the trust fund promptly (but not more often than once each calendar quarter) shall prepare and submit to the Court of Appeals a proposed interim Decertification Order stating the name and account number of each lawyer who remains in default of payment for a dishonored check and related charges. The Court of Appeals shall enter an interim Decertification Order prohibiting the practice of law in the State by each lawyer as to whom it is satisfied that the treasurer has made reasonable and good faith efforts to give notice concerning the dishonored check. The treasurer shall mail by first class mail a copy of the interim Decertification Order to each lawyer named in the order at the lawyer's last address as it appears on the records of the trustees, and the mailing of the copy shall constitute service of the order. (Amended June 5, 1995, effective July 1, 1995.)

7. Notices to clerks. The Clerk of the Court of Appeals shall send a copy of a Decertification Order and rescission order entered pursuant to this Rule to the clerk of the Court of Special Appeals, the clerk of each Circuit Court, the Chief Clerk of the District Court, and the Register of Wills for each county. (Amended Oct. 12, 1970; June 30, 1973, effective July 1, 1973; Nov. 8, 1982, effective Jan. 1, 1983; Dec. 8, 1992; June 7, 1994, effective Oct. 1, 1994.)

h. *Treasurer's duties.* 1. Separate account. The trust fund shall be maintained by the treasurer in a separate account.

2. Disbursements. The treasurer shall disburse monies from the trust fund only upon the action of the trustees pursuant to this Rule.

3. Bond. The treasurer shall file annually with the trustees a bond for the proper execution of the duties of the office of treasurer of the trust fund in an amount established from time to time by the trustees and with such surety as may be approved by the trustees. (Amended Nov. 20, 1984, effective Jan. 1, 1985; Dec. 8, 1992.)

i. *Claims.* 1. Power of trustees. The trustees are invested with the power to determine whether a claim merits reimbursement from the trust fund, and if so, the amount of such reimbursement, the time, place, and manner of its payment, the conditions upon which payment shall be made, and the order in which payments shall be made. The trustees' powers under this section may be exercised only by the affirmative vote of at least five trustees.

2. No rights in fund. No claimant or other person or organization has any right in the trust fund as beneficiary or otherwise.

3. Exercise of discretion — Factors. In exercising their discretion the trustees may consider, together with such other factors as they deem appropriate, the following:

(i) The amounts available and likely to become available to the trust fund for payment of claims.

(ii) The size and number of claims which are likely to be presented in the future.

(iii) The total amount of losses caused by defalcations of any one attorney or associated groups of attorneys.

(iv) The unreimbursed amounts of claims recognized by the trustees in the past as meriting reimbursement, but for which reimbursement has not been made in the total amount of the loss sustained.

(v) The amount of the claimant's loss as compared with the amount of the losses sustained by others who may merit reimbursement from the trust fund.

(vi) The degree of hardship the claimant has suffered by the loss.

(vii) Any negligence of the claimant which may have contributed to the loss.

4. Additional powers of trustees. In addition to other conditions and requirements the trustees may require each claimant, as a condition of payment, to execute such instruments, to take such action, and to enter such agreements as the trustees may desire, including assignments, subrogation agreements, trust agreements and promises to cooperate with the trustees in making and prosecuting claims or charges against any person.

5. Investigation of claims — Assistance. The trustees may request individual lawyers, bar associations, and other organizations of lawyers to assist the trustees in the investigation of claims. (Amended Sept. 15, 1976; July 3, 1980; Dec. 8, 1992.)

j. *Powers of Court of Appeals.* 1. To change rule. This Court may amend, modify, or repeal this Rule at any time without prior notice, and may provide for the dissolution and winding up of the affairs of the trust.

2. Judicial review. A claimant aggrieved by a final determination of the trustees denying his claim may, within 15 days thereafter, file exceptions in the Court of Appeals. The decision of the trustees shall be deemed prima facie correct and the exceptions shall be denied unless it is shown that the decision was arbitrary or capricious, or unsupported by substantial evidence on the

record considered as a whole, or was not within the authority vested in the trustees, or was made upon unlawful procedure, or was unconstitutional or otherwise illegal. In any case in which the Court does not deny the exceptions, it may, with or without a hearing, vacate the decision of the trustees and remand the matter thereto for further proceedings, including where appropriate the taking of additional evidence, as may be specified in the Court's remand order.

3. Arrange audit. The trustees shall arrange for auditing of the accounts of the trust fund by state or private auditors, and this Court may at any time arrange for such an audit to be made. The cost of any such audit shall be paid by the trust fund if no other source of funds is available.

4. Interpret rule. The trustees may apply to this Court for interpretation of this Rule and for advice as to their powers and as to the proper administration of the trust. Any final order issued by this Court in response to any such application shall finally bind and determine all rights with respect to the matters covered therein. (Amended Sept. 15, 1976; June 5, 1996, effective Jan. 1, 1997; Dec. 10, 1996, effective Jan. 1, 1997.)

Source. — This Rule is former Rule 1228.

Effect of amendments. — The first 1996 amendment, in f.1., substituted "Title 16, Chapter 700" for "Subtitle BV" and substituted "Rule 16-701 b" for "Rule BV1 b"; substituted "Title 15, Chapter 200" for "Subtitle P" in g.4.(ii); and added the Source note.

The second 1996 amendment substituted "nine" for "eight" in the first sentence of b 2.

Editor's note. — An Order dated June 5, 1996, effective Jan. 1, 1997, renumbered this Rule, which was formerly Rule 1228.

Maryland Law Review. — For note on rules governing the administration of Clients' Security Trust Fund in Maryland, see 26 Md. L. Rev. 369 (1966).

University of Baltimore Law Review. — For article, "The Maryland Rules — A Time for Overhaul," see 9 U. Balt. L. Rev. 1 (1979).

Narrow interpretation. — The history of the Clients' Security Trust Fund suggests a carefully tailored and rather narrow expansion of the desire to provide some protection to clients from defalcations by their attorneys, rather than a broad-brush attempt to compensate for any type of loss caused by an attorney. Monumental Life Ins. Co. v. Trustees of Clients' Sec. Trust Fund, 322 Md. 442, 588 A.2d 340 (1991).

Eligibility for reimbursement. — To be eligible for reimbursement by the Clients' Security Trust Fund a claimant must be the client of, or in a fiduciary relationship with, the defaulting attorney. Monumental Life Ins. Co. v. Trustees of Clients' Sec. Trust Fund, 322 Md. 442, 588 A.2d 340 (1991).

Fiduciary for non-client. — An attorney acts as a fiduciary for a non-client within the meaning of § 10-312 (b) (1) of the Business Occupations and Professions Article and section (b) (3) of this Rule when the attorney disburses client funds from the attorney's trust account to a non-client, at the instructions of the client and pursuant to the obligations recognized in Rule 1.15 of the Rules of Professional Conduct. Advance Fin. Co. v. Trustees of Clients' Sec. Trust Fund, 337 Md. 195, 652 A.2d 660 (1995).

Claim that former Rule BV2 (now Rule 16-702) and this Rule are impermissible taxes may or may not be correct, but even if the point is well taken, it would not be an excuse for unethical conduct on the part of a member of the bar, nor would it be a defense to charges relative to such conduct. Attorney Grievance Comm'n v. Kerpelman, 288 Md. 341, 420 A.2d 940 (1980), cert. denied, 450 U.S. 970, 101 S. Ct. 1492, 67 L. Ed. 2d 621 (1981).

Trustees are granted wide discretion. Folly Farms I, Inc. v. Trustees of Clients' Sec. Trust Fund, 282 Md. 659, 387 A.2d 248 (1978).

In exercising their discretion, the trustees are to consider a number of factors, including the amounts available and likely to become available to the trust fund for payment of claims, the size and number of claims likely to be presented, the total amount of losses caused by defalcations of any one attorney, the unreimbursed amounts of claims recognized by the trustees in the past as meriting reimbursement but for which reimbursement has not been made in the total amount of the loss sustained, the amount of the claimant's loss as compared with the amount of the losses sustained by others who may merit reimbursement from the trust fund, the degree of hardship the claimant has suffered by the loss, and any negligence of the claimant which may have contributed to the loss. Folly Farms I, Inc. v. Trustees of Clients' Sec. Trust Fund, 282 Md. 659, 387 A.2d 248 (1978).

It is not negligence under subsection i 3 of this Rule to trust one's attorney in the absence of facts which put one on notice or ought to put the client on notice that inquiry should be made. Folly Farms I, Inc. v. Trustees of Clients' Sec. Trust Fund, 282 Md. 659, 387 A.2d 248 (1978).

Deprivation of right to counsel. — Defendant was not deprived of his constitutional right to counsel because the lawyer who conducted his defense was then under suspension from the practice of law in Maryland for fail-

ure to pay an annual assessment required by law. Jones v. State, 328 Md. 654, 616 A.2d 422 (1992).

"Defalcation." — Converting the funds of a client, or the funds held for another in a fiduciary capacity, clearly comes within the meaning of "defalcation"; however, obtaining money from a third party by means of a fraud does not. Monumental Life Ins. Co. v. Trustees of Clients' Sec. Trust Fund, 322 Md. 442, 588 A.2d 340 (1991).

Standard of judicial review. — The standard of judicial review of decisions of the trustees of the Clients' Security Trust Fund set forth in section (j) (2) of this Rule is analogous to the standard of review applicable to administrative agencies: whether a reasonable mind could have reached the factual conclusion the agency reached. Advance Fin. Co. v. Trustees of Clients' Sec. Trust Fund, 337 Md. 195, 652 A.2d 660 (1995).

Rule 16-812. Maryland Rules of Professional Conduct.

The Maryland Rules of Professional Conduct, as set forth in Appendix: Rules of Professional Conduct of the Maryland Rules, are hereby adopted. (Added Oct. 13, 1970; amended Dec. 9, 1976, effective Jan. 1, 1977; Mar. 8, 1978, effective May 1, 1978; Apr. 15, 1986, effective Jan. 1, 1987; amended June 5, 1996, effective Jan. 1, 1997.)

Source. — This Rule is former Rule 1230.

Effect of amendments. — The 1996 amendment added the Source note.

Editor's note. — An Order dated June 5, 1996, effective Jan. 1, 1997, renumbered this Rule, which was formerly Rule 1230.

Maryland Law Review. — For article, "Group Legal Services and Canon II," see 34 Md. L. Rev. 541 (1974).

For note, "Applying the Sherman Act to Restrictive Practices of the Legal Profession," see 34 Md. L. Rev. 571 (1974).

For comment, "Discipline of Attorneys in Maryland," see 35 Md. L. Rev. 236 (1975).

For article, "The Law of Disbarment and Reinstatement in Maryland," see 36 Md. L. Rev. 703 (1977).

For article, "Survey of Developments in Maryland Law, 1987-88," see 48 Md. L. Rev. 551 (1989).

University of Baltimore Law Review. — For article on fee schedules and prepaid legal services, see 4 U. Balt. L. Rev. 80 (1974).

For article, "The Maryland Rules — A Time for Overhaul," see 9 U. Balt. L. Rev. 1 (1979).

Purpose of sanctions imposed in disciplinary proceedings. — Sanctions imposed

in disciplinary proceedings against an attorney are not for the purpose of punishing the individual, but are intended as protection to the public. Attorney Grievance Comm'n v. Pattison, 292 Md. 599, 441 A.2d 328 (1982).

Professional service corporations. — When the conduct of a lawyer in a professional service corporation is called into question with reference to the attorney-client relationship, the Rules of Professional Conduct will apply and not those of an ordinary business corporation. Where, however, the situation involves a dispute between shareholders of the professional service corporation, the corporate law should not be disregarded in favor of partnership law. Langhoff v. Marr, 81 Md. App. 438, 568 A.2d 844 (1990), vacated on other grounds and remanded, 322 Md. 657, 589 A.2d 470 (1991).

Attorney accepts clients' moneys and properties in trust. — The relationship existing between an attorney and his client is one that of necessity requires mutual trust and confidence. An attorney accepts moneys and properties belonging to his clients in trust and is strictly accountable for his conduct in administering that trust, so he dares not appropriate those funds and properties for his personal use. The misappropriation by an attorney of funds of others entrusted to his care, be the amount small or large, is of great concern and represents the gravest form of professional misconduct. Attorney Grievance Comm'n v. Pattison, 292 Md. 599, 441 A.2d 328 (1982).

Fiduciary may not make loan to himself. — It is fundamental that a fiduciary, including an attorney administering a decedent's estate, may not make a loan secured or unsecured, unto himself. Attorney Grievance Comm'n v. Pattison, 292 Md. 599, 441 A.2d 328 (1982).

Disbarment sanction for converting funds. — Absent extenuating circumstances, disbarment is the sanction which should be imposed upon an attorney for converting the funds of his client to his own use, even if he intended to repay the funds. Attorney Grievance Comm'n v. Pattison, 292 Md. 599, 441 A.2d 328 (1982).

When defendant tells his attorney before trial that he committed crime charged and the attorney is convinced that his client is telling the truth, the attorney is precluded under this Rule from calling or presenting alibi witnesses who would offer perjured testimony. State v. Lloyd, 48 Md. App. 535, 429 A.2d 244 (1981).

Rule 16-813. Maryland Code of Judicial Conduct.

CANON 1

Integrity and Independence of the Judiciary

An independent and honorable judiciary is indispensable to justice in our society. A judge should observe high standards of conduct so that the integrity and independence of the judiciary may be preserved. The provisions of this Code should be construed and applied to further that objective.

Committee note. — The American Bar Association Model Code of Judicial Conduct ("ABA Code") states that a judge should "participate in establishing, maintaining, and enforcing, and should himself" observe, high standards of conduct so that the integrity and independence of the judiciary may be preserved. The Committee believes that even though desirable, a judge should not be obligated to participate in "establishing" standards of conduct. "Maintaining" and "enforcing" high standards of conduct are dealt with in Canon 3 B (3).

CANON 2

Avoidance of Impropriety and the Appearance of Impropriety

A. A judge should behave with propriety and should avoid even the appearance of impropriety. A judge should respect and comply with the law and should act at all times in a manner that promotes public confidence in the integrity and impartiality of the judiciary. The personal behavior of a judge in both the performance of judicial duties, and in everyday life, should be beyond reproach.

B. A judge should not allow judicial conduct to be improperly influenced by family, social, or other relationships. A judge should not use the prestige of judicial office to advance the private interests of others; nor should a judge convey or permit others to convey the impression that they are in a special position to influence judicial conduct. A judge should not testify voluntarily as a character witness.

COMMENT

Public confidence in the judiciary is eroded by irresponsible or improper conduct by judges. A judge must expect to be the subject of constant public scrutiny. A judge must therefore accept restrictions on his or her conduct that might be viewed as burdensome by the ordinary citizen and should do so freely and willingly.

The testimony of a judge as a character witness injects the prestige of judicial office into the proceeding in which a judge testifies and may be misunderstood to be an official testimonial. This Canon, however, does not afford a judge the privilege against testifying in response to an official summons.

Committee note. — The first and third sentences of Sec. 2A are derived from current Md. Canon IV. ABA Canon 2 relegates the first sentence of Section 2A to Commentary; but the Committee believes that it is sufficiently important to retain its status as part of the Canon. The second sentence of Sec. 2A is derived from ABA Canon 2A.

The first sentence and the second clause of the second sentence of Section 2B are derived from ABA Canon 2B and current Md. Canon XXXII. The first clause of the second sentence of Sec. 2B is derived from ABA Canon 2B and prohibits a judge from advancing the "private interests" of others, while current Md. Ethics Rule 9 applies the prohibition only to "private business interests" of others, which is somewhat narrower in scope. The broader prohibitory language in the ABA Canon is not meant to preclude a judge from writing a letter of recommendation or the like under appropriate circumstances, as discussed in Md. Judicial Ethics Opinion No. 98 (issued 7/16/82).

The last sentence of Sec. 2B is derived from ABA Canon 2B and current Md. Canon XIII.

The first paragraph of the Commentary is derived from a Commentary to ABA Section 2A of Canon 2.

The last paragraph of the Commentary is derived from a Commentary to ABA Canon 2 and is consistent with Md. Judicial Ethics Opinion No. 31 (issued 5/7/75).

C. A judge shall not hold membership in any organization that practices invidious discrimination on the basis of race, sex, religion or national origin.

COMMENT

Membership of a judge in an organization that practices invidious discrimination on the basis of race, sex, religion, or national origin may give rise to perceptions that the judge's impartiality is impaired. It is therefore inappropriate for a judge to continue to hold membership in an organization that the judge knows or reasonably should know, practices and will continue to practice such invidious discrimination so as to give rise to the perception that the judge's impartiality is impaired. Whether an organization practices and will continue to practice that kind of invidious discrimination is often a complex question to which judges should be sensitive. The answer cannot be determined merely from an examination of an organization's current membership rolls but may depend on (1) the nature and purpose of the organization, (2) any restrictions on membership, (3) the history of the organization's selection of members, and (4) other relevant factors such as that the organization is dedicated to the preservation of religious, ethnic or cultural values of legitimate common interests to its members, or that it is in fact, an intimate, purely private organization whose membership limitations could not be constitutionally prohibited. Absent such factors, an organization is generally said to discriminate invidiously if it arbitrarily ex-

cludes from membership on the basis of race, religion, sex or national origin persons who would otherwise be admitted to membership. See New York State Club Ass'n. Inc. v. City of New York, 108 S. Ct. 2225, 101 L. Ed. 2d 1 (1988); Board of Directors of Rotary International v. Rotary Club of Duarte, 481 U.S. 537, 107 S. Ct. 1940 (1987), 95 L. Ed. 2d 474; Roberts v. United States Jaycees, 468 U.S. 609, 104 S. Ct. 3244, 82 L. Ed. 2d 462 (1984).

Although Section 2C relates only to membership in organizations that invidiously discriminate on the basis of race, sex, religion or national origin, a judge's membership in an organization that engages in any discriminatory membership practices prohibited by the law of the jurisdiction also violates Canon 2 and Section 2A and gives the appearance of impropriety. In addition, it would be a violation of Canon 2 and Section 2A for a judge to arrange a meeting at a club that the judge knows practices invidious discrimination on the basis of race, sex, religion or national origin in its membership or other policies, or for the judge to regularly use such a club. Moreover, public manifestation by a judge of the judge's knowing approval of invidious discrimination on any basis gives the appearance of impropriety under Canon 2 and diminishes public confidence in the integrity and impartiality of the judiciary, in violation of Section 2A.

When a person who is a judge on the date this code becomes effective learns that an organization to which the judge belongs engages in invidious discrimination that would preclude membership under Section 2C or under Canon 2 and Section 2A, the judge is permitted, in lieu of resigning, to make immediate efforts to have the organization discontinue its invidiously discriminatory practices, but is required to suspend participation in any other activities of the organization. If the organization fails to discontinue its invidiously discriminatory practices as promptly as possible (and in all events within two years of the judge's first learning of the practices), the judge is required to resign immediately from the organization.

Committee note. — After careful consideration, the Committee decided to make membership in organizations that practice invidious discrimination a violation of the Code. New Section 2C moves to black-letter text a principle that had been in the Commentary to Canon 2 of the 1989 Code. It was determined that it was neither appropriate nor workable to leave to each individual judge's conscience the determination whether an organization practices invidious discrimination, and this discretionary standard was removed from the Commentary.

The Commentary incorporates most of the Commentary to ABA Section 2C of Canon 2. The second sentence of the first paragraph is derived from the Commentary to current Md. Canon 2B and has been retained to make clear that membership in an organization would not be prohibitive unless that membership would reasonably give rise to a perception of partiality. Certain organizations — such as congregational brotherhoods, sisterhoods, bowling leagues, etc. — may well be restricted to persons belonging to the particular congregation and therefore to those sharing a particular religious belief, but it is hardly likely that membership in such an organization would cause people reasonably to believe that the judge is partial.

CANON 3

Impartial and Diligent Performance of Judicial Duties

In the performance of judicial duties, the following standards apply:

A. ADJUDICATIVE RESPONSIBILITIES. (1) A judge should be faithful to the law and maintain professional competence in it.

(2) A judge should be unswayed by partisan interests, public clamor or fear of criticism.

(3) A judge should maintain order and decorum in proceedings before the judge.

(4) A judge should be patient, dignified, and courteous to litigants, jurors, witnesses, lawyers, and others with whom the judge deals in an official capacity and should require similar conduct of lawyers, and of staff, court officials and others subject to the judge's direction and control.

(5) A judge should accord to every person who is legally interested in proceedings, or the person's lawyer, full right to be heard according to law, and, except as authorized by law, neither initiate nor consider ex parte or other communications concerning a pending or impending proceeding. A judge, however, may obtain the advice of a disinterested expert on the law applicable to a proceeding before the judge if the judge gives notice to the parties of the name of the person consulted and the substance of the advice, and affords the parties reasonable opportunity to respond.

COMMENT

The proscription against communications concerning a proceeding includes communications from lawyers, law teachers, and other persons who are not participants in the proceeding, except to the limited extent permitted. It does not preclude a judge from consulting with other judges, or with court personnel whose function is to aid the judge in carrying out adjudicative responsibilities.

An appropriate and often desirable procedure for a court to obtain the advice of a disinterested expert on legal issues is to invite the expert to file a brief *amicus curiae*.

(6) A judge should dispose promptly of the business of the court.

COMMENT

Prompt disposition of the court's business requires a judge to devote adequate time to judicial duties, to be punctual in attending court and expeditious in determining matters under submission, and to insist that court officials, litigants and their lawyers cooperate to that end.

(7) A judge should abstain from public comment about a pending or impending proceeding in any court, and should require similar abstention on the part of court personnel subject to the judge's direction and control. This subsection does not prohibit a judge from making public statements in the course of official duties or from explaining for public information the procedures of the court.

COMMENT

"Court personnel" does not include the lawyers in a proceeding before a judge. The conduct of lawyers in this regard is governed by Rule 3.6 of the Maryland [Lawyers'] Rules of Professional Conduct.

(8) At the conclusion of a jury trial, the judge should neither praise nor criticize the verdict but may thank the jurors for their public service.

(9) A judge shall perform judicial duties without bias or prejudice. A judge shall not, in the performance of judicial duties, by words or conduct manifest bias or prejudice, including but not limited to bias or prejudice based upon race, sex, religion, national origin, disability, age, sexual orientation or socioeconomic status, and shall not permit staff, court officials and others subject to the judge's direction and control to do so.

COMMENT

A judge must refrain from speech, gestures or other conduct that could reasonably be perceived as sexual harassment and must require the same standard of conduct of others subject to the judge's direction and control.

A judge must perform judicial duties impartially and fairly. A judge who manifests bias on any basis in a proceeding impairs the fairness of the proceeding and brings the judiciary into disrepute. Facial expression and body language, in addition to oral communication, can give to parties or lawyers in the proceeding, jurors, the media and others an appearance of judicial bias. A judge must be alert to avoid behavior that may be perceived as prejudicial.

(10) A judge shall require lawyers in proceedings before the judge to refrain from manifesting, by words or conduct, bias or prejudice based upon race, sex, religion, national origin, disability, age, sexual orientation or socioeconomic status, against parties, witnesses, counsel or others. This Section 3B(10) does not preclude legitimate advocacy when race, sex, religion, national origin, disability, age, sexual orientation or socioeconomic status, or other similar factors, are issues in the proceeding.

361

Committee note. — Secs. 3 A (1) and (2) are derived from ABA Canon 3 A (1) and current Md. Canon XIV.

Sec. 3 A (3) is derived from ABA Canon 3 A (2) and current Md. Canon XV.

Sec. 3 A (4) is derived from ABA Canon 3 A (3) and current Md. Canons IX and X.

Sec. 3 A (5) is derived from ABA Canon 3 A (4) and current Md. Canon XVI.

The Commentary to sec. 3 A (5) is derived from the Commentary to ABA Canon 3 A (4) and the Committee note to current Md. Canon XVI.

Sec. 3 A (6) is derived from ABA Canon 3 A (5) and current Md. Canon VII.

The Commentary to sec. 3 A (6) is derived from the Commentary to ABA Canon 3 A (5) and from current Md. Canon VII.

Sec. 3 A (7) is derived from ABA Canon 3 A (6) and current Md. Ethics Rule 12.

The Commentary to sec. 3 A (7) is derived from the Commentary to ABA Canon 3 A (6).

Sec. 3 A (8) is derived from current Md. Ethics Rule 13. There is no ABA provision on this subject.

ABA Canon 3 A (7), current Md. Canon XXXIV, and current Md. Ethics Rule 11 contain provisions governing broadcasting, televising, recording or photographing in courtrooms and adjacent areas. Several states have deleted that provision on the ground that it addresses a question of court administration rather than ethics. The Committee agrees, especially since Rule 1209 of the Md. Rules of Procedure governs media coverage of civil actions, and Md. Code, Art. 27, sec. 467B prohibits (with limited exceptions) media coverage of criminal trials.

Sec. 3A(9) and the Commentary to Sec. 3A(9) are derived from ABA Canon 3B(5) and the Commentary to the Canon of the 1990 ABA Code of Judicial Conduct.

Section 3A(10) is derived from ABA Canon 3B(6) of the 1990 Code.

Section 3A(9) and 3A(10) were added to emphasize the requirements of impartial decision-making and the appearance of fairness in the courtroom.

B. ADMINISTRATIVE RESPONSIBILITIES. (1) A judge shall diligently discharge the judge's administrative responsibilities without bias or prejudice and maintain professional competence in judicial administration, and should cooperate with other judges and court officials in the administration of court business.

COMMENT

Former Section 3B(1) was revised to prohibit a judge from manifesting bias or prejudice in the performance of administrative duties and to encourage, rather than to require, the more practicable duty of cooperation rather than facilitation.

(2) A judge shall require staff, court officials and others subject to direction and control to observe the standards of fidelity and diligence that apply to the judge and to refrain from manifesting bias or prejudice in the performance of their official duties.

COMMENT

Former Section 3B(2) was revised to add the requirement that a judge exercise reasonable direction and control over judicial personnel to assure that they do not manifest bias or prejudice in the performance of their official duties.

(3) A judge should take or initiate appropriate corrective measures against a judge or lawyer for unprofessional conduct of which the judge may be aware.

COMMENT

Corrective measures may include a private admonition or reporting misconduct to the appropriate disciplinary body or a bar association counseling program.

(4) In exercising a power of appointment, a judge should appoint only qualified persons and should avoid nepotism and favoritism. No unnecessary appointments should be made. A judge should not approve compensation of appointees beyond the fair value of services rendered.

COMMENT

Consent by the parties to an appointment or an award of compensation does not relieve the judge of the obligation prescribed by this section.

Committee note. — Sec. 3B(1) is derived from ABA Canon [3B(1)] C(1) of the 1990 Code of Judicial Conduct and current Md. Canon VIII.

Sec. 3B(2) is derived from ABA Canon [3B(2)] 3C(2) of the 1990 Code of Judicial Conduct and current Md. Canon VIII.

The Commentary to Sections 3B(1) and (2) is derived from the Commentary to ABA Canons 3C(1) and (2) of the 1990 Code of Judicial Conduct.

Sec. 3 B (3) is derived from ABA Canon 3 B (3) and current Md. Canon XI, except that those provisions require the judge to take

appropriate "disciplinary" measures. The Committee believes that there may be instances of professional misconduct which would warrant a private admonition or referral to a bar association counseling service, actions which are less drastic than "disciplinary" measures. Requiring a judge to take "corrective" measures, therefore, gives the judge a wider range of options to deal with unprofessional conduct.

The Commentary to sec. 3 B (3) is derived from the Commentary to ABA Canon 3 B (3), but is modified in accordance with the Committee's changes to ABA Canon 3 B (3).

Sec. 3 B (4) is derived from ABA Canon 3 B (4) and current Md. Canon XII.

The Commentary to sec. 3 B (4) is derived from the Commentary to ABA Canon 3 B (4) and from current Md. Canon XII.

C. RECUSAL. (1) A judge should not participate in a proceeding in which the judge's impartiality might reasonably be questioned, including but not limited to instances where:

(a) the judge has a personal bias or prejudice concerning a party, or personal knowledge of disputed evidentiary facts concerning the proceeding;

(b) the judge served as lawyer in the matter in controversy, or a lawyer with whom the judge previously practiced law served during such association as a lawyer concerning the matter, or the judge or lawyer has been a material witness concerning it;

COMMENT

A lawyer in a governmental agency does not necessarily have an association with other lawyers employed by that agency within the meaning of this subsection; a judge formerly

employed by a governmental agency, however, should not participate in a proceeding if the judge's impartiality might reasonably be questioned because of such association.

(c) the judge knows that he or she, individually or as a fiduciary, or the judge's spouse or minor child of the judge residing in the judge's household, has a significant financial interest in the subject matter in controversy or in a party to the proceeding, or any other interest that could be substantially affected by the outcome of the proceeding;

COMMENT

As a minimum standard for determining what constitutes a "significant financial interest," the judge should apply the definition of "financial interest" provided in the Maryland

Public Ethics Law, Md. Code, State Government Article, § 15-102 (n): "(1) Ownership of an interest as the result of which the owner has received within the past 3 years, is currently receiving, or in the future is entitled to receive, more than $1,000 per year; or (2) (i) ownership of more than 3% of a business entity; or (ii) ownership of securities of any kind that represent, or are convertible into, ownership of more than 3% of a business entity."

Moreover, there may be situations involving a lesser financial interest which also require recusal because of the judge's own sense of propriety. Conversely, there are situations where participation may be appropriate even though the "financial interest" threshold is present. In the latter case, the judge must first obtain an opinion from the Judicial Ethics Committee to obtain an exemption, except as provided in Canon 3 D (Non-recusal by Agreement).

(d) the judge, the spouse of the judge, a person within the third degree of relationship to either of them, or the spouse of such a person:

(i) is a party to the proceeding, or is known by the judge to be an officer, director, or trustee of a party;

(ii) is acting as lawyer in the proceeding;

COMMENT

The fact that a lawyer in a proceeding is affiliated with a law firm with which a lawyer-relative of the judge is affiliated does not of itself require recusal of the judge. Under appropriate circumstances, the fact that "the judge's impartiality might reasonably be questioned" under Canon 3 C (1), or that the lawyer-relative is known by the judge to have an interest in the law firm that could be "substantially affected by the outcome of the proceeding" under Canon 3 C (1) (d) (iii) may require the judge's recusal.

(iii) is known by the judge to have an interest that could be substantially affected by the outcome of the proceeding;

(iv) is to the judge's knowledge likely to be a material witness in the proceeding.

(2) A judge should keep informed about his or her personal and fiduciary financial interests, and make a reasonable effort to keep informed about the personal financial interests of the judge's spouse and minor children residing in the judge's household.

(3) For the purposes of this section:

(a) the degree of relationship is calculated according to the civil law system;

COMMENT

The following persons are within three degrees of relationship according to the civil law system: parent, grandparent, sibling, child, grandchild, uncle, aunt, niece, and nephew.

(b) "fiduciary" includes such relationships as personal representative, executor, administrator, trustee, custodian, attorney in fact by power of attorney, and guardian;

(c) "financial interest" means ownership of a legal or equitable interest, or a relationship as director, advisor, or other active participant in the affairs of a party, except that:

(i) ownership in a mutual or common investment fund that holds securities is not a "financial interest" in such securities unless the judge participates in the management of the fund;

(ii) an office in an educational, religious, charitable, fraternal, or civic organization is not a "financial interest" in securities held by the organization;

(iii) the proprietary interest of a policy holder in a mutual insurance company, of a depositor in a mutual savings association, or a similar proprietary interest, is a "financial interest" in the issuer only if the outcome of the proceeding could substantially affect the value of the interest;

(iv) ownership of government securities is a "financial interest" in the issuer only if the outcome of the proceeding could substantially affect the value of the securities.

Committee note. — Sec. 3 C (1) (a) is derived from ABA Canon 3 C (1) (a).

Sec. 3 C (1) (b) is derived from ABA Canon 3 C (1) (b). Current Md. Ethics Rule 2 requires recusal in any matter in which the judge previously acted as a lawyer. Sec. 3 C (1) (b) extends the recusal requirement to any matter in which the judge's former partner or associate acted while the judge was in practice.

The Commentary to sec. 3 C (1) (b) is derived from the Commentary to ABA Canon 3 C (1) (b) and is consistent with Md. Judicial Ethics Opinion No. 1 (issued 9/13/71).

Sec. 3 C (1) (c) is derived from ABA Canon 3 C (1) (c) and current Md. Ethics Rule 2. That ABA Canon requires recusal if any financial interest, "however small," is present; current Md. Ethics Rule 2 mandates recusal if a judge has a "significant" financial interest in the matter, which means a value in excess of $1,000. See Md. Judicial Ethics Opinion No. 78 (issued 10/29/80). The Committee believes that *de minimis* financial interests should not automatically require recusal. As a result, the Committee favors the use of the definition of "financial interest" provided in the Maryland Public Ethics Law. Accordingly, this standard is set forth in the Commentary to sec. 3 C (1) (c).

The first sentence of the last paragraph of the Commentary to sec. 3 C (1) (c) is derived from the Committee note to current Md. Ethics Rule 2. The last two sentences of this Commentary are new and allow some flexibility to mandatory recusal even where the financial interest threshold exists. Such exemptions can be determined by the Committee on an *ad hoc* basis.

The first clause of sec. 3 C (1) (d) (i) is derived from ABA Canon 3 C (1) (d) (i), current Md. Canon XIII, and current Md. Ethics Rule 2. The second clause is derived from the same ABA Canon, which does not, however, require knowledge by the judge of the relative's position. The Committee believes that such knowledge should be actual, not imputed.

Sec. 3 C (1) (d) (ii) is derived from ABA Canon 3 C (1) (d) (ii).

The Commentary to sec. 3 C (1) (d) (ii) is derived from ABA Canon 3 C (1) (d) (ii) and is consistent with Md. Judicial Ethics Opinion No. 53 (issued 6/16/77) and No. 25 (issued 12/26/74).

Sec. 3 C (1) (d) (iii) is derived from ABA Canon 3 C (1) (d) (iii).

Sec. 3 C (1) (d) (iv) is derived from ABA Canon 3 C (1) (d) (iv).

Sec. 3 C (2) is derived from ABA Canon 3 C (2) and current Md. Canon XXV.

Sec. 3 C (3) (a) is derived from ABA Canon 3 C (3) (a). Current Md. Ethics Rule 2 uses the common law system, which counts down from the common ancestor, a method which would extend the disqualification where the judge's first cousins are involved. Thirty-seven states have adopted the ABA Code provision, as does Md. Code, sec. 1-203 of the Estates and Trusts Article for purposes of estate distribution and administration.

The Commentary to sec. 3 C (3) (a) is derived from the Commentary to ABA Canon 3 C (3) (a).

Sec. 3 C (3) (b) is derived from ABA Canon 3 C (3) (b).

Sec. 3 C (3) (c) is derived from ABA Canon 3 C (3) (c), but is modified as explained in the Committee note to sec. 3 C (1) (c).

Sec. 3 C (3) (c) (i) is derived from ABA Canon 3 C (1) (c) (i). This provision would, superficially at least, negate Md. Judicial Ethics Opinion No. 81 (issued 11/20/80). That opinion required recusal because the judge had invested in an unusual type of mutual fund, where the investments were unchanging and the judge knew of each company in which the fund had invested. Under those particular facts, however, the judge's recusal would still be required under Canon 3 C (1) (c) ("an interest that could be substantially affected by the outcome of the proceeding") or under the broad test of Canon 3 C (1) (where the judge's "impartiality might reasonably be questioned").

Secs. 3 C (3) (c) (ii), (iii) and (iv) are derived from ABA Canon 3 C (3) (ii), (iii), and (iv), respectively.

D. NON-RECUSAL BY AGREEMENT. Where recusal would be required by Canon 3 C (1) (c) or Canon 3 C (1) (d), the judge may disclose on the record the basis of the recusal. If the lawyers, after consultation with their clients and independently of the judge's participation, all agree on the record that the judge ought to participate notwithstanding the basis for recusal, the judge may participate in the proceeding.

COMMENT

This procedure is designed to minimize the chance that a party or lawyer will feel coerced into an agreement. A pro se party may agree to allow participation by the judge.

Committee note. — Sec. 3 D and the Commentary thereto are derived from ABA Canon 3 D and the Commentary thereto; however, those provisions require written approval of the parties. Because a party may not be readily available to sign, the Committee believes that the lawyer's agreement, after consultation with the client, should suffice. Non-recusal by agreement is not permitted under current Md. Ethics Rule 2, as interpreted by Md. Judicial Ethics Opinion No. 78 (issued 10/29/80) and No. 50 (issued 1/17/77).

CANON 4

Extra-Judicial Activities

Except as otherwise prohibited or limited by law or these canons, a judge may engage in the following activities, if doing so does not interfere with the proper performance of judicial duties, does not reflect adversely upon the judge's impartiality, and does not detract from the dignity of the office.

Committee note. — This Canon combines ABA Canons 4 (Quasi-judicial Activities) and 5 (Extra-judicial Activities) and 6 A and B (Compensation and Expense Reimbursement) and is consistent with the ABA Code, unless specifically noted otherwise.

A. AVOCATIONAL ACTIVITIES. A judge may speak, write, lecture, and teach on both legal and non-legal subjects. A judge may participate in other activities concerning the law, the legal system and the administration of justice. A judge may engage in social and recreational activities.

COMMENT

Complete separation of a judge from extra-judicial activities is neither possible nor wise; a judge should not become isolated from the society in which he or she may live.

Committee note. — Sec. 4 A is derived from ABA Canons 4 A and 5 A and current Md. Canon XXX.

The Commentary to sec. 4 A is derived from the Commentary to ABA Canon 5 A and from current Md. Canon XXXII.

B. GOVERNMENT ACTIVITIES. (1) A judge may appear before and confer with public bodies or officials on matters concerning the judiciary or the administration of justice.

COMMENT

As suggested in the *Reporter's Notes to the ABA Code of Judicial Conduct,* the "administration of justice" is not limited to "matters of judicial administration" but is broad enough to include other matters relating to the judiciary.

(2) A judge may serve on governmental advisory bodies devoted to the improvement of the law, the legal system or the administration of justice and may represent his or her country, state or locality on ceremonial occasions or in connection with historical, educational and cultural activities.

COMMENT

Valuable services have been rendered in the past to the states and the nation by judges appointed by the executive to undertake extra-judicial assignments. The appropriateness of conferring these assignments on judges must be reassessed, however, in light of the demands on judicial time created by today's crowded dockets and the need to protect the courts from involvement in extra-judicial matters that may prove to be controversial. Judges should not be expected or permitted to accept governmental appointments that could interfere with the effectiveness and independence of the judiciary. Nor can a judge assume or discharge the legislative or executive powers of government (Article 8 of the Md. Declaration of Rights) or hold an "office" under the constitution or laws of the United States or State of Maryland (Article 33 of the Md. Declaration of Rights).

(3) As a private citizen, a judge may appear before or confer with public bodies or officials on matters that directly relate to a judge's person, immediate family or property so long as the judge does not use, and avoids the appearance of using, the prestige of the judge's office to influence decision-making.

Committee note. — Sec. 4 B (1) is derived from ABA Canon 4 B, which provides as follows:

[A judge] may appear at a public hearing before an executive or legislative body or official on matters concerning the law, the legal system, and the administration of justice, and he may otherwise consult with an executive or legislative body or official, but only on matters concerning the administration of justice.

The Committee believes that the phrase "matters concerning the law" is overly broad, and that a judge's participation, as a judge, before public bodies or officials should be limited to matters involving the judiciary or administration of justice. Current Md. Canon XXII allows a judge's participation in executive and legislative matters to "improve the administration of justice."

The Commentary to sec. 4 B (1) is from the stated source.

Sec. 4 B (2) is derived from ABA Canon 5 G. Current Md. Ethics Rule 3 and Article 33 of the Md. Declaration of Rights prohibit a judge from holding any "office," civil, military or political, under the constitution or laws of the United States or State of Maryland. An "office" is one which calls for the exercise of some portion of the sovereign power of government. See, *e.g.,* Howard County Comm. v. Westphal, 232 Md. 334, 340 (1963) and Judicial Ethics Opinion No. 77 (issued 9/14/79) and No. 97 (issued 4/21/82). Service on a government "advisory" commission would not be prohibited. See Judicial Ethics Opinion No. 75 (issued 9/13/79) and No. 90 (11/28/80) and Unreported Opinion No. 82-16 (issued 9/7/82), No. 81-3 (issued 4/1/81) and No. 80-1 (issued 6/13/80).

The Commentary to sec. 4 B (2) is derived from the Commentary to ABA Canon 5 G, except that the last sentence thereof is added to reflect the provisions of Articles 8 and 33 of the Md. Declaration of Rights.

Sec. 4 B (3) appears to be prohibited by ABA Canon 4 B. However, within proper bounds and with appropriate restraint, such conduct has been permitted by Maryland judges in their personal affairs. See Judicial Ethics Opinion No. 99 (issued 7/12/82) and In Re Foster, 271 Md. 449 (1974).

C. CIVIC AND CHARITABLE ACTIVITIES. A judge may participate and serve as a member, officer, director, trustee, or non-legal advisor of an educational, religious, charitable, fraternal, law-related or civic organization not conducted for the economic or political advantage of its members, subject to the following provisions:

(1) A judge should not participate and serve if it is likely that the organization: (a) will be engaged in proceedings that would ordinarily come before the judge; (b) will be regularly engaged in adversary proceedings in any court; or

(c) deals with people who are referred to the organization by the court on which the judge serves or who otherwise may likely come before that court.

COMMENT

The changing nature of some organizations and of their relationship to the law makes it necessary for a judge regularly to reexamine the activities of each organization with which a judge is affiliated to determine if it is proper to continue a relationship with it. For example, in many jurisdictions charitable organizations are now more frequently in court than in the past or make policy decisions that may have political significance or imply commitment to causes that may come before the courts for adjudication.

As a judicial officer and person specially learned in the law, a judge is in a unique position to contribute to the improvement of the law, the legal system, and the administration of justice, including revision of substantive and procedural law and the improvement of criminal and juvenile justice. To the extent that time permits, a judge is encouraged to do so, either independently or through a bar association, judicial conference or other organization dedicated to the improvement of the law.

(2) A judge should not solicit funds for any such organization, or use or permit the use of the prestige of the judge's office for that purpose, but a judge may be listed as an officer, director, or trustee of the organization. A judge may make recommendations to public and private fund granting agencies on projects and programs of which the judge has personal knowledge and which concern the law, the legal system, or the administration of justice. A judge should not be a speaker or the guest of honor at an organization's fund raising events, but may attend such events.

Committee note. — The first paragraph of sec. C is derived from ABA Canons 4 C and 5 B, current Md. Ethics Rule 9 and the Committee note to current Md. Ethics Rule 9.

Secs. 4 C (1) (a) and (b) are derived from ABA Canon 5 B (1).

Sec. 4 C (1) (c) is derived from a series of rulings by the Md. Judicial Ethics Committee. See Opinion No. 6 (issued 3/1/72), No. 35 (issued 10/3/75), and No. 75 (issued 9/13/79) and Unreported Opinion No. 81-15 (issued 2/16/82) and No. 82-7 (issued 4/26/82).

The first paragraph of the Commentary to sec. 4 C (1) is derived from the Commentary to ABA Canon 5 B.

The second paragraph of the Commentary to sec. 4 C (1) is derived from the Commentary to ABA Canon 4 C.

Sec. 4 C (2) is derived from ABA Canon 5 B (2), ABA Canon 4 C, current Md. Canon XXIV, current Md. Ethics Rule 9 and is consistent with numerous opinions issued by the Judicial Ethics Committee, with one exception: Judicial Ethics Opinion No. 6 (issued 3/1/72) and No. 59 (issued 11/30/77) require that the name of the judge be omitted as an officer or director in any campaign literature for that organization. ABA Canon 4 C permits a judge to assist in fund raising for a law-related organization, provided the judge does not personally participate in "public" fund raising activities. The Committee believes that the dangers inherent in a judge's participation in civic and charitable fund raising are equally applicable to fund raising, public or private, for law-related organizations. Notwithstanding these prohibitions, the judge may still participate in "purely internal discussions and decisions within the confines of the governing board" relating to fund raising activities. Judicial Ethics Opinion No. 89 (issued 11/25/80).

ABA Canon 5 B (3) provides that a judge should not give investment advice to a nonprofit organization, but may serve on its board of directors or trustees even though it has the responsibility for approving investment decisions. The ABA rationale for this prohibition is to avoid attributing to the judge a fiduciary's interest in the organization's investment portfolio, which could result in the judge's recusal in a case involving such investments. This provision is unnecessary, since proposed Maryland Canon 3 C (3) (c) (ii) provides that a judge's office in a non-profit organization is not a "financial interest" in securities held by the organization. Moreover, there are many other types of decisions that a judge would make as a board member which would require recusal in a particular matter, but which are not specifically dealt with in these canons.

D. FINANCIAL ACTIVITIES. (1) A judge should refrain from financial and business dealings that use the judge's position or involve the judge in frequent transactions with lawyers or persons likely to come before the court on which the judge serves.

(2) A judge may hold and manage investments, including real estate, and engage in other remunerative activity except that a full-time judge shall not hold any office or directorship in any public utility, bank, savings and loan association, lending institution, insurance company, or any other business corporation or enterprise or venture which is affected with a public interest.

(3) A judge should manage investments and other financial interests to minimize the number of cases in which recusal would be required. As soon as practicable without serious financial detriment, the judge should dispose of investments and other financial interests that might require frequent recusal.

(4) Information acquired by a judge in his or her judicial capacity should not be used or disclosed by the judge in financial dealings or for any other purpose not related to the judge's judicial duties.

Committee note. — Sec. 4 D (1) is derived from ABA Canon 5 C (1) and current Md. Canon XXV.

Sec. 4 D (2) is derived from ABA Canon 5 C (2) and current Md. Ethics Rule 6. However, ABA Canon 5 C (2) prohibits a judge from serving as an officer, director, manager, advisor, or employee of *any* business. Only 8 states have adopted that version without any change, and 7 states have adopted a slightly modified version. Sec. 4 D (2) continues the present practice provided in current Md. Ethics Rule 6 and has been substantially adopted in at least 15 states. At least 2 other states are more permissive. Seven states only allow a judge to participate in a "family" business or "closely held business."

Sec. 4 D (3) is derived from ABA Canon 5 C (3) and current Md. Canon XXV.

Sec. 4 D (4) is derived from ABA Canon 5 C (7) and current Md. Canon XXV.

E. COMPENSATION AND EXPENSE REIMBURSEMENT. A judge may receive compensation and reimbursement of expenses for activities permitted by this Code, subject to the following restrictions:

(1) Compensation should not exceed a reasonable amount nor should it exceed what a person who is not a judge would receive for the same activity.

(2) Expense reimbursement should be limited to the actual cost of travel, food and lodging reasonably incurred by the judge and, where appropriate to the occasion, by the judge's spouse. Any payment in excess of such an amount is compensation.

Committee note. — This is found in ABA Canon 6 A and 6 B but is placed here because it is related to the financial activities of a judge.

F. GIFTS. (1) A judge must be especially careful in accepting gifts, favors, and loans from persons not in the judge's immediate family. However innocently intended, gifts and favors from such persons, especially gifts and favors having substantial monetary value, may create an appearance that the judge could be improperly beholden to the donor. Subject to this caveat, and except as otherwise prohibited or limited by law or these canons, a judge may accept:

(a) a gift incident to a public testimonial or books supplied by publishers on a complimentary basis for official use;

(b) ordinary social hospitality;

(c) a gift from a friend or relative by reason of some special occasion, such as a wedding, anniversary, birthday, and the like, if the gift is fairly commensurate with the nature of the occasion and the friendship or relationship;

(d) a gift, favor, or loan from a relative or close personal friend whose appearance before the judge or whose interest in a case would require a recusal under Canon 3 C;

(e) a scholarship or fellowship awarded on the same terms applied to other applicants;

(f) a loan from a lending institution in its regular course of business on the same terms generally available to persons who are not judges.

(2) The standards set forth in subsection (1) of this section also apply to gifts, favors, and loans offered to members of the judge's family who reside in the judge's household. For purposes of this Canon and absent extraordinary circumstances, gifts, favors and loans accepted by such family members shall be considered to be accepted by the judge.

COMMENT

This section relating to gifts does not apply to contributions to a judge's campaign for judicial office, a matter governed by Canon 5.

Judges are often invited by lawyers or other persons to attend social, educational, or recreational functions. In most cases, such invitations would fall within the realm of ordinary social hospitality and may be accepted by the judge. If there is more than a token fee for admission to the function, however, unless the fee is waived by the organization, the judge should pay the fee and not permit a lawyer or other person to pay it on the judge's behalf.

Committee note. — Sec. 4 F (1) is new language not found in either the ABA Code or the current Md. Canons.

Sec. 4 F (1) (a) is derived from ABA Canon 5 C (4) (a).

Sec. 4 F (1) (b) is derived from ABA Canon 5 C (4) (b).

Sec. 4 F (1) (c) is derived from ABA Canon 5 C (4) (b); but that provision allows a judge to receive a wedding or engagement gift from anyone, which the Committee believes is overly broad.

Sec. 4 F (1) (d) is derived from ABA Canon 5 C (4) (c), current Md. Canon XXXI, and current Md. Ethics Rule 7. Those ABA and Md. provisions allow a judge to receive any gift from any donor who is not a party or other person whose interests have come or are likely to come before the judge. The Committee believes these provisions are too permissive, since it is difficult to know if a person's interests will be submitted to the judge in the future, and since it is unseemly and perhaps suspicious for a

judge to accept gifts for no apparent reason from persons with whom the judge has little or no connection or relationship. This provision allows a judge to receive any type of gift from relatives and close personal friends who could not appear before the judge.

Sec. 4 F (1) (e) is derived from ABA Canon 5 C (4) (b).

Sec. 4 F (1) (f) is derived from ABA Canon 5 C (4) (b).

Sec. 4 F (2) is derived from ABA Canon 5 C (4) (b), except that the phrase "absent extraordinary circumstances" has been added.

The first sentence of the Commentary following sec. 4 F (2) is derived from the Commentary to ABA Canon 5 C (4) and from current Md. Ethics Rule 7. The remainder of that Commentary is new and provides guidance as to the scope of "ordinary social hospitality" as used in sec. 4 F (1) (b). It is consistent with Md. Judicial Ethics Opinion No. 91 (issued 3/2/81), which permits a judge to accept an invitation by a bar association to a bar association function which otherwise requires a paid ticket of admission; and Md. Judicial Ethics Opinion No. 102 (issued 3/21/84), which allows a judge to accept an invitation of an attorney to a bar association or other social function where an admission fee is not charged provided that "there is no reason to suspect that the attorney will attempt to use the judge's presence for any inappropriate purpose." ABA Canon 5 C (4) (a) allows a judge to accept an invitation from anyone to a bar-related function or activity even if the inviter pays the admission fee for the judges.

G. FIDUCIARY ACTIVITIES. A judge should not serve as a fiduciary except in the following instances. A judge may serve as a personal representative (executor or administrator) or special administrator of the estate of a decedent, as a trustee of a trust, as a custodian, as a guardian, or as an attorney in fact but only where the judge is spouse, the surviving spouse or is related within the third degree (according to the civil law system) to the decedent, grantor, minor or disabled person. A judge actually serving as a trustee of a trust on December 31, 1969, may continue to serve even if not within the required degree of relationship. In extraordinary cases, a judge may serve as guardian or attorney in fact for any other person with whom the judge maintains a close familial relationship, but only if there is no other person ready, willing and able to serve in that capacity. While acting as a fiduciary a judge is subject to the same restrictions on financial activities that apply to the judge personally.

COMMENT

A judge's obligation under this canon and as a fiduciary may come into conflict. For example, a judge should resign as trustee if it would result in detriment to the trust to divest it of holdings whose retention would place the judge in violation of Canon 4 D (3).

Committee note. — Sec. 4 G is derived from ABA Canon 5 D, with substantial modifications. Secs. 5-105 (b) (5) and 14-104 of Md. Code Ann., Estates and Trusts Article, prohibit a judge from serving as a personal representative or trustee for someone who is not a spouse or related within the third degree (although a judge serving as trustee as of 12/31/69 is allowed to continue in that capacity). Maryland law and the existing Maryland canons do not prohibit a judge from serving as any other type of fiduciary for anyone. (Judicial Ethics Opinion No. 60 erroneously assumes that Maryland statutory law prohibits a judge from serving as a guardian of the property of a disabled person. But see Unreported Opinion Docket No. 82-10). ABA Canon 5 D allows a judge to serve as a fiduciary only for a "spouse, child, grandchild, parent, grandparent, or other relative or person with whom the judge maintains a close familial relationship." As can be seen, the ABA canon is more permissive than Maryland law as to personal representatives and trustees, but is more restrictive than Maryland law or existing Maryland canons as to other types of fiduciaries. The Committee

believes that a judge's eligibility as a fiduciary should be very limited, because of the necessity or likelihood of the judge having to appear in court or be under court supervision as a representative of a party. The limitations imposed by the legislature as to personal representatives and trustees appeared to the Committee to be appropriate for guardians and custodians. The Committee recognizes the exceptional situation where the judge should be allowed to act as a guardian or attorney in fact for a disabled person who is not a near relative but with whom the judge has a close relationship, and no one else is willing to undertake that personal responsibility.

ABA Canon 5 D (1) provides that a judge "should not serve if it is likely that as a fiduciary he will be engaged in proceedings that would ordinarily come before him, or if the estate, trust, or ward becomes involved in adversary proceedings in the court on which he serves or one under its appellate jurisdiction." The Committee agrees that ordinarily a judge should not undertake a fiduciary position if adversary proceedings in the judge's court are likely to occur; however, the Committee believes that this ABA provision, which would require resignation whenever the estate or trust became involved in adversary proceedings, is too inflexible.

The Commentary to sec. 4 G is derived from the Commentary to ABA Canon 5 D.

H. ARBITRATION. A judge should not act as an arbitrator or mediator.

COMMENT

This does not preclude a judge from participating in settlement conferences. If by reason of disclosure made during or as a result of the conference, the judge's impartiality might rea-

sonably be questioned, the judge should not further participate in the matter. See Canon 3 C (1).

Sec. H is derived from ABA Canon 5 E.

Current Md. Canon XXX allows a judge to act as an arbitrator or mediator pursuant to a contract in force on January 1, 1975. The Committee assumes that no such contract is still operative. If otherwise, the judge should make this known to the Committee.

Committee note. — The Commentary to sec. H is new.

I. PRACTICE OF LAW. (1)(a) Except as provided in subsection (b), a judge should not practice law.

(b) A part-time judge of the Orphans' Court may practice law to the extent permitted by law, except that the judge shall avoid conduct whereby such judicial position is used or seems to be used to further success in the practice of law; and in no event should the judge practice in the court in which the judge sits, even when presided over by another judge, nor appear therein pro se in any controversy.

(2) Prior to qualification for judicial office, a judge who intends to enter into an agreement under § 1-203 (b) of the Md. Code Ann., Courts and Judicial Proceedings Article, for payments relating to the judge's former law practice should submit the agreement to the Judicial Ethics Committee so that the Committee may review it as to the reasonableness of the time provided for payments to be made under the agreement. A payment period limited to a maximum of five years or less is presumptively reasonable. A longer payment period is permitted only with the Committee's prior approval as to its reasonableness.

(3) An agreement entered into under § 1-203 (b) of Md. Code Ann., Courts and Judicial Proceedings Article, may not be amended without the prior approval of the Judicial Ethics Committee.

(4) These subsections are applicable to any agreement entered into under § 1-203 (b) of Md. Code Ann., Courts and Judicial Proceedings Article, on and after July 1, 1981.

Committee note. — Sec. 4 I (a) is derived from ABA Canon 5 F and current Md. Canon XXX.

Sec. 4 I (b) is derived from paragraph A of the Compliance Section of the ABA Code and current Md. Canon XXX.

Secs. 4 I (2), (3), and (4) are derived from current Md. Ethics Rule 5A. a., b., and c., respectively.

CANON 5

Political Activity

A. POLITICAL CONDUCT OF A JUDGE WHO IS NOT A CANDIDATE. A judge who is not a candidate for election, re-election, or retention to judicial office should not engage in any partisan political activity and should resign judicial office when becoming a candidate for a non-judicial office, except that the judge may continue to hold judicial office while a candidate for election to or serving as a delegate in a state constitutional convention.

Committee note. — ABA Canon 7 A, current Md. Canon XXVII, and current Md. Ethics Rule 3 generally prohibit partisan political activity by a judge who is not a candidate for judicial office. The resignation requirement is found in ABA Canon 7 A (3), current Md.

Canon XXIX, and current Md. Ethics Rule 4. ABA Canon 7 A (3) allows a judge to serve as a state constitutional convention delegate if allowed by law. Such a delegate is not an "office" which Article 33 of the Md. Declaration of Rights prohibits a judge from holding. Board v. Attorney General, 246 Md. 417 (1967).

B. POLITICAL CONDUCT OF A JUDGE WHO IS CANDIDATE. A judge who is a candidate for election, re-election, or retention to judicial office may engage in partisan political activity allowed by law with respect to such candidacy, except that the judge

(1) should not act as a leader or hold any office in a political organization;

(2) should not make speeches for a political organization or candidate or publicly endorse a candidate for non-judicial office;

COMMENT

A judge does not publicly endorse a candidate for public office by having the judge's name on the same ticket.

(3) should maintain the dignity appropriate to judicial office;

(4) should not allow any other person to do for the judge what the judge is prohibited from doing;

(5) should not make pledges or promises of conduct in office other than the faithful and impartial performance of the duties of the office, announce the judge's views on disputed legal or political issues, or misrepresent the judge's identity, qualifications, or other fact.

Committee note. — Sec. 5 B (1) is derived from ABA Canon 7 A (1) (a), current Md. Canon XXVII, and current Md. Ethics Rule 3.

Sec. 5 B (2) is derived from ABA Canon 7 A (1) (b) and current Md. Canon XXVII, although the ABA language probably is broad enough even to prohibit a judge from endorsing another judge who is also a candidate. However, public endorsement by one judicial candidate of another judicial candidate has long been permitted in Maryland. See Md. Judicial Ethics Opinion No. 20 (issued 4/25/74).

The Commentary to sec. 5 B (2) is derived from the Commentary to ABA Canon 7 A (1) (b) and is consistent with Md. Judicial Ethics Opinion No. 109 (issued 2/14/86).

Sec. 5 B (3) is derived from ABA Canon 7 B (1) (a). That canon also provides that a judge should encourage family members to adhere to the same standards of political conduct that apply to the judge. The Committee disagrees with this proposition; it believes that family members should be free to engage in political activity in their own right which is not related to the judge's office.

Sec. 5 B (4) is derived from ABA Canon 7 B (1) (b) and is generally implied in current Md. Canon XXIX and current Md. Ethics Rule 10. ABA Canon 7 B (1) (b) also provides that a judge should prohibit public officials or employees subject to the judge's direction and control for doing for the judge what the judge is prohibited from doing. The Committee believes that this is redundant to the remainder of the subsection and may even imply that a judge must terminate the employment of a person who does not follow the judge's admonitions — a result which may be unreasonable under the circumstances.

Sec. 5 B (5) is derived from ABA Canon 7 B (1) (c) and current Md. Canon XXIX.

ABA Canon 7 B (2) prohibits a judge from personally soliciting or accepting campaign funds or soliciting publicly stated support; however, the judge may establish "committees of responsible persons" to do these things for the judge. The Committee believes that this is too restrictive and politically unrealistic, since it puts the judge at a distinct disadvantage to active opposition. Maryland law does require all campaign funds to be publicly reported by the campaign treasurer.

ABA Canon 7 permits partisan political activity by a judge who is a candidate for retention without a competing candidate only if the judge's candidacy has drawn "active opposition." However, Md. Judicial Ethics Opinion No. 88 (issued 8/29/80) stated that such a view "would not be realistic, since ... even in the absence of an active campaign against the

373

judge, negative votes might be cast against the judge's continuance in office, as was the case in the 1978 general election." The opinion concluded that the exception in the canons which permitted political activity by judges seeking election is "equally applicable" to appellate judges standing for retention under non-competitive election procedures. The Committee supports this conclusion.

C. STATUS OF A JUDGE AS A CANDIDATE. A newly appointed judge is a "candidate" for judicial office from the date of taking office until the general election pertaining to that judge's election or initial retention. Any other incumbent judge is a "candidate" for a period commencing two years prior to the general election pertaining to that judge's re-election or subsequent retention, or when a newly appointed judge to that court becomes a "candidate" in the same general election, whichever first occurs. A judge who is seeking election to another judicial office is a "candidate" for that office when the judge files a certificate of candidacy in accordance with the state election laws, but no earlier than two years prior to the general election for that office, or when a newly appointed judge to that court becomes a "candidate" in the same general election, whichever first occurs.

Committee note. — Md. Judicial Ethics Opinion No. 14 (issued 5/23/74) allows a judge to begin campaigning as a candidate immediately upon assumption of office. The longest possible campaign period would be one day less than three years. See Article IV, sec. 5 of the Constitution of Maryland. Md. Judicial Ethics Opinion No. 34 (issued 7/7/75) allowed an incumbent judge to begin campaigning for re-election only from January 1 of the year of the election. This was found to be too restrictive, so the campaign period was changed to "times which are reasonable under the particular circumstances of each case." Md. Judicial Ethics Opinion No. 57 (issued 11/28/77). The Committee believes that the latter standard is too vague, and that an incumbent judge should be permitted to campaign as soon as the preceding general election has ended, which is a two-year period, or earlier if a newly appointed judge, who will be a running mate of the incumbent judge, has already become a candidate. ABA Canon 7 A (2) considers an incumbent judge whose office is filled by election between competing candidates as *always* a candidate for re-election. While this may be a political necessity for judges in some states who must stand for re-election frequently, the Committee believes this is inappropriate in Maryland, where circuit court judges are elected for 15-year terms and appellate judges are retained for 10-year terms.

A judge should be permitted to engage in political activity regarding the judge's candidacy for judicial office only if the judge's intention to pursue that candidacy is clear. An incumbent judge's candidacy for election or re-election is fairly obvious, but a judge's intention to seek another judicial office is not as clear; therefore, the filing of a certificate of candidacy is required in the latter situation.

CANON 6

Compliance

A. This Code of Judicial Conduct applies to each judge of the Court of Appeals, the Court of Special Appeals, the Circuit Courts, the District Court and the Orphans' Courts.

Committee note. — Sec. 6 A is derived from current Md. Ethics Rule 14 a.

B. Violation of any of the provisions of this Code of Judicial Conduct by a judge may be regarded as conduct prejudicial to the proper administration of justice within the meaning of Maryland Rule 16-803 (g) of the Rules concerning the Commission on Judicial Disabilities.

Committee note. — Sec. 6 B is derived from current Md. Ethics Rule 15, which provides that a violation of an Ethics Rule *is* conduct prejudicial to the proper administration of justice. Whether the violation actually is or is not prejudicial conduct is to be determined by the Court of Appeals of Maryland.

Article IV, Sec. 4B of the Md. Constitution gives that Court the authority to discipline any judge upon recommendation of the Commission on Judicial Disabilities. This disciplinary power is alternative to and cumulative with the impeachment authority of the General Assembly.

C. This Code of Judicial Conduct applies to each judge of one of those courts who has resigned or retired, if the judge is subject to and approved for recall for temporary service under Article IV, Section 3A of the Constitution, except that Canon 4 C (Civil and Charitable Activities); Canon 4 D (Financial Activities) — paragraphs (1), (2), and (3); Canon 4 G (Fiduciary Activities); and Canon 4 H (Arbitration) do not apply to any such former judge.

Committee note. — Sec. 6 C is derived from current Md. Ethics Rule 14 b. (1).

Paragraph C of the Compliance Section of the ABA Code exempts a retired judge subject to recall from only one provision of the ABA

Code: The provision which prohibits a judge from serving on a governmental commission concerned with matters other than improvement of the law, legal system, or the administration of justice.

CANON 7

Judicial Ethics Committee

A. The Chief Judge of the Court of Appeals shall appoint annually an Ethics Committee consisting of not less than seven and not more than nine members. One member shall be appointed from each of the Court of Special Appeals, the Circuit Courts, and the District Court. Three members may not be judges and of these one may not be a lawyer or an employee or officer within the judicial branch of government. The remaining members shall be judges appointed from any of the above courts, but not from the Court of Appeals. The Chief Judge shall designate one of the members as chairperson.

In addition to its other duties, the Committee

(1) is designated as the body to give advice with respect to the application of the provisions of Subtitles 5 and 6 of Title 15 of the State Government Article, Annotated Code of Maryland, to State officials of the Judicial Branch as defined in Title 15 of the State Government Article; and

(2) shall from time to time submit to the Court of Appeals recommendations for necessary or desirable changes in the Code of Judicial Conduct, and the Code of Conduct for Judicial Appointees.

B. Any judge may in writing request the opinion of the Committee on the proper interpretation of the Code of Judicial Conduct as contained in Rule 16-813, or as to the provisions of Subtitle 5 or 6 of Title 15 of the State Government Article, Annotated Code of Maryland. A judge who has requested an opinion and who is in compliance with that opinion is protected from a charge of violation of Code or statute construed in that opinion.

C. A judge or any person who is subject to the Code of Conduct for Judicial Appointees as contained in Rule 16-814 may in writing request the opinion of the Committee on the proper interpretation of the rules of conduct. A person who has requested an opinion and who is in compliance with it is protected from a charge of violation of the Code construed in that opinion.

D. Any person, other than a judge, who is a State official of the Judicial Branch within the meaning of that term as used in § 15-104 (2) of the State Government Article, Annotated Code of Maryland, may in writing request the opinion of the Committee on the proper interpretation of Subtitle 5 or 6 of Title 15 of the State Government Article. The person who requests an opinion and who is in compliance with it is protected from a charge of violation of the statute construed in that opinion.

E. Every opinion issued pursuant to this rule shall be filed with the Secretary of the Maryland Judicial Conference. The filed opinion is confidential and not public information unless the Court of Appeals otherwise directs. However, the Secretary shall prepare an edited version of each opinion, in which the identity of the person who has requested the opinion, the specific court or geographical location of that person, and the identity of other individuals, organizations or groups mentioned in the opinion, may not be disclosed. Edited opinions shall be published in the manner the Secretary deems proper.

Committee note. — Canon 7 is derived from current Md. Ethics Rule 16. (Added May 4, 1971, effective July 1, 1971; amended Feb. 15, 1974; July 1, 1974; June 16, 1975, effective July 1, 1975; Jan. 31, 1977, effective July 1, 1977; Feb. 28, 1977, effective July 1, 1977; Dec. 5, 1977, effective Jan. 1, 1978; Dec. 8, 1977, effective Jan. 1, 1978; May 2, 1979, effective July 1, 1979; Oct. 5, 1979; Aug. 11, 1980, effective Sept. 1, 1980; June 26, 1981, effective July 1, 1981; revised Nov. 21, 1986, effective July 1, 1987; amended June 15, 1988; Jan. 11, 1993, effective Feb. 1, 1993; Nov. 21, 1995, effective Dec. 1, 1995; June 5, 1996, effective Jan. 1, 1997; Dec. 10, 1996, effective Jan. 1, 1997.)

Cross references. — See Rule 16-802 (The Maryland Judicial Conference).

Source. — This Rule is former Rule 1231.

Effect of amendments. — The first 1996 amendment substituted "Rule 16-803 g" for "Rule 1227 g" in Canon 6 B; substituted "Rule 16-813" for "Rule 1231" in the first sentence of Canon 7B; substituted "Rule 16-814" for "Rule 1232" in the first sentence of Canon 7C; substituted "Rule 16-802" for "Rule 1226 a" in the Cross reference note; and added the Source note.

The second 1996 amendment substituted "Judicial Appointees" for "Masters, Examiners, Auditors, Referees and District Court Commissioners" in Canon 7A(2); and substituted "Judicial Appointees" for "Masters, Examiners, Auditors, Referees and District Court Commissioners and the Rules of Conduct" in the first sentence of Canon 7C.

Editor's note. — An Order dated June 5, 1996, effective Jan. 1, 1997, renumbered this Rule, which was formerly Rule 1231.

Maryland Law Review. — For note, "Dis-cipline of Judges in Maryland," see 34 Md. L. Rev. 612 (1974).

University of Baltimore Law Review. — For article, "Report of the Special Joint Committee on Gender Bias in the Courts," see 20 U. Balt. L. Rev. 1 (1990).

Canons do not have same legal status as Rules. — The Canons of Judicial Ethics do not have the same operative or legal status as do the Rules of Judicial Ethics, in governing the activities of judges. 65 Op. Att'y Gen. 285 (1980).

Judges may teach part-time at State institutions. — With the possible exception of Judicial Ethics Rule 3 (now Canon 5 B of this Rule), the Constitution and laws of Maryland do not preclude judges from teaching part-time at State institutions. 65 Op. Att'y Gen. 285 (1980).

Rule applicable to orphans' court judges. — The Canons and Rules of Judicial

Ethics, promulgated by the Court of Appeals as this Rule, are applicable to orphans' court judges. 63 Op. Att'y Gen. 498 (1978).

Service as expert witness. — An orphan's court judge does not violate the Code of Judicial Conduct by testifying as an expert witness on projected damages, when his public office is unrevealed to the fact finders, when he was retained as an expert before he became a judge, and when there is no suggestion that his appearance in court in any way affected his judicial duties. K & K Mgt., Inc. v. Lee, 316 Md. 137, 557 A.2d 965 (1989).

Testimony elicited from witness judge that did not concern any judicial activity and which was limited to factual matters that were relevant to the case and that occurred while he was practicing law was deemed not prejudicial. Ginsberg v. McIntire, 348 Md. 526, 704 A.2d 1246 (1998).

Recusal. — Canon 3 C (1) (a) of the ABA Code of Judicial Conduct — which, since July 1, 1987, is in force as part of this Rule — requires recusal of a judge when the judge has "personal knowledge of disputed evidentiary facts concerning the proceeding." Wiseman v. State, 72 Md. App. 605, 531 A.2d 1311 (1987).

A trial judge was not disqualified from presiding at a subsequent capital sentencing hearing because he had previously expressed his opinion that death was not the appropriate sentence in his report following an earlier sentencing hearing before a jury. Doering v. Fader, 316 Md. 351, 558 A.2d 733 (1989).

When bias, prejudice or lack of impartiality is alleged, the decision to recuse is a discretionary one, unless the basis asserted is grounds for mandatory recusal, and will be overturned only upon a showing of abuse of discretion. Surratt v. Prince George's County, 320 Md. 439, 578 A.2d 745 (1990).

Conduct held not improper. — Although the trial judge was clearly involved, and revealed to both counsel how he was reacting to the evidence, his doing so did not come close to trespassing into the area where his conduct violated the rights of either litigant. Ricker v. Ricker, 114 Md. App. 583, 691 A.2d 283 (1997).

Bias or prejudice required for recusal. — A trial judge has broad discretion in deciding whether to recuse himself, and a successful motion must be supported by an affirmative showing of bias or prejudice; thus, where there was no affirmative showing of bias or prejudice, judge's failure to recuse himself was not an abuse of discretion. Pearlstein v. Maryland Deposit Ins. Fund, 78 Md. App. 8, 552 A.2d 51 (1989).

The accused has a right to a trial in which the judge is not only impartial and disinterested, but who also has the appearance of being impartial and disinterested. Chapman v. State, 115 Md. App. 626, 694 A.2d 480 (1997).

Adversarial representation requires recusal. — When a judge has appeared as counsel in an earlier stage of the same adversarial proceeding, there is no question that the judge has advocated the client's cause, and recusal is automatic because of the danger of an appearance of partiality. Sharp v. Howard County, 327 Md. 17, 607 A.2d 545 (1992).

Recusal required for nonadversarial advice or work. — When a judge has given legal advice or performed legal work in a nonadversarial setting, recusal is required only if the underlying purpose of the advice or work was to achieve the goal that is at issue in the later proceeding before the judge. Sharp v. Howard County, 327 Md. 17, 607 A.2d 545 (1992).

A recusal motion alleging personal misconduct must set forth facts in reasonable detail sufficient to show the purported personal misconduct; mere conclusions as to lack of impartiality will not suffice, and it should be supported by affidavit or testimony, or both. Surratt v. Prince George's County, 320 Md. 439, 578 A.2d 745 (1990).

Burden on defendant to show actual bias. — Where an allegation of actual bias or prejudice is made, the burden is upon the defendant to make that showing from the record. Boyd v. State, 321 Md. 69, 581 A.2d 1 (1990).

A party attempting to demonstrate that a judge is not impartial or disinterested has a high burden to meet; a party attempting to demonstrate that a judge does not have the 'appearance' of disinterestedness or impartiality carries a slightly lesser burden. Chapman v. State, 115 Md. App. 626, 694 A.2d 480 (1997).

Personal bias or prejudice. — The word "personal" as used in Canon 3 C means knowledge acquired from extra-judicial sources. Boyd v. State, 321 Md. 69, 581 A.2d 1 (1990).

Information acquired during prior judicial proceedings, involving codefendants, is "judicial" and not personal knowledge or bias requiring disqualification. Boyd v. State, 321 Md. 69, 581 A.2d 1 (1990).

The standard to be applied in evaluating a motion for recusal is an objective one — "whether a reasonable member of the public knowing all the circumstances would be led to the conclusion that the judge's impartiality might reasonably be questioned." Surratt v. Prince George's County, 320 Md. 439, 578 A.2d 745 (1990).

The standard for assessing the facts put forth by a complainant in a recusal motion alleging personal misconduct will be the objective standard currently used in Maryland for other types of recusal motions. Using an objective standard precludes the necessity of delving into the subjective mindset of the challenged judge. Surratt v. Prince George's County, 320 Md. 439, 578 A.2d 745 (1990).

Timeliness of filing of motion to recuse. — To trigger the recusal procedure, a motion alleging personal misconduct must be timely filed. To avoid disruption of a trial, or the possible withholding of a recusal motion as a weapon to use only in the event of some unfavorable ruling, the motion generally should be filed as soon as the basis for it becomes known and relevant. Surratt v. Prince George's County, 320 Md. 439, 578 A.2d 745 (1990).

Judicial decision on motion to recuse. — The question of recusal ordinarily is decided, in the first instance, by the judge whose recusal is sought. Surratt v. Prince George's County, 320 Md. 439, 578 A.2d 745 (1990).

Bench trial vs. jury trial. — There was no abuse of discretion on the part of the judge in drawing a distinction between a bench trial and a jury trial in case where defendant requested that judge recuse himself and judge agreed to do so if defendant elected a bench trial. Chapman v. State, 115 Md. App. 626, 694 A.2d 480 (1997).

When the asserted basis for recusal is personal conduct of the trial judge that generates serious issues about his or her personal misconduct, then the trial judge must permit another judge to decide the motion for recusal. Surratt v. Prince George's County, 320 Md. 439, 578 A.2d 745 (1990).

Appellate intervention may be warranted regarding recusal provisions. — The canonical provisions dealing with recusal may warrant appellate intervention if their prohibitions are disregarded. Surratt v. Prince George's County, 320 Md. 439, 578 A.2d 745 (1990).

Denial of motion to recuse proper. —

Denial of a motion to recuse did not constitute an abuse of discretion, although the trial judge's impartiality might reasonably be questioned given the incriminating statement of a co-defendant in a trial three weeks earlier, before the same judge. Boyd v. State, 79 Md. App. 53, 555 A.2d 535 (1989), aff'd, 321 Md. 69, 581 A.2d 1 (1990).

Ex parte communication concerning sentencing of codefendants. — Where trial judge and prosecutor conferred, in absence of defense counsel, to discuss the sentencing of appellant's codefendants, and the interrelationship of the various defendants' culpability influenced the judge in determining the sentence to be imposed on each codefendant, appellant's sentence was vacated and the case was remanded to a different trial judge for resentencing. Caldwell v. State, 51 Md. App. 703, 445 A.2d 1069 (1982).

Judge acting as auctioneer. — Where a judge on the Orphans' Court of Cecil County continued as a part-time auctioneer during his tenure as judge, and in that capacity handled at least three public auction sales involving estates administered through the Orphans' Court of Cecil County, the judge violated the ethical canons and rules, and his conduct was prejudicial to the proper administration of justice. In re Welch, 283 Md. 68, 388 A.2d 535 (1978).

Forgery held "conduct prejudicial to the proper administration of justice." — Forgery of another judge's name to the change of a disposition in a traffic case constitutes "conduct prejudicial to the proper administration of justice," in violation of Rule 15 of the Rules of Judicial Ethics (now Canon 6 B of this Rule), warranting removal of the judge from office. In re Bennett, 301 Md. 517, 483 A.2d 1242 (1984).

Rule 16-814. Code of Conduct for Judicial Appointees.

The Code of Conduct for Judicial Appointees as set forth in this Rule is adopted as a Rule of this Court governing the conduct of all judicial appointees. For purposes of this Rule, judicial appointees are defined as: a master, examiner, auditor, referee appointed by the Court of Appeals of Maryland, the Court of Special Appeals of Maryland, a circuit court or an Orphans' Court; or a commissioner appointed by the Administrative Judge of the District Court of Maryland subject to the approval of the Chief Judge of the District Court of Maryland.

Committee note. — (1) These are minimum standards and are not intended as a limitation on the appointing authority's power to impose additional requirements; and (2) This Code of Conduct is generally patterned after Maryland Rule 16-813, the Code of Judicial Conduct. The Committee notes found appended thereto explain many provisions of the Code of Judicial Conduct and may be used to assist in the interpretation of parallel provisions of this Code of Conduct.

CANON 1

Integrity and Independence

An independent and honorable judicial system is indispensable to justice in our society. A judicial appointee should observe high standards of conduct so that the integrity and independence of the judicial system may be preserved. The provisions of this Code should be construed and applied to further that objective.

CANON 2

Avoidance of Impropriety and the Appearance of Impropriety

A. A judicial appointee should behave with propriety and should avoid even the appearance of impropriety. A judicial appointee should respect and comply with the law and should act at all times in a manner that promotes public confidence in the integrity and impartiality of the judicial system. The personal behavior of a judicial appointee in both the performance of official duties, and in everyday life, should be beyond reproach.

B. A judicial appointee should not allow official conduct to be improperly influenced by family, social, or other relationships. A judicial appointee should not use the prestige of the position to advance the private interests of others; nor should a judicial appointee convey or permit others to convey the impression that they are in a special position to influence official conduct. A judicial appointee should not testify voluntarily as a character witness.

COMMENT

Public confidence in the judicial system is eroded by irresponsible or improper conduct by judicial appointees. A judicial appointee must expect to be the subject of constant public scrutiny. A judicial appointee must therefore accept restrictions on his or her conduct that might be viewed as burdensome by the ordinary citizen and should do so freely and willingly.

Membership of a judicial appointee in an organization that practices invidious discrimination on the basis of race, sex, religion, or national origin may give rise to perceptions that the judicial appointee's impartiality is impaired. It is therefore inappropriate for a judicial appointee to continue to hold membership in an organization that the judicial appointee knows or reasonably should know, practices and will continue to practice such invidious discrimination so as to give rise to the perception that the judicial appointee's impartiality is impaired. Whether an organization practices and will continue to practice that kind of invidious discrimination is often a complex question to which judicial appointees should be sensitive. The answer cannot be determined merely from an examination of an organization's current membership rolls but may depend on the nature and purpose of the organization, and of any restrictions on membership, the history of the organization's selection of members, and other relevant factors. Ultimately, each judicial appointee must determine in the judicial appointee's own conscience whether an organization of which the judicial appointee is a member practices invidious discrimination.

The testimony of a judicial appointee as a character witness injects the prestige of the appointment into the proceeding in which a judicial appointee testifies and may be misunderstood to be an official testimonial. This Canon, however, does not afford a judicial appointee the privilege against testifying in response to an official summons.

CANON 3

Impartial and Diligent Performance
of Official Duties

In the performance of official duties, the following standards apply:

A. ADJUDICATIVE RESPONSIBILITIES. (1) A judicial appointee should be faithful to the law and maintain professional competence in it.

(2) A judicial appointee should be unswayed by partisan interests, public clamor, or fear of criticism.

(3) A judicial appointee should maintain order and decorum in proceedings before the judicial appointee.

(4) A judicial appointee should be patient, dignified, and courteous to litigants, witnesses, lawyers, and others with whom the judicial appointee deals in an official capacity and should require similar conduct of lawyers, and of staff, and others subject to the judicial appointee's direction and control.

(5) A judicial appointee should accord to every person who is legally interested in a proceeding, or the person's lawyer, full right to be heard according to law, and, except as authorized by law, neither initiate nor consider ex parte or other communications concerning a pending or impending proceeding. A judicial appointee, however, may obtain the advice of a disinterested expert on the law applicable to a proceeding before the judicial appointee if the judicial appointee gives notice to the parties of the name of the person consulted and the substance of the advice, and affords the parties reasonable opportunity to respond.

COMMENT

The proscription against communications concerning a proceeding includes communications from lawyers, law teachers, and other persons who are not participants in the proceeding, except to the limited extent permitted. It does not preclude a judicial appointee from consulting with judges, other judicial appointees, or with court personnel whose function is to aid the judicial appointee in carrying out adjudicative responsibilities.

(6) A judicial appointee should dispose promptly of official business.

COMMENT

Prompt disposition of official business requires a judicial appointee to devote adequate time to official duties, to be punctual in attending hearings and expeditious in determining matters under submission, and to insist that officials, litigants and their lawyers cooperate to that end.

(7) A judicial appointee should abstain from public comment about a pending or impending proceeding in any court, and should require similar abstention on the part of personnel subject to the judicial appointee's direction and control. This subsection does not prohibit a judicial appointee from making public statements in the course of official duties or from explaining for public information the procedures of a court.

COMMENT

Personnel subject to the judicial appointee's direction and control does not include the lawyers in a proceeding before a judicial appointee. The conduct of lawyers in this regard is governed by Rule 3.6 of the Maryland Rules of Professional Conduct.

B. ADMINISTRATIVE RESPONSIBILITIES. (1) A judicial appointee should diligently discharge his or her administrative responsibilities, maintain professional competence in judicial administration, and facilitate the performance of the administrative responsibilities of other judicial appointees and court officials.

(2) A judicial appointee should require staff and court officials subject to the judicial appointee's direction and control to observe the standards of fidelity and diligence that apply to the judicial appointee.

(3) A judicial appointee should take or initiate appropriate corrective measures against a judge, a judicial appointee, or a lawyer for unprofessional conduct of which the judicial appointee may be aware.

COMMENT

Corrective measures may include a private admonition or reporting misconduct to the appropriate disciplinary body or a bar association counseling program.

(4) A judicial appointee should not make unnecessary appointments. A judicial appointee should exercise the power of appointment only on the basis of merit, avoiding nepotism and favoritism. The judicial appointee should not approve compensation of appointees beyond the fair value of services rendered.

COMMENT

Consent by the parties to an appointment or an award of compensation does not relieve the judicial appointee of the obligation prescribed by this section.

C. RECUSAL. (1) A judicial appointee should not participate in a proceeding in which the judicial appointee's impartiality might reasonably be questioned, including but not limited to instances where:

(a) the judicial appointee has a personal bias or prejudice concerning a party, or personal knowledge of disputed evidentiary facts concerning the proceeding;

(b) the judicial appointee served as lawyer in the matter in controversy, or a lawyer with whom the judicial appointee previously practiced law served during such association as a lawyer concerning the matter, or the judicial appointee or lawyer has been a material witness concerning it;

COMMENT

A lawyer in a governmental agency does not necessarily have an association with other lawyers employed by that agency within the meaning of this subsection; a judicial appointee formerly employed by a governmental agency, however, should not participate in a proceeding if the judicial appointee's impartiality might reasonably be questioned because of such association.

(c) if a judicial appointee is part-time, the judicial appointee or any attorney with whom the judicial appointee is associated, represents a party or otherwise has an interest in the proceeding;

(d) the judicial appointee knows that he or she, individually or as a fiduciary, or the judicial appointee's spouse or minor child of the judicial appointee residing in the judicial appointee's household, has a significant financial interest in the subject matter in controversy or in a party to the proceeding, or any other interest that could be substantially affected by the outcome of the proceeding;

COMMENT

As a minimum standard for determining what constitutes a "significant financial interest," the judge should apply the definition of "financial interest" provided in the Maryland Public Ethics Law, Md. Code, State Government Article, § 15-102 (n): "(1) Ownership of an interest as the result of which the owner has received within the past 3 years, is currently receiving, or in the future is entitled to receive, more than $1,000 per year; or (2)(i) ownership of more than 3% of a business entity; or (ii) ownership of securities of any kind that represent, or are convertible into,

ownership of more than 3% of a business entity."

Moreover, there may be situations involving a lesser financial interest which also require recusal because of the judicial appointee's own sense of propriety. Conversely, there are situations where participation may be appropriate even though the "financial interest" threshold is present. In the latter case, the judicial appointee must first obtain an opinion from the Judicial Ethics Committee to obtain an exemption, except as provided in Canon 3 D (Non-recusal by Agreement).

(e) the judicial appointee, the spouse of the judicial appointee, a person within the third degree of relationship to either of them, or the spouse of such a person:

(i) is a party to the proceeding, or is known by the judicial appointee to be an officer, director, or trustee of a party;

(ii) is acting as lawyer in the proceeding;

COMMENT

The fact that a lawyer in a proceeding is affiliated with a law firm with which a lawyer-relative of the judicial appointee is affiliated does not of itself require recusal of the judicial appointee. Under appropriate circumstances, the fact that "the judicial appointee's impartiality might reasonably be questioned" under

Canon 3 C (1), or that the lawyer-relative is known by the judicial appointee to have an interest in the law firm that could be "substantially affected by the outcome of the proceeding" under Canon 3 C (1) (d) (iii) may require the judicial appointee's recusal.

(iii) is known by the judicial appointee to have an interest that could be substantially affected by the outcome of the proceeding;

(iv) is to the judicial appointee's knowledge likely to be a material witness in the proceeding.

(2) A judicial appointee should keep informed about his or her personal and fiduciary financial interests, and make a reasonable effort to keep informed about the personal financial interests of the judicial appointee's spouse and minor children residing in the judicial appointee's household.

(3) For the purposes of this section:

(a) the degree of relationship is calculated according to the civil law system;

COMMENT

The following persons are within three degrees of relationship according to the civil law system: parent, grandparent, sibling, child, grandchild, uncle, aunt, niece, and nephew.

(b) "fiduciary" includes such relationships as personal representative, executor, administrator, trustee, custodian, attorney in fact by power of attorney, and guardian;

(c) "financial interest" means ownership of a legal or equitable interest, or a relationship as director, advisor, or other active participant in the affairs of a party, except that:

(i) ownership in a mutual or common investment fund that holds securities is not a "financial interest" in such securities unless the judicial appointee participates in the management of the fund;

(ii) an office in an educational, religious, charitable, fraternal, or civic organization is not a "financial interest" in securities held by the organization.

(iii) the proprietary interest of a policy holder in a mutual insurance company, of a depositor in a mutual savings association, or a similar proprietary interest, is a "financial interest" in the issuer only if the outcome of the proceeding could substantially affect the value of the interest;

(iv) ownership of government securities is a "financial interest" in the issuer only if the outcome of the proceeding could substantially affect the value of the securities.

D. NON-RECUSAL BY AGREEMENT. Where recusal would be required by Canon 3 C (1) (c) or Canon 3 C (1) (d), the judicial appointee may disclose on the record the basis of the recusal. If the lawyers, after consultation with their clients and independently of the judicial appointee's participation, all agree on the record that the judicial appointee ought to participate notwithstanding the basis for recusal, the judicial appointee may participate in the proceeding.

COMMENT

This procedure is designed to minimize the chance that a party or lawyer will feel coerced into an agreement. A pro se party may agree to allow participation by the judicial appointee.

CANON 4

Extra-Official Activities

Except as otherwise prohibited or limited by law or these canons, a judicial appointee may engage in the following activities, if doing so does not interfere with the proper performance of official duties, does not reflect adversely upon the judicial appointee's impartiality, and does not detract from the dignity of the position.

A. AVOCATIONAL ACTIVITIES. A judicial appointee may speak, write, lecture, and teach on both legal and non-legal subjects. A judicial appointee may participate in other activities concerning the law, the legal system and the administration of justice. A judicial appointee may engage in social and recreational activities.

COMMENT

Complete separation of a judicial appointee from extra-official activities is neither possible nor wise; a judicial appointee should not be-come isolated from the society in which he or she may live.

B. GOVERNMENT ACTIVITIES.

(1) A judicial appointee may appear before and confer with public bodies or officials on matters concerning the judicial system or the administration of justice.

COMMENT

As suggested in the *Reporter's Notes to the ABA Code of Judicial Conduct,* the "administration of justice" is not limited to "matters of judicial administration" but is broad enough to include other matters relating to a judicial system.

(2) A judicial appointee may serve on governmental advisory bodies devoted to the improvement of the law, the legal system or the administration of justice and may represent his or her country, state or locality on ceremonial occasions or in connection with historical, educational and cultural activities.

COMMENT

Valuable services have been rendered in the past to the states and the nation by judicial appointees who may be appointed by the executive to undertake additional assignments. The appropriateness of conferring these assignments on judicial appointees must be reassessed, however, in light of the demands on time created by today's crowded dockets and the need to protect the judicial appointees from involvement in matters that may prove to be controversial. Judicial appointees should not be expected or permitted to accept governmental appointments that could interfere with their effectiveness and independence. Nor can a judicial appointee assume or discharge the legislative or executive powers of government or hold an "office" under the constitution or laws of the United States or State of Maryland.

(3) As a private citizen, a judicial appointee may appear before or confer with public bodies or officials on matters that directly relate to a judicial appointee's person, immediate family or property so long as the judicial appointee does not use, and avoids the appearance of using, the prestige of the judicial appointment to influence decision-making.

C. CIVIC AND CHARITABLE ACTIVITIES. A judicial appointee may participate and serve as a member, officer, director, trustee, or non-legal advisor of an educational, religious, charitable, fraternal, law-related or civic organization not conducted for the economic or political advantage of its members, subject to the following provisions:

(1) A judicial appointee should not participate and serve if it is likely that the organization: (a) will be engaged in proceedings that would ordinarily come before the judicial appointee; (b) will be regularly engaged in adversary proceedings in any court; or (c) deals with people who are referred to the organization by the court on recommendation of the judicial appointee or other judicial appointees of that court exercising similar authority.

COMMENT

The changing nature of some organizations and of their relationship to the law makes it necessary for a judicial appointee regularly to reexamine the activities of each organization with which a judicial appointee is affiliated to determine if it is proper to continue a relationship with it. For example, in many jurisdictions charitable organizations are now more frequently in court than in the past or make policy decisions that may have political significance or imply commitment to causes that may come before the courts for adjudication.

As a judicial officer and person specially learned in the law, a judicial appointee is in a unique position to contribute to the improvement of the law, the legal system, and the administration of justice, including revision of substantive and procedural law and the improvement of criminal and juvenile justice. To the extent that time permits, a judicial appointee is encouraged to do so, either independently or through a bar association or other organization dedicated to the improvement of the law.

(2) A judicial appointee should not solicit funds for any such organization, or use or permit the use of the prestige of his or her position for that purpose, but a judicial appointee may be listed as an officer, director, or trustee of the organization. A judicial appointee may make recommendations to public and private fund granting agencies on projects and programs of which the judicial appointee has personal knowledge and which concern the law, the legal system, or the administration of justice. A judicial appointee should not be a speaker or the guest of honor at an organization's fund raising events, but may attend such events.

D. FINANCIAL ACTIVITIES. (1) A judicial appointee should refrain from financial and business dealings that use the judicial appointee's position or involve the judicial appointee in frequent transactions with lawyers or persons likely to come before the judicial appointee or the appointing court in matters relating to the judicial appointee's duties and authority.

COMMENT

This section is not intended to apply to the practice of law of part-time judicial appointees, which is covered by Canon 4I (2).

(2) A judicial appointee may hold and manage investments, including real estate, and engage in other remunerative activity except that a full-time judicial appointee shall not hold any office or directorship in any public utility, bank, savings and loan association, lending institution, insurance company, or any other business corporation or enterprise or venture which is affected with a public interest.

(3) A judicial appointee should manage investments and other financial interests to minimize the number of cases in which recusal would be required. As soon as practicable without serious financial detriment, the judicial appointee should dispose of investments and other financial interests that might require frequent recusal.

(4) Information acquired by a judicial appointee in his or her judicial capacity should not be used or disclosed by the judicial appointee in financial dealings or for any other purpose not related to the judicial appointee's official duties.

E. COMPENSATION AND EXPENSE REIMBURSEMENT. A judicial appointee may receive compensation and reimbursement of expenses for activities permitted by this Code, subject to the following restrictions:

(1) Compensation should not exceed a reasonable amount nor should it exceed what a person who is not a judicial appointee would receive for the same activity.

(2) Expense reimbursement should be limited to the actual cost of travel, food and lodging reasonably incurred by the judicial appointee and, where appropriate to the occasion, by the judicial appointee's spouse. Any payment in excess of such an amount is compensation.

F. GIFTS. (1) A judicial appointee must be especially careful in accepting gifts, favors, and loans from persons not in the judicial appointee's immediate family. However innocently intended, gifts and favors from such persons, especially gifts and favors having substantial monetary value, may create an appearance that the judicial appointee could be improperly beholden to the donor. Subject to this caveat, and except as otherwise prohibited or limited by law or these canons, a judicial appointee may accept:

(a) a gift incident to a public testimonial or books supplied by publishers on a complimentary basis for official use;

(b) ordinary social hospitality;

(c) a gift from a friend or relative by reason of some special occasion, such as a wedding, anniversary, birthday, and the like, if the gift is fairly commensurate with the nature of the occasion and the friendship or relationship;

(d) a gift, favor, or loan from a relative or close personal friend whose appearance before the judicial appointee or whose interest in a case would require a recusal under Canon 3 C;

(e) a scholarship or fellowship awarded on the same terms applied to other applicants;

(f) a loan from a lending institution in its regular course of business on the same terms generally available to persons who are not judicial appointees.

(2) The standards set forth in subsection (1) of this section also apply to gifts, favors, and loans offered to members of the judicial appointee's family who reside in the judicial appointee's household. For purposes of this Canon and absent extraordinary circumstances, gifts, favors and loans accepted by such family members shall be considered to be accepted by the judicial appointee.

Judicial appointees are often invited by lawyers or other persons to attend social, educational, or recreational functions. In most cases, such invitations would fall within the realm of ordinary social hospitality and may be accepted by the judicial appointee. If there is more than a token fee for admission to the function, however, unless the fee is waived by the organization, the judicial appointee should pay the fee and not permit a lawyer or other person to pay it on the judicial appointee's behalf.

G. FIDUCIARY ACTIVITIES. While a judicial appointee is not absolutely disqualified from holding a fiduciary position, a judicial appointee should not accept or continue to hold such position if the holding of it would interfere or seem to interfere with the proper performance of official duties, or if the business interests of those represented require investments in enterprises that are apt to come before the judicial appointee officially or tend to be involved in questions to be determined by the judicial appointee.

H. ARBITRATION. A full-time judicial appointee should not act as an arbitrator or mediator.

COMMENT

This does not preclude a judicial appointee from participating in settlement conferences. If by reason of disclosure made during or as a result of the conference, the judicial appoin-tee's impartiality might reasonably be questioned, the judicial appointee should not further participate in the matter. See Canon 3 C (1).

I. PRACTICE OF LAW. (1) Except as provided in subsection (2), a judicial appointee should not practice law.

(2) A part-time judicial appointee may practice law to the extent permitted by the appointing authority, but the judicial appointee shall not use or appear to use the appointee's position to further that practice.

(3) Prior to assuming official duties, a full-time judicial appointee should enter into an agreement for payments relating to the judicial appointee's former law practice and should submit the agreement to the Judicial Ethics Committee so that the Committee may review it as to the reasonableness of the time provided for payments to be made under the agreement. A payment period limited to a maximum of five years or less is presumptively reasonable. A longer payment period is permitted only with the Committee's prior approval as to its reasonableness. An agreement entered into under this provision may not be amended without the prior approval of the Judicial Ethics Committee.

CANON 5

Political Activity

A. POLITICAL CONDUCT OF A JUDICIAL APPOINTEE WHO IS NOT A CANDIDATE. A judicial appointee who is not a candidate for election to judicial office should not engage in any partisan political activity and should resign the appointed position when becoming a candidate for a non-judicial office, except that a judicial appointee may continue to hold the appointment while a candidate for election to or serving as a delegate in a State constitutional convention.

B. POLITICAL CONDUCT OF A JUDICIAL APPOINTEE WHO IS A CANDIDATE. A judicial appointee who is a candidate for election to judicial office may engage in partisan political activity allowed by law with respect to such candidacy, except that the judicial appointee

(1) should not act as a leader or hold any office in a political organization;

(2) should not make speeches for a political organization or candidate or publicly endorse a candidate for non-judicial office;

387

COMMENT

A judicial appointee does not publicly endorse a candidate for public office by having the judicial appointee's name on the same ticket.

(3) should maintain the dignity appropriate to the appointed position;

(4) should not allow any other person to do for the judicial appointee what the judicial appointee is prohibited from doing;

(5) should not make pledges or promises of conduct in office other than the faithful and impartial performance of the duties of the office, announce the judicial appointee's views on disputed legal or political issues, or misrepresent the judicial appointee's identity, qualifications, or other fact.

C. STATUS OF A JUDICIAL APPOINTEE AS A CANDIDATE. A judicial appointee who is seeking election to a judicial office is a "candidate" for that office when the judicial appointee files a certificate of candidacy in accordance with the State election laws, but no earlier than two years prior to the general election for that office, or when a newly appointed judge to that court becomes a "candidate" in the same general election, whichever first occurs.

CANON 6

Compliance

Violation of any of the canons of this Code of Conduct for Judicial Appointees is grounds for disciplinary action, including removal by the appointing authority. (Added Oct. 14, 1988, effective Jan. 1, 1989; amended Nov. 21, 1995, effective Dec. 1, 1995; June 5, 1996, effective Jan. 1, 1997; Dec. 10, 1996, effective Jan. 1, 1997.)

Source. — This Rule is former Rule 1232.

Effect of amendments. — The first 1996 amendment substituted "Rule 16-813" for "Rule 1231" in the Committee note to the introductory paragraph; and added the Source note.

The second 1996 amendment substituted "Conduct" for "Responsibility" in the Commentary to Canon 3 A (7).

Editor's note. — An Order dated June 5, 1996, effective Jan. 1, 1997, renumbered this Rule, which was formerly Rule 1232.

University of Baltimore Law Review. — For article, "Report of the Special Joint Committee on Gender Bias in the Courts," see 20 U. Balt. L. Rev. 1 (1990).

Recusal decision is discretionary. — Canon 3 C has not been interpreted to require a trial judge, who has presided over a prior case involving the same defendant or incident, automatically to recuse him or herself from presiding over a subsequent trial involving the defendant. The recusal decision, therefore, is discretionary, and the exercise of that discretion will not be overturned except for abuse. Jefferson-El v. State, 330 Md. 99, 622 A.2d 737 (1993).

Presumption of impartiality. — There is a strong presumption in Maryland that judges are impartial participants in the legal process, whose duty to preside when qualified is as strong as their duty to refrain from presiding when not qualified. Jefferson-El v. State, 330 Md. 99, 622 A.2d 737 (1993).

To overcome the presumption of impartiality, a party requesting recusal must prove that the trial judge has a personal bias or prejudice concerning him or personal knowledge of disputed evidentiary facts concerning the proceedings. Jefferson-El v. State, 330 Md. 99, 622 A.2d 737 (1993).

Recusal motion erroneously denied. — Trial judge, who in an earlier proceeding called defendant's acquittal on rape and burglary charge an "abomination" and subsequently brought defendant before court on charges of probation violation, should have granted the defendant's recusal motion to avoid the ap-

pearance of impropriety. Jefferson-El v. State, 330 Md. 99, 622 A.2d 737 (1993).

Rule 16-815. Financial disclosure statement.

a. Every judge shall file with the State Court Administrator an annual financial disclosure statement on the form prescribed by the Court of Appeals. When filed, a financial disclosure statement is a public record.

b. Except as provided in paragraph c of this Rule:

1. The initial financial disclosure statement shall be filed on or before April 15, 1987 and shall cover the period beginning on January 1, 1986 and ending on December 31, 1986.

2. A subsequent statement shall be filed annually on or before April 15 of each year and shall cover the preceding calendar year or that portion of the preceding calendar year during which the judge held office.

3. A financial disclosure statement is presumed to have been filed unless the State Court Administrator, on April 16, notifies a judge that the judge's statement for the preceding calendar year or portion thereof has not been received.

c. If a judge or other person who files a certificate of candidacy for nomination for an election to an elected judgeship has filed a statement pursuant to § 15-610 (b) of the State Government Article, Annotated Code of Maryland, the person need not file for the same period of time the statement required by paragraph b of this Rule.

d. The State Court Administrator is designated as the person to receive statements from the State Administrative Board of Election Laws pursuant to § 15-610 (b) of the State Government Article.

e. *Extention of time for filing.* 1. Except when the judge is required to file a statement pursuant to § 15-610 (b) of the State Government Article, Annotated Code of Maryland, a judge may apply to the State Court Administrator for an extension of time for filing the statement. The application shall be submitted prior to the deadline for filing the statement, and shall set forth in detail the reasons an extension is requested and the date upon which a completed statement will be filed.

2. For good cause shown, the State Court Administrator may grant a reasonable extension of time for filing the statement. Whether he grants or denies the request, the State Court Administrator shall furnish the judge and the Judicial Ethics Committee with a written statement of his reasons, and the facts upon which this decision is based.

3. A judge who is dissatisfied with the State Court Administrator's decision may seek review by the Judicial Ethics Committee by filing with the Committee a statement of reasons for the judge's dissatisfaction within ten days from the date of the State Court Administrator's decision. The Committee may take the action it deems appropriate with or without a hearing or the consideration of additional documents.

f. *Failure to file statement — Incomplete statement.* 1. A judge who fails to file a timely statement, or who files an incomplete statement, shall be notified in writing by the State Court Administrator, and given a reasonable time, not to exceed ten days, within which to correct the deficiency. If the deficiency has not been corrected within the time allowed, the State Court Administrator shall report the matter to the Committee on Judicial Ethics.

2. If the Committee finds, after inquiry, that the failure to file or the omission of information was either inadvertent or in a good faith belief that the omitted information was not required to be disclosed, the Committee shall give the judge a reasonable period, not to exceed 15 days, within which to correct the deficiency. Otherwise, the Committee shall refer the matter to the Commission on Judicial Disabilities. If a judge who has been allowed additional time within which to correct a deficiency fails to do so within that time, the matter shall also be referred to the Commission on Judicial Disabilities.

g. This rule applies to any judge of a court named in Canon 6 A who has resigned or retired in any calendar year, with respect to the portion of that calendar year prior to his resignation or retirement. (Added Nov. 21, 1986, effective July 1, 1987; amended Nov. 21, 1995, effective Dec. 1, 1995; June 5, 1996, effective Jan. 1, 1997.)

Source. — This Rule is former Rule 1233.

Effect of amendments. — The 1996 amendment rewrote the Source note.

Editor's note. — An Order dated June 5, 1996, effective Jan. 1, 1997, renumbered this Rule, which was formerly Rule 1233.

Canon 6 A, which is referred to in section g, is incorporated as part of Rule 16-813.

Rule 16-816. Financial disclosure statement — Judicial appointees.

a. In this Rule, "judicial appointee" includes a full-time judicial appointee as defined in Maryland Rule 16-814 and any master, examiner, auditor, referee, or District Court commissioner as defined in that Rule who earns in any calendar year, by reason of the judicial appointee's official position, compensation at least equal to the pay provided for the base step of State Pay Grade 16, as in effect on July 1 of that calendar year. If a judicial appointee has served as such for only a portion of a calendar year, a pro rata determination of compensation shall be applied.

b. Every appointee shall file with the State Court Administrator an annual financial statement on the form prescribed by the Court of Appeals. When filed, a financial disclosure statement is a public record.

c. Except as provided in paragraph d of this Rule:

(i) The initial financial disclosure statement shall be filed on or before April 15, 1989, and shall cover the period beginning on January 1, 1988, and ending on December 31, 1988.

(ii) A subsequent statement shall be filed annually on or before April 15 of each year, and shall cover the preceding calendar year or that portion of the preceding calendar year during which the judicial appointee held office.

(iii) A financial disclosure statement is presumed to have been filed unless the State Court Administrator, on April 16, notifies a judicial appointee that the judicial appointee's statement for the preceding calendar year or portion thereof has not been received.

d. If an appointee who files a certificate of candidacy for nomination for an elected office has filed a statement pursuant to § 15-605 or § 15-610 (b) of the State Government Article, Annotated Code of Maryland, the judicial appointee need not file for the same period of time the statement required by paragraph c of this Rule.

e. The State Court Administrator is designated as the person to receive statements from the State Administrative Board of Election Laws pursuant to § 15-610 (b) of the State Government Article.

f.(i) Except when the judicial appointee is required to file a statement pursuant to § 15-605 or § 15-610 (b) of the State Government Article, Annotated Code of Maryland, a judicial appointee may apply to the State Court Administrator for an extension of time for filing the judicial appointee's statement. The application shall be submitted prior to the deadline for filing the statement, and shall set forth in detail the reasons an extension is requested and the date upon which a completed statement will be filed.

(ii) For good cause shown, the State Court Administrator may grant a reasonable extension of time for filing the statement. Whether the request is denied or approved, the State Court Administrator shall furnish the judicial appointee and the Judicial Ethics Committee with a written statement of the State Court Administrator's reasons, and the facts upon which this decision is based.

(iii) A judicial appointee who is dissatisfied with the State Court Administrator's decision may seek review by the Judicial Ethics Committee by filing with the Committee a statement of reasons for the judicial appointee's dissatisfaction within ten days from the date of the State Court Administrator's decision. The Committee may take the action it deems appropriate with or without a hearing or the consideration of additional documents.

g.(i) A judicial appointee who fails to file a timely statement, or who files an incomplete statement, shall be notified in writing by the State Court Administrator, and given a reasonable time, not to exceed ten days, within which to correct the deficiency. If the deficiency has not been corrected within the time allowed, the State Court Administrator shall report the matter to the Committee on Judicial Ethics.

(ii) If the Committee finds, after inquiry, that failing to file or the omission of information was either inadvertent or in good faith belief that the omitted information was not required to be disclosed, the Committee shall give the appointee a reasonable period, not to exceed 15 days, within which to correct the deficiency. Otherwise, the Committee shall refer the matter to the State Ethics Commission. If an appointee who has been allowed additional time within which to correct a deficiency fails to do so within that time, the matter shall also be referred to the State Ethics Commission.

h. Violation of this Rule is grounds for disciplinary action, including removal, by the appointing authority. (Added Oct. 14, 1988, effective Jan. 1, 1989; amended Nov. 21, 1995, effective Dec. 1, 1995; June 5, 1996, effective Jan. 1, 1997.)

Source. — This Rule is former Rule 1234.

Effect of amendments. — The 1996 amendment substituted "Rule 16-814" for "Rule 1233" in the first sentence of a.; and added the Source note.

Editor's note. — An Order dated June 5, 1996, effective Jan. 1, 1997, renumbered this Rule, which was formerly Rule 1234.

Rule 16-817. Appointment of bail bond commissioner — Licensing and regulation of bail bondsmen.

A majority of the judges of any judicial circuit may appoint a bail bond commissioner and license and regulate bail bondsmen and acceptance of bail bonds.

Each bail bond commissioner appointed pursuant to this Rule shall prepare, maintain and periodically distribute to all District Court commissioners and clerks within his jurisdiction for posting in their respective offices, and to the State Court Administrator, an alphabetical list of bail bondsmen licensed to write bail bonds within the judicial circuit, showing the bail bondsman's name, business address and telephone number, and any limit on the amount of any one bond, and the aggregate limit on all bonds, each bail bondsman is authorized to write. (Added Jan. 1, 1977, effective July 1, 1977; amended June 5, 1996, effective Jan. 1, 1997.)

Source. — This Rule is former Rule 1285.

Effect of amendments. — The 1996 amendment added the Source note.
Editor's note. — An Order dated June 5,

1996, effective Jan. 1, 1997, renumbered this Rule, which was formerly Rule 1285.

Rule 16-818. Disposition of records.

a. *Definitions.* In this Rule, unless the context or subject matter otherwise requires:

1. Dispose. "Dispose" means to either destroy or remove records.

2. Records. "Records" mean any original papers, official books, documents, files, including but not limited to dockets, electronic recordings of testimony and exhibits within the custody of the clerk of the court.

Cross references. — See Code, §§ 9-1009 and 10-639 through 10-642 of the State Government Article.

3. Schedule. "Schedule" means the form known as the "Records Retention and Disposal Schedule" used by the Records Management Division of the Hall of Records Commission.

b. *Authority.* Subject to the provisions of this Rule, the clerk of the court, with the written approval of the County Administrative Judge and in cooperation with the Hall of Records Commission, may dispose of records within his custody.

Cross references. — See § 2-205 of the Courts Article.

c. *Procedure.* 1. Schedule preparation — Hall of Records recommendation. The clerk of the court shall prepare a schedule for the disposition of court records and submit it to the Hall of Records Commission for its recommendation.

2. Administrative judge — Approval. The schedule, together with the recommendation of the Hall of Records Commission, shall be submitted for the written approval of the County Administrative Judge who may approve it in whole or in part, amend it or disapprove it.

3. Court order. Approval of the schedule by the County Administrative Judge shall be deemed an order of court providing for disposal of the records.

4. Contents of schedule. The schedule, as approved, shall set forth:

(i) The identification of the records.

(ii) The length of time the records are to be retained by the clerk of the court before disposition.

(iii) Whether the Hall of Records Commission declines to accept the records for preservation.

(iv) Whether the records are to be destroyed or removed.

(v) The place to which the records would be removed.

(vi) Whether the schedule shall be "standing" viz., operative until changed by further order of court.

5. Removal procedures — Hall of Records. In those cases where the Hall of Records Commission accepts records, they shall be removed according to the Hall of Records Commission procedures.

6. Disposal if Hall of Records declines custody. In those cases where the Hall of Records Commission declines records, disposition shall be according to the terms set forth in the schedule as approved. If the records are to be destroyed the clerk shall obtain the approval of the Board of Public Works and upon destruction shall file a certificate of destruction with the Hall of Records Commission.

Cross references. — See Code, § 10-642 of the State Government Article.

Committee note. — This Rule is meant to allow periodic destruction of records without the necessity of obtaining Board of Public Works approval each time if such destruction of records or classes of records had been clearly approved by the Board of Public Works in a standing schedule.

d. *Limitations upon disposal of records.* 1. Permanent retention — Clerks or Hall of Records. Records which shall be retained permanently either by the clerks or the Hall of Records Commission:

(i) Permanent books of account.

(ii) Indices and dockets maintained by the clerks.

(iii) Other records as designated on a schedule as approved.

2. Permanent retention — Clerks. Records which shall be retained permanently by the clerk:

(i) Records affecting title to real estate.

3. Records destruction after certain periods. Records which may be destroyed by the clerk after the following minimum periods of time:

(i) Motor vehicle and natural resources cases — three years after case is closed and audit performed, if required; except for convictions of offenses which carry subsequent offender penalties which cases shall be retained as permanent records.

(ii) Landlord/Tenant cases — three years in cases involving restitution of premises where there is no money judgment.

(iii) Other records — according to times designated on a schedule as approved — twelve years.

4. Disposal if photographed, photocopied, or microphotographed. Any of the records set forth in subsections 1, 2, and 3 of this section may be disposed of at any time provided that the records have been photographed, photocopied or microphotographed in accordance with the Hall of Records Commission procedures and copies have been substituted therefor. (Added June 16, 1975, effective July 1, 1975; amended Dec. 17, 1975, effective Jan. 1, 1976; May 6, 1977, effective July 1, 1977; June 5, 1996, effective Jan. 1, 1997.)

Source. — This Rule is former Rule 1299.

Effect of amendments. — The 1996 amendment added the Source note.

Editor's note. — An Order dated June 5, 1996, effective Jan. 1, 1997, renumbered this Rule, which was formerly Rule 1299.

TITLE 17. ALTERNATIVE DISPUTE RESOLUTION

CHAPTER 100. PROCEEDINGS IN CIRCUIT COURT.

Editor's note. — This Chapter was added Oct. 9, 1998, effective January 1, 1999.

Rule 17-101. Applicability.

(a) *Generally.* The rules in this Chapter apply only to civil actions in a circuit court. The rules in this Chapter do not apply to actions or orders to enforce a contractual agreement to submit a dispute to alternative dispute resolution.

(b) *Rules governing qualifications and selection.* The rules governing the qualifications and selection of a person designated to conduct court-ordered alternative dispute resolution proceedings apply only to a person designated by the court in the absence of an agreement by the parties. They do not apply to a master, examiner, or auditor appointed under Rules 2-541, 2-542, or 2-543.

Source. — This Rule is new.

Rule 17-102. Definitions.

In this Chapter, the following definitions apply except as expressly otherwise provided or as necessary implication requires:

(a) *Alternative dispute resolution.* "Alternative dispute resolution" means the process of resolving matters in pending litigation through a settlement conference, neutral case evaluation, neutral fact finding, arbitration, mediation, other non-judicial dispute resolution process, or combination of those processes.

(b) *Arbitration.* "Arbitration" means a process in which (1) the parties appear before one or more arbitrators and present evidence and argument supporting their respective positions, and (2) the arbitrators render a decision in the form of an award that, unless the parties otherwise agree in writing, is not binding.

(c) *Fee-for-service.* "Fee-for-service" means that a party will be charged a fee by the person or persons conducting the alternative dispute resolution proceeding.

(d) *Mediation.* "Mediation" means a process in which the parties appear before an impartial mediator who, through the application of standard mediation techniques generally accepted within the professional mediation

395

community and without providing legal advice, assists the parties in reaching their own voluntary agreement for the resolution of all or part of their dispute. A mediator may identify issues, explore settlement alternatives, and discuss candidly with the parties or their attorneys the basis and practicality of their respective positions, but, unless the parties agree otherwise, the mediator does not engage in arbitration, neutral case evaluation, or neutral fact-finding and does not recommend the terms of an agreement.

(e) *Neutral case evaluation.* "Neutral case evaluation" means a process in which (1) the parties, their attorneys, or both appear before an impartial person and present in summary fashion the evidence and arguments supporting their respective positions, and (2) the impartial person renders an evaluation of their positions and an opinion as to the likely outcome if the action is tried.

(f) *Neutral fact-finding.* "Neutral fact-finding" means a process in which (1) the parties, their attorneys, or both appear before an impartial person and present evidence and arguments supporting their respective positions as to particular disputed factual issues, and (2) the impartial person makes findings of fact as to those issues. Unless the parties otherwise agree in writing, those findings are not binding.

(g) *Settlement conference.* "Settlement conference" means a conference at which the parties, their attorneys, or both appear before an impartial person to discuss the issues and positions of the parties in the action in an attempt to resolve the dispute or issues in the dispute by agreement or by means other than trial. A settlement conference may include neutral case evaluation and neutral fact-finding, and the impartial person may recommend the terms of an agreement.

Source. — This Rule is new.

Rule 17-103. General procedures and requirements.

(a) *In general.* A court may not require a party or the party's attorney to participate in an alternative dispute resolution proceeding except in accordance with this Rule.

(b) *Minimum qualifications required for court designees.* A court may not require a party or the party's attorney to participate in an alternative dispute resolution proceeding conducted by a person designated by the court unless (1) that person possesses the minimum qualifications prescribed in the applicable rules in this Chapter, or (2) the parties agree to participate in the process conducted by that person.

(c) *Procedure.* (1) Inapplicable to Child Access Disputes. This section does not apply to proceedings under Rule 9-205.

(2) Objection. If the court enters an order or determines to enter an order referring a matter to an alternative dispute resolution process, the court shall give the parties a reasonable opportunity (A) to object to the referral, (B) to offer an alternative proposal, and (C) to agree on a person to conduct the proceeding. The court may provide that opportunity before the order is entered or upon request of a party filed within 30 days after the order is entered.

(3) Ruling on Objection. The court shall give fair consideration to an objection to a referral and to any alternative proposed by a party. The court may not require an objecting party or the attorney of an objecting party to participate in an alternative dispute resolution proceeding other than a non-fee-for-service settlement conference.

(4) Designation of Person to Conduct Procedure. In an order referring an action to an alternative dispute resolution proceeding, the court may tentatively designate any person qualified under these rules to conduct the proceeding. The order shall set a reasonable time within which the parties may inform the court that (A) they have agreed on another person to conduct the proceeding, and (B) that person is willing and able to conduct the proceeding. If, within the time allowed by the court, the parties inform the court of their agreement on another person willing and able to conduct the proceeding, the court shall designate that person. Otherwise, the referral shall be to the person designated in the order. In making a designation when there is no agreement by the parties, the court is not required to choose at random or in any particular order from among the qualified persons. Although the court should endeavor to use the services of as many qualified persons as possible, the court may consider whether, in light of the issues and circumstances presented by the action or the parties, special training, background, experience, expertise, or temperament may be helpful and may designate a person possessing those special qualifications.

Source. — This Rule is new.

Rule 17-104. Qualifications and selection of mediators.

(a) *Qualifications in general.* To be designated by the court as a mediator, other than by agreement of the parties, a person must:

(1) be at least 21 years old;

(2) unless waived by the court for good cause in connection with a particular action, have at least a bachelor's degree from an accredited college or university;

(3) have completed at least 40 hours of mediation training in a program meeting the requirements of Rule 17-106;

(4) agree to abide by a code of ethics approved by the Court of Appeals;

(5) agree to submit to periodic monitoring of court-ordered mediations by a qualified mediator designated by the county administrative judge; and

(6) agree to comply with reasonable procedures and requirements prescribed in the court's case management plan filed under Rule 16-203 b. relating to diligence, quality assurance, and a willingness to accept a reasonable number of referrals on a reduced-fee or pro bono basis upon request by the court.

(b) *Additional qualifications for mediators of child access disputes.* To be designated by the court as a mediator with respect to issues concerning child custody or visitation, the person must:

(1) have the qualifications prescribed in section (a) of this Rule;

(2) have completed at least 20 hours of training in a family mediation training program meeting the requirements of Rule 17-106; and

(3) have observed at least two custody or visitation mediations conducted by a person approved by the county administrative judge, in addition to any observations during the training program.

Source. — This Rule is new.

Rule 17-105. Qualifications and selections of persons other than mediators.

(a) *Generally.* Except as provided in section (b) of this Rule, to be designated by the Court to conduct an alternative dispute resolution proceeding other than mediation, a person, unless the parties agree otherwise, must:

(1) agree to abide by a code of ethics approved by the Court of Appeals;

(2) agree to submit to periodic monitoring of court-ordered alternative dispute resolution proceedings by a qualified person designated by the county administrative judge;

(3) agree to comply with reasonable procedures and requirements prescribed in the court's case management plan filed under Rule 16-203 b. relating to diligence, quality assurance, and a willingness to accept a reasonable number of referrals on a reduced-fee or pro bono basis upon request by the court;

(4) either (A) be a member in good standing of the Maryland bar and have at least five years experience in the active practice of law as (i) a judge, (ii) a practitioner, (iii) a full-time teacher of law at a law school accredited by the American Bar Association, or (iv) a Federal or Maryland administrative law judge, or (B) have equivalent or specialized knowledge and experience in dealing with the issues in dispute; and

(5) have either completed a training program specified by the circuit administrative judge or conducted at least two alternative dispute resolution proceedings with respect to actions pending in a circuit court.

(b) *Judges and masters.* A judge or master of the court may conduct a non-fee-for-service settlement conference.

Cross references. — See Rules 16-813, Canon 4H and 16-814, Canon 4H.
Source. — This Rule is new.

Rule 17-106. Mediation training programs.

(a) *In general.* To qualify under Rule 17-104 (a)(3), a mediation training program must include the following:

(1) conflict resolution and mediation theory, including causes of conflict, interest-based versus positional bargaining, and models of conflict resolution;

(2) mediation skills and techniques, including information gathering skills, communication skills, problem solving skills, interaction skills, conflict management skills, negotiation techniques, caucusing, cultural and gender issues, and power balancing;

(3) mediator conduct, including conflicts of interest, confidentiality, neutrality, ethics, and standards of practice;

(4) rules, statutes, and practice governing mediation in the circuit courts; and

(5) rules, statutes, and practice governing mediation in the circuit courts; and

(b) *Child access mediation training.* To qualify under Rule 17-104 (b)(2), a mediation training program must include the following:

(1) Maryland law relating to separation, divorce, annulment, child custody and visitation, child and spousal support;

(2) emotional aspects of separation and divorce on adults and children;

(3) screening for and addressing domestic violence;

(4) introduction to family systems and child development theory; and

(5) inter-relationship of custody and child support.

Source. — This Rule is new.

Rule 17-107. Procedure for approval.

(a) *Application.* A person seeking designation to conduct alternative dispute resolution proceedings pursuant to Rule 2-504 shall file an application with the clerk of the circuit court from which the person is willing to accept referrals. The application shall be substantially in the form approved by the State Court Administrator and shall be accompanied by documentation demonstrating that the applicant has the qualifications required by Rule 17-104, if the person is applying for designation as a mediator, or Rule 17-105 (a), if the person is applying for designation to conduct alternative dispute resolution proceedings other than mediation. The State Court Administrator may require the application and documentation to be in a form that can be stored in a computer.

(b) *Approved lists.* After any investigation that the county administrative judge chooses to make, the county administrative judge shall notify each applicant of the approval or disapproval of the application and the reasons for a disapproval. The clerk shall prepare a list of mediators found by the county administrative judge to meet the qualifications required by Rule 17-104 and a separate list of persons found by the county administrative judge to meet the qualifications required by Rule 17-105 (a) for conducting other alternative dispute resolution proceedings. Those lists, together with the applications of the persons on the lists, shall be kept current by the clerk and be available in the clerk's office to the public.

(c) *Removal from list.* After notice and a reasonable opportunity to respond, the county administrative judge shall remove a person from a list if the person ceases to meet the applicable qualifications of Rule 17-104 or Rule 17-105 (a) and may remove a person for other good cause.

Source. — This Rule is new.

Rule 17-108. Fee schedules.

Subject to the approval of the Chief Judge of the Court of Appeals, the county administrative judge of each circuit court may develop and adopt maximum fee schedules for persons conducting each type of alternative dispute resolution proceeding other than on a volunteer basis. In developing the fee schedules, the county administrative judge shall take into account the availability of qualified persons willing to provide those services and the ability of litigants to pay for those services. A person designated by the court, other than on the agreement of the parties, to conduct an alternative dispute resolution proceeding under Rule 2-504 may not charge or accept a fee for that proceeding in excess of that allowed by the schedule. Violation of this Rule shall be cause for removal from all lists.

Source. — This Rule is new.

APPENDIX: FORMS

Introductory statement.

Form
1 to 21. [Rescinded].
22. Notice of appeal.
22a to 26. [Rescinded].
27 to 36. Juvenile causes.
611. [Rescinded].
1-332. Notification under Rule 1-332 of need
    for accommodation.

Forms for Juvenile Causes.

903-P/C. Juvenile petition — Child.
903-P/A. Juvenile petition — Adult.
904-R. Recognizance of parent, guardian, or
    custodian.
904-S. Summons.
904-R/WS. Request for witness subpoena.
904-WS. Witness subpoena.
904-WA. Writ of attachment.
905-OE. Order for physical or mental exami-
    nation of respondent.
912-A. Authorization for emergency detention
    or shelter care pending hearing.
912-N. Notice of emergency detention/shelter
    care and notice of hearing.
912-P/CDSC. Petition for continued detention
    or shelter care.
912-O/CDSC. Order for continued detention
    or shelter care.
913-P/W. Petition for waiver of juvenile juris-
    diction.
913-O/W. Order waiving juvenile jurisdiction.
914-O/A. Order of adjudication.
915-O/PDC. Order for probation of delinquent
    child.
915-O/CJ. Order for commitment of juvenile.
915-O/PS. Order for protective supervision.
915-O/PA. Order for probation — Adult.

Form
916-P/RPC. Petition for revocation of proba-
    tion and for commitment of delin-
    quent child.
916-P/RPSC. Petition for revocation of protec-
    tive supervision and for commitment.
916-SCO. Show cause order.
916-O/RCAS. Order rescinding commitment
    and for aftercare supervision.
916-O/TPPS. Order terminating probation/
    protective supervision.
918-O/S. Order for support.
918-O/JR. Order for judgment of restitution.
920-FOT. Final order of termination.

Forms for Expungement of Records.
[Rescinded].

Bail Bond Forms.
[Rescinded].

Forms for Special Admission of Out-of-
State Attorney.

RGAB-14/M. Motion for special admission of
    out-of-state attorney under Rule 14 of
    the Rules Governing Admission to the
    Bar of Maryland.
RGAB-14/O. Order.

Form Interrogatories.

1. Instructions.
2. General definitions.
3. General interrogatories.
4. Domestic relations definitions.
5. Domestic relations interrogatories.
6. Motor vehicle tort definitions.
7. Motor vehicle tort interrogatories.
8. Personal injury interrogatories.

Introductory statement.

The forms contained in this Appendix are limited in number and intended to illustrate some of the more commonly used forms in modern practice. Rule 1-302 provides that the forms in this Appendix are not mandatory except as otherwise expressly provided by rule or statute.

Forms 1 to 21.

Rescinded April 6, 1984, effective July 1, 1984.

Form 22. Notice of appeal.
(Rule 8-201)

(Caption)

NOTICE OF APPEAL

_____ notes an appeal to the Court of Special Appeals in the above-captioned action.

(Signature and Certificate of Service)

Editor's note. — This form was amended Feb. 10, 1998, effective July 1, 1998.

Forms 22a to 26.
Rescinded June 5, 1996, effective January 1, 1997.

Forms 27 to 36. Juvenile causes.
New forms substituted.

Editor's note. — Forms 903-P/C to 920-FOT were substituted for Forms 27 to 36 by Order of the Court of Appeals dated June 18, 1975.

Form 611. Notice of judgment by default or decree pro confesso.
Rescinded April 6, 1984, effective July 1, 1984.

Form 1-332. Notification under Rule 1-332 of need for accommodation.
Court: _____

Case Name: _____

Case Number: _____

Trial or Hearing Date, if known: _____

NOTIFICATION UNDER RULE 1-332 OF NEED FOR ACCOMMODATION

☐ Assistive Listening Device _____ (specify type)
☐ Computer Assisted Technology
☐ Documents ☐ in large print _____ (specify size)
     or ☐ in Braille or ☐ in digital form or ☐ on cassette
☐ Communication board
☐ Electrical outlet for, e.g., assistive notetaking device
☐ Escort
☐ Familiarization with courtroom layout
☐ Guide dog accommodations _____ (specify)
☐ Interpreter (in connection with disability) _____ (specify language)
☐ Lighting _____ (specify)
☐ Quiet room

402

- ☐ Recesses at _____ intervals (specify time or other interval)
- ☐ Scheduling of proceedings in ☐ a.m. or ☐ p.m.
- ☐ Small room
- ☐ Stair-free access to facility
- ☐ Use of personal tape recorder
- ☐ Videotaped testimony
- ☐ Visual aid machine _____ (specify)
- ☐ Wheel-chair accessible facilities, including ☐ raised/lowered counsel table; ☐ accessible witness stand
- ☐ Other _____

_____

_____

Name of person needing assistance: _____
Attorney's name, address, and telephone number: _____
_____

Date: _____

Form effective October 1, 1994. — This form was added June 7, 1994, effective October 1, 1994.

FORMS FOR JUVENILE CAUSES.

Form 903-P/C. Juvenile petition — Child.
MATTER OF

....
     (Respondent)

IN THE .... COURT
FOR .... CITY/COUNTY
SITTING AS A JUVENILE
COURT
     Case Number ....

JUVENILE PETITION — CHILD

TO THE HONORABLE JUDGE OF THE COURT:

The Petition of the State of Maryland respectfully shows:
1. That:
(a) The Respondent's home address is ....
....
(b) He resides with ....
     at that address.
(c) The name and address of his parent, guardian, or custodian is ....
....
(d) The Respondent's date of birth is ....

2. That the State alleges the Respondent is
   ☐ Delinquent   ☐ In need of supervision
   ☐ In need of assistance

3. That the facts on which the allegation is based are as follows: ....
   ....
   in violation of ....
   (specify law violated, if applicable)

4. That pending these proceedings, the Respondent:
   ☐ was released in the custody of ....
   ....
   (name and address)
   ☐ has been in detention/shelter care since ....
   (date)

and that his parent, guardian, or custodian has/has not been notified of the
detention or shelter care.

WHEREFORE, the State asks that the Court make appropriate findings and
dispositions under the Juvenile Causes Law (Title 3, Subtitle 8, Courts Article,
Annotated Code of Maryland).

STATE OF MARYLAND
by ....
State's Attorney/Intake Officer
for .... City/County
Petitioner

The names of each witness to be summoned in support of this petition are:

Rev. 9/76

Editor's note. — By Order dated Nov. 5, 1976, effective Jan. 1, 1977, the Court of Appeals adopted the Fifty-sixth Report of the Standing Committee on Rules of Practice and Procedure, including the present Forms for juvenile causes.

Form 903-P/A. Juvenile petition — Adult.

(Caption)

JUVENILE PETITION — ADULT

TO THE HONORABLE JUDGE OF THE COURT:

The Petition of the State of Maryland respectfully shows:

1. That the Respondent was born on .... and is an adult residing at
....

2. That your petitioner alleges that the Respondent has willfully committed
an act, omission, or condition which contributed to, encouraged, caused or

tended to cause .... to be brought within the jurisdiction of the Courts as a

        ☐ delinquent child.
        ☐ child in need of supervision.
        ☐ child in need of assistance.

3. That the facts on which the allegation is based are as follows:
....
in violation of section 3-831 of the Courts Article of the Annotated Code of Maryland.

4. That pending these proceedings, the Respondent was
        ☐ not arrested on this charge
        ☐ released on recognizance
        ☐ detained in default of $...... bail.

WHEREFORE, the State asks that the Court make appropriate findings and dispositions under the Juvenile Causes Law (Title 3, Subtitle 8, Courts Article, Annotated Code of Maryland).

                     STATE OF MARYLAND
                     By ....
                     State's Attorney for
                     .... City/County
                     Petitioner

The names of each witness to be summoned in support of this petition are:
Rev. 9/76

Form 904-R. Recognizance of parent, guardian, or custodian.

RECOGNIZANCE OF PARENT, GUARDIAN, OR CUSTODIAN

I hereby acknowledge:

1. That I am the parent, guardian, or custodian of ....;
2. That the child was released into my custody at .... o'clock on ...., 19 ..., pending possible proceedings in the .... Court for .... City/County, sitting as a Juvenile Court;
3. That, as a condition of the child's release, I hereby assume the responsibility for retaining custody and control of the child and for bringing him before the court when ordered to do so;
4. That I have posted $ ...... as security for the child's appearance in court, and that all or part of it may be forfeited if I fail to produce the child when ordered to do so;
5. That the child may be taken into custody and I may be proceeded against for contempt of court if I fail to produce the child before the court when ordered to do so.
6. That I will immediately notify the Clerk of the Juvenile Court at ...., ..., of any new address for me or the child.

Address   Telephone

....

Witness   Parent/Guardian/Custodian

            ....

            Address

....

Date   Telephone Number

Rev. 9/76

Form 904-S. Summons.

(Caption)

SUMMONS

STATE OF MARYLAND ....   City/County

TO: ....

....

(Address)

....

....

You are hereby summoned to attend a ....

(specify type)

hearing in this case at ...., 19 ..., at ....., Maryland.

IF YOU FAIL TO ATTEND, YOU MAY BE ARRESTED.

ISSUED the .... day of .... , 19 ....

WITNESS the Honorable .... Judge of the ....

(place)

Court for .... City/County, Maryland.

            ....

(SEAL)   Clerk

TO THE PERSON SUMMONED: TAKE NOTICE that the Court may, at this or any later hearings, consider and pass orders concerning but not limited to the detention, shelter care, commitment, custody, treatment, and supervision of the respondent child; responsibility for his support; restitution by the respondent and/or his parents in an amount not to exceed $10,000; controlling the conduct of persons before the court; and assessment of court costs.

You may, if you wish, retain a lawyer to represent you or the child; if you do, be sure to show this Summons to him. If you cannot afford a lawyer, contact the Office of the Public Defender on any weekday between 8:30 and 4:30 at: .... Telephone Number: .... A postponement will NOT be granted because you fail to contact a lawyer.

If you do not want a lawyer, but you wish to subpoena witnesses on your behalf or on behalf of the respondent child, you must list their names and addresses neatly on the enclosed Request for Witness Subpoena Form, and mail it promptly to the Clerk at the address shown on the form.

RETURN OF SERVICE

SUMMONED ....
by personal service and delivering
a copy of this Summons and the
attached ....
....
to the said
.... at
....
this .... day of ....
19 ...

Non Est: ....
Other ....
....
ATTEMPTS AT SERVICE
....
Date   Time   Date   Time
....
....
By: ....
                          Sheriff

Rev. 9/76, 7/87, 12/95

Editor's note. — This form was amended April 6, 1984, effective July 1, 1984; March 3, 1987, effective July 1, 1987; and Nov. 21, 1995, effective Dec. 1, 1995.

Form 904-R/WS. Request for witness subpoena.

(Caption)

REQUEST FOR WITNESS SUBPOENA

Clerk, Juvenile Court for .... City/County
....
(address)
....

Please subpoena the following:

Name: ....   Address: ....
       ....
       ....
       ....
       ....

to testify for the respondent at the hearing in this case.

                          Signed ....
                          Respondent, Parent, Guardian,
                          Custodian or Attorney
                          (Circle appropriate status)

Rev. 9/76

Editor's note. — This form was amended April 6, 1984, effective July 1, 1984.

Form 904-WS. Witness subpoena.

(Caption)

WITNESS SUBPOENA

STATE OF MARYLAND .... City/County:

TO: ....

....

(Address)

....

You are hereby subpoenaed to attend a hearing in this case at .... M. on

(time)

.... at ...., Maryland, to testify on behalf of the

date   place

State/Respondent.

IF YOU FAIL TO ATTEND, YOU MAY BE ARRESTED.

ISSUED the ...... day of ...., 19 ....

WITNESS the Honorable ...., Judge of the .... Court for
.... City/County, Maryland.

....

(SEAL)   Clerk

RETURN OF SERVICE

SUBPOENAED ....   Non Est: ....
by personal service of a copy   Other: ....
of this Subpoena
Subpoenaed on the said   Date   Time   Date   Time
.... at   ....
....
this ...... day of ....   By: ....
19 ...   Sheriff

Rev. 9/76

Editor's note. — This form was amended
April 6, 1984, effective July 1, 1984.

Form 904-WA. Writ of attachment.

(Caption)

WRIT OF ATTACHMENT

TO THE SHERIFF OF .... CITY/COUNTY

WHEREAS, the Respondent ...., was released in the custody of his parent, guardian or custodian on recognizance pending further proceedings, and his parent, guardian or custodian has failed to produce the Respondent at a hearing before the Court, you are commanded to take the said Respondent into custody and deliver him before the Court.

ISSUED this ...... day of ...., 19 ... by the .... Court for .... City/County, Maryland.

....
Clerk

CIPI this ...... day of ...., 19 ..., at ...M. and copy of writ delivered.
NON EST ....

....
Sheriff

Rev. 9/76

Form 905-OE. Order for physical or mental examination of respondent.

(Caption)

ORDER FOR PHYSICAL OR MENTAL EXAMINATION
OF RESPONDENT

WHEREAS, the Respondent is before this Court on a Juvenile Petition alleging that he is:

☐ delinquent
☐ in need of supervision
☐ in need of assistance; and

The Court believing that the Respondent should be examined in order to assist the Court in making a proper adjudication and disposition, it is thereupon

ORDERED, this ...... day of ...., 19 ..., by the .... Court for .... City/County, Maryland, sitting as a Juvenile Court, that the Respondent .... be examined by a qualified .... at .... on or before ...., 19 ..., for the purpose of advising the Court as to

☐ his competence to participate in these proceedings
☐ his responsibility for the alleged acts
☐ his general mental and physical condition
☐ the propriety of the Court waiving its jurisdiction
☐ any physical or mental condition that may require treatment

and it is further

ORDERED, that the Report of the examination be delivered to Court; and it is further

409

ORDERED, that the cost of the examination be paid by ....; and it is further

ORDERED, that a copy of this Order be served on the Respondent and on ....

Recommended:

....
Master for Juvenile Causes

....
Judge

Rev. 9/76

Form 912-A. Authorization for emergency detention or shelter care pending hearing.

(Caption)

AUTHORIZATION FOR EMERGENCY DETENTION OR
SHELTER CARE PENDING HEARING

TO: ....
....
(Address)
....

WHEREAS, it has been determined that .... requires emergency

☐ detention, having been alleged delinquent;
☐ shelter care, having been alleged to be delinquent, in need of supervision, or in need of assistance

you are hereby authorized to receive and keep the child in your care and custody pending a hearing in this case on ....
(Date)

Dated ...., 19 ....

STATE OF MARYLAND
By ....
Juvenile Services Intake Officer
for .... City/County

Rev. 9/76

Form 912-N. Notice of emergency detention/shelter care and notice of hearing.

(Caption)

NOTICE OF EMERGENCY DETENTION/SHELTER CARE
AND NOTICE OF HEARING

TO: ....

....

(Address)

....

Parent, Guardian or Custodian

of ....

TAKE NOTICE that .... has been taken into custody for the reason that he is alleged to be

☐ delinquent

☐ in need of supervision

☐ in need of assistance

and that he was at ...M. on .... placed in emergency detention/shelter care at ...., Maryland, for the reasons indicated below:

☐ to protect the child, or the person and property of others;

☐ the child is believed likely to leave the jurisdiction of the Court;

☐ there appears to be no parent, guardian or custodian able to provide supervision and care for the child when required.

A hearing has been scheduled for ... M. on ...., 19 ..., before the .... Court for .... City/County, Maryland, to determine whether the said child should remain in detention or shelter care.

AS THE PARENT, GUARDIAN, OR CUSTODIAN OF THE CHILD, YOU ARE DIRECTED TO BE PRESENT AT THE HEARING.

If you wish, you may contact the Juvenile Services Agency Intake Officer at .... Maryland, Telephone No. ....

STATE OF MARYLAND

By ....

Juvenile Services Intake Officer

for .... City/County

Rev. 9/76, 8/87

Editor's note. — This form was amended July 27, 1987, effective August 17, 1987.

Form 912-P/CDSC. Petition for continued detention or shelter care.

(Caption)

PETITION FOR CONTINUED DETENTION OR SHELTER CARE

TO THE HONORABLE JUDGE OF THE COURT:

The Petition of the State of Maryland respectfully shows:

1. That the Respondent was taken into custody as the result of certain facts and conditions that indicate that he may be a

    ☐ delinquent child
    ☐ child in need of supervision
    ☐ child in need of assistance

2. That the Respondent was placed in emergency detention or shelter care at ... M. on ...., 19 ..., at ....
(place)

3. That an investigation is now being made to determine whether a Juvenile Petition should be filed with respect to the Respondent.

4. That pending the possible filing of Juvenile Petition, the Respondent should remain in detention or shelter care

    ☐ to protect the child, or the person and property of others;
    ☐ the child is believed likely to leave the jurisdiction of the Court;
    ☐ there appears to be no parent, guardian, or custodian able to provide supervision and care for the child and to return him to Court when required.

WHEREFORE, the State asks that the Court pass an Order continuing the detention or shelter care of the Respondent for a period not to exceed ...... days.

                          STATE OF MARYLAND
                          By ....
                          Juvenile Services Intake Officer
                          for ....City/County

Rev. 9/76

Form 912-O/CDSC. Order for continued detention or shelter care.

(Caption)

ORDER FOR CONTINUED DETENTION OR SHELTER CARE

WHEREAS, the Respondent having been alleged/adjudicated to be delinquent/in need of supervision/in need of assistance, and the Court, after a hearing, having found that the respondent's continued detention or shelter care is necessary pending further proceedings in this case; it is

ORDERED, this .... day of ...., 19 ..., by the .... Court for .... City/County, Maryland, sitting as a Juvenile Court, that the detention/shelter care of the Respondent at .... Maryland be continued pending the further order of this Court or the expiration of 30 days from the date of this Order, whichever first occurs; and it is further

ORDERED, that .... be, and hereby is, authorized and directed to retain the Respondent in its care and custody, with the right to consent to such medical, surgical and hospital care and treatment as may from time to time be determined to be in Respondent's best interests, subject to the further order of this Court; and it is further

ORDERED, that .... deliver the Respondent to the appropriate detention/shelter care facility and it is further

ORDERED, that a copy of this Order be served on the Respondent .... and ....

Recommended:

....
Master for Juvenile Causes

....
Judge

Form 913-P/W. Petition for waiver of juvenile jurisdiction.

(Caption)

PETITION FOR WAIVER OF JUVENILE JURISDICTION

TO THE HONORABLE JUDGE OF THE COURT:

The Petition of the State of Maryland respectfully shows:

1. That the Respondent was born on ....

2. That the petition filed in these proceedings alleges that the respondent is a delinquent child.

3. That the Respondent is an unfit subject for juvenile rehabilitative measures because:

☐   he is .... years of age and

☐   by reason of his physical and mental condition or past experience, he is not amenable to treatment in any institution, facility, or program available to delinquents;

☐   of the seriousness of the alleged offense;

☐   of the degree of his alleged participation in the offense;

☐   of the requirements of public safety;

☐   the Court has previously waived its jurisdiction with respect to the Respondent on another petition alleging delinquency.

WHEREFORE, the State asks that the Court waive its exclusive original jurisdiction so that the Respondent may be tried in the criminal court.

STATE OF MARYLAND

By ....

State's Attorney

for ....City/County

Rev. 9/76

Form 913-O/W. Order waiving juvenile jurisdiction.

(Caption)

ORDER WAIVING JUVENILE JURISDICTION

WHEREAS,

☐   a waiver hearing having been held, upon petition by the State of Maryland/Motion of the Court,

☐   after summary review pursuant to § 3-817 of the Courts Article, it is ORDERED, this .... day of ...., 19 ..., by the .... Court for .... City/County, Maryland, sitting as a Juvenile Court, that this Court's exclusive original jurisdiction over the Respondent .... be, and it hereby is, waived; and it is further

ORDERED, that the Respondent be held for action under the appropriate criminal procedure; and it is further

ORDERED, that the Respondent be placed in the custody of the sheriff or other appropriate officer in an adult detention facility pending a bail hearing pursuant to Rule 4-222; and it is further

ORDERED, that a copy of this Order be served upon the Respondent, the State's Attorney for .... City/County, Maryland, and the sheriff or other custodian of the adult detention facility.

....

Judge

Rev. 9/76

Form 914-O/A. Order of adjudication.

(Caption)

ORDER OF ADJUDICATION

THIS cause having come on for an adjudicatory hearing on notice to all parties, the Court finds that the allegations of the petition have been proved

☐   beyond a reasonable doubt, that the respondent is a delinquent child;

☐   by a preponderance of the evidence, that the respondent is a child in need of supervision;

☐   by a preponderance of the evidence, that the respondent is a child in need of assistance;

and it is thereupon

ADJUDGED, ORDERED and DECREED, this .... day of ....,
19 ..., by the .... Court for .... City/County, Maryland, sitting as
a Juvenile Court, that the Respondent .... be and hereby is made and
declared to be a ward of this Court; and it is further

ORDERED, that a copy of   this Order   be served upon the Respondent
and ....

Recommended:

....
Master for Juvenile Causes

                                        ....
                                                  Judge

Rev. 9/76

Form 915-O/PDC. Order for probation of delinquent child.

(Caption)

ORDER FOR PROBATION OF DELINQUENT CHILD

WHEREAS, the Respondent has been adjudicated as a delinquent child, and
the Court believes that the Respondent should be placed on probation, it is

ORDERED, this .... day of ...., 19 ..., by the .... Court for
.... City/County, Maryland, sitting as a Juvenile Court, that the Respondent .... be, and hereby is placed on probation in the custody of
.... but under the supervision of .... and subject to the following
special conditions:

....
....

and to the further order of this Court; and it is further

ORDERED, that a copy of this Order be served on the Respondent and

Recommended:
....
Master for Juvenile Causes

                                        ....
                                                  Judge

Rev. 9/76

Form 915-O/CJ. Order for commitment of juvenile.

(Caption)

ORDER FOR COMMITMENT OF JUVENILE

WHEREAS, the Respondent was made a ward of this Court on ....,
19 ..., and the Court finds that the best interests of both the Respondent and

415

the public would be served by removing the Respondent from his present environment, it is thereupon

ORDERED, this .... day of ...., 19 ..., by the .... Court for .... City/County, Maryland, sitting as a Juvenile Court, that the Respondent .... be, and hereby is committed to the care and custody of .... with the right of the custodian to consent to such medical, surgical, and hospital care and treatment as may from time to time be determined to be in the Respondent's best interest, subject to the further Order of this Court; and it is further

ORDERED, that .... shall deliver the Respondent to the appropriate detention/shelter care facility; and it is further

ORDERED, that a copy of this Order be served upon the Respondent and ....

Recommended:

....
Master for Juvenile Causes

....
                                                                    Judge

Rev. 9/76

Form 915-O/PS. Order for protective supervision.

(Caption)

ORDER FOR PROTECTIVE SUPERVISION

WHEREAS, the Respondent has been adjudicated as a child in need of supervision/assistance, and the Court believes that the Respondent should be placed in protective supervision, it is thereupon,

ORDERED, this .... day of ...., 19 ..., by the .... Court for .... City/County, Maryland, sitting as a Juvenile Court, that the Respondent .... be, and hereby is, placed in protective supervision in the custody of .... but under the supervision of .... subject to the following special conditions: ....
....
and to the further order of this Court; and it is further

ORDERED, that a copy of this Order be served upon the Respondent and ....

Recommended:

....
Master for Juvenile Causes

....
                                                                    Judge

Rev. 9/76

Form 915-O/PA. Order for probation — Adult.

(Caption)

ORDER FOR PROBATION — ADULT

WHEREAS, the Respondent has been convicted of violating Section 3-831 of the Courts Article, and the Court believes that the Respondent should be placed on probation under the conditions set forth in this Order, it is thereupon ORDERED, this .... day of ...., 19 ..., by the .... Court for .... City/County, Maryland, sitting as a Juvenile Court, that the Respondent .... be, and hereby is, placed on probation for a period of .... under the supervision of .... subject to the following special conditions:
....
....
and to the further order of this Court; and it is further

ORDERED, that a copy of this Order be served upon the Respondent and
....

Recommended:

....
Master for Juvenile Causes

                                    ....
                                                            Judge

Rev. 9/76

Form 916-P/RPC. Petition for revocation of probation and for commitment of delinquent child.

(Caption)

PETITION FOR REVOCATION OF PROBATION
AND FOR COMMITMENT OF DELINQUENT CHILD

TO THE HONORABLE JUDGE OF THE COURT:

The Petition of the State of Maryland respectfully shows:

1. That the Respondent was placed on probation in the custody of and under supervision of .... by Order of this Honorable Court dated ...., 19 ..., subject to the following special conditions .... and to the further Order of the Court.

2. That the Respondent has violated the following conditions of probation
....
....

WHEREFORE, the State asks that an Order be passed directing the Respondent to appear and show cause why his probation should not be revoked and why he should not be committed.

STATE OF MARYLAND

By ....

....

(Agency)

Petitioner

Rev. 9/76

Form 916-P/RPSC. Petition for revocation of protective supervision and for commitment.

(Caption)

PETITION FOR REVOCATION OF PROTECTIVE SUPERVISION AND FOR COMMITMENT

TO THE HONORABLE JUDGE OF THE COURT:

The Petition of the State of Maryland respectfully shows:

1. That the Respondent was placed in protective supervision in the custody of .... and under supervision of .... by Order of this Honorable Court on ...., 19 ..., subject to the following special conditions .... and subject to the further Order of the Court.

2. That the following conditions of protective supervision have been violated

....

WHEREFORE, the State asks that an Order be passed directing the Respondent to appear and show cause why the protective supervision should not be revoked and why he should not be committed.

STATE OF MARYLAND

By ....

....

(Agency)

Petitioner

Rev. 9/76

Form 916-SCO. Show cause order.

(Caption)

SHOW CAUSE ORDER

UPON consideration of the petition of the State of Maryland/the Motion of the Court, it is

ORDERED, this .... day of ...., 19 ..., by the .... Court for .... City/County, sitting as a Juvenile Court, that the Respondent ....

be, and hereby is, directed to appear in this Court at ..... .M. on .... 19 ...,
and show cause why the Order for Probation or Protective Supervision passed
on ...., 19 ..., should not be rescinded and why the Respondent should not
be committed; provided that a copy of this Order and the petition of the State,
if any, be served upon the Respondent and on .... on or before ....,
19 ...

Recommended:

....
Master for Juvenile Causes

                                        ....
                                                    Judge

Rev. 9/76

Form 916-O/RCAS. Order rescinding commitment and for aftercare supervision.

(Caption)

ORDER RESCINDING COMMITMENT AND FOR AFTERCARE SUPERVISION

WHEREAS, the Respondent was committed by this Court to .... on
............, 19 ..., and the Court having found, upon the petition of ....,
that the interests of the Respondent and the public would best be served by the
Respondent's release from commitment and placement in protective supervision, it is thereupon

ORDERED, this ...... day of ...., 19 ..., by the .... Court for
.... City/County, Maryland, sitting as a Juvenile Court, that the commitment of the Respondent .... be, and it hereby is, rescinded, and that the
Respondent be released into the custody of .... effective ...., 19 ...;
and it is further

ORDERED, that the Respondent be, and hereby is, placed under the
supervision of .... subject to the following special conditions
....
and subject to the further Order of this Court; and it is further

ORDERED, that a copy of this Order be served on the Respondent, and on
....

Recommended:

....
Master for Juvenile Causes

                                        ....
                                                    Judge

Rev. 9/76

Form 916-O/TPPS. Order terminating probation/protective supervision.

(Caption)

ORDER TERMINATING PROBATION/PROTECTIVE SUPERVISION

WHEREAS, the Respondent was placed on probation/in protective supervision by Order of this Court on ...., 19 ..., and the Court having found that the interests of the Respondent and the public would best be served by releasing the Respondent from that status, it is thereupon

ORDERED, this .... day of ...., 19 ..., by the .... Court for .... City/County, Maryland, sitting as a Juvenile Court, that the afore-mentioned Order for Probation/Protective Supervision be, and hereby is, rescinded, and the Respondent be, and hereby is, released from Probation/Protective Supervision; and it is further

ORDERED, that a copy of this Order be served on the Respondent and on

....

Recommended:

....

Master for Juvenile Causes

....
                                                                                Judge

Rev. 9/76

Form 918-O/S. Order for support.

(Caption)

ORDER FOR SUPPORT

ORDERED, this .... day of ...., 19 ..., by the .... Court for .... City/County, Maryland, sitting as a Juvenile Court, that .... be, and hereby is, directed to pay the sum of $.........per .... toward the support and maintenance of ...., a child subject to the jurisdiction of this Court, subject to the further Order of the Court; and it is further

ORDERED, that this sum be paid to ....; and it is further

ORDERED, that a copy of this Order be served on .... and ....

Recommended:

....

Master for Juvenile Causes

....
                                                                                Judge

Rev. 9/76

Form 918-O/JR. Order for judgment of restitution.

(Caption)

ORDER FOR JUDGMENT OF RESTITUTION

WHEREAS, the Court having found that the Respondent child

☐   stole, damaged, destroyed, converted, unlawfully obtained, or substantially decreased the value of the property of .in the amount of $ ....;

☐   inflicted personal injury on ....
requiring that person to incur medical, dental, hospital, funeral or burial expenses in the amount of $ ....;

and that .... is the Respondent child or the parent of the Respondent child, it is thereupon

ORDERED, this .... day of ...., 19 ..., by the Court for .... City/County, Maryland, sitting as a Juvenile Court, that Judgment of Restitution in the amount of $ .... be, and it hereby is, entered against .... jointly and severally in favor of ...., pursuant to Section 3-829 of the Courts Article, and that the judgment debtor pay the costs of this proceeding; and it is further

ORDERED, that a copy of this Order be served on the Respondent, on .... and on ....

Recommended:

....

Master for Juvenile Causes

....
Judge

Rev. 9/76, 7/87, 8/87

Editor's note. — This form was amended March 3, 1987, effective July 1, 1987, and July 27, 1987, effective August 17, 1987.

Form 920-FOT. Final order of termination.

(Caption)

FINAL ORDER OF TERMINATION

ORDERED, this .... day of ...., 19 ..., by the .... Court for .... City/County, Maryland, sitting as a Juvenile Court, that this proceeding be, and it hereby is, terminated; and it is further

ORDERED, that a copy of this Order be served on the Respondent and on

....

Recommended:

....

Master for Juvenile Causes

....
Judge

Rev. 9/76

FORMS FOR EXPUNGEMENT OF RECORDS.

Rescinded April 6, 1984, effective July 1, 1984.

Editor's note. — Forms 4-503.1 through 4-503.4, 4-504.1 through 4-504.3, and 4-508.1 through 4-508.3, the present forms for expungement of records, appear in Volume 1 of the Maryland Rules, following revised Title 4 and the Bail Bond forms.

BAIL BOND FORMS.

Rescinded April 6, 1984, effective July 1, 1984.

Editor's note. — Forms 4-217.1 and 4-217.2, the present bail bond forms, appear in Volume 1 of the Maryland Rules, following revised Title 4.

FORMS FOR SPECIAL ADMISSION OF OUT-OF-STATE ATTORNEY.

Form RGAB-14/M. Motion for special admission of out-of-state attorney under Rule 14 of the Rules Governing Admission to the Bar of Maryland.

(Caption)

MOTION FOR SPECIAL ADMISSION OF OUT-OF-STATE ATTORNEY
UNDER RULE 14 OF THE RULES GOVERNING
ADMISSION TO THE BAR OF MARYLAND

I, ..., attorney of record in this case, move that the court admit, ... of ...., an out-of-state attorney who is a member
(name)   (address)
in good standing of the Bar of ....,
for the limited purpose of appearing and participating in this case as co-counsel with me.

I □ do □ do not request that my presence be waived under Rule 14 (d) of the Rules Governing Admission to the Bar of Maryland.

....
Signature of Moving Attorney
....
Name
....
Address
....
Telephone

Attorney for ....

CERTIFICATE AS TO SPECIAL ADMISSIONS

I, ..., certify on this .... day of ...., ..., that during the preceding twelve months, I have been specially admitted in the State of Maryland .... times.

....
Signature of
Out-of-State Attorney

....
Name

....
Address

....
Telephone

(Certificate of Service)

Editor's note. — This form was renumbered (formerly appeared as Form RGAB-20/M) and amended Feb. 10, 1998, effective July 1, 1998.

Form RGAB-14/O. Order.

(Caption)

ORDER

ORDERED, this ...... day of ...., ..., by the .... Court for ...., Maryland, that

☐ .... is admitted specially for the limited purpose of appearing and participating in this case as co-counsel for .... The presence of the Maryland lawyer ☐ is ☐ is not waived.

☐ That the Special Admission of .... is denied for the following reasons: ....
.... and it is further

ORDERED, that the Clerk forward a true copy of the Motion and of this Order to the State Court Administrator.

....
Judge

Editor's note. — This form was renumbered (formerly appeared as Form RGAB-20/O) and amended Feb. 10, 1998, effective July 1, 1998.

FORM INTERROGATORIES.

Committee note. — The following forms have been prepared to facilitate the exchange of meaningful information with a minimum of controversy. They are designed to be appropriate in a large percentage of cases, and the Committee encourages their use. In the context of some cases, however, they may be overly burdensome or otherwise inappropriate. The forms are not designed to limit the parties' right to frame their own interrogatories.

Rule 2-421 (a) provides that each form interrogatory contained in the appendix to these rules shall count as a single interrogatory even though some of the interrogatories, were it not for the rule, might constitute more than a single interrogatory for counting purposes. While use of the form interrogatories contained in this appendix may provide a safe harbor from the counting rules, that protection may be lost if any change is made to the interrogatory or in any of the instructions or definitions contained in this appendix.

It is suggested that when a form contained in this appendix is being used, that fact should be indicated in a parenthetical reference at the end of the form so that opposing counsel and the court may be aware that a form interrogatory is being used.

Editor's note. — Interrogatories, Forms 1 through 8 were adopted by Order of the Court of Appeals, dated January 18, 1996 and effective July 1, 1996.

Form 1. Instructions.
TO: [Name of party to answer interrogatories]
FROM: [Name of party propounding interrogatories]

Instructions

Pursuant to Rule 2-421, you are required to answer the following interrogatories within 30 days or within the time otherwise required by court order or by the Maryland Rules:

(a) In accordance with Rule 2-421 (b), your response shall set forth the interrogatory, and shall set forth the answer to the interrogatory "separately and fully in writing under oath" or "shall state fully the grounds for refusal to answer any interrogatory." The response shall be signed by you. (Standard Instruction (a).)

(b) Also in accordance with Rule 2-421 (b), your answers "shall include all information available" to you "directly or through agents, representatives, or attorneys." (Standard Instruction (b).)

(c) Pursuant to Rule 2-401 (e), these interrogatories are continuing. If you obtain further material information before trial you are required to supplement your answers promptly. (Standard Instruction (c).)

(d) If pursuant to Rule 2-421 (c), you elect to specify and produce business records of yours in answer to any interrogatory, your specification shall be in sufficient detail to enable the interrogating party to locate and identify the records from which the answer may be ascertained. (Standard Instruction (d).)

(e) If you perceive any ambiguities in a question, instruction, or definition, set forth the matter deemed ambiguous and the construction used in answering. (Standard Instruction (e).)

Committee note. — These instructions are designed to be used in virtually all cases.

Form 2. General definitions.

Definitions

In these interrogatories, the following definitions apply:

(a) **Document** includes a writing, drawing, graph, chart, photograph, recording, and other data compilation from which information can be obtained, translated, if necessary, through detection devices into reasonably usable form. (Standard General Definition (a).)

(b) **Identify, identity,** or **identification**, (1) when used in reference to a natural **person**, means that **person's** full name, last known address, home and business telephone numbers, and present occupation or business affiliation; (2) when used in reference to a **person** other than a natural **person**, means that **person's** full name, a description of the nature of the **person** (that is, whether it is a corporation, partnership, etc. under the definition of **person** below), and the **person's** last known address, telephone number, and principal place of business; (3) when used in reference to any **person** after the **person** has been properly **identified** previously means the **person's** name; and (4) when used in reference to a **document**, requires you to state the date, the author (or, if different, the signer or signers), the addressee, and the type of **document** (e.g. letter, memorandum, telegram, chart, etc.) or to attach an accurate copy of the **document** to your answer, appropriately labeled to correspond to the interrogatory. (Standard General Definition (b).)

(c) **Person** includes an individual, general or limited partnership, joint stock company, unincorporated association or society, municipal or other corporation, incorporated association, limited liability partnership, limited liability company, the State, an agency or political subdivision of the State, a court, and any other governmental entity. (Standard General Definition (c).) (Amended June 10, 1997, effective July 1, 1997.)

Committee note. — These definitions are designed to be used in virtually all cases. In order to flag the use of a defined term in the actual interrogatories and alert the responding party to the need to consult the definition, defined terms have been printed in bold type.

Effect of amendments. — The 1997 amendment substituted "means that **person's** full name, a description of the nature of the **person**" for "includes a description of the nature of the **person**" in (b) (2).

Form 3. General interrogatories.

Interrogatories

1. **Identify** each **person**, other than a **person** intended to be called as an expert witness at trial, having discoverable information that tends to support a position that you have taken or intend to take in this action, including any claim for damages, and state the subject matter of the information possessed by that **person**. (Standard General Interrogatory No. 1.)

2. **Identify** each **person** whom you expect to call as an expert witness at trial, state the subject matter on which the expert is expected to testify, state

the substance of the findings and opinions to which the expert is expected to testify and a summary of the grounds for each opinion, and attach to your answers any written report made by the expert concerning those findings and opinions. (Standard General Interrogatory No. 2.)

3. If you intend to rely upon any **documents** or other tangible things to support a position that you have taken or intend to take in the action, including any claim for damages, provide a brief description, by category and location, of all such **documents** and other tangible things, and **identify** all **persons** having possession, custody, or control of them. (Standard General Interrogatory No. 3.)

4. Itemize and show how you calculate any economic damages claimed by you in this action, and describe any non-economic damages claimed. (Standard General Interrogatory No. 4.)

5. If any **person** carrying on an insurance business might be liable to satisfy part or all of a judgment that might be entered in this action or to indemnify or reimburse for payments made to satisfy the judgment, **identify** that **person**, state the applicable policy limits of any insurance agreement under which the **person** might be liable, and describe any question or challenge raised by the **person** relating to coverage for this action. (Standard General Interrogatory No. 5.)

Committee note. — These interrogatories are general in nature and are designed to be used in a broad range of cases.

Form 4. Domestic relations definitions.

Definitions

(a) **Employer** means any **person** that has compensated, or is obligated to compensate, you for services. (Standard Domestic Relations Definition (a).)

(b) **Fringe benefits** include: (1) contributions made by your **employer** to health insurance, life insurance, disability insurance, pension, profit sharing, or retirement plans; and (2) **employer** reimbursements or payments that reduce your personal living expenses such as use of a company car, expense accounts, and housing. (Standard Domestic Relations Definition (b).)

(c) **Property** includes:

(1) accounts in any financial institution or brokerage, including certificates of deposit;

(2) cash;

(3) debts owed to you, secured or unsecured, actual or contingent;

(4) home furnishings, jewelry, furs, stamp or coin collections, antiques, and works of art;

(5) intellectual property, including patents, royalties, and copyrights;

(6) interests in any entity, including partnerships, joint ventures, and corporations;

(7) interest in improved or unimproved real property, including leaseholds, condominiums, and time share interests; .

(8) life insurance and annuities;

(9) military or federal retirement benefits;

(10) pension plans, profit sharing plans, individual retirement accounts, and retirement plans;

(11) securities, including stocks, bonds, mutual funds, United States Government obligations, options, and debentures;

(12) vehicles, boats, aircraft, equipment, machinery, crops, livestock, and poultry;

(13) workers' compensation claims and tort or contract claims against another; and

(14) any other interest or asset. (Standard Domestic Relations Definition (c).)

(d) **Wages** include hourly **wages**, salary, bonuses, tips, incentive awards, fees, commissions, self-employment income, and overtime pay. (Standard Domestic Relations Definition (d).)

Committee note. — These definitions, in addition to the General Definitions, are designed to be used in domestic relations cases.

Form 5. Domestic relations interrogatories.

Interrogatories

1. **Identify** yourself and all individuals with whom you reside. For each individual other than yourself, state that individual's age, relationship to you, and marital status. State your own birth date and social security number. (Standard Domestic Relations Interrogatory No. 1.)

2. Describe your educational background. Include in your answer the highest grade you completed; the name and date of any degree, diploma, or certificate you received, and the name of the institution conferring the degree, diploma, or certificate; and any specialized training you have received. (Standard Domestic Relations Interrogatory No. 2.)

3. If you are currently employed in any capacity, **identify** each current **employer** and, for each employment, state: (a) your job title, (b) your duties, (c) the number of hours in your average work week, (d) your regular pay period, (e) your gross **wages** per pay period, and (f) the deductions per pay period made by your **employer** from your **wages**. If overtime work was available to you during the past 12 months, state: (a) the number of overtime hours you worked during the 12 months and your rate of pay for those hours and (b) the number of overtime hours that were available to you during the 12 months but that you did not work and the rate of pay you would have received if you had worked those hours. (Standard Domestic Relations Interrogatory No. 3.)

4. Describe the nature and amount of any **fringe benefits** that you receive as a result of your employment. (Standard Domestic Relations Interrogatory No. 4.)

5. If you are unemployed, describe your efforts to obtain employment since you became unemployed, **identify** each prospective **employer** and employment agency you have contacted while seeking employment and state the date of each contact. (Standard Domestic Relations Interrogatory No. 5.)

6. If you claim you are physically or mentally unable to work or your capacity to work is limited, state the facts upon which your claim is based and **identify** all **persons** with personal knowledge of those facts. (Standard Domestic Relations Interrogatory No. 6.)

7. For each employment that you have had during the past five years other than any current employment, **identify** each **employer** and for each employment state: (a) the dates of employment, (b) your duties, (c) your **wages**, and (d) your reason for leaving the job. If you were unemployed for any period of time, specify the amount and source of any income that you received while unemployed. (Standard Domestic Relations Interrogatory No. 7.)

8. **Identify** the sources and amounts of all taxable and non-taxable income you received during the past five years. (Standard Domestic Relations Interrogatory No. 8.)

9. **Identify** the sources and amounts of any other moneys and credit(s) you received during the past five years with an aggregate value in excess of $250 in any one year, including gifts, loans from others, loans repaid to you by others, sales of assets, and untaxed distributions. (Standard Domestic Relations Interrogatory No. 9.)

10. List each item of **property** in which you have any interest. For each item listed, state how it is titled, its value, the amount of any present lien or mortgage on the **property**, the date of acquisition of the **property**, and the **identity** of any other **person** with an interest in the **property**. If you claim that any **property** listed is not marital **property**, state the facts upon which you base your claim, including all sources of funds used for the acquisition of the **property** and **identify** all **persons** with personal knowledge of those facts. (Standard Domestic Relations Interrogatory No. 10.)

11. If you, either alone or with anyone other than your spouse, transferred **property** during the last five years of your marriage with a value in excess of $250 to any **person** other than your spouse without receiving full consideration in money or money's worth for the **property** transferred, **identify** each **person** to whom a transfer was made and the **property** transferred, giving the date and method of transfer and the value of the **property** at the time of transfer. (Standard Domestic Relations Interrogatory No. 11.)

12. If the information contained on your financial statement submitted pursuant to Rule S72 f. has changed, describe each change. (Standard Domestic Relations Interrogatory No. 12.)

13. State by type and amount all support provided by you for your spouse and children since the date of your separation. (Standard Domestic Relations Interrogatory No. 13.)

14. State the date on which you separated from your spouse and describe the circumstances of the separation. (Standard Domestic Relations Interrogatory No. 14.)

15. If you contend that your spouse's conduct was excessively vicious or that your spouse acted with extreme cruelty or constructively deserted you, describe your spouse's conduct and state the date and nature of any injuries sustained by you and the date, nature, and provider of health care services rendered to you. **Identify** all **persons** with personal knowledge of your

428

spouse's conduct and all **persons** with knowledge of any injuries you sustained as a result of that conduct. (Standard Domestic Relations Interrogatory No. 15.)

16. State the date on which you and your spouse last had sexual relations with each other. (Standard Domestic Relations Interrogatory No. 16.)

17. If you have had sexual relations with a **person** other than your spouse during your marriage, **identify** the **person(s)** with whom you have had sexual relations, state the date of each act of sexual relations, and state the location where each act took place. If you refuse to answer this interrogatory as framed because the answer would tend to incriminate you, so state and answer for the period ending one year prior to the date of your answers. (Standard Domestic Relations Interrogatory No. 17.)

18. If you have had sexual relations with a **person** other than your spouse during the marriage and you contend that your spouse has forgiven or condoned your actions, state the facts upon which your contention is based. (Standard Domestic Relations Interrogatory No. 18.)

19. If you contend that your spouse is unfit to have custody of the children, state the facts upon which your contention is based and **identify** all **persons** having personal knowledge of these facts. If your contention is based on the use of controlled dangerous substances or the abuse of alcohol on specific occasions, **identify** the substance used, the other **persons** present at the time of the use, and the date, time, and place of the use. If your contention is based on the repeated use of controlled dangerous substances or the repeated abuse of alcohol, **identify** the substance and all **persons** with personal knowledge of the repeated use or abuse. (Standard Domestic Relations Interrogatory No. 19.)

20. If you have sought or received treatment or therapy at any time during the past 10 years for any physical, mental, or emotional condition, including drug addiction or alcoholism, describe the condition and the treatment or therapy provided, state the date or dates of treatment or therapy, and **identify** all **persons** providing treatment or therapy. (Standard Domestic Relations Interrogatory No. 20.)

21. If you contend that placing the children in your sole, shared, or joint custody will be in their best interest, specify the facts and circumstances upon which you rely. (Standard Domestic Relations Interrogatory No. 21.)

22. Describe the child care plan you intend to follow when the children are with you. Include in your answer a description of the place where the children will reside, specifying the number of bedrooms, bathrooms, and other rooms, the distance to the school which the children will attend, and the **identity** of all other **persons** who will be residing in that household. **Identify** all **persons** who will care for the children in your absence, state the hours during which they will care for the children, and the location where the care will be provided. (Standard Domestic Relations Interrogatory No. 22.)

Form 6. Motor vehicle tort definitions.

Definitions

(a) The term **occurrence**, unless otherwise indicated, means the collision or other event complained of in the pleadings. (Standard Motor Vehicle Tort Definition (a).)

(b) The phrase **in [a, the, or that] vehicle** includes entering, exiting, and being in or on a vehicle. (Standard Motor Vehicle Tort Definition (b).)

(c) The term **possession** includes possession, custody, or control. (Standard Motor Vehicle Tort Definition (c).)

Committee note. — These definitions, in addition to the General Definitions, are designed to be used in motor vehicle tort cases.

Form 7. Motor vehicle tort interrogatories.

Interrogatories

1. **Identify** yourself and state all names by which you have been known, your date of birth, your marital status, and the **identity** of your spouse. (Standard Motor Vehicle Tort Interrogatory No. 1.)

2. State all addresses at which you have resided for the past five years and the date that you resided at each. (Standard Motor Tort Interrogatory No. 2.)

3. Describe in detail how the **occurrence** took place. (Standard Motor Vehicle Tort Interrogatory No. 3.)

4. **Identify** all **persons** who were witnesses to the **occurrence** and state their location at the time of the **occurrence**.

5. **Identify** all **persons** who were at or near the scene at the time of the **occurrence**. (Standard Motor Vehicle Tort Interrogatory No. 5.)

6. If you were **in a vehicle** at the time of the **occurrence**, **identify** all other **persons** who were **in that vehicle**. (Standard Motor Vehicle Tort Interrogatory No. 6.)

7. **Identify** all **persons** who arrived at the scene within two hours after the **occurrence**. (Standard Motor Vehicle Tort Interrogatory No. 7.)

8. If you were **in a vehicle** at the time of the **occurrence**, state the itinerary of the vehicle, including the time and place of the beginning of the trip, the time and duration of each stop, the destination, and the expected time of arrival. (Standard Motor Vehicle Tort Interrogatory No. 8.)

9. If you were engaged in any activity for an employer or other **person** at the time of the **occurrence**, state the nature of the activity and **identify** the employer or other **person**. (Standard Motor Vehicle Tort Interrogatory No. 9.)

10. If a report with respect to the **occurrence** was made in the ordinary course of business, state the date of the report and **identify** the **person** who made the report and the custodian. (Standard Motor Vehicle Tort Interrogatory No. 10.)

11. **Identify** all photographs, videotapes, plats, diagrams, or other depictions of the scene or of things connected with the **occurrence** that are in your **possession**. (Standard Motor Vehicle Tort Interrogatory No. 11.)

12. **Identify** all **persons** who have given you "statements," as that term is defined in Rule 2-402 (d), concerning the action or its subject matter. For each statement, state the date on which it was given and **identify** the custodian. (Standard Motor Vehicle Tort Interrogatory No. 12.)

13. If you were charged with any offenses arising out of the **occurrence**, state the nature of the charges, the court and case number, and the disposition of the charges. (Standard Motor Vehicle Tort Interrogatory No. 13.)

14. If you contend that any party to this action caused or contributed to the **occurrence**, state concisely the facts on which you rely. (Standard Motor Vehicle Tort Interrogatory No. 14.)

15. If you contend that a **person** not a party to this action caused or contributed to the **occurrence**, **identify** each such **person** and state concisely the facts upon which you rely. (Standard Motor Vehicle Tort Interrogatory No. 15.)

16. If you owned or were **in a vehicle** damaged as a result of the **occurrence**, describe any damage to the vehicle. If the vehicle was repaired, **identify** the **person** who performed the repairs, the dates of the repairs, and the cost. If the vehicle is unrepaired, state the address where and the hours when it may be seen. (Standard Motor Vehicle Tort Interrogatory No. 16.)

17. If you owned or were **in a vehicle** involved in the **occurrence**, state: when the vehicle was last repaired before the **occurrence**; the nature, dates, and costs of the repairs; the **identity** of the **persons** making the repairs; and the extent of any unrepaired damage to the vehicle immediately prior to the **occurrence**. (Standard Motor Vehicle Tort Interrogatory No. 17.)

18. If you contend that mechanical failure caused or contributed to the **occurrence**, state concisely the facts upon which you rely. (Standard Motor Vehicle Tort Interrogatory No. 18.)

19. If you were **in a vehicle** at the time of the **occurrence**, **identify** the owner and the driver of the vehicle. If you were not the owner, state whether you had the permission of the owner to be **in the vehicle** and the purpose for which permission was given. (Standard Motor Vehicle Tort Interrogatory No. 19.)

20. If you were the driver of a vehicle involved in the **occurrence**, state whether you have or have ever had any disability, illness, disease, or injury that could affect your ability to operate a motor vehicle, and describe its nature and extent. If treated or evaluated, **identify** all treating or examining health care providers and the approximate date of each examination or treatment. (Standard Motor Vehicle Tort Interrogatory No. 20.)

21. State whether you used any alcoholic beverages or drugs, whether controlled or otherwise, within 24 hours before the **occurrence**, the places where they were obtained, the places where they were used, and the nature and amount used. (Standard Motor Vehicle Tort Interrogatory No. 21.)

22. State the substance of all discussions concerning the **occurrence** that you or others in your presence had with any party to this case. State when and where each discussion took place and **identify** all **persons** who were present. (Standard Motor Vehicle Tort Interrogatory No. 22.)

23. State whether you have **possession** or knowledge of any recordings or transcripts of testimony in any proceeding arising out of the **occurrence**. If so,

state the date and subject matter, and **identify** each **person** who recorded the testimony and the custodian of each recording or transcript. (Standard Motor Vehicle Tort Interrogatory No. 23.)

24. If you were **in a vehicle** involved in the **occurrence**, state whether the driver of the vehicle has a current driver's license. If so, state when and where the license was issued, the nature of any restrictions on the license, and whether the license was ever suspended or revoked. (Standard Motor Vehicle Tort Interrogatory No. 24.)

25. State whether, at any time during the fifteen year period preceding the date of your answers to these interrogatories, you have been convicted of any crime other than a minor traffic offense. If so, for each conviction **identify** the court in which you were convicted and state the amount of any fine and the date and length of any incarceration imposed. For purposes of this interrogatory, a conviction includes a plea of *nolo contendere* followed by a sentence, whether or not the sentence is suspended. (Standard Motor Vehicle Tort Interrogatory No. 25.)

Form 8. Personal injury interrogatories.

Interrogatories

1. Describe each injury sustained by you as a result of the **occurrence**, and state whether the injury was temporary or is permanent. (Standard Personal Injury Interrogatory No. 1.)

2. Describe all current symptoms, handicaps, and other physical or mental conditions that you claim are a result of the **occurrence**. (Standard Personal Injury Interrogatory No. 2.)

3. **Identify** each health care provider who has examined or treated you as a result of the **occurrence**, and for each provider state the date and purpose of each examination or treatment. (Standard Personal Injury Interrogatory No. 3.)

4. **Identify** all hospitals or other facilities at which you have been examined or treated as a result of the **occurrence**, and for each state the dates of your examinations or treatments and, if you were admitted, the dates of your admissions and discharges. (Standard Personal Injury Interrogatory No. 4.)

5. **Identify** all health care providers, other than those otherwise **identified** in your answers, who have examined or treated you during the period commencing five years before the **occurrence** and extending to the present, **identify** all hospitals and other facilities at which you were examined or treated, and describe the condition for which you were examined or treated. (Standard Personal Injury Interrogatory No. 5.)

6. State whether you claim past or future loss of earnings or earning capacity as a result of the **occurrence** and, if so, state for each category the amount claimed, the method by which you computed that amount, the figures used in that computation, and the facts and assumptions upon which your claim is based. (Standard Personal Injury Interrogatory No. 6.)

7. State the amount you reported as earned income on your federal income tax returns for each of the past three years and whether you have a copy of the returns. (Standard Personal Injury Interrogatory No. 7.)

8. Itemize all expenses and other economic damages, past and future, that you claim are a result of the **occurrence** and as to each item claimed **identify** the item, the amount claimed for that item, the method, if any, by which you computed the amount, the figures used in that computation, and the facts and assumptions upon which your claim is based. (Standard Personal Injury Interrogatory No. 8.)

9. State whether prior or subsequent to the **occurrence** you have sustained any accidental injury for which you received medical care or treatment. If so, describe the date and circumstances of the accidental injury and **identify** all health care providers, including hospitals and other institutions, that furnished care to you. (Standard Personal Injury Interrogatory No. 9.)

APPENDIX: THE MARYLAND RULES OF PROFESSIONAL CONDUCT

Preamble: A lawyer's responsibilities.
Scope.
Terminology.

Client-Lawyer Relationship.

Rule
1.1. Competence.
1.2. Scope of representation.
1.3. Diligence.
1.4. Communication.
1.5. Fees.
1.6. Confidentiality of information.
1.7. Conflict of interest: General rule.
1.8. Conflict of interest: Prohibited transactions.
1.9. Conflict of interest: Former client.
1.10. Imputed disqualification: General rule.
1.11. Successive government and private employment.
1.12. Former judge or arbitrator.
1.13. Organization as client.
1.14. Client under a disability.
1.15. Safekeeping property.
1.16. Declining or terminating representation.

Counselor.

2.1. Advisor.
2.2. Intermediary.
2.3. Evaluation for use by third persons.

Advocate.

3.1. Meritorious claims and contentions.
3.2. Expediting litigation.
3.3. Candor toward the tribunal.
3.4. Fairness to opposing party and counsel.
3.5. Impartiality and decorum of the tribunal.
3.6. Trial publicity.
3.7. Lawyer as witness.
3.8. Special responsibilities of a prosecutor.
3.9. Advocate in nonadjudicative proceedings.

Transactions With Persons Other Than Clients.

4.1. Truthfulness in statements to others.
4.2. Communication with person represented by counsel.

Rule
4.3. Dealing with unrepresented person.
4.4. Respect for rights of third persons.

Law Firms and Associations.

5.1. Responsibilities of a partner or supervisory lawyer.
5.2. Responsibilities of a subordinate lawyer.
5.3. Responsibilities regarding nonlawyer assistants.
5.4. Professional independence of a lawyer.
5.5. Unauthorized practice of law.
5.6. Restrictions on right to practice.

Public Service.

6.1. Pro bono publico service.
6.2. Accepting appointments.
6.3. Membership in legal services organization.
6.4. Law reform activities affecting client interests.

Information About Legal Services.

7.1. Communications concerning a lawyer's services.
7.2. Advertising.
7.3. Direct contact with prospective clients.
7.4. Communication of fields of practice.
7.5. Firm names and letterheads.

Maintaining the Integrity of the Profession.

8.1. Bar admission and disciplinary matters.
8.2. Judicial and legal officials.
8.3. Reporting professional misconduct.
8.4. Misconduct.
8.5. Jurisdiction.

Editor's note. — The Court of Appeals, by Order dated April 15, 1986, adopted the Maryland Rules of Professional Conduct, effective January 1, 1987. The Order provides that "the Maryland Rules of Professional Conduct shall govern the conduct of attorneys from and after said date; provided, however, that the Code of Professional Responsibility as set forth in Appendix F of the Maryland Rules shall continue in full force and effect and shall govern the conduct of attorneys until January 1, 1987." Annotations from cases appearing under the new Rules were decided under the former Code of Professional Responsibility, and have been retained where it is thought they will be of value in construing the new Rules.

Preamble: A lawyer's responsibilities.

A lawyer is a representative of clients, an officer of the legal system and a public citizen having special responsibility for the quality of justice.

As a representative of clients, a lawyer performs various functions. As advisor, a lawyer provides a client with an informed understanding of the client's legal rights and obligations and explains their practical implications. As advocate, a lawyer zealously asserts the client's position under the rules of the adversary system. As negotiator, a lawyer seeks a result advantageous to the client but consistent with requirements of honest dealing with others. As intermediary between clients, a lawyer seeks to reconcile their divergent interests as an advisor and, to a limited extent, as a spokesperson for each client. A lawyer acts as evaluator by examining a client's legal affairs and reporting about them to the client or to others.

In all professional functions a lawyer should be competent, prompt and diligent. A lawyer should maintain communication with a client concerning the representation. A lawyer should keep in confidence information relating to representation of a client except so far as disclosure is required or permitted by the Rules of Professional Conduct or other law.

A lawyer's conduct should conform to the requirements of the law, both in professional service to clients and in the lawyer's business and personal affairs. A lawyer should use the law's procedures only for legitimate purposes and not to harass or intimidate others. A lawyer should demonstrate respect for the legal system and for those who serve it, including judges, other lawyers and public officials. While it is a lawyer's duty, when necessary, to challenge the rectitude of official action, it is also a lawyer's duty to uphold legal process.

As a public citizen, a lawyer should seek improvement of the law, the administration of justice and the quality of service rendered by the legal profession. As a member of a learned profession, a lawyer should cultivate knowledge of the law beyond its use for clients, employ that knowledge in reform of the law and work to strengthen legal education. A lawyer should be mindful of deficiencies in the administration of justice and of the fact that the poor, and sometimes persons who are not poor, cannot afford adequate legal assistance, and should therefore devote professional time and civic influence in their behalf. A lawyer should aid the legal profession in pursuing these objectives and should help the bar regulate itself in the public interest.

Many of a lawyer's professional responsibilities are prescribed in the Rules of Professional Conduct, as well as substantive and procedural law. However, a lawyer is also guided by personal conscience and the approbation of professional peers. A lawyer should strive to attain the highest level of skill, to improve the law and the legal profession and to exemplify the legal profession's ideals of public service.

A lawyer's responsibilities as a representative of clients, an officer of the legal system and a public citizen are usually harmonious. Thus, when an opposing party is well represented, a lawyer can be a zealous advocate on behalf of a client and at the same time assume that justice is being done. So also, a lawyer can be sure that preserving client confidences ordinarily serves the public interest because people are more likely to seek legal advice, and thereby heed their legal obligations, when they know their communications will be private.

In the nature of law practice, however, conflicting responsibilities are encountered. Virtually all difficult ethical problems arise from conflict between a lawyer's responsibilities to clients, to the legal system and to the lawyer's own interest in remaining an upright person while earning a satisfactory living. The Rules of Professional Conduct prescribe terms for resolving such conflicts. Within the framework of these Rules many difficult issues of professional discretion can arise. Such issues must be resolved through the exercise of sensitive professional and moral judgment guided by the basic principles underlying the Rules.

The legal profession is largely self-governing. Although other professions also have been granted powers of self-government, the legal profession is unique in this respect because of the close relationship between the profession and the processes of government and law enforcement. This connection is manifested in the fact that ultimate authority over the legal profession is vested largely in the courts.

To the extent that lawyers meet the obligations of their professional calling, the occasion for government regulation is obviated. Self-regulation also helps maintain the legal profession's independence from government domination. An independent legal profession is an important force in preserving government under law, for abuse of legal authority is more readily challenged by a profession whose members are not dependent on government for the right to practice.

The legal profession's relative autonomy carries with it special responsibilities of self-government. The profession has a responsibility to assure that its regulations are conceived in the public interest and not in furtherance of parochial or self-interested concerns of the bar. Every lawyer is responsible for observance of the Rules of Professional Conduct. A lawyer should also aid in securing their observance by other lawyers. Neglect of these responsibilities compromises the independence of the profession and the public interest which it serves.

Lawyers play a vital role in the preservation of society. The fulfillment of this role requires an understanding by lawyers of their relationship to our legal system. The Rules of Professional Conduct, when properly applied, serve to define that relationship.

Scope.

The Rules of Professional Conduct are rules of reason. They should be interpreted with reference to the purposes of legal representation and of the law itself. Some of the Rules are imperatives, cast in the terms "shall" or "shall not." These define proper conduct for purposes of professional discipline.

Others, generally cast in the term "may," are permissive and define areas under the Rules in which the lawyer has professional discretion. No disciplinary action should be taken when the lawyer chooses not to act or acts within the bounds of such discretion. Other Rules define the nature of relationships between the lawyer and others. The Rules are thus partly obligatory and disciplinary and partly constitutive and descriptive in that they define a lawyer's professional role. Many of the Comments use the term "should." Comments do not add obligations to the Rules but provide guidance for practicing in compliance with the Rules.

The Rules presuppose a larger legal context shaping the lawyer's role. That context includes court rules and statutes relating to matters of licensure, laws defining specific obligations of lawyers and substantive and procedural law in general. Compliance with the Rules, as with all law in an open society, depends primarily upon understanding and voluntary compliance, secondarily upon reinforcement by peer and public opinion and finally, when necessary, upon enforcement through disciplinary proceedings. The Rules do not, however, exhaust the moral and ethical considerations that should inform a lawyer, for no worthwhile human activity can be completely defined by legal rules. The Rules simply provide a framework for the ethical practice of law.

Furthermore, for purposes of determining the lawyer's authority and responsibility, principles of substantive law external to these Rules determine whether a client-lawyer relationship exists. Most of the duties flowing from the client-lawyer relationship attach only after the client has requested the lawyer to render legal services and the lawyer has agreed to do so. But there are some duties, such as that of confidentiality under Rule 1.6 that may attach when the lawyer agrees to consider whether a client-lawyer relationship shall be established. Whether a client-lawyer relationship exists for any specific purpose can depend on the circumstances and may be a question of fact.

Under various legal provisions, including constitutional, statutory and common law, the responsibilities of government lawyers may include authority concerning legal matters that ordinarily reposes in the client in private client-lawyer relationships. For example, a lawyer for a government agency may have authority on behalf of the government to decide upon settlement or whether to appeal from an adverse judgment. Such authority in various respects is generally vested in the attorney general and the state's attorney in state government, and their federal counterparts, and the same may be true of other government law officers. Also, lawyers under the supervision of these officers may be authorized to represent several government agencies in intragovernmental legal controversies in circumstances where a private lawyer could not represent multiple private clients. They also may have authority to represent the "public interest" in circumstances where a private lawyer would not be authorized to do so. These Rules do not abrogate any such authority.

Failure to comply with an obligation or prohibition imposed by a Rule is a basis for invoking the disciplinary process. The Rules presuppose that disciplinary assessment of a lawyer's conduct will be made on the basis of the facts and circumstances as they existed at the time of the conduct in question and in recognition of the fact that a lawyer often has to act upon uncertain or incomplete evidence of the situation. Moreover, the Rules presuppose that whether or not discipline should be imposed for a violation, and the severity of a sanction, depend on all the circumstances, such as the willfulness and seriousness of the violation, extenuating factors and whether there have been previous violations.

Violation of a Rule should not give rise to a cause of action nor should it create any presumption that a legal duty has been breached. The Rules are designed to provide guidance to lawyers and to provide a structure for regulating conduct through disciplinary agencies. They are not designed to be a basis for civil liability. Furthermore, the purpose of the Rules can be subverted when they are invoked by opposing parties as procedural weapons. The fact that a Rule is a just basis for a lawyer's self-assessment, or for sanctioning a lawyer under the administration of a disciplinary authority, does not imply that an antagonist in a collateral proceeding or transaction has standing to seek enforcement of the Rule. Accordingly, nothing in the Rules should be deemed to augment any substantive legal duty of lawyers or the extra-disciplinary consequences of violating such a duty.

Moreover, these Rules are not intended to govern or affect judicial application of either the attorney-client or work product privilege. Those privileges were developed to promote compliance with law and fairness in litigation. In reliance on the attorney-client privilege, clients are entitled to expect that communications within the scope of the privilege will be protected against compelled disclosure. The attorney-client privilege is that of the client and not of the lawyer. The fact that in exceptional situations the lawyer under the Rules has a limited discretion to disclose a client confidence does not vitiate the proposition that, as a general matter, the client has a reasonable expectation that information relating to the client will not be voluntarily disclosed and that disclosure of such information may be judicially compelled only in accordance with recognized exceptions to the attorney-client and work product privileges.

The lawyer's exercise of discretion not to disclose information under Rule 1.6 should not be subject to reexamination. Permitting such reexamination would be incompatible with the general policy of promoting compliance with law through assurances that communications will be protected against disclosure.

The Comment accompanying each Rule explains and illustrates the meaning and purpose of the Rule. The Preamble and this note on Scope provide general orientation. The Comments are intended as guides to interpretation, but the text of each Rule is authoritative. The Code comparison following each Rule has not been adopted, does not constitute part of the Rules, and is not intended to affect the application or interpretation of the Rules and Comments.

Terminology.

"Belief" or "Believes" denotes that the person involved actually supposed the fact in question to be true. A person's belief may be inferred from circumstances.

"Consult" or "Consultation" denotes communication of information reasonably sufficient to permit the client to appreciate the significance of the matter in question.

"Firm" or "Law firm" denotes a lawyer or lawyers in a private firm, lawyers employed in the legal department of a corporation or other organization and lawyers employed in a legal services organization. See Comment, Rule 1.10.

"Fraud" or "Fraudulent" denotes conduct having a purpose to deceive and not merely negligent misrepresentation or failure to apprise another of relevant information.

"Knowingly," "Known," or "Knows" denotes actual knowledge of the fact in question. A person's knowledge may be inferred from circumstances.

"Partner" denotes a member of a partnership and a shareholder in a law firm organized as a professional corporation.

"Reasonable" or "Reasonably" when used in relation to conduct by a lawyer denotes the conduct of a reasonably prudent and competent lawyer.

"Reasonable belief" or "Reasonably believes" when used in reference to a lawyer denotes that the lawyer believes the matter in question and that the circumstances are such that the belief is reasonable.

"Reasonably should know" when used in reference to a lawyer denotes that a lawyer of reasonable prudence and competence would ascertain the matter in question.

"Substantial" when used in reference to degree or extent denotes a material matter of clear and weighty importance.

CLIENT-LAWYER RELATIONSHIP.

Rule 1.1. Competence.

A lawyer shall provide competent representation to a client. Competent representation requires the legal knowledge, skill, thoroughness and preparation reasonably necessary for the representation.

COMMENT

Legal knowledge and skill. — In determining whether a lawyer employs the requisite knowledge and skill in a particular matter, relevant factors include the relative complexity and specialized nature of the matter, the lawyer's general experience, the lawyer's training and experience in the field in question, the preparation and study the lawyer is able to give the matter and whether it is feasible to refer the matter to, or associate or consult with, a lawyer of established competence in the field in question. In many instances, the required proficiency is that of a general practitioner. Expertise in a particular field of law may be required in some circumstances.

A lawyer need not necessarily have special training or prior experience to handle legal problems of a type with which the lawyer is unfamiliar. A newly admitted lawyer can be as competent as a practitioner with long experience. Some important legal skills, such as the analysis of precedent, the evaluation of evidence and legal drafting, are required in all legal problems. Perhaps the most fundamental legal skill consists of determining what kind of legal problems a situation may involve, a skill that necessarily transcends any particular specialized knowledge. A lawyer can provide adequate representation in a wholly novel field through necessary study. Competent representation can also be provided through the association of a lawyer of established competence in the field in question.

In an emergency a lawyer may give advice or assistance in a matter in which the lawyer does not have the skill ordinarily required where referral to or consultation or association with another lawyer would be impractical. Even in an emergency, however, assistance should be limited to that reasonably necessary in the circumstances, for ill-considered action under emergency conditions can jeopardize the client's interest.

A lawyer may accept representation where the requisite level of competence can be achieved by reasonable preparation. This applies as well to a lawyer who is appointed as counsel for an unrepresented person. See also Rule 6.2.

Thoroughness and preparation. — Competent handling of a particular matter includes inquiry into and analysis of the factual and legal elements of the problem, and use of methods and procedures meeting the standards of competent practitioners. It also includes adequate preparation. The required attention and preparation are determined in part by what is at stake; major litigation and complex transactions ordinarily require more elaborate treatment than matters of lesser consequence.

Maintaining competence. — To maintain the requisite knowledge and skill, a lawyer should engage in continuing study and education. If a system of peer review has been established, the lawyer should consider making use of it in appropriate circumstances.

Code Comparison. — DR 6-101 (A) (1) provides that a lawyer shall not handle a matter "which he knows or should know that he is not competent to handle, without associating himself with a lawyer who is competent to handle it." DR 6-101 (A) (2) requires "preparation adequate in the circumstances"; Rule 1.1 more fully particularizes the elements of competence.

Maryland Law Review. — For symposium, expanding pro bono legal assistance in civil cases to Maryland's poor, see 49 Md. L. Rev. 1 (1990).

University of Baltimore Law Forum. — For discussion of the code of ethics, see 17, No. 1 U. Balt. Law Forum 31 (1986).

In general. — Where clients consulted him with the knowledge that he was a practicing attorney and he made no attempt to inform them that he was dealing with them in any restricted capacity, the attorney will be held accountable to the ethical and performance standards of his profession. Attorney Grievance Comm'n v. Martin, 308 Md. 272, 518 A.2d 1050 (1987).

Thoroughness and preparation. — Absent some compelling extenuating circumstance, it is ordinarily unacceptable for a lawyer to appear in court for a trial or other proceeding unprepared, and doing so may constitute a violation of this rule. Attorney Grievance Comm'n v. Ficker, 349 Md. 13, 706 A.2d 1045 (1998).

Professional service corporations. — When the conduct of a lawyer in a professional service corporation is called into question with reference to the attorney-client relationship, the Rules of Professional Conduct will apply and not those of an ordinary business corporation. Where, however, the situation involves a dispute between shareholders of the professional service corporation, the corporate law should not be disregarded in favor of partnership law. Langhoff v. Marr, 81 Md. App. 438, 568 A.2d 844 (1990), vacated on other grounds and remanded, 322 Md. 657, 589 A.2d 470 (1991).

Competence in specialty areas. — Each member of the Bar should be on notice to consider his or her own competence prior to undertaking employment involving a particularly complex area of the law and should, if deemed appropriate, either decline the employment, or with the consent of the client, accept the employment and associate a lawyer who is competent in the matter. Attorney Grievance Comm'n v. Brown, 308 Md. 219, 517 A.2d 1111 (1986).

Numerous trivial and inconsequential errors. — Seven errors, each taken separately trivial and inconsequential, taken together amounted to collective incompetence and violations of former disciplinary rules. Attorney Grievance Comm'n v. Brown, 308 Md. 219, 517 A.2d 1111 (1986).

Mishandling escrow account. — Indefinite suspension was appropriate sanction for attorneys mishandling of escrow account, including the failure to pay claims due from the account and the failure to refund moneys to clients. Attorney Grievance Comm'n v. Singleton, 311 Md. 1, 532 A.2d 157 (1987); Attorney Grievance Comm'n v. Bakas, 323 Md. 395, 593 A.2d 1087 (1991).

Failure to file affidavit. — A lawyer engaged in default judgment proceedings who fails to file a military affidavit or to adequately comply with the content requirements of Maryland Rule 2-613(a) is not incompetent; such failure is, at best, indicative of the lawyer's carelessness or negligence. Attorney Grievance Comm'n v. Kemp, 335 Md. 1, 641 A.2d 510 (1994).

Alcoholism, drug addiction or mental disorder. — When a lawyer's misconduct is caused by alcoholism, drug addiction, or a mental disorder, the usual sanction is indefinite suspension. This provides the requisite protection for the public, for it prevents the lawyer from practicing law until such time (if ever) that he or she can demonstrate that he or she is free from the effects of the ailment and able to practice competently. At the same time, the lawyer is spared the ultimate sanction of disbarment, a sanction which would be unfair to apply where the lawyer's conduct is caused by factors beyond his or her control. Attorney Grievance Comm'n v. Powers, 314 Md. 484, 551 A.2d 465 (1989).

An indefinite suspension was the proper sanction in the case of a misappropriation of client funds caused by alcoholism; however, in the future, absent truly compelling circumstances, alcoholism will usually not be permitted to mitigate where an attorney commits a violation of ethical or legal rules which would ordinarily warrant disbarment. Attorney Grievance Comm'n v. Kenney, 339 Md. 578, 664 A.2d 854 (1995).

Incompetence found. — Attorney's professed inability to render an accounting of what happened in his law practice and his escrow account, coupled with his loss of memory on everything from money entrusted to him to the names of his secretaries, cast doubt on his ability to adequately carry out the functions of an attorney. Attorney Grievance Comm'n v. Kramer, 325 Md. 39, 599 A.2d 100 (1991).

Maryland law refuses to impose liability for a breach of a rule of professional conduct; violation of a rule does not give rise to a cause of action and does not create a presumption that a legal duty has been breached. Maryland Nat'l Bank v. Resolution Trust Corp., 895 F. Supp. 762 (D. Md. 1995).

Disbarment was proper sanction. — Attorney was properly disbarred for violating Maryland Rules of Professional Conduct 1.1, 1.3, 1.4(a) and (b), 1.15(a), 3.3(a)(1), and 8.4(b) and (c), § 10-306 of the Business Occupations and Professions Article, and Rule BU9 (now Rule 16-609) of the Maryland Rules of Procedure. Attorney Grievance Comm'n v. Williams, 335 Md. 458, 644 A.2d 490 (1994).

Disbarment of attorney was appropriate where there were serious and repeated violations of this Rule and other provisions of the Maryland Rules of Professional Conduct. At-

torney Grievance Comm'n v. Milliken, 348 Md. 486, 704 A.2d 1225 (1998).

Indefinite suspension was proper sanction. — Where respondent attorney's representation of four clients was marked by serious neglect and inattention; where he failed to return a fee which was unearned for a period of nine months; where he failed to timely remit funds he received on behalf of a client; where he failed to communicate with his clients; and in connection with the investigation of three of the complaints, where respondent failed to answer Bar Counsel's requests for information, the proper sanction was that the attorney be indefinitely suspended from the practice of law, with the right to apply for reinstatement after the suspension had been in effect for six months, conditioned upon his payment of all costs and upon the monitoring of respondent's practice. Attorney Grievance Comm'n v. David, 331 Md. 317, 628 A.2d 178 (1993).

An attorney's practice of assigning and handling cases in such a manner that the lawyer ultimately charged with actually representing the client went into court unprepared, or missed scheduled trial dates entirely, resulted in clients not being afforded competent representation, and justified an indefinite suspension from the practice of law. Attorney Grievance Comm'n v. Ficker, 349 Md. 13, 706 A.2d 1045 (1998).

Applied in Gantt v. State, 81 Md. App. 653, 569 A.2d 220 (1990); Attorney Grievance Comm'n v. Keister, 327 Md. 56, 607 A.2d 909 (1992).

Quoted in Massey v. Prince George's County, 907 F. Supp. 138 (D. Md. 1995); Attorney Grievance Comm'n v. Sachse, 345 Md. 578, 693 A.2d 806 (1997).

Stated in Attorney Grievance Comm'n v. Montgomery, 318 Md. 154, 567 A.2d 112 (1989).

Cited in Attorney Grievance Comm'n v. Tahir, 330 Md. 297, 623 A.2d 1296 (1993); Attorney Grievance Comm'n v. Drew, 341 Md. 139, 669 A.2d 1344 (1996); Attorney Grievance Comm'n v. Hallmon, 343 Md. 390, 681 A.2d 510 (1996); Attorney Grievance Comm'n v. Williams, 348 Md. 196, 702 A.2d 1271 (1997).

Rule 1.2. Scope of representation.

(a) A lawyer shall abide by a client's decisions concerning the objectives of representation, subject to paragraphs (c), (d) and (e), and, when appropriate, shall consult with the client as to the means by which they are to be pursued. A lawyer shall abide by a client's decision whether to accept an offer of settlement of a matter. In a criminal case, the lawyer shall abide by the client's decision, after consultation with the lawyer, as to a plea to be entered, whether to waive jury trial and whether the client will testify.

(b) A lawyer's representation of a client, including representation by appointment, does not constitute an endorsement of the client's political, economic, social or moral views or activities.

(c) A lawyer may limit the objectives of the representation if the client consents after consultation.

(d) A lawyer shall not counsel a client to engage, or assist a client, in conduct that the lawyer knows is criminal or fraudulent, but a lawyer may discuss the legal consequences of any proposed course of conduct with a client and may counsel or assist a client to make a good faith effort to determine the validity, scope, meaning or application of the law.

(e) When a lawyer knows that a client expects assistance not permitted by the Rules of Professional Conduct or other law, the lawyer shall consult with the client regarding the relevant limitations on the lawyer's conduct.

COMMENT

Scope of representation. — Both lawyer and client have authority and responsibility in the objectives and means of representation. The client has ultimate authority to determine the purposes to be served by legal representation, within the limits imposed by law and the lawyer's professional obligations. Within those limits, a client also has a right to consult with the lawyer about the means to be used in pursuing those objectives. At the same time, a lawyer is not required to pursue objectives or employ means simply because a client may wish that the lawyer do so. A clear distinction between objectives and means sometimes cannot be drawn, and in many cases the client-lawyer relationship partakes of a joint undertaking. In questions of means, the lawyer should assume responsibility for technical and legal tactical issues, but should defer to the client regarding such questions as the expense to be incurred and concern for third persons who might be adversely affected. Law defining the lawyer's scope of authority in litigation varies among jurisdictions.

In a case in which the client appears to be suffering mental disability, the lawyer's duty to abide by the client's decisions is to be guided by reference to Rule 1.14.

Independence from client's views or activities. — Legal representation should not be denied to people who are unable to afford legal services, or whose cause is controversial or the subject of popular disapproval. By the same token, representing a client does not constitute approval of the client's views or activities.

Services limited in objectives or means. — The objectives or scope of services provided by a lawyer may be limited by agreement with the client or by the terms under which the lawyer's services are made available to the client. For example, a retainer may be for a specifically defined purpose. Representation provided through a legal aid agency may be subject to limitations on the types of cases the agency handles. When a lawyer has been retained by an insurer to represent an insured, the representation may be limited to matters related to the insurance coverage. The terms upon which representation is undertaken may exclude specific objectives or means. Such limitations may exclude objectives or means that the lawyer regards as repugnant or imprudent.

An agreement concerning the scope of representation must accord with the Rules of Professional Conduct and other law. Thus, the client may not be asked to agree to representation so limited in scope as to violate Rule 1.1, or to surrender the right to terminate the lawyer's services or the right to settle litigation that the lawyer might wish to continue.

Criminal, fraudulent and prohibited transactions. — A lawyer is required to give an honest opinion about the actual consequences that appear likely to result from a client's conduct. The fact that a client uses advice in a course of action that is criminal or fraudulent does not, of itself, make a lawyer a party to the course of action. However, a lawyer may not knowingly assist a client in criminal or fraudulent conduct. There is a critical distinction between presenting an analysis of legal aspects of questionable conduct and recommending the means by which a crime or fraud might be committed with impunity.

When the client's course of action has already begun and is continuing, the lawyer's responsibility is especially delicate. The lawyer is not permitted to reveal the client's wrongdoing, except where permitted by Rule 1.6. However, the lawyer is required to avoid furthering the purpose, for example, by suggesting how it might be concealed. A lawyer may not continue assisting a client in conduct that the lawyer originally supposes is legally proper but then discovers is criminal or fraudulent. Withdrawal from the representation, therefore, may be required. *See Rule 1.16.*

Where the client is a fiduciary, the lawyer may be charged with special obligations in dealings with a beneficiary.

Paragraph (d) applies whether or not the defrauded party is a party to the transaction. Hence, a lawyer should not participate in a sham transaction; for example, a transaction to effectuate criminal or fraudulent escape of tax liability. Paragraph (d) does not preclude undertaking a criminal defense incident to a general retainer for legal services to a lawful enterprise. The last clause of paragraph (d) recognizes that determining the validity or interpretation of a statute or regulation may require a course of action involving disobedience of the statute or regulation or of the interpretation placed upon it by governmental authorities.

Code Comparison. — Rule 1.2 (a) has no counterpart in the Disciplinary Rules of the Code. EC 7-7 states that "In certain areas of legal representation not affecting the merits of the cause or substantially prejudicing the rights of a client, a lawyer is entitled to make decisions on his own. But otherwise the authority to make decisions is exclusively that of the client ..." EC 7-8 states that "In the final analysis, however, the ... decision whether to forego legally available objectives or methods because of nonlegal factors is ultimately for the client .... In the event that the client in a nonadjudicatory matter insists upon a course of conduct that is contrary to the judgment and

advice of the lawyer but not prohibited by Disciplinary Rules, the lawyer may withdraw from the employment." DR 7-101 (A) (1) provides that "A lawyer shall not intentionally ... fail to seek the lawful objectives of his client through reasonably available means permitted by law .... A lawyer does not violate this Disciplinary Rule, however, by ... avoiding offensive tactics ...."

Rule 1.2 (b) has no counterpart in the Code.

Rule 1.2 (c) has no counterpart in the Code.

With regard to paragraph (d), DR 7-102 (A) (7) provides that a lawyer shall not "counsel or assist his client in conduct that the lawyer knows to be illegal or fraudulent." DR 7-102 (A) (6) provides that a lawyer shall not "participate in the creation or preservation of evidence when he knows or it is obvious that the evidence is false." DR 7-106 provides that "A lawyer shall not ... advise his client to disregard a standing rule of a tribunal or a ruling of a tribunal ... but he may take appropriate steps in good faith to test the validity of such rule or ruling." EC 7-5 states that "A lawyer should never encourage or aid his client to commit criminal acts or counsel his client on how to violate the law and avoid punishment therefor."

With regard to Rule 1.2 (e), DR 2-110 (C) (1) (c) provides that a lawyer may withdraw from representation if a client "insists" that the lawyer engage in "conduct that is illegal or that is prohibited under the Disciplinary Rules." DR 9-101 (C) provides that "A lawyer shall not state or imply that he is able to influence improperly ... any tribunal, legislative body or public official."

Maryland Law Review. — For symposium, expanding pro bono legal assistance in civil cases to Maryland's poor, see 49 Md. L. Rev. 1 (1990).

Assisting client in criminal conduct. — Although attorney's conduct in assisting a former client in breaking into the home of his wife was an aberration, the egregious nature of that conduct warranted the imposition of a significant sanction such that the attorney was suspended indefinitely from the practice of law with the right to apply for reinstatement not less than one year from the date of filing the opinion. Attorney Grievance Comm'n v. Protokowicz, 329 Md. 252, 619 A.2d 100 (1993).

Defense of criminal responsibility. — A defendant who is competent is entitled to decide whether the defense of criminal responsibility is to be interposed at that trial, and absent the most unusual circumstances, this decision binds both counsel and the trial judge. Treece v. State, 313 Md. 665, 547 A.2d 1054 (1988).

Applied in Attorney Grievance Comm'n v. Rohrback, 323 Md. 79, 591 A.2d 488 (1991).

Quoted in Unnamed Att'y v. Attorney Grievance Comm'n, 349 Md. 391, 708 A.2d 667 (1998).

Cited in Schlossberg v. Epstein, 73 Md. App. 415, 534 A.2d 1003 (1988); Wilson v. Stanbury, 118 Md. App. 209, 702 A.2d 436 (1997).

Rule 1.3. Diligence.

A lawyer shall act with reasonable diligence and promptness in representing a client.

COMMENT

A lawyer should pursue a matter on behalf of a client despite opposition, obstruction or personal inconvenience to the lawyer, and may take whatever lawful and ethical measures are required to vindicate a client's cause or endeavor. A lawyer should act with commitment and dedication to the interests of the client and with zeal in advocacy upon the client's behalf. However, a lawyer is not bound to press for every advantage that might be realized for a client. A lawyer has professional discretion in determining the means by which a matter should be pursued. See Rule 1.2. A lawyer's workload should be controlled so that each matter can be handled adequately.

Perhaps no professional shortcoming is more widely resented than procrastination. A client's interests often can be adversely affected by the passage of time or the change of conditions; in extreme instances, as when a lawyer overlooks a statute of limitations the client's legal position may be destroyed. Even when the client's interests are not affected in substance, however, unreasonable delay can cause a client needless anxiety and undermine confidence in the lawyer's trustworthiness.

Unless the relationship is terminated as provided in Rule 1.16, a lawyer should carry through to conclusion all matters undertaken for a client. If a lawyer's employment is limited to a specific matter, the relationship terminates when the matter has been resolved. If a lawyer has served a client over a substantial period in a variety of matters, the client sometimes may assume that the lawyer will continue to serve on a continuing basis unless the lawyer gives notice of withdrawal. Doubt about whether a client-lawyer relationship still exists should be clarified by the lawyer, preferably in writing, so that the client will not mistakenly suppose the lawyer is looking after the client's affairs when the lawyer has ceased to do so. For example, if a lawyer has handled a judicial or administrative proceeding that produced a result adverse to the client but has not been specifically instructed concerning pursuit of an appeal, the lawyer should advise the client of the possibility of appeal before relinquishing responsibility for the matter.

Code Comparison. — DR 6-101 (A) (3) requires that a lawyer not "neglect a matter entrusted to him." EC 6-4 states that a lawyer should "give appropriate attention to his legal work." Canon 7 states that "a lawyer should represent a client zealously within the bounds of law." DR 7-101 (A) (1) provides that "a lawyer shall not intentionally ... fail to seek the lawful objectives of his client through reasonably available means permitted by law and the Disciplinary Rules ...." DR 7-101 (A) (3) provides that "a lawyer shall not intentionally ... prejudice or damage his client during the course of the relationship ...."

Maryland Law Review. — For note discussing whether, under third-party beneficiary theory, a nonclient can sue attorney for negligent misrepresentation without proof of privity of contract, see 16 U. Balt. L. Rev. 354 (1987).

For symposium, expanding pro bono legal assistance in civil cases to Maryland's poor, see 49 Md. L. Rev. 1 (1990).

University of Baltimore Law Forum. — For article, "Code of Ethics Revisited," see 19.2 U. Balt. Law Forum 14 (1989).

Alcoholism, drug addiction or mental disorder. — When alcoholism is, to a substantial extent, the cause of the misconduct by an attorney, we view the misconduct in a somewhat different light; under this circumstance the appropriate sanction is indefinite suspension and the focus shifts to questions of rehabilitation and the imposition of conditions sufficient to protect the public if the lawyer is allowed to resume practice. Attorney Grievance Comm'n v. Reid, 308 Md. 646, 521 A.2d 743 (1987).

When a lawyer's misconduct is caused by alcoholism, drug addiction, or a mental disorder, the usual sanction is indefinite suspension. This provides the requisite protection for the public, for it prevents the lawyer from practicing law until such time (if ever) that he or she can demonstrate that he or she is free from the effects of the ailment and able to practice competently. At the same time, the lawyer is spared the ultimate sanction of disbarment, a sanction which would be unfair to apply where the lawyer's conduct is caused by factors beyond his or her control. Attorney Grievance Comm'n v. Powers, 314 Md. 484, 551 A.2d 465 (1989).

An indefinite suspension was the proper sanction in the case of a misappropriation of client funds caused by alcoholism; however, in the future, absent truly compelling circumstances, alcoholism will usually not be permitted to mitigate where an attorney commits a violation of ethical or legal rules which would ordinarily warrant disbarment. Attorney Grievance Comm'n v. Kenney, 339 Md. 578, 664 A.2d 854 (1995).

Workaholism. — Acceptance of "workaholism" as an excuse for lack of diligence would effectively gut this Rule. Attorney Grievance Comm'n v. Drew, 341 Md. 139, 669 A.2d 1344 (1996).

Failure to carry out contract of employment. — Ninety-day suspension was appropriate sanction for attorney's failure to timely file or adequately investigate action on behalf of her client, and for misrepresenting to her client that the suit had been filed on her behalf and was proceeding to trial where the client paid the attorney only part of the costs involved in the work the attorney did do and the attorney did not consider the gratuitous client to be a client; an attorney-client relationship did exist and, thus, the attorney failed to carry out her contract of employment. Attorney Grievance Comm'n v. Pinkney, 311 Md. 137, 532 A.2d 1367 (1987).

Failure to pursue applicable legal authority in timely fashion may well constitute a violation of this Rule. Massey v. Prince George's County, 907 F. Supp. 138 (D. Md. 1995).

This Rule's requirement of diligence includes pursuing applicable legal authority in timely fashion. Massey v. Prince George's County, 918 F. Supp. 905 (D. Md. 1996).

Tardiness or absence from trial. — Since being late for a scheduled court appearance interferes with the administration of justice, it is obvious that being altogether absent from a scheduled trial does so as well; however, the circumstances surrounding the failure to appear and the actual consequences of that failure are matters that go to the question of sanction. Attorney Grievance Comm'n v. Ficker, 319 Md. 305, 572 A.2d 501 (1990).

Given the duty of zealous representation that a lawyer owes the client, a failure to appear caused by poor office practices or simple forgetfulness may constitute neglect. Attorney Grievance Comm'n v. Ficker, 319 Md. 305, 572 A.2d 501 (1990).

A single inadvertent failure to appear may constitute neglect of a legal matter. Attorney Grievance Comm'n v. Ficker, 319 Md. 305, 572 A.2d 501 (1990).

Mishandling escrow account. — Indefinite suspension was appropriate sanction for attorney's mishandling of escrow account, including the failure to pay claims due from the account and the failure to refund moneys to clients. Attorney Grievance Comm'n v. Singleton, 311 Md. 1, 532 A.2d 157 (1987); Attorney

Grievance Comm'n v. Bakas, 323 Md. 395, 593 A.2d 1087 (1991).

Ninety-day suspension was appropriate sanction for attorney's neglect of client's cases, falsifying client's signature on a complaint, and causing the complaint with the false signature to be notarized and filed. Attorney Grievance Comm'n v. Parsons, 310 Md. 132, 527 A.2d 325 (1987).

One-year suspension was warranted where attorney's neglect of case was continuous over three-year period and his misconduct ultimately prejudiced his client's right to seek damages for her injuries. Attorney Grievance Comm'n v. Sinclair, 302 Md. 581, 490 A.2d 236 (1985).

Three-year suspension was warranted where attorney prepared defective will for his client and later excoriated her and attempted to mislead an investigator and inquiry panel for the Attorney Grievance Commission. Attorney Grievance Comm'n v. Myers, 302 Md. 571, 490 A.2d 231 (1985).

Disbarment was proper sanction. — Attorney was properly disbarred for violating Maryland Rules of Professional Conduct 1.1, 1.3, 1.4(a) and (b), 1.15(a), 3.3(a)(1), and 8.4(b) and (c), § 10-306 of the Business Occupations and Professions Article, and Rule BU9 (now Rule 16-609) of the Maryland Rules of Procedure. Attorney Grievance Comm'n v. Williams, 335 Md. 458, 644 A.2d 490 (1994).

Disbarment of attorney was appropriate where there were serious and repeated violations of this Rule and other provisions of the Maryland Rules of Professional Conduct. Attorney Grievance Comm'n v. Milliken, 348 Md. 486, 704 A.2d 1225 (1998).

Indefinite suspension was proper sanction. — Where respondent attorney's representation of four clients was marked by serious neglect and inattention; where he failed to return a fee which was unearned for a period of nine months; where he failed to timely remit funds he received on behalf of a client; where he failed to communicate with his clients; and in connection with the investigation of three of the complaints, where respondent failed to answer Bar Counsel's requests for information, the proper sanction was that the attorney be indefinitely suspended from the practice of law, with the right to apply for reinstatement after the suspension had been in effect for six months, conditioned upon his payment of all costs and upon the monitoring of respondent's practice. Attorney Grievance Comm'n v. David, 331 Md. 317, 628 A.2d 178 (1993).

Failure to file affidavit. — A lawyer engaged in default judgment proceedings who fails to file a military affidavit or to adequately comply with the content requirements of former Maryland Rule 2-613 (a) (now Rule 2-613 (b)) is not incompetent; such failure is, at best, indicative of the lawyer's carelessness or negligence. Attorney Grievance Comm'n v. Kemp, 335 Md. 1, 641 A.2d 510 (1994).

Failure to include attestation clause and witness signature lines on will and neglecting to inform the client of these necessities constitute neglect of a legal matter. Attorney Grievance Comm'n v. Myers, 302 Md. 571, 490 A.2d 231 (1985).

Evidence justified findings of misconduct, and disbarment was warranted. Attorney Grievance Comm'n v. Mazelis, 309 Md. 50, 522 A.2d 913 (1987); Attorney Grievance Comm'n v. Manning, 318 Md. 697, 569 A.2d 1250 (1990).

Applied in Gantt v. State, 81 Md. App. 653, 569 A.2d 220 (1990); Attorney Grievance Comm'n v. Berger, 323 Md. 428, 593 A.2d 1103 (1991); Attorney Grievance Comm'n v. Ficker, 349 Md. 13, 706 A.2d 1045 (1998).

Stated in Attorney Grievance Comm'n v. Montgomery, 318 Md. 154, 567 A.2d 112 (1989); Unnamed Att'y v. Attorney Grievance Comm'n, 349 Md. 391, 708 A.2d 667 (1998).

Cited in Attorney Grievance Comm'n v. Noble, 324 Md. 42, 595 A.2d 468 (1991); Attorney Grievance Comm'n v. Powell, 328 Md. 276, 614 A.2d 102 (1992); Attorney Grievance Comm'n v. Tahir, 330 Md. 297, 623 A.2d 1296 (1993); Attorney Grievance Comm'n v. Williams, 348 Md. 196, 702 A.2d 1271 (1997).

Rule 1.4. Communication.

(a) A lawyer shall keep a client reasonably informed about the status of a matter and promptly comply with reasonable requests for information.

(b) A lawyer shall explain a matter to the extent reasonably necessary to permit the client to make informed decisions regarding the representation.

COMMENT

The client should have sufficient information to participate intelligently in decisions concerning the objectives of the representation and the means by which they are to be pursued, to the extent the client is willing and able to do so. For example, a lawyer negotiating on behalf of a client should provide the client with facts relevant to the matter, inform the client of communications from another party and take other reasonable steps that permit the client to make a decision regarding a serious offer from another party. A lawyer who receives from opposing counsel an offer of settlement in a civil controversy or a proffered plea bargain in a criminal case should promptly inform the client of its substance unless prior discussions with the client have left it clear that the proposal will be unacceptable. See Rule 1.2 (a). Even when a client delegates authority to the lawyer, the client should be kept advised of the status of the matter.

Adequacy of communication depends in part on the kind of advice or assistance involved. For example, in negotiations where there is time to explain a proposal, the lawyer should review all important provisions with the client before proceeding to an agreement. In litigation a lawyer should explain the general strategy and prospects of success and ordinarily should consult the client on tactics that might injure or coerce others. On the other hand, a lawyer ordinarily cannot be expected to describe trial or negotiation strategy in detail. The guiding principle is that the lawyer should fulfill reasonable client expectations for information consistent with the duty to act in the client's best interests, and the client's overall requirements as to the character of representation.

Ordinarily, the information to be provided is that appropriate for a client who is a comprehending and responsible adult. However, fully informing the client according to this standard may be impracticable, for example, where the client is a child or suffers from mental disability. See Rule 1.14. When the client is an organization or group, it is often impossible or inappropriate to inform every one of its members about its legal affairs; ordinarily, the lawyer should address communications to the appropriate officials of the organization. See Rule 1.13. Where many routine matters are involved, a system of limited or occasional reporting may be arranged with the client. Practical exigency may also require a lawyer to act for a client without prior consultation.

Withholding information. — In some circumstances, a lawyer may be justified in delaying transmission of information when the client would be likely to react imprudently to an immediate communication. Thus, a lawyer might withhold a psychiatric diagnosis of a client when the examining psychiatrist indicates that disclosure would harm the client. A lawyer may not withhold information to serve the lawyer's own interest or convenience. Rules or court orders governing litigation may provide that information supplied to a lawyer may not be disclosed to the client. Rule 3.4 (c) directs compliance with such rules or orders.

Code Comparison. — This Rule has no

direct counterpart in the Disciplinary Rules of the Code. DR 6-101 (A) (3) provides that a lawyer shall not "neglect a legal matter entrusted to him." DR 9-102 (B) (1) provides that a lawyer "shall promptly notify a client of the receipt of his funds, securities, or other properties." EC 7-8 states that "a lawyer should exert his best efforts to insure that decisions of his client are made only after the client has been informed of relevant considerations." EC 9-2 states that "a lawyer should fully and promptly inform his client of material developments in the matters being handled for the client."

Misrepresentation of status of case to client. — Ninety-day suspension was appropriate sanction for attorney's failure to timely file or adequately investigate action on behalf of her client, and for misrepresenting to her client that the suit had been filed on her behalf and was proceeding to trial where the client paid the attorney only part of the costs involved in the work the attorney did do and the attorney did not consider the gratuitous client to be a client; an attorney-client relationship did exist and, thus, the attorney failed to carry out her contract of employment. Attorney Grievance Comm'n v. Pinkney, 311 Md. 137, 532 A.2d 1367 (1987).

Professional obligation in advising about merits of claim. — A client may certainly consent to an action that has only a modest chance of success in court; nonetheless, an attorney has both professional and contractual obligations to exercise reasonable care in advising his or her client about the merits of a claim. Taylor v. Feissner, 103 Md. App. 356, 653 A.2d 947 (1995).

Mishandling escrow account. — Indefinite suspension was appropriate sanction for attorney's mishandling of escrow account, including the failure to pay claims due from the account and the failure to refund moneys to clients. Attorney Grievance Comm'n v. Singleton, 311 Md. 1, 532 A.2d 157 (1987).

Use of expert testimony in establishing likely conclusions of reasonable attorney. — Expert testimony was indispensable in establishing what conclusions a reasonably competent workers' compensation attorney would have reached under all the facts and circumstances, including the state of Maryland law at the time of the representation, to determine whether the attorney was negligent in advising his client not to appeal. Ankney v. Franch, 103 Md. App. 83, 652 A.2d 1138 (1995).

Ninety-day suspension was appropriate sanction for attorney's neglect of client's cases, falsifying client's signature on a complaint, and causing the complaint with the false signature to be notarized and filed. Attorney Grievance Comm'n v. Parsons, 310 Md. 132, 527 A.2d 325 (1987).

Disbarment was proper sanction. — Attorney was properly disbarred for violating Maryland Rules of Professional Conduct 1.1, 1.3, 1.4(a) and (b), 1.15(a), 3.3(a)(1), and 8.4(b) and (c), § 10-306 of the Business Occupations and Professions Article, and former Rule BU9 (now Rule 16-609) of the Maryland Rules of Procedure. Attorney Grievance Comm'n v. Williams, 335 Md. 458, 644 A.2d 490 (1994).

Disbarment of attorney was appropriate where there were serious and repeated violations of this Rule and other provisions of the Maryland Rules of Professional Conduct. Attorney Grievance Comm'n v. Milliken, 348 Md. 486, 704 A.2d 1225 (1998).

Indefinite suspension was proper sanction. — Where respondent attorney's representation of four clients was marked by serious neglect and inattention; where he failed to return a fee which was unearned for a period of nine months; where he failed to timely remit funds he received on behalf of a client; where he failed to communicate with his clients; and in connection with the investigation of three of the complaints, where respondent failed to answer Bar Counsel's requests for information, the proper sanction was that the attorney be indefinitely suspended from the practice of law, with the right to apply for reinstatement after the suspension had been in effect for six months, conditioned upon his payment of all costs and upon the monitoring of respondent's practice. Attorney Grievance Comm'n v. David, 331 Md. 317, 628 A.2d 178 (1993).

Alcoholism, drug addiction or mental disorder. — When a lawyer's misconduct is caused by alcoholism, drug addiction, or a mental disorder, the usual sanction is indefinite suspension. This provides the requisite protection for the public, for it prevents the lawyer from practicing law until such time (if ever) that he or she can demonstrate that he or she is free from the effects of the ailment and able to practice competently. At the same time, the lawyer is spared the ultimate sanction of disbarment, a sanction which would be unfair to apply where the lawyer's conduct is caused by factors beyond his or her control. Attorney Grievance Comm'n v. Powers, 314 Md. 484, 551 A.2d 465 (1989).

An indefinite suspension was the proper sanction in the case of a misappropriation of client funds caused by alcoholism; however, in the future, absent truly compelling circumstances, alcoholism will usually not be permitted to mitigate where an attorney commits a violation of ethical or legal rules which would ordinarily warrant disbarment. Attorney Grievance Comm'n v. Kenney, 339 Md. 578, 664 A.2d 854 (1995).

Applied in Attorney Grievance Comm'n v. Trilling, 311 Md. 711, 537 A.2d 269 (1988); Attorney Grievance Comm'n v. Werner, 315 Md. 172, 553 A.2d 722 (1989); Attorney Grievance Comm'n v. Berger, 323 Md. 428, 593 A.2d 1103 (1991).

Stated in Attorney Grievance Comm'n v. Ficker, 349 Md. 13, 706 A.2d 1045 (1998); Unnamed Att'y v. Attorney Grievance Comm'n, 349 Md. 391, 708 A.2d 667 (1998).

Cited in Attorney Grievance Comm'n v. Kerpelman, 323 Md. 136, 591 A.2d 516 (1991), cert. denied, 502 U.S. 939, 112 S. Ct. 374, 116 L. Ed. 2d 326 (1991); Attorney Grievance Comm'n v. Powell, 328 Md. 276, 614 A.2d 102 (1992); Attorney Grievance Comm'n v. Cannon, 329 Md. 306, 619 A.2d 531 (1993); Attorney Grievance Comm'n v. Drew, 341 Md. 139, 669 A.2d 1344 (1996).

Rule 1.5. Fees.

(a) A lawyer's fee shall be reasonable. The factors to be considered in determining the reasonableness of a fee include the following:

(1) the time and labor required, the novelty and difficulty of the questions involved, and the skill requisite to perform the legal service properly;

(2) the likelihood, if apparent to the client, that the acceptance of the particular employment will preclude other employment by the lawyer;

(3) the fee customarily charged in the locality for similar legal services;

(4) the amount involved and the results obtained;

(5) the time limitations imposed by the client or by the circumstances;

(6) the nature and length of the professional relationship with the client;

(7) the experience, reputation, and ability of the lawyer or lawyers performing the services; and

(8) whether the fee is fixed or contingent.

(b) When the lawyer has not regularly represented the client, the basis or rate of the fee shall be communicated to the client, preferably in writing, before or within a reasonable time after commencing the representation.

(c) A fee may be contingent on the outcome of the matter for which the service is rendered, except in a matter in which a contingent fee is prohibited by paragraph (d) or other law. The terms of a contingent fee agreement shall be communicated to the client in writing. The communication shall state the method by which the fee is to be determined, including the percentage or percentages that shall accrue to the lawyer in the event of settlement, trial or appeal, litigation and other expenses to be deducted from the recovery, and whether such expenses are to be deducted before or after the contingent fee is calculated. Upon conclusion of a contingent fee matter, the lawyer shall provide the client with a written statement stating the outcome of the matter, and, if there is a recovery, showing the remittance to the client and the method of its determination.

(d) A lawyer shall not enter into an arrangement for, charge, or collect:

(1) any fee in a domestic relations matter, the payment or amount of which is contingent upon the securing of a divorce or custody of a child or upon the amount of alimony or support or property settlement, or upon the amount of an award pursuant to Sections 8-201 through 213 of Family Law Article, Annotated Code of Maryland; or

(2) a contingent fee for representing a defendant in a criminal matter.

(e) A division of fee between lawyers who are not in the same firm may be made only if:

(1) the division is in proportion to the services performed by each lawyer or, by written agreement with the client, each lawyer assumes joint responsibility for the representation;

(2) the client is advised of and does not object to the participation of all the lawyers involved; and

(3) the total fee is reasonable.

COMMENT

Basis or rate of fee. — When the lawyer has regularly represented a client, they ordinarily will have evolved an understanding concerning the basis or rate of the fee. In a new client-lawyer relationship, however, an understanding as to the fee should be promptly established. It is not necessary to recite all the factors that underlie the basis of the fee, but only those that are directly involved in its computation. It is sufficient, for example, to state that the basic rate is an hourly charge or a fixed amount or an estimated amount, or to identify the factors that may be taken into account in finally fixing the fee. When developments occur during the representation that render an earlier estimate substantially inaccurate, a revised estimate should be provided to the client. A written statement concerning the fee reduces the possibility of misunderstanding. Furnishing the client with a simple memorandum or a copy of the lawyer's customary fee schedule is sufficient if the basis or rate of the fee is set forth.

Terms of payment. — A lawyer may require advance payment of a fee, but is obliged to return any unearned portion. See Rule 1.16 (d). A lawyer may accept property in payment for services, such as an ownership interest in an enterprise, providing this does not involve acquisition of a proprietary interest in the cause of action or subject matter of the litigation contrary to Rule 1.8 (j). However, a fee paid in property instead of money may be subject to special scrutiny because it involves questions concerning both the value of the services and the lawyer's special knowledge of the value of the property.

An agreement may not be made whose terms might induce the lawyer improperly to curtail services for the client or perform them in a way contrary to the client's interest. For example, a lawyer should not enter into an agreement whereby services are to be provided only up to a stated amount when it is foreseeable that more extensive services probably will be required, unless the situation is adequately explained to the client. Otherwise, the client might have to bargain for further assistance in the midst of a proceeding or transaction. However, it is proper to define the extent of services in light of the client's ability to pay. A lawyer should not exploit a fee arrangement based primarily on hourly charges by using wasteful procedures. When there is doubt whether a contingent fee is consistent with the client's best interest, the lawyer should offer the client alternative bases for the fee and explain their implications. Applicable law may impose limitations on contingent fees, such as a ceiling on the percentage.

Contingent fees. — For purposes of Rules 1.5 (c) and 1.5 (d), a contingent fee arrangement means an agreement for legal services (1) made before the services are completed, and (2) providing compensation of the lawyer which is contingent in whole or in part upon the successful accomplishment or disposition of the legal matter and which is either in a fixed amount or in an amount determined under a specified formula.

Division of fee. — A division of fee is a single billing to a client covering the fee of two or more lawyers who are not in the same firm. A division of fee facilitates association of more than one lawyer in a matter in which neither alone could serve the client as well, and most often is used when the fee is contingent and the division is between a referring lawyer and a trial specialist. Paragraph (e) permits the lawyers to divide a fee on either the basis of the proportion of services they render or by agreement between the participating lawyers if all assume responsibility for the representation as a whole and the client is advised and does not object. It does not require disclosure to the client of the share that each lawyer is to receive. Joint responsibility for the representation entails the obligations stated in Rule 5.1 for purposes of the matter involved.

Disputes over fees. — If a procedure has been established for resolution of fee disputes, such as an arbitration or mediation procedure established by the bar, the lawyer should conscientiously consider submitting to it. Law may prescribe a procedure for determining a lawyer's fee, for example, in representation of an executor or administrator, a class or a person entitled to a reasonable fee as part of the measure of damages. The lawyer entitled to such a fee and a lawyer representing another party concerned with the fee should comply with the prescribed procedure.

Code Comparison. — DR 2-106 (A) provides that "A lawyer shall not enter into an agreement for, charge, or collect an illegal or clearly excessive fee." DR 2-106 (B) provides that "A fee is clearly excessive when, after a review of the facts, a lawyer of ordinary prudence would be left with a definite and firm conviction that the fee is in excess of a reasonable fee." DR 2-106 (B) further provides that "Factors to be considered ... determining ... reasonableness ... include ... (1) The time and labor required, the novelty and difficulty of the questions involved and the skill requisite to perform the legal service properly. (2) The likelihood, if apparent to the client, that the acceptance of the particular employment will preclude other employment by the lawyer. (3) The fee customarily charged in the locality for similar services. (4) The amount involved and the results obtained. (5) The time limitations imposed by the client or by the circumstances. (6) The nature and length of the professional relationship with the client. (7) The experience, reputation, and ability of the lawyer or lawyers performing the services. (8) Whether the fee is fixed or contingent." The Rule includes the factor of ability to pay; a person of ample means may justly be charged more for a service, and a person of limited means less, other factors being the same. EC 2-17 states that "A lawyer should not charge more than a reasonable fee ...."

There is no counterpart to Rule 1.5 (b) in the Disciplinary Rules of the Code. EC 2-19 states that "It is usually beneficial to reduce to writing the understanding of the parties regarding the fee, particularly when it is contingent."

With regard to Rule 1.5 (c), DR 2-106 (C) prohibits "a contingent fee in a criminal case."

With regard to Rule 1.5 (d), DR 2-107 (A) permits division of fees only if:

"(1) The client consents to employment of the other lawyer after a full disclosure that a division of fees will be made. (2) The division is in proportion to the services performed and responsibility assumed by each. (3) The total fee does not exceed clearly reasonable compensation ...." Rule 1.5 (d) permits division without regard to the services rendered by each lawyer if they assume joint responsibility for the representation.

Maryland Law Review. — For article, "Survey of Developments in Maryland Law, 1987-88," see 48 Md. L. Rev. 551 (1989).

For note, "Recent Decisions, The Maryland Court of Appeals," see 54 Md. L. Rev. 670 (1995).

University of Baltimore Law Forum. — For article, "Code of Ethics Revisited," see 19.2 U. Balt. Law Forum 14 (1989).

Focus of Rule. — The focus of this Rule is clearly upon excessive fees. Attorney Grievance Comm'n v. Eisenstein, 333 Md. 464, 635 A.2d 1327 (1994).

"Excessive fee." — Receipt of one-third of $5,000 paid under an insured client's medical payment coverage as a contingency fee was clearly an "excessive fee." Attorney Grievance Comm'n v. Kemp, 303 Md. 664, 496 A.2d 672 (1985).

A fee based on results in a domestic relations case which is one and one-half times the lodestar fee was excessive. Head v. Head, 66 Md. App. 655, 505 A.2d 868 (1986).

If attorney's contingent fee was clearly excessive in violation of former DR 2-106, then he also failed to stay within the exception to the prohibition of former DR 5-103(A) against acquiring a proprietary interest in the clients' causes of action. Attorney Grievance Comm'n v. Korotki, 318 Md. 646, 569 A.2d 1224 (1990).

A $20,000, nonrefundable engagement retainer that was not intended to pay for future services was excessive and therefore unreasonable under section (a) of this Rule. In re Printing Dimensions, Inc., 153 Bankr. 715 (Bankr. D. Md. 1993).

Agreements for division of fees. — Compliance with subsection (e) of this Rule is not implied in every fee-sharing agreement between attorneys. Post v. Bregman, 112 Md. App. 738, 686 A.2d 665 (1996).

Applicability to agreements between attorneys. — This Rule does not apply to a case involving one lawyer's attempt to enforce an agreement he made with another. Vogelhut v. Kandel, 66 Md. App. 170, 502 A.2d 1120, aff'd, 308 Md. 183, 517 A.2d 1092 (1986).

Subsection (e) of this Rule constitutes a supervening statement of public policy to which fee-sharing agreements by lawyers are subject; its enforcement is not limited to disciplinary proceedings, and may render fee-sharing arrangements in clear and flagrant violation of this Rule unenforceable. Post v. Bregman, 349 Md. 142, 707 A.2d 806 (1998).

It is inappropriate for attorney to ask court to set attorney's fees as the attorney is in the best position to assess the skill, time, labor and effort the case requires and set the value of his or her own services. Head v. Head, 66 Md. App. 655, 505 A.2d 868 (1986).

Unilateral increase of attorney's fees by the attorney after a fee arrangement is agreed upon by client is inappropriate. Head v. Head, 66 Md. App. 655, 505 A.2d 868 (1986).

Modification of fee arrangement permissible. — Where an attorney and client have a special fee arrangement they may, after disclosures appropriate to the existing confidential relationship, agree on a modification of that arrangement. Attorney Grievance Comm'n v. Wright, 306 Md. 93, 507 A.2d 618 (1986).

Fees based on preclusion of other employment. — In the relation of attorney and client, if a fee for work requiring only modest legal ability is to be based on the higher value of more complex legal work which the attorney is capable of performing, but which he is unable to perform because of the employment, then some kind of effective disclosure to the client is required as part of the terms of the engagement. Attorney Grievance Comm'n v. Wright, 306 Md. 93, 507 A.2d 618 (1986).

Where a default judgment directly resulted from attorney's violations, at a minimum, the loss suffered by a client included the expense incurred by her in engaging counsel to appeal the default judgment and to appear in circuit court where successor counsel was able to have that default judgment vacated. Attorney Grievance Comm'n v. Dietz, 331 Md. 637, 629 A.2d 678 (1993).

Unreasonableness argument not considered absent findings of fact. — Appellate court refused to consider insurance company's argument that insured's legal fees were unreasonable where, even assuming the insurer had standing to question the fee's reasonableness, such a determination would require a factual hearing and findings of fact, neither of which had occurred. Medical Mut. Liab. Ins. Soc'y v. Evans, 330 Md. 1, 622 A.2d 103 (1993).

Fee-sharing violations. — A violation of subsection (e) of this Rule, whether regarded as an external defense or as incorporated into the contract itself, is an equitable defense and the principles of equity ought to be applied. Post v. Bregman, 349 Md. 142, 707 A.2d 806 (1998).

Cumulative violations. — Although a fee that is not permitted by law is by definition an unreasonable fee, where other rules more specifically and completely address the specifically and completely address the improper conduct, adding a cumulative violation for the same conduct will serve no useful purpose. Attorney Grievance Comm'n v. Eisenstein, 333 Md. 464, 635 A.2d 1327 (1994).

Evidence justified findings of misconduct, and disbarment was warranted. Attorney Grievance Comm'n v. Mazelis, 309 Md. 50, 522 A.2d 913 (1987); Attorney Grievance Comm'n v. Manning, 318 Md. 697, 569 A.2d 1250 (1990).

Indefinite suspension was proper sanction. — Where respondent attorney's representation of four clients was marked by serious neglect and inattention; where he failed to return a fee which was unearned for a period of nine months; where he failed to timely remit funds he received on behalf of a client; where he failed to communicate with his clients; and in connection with the investigation of three of the complaints, where respondent failed to answer Bar Counsel's requests for information, the proper sanction was that the attorney be indefinitely suspended from the practice of law, with the right to apply for reinstatement after the suspension had been in effect for six months, conditioned upon his payment of all costs and upon the monitoring of respondent's practice. Attorney Grievance Comm'n v. David, 331 Md. 317, 628 A.2d 178 (1993).

Quoted in Reisterstown Plaza Assocs. v. General Nutrition Ctr., Inc., 89 Md. App. 232, 597 A.2d 1049 (1991); Attorney Grievance Comm'n v. James, 333 Md. 174, 634 A.2d 48 (1993); Kilsheimer v. Dewberry & Davis, 106 Md. App. 600, 665 A.2d 723 (1995); Attorney Grievance Comm'n v. James, 340 Md. 318, 666 A.2d 1246 (1995); Attorney Grievance Comm'n v. Awuah, 346 Md. 420, 697 A.2d 446 (1997).

Cited in Collins v. United Pac. Ins. Co., 315 Md. 141, 553 A.2d 707 (1989); Attorney Grievance Comm'n v. Kerpelman, 323 Md. 136, 591 A.2d 516 (1991), cert. denied, 502 U.S. 939, 112 S. Ct. 374, 116 L. Ed. 2d 326 (1991); Attorney Grievance Comm'n v. Powell, 328 Md. 276, 614 A.2d 102 (1992); In re Attorney's Use of Trade Name, 333 Md. 488, 635 A.2d 1338 (1994); Son v. Margolius, Mallios, Davis, Rider & Tomar, 114 Md. App. 190, 689 A.2d 645 (1997); Philip Morris, Inc. v. Glendening, 349 Md. 660, 709 A.2d 1230 (1998).

Rule 1.6. Confidentiality of information.

(a) A lawyer shall not reveal information relating to representation of a client unless the client consents after consultation, except for disclosures that are impliedly authorized in order to carry out the representation, and except as stated in paragraph (b).

(b) A lawyer may reveal such information to the extent the lawyer reasonably believes necessary:

(1) to prevent the client from committing a criminal or fraudulent act that

the lawyer believes is likely to result in death or substantial bodily harm or in substantial injury to the financial interests or property of another;

(2) to rectify the consequences of a client's criminal or fraudulent act in the furtherance of which the lawyer's services were used;

(3) to establish a claim or defense on behalf of the lawyer in a controversy between the lawyer and the client, or to establish a defense to a criminal charge, civil claim, or disciplinary complaint against the lawyer based upon conduct in which the client was involved or to respond to allegations in any proceedings concerning the lawyer's representation of the client.

(4) to comply with these Rules, a court order or other law.

COMMENT

The lawyer is part of a judicial system charged with upholding the law. One of the lawyer's functions is to advise clients so that they avoid any violation of the law in the proper exercise of their rights.

The observance of the ethical obligation of a lawyer to hold inviolate confidential information of the client not only facilitates the full development of facts essential to proper representation of the client but also encourages people to seek early legal assistance.

Almost without exception, clients come to lawyers in order to determine what their rights are and what is, in the maze of laws and regulations, deemed to be legal and correct. The common law recognizes that the client's confidences must be protected from disclosure. Based upon experience, lawyers know that almost all clients follow the advice given, and the law is upheld.

A fundamental principle in the client-lawyer relationship is that the lawyer maintain confidentiality of information relating to the representation. The client is thereby encouraged to communicate fully and frankly with the lawyer even as to embarrassing or legally damaging subject matter.

The principle of confidentiality is given effect in two related bodies of law, the attorney-client privilege (which includes the work product doctrine) in the law of evidence and the rule of confidentiality established in professional ethics. The attorney-client privilege applies in judicial and other proceedings in which a lawyer may be called as a witness or otherwise required to produce evidence concerning a client. The rule of client-lawyer confidentiality applies in situations other than those where evidence is sought from the lawyer through compulsion of law. The confidentiality rule applies not merely to matters communicated in confidence by the client but also to all information relating to the representation, whatever its source. A lawyer may not disclose such information except as authorized or required by the Rules of Professional Con-

duct or other law. See also Scope.

The requirement of maintaining confidentiality of information relating to representation applies to government lawyers who may disagree with the policy goals that their representation is designed to advance.

Information relating to representation. — "Information relating to representation" protected under paragraph (a) includes revelations made to a lawyer by a person seeking to engage the lawyer's services. The revelations are protected even if the prospective client decides not to engage the services of the lawyer or the lawyer does not agree to undertake the representation.

Authorized disclosure. — A lawyer is impliedly authorized to make disclosures about a client when appropriate in carrying out the representation, except to the extent that the client's instructions or special circumstances limit that authority. In litigation, for example, a lawyer may disclose information by admitting a fact that cannot properly be disputed, or in negotiation by making a disclosure that facilitates a satisfactory conclusion.

Lawyers in a firm may, in the course of the firm's practice, disclose to each other information relating to a client of the firm, unless the client has instructed that particular information be confined to specified lawyers.

Disclosure adverse to client. — The confidentiality rule is subject to limited exceptions. In becoming privy to information about a client, a lawyer may foresee that the client intends serious harm to another person. However, to the extent a lawyer is required or permitted to disclose a client's purposes, the client will be inhibited from revealing facts which would enable the lawyer to counsel against a wrongful course of action. The public is better protected if full and open communication by the client is encouraged than if it is inhibited.

Several situations must be distinguished.

First, the lawyer may not counsel or assist a client in conduct that is criminal or fraudulent. See Rule 1.2 (d). There can be situations where the lawyer may have to reveal information relating to the representation in order to avoid assisting a client's criminal or fraudulent conduct. Similarly, a lawyer has a duty under Rule 3.3 (a)(4) not to use false evidence. This duty is essentially a special instance of the duty prescribed in Rule 1.2 (d) to avoid assisting a client in criminal or fraudulent conduct. The same is true of compliance with Rule 4.1 concerning truthfulness of a lawyer's own representations.

Second, the lawyer may have been innocently involved in past conduct by the client that was criminal or fraudulent. In such a situation the lawyer has not violated Rule 1.2 (d), because to "counsel or assist" criminal or fraudulent conduct requires knowing that the conduct is of that character. Even if the involvement was innocent, however, the fact remains that the lawyer's professional services were made the instrument of the client's crime or fraud. The lawyer, therefore, has a legitimate interest in being able to rectify the consequences of such conduct, and has the professional right although not a professional duty to rectify the situation. Exercising that right may require revealing information relating to the representation. Paragraph (b) (2) gives the lawyer professional discretion to reveal such information to the extent necessary to accomplish rectification.

Third, the lawyer may learn that a client intends prospective conduct that is criminal and likely to result in death or substantial bodily harm or in substantial injury to the financial interests or property of another. As stated in paragraph (b) (1), the lawyer has professional discretion to reveal information in order to prevent such consequences. The lawyer may make a disclosure in order to prevent homicide or serious bodily injury or substantial injury to the financial interests or property of another which the lawyer reasonably believes is intended by a client. It is very difficult for a lawyer to "know" when such a heinous purpose will actually be carried out, for the client may have a change of mind.

The lawyer's exercise of discretion requires consideration of such factors as the nature of the lawyer's relationship with the client and with those who might be injured by the client, the lawyer's own involvement in the transaction and factors that may extenuate the conduct in question. Where practical, the lawyer should seek to persuade the client to take suitable action. In any case, a disclosure adverse to the client's interest should be no greater than the lawyer reasonably believes necessary to the purpose. A lawyer's decision not to take preventive action permitted by paragraph (b) (1) does not violate this Rule. Paragraph (b) (2) does not apply where a lawyer is employed after a crime or fraud has

been committed to represent the client in matters ensuing therefrom.

Withdrawal. — If the lawyer's services will be used by the client in materially furthering a course of criminal or fraudulent conduct, the lawyer must withdraw, as stated in Rule 1.16 (a) (1).

After withdrawal the lawyer is required to refrain from making disclosure of the client's confidences, except as otherwise provided in Rule 1.6. If the lawyer knows that despite the withdrawal the client is continuing in conduct that is criminal or fraudulent, and is making use of the fact that the lawyer was involved in the matter, the lawyer may have to take positive steps to avoid being held to have assisted the conduct. See Rules 1.2 (d) and 4.1. In other situations not involving such assistance, the lawyer has discretion to make disclosure of otherwise confidential information only in accordance with Rules 1.6 and 1.13 (c). Neither this Rule nor Rule 1.8 (b) nor Rule 1.16 (d) prevents the lawyer from giving notice of the fact of withdrawal, and the lawyer may also withdraw or disaffirm any opinion, document, affirmation, or the like.

Where the client is an organization, the lawyer may be in doubt whether contemplated conduct will actually be carried out by the organization. Where necessary to guide conduct in connection with this Rule, the lawyer may make inquiry within the organization as indicated in Rule 1.13 (b).

Dispute concerning lawyer's conduct. — Where a legal claim or disciplinary charge alleges complicity of the lawyer in a client's conduct or other misconduct of the lawyer involving representation of the client, the lawyer may respond to the extent the lawyer reasonably believes necessary to establish a defense. The same is true with respect to a claim involving the conduct or representation of a former client. The lawyer's right to respond arises when an assertion of such complicity has been made. Paragraph (b) (3) does not require the lawyer to await the commencement of an action or proceeding that charges such complicity, so that the defense may be established by responding directly to a third party who has made such an assertion. The right to defend, of course, applies where a proceeding has been commenced. Where practicable and not prejudicial to the lawyer's ability to establish the defense, the lawyer should advise the client of the third party's assertion and request that the client respond appropriately. In any event, disclosure should be no greater than the lawyer reasonably believes is necessary to vindicate innocence, the disclosure should be made in a manner which limits access to the information to the tribunal or other persons having a need to know it, and appropriate protective orders or other arrangements should be sought by the lawyer to the fullest extent practicable.

If the lawyer is charged with wrongdoing in which the client's conduct is implicated, the rule of confidentiality should not prevent the lawyer from defending against the charge. Such a charge can arise in a civil, criminal or professional disciplinary proceeding, and can be based on a wrong allegedly committed by the lawyer against the client, or on a wrong alleged by a third person; for example, a person claiming to have been defrauded by the lawyer and client acting together. A lawyer entitled to a fee is permitted by paragraph (b) (3) to prove the services rendered in an action to collect it. This aspect of the rule expresses the principle that the beneficiary of a fiduciary relationship may not exploit it to the detriment of the fiduciary. As stated above, the lawyer must make every effort practicable to avoid unnecessary disclosure of information relating to a representation, to limit disclosure to those having the need to know it, and to obtain protective orders or make other arrangements minimizing the risk of disclosure.

Disclosures otherwise required or authorized. — The attorney-client privilege is differently defined in various jurisdictions. If a lawyer is called as a witness to give testimony concerning a client, absent waiver by the client, Rule 1.6 (a) requires the lawyer to invoke the privilege when it is applicable. The lawyer must comply with the final orders of a court or other tribunal of competent jurisdiction requiring the lawyer to give information about the client.

The Rules of Professional Conduct in various circumstances permit or require a lawyer to disclose information relating to the representation. See Rules 1.13, 2.2, 2.3, 3.3 and 4.1. In addition to these provisions, a lawyer may be obligated or permitted by other provisions of law to give information about a client.

Former client. — The duty of confidentiality continues after the client-lawyer relationship has terminated. See Rule 1.9.

Code Comparison. — The principle of confidentiality is enlarged in several respects and narrowed in a few respects compared with the corresponding provisions of the Code.

The general principle is enlarged in the following respects: First, the confidentiality requirement applies to all information about a client "relating to the representation." Under the Code, DR 4-101, the requirement applies only to information governed by the attorney-client privilege and to information "gained in" the professional relationship that "the client has requested be held inviolate or the disclosure of which would be embarrassing or would be likely to be detrimental to the client." Rule

1.6 thus imposes confidentiality on information relating to the representation even if it is acquired before or after the relationship existed. It does not require the client to indicate information that is to be confidential, or permit the lawyer to speculate whether particular information might be embarrassing or detrimental. Furthermore, this definition avoids the constricted definition of "confidence" that appears in some decisions.

See Allegaert v. Perot, 434 F. Supp. 790 (S.D.N.Y. 1977); Mortiz v. Medical Protection Co., 428 F. Supp. 865 (W.D. Wis. 1977); City of Wichita v. Chapman, 521 P.2d 589 (Kan. 1974).

Rule 1.6 (a) permits a lawyer to disclose information where impliedly authorized in order to carry out the representation. Under DR 4-101 (B) and (C), a lawyer cannot disclose "confidences" unless the client first expressly consents after disclosure.

Second, paragraph (b) redefines the exceptions to the requirement of confidentiality. Under the Code, DR 4-101 (C) (3), a lawyer "may reveal the intention of his client to commit a crime and the information necessary to prevent the crime." This option exists regardless of the seriousness of the proposed crime. Rule 1.6 (b) (1) permits the lawyer to reveal information about a client to prevent the client from committing a crime or fraud that is likely to result in the specified serious consequences.

Under DR 7-102 (B), the lawyer is required to reveal information necessary to "rectify" a "fraud upon a person or tribunal." DR 7-102 (B) applies to past frauds and presumably to future frauds if the client goes on to commit them.

Rule 1.6 (b) (2) permits the lawyer to reveal such information.

With regard to Rule 1.6 (b) (3), DR 4-101 (C) (4) provides that a lawyer may reveal "confidences or secrets necessary to establish or collect his fee or to defend himself or his employers or associates against an accusation of wrongful conduct." Rule 1.6 (b) (3) enlarges the exception to include disclosure of information relating to claims by the lawyer other than for his fee; for example, recovery of property from the client. It narrows the exception dealing with defense against claims of wrongful conduct to situations where the client's conduct was involved.

Under DR 4-101 (C) the lawyer may reveal confidences or secrets when permitted under Disciplinary Rules or required by law or court order. Rule 1.6 (b) (4) permits the lawyer to reveal information relating to the representation to the extent the lawyer reasonably believes necessary to comply with the Rules of Professional Conduct, a court order or other law.

Maryland Law Review. — For comment discussing the need for a consensus on the proper scope of the attorney-client privilege where a client attempts to use an attorney's services for fraudulent or illegal purposes, see 46 Md. L. Rev. 436 (1987).

For article, "Conducting Informal Discovery of a Party's Former Employees: Legal and Ethical Concerns and Constraints," see 51 Md. L. Rev. 239 (1992).

For survey, "Developments in Maryland Law, 1991-92," see 52 Md. L. Rev. 530 (1993).

For survey, "Developments in Maryland Law, 1992-93," see 53 Md. L. Rev. 616 (1994).

University of Baltimore Law Forum. — For article, "Code of Ethics Revisited," see 19.2 U. Balt. Law Forum 14 (1989).

This Rule is permissive. — This Rule is permissive; failure to reveal that which may be revealed, as opposed to that which must be revealed, is not a basis for disciplinary action. Attorney Grievance Comm'n v. Rohrback, 323 Md. 79, 591 A.2d 488 (1991).

Public defenders. — Public defenders owe their clients the same duty to maintain confidentiality of information that all lawyers owe to their clients under this Rule. Harris v. Baltimore Sun Co., 330 Md. 595, 625 A.2d 941 (1993).

Allegations of breach insufficient. — With respect to allegations that an attorney communicated information to various government organizations, the plaintiff's amended complaint failed to allege facts which would explain how that attorney breached his duty by speaking to these government organizations; the bald allegation that the attorney's revelations to government agencies constituted a breach of duty was clearly insufficient. Alleco Inc. v. Harry & Jeanette Weinberg Found., Inc., 340 Md 176, 665 A.2d 1038 (1995).

Prohibition against disclosure. — Under the structure of this Rule, the lawyer who reveals confidential information, reasonably believing the revelation to be necessary in order to comply with other law, is not in violation of the general prohibition against disclosure and is not subject to professional discipline. Harris v. Baltimore Sun Co., 330 Md. 595, 625 A.2d 941 (1993).

A lawyer can never violate the section (a) prohibition against disclosure by refusing to produce requested public records, even if production would not violate section (a) because of the permissive disclosure of section (b). Harris v. Baltimore Sun Co., 330 Md. 595, 625 A.2d 941 (1993).

Failure to inform authorities of completed crimes. — When client revealed to attorney that he had operated a motor vehicle when his license was expired, and that, unbeknownst to the arresting officer, he had given a fictitious name when arrested on DWI charge, attorney had no duty to inform authorities, as these were completed crimes; the attorney had a duty not to disclose them. Attorney Grievance Comm'n v. Rohrback, 323 Md. 79, 591 A.2d 488 (1991).

Attorney's previous work with corporation as labor attorney and labor relations lawyer which made him familiar with the corporation's personnel policies and procedures held sufficiently related to his representation of employee in an age discrimination case to work to the corporation's disadvantage; therefore attorney held disqualified from further participation in the age discrimination case. Stitz v. Bethlehem Steel Corp., 650 F. Supp. 914 (D. Md. 1987).

Disclosure of fee arrangement. — Whether a fee arrangement is protected from disclosure in judicial proceedings is governed by the attorney-client privilege, and not by the Rules of Professional Conduct. In re Criminal Investigation No. 1/242Q, 326 Md. 1, 602 A.2d 1220 (1992).

The attorney-client privilege is generally not violated by requiring disclosure of the payment of attorney's fees and expenses. In re Criminal Investigation No. 1/242Q, 326 Md. 1, 602 A.2d 1220 (1992).

Stated in Noble v. Bruce, 349 Md. 730, 709 A.2d 1264 (1998).

Cited in Post v. Bregman, 349 Md. 142, 707 A.2d 806 (1998).

Rule 1.7. Conflict of interest: General rule.

(a) A lawyer shall not represent a client if the representation of that client will be directly adverse to another client, unless:

(1) the lawyer reasonably believes the representation will not adversely affect the relationship with the other client; and

(2) each client consents after consultation.

(b) A lawyer shall not represent a client if the representation of that client may be materially limited by the lawyer's responsibilities to another client or to a third person, or by the lawyer's own interests, unless:

(1) the lawyer reasonably believes the representation will not be adversely affected; and

(2) the client consents after consultation.

(c) The consultation required by paragraphs (a) and (b) shall include explanation of the implications of the common representation and any limitations resulting from the lawyer's responsibilities to another, or from the lawyer's own interests, as well as the advantages and risks involved. (Amended Dec. 10, 1996, effective July 1, 1997.)

COMMENT

Loyalty to a client. — Loyalty is an essential element in the lawyer's relationship to a client. An impermissible conflict of interest may exist before representation is undertaken, in which event the representation should be declined. If such a conflict arises after representation has been undertaken, the lawyer should withdraw from the representation. See Rule 1.16. Where more than one client is involved and the lawyer withdraws because a conflict arises after representation, whether the lawyer may continue to represent any of the clients is determined by Rule 1.9. See also Rule 2.2 (c). As to whether a client-lawyer relationship exists or, having once been established, is continuing, see Comment to Rule 1.3 and Scope.

As a general proposition, loyalty to a client prohibits undertaking representation directly adverse to that client without that client's consent. Paragraph (a) expresses that general rule. Thus, a lawyer ordinarily may not act as advocate against a person the lawyer represents in some other matter, even if it is wholly unrelated. On the other hand, simultaneous representation in unrelated matters of clients whose interests are only generally adverse, such as competing economic enterprises, does not require consent of the respective clients. Paragraph (a) applies only when the representation of one client would be directly adverse to the other.

Loyalty to a client is also impaired when a lawyer cannot consider, recommend or carry out an appropriate course of action for the client because of the lawyer's other responsibilities or interests. The conflict in effect forecloses alternatives that would otherwise be available to the client. Paragraph (b) addresses such situations. A possible conflict does not itself preclude the representation. The critical questions are the likelihood that a conflict will eventuate and, if it does, whether it will materially interfere with the lawyer's independent professional judgment in considering alternatives or foreclose courses of action that reasonably should be pursued on behalf of the client. Consideration should be given to whether the client wishes to accommodate the other interest involved.

Consultation and consent. — A client may consent to representation notwithstanding a conflict. However, as indicated in paragraph (a) (1) with respect to representation directly adverse to a client, and paragraph (b) (1) with respect to material limitations on representation of a client, when a disinterested lawyer would conclude that the client should not agree to the representation under the circumstances, the lawyer involved cannot properly ask for such agreement or provide representation on the basis of the client's consent. When more than one client is involved, the question of conflict must be resolved as to each client. Moreover, there may be circumstances where it is impossible to make the disclosure necessary to obtain consent. For example, when the lawyer represents different clients in related matters and one of the clients refuses to consent to the disclosure necessary to permit the other client to make an informed decision, the lawyer cannot properly ask the latter to consent.

Lawyer's interests. — The lawyer's own interests should not be permitted to have adverse effect on representation of a client. For example, a lawyer's need for income should not lead the lawyer to undertake matters that cannot be handled competently and at a reasonable fee. See Rules 1.1 and 1.5. If the probity of a lawyer's own conduct in a transaction is in serious question, it may be difficult or impossible for the lawyer to give a client detached advice. A lawyer may not allow related business interests to affect representation, for example, by referring clients to an enterprise in which the lawyer has an undisclosed interest.

A sexual relationship with a client, whether or not in violation of criminal law, will create an impermissible conflict between the interests of the client and those of the lawyer if (1) the representation of the client would be materially limited by the sexual relationship and (2) it is unreasonable for the lawyer to believe otherwise. Under those circumstances, client consent after consultation is ineffective. See also Rule 8.4.

Conflicts in litigation. — Paragraph (a) prohibits representation of opposing parties in litigation. Simultaneous representation of parties whose interests in litigation may conflict, such as co-plaintiffs or co-defendants, is governed by paragraph (b). An impermissible conflict may exist by reason of substantial discrepancy in the parties' testimony, incompatibility in positions in relation to an opposing party or the fact that there are substantially different possibilities of settlement of the claims or liabilities in question. Such conflicts can arise in criminal cases as well as civil. The potential for conflict of interest in representing multiple defendants in a criminal case is so grave that ordinarily a lawyer should decline to represent more than one co-defendant. On the other hand, common representation of persons having similar interests is proper if the risk of adverse effect is minimal and the requirements of paragraph (b) are met. Compare Rule 2.2 involving intermediation between clients.

Ordinarily, a lawyer may not act as advocate against a client the lawyer represents in some other matter, even if the other matter is wholly unrelated. However, there are circumstances in which a lawyer may act as advocate against a client. For example, a lawyer representing an enterprise with diverse operations may accept employment as an advocate against the enterprise in an unrelated matter if doing so will not adversely affect the lawyer's relationship with the enterprise or conduct of the suit and if both clients consent upon consultation. By the same token, government lawyers in some circumstances may represent government employees in proceedings in which a government agency is the opposing party. The propriety of concurrent representation can depend on the nature of the litigation. For example, a suit charging fraud entails conflict to a degree not involved in a suit for a declaratory judgment concerning statutory interpretation.

A lawyer may represent parties having antagonistic positions on a legal question that has arisen in different cases, unless representation of either client would be adversely affected. Thus, it is ordinarily not improper to assert such positions in cases pending in different trial courts, but it may be improper to do so in cases pending at the same time in an appellate court.

Interest of person paying for a lawyer's service. — A lawyer may be paid from a source other than the client, if the client is informed of that fact and consents and the arrangement does not compromise the lawyer's duty of loyalty to the client. See Rule 1.8 (f). For example, when an insurer and its insured have conflicting interests in a matter arising from a liability insurance agreement, and the insurer is required to provide special counsel for the insured, the arrangement should assure the special counsel's professional independence.

So also, when a corporation and its directors or employees are involved in a controversy in which they have conflicting interests, the corporation may provide funds for separate legal representation of the directors or employees, if the clients consent after consultation and the arrangement ensures the lawyer's professional independence.

Other conflict situations. — Conflicts of interest in contexts other than litigation sometimes may be difficult to assess. Relevant factors in determining whether there is potential for adverse effect include the duration and intimacy of the lawyer's relationship with the client or clients involved, the functions being performed by the lawyer, the likelihood that actual conflict will arise and the likely prejudice to the client from the conflict if it does arise. The question is often one of proximity and degree.

For example, a lawyer may not represent multiple parties to a negotiation whose interests are fundamentally antagonistic to each other, but common representation is permissible where the clients are generally aligned in interest even though there is some difference of interest among them.

Conflict questions may also arise in estate planning and estate administration. A lawyer may be called upon to prepare wills for several family members, such as husband and wife, and, depending upon the circumstances, a conflict of interest may arise. In estate administration the identity of the client may be unclear under the law of a particular jurisdiction. Under one view, the client is the fiduciary; under another view the client is the estate or trust, including its beneficiaries. The lawyer should make clear the relationship to the parties involved.

A lawyer for a corporation or other organization who is also a member of its board of directors should determine whether the responsibilities of the two roles may conflict. The lawyer may be called on to advise the corporation in matters involving actions of the directors. Consideration should be given to the frequency with which such situations may arise, the potential intensity of the conflict the effect of the lawyer's resignation from the board and the possibility of the corporation's obtaining legal advice from another lawyer in such situations. If there is material risk that the dual role will compromise the lawyer's independence of professional judgment, the lawyer should not serve as a director.

Conflict charged by an opposing party. — Resolving questions of conflict of interest is primarily the responsibility of the lawyer undertaking the representation. In litigation, a court may raise the question when there is reason to infer that the lawyer has neglected the responsibility. In a criminal case, inquiry by the court is generally required when a lawyer represents multiple defendants. Where the conflict is such as clearly to call in question the fair or efficient administration of justice, opposing counsel may properly raise the question. Such an objection should be viewed with caution, however, for it can be misused as a technique of harassment. See Scope.

Code Comparison. — DR 5-101 (A) provides that "Except with the consent of his client after full disclosure, a lawyer shall not accept employment if the exercise of his professional judgment on behalf of the client will be or reasonably may be affected by his own financial, business, property, or personal interests." DR 5-105 (A) provides that "A lawyer shall decline proffered employment if the exercise of his independent professional judgment in behalf of a client will be or is likely to be adversely affected by the acceptance of the proffered employment, or if it would be likely to involve him in representing differing interests, except to the extent permitted under DR 5-105 (C)." DR 5-105 (C) provides that "In the situations covered by DR 5-105 (A) and (B), a lawyer may represent multiple clients if it is obvious that he can adequately represent the interest of each and if each consents to the representation after full disclosure of the possible effect of such representation on the exercise of his independent professional judgment on behalf of each." DR 5-107 (B) provides that "A lawyer shall not permit a person who recommends, employs, or pays him to render legal services for another to direct or regulate his professional judgment in rendering such services."

Rule 1.7 goes beyond DR 5-105 (A) in requiring that, when the lawyer's other interests are involved, not only must the client consent after consultation but also that, independent of such consent, the representation reasonably appears not be adversely affected by the lawyer's other interests. This requirement appears to be the intended meaning of the provision in DR 5-105 (C) that "it is obvious that he can adequately represent" the client, and is implicit in EC 5-2, which states that "A lawyer should not accept proffered employment if his personal interests or desires will, or there is a reasonable possibility that they will, adversely affect the advice to be given or services to be rendered the prospective client."

Effect of amendments. — The 1996 amendment added the second paragraph under "Lawyer's interests" in the Comment.

Maryland Law Review. — For note discussing whether, under third-party beneficiary theory, a nonclient can sue attorney for negligent misrepresentation without proof of privity of contract, see 16 U. Balt. L. Rev. 354 (1987).

Office of public defender. — Attorneys employed by a public defender who are required to practice their profession side by side are, literally and figuratively, members of a "firm"; where the practice of each attorney is so separated from the other's that the interchange of confidential information can be avoided or where it is possible to create such a separation, there need be no relationship between them analogous to that of a law firm and there would be no inherent ethical bar to their representation of antagonistic interests. Graves v. State, 94 Md. App. 649, 619 A.2d 123 (1993), rev'd on other grounds, 334 Md. 30, 637 A.2d 1197 (1994).

Public defender (or assistant public defender representing a particular defendant) is required to do no more than merely ascertain that there is hostility or adversity between defendants represented by his office before filing a motion to withdraw; it is also his duty to ascertain, as a condition precedent to the filing of that motion, that counseling of such defendants by different members of the staff cannot be done without conflict of interest. Graves v. State, 94 Md. App. 649, 619 A.2d 123 (1993), rev'd on other grounds, 334 Md. 30, 637 A.2d 1197 (1994).

Where a public defender concludes that a potential conflict of interest is such that it is required that other counsel be assigned, the case may be assigned to a panel attorney, or the court may be requested to assign counsel; in addition, the case may be transferred to another district public defender's office. Graves v. State, 94 Md. App. 649, 619 A.2d 123 (1993), rev'd on other grounds, 334 Md. 30, 637 A.2d 1197 (1994).

The public defender may make changes within a specific office that could sufficiently insulate, from each other, assistant public defenders who operate from the same office and who are simultaneously representing co-defendants. These institutional changes could include early screening of the cases, structural and procedural separation of the units, assignments to completely separate units in the same office, and other innovations in the handling of cases involving co-defendants that would be conducive to the avoidance of any conflict of interest. Graves v. State, 94 Md. App. 649, 619 A.2d 123 (1993), rev'd on other grounds, 334 Md. 30, 637 A.2d 1197 (1994).

When representation is not simultaneous, this Rule's prohibition is not abso-

lute; a lawyer is not necessarily prohibited from representing a client whose interests are adverse to a former client. Gaumer v. McDaniel, 811 F. Supp. 1113 (D. Md. 1991), aff'd, 23 F.3d 400 (4th Cir. 1994).

Representation of multiple defendants in a criminal case by the same attorney or law partners is not per se an actual conflict of interest; the potential, however, for conflict of interest is present. Graves v. State, 94 Md. App. 649, 619 A.2d 123 (1993), rev'd on other grounds, 334 Md. 30, 637 A.2d 1197 (1994).

The trial court had no affirmative duty to inquire or determine whether there was a conflict of interest in joint representation where there was no objection by defense counsel to the multiple representation and where the conflict, if any, was merely a potential one. Pugh v. State, 103 Md. App. 624, 654 A.2d 888 (1995).

An attorney's contact with his client's represented criminal codefendant was deemed a violation of this Rule and resulted in disbarment. Attorney Grievance Comm'n v. Kent, 337 Md. 361, 653 A.2d 909 (1995).

Representation of co-defendants by members of a single law firm is treated the same, for purposes of conflict of interest analysis, as representation of co-defendants by one attorney. Graves v. State, 94 Md. App. 649, 619 A.2d 123 (1993), rev'd on other grounds, 334 Md. 30, 637 A.2d 1197 (1994).

Consent to multiple representation. — Where the record revealed an affidavit from both represented parties, stating that they were apprised of the alleged conflict that could arise concerning the planned scope of employment defense, and where they consented to the continued joint representation by counsel, any conflict of interest that may have occurred was consented to by the parties. Fearnow v. C & P Tel. Co., 104 Md. App. 1, 655 A.2d 1 (1995).

Appointment of substitute counsel. — Although it was proper for court to prohibit attorney from representing the corporation, the directors and the majority stockholders because of a conflict of interest, it was error for the court to appoint counsel for the corporation and prohibit the corporation from selecting its own counsel. Tydings v. Berk Enters., 80 Md. App. 634, 565 A.2d 390 (1989).

Requirement that borrower use and pay for specific lawyer at settlement. — Pertinent rules of legal ethics do not bar a lender from requiring that a specific settlement lawyer be used and that the borrower pay for the lawyer's settlement services. 72 Op. Att'y Gen. 72 (1987).

Separation agreement, or divorce. — Where husband and wife are contemplating a separation agreement or divorce, it should be obvious to an attorney that he cannot adequately represent the interests of both parties; attorney should not attempt to represent both parties in these matters. Hale v. Hale, 74 Md. App. 555, 539 A.2d 247, cert. denied, 313 Md. 30, 542 A.2d 857 (1988).

Representation of indigent defendants. — If the public defender's office is unable to represent an indigent defendant because of a conflict, and if funds for the provision of panel attorneys are unavailable, the defendant would be represented by an attorney appointed by the court. To the extent of available funds, the county in which the prosecution is brought would be responsible for paying the fees set by the court for the appointed attorney's services. 76 Op. Att'y Gen. (October 4, 1991).

An actual conflict of interest was not shown where appellants' defenses were not necessarily incompatible or inconsistent. Pugh v. State, 103 Md. App. 624, 654 A.2d 888 (1995).

Sanction held proper. — The appropriate sanction for an attorney's improper administration of a trust in violation of this Rule and § 10-306 of the Business Occupations and Professions Article would be indefinite suspension from the practice of law for not less than one year with the right to reapply, conditioned upon restitution and appropriate monitoring. Attorney Grievance Comm'n v. Sachse, 345 Md. 578, 693 A.2d 806 (1997).

Quoted in Watson v. Watson, 73 Md. App. 483, 534 A.2d 1365 (1988); Reilly v. Newman, 74 Md. App. 281, 314 Md. 364, 536 A.2d 1230 modified, 550 A.2d 959 (1988); Newman v. Reilly, 314 Md. 364, 550 A.2d 959 (1988); Attorney Grievance Comm'n v. Webster, 348 Md. 662, 705 A.2d 1135 (1998); Attorney Grievance Comm'n v. Sabghir, 350 Md. 67, 710 A.2d 926 (1998).

Cited in Stueber v. Arrowhead Farm Estates Ltd. Partnership, 69 Md. App. 775, 519 A.2d 816 (1987); Walton v. Davy, 86 Md. App. 275, 586 A.2d 760, cert. denied, 323 Md. 309, 593 A.2d 669 (1991); Attorney Grievance Comm'n v. Powell, 328 Md. 276, 614 A.2d 102 (1992); In re Printing Dimensions, Inc., 153 Bankr. 715 (Bankr. D. Md. 1993); Post v. Bregman, 349 Md. 142, 707 A.2d 806 (1998).

Rule 1.8. Conflict of interest: Prohibited transactions.

(a) A lawyer shall not enter into a business, financial or property transaction with a client unless:

(1) the transaction is fair and equitable to the client; and

(2) the client is advised to seek the advice of independent counsel in the transaction and is given a reasonable opportunity to do so.

(b) A lawyer shall not use information relating to representation of a client to the disadvantage of the client unless the client consents after consultation.

(c) A lawyer shall not prepare an instrument giving the lawyer or a person related to the lawyer as parent, child, sibling, or spouse any substantial gift from a client, including a testamentary gift, except where:

(1) the client is related to the donee; or

(2) the client is represented by independent counsel in connection with the gift.

(d) Prior to the conclusion of representation of a client, a lawyer shall not make or negotiate an agreement giving the lawyer literary or media rights to a portrayal or account based in substantial part on information relating to the representation.

(e) A lawyer shall not provide financial assistance to a client in connection with pending or contemplated litigation, except that:

(1) a lawyer may advance court costs and expenses of litigation, the repayment of which may be contingent on the outcome of the matter; and

(2) a lawyer representing an indigent client may pay court costs and expenses of litigation on behalf of the client.

(f) A lawyer shall not accept compensation for representing a client from one other than the client unless:

(1) the client consents;

(2) there is no interference with the lawyer's independence of professional judgment or with the client-lawyer relationship; and

(3) information relating to representation of a client is protected as required by Rule 1.6.

(g) A lawyer who represents two or more clients shall not participate in making an aggregate settlement of the claims of or against the clients, or in a criminal case an aggregated agreement as to guilty or nolo contendere pleas, unless each client consents after consultation, including disclosure of the existence and nature of all the claims or pleas involved and of the participation of each person in the settlement.

(h) A lawyer shall not make an agreement prospectively limiting the lawyer's liability to a client for malpractice unless permitted by law and the client is independently represented in making the agreement, or settle a claim for such liability with an unrepresented client or former client without first advising that person in writing that independent representation is appropriate in connection therewith.

(i) A lawyer related to another lawyer as parent, child, sibling or spouse shall not represent a client in a representation directly adverse to a person who the lawyer knows is represented by the other lawyer except upon consent by the client after consultation regarding the relationship.

(j) A lawyer shall not acquire a proprietary interest in the cause of action or subject matter of litigation the lawyer is conducting for a client, except that the lawyer may:

(1) acquire a lien granted by law to secure the lawyer's fee or expenses; and

(2) subject to Rule 1.5 contract with a client for a reasonable contingent fee in a civil case.

COMMENT

Transactions between client and lawyer. — As a general principle, all transactions between client and lawyer must be fair and reasonable to the client. In such transactions a review by independent counsel on behalf of the client is often advisable. The lawyer is required by paragraph (a) (2) to advise the client to seek advice of independent counsel and to give the client a reasonable opportunity to do so. Furthermore, a lawyer may not exploit information relating to the representation to the client's disadvantage. See paragraph (b). For example, a lawyer who has learned that the client is investing in specific real estate may not, without the client's consent, seek to acquire nearby property where doing so would adversely affect the client's plan for investment. Paragraphs (a) and (b) do not, however, apply to standard commercial transactions between the lawyer and the client for products or services that the client generally markets to others, for example, banking or brokerage services, medical services, products manufactured or distributed by the client, and utilities services. In such transactions, the lawyer has no advantage in dealing with the client, and the restrictions in paragraph (a) are unnecessary and impracticable.

A lawyer may accept a gift from a client, if the transaction meets general standards of fairness. For example, a simple gift such as a present given at a holiday or as a token of appreciation is permitted. If effectuation of a substantial gift requires preparing a legal instrument such as a will or conveyance, however, the client must be offered the opportunity to have the detached advice that another lawyer can provide. Paragraph (c) recognizes an exception where the client is a relative of the donee or the gift is not substantial.

Literary rights. — An agreement by which a lawyer acquires literary or media rights concerning the conduct of the representation creates a conflict between the interests of the client and the personal interests of the lawyer. Measures suitable in the representation of the client may detract from the publication value of an account of the representation. Paragraph (d) does not prohibit a lawyer representing a client in a transaction concerning literary property from agreeing that the lawyer's fee shall consist of a share in ownership in the property, if the arrangement conforms to Rule 1.5 and paragraph (j).

Person paying for lawyer's services. — Rule 1.8 (f) requires disclosure of the fact that the lawyer's services are being paid for by a third party. Such an arrangement must also conform to the requirements of Rule 1.6 concerning confidentiality and Rule 1.7 concerning conflict of interest. Where the client is a class, consent may be obtained on behalf of the class by court-supervised procedure.

Limitation of liability. — Rule 1.8 (h) is not intended to apply to customary qualifications and limitations in legal opinions and memoranda.

Family relationships between lawyers. — Rule 1.8 (i) applies to related lawyers who are in different firms. Related lawyers in the same firm are governed by Rules 1.7, 1.9, and 1.10. The disqualification stated in Rule 1.8 (i) is personal and is not imputed to members of firms with whom the lawyers are associated.

Acquisition of interest in litigation. — Paragraph (j) states the traditional general rule that lawyers are prohibited from acquiring a proprietary interest in litigation. This general rule, which has its basis in common law champerty and maintenance, is subject to specific exceptions developed in decisional law and continued in these Rules, such as the exception for reasonable contingent fees set forth in Rule 1.5 and the exception for certain advances of the costs of litigation set forth in paragraph (e).

Code Comparison. — This Rule deals with certain transactions that per se involve conflict of interest.

With regard to Rule 1.8 (a), DR 5-104 (A) provides that "A lawyer shall not enter into a business transaction with a client if they have differing interests therein and if the client expects the lawyer to exercise his professional judgment therein for the protection of the client, unless the client has consented after full disclosure." EC 5-3 states that "A lawyer should not seek to persuade his client to permit him to invest in an undertaking of his client nor make improper use of his professional relationship to influence his client to invest in an enterprise in which the lawyer is interested."

With regard to Rule 1.8 (b), DR 4-101 (B) (3)

provides that a lawyer shall not "use a confidence or secret of his client for the advantage of himself, or of a third person, unless the client consents after full disclosure."

There is no counterpart to Rule 1.8 (c) in the Disciplinary Rules of the Code. EC 5-5 states that "A lawyer should not suggest to his client that a gift be made to himself or for his benefit. If a lawyer accepts a gift from his client, he is peculiarly susceptible to the charge that he unduly influenced or overreached the client. If a client voluntarily offers to make a gift to his lawyer, the lawyer may accept the gift, but before doing so, he should urge that the client secure disinterested advice from an independent, competent person who is cognizant of all the circumstances. Other than in exceptional circumstances, a lawyer should insist that an instrument in which his client desires to name him beneficially be prepared by another law-

yer selected by the client.

Rule 1.8 (d) is substantially similar to DR 5-104 (B), but refers to "literary or media" rights, a more generally inclusive term than "publication" rights.

Rule 1.8 (e) (1) is similar to DR 5-103 (B), but eliminates the requirement that "the client remain ultimately liable for such expenses."

Rule 1.8 (e) (2) has no counterpart in the Code.

Rule 1.8 (f) is substantially identical to DR 5-107 (A) (1).

Rule 1.8 (g) is substantially identical to DR 5-106.

The first clause of Rule 1.8 (h) deals with the same subject as DR 6-102 (A). There is no counterpart in the Code to the second clause of Rule 1.8 (h).

Rule 1.8 (i) has no counterpart in the Code.

Limitations on the purposes of advances. — Although there are differences between the former DR 5-1038 and paragraph (e) of this Rule, the limitations on the purposes for which advances may be made remain essentially the same. Attorney Grievance Comm'n v. Eisenstein, 333 Md. 464, 635 A.2d 1327 (1994).

Excessive fee. — If attorney's contingent fee was clearly excessive in violation of former DR 2-106, then he also failed to stay within the exception to the prohibition of former DR 5-103(A) against acquiring a proprietary interest in the clients' causes of action. Attorney Grievance Comm'n v. Korotki, 318 Md. 646, 569 A.2d 1224 (1990).

Requirement that borrower use and pay for specific lawyer at settlement. — Pertinent rules of legal ethics do not bar a lender from requiring that a specific settlement lawyer be used and that the borrower pay for the lawyer's settlement services. 72 Op. Att'y Gen. 72 (1987).

Client loan to attorney not violative of this Rule. — Trial court's finding that client's loan to her attorney was a fair and equitable personal loan to a close friend which did not violate this rule was not clearly erroneous.

Attorney Grievance Comm'n v. Powell, 328 Md. 276, 614 A.2d 102 (1992).

Attorney's advancement of funds to client for medical treatment, or for transportation to a medical office for treatment, violated former DR 5-103 (B). Attorney Grievance Comm'n v. Kandel, 317 Md. 274, 563 A.2d 387 (1989).

Advancement of living expenses violation of Rule. — Attorney suspended for 2 years for violating paragraph (e) of this Rule, inter alia, by advancing certain living expenses to the claimant during the pendency of the litigation. Attorney Grievance Comm'n v. Eisenstein, 333 Md. 464, 635 A.2d 1327 (1994).

Applied in Attorney Grievance Comm'n v. Singleton, 311 Md. 1, 532 A.2d 157 (1987); Attorney Grievance Comm'n v. Werner, 315 Md. 172, 553 A.2d 722 (1989).

Quoted in Medical Mut. Liab. Ins. Soc'y v. Evans, 330 Md. 1, 622 A.2d 103 (1993); Attorney Grievance Comm'n v. Webster, 348 Md. 662, 705 A.2d 1135 (1998).

Cited in Stueber v. Arrowhead Farm Estates Ltd. Partnership, 69 Md. App. 775, 519 A.2d 816 (1987).

Rule 1.9. Conflict of interest: Former client.

A lawyer who has formerly represented a client in a matter shall not thereafter:

(a) represent another person in the same or a substantially related matter in which that person's interests are materially adverse to the interests of the former client unless the former client consents after consultation; or

(b) use information relating to the representation to the disadvantage of the former client except as Rule 1.6 would permit with respect to a client or when the information has become generally known.

COMMENT

After termination of a client-lawyer relationship, a lawyer may not represent another client except in conformity with this Rule. The principles in Rule 1.7 determine whether the interests of the present and former client are adverse. Thus, a lawyer could not properly seek to rescind on behalf of a new client a contract drafted on behalf of the former client. So also a lawyer who has prosecuted an accused person could not properly represent the accused in a subsequent civil action against the government concerning the same transaction.

The scope of a "matter" for purposes of Rule 1.9 (a) may depend on the facts of a particular situation or transaction. The lawyer's involvement in a matter can also be a question of degree. When a lawyer has been directly involved in a specific transaction, subsequent representation of other clients with materially adverse interests clearly is prohibited. On the other hand, a lawyer who recurrently handled a type of problem for a former client is not precluded from later representing another client in a wholly distinct problem of that type even though the subsequent representation involves a position adverse to the prior client. Similar considerations can apply to the reassignment of military lawyers between defense and prosecution functions within the same military jurisdiction. The underlying question is whether the lawyer was so involved in the matter that the subsequent representation can be justly regarded as a changing of sides in the matter in question.

Information acquired by the lawyer in the course of representing a client may not subsequently be used by the lawyer to the disadvantage of the client. However, the fact that a lawyer has once served a client does not preclude the lawyer from using generally known information about that client when later representing another client.

Disqualification from subsequent representation is for the protection of clients and can be waived by them. A waiver is effective only if there is disclosure of the circumstances, including the lawyer's intended role in behalf of the new client.

With regard to an opposing party's raising a question of conflict of interest, see Comment to Rule 1.7. With regard to disqualification of a firm with which a lawyer is associated, see Rule 1.10.

Code Comparison. — There is no counterpart to Rule 1.9 (a) or (b) in the Disciplinary Rules of the Code. The problem addressed in Rule 1.9 (a) sometimes has been dealt with under the rubric of Canon 9 of the Code, which provides that "A lawyer should avoid even the appearance of impropriety." EC 4-6 states that "The obligation of a lawyer to preserve the confidences and secrets of his client continues after the termination of his employment."

The exception in the last sentence of Rule 1.9 (b) permits a lawyer to use information relating to a former client that is in the "public domain," a use that is also not prohibited by the Code. Since the scope of Rule 1.6 (a) is much broader than "confidences and secrets," it is necessary to define when a lawyer may make use of information about a client after the client-lawyer relationship has terminated.

The provision for waiver by the former client is in effect similar to DR 5-105 (C).

Duty of court. — Under this Rule, a court must examine the nature and scope of the prior and present representation and determine whether confidences might have been disclosed in the course of the prior representation which could be relevant to the present action. Buckley v. Airshield Corp., 908 F. Supp. 299 (D. Md. 1995), appeal dismissed, 86 F.3d 1175 (Fed. Cir. 1996).

Same or substantially related matter. — In order to show a substantial relationship for the purposes of this rule it is not necessary that two lawsuits involve the same operative facts, so long as there is a sufficient similarity of issues. Buckley v. Airshield Corp., 908 F. Supp. 299 (D. Md. 1995), appeal dismissed, 86 F.3d 1175 (Fed. Cir. 1996).

Attorney's previous work with corporation as labor attorney and labor relations lawyer which made him familiar with the corporation's personnel policies and procedures held sufficiently related to his representation of employee in an age discrimination case to work to the corporation's disadvantage; therefore attorney held disqualified from further participation in the age discrimination case. Stitz v. Bethlehem Steel Corp., 650 F. Supp. 914 (D. Md. 1987).

Applied in Blumenthal Power Co. v. Browning-Ferris, Inc., 903 F. Supp. 901 (D. Md. 1995).

Cited in In re Printing Dimensions, Inc.,

153 Bankr. 715 (Bankr. D. Md. 1993); Post v. Bregman, 349 Md. 142, 707 A.2d 806 (1998).

Rule 1.10. Imputed disqualification: General rule.

(a) While lawyers are associated in a firm, none of them shall knowingly represent a client when any one of them practicing alone would be prohibited from doing so by Rules 1.7, 1.8 (c), 1.9 or 2.2.

(b) When a lawyer becomes associated with a firm, the firm may not knowingly represent a person in the same or a substantially related matter in which that lawyer, or a firm with which the lawyer was associated, had previously represented a client whose interests are materially adverse to that person and about whom the lawyer had acquired information protected by Rules 1.6 and 1.9 (b) that is material to the matter.

(c) When a lawyer has terminated an association with a firm, the firm is not prohibited from thereafter representing a person with interests materially adverse to those of a client represented by the formerly associated lawyer unless:

(1) the matter is the same or substantially related to that in which the formerly associated lawyer represented the client; and

(2) any lawyer remaining in the firm has information protected by Rules 1.6 and 1.9 (b) that is material to the matter.

(d) A disqualification prescribed by this Rule may be waived by the affected client under the conditions stated in Rule 1.7.

COMMENT

Definition of "firm". — For the purposes of the Rules of Professional Conduct, the term "firm" includes lawyers in a private firm, and lawyers employed in the legal department of a corporation or other organization, or in a legal services organization. Whether two or more lawyers constitute a firm within this definition can depend on the specific facts. For example, two practitioners who share office space and occasionally consult or assist each other ordinarily would not be regarded as constituting a firm. However, if they present themselves to the public in a way suggesting that they are a firm or conduct themselves as a firm, they should be regarded as a firm for purposes of the Rules. The terms of any formal agreement between associated lawyers are relevant in determining whether they are a firm, as is the fact that they have mutual access to confidential information concerning the clients they serve. Furthermore, it is relevant in doubtful cases to consider the underlying purpose of the rule that is involved. A group of lawyers could be regarded as a firm for purposes of the rule that the same lawyer should not represent opposing parties in litigation, while it might not be so regarded for purposes of the rule that information acquired by one lawyer is attributed to another.

With respect to the law department of an organization, there is ordinarily no question that the members of the department constitute a firm within the meaning of the Rules of Professional Conduct. However, there can be uncertainty as to the identity of the client. For example, it may not be clear whether the law department of a corporation represents a subsidiary or an affiliated corporation, as well as the corporation by which the members of the department are directly employed. A similar question can arise concerning an unincorporated association and its local affiliates.

Similar questions can also arise with respect to lawyers in legal aid. Lawyers employed in the same unit of a legal service organization constitute a firm, but not necessarily those employed in separate units. As in the case of independent practitioners, whether the lawyers should be treated as associated with each other can depend on the particular rule that is involved, and on the specific facts of the situation.

Where a lawyer has joined a private firm after having represented the government, the situation is governed by Rule 1.11 (a) and (b); where a lawyer represents the government after having served private clients, the situation is governed by Rule 1.11 (c) (1). The

464

individual lawyer involved is bound by the Rules generally, including Rules 1.6, 1.7, and 1.9.

Different provisions are thus made for movement of a lawyer from one private firm to another and for movement of a lawyer between a private firm and the government. The government is entitled to protection of its client confidences, and therefore to the protections provided in Rules 1.6, 1.9, and 1.11. However, if the more extensive disqualification in Rule 1.10 were applied to former government lawyers, the potential effect on the government would be unduly burdensome. The government deals with all private citizens and organizations, and thus has a much wider circle of adverse legal interests than does any private law firm. In these circumstances, the government's recruitment of lawyers would be seriously impaired if Rule 1.10 were applied to the government. On balance, therefore, the government is better served in the long run by the protections stated in Rule 1.11.

Principles of Imputed Disqualification. — The rule of imputed disqualification stated in paragraph (a) gives effect to the principle of loyalty to the client as it applies to lawyers who practice in a law firm. Such situations can be considered from the premise that a firm of lawyers is essentially one lawyer for purposes of the rules governing loyalty to the client, or from the premise that each lawyer is vicariously bound by the obligation of loyalty owed by each lawyer with whom the lawyer is associated. Paragraph (a) operates only among the lawyers currently associated in a firm. When a lawyer moves from one firm to another, the situation is governed by paragraphs (b) and (c).

Lawyers moving between firms. — When lawyers have been associated in a firm but then end their association, however, the problem is more complicated. The fiction that the law firm is the same as a single lawyer is no longer wholly realistic. There are several competing considerations. First, the client previously represented must be reasonably assured that the principle of loyalty to the client is not compromised. Second, the rule of disqualification should not be so broadly cast as to preclude other persons from having reasonable choice of legal counsel. Third, the rule of disqualification should not unreasonably hamper lawyers from forming new associations and taking on new clients after having left a previous association. In this connection, it should be recognized that today many lawyers practice in firms, that many to some degree limit their practice to one field or another, and that many move from one association to another several times in their careers. If the concept of imputed disqualification were defined with unqualified rigor, the result would be radical

curtailment of the opportunity of lawyers to move from one practice setting to another and of the opportunity of clients to change counsel.

Reconciliation of these competing principles in the past has been attempted under two rubrics. One approach has been to seek per se rules of disqualification. For example, it has been held that a partner in a law firm is conclusively presumed to have access to all confidences concerning all clients of the firm. Under this analysis, if a lawyer has been a partner in one law firm and then becomes a partner in another law firm, there is a presumption that all confidences known by a partner in the first firm are known to all partners in the second firm. This presumption might properly be applied in some circumstances, especially where the client has been extensively represented, but may be unrealistic where the client was represented only for limited purposes. Furthermore, such a rigid rule exaggerates the difference between a partner and an associate in modern law firms.

The other rubric formerly used for dealing with vicarious disqualification is the appearance of impropriety proscribed in Canon 9 of the Maryland Code of Professional Responsibility. This rubric has a two-fold problem. First, the appearance of impropriety can be taken to include any new client-lawyer relationship that might make a former client feel anxious. If that meaning were adopted, disqualification would become little more than a question of subjective judgment by the former client. Second, since "impropriety" is undefined, the term "appearance of impropriety" is question-begging. It therefore has to be recognized that the problem of imputed disqualification cannot be properly resolved either by simple analogy to a lawyer practicing alone or by the very general concept of appearance of impropriety.

A rule based on a functional analysis is more appropriate for determining the question of vicarious disqualification. Two functions are involved: preserving confidentiality and avoiding positions adverse to a client.

Confidentiality. — Preserving confidentiality is a question of access to information. Access to information, in turn, is essentially a question of fact in particular circumstances, aided by inferences, deductions or working presumptions that reasonably may be made about the way in which lawyers work together. A lawyer may have general access to files of all clients of a law firm and may regularly participate in discussions of their affairs; it should be inferred that such a lawyer in fact is privy to all information about all the firm's clients. In contrast, another lawyer may have access to the files of only a limited number of clients and participate in discussion of the affairs of no other clients; in the absence of information to the contrary, it should be inferred that such a lawyer in fact is privy to information about the clients actually served but not those of other clients.

Application of paragraphs (b) and (c) depends on a situation's particular facts. In any such inquiry, the burden of proof should rest upon the firm whose disqualification is sought.

Paragraphs (b) and (c) operate to disqualify the firm only when the lawyer involved has actual knowledge of information protected by Rules 1.6 and 1.9 (b). Thus, if a lawyer while with one firm acquired no knowledge of information relating to a particular client of the firm, and that lawyer later joined another firm, neither the lawyer individually nor the second firm is disqualified from representing another client in the same or a related matter even though the interests of the two clients conflict.

Independent of the question of disqualification of a firm, a lawyer changing professional association has a continuing duty to preserve confidentiality of information about a client formerly represented. See Rules 1.6 and 1.9.

Adverse Positions. — The second aspect of loyalty to client is the lawyer's obligation to decline subsequent representations involving positions adverse to a former client arising in substantially related matters. This obligation requires abstention from adverse representation by the individual lawyer involved, but does not properly entail abstention of other lawyers through imputed disqualification. Hence, this aspect of the problem is governed by Rule 1.9 (a). Thus, if a lawyer left one firm for another, the new affiliation would not preclude the firms involved from continuing to represent clients with adverse interests in the same or related matters, so long as the conditions of Rule 1.10 (b) and (c) concerning confidentiality have been met.

Code Comparison. — DR 5-105 (D) provides that "If a lawyer is required to decline or to withdraw from employment under a Disciplinary Rule, no partner, or associate, or affiliate with him or his firm, may accept or continue such employment."

An "unrelated" law firm must be disqualified when there is some evidence of the possibility that the tainted lawyer, either consciously or unconsciously, transmitted some confidence to a previously untainted firm; however, where law firm had met only briefly with the disqualified attorney and it was unlikely that tainted information was discussed at that meeting, the law firm was not disqualified. Stitz v. Bethlehem Steel Corp., 650 F. Supp. 914 (D. Md. 1987).

Representation of multiple defendants in a criminal case, by the same attorney or law partners, is not per se an actual conflict of interest; however, an actual conflict of interest exists where an attorney, or law partners, represent, in the same criminal case, both the defendant and a codefendant (or other individual) who testifies adversely to the defendant. Austin v. State, 327 Md. 375, 609 A.2d 728 (1992).

Cited in In re Printing Dimensions, Inc., 153 Bankr. 715 (Bankr. D. Md. 1993).

Rule 1.11. Successive government and private employment.

(a) Except as law may otherwise expressly permit, a lawyer shall not represent a private client in connection with a matter in which the lawyer participated personally and substantially as a public officer or employee, unless the appropriate government agency consents after consultation. No lawyer in a firm with which that lawyer is associated may knowingly undertake or continue representation in such a matter unless:

(1) the disqualified lawyer is screened from any participation in the matter and is apportioned no part of the fee therefrom; and

(2) written notice is promptly given to the appropriate government agency to enable it to ascertain compliance with the provisions of this rule.

(b) Except as law may otherwise expressly permit, a lawyer having information that the lawyer knows is confidential government information about a person acquired when the lawyer was a public officer or employee, may not represent a private client whose interests are adverse to that person in a matter in which the information could be used to the material disadvantage of that person. A firm with which that lawyer is associated may undertake or continue representation in the matter only if the disqualified lawyer is screened from any participation in the matter and is apportioned no part of the fee therefrom.

(c) Except as law may otherwise expressly permit, a lawyer serving as a public officer or employee shall not:

(1) participate in a matter in which the lawyer participated personally and substantially while in private practice or nongovernmental employment, unless under applicable law no one is, or by lawful delegation may be, authorized to act in the lawyer's stead in the matter; or

(2) negotiate for private employment with any person who is involved as a party or as attorney for a party in a matter in which the lawyer is participating personally and substantially.

(d) As used in this Rule, the term "matter" includes:

(1) any judicial or other proceeding, application, request for a ruling or other determination, contract, claim, controversy, investigation, charge, accusation, arrest or other particular matter involving a specific party or parties; and

(2) any other matter covered by the conflict of interest rules of the appropriate government agency.

(e) As used in this Rule, the term "confidential government information" means information which has been obtained under governmental authority and which, at the time this Rule is applied, the government is prohibited by law from disclosing to the public or has a legal privilege not to disclose, and which is not otherwise available to the public.

COMMENT

This Rule prevents a lawyer from exploiting public office for the advantage of a private client. It is a counterpart of Rule 1.10 (b), which applies to lawyers moving from one firm to another.

A lawyer representing a government agency, whether employed or specially retained by the government, is subject to the Rules of Professional Conduct, including the prohibition against representing adverse interests stated in Rule 1.7 and the protections afforded former clients in Rule 1.9. In addition, such a lawyer is subject to Rule 1.11 and to statutes and government regulations regarding conflict of interest. Such statutes and regulations may circumscribe the extent to which the government agency may give consent under this Rule.

Where the successive clients are a public agency and a private client, the risk exists that power or discretion vested in public authority might be used for the special benefit of a private client. A lawyer should not be in a position where benefit to a private client might affect performance of the lawyer's professional functions on behalf of public authority. Also, unfair advantage could accrue to the private client by reason of access to confidential government information about the client's adver-

sary obtainable only through the lawyer's government service. However, the rules governing lawyers presently or formerly employed by a government agency should not be so restrictive as to inhibit transfer of employment to and from the government. The government has a legitimate need to attract qualified lawyers as well as to maintain high ethical standards. The provisions for screening and waiver are necessary to prevent the disqualification rule from imposing too severe a deterrent against entering public service.

When the client is an agency of one government, that agency should be treated as a private client for purposes of this Rule if the lawyer thereafter represents an agency of another government, as when a lawyer represents a city and subsequently is employed by a federal agency.

Paragraphs (a) (1) and (b) do not prohibit a lawyer from receiving a salary or partnership share established by prior independent agreement. They prohibit directly relating the attorney's compensation to the fee in the matter in which the lawyer is disqualified.

Paragraph (a) (2) does not require that a lawyer give notice to the government agency at a time when premature disclosure would injure the client; a requirement for premature disclosure might preclude engagement of the lawyer. Such notice is, however, required to be given as soon as practicable in order that the government agency will have a reasonable opportunity to ascertain that the lawyer is complying with Rule 1.11 and to take appropriate action if it believes the lawyer is not complying.

Paragraph (b) operates only when the lawyer in question has knowledge of the information, which means actual knowledge; it does not operate with respect to information that merely could be imputed to the lawyer.

Paragraphs (a) and (c) do not prohibit a lawyer from jointly representing a private party and a government agency when doing so is permitted by Rule 1.7 and is not otherwise prohibited by law.

Paragraph (c) does not disqualify other lawyers in the agency with which the lawyer in question has become associated.

Code Comparison. — Rule 1.11 (a) is similar to DR 9-101 (B), except that the latter uses of the terms "in which he had substantial responsibility while he was a public employee."

Rules 1.11 (b), (c), (d) and (e) have no counterparts in the Code.

Rule 1.12. Former judge or arbitrator.

(a) Except as stated in paragraph (d), a lawyer shall not represent anyone in connection with a matter in which the lawyer participated personally and substantially as a judge or other adjudicative officer, arbitrator or law clerk to such a person, unless all parties to the proceeding consent after disclosure.

(b) A lawyer shall not negotiate for employment with any person who is involved as a party or as attorney for a party in a matter in which the lawyer is participating personally and substantially as a judge or other adjudicative officer, or arbitrator. A lawyer serving as a law clerk to a judge, other adjudicative officer or arbitrator may negotiate for employment with a party or attorney involved in a matter in which the clerk is participating personally and substantially, but only after the lawyer has notified the judge, other adjudicative officer or arbitrator.

(c) If a lawyer is disqualified by paragraph (a), no lawyer in a firm with which that lawyer is associated may knowingly undertake or continue representation in the matter unless:

(1) the disqualified lawyer is screened from any participation in the matter and is apportioned no part of the fee therefrom; and

(2) written notice is promptly given to the appropriate tribunal to enable it to ascertain compliance with the provisions of this rule.

(d) An arbitrator selected as a partisan of a party in a multi-member arbitration panel is not prohibited from subsequently representing that party.

COMMENT

This Rule generally parallels Rule 1.11. The term "personally and substantially" signifies that a judge who was a member of a multi-member court, and thereafter left judicial office to practice law, is not prohibited from representing a client in a matter pending in the court, but in which the former judge did not participate. So also the fact that a former judge exercised administrative responsibility in a court does not prevent the former judge from acting as a lawyer in a matter where the judge had previously exercised remote or incidental administrative responsibility that did not affect the merits. Compare the Comment to Rule 1.11. The term "adjudicative officer" includes such officials as judges pro tempore, referees, special masters, hearing officers and other parajudicial officers, and also lawyers who serve as part-time judges.

Code Comparison. — Paragraph (a) is substantially similar to DR 9-101 (A), which provides that "A lawyer shall not accept employment in a matter upon the merits of which he has acted in a judicial capacity." Paragraph (a) differs, however, in that it is broader in scope and states more specifically the persons to whom it applies. There is no counterpart in the Code to paragraphs (b), (c) or (d).

With regard to arbitrators, EC 55-20 states that "a lawyer who has undertaken to act as an impartial arbitrator or mediator ... should not thereafter represent in the dispute any of the parties involved." DR 9-101 (A) does not provide a waiver of the disqualification applied to former judges by consent of the parties. However, DR 5-105 (C) is similar in effect and could be construed to permit waiver.

Rule 1.13. Organization as client.

(a) A lawyer employed or retained by an organization represents the organization acting through its duly authorized constituents.

(b) If a lawyer for an organization knows that an officer, employee or other person associated with the organization is engaged in action, intends to act or refuses to act in a matter related to the representation that is a violation of a legal obligation to the organization, or a violation of law which reasonably might be imputed to the organization, and is likely to result in substantial injury to the organization, the lawyer shall proceed as is reasonably necessary in the best interest of the organization. In determining how to proceed, the lawyer shall give due consideration to the seriousness of the violation and its consequences, the scope and nature of the lawyer's representation, the responsibility in the organization and the apparent motivation of the person involved, the policies of the organization concerning such matters and any other relevant considerations. Any measures taken shall be designed to minimize disruption of the organization and the risk of revealing information relating to the representation to persons outside the organization. Such measures may include among others:

(1) asking reconsideration of the matter;

(2) advising that a separate legal opinion on the matter be sought for presentation to appropriate authority in the organization; and

(3) referring the matter to higher authority in the organization, including, if warranted by the seriousness of the matter, referral to the highest authority that can act in behalf of the organization as determined by applicable law.

(c) When the organization's highest authority insists upon action, or refuses to take action, that is clearly a violation of a legal obligation to the organization, or a violation of law which reasonably might be imputed to the organization, and is likely to result in substantial injury to the organization, the lawyer may take further remedial action that the lawyer reasonably believes to be in the best interest of the organization. Such action may include revealing information otherwise protected by Rule 1.6 only if the lawyer reasonably believes that:

(1) the highest authority in the organization has acted to further the personal or financial interests of members of the authority which are in conflict with the interests of the organization; and

(2) revealing the information is necessary in the best interest of the organization.

(d) In dealing with an organization's directors, officers, employees, members, shareholders or other constituents, a lawyer shall explain the identity of the client when it is apparent that the organization's interests are adverse to those of the constituents with whom the lawyer is dealing.

(e) A lawyer representing an organization may also represent any of its directors, officers, employees, members, shareholders or other constituents, subject to the provisions of Rule 1.7. If the organization's consent to the dual representation is required by Rule 1.7, the consent shall be given by an appropriate official of the organization other than the individual who is to be represented, or by the shareholders.

COMMENT

The entity as the client. — An organizational client is a legal entity, but it cannot act except through its officers, directors, employees, shareholders and other constituents.

Officers, directors, employees and shareholders are the constituents of the corporate organizational client. The duties defined in this Comment apply equally to unincorporated associations. "Other constituents" as used in this Comment means the positions equivalent to officers, directors, employees and shareholders held by persons acting for organizational clients that are not corporations.

When one of the constituents of an organizational client communicates with the organization's lawyer in that person's organizational capacity, the communication is protected by Rule 1.6. Thus, by way of example, if an organizational client requests its lawyer to investigate allegations of wrongdoing, interviews made in the course of that investigation between the lawyer and the client's employees or other constituents are covered by Rule 1.6. This does not mean, however, that constituents of an organizational client are the clients of the lawyer. The lawyer may not disclose to such constituents information relating to the representation except for disclosures explicitly or impliedly authorized by the organizational client in order to carry out the representation or as otherwise permitted by Rule 1.6.

When constituents of the organization make decisions for it, the decisions ordinarily must be accepted by the lawyer even if their utility or prudence is doubtful. Decisions concerning policy and operations, including ones entailing serious risk, are not as such in the lawyer's province. However, different considerations arise when the lawyer knows that the organization may be substantially injured by action of a constituent that is in violation of law. In such a circumstance, it may be reasonably necessary for the lawyer to ask the constituent to reconsider the matter. If that fails, or if the matter is of sufficient seriousness and importance to the organization, it may be reasonably necessary for the lawyer to take steps to have the matter reviewed by a higher authority in the organization. Clear justification should exist for seeking review over the head of the constituent normally responsible for it. The stated policy of the organization may define circumstances and prescribe channels for such review, and a lawyer should encourage the formulation of such a policy. Even in the absence of organization policy, however, the lawyer may have an obligation to refer a matter to higher authority, depending on the seriousness of the matter and whether the constituent in question has apparent motives to act at variance with the organization's interest. Review by the chief executive officer or by the board of directors may be required when the matter is of importance commensurate with their authority. At some point it may be useful or essential to obtain an independent legal opinion.

In an extreme case, it may be reasonably necessary for the lawyer to refer the matter to the organization's highest authority. Ordinarily, that is the board of directors or similar governing body. However, applicable law may prescribe that under certain conditions highest authority reposes elsewhere; for example, in the independent directors of a corporation.

In such a situation, if the lawyer can take remedial action without a disclosure of information that might adversely affect the organization, the lawyer as a matter of professional discretion may take such action as the lawyer reasonably believes to be in the best interest of the organization. For example, a lawyer for a close corporation may find it reasonably necessary to disclose misconduct by the Board to the shareholders. However, taking such action could entail disclosure of information relating to the representation with consequent risk of injury to the client; when such is the case, the organization is threatened by alternative injuries; the injury that may result from the governing Board's action or refusal to act, and the injury that may result if the lawyer's remedial efforts entail disclosure of confidential information. The lawyer may pursue remedial efforts even at the risk of disclosure in the circumstances stated in paragraphs (c) (1) and (c) (2).

Relation to other rules. — The authority and responsibility provided in paragraphs (b) and (c) are concurrent with the authority and responsibility provided in other Rules. In particular, this Rule does not limit [or expand] the lawyer's responsibility under Rules 1.6, 1.8, and 1.16, 3.3 or 4.1. If the lawyer's services are being used by an organization to further a crime or fraud by the organization, Rule 1.2 (d) can be applicable.

Government agency. — The duty defined in

this Rule applies to governmental organizations. However, when the client is a governmental organization, a different balance may be appropriate between maintaining confidentiality and assuring that the wrongful official act is prevented or rectified, for public business is involved. In addition, duties of lawyers employed by the government or lawyers in military service may be defined by statutes and regulation. Therefore, defining precisely the identity of the client and prescribing the resulting obligations of such lawyers may be more difficult in the government context. Although in some circumstances the client may be a specific agency, it is generally the government as a whole. For example, if the action or failure to act involves the head of a bureau, either the department of which the bureau is a part or the government as a whole may be the client for purpose of this Rule. Moreover, in a matter involving the conduct of government officials, a government lawyer may have authority to question such conduct more extensively than that of a lawyer for a private organization in similar circumstances. This Rule does not limit that authority. See note on Scope.

Clarifying the lawyer's role. — There are times when the organization's interest may be or become adverse to those of one or more of its constituents. In such circumstances the lawyer should advise any constituent, whose interest the lawyer finds adverse to that of the organization of the conflict or potential conflict of interest, that the lawyer cannot represent such constituent, and that such person may wish to obtain independent representation. Care must be taken to assure that the individual understands that, when there is such adversity of interest, the lawyer for the organization cannot provide legal representation for that constituent individual, and that discussions between the lawyer for the organization and the individual may not be privileged.

Whether such a warning should be given by the lawyer for the organization to any constituent individual may turn on the facts of each case.

Dual representation. — Paragraph (e) recognizes that a lawyer for an organization may also represent a principal officer or major shareholder.

Derivative actions. — Under generally pre-

vailing law, the shareholders or members of a corporation may bring suit to compel the directors to perform their legal obligations in the supervision of the organization. Members of unincorporated associations have essentially the same right. Such an action may be brought nominally by the organization, but usually is, in fact, a legal controversy over management of the organization.

The question can arise whether counsel for the organization may defend such an action. The proposition that the organization is the lawyer's client does not alone resolve the issue. Most derivative actions are a normal incident of an organization's affairs, to be defended by the organization's lawyer like any other suit. However, if the claim involves serious charges of wrongdoing by those in control of the organization, a conflict may arise between the lawyer's duty to the organization and the lawyer's relationship with the board. In those circumstances, Rule 1.7 governs who should represent the directors and the organization.

Code Comparison. — There is no counterpart to this Rule in the Disciplinary Rules of the Code. EC 5-18 states that "A lawyer employed or retained by a corporation or similar entity owes his allegiance to the entity and not to a stockholder, director, officer, employee, representative, or other person connected with the entity. In advising the entity, a lawyer should keep paramount its interests and his professional judgment should not be influenced by the personal desires of any person or organization. Occasionally, a lawyer for an entity is requested by a stockholder, director, officer, employee, representative, or other person connected with the entity to represent him in an individual capacity; in such a case the lawyer may serve the individual only if the lawyer is convinced that differing interests are not present." EC 5-24 states "although a lawyer may be employed by a business corporation with non-lawyers serving as directors or officers, and they necessarily have the right to make decisions of business policy, a lawyer must decline to accept direction of his professional judgment from any layman." DR 5-107 (B) provides that "a lawyer shall not permit a person who ... employs ... him to render legal services for another to direct or regulate his professional judgment in rendering such legal services."

Relationship of county attorney with citizens of county served. — St. Mary's County, as a corporate entity, is the client of the St. Mary's County Attorney, and the County Attorney may, under appropriate circumstances, invoke the attorney-client and other privileges to maintain the confidentiality

of documents encompassed by those privileges; although the County Attorney should act with due regard for the public interest, an attorney-client relationship as such does not ordinarily exist between the County Attorney and the citizens of the County. 82 Op. Att'y Gen. (December 16, 1997).

Cited in Attorney Grievance Comm'n v. Glenn, 341 Md. 448, 671 A.2d 463 (1996).

Rule 1.14. Client under a disability.

(a) When a client's ability to make adequately considered decisions in connection with the representation is impaired, whether because of minority, mental disability or for some other reason, the lawyer shall, as far as reasonably possible, maintain a normal client-lawyer relationship with the client.

(b) A lawyer may seek the appointment of a guardian or take other protective action with respect to a client, only when the lawyer reasonably believes that the client cannot adequately act in the client's own interest.

COMMENT

The normal client-lawyer relationship is based on the assumption that the client, when properly advised and assisted, is capable of making decisions about important matters. When the client is a minor or suffers from a mental disorder or disability, however, maintaining the ordinary client-lawyer relationship may not be possible in all respects. In particular, an incapacitated person may have no power to make legally binding decisions. Nevertheless, a client lacking legal competence often has the ability to understand, deliberate upon, and reach conclusions about matters affecting the client's own well-being. Furthermore, to an increasing extent the law recognizes intermediate degrees of competence. For example, children as young as five or six years of age, and certainly those of ten or twelve, are regarded as having opinions that are entitled to weight in legal proceedings concerning their custody. So also, it is recognized that some persons of advanced age can be quite capable of handling routine financial matters while needing special legal protection concerning major transactions.

The fact that a client suffers a disability does not diminish the lawyer's obligation to treat the client with attention and respect. If the person has no guardian or legal representative, the lawyer often must act as de facto guardian. Even if the person does have a legal representative, the lawyer should as far as possible accord the represented person the status of client, particularly in maintaining communication.

If a legal representative has already been appointed for the client, the lawyer should ordinarily look to the representative for decisions on behalf of the client. If a legal representative has not been appointed, the lawyer should see to such an appointment where it would serve the client's best interests. Thus, if a disabled client has substantial property that should be sold for the client's benefit, effective completion of the transaction ordinarily requires appointment of a legal representative. In many circumstances, however, appointment of a legal representative may be expensive or traumatic for the client. Evaluation of these considerations is a matter of professional judgment on the lawyer's part.

If the lawyer represents the guardian as distinct from the ward, and is aware that the guardian is acting adversely to the ward's interest, the lawyer may have an obligation to prevent or rectify the guardian's misconduct. See Rule 1.2 (d).

Disclosure of the client's condition. — Rules of procedure in litigation generally provide that minors or persons suffering mental disability shall be represented by a guardian or next friend if they do not have a general guardian. However, disclosure of the client's disability can adversely affect the client's interests. For example, raising the question of disability could, in some circumstances, lead to proceedings for involuntary commitment. The lawyer's position in such cases is an unavoidably difficult one. The lawyer may seek guidance from an appropriate diagnostician.

Code Comparison. — There is no counterpart to this Rule in the Disciplinary Rules of the Code. EC 7-12 states that "Any mental or physical condition of a client that renders him incapable of making a considered judgment on his own behalf casts additional responsibilities upon his lawyer. Where an incompetent is acting through a guardian or other legal representative, a lawyer must look to such representative for those decisions which are normally the prerogative of the client. If a client under disability has no legal representative, his lawyer may be compelled in court proceedings to make decisions on behalf of the client. If the client is capable of understanding the matter in question or of contributing to the advancement of his interests, regardless of whether he is legally disqualified from performing certain acts, the lawyer should obtain from him all possible aid. If the disability of a client and the lack of legal representative compel the lawyer to make decisions for his client, the lawyer should consider all circumstances then prevailing and act with care to safeguard and advance the interests of his client. But obviously a lawyer cannot perform any act or make any decision which the law requires his client to perform or make, either acting for himself if competent, or by a duly constituted representative if legally incompetent."

Cited in John O. v. Jane O., 90 Md. App. 406, 601 A.2d 149 (1992).

Rule 1.15. Safekeeping property.

(a) A lawyer shall hold property of clients or third persons that is in a lawyer's possession in connection with a representation separate from the lawyer's own property. Funds shall be kept in a separate account maintained pursuant to Title 16, Chapter 600 of the Maryland Rules. Other property shall be identified as such and appropriately safeguarded. Complete records of such account funds and of other property shall be kept by the lawyer and shall be preserved for a period of five years after termination of the representation.

(b) Upon receiving funds or other property in which a client or third person has an interest, a lawyer shall promptly notify the client or third person. Except as stated in this Rule or otherwise permitted by law or by agreement with the client, a lawyer shall promptly deliver to the client or third person any funds or other property that the client or third person is entitled to receive and, upon request by the client or third person, shall promptly render a full accounting regarding such property.

(c) When in the course of representation a lawyer is in possession of property in which both the lawyer and another person claim interests, the property shall be kept separate by the lawyer until there is an accounting and severance of their interests. If a dispute arises concerning their respective interests, the portion in dispute shall be kept separate by the lawyer until the dispute is resolved. (Amended Nov. 23, 1988, effective Jan. 1, 1989; June 5, 1996, effective Jan. 1, 1997.)

COMMENT

A lawyer should hold property of others with the care required of a professional fiduciary. Securities should be kept in a safe deposit box, except when some other form of safekeeping is warranted by special circumstances. All property which is the property of clients or third persons should be kept separate from the lawyer's business and personal property and, if monies, in one or more trust accounts. Separate trust accounts may be warranted when administering estate monies or acting in similar fiduciary capacities.

Lawyers often receive funds from third parties from which the lawyer's fee will be paid. If there is risk that the client may divert the funds without paying the fee, the lawyer is not required to remit the portion from which the fee is to be paid. However, a lawyer may not hold funds to coerce a client into accepting the lawyer's contention. The disputed portion of the funds should be kept in trust and the lawyer should suggest means for prompt resolution of the dispute, such as arbitration. The undisputed portion of the funds shall be promptly distributed.

Third parties, such as client's creditors, may have just claims against funds or other property in a lawyer's custody. A lawyer may have a duty under applicable law to protect such third-party claims against wrongful interference by the client, and accordingly may refuse to surrender the property to the client. However, a lawyer should not unilaterally assume to arbitrate a dispute between the client and the third party.

The obligations of a lawyer under this Rule are independent of those arising from activity other than rendering legal services. For example, a lawyer who serves as an escrow agent is governed by the applicable law relating to fiduciaries even though the lawyer does not render legal services in the transaction.

A "client's security fund" provides a means through the collective efforts of the bar to reimburse persons who have lost money or property as a result of dishonest conduct of a lawyer.

Code Comparison. — With regard to Rule 1.15 (a), DR 9-102 (A) provides that "funds of clients" are to be kept in a trust account in the state in which the lawyer's office is situated. DR 9-102 (B) (2) provides that a lawyer shall "identify and label securities and properties of a client ... and place them in ... safekeeping...." DR 9-102 (B) (3) requires that a lawyer "maintain complete records of all funds, securities and other properties of a client ... ." Rule 1.15 (a) extends these requirements to property of a third person that is in the lawyer's possession in connection with the representation.

Rule 1.15 (b) is substantially similar to DR 9-102 (B) (1) and (4).

Rule 1.15 (c) is substantially similar to DR 9-102 (A) (2), except that the requirement regarding disputes applies to property concerning which an interest is claimed by a third person as well as by a client.

Effect of amendments. — The 1988 amendment substituted "pursuant to Subtitle BU of the Maryland Rules" for "in the state where the lawyer's office is situated, or elsewhere with the consent of the client or third person" in the second sentence of section (a).

The 1996 amendment substituted "Title 16, Chapter 600" for "Subtitle BU" in the second sentence of (a).

University of Baltimore Law Forum. — For article "The Regulation of Attorney Escrow Accounts ... Boon or Overkill?", see 17, No. 3 U. Balt. Law Forum 9 (1987).

Misappropriation of client's funds involves conduct constituting moral turpitude. Attorney Grievance Comm'n v. Moore, 301 Md. 169, 482 A.2d 497 (1984).

What constitutes commingling. — Deposit of a check from a client's insurer, payable to the client and attorney, into the attorney's personal account constituted a prohibited commingling of funds, even though the attorney disbursed funds to the client less than three weeks later. Attorney Grievance Comm'n v. Kemp, 303 Md. 664, 496 A.2d 672 (1985).

Mishandling escrow account. — Indefinite suspension was appropriate sanction for attorneys mishandling of escrow account, including the failure to pay claims due from the account and the failure to refund moneys to clients. Attorney Grievance Comm'n v. Singleton, 311 Md. 1, 532 A.2d 157 (1987).

Fiduciary for non-client. — An attorney acts as a fiduciary for a non-client within the meaning of § 10-312 (b) (1) of the Business Occupations and Professions Article and of former Md. Rule 1228 b 3 (now Rule 16-811 b 3), relating to the Clients' Security Trust Fund, when the attorney disburses client funds from the attorney's trust account to a non-client, at the instructions of the client and pursuant to the obligations recognized in this Rule. Advance Fin. Co. v. Trustees of Clients' Sec. Trust Fund, 337 Md. 195, 652 A.2d 660 (1995).

Unapproved accounts. — Respondent violated § 10-302 of the Business Occupations & Professions Article of the Annotated Code, paragraph (a) of this Rule and Rule 8.4 by placing trust account money in an unapproved account. Attorney Grievance Comm'n v. Boyd, 333 Md. 298, 635 A.2d 382 (1994).

Alcoholism, drug addiction or mental disorder. — When alcoholism is, to a substantial extent, the cause of the misconduct by an attorney, we view the misconduct in a somewhat different light; under this circumstance the appropriate sanction is indefinite suspension and the focus shifts to questions of rehabilitation and the imposition of conditions sufficient to protect the public if the lawyer is allowed to resume practice. Attorney Grievance Comm'n v. Reid, 308 Md. 646, 521 A.2d 743 (1987).

When a lawyer's misconduct is caused by alcoholism, drug addiction, or a mental disorder, the usual sanction is indefinite suspension. This provides the requisite protection for the public, for it prevents the lawyer from practicing law until such time (if ever) that he or she can demonstrate that he or she is free from the effects of the ailment and able to practice competently. At the same time, the lawyer is spared the ultimate sanction of disbarment, a sanction which would be unfair to apply where the lawyer's conduct is caused by factors beyond his or her control. Attorney Grievance Comm'n v. Powers, 314 Md. 484, 551 A.2d 465 (1989).

Where alcoholism is allegedly implicated in cases involving misappropriation of trust or client funds, a sanction less severe than disbarment may be imposed if the evidence discloses that the alcoholism, to a substantial extent, was the responsible, precipitating, and root cause of the misappropriation. Attorney Grievance Comm'n v. White, 328 Md. 412, 614 A.2d 955 (1992).

Simply to show that an attorney was in the throes of alcoholism at the time he misappropriated client funds and that his thinking was "alcoholically impaired" to the point where he rationalized his behavior as acceptable, even though he knew it was not, is insufficient mitigation in and of itself to justify a sanction less than disbarment. Attorney Grievance Comm'n v. White, 328 Md. 412, 614 A.2d 955 (1992).

An indefinite suspension was the proper sanction in the case of a misappropriation of client funds caused by alcoholism; however, in the future, absent truly compelling circumstances, alcoholism will usually not be permitted to mitigate where an attorney commits a violation of ethical or legal rules which would ordinarily warrant disbarment. Attorney Grievance Comm'n v. Kenney, 339 Md. 578, 664 A.2d 854 (1995).

Prima facie showing of violation. — The mere fact that the balance in an attorney trust account falls below the total amounts held in trust supports a prima facie finding of violation of the Rule. Attorney Grievance Comm'n v. Glenn, 341 Md. 448, 671 A.2d 463 (1996).

Unintentional violations. — An unintentional violation of this Rule, with certain limited exceptions is still a violation of the attorney's affirmative duties imposed by the Rule. Attorney Grievance Comm'n v. Glenn, 341 Md. 448, 671 A.2d 463 (1996).

Bar Counsel failed to prove by clear and convincing evidence violations of this Rule or Rule 8.4(c), or § 10-306 of the Business Occupations and Professions Article, where judge found lawyer's use of funds from trust account for operating expenses was motivated by ignorance of his obligations and not by fraud, dishonesty or deceit. Attorney Grievance Comm'n v. Awuah, 346 Md. 420, 697 A.2d 446 (1997).

Disbarment was proper sanction. — Attorney was properly disbarred for violating Maryland Rules of Professional Conduct 1.1, 1.3, 1.4 (a) and (b), 1.15 (a), 3.3 (a) (1), and 8.4 (b) and (c), § 10-306 of the Business Occupations and Professions Article, and former Rule BU9 (now Rule 16-609) of the Maryland Rules of Procedure. Attorney Grievance Comm'n v. Williams, 335 Md. 458, 644 A.2d 490 (1994).

Disbarment of attorney was appropriate where there were serious and repeated violations of this Rule and other provisions of the Maryland Rules of Professional Conduct. Attorney Grievance Comm'n v. Milliken, 348 Md. 486, 704 A.2d 1225 (1998).

Indefinite suspension was proper sanc-tion. — Where respondent attorney's representation of four clients was marked by serious neglect and inattention; where he failed to return a fee which was unearned for a period of nine months; where he failed to timely remit funds he received on behalf of a client; where he failed to communicate with his clients; and in connection with the investigation of three of the complaints, where respondent failed to answer Bar Counsel's requests for information, the proper sanction was that the attorney be indefinitely suspended from the practice of law, with the right to apply for reinstatement after the suspension had been in effect for six months, conditioned upon his payment of all costs and upon the monitoring of respondent's practice. Attorney Grievance Comm'n v. David, 331 Md. 317, 628 A.2d 178 (1993).

Two-year suspension justified. — Attorney suspended for 2 years for violating paragraph (a) of this Rule, inter alia, and by the manner in which he collected fees and handled the funds of a client. Attorney Grievance Comm'n v. Eisenstein, 333 Md. 464, 635 A.2d 1327 (1994).

Evidence justified findings of misconduct, and disbarment was warranted. Attorney Grievance Comm'n v. Mazelis, 309 Md. 50, 522 A.2d 913 (1987); Attorney Grievance Comm'n v. Kolodner, 321 Md. 545, 583 A.2d 724 (1991).

Attorney's professed inability to render an accounting of what happened in his law practice and his escrow account, coupled with his loss of memory on everything from money entrusted to him to the names of his secretaries, cast doubt on his ability to adequately carry out the functions of an attorney. Attorney Grievance Comm'n v. Kramer, 325 Md. 39, 599 A.2d 100 (1991).

Applied in Attorney Grievance Comm'n v. Trilling, 311 Md. 711, 537 A.2d 269 (1988); Attorney Grievance Comm'n v. Dacy, 313 Md. 1, 542 A.2d 841 (1988); Attorney Grievance Comm'n v. Berger, 323 Md. 428, 593 A.2d 1103 (1991); Attorney Grievance Comm'n v. Keister, 327 Md. 56, 607 A.2d 909 (1992); Attorney Grievance Comm'n v. Drew, 341 Md. 139, 669 A.2d 1344 (1996); Attorney Grievance Comm'n v. Hollis, 347 Md. 547, 702 A.2d 223 (1997); Attorney Grievance Comm'n v. Adams, 349 Md. 86, 706 A.2d 1080 (1998).

Quoted in Unnamed Att'y v. Attorney Grievance Comm'n, 349 Md. 391, 708 A.2d 667 (1998); Roberts v. Total Health Care, Inc., 349 Md. 499, 709 A.2d 142 (1998).

Stated in Attorney Grievance Comm'n v. Montgomery, 318 Md. 154, 567 A.2d 112 (1989).

Cited in Attorney Grievance Comm'n v. Powell, 328 Md. 276, 614 A.2d 102 (1992); Medical Mut. Liab. Ins. Soc'y v. Azzato, 94 Md. App. 632, 618 A.2d 274, cert. denied, 330 Md.

319, 624 A.2d 491 (1993); Attorney Grievance Comm'n v. Gregory, 346 Md. 600, 697 A.2d 898 (1997); Attorney Grievance Comm'n v. Haar, 347 Md. 124, 699 A.2d 434 (1997); Post v. Bregman, 349 Md. 142, 707 A.2d 806 (1998).

Rule 1.16. Declining or terminating representation.

(a) Except as stated in paragraph (c), a lawyer shall not represent a client or, where representation has commenced, shall withdraw from the representation of a client if:

(1) the representation will result in violation of the Rules of Professional Conduct or other law;

(2) the lawyer's physical or mental condition materially impairs the lawyer's ability to represent the client; or

(3) the lawyer is discharged.

(b) Except as stated in paragraph (c), a lawyer may withdraw from representing a client if withdrawal can be accomplished without material adverse effect on the interests of the client, or if:

(1) the client persists in a course of action involving the lawyer's services that the lawyer reasonably believes is criminal or fraudulent;

(2) the client has used the lawyer's services to perpetrate a crime or fraud;

(3) a client insists upon pursuing an objective that the lawyer considers repugnant or imprudent;

(4) the client fails substantially to fulfill an obligation to the lawyer regarding the lawyer's services and has been given reasonable warning that the lawyer will withdraw unless the obligation is fulfilled;

(5) the representation will result in an unreasonable financial burden on the lawyer or has been rendered unreasonably difficult by the client; or

(6) other good cause for withdrawal exists.

(c) When ordered to do so by a tribunal, a lawyer shall continue representation notwithstanding good cause for terminating the representation.

(d) Upon termination of representation, a lawyer shall take steps to the extent reasonably practicable to protect a client's interests, such as giving reasonable notice to the client, allowing time for employment of other counsel, surrendering papers and property to which the client is entitled and refunding any advance payment of fee that has not been earned. The lawyer may retain papers relating to the client to the extent permitted by other law.

COMMENT

A lawyer should not accept representation in a matter unless it can be performed competently, promptly, without improper conflict of interest and to completion.

Mandatory withdrawal. — A lawyer ordinarily must decline or withdraw from representation if the client demands that the lawyer engage in conduct that is illegal or violates the Rules of Professional Conduct or other law. The lawyer is not obliged to decline or withdraw simply because the client suggests such a course of conduct; a client may make such a suggestion in the hope that a lawyer will not be constrained by a professional obligation.

When a lawyer has been appointed to represent a client, withdrawal ordinarily requires approval of the appointing authority. See also Rule 6.2. Difficulty may be encountered if withdrawal is based on the client's demand that the lawyer engage in unprofessional conduct. The court may wish an explanation for the withdrawal, while the lawyer may be bound to keep confidential the facts that would constitute such an explanation. The lawyer's statement that professional considerations require termination of the representation ordinarily should be accepted as sufficient.

Discharge. — A client has a right to discharge a lawyer at any time, with or without cause, subject to liability for payment for the lawyer's services. Where future dispute about the withdrawal may be anticipated, it may be advisable to prepare a written statement reciting the circumstances.

Whether a client can discharge appointed counsel may depend on applicable law. A client seeking to do so should be given a full explanation of the consequences. These consequences may include a decision by the appointing authority that appointment of successor counsel is unjustified, thus requiring the client to represent himself.

If the client is mentally incompetent, the client may lack the legal capacity to discharge the lawyer, and in any event the discharge may be seriously adverse to the client's interests. The lawyer should make special effort to help the client consider the consequences and, in an extreme case, may initiate proceedings for a conservatorship or similar protection of the client. See Rule 1.14.

Optional withdrawal. — A lawyer may withdraw from representation in some circumstances. The lawyer has the option to withdraw if it can be accomplished without material adverse effect on the client's interests. Withdrawal is also justified if the client persists in a course of action that the lawyer reasonably believes is criminal or fraudulent, for a lawyer is not required to be associated with such conduct even if the lawyer does not further it. Withdrawal is also permitted if the lawyer's services were misused in the past even if that would materially prejudice the client. The lawyer also may withdraw where the client insists on a repugnant or imprudent objective.

A lawyer may withdraw if the client refuses to abide by the terms of an agreement relating to the representation, such as an agreement concerning fees or court costs or an agreement limiting the objectives of the representation.

Assisting the client upon withdrawal. — Even if the lawyer has been unfairly discharged by the client, a lawyer must take all reasonable steps to mitigate the consequences to the client. The lawyer may retain papers as security for a fee only to the extent permitted by law.

Whether or not a lawyer for an organization may under certain unusual circumstances have a legal obligation to the organization after withdrawing or being discharged by the organization's highest authority is beyond the scope of these Rules.

Code Comparison. — With regard to paragraph (a), DR 2-109 (A) provided that a lawyer "shall not accept employment ... if he knows or it is obvious that [the prospective client] wishes to ... [b]ring a legal action ... or otherwise have steps taken for him, merely for the purpose of harassing or maliciously injuring any person ... ." Nor may a lawyer accept employment if the lawyer is aware that the prospective client wishes to "[p]resent a claim or defense ... that is not warranted under existing law, unless it can be supported by good faith argument for an extension, modification, or reversal of existing law." DR 2-110 (B) provided that a lawyer "shall withdraw from employment ... if:

"(1) He knows or it is obvious that his client is bringing the legal action ... or is otherwise having steps taken for him, merely for the purpose of harassing or maliciously injuring any person.

"(2) He knows or it is obvious that his continued employment will result in violation of a Disciplinary Rule.

"(3) His mental or physical condition renders it unreasonably difficult for him to carry out the employment effectively.

"(4) He is discharged by his client."

With regard to paragraph (b), DR 2-110 (C) permitted withdrawal regardless of the effect on the client if:

"(1) His client: (a) Insists upon presenting a claim or defense that is not warranted under existing law and cannot be supported by good faith argument for an extension, modification, or reversal of existing law; (b) Personally seeks to pursue an illegal course of conduct; (c) Insists that the lawyer pursue a course of conduct that is illegal or that is prohibited under the Disciplinary Rules; (d) By other conduct renders it unreasonably difficult for the lawyer to carry out his employment effectively; (e) Insists, in a matter not pending before a tribunal, that the lawyer engage in conduct that is contrary to the judgment and advice of the lawyer but not prohibited under the Disciplinary Rules; (f) Deliberately disregards an agreement or obligation to the lawyer as to expenses and fees.

"(2) His continued employment is likely to result in a violation of a Disciplinary Rule.

"(3) His inability to work with co-counsel indicates that the best interest of the client likely will be served by withdrawal.

"(4) His mental or physical condition renders it difficult for him to carry out the employment effectively.

"(5) His client knowingly and freely assents to termination of his employment.

"(6) He believes in good faith, in a proceeding pending before a tribunal, that the tribunal will find the existence of other good cause for withdrawal."

With regard to paragraph (c), DR 2-110 (A) (1) provided: "If permission for withdrawal from employment is required by the rules of a tribunal, the lawyer shall not withdraw ... without its permission."

The provisions of paragraph (d) are substantially identical to DR 2-110 (A) (2) and (3).

Maryland Law Review. — For comment discussing the need for a consensus on the proper scope of the attorney-client privilege where a client attempts to use an attorney's services for fraudulent or illegal purposes, see 46 Md. L. Rev. 436 (1987).

Advance payment fees. — Most courts that have considered the issue have determined that advance payment fees must be placed in a trust account as opposed to an operating account; it is beyond question that section (d) of this Rule requires that any portion of an advance payment fee that is unearned must be returned to the client. Attorney Grievance Comm'n v. Milliken, 348 Md. 486, 704 A.2d 1225 (1998).

Disbarment was proper sanction. — Disbarment of attorney was appropriate where there were serious and repeated violations of this Rule and other provisions of the Maryland Rules of Professional Conduct. Attorney Grievance Comm'n v. Milliken, 348 Md. 486, 704 A.2d 1225 (1998).

Indefinite suspension was proper sanction. — Where respondent attorney's representation of four clients was marked by serious neglect and inattention; where he failed to return a fee which was unearned for a period of nine months; where he failed to timely remit funds he received on behalf of a client; where he failed to communicate with his clients; and

in connection with the investigation of three of the complaints, where respondent failed to answer Bar Counsel's requests for information, the proper sanction was that the attorney be indefinitely suspended from the practice of law, with the right to apply for reinstatement after the suspension had been in effect for six months, conditioned upon his payment of all costs and upon the monitoring of respondent's practice. Attorney Grievance Comm'n v. David, 331 Md. 317, 628 A.2d 178 (1993).

Applied in Attorney Grievance Comm'n v. Keister, 327 Md. 56, 607 A.2d 909 (1992); Baltimore Gas & Elec. Co. v. Commercial Union Ins. Co., 113 Md. App. 540, 688 A.2d 496 (1997).

Quoted in Attorney Grievance Comm'n v. Protokowicz, 329 Md. 252, 619 A.2d 100 (1993); Attorney Grievance Comm'n v. James, 340 Md. 318, 666 A.2d 1246 (1995); Unnamed Att'y v. Attorney Grievance Comm'n, 349 Md. 391, 708 A.2d 667 (1998).

Stated in Attorney Grievance Comm'n v. Montgomery, 318 Md. 154, 567 A.2d 112 (1989).

Cited in Attorney Grievance Comm'n v. Kerpelman, 323 Md. 136, 591 A.2d 516 (1991), cert. denied, 502 U.S. 939, 112 S. Ct. 374, 116 L. Ed. 2d 326 (1991); Attorney Grievance Comm'n v. Noble, 324 Md. 42, 595 A.2d 468 (1991).

COUNSELOR.

Rule 2.1. Advisor.

In representing a client, a lawyer shall exercise independent professional judgment and render candid advice. In rendering advice, a lawyer may refer not only to law but to other considerations such as moral, economic, social and political factors, that may be relevant to the client's situation.

COMMENT

Scope of advice. — A client is entitled to straightforward advice expressing the lawyer's honest assessment. Legal advice often involves unpleasant facts and alternatives that a client may be disinclined to confront. In presenting advice, a lawyer endeavors to sustain the client's morale and may put advice in as acceptable a form as honesty permits. However, a lawyer should not be deterred from giving candid advice by the prospect that the advice will be unpalatable to the client.

Advice couched in narrowly legal terms may be of little value to a client, especially where

practical considerations, such as cost or effects on other people, are predominant. Purely technical legal advice, therefore, can sometimes be inadequate. It is proper for a lawyer to refer to relevant moral and ethical considerations in giving advice. Although a lawyer is not a moral advisor as such, moral and ethical considerations impinge upon most legal questions and may decisively influence how the law will be applied.

A client may expressly or impliedly ask the lawyer for purely technical advice. When such a request is made by a client experienced in legal matters, the lawyer may accept it at face value. When such a request is made by a client inexperienced in legal matters, however, the lawyer's responsibility as advisor may include indicating that more may be involved than strictly legal considerations.

Matters that go beyond strictly legal questions may also be in the domain of another profession. Family matters can involve problems within the professional competence of psychiatry, clinical psychology or social work; business matters can involve problems within the competence of the accounting profession or of financial specialists. Where consultation with a professional in another field is itself something a competent lawyer would recommend, the lawyer should make such a recommendation. At the same time, a lawyer's advice at its best often consists of recommending a course of action in the face of conflicting recommendations of experts.

Offering advice. — In general, a lawyer is not expected to give advice until asked by the client. However, when a lawyer knows that a client proposes a course of action that is likely to result in substantial adverse legal consequences to the client, duty to the client under

Rule 1.4 may require that the lawyer act if the client's course of action is related to the representation. A lawyer ordinarily has no duty to initiate investigation of a client's affairs or to give advice that the client has indicated is unwanted, but a lawyer may initiate advice to a client when doing so appears to be in the client's interest.

Code Comparison. — There is no direct counterpart to Rule 2.1 in the Disciplinary Rules of the Code. DR 5-107 (B) provides that "A lawyer shall not permit a person who recommends, employs, or pays him to render legal services for another to direct or regulate his professional judgment in rendering such legal services." EC 7-8 states that "Advice of a lawyer to his client need not be confined to purely legal considerations .... In assisting his client to reach a proper decision, it is often desirable for a lawyer to point out those factors which may lead to a decision that is morally just as well as legally permissible .... In the final analysis, however ... the decision whether to forego legally available objectives or methods because of nonlegal factors is ultimately for the client ...."

University of Baltimore Law Forum. — For discussion of the code of ethics, see 17, No. 1 U. Balt. Law Forum 31 (1986).

Rule 2.2. Intermediary.

(a) A lawyer may act as intermediary between clients if:

(1) the lawyer consults with each client concerning the implications of the common representation, including the advantages and risks involved, and the effect on the attorney-client privileges, and obtains each client's consent to the common representation;

(2) the lawyer reasonably believes that the matter can be resolved on terms compatible with the clients' best interests, that each client will be able to make adequately informed decisions in the matter and that there is little risk of material prejudice to the interests of any of the clients if the contemplated resolution is unsuccessful; and

(3) the lawyer reasonably believes that the common representation can be undertaken impartially and without improper effect on other responsibilities the lawyer has to any of the clients.

(b) While acting as intermediary, the lawyer shall consult with each client concerning the decisions to be made and the considerations relevant in making them, so that each client can make adequately informed decisions.

(c) A lawyer shall withdraw as intermediary if any of the clients so requests, or if any of the conditions stated in paragraph (a) is no longer satisfied. Upon withdrawal, the lawyer shall not continue to represent any of the clients in the matter that was the subject of the intermediation.

COMMENT

A lawyer acts as intermediary under this Rule when the lawyer represents two or more parties with potentially conflicting interests. A key factor in defining the relationship is whether the parties share responsibility for the lawyer's fee, but the common representation may be inferred from other circumstances. Because confusion can arise as to the lawyer's role where each party is not separately represented, it is important that the lawyer make clear the relationship.

The Rule does not apply to a lawyer acting as arbitrator or mediator between or among parties who are not clients of the lawyer, even where the lawyer has been appointed with the concurrence of the parties. In performing such a role the lawyer may be subject to applicable codes of ethics, such as the Code of Ethics for Arbitration in Commercial Disputes prepared by a joint Committee of the American Bar Association and the American Arbitration Association.

A lawyer acts as intermediary in seeking to establish or adjust a relationship between clients on an amicable and mutually advantageous basis; for example, in helping to organize a business in which two or more clients are entrepreneurs, working out the financial reorganization of an enterprise in which two or more clients have an interest, arranging a property distribution in settlement of an estate or mediating a dispute between clients. The lawyer seeks to resolve potentially conflicting interests by developing the parties' mutual interests. The alternative can be that each party may have to obtain separate representation, with the possibility in some situations of incurring additional cost, complication or even litigation. Given these and other relevant factors, all the clients may prefer that the lawyer act as intermediary.

In considering whether to act as intermediary between clients, a lawyer should be mindful that if the intermediation fails the result can be additional cost, embarrassment and recrimination. In some situations the risk of failure is so great that intermediation is plainly impossible. For example, a lawyer cannot undertake common representation of clients between whom contentious litigation is imminent or who contemplate contentious negotiations. More generally, if the relationship between the parties has already assumed definite antagonism, the possibility that the clients' interests can be adjusted by intermediation ordinarily is not very good.

The appropriateness of intermediation can depend on its form. Forms of intermediation range from informal arbitration, where each client's case is presented by the respective client and the lawyer decides the outcome, to mediation, to common representation where the clients' interests are substantially though not entirely compatible. One form may be appropriate in circumstances where another would not. Other relevant factors are whether the lawyer subsequently will represent both parties on a continuing basis and whether the situation involves creating a relationship between the parties or terminating one.

Confidentiality and privilege. — A particularly important factor in determining the appropriateness of intermediation is the effect on client-lawyer confidentiality and the attorney-client privilege. In a common representation, the lawyer is still required both to keep each client adequately informed and to maintain confidentiality of information relating to the representation. See Rules 1.4 and 1.6. Complying with both requirements while acting as intermediary requires a delicate balance. If the balance cannot be maintained, the common representation is improper. With regard to the attorney-client privilege, the prevailing rule is that as between commonly represented clients the privilege does not attach. Hence, it must be assumed that if litigation eventuates between the clients, the privilege will not protect any such communications, and the clients should be so advised.

Since the lawyer is required to be impartial between commonly represented clients, intermediation is improper when that impartiality cannot be maintained. For example, a lawyer who has represented one of the clients for a long period and in a variety of matters might have difficulty being impartial between that client and one to whom the lawyer has only recently been introduced.

Consultation. — In acting as intermediary between clients, the lawyer is required to consult with the clients on the implications of doing so, and proceed only upon consent based on such a consultation. The consultation should make clear that the lawyer's role is not that of partisanship normally expected in other circumstances.

Paragraph (b) is an application of the principle expressed in Rule 1.4. Where the lawyer is intermediary, the clients ordinarily must assume greater responsibility for decisions than when each client is independently represented.

Withdrawal. — Common representation does not diminish the rights of each client in the client-lawyer relationship. Each has the right to loyal and diligent representation, the right to discharge the lawyer as stated in Rule 1.16, and the protection of Rule 1.9 concerning obligations to a former client.

Code Comparison. — There is no direct counterpart to Rule 2.2 in the Disciplinary Rules of the Code. EC 5-20 states that "A lawyer is often asked to serve as an impartial arbitrator or mediator in matters which involve present or former clients. He may serve in either capacity if he first discloses such present or former relationships." DR 5-105 (B) provides that "A lawyer shall not continue multiple employment if the exercise of his independent judgment in behalf of a client will be or is likely to be adversely affected by his representation of another client, or if it would involve him in representation of differing interests, except to the extent permitted under DR 5-105 (C)." DR 5-105 (C) provides that "a lawyer may represent multiple clients if it is obvious that he can adequately represent the interests of each and if each consents to the representation after full disclosure of the possible effect of such representation on the exercise of his independent professional judgment on behalf of each."

Rule 2.3. Evaluation for use by third persons.

(a) A lawyer may undertake an evaluation of a matter affecting a client for the use of someone other than the client if:

(1) the lawyer reasonably believes that making the evaluation is compatible with other aspects of the lawyer's relationship with the client; and

(2) the client consents after consultation.

(b) Except as disclosure is required in connection with a report of an evaluation, information relating to the evaluation is otherwise protected by Rule 1.6.

COMMENT

Definition. — An evaluation may be performed at the client's direction but for the primary purpose of establishing information for the benefit of third parties; for example, an opinion concerning the title of property rendered at the behest of a vendor for the information of a prospective purchaser, or at the behest of a borrower for the information of a prospective lender. In some situations, the evaluation may be required by a government agency; for example, an opinion concerning the legality of the securities registered for sale under the securities laws. In other instances, the evaluation may be required by a third person, such as a purchaser of a business.

Lawyers for the government may be called upon to give a formal opinion on the legality of contemplated government agency action. In making such an evaluation, the government lawyer acts at the behest of the government as the client but for the purpose of establishing the limits of the agency's authorized activity. Such an opinion is to be distinguished from confidential legal advice given agency officials. The critical question is whether the opinion is to be made public.

A legal evaluation should be distinguished from an investigation of a person with whom the lawyer does not have a client-lawyer relationship. For example, a lawyer retained by a purchaser to analyze a vendor's title to property does not have a client-lawyer relationship with the vendor. So also, an investigation into a person's affairs by a government lawyer, or by special counsel employed by the government, is not an evaluation as that term is used in this Rule. The question is whether the lawyer is retained by the person whose affairs are being examined. When the lawyer is retained by that person, the general rules concerning loyalty to client and preservation of confidences apply, which is not the case if the lawyer is retained by someone else. For this reason, it is essential to identify the person by whom the lawyer is retained. This should be made clear not only to the person under examination, but also to others to whom the results are to be made available.

Duty to third person. — When the evaluation is intended for the information or use of a third person, a legal duty to that person may or may not arise. That legal question is beyond the scope of this Rule. However, since such an evaluation involves a departure from the normal client-lawyer relationship, careful analysis of the situation is required. The lawyer must be satisfied as a matter of professional judgment that making the evaluation is compatible with other functions undertaken in behalf of the client. For example, if the lawyer is acting as advocate in defending the client against charges of fraud, it would normally be incompatible with that responsibility for the lawyer to perform an evaluation for others concerning the same or a related transaction. Assuming no such impediment is apparent, however, the lawyer should advise the client of the implications of the evaluation, particularly the lawyer's responsibilities to third persons and the duty to disseminate the findings.

Access to and disclosure of information. — The quality of an evaluation depends on the freedom and extent of the investigation upon which it is based. Ordinarily a lawyer should have whatever latitude of investigation seems necessary as a matter of professional judgment. Under some circumstances, however, the terms of the evaluation may be limited. For example, certain issues or sources may be categorically excluded, or the scope of search may be limited by time constraints or the noncooperation of persons having relevant information. Any such limitations which are material to the evaluation should be described in the report. If after a lawyer has commenced an evaluation, the client refuses to comply with the terms upon which it was understood the evaluation was to have been made, the lawyer's obligations are determined by law, having reference to the terms of the client's agreement and the surrounding circumstances.

Financial auditors' requests for information. — When a question concerning the legal situation of a client arises at the instance of the client's financial auditor and the question is referred to the lawyer, the lawyer's response may be made in accordance with procedures recognized in the legal profession. Such a procedure is set forth in the American Bar Association Statement of Policy Regarding Lawyers' Responses to Auditors' Requests for Information, adopted in 1975.

Code Comparison. — There is no counterpart to Rule 2.3 in the Code.

ADVOCATE.

Rule 3.1. Meritorious claims and contentions.

A lawyer shall not bring or defend a proceeding, or assert or controvert an issue therein, unless there is a basis for doing so that is not frivolous, which includes a good faith argument for an extension, modification or reversal of existing law. A lawyer may nevertheless so defend the proceeding as to require that every element of the moving party's case be established.

COMMENT

The advocate has a duty to use legal procedure for the fullest benefit of the client's cause, but also a duty not to abuse legal procedure. The law, both procedural and substantive, establishes the limits within which an advocate may proceed. However, the law is not always clear and never is static. Accordingly, in determining the proper scope of advocacy, account must be taken of the law's ambiguities and potential for change.

The filing of an action or defense or similar action taken for a client is not frivolous merely because the facts have not first been fully substantiated or because the lawyer expects to develop vital evidence only by discovery. Such action is not frivolous even though the lawyer believes that the client's position ultimately will not prevail. The action is frivolous, however, if the client desires to have the action taken primarily for the purpose of harassing or maliciously injuring a person or if the lawyer is unable either to make a good faith argument on the merits of the action taken or to support the action taken by a good faith argument for an extension, modification or reversal of existing law.

Code Comparison. — DR 7-102 (A) (1) provides that a lawyer may not "file a suit, assert a position, conduct a defense, delay a trial, or take other action on behalf of his client when he knows or when it is obvious that such action would serve merely to harass or maliciously injure another." Rule 3.1 is to the same general effect as DR 7-102 (A) (1), with two qualifications. First, the test of improper conduct is changed from "merely to harass or maliciously injure another" to the requirement that there be a basis for the litigation measure involved that is "not frivolous." This includes the concept stated in DR 7-102 (A) (2) that a lawyer may advance a claim or defense unwarranted by existing law if "it can be supported by good faith argument for an extension, modification, or reversal of existing law." Second, the test in Rule 3.1 is an objective test, whereas DR 7-102 (A) (1) applies only if the lawyer "knows or when it is obvious" that the litigation is frivolous.

Maryland Law Review. — For symposium, expanding pro bono legal assistance in civil cases to Maryland's poor, see 49 Md. L. Rev. 1 (1990).

For article, "The Devolution of the Legal Profession: A Demand Side Perspective," see 49 Md. L. Rev. 869 (1990).

University of Baltimore Law Forum. — For discussion of the code of ethics, see 17, No. 1 U. Balt. Law Forum 31 (1986).

For article, "Code of Ethics Revisited," see 19.2 U. Balt. Law Forum 14 (1989).

Frivolous or unjustified motions. — The frivolous and unjustified filing of any motion, including one under Md. Rule 1-341, may not only be grounds for sanctions under that rule, but may also constitute a violation of this Rule. Gunther v. Smith, 78 Md. App. 508, 553 A.2d 1314 (1989).

Violations. — Sanctions warranted where the actions of an attorney, including pressing claims that were completely without founda-tion, keeping a party in a suit for no other reason except to unnecessarily burden them, and knowingly failing to respond to a lawful demand for information from a disciplinary authority. Attorney Grievance Comm'n v. Alison, 349 Md. 623, 709 A.2d 1212 (1998).

Cited in Legal Aid Bureau, Inc. v. Bishop's Garth Assocs., 75 Md. App. 214, 540 A.2d 1175, cert. denied, 313 Md. 611, 547 A.2d 188 (1988); Stinnett v. Cort Furn. Rental, 315 Md. 448, 554 A.2d 1226 (1989); Needle v. White, Mindel, Clarke & Hill, 81 Md. App. 463, 568 A.2d 856 (1990); Surratt v. Prince George's County, 320 Md. 439, 578 A.2d 745 (1990); Major v. First Va. Bank, 97 Md. App. 520, 631 A.2d 127, cert. denied, 331 Md. 480, 628 A.2d 1067 (1993); Seney v. Seney, 97 Md. App. 544, 631 A.2d 139 (1993); In re Attorney's Use of Trade Name, 333 Md. 488, 635 A.2d 1338 (1994); Wilson v. Stanbury, 118 Md. App. 209, 702 A.2d 436 (1997).

Rule 3.2. Expediting litigation.

A lawyer shall make reasonable efforts to expedite litigation consistent with the interests of the client.

COMMENT

Dilatory practices bring the administration of justice into disrepute. Delay should not be indulged merely for the convenience of the advocates, or for the purpose of frustrating an opposing party's attempt to obtain rightful redress or repose. It is not a justification that similar conduct is often tolerated by the bench and bar. The question is whether a competent lawyer acting in good faith would regard the course of action as having some substantial purpose.

Code Comparison. — DR 7-102 (A) (1) provides that "A lawyer shall not ... file a suit, assert a position, conduct a defense (or) delay a trial ... when he knows or when it is obvious that such action would serve merely to harass or maliciously injure another."

Failure to timely file or adequately investigate action. — Ninety day suspension was appropriate sanction for attorney's failure to timely file or adequately investigate action on behalf of her client, and for misrepresenting to her client that the suit had been filed on her behalf and was proceeding to trial where the client paid the attorney only part of the costs involved in the work the attorney did do and the attorney did not consider the gratuitous client to be a client; an attorney-client relationship did exist and, thus, the attorney failed to carry out her contract of employment. Attorney Grievance Comm'n v. Pinkney, 311 Md. 137, 532 A.2d 1367 (1987).

Violation of Rule shown. — Bar Counsel's exception to judge's failure to find a violation of this Rule, requiring a lawyer to make reasonable efforts to expedite litigation consistent with the interests of the client, was granted. Attorney Grievance Comm'n v. Dietz, 331 Md. 637, 629 A.2d 678 (1993).

Disbarment was proper sanction. — Disbarment of attorney was appropriate where there were serious and repeated violations of this Rule and other provisions of the Maryland Rules of Professional Conduct. Attorney Grievance Comm'n v. Milliken, 348 Md. 486, 704 A.2d 1225 (1998).

Cited in Stinnett v. Cort Furn. Rental, 315 Md. 448, 554 A.2d 1226 (1989); Surratt v. Prince George's County, 320 Md. 439, 578 A.2d 745 (1990).

Rule 3.3. Candor toward the tribunal.

(a) A lawyer shall not knowingly:

(1) make a false statement of material fact or law to a tribunal;

(2) fail to disclose a material fact to a tribunal when disclosure is necessary to avoid assisting a criminal or fraudulent act by the client;

(3) fail to disclose to the tribunal legal authority in the controlling jurisdiction known to the lawyer to be directly adverse to the position of the client and not disclosed by opposing counsel; or

(4) offer evidence that the lawyer knows to be false. If a lawyer has offered material evidence and comes to know of its falsity, the lawyer shall take reasonable remedial measures.

(b) The duties stated in paragraph (a) continue to the conclusion of the proceeding, and apply even if compliance requires disclosure of information otherwise protected by Rule 1.6.

(c) A lawyer may refuse to offer evidence that the lawyer reasonably believes is false.

(d) In an ex parte proceeding, a lawyer shall inform the tribunal of all material facts known to the lawyer which will enable the tribunal to make an informed decision, whether or not the facts are adverse.

(e) Notwithstanding paragraphs (a) through (d), a lawyer for an accused in a criminal case need not disclose that the accused intends to testify falsely or has testified falsely if the lawyer reasonably believes that the disclosure would jeopardize any constitutional right of the accused.

COMMENT

The advocate's task is to present the client's case with persuasive force. Performance of that duty while maintaining confidences of the client is qualified by the advocate's duty of candor to the tribunal. However, an advocate does not vouch for the evidence submitted in a cause; the tribunal is responsible for assessing its probative value.

Representations by a lawyer. — An advocate is responsible for pleadings and other documents prepared for litigation, but is usually not required to have personal knowledge of matters asserted therein, for litigation documents ordinarily present assertions by the client, or by someone on the client's behalf, and not assertions by the lawyer. Compare Rule 3.1. However, an assertion purporting to be on the lawyer's own knowledge, as in an affidavit by the lawyer or in a statement in open court, may properly be made only when the lawyer knows the assertion is true or believes it to be true on the basis of a reasonably diligent inquiry. There are circumstances where failure to make a disclosure is the equivalent of an affirmative misrepresentation. The obligation prescribed in Rule 1.2 (d) not to counsel a client to commit or assist the client in committing a fraud applies in litigation. Regarding compliance with Rule 1.2 (d), see the Comment to that Rule. See also the Comment to Rule 8.4 (b).

Misleading legal argument. — Legal argument based on a knowingly false representation of law constitutes dishonesty toward the tribunal. A lawyer is not required to make a disinterested exposition of the law, but must recognize the existence of pertinent legal authorities. Furthermore, as stated in paragraph (a) (3), an advocate has a duty to disclose directly adverse authority in the controlling jurisdiction which has not been disclosed by the opposing party. The underlying concept is that legal argument is a discussion seeking to determine the legal premises properly applicable to the case.

False evidence. — When evidence that a lawyer knows to be false is provided by a person who is not the client, the lawyer must refuse to offer it regardless of the client's wishes.

When false evidence is offered by the client, however, a conflict may arise between the lawyer's duty to keep the client's revelations confidential and the duty of candor to the court. Upon ascertaining that material evidence is false, the lawyer should seek to persuade the client that the evidence should not be offered or, if it has been offered, that its false character should immediately be disclosed. If the persuasion is ineffective, the lawyer must take reasonable remedial measures.

Except in the defense of a criminal accused, the rule generally recognized is that, if necessary to rectify the situation, an advocate must disclose the existence of the client's deception to the court or to the other party. Such a disclosure can result in grave consequences to the client, including not only a sense of betrayal but also loss of the case and perhaps a prosecution for perjury. But the alternative is that the lawyer cooperate in deceiving the court, thereby subverting the truth-finding process which the adversary system is designed to implement. See Rule 1.2 (d). Futhermore, unless it is clearly understood that the lawyer will act upon the duty to disclose the existence of false evidence, the client can simply reject the lawyer's advice to reveal the false evidence and insist that the lawyer keep silent. Thus the client could in effect coerce the lawyer into being a party to fraud on the court.

Perjury by a criminal defendant. — Whether an advocate for a criminally accused has the same duty of disclosure has been intensely debated. While it is agreed that the lawyer should seek to persuade the client to refrain from perjurious testimony, there has been dispute concerning the lawyer's duty when that persuasion fails. If the confrontation with the client occurs before trial, the lawyer ordinarily can withdraw. Withdrawal before trial may not be possible, however, either because trial is imminent, or because the confrontation with the client does not take place until the trial itself, or because no other counsel is available.

The most difficult situation, therefore, arises in a criminal case where the accused insists on testifying when the lawyer knows that the testimony is perjurious. The lawyer's effort to rectify the situation can increase the likelihood of the client's being convicted as well as opening the possibility of a prosecution for perjury. On the other hand, if the lawyer does not exercise control over the proof, the lawyer participates, although in a merely passive way, in deception of the court.

Three resolutions of this dilemma have been proposed. One is to permit the accused to testify by a narrative without guidance through the lawyer's questioning. This compromises both contending principles; it exempts the lawyer from the duty to disclose false evidence but subjects the client to an implicit disclosure of information imparted to counsel. Another suggested resolution, of relatively recent origin, is that the advocate be entirely excused from the duty to reveal perjury if the perjury is that of the client. This a coherent solution but makes the advocate a knowing instrument of perjury.

The other resolution of the dilemma is that the lawyer must reveal the client's perjury if necessary to rectify the situation. A criminal accused has a right to the assistance of an advocate, a right to testify and a right of confidential communication with counsel. However, an accused should not have a right to assistance of counsel in committing perjury. Furthermore, an advocate has an obligation, not only in professional ethics but under the law as well, to avoid implication in the commission of perjury or other falsification of evidence. See Rule 1.2 (d).

Remedial measures. — If perjured testimony or false evidence has been offered, the advocate's proper course ordinarily is to remonstrate with the client confidentially. If that fails, the advocate should seek to withdraw if that will remedy the situation. If withdrawal will not remedy the situation or is impossible, the advocate should make disclosure to the court. It is for the court then to determine what should be done — making a statement about the matter to the trier of fact, ordering a mistrial or perhaps nothing. If the false testimony was that of the client, the client may controvert the lawyer's version of their communication when the lawyer discloses the situation to the court. If there is an issue whether the client has committed perjury, the lawyer cannot represent the client in resolution of the issue, and a mistrial may be unavoidable. An unscrupulous client might in this way attempt to produce a series of mistrials and thus escape prosecution. However, a second such encounter could be construed as a deliberate abuse of the right to counsel and as such a waiver of the right to further representation.

Constitutional requirements. — The general rule — that an advocate must disclose the existence of perjury with respect to a material fact, even that of a client — applies to defense counsel in criminal cases, as well as in other instances. However, the definition of the lawyer's ethical duty in such a situation may be qualified by constitutional provisions for due process and the right to counsel in criminal cases. Paragraph (3) (e) is intended to protect from discipline the lawyer who does not make disclosures mandated by paragraphs (a) through (d) only when the lawyer acts in the "reasonable belief" that disclosure would jeopardize a constitutional right of the client. See the definition of this term under the TERMINOLOGY section of these Rules, *supra*.

Duration of obligation. — A practical time limit on the obligation to rectify the presentation of false evidence has to be established. The conclusion of the proceeding is a reasonably definite point for the termination of the obligation. After that point, however, the lawyer may rectify the consequences as provided in Rule 1.6 (b) (2).

Refusing to offer proof believed to be false. — Generally speaking, a lawyer has authority to refuse to offer testimony or other proof that the lawyer believes is untrustworthy. Offering such proof may reflect adversely on the lawyer's ability to discriminate in the quality of evidence and thus impair the lawyer's effectiveness as an advocate. In criminal cases, however, a lawyer may, in some jurisdictions, be denied this authority by constitutional requirements governing the right to counsel.

Ex parte proceedings. — Ordinarily, an advocate has the limited responsibility of presenting one side of the matters that a tribunal should consider in reaching a decision; the conflicting position is expected to be presented by the opposing party. However, in an ex parte proceeding, such as an application for a temporary restraining order, there is no balance of presentation by opposing advocates. The object of an ex parte proceeding is nevertheless to yield a substantially just result. The judge has an affirmative responsibility to accord the absent party just consideration. The lawyer for the represented party has the correlative duty to make disclosures of material facts known to the lawyer and that the lawyer reasonably believes are necessary to an informed decision.

Code Comparison. — Rule 3.3 (a) (1) is substantially identical to DR 7-102 (A) (5), which provides that a lawyer shall not "knowingly make a false statement of law or fact."

Rule 3.3 (a) (2) is implicit in DR 7-102 (A) (3), which provides that "a lawyer shall not ... knowingly fail to disclose that which he is required by law to reveal."

Rule 3.3 (a) (3) is identical to DR 7-106 (B) (1).

With regard to rule 3.3 (a) (4), the first sentence of this subparagraph is similar to DR 7-102 (A) (4), which provides that a lawyer shall not "knowingly use" perjured testimony or false evidence. The second sentence of Rule 3.3 (a) (4) resolves an ambiguity in the Code concerning the action required of a lawyer when he discovers that he has offered perjured testimony or false evidence. DR 7-102 (A) (4), quoted above, does not expressly deal with this situation, but the prohibition against "use" of false evidence can be construed to preclude carrying through with a case based on such evidence when that fact has become known during the trial. DR 7-102 (B) (1), also noted in connection with Rule 1.6, provides that "a lawyer who receives information clearly establishing that ... his client has ... perpetrated a fraud upon ... a tribunal shall if the client does not rectify the situation ... reveal the fraud to the ... tribunal ...." Since use of perjured testimony or false evidence is usually regarded as "fraud" upon the court, DR 7-102 (B) (1) requires disclosure by the lawyer in such circumstances. However, some states, but not Maryland, amended DR 7-102 (B) (1) in conformity with an ABA recommended amendment to provide that the duty of disclosure does not apply when the "information is protected as a privileged communication." This qualification may have been empty, for the rule of attorney-client privilege has been construed to exclude communications that further a crime, including the crime of perjury. On this interpretation of DR 7-102 (B) (1), the lawyer has a duty to disclose the perjury.

Rule 3.3 (c) confers discretion on the lawyer to refuse to offer evidence that he "reasonably believes" is false. This gives the lawyer more latitude than DR 7-102 (A) (4), which prohibits the lawyer from offering evidence the lawyer "knows" is false.

There is no counterpart in the Code to paragraph (d).

Paragraph (e) also has no counterpart in the Code, but recognizes an implicit exception to making disclosures which would result in violating the constitutional rights of an accused.

Maryland Law Review. — For article, "The Devolution of the Legal Profession: A Demand Side Perspective," see 49 Md. L. Rev. 869 (1990).

Nature of practice. — Fact that attorney had nonlawyers working for him did not transform his business from that of a law practice to a title business. Prahinski v. Prahinski, 75 Md. App. 113, 540 A.2d 833 (1988), aff'd, 321 Md. 227, 582 A.2d 784 (1990).

Important character traits. — Candor and truthfulness are two of the most important moral character traits of a lawyer. Attorney Grievance Comm'n v. Myers, 333 Md. 440, 635 A.2d 1315 (1994).

Comments from bench may be reversible error, even if counsel violates his ethical duty toward the court. Spencer v. State, 76 Md. App. 71, 543 A.2d 851 (1988).

Citation of relevant Fourth Circuit cases. — In this district, whenever a case from the Fourth Circuit comes anywhere close to being relevant to a disputed issue, the better part of wisdom is to cite it and attempt to distinguish it, and the matter will then be left for the judge to decide. While attorneys may still in time be judged unsuccessful in their attempt to distinguish the case, they will never be judged ethically omissive for failing to cite it. Massey v. Prince George's County, 918 F. Supp. 905 (D. Md. 1996).

Failure to inform authorities of completed crimes. — When client revealed to attorney that he had operated a motor vehicle when his license was expired, and that, unbeknownst to the arresting officer, he had given a fictitious name when arrested on DWI charge, attorney had no duty to inform authorities, as these were completed crimes; the attorney had a duty not to disclose them. Attorney Grievance Comm'n v. Rohrback, 323 Md. 79, 591 A.2d 488 (1991).

Failure to disclose client's use of fictitious name at presentence investigation interview. — A client awaiting sentencing has no constitutional right to counsel at presentence investigation interview; therefore, attorney's failure to disclose client's use of a fictitious name to the agent conducting the presentence investigation did not fall within the exception under paragraph (e) of this Rule, to the requirement of candor toward a tribunal. Attorney Grievance Comm'n v. Rohrback, 323 Md. 79, 591 A.2d 488 (1991).

Representation of multiple defendants in a criminal case. — An attorney's contact with his client's represented criminal codefendant was deemed a violation of this Rule and resulted in disbarment. Attorney Grievance Comm'n v. Kent, 337 Md. 361, 653 A.2d 909 (1995).

Respondent was deemed to have displayed a lack of candor to the tribunal where subsequent testimony to an inquiry board contradicted his testimony to the hearing court. Attorney Grievance Comm'n v. Kent, 337 Md. 361, 653 A.2d 909 (1995).

Fraud action. — One may not use the Maryland Rules of Professional Conduct as the basis of a fraud action. Maryland Nat'l Bank v. Resolution Trust Corp., 895 F. Supp. 762 (D. Md. 1995).

Maryland law refuses to impose liability for a breach of a rule of professional conduct; violation of a rule does not give rise to a cause of action and does not create a presumption that a legal duty has been breached. Maryland Nat'l Bank v. Resolution Trust Corp., 895 F. Supp. 762 (D. Md. 1995).

Disbarment appropriate. — Where an attorney violated paragraph (a)(1) of this Rule and Rule 8.4 (c) when he gave a false response to a question posed by a District Court judge concerning his traffic record due to his previous history of misconduct, he was disbarred. Attorney Grievance Comm'n v. Myers, 333 Md. 440, 635 A.2d 1315 (1994).

Ninety-day suspension was appropriate sanction for attorney's neglect of client's cases, falsifying client's signature on a complaint, and causing the complaint with the false signature to be notarized and filed. Attorney Grievance Comm'n v. Parsons, 310 Md. 132, 527 A.2d 325 (1987).

Disbarment was proper sanction. — Attorney was properly disbarred for violating Maryland Rules of Professional Conduct 1.1, 1.3, 1.4 (a) and (b), 1.15 (a), 3.3 (a)(1), and 8.4 (b) and (c), § 10-306 of the Business Occupations and Professions Article, and former Rule BU9 (now Rule 16-609) of the Maryland Rules of Procedure. Attorney Grievance Comm'n v. Williams, 335 Md. 458, 644 A.2d 490 (1994).

Applied in Massey v. Prince George's County, 907 F. Supp. 138 (D. Md. 1995).

Quoted in Magness v. Magness, 79 Md. App. 668, 558 A.2d 807 (1989); Gindes v. Khan, 346 Md. 143, 695 A.2d 163 (1997); Wilson v. Stanbury, 118 Md. App. 209, 702 A.2d 436 (1997).

Cited in In re Adoption No. 85365027, 71 Md. App. 362, 525 A.2d 1081 (1987); Stinnett v. Cort Furn. Rental, 315 Md. 448, 554 A.2d 1226 (1989); Gray v. State, 317 Md. 250, 562 A.2d 1278 (1989); Surratt v. Prince George's County, 320 Md. 439, 578 A.2d 745 (1990); Attorney Grievance Comm'n v. Protokowicz, 329 Md. 252, 619 A.2d 100 (1993); Venable v. State, 108 Md. App. 395, 672 A.2d 123 (1996); Attorney Grievance Comm'n v. Paugh, 345 Md. 692, 694 A.2d 106 (1997).

Rule 3.4. Fairness to opposing party and counsel.

A lawyer shall not:

(a) unlawfully obstruct another party's access to evidence or unlawfully alter, destroy or conceal a document or other material having potential evidentiary value. A lawyer shall not counsel or assist another person to do any such act;

(b) falsify evidence, counsel or assist a witness to testify falsely, or offer an inducement to a witness that is prohibited by law;

(c) knowingly disobey an obligation under the rules of a tribunal except for an open refusal based on an assertion that no valid obligation exists;

(d) in pretrial procedure, make a frivolous discovery request or fail to make reasonably diligent effort to comply with a legally proper discovery request by an opposing party;

(e) in trial, allude to any matter that the lawyer does not reasonably believe is relevant or that will not be supported by admissible evidence, assert personal knowledge of facts in issue except when testifying as a witness, or state a personal opinion as to the justness of a cause, the credibility of a witness, the culpability of a civil litigant or the guilt or innocence of an accused; or

(f) request a person other than a client to refrain from voluntarily giving relevant information to another party unless:

(1) the person is a relative or an employee or other agent of a client; and

(2) the lawyer reasonably believes that the person's interests will not be adversely affected by refraining from giving such information.

COMMENT

The procedure of the adversary system contemplates that the evidence in a case is to be marshalled competitively by the contending parties. Fair competition in the adversary system is secured by prohibitions against destruction or concealment of evidence, improperly influencing witnesses, obstructive tactics in discovery procedure, and the like.

Documents and other items of evidence are often essential to establish a claim or defense. Subject to evidentiary privileges, the right of an opposing party, including the government, to obtain evidence through discovery or subpoena is an important procedural right. The exercise of that right can be frustrated if relevant material is altered, concealed or destroyed. Applicable law in many jurisdictions makes it an offense to destroy material for purpose of impairing its availability in a pending proceeding or in one whose commencement can be foreseen. Falsifying evidence is also generally a criminal offense. Paragraph (a) applies to evidentiary material generally, including computerized information.

With regard to paragraph (b), it is not improper to pay a witness's expenses or to compensate an expert witness on terms permitted by law. The common law rule in most jurisdictions is that it is improper to pay an occurrence witness any fee for testifying and that it is improper to pay an expert witness a contingent fee.

Paragraph (f) permits a lawyer to advise employees of a client to refrain from giving information to another party, for the employees may identify their interests with those of the client. See also Rule 4.2.

Code Comparison. — With regard to Rule 3.4 (a), DR 7-109 (A) provides that "a lawyer shall not suppress any evidence that he or his client has a legal obligation to reveal." DR 7-109 (B) provides that "a lawyer shall not advise or cause a person to secrete himself ... for the purpose of making him unavailable as a witness...." DR 7-106 (C) (7) provides that a lawyer shall not "intentionally or habitually

violate any established rule of procedure or of evidence."

With regard to Rule 3-4 (b), DR 7-102 (B) (6) provides that a lawyer shall not "participate in the creation or preservation of evidence when he knows or it is obvious that the evidence is false." DR 7-109 provides that "a lawyer shall not pay, offer to pay, or acquiesce in the payment of compensation to a witness contingent on the content of his testimony or the outcome of the case. But a lawyer may advance, guarantee or acquiesce in the payment of: (1) expenses reasonably incurred by a witness in attending or testifying; (2) reasonable compensation to a witness for his loss of time in attending or testifying; (or) (3) a reasonable fee for the professional services of an expert witness." EC 7-28 states that "witnesses should always testify truthfully and should be free from any financial inducements that might tempt them to do otherwise."

Rule 3.4 (c) is substantially similar to DR 7-106 (A), which provides that "A lawyer shall not disregard ... a standing rule of a tribunal or a ruling of a tribunal made in the course of a proceeding, but he may take appropriate steps in good faith to test the validity of such rule or ruling."

Rule 3.4 (d) has no counterpart in the Code.

Rule 3.4 (e) substantially incorporates DR 7-106 (C) (1), (2), (3) and (4). DR 7-106 (C) (2) proscribes asking a question "intended to degrade a witness or other person," a matter dealt with in Rule 4.4. DR 7-106 (C) (5), providing that a lawyer shall not "fail to comply with known local customs of courtesy or practice," is too vague to be a rule of conduct enforceable as law.

With regard to Rule 3.4 (f), DR 7-104 (A) (2) provides that a lawyer shall not "give advice to a person who is not represented ... other than the advice to secure counsel, if the interests of such person are or have a reasonable possibility of being in conflict with the interests of his client."

Failure to report to a D.W.I. facility following a D.W.I. conviction was conduct prejudicial to the administration of justice and in violation of the Rules of Professional Conduct. Attorney Grievance Comm'n v. Garland, 345 Md. 383, 692 A.2d 465 (1997).

Representation of multiple defendants in a criminal case. — An attorney's contact with his client's represented criminal codefendant was deemed a violation of this Rule and resulted in disbarment. Attorney Grievance Comm'n v. Kent, 337 Md. 361, 653 A.2d 909 (1995).

Professional obligation to meet agreed upon extended deadline. — A lawyer who has requested and received an extension of time in which to answer interrogatories has a concomitant professional obligation to meet the agreed upon extended deadline, and failure to do so absent extenuating circumstances may well violate this Rule. Jayne H. Lee, Inc. v. Flagstaff Indus. Corp., 173 F.R.D. 651 (D. Md. 1997).

Rule not violated — This Rule was not violated where an attorney stated that "one learns to expect to get jerked around" when dealing with an insurance company, and called a driver in the case an "idiot." Attorney Grievance Comm'n v. Alison, 349 Md. 623, 709 A.2d 1212 (1998).

Acts not resulting in criminal conviction. — An attorney may be disciplined for acts which are criminal but do not result in a criminal conviction if Bar Counsel proves the underlying conduct at the disciplinary hearing. Attorney Grievance Comm'n v. Garland, 345 Md. 383, 692 A.2d 465 (1997).

Suspension warranted. — Although attorney's conduct was an aberration, the egregious nature of assisting a former client in breaking into the home of his wife in an attempt to recover evidence warranted the imposition of a significant sanction such that the attorney was suspended indefinitely from the practice of law with the right to apply for reinstatement not less than one year from the date of filing the opinion. Attorney Grievance Comm'n v. Protokowicz, 329 Md. 252, 619 A.2d 100 (1993).

Applied in Attorney Grievance Comm'n v. Ficker, 349 Md. 13, 706 A.2d 1045 (1998).

Quoted in Magness v. Magness, 79 Md. App. 668, 558 A.2d 807 (1989).

Cited in Carter v. State, 73 Md. App. 437, 534 A.2d 1015 (1988); Stinnett v. Cort Furn. Rental, 315 Md. 448, 554 A.2d 1226 (1989); Attorney Grievance Comm'n v. Dietz, 331 Md. 637, 629 A.2d 678 (1993); Attorney Grievance Comm'n v. Zeiger, 347 Md. 107, 698 A.2d 1115 (1997).

Rule 3.5. Impartiality and decorum of the tribunal.

(a) A lawyer shall not:

(1) seek to influence a judge, juror, prospective juror, or other official by means prohibited by law;

(2) before the trial of a case with which the lawyer is connected, communicate outside the course of official proceedings with anyone known to the lawyer to be on the list from which the jurors will be selected for the trial of the case;

(3) during the trial of a case with which the lawyer is connected, communicate outside the course of official proceedings with any member of the jury;

(4) during the trial of a case with which the lawyer is not connected, communicate outside the course of official proceedings with any member of the jury about the case;

(5) after discharge of a jury from further consideration of a case with which the lawyer is connected, ask questions of or make comments to a member of that jury that are calculated to harass or embarrass the juror or to influence the juror's actions in future jury service;

(6) conduct a vexatious or harassing investigation of any juror or prospective juror;

(7) communicate ex parte about an adversary proceeding with the judge or other official before whom the proceeding is pending, except as permitted by law; or

(8) engage in conduct intended to disrupt a tribunal.

(b) A lawyer who has knowledge of any violation of section (a) of this Rule, any improper conduct by a juror or prospective juror, or any improper conduct by another towards a juror or prospective juror, shall report it promptly to the court or other appropriate authority.

COMMENT

Many forms of improper influence upon a tribunal are proscribed by criminal law. Others are specified in the Maryland Canons and Rules of Judicial Ethics, with which an advocate should be familiar. A lawyer is required to avoid contributing to a violation of such provisions.

The advocate's function is to present evidence and argument so that the cause may be decided according to law. Refraining from abusive or obstreperous conduct is a corollary of the advocate's right to speak on behalf of litigants. A lawyer may stand firm against abuse by a judge but should avoid reciprocation; the judge's default is no justification for similar dereliction by an advocate. An advocate can present the cause, protect the record for subsequent review and preserve professional integrity by patient firmness no less effectively than by belligerence or theatrics.

With regard to the prohibition in subsection (a) (2) of this Rule against communications with anyone on "the list from which the jurors will be selected," see Rules 2-512 (c) and 4-312 (c) of the Maryland Rules of Procedure.

Code Comparison. — With regard to Rule 3.5 (a) and (b), DR 7-108 (A) provides that "before the trial of a case a lawyer ... shall not communicate with ... anyone he knows to be a member of the venire...." DR 7-108 (B) provides that "during the trial of a case ... a lawyer ... shall not communicate with ... a juror concerning the case." DR 7-109 (C) provides that a lawyer shall not "communicate ... as to the merits of the cause with a judge or an official before whom the proceeding is pending except ... upon adequate notice to opposing counsel ... (or) as otherwise authorized by law."

With regard to Rule 3.5 (a) (8), DR 7-106 (C) (6) provides that a lawyer shall not "engage in undignified or discourteous conduct which is degrading to a tribunal."

Ex parte communications. — Counsel's discussion with dentist member of arbitration panel, which occurred within the 30-day period during which a party may ask the arbitration panel to modify or correct an award, did not constitute an ex parte communication in violation of both the regulations of the Health Claims Arbitration Office and the Maryland Rules of Professional Conduct. Counsel's contact with dentist came subsequent to the pendency of the arbitration, at least as it concerned dentist. Carrion v. Linzey, 342 Md. 266, 675 A.2d 527 (1996).

Quoted in Magness v. Magness, 79 Md. App. 668, 558 A.2d 807 (1989).

Cited in Carter v. State, 73 Md. App. 437, 534 A.2d 1015 (1988); Attorney Grievance Comm'n v. Kerpelman, 323 Md. 136, 591 A.2d 516 (1991), cert. denied, 502 U.S. 939, 112 S. Ct. 374, 116 L. Ed. 2d 326 (1991).

Rule 3.6. Trial publicity.

(a) A lawyer shall not make an extrajudicial statement that a reasonable person would expect to be disseminated by means of public communication if the lawyer knows or reasonably should know that it will have a substantial likelihood of materially prejudicing an adjudicative proceeding.

(b) A statement referred to in paragraph (a) ordinarily is likely to have such an effect when it refers to a civil matter triable to a jury, a criminal matter, or any other proceeding that could result in incarceration, and the statement relates to:

(1) the character, credibility, reputation or criminal record of a party, suspect in a criminal investigation or witness, or the identity of a witness, or the expected testimony of a party or witness;

(2) in a criminal case or proceeding that could result in incarceration, the possibility of a plea of guilty to the offense or the existence or contents of any confession, admission, or statement given by a defendant or suspect or that person's refusal or failure to make a statement;

(3) the performance or results of any examination or test or the refusal or failure of a person to submit to an examination or test, or the identity or nature of physical evidence expected to be presented;

(4) any opinion as to the guilt or innocence of a defendant or suspect in a criminal case or proceeding that could result in incarceration;

(5) information the lawyer knows or reasonably should know is likely to be inadmissible as evidence in a trial and would if disclosed create a substantial risk of prejudicing an impartial trial; or

(6) the fact that a defendant has been charged with a crime, unless there is included therein a statement explaining that the charge is merely an accusation and that the defendant is presumed innocent until and unless proven guilty.

(c) Notwithstanding paragraph (a) and (b) (1-5), a lawyer involved in the investigation or litigation of a matter may state without elaboration:

(1) the general nature of the claim or defense;

(2) the information contained in a public record;

(3) that an investigation of the matter is in progress, including the general scope of the investigation, the offense or claim or defense involved and, except when prohibited by law, the identity of the persons involved;

(4) the scheduling or result of any step in litigation;

(5) a request for assistance in obtaining evidence and information necessary thereto;

(6) a warning of danger concerning the behavior of a person involved, when there is reason to believe that there exists the likelihood of substantial harm to an individual or to the public interest; and

(7) in a criminal case:

(i) the identity, residence, occupation and family status of the accused;

(ii) if the accused has not been apprehended, information necessary to aid in apprehension of that person;

(iii) the fact, time and place of arrest; and

(iv) the identity of investigating and arresting officers or agencies and the length of the investigation.

COMMENT

It is difficult to strike a balance between protecting the right to a fair trial and safeguarding the right of free expression. Preserving the right to a fair trial necessarily entails some curtailment of the information that may be disseminated about a party prior to trial, particularly where trial by jury is involved. If there were no such limits, the result would be the practical nullification of the protective effect of the rules of forensic decorum and the exclusionary rules of evidence. On the other hand, there are vital social interests served by the free dissemination of information about events having legal consequences and about legal proceedings themselves. The public has a right to know about threats to its safety and measures aimed at assuring its security. It also has a legitimate interest in the conduct of judicial proceedings, particularly in matters of general public concern. Furthermore, the subject matter of legal proceedings is often of direct significance in debate and deliberation over questions of public policy.

No body of rules can simultaneously satisfy all interests of fair trial and all those of free expression. The formula in this Rule is based upon the Code of Professional Responsibility and the ABA Standards Relating to Fair Trial and Free Press, as amended in 1978.

Special rules of confidentiality may validly govern proceedings in juvenile, domestic relations and mental disability proceedings, and perhaps other types of litigation. Rule 3.4 (c) requires compliance with such Rules.

491

Code Comparison. — Rule 3.6 is similar to DR 7-107, except as follows: First, Rule 3.6 adopts the general criteria of "substantial likelihood of materially prejudicing an adjudicative proceeding" to describe impermissible conduct. Second, Rule 3.6 transforms the particulars in DR 7-107 into an illustrative compilation that gives fair notice of conduct ordinarily posing unacceptable dangers to the fair administration of justice. Finally, Rule 3.6 omits DR 7-107 (C) (7), which provides that a lawyer may reveal "at the time of seizure, a description of the physical evidence seized, other than a confession, admission or statement." Such revelations may be substantially prejudicial and are frequently the subject of pretrial suppression motions, which, if successful, may be circumvented by prior disclosure to the press.

Rule 3.7. Lawyer as witness.

(a) A lawyer shall not act as advocate at a trial in which the lawyer is likely to be a necessary witness except where:

(1) the testimony relates to an uncontested issue;

(2) the testimony relates to the nature and value of legal services rendered in the case; or

(3) disqualification of the lawyer would work substantial hardship on the client.

(b) A lawyer may act as advocate in a trial in which another lawyer in the lawyer's firm is likely to be called as a witness unless precluded from doing so by Rule 1.7 or Rule 1.9.

COMMENT

Combining the roles of advocate and witness can prejudice the opposing party and can involve a conflict of interest between the lawyer and client.

The opposing party has proper objection where the combination of roles may prejudice that party's rights in the litigation. A witness is required to testify on the basis of personal knowledge, while an advocate is expected to explain and comment on evidence given by others. It may not be clear whether a statement by an advocate-witness should be taken as proof or as an analysis of the proof.

Paragraph (a) (1) recognizes that if the testimony will be uncontested, the ambiguities in the dual role are purely theoretical. Paragraph (a) (2) recognizes that where the testimony concerns the extent and value of legal services rendered in the action in which the testimony is offered, permitting the lawyers to testify avoids the need for a second trial with new counsel to resolve that issue. Moreover, in such a situation the judge has first hand knowledge of the matter in issue; hence, there is less dependence on the adversary process to test the credibility of the testimony.

Apart from these two exceptions, paragraph (a) (3) recognizes that a balancing is required between the interests of the client and those of the opposing party. Whether the opposing party is likely to suffer prejudice depends on the nature of the case, the importance and probable tenor of the lawyer's testimony, and the probability that the lawyer's testimony will conflict with that of other witnesses. Even if there is risk of such prejudice, in determining whether the lawyer should be disqualified due regard must be given to the effect of disqualification on the lawyer's client. It is relevant that one or both parties could reasonably foresee that the lawyer would probably be a witness. The principle of imputed disqualification stated in Rule 1.10 has no application to this aspect of the problem.

Whether the combination of roles involves an improper conflict of interest with respect to the client is determined by Rule 1.7 or 1.9. For example, if there is likely to be substantial conflict between the testimony of the client and that of the lawyer or a member of the lawyer's firm, the representation is improper. The problem can arise whether the lawyer is called as a witness on behalf of the client or is called by the opposing party. Determining whether or not such a conflict exists is primarily the responsibility of the lawyer involved. See Comment to Rule 1.7. If a lawyer who is a member of a firm may not act as both advocate and witness by reason of conflict of interest, Rule 1.10 disqualifies the firm also.

Code Comparison. — DR 5-102 (A) prohibits a lawyer, or the lawyer's firm, from serving as advocate if the lawyer "learns or it is obvious that he or a lawyer in his firm ought to be called as a witness on behalf of his client." DR 5-102 (B) provides that a lawyer, and the lawyer's firm, may continue representation if the "lawyer learns or it is obvious that he or a lawyer in his firm may be called as a witness other than on behalf of his client ... until it is apparent that his testimony is or may be prejudicial to his client." DR 5-101 (B) permits a lawyer to testify while representing a client: "(1) If the testimony will relate solely to an uncontested matter; (2) If the testimony will relate solely to a matter of formality and there is no reason to believe that substantial evidence will be offered in opposition to the testimony; (3) If the testimony will relate solely to

the nature and value of legal services rendered in the case by the lawyer or his firm to the client; (4) As to any matter if refusal would work a substantial hardship on the client because of the distinctive value of the lawyer or his firm as counsel in the particular case."

The exception stated in (a) (1) consolidates provisions of DR 5-101 (B) (1) and (2). Testimony relating to a formality, referred to in DR 5-101 (B) (2), in effect defines the phrase "uncontested issue," and is redundant.

Defense counsel as State's witness. — Allowing defense counsel to be called as State's witness does not constitute a per se violation of either this section or the Constitution. Venable v. State, 108 Md. App. 395, 672 A.2d 123 (1996).

Although the issue of whether a party can call opposing counsel to testify is ordinarily within the discretion of the trial judge, in exercising that discretion during a criminal trial the judge must weigh the materiality of defense counsel's testimony versus the defendant's constitutional rights, and must also consider the extent to which defense counsel's credibility as an advocate will be adversely affected. Venable v. State, 108 Md. App. 395, 672 A.2d 123 (1996).

Whenever the prosecutor calls defense counsel to the stand, the trial judge must (1) require that the prosecutor make a detailed and complete proffer of what he or she expects defense counsel's testimony will be; (2) afford defense counsel an opportunity to respond; and (3) consider alternate methods of presenting any evidence that the prosecutor is entitled to introduce through defense counsel's testimony. If the court determines that the State is entitled to defense counsel's testimony, the court must next determine whether the defendant — not defense counsel — wants the assistance of another lawyer while defense counsel is on the stand. Venable v. State, 108 Md. App. 395, 672 A.2d 123 (1996).

Putting a defense counsel in the position of a prosecution witness is something that should be avoided whenever possible because defense counsel is called to testify as a State's witness,

(1) it is impossible for the defendant to consult with the attorney; (2) the defendant cannot call attention to any inaccuracy in the attorney's testimony or suggest proper questions for cross-examination; (3) it is difficult, to say the least, for the lawyer, as a witness, to determine what objections should be made to questions asked him; (4) it is difficult for the lawyer to determine what questions to ask himself on cross-examination, and if he attempts to cross-examine himself the proceedings may take on a ludicrous appearance, and (5) it is difficult for the lawyer to answer questions so as to not antagonize the jury and still maintain a favorable impression. Venable v. State, 108 Md. App. 395, 672 A.2d 123 (1996).

Where prosecutor testifies as to exercise of peremptory juror challenges. — Although this rule may suggest the advisability of having a second prosecutor available, whenever practicable, to argue the matter of alleged racial discrimination in exercising peremptory juror challenges when another prosecutor has been required to formally testify, this rule would in no way impair the ability of the testifying prosecutor to proceed with the trial on the merits. Gray v. State, 317 Md. 250, 562 A.2d 1278 (1989).

Quoted in Harris v. Harris, 310 Md. 310, 529 A.2d 356 (1987); Medical Mut. Liab. Ins. Soc'y v. Evans, 330 Md. 1, 622 A.2d 103 (1993).

Stated in In re Criminal Investigation No. 1/296X, 336 Md. 1, 646 A.2d 389 (1994).

Cited in Attorney Grievance Comm'n v. Hallmon, 343 Md. 390, 681 A.2d 510 (1996); Post v. Bregman, 349 Md. 142, 707 A.2d 806 (1998).

Rule 3.8. Special responsibilities of a prosecutor.

The prosecutor in a criminal case shall:

(a) refrain from prosecuting a charge that the prosecutor knows is not supported by probable cause;

(b) make reasonable efforts to assure that the accused has been advised of the right to, and the procedure for obtaining, counsel and has been given reasonable opportunity to obtain counsel;

(c) not seek to obtain from an unrepresented accused a waiver of important pretrial rights, such as the right to a preliminary hearing;

(d) make timely disclosure to the defense of all evidence or information known to the prosecutor that tends to negate the guilt of the accused or mitigates the offense, and, in connection with sentencing, disclose to the defense and to the tribunal all unprivileged mitigating information known to the prosecutor, except when the prosecutor is relieved of this responsibility by a protective order of the tribunal; and

(e) exercise reasonable care to prevent an employee or other person under the control of the prosecutor in a criminal case from making an extrajudicial statement that the prosecutor would be prohibited from making under Rule 3.6.

COMMENT

A prosecutor has the responsibility of a minister of justice and not simply that of an advocate. This responsibility carries with it specific obligations to see that the defendant is accorded procedural justice and that guilt is decided upon the basis of sufficient evidence. Precisely how far the prosecutor is required to go in this direction is a matter of debate and varies in different jurisdictions. Many jurisdictions have adopted the ABA Standards of Criminal Justice Relating to Prosecution Function, which in turn are the product of prolonged and careful deliberation by lawyers experienced in both criminal prosecution and defense. See also Rule 3.3 (d), governing ex parte proceedings, among which grand jury proceedings are included. Applicable law may require other measures by the prosecutor and knowing disregard of those obligations or a systematic abuse of prosecutorial discretion could constitute a violation of Rule 8.4.

Paragraph (c) does not apply to an accused appearing pro se with the approval of the tribunal. Nor does it forbid the lawful questioning of a suspect who has knowingly waived the rights to counsel and silence.

The exception in paragraph (d) recognizes that a prosecutor may seek an appropriate protective order from the tribunal if disclosure of information to the defense could result in substantial harm to an individual or to the public interest.

Code Comparison. — DR 7-103 (A) provides that "A public prosecutor ... shall not institute ... criminal charges when he knows or it is obvious that the charges are not supported by probable cause." DR 7-103 (B) provides that "A public prosecutor ... shall make timely disclosure ... of the existence of evidence, known to the prosecutor ... that tends to negate the guilt of the accused, mitigate the degree of the offense, or reduce the punishment."

Rule 3.9. Advocate in nonadjudicative proceedings.

A lawyer representing a client before a legislative or administrative tribunal in a nonadjudicative proceeding shall disclose that the appearance is in a representative capacity and shall conform to the provisions of Rules 3.3 (a) through (c), 3.4 (a) through (c), and 3.5.

COMMENT

In representation before bodies such as legislatures, municipal councils, and executive and administrative agencies acting in a rule-making or policy-making capacity, lawyers present facts, formulate issues and advance argument in the matters under consideration. The decision-making body, like a court, should be able to rely on the integrity of the submissions made to it. A lawyer appearing before such a body should deal with the tribunal honestly and in conformity with applicable rules of procedure.

Lawyers have no exclusive right to appear before nonadjudicative bodies, as they do before a court. The requirements of this Rule therefore may subject lawyers to regulations inapplicable to advocates who are not lawyers. However, legislatures and administrative agencies have a right to expect lawyers to deal with them as they deal with courts.

This Rule does not apply to representation of a client in a negotiation or other bilateral transaction with a governmental agency; representation in such a transaction is governed by Rules 4.1 through 4.4.

Code Comparison. — EC 7-15 states that "A lawyer appearing before an administrative agency, regardless of the nature of the proceeding it is conducting, has the continuing duty to advance the cause of his client within the bounds of the law." EC 7-16 states that "When a lawyer appears in connection with proposed legislation, he ... should comply with applicable laws and regulations." EC 8-5 states that "Fraudulent, deceptive, or otherwise illegal conduct by a participant in a proceeding before a ... legislative body should never be participated in ... by lawyers." DR 7-106 (B) (1) provides that "In presenting a matter to a tribunal, a lawyer shall disclose ... unless privileged or irrelevant, the identity of the clients he represents and of the persons who employed him."

TRANSACTIONS WITH PERSONS OTHER THAN CLIENTS.

Rule 4.1. Truthfulness in statements to others.

(a) In the course of representing a client a lawyer shall not knowingly:

(1) make a false statement of material fact or law to a third person; or

(2) fail to disclose a material fact to a third person when disclosure is necessary to avoid assisting a criminal or fraudulent act by a client.

(b) The duties stated in this Rule apply even if compliance requires disclosure of information otherwise protected by Rule 1.6.

COMMENT

Misrepresentation. — A lawyer is required to be truthful when dealing with others on a client's behalf, but generally has no affirmative duty to inform an opposing party of relevant facts. A misrepresentation can occur if the lawyer incorporates or affirms a statement of another person that the lawyer knows is false. Misrepresentations can also occur by failure to act.

Statements of fact. — This Rule refers to statements of fact. Whether a particular statement should be regarded as one of fact can depend on the circumstances. Under generally accepted conventions in negotiation, certain types of statements ordinarily are not taken as statements of material fact. Estimates of price or value placed on the subject of a transaction and a party's intentions as to an acceptable settlement of a claim are in this category, and so is the existence of an undisclosed principal except where nondisclosure of the principal would constitute fraud.

Fraud by client. — This Rule governs representation by a lawyer. The critical elements under paragraph (a) (1) are the making of a statement by the lawyer and the lawyer's knowledge that the statement is false. Paragraph (a) (2) is essentially a special instance of the duty under Rule 1.2 (d), which forbids a lawyer to assist a client in conduct that is criminal or fraudulent.

Disclosure. — As noted in the Comment to Rule 1.6, the duty imposed by Rule 4.1 may require a lawyer to disclose information that otherwise is confidential and to correct or withdraw a statement. However, the constitutional rights of defendants in criminal cases may limit the extent to which counsel for a defendant may correct a misrepresentation that is based on information provided by the client. See Comment to Rule 3.3.

Code Comparison. — Rule 4.1 (a) (1) is substantially similar to DR 7-102 (A) (5), which states that "In his representation of a client, a lawyer shall not ... knowingly make a false statement of law or fact."

With regard to Rules 4.1 (a) (2) and 4.1 (b), DR 7-102 (A) (3) provides that a lawyer shall not "conceal or knowingly fail to disclose that which he is required by law to reveal."

University of Baltimore Law Forum. — For discussion of the code of ethics, see 17, No. 1 U. Balt. Law Forum 31 (1986).

Failure to inform authorities of completed crimes. — When client revealed to attorney that he had operated a motor vehicle when his license was expired, and that, unbeknownst to the arresting officer, he had given a fictitious name when arrested on DWI charge, attorney had no duty to inform authorities, as these were completed crimes; the attorney had a duty not to disclose them. Attorney Grievance Comm'n v. Rohrback, 323 Md. 79, 591 A.2d 488 (1991).

Failure to disclose client's use of fictitious name at presentence investigation interview. — A client awaiting sentencing has no constitutional right to counsel at presentence investigation interview; therefore, attorney's failure to disclose client's use of a fictitious name to the agent conducting the presentence investigation did not fall within the exception under paragraph (e) of Rule 3.3 to the requirement of candor toward a tribunal. Attorney Grievance Comm'n v. Rohrback,

323 Md. 79, 591 A.2d 488 (1991).

Ninety-day suspension was appropriate sanction for attorney's neglect of client's cases, falsifying client's signature on a complaint, and causing the complaint with the false signature to be notarized and filed. Attorney Grievance Comm'n v. Parsons, 310 Md. 132, 527 A.2d 325 (1987).

Quoted in Attorney Grievance Comm'n v. Awuah, 346 Md. 420, 697 A.2d 446 (1997); Attorney Grievance Comm'n v. Webster, 348 Md. 662, 705 A.2d 1135 (1998).

Cited in Attorney Grievance Comm'n v. Zeiger, 347 Md. 107, 698 A.2d 1115 (1997); Wilson v. Stanbury, 118 Md. App. 209, 702 A.2d 436 (1997).

Rule 4.2. Communication with person represented by counsel.

In representing a client, a lawyer shall not communicate about the subject of the representation with a party the lawyer knows to be represented by another lawyer in the matter, unless the lawyer has the consent of the other lawyer or is authorized by law to do so.

COMMENT

This Rule does not prohibit communication with a party, or an employee or agent of a party, concerning matters outside the representation. For example, the existence of a controversy between a government agency and a private party, or between two organizations, does not prohibit a lawyer for either from communicating with nonlawyer representatives of the other regarding a separate matter. Also, parties to a matter may communicate directly with each other and a lawyer having independent justification for communicating with the other party is permitted to do so. Communications authorized by law include, for example, the right of a party to a controversy with a government agency to speak with government officials about the matter.

In the case of an organization, this Rule prohibits communications by a lawyer for one party concerning the matter in representation with persons having a managerial responsibility on behalf of the organization, and with any other person whose act or omission in connection with that matter may be imputed to the organization for purposes of civil or criminal liability or whose statement may constitute an admission on the part of the organization. If an agent or employee of the organization is represented in the matter by his or her own counsel, the consent by that counsel to a communication will be sufficient for purposes of this Rule. Compare Rule 3.4 (f).

This Rule also covers any person, whether or not a party to a formal proceeding, who is represented by counsel concerning the matter in question.

Code Comparison. — This Rule is substantially identical to DR 7-104 (A) (1).

Maryland Law Review. — For article, "Conducting Informal Discovery of a Party's Former Employees: Legal and Ethical Concerns and Constraints," see 51 Md. L. Rev. 239 (1992).

Purpose of Rule. — Protection of information covered by the attorney-client privilege (as well as the work product privilege) has been traditionally cited as one of the prime objectives of the no-contact rule. Camden v. Maryland, 910 F. Supp. 1115 (D. Md. 1996).

Representation of multiple defendants in a criminal case. — An attorney's contact

with his client's represented criminal codefendant was deemed a violation of this Rule and resulted in disbarment. Attorney Grievance Comm'n v. Kent, 337 Md. 361, 653 A.2d 909 (1995).

Other interested parties. — Other interested parties, for purposes of determining whether a lawyer may have ex parte contact with a former employee of an interested party, include corporations and other organizations. Camden v. Maryland, 910 F. Supp. 1115 (D. Md. 1996).

Plaintiff's counsel violated rule by engaging

in ex parte contact with a former employee of the defendants whom plaintiff's counsel well knew had been extensively exposed to confidential information; accordingly, appropriate remedy for violation of rule was disqualification of counsel from any further representation in the matters covered by lawsuit. Zachair, Ltd. v. Driggs, 965 F. Supp. 741 (D. Md. 1997), aff'd, 141 F.3d 1162 (4th Cir. 1998). **This Rule did not apply to criminal investigation of corporation and certain of its employees** where corporation sought ex parte injunction to prevent interviews of any of its employees by Attorney General's office without consent and presence of corporation counsel. In re Criminal Investigation No. 13, 82 Md. App. 609, 573 A.2d 51 (1990).

A prosecutor's use of a wired informant for the purpose of recording conversations with the represented target of a criminal investigation, even to the point of suggesting topics to be discussed, does not violate professional disciplinary rules. United States v. Marcus, 849 F. Supp. 417 (D. Md. 1994), aff'd, 82 F.3d 606 (4th Cir. 1996).

Applied in Davidson Supply Co. v. P.P.E., Inc., 986 F. Supp. 956 (D. Md. 1997).

Rule 4.3. Dealing with unrepresented person.

In dealing on behalf of a client with a person who is not represented by counsel, a lawyer shall not state or imply that the lawyer is disinterested. When the lawyer knows or reasonably should know that the unrepresented person misunderstands the lawyer's role in the matter, the lawyer shall make reasonable efforts to correct the misunderstanding.

COMMENT

An unrepresented person, particularly one not experienced in dealing with legal matters, might assume that a lawyer is disinterested in loyalties or is a disinterested authority on the law even when the lawyer represents a client. During the course of a lawyer's representation of a client, the lawyer should not give advice to an unrepresented person other than the advice to obtain counsel.

Code Comparison. — There is no direct counterpart to this Rule in the Code. DR 7-104 (A) (2) provides that a lawyer shall not "[g]ive advice to a person who is not represented by a lawyer, other than the advice to secure counsel...."

Rule 4.4. Respect for rights of third persons.

In representing a client, a lawyer shall not use means that have no substantial purpose other than to embarrass, delay, or burden a third person, or use methods of obtaining evidence that the lawyer knows violate the legal rights of such a person.

COMMENT

Responsibility to a client requires a lawyer to subordinate the interests of others to those of the client, but that responsibility does not imply that a lawyer may disregard the rights of third persons. It is impractical to catalogue all such rights, but they include legal restrictions on methods of obtaining evidence from third persons.

Code Comparison. — DR 7-106 (C) (2) provides that a lawyer shall not "ask any question that he has no reasonable basis to believe is relevant to the case and that is intended to degrade a witness or other person."

DR 7-102 (A) (1) provides that a lawyer shall not "take ... action on behalf of his client when he knows or when it is obvious that such action would serve merely to harass or maliciously injure another." DR 7-108 (D) provides that "after discharge of the jury ... the lawyer shall not ask questions or make comments to a member of that jury that are calculated merely to harass or embarrass the juror...." DR 7-108 (E) provides that "a lawyer shall not conduct ... a vexatious or harassing investigation of either a venireman or a juror."

Cited in Attorney Grievance Comm'n v. Protokowicz, 329 Md. 252, 619 A.2d 100 (1993).

LAW FIRMS AND ASSOCIATIONS.

Rule 5.1. Responsibilities of a partner or supervisory lawyer.

(a) A partner in a law firm shall make reasonable efforts to ensure that the firm has in effect measures giving reasonable assurance that all lawyers in the firm conform to the rules of professional conduct.

(b) A lawyer having direct supervisory authority over another lawyer shall make reasonable efforts to ensure that the other lawyer conforms to the rules of professional conduct.

(c) A lawyer shall be responsible for another lawyer's violation of the rules of professional conduct if:

(1) the lawyer orders or, with knowledge of the specific conduct, ratifies the conduct involved; or

(2) the lawyer is a partner in the law firm in which the other lawyer practices, or has direct supervisory authority over the other lawyer, and knows of the conduct at a time when its consequences can be avoided or mitigated but fails to take reasonable remedial action.

COMMENT

Paragraphs (a) and (b) refer to lawyers who have supervisory authority over the professional work of a firm or legal department of a government agency. This includes members of a partnership and the shareholders in a law firm organized as a professional corporation; lawyers having supervisory authority in the law department of an enterprise or government agency; and lawyers who have intermediate managerial responsibilities in a firm.

The measures required to fulfill the responsibility prescribed in paragraphs (a) and (b) can depend on the firm's structure and the nature of its practice. In a small firm, informal supervision and occasional admonition ordinarily might be sufficient. In a large firm, or in practice situations in which intensely difficult ethical problems frequently arise, more elaborate procedures may be necessary. Some firms, for example, have a procedure whereby junior lawyers can make confidential referral of ethical problems directly to a designated senior partner or special committee. See Rule 5.2. Firms, whether large or small, may also rely on continuing legal education in professional ethics. In any event, the ethical atmosphere of a firm can influence the conduct of all its members and a lawyer having authority over the work of another may not assume that the subordinate lawyer will inevitably conform to the Rules.

Paragraph (c) (1) expresses a general principle of responsibility for acts of another. See also Rule 8.4 (a).

Paragraph (c) (2) defines the duty of a lawyer having direct supervisory authority over performance of specific legal work by another lawyer. Whether a lawyer has such supervisory authority in particular circumstances is a question of fact. Partners of a private firm have at least indirect responsibility for all work being done by the firm, while a partner in charge of a particular matter ordinarily has direct authority over other firm lawyers engaged in the matter. Appropriate remedial action by a partner would depend on the immediacy of the partner's involvement and the seriousness of the misconduct. The supervisor is required to intervene to prevent avoidable consequences of misconduct if the supervisor knows that the misconduct occurred. Thus, if a supervising lawyer knows that a subordinate misrepresented a matter to an opposing party in negotiation, the supervisor as well as the subordinate has a duty to correct the resulting misapprehension.

Professional misconduct by a lawyer under supervision could reveal a violation of paragraph (b) on the part of the supervisory lawyer even though it does not entail a violation of paragraph (c) because there was no direction, ratification or knowledge of the violation.

Apart from this Rule and Rule 8.4 (a), a lawyer does not have disciplinary liability for the conduct of a partner, associate or subordinate. Whether a lawyer may be liable civilly or criminally for another lawyer's conduct is a question of law beyond the scope of these Rules.

Code Comparison. — There is no direct counterpart to this Rule in the Code. DR 1-103 (A) provides that "A lawyer possessing unprivileged knowledge of a violation of DR 1-102 shall report such knowledge to ... authority empowered to investigate or act upon such violation."

University of Baltimore Law Forum. — For discussion of the code of ethics, see 17, No. 1 U. Balt. Law Forum 31 (1986).

For article, "Recent Developments," see 18.3 U. Balt. Law Forum 32 (1988).

Delegation of workload. — An attorney's practice of assigning and handling cases in such a manner that the lawyer ultimately charged with actually representing the client went into court unprepared, or missed scheduled trial dates entirely, resulted in clients not being afforded competent representation, and justified an indefinite suspension from the practice of law. Attorney Grievance Comm'n v. Ficker, 349 Md. 13, 706 A.2d 1045 (1998).

Rule 5.2. Responsibilities of a subordinate lawyer.

(a) A lawyer is bound by the rules of professional conduct notwithstanding that the lawyer acted at the direction of another person.

(b) A subordinate lawyer does not violate the rules of professional conduct if that lawyer acts in accordance with a supervisory lawyer's reasonable resolution of an arguable question of professional duty.

COMMENT

Although a lawyer is not relieved of responsibility for a violation by the fact that the lawyer acted at the direction of a supervisor, that fact may be relevant in determining whether a lawyer had the knowledge required to render conduct a violation of the Rules. For example, if a subordinate filed a frivolous pleading at the direction of a supervisor, the subordinate would not be guilty of a professional violation unless the subordinate knew of the document's frivolous character.

When lawyers in a supervisor-subordinate relationship encounter a matter involving professional judgment as to ethical duty, the supervisor may assume responsibility for making the judgment. Otherwise a consistent course of action or position could not be taken. If the question can reasonably be answered only one way, the duty of both lawyers is clear and they are equally responsible for fulfilling it. However, if the question is reasonably arguable, someone has to decide upon the course of action. That authority ordinarily reposes in the supervisor, and a subordinate may be guided accordingly. For example, if a question arises whether the interests of two clients conflict under Rule 1.7, the supervisor's reasonable resolution of the question should protect the subordinate professionally if the resolution is subsequently challenged.

Code Comparison. — There is no counterpart to this Rule in the Code.

Rule 5.3. Responsibilities regarding nonlawyer assistants.

With respect to a nonlawyer employed or retained by or associated with a lawyer:

(a) a partner in a law firm shall make reasonable efforts to ensure that the firm has in effect measures giving reasonable assurance that the person's conduct is compatible with the professional obligations of the lawyer;

(b) a lawyer having direct supervisory authority over the nonlawyer shall make reasonable efforts to ensure that the person's conduct is compatible with the professional obligations of the lawyer; and

(c) a lawyer shall be responsible for conduct of such a person that would be a violation of the rules of professional conduct if engaged in by a lawyer if:

(1) the lawyer orders or, with the knowledge of the specific conduct, ratifies the conduct involved; or

(2) the lawyer is a partner in the law firm in which the person is employed, or has direct supervisory authority over the person, and knows of the conduct at a time when its consequences can be avoided or mitigated but fails to take reasonable remedial action.

COMMENT

Lawyers generally employ assistants in their practice, including secretaries, investigators, law student interns, and paraprofessionals. Such assistants, whether employees or independent contractors, act for the lawyer in rendition of the lawyer's professional services. A lawyer should give such assistants appropriate instruction and supervision concerning the ethical aspects of their employment, particularly regarding the obligation not to disclose information relating to representation of the client, and should be responsible for their work product. The measures employed in supervising nonlawyers should take account of the fact that they do not have legal training and are not subject to professional discipline.

Code Comparison. — There is no direct counterpart to this Rule in the Code. DR 4-101 (D) provides that "A lawyer shall exercise reasonable care to prevent his employees, associates, and others whose services are utilized by him from disclosing or using confidences or secrets of a client...." DR 7-107 (J) provides that "a lawyer shall exercise reasonable care to prevent his employees and associates from making an extrajudicial statement that he would be prohibited from making under DR 7-107."

Indefinite suspension was proper sanction. — Where respondent attorney's representation of four clients was marked by serious neglect and inattention; where he failed to return a fee which was unearned for a period of nine months; where he failed to timely remit funds he received on behalf of a client; where he failed to communicate with his clients; and where, in connection with the investigation of three of the complaints, respondent failed to answer Bar Counsel's requests for information, the proper sanction was that the attorney be indefinitely suspended from the practice of law, with the right to apply for reinstatement after the suspension had been in effect for six months, conditioned upon his payment of all costs and upon the monitoring of respondent's practice. Attorney Grievance Comm'n v. David, 331 Md. 317, 628 A.2d 178 (1993).

Disbarment was proper sanction. — Disbarment of attorney was appropriate where there were serious and repeated violations of this Rule and other provisions of the Maryland Rules of Professional Conduct. Attorney Grievance Comm'n v. Milliken, 348 Md. 486, 704 A.2d 1225 (1998).

Duty to determine that employees perform competently. — An attorney may not escape responsibility to his clients by blithely saying that any shortcomings are solely the fault of his employee; an attorney must ascertain that his or her employees perform their responsibilities in a competent manner. Attorney Grievance Comm'n v. Glenn, 341 Md. 448, 671 A.2d 463 (1996).

Stated in Attorney Grievance Comm'n v. Ficker, 349 Md. 13, 706 A.2d 1045 (1998).

Cited in Prahinski v. Prahinski, 321 Md. 227, 582 A.2d 784 (1990); Attorney Grievance Comm'n v. Drew, 341 Md. 139, 669 A.2d 1344 (1996); Attorney Grievance Comm'n v. Gregory, 346 Md. 600, 697 A.2d 898 (1997).

Rule 5.4. Professional independence of a lawyer.

(a) A lawyer or law firm shall not share legal fees with a nonlawyer, except that:

(1) an agreement by a lawyer with the lawyer's firm, partner, or associate may provide for the payment of money, over a reasonable period of time after the lawyer's death, to the lawyer's estate or to one or more specified persons;

(2) a lawyer who undertakes to complete unfinished legal business of a deceased lawyer may pay to the estate of the deceased lawyer that proportion

of the total compensation which fairly represents the services rendered by the deceased lawyer; and

(3) a lawyer or law firm may include nonlawyer employees in a compensation or retirement plan, even though the plan is based in whole or in part on a profit-sharing arrangement.

(b) A lawyer shall not form a partnership with a nonlawyer if any of the activities of the partnership consist of the practice of law.

(c) A lawyer shall not permit a person who recommends, employs, or pays the lawyer to render legal services for another to direct or regulate the lawyer's professional judgment in rendering such legal services.

(d) A lawyer shall not practice with or in the form of a professional corporation or association authorized to practice law for a profit, if:

(1) a nonlawyer owns any interest therein, except that a fiduciary representative of the estate of a lawyer may hold the stock or interest of the lawyer for a reasonable time during administration;

(2) a nonlawyer is a corporate director or officer thereof; or

(3) a nonlawyer has the right to direct or control the professional judgment of a lawyer.

COMMENT

The provisions of this Rule express traditional limitations on sharing fees. These limitations are to protect the lawyer's professional independence of judgment. Where someone other than the client pays the lawyer's fee or salary, or recommends employment of the lawyer, that arrangement does not modify the lawyer's obligation to the client. As stated in paragraph (c), such arrangements should not interfere with the lawyer's professional judgment.

Code Comparison. — DR 3-102 (A) provides that "A lawyer or law firm shall not share legal fees with a nonlawyer... ." DR 3-103 (A) provides that "A lawyer shall not form a partnership with a nonlawyer if any of the activities of the partnership consist of the practice of law." DR 5-107 (B) provides that "A lawyer shall not permit a person who recommends, employs, or pays him to render legal services for another to direct or regulate his professional judgment in rendering such legal services." DR 5-107 (C) provides that "A lawyer shall not practice with or in the form of a professional corporation or association authorized to practice law for a profit, if: (1) A nonlawyer owns any interests therein, except that a fiduciary representative of the estate of a lawyer may hold the stock or interest of the lawyer for a reasonable time during administration; (2) A nonlawyer is a corporate director or officer

thereof; or (3) A nonlawyer has the right to direct or control the professional judgment of the lawyer." EC 5-24 states that "A lawyer should not practice with or in the form of a professional legal corporation, even though the corporate form is permitted by law, if any director, officer, or stockholder of it is a nonlawyer. Although a lawyer may be employed by a business corporation with nonlawyers serving as directors or officers, and they necessarily have the right to make decisions of business policy, a lawyer must decline to accept direction of his professional judgment from any layman. Various types of legal aid offices are administered by boards of directors composed of lawyers and laymen. A lawyer should not accept employment from such an organization unless the board sets only broad policies and there is no interference in the relationship of the lawyer and the individual client he serves. Where a lawyer is employed by an organization, a written agreement that defines the relationship between him and the organization and provides for his independence is desirable since it may serve to prevent misunderstanding as to their respective roles. Although other innovations in the means of supplying legal counsel may develop, the responsibility of the lawyer to maintain his professional independence remains constant...."

501

Professional service corporations. — When the conduct of a lawyer in a professional service corporation is called into question with reference to the attorney-client relationship, the Rules of Professional Conduct will apply and not those of an ordinary business corporation. Where, however, the situation involves a dispute between shareholders of the professional service corporation, the corporate law should not be disregarded in favor of partnership law. Langhoff v. Marr, 81 Md. App. 438, 568 A.2d 844 (1990), vacated and remanded, 322 Md. 657, 589 A.2d 470 (1991).

Agent of nonlawyer. — Defendant was an agent for Burrus trading as Life Investors. Although he improperly participated in a referral arrangement, this does not amount to a partnership with a nonlawyer. Attorney Grievance Comm'n v. Martin, 308 Md. 272, 518 A.2d 1050 (1987).

Nonlawyer spouse as partner. — Because nonlawyer spouse could not be a partner in the attorney's spouse's practice, she could not claim a partner's interest in the practice upon her divorce from her lawyer husband, and therefore the goodwill of the practice could not be included as marital property. Prahinski v. Prahinski, 321 Md. 227, 582 A.2d 784 (1990).

Illegal contract claims. — The Rules of Professional Conduct are not statements of public policy on which an illegal contract claim may be founded. Son v. Margolius, Mallios, Davis, Rider & Tomar, 114 Md. App. 190, 689 A.2d 645 (1997).

Disbarment was proper sanction. — Disbarment of attorney was appropriate where there were serious and repeated violations of this Rule and other provisions of the Maryland Rules of Professional Conduct. Attorney Grievance Comm'n v. Milliken, 348 Md. 486, 704 A.2d 1225 (1998).

Applied in Son v. Margolius, Mallios, Davis, Rider & Tomar, 349 Md. 441, 709 A.2d 112 (1998).

Quoted in Hollander v. Hollander, 89 Md. App. 156, 597 A.2d 1012 (1991).

Cited in Post v. Bregman, 349 Md. 142, 707 A.2d 806 (1998).

Rule 5.5. Unauthorized practice of law.

A lawyer shall not:

(a) practice law in a jurisdiction where doing so violates the regulation of the legal profession in that jurisdiction; or

(b) assist a person who is not a member of the bar in the performance of activity that constitutes the unauthorized practice of law.

COMMENT

The definition of the practice of law is established by law and varies from one jurisdiction to another. Whatever the definition, limiting the practice of law to members of the bar protects the public against rendition of legal services by unqualified persons. Paragraph (b) does not prohibit a lawyer from employing the services of paraprofessionals and delegating functions to them, so long as the lawyer supervises the delegated work and retains responsibility for their work. See Rule 5.3. Likewise, it does not prohibit lawyers from providing professional advice and instruction to nonlawyers whose employment requires knowledge of law; for example, claims adjusters, employees of financial or commercial institutions, social workers, accountants and persons employed in government agencies. In addition, a lawyer may counsel nonlawyers who wish to proceed pro se.

Code Comparison. — With regard to Rule 5.5 (a), DR 3-101 (B) of the Model Code provides that "a lawyer shall not practice law in a jurisdiction where to do so would be in violation of regulations of the profession in that jurisdiction."

With regard to Rule 5.5 (b), DR 3-101 (A) of the Model Code provides that "a lawyer shall not aid a nonlawyer in the unauthorized practice of law."

The purpose of this Rule is to protect the public from being preyed upon by those not competent to practice law – from incompetent, unethical, or irresponsible representation; that goal is achieved by emphasizing the insulation of the unlicensed person from the public and from tribunals such as courts and certain administrative agencies. Attorney Grievance Comm'n v. Hallmon, 343 Md. 390, 681 A.2d 510 (1996).

To determine whether an individual has engaged in the practice of law, the focus of the inquiry should be on whether the activity in question required legal knowledge and skill in order to apply legal principles and precedent; where trial work is not involved but the preparation of legal documents, their interpretation, the giving of legal advice, or the application of legal principles to problems of any complexity is involved, these activities are still the practice of law. Attorney Grievance Comm'n v. Hallmon, 343 Md. 390, 681 A.2d 510 (1996).

Lay advocates. — A lay advocate who provides certain services to victims of domestic violence may provide basic information about the existence of legal rights and remedies; may provide basic information about the manner in which judicial proceedings are conducted; may assist victims in preparing legal pleadings or other legal documents on her own behalf by defining unfamiliar terms on a form, explaining where on a form the victim is to provide certain information, and if necessary transcribing or otherwise recording the victim's own words verbatim; may sit with a victim at trial table, if permitted by the court; and may engage in the general advocacy of the rights of battered women as a group. 80 Op. Att'y Gen. (Dec. 19, 1995).

Except under the supervision of an attorney, a lay advocate may not provide any advice relating to a victim's rights or remedies, including whether a victim's particular circumstances suggest that she should pursue a particular remedy; may not provide information about the legal aspects of judicial proceedings, such as how to present a case, call witnesses, introduce evidence, and the like; may not use the advocate's own language in preparing or filling out form pleadings or other legal documents; or may not engage in advocacy before any governmental representative on behalf of an individual victim. 80 Op. Att'y Gen. (Dec. 19, 1995).

Law clerks and paralegals. — Law clerks and paralegals perform a variety of services for attorneys but they may not give legal advice, accept cases, set fees, appear in court, plan strategy, make legal decisions, or chart the direction of a case. Attorney Grievance Comm'n v. Hallmon, 343 Md. 390, 681 A.2d 510 (1996).

Adequate supervision of legal assistants is an ethical requirement. Attorney Grievance Comm'n v. Hallmon, 343 Md. 390, 681 A.2d 510 (1996).

Hearing record demonstrated by clear and convincing evidence an abdication of supervision by subject attorney and that a lay legal assistant was unauthorizedly practicing law. Attorney Grievance Comm'n v. Hallmon, 343 Md. 390, 681 A.2d 510 (1996).

Cited in In re R.G.S., 312 Md. 626, 541 A.2d 977 (1988); Attorney Grievance Comm'n v. Willis, 348 Md. 633, 705 A.2d 1121 (1998).

Rule 5.6. Restrictions on right to practice.

A lawyer shall not participate in offering or making:

(a) a partnership or employment agreement that restricts the rights of a lawyer to practice after termination of the relationship, except an agreement concerning benefits upon retirement; or

(b) an agreement in which a restriction on the lawyer's right to practice is part of the settlement of a controversy between private parties.

COMMENT

An agreement restricting the right of partners or associates to practice after leaving a firm not only limits their professional autonomy but also limits the freedom of clients to choose a lawyer. Paragraph (a) prohibits such agreements except for restrictions incident to provisions concerning retirement benefits for service with the firm.

Paragraph (b) prohibits a lawyer from agreeing not to represent other persons in connection with settling a claim on behalf of a client.

Code Comparison. — Rule 5.6 is substantially similar to DR 2-108.

Maryland Law Review. — For survey, "Developments in Maryland Law, 1990-91," see 51 Md. L. Rev. 507 (1992).

Quoted in Holloway v. Faw, Casson & Co., 78 Md. App. 205, 552 A.2d 1311 (1989), modified, 319 Md. 324, 572 A.2d 510 (1990); Marr v.

Langhoff, 322 Md. 657, 589 A.2d 470 (1991).

Cited in Prahinski v. Prahinski, 75 Md. App. 113, 540 A.2d 833 (1988), aff'd, 321 Md. 227, 582 A.2d 784 (1990); Holloway v. Faw, Casson & Co., 319 Md. 324, 572 A.2d 510 (1990).

PUBLIC SERVICE.

Rule 6.1. Pro bono publico service.

A lawyer should render public interest legal service. A lawyer may discharge this responsibility by providing professional services at no fee or a reduced fee to persons of limited means or to public service or charitable groups or organizations, by service in activities for improving the law, the legal system or the legal profession, or by financial support for organizations that provide legal services to persons of limited means.

COMMENT

The ABA House of Delegates has formally acknowledged "the basic responsibility of each lawyer engaged in the practice of law to provide public interest legal services" without fee, or at a substantially reduced fee, in one or more of the following areas: poverty law, civil rights law, public rights law, charitable organization representation and the administration of justice. This Rule expresses that policy but is not intended to be enforced through disciplinary process.

The rights and responsibilities of individuals and organizations in the United States are increasingly defined in legal terms. As a consequence, legal assistance in coping with the web of statutes, rules and regulations is imperative for persons of modest and limited means, as well as for the relatively well-to-do.

The basic responsibility for providing legal services for those unable to pay ultimately rests upon the individual lawyer, and personal involvement in the problems of the disadvantaged can be one of the most rewarding experiences in the life of a lawyer. Every lawyer, regardless of professional prominence or professional workload, should find time to participate in or otherwise support the provision of legal services to the disadvantaged. The provision of free legal services to those unable to pay reasonable fees continues to be an obligation of each lawyer as well as the profession generally, but the efforts of individual lawyers are often not enough to meet the need. Thus, it has been necessary for the profession and government to institute additional programs to provide legal services. Accordingly, legal aid offices, lawyer referral services and other related programs have been developed, and others will be developed by the profession and government. Every lawyer should support all proper efforts to meet this need for legal services.

Code Comparison. — There is no counterpart of Rule 6.1 in the Disciplinary Rules of the Code. EC 2-25 states that "The basic responsibility for providing legal services for those unable to pay ultimately rests upon the individual lawyer.... Every lawyer, regardless of professional prominence or professional workload, should find time to participate in serving the disadvantaged." EC 8-9 states that "The advancement of our legal system is of vital importance in maintaining the rule of law ... and lawyers should encourage, and should aid in making needed changes and improvements." EC 8-3 states that "Those persons unable to pay for legal services should be provided needed services."

Maryland Law Review. — For symposium, expanding pro bono legal assistance in civil cases to Maryland's poor, see 49 Md. L. Rev. 1 (1990).

University of Baltimore Law Forum. — For discussion of the code of ethics, see 17, No.

1 U. Balt. Law Forum 31 (1986).

For article, "Code of Ethics Revisited," see 19.2 U. Balt. Law Forum 14 (1989).

For article, "Pro Bono for the Non-Litigator," see 20.2 U. Balt. Law Forum 13 (1990).

Rule 6.2. Accepting appointments.

A lawyer shall not seek to avoid appointment by a tribunal to represent a person except for good cause, such as:

(a) representing the client is likely to result in violation of the rules of professional conduct or other law;

(b) representing the client is likely to result in an unreasonable financial burden on the lawyer; or

(c) the client or the cause is so repugnant to the lawyer as to be likely to impair the client-lawyer relationship or the lawyer's ability to represent the client.

COMMENT

A lawyer ordinarily is not obliged to accept a client whose character or cause the lawyer regards as repugnant. The lawyer's freedom to select clients is, however, qualified. All lawyers have a responsibility to assist in providing pro bono publico service. See Rule 6.1. An individual lawyer fulfills this responsibility by accepting a fair share of unpopular matters or indigent or unpopular clients. A lawyer may also be subject to appointment by a court to serve unpopular clients or persons unable to afford legal services.

Appointed counsel. — For good cause a lawyer may seek to decline an appointment to represent a person who cannot afford to retain counsel or whose cause is unpopular. Good cause exists if the lawyer could not handle the matter competently, see Rule 1.1, or if undertaking the representation would result in an improper conflict of interest, for example, when the client or the cause is so repugnant to the lawyer as to be likely to impair the client-lawyer relationship or the lawyer's ability to represent the client. A lawyer may also seek to decline an appointment if acceptance would be unreasonably burdensome, for example, when it would impose a financial sacrifice so great as to be unjust.

An appointed lawyer has the same obligations to the client as retained counsel, including the obligations of loyalty and confidentiality, and is subject to the same limitations on the client-lawyer relationship, such as the obligation to refrain from assisting the client in violation of the Rules.

Code Comparison. — There is no counterpart to Rule 6.2 in the Disciplinary Rules of the Code. EC 2-29 states that "When a lawyer is appointed by a court or requested by a bar association to undertake representation of a person unable to obtain counsel, whether for financial or other reasons, he should not seek to be excused from undertaking the representation except for compelling reason. Compelling reasons do not include such factors as the repugnance of the subject matter of the proceeding, the identity or position of a person involved in the case, the belief of the lawyer that the defendant in a criminal proceeding is guilty, or the belief of the lawyer regarding the merits of the civil case." EC 2-30 states that "a lawyer should decline employment if the intensity of his personal feelings, as distinguished from a community attitude, may impair his effective representation of a prospective client."

Maryland Law Review. — For symposium, expanding pro bono legal assistance in civil cases to Maryland's poor, see 49 Md. L. Rev. 1 (1990).

Rule 6.3. Membership in legal services organization.

A lawyer may serve as a director, officer or member of a legal services organization, apart from the law firm in which the lawyer practices, notwithstanding that the organization serves persons having interests adverse to a client of the lawyer. The lawyer shall not knowingly participate in a decision or action of the organization:

(a) if participating in the decision would be incompatible with the lawyer's obligations to a client under Rule 1.7; or

(b) where the decision could have a material adverse effect on the representation of a client of the organization whose interests are adverse to a client of the lawyer.

COMMENT

Lawyers should be encouraged to support and participate in legal service organizations. A lawyer who is an officer or a member of such an organization does not thereby have a client-lawyer relationship with persons served by the organization. However, there is potential conflict between the interests of such persons and the interests of the lawyer's clients. If the possibility of such conflict disqualified a lawyer from serving on the board of a legal services organization, the profession's involvement in such organizations would be severely curtailed.

It may be necessary in appropriate cases to reassure a client of the organization that the representation will not be affected by conflicting loyalties of a member of the board. Established, written policies in this respect can enhance the credibility of such assurances.

Code Comparison. — There is no counterpart to this Rule in the Code.

Rule 6.4. Law reform activities affecting client interests.

A lawyer may serve as a director, officer or member of an organization involved in reform of the law or its administration notwithstanding that the reform may affect the interests of a client of the lawyer. When the lawyer knows that the interests of a client may be materially benefitted by a decision in which the lawyer participates, the lawyer shall disclose that fact but need not identify the client.

COMMENT

Lawyers involved in organizations seeking law reform generally do not have a client-lawyer relationship with the organization. Otherwise, it might follow that a lawyer could not be involved in a bar association law reform program that might indirectly affect a client. See also Rule 1.2 (b). For example, a lawyer specializing in antitrust litigation might be regarded as disqualified from participating in drafting revisions of rules governing that subject. In determining the nature and scope of participation in such activities, a lawyer should be mindful of obligations to clients under other Rules, particularly Rule 1.7. A lawyer is professionally obligated to protect the integrity of the program by making an appropriate disclosure within the organization when the lawyer knows a private client might be materially benefitted.

Code Comparison. — There is no counterpart to this Rule in the Code.

INFORMATION ABOUT LEGAL SERVICES.

Rule 7.1. Communications concerning a lawyer's services.

A lawyer shall not make a false or misleading communication about the lawyer or the lawyer's services. A communication is false or misleading if it:

(a) contains a material misrepresentation of fact or law, or omits a fact necessary to make the statement considered as a whole not materially misleading;

(b) is likely to create an unjustified expectation about results the lawyer can achieve, or states or implies that the lawyer can achieve results by means that violate the rules of professional conduct or other law; or

(c) compares the lawyer's services with other lawyers' services, unless the comparison can be factually substantiated. (Amended May 14, 1992, effective July 1, 1992.)

COMMENT

This Rule governs all communications about a lawyer's services, including advertising and direct personal contact with potential clients permitted by Rules 7.2 and 7.3. Whatever means are used to make known a lawyer's services, statements about them should be truthful. The prohibition in paragraph (b) of statements that may create "unjustified expectations" would ordinarily preclude advertisements about results obtained on behalf of a client, such as the amount of a damage award or the lawyer's record in obtaining favorable verdicts, and advertisements containing client endorsements. Such information may create the unjustified expectation that similar results can be obtained for others without reference to the specific factual and legal circumstances.

A communication will be regarded as false or misleading if it (1) asserts the lawyer's record in obtaining favorable awards, verdicts, judgments, or settlements in prior cases, unless it also expressly and conspicuously states that each case is different and that the past record is no assurance that the lawyer will be successful in reaching a favorable result in any future case, or (2) contains an endorsement or testimonial as to the lawyer's legal services or abilities by a person who is not a bona fide pre-existing client of the lawyer and has not in fact benefited as such from those services or abilities.

Code Comparison. — Rules 7.1 (a) and 7.1. (b) are substantially similar to DR 2-101 (A) 1 to 4 in effect in Maryland. DR 2-101 (A) 5 (prohibiting publicity which is part of an unlawful act) is omitted from Rule 7.1. See, however, Rules 8.4 (b) and (c) (professional misconduct includes: committing a criminal act reflecting "on the lawyer's honesty, trustworthiness or fitness as a lawyer;" or engaging "in conduct involving dishonesty, fraud, deceit or misrepresentation").

Rule 7.1 (c) has no counterpart in the Maryland Disciplinary Rules.

Effect of amendments. — The 1992 amendment added the second paragraph of the comment.

Editor's note. — The Order of the Court of Appeals dated May 14, 1992, provided, in part, that "the amendments to Maryland Rules of Professional Conduct 7.1, 7.2, and 7.4 shall take effect on July 1, 1992 and shall apply to all advertising and communications published on television, radio, or through any other electronic medium on or after September 1, 1992, and to all other advertising and communications published on or after January 1, 1993...."

University of Baltimore Law Forum. — For discussion of the code of ethics, see 17, No. 1 U. Balt. Law Forum 31 (1986).

For article, "Code of Ethics Revisited," see 19.2 U. Balt. Law Forum 14 (1989).

Trade names. — The Court of Appeals lacks the jurisdiction to render advisory ethics opinions, and has no authority either to approve of or disapprove a contemplated trade name. In re Attorney's Use of Trade Name, 333 Md. 488, 635 A.2d 1338 (1994).

Tasteless advertisement did not violate Rule. — Attorney's advertisements regarding palimony suits, although deemed to be tasteless, were not in violation of this Rule. Attorney Grievance Comm'n v. Ficker, 319 Md. 305, 572 A.2d 501 (1990).

Applied in Ex parte Lord & Whip, 309 Md. 222, 522 A.2d 1347 (1987).

Cited in In re R.G.S., 312 Md. 626, 541 A.2d 977 (1988).

Rule 7.2. Advertising.

(a) Subject to the requirements of Rules 7.1 and 7.3 (b), a lawyer may advertise services through public media, such as a telephone directory, legal directory, newspaper or other periodical, outdoor, radio or television advertising, or through communications not involving in person contact.

(b) A copy or recording of an advertisement or such other communication shall be kept for at least three years after its last dissemination along with a record of when and where it was used.

(c) A lawyer shall not give anything of value to a person for recommending the lawyer's services, except that a lawyer may pay the reasonable cost of advertising or written communication permitted by this Rule and may pay the usual charges of a not-for-profit lawyer referral service or other legal service organization.

(d) Any communication made pursuant to this Rule shall include the name of at least one lawyer responsible for its content.

(e) An advertisement or communication indicating that no fee will be charged in the absence of a recovery shall also disclose whether the client will be liable for any expenses.

Cross references. — Maryland Rule of Professional Conduct 1.8 (e).

(f) A lawyer, including a participant in an advertising group or lawyer referral service or other program involving communications concerning the lawyer's services, shall be personally responsible for compliance with the provisions of Rules 7.1, 7.2, 7.3, 7.4, and 7.5 and shall be prepared to substantiate such compliance. (Amended May 14, 1992, effective July 1, 1992.)

COMMENT

To assist the public in obtaining legal services, lawyers should be allowed to make known their services not only through reputation but also through organized information campaigns in the form of advertising. Advertising involves an active quest for clients, contrary to the tradition that a lawyer should not seek clientele. However, the public's need to know about legal services can be fulfilled in part through advertising. This need is particularly acute in the case of persons of moderate means who have not made extensive use of legal services. The interest in expanding public information about legal services ought to prevail over considerations of tradition. Nevertheless, advertising by lawyers entails the risk of practices that are misleading or overreaching.

This Rule permits public dissemination of information concerning a lawyer's name or firm name, address and telephone number; the kinds of services the lawyer will undertake; the basis on which the lawyer's fees are determined, including prices for specific services and payment and credit arrangements; a lawyer's foreign language ability; names of references and, with their consent, names of clients regularly represented; and other information that might invite the attention of those seeking legal assistance.

Questions of effectiveness and taste in advertising are matters of speculation and subjective judgment. Some jurisdictions have had extensive prohibitions against television advertising, against advertising going beyond specified facts about a lawyer, or against "undignified" advertising. Television is now one of the most powerful media for getting information to the public, particularly persons of low and moderate income; prohibiting television advertising, therefore, would impede the flow of information about legal services to many sectors of the public. Limiting the information that may be advertised has a similar effect and assumes that the bar can accurately forecast the kind of information that the public would regard as relevant.

Neither this Rule nor Rule 7.3 prohibits communications authorized by law, such as notice to members of a class in class action litigation.

Paragraph (a) permits communication by mail to a specific individual as well as general mailings, but does not permit contact by telephone or in person delivery of written material except through the postal service or other delivery service.

Record of advertising. — Paragraph (b) requires that a record of the content and use of advertising be kept in order to facilitate enforcement of this Rule. It does not require that advertising be subject to review prior to dissemination. Such a requirement would be burdensome and expensive relative to its possible benefits, and may be of doubtful constitutionality.

Paying others to recommend a lawyer. — A lawyer is allowed to pay for advertising permitted by this Rule, but otherwise is not permitted to pay another person for channeling professional work. This restriction does not prevent an organization or person other than the lawyer from advertising or recommending the lawyer's services. Thus, a legal aid agency or prepaid legal services plan may pay to advertise legal services provided under its auspices. Likewise, a lawyer may participate in not-for-profit lawyer referral programs and pay the usual fees charged by such programs. Paragraph (c) does not prohibit paying regular compensation to an assistant, such as a secretary, to prepare communications permitted by this Rule.

Responsibility for compliance. — Every lawyer who participates in communications concerning the lawyer's services is responsible for assuring that the specified Rules are complied with and must be prepared to substantiate compliance with those Rules. That may require retaining records for more than the three years specified in paragraph (b) of this Rule.

Code Comparison. — Rule 7.2 (a) has no counterpart in the Maryland Disciplinary Rules, which spoke in terms of what advertising is prohibited rather than in terms of what is permitted. DR 2-103 (B) prohibits a lawyer from recommending to a nonlawyer the employment of the lawyer, "his partner ... or associate," except for "commercial advertising which complies with DR 2-101." DR 2-103 (A). See also DR 2-104 (A). This could have been construed as prohibiting all direct mailings seeking legal employment sent to those known to need legal services in specific matters. Such direct mailings are specifically permitted by Rule 7.2 (a), but are subject to Rule 7.3 (b) as well as Rule 7.1.

With regard to Rule 7.2 (b), DR 2-101 (D) provides that "If the advertisement is communicated over television or radio ..., a recording of the actual transmission shall be retained by the lawyer."

With regard to Rule 7.2 (c), DR 2-101 (B) provides that "A lawyer shall not compensate or give anything of value to representatives of the press, radio, television, or other communication medium in anticipation of or in return for professional publicity in a news item." DR 2-103 (C) provides that "A lawyer shall not compensate or give anything of value to a person or organization to recommend or secure his employment ... except that he may pay the usual and reasonable fees or dues charged by any of the organizations listed in DR 2-103 (D)." (DR 2-103 (D) refers to legal aid and other legal services organizations.)

There is no counterpart to Rule 7.2 (d) in the Code.

There is no counterpart to Rule 7.2 (e) in the Code.

Rule 7.2 (f) is substantially the same as the last paragraph of DR 2-101 (A).

Effect of amendments. — The 1992 amendment inserted present (e) and redesignated former (e) as (f); and, in the Code Comparison note, inserted the present next-to-last paragraph, and substituted "(f)" for "(e)" in the last paragraph.

Editor's note. — The Order of the Court of Appeals dated May 14, 1992, provided, in part, that "the amendments to Maryland Rules of Professional Conduct 7.1, 7.2, and 7.4 shall take effect on July 1, 1992, and shall apply to all advertising and communications published on television, radio, or through any other electronic medium on or after September 1, 1992, and to all other advertising and communications published on or after January 1, 1993...."

University of Baltimore Law Forum. — For article, "Code of Ethics Revisited," see 19.2 U. Balt. Law Forum 14 (1989).

For comment, "Lawyer Television Advertising—What's the Big Deal?," see 19.3 U. Balt. Law Forum 31 (1989).

Illegal contract claims. — The Rules of Professional Conduct are not statements of public policy on which an illegal contract claim may be founded. Son v. Margolius, Mallios, Davis, Rider & Tomar, 114 Md. App. 190, 689 A.2d 645 (1997).

Application of prohibition against solicitation must not offend constitutional guarantees. — A general prohibition against solicitation must be tested against the individual facts of each case to determine whether the application of that prohibition would offend constitutional guarantees of free speech and the right of association. Attorney Grievance Comm'n v. Gregory, 311 Md. 522, 536 A.2d 646 (1988).

Prohibition of in-person solicitation for pecuniary gain does not offend constitutional guarantees of free speech and the right of association. Attorney Grievance Comm'n v. Gregory, 311 Md. 522, 536 A.2d 646 (1988).

Referrals by nonlawyers. — Referrals by nonlawyers are permitted under certain conditions, but not where an attorney accepts a referral from a profit-making organization where the attorney is employed or selected by the organization, except where the organization has ultimate legal responsibility for the person referred. Attorney Grievance Comm'n v. Martin, 308 Md. 272, 518 A.2d 1050 (1987).

Law firm employees. — There is no violation of the prohibition in section (c) against a lawyer's giving "anything of value to a person for recommending the lawyer's services" if the lawyer's employee engages in conduct in which the lawyer permissibly may directly engage. Attorney Grievance Comm'n v. Willis, 348 Md. 633, 705 A.2d 1121 (1998).

Improper solicitation of defendants in criminal cases. — Ninety-day suspension was warranted where attorney engaged in improper solicitation of defendants in criminal cases by in-person solicitation where attorney had earlier received a reprimand for similar conduct. Attorney Grievance Comm'n v. Gregory, 311 Md. 522, 536 A.2d 646 (1988).

Attorney's practice of initiating personal contacts with criminal defendants outside courtrooms where those defendants had just been advised of their right to counsel, and then introducing himself as an attorney, handing the defendants a letter soliciting their business, suggesting that they call him, and accepting employment from these defendants was improper. Attorney Grievance Comm'n v. Gregory, 311 Md. 522, 536 A.2d 646 (1988).

Applied in Son v. Margolius, Mallios, Davis, Rider & Tomar, 349 Md. 441, 709 A.2d 112 (1998).

Quoted in In re Attorney's Use of Trade Name, 333 Md. 488, 635 A.2d 1338 (1994).

Rule 7.3. Direct contact with prospective clients.

(a) A lawyer may initiate in person contact with a prospective client for the purpose of obtaining professional employment only in the following circumstances and subject to the requirements of paragraph (b):

(1) if the prospective client is a close friend, relative, former client or one whom the lawyer reasonably believes to be a client;

(2) under the auspices of a public or charitable legal services organization; or

(3) under the auspices of a bona fide political, social, civic, fraternal, employee or trade organization whose purposes include but are not limited to providing or recommending legal services, if the legal services are related to the principal purposes of the organization.

(b) A lawyer shall not contact, or send a communication to, a prospective client for the purpose of obtaining professional employment if:

(1) the lawyer knows or reasonably should know that the physical, emotional or mental state of the person is such that the person could not exercise reasonable judgment in employing a lawyer;

(2) the person has made known to the lawyer a desire not to receive communications from the lawyer; or

(3) the communication involves coercion, duress, or harassment.

COMMENT

Unrestricted solicitation involves definite social harms. Among these are harassment, overreaching, provocation of nuisance litigation and schemes for systematic fabrication of claims, all of which were experienced prior to adoption of restrictions on solicitation. Measures reasonably designed to suppress these harms are constitutionally legitimate. At the same time, measures going beyond realization of such objectives would appear to be invalid under relevant decisions of the United States Supreme Court.

In determining whether a contact is permissible under Rule 7.3 (b), it is relevant to consider the time and circumstances under which the contact is initiated. For example, a person undergoing active medical treatment for traumatic injury is unlikely to be in an emotional state in which reasonable judgment about employing a lawyer can be exercised.

Code Comparison. — With regard to Rule 7.3 (a), DR 2-104 (A) provides with certain exceptions that "a lawyer who has given unsolicited advice to a layperson that he should obtain counsel or take legal action shall not accept employment resulting from that advice...." The exceptions include DR 2-104 (A) (1), which provides that "A lawyer may accept employment by a close friend, relative, former client (if the advice is germane to the former employment), or one whom the lawyer reasonably believes to be a client." DR 2-104 (A) (2) through DR 2-104 (A) (5) provide other exceptions relating, respectively, to employment resulting from public educational programs, recommendation by a legal assistance organization, public speaking or writing and representing members of a class in class action litigation.

Rule 7.3 (b) has no counterpart in the Maryland Disciplinary Rules.

University of Baltimore Law Forum. — For article, "Recent Developments," see 19.1 U. Balt. Law Forum 29 (1988).

For article, "Code of Ethics Revisited," see 19.2 U. Balt. Law Forum 14 (1989).

Application of prohibition must not offend constitutional guarantees. — A general prohibition against solicitation must be tested against the individual facts of each case to determine whether the application of that prohibition would offend constitutional guarantees of free speech and the right of association. Attorney Grievance Comm'n v. Gregory, 311 Md. 522, 536 A.2d 646 (1988).

Validity. — Section (b) (1), which improperly focuses solely on the condition of the recipient of the solicitation, has questionable validity. Unnamed Att'y v. Attorney Grievance Comm'n, 313 Md. 357, 545 A.2d 685 (1988).

Written modes of solicitation (as opposed to in-person solicitation) are protected by the First Amendment, regardless of the recipient's condition, so long as such communication is neither false, misleading, nor overreaching. Unnamed Att'y v. Attorney Grievance Comm'n, 313 Md. 357, 545 A.2d 685 (1988).

Insofar as former Code of Professional Responsibility DR 2-103 (B) constituted a blanket prohibition against targeted direct mail solicitation, it was unconstitutional. Unnamed Att'y v. Attorney Grievance Comm'n, 313 Md. 357, 545 A.2d 685 (1988).

Improper solicitation of criminal defendants. — Ninety-day suspension was warranted where attorney engaged in improper solicitation of defendants in criminal cases by in-person solicitation where attorney had earlier received a reprimand for similar conduct. Attorney Grievance Comm'n v. Gregory, 311 Md. 522, 536 A.2d 646 (1988).

Cited in Attorney Grievance Comm'n v. Willis, 348 Md. 633, 705 A.2d 1121 (1998).

Rule 7.4. Communication of fields of practice.

A lawyer may communicate the fact that the lawyer does or does not practice in particular fields of law, subject to the requirements of Rule 7.1. A lawyer shall not hold himself or herself out publicly as a specialist. (Amended May 14, 1992, effective July 1, 1992.)

COMMENT

This Rule permits a lawyer to indicate areas of practice in communications about the lawyer's services; for example, in a telephone directory or other advertising. If a lawyer practices only in certain fields, or will not accept matters except in such fields, the lawyer is permitted so to indicate.

Code Comparison. — Rule 7.4 is substantially the same as former DR 2-105.

Effect of amendments. — The 1992 amendment added the second sentence; and, in the Code Comparison note, substituted "former DR 2-105" for "DR 2-105 which provides that 'A lawyer shall not hold himself out publicly as a specialist, or as limiting his practice except as permitted under DR 2-101.'"

Editor's note. — The Order of the Court of Appeals dated May 14, 1992, provided, in part, that "the amendments to Maryland Rules of Professional Conduct 7.1, 7.2, and 7.4 shall take effect on July 1, 1992 and shall apply to all advertising and communications published on television, radio, or through any other electronic medium on or after September 1, 1992, and to all other advertising and communications published on or after January 1, 1993...."

Rule 7.5. Firm names and letterheads.

(a) A lawyer shall not use a firm name, letterhead or other professional designation that violates Rule 7.1. A trade name may be used by a lawyer in private practice if it does not imply a connection with a government agency or with a public or charitable legal services organization and is not otherwise in violation of Rule 7.1.

(b) A law firm with offices in more than one jurisdiction may use the same name in each jurisdiction, but identification of the lawyers in an office of the firm shall indicate the jurisdictional limitations on those not licensed to practice in the jurisdiction where the office is located.

(c) The name of a lawyer holding a public office shall not be used in the name of a law firm, or in communications on its behalf, during any substantial period in which the lawyer is not actively and regularly practicing with the firm.

(d) Lawyers may state or imply that they practice in a partnership or other organization only when that is the fact.

COMMENT

A firm may be designated by the names of all or some of its members, by the names of deceased or retired members where there has been a continuing succession in the firm's identity or by a trade name such as the "ABC Legal Clinic." Although the United States Supreme Court has held that legislation may prohibit the use of trade names in professional practice, use of such names in law practice is acceptable so long as it is not misleading. It may be observed that any firm name including the name of a deceased partner is, strictly speaking, a trade name. The use of such names to designate law firms has proven a useful means of identification. However, it is misleading to use the name of a lawyer not associated with the firm or a predecessor of the firm.

A lawyer in private practice may not practice under a name which implies any connection with the government or any agency of the federal government, any state or any political subdivision, or with a public or charitable legal services organization. This is to prevent a situation where nonlawyers might conclude that they are dealing with an agency established or sanctioned by the government, or one funded by either the government or public contributions and thus charging lower fees. The use of any of the following ordinarily would violate this Rule:

1. The proper name of a government unit, whether or not identified with the type of unit. Thus, a name could be the basis of a disciplinary proceeding if it included the designation "Annapolis" or "City of Annapolis," "Baltimore," or "Baltimore County," "Maryland," or "Maryland State" (which could be a violation as a confusing although mistaken reference to the state or under the third application of this instruction below).

2. The generic name of any form of government unit found in the same area where the firm practices, e.g., national, state, county, or municipal.

3. The name of or a reference to a college, university, or other institution of higher learning, regardless of whether it has a law school, unless the provider of legal higher learning. For example, the names "Georgetown Legal Clinic (or "Law Office," etc.)" and "U.B. Legal Clinic (or "Law Office," etc.)" could both violate this Rule if used by unaffiliated organizations.

4. The words "public," "government," "civic," "legal aid," "community," "neighborhood," or other words of similar import suggesting that the legal services offered are at least in part publicly funded. Although names such as "Neighborhood Legal Clinic of John Doe" might otherwise appear unobjectionable, the terms "legal aid," "community" and "neighborhood" have become so associated with public or charitable legal services organizations as to form the basis of disciplinary proceedings.

Firm names which include geographical names which are not also government units, or adjectives merely suggesting the context of the practice (e.g., "urban", "rural") ordinarily would not violate Rule 7.5. The acceptability of the use of a proper or generic name of a government unit when coupled with an adjective or further description (beyond mere reference to the provision of legal services) should be judged by the general policy underlying Rule 7.5, and any doubt regarding the misleading connotations of a name may be resolved against use of the name.

With regard to paragraph (d), lawyers sharing office facilities, but who are not in fact partners, may not denominate themselves as, for example, "Smith and Jones," for that title suggests partnership in the practice of law.

Code Comparison. — With regard to Rule 7.5 (a), DR 2-102 (A) provides that "A lawyer in private practice shall not practice under a trade name, a name that is misleading as to the identity of the lawyer or lawyers practicing under such name, or a firm name containing names other than those of one or more of the lawyers in the firm, except that ... a firm may use as ... its name the name or names of one or more deceased or retired members of the firm or of a predecessor firm in a continuing line of succession."

With regard to Rule 7.5 (b), DR 2-102 (C) provides that "A partnership shall not be formed or continued between or among lawyers licensed in different jurisdictions unless all enumerations of the members and associates of the firm on its letterhead and in other permissible listings make clear the jurisdictional limitations on those members and associates of the firm not licensed to practice in all listed jurisdictions; however, the same firm name may be used in each jurisdiction."

With regard to Rule 7.5 (c), DR 2-102 (A) provides that "A lawyer who assumes a judicial, legislative, or public executive or administrative post or office shall not permit his name to remain in the name of a law firm ... during any significant period in which he is not actively and regularly practicing law as a member of the firm ...."

Rule 7.5 (d) is substantially similar to DR 2-102 (B).

Trade names. — The Court of Appeals lacks the jurisdiction to render advisory ethics opinions, and has no authority either to approve of or disapprove a contemplated trade name. In re Attorney's Use of Trade Name, 333 Md. 488, 635 A.2d 1338 (1994).

Applied in Ex parte Lord & Whip, 309 Md. 222, 522 A.2d 1347 (1987).

Quoted in Prahinski v. Prahinski, 75 Md. App. 113, 540 A.2d 833 (1988), aff'd, 321 Md. 227, 582 A.2d 784 (1990).

Cited in In re R.G.S., 312 Md. 626, 541 A.2d 977 (1988).

MAINTAINING THE INTEGRITY OF THE PROFESSION.

Rule 8.1. Bar admission and disciplinary matters.

An applicant for admission or reinstatement to the bar, or a lawyer in connection with a bar admission application or in connection with a disciplinary matter, shall not:

(a) knowingly make a false statement of material fact; or

(b) fail to disclose a fact necessary to correct a misapprehension known by the person to have arisen in the matter, or knowingly fail to respond to a lawful demand for information from an admissions or disciplinary authority, except that this Rule does not require disclosure of information otherwise protected by Rule 1.6.

COMMENT

The duty imposed by this Rule extends to persons seeking admission or reinstatement to the bar as well as to lawyers. Hence, if a person makes a material false statement in connection with an application for admission or for reinstatement, it may be the basis for subsequent disciplinary action if the person is admitted or reinstated, and in any event may be relevant in a subsequent admission application. The duty imposed by this Rule applies to a lawyer's own admission or discipline as well as that of others. Thus, it is a separate professional offense for a lawyer to knowingly make a misrepresentation or omission in connection with a disciplinary investigation of the lawyer's own conduct. This Rule also requires affirmative clarification of any misunderstanding on the part of the admissions or disciplinary authority of which the person involved becomes aware.

This Rule is subject to the provisions of the Fifth Amendment of the United States Constitution and corresponding provisions of state constitutions. A person relying on such a provision in response to a question, however, should do so openly and not use the right of nondisclosure as a justification for failure to comply with this Rule.

A lawyer representing an applicant for admission to the bar, or representing a lawyer who is the subject of a disciplinary inquiry or proceeding, is governed by the rules applicable to the client-lawyer relationship.

Code Comparison. — DR 1-101 (A) provides that "A lawyer is subject to discipline if he has made a materially false statement in, or if he has deliberately failed to disclose a material fact requested in connection with his application for admission to the bar." DR 1-101 (B) provides that "A lawyer shall not further the application for admission to the bar of another person known by him to be unqualified in respect to character, education, or other relevant attribute." With respect to paragraph (b) of Rule 8.1, DR 1-102 (A) (5) provides that "a lawyer shall not engage in conduct that is prejudicial to the administration of justice."

University of Baltimore Law Forum. — For discussion of the code of ethics, see 17, No. 1 U. Balt. Law Forum 31 (1986).

For note, *"Attorney Grievance Commission v. Gilbert:* Attorney Disbarred for Failure to Disclose Material Information on His Bar Application", see 17, No. 3 U. Balt. Law Forum 27 (1987).

Comparison with Rule 8.4 (c). — Dishonesty before disciplinary authorities could fall under both the narrow proscription of this Rule as well as under the broader proscription of Rule 8.4 (c). Attorney Grievance Comm'n v. Goldsborough, 330 Md. 342, 624 A.2d 503 (1993).

Bar admission applications. — For determining the materiality under former DR 1-101 (A) of an omission or false statement on a bar admission application, the standard was whether the omission had the effect of inhibiting the efforts of the bar to determine an applicant's fitness to practice law. Attorney Grievance Comm'n v. Gilbert, 307 Md. 481, 515 A.2d 454 (1986).

Material, deliberate omission. — Attorney's failure to disclose in his application for admission to the Maryland Bar that, although he had a Pennsylvania license and a Pennsylvania office, he worked full-time for a Baltimore corporation and only worked at his legal practice 10-15 hours per week was material, deliberate omission for which disbarment was the appropriate sanction. Attorney Grievance Comm'n v. Keehan, 311 Md. 161, 533 A.2d 278 (1987).

Mishandling escrow account. — Indefinite suspension was appropriate sanction for attorney's mishandling of escrow account, including the failure to pay claims due from the account and the failure to refund moneys to clients. Attorney Grievance Comm'n v. Singleton, 311 Md. 1, 532 A.2d 157 (1987).

Alcoholism, drug addiction and mental disorders. — An indefinite suspension was the proper sanction in the case of a misappropriation of client funds caused by alcoholism; however, in the future, absent truly compelling circumstances, alcoholism will usually not be permitted to mitigate where an attorney commits a violation of ethical or legal rules which would ordinarily warrant disbarment. Attorney Grievance Comm'n v. Kenney, 339 Md. 578, 664 A.2d 854 (1995).

Indefinite suspension was proper sanction. — Where respondent attorney's representation of four clients was marked by serious neglect and inattention; where he failed to return a fee which was unearned for a period of nine months; where he failed to timely remit funds he received on behalf of a client; where he failed to communicate with his clients; and where, in connection with the investigation of three of the complaints, respondent failed to answer Bar Counsel's requests for information, the proper sanction was that the attorney be indefinitely suspended from the practice of law, with the right to apply for reinstatement after the suspension had been in effect for six months, conditioned upon his payment of all costs and upon the monitoring of respondent's practice. Attorney Grievance Comm'n v. David, 331 Md. 317, 628 A.2d 178 (1993).

Disbarment required. — Willful misconduct of attorney where there was no causal relation between the misconduct and alcoholism and no evidence of any extenuating circumstances for misconduct warranted disbarment. Attorney Grievance Comm'n v. Kolodner, 321 Md. 545, 583 A.2d 724 (1991).

Representations and omissions made by an attorney in connection with his application for admission to the Bar of this State violated Rules 8.1, 8.4(b), 8.4(c), and 8.4(d) of the Maryland Rules of Professional Conduct and warranted disbarment. Attorney Grievance Comm'n v. Joehl, 335 Md. 83, 642 A.2d 194 (1994).

Disbarment of attorney was appropriate where there were serious and repeated violations of this Rule and other provisions of the Maryland Rules of Professional Conduct. Attorney Grievance Comm'n v. Milliken, 348 Md. 486, 704 A.2d 1225 (1998).

Four principal criteria have to be evaluated in a petition for readmission to the Maryland Bar: (1) the nature and circumstances of petitioner's original misconduct; (2) petitioner's subsequent conduct and reformation; (3) petitioner's present character; and (4) petitioner's present qualifications and competence to practice law. In re Keehan, 342 Md. 121, 674 A.2d 510 (1996).

Disbarred attorney, in light of evidence exhibiting compliance with readmission criteria except as to his present qualifications and competence to practice law, demonstrated his fitness to become a member of the Maryland Bar, but only after taking and passing the regular comprehensive Maryland Bar examination. In re Keehan, 342 Md. 121, 674 A.2d 510 (1996).

Rule violation not shown. — While less than cooperative and reasonable in his responses to Bar Counsel's investigation of the charges against him, an attorney's conduct fell short of a violation of the provisions of this Rule. Attorney Grievance Comm'n v. Powell, 328 Md. 276, 614 A.2d 102 (1992).

Applied in Attorney Grievance Comm'n v. Werner, 315 Md. 172, 553 A.2d 722 (1989); Attorney Grievance Comm'n v. Nisbet, 316 Md. 464, 560 A.2d 18 (1989); Attorney Grievance Comm'n v. Boyd, 333 Md. 298, 635 A.2d 382 (1994); Attorney Grievance Comm'n v. Hallmon, 343 Md. 390, 681 A.2d 510 (1996); Attorney Grievance Comm'n v. Hollis, 347 Md.

547, 702 A.2d 223 (1997); Attorney Grievance Comm'n v. Lilly, 347 Md.506, 701 A.2d 847 (1997).

Quoted in Attorney Grievance Comm'n v. Willis, 348 Md. 633, 705 A.2d 1121 (1998); Attorney Grievance Comm'n v. Webster, 348 Md. 662, 705 A.2d 1135 (1998).

Cited in Attorney Grievance Comm'n v. Kerpelman, 323 Md. 136, 591 A.2d 516 (1991),

cert. denied, 502 U.S. 939, 112 S. Ct. 374, 116 L. Ed. 2d 326 (1991); Attorney Grievance Comm'n v. Noble, 324 Md. 42, 595 A.2d 468 (1991); Attorney Grievance Comm'n v. Protokowicz, 329 Md. 252, 619 A.2d 100 (1993); Attorney Grievance Comm'n v. Sachse, 345 Md. 578, 693 A.2d 806 (1997); Attorney Grievance Comm'n v. Lilly, 347 Md.506, 701 A.2d 847 (1997).

Rule 8.2. Judicial and legal officials.

(a) A lawyer shall not make a statement that the lawyer knows to be false or with reckless disregard as to its truth or falsity concerning the qualifications or integrity of a judge, adjudicatory officer or public legal officer, or of a candidate for election or appointment to judicial or legal office.

(b) A candidate for judicial position shall not make or suffer others to make for him, promises of conduct in office which appeal to the cupidity or prejudices of the appointing or electing power; he shall not announce in advance his conclusions of law on disputed issues to secure class support, and he shall do nothing while a candidate to create the impression that if chosen, he will administer his office with bias, partiality or improper discrimination. (Amended Dec. 5, 1986.)

COMMENT

Assessments by lawyers are relied on in evaluating the professional or personal fitness of persons being considered for election or appointment to judicial office and to public legal offices, such as attorney general, prosecuting attorney and public defender. Expressing honest and candid opinions on such matters contributes to improving the administration of justice. Conversely, false statements by a lawyer can unfairly undermine public confidence in the administration of justice.

To maintain the fair and independent administration of justice, lawyers are encouraged to continue traditional efforts to defend judges and courts unjustly criticized.

Code Comparison. — With regard to Rule 8.2 (a), DR 8-102 (A) provides that "A lawyer shall not knowingly make false statements of fact concerning the qualifications of a candidate for election or appointment to a judicial office." DR 8-102 (B) provides that "A lawyer shall not knowingly make false accusations against a judge or other adjudicatory officer."

Rule 8.2 (b) is identical to Canon XXIX of the Canons and Rules of Judicial Ethics, which is applicable to judges who are candidates for judicial office. Although the Maryland Disciplinary Rules have no counterpart to Rule 8.2 (b), DR 8-103 of the Model Code, adopted by the ABA after the Code was adopted in Maryland, is the same as Rule 8.2 (b) in substance.

Effect of amendments. — The 1986 amendment substituted "shall" for "should" three times in subsection (b).

Cited in Attorney Grievance Comm'n v.

Kerpelman, 323 Md. 136, 591 A.2d 516 (1991), cert. denied, 502 U.S. 939, 112 S. Ct. 374, 116 L. Ed. 2d 326 (1991).

Rule 8.3. Reporting professional misconduct.

(a) A lawyer having knowledge that another lawyer has committed a violation of the Rules of Professional Conduct that raises a substantial question as to that lawyer's honesty, trustworthiness or fitness as a lawyer in other respects, shall inform the appropriate professional authority.

(b) A lawyer having knowledge that a judge has committed a violation of applicable rules of judicial conduct that raises a substantial question as to the judge's fitness for office shall inform the appropriate authority.

(c) This rule does not require disclosure of information otherwise protected by Rule 1.6.

COMMENT

Self-regulation of the legal profession requires that members of the profession initiate disciplinary investigation when they know of a violation of the Rules of Professional Conduct. Lawyers have a similar obligation with respect to judicial misconduct. An apparently isolated violation may indicate a pattern of misconduct that only a disciplinary investigation can uncover. Reporting a violation is especially important where the victim is unlikely to discover the offense.

A report about misconduct is not required where it would involve violation of Rule 1.6. However, a lawyer should encourage a client to consent to disclosure where prosecution would not substantially prejudice the client's interests.

If a lawyer were obliged to report every violation of the Rules, the failure to report any violation would itself be a professional offense. Such a requirement existed in many jurisdictions but proved to be unenforceable. This Rule limits the reporting obligation to those offenses that a self-regulating profession must

vigorously endeavor to prevent. A measure of judgment is, therefore, required in complying with the provisions of this Rule. The term "substantial" refers to the seriousness of the possible offense and not the quantum of evidence of which the lawyer is aware. A report should be made to the bar disciplinary agency unless some other agency, such as a peer review agency, is more appropriate in the circumstances. Similar considerations apply to the reporting of judicial misconduct.

The duty to report professional misconduct does not apply to a lawyer retained to represent a lawyer whose professional conduct is in question. Such a situation is governed by the rules applicable to the client-lawyer relationship.

Code Comparison. — DR 1-103 (A) provides that "A lawyer possessing unprivileged knowledge of a violation of a Disciplinary Rule shall report such knowledge to ... authority empowered to investigate or act upon such violation."

Charges filed must embody rule most probably violated. — See Attorney Grievance Comm'n v. Wright, 306 Md. 93, 507 A.2d 618 (1986).

Cited in Magness v. Magness, 79 Md. App. 668, 558 A.2d 807 (1989).

Rule 8.4. Misconduct.

It is professional misconduct for a lawyer to:

(a) violate or attempt to violate the Rules of Professional Conduct, knowingly assist or induce another to do so, or do so through the acts of another;

(b) commit a criminal act that reflects adversely on the lawyer's honesty, trustworthiness or fitness as a lawyer in other respects;

(c) engage in conduct involving dishonesty, fraud, deceit or misrepresentation;

(d) engage in conduct that is prejudicial to the administration of justice;

(e) state or imply an ability to influence improperly a government agency or official; or

(f) knowingly assist a judge or judicial officer in conduct that is a violation of applicable rules of judicial conduct or other law. (Amended Dec. 10, 1996, effective July 1, 1997.)

COMMENT

Many kinds of illegal conduct reflect adversely on fitness to practice law, such as offenses involving fraud and the offense of willful failure to file an income tax return. However, some kinds of offense carry no such implication. Traditionally, the distinction was drawn in terms of offenses involving "moral turpitude." That concept can be construed to include offenses concerning some matters of personal morality, such as adultery and comparable offenses, that have no specific connection to fitness for the practice of law. Although a lawyer is personally answerable to the entire criminal law, a lawyer should be professionally answerable only for offenses that indicate lack of those characteristics relevant to law practice. Offenses involving violence, dishonesty, or breach of trust, or serious interference with the administration of justice are in that category. A pattern of repeated offenses, even ones of minor significance when considered separately, can indicate indifference to legal obligation.

Sexual misconduct or sexual harassment involving colleagues, clients, or co-workers may violate paragraph (d). This could occur, for example, where coercion or undue influence is used to obtain sexual favor in exploitation of these relationships. See also *Attorney Grievance Commission v. Goldsborough*, 330 Md. 342 (1993). See also Rule 1.7.

A lawyer may refuse to comply with an obligation imposed by law upon a good faith belief that no valid obligation exists. The provisions of Rule 1.2 (d) concerning a good faith challenge to the validity, scope, meaning or application of the law apply to challenges of legal regulation of the practice of law.

Lawyers holding public office assume legal responsibilities going beyond those of other citizens. A lawyer's abuse of public office can suggest an inability to fulfill the professional role of attorney. The same is true of abuse of positions of private trust such as trustee, executor, administrator, guardian, agent and officer, director or manager of a corporation or other organization.

Code Comparison. — With regard to Rule 8.4 (a)-(d), DR 1-102 (A) provides that "A lawyer shall not:

"(1) Violate a Disciplinary Rule.

"(2) Circumvent a Disciplinary Rule through actions of another.

"(3) Engage in illegal conduct involving moral turpitude.

"(4) Engage in conduct involving dishonesty, fraud, deceit, or misrepresentation.

"(5) Engage in conduct that is prejudicial to the administration of justice.

"(6) Engage in any other conduct that adversely reflects on his fitness to practice law."

Rule 8.4 (e) is substantially similar to DR 9-101 (C).

There is no direct counterpart to Rule 8.4 (f) in the Disciplinary Rules of the Code. EC 7-34 states in part that "A lawyer ... is never justified in making a gift or a loan to a judicial officer except as permitted by ... the Code of Judicial Conduct." EC 9-1 states that "A lawyer should promote public confidence in our legal system and in the legal profession."

Effect of amendments. — The 1996 amendment inserted the present second paragraph in the Comment.

Comparison with Rule 8.1. — Dishonesty before disciplinary authorities could fall under both the narrow proscription of Rule 8.1 as well as under the broader proscription of section (c) of this Rule. Attorney Grievance Comm'n v. Goldsborough, 330 Md. 342, 624 A.2d 503 (1993).

Imposition of sanctions protects the public interest. — The imposition of a sanction for misconduct protects the public interest because it demonstrates to members of the legal profession the type of conduct which will not be tolerated. Attorney Grievance Comm'n v. Hamby, 322 Md. 606, 589 A.2d 53 (1991).

Purpose of disciplinary proceedings. — The purpose of disciplinary proceedings is to protect the public rather then to punish the erring attorney, although concepts of general and specific deterrence are consistent with that primary goal. Attorney Grievance Comm'n v. Owrutsky, 322 Md. 334, 587 A.2d 511 (1991).

Actions reflecting adversely on fitness to practice law. — Lawyer's neglect of divorce matter prior to his suspension from the practice of law, and his subsequent failure to advise client to obtain other counsel after suspension, constituted conduct prejudicial to the administration of justice reflecting adversely on his fitness to practice in violation of former DR 1-102 (A) (5) (6). Attorney Grievance Comm'n v. Singleton, 315 Md. 1, 553 A.2d 222 (1989).

Criminal prosecution not required to find violation. — Although criminal prosecution is certainly a factor weighing heavily in favor of finding a violation of this Rule, its absence does not necessarily mean the Rule has not been violated. Attorney Grievance

Comm'n v. Breschi, 340 Md. 590, 667 A.2d 659 (1995).

Criminal conviction is not required to find a violation. What is required is clear and convincing evidence of conduct that constitutes a commission of the offense. Attorney Grievance Comm'n v. Proctor, 309 Md. 412, 524 A.2d 773 (1987).

An attorney may be disciplined for acts which are criminal but do not result in a criminal conviction if Bar Counsel proves the underlying conduct at the disciplinary hearing. Attorney Grievance Comm'n v. Garland, 345 Md. 383, 692 A.2d 465 (1997).

Moral turpitude irrelevant under current Rule. — The only difference under this Rule and the rule that existed before 1987 is that a crime's moral turpitude now irrelevant to whether a lawyer is guilty of misconduct; under the current rule, a lawyer's commission of a crime or conduct enumerated therein will subject that lawyer to discipline irrespective of whether the crime is also one of moral turpitude. Attorney Grievance Comm'n v. Casalino, 335 Md. 446, 644 A.2d 43 (1994).

Violation of Article 27, § 286. — Although conduct in violation of Article 27, § 286 will ordinarily involve moral turpitude, each case must be decided on its own facts. Attorney Grievance Comm'n v. Proctor, 309 Md. 412, 524 A.2d 773 (1987).

Violation not found by Review Board. — It was not improper for Bar Counsel to charge in a disciplinary petition a number of rule violations not specifically found by the Review Board. Attorney Grievance Comm'n v. Goldsborough, 330 Md. 342, 624 A.2d 503 (1993).

Providing false information. — Where attorney was aware that clients were declining disbursement for the purpose of secreting the settlement funds, and where he willfully complied with their plan to provide false information by withholding their funds, attorney engaged in dishonest and deceitful conduct prohibited by this Rule. Attorney Grievance Comm'n v. Glenn, 341 Md. 448, 671 A.2d 463 (1996).

Bar Counsel's failure to present evidence that attorney's clients actually filed a false financial aid application, that the false information was relied upon, or that their son actually received a benefit from such a representation was immaterial to finding that attorney was in violation of this Rule as it was sufficient if attorney aided the clients in their efforts to defraud or mislead college authorities in assessing their financial picture. Attorney Grievance Comm'n v. Glenn, 341 Md. 448, 671 A.2d 463 (1996).

Where the case was a disciplinary proceeding and not a criminal case, Bar Counsel did not need to prove fraud or false pretenses, nor prove that attorney specifically intended to defraud the college authorities in order to establish that attorney's conduct was dishonest or deceitful. Attorney Grievance Comm'n v. Glenn, 341 Md. 448, 671 A.2d 463 (1996).

Section (c) is broad enough to include intentionally deceptive or misleading testimony, even if it does not relate to a material matter. Attorney Grievance Comm'n v. Willis, 348 Md. 633, 705 A.2d 1121 (1998).

Federal theft charges. — Attorney who pleaded guilty to federal theft charges violated sections (b) and (c) of this Rule, and engaged in misconduct as defined in former Rule BV1k (see now Maryland Rule 16-701). Attorney Grievance Comm'n v. Gittens, 346 Md. 316, 697 A.2d 83 (1997).

Wilful tax evasion is a crime involving moral turpitude and dishonesty; accordingly, the court held that disbarment was the appropriate sanction. Attorney Grievance Comm'n v. Clinton, 308 Md. 701, 521 A.2d 1202 (1987).

Wilful tax evasion is a crime infested with fraud, deceit and dishonesty, and will result in automatic disbarment absent clear and convincing evidence of a compelling reason to the contrary; the exemplary character or activities of an attorney is not sufficient to avoid disbarment. Attorney Grievance Comm'n v. Casalino, 335 Md. 446, 644 A.2d 43 (1994).

Wilful failure to file withholding tax returns may seriously impair public confidence in the entire profession; therefore, where there were no extenuating circumstances, and the defendant had previously been reprimanded and suspended, the defendant's conduct was prejudicial to the administration of justice. Attorney Grievance Comm'n v. Baldwin, 308 Md. 397, 519 A.2d 1291 (1987).

Failure to report and remit income taxes withheld from employees' wages did not show dishonesty or conduct involving moral turpitude, due to the effect the defendant's financial and family problems and alcoholism had on his intent, together with the absence of any evidence that defendant falsified or did not maintain records. Attorney Grievance Comm'n v. Baldwin, 308 Md. 397, 519 A.2d 1291 (1987).

While an attorney's failure to file timely withholding tax returns was a "criminal act" within the meaning of the Rule, it did not "adversely reflect on his fitness" as an attorney within the meaning of the Rule. Attorney Grievance Comm'n v. Post, 350 Md. 85, 710 A.2d 935 (1998).

The proper sanction for an attorney found to have willfully failed to make required withholding tax payments was indefinite suspension with the right to apply for re-admission after 30 days. Attorney Grievance Comm'n v. Post, 350 Md. 85, 710 A.2d 935 (1998).

Knowingly falsifying income tax returns is illegal conduct involving moral

turpitude. Attorney Grievance Comm'n v. Jacob, 303 Md. 172, 492 A.2d 905, cert. denied, 474 U.S. 905, 106 S. Ct. 272, 88 L. Ed. 2d 234 (1985).

A conviction of making a fraudulent return with the intent to defeat the payment of taxes is a crime of moral turpitude and warrants disbarment. Attorney Grievance Comm'n v. Osburn, 304 Md. 179, 498 A.2d 276 (1985).

Willful delay in correcting tax delinquencies amounted to Rule violation. — An attorney's willful delay in correcting tax delinquencies spanning from two to six years from the date he first became aware of them constituted "conduct prejudicial to the administration of justice," and thus violated Rule of Professional Conduct 8.4. Attorney Grievance Comm'n v. Gavin, 350 Md. 176, 711 A.2d 193 (1998).

Eventual payment of moneys due. — Eventual late payment of all monies due to a taxing authority does not preclude disciplinary action under section (d) of this Rule consequences of the illegal action, but does not mitigate the act itself and therefore does not erase a potential disciplinary violation. Attorney Grievance Comm'n v. Breschi, 340 Md. 590, 667 A.2d 659 (1995).

Acceptance of unapproved fees was criminal conduct. — Attorney's act in taking unapproved worker's compensation fees in violation of 33 U.S.C. § 928(e) amounted to "criminal conduct" within the meaning of paragraph (b) of this Rule. Attorney Grievance Comm'n v. Eisenstein, 333 Md. 464, 635 A.2d 1327 (1994).

Misrepresentation of endorsement. — An attorney's misrepresentation of an endorsement constituted forgery which warranted suspension. Attorney Grievance Comm'n v. James, 333 Md. 174, 634 A.2d 48 (1993).

Attestation of false signature. — Ninety-day suspension was proper sanction for deliberate falsification of the notary certificate and knowing attestation of a false signature on a deed as genuine. Attorney Grievance Comm'n v. Maxwell, 307 Md. 600, 516 A.2d 570 (1986).

Forging another judge's name to change of disposition in a traffic case in return for political support warranted disbarment. Attorney Grievance Comm'n v. Bennett, 304 Md. 120, 497 A.2d 1140 (1985).

Misappropriation of client's funds involves conduct constituting "moral turpitude." Attorney Grievance Comm'n v. Moore, 301 Md. 169, 482 A.2d 497 (1984); Attorney Grievance Comm'n v. Short, 303 Md. 317, 493 A.2d 362 (1985).

Subsequent approval of unauthorized advance. — Arguing that an unauthorized "advance" from estate funds was later approved as a fee is little better than arguing that a fiduciary may dip into the client's funds

for a "loan" as long as the money is later repaid. Attorney Grievance Comm'n v. Owrutsky, 322 Md. 334, 587 A.2d 511 (1991).

It is a breach of trust for a trustee to lend trust funds to himself. Attorney Grievance Comm'n v. Owrutsky, 322 Md. 334, 587 A.2d 511 (1991).

Placing trust account money in unapproved account. — Respondent violated § 10-302 of the Business Occupations & Professions Article of the Annotated Code, Rule 1.15 (a) and this Rule, by placing trust account money in an unapproved account. Attorney Grievance Comm'n v. Boyd, 333 Md. 298, 635 A.2d 382 (1994).

Neglect of administration of estate which was continuous over several years and which ultimately prejudiced the right of at least one legatee under the will from receiving a monetary bequest was sufficient to warrant a 45-day suspension. Attorney Grievance Comm'n v. Gallagher, 306 Md. 107, 507 A.2d 625 (1986).

Failure to carry out contract of employment. — Ninety-day suspension was appropriate sanction for attorney's failure to timely file or adequately investigate action on behalf of her client, and for misrepresenting to her client that the suit had been filed on her behalf and was proceeding to trial where the client paid the attorney only part of the costs involved in the work the attorney did do and the attorney did not consider the gratuitous client to be a client; an attorney-client relationship did exist and, thus, the attorney failed to carry out her contract of employment. Attorney Grievance Comm'n v. Pinkney, 311 Md. 137, 532 A.2d 1367 (1987).

Unwarranted claims. — Evidence that a lawyer had filed a RICO action that had "absolutely no foundation of facts" in the hope of obtaining treble damages was sufficient to justify sanction. Attorney Grievance Comm'n v. Alison, 349 Md. 623, 709 A.2d 1212 (1998).

Delegation of responsibility. — An attorney's practice of assigning and handling cases in such a manner that the lawyer ultimately charged with actually representing the client went into court unprepared or missed scheduled trial dates entirely, resulted in clients not being afforded competent representation, and justified an indefinite suspension from the practice of law. Attorney Grievance Comm'n v. Ficker, 349 Md. 13, 706 A.2d 1045 (1998).

Tardiness or absence from trial. — Since being late for a scheduled court appearance interferes with the administration of justice, it is obvious that being altogether absent from a scheduled trial does so as well; however, the circumstances surrounding the failure to appear and the actual consequences of that failure are matters that go to the question of sanction. Attorney Grievance Comm'n v.

Ficker, 319 Md. 305, 572 A.2d 501 (1990).

Clients of other attorneys. — It was not a violation of former DR 1-102 (A) (4) for attorney not to have advised the clients of other attorneys that the recording undertaken by those attorneys was possibly ineffective. Attorney Grievance Comm'n v. Clements, 319 Md. 289, 572 A.2d 174 (1990).

Unintentional commingling of funds. — Lawyer was indefinitely suspended from the practice of law where he failed to maintain a trust account, commingled client funds and his own, and failed to keep proper records regarding such funds; but, the violations were unintentional, resulting from lawyer's ignorance of his obligation to refrain from commingling, and he was not motivated to use client funds for his own benefit. Attorney Grievance Comm'n v. Awuah, 346 Md. 420, 697 A.2d 446 (1997).

Bar Counsel failed to prove by clear and convincing evidence violations of section (c), Rule 1.15, or § 10-306 of the Business Occupations and Professions Article, where lawyer's use of funds from trust account for operating expenses was motivated by ignorance of his obligations and not by fraud, dishonesty or deceit. Attorney Grievance Comm'n v. Awuah, 346 Md. 420, 697 A.2d 446 (1997).

Mishandling of escrow account. — Indefinite suspension was appropriate sanction for attorney's mishandling of escrow account, including the failure to pay claims due from the account and the failure to refund moneys to clients. Attorney Grievance Comm'n v. Singleton, 311 Md. 1, 532 A.2d 157 (1987).

Escrow account violations. — An attorney who failed to observe the requirements with regard to an escrow account violated this Rule and Rule 1.15 of the Rules of Professional Conduct, former Rule BV9 (now Rule 16-709) and § 10-306 of the Business Occupations and Professions Article, and was suspended for a minimum of one year. Attorney Grievance Comm'n v. Drew, 341 Md. 139, 669 A.2d 1344 (1996).

The nonconsensual kissing of clients and spanking of clients and employees was "relevant to law practice" within the meaning of this Rule. Attorney Grievance Comm'n v. Goldsborough, 330 Md. 342, 624 A.2d 503 (1993).

Claimed ignorance of ethical duties and bookkeeping requirements is not a defense in disciplinary proceedings, but a finding with respect to the intent with which a violation was committed is relevant on the issue of the appropriate sanction. Attorney Grievance Comm'n v. Awuah, 346 Md. 420, 697 A.2d 446 (1997).

Use of colorful language. — This Rule was not violated where an attorney stated that "one learns to expect to get jerked around" when dealing with an insurance company, and called a driver in the case an idiot. Attorney Grievance Comm'n v. Alison, 349 Md. 623, 709 A.2d 1212 (1998).

Violations may show intent with regard to good faith or honest belief defense. Where the defendant in a criminal proceeding introduces evidence of possible Disciplinary Code violations as evidence of a good faith or honest belief defense, whether a violation in fact occurred is relevant to the jury's determination of the defendant's intent or lack thereof; thus, instructions to that effect were correct. Cardin v. State, 73 Md. App. 200, 533 A.2d 928 (1987), cert. denied, 488 U.S. 827, 109 S. Ct. 78, 102 L. Ed. 2d 55 (1988).

Representation of multiple defendants in a criminal case. — An attorney's contact with his client's represented criminal codefendant was deemed a violation of this Rule and resulted in disbarment. Attorney Grievance Comm'n v. Kent, 337 Md. 361, 653 A.2d 909 (1995).

Mitigating circumstances. — While disbarment usually follows a conviction of a crime of moral turpitude which involves fraud or dishonesty, a lesser sanction may be justified when compelling mitigating circumstances exist. Attorney Grievance Comm'n v. Mandel, 316 Md. 197, 557 A.2d 1329 (1989).

The traumatic events in attorney's life during the period for which he failed to file tax returns, together with the fact he acknowledged and regretted his errors and felt tremendous remorse, warranted the unusually lenient sanction of a six-month suspension. Attorney Grievance Comm'n v. Breschi, 340 Md. 590, 667 A.2d 659 (1995).

Alcoholism, drug addiction or mental disorder. — When alcoholism is, to a substantial extent, the cause of the misconduct by an attorney, we view the misconduct in a somewhat different light; under this circumstance the appropriate sanction is indefinite suspension and the focus shifts to questions of rehabilitation and the imposition of conditions sufficient to protect the public if the lawyer is allowed to resume practice. Attorney Grievance Comm'n v. Reid, 308 Md. 646, 521 A.2d 743 (1987).

When a lawyer's misconduct is caused by alcoholism, drug addiction, or a mental disorder, the usual sanction is indefinite suspension. This provides the requisite protection for the public, for it prevents the lawyer from practicing law until such time (if ever) that he or she can demonstrate that he or she is free from the effects of the ailment and able to practice competently. At the same time, the lawyer is spared the ultimate sanction of disbarment, a sanction which would be unfair to apply where the lawyer's conduct is caused by factors beyond his or her control. Attorney

520

Grievance Comm'n v. Powers, 314 Md. 484, 551 A.2d 465 (1989).

Where alcoholism is allegedly implicated in cases involving misappropriation of trust or client funds, a sanction less severe than disbarment may be imposed if the evidence discloses that the alcoholism, to a substantial extent, was the responsible, precipitating, and root cause of the misappropriation. Attorney Grievance Comm'n v. White, 328 Md. 412, 614 A.2d 955 (1992).

Simply to show that an attorney was in the throes of alcoholism at the time he misappropriated client funds and that his thinking was "alcoholically impaired" to the point where he rationalized his behavior as acceptable, even though he knew it was not, is insufficient mitigation in and of itself to justify a sanction less than disbarment. Attorney Grievance Comm'n v. White, 328 Md. 412, 614 A.2d 955 (1992).

An indefinite suspension was the proper sanction in the case of a misappropriation of client funds caused by alcoholism; however, in the future, absent truly compelling circumstances, alcoholism will usually not be permitted to mitigate where an attorney commits a violation of ethical or legal rules which would ordinarily warrant disbarment. Attorney Grievance Comm'n v. Kenney, 339 Md. 578, 664 A.2d 854 (1995).

Failure to report to a D.W.I. facility following a D.W.I. conviction was conduct prejudicial to the administration of justice and in violation of the Rules of Professional Conduct. Attorney Grievance Comm'n v. Garland, 345 Md. 383, 692 A.2d 465 (1997).

Lawyer's criminal behavior, which was causally related to psychiatric disorder, warranted imposition of indefinite suspension. Attorney Grievance Comm'n v. Mitchell, 308 Md. 653, 521 A.2d 746 (1987).

Evidence justified findings of misconduct, and disbarment was warranted. Attorney Grievance Comm'n v. Mazelis, 309 Md. 50, 522 A.2d 913 (1987).

Sanctions for misrepresentation. — A misrepresentation need not involve fraud or deceit; and in such a circumstance a sanction other than disbarment is justified and has been imposed; when, in addition to the misrepresentation, a finding of fraud is made and is supported by the evidence, disbarment would follow as a matter of course absent compelling extenuating circumstances. Attorney Grievance Comm'n v. Myers, 333 Md. 440, 635 A.2d 1315 (1994).

Ninety-day suspension was appropriate sanction for attorney's neglect of client's cases, falsifying client's signature on a complaint, and causing the complaint with the false signature to be notarized and filed. Attorney Grievance Comm'n v. Parsons, 310 Md.

132, 527 A.2d 325 (1987).

Indefinite suspension with leave to apply for reinstatement in one year was warranted where the attorney had served sentence for federal offenses in California, had been suspended and reinstated by the California Bar, and had, both prior to and after the federal charges, no other misconduct or disciplinary problems. Attorney Grievance Comm'n v. Sparrow, 314 Md. 421, 550 A.2d 1150 (1988).

Indefinite suspension with leave to apply for reinstatement after 90 days was warranted, where defendant pleaded guilty to possessing cocaine and drug paraphernalia, resisting arrest, and assault and battery upon an officer, and had a long history of abuse of controlled substances. Attorney Grievance Comm'n v. Hamby, 322 Md. 606, 589 A.2d 53 (1991).

Indefinite suspension was proper sanction. — Where respondent attorney's representation of four clients was marked by serious neglect and inattention; where he failed to return a fee which was unearned for a period of nine months; where he failed to timely remit funds he received on behalf of a client; where he failed to communicate with his clients; and where in connection with the investigation of three of the complaints, respondent failed to answer Bar Counsel's requests for information, the proper sanction was that the attorney be indefinitely suspended from the practice of law, with the right to apply for reinstatement after the suspension had been in effect for six months, conditioned upon his payment of all costs and upon the monitoring of respondent's practice. Attorney Grievance Comm'n v. David, 331 Md. 317, 628 A.2d 178 (1993).

Suspension of one year required, disbarment was not appropriate sanction considering the nature of the controlled dangerous substances involved, the absence of a finding of actual distribution, and all other surrounding circumstances. Attorney Grievance Comm'n v. Proctor, 309 Md. 412, 524 A.2d 773 (1987).

One-year suspension appropriate. — Although attorney's conduct in assisting a former client in breaking into the home of his wife was an aberration, the egregious nature of that conduct warranted the imposition of a significant sanction such that the attorney was suspended indefinitely from the practice of law with the right to apply for reinstatement not less than one year from the date of filing the opinion. Attorney Grievance Comm'n v. Protokowicz, 329 Md. 252, 619 A.2d 100 (1993).

Two-year suspension appropriate. — Attorney suspended for 2 years for violating paragraphs (b), (c), and (d) of this Rule, inter alia, by the manner in which he collected fees and handled the funds of a client. Attorney

Grievance Comm'n v. Eisenstein, 333 Md. 464, 635 A.2d 1327 (1994).

Three-year suspension appropriate. — Where an attorney, who had been practicing for nearly 30 years and had no record of previous misconduct, had been negligent and careless in handling estates and trusts, had taken fees from the estates before, and in some cases without, approval of the Orphans' Court and had made a loan to himself from the trust funds, a three-year suspension from the practice of law was the appropriate sanction. Attorney Grievance Comm'n v. Owrutsky, 322 Md. 334, 587 A.2d 511 (1991).

Three-year suspension was warranted where attorney prepared defective will for his client and later excoriated her and attempted to mislead an investigator and inquiry panel for the Attorney Grievance Commission. Attorney Grievance Comm'n v. Myers, 302 Md. 571, 490 A.2d 231 (1985).

Disbarment required. — Illegal conduct involving moral turpitude, dishonesty, fraud, deceit, or misrepresentation; and conduct prejudicial to the administration of justice, adversely reflected on attorney's fitness to practice law and warranted disbarment. Attorney Grievance Comm'n v. Ezrin, 312 Md. 603, 541 A.2d 966 (1988).

Misappropriation of funds by an attorney involves moral turpitude; it is an act infected with deceit and dishonesty and will result in disbarment in the absence of compelling extenuating circumstances justifying a lesser sanction. Attorney Grievance Comm'n v. Ezrin, 312 Md. 603, 541 A.2d 966 (1988).

Absent compelling extenuating circumstances justifying a lesser sanction, misappropriation by an attorney of funds entrusted to the attorney's care warrants disbarment, and this is true even where the misappropriation is committed in a nonprofessional capacity, since it involves a breach of trust or a fiduciary relationship and bears upon the fitness of a lawyer to practice his profession. Attorney Grievance Comm'n v. Lazerow, 320 Md. 507, 578 A.2d 779 (1990); Attorney Grievance Comm'n v. Kolodner, 321 Md. 545, 583 A.2d 724 (1991).

Disbarment was appropriate sanction where attorney executed documents without ex-spouse's authority in order to obtain for himself the proceeds of the sale of property. Attorney Grievance Comm'n v. Pearson, 322 Md. 154, 586 A.2d 25 (1991).

Representations and omissions made by an attorney in connection with his application for admission to the Bar of this State violated Rules 8.1, 8.4 (b), 8.4 (c), and 8.4 (d) of the Maryland Rules of Professional Conduct and warranted disbarment. Attorney Grievance Comm'n v. Joehl, 335 Md. 83, 642 A.2d 194 (1994).

Attorney was properly disbarred for violating Maryland Rules of Professional Conduct 1.1, 1.3, 1.4 (a) and (b), 1.15 (a), 3.3 (a) (1), and 8.4 (b) and (c), § 10-306 of the Business Occupations and Professions Article, and former Rule BU9 (now Rule 16-609) of the Maryland Rules of Procedure. Attorney Grievance Comm'n v. Williams, 335 Md. 458, 644 A.2d 490 (1994).

Where an attorney violated Rule 3.3 (a) (1) and paragraph (c) of the Rule when he gave a false response to a question posed by a District Court judge concerning his traffic record, due to his previous history of misconduct, he was disbarred. Attorney Grievance Comm'n v. Myers, 333 Md. 440, 635 A.2d 1315 (1994).

Disbarment of attorney was appropriate where there were serious and repeated violations of this Rule and other provisions of the Maryland Rules of Professional Conduct. Attorney Grievance Comm'n v. Milliken, 348 Md. 486, 704 A.2d 1225 (1998).

Reinstatement proceedings. — The essential factors to be considered in any reinstatement proceeding are: (1) the nature and circumstances of the petitioner's original misconduct; (2) the petitioner's subsequent conduct and reformation; (3) the petitioner's present character; and (4) the petitioner's present qualifications and competence to practice. In re Blondes, 335 Md. 456, 644 A.2d 489 (1994).

Applied in Attorney Grievance Comm'n v. Martin, 308 Md. 272, 518 A.2d 1050 (1987); Attorney Grievance Comm'n v. Trilling, 311 Md. 711, 537 A.2d 269 (1988); Attorney Grievance Comm'n v. Dacy, 313 Md. 1, 542 A.2d 841 (1988); Attorney Grievance Comm'n v. Greenspan, 313 Md. 180, 545 A.2d 12 (1988); Attorney Grievance Comm'n v. Werner, 315 Md. 172, 553 A.2d 722 (1989); Attorney Grievance Comm'n v. Keister, 327 Md. 56, 607 A.2d 909 (1992); Attorney Grievance Comm'n v. Hollis, 347 Md. 547, 702 A.2d 223 (1997); Post v. Bregman, 349 Md. 142, 707 A.2d 806 (1998).

Quoted in Attorney Grievance Comm'n v. Sachse, 345 Md. 578, 693 A.2d 806 (1997); Attorney Grievance Comm'n v. Sabghir, 350 Md. 67, 710 A.2d 926 (1998).

Stated in Attorney Grievance Comm'n v. Montgomery, 318 Md. 154, 567 A.2d 112 (1989).

Cited in Attorney Grievance Comm'n v. Kerpelman, 323 Md. 136, 591 A.2d 516 (1991), cert. denied, 502 U.S. 939, 112 S. Ct. 374, 116 L. Ed. 2d 326 (1991); Attorney Grievance Comm'n v. Berger, 323 Md. 428, 593 A.2d 1103 (1991); Medical Mut. Liab. Ins. Soc'y v. Azzato, 94 Md. App. 632, 618 A.2d 274, cert. denied, 330 Md. 319, 624 A.2d 419 (1993); Attorney Grievance Comm'n v. Paugh, 345 Md. 692, 694 A.2d 106 (1997); Attorney Grievance Comm'n v. Zeiger, 347 Md. 107, 698 A.2d 1115 (1997).

Rule 8.5. Jurisdiction.

(a) A lawyer admitted by the Court of Appeals to practice in this State is subject to the disciplinary authority of this State for a violation of these rules in this or any other jurisdiction.

(b) A lawyer not admitted by the Court of Appeals to practice in this State is subject to the disciplinary authority of this State for conduct that constitutes a violation of these Rules and that:

(1) involves the practice of law in this State by that lawyer, or

(2) involves that lawyer holding himself or herself out as practicing law in this State, or

(3) involves the practice of law in this State by another lawyer over whom that lawyer has the obligation of supervision or control.

Code Comparison. — There is no counterpart to this Rule in the Code. See, however, Rule 16-701 a of the Maryland Rules of Procedure.

Quoted in Attorney Grievance Comm'n v. Hopp, 330 Md. 177, 623 A.2d 193 (1993).

Cited in Kennedy v. Bar Ass'n, 316 Md. 646, 561 A.2d 200 (1989).

APPENDIX: TABLES OF COMPARABLE RULES

TABLE I — 1984 Revision

(Table II — 1997 Revision follows)

THIS TABLE SHOWS THOSE FORMER MARYLAND RULES OF PROCEDURE AND MARYLAND DISTRICT RULES RESCINDED EFFECTIVE JULY 1, 1984, FROM WHICH CORRESPONDING MARYLAND RULES IN TITLE 1 THROUGH TITLE 4 HAVE BEEN DERIVED

RESCINDED RULE	REVISED RULE
CJ § 7-201	1-325
1 f	1-102
1 g	1-201 (c)
1 h, i	1-201 (b)
2 b	1-201 (e)
2 c	1-201 (d)
3	1-312 (a)
3 a	1-331
3 d	1-103
5 a	1-202 (a)
5 c	1-202 (b), 1-303, 1-304
5 e	1-202 (e)
5 f	1-202 (f)
5 g	1-202 (g)
5 h	1-202 (h)
5 m	1-202 (j)
5 n	1-202 (l)
5 o	1-202 (m)
5 q	1-202 (p)
5 r	1-202 (k)
5 v	1-202 (o)
5 w	1-202 (r)
5 y	1-202 (s)
5 z	1-202 (t)
5 aa	1-202 (d)
5 cc	1-202 (v)
5 ee	1-202 (w)
5 ff	1-202 (y)
8 a	1-203 (a)
8 b	1-203 (b)
18 (b)	2-522 (a)
21	1-303
103 b	2-111 (b)
103 c	2-112 (a)
103 e	2-112 (a)
103 f	2-114
103 g	2-111 (a)
103 j	2-112 (b), 3-112 (b)
104 a	2-510 (d)
104 a (2)	2-126 (f)
104 a (4)	2-645 (d)
104 b	2-510 (d)
104 b 1	2-121 (a), 2-123 (a)
104 b 1 (i), (ii)	2-124 (a)

RESCINDED RULE	REVISED RULE
104 b 2	2-121 (a), 2-126 (a)
104 c	2-125
104 h 1	2-121 (b)
104 h 2	2-123 (a)
104 h 3 (c)	2-126 (g)
104 i	2-121 (d)
105 a	2-121 (a)
105 b	2-122 (a)
105 b 1 (a)	2-126 (b), 3-126 (b)
105 b 2	2-122 (b), 2-126 (b), 3-126 (b)
106 b, c	2-124 (c)
106 e 1, 2	2-124 (c)
106 e 3	2-321 (b) (3)
107 a 1	2-121 (a)
107 a 2	2-121 (a), 2-126 (a)
107 a 3	2-121 (b)
107 a 4	2-121 (a)
107 b	2-321 (b) (1), (5)
107 c	2-121 (d)
108 a	2-124 (f), 3-124 (f)
108 b	2-124 (g), 3-124 (g)
108 d	2-321 (b) (4)
111 a	2-122 (a)
114 a, b	2-510 (c)
114 d	2-510 (h)
115 a	2-510 (c)
115 b	2-510 (e)
116 a	2-123 (a), (b)
116 b	2-510 (d)
116 c 1, 2	2-126 (a)
116 c 3	2-126 (g)
117 a, b	2-123 (c)
119	2-124 (b)
124	2-131, 3-131
125 a	2-132 (b)
125 c 2	2-132 (b)
125 d	2-132 (c)
125 e	2-132 (d)
140 a	2-101
170 a	2-101
203 a-c	2-201
205 c, d	2-202 (b)
205 e 1, 2	2-202 (c)
208 b 1	2-214 (b) (1)
208 b 2	2-214 (b) (2)
208 c	2-214 (c)
209 a	2-231 (a)
209 d	2-231 (h)
220	2-241 (a)
220 c-e	2-241 (b)
220 f	2-241 (d)
222	2-241 (a), 3-241 (a)
240	2-241 (a)
301 b	2-303 (b), (d), 3-303 (d)
301 c	2-304 (c), 2-305
301 d	2-303 (c), 3-303 (c)
301 e	1-301 (a)

RESCINDED RULE	REVISED RULE	RESCINDED RULE	REVISED RULE
301 f	1-311 (a)	400 d	2-402 (c)
301 g	1-313	400 e	2-402 (d), 2-432 (c)
301 h	1-301 (a)	400 f	2-402 (c) (1)
301 j	2-322 (e)	401	2-411
301 k	1-301 (f)	402	2-404 (a) (1)
301 l	1-302	403 a	2-414 (a)
302 a	1-311 (a)	403 b	2-414 (b)
302 b	1-311 (b)	403 c	2-414 (c)
302 c 1	1-312 (b)	403 d	2-414 (d)
302 c 2, 3	1-312 (a)	404	2-401 (e)
303 a	1-301 (f)	405 a 1	2-412 (a)
306 a 1	1-321 (a)	405 a 2 (a)	2-412 (a)
306 a 2	1-323	405 a 2 (b)	2-412 (d), 2-510 (c)
306 b	1-321 (b)	405 b 1, 2	2-417 (a)
306 c	1-321 (a)	406 a	2-403 (a)
306 d	1-323	407 a	3-510 (a)
307 a 2	2-321 (b) (2)	408	2-413
307 c (4)	2-321 (b) (1)	409 a	2-415 (b)
309	1-204 (a)	409 b	2-417 (b)
311 a	2-323 (f)	409 c	2-415 (a)
312 b	2-323 (e)	409 c 2	2-415 (g), 2-416 (g)
313 a	2-212 (a), 2-303 (c),	410	2-416 (a)-(f), (h), (i)
	3-212 (a), 3-303 (c)	410 c	2-412 (b)
313 c-e	2-212 (a), 3-212 (a)	411 a	2-415 (d)
314 a 1, 2	2-331 (a)	411 b 1, 2	2-415 (e)
314 b	2-331 (b)	411 b 3	2-415 (c)
314 c	2-331 (c), 3-331 (c)	411 b 4	2-415 (f)
314 d 2	2-331 (d)	411 b 5	2-415 (e)
314 d 3	2-331 (c), 3-331 (c)	412 a	2-412 (e)
315 a	2-332 (a)	412 b	2-414 (e)
315 b	2-332 (e)	412 c 1, 2	2-415 (g)
315 c 1, 2	2-332 (b)	412 c 3	2-417 (c)
315 d	2-332 (c), 3-332 (c)	412 d	2-415 (i)
315 d 1	2-332 (b)	412 e	2-415 (d), (i)
315 f 1, 2	2-332 (d), 3-332 (d)	413	2-419
317	2-327 (b)	413 a 5	2-401 (d)
319	2-311 (c)	413 c	2-416 (g)
320	2-341 (a), 3-341 (a)	414	2-434
320 a 2-4	2-341 (c), 3-341 (c)	417 a 1, 2	2-421 (a)
320 b 1	2-341 (c), 3-341 (c)	417 a 3	2-401 (c)
320 d 5	2-341 (c), 3-341 (c)	417 b 1, 2	2-421 (b)
321 a	2-311 (a)	417 c 1	2-432 (d)
321 b	2-311 (d)	417 d	2-421 (d)
321 d	2-311 (e)	417 f	2-421 (c)
322	2-322 (e)	419	2-422
323 a 1-4	2-322 (a)	420	2-423
323 a 5	2-323 (f)	421 a	2-424 (a)
323 b	2-322 (a), 2-324 (a)	421 b 1, 2	2-424 (b)
340 a	2-305	421 c	2-424 (d)
342 b 1, 2	2-323 (d)	421 d	2-424 (c)
342 c 1, 2	2-323 (f), (g)	421 e	2-424 (e)
343 a	2-325 (a)	421 f	2-424 (d)
343 d	2-325 (d)	422 a 1	2-432 (e)
343 e	2-325 (f)	422 a 2	2-415 (h), 2-432 (b)
370 a 3	2-305	422 a 3, 4	2-432 (b)
372 a 2	2-323 (c)	422 a 5-7	2-433 (c)
372 b	2-323 (e)	422 b	2-433 (b)
372 b 1	2-323 (e)	422 c 1	2-432 (a), 2-433 (a)
379	2-341 (c), 3-341 (c)	422 c 2	2-433 (a)
400 c	2-402 (a)	422 c 3	2-432 (a)

RESCINDED RULE	REVISED RULE	RESCINDED RULE	REVISED RULE
422 d	2-431	580 m 1	2-542 (f)
501 a	2-503 (b)	580 n	2-542 (f)
501 b	2-212 (b)	580 q	2-542 (i)
502	2-502	582 b	2-506 (d), 3-506 (e)
503	2-503 (a)	595 a	2-543 (c)
504 a-c	2-504	595 d	2-543 (d) (1)
515 a	2-327 (a)	595 e	2-543 (c)
517	2-511 (d)	595 h	2-543 (h)
521	2-514, 3-514	596 b	2-541 (a), 2-542 (a), 2-543 (a)
522 a	2-517 (d), 3-517 (d)	596 c	2-541 (b)
522 b, c	2-517 (c), 3-517 (c)	596 d	2-541 (d), 2-542 (c), 2-543 (c)
522 d	2-517 (a), 3-517 (a)	596 e	2-541 (e)
526	2-508 (b)	596 e 1	2-542 (d) (2), 2-543 (d) (2)
527 a 1	2-508 (a)	596 e 2	2-543 (d) (3)
527 b	2-508 (d), 3-508 (c)	596 f	2-541 (f)
527 c 1-4	2-508 (c)	596 g	2-541 (g)
527 e	2-508 (e), 3-508 (d)	596 h 1, 2	2-541 (h), 2-543 (f)
528	2-536, 3-536	596 h 3	2-541 (h)
530	2-507	596 h 3 (c), (d)	2-543 (f)
536	2-513 (a), 3-513 (a)	596 h 4	2-541 (h), 2-543 (f)
541 b	2-506 (b), 3-506 (b), (d)	596 h 5, 6	2-541 (i), 2-543 (g)
541 c	2-506 (c)	596 h 7	2-541 (h)
541 d	2-506 (d), 3-506 (e)	596 h 8	2-541 (j), 2-542 (i), 2-543 (h)
542 a 1, 2	2-505 (a)	596 i	2-541 (j)
542 c 1	2-505 (b)	604 a	2-603 (a), (b)
542 c 4	2-505 (b)	604 b	1-341
542 d 1	2-505 (c)	604 c	2-603 (d), 3-603 (c)
542 g	2-505 (d)	605 a	2-602
542 i	2-505 (e)	605 b	2-615, 3-615
543 a 3, 4	2-512 (h)	605 d	2-614
543 a 8	2-511 (c)	606	2-503 (a)
543 d	2-512 (d)	607	2-632 (c)
544	2-511 (b)	610 a 1	2-501 (a)
545	2-325 (e)	610 a 3	2-501 (a)
548	2-509	610 b	2-501 (c)
550 a	2-515 (a)	610 d 1	2-501 (e)
550 d	2-515 (c)	610 d 2	2-501 (d)
554 a	2-520 (b)	610 d 4	2-501 (f)
554 b 1	2-520 (c)	619 a	2-623
554 b 2	2-520 (d)	620 a	2-621 (a)
554 d	2-520 (e)	622 e	2-641 (a)
558 a, b	2-521 (a)	622 h 1	2-641 (b)
558 d	2-521 (a)	622 h 2	2-126 (f), 2-642 (e)
560	2-522 (c)	622 h 3	2-641 (b)
561	2-503 (a)	625 a	2-535 (a), (b)
563 a	2-532 (a)	625 b	2-535 (c)
563 a 2	2-532 (b)	627	2-633 (a)
563 a 3	2-532 (c)	628 b	2-633 (b)
563 a 4	2-532 (d)	635 b	2-516, 3-516
563 b	2-532 (e)	645	2-115 (d)
563 b 3	2-533 (c)	645 a	2-611 (a)
563 c	2-532 (f)	645 c	2-611 (c)
567 b	2-533 (b)	645 d	2-611 (d)
567 c	2-533 (c)	659	2-115 (k)
567 e	2-533 (d)	681	2-535 (d), 3-535 (d)
580 a, b	2-542 (a)	685 a	2-648, 3-648
580 c	2-542 (c)	701	1-201 (a), (c), 4-101
580 d	2-542 (d) (1)	702 a	4-102 (a)
580 g 1	2-542 (d) (5)	702 b	4-102 (c)
580 l 1, 2	2-542 (d) (3)	702 c	4-102 (d)

RESCINDED RULE	REVISED RULE	RESCINDED RULE	REVISED RULE
702 d	4-102 (e)	741 a 1, 2	4-263 (a)
702 e	4-102 (g)	741 a 3	4-263 (g)
702 f	4-102 (j)	741 b	4-263 (b)
702 g	4-102 (k)	741 c	4-263 (c)
702 h	4-102 (l)	741 d	4-263 (d)
710 a	4-201 (a)	741 e 1	4-263 (e)
710 e	4-201 (d)	741 e 2	4-263 (f)
711 a	4-202 (a)	741 f	4-263 (h)
711 b	4-202 (c)	741 g	4-263 (i)
711 c	4-202 (b)	742 a	4-264
711 d, e	4-202 (d)	742 b	4-265
712 a	4-203 (a)	742 c	4-266 (a)
712 b	4-203 (b)	742 d	4-266 (c)
713 a	4-204	742 e	2-510 (h), 4-266 (d)
713 c	4-204	743	4-267 (a)-(d)
720 a	4-212 (a), (b)	744	4-254 (b)
720 b	4-212 (c)	745 b	4-253 (b)
720 c	4-212 (d)	745 c	4-253 (c)
720 d, e	4-212 (e)	746 a, b	4-271 (a)
720 f	4-212 (f)	750 a	4-361 (b)
721 a	4-216 (a)	750 b	4-361 (a)
721 b	4-216 (d)	751 a	4-311 (b)
721 c	4-216 (e)	751 b	2-512 (b), 4-312 (b)
721 d	4-216 (f)	751 c	4-312 (b)
721 e	4-216 (h)	751 d	2-512 (i), 4-312 (h)
721 f	4-216 (i)	751 e	4-311 (c)
721 g	4-216 (j)	752	2-512 (d), 4-312 (d)
722	4-217	753	4-313
723	4-215 (b)	753 b 1	2-512 (g), 4-312 (g)
723 a	4-213 (c)	753 b 3	2-512 (i)
723 b 1-3	4-215 (a)	754 a	2-512 (a), 4-312 (a)
723 b 7	4-215 (a)	754 b	2-512 (e), 4-312 (b), (e)
723 c 1	4-215 (a)	755 a	4-321 (a)
724	4-231	755 b	2-513 (b), 3-513 (b), 4-321 (b)
725	4-214	755 c	4-321 (a)
730	4-241	755 d	2-513 (c), 3-513 (c), 4-321 (c)
731 a	4-242 (a)	756	4-324
731 b 1	4-242 (b) (1)	757 a	4-325 (b)
731 b 2	4-242 (b) (3)	757 b	4-325 (c)
731 b 3	4-242 (b) (4)	757 c	2-520 (d), 4-325 (d)
731 c	4-242 (c)	757 d	4-325 (a)
731 d	4-242 (d)	757 e	4-326 (a)
731 e	4-242 (e)	757 f	4-325 (e)
731 f	4-242 (f)	757 g	4-325 (f)
732	4-244	757 h	4-325 (e)
733	4-243	758 a	4-326 (a)
734	4-245	758 b	2-521 (a), 4-326 (a)
735	4-246	758 c	2-521 (b), 4-326 (b)
736	4-252	758 d	2-521 (c), 4-326 (c)
737 b	4-266 (b)	759	4-327
740 a	4-261 (b)	759 a	2-522 (a)
740 b	4-267 (e)	759 e	2-522 (b)
740 c	4-261 (c)	760	4-328
740 d	4-261 (d)	764	4-353
740 e	4-261 (e)	770	4-331
740 f	4-261 (f)	771	4-341
740 g	4-261 (g)	772 a	4-342 (a)
740 h	4-261 (h)	772 b	4-342 (b)
740 i	4-261 (i)	772 c	4-342 (c)
740 j	4-261 (b)	772 d	4-342 (d), 4-343 (d)

RESCINDED RULE	REVISED RULE	RESCINDED RULE	REVISED RULE
772 e	4-342 (e)	BK41 d	4-402 (c)
772 f	4-342 (f)	BK41 e	4-403
772 h	4-342 (g)	BK43 a	4-404
772 A	4-343 (a)-(c), (e)-(g)	BK43 b	4-404, 4-405
773	4-344	BK44 c	4-406 (b)
774	4-345	BK44 d	4-406 (c)
775	4-346	BK44 e	4-406 (d)
776 a	4-348 (a)	BK45 a	4-407 (b)
776 b	4-348 (c)	BK45 b	4-407 (a)
776 c	4-348 (b)	BK45 c	4-407 (d)
777	4-351	BK45 d	4-407 (c)
778 a	4-347	BK46	4-408
778 b	4-348 (c)	BU70	2-221 (a)
780	4-601	BU72	2-221 (b)
781	4-611	BU73	2-221 (c)
782 a, b	4-247	BU74	2-221 (d)
782 c, d	4-248	EX1	4-502
784	4-621	EX2	4-501
785	4-631	EX3 a	4-503
F6 a	2-646 (a)	EX3 b	4-504
F6 b	2-646 (c)	EX3 c	4-504
F6 c	2-645 (d), 2-646 (d)	EX3 c 1, 2	4-503
F6 d	2-646 (e)	EX4	4-505
F6 e	2-646 (g)	EX5	4-506
F6 f	2-646 (f)	EX6	4-507
F6 g	2-646 (h)	EX7	4-508
F6 h	2-646 (i)	EX8	4-509
F6 i	2-646 (k)	EX9	4-510
F6 j	2-646 (j)	EX10	4-511
F6 k	2-646 (e)	EX11	4-512
G40 a, b	2-115 (a)	1219	1-324
G40 b 4	2-641 (a)	M.D.R. 1 b	3-711
G43	2-115 (b)	M.D.R. 100	3-101
G44	2-115 (c)	M.D.R. 101 a	3-102 (a)
G45	2-115 (d)	M.D.R. 102	1-325
G49 a	2-641 (a), 2-642 (a), (b)	M.D.R. 103 b	3-111 (b)
G51	2-115 (g), 2-643 (b), (c)	M.D.R. 103 c	3-112 (a)
G52 a, b	2-645 (e)	M.D.R. 103 d 2	3-126 (d)
G56	2-645 (h)	M.D.R. 103 e	3-102 (b), 3-112 (a)
G59	2-115 (k)	M.D.R. 103 f	3-114
G60	2-115 (i)	M.D.R. 103 g	3-102 (c)
H1	1-401	M.D.R. 103 h	3-111 (a)
H2 a	1-402 (a), (f)	M.D.R. 104 a	3-510 (a)
H2 b 1, 2	1-402 (b)	M.D.R. 104 a (ii)	3-126 (f)
H3 a 2	1-402 (e)	M.D.R. 104 a (iii)	3-645 (d)
H3 b	1-402 (e)	M.D.R. 104 b	3-510 (d)
H4 a, b	1-402 (d)	M.D.R. 104 b 1	3-121 (a), 3-123 (a)
H5	1-406	M.D.R. 104 b 1 (i), (ii)	3-124 (a)
H6 a	1-403 (a)	M.D.R. 104 b 2	3-121 (a), 3-126 (a)
H6 b	1-403 (b)	M.D.R. 104 c	3-125
H6 c 1, 2	1-403 (a), (b)	M.D.R. 104 h 1	3-121 (b)
H7 a, b	1-402 (c)	M.D.R. 104 h 2	3-123 (a)
H8	1-405	M.D.R. 104 h 3 (a)	3-126 (a)
U12 b	2-402 (e) (2)	M.D.R. 104 h 3 (c)	3-126 (g)
U18 a	2-515 (a)	M.D.R. 104 i	3-121 (d)
U18 b	2-515 (c)	M.D.R. 106 b, c	3-124 (c)
U18 c-e	2-515 (a)	M.D.R. 106 e 1, 2	3-124 (c)
BK40	4-401	M.D.R. 106 f	3-124 (h)
BK41 a	4-402 (a)	M.D.R. 107 a 1	3-121 (a)
BK41 c	4-402 (b)	M.D.R. 107 a 2	3-121 (a), 3-126 (a)

APPENDIX: TABLES OF COMPARABLE RULES

RESCINDED RULE	REVISED RULE
M.D.R. 107 a 3	3-121 (b)
M.D.R. 107 b	3-121 (d)
M.D.R. 114 a, b	3-510 (c)
M.D.R. 114 d	3-510 (h)
M.D.R. 115 a	3-510 (c)
M.D.R. 115 b	3-510 (e)
M.D.R. 116 a	3-123 (a), (b)
M.D.R. 116 b	3-510 (d)
M.D.R. 116 c 1, 2	3-126 (a)
M.D.R. 116 c 3	3-126 (g)
M.D.R. 117 a, b	3-123 (c)
M.D.R. 119	3-124 (b)
M.D.R. 125 a	3-132 (a), (b)
M.D.R. 125 b	3-132 (c)
M.D.R. 203	3-201
M.D.R. 205 c, d	3-202 (b)
M.D.R. 205 e	3-202 (c)
M.D.R. 208 b 1	3-214 (b) (1)
M.D.R. 208 b 2	3-214 (b) (2)
M.D.R. 208 c	3-214 (c)
M.D.R. 220	3-241 (a)
M.D.R. 220 b-d	3-241 (d)
M.D.R. 220 e	3-241 (d)
M.D.R. 240	3-241 (a)
M.D.R. 300 b	3-303 (a)
M.D.R. 301 a	3-303 (b)
M.D.R. 301 a (i)	3-304
M.D.R. 301 a (ii)	3-305
M.D.R. 302	3-307
M.D.R. 302 a	3-308, 3-332 (b)
M.D.R. 314 a	3-331 (a)
M.D.R. 314 b	3-331 (b)
M.D.R. 314 c	3-331 (d)
M.D.R. 314 g	3-331 (e)
M.D.R. 314 h	3-331 (f)
M.D.R. 315 a	3-332 (a), (e)
M.D.R. 315 b	3-332 (a)
M.D.R. 317	3-326
M.D.R. 321 a	3-311 (a), (b)
M.D.R. 321 b	3-311 (d)
M.D.R. 321 d	3-311 (c)
M.D.R. 343 a	3-325 (b)
M.D.R. 343 b, c	3-325 (a)
M.D.R. 343 d	3-325 (c)
M.D.R. 401 a	3-701, 3-711
M.D.R. 401 b	3-401
M.D.R. 402	3-431
M.D.R. 405	3-401
M.D.R. 417 a	3-421 (b)
M.D.R. 417 b	3-421 (d)
M.D.R. 417 c	3-421 (g)
M.D.R. 417 d	3-421 (h)
M.D.R. 417 e	3-421 (a)
M.D.R. 417 e 4	3-421 (e)
M.D.R. 417 f	3-421 (c)
M.D.R. 417 g	3-421 (i)
M.D.R. 501	3-503
M.D.R. 504	3-504
M.D.R. 526	3-508 (b)
M.D.R. 527	3-508 (a)
M.D.R. 530	3-507
M.D.R. 541 b	3-506 (c)
M.D.R. 542	3-505
M.D.R. 564 c	3-522
M.D.R. 567 b	3-533 (b)
M.D.R. 567 c	3-533 (c)
M.D.R. 567 d	3-533 (d)
M.D.R. 568	3-701
M.D.R. 604	3-603 (a)
M.D.R. 605 a	3-602
M.D.R. 605 b	3-632 (c)
M.D.R. 605 d	3-614
M.D.R. 610 a	3-306 (a)
M.D.R. 610 b, c	3-306 (b)
M.D.R. 610 d	3-306 (b), (d)
M.D.R. 610 e	3-306 (c)
M.D.R. 619 b	3-601 (c)
M.D.R. 620 a	4-354
M.D.R. 620 b	3-621 (a)
M.D.R. 620 c	3-621 (b)
M.D.R. 621 b, c	3-621 (c)
M.D.R. 622 e	3-641 (a)
M.D.R. 622 h 1	3-641 (b)
M.D.R. 622 h 2	3-126 (f), 3-642 (e)
M.D.R. 622 h 3	3-641 (b)
M.D.R. 622 i	3-641 (a)
M.D.R. 625 a	3-535 (a), (b)
M.D.R. 625 b	3-535 (c)
M.D.R. 627	3-633 (a)
M.D.R. 628 b	3-633 (b)
M.D.R. 645 a	3-611 (a)
M.D.R. 645 c	3-611 (c)
M.D.R. 645 d	3-611 (d)
M.D.R. 645 j	3-611 (f)
M.D.R. 648	3-509
M.D.R. 701	4-101
M.D.R. 702 a	4-102 (a)
M.D.R. 702 c	4-102 (b)
M.D.R. 702 d	4-102 (c)
M.D.R. 702 e	4-102 (e)
M.D.R. 702 f	4-102 (f)
M.D.R. 702 g	4-102 (g)
M.D.R. 702 h	4-102 (h)
M.D.R. 702 i	4-102 (i)
M.D.R. 702 j	4-102 (j)
M.D.R. 702 l	4-102 (k)
M.D.R. 702 m	4-102 (l)
M.D.R. 710 a	4-201 (a)
M.D.R. 710 b-d	4-201 (b), (c)
M.D.R. 710 e	4-201 (d)
M.D.R. 711 a	4-202 (a)
M.D.R. 711 b 1	4-202 (c)
M.D.R. 711 b 2	4-202 (b)
M.D.R. 711 c, d	4-202 (d)
M.D.R. 712	4-203 (a)
M.D.R. 713 a, b	4-204
M.D.R. 720 a, b	4-211 (b)
M.D.R. 720 c	4-212 (a), (b)
M.D.R. 720 d	4-212 (c)
M.D.R. 720 e	4-212 (d)

RESCINDED RULE	REVISED RULE	RESCINDED RULE	REVISED RULE
M.D.R. 720 f	4-212 (e)	M.D.R. 756	4-324
M.D.R. 720 g	4-212 (g)	M.D.R. 760	4-328
M.D.R. 720 h	4-212 (f)	M.D.R. 764	4-353
M.D.R. 720 i	4-211 (a), 4-212 (h)	M.D.R. 770	4-331
M.D.R. 721 a	4-216 (a)	M.D.R. 771	4-341
M.D.R. 721 b	4-216 (b)	M.D.R. 772 a	4-342 (b)
M.D.R. 721 c	4-216 (d)	M.D.R. 772 b	4-342 (c)
M.D.R. 721 d	4-216 (e)	M.D.R. 772 c	4-342 (d), 4-343 (d)
M.D.R. 721 e	4-216 (f)	M.D.R. 772 d	4-342 (e)
M.D.R. 721 f	4-216 (g)	M.D.R. 772 e	4-342 (f)
M.D.R. 721 g	4-216 (i)	M.D.R. 772 g	4-342 (g)
M.D.R. 721 h	4-216 (j)	M.D.R. 774	4-345
M.D.R. 722	4-217	M.D.R. 775	4-346
M.D.R. 723	4-213 (a)	M.D.R. 776 a	4-348 (a)
M.D.R. 723 a	4-212 (e)	M.D.R. 776 b	4-348 (c)
M.D.R. 723 b 4	4-216 (c)	M.D.R. 776 c	4-348 (b)
M.D.R. 724	4-231	M.D.R. 777	4-351
M.D.R. 725	4-214	M.D.R. 778 a	4-347
M.D.R. 726 d	4-215 (c)	M.D.R. 778 b	4-348 (c)
M.D.R. 727	4-221	M.D.R. 780	4-601
M.D.R. 728	4-222	M.D.R. 782 a, b	4-247
M.D.R. 731 a	4-242 (a)	M.D.R. 782 c, d	4-248
M.D.R. 731 b 1	4-242 (b) (1)	M.D.R. 784	4-621
M.D.R. 731 b 2	4-242 (b) (4)	M.D.R. 785	4-631
M.D.R. 731 c	4-242 (c)	M.D.R. F6 a	3-646 (a)
M.D.R. 731 d	4-242 (d)	M.D.R. F6 b	3-646 (c)
M.D.R. 731 e	4-242 (f)	M.D.R. F6 c	3-645 (d), 3-646 (d)
M.D.R. 732	4-244	M.D.R. F6 d	3-646 (e)
M.D.R. 733	4-243	M.D.R. F6 e	3-646 (g)
M.D.R. 734	4-245	M.D.R. F6 f	3-646 (f)
M.D.R. 736	4-251	M.D.R. F6 g	3-646 (h)
M.D.R. 737 b	4-266 (b)	M.D.R. F6 h	3-646 (i)
M.D.R. 742 a	4-265	M.D.R. F6 i	3-646 (k)
M.D.R. 742 b	4-266 (a)	M.D.R. F6 j	3-646 (j)
M.D.R. 742 c	4-266 (c)	M.D.R. F6 k	3-646 (e)
M.D.R. 742 d	3-510 (h), 4-266 (d)	M.D.R. G40 a, b	3-115 (a)
M.D.R. 743	4-267 (a)-(d)	M.D.R. G40 b 4	3-641 (a)
M.D.R. 744	4-254 (a)	M.D.R. G43	3-115 (b)
M.D.R. 745 a	4-253 (a)	M.D.R. G44	3-115 (c)
M.D.R. 745 b	4-253 (b)	M.D.R. G45	3-115 (d)
M.D.R. 745 c	4-253 (c)	M.D.R. G47 c	3-115 (e)
M.D.R. 746	4-271 (b)	M.D.R. G49 a	3-641 (a), 3-642 (a), (b)
M.D.R. 750	4-361 (a)	M.D.R. G51	3-115 (h), 3-643 (b), (c)
M.D.R. 751	4-301 (a)	M.D.R. G52 a, b	3-645 (e)
M.D.R. 755 a	4-321 (a)	M.D.R. G56	3-645 (h)
M.D.R. 755 b	4-321 (b)	M.D.R. G59	3-115 (l)
M.D.R. 755 c	4-321 (a)	M.D.R. G60	3-115 (j)
M.D.R. 755 d	4-321 (c)		

Table II — 1997 Revision

(Table I — 1984 Revision precedes this table)

THIS TABLE SHOWS THOSE FORMER MARYLAND RULES OF PROCEDURE AND MARYLAND DISTRICT RULES RESCINDED EFFECTIVE JANUARY 1, 1997, FROM WHICH CORRESPONDING MARYLAND RULES IN TITLE 9 THROUGH TITLE 16 HAVE BEEN DERIVED.

RESCINDED RULE	REVISED RULE
901	11-101
902	11-102
902A	11-102A
903	11-103
904	11-104
905	11-105
906	11-106
907	11-107
908	11-108
909	11-109
910	11-110
911	11-111
912	11-112
913	11-113
914	11-114
915	11-115
916	11-116
917	11-117
918	11-118
919	11-119
920	11-120
921	11-121
922	11-122
D71	9-101
D72	9-103
D73	9-102
D74	9-105
D75	9-106
D76	9-107
D77	9-109
D78(d)	9-108
D79	9-111
D80	9-103; 9-112
E2	15-101
E3	15-101
E4	15-101
J70	14-401 (b)
J71	14-401 (a)
J72	14-401 (c)
J73	14-401 (d)
P1	15-202
P2 a & c	15-201
P3	15-203

RESCINDED RULE	REVISED RULE
P4 c & d 2	15-207
P5	15-208
Q40	15-1001 (a)
Q41 a	15-1001 (b)
Q42	15-1001 (d)
R70 a	10-103 (a)
R70 b	10-103 (b)
R70 c	10-103 (e)
R70 d	10-103 (f) (1)
R70 e	10-103 (g)
R70 f	10-105
R71 a	10-110, 10-201 (a), 10-301 (a)
R72 a & b	10-201 (b), 10-207 (b), 10-208 (b), 10-210, 10-301 (b), 10-711 (b) (1), 10-712 (c) (1)
R72 d	10-109
R73 a	10-201 (c), 10-301 (c)
R73 b 1	10-202
R74	10-203, 10-302
R76	10-106
R77	10-205, 10-304, 10-601
R77 b 2	10-503, 10-603
R78 b	10-108 (d)
R80 c 1	15-601
S70	9-201
S71	9-202
S72	9-203
S73	9-204
S73A	9-205
S74	9-206
S74A	9-207
S75	9-208
S76	9-209
S77	9-210
T44	12-101
U1	12-201
U2	12-202
U4 b	12-203
U5	12-204
U6	12-205
U12 b	12-206
U15	12-207
U17	12-207
U18	12-207
U19	12-208
U21	12-209
U22	12-212
U23	12-210
U24 b	12-212
U25	12-209
U26	12-211
U27	12-213
V70 b	10-103 (c)
V70 c	10-103 (f) (2)
V71	10-101, 10-106, 10-601
V71 a & b 1	10-501
V71 c	10-201 (c), 10-501
V71 d	10-502, 10-702 (b) (3)
V71 f 1 & f 2	10-108 (c)

RESCINDED RULE	REVISED RULE	RESCINDED RULE	REVISED RULE
V72	10-505	Z42	15-302
V73	10-702, 13-107	Z43	15-303
V74	10-706	Z44	15-303
V74 b 1 & 2	10-707 (a)	Z45	15-305
V74 b 3	10-707 (b)	Z46	15-306
V74 c 2 (b)	10-206 (a) & (b)	Z46 b	15-309, 15-310
V74 c 2 (e)	10-705 (d)	Z47	15-306
V74 e 1 (a)	10-208 (a) & (c), 10-712 (a) & (d)	Z48	15-309
		Z49	15-307
V74 e 2	10-208 (e), 10-712 (g)	Z50	15-308
V75 a & b	10-705 (a)	Z51	15-310
V75 c	10-705 (b)	Z52	15-303
V75 d	10-705 (c)	Z53	15-311
V76 a	10-704, 10-704 (a) (1)	Z54	15-303
V76 c	10-704 (a) (2)	Z55	15-304
V77 b 1	10-703, 13-403	Z56	15-312
V77 c 3	10-108 (b)	Z47	14-203
V78	10-209, 10-710	Z48 c-e	14-204
V78 b 5	10-207 (e), 10-711 (f)	Z51	14-205
V79	10-601	Z52	14-206
V79 b & c	10-602	Z53 b-g	14-207
V79 d	10-604	Z54 a	14-208
V79 e	10-605	Z55	14-209
V80	10-709	BB70	15-501
V81	13-702	BB71	15-502
V81 a	10-207 (a), 10-711 (a) & (b) (2)	BB72	15-504
V81 b 1	10-711 (c)	BB73	15-504
V81 c 1	10-207 (c), 10-711 (d)	BB74	15-505
V81 e	10-207 (f), 10-711 (i)	BB75	15-503
V82 a	10-207 (a), 10-711 (a), 13-703	BB76	15-502
V82 e	10-711 (h)	BB77	15-502
V84	13-701	BB78	15-502
V84 c	10-712 (c) (2)	BB79	15-502, 15-504
V84 d	10-208 (a), 10-712 (a)	BD1	12-102(b)
V84 d 1 & 2	10-208 (b), 10-712 (b)	BD2	12-102(b)
V84 e	10-208 (c), 10-712 (d)	BD3	12-102(c)
V84 f	10-712 (f)	BE40	15-701
W70 a	14-201(b)	BE41	15-701
W70 b	14-201(a)	BE43	15-701
W71	14-202	BE44	15-701
W72	14-203	BE45	15-701
W72 c-e	14-204	BE46	15-701
W73	14-205	BG70	12-301
W74	14-206	BG71	12-302
W74 b-g	14-207	BG72	12-303
W75 a	14-208	BG73	12-304
W76	14-209	BG74	12-305
W77 b	14-202(c)	BG75	12-306
W77 d	14-210	BG76	12-307
W79	14-203	BG77	12-308
W79 c	14-201(a)	BH70	15-901
Y70	12-501 (a)	BH71	15-901
Y71	12-501 (a), (b)	BH72	15-901
Y72	12-501 (b)	BH73	15-901
Y73	12-501 (b)	BH74	15-901
Y74	12-501 (c)	BH75	15-901
Y76	12-501 (d)	BJ71	12-401 (b)
Y77	12-501 (e)	BJ72	12-401 (c)
Y78	12-501 (f)	BJ73	12-401 (c)
Y79	12-501 (g)	BP1 a	13-101

RESCINDED RULE	REVISED RULE	RESCINDED RULE	REVISED RULE
BP1 b	13-102	BW2	15-804
BP2 a & b	13-203	BW3	15-804
BP3 a, b & d	13-302	BW4	15-803
BP3 a & c	13-105	BW5	15-804
BP4 a 1	13-201	BW6	15-803
BP4 a 2	13-202	BW7	15-805
BP4 b & c	13-401	BY2	15-403
BP4 d	13-402	BY3	15-403
BP5	13-103	BY4	15-403
BP6 a & b	13-301	1200	16-101
BP7	13-303	1201	16-102
BP8	13-601	1202	16-103
BP9 a, b, d-g	13-501	1203	16-104
BP9 b & c	13-401	1204	16-105
BP9 b 2	13-503	1205	16-106
BP10	13-502	1206	16-107
BP10 b	13-503	1207	16-108
BR1	14-301	1209	16-109
BR2	14-302	1210	16-201
BR3	14-303	1211	16-202
BR4	14-304	1211A	16-203
BR5	14-306	1212	16-301
BR6	14-305	1213	16-302
BQ41-45	12-601	1214	16-303
BQ49	12-601	1215	16-304
BQ51	12-602	1216	16-305
BQ53	12-602	1217	16-306
BU1	16-601	1217A	16-307
BU2	16-602	1218	16-308
BU3	16-603	1219	16-309
BU4	16-604	1220	16-401
BU5	16-605	1221	16-402
BU6	16-606	1223	16-403
BU7	16-607	1224	16-404
BU8	16-608	1224A	16-405
BU9	16-609	1224B	16-406
BU10	16-610	1225	16-801
BU11	16-611	1226	16-802
BU12	16-612	1227	16-803
BV1	16-701	1227A	16-804
BV2	16-702	1227B	16-805
BV3	16-703	1227C	16-806
BV4	16-704	1227D	16-807
BV5	16-705	1227E	16-808
BV6	16-706	1227F	16-809
BV7	16-707	1227G	16-810
BV8	16-708	1228	16-811
BV9	16-709	1230	16-812
BV10	16-710	1231	16-813
BV11	16-711	1232	16-814
BV12	16-712	1233	16-815
BV13	16-713	1234	16-816
BV14	16-714	1285	16-817
BV15	16-715	1299	16-818
BV16	16-716	M.D.R. 1214	16-502
BV17	16-717	M.D.R. 1218	16-503
BV18	16-718	M.D.R. 1224	16-504
BW1 a	15-802	M.D.R. 1299	16-505
BW1 b	15-801		

Index to Maryland Rules

ADMINISTRATION OF COURTS —Cont'd
Orders —Cont'd
Promulgation of rules.
Promulgation by rules order, Rule 16-801.
Payment of money into court, Rule
16-303.
Personal leave by judges, Rule 16-104.
Photographing, recording, broadcasting
or televising in courthouses.
Definitions, Rule 16-109.
Generally, Rule 16-109.
Pleadings.
Electronic filing of pleadings and papers,
Rule 16-307.
Promulgation of rules, Rule 16-801.
Proscribed activities.
Attorneys, officers of court, etc., Rule
16-401.
Radio.
Broadcasting in courthouses, Rule 16-109.
Recording in courthouses, Rule 16-109.
Records.
Court reporters.
Circuit court reporters.
Maintenance and filing of
administrative records, Rule
16-404.
District courts, Rule 16-504.
Disposition of records, Rule 16-818.
District courts, Rule 16-505.
Reporters. See within this heading, "Court
reporters."
Reports.
Information system.
Criminal history record information, Rule
16-308.
District courts, Rule 16-503.
Judges, Rule 16-105.
Responsibility for administration, Rule
16-101.
Rules and regulations.
Promulgation of rules, Rule 16-801.
Rules of professional conduct.
Adoption, Rule 16-812.
Sessions.
Holidays, Rule 16-106.
Judicial conference, Rule 16-802.
Time for convening, Rule 16-106.
Sick leave by judges, Rule 16-104.
Tape recordings.
Photographing, recording, broadcasting or
televising in courthouses, Rule 16-109.
Televising in courthouses, Rule 16-109.
Terms of circuit court and juries, Rule
16-107.
Trial.
Assignment of actions for trial, Rule 16-202.
Trust clerks.
Designation, Rule 16-403.
Trust funds.
Clients' security fund, Rule 16-811.

ADMINISTRATION OF COURTS —Cont'd
Videotape recording.
Circuit court proceedings, Rule 16-405.
Access to videotape recordings, Rule
16-406.

ADMINISTRATION OF ESTATES.
Executors and administrators.
Settlement of decedents' estates.
General provisions, Rules 6-101 to 6-501.
See EXECUTORS AND
ADMINISTRATORS.

ADMINISTRATIVE AGENCY DECISIONS,
JUDICIAL REVIEW, Rules 7-201 to
7-210.
Administrative agency defined, Rule
7-201.
Affirmance, reversal or remand.
Disposition, Rule 7-209.
Answering memoranda, Rule 7-207.
Applicability, Rule 7-201.
Caption of petition, Rule 7-202.
Certificate of compliance.
Notice requirements, Rule 7-202.
Contents of petition, Rule 7-202.
Dismissal of action.
Disposition, Rule 7-209.
Late filing of memoranda, Rule 7-207.
Disposition, Rule 7-209.
Evidence in support of or against
decision.
Additional evidence, Rule 7-208.
Hearing, Rule 7-208.
Memoranda.
Setting forth questions presented for
review, Rule 7-207.
Method of securing review, Rule 7-202.
Notice to agencies named in petitions,
Rule 7-202.
Notice to parties by agencies, Rule 7-202.
Petition.
Filing by other party, Rule 7-203.
Time for filing, Rule 7-203.
Petitions, Rule 7-202.
Preliminary motions.
Filed with response to petition, Rule 7-204.
Record, Rule 7-206.
Return of agency record, Rule 7-210.
Response, Rule 7-204.
Response to petition, Rules 7-202, 7-204.
Return of agency record, Rule 7-210.
Sanctions for late filing of memoranda,
Rule 7-207.
Scheduling of hearing, Rule 7-208.
Service of response to petition, Rule
7-204.
Statement in lieu of record, Rule 7-206.
Stays, Rule 7-205.
Time for filing action, Rule 7-203.
Time for filing memoranda, Rule 7-207.
Time for filing response to petition, Rules
7-202, 7-204.
Time for hearing, Rule 7-208.

ADMINISTRATIVE AGENCY DECISIONS, JUDICIAL REVIEW —Cont'd
Time for transmitting record, Rule 7-206.
Time of filing certificate of compliance to notice requirements, Rule 7-202.
Transcript expenses, Rule 7-206.
ADMISSIONS.
Answers.
Specific admissions or denials.
Circuit courts, Rule 2-323.
Mechanics' liens.
Affidavit or verified answer.
Failure to file deemed admission, Rule 12-304.
Motions.
Mandatory motions in circuit courts.
Criminal rules, Rule 4-252.
Request for admission of facts and genuineness of documents.
Generally.
Circuit courts, Rule 2-424.
ADOPTION.
Accounting report, Rule 9-110.
Adults.
Show cause order.
Service of show cause order where adult adopted, Rule 9-105.
Appeals from proceedings for adoption, Rule 8-122.
Applicability of rules, Rule 1-101.
Attorneys at law.
Appointment, Rule 9-106.
Show cause order.
Service.
Court appointed attorney, Rule 9-105.
Change of name.
Notice, Rule 9-105.
Consent, Rule 9-102.
Notice to consenting persons, Rule 9-104.
Definitions, Rule 9-101.
Dockets.
Clerk to keep, Rule 9-112.
Family division and support services, Rule 16-204.
Filing.
Objections.
Notice of objection, Rule 9-107.
Final decree of adoption.
Generally, Rule 9-111.
Spouse of natural parent, Rule 9-111.
Guardian and ward.
Consent, Rule 9-102.
Notice to consenting persons, Rule 9-104.
Notice.
Additional notice of guardianship proceeding, Rule 9-105.
Petition for guardianship, Rules 9-103, 11-501.
Hearings.
Procedure, Rule 9-109.
Investigations.
Court investigation, Rule 9-106.
Report, Rule 9-106.

ADOPTION —Cont'd
Medical history of child, Rule 9-113.
Names.
Change of name.
Notice, Rule 9-105.
Notice.
Change of name, Rule 9-105.
Objections.
Filing notice of objection, Rule 9-107.
Show cause order, Rule 9-105.
Objections, Rule 9-107.
Orders.
Show cause order.
Content, Rule 9-105.
Notice, Rule 9-105.
Petition, Rule 11-501. Rule 9-103.
Records.
Clerk to keep, Rule 9-112.
Medical history of child, Rule 9-113.
Notice of objection.
Access to records, Rule 9-107.
Sealing, Rule 9-112.
Reports, Rule 9-106.
Accounting report, Rule 9-110.
Seals.
Records to be sealed, Rule 9-112.
Service of process.
Show cause order.
Adult adopted, Rule 9-105.
Court appointed attorney, Rule 9-105.
Minor child, Rule 9-105.
Show cause order.
Content, Rule 9-105.
Notice, Rule 9-105.
Service of process.
Adult adopted, Rule 9-105.
Court appointed attorney, Rule 9-105.
Minor child, Rule 9-105.
Temporary custody award, Rule 9-108.

ADVERTISING.
Attorneys at law.
Rules of professional conduct, Prof. Cond. R. 7.2.
Judicial sales.
Public sale, Rule 14-303.
Rules of professional conduct, Prof. Cond. R. 7.2.

AFFIDAVITS.
Appeals.
Dismissal of appeals.
Motion to dismiss, Rule 8-603.
Injunction pending appeal.
Affidavit to accompany motion, Rule 8-425.
Motions.
Requirement that affidavit accompany or support motion, Rule 8-431.
Definitions, Rule 1-202.
Divorce.
Ne exeat.
Requirement of affidavit, Rule 9-203.

541

APPEALS —Cont'd
Circuit courts.
Certiorari in circuit court, Rule 7-301.
Form of court papers, Rule 1-301.
From District Court to circuit court, Rules 7-101 to 7-116.
See APPEALS FROM DISTRICT COURT TO CIRCUIT COURT.
Judicial review of administrative agency decisions, Rules 7-201 to 7-210.
See ADMINISTRATIVE AGENCY DECISIONS, JUDICIAL REVIEW.
Confidentiality.
Adoption proceedings, Rule 8-122.
Court of special appeals.
Information reports, Rule 8-205. Rule 8-206.
Criminal investigations, Rule 8-123.
Guardianship appeals, Rule 8-122.
Juvenile causes.
Appeals from courts exercising juvenile jurisdiction, Rule 8-121.
Consideration of appeal on brief, Rule 8-523.
Corporations.
Appearance of counsel.
Requirement of appearance of counsel, Rule 8-402.
Costs.
Allocation, Rule 8-607.
Allowance, Rule 8-607.
Amicus curiae, Rule 8-607.
Appeals from District Court to circuit court.
Assessment, Rule 7-116.
Preparation of transcript.
Payment by appellant, Rule 7-103.
Assessment, Rule 8-607.
Computation, Rule 8-608.
Dismissal of appeals.
Appellant dismissing, Rule 8-601.
Excluded costs, Rule 8-608.
Generally allowable costs, Rule 8-608.
Mandate.
Statement of costs contained in mandate, Rule 8-606.
Record on appeal.
Unnecessary correction of record.
Disallowance of costs, Rule 8-607.
Reproduction allowance, Rule 8-608.
State.
Assessment of costs against state, Rule 8-607.
Unnecessary material.
Disallowance of costs for reproduction of unnecessary material, Rule 8-607.
Court of appeals.
Applicability of rules, Rules 1-101, 8-101.
Application for leave to appeal.
Applicability of certain rules to court of appeals procedure, Rule 8-306.
Methods of securing review, Rule 8-301.
When available, Rule 8-301.

APPEALS —Cont'd
Court of appeals —Cont'd
Automatic appeals.
Capital cases, Rule 8-306.
Briefs.
Certification from court of special appeals, Rule 8-304.
Consideration on brief.
Submission on brief by party, Rule 8-523.
Capital cases reviewed by court of appeals.
Applicability of other provisions, Rule 8-306.
Automatic appeal from judgment, Rule 8-306.
Scope of review, Rule 8-306.
Transcript in lieu of record extract, Rule 8-306.
Certification procedure.
Appearance of counsel, Rule 8-402.
Applicable provisions, Rule 8-301.
Court of special appeals as certifying court, Rule 8-304.
Federal courts or other state courts as certifying courts, Rule 8-305.
Method of securing review, Rule 8-301.
Certiorari.
Method of securing review, Rule 8-301.
Petition for writ, Rule 8-303.
Time for filing, Rule 8-302.
Direct appeals.
Capital cases, Rule 8-306.
Methods of securing review, Rule 8-301.
When available, Rule 8-301.
Injunction pending appeal.
Decision of court, Rule 8-425.
Obtaining appellate review in court of appeals.
Capital cases, Rule 8-306.
Certification from court of special appeals, Rule 8-304.
Certification from federal courts and other state courts, Rule 8-305.
Certiorari.
Procedure on petition for writ, Rule 8-303.
Time for filing petition for writ, Rule 8-302.
Method, Rule 8-301.
Reconsiderations.
Motions in court, Rule 8-605.
Record on appeal.
Capital cases.
Transcript in lieu of record extract, Rule 8-306.
Certification from court of special appeals.
Record extract and brief, Rule 8-304.
Extract.
Capital cases.
Transcript in lieu of record extract, Rule 8-306.

543

APPEARANCE —Cont'd
Charging documents.
Initial appearance of defendant.
District Court following arrest.
Advice of charges, Rule 4-213.
Clerks.
Initial appearance of defendant.
Transfer of papers by clerk, Rule 4-213.
Corporations.
Circuit courts.
Appearance by attorney only, Rule 2-131.
District Court, Rule 3-131.
Criminal rules, Rule 4-213.
Defendants.
Initial appearance of defendant, Rule 4-213.
Effect.
Circuit courts, Rule 2-131.
District Court, Rule 3-131.
Entry of appearance.
How entered.
Circuit courts, Rule 2-131.
Executors and administrators.
Settlement of decedents' estates.
Presence of personal representative, Rule 6-131.
How appearance entered.
District Court, Rule 3-131.
Initial appearance of defendant, Rule 4-213.
Juvenile causes.
Right to counsel.
Out-of-state attorney, Rule 11-106.
Motions.
Striking attorney's appearance.
Circuit courts, Rule 2-132.
District Court, Rule 3-132.
Notice.
Striking attorney's appearance.
Circuit courts, Rule 2-132.
District Court, Rule 3-132.
Preliminary hearings.
Initial appearance of defendant.
Advice of preliminary hearing, Rule 4-213.
Pretrial release.
Initial appearance of defendant.
Determination of pretrial release, Rule 4-213.
Proper person.
Circuit courts, Rule 2-131.
District Court, Rule 3-131.
Striking of attorney's appearance.
Circuit courts, Rule 2-132.
District Court, Rule 3-132.
Summons and process.
Initial appearance of defendant.
Circuit court following arrest or summons, Rule 4-213.
District Court following summons, Rule 4-213.
Termination of appearance.
Automatic termination.
District Court, Rule 3-132.

APPRAISALS.
Appraisers.
Receivers.
Compensation and fees, Rule 13-303.
Employment, Rule 13-301.
Executors and administrators.
Settlement of decedents' estates.
Application to fix inheritance tax on non-probate assets.
Form, Rule 6-405.
Basis, Rule 6-403.
Content.
Required content, Rule 6-403.
Forms, Rule 6-403.
Application to fix inheritance tax on non-probate assets, Rule 6-405.
Forms.
Executors and administrators.
Settlement of decedents' estates.
Application to fix inheritance tax on non-probate assets, Rule 6-405.
Inventory, Rule 6-403.

ARBITRATION AND AWARD.
Alternative dispute resolution generally, Rules 17-101 to 17-108.
See ALTERNATIVE DISPUTE RESOLUTION.
Code of judicial conduct.
Judge not to act as arbitrator, Rule 16-813, Canon 4.
Health care malpractice claims, Rules 15-401 to 15-403.
See MALPRACTICE.
Uniform arbitration act.
Applicability to certain proceedings, Rule 15-101.

ARRAY.
Jury trial.
Challenge to the array.
Circuit courts, Rule 2-512.

ARREST.
Circuit courts.
Initial appearance of defendant, Rule 4-213.
Procedure when defendant in custody.
Other offenses, Rule 4-212.
Same offense, Rule 4-212.
Statement of charges.
Filing, Rule 4-211.
District Courts.
Initial appearance after arrest, Rule 4-213.

ASBESTOS DOCKET, Rule 16-203.

ASSAULT.
Spousal privilege.
Record of assertion, Rule 4-632.

ASSETS.
Executors and administrators.
Settlement of decedents' estates.
Application to fix inheritance tax on non-probate assets, Rule 6-405.

ATTORNEYS AT LAW —Cont'd
Disbarment or suspension —Cont'd
Suspension —Cont'd
Termination or modification, Rule 16-714.
Costs, Rule 16-715.
Termination or modification of suspension
or inactive status.
Costs, Rule 16-715.
Petition, Rule 16-714.
Procedure, Rule 16-714.
Discovery.
Hearing.
Disbarment or suspension, Rule 16-710.
Trial preparation.
Scope of discovery.
Circuit courts, Rule 2-402.
Divorce.
Pleadings.
Mentally incompetent defendant.
Answer, Rule 9-203.
Appointment of attorney for guardian,
Rule 9-203.
Ethics.
Rules of professional conduct.
Adoption, Rule 16-812.
Evidence.
Disbarment or suspension.
Hearings.
Conviction of crime or adjudication of
misconduct, Rule 16-710.
Examinations.
Petition to take.
Certification by law school, Bar Adm.
Rule 6.
Executors and administrators.
Settlement of decedents' estates.
See EXECUTORS AND
ADMINISTRATORS.
Fees.
Divorce, annulment and alimony.
Pleadings.
Mentally incompetent defendant, Rule
9-203.
Eminent domain.
Appeals, Rule 12-209.
Executors and administrators.
Settlement of decedent's estate, Rule
6-416.
Fiduciaries.
Absent or unknown persons, Rule 10-604.
Assumption of jurisdiction.
Appointment, Rule 10-501.
Filing.
Disbarment or suspension.
Charges.
Bar counsel to file, Rule 16-709.
Funds.
Disbarment or suspension.
Attorney grievance commission.
Disciplinary fund, Rule 16-702.
Grievance commission. See within this
heading, "Attorney grievance
commission."

ATTORNEYS AT LAW —Cont'd
Hearings.
Disbarment or suspension.
Generally, Rule 16-710.
Inactive status.
Disbarment or suspension, Rules 16-701 to
16-718. See within heading,
"Disbarment or suspension."
Investigations.
Disbarment or suspension.
Complaints and investigations, Rule
16-706.
Judges.
Disbarment or suspension.
Hearings.
Number of judges, Rule 16-710.
Juvenile causes, Rule 11-106.
Liens.
Enforcement of attorneys' liens, Rule 2-652.
Motions.
Admission to the bar.
Pro hac vice.
Form, Form RGAB 20/M.
Notice.
Disbarment or suspension.
Audit of attorney's accounts and records,
Rule 16-718.
Trust accounts.
Approved institutions, Rule 16-611.
Duty of attorney to notify institution,
Rule 16-605.
Orders.
Admission to the bar.
Pro hac vice.
Orders, Form RGAB 20/O.
Disbarment or suspension.
Conservator of clients' affairs, Rule
16-717.
Parole and probation.
Revocation of probation.
Waiver of counsel, Rule 4-347.
Parties.
Attorney may act for party, Rule 1-331.
Individuals not in being.
Property interest of individuals not in
being.
Appointment of attorney to represent,
Rule 2-203.
Petitions.
Disbarment or suspension.
Conservator of clients' affairs, Rule
16-717.
Pleadings.
Notice of intention to defend.
Identity of attorney.
District Court, Rule 3-307.
Professional conduct.
See RULES OF PROFESSIONAL
CONDUCT.
Pro hac vice.
Forms.
Motions, Form RGAB 20/M.
Orders, Form RGAB 20/O.

BONDS, SURETY —Cont'd
Replevin.
Action on replevin bond, Rule 12-601.
Securities.
Security instead of surety, Rule 1-402.
Small estates.
Personal representative, Rule 6-222.
State of Maryland.
Bond in name of state, Rule 1-402.
Supersedeas bond.
Appeals, Rule 8-423.
Appeals from District Court to circuit court, Rule 7-111.

BOUNDARIES.
Hearsay exceptions, Rule 5-803.
Mechanics' liens.
Establishment generally, Rule 12-308.

BRIEFS.
Appeals.
General provisions.
See APPEALS.

BUDGETS.
Clerks of court.
Submission, Rule 16-302.

BURDEN OF PROOF.
Contempt for failure to pay spousal or child support, Rule 15-207.

BURIAL GROUNDS.
Eminent domain.
Acquisition of cemetery, Rule 12-204.
Sales.
Sale for other use, Rule 14-401.

BUSINESS RECORDS.
Hearsay exceptions, Rule 5-803.
Interrogatories.
Interrogatories to parties.
Option to produce business records, Rule 2-421.
District Court, Rule 3-421.

C

CAPACITY.
Parties.
Circuit courts, Rule 2-202.
District Court, Rule 3-202.
Pleadings.
Circuit courts, Rule 2-304.

CAPITAL CASES.
See DEATH PENALTY.

CAPTION.
Administrative agency decisions, judicial review.
Petition, Rule 7-202.

CEMETERIES.
Burial grounds.
Sale for other use, Rule 14-401.

CEMETERIES —Cont'd
Eminent domain.
Acquisition of cemetery, Rule 12-204.

CERTIFICATION OF QUESTIONS OF LAW.
Court of appeals.
Procedure in court of appeals, Rules 8-304, 8-305.

CERTIFIED MAIL.
Definitions, Rule 1-202.

CERTIORARI.
Appeals.
Court of appeals.
Method of securing review, Rule 8-301.
Petition for writ.
Procedure on petition, Rule 8-303.
Time for filing, Rule 8-302.
Circuit courts, Rule 7-301.

CERTIORARI IN CIRCUIT COURT, Rule 7-301.

CHANGE OF NAME.
Action for, Rule 15-901.
Family division and support services, Rule 16-204.

CHARACTER EVIDENCE.
Accused, Rule 5-404.
Conduct.
Admissibility to prove character, Rule 5-404.
Specific instances of conduct, Rule 5-405.
Definitions, Rule 5-404.
Methods of proving character, Rule 5-405.
Opinion, Rule 5-405.
Other crimes, wrongs or acts, Rule 5-404.
Reputation, Rule 5-405.
Hearsay exceptions, Rule 5-803.
Specific instances of conduct, Rule 5-405.
Victims, Rule 5-404.
Witnesses, Rule 5-404.
Rehabilitation, Rule 5-608.

CHARGING DOCUMENTS.
Appearances.
Initial appearance of defendant.
District Court following arrest.
Advice of charges, Rule 4-213.
Circuit courts.
Motions in circuit courts in criminal cases, Rule 4-252.
Use, Rule 4-201.
Citations.
Content, Rule 4-202.
Defined, Rule 4-102.
Docket in place of citation, Rule 4-201.
Content.
Citations, Rule 4-202.
Indictments, Rule 4-202.
Matters not required, Rule 4-202.
Requirements.
General requirements, Rule 4-202.
Signatures, Rule 4-202.

CIVIL PROCEDURE —Cont'd
Summons —Cont'd
Copies to be furnished.
Circuit courts, Rule 2-111.
District Court, Rule 3-111.
Delivery to another county.
Circuit courts, Rule 2-112.
District Court, Rule 3-112.
Duration, dormancy and renewal of
summons.
Circuit courts, Rule 2-113.
District Court, Rule 3-113.
Issuance.
Circuit courts, Rule 2-112.
District Court, Rule 3-112.
Requirements preliminary to summons.
Circuit courts, Rule 2-111.
District Court, Rule 3-111.
Sheriffs.
Instructions for sheriff.
Circuit courts, Rule 2-111.
District Court, Rule 3-111.
Sundays and holidays.
Service of process.
Circuit courts, Rule 2-125.
District Court, Rule 3-125.
Third-party practice.
Circuit courts, Rule 2-332.
District Court, Rule 3-332.
Trial.
General provisions.
See TRIAL.

CLAIMS.
Administration of courts.
Clients' security fund.
Disposition, Rule 16-811.
Circuit courts, Rule 2-305.
District Court, Rule 3-305.
Health care malpractice claims, Rules
15-401 to 15-403.
See MALPRACTICE.
Judgments.
Judgment on claim and counterclaim.
Circuit courts, Rule 2-615.
District Court, Rule 3-615.
Multiple claims.
Circuit courts, Rule 2-602.
Stay.
Circuit courts, Rule 2-632.
District Court, Rule 3-632.
Levy.
Release of property from levy.
Third person claim.
Circuit courts, Rule 2-643.
District Court, Rule 3-643.
Motions.
Defense of failure to state claim for relief
not waived.
Circuit courts, Rule 2-324.
Preliminary motions.
Permissive motions.
Circuit courts, Rule 2-322.

CLAIMS —Cont'd
Pleadings.
Circuit courts, Rule 2-305.
Defense of failure to state claim not waived.
Circuit courts, Rule 2-324.
Receivers.
Compromise of claim or dispute, Rule
13-403.
Objections to claims, Rule 13-402.
Proof of claim, Rule 13-401.
Third parties.
Circuit courts, Rule 2-332.
District Court, Rule 3-332.
Trial.
Voluntary dismissal.
Circuit courts, Rule 2-506.
Effect on claim.
District Court, Rule 3-506.

CLASS ACTIONS, Rule 2-231.

CLERKS OF COURT.
Administration of courts.
Clients' security fund.
Notice to clerk, Rule 16-811.
Disposition of records.
Permanent retention, Rule 16-818.
Dockets, Rule 16-305.
Filing and removal of papers, Rule 16-306.
Hours, Rule 16-304.
Offices, Rule 16-304.
Payment of money into court, Rule 16-303.
District Court.
District Rule 1214.
Trust clerk.
Designation, Rule 16-403.
Appearances.
Initial appearance of defendant.
Transfer of papers by clerk, Rule 4-213.
Attorneys at law.
Discipline and inactive status.
Audit of attorney's accounts and records,
Rule 16-718.
Audits, Rule 16-302.
Bail and recognizance.
Defined, Rule 4-217.
Bonds, surety.
Recordation, Rule 1-402.
Budgets.
Submission, Rule 16-302.
Definitions, Rule 1-202.
Deputy clerks, Rule 16-301.
Eminent domain.
Board of property review.
Certification to board.
Duty of clerk, Rule 12-213.
Employees.
Personnel system, Rule 16-301.
Fiduciaries.
Trust clerks.
See FIDUCIARIES.
General operations of office, Rule 16-302.
Judgments.
Costs.
Assessment by clerk.
Circuit courts, Rule 2-603.

563

CONTEMPT —Cont'd

Direct contempt —Cont'd
Summary imposition of sanctions, Rules 15-203, 15-204.

Enforcement of judgment prohibiting or mandating action.
District Court, Rule 3-648.

Jury.
Constructive criminal contempt proceedings.
Jury trial, Rule 15-205.

Juvenile causes.
Hearings.
Controlling conduct of person before court, Rule 11-110.

Masters.
Time of entry of order.
Circuit courts, Rule 2-541.

Searches and seizures.
Warrants, Rule 4-601.

Service of process.
Constructive civil contempt, Rule 15-206.

Spousal support nonpayment, Rule 15-207.

Subpoenas.
Criminal rules, Rule 4-266.

Summary imposition of sanctions, Rules 15-203, 15-204.

CONTINUANCE.

Circuit courts, Rule 2-508.

District Court, Rule 3-508.

Juvenile causes.
Juvenile petitions or pleadings.
Amendment.
Amended pleadings or petitions, Rule 11-108.

CONTRACTORS.

Mechanics' liens.
Defined, Rule 12-301.

CONTRACTS.

Answers.
General denials in specified causes.
Circuit courts, Rule 2-323.

Mechanics' liens.
Defined, Rule 12-301.

CONTRIBUTING TO THE DELINQUENCY OF A MINOR.

Juvenile causes.
See JUVENILE CAUSES.

CONTRIBUTION.

Judgments.
Judgment of contribution or recovery over.
Circuit courts, Rule 2-614.
District Court, Rule 3-614.

CONTROLLED SUBSTANCES.

Convictions.
Reporting to licensing agency, Rule 4-340.

CONVEYANCES.

Ground rents.
Order of conveyances, Rule 12-501.

CONVICTIONS.

Impeachment, Rule 5-609.
Extrinsic evidence, Rule 5-616.
Nolo contendere.
Effect, Rule 5-609.

Post conviction procedure, Rules 4-401 to 4-408.
See POST-CONVICTION PROCEDURE.

Sentence and punishment.
See SENTENCE AND PUNISHMENT.

Witnesses.
Impeachment by evidence of conviction of crime, Rules 5-609, 5-616.

COPIES.

Decedents' estates.
Photocopies of pleadings or papers, Rule 6-108.

Depositions.
Furnishing copies.
Circuit courts, Rule 2-415.

Expungement of records.
Applications.
No charges filed, Rule 4-503.
Petitions.
Charges filed, Rule 4-504.

Post conviction procedures.
Copy of order and statement of court, Rule 4-407.

Summons and process.
Requirements preliminary to summons.
District Court, Rule 3-111.

CORPORATIONS.

Appeals.
Appearance of counsel.
Requirement of appearance of counsel, Rule 8-402.

Appearance.
Circuit courts.
Appearance by attorney only, Rule 2-131.
District Court, Rule 3-131.

Attorneys at law.
Circuit courts.
Appearance by attorney only, Rule 2-131.

Depositions.
Designation of person to testify for organization.
Notice.
Circuit courts, Rule 2-412.

Fiduciaries.
Bond of fiduciary, Rule 10-702.

Parties.
Capacity.
Circuit courts, Rule 2-202.

Service of process.
Persons to be served.
Circuit courts, Rule 2-124.
District Court, Rule 3-124.

COSTS.

Amicus curiae, Rule 8-607.

Appeals.
Allocation, Rule 8-607.
Allowance, Rule 8-607.

568

CRIMINAL RULES —Cont'd

Expungement of records, Rules 4-501 to 4-512.
See RECORDS.

Filing, Rule 4-211.

Guilty pleas.
Disclosure of notice of mandatory or additional penalties, Rule 4-245.
Permitted pleas, Rule 4-242.
Pleas generally.
See PLEAS.
Pleas to other offenses, Rule 4-244.
Plea to a degree, Rule 4-242.
Requirements for court to accept, Rule 4-242.
Subsequent offenders.
Disclosure of notice of additional or mandatory penalties, Rule 4-245.
Types of pleas, Rule 4-242.

Habitual offenders.
Subsequent offenders, Rule 4-245.

Immunity.
Compelling testimony on condition of immunity, Rule 4-631.

Indictments.
Charging documents generally.
See CHARGING DOCUMENTS.
Defined, Rule 4-102.
Filing, Rule 4-211.

Informations.
Charging documents generally.
See CHARGING DOCUMENTS.
Defined, Rule 4-102.
Filing, Rule 4-211.

Instructions to jury, Rule 4-325.

Interception of wire or oral communications, Rule 4-611.

Investigations.
Applicability, Rule 4-641.
Court records.
Secrecy, Rule 4-642.
Enforcement of subpoenas, Rule 4-643.
File.
Maintenance, Rule 4-644.
Grand jury.
Subpoenas to appear before grand jury, Rule 4-643.
Hearings.
Secrecy, Rule 4-642.
Motion for disclosure.
Secrecy, Rule 4-642.
Orders.
Protective orders, Rule 4-643.
Secrecy, Rule 4-642.
Subpoenas, Rule 4-643.
Record of subpoena, Rule 4-644.

Joinder.
Multiple defendants, Rule 4-203.

Judges.
Disability of judge, Rule 4-361.

Judgments.
Enforcement of money judgment, Rule 4-354.

CRIMINAL RULES —Cont'd

Judicial officers.
Defined, Rule 4-102.

Jury trial.
Challenges.
Array, Rule 4-312.
Peremptory challenges, Rule 4-313.
Communications, Rule 4-326.
Demand for jury trial, Rule 4-301.
Exhibits, Rule 4-322.
Instructions to jury, Rule 4-325.
Number of jurors, Rule 4-311.
Objections.
Method of making, Rule 4-323.
Peremptory challenges, Rule 4-313.
Review of evidence, Rule 4-326.
Right preserved, Rule 4-311.
Selection, Rule 4-312.
Separation of jury, Rule 4-311.
Verdicts, Rule 4-327.
Waiver.
Circuit courts, Rule 4-246.

Juvenile courts.
Jurisdiction.
Waiver.
Procedure.
District Court, Rule 4-222.

Mistake.
Correction of clerical mistakes, Rule 4-621.

Motions.
Circuit court motions, Rule 4-252.
District Court motions, Rule 4-251.
New trial, Rule 4-331.

New trial.
Motions for new trial, Rule 4-331.

Nolle prosequi.
Disposition by nolle prosequi, Rule 4-247.
Effect of nolle prosequi, Rule 4-247.
Expungement of records.
Petition for expungement of records.
Form, Title 4, Form 4-504.1.

Nolo contendere.
See PLEAS.

Offenses.
Defined, Rule 4-102.
Petty offenses.
Defined, Rule 4-102.

Petty offenses.
Defined, Rule 4-102.

Plea bargains, Rule 4-243.

Pleas.
See PLEAS.

Post conviction procedure, Rules 4-401 to 4-408.
See POST-CONVICTION PROCEDURE.

Preliminary hearings.
Appearances.
Initial appearance of defendant.
Advice of preliminary hearing, Rule 4-213.
District Court, Rule 4-221.

Presence of defendants, Rule 4-231.
Depositions, Rule 4-261.

570

DECREES —Cont'd
Orders generally.
See INTERLOCUTORY ORDERS.
DEFAULT JUDGMENTS.
Circuit courts, Rule 2-613.
District Court, Rule 3-509.
Divorce, annulment and alimony, Rule 9-208.
Service of pleadings.
Nonoriginal pleadings, Rule 1-321.
DEFENDANTS.
Appearances.
Initial appearance of defendant, Rule 4-213.
Attachment.
Prejudgment attachment.
Judgment for defendant.
Circuit courts, Rule 2-115.
District Court, Rule 3-115.
Criminal rules.
Defined, Rule 4-102.
Presence of defendants, Rule 4-231.
Definitions.
Criminal rules, Rule 4-102.
Depositions.
Presence of defendant.
Criminal rules, Rule 4-261.
Discovery.
Matters not subject to discovery by defendant.
Criminal rules, Rule 4-263.
Property of defendant.
Disclosure upon request.
Criminal rules, Rule 4-263.
Statements of codefendants.
Disclosure upon request.
Criminal rules, Rule 4-263.
Statements of the defendant.
Disclosure upon request.
Criminal rules, Rule 4-263.
Joinder.
Charging documents, Rule 4-203.
Circuit courts, Rule 4-203.
Depositions.
Criminal rules, Rule 4-261.
Pleas.
Pleas to other offenses.
Request of defendant, Rule 4-244.
DEFENSES.
Answers.
Affirmative defenses.
Circuit courts, Rule 2-323.
Negative defenses.
Circuit courts, Rule 2-323.
Civil procedure.
Preservation of certain defenses.
Circuit courts, Rule 2-324.
Motions.
Consolidation of defenses in motion.
Circuit courts, Rule 2-322.
Motion to dismiss.
Circuit courts.
Defenses which may be made by motion to dismiss, Rule 2-322.

DEFENSES —Cont'd
Motions —Cont'd
Preservation of certain defenses.
Circuit courts, Rule 2-324.
Pleadings.
Answers, Rule 2-323.
Form of pleadings.
Circuit courts, Rule 2-303.
Preservation of certain defenses.
Circuit courts, Rule 2-324.
Tax sales.
Invalidity, Rule 14-505.

DEFINITIONS.
Actions, Rule 1-202.
Administration of courts.
Disposition of records, Rule 16-818.
Judicial disability and sanctionable conduct, Rule 16-803.
Judicial leave.
Judge, Rule 16-104.
Photographing, recording, broadcasting or televising in courthouses, Rule 16-109.
Administrative agency, Rule 7-201.
Adoption, Rule 9-101.
Affidavits, Rule 1-202.
Alternative dispute resolution, Rule 17-102.
Appeals.
Court of appeals.
Certification from federal courts and other state courts.
Certifying courts, Rule 8-305.
Date of entry.
Appeals from District Court to circuit court, Rule 7-104.
Application.
Expungement of records, Rule 4-502.
Arbitration.
Alternative dispute resolution, Rule 17-102.
Asbestos docket, Rule 16-203.
Attachment.
Body attachment, Rule 1-202.
Attorneys at law.
Discipline and inactive status, Rule 16-701.
Trust accounts, Rule 16-602.
Automobile insurance fund, Rule 15-802.
Bail and recognizance, Rule 4-217.
Body attachment, Rule 1-202.
Central repository.
Expungement of records, Rule 4-502.
Certified mail, Rule 1-202.
Charging documents, Rule 4-102.
Circuits, Rule 1-202.
Clerks, Rule 1-202.
Code, Rule 1-202.
Computer-generated evidence, Rule 2-504.3.
Contempt, Rule 15-202.
Counties.
Maryland rules, Rule 1-202.
Court.
Expungement of records, Rule 4-502.

573

DOCKETS.
Administration of courts, Rule 16-305.
  Asbestos docket, Rule 16-203.
  Filing and removal of papers, Rule 16-306.
  Information system.
    District courts, Rule 16-503.
    Report of docketing and disposition of
      cases, Rule 16-308.
Adoption.
  Clerk to keep, Rule 9-112.
Appeals.
  Dismissal of appeals.
    Reconsideration of dismissal.
      Reinstatement on docket, Rule 8-602.
  Docketing of appeals, Rule 8-421.
**Appeals from District Court to circuit
  court.**
  Docket for appeals, Rule 7-110.
  Separate appeals docketed as one action,
    Rule 7-110.
Charging documents.
  Citations.
    Docket in place of citation, Rule 4-201.
Expungement of records, Rule 4-511.
Juvenile causes.
  Separate docket.
    Duties of clerk, Rule 11-104.

DOCUMENTS.
**Admission of facts and genuineness of
  documents,** Rule 2-424.
Charging documents.
  See CHARGING DOCUMENTS.
Court papers.
  Form of court papers, Rule 1-301.
Depositions.
  Production of documents and tangible
    things.
    Circuit courts, Rule 2-415.
  Generally.
    Circuit courts, Rule 2-422.
  Notice, Rule 2-412.
Discovery.
  Admission of facts and genuineness of
    documents.
    Circuit courts, Rule 2-424.
  Circuit courts, Rule 2-422.
Forms.
  Court papers, Rule 1-301.
Interrogatories.
  Parties.
    Scope of discovery.
      District Court, Rule 3-421.

DOMESTIC RELATIONS.
Annulment of marriage.
  See ANNULMENT OF MARRIAGE.
Costs.
  Waiver of cost, Rule 2-603.
Divorce, Rules 9-201 to 9-210.
  See DIVORCE.
Family division and support services,
  Rule 16-204.

DOMESTIC RELATIONS —Cont'd
Interrogatories, Interrogatories Forms Nos.
  4, 5.
Parent and child.
  See PARENT AND CHILD.

DYING DECLARATIONS.
Hearsay exceptions, Rule 5-804.

E

EAVESDROPPING.
**Interception of wire or oral
  communications,** Rule 4-611.
  Mandatory motions in circuit courts.
    Criminal rules, Rule 4-252.

EJECTMENT.
Execution.
  Warrant of resurvey, Rule 12-101.
Filing.
  Warrant of resurvey.
    Plat to be filed, Rule 12-101.
Plats.
  Warrant of resurvey.
    Filing plat, Rule 12-101.
Summary ejectment.
  District Court, Rule 3-711.
Surveyors.
  Warrant of resurvey, Rule 12-101.
Warrant of resurvey.
  Execution, Rule 12-101.
  Plat.
    Filing, Rule 12-101.
  Requirements, Rule 12-101.

ELECTION OF RIGHTS AND REMEDIES.
Appeals.
  Court of special appeals.
    Expedited appeals, Rule 8-207.
Eminent domain.
  Trial by court, Rule 12-207.
Executions.
  Levy.
    Release of property from levy.
      Election of exemption by judgment
        debtor.
        Circuit courts, Rule 2-643.
        District Court, Rule 3-643.
Jury trial.
  Effect of election.
    Circuit courts, Rule 2-325.
  Withdrawal of election.
    Circuit courts, Rule 2-325.
Levies.
  Release of property from levy.
    Election of exemption by judgment
      debtor.
      Circuit courts, Rule 2-643.
      District Court, Rule 3-643.

ELECTIONS.
Administration of courts.
  Judicial conference.
    Executive committee, Rule 16-802.

583

EVIDENCE —Cont'd
Family history.
Hearsay exceptions.
Declarant unavailable, Rule 5-804.
Unavailability of declarant not required,
Rule 5-803.
Family records.
Hearsay exceptions, Rule 5-803.
Former testimony.
Hearsay exceptions, Rule 5-804.
Guilty pleas.
Withdrawn or unaccepted pleas.
Admissibility, Rule 5-410.
Habit, Rule 5-406.
Handwriting.
Authentication or identification.
Nonexpert opinion, Rule 5-901.
Hearsay.
Credibility of declarant.
Attacking and supporting, Rule 5-806.
Definition, Rule 5-801.
Unavailability as a witness, Rule 5-804.
Exceptions.
Declarant unavailable, Rule 5-804.
Definition of unavailability, Rule 5-804.
Prior statements by witnesses, Rule
5-802.1.
Unavailability of declarant not required,
Rule 5-803.
General rule, Rule 5-802.
Prior statements by witnesses.
Hearsay exceptions, Rule 5-802.1.
Within hearsay, Rule 5-805.
History.
Family or personal history.
Hearsay exceptions.
Declarant unavailable, Rule 5-804.
Unavailability of declarant not
required, Rule 5-803.
Hearsay exceptions, Rule 5-803.
Hospital expenses.
Payment of expenses.
Admissibility, Rule 5-409.
Impeachment, Rule 5-616.
Bias, Rule 5-616.
Capacity, Rule 5-616.
Character evidence, Rule 5-608.
Computer-generated evidence used to
impeach, Rule 2-504.3.
Conduct of witness, Rules 5-608, 5-616.
Nonwaiver of privilege against
self-incrimination, Rule 5-608.
Conviction of crime, Rule 5-609.
Extrinsic evidence, Rule 5-616.
Personal knowledge, Rule 5-616.
Prejudice, Rule 5-616.
Prior statements of witnesses, Rules 5-613,
5-616.
Rehabilitation, Rule 5-616.
Religious beliefs or opinions, Rule 5-610.
Who may impeach, Rule 5-607.
Inconsistent statements.
Witnesses, Rule 5-613.

EVIDENCE —Cont'd
Injuries.
Payment of medical, hospital or similar
expenses.
Admissibility to prove liability for injury,
Rule 5-409.
Instructions to the jury.
Reference to evidence.
Circuit courts, Rule 2-520.
Criminal rules, Rule 4-325.
Insurance.
Liability insurance.
Admissibility, Rule 5-411.
Interpreters.
Oath or affirmation, Rule 5-604.
Qualification as expert, Rule 5-604.
Interrogation of witnesses.
By court, Rule 5-614.
Mode and order, Rule 5-611.
Prior statements, Rule 5-613.
Irrelevant evidence.
Inadmissible, Rule 5-402.
Judges.
Competency as witness, Rule 5-605.
Explanation of ruling on evidence, Rule
5-103.
Functions of court and jury.
Writings, recordings or photographs, Rule
5-1008.
Judgments.
Boundaries.
Hearsay exceptions, Rule 5-803.
General history.
Hearsay exceptions, Rule 5-803.
Personal or family history.
Hearsay exceptions, Rule 5-803.
Judgments and decrees.
Revisory power of court.
Newly-discovered evidence.
District Court, Rule 3-535.
Judicial notice, Rule 5-201.
Jury.
Competency of juror as witness, Rule 5-606.
Functions of court and jury.
Writings, recordings or photographs, Rule
5-1008.
Hearing of jury.
Inadmissible evidence suggested to the
jury, Rule 5-103.
Preliminary questions, Rule 5-104.
Judicial notice.
Instructing jury, Rule 5-201.
Limited admissibility.
Instructing jury, Rule 5-105.
Misleading the jury.
Relevance.
Exclusion of relevant evidence on
grounds of misleading the jury,
Rule 5-403.
Writings, recordings or photographs.
Functions of court and jury, Rule 5-1008.
Jury trial.
Exhibits.
Circuit courts, Rule 2-516.

603

607

FORMS —Cont'd
Interrogatories —Cont'd
Domestic relations, Interrogatories Forms
Nos. 4, 5.
General interrogatories, Interrogatories
Form No. 3.
Instructions, Interrogatories Form No. 1.
Motor vehicle tort actions, Interrogatories
Forms Nos. 6, 7.
Personal injury actions, Interrogatories
Form No. 8.
Juvenile causes.
Adjudication.
Order of adjudication, Form 914-O/A.
Attachment.
Writ of attachment, Form 904-WA.
Commitment.
Order rescinding commitment and for
aftercare supervision, Form
916-O/RCAS.
Petition for revocation of protective
supervision and for commitment,
Form 916-P/RPSC.
Commitment of delinquent child.
Petition for revocation of probation and
commitment of delinquent child,
Form 916-P/RPC.
Commitment of juvenile.
Order, Form 915-O/CJ.
Delinquent child.
Order, Form 915-O/PDC.
Order terminating probation or protective
supervision, Form 916-O/TPPS.
Petition for revocation of probation and
commitment of delinquent child,
Form 916-P/RPC.
Emergency detention or shelter care.
Authorization, Form 912-A.
Continued detention or shelter care.
Order, Form 912-O/CDSC.
Notice, Form 912-N.
Judgments.
Restitution.
Order for judgment of restitution, Form
918-O/JR.
Petitions, Form 903-P/C.
Adults, Form 903-P/A.
Physical and mental examination of
respondent.
Order, Form 905-OE.
Probation.
Adult.
Order, Form 915-O/PA.
Protective supervision.
Order, Form 915-O/PS.
Order terminating probation or protective
supervision, Form 916-O/TPPS.
Petition for revocation of protective
supervision and for commitment,
Form 916-P/RPSC.
Recognizance of parent, guardian or
custodian, Form 904-R.

FORMS —Cont'd
Juvenile causes —Cont'd
Restitution.
Order for judgment of restitution, Form
918-O/JR.
Show cause order, Form 916-SCO.
Subpoenas.
Request for witness subpoena, Form
904-R/WS.
Summons, Form 904-S.
Supervision.
Order rescinding commitment and for
aftercare supervision, Form
916-O/RCAS.
Support.
Order for support, Form 918-O/S.
Termination of proceedings.
Final order, Form 920-FOT.
Waiver of juvenile jurisdiction.
Order, Form 913-O/W.
Petition, Form 913-P/W.
Motor vehicle tort actions.
Interrogatories, Interrogatories Forms Nos.
6, 7.
New trial.
Motion for new trial.
Form of motion.
Criminal rules, Rule 4-331.
Oaths, Rule 1-303.
Order for appeal, Form 22.
Parties.
Court papers.
Appeals to circuit court.
Designation of parties, Rule 1-301.
Original claim.
Designation of parties, Rule 1-301.
Subsequent claims.
Designation of parties, Rule 1-301.
Personal injury actions, Interrogatories
Form No. 8.
Petitions.
Administrative agency decisions, judicial
review, Rule 7-202.
Pleadings.
Circuit courts, Rule 2-303.
District Court, Rule 3-303.
Probate, petition, Rule 6-122.
Pro hac vice admission.
Motions, Form RGAB 20/M.
Orders, Form RGAB 20/O.
Sentencing.
Review of sentence.
Application, Rule 4-344.
Small claim actions.
District Court, Rule 3-701.
Subpoenas.
Circuit courts, Rule 2-510.
Criminal rules, Rule 4-266.
District Court, Rule 3-510.
Summary judgment.
Affidavits.
Circuit courts, Rule 2-501.

HEARINGS —Cont'd
Juvenile causes —Cont'd
Recording proceedings, Rule 11-110.
Scheduling of hearing.
Duties of clerk, Rule 11-104.
Waiver of jurisdiction, Rule 11-113.
Pretrial release hearing, Rule 4-222.
Juvenile courts.
Waiver of jurisdiction.
Pretrial release hearing, Rule 4-222.
Levy.
Release of property from levy.
District Court, Rule 3-643.
Masters.
Attendance of witnesses.
Circuit courts, Rule 2-541.
Notice, Rule 2-541.
Records.
Circuit courts, Rule 2-541.
Mechanics' liens, Rule 12-304.
Motions.
Amendment of judgments.
District Court, Rule 3-311.
Circuit courts, Rule 2-311.
District Court, Rule 3-311.
New trial.
Circuit courts, Rule 2-311.
District Court, Rule 3-311.
Requests for hearings.
Circuit courts, Rule 2-311.
Post conviction procedures, Rule 4-406.
Probation.
Revocation, Rule 4-347.
Sentencing.
Revisory power of court, Rule 4-345.
Subpoenas.
Preparation by clerk.
Criminal rules, Rule 4-265.
Preparation by parties.
Criminal rules, Rule 4-265.

HEARSAY, Rules 5-801 to 5-805.
See EVIDENCE.

HISTORY.
Family or personal history.
Hearsay exceptions, Rules 5-803, 5-804.

HOLIDAYS.
Administration of courts.
Sessions of court, Rule 16-106.
Definition, Rule 1-202.
Service of process.
Circuit courts, Rule 2-125.
District Court, Rule 3-125.

HOSPITALS.
Payment of hospital expenses.
Evidentiary effect, Rule 5-409.
Records.
Subpoenas.
Circuit courts, Rule 2-510.
District Court, Rule 3-510.

HUSBAND AND WIFE.
Divorce.
See DIVORCE.

HUSBAND AND WIFE —Cont'd
Spousal privilege.
Record of assertion, Rule 4-632.

I

IDENTIFICATION.
Authentication and identification.
See EVIDENCE.
Discovery.
Discovery by the state.
Criminal rules, Rule 4-263.
Motions.
Mandatory motions in circuit courts.
Criminal rules, Rule 4-252.

IMMUNITY.
Sovereign immunity.
Motions.
Preliminary motions.
Permissive motions.
Circuit courts, Rule 2-322.
Pleadings.
Defenses not waived.
Circuit courts, Rule 2-324.
Witnesses.
Compelling testimony on condition of
immunity.
Court order, Rule 4-631.
Investigation of judge, Rule 16-806.
Requested by state, Rule 4-631.

IMPEACHMENT, Rule 5-616.
Character evidence, Rule 5-608.
**Computer-generated evidence used to
impeach,** Rule 2-504.3.
Conduct of witness, Rules 5-608, 5-616.
Self-incrimination.
Privilege not waived, Rule 5-608.
Convictions, Rule 5-609.
Depositions.
Criminal rules, Rule 4-261.
Use of depositions.
Circuit courts, Rule 2-419.
Extrinsic evidence, Rule 5-616.
Personal knowledge, Rule 5-616.
Prejudice, Rule 5-616.
Prior statements, Rules 5-613, 5-616.
Rehabilitation, Rule 5-616.
Religious beliefs or opinions, Rule 5-610.
Who may impeach, Rule 5-607.

INACTIVE STATUS OF ATTORNEYS.
**Discipline and inactive status of
attorneys,** Rules 16-701 to 16-718.
See ATTORNEYS AT LAW.

IN BANC REVIEW.
Decision.
Circuit courts, Rule 2-551.
Dismissal.
Circuit courts, Rule 2-551.
Further review.
Circuit courts, Rule 2-551.

JUDGES —Cont'd
Investigation of complaints —Cont'd
Preliminary investigation, Rule 16-805.
Judgments.
Discovery in aid of enforcement.
Examination before judge or examiner.
Circuit courts, Rule 2-633.
District Court, Rule 3-633.
Judicial conference, Rule 16-802.
Judicial notice, Rule 5-201.
Jury trial.
Disability of judge.
Criminal rules, Rule 4-361.
Juvenile causes.
Disposition hearing, Rule 11-115.
Leaves, Rule 16-104.
Personal leave, Rule 16-104.
Pleas.
Disability of judge.
After verdict of acceptance of plea.
Criminal rules, Rule 4-361.
Post conviction procedures.
Hearings, Rule 4-406.
Private reprimand, Rule 16-807.
Recusal.
Circuit courts, Rule 2-505.
Code of judicial conduct, Rule 16-813,
Canon 3.
District Court, Rule 3-505.
Reprimand, Rule 16-807.
Rulings on evidence.
Explanation, Rule 5-103.
Sales.
Judicial sales, Rules 14-301 to 14-306.
See JUDICIAL SALES.
Sanctionable conduct, Rules 16-803 to
16-810.
Sentence and punishment.
Capital cases, Rule 4-343.
Advice of the judge, Rule 4-343.
Report of judge, Rule 4-343.
Service of process upon judge.
Charge of disability or sanctionable
conduct, Rule 16-808.
Sick leave, Rule 16-104.
Trial.
Decision of judge.
District Court, Rule 3-522.
Disability of judge.
Circuit courts, Rule 2-536.
Criminal rules, Rule 4-361.
Effect.
District Court, Rule 3-536.
Disqualification of judge.
District Court, Rule 3-505.
Further reassignment by another party.
District Court, Rule 3-505.
Motion and affidavit.
District Court, Rule 3-505.
Removal of trial.
Grounds.
Circuit courts, Rule 2-505.

JUDGES —Cont'd
Trial —Cont'd
Disqualification of judge —Cont'd
Request for recusal.
District Court, Rule 3-505.
Verdicts.
Disability of judge.
After verdict or acceptance of plea.
Criminal rules, Rule 4-361.
Writings, recordings or photographs.
Evidence.
Functions of court and jury, Rule 5-1008.

**JUDGMENT NOTWITHSTANDING THE
VERDICT.**
Appeals.
Effect of reversal on appeal.
Circuit courts, Rule 2-532.
Disposition.
Circuit courts, Rule 2-532.
Effect of failure to make motion.
Circuit courts, Rule 2-532.
Filing.
Time for filing.
Circuit courts, Rule 2-532.
Shortening or extending time prohibited,
Rule 1-204.
Jury trial.
Appeals.
Effect of reversal on appeal.
Circuit courts, Rule 2-532.
Motion.
Disposition.
Circuit courts, Rule 2-532.
Effect of failure to make.
Circuit courts, Rule 2-532.
Joinder with motion for new trial.
Circuit courts, Rule 2-532.
When permitted.
Circuit courts, Rule 2-532.
Motions.
Hearing.
Circuit courts, Rule 2-311.
New trial.
Joinder with motion for new trial.
Circuit courts, Rule 2-532.
Time.
Circuit courts, Rule 2-532.
Shortening or extending time for filing
motion prohibited, Rule 1-204.
When permitted.
Circuit courts, Rule 2-532.

JUDGMENTS AND DECREES.
Affidavits.
Judgment on affidavit.
Pleading.
District Court, Rule 3-306.
Amendments.
Motion to alter or amend judgment.
District Court, Rule 3-534.
Ancillary relief in aid of enforcement.
Circuit courts, Rule 2-651.

627

JURISDICTION —Cont'd
Transfer of action.
Circuit courts, Rule 2-327.
Trial.
Dismissal for lack of jurisdiction.
Circuit courts, Rule 2-507.
District Court, Rule 3-507.
Waiver.
Juvenile courts.
Procedure upon waiver, Rule 4-222.

JURY.
Acquittal.
Motion for judgment of acquittal, Rule 4-324.
Additional jurors.
Circuit courts, Rule 2-512.
Criminal rules, Rule 4-312.
Advisory verdicts disallowed.
Circuit courts, Rule 2-511.
Alternate jurors.
Circuit courts, Rule 2-512.
Criminal rules, Rule 4-312.
Peremptory challenges.
Number.
Criminal rules, Rule 4-313.
Appeals.
Administrative agencies.
Circuit courts, Rule 2-325.
Array.
Challenge to the array.
Circuit courts, Rule 2-512.
Criminal rules, Rule 4-312.
Cause.
Challenges for cause.
Circuit courts, Rule 2-512.
Criminal rules, Rule 4-312.
Challenges.
Array.
Circuit courts, Rule 2-512.
Criminal rules, Rule 4-312.
Cause.
Circuit courts, Rule 2-512.
Criminal rules, Rule 4-312.
Peremptory challenges, Rule 2-512.
Criminal rules, Rule 4-313.
Circuit courts.
Demand for jury trial.
Transfers from District Court, Rules 2-325, 2-326.
Transmittal of record from District Court to circuit court upon timely demand for jury trial, Rule 2-325.
Communications with jury.
Circuit courts, Rule 2-521.
Criminal rules, Rule 4-326.
Competency of juror as witness, Rule 5-606.
Contempt.
Constructive criminal contempt proceedings.
Jury trial, Rule 15-205.

JURY —Cont'd
Costs.
Criminal rules, Rule 4-353.
Special costs in first, second and fourth judicial circuits, Rule 2-509.
Criminal procedure.
Challenges.
Array, Rule 4-312.
Communications, Rule 4-326.
Demand for jury trial, Rule 4-301.
Exhibits, Rule 4-322.
Instructions to jury, Rule 4-325.
Number of jurors, Rule 4-311.
Objections.
Method of making, Rule 4-323.
Peremptory challenges, Rule 4-313.
Review of evidence, Rule 4-326.
Right preserved, Rule 4-311.
Selection, Rule 4-312.
Separation of jury, Rule 4-311.
Verdicts, Rule 4-327.
Waiver.
Circuit courts, Rule 4-246.
Demand for jury trial.
Circuit courts, Rule 2-325.
Transfers from District Court on demand for jury trial, Rule 2-326.
Designation of list of qualified jurors.
Criminal rules, Rule 4-312.
District Court.
Demand for jury trial.
Transfer from District Court, Rule 2-326.
New demand upon transfer not required, Rule 2-325.
Transferred actions from District Court.
New demand not required, Rule 2-325.
Election of rights and remedies.
Effect of election.
Circuit courts, Rule 2-325.
Withdrawal of election.
Circuit courts, Rule 2-325.
Eminent domain.
Method of trial, Rule 12-207.
Opening statement, Rule 12-207.
Verdicts, Rule 12-208.
View, Rule 12-207.
Evidence.
Competency of juror as witness, Rule 5-606.
Exhibits.
Circuit courts, Rule 2-516.
Criminal rules, Rule 4-322.
Hearing of jury.
Proceedings out of hearing of jury, Rules 5-103, 5-104.
Instructions to jury.
Reference to evidence.
Circuit courts, Rule 2-520.
Criminal rules, Rule 4-325.
Items taken to jury room.
Review of evidence.
Circuit courts, Rule 2-521.
Criminal rules, Rule 4-326.
Judicial notice, Rule 5-201.

JUVENILE CAUSES —Cont'd
Forms —Cont'd
Attachment.
Writ of attachment, Form 904-WA.
Commitment.
Delinquent child.
Petition for revocation of probation and commitment of delinquent child, Form 916-P/RPC.
Juvenile.
Order, Form 915-O/CJ.
Order rescinding commitment and for aftercare supervision, Form 916-O/RCAS.
Petition for revocation of protective supervision and for commitment, Form 916-P/RPSC.
Delinquent child.
Order, Form 915-O/PDC.
Order terminating probation or protective supervision, Form 916-O/TPPS.
Petition for revocation of probation and commitment of delinquent child, Form 916-P/RPC.
Emergency detention or shelter care.
Authorization, Form 912-A.
Continued detention or shelter care.
Order, Form 912-O/CDSC.
Notice, Form 912-N.
Judgments.
Restitution.
Order for judgment of restitution, Form 918-O/JR.
Petitions, Form 903-P/C.
Adults, Form 903-P/A.
Physical and mental examination of respondent.
Order, Form 905-OE.
Probation.
Adult.
Order, Form 915-O/PA.
Delinquent child.
Order, Form 915-O/PDC.
Petition for revocation of probation and commitment of delinquent child, Form 916-P/RPC.
Order terminating probation or protective supervision, Form 916-O/TPPS.
Protective supervision.
Order, Form 915-O/PS.
Terminating probation or protective supervision, Form 916-O/TPPS.
Petition for revocation of protective supervision and for commitment, Form 916-P/RPSC.
Recognizance of parent, guardian or custodian, Form 904-R.
Restitution.
Order for judgment of restitution, Form 918-O/JR.
Show cause order, Form 916-SCO.
Subpoenas.
Request for witness subpoena, Form 904-R/WS.

JUVENILE CAUSES —Cont'd
Forms —Cont'd
Summons, Form 904-S.
Supervision.
Order rescinding commitment and for aftercare supervision, Form 916-O/RCAS.
Support.
Order for support, Form 918-O/S.
Termination of proceedings.
Final order, Form 920-FOT.
Waiver of juvenile jurisdiction.
Order, Form 913-O/W.
Petition, Form 913-P/W.
Guardians.
Appointment of guardian, Rule 11-117.
Recognizance of parent, guardian or custodian, Form 904-R.
Hearings.
Adjudicatory hearing, Rule 11-114.
Controlling conduct of person before court, Rule 11-110.
Disposition hearing, Rule 11-115.
Emergency detention or shelter care, Rule 11-112.
Generally, Rule 11-110.
Liability of parents, Rule 11-118.
Modification or vacation of order.
When hearing required, Rule 11-116.
Notice, Rule 11-110.
Open hearings, list, Rule 11-104.
Petitions.
Multiple petitions, Rule 11-110.
Place, Rule 11-110.
Recording proceedings, Rule 11-110.
Scheduling of hearing.
Duties of clerk, Rule 11-104.
Waiver of jurisdiction, Rule 11-113.
Pretrial release hearing, Rule 4-222.
Indigent persons.
Right to counsel, Rule 11-106.
Intake procedures, Rule 11-102.
Interstate compact on juveniles.
Petition under interstate compact, Rule 11-103.
Intervention.
Leave of court, Rule 11-122.
Of right, Rule 11-122.
Investigations.
Waiver of jurisdiction, Rule 11-113.
Judgments and decrees.
Hearings, Rule 11-110.
Jurisdiction.
Transfer from court exercising criminal jurisdiction, Rule 11-102A.
Transfer of jurisdiction.
Court exercising criminal jurisdiction.
Motions, Rule 4-251.
Waiver of jurisdiction.
Form of petition, Form 913-P/W.
Order.
Forms, Form 913-O/W.

641

NOLO CONTENDERE.
Impeachment of witness, Rule 5-609.
Pleas.
See PLEAS.
Subsequent offenders.
Disclosure of notice of additional or
mandatory penalties, Rule 4-245.
Withdrawn or unaccepted pleas.
Admissibility in evidence, Rule 5-410.

NONJOINDER.
Motions.
Preliminary motions.
Permissive motions.
Circuit courts, Rule 2-322.
Parties.
Circuit courts, Rule 2-213.
District Court, Rule 3-211.
Effect.
District Court, Rule 3-213.
Reasons for nonjoinder.
Circuit courts, Rule 2-211.

NONRESIDENTS.
Executors and administrators.
Settlement of decedents' estates.
Foreign personal representative.
Application to set inheritance tax, Rule
6-501.
Forms.
Executors and administrators.
Settlement of decedents' estates.
Foreign personal representative.
Application to set inheritance tax,
Rule 6-501.
Signatures.
Certification by signing attorney with
out-of-state office, Rule 1-313.

NOTICE.
Actions.
Dismissal for lack of jurisdiction or
prosecution.
Circuit courts, Rule 2-507.
District Court, Rule 3-507.
Administration of courts.
Clients' security fund.
Decertification orders.
Notice to clerks, Rule 16-811.
Information system.
Court of special appeals, Rule 16-309.
Motion day.
Hearings.
Lengthy hearing, Rule 16-201.
Administrative agency decisions, judicial
review, Rule 7-202.
Certificate of compliance, Rule 7-202.
Adoption.
See ADOPTION.
Appeals.
General provisions.
See APPEALS.
Appeals from District Court to circuit
court.
Appeals heard on record, Rule 7-113.

NOTICE —Cont'd
Appeals from District Court to circuit
court —Cont'd
Notice of appeal.
Method of securing review, Rule 7-103.
Striking of notice by District Court, Rule
7-105.
Notice of striking of notice of appeal, Rule
7-105.
Appearances.
Striking attorney's appearance.
Circuit courts, Rule 2-132.
District Court, Rule 3-132.
Attachment.
Prejudgment attachment.
Lien of attachment.
District Court, Rule 3-115.
Attorneys at law.
Discipline and inactive status.
Audit of attorney's accounts and records,
Rule 16-718.
Trust accounts.
Approved institutions, Rule 16-611.
Duty of attorney to notify institution,
Rule 16-605.
Auditors.
Hearings.
Circuit courts, Rule 2-543.
Burial grounds.
Sale for other use, Rule 14-401.
Certiorari in circuit court, Rule 7-301.
Class actions.
Circuit courts, Rule 2-231.
Computer-generated evidence, Rule
2-504.3.
Confessed judgments.
Circuit courts, Rule 2-611.
District Court, Rule 3-611.
Default judgments.
Circuit courts, Rule 2-613.
Depositions.
Certification and filing of deposition.
Circuit courts, Rule 2-415.
Criminal rules, Rule 4-212.
Failure of party giving notice to attend.
Expenses for failure to pursue deposition,
Rule 2-434.
Written questions.
Circuit courts, Rule 2-417.
Disabled persons.
Need for accomodation, Rule 1-332.
Form, Form 1-332.
Discovery.
Perpetuation of evidence.
Before action instituted.
Circuit courts, Rule 2-404.
Eminent domain.
Board of property review procedures, Rule
12-213.
Cemeteries.
Publication.
Acquisition of cemetery, Rule 12-204.

643

O

OATHS.
Depositions.
Officer before whom deposition taken.
  In state, Rule 2-414.
Procedure.
  Circuit courts, Rule 2-415.
Forms, Rule 1-303.
Interpreters, Rule 5-604.
Witnesses, Rule 5-603.

OPENING ESTATES, Rules 6-301 to 6-351.
See EXECUTORS AND ADMINISTRATORS.

OPINIONS.
Appeals.
General provisions.
  See APPEALS.
Appeals from District Court to circuit court.
Appeals heard on the record, Rule 7-113.

OPINION TESTIMONY.
Experts.
Bases of opinion, Rule 5-703.
Mental state of criminal defendant, Rule 5-704.
Right to challenge, Rule 5-703.
Underlying facts or data, Rule 5-705.
Handwriting, Rule 5-901.
Impeachment, Rule 5-616.
Lay witnesses, Rule 5-701.
Ultimate issue, Rule 5-704.

ORAL ARGUMENTS.
Appeals from District Court to circuit court.
Appeals heard on the record, Rule 7-113.
Death penalty cases, Rule 8-306.

ORDERS.
Interlocutory orders.
See INTERLOCUTORY ORDERS.

ORDERS OF COURT.
Administration of courts.
Clients' security fund.
  Show cause order, Rule 16-811.
Disposition of records.
  Court order, Rule 16-818.
Promulgation of rules.
  Promulgation by rules order, Rule 16-801.
Adoption.
Show cause order, Rule 9-105.
Appeals.
Court of appeals.
  Certification procedure.
    Federal courts and other state courts as certifying courts, Rule 8-305.
Emergency orders.
  Authority of court to rule on party's motion before expiration of time for response, Rule 8-431.
Entry of order.
  Clerk entering, Rule 8-432.
  Court entering, Rule 8-432.

ORDERS OF COURT —Cont'd
Appeals —Cont'd
Entry of order —Cont'd
  Time extensions in court of special appeals, Rule 8-432.
Forms, Form 22.
Mandate.
  Evidence of order of court, Rule 8-606.
Attorneys at law.
Discipline and inactive status.
  Audit of attorney's accounts and records.
    Show cause order, Rule 16-718.
  Conservator of clients' affairs, Rule 16-717.
  Suspension upon conviction of certain crimes, Rule 16-716.
Auditors.
Referral by order.
  Circuit courts, Rule 2-543.
Automobile insurance fund.
Judgments.
  Actions against fund.
    Payment of judgments.
      Show cause order, Rule 15-804.
Bail and recognizance.
Pretrial release.
  Amendment of pretrial release order, Rule 4-216.
  Review of order, Rule 4-216.
Bar admissions.
Out-of-state attorneys.
  Special admission.
    Form, Form RGAB 20/O.
Certiorari in circuit court.
Show cause orders, Rule 7-301.
Class actions.
Conduct of class actions.
  Circuit courts, Rule 2-231.
Computer-generated evidence, Rule 2-504.3.
Contempt, Rules 15-203, 15-204.
Child or spousal support nonpayment, Rule 15-207.
Default judgments.
Orders of default.
  Circuit courts, Rule 2-613.
Depositions.
Contents.
  Criminal rules, Rule 4-261.
Protective orders.
  Criminal rules, Rule 4-261.
Discovery.
Compelling discovery.
  Circuit courts, Rule 2-432.
  Sanction for failure to comply.
    Circuit courts, Rule 2-433.
Perpetuation of evidence.
  Before action instituted.
    Court order.
      Circuit courts, Rule 2-404.
Protective orders.
  Circuit courts, Rule 2-403.

ORDERS OF COURT —Cont'd

Pretrial conference.

Pretrial order.

Circuit courts, Rules 2-504, 2-504.2.

District Court, Rule 3-504.

Probation.

Modification of probation order, Rule 4-346.

Receivers.

Removal, Rule 13-701.

Schedule of debtor's property and debts, Rule 13-203.

Scheduling conferences.

Circuit courts, Rule 2-504.1.

Scheduling orders.

Circuit courts, Rule 2-504.

Sentencing.

Release after conviction.

Amendment of order of release, Rule 4-349.

Service of process.

Order of court.

District Court, Rule 3-121.

Subpoenas.

Protective orders.

Criminal rules, Rule 4-266.

Summary judgment.

Order specifying issues or facts not in dispute.

Circuit courts, Rule 2-501.

Time.

Motion to shorten or extend time requirements.

Ex parte order, Rule 1-204.

Generally, Rule 1-204.

Service of order, Rule 1-204.

Trial.

Objections to other rulings or orders.

Circuit courts, Rule 2-517.

Criminal rules, Rule 4-323.

District Court, Rule 3-517.

Pretrial conference.

Pretrial order, Rules 2-504, 2-504.2.

District Court, Rule 3-504.

Production of evidence.

When court may require.

Circuit courts, Rule 2-514.

District Court, Rule 3-514.

Removal of trial.

Order by court to which removed, Rule 2-505.

Striking order of removal.

Circuit courts, Rule 2-505.

Scheduling conferences.

Circuit courts, Rule 2-504.1.

Scheduling orders, Rule 2-504.

Voluntary dismissal.

Circuit courts, Rule 2-506.

District Court, Rule 3-506.

Witnesses.

Body attachment of material witnesses.

Criminal rules, Rule 4-267.

ORDERS OF COURT —Cont'd

Witnesses —Cont'd

Immunity.

Compelling testimony on condition of immunity.

Court order, Rule 4-631.

ORPHANS' COURT.

Applicability of rules, Rule 1-101.

Executors and administrators.

Settlement of decedents' estates.

See EXECUTORS AND ADMINISTRATORS.

P

PAPERS.

Court papers.

Filing, Rule 1-322.

Form of court papers, Rule 1-301.

Service of process, Rule 1-321.

Proof of service, Rule 1-323.

Signatures, Rule 1-311.

PARDONS.

Evidence.

Impeachment by evidence of conviction of crime.

Effect of pardon, Rule 5-609.

Expungement of records.

Petition for expungement of records.

Form, Title 4, Form 4-504.1.

PARENT AND CHILD.

Adoption.

General provisions, Rules 9-101 to 9-113.

See ADOPTION.

Divorce.

Custody.

Pleadings, Rule 9-203.

Family division and support services, Rule 16-204.

Juvenile causes, Rules 11-101 to 11-122.

See JUVENILE CAUSES.

PAROLE AND PROBATION.

Attorneys at law.

Revocation of probation.

Waiver of counsel, Rule 4-347.

Expungement of records.

Petition, Title 4, Form 4-504.1.

Hearings.

Probation.

Revocation of probation, Rule 4-347.

Notices.

Revocation of probation.

Notice of proceedings, Rule 4-347.

Probation.

Expungement of records.

Petition, Title 4, Form 4-504.1.

Hearings.

Revocation of probation, Rule 4-347.

Imposition.

Manner, Rule 4-346.

Modification of order, Rule 4-346.

651

653

PLEAS —Cont'd
Verdicts.
Guilty verdict.
Pleas to other offenses before sentencing, Rule 4-244.
Withdrawal.
Generally, Rule 4-242.
Plea agreements.
Agreements on sentencing, disposition or other judicial action, Rule 4-243.
Pleas to other offenses.
Objection or withdrawal of plea, Rule 4-244.

POOR.
Appeals.
Briefs.
Costs paid by state, Rule 8-505.
Juvenile causes.
Right to counsel, Rule 11-106.

POST-CONVICTION PROCEDURE.
Amendments.
Petitions, Rule 4-402.
Appeals.
Application.
Leave to appeal, Rule 4-408.
Application for leave to appeal, Rule 4-408.
Commencement.
How commenced, Rule 4-401.
Copies.
Copy of order and statement of court, Rule 4-407.
Evidence.
Hearings, Rule 4-406.
Habeas corpus.
Alternative remedy to writ, Rule 15-304.
Hearings.
Evidence, Rule 4-406.
Judge, Rule 4-406.
Presence of petitioner, Rule 4-406.
When required, Rule 4-406.
Judges.
Hearings, Rule 4-406.
Judgments.
Finality of statement and order, Rule 4-407.
Notice.
Petition, Rule 4-403.
Orders, Rule 4-407.
Copy to parties, Rule 4-407.
Finality, Rule 4-407.
Parties.
Statement and order of court.
Copy to parties, Rule 4-407.
Petitions.
Amendment, Rule 4-402.
Arguments or citations, Rule 4-402.
Citation of authority, Rule 4-402.
Commencement of action, Rule 4-401.
Content, Rule 4-402.
Notice, Rule 4-403.
Response, Rule 4-404.
Withdrawal, Rule 4-405.

POST-CONVICTION PROCEDURE —Cont'd
Statement of court, Rule 4-407.
Copy to parties, Rule 4-407.
Finality, Rule 4-407.
State's attorney.
Response to petition, Rule 4-404.
Venue, Rule 4-401.

POSTING.
Publication.
See PUBLICATION.

PRISONERS.
Depositions.
Right to take.
Circuit courts, Rule 2-411.
Habeas corpus.
See HABEAS CORPUS.
Imprisonment.
Sentencing, Rule 4-351.
Stay of execution, Rule 4-348.

PRIVILEGED COMMUNICATIONS.
Attorney at law.
Discipline and inactive status, Rule 16-708.
Audit of attorney's accounts and records, Rule 16-718.
Conservator of clients' affairs, Rule 16-717.
Continuances.
Legislative privilege.
Circuit courts, Rule 2-508.
Grounds for continuance.
District Court, Rule 3-508.
Investigations.
Motion for disclosure.
Criminal rules, Rule 4-642.
Secrecy of court records, Rule 4-642.
Secrecy of hearings, Rule 4-642.
Judicial disabilities and sanctionable conduct.
Confidentiality of complaints, investigation, etc., Rule 16-810.
Juvenile causes.
Court records.
Sealing of records, Rule 11-121.
Rules of professional conduct, Prof. Cond. R. 1.6.
Searches and seizures.
Warrants.
Retention of application and affidavits, Rule 4-601.
Spousal privilege.
Record of assertion, Rule 4-632.
Trial.
Continuances.
Legislative privileges.
Circuit courts, Rule 2-508.
District Court, Rule 3-508.

PRIVILEGES, EVIDENCE.
Preliminary questions, Rule 5-104.
Self-incrimination, Rule 5-608.

Q

QUASI IN REM SERVICE OF PROCESS.
Circuit courts, Rule 2-122.
Returns, Rule 2-126.

R

RADIO.
Administration of courts.
Photographing, recording, broadcasting or
televising in courthouses, Rule 16-109.

RAPE SHIELD LAW, Rule 5-412.

REAL PARTY IN INTEREST.
Circuit courts, Rule 2-201.
District Court, Rule 3-201.

REAL PROPERTY.
Actions regarding.
Applicability of rules, Rule 1-101.
Definitions, Rule 1-202.
Executions.
Levy.
Circuit courts, Rule 2-642.
District Court, Rule 3-642.
Sale of property under levy.
Circuit courts, Rule 2-644.
District Court, Rule 3-644.
Fiduciaries.
Applicability of rules, Rule 10-701.
Bond of fiduciary, Rule 10-702.
Foreclosures.
Location of public sale, Rule 14-101.
Guardian and ward.
Administration of guardianship, Rule
10-305.
Advice of rights, Rule 10-303.
Hearings, Rule 10-304.
Petition for appointment of guardian, Rule
10-301.
Service of show cause order, Rule 10-302.
Judgments and decrees.
Transfer of property in violation of
judgment, Rule 2-648.
Judicial sales.
Ratification of sale.
Affidavit by purchaser, Rule 14-305.
Recordation, Rule 14-306.
Levy.
Sale of property under levy.
Transfer of real property following sale.
Circuit courts, Rule 2-644.
District Court, Rule 3-644.
Mechanics' liens.
Land.
Defined, Rule 12-301.
Tax sales, Rules 14-501 to 14-505.
See TAX SALES.
**Transfer of property in violation of
judgment,** Rule 2-648.

RECEIVERS.
Abandonment of property and records,
Rule 13-601.

RECEIVERS —Cont'd
Accountants.
Compensation and fees, Rule 13-303.
Employment, Rule 13-301.
Applicability of other rules, Rule 13-103.
Applicability of provisions, Rule 13-102.
Appraisers.
Compensation and fees, Rule 13-303.
Employment, Rule 13-301.
Assignees.
Compensation and fees, Rule 13-303.
Assumption of jurisdiction.
Ineligibility as receiver, Rule 13-105.
Petition, Rule 13-106.
Attorneys at law.
Compensation and fees, Rule 13-303.
Employment, Rule 13-301.
Special counsel, Rule 13-105.
Auctioneers.
Compensation and fees, Rule 13-303.
Employment, Rule 13-301.
Auditors.
Referral to auditor, Rule 13-502.
Bonds, surety.
Requirements, Rule 13-107.
Claims.
Compromise of claim or dispute, Rule
13-403.
Objections to claims, Rule 13-402.
Proof of claim, Rule 13-401.
Compensation and fees, Rule 13-303.
Definitions, Rule 13-101.
Disclosures required, Rule 13-302.
Discovery.
When authorized, Rule 13-103.
Disposition of unclaimed distributions,
Rule 13-503.
Distribution of property, Rule 13-503.
Eligibility for service, Rule 13-105.
**Employment of attorney, accountant,
auctioneer or appraiser.**
Compensation and fees, Rule 13-303.
Forfeiture of compensation.
Appointment of successor, Rule 13-703.
Notice.
Mailing of notice to creditors, Rule 13-202.
Publication of notice to creditors, Rule
13-201.
Orders.
Schedule of debtor's property and debts.
Order of debtor to disclose information,
Rule 13-203.
Petitions.
Assumption of jurisdiction, Rule 13-106.
Publication of notice to creditors, Rule
13-201.
Records.
Abandonment of property and records, Rule
13-601.
Referral to auditor, Rule 13-502.
Removal, Rule 13-701.
Reports.
Annual reports, Rule 13-501.
Required disclosures, Rule 13-302.

RECEIVERS —Cont'd
Resignation, Rule 13-702.
Schedule of debtor's property and debts, Rule 13-203.
Scope of provisions, Rule 13-102.
Service of process.
Requirements, Rule 13-104.
Show cause orders.
Removal proceedings, Rule 13-701.
Successors, Rule 13-703.

RECIDIVISM.
Subsequent offenders.
Generally, Rule 4-245.

RECORDATION.
Adoption judgments, Rule 11-501.
Bonds, surety.
Clerks to record bond, Rule 1-402.
Eminent domain.
Inquisition, Rule 12-212.
Recording inquisition in other county, Rule 12-212.
Judgments.
Adoption judgments, Rule 11-501.
Entry of judgment.
Circuit courts, Rule 2-601.
District Court, Rule 3-601.
Lien of judgment.
County where recorded.
Circuit courts, Rule 2-621.
District Court notice of lien, Rule 2-623.
Recording of judgment of another court.
Circuit courts, Rule 2-623.
Judicial sales.
Real property, Rule 14-306.
Juvenile causes.
Liability of parents, Rule 11-118.
Liens.
District Court notice of lien, Rule 2-623.
Mechanics' liens.
Boundaries.
Designation after commencement of construction, Rule 12-308.

RECORDS.
Administration of courts.
Commission on judicial disabilities, Rule 16-804.
Proceedings before commission, Rule 16-808.
Court reporters.
Circuit court reporters.
Maintenance and filing of administrative records, Rule 16-404.
District courts, Rule 16-504.
Disposition of records, Rule 16-818.
District courts, Rule 16-505.
Promulgation of rules.
Record of rules, Rule 16-801.
Administrative agency decisions, judicial review, Rule 7-206.
Return to agency, Rule 7-210.

RECORDS —Cont'd
Adoption.
Clerk to keep, Rule 9-112.
Medical history of child, Rule 9-113.
Notice of objection.
Access to records, Rule 9-107.
Sealing, Rule 9-112.
Appeals from District Court to circuit court.
Contents and form generally, Rule 7-109.
Record on appeal.
Generally.
See APPEALS FROM DISTRICT COURT TO CIRCUIT COURT.
Transmittal, Rule 7-103.
Time for, Rule 7-108.
Appeals to court of special appeals.
Record on appeal.
See APPEALS.
Attorneys at law.
Discipline and inactive status.
Audit of attorney's accounts and records, Rule 16-718.
Charges, Rule 16-711.
Auditors.
Hearings.
Record of hearing.
Circuit courts, Rule 2-543.
Commission on judicial disabilities, Rule 16-804.
Proceedings before commission, Rule 16-808.
Confidentiality.
Juvenile causes.
Court records, Rule 11-121.
Criminal rules.
Expungement of records, Rules 4-501 to 4-512.
See RECORDS.
Spousal privilege.
Record of assertion, Rule 4-632.
Depositions.
Testimony.
Circuit courts, Rule 2-415.
Eminent domain.
Abandonment.
Effect on records, Rule 12-211.
Evidence.
See EVIDENCE.
Examiners.
Hearing.
Circuit courts, Rule 2-542.
Record of hearing.
Exceptions.
Circuit courts, Rule 2-542.
Hearing on exceptions, Rule 2-542.
Filing.
Circuit courts, Rule 2-542.
Expungement.
Amendments.
Applications, petitions or answers, Rule 4-506.

660

REFEREES.
Administration of courts.
Code of conduct for judicial appointees.
Adoption, Rule 16-814.
Financial disclosure statements, Rule
16-816.

REGISTERS OF WILLS.
Executors and administrators.
Settlement of decedents' estate.
See EXECUTORS AND
ADMINISTRATORS.

RELEVANT EVIDENCE.
See EVIDENCE.

RELIGION.
Records.
Hearsay exceptions for records of religious
organizations, Rule 5-803.
Witnesses.
Beliefs or opinions or witness, Rule 5-610.

REMOVAL OF CAUSES.
Civil procedure.
Circuit courts, Rule 2-505.
Criminal procedure.
Circuit courts, Rule 4-254.

RENT.
Ground rent, Rule 12-501.

RENUNCIATION.
Executors and administrators.
Settlement of decedents' estates.
See EXECUTORS AND
ADMINISTRATORS.

REPAIRS.
Subsequent remedial measures.
Evidentiary considerations, Rule 5-407.

REPEAT OFFENDERS.
Generally, Rule 4-245.

REPLEVIN.
Actions.
Replevin bond, Rule 12-601.
Bonds, surety.
Action on replevin bond, Rule 12-601.
**Enforcement of judgment awarding
possession.**
Circuit courts, Rule 2-647.
Verdicts, Rule 12-601.

REPORTERS.
Administration of courts.
Court reporters.
See ADMINISTRATION OF COURTS.

REPORTS.
Administration of courts.
Clients' security fund.
Filing, Rule 16-811.
Commission on judicial disabilities, Rule
16-804.
Information system.
Criminal history record information, Rule
16-308.

REPORTS —Cont'd
Administration of courts —Cont'd
Information system —Cont'd
District courts, Rule 16-503.
Judges, Rule 16-105.
Adoption, Rule 9-106.
Accounting report, Rule 9-110.
Auditors.
Circuit courts, Rule 2-543.
Time of entry of order ratifying report,
Rule 2-543.
Exceptions.
Circuit courts, Rule 2-543.
Commission on judicial disabilities, Rule
16-804.
Evidence.
Market reports.
Hearsay exceptions, Rule 5-803.
Public records and reports.
Certified copies, Rule 5-1005.
Hearsay exceptions, Rule 5-803.
Executions.
Levy.
Sale of property under levy.
Report to the court.
Circuit courts, Rule 2-644.
District Court, Rule 3-644.
Executors and administrators.
Settlement of decedents' estates.
Information report.
Form, Rule 6-404.
Fiduciaries.
Inventory and information report, Rule
10-707.
Guardian and ward.
Annual report, Rule 10-206.
Judicial sales.
Procedure following sale, Rule 14-305.
Juvenile causes.
Emergency detention or shelter care, Rule
11-112.
Masters, Rule 11-111.
Physical and mental examinations, Rule
11-105.
Levy.
Sale of property under levy.
Circuit courts, Rule 2-644.
District Court, Rule 3-644.
Masters.
Circuit courts, Rule 2-541.
Mechanics' liens.
Boundaries.
Designation after commencement of
construction.
Surveyor's report, Rule 12-308.
Partition.
Commissioner's report.
Service of process, Rule 12-401.
Receivers.
Annual reports, Rule 13-501.
Sentence and punishment.
Capital cases.
Judge's report, Rule 4-343.

663

SERVICE OF PROCESS —Cont'd
Forms.
Executors and administrators.
Settlement of decedents' estates.
Certificate of service, Rule 6-125.
Garnishment.
Property.
Circuit courts, Rule 2-645.
District Court, Rule 3-645.
Wages.
Circuit courts, Rule 2-646.
District Court, Rule 3-646.
Generally.
District Court, Rule 3-121.
Guardian and ward.
See GUARDIAN AND WARD.
Habeas corpus, Rule 15-303.
Issuance of writ.
Procedure following issuance of writ, Rule 15-306.
Health care malpractice claims, Rule 15-403.
Holidays.
Circuit courts, Rule 2-125.
District Court, Rule 3-125.
Individuals.
Persons to be served.
Circuit courts, Rule 2-124.
District Court, Rule 3-124.
In personam service.
Circuit courts, Rule 2-121.
District Court, Rule 3-121.
Evasion of service.
Circuit courts, Rule 2-121.
Exclusivity of methods.
Nonexclusive.
Circuit courts, Rule 2-121.
Order of court.
Circuit courts, Rule 2-121.
In rem or quasi in rem service of process.
Content of notice.
Circuit courts, Rule 2-122.
Notice.
Content of notice.
Circuit courts, Rule 2-122.
Posting.
Circuit courts, Rule 2-122.
Publication.
Circuit courts, Rule 2-122.
Return.
Circuit courts, Rule 2-126.
Time.
Circuit courts, Rule 2-122.
Judicial disabilities and sanctionable conduct.
Service of charges upon judge, Rule 16-808.
Juvenile causes.
Duties of clerk, Rule 11-104.
Hearings.
Notice of hearing, Rule 11-110.
Intervention.
Motion to intervene, Rule 11-122.

SERVICE OF PROCESS —Cont'd
Juvenile causes —Cont'd
Physical and mental examination.
Service of copies of report, Rule 11-105.
Legal disabilities.
Persons to be served.
Circuit courts, Rule 2-124.
District Court, Rule 3-124.
Limited liability companies.
Persons to be served.
Circuit courts, Rule 2-124.
District Court, Rule 3-124.
Limited liability partnerships.
Persons to be served.
Circuit courts, Rule 2-124.
District court, Rule 3-124.
Mail.
Return.
Circuit courts, Rule 2-126.
District Court, Rule 3-126.
Time.
Additional time after service by mail, Rule 1-203.
Masters.
Reports.
Circuit courts, Rule 2-541.
Methods.
Nonexclusivity.
Circuit courts, Rule 2-121.
District Court, Rule 3-121.
Motions.
Preliminary motions.
Mandatory motions.
Circuit courts, Rule 2-322.
Officers and employees.
Persons to be served.
District Court, Rule 3-124.
Orders.
Order of court.
District Court, Rule 3-121.
Papers, Rule 1-321.
Proof of service, Rule 1-323.
Partition.
Report of commissioners, Rule 12-401.
Partnerships.
Persons to be served.
Circuit courts, Rule 2-124.
District Court, Rule 3-124.
Personal service.
Circuit courts, Rule 2-121.
District Court, Rule 3-121.
Persons to be served.
Circuit courts, Rule 2-124.
District Court, Rule 3-124.
Pleadings.
Amendment of pleadings.
Additional parties.
Circuit courts, Rule 2-341.
District court, Rule 3-341.
Nonoriginal pleadings.
Defaulting party.
Exceptions, Rule 1-321.
Generally, Rule 1-321.

SHERIFFS —Cont'd
Levy.
Sale of property under levy.
Circuit courts, Rule 2-644.
District Court, Rule 3-644.
Service of process.
By whom served, Rule 2-123.
District Court, Rule 3-123.
Summons and process.
Requirements preliminary to summons.
Instructions to sheriff.
Circuit courts, Rule 2-111.
District Court, Rule 3-111.

SHOW CAUSE ORDERS.
Certiorari in circuit court, Rule 7-301.

SIGNATURES.
Attorneys at law.
Certification by signing attorney with
out-of-state office, Rule 1-313.
Requirements of signing attorney, Rule
1-312.
Charging documents, Rule 4-202.
Definitions.
Requirements of signing attorney.
Office for the practice of law, Rule 1-312.
Depositions.
Correction and signature.
Circuit courts, Rule 2-415.
Divorce.
Pleadings, Rule 9-203.
Eminent domain.
Verdicts, Rule 12-208.
Juvenile causes.
Juvenile petition, Rule 11-103.
Nonresidents.
Certification by signing attorney with
out-of-state office, Rule 1-313.
Papers, Rule 1-311.
Pleadings.
Effect, Rule 1-311.
Requirement, Rule 1-311.
Requirements of signing attorney.
Certification by signing attorney with
out-of-state office, Rule 1-313.
Definition of "office for the practice of
law," Rule 1-312.
Sanctions for failure, Rule 1-311.

SMALL CLAIM ACTIONS.
Applicability of rules.
District Court, Rule 3-701.
Counterclaims.
District Court, Rule 3-701.
Cross-claims.
District Court, Rule 3-701.
Discovery.
Nonavailability of discovery.
District Court, Rule 3-701.
Forms.
District Court, Rule 3-701.
Third parties.
Claims.
District Court, Rule 3-701.

SMALL CLAIM ACTIONS —Cont'd
Time.
Trial date and time.
District Court, Rule 3-701.
Trial.
Conduct of trial.
District Court, Rule 3-701.
Date and time.
District Court, Rule 3-701.

SMALL ESTATES, Rules 6-201 to 6-221.
See EXECUTORS AND ADMINISTRATORS.

SOCIAL SERVICES.
Juvenile causes.
Disposition hearing.
Commitment to department of social
services, Rule 11-115.

SOVEREIGN IMMUNITY.
Motions.
Preliminary motions.
Permissive motions.
Circuit courts, Rule 2-322.
Pleadings.
Defenses not waived.
Circuit courts, Rule 2-324.

SPECIAL PROCEEDINGS.
Adoption.
See ADOPTION.
Arbitration and award, Rule 15-101.
Attorneys at law.
Discipline and inactive status.
See ATTORNEYS AT LAW.
Automobile insurance fund.
See AUTOMOBILE INSURANCE FUND.
Burial grounds.
See BURIAL GROUNDS.
Certiorari.
See CERTIORARI.
Contempt.
See CONTEMPT.
Detinue.
See DETINUE.
Divorce.
See DIVORCE.
Ejectment.
See EJECTMENT.
Eminent domain.
See EMINENT DOMAIN.
Expungement of records.
See RECORDS.
Fiduciaries.
See FIDUCIARIES.
Foreclosures.
See FORECLOSURES.
Ground rent.
See GROUND RENT.
Habeas corpus.
See HABEAS CORPUS.
Health care malpractice claims.
See MALPRACTICE.
Injunctions.
See INJUNCTIONS.

STIPULATIONS.
Appeals.
Expedited appeals.
Extension for filing statement of the case,
Rule 8-207.
Automobile insurance fund.
Actions against uninsured motorists, Rule
15-803.
Commencement of action against fund, Rule
15-804.
Settlements by fund, Rule 15-805.
Depositions.
Stipulations regarding discovery procedure.
Circuit courts, Rule 2-401.
Discovery.
Stipulations regarding discovery procedure,
Rule 2-401.
Interrogatories.
Stipulations regarding discovery procedure.
Circuit courts, Rule 2-401.
Trial.
Voluntary dismissal.
Circuit courts, Rule 2-506.
District Court, Rule 3-506.

SUBPOENAS.
Attorneys at law.
Discipline and inactive status.
Inquiry panel.
Complaints and investigations, Rule
16-706.
Body attachment.
Circuit courts, Rule 2-510.
Criminal rules, Rule 4-266.
Definitions, Rule 1-202.
District Court, Rule 3-510.
Circuit court civil rules, Rule 2-510.
Clerks.
Trial or hearing.
Preparation by clerk.
Criminal rules, Rule 4-265.
Court proceedings.
Objection to subpoena.
Circuit courts, Rule 2-510.
Criminal rules.
Evidence.
Tangible evidence before trial in circuit
court, Rule 4-264.
Generally, Rule 4-266.
Investigations, Rule 4-643.
Record of subpoena, Rule 4-644.
Trial or hearing, Rule 4-265.
Definitions, Rule 1-202.
Depositions.
Criminal rules, Rule 4-261.
Failure to subpoena witnesses.
Expenses for failure to pursue deposition.
Circuit courts, Rule 2-434.
Objections to subpoena for deposition.
Circuit courts, Rule 2-510.
District Court, Rule 3-510.

SUBPOENAS —Cont'd
Discovery.
Perpetuation of evidence.
Before action instituted.
Circuit courts, Rule 2-404.
District Court civil rules, Rule 3-510.
Evidence.
Exclusion of evidence for improper use of
subpoenas.
Circuit court, Rule 2-510.
District Court, Rule 3-510.
Perpetuation of evidence.
Before action instituted.
Circuit courts, Rule 2-404.
Subpoena for tangible evidence before trial
in circuit courts, Rule 4-264.
Executors and administrators.
Settlement of decedents' estates, Rule
6-161.
Forms.
Circuit courts, Rule 2-510.
Criminal rules, Rule 4-266.
District Court, Rule 3-510.
Hearings.
Preparation by clerk.
Criminal rules, Rule 4-265.
Preparation by parties.
Criminal rules, Rule 4-265.
Hospitals.
Records.
Circuit courts, Rule 2-510.
District Court, Rule 3-510.
Investigations.
Enforcement.
Criminal rules, Rule 4-643.
Grand jury.
Criminal rules, Rule 4-643.
Judicial disabilities and sanctionable
conduct.
Further investigation, Rule 16-806.
Preliminary investigation, Rule 16-805.
Record and file.
Criminal rules, Rule 4-644.
Issuance.
Circuit courts, Rule 2-510.
District Court, Rule 3-510.
**Judicial disabilities and sanctionable
conduct.**
Further investigation, Rule 16-806.
Preliminary, Rule 16-805.
Juvenile causes.
Duties of clerk, Rule 11-104.
Request for witness subpoena, Form
904-R/WS.
Witness subpoena.
Forms, Form 904-WS.
Objections to subpoena.
Court proceedings.
Circuit courts, Rule 2-510.
District Court, Rule 3-510.
Depositions.
Circuit courts, Rule 2-510.
District Court, Rule 3-510.

TRIAL —Cont'd
Examiners.
Circuit courts, Rule 2-542.
Exhibits.
Circuit courts, Rule 2-516.
District Court, Rule 3-516.
Formal exceptions unnecessary.
Circuit courts, Rule 2-517.
Criminal rules, Rule 4-323.
District Court, Rule 3-517.
Forms.
Subpoenas.
Circuit courts, Rule 2-510.
In banc review.
Circuit courts, Rule 2-551.
Criminal rules, Rule 4-352.
Initial procedures.
District Court.
Criminal rules, Rule 4-301.
Insanity.
Defense of not criminally responsible by
reason of insanity.
Bifurcation of trial, Rule 4-314.
Joinder.
Circuit courts, Rule 2-311.
Defendants.
Criminal rules, Rule 4-253.
District Court, Rule 3-311.
Offenses.
Criminal rules, Rule 4-253.
Prejudicial joinder.
Criminal rules, Rule 4-253.
Judges.
Decision of judge.
District Court, Rule 3-522.
Disability of judge.
Circuit courts, Rule 2-536.
Criminal rules, Rule 4-361.
District Court, Rule 3-536.
Disqualification of judge.
All judges disqualified.
Removal of trial.
Circuit courts, Rule 2-505.
District Court, Rule 3-505.
Further reassignment by another party.
District Court, Rule 3-505.
Motion and affidavit.
District Court, Rule 3-505.
Request for recusal.
District Court, Rule 3-505.
Judgments.
Acquittal.
Motion for judgment of acquittal, Rule
4-324.
Consolidation of trial.
Circuit courts, Rule 2-503.
Default.
Notice of judgment.
District Court, Rule 3-509.
Motion for judgment.
District Court, Rule 3-519.
Motion to alter or amend.
Circuit courts, Rule 2-534.
District Court, Rule 3-534.

TRIAL —Cont'd
Judgments —Cont'd
Revisory power of court.
Circuit courts, Rule 2-535.
District Court, Rule 3-535.
Jurisdiction.
Dismissal for lack of jurisdiction.
Circuit courts, Rule 2-507.
District Court, Rule 3-507.
Jury.
See JURY.
Masters.
Circuit courts, Rule 2-541.
Mechanics' liens, Rule 12-304.
Motion for judgment.
Denial.
Effect.
District Court, Rule 3-519.
Disposition.
District Court, Rule 3-519.
Generally.
District Court, Rule 3-519.
Motions.
Acquittal.
Motion for judgment of acquittal, Rule
4-324.
Disqualification of judge.
Circuit courts, Rule 2-505.
District Court, Rule 3-505.
Judgments.
Altering or amending judgments.
Court decisions, Rule 2-534.
District Court, Rule 3-519.
Mandatory motions in circuit courts.
Joint or separate trial of defendants or
offenses.
Criminal rules, Rule 4-252.
Motion for judgment.
District Court, Rule 3-519.
New trial.
General provisions.
See NEW TRIAL.
Notice.
Default.
Judgment.
District Court, Rule 3-509.
Dismissal.
Lack of jurisdiction or prosecution.
Circuit courts, Rule 2-507.
District Court, Rule 3-507.
Voluntary dismissal.
Circuit courts, Rule 2-506.
District Court, Rule 3-506.
Objections.
Evidence.
Continuing objections to evidence.
Circuit courts, Rule 2-517.
District Court, Rule 3-517.
Method of making.
Circuit courts, Rule 2-517.
District Court, Rule 3-517.
Formal exceptions unnecessary.
Circuit courts, Rule 2-517.
Criminal rules, Rule 4-323.

TRIAL —Cont'd
Objections —Cont'd
Formal exceptions unnecessary —Cont'd
District Court, Rule 3-517.
Method of making.
Circuit courts, Rule 2-517.
Criminal rules, Rule 4-323.
District Court, Rule 3-517.
Orders.
Objections to other rulings or orders.
Circuit courts, Rule 2-517.
Criminal rules, Rule 4-323.
District Court, Rule 3-517.
Pretrial conference.
Pretrial order, Rules 2-504, 2-504.2.
District Court, Rule 3-504.
Production of evidence.
When court may require.
Circuit courts, Rule 2-514.
District Court, Rule 3-514.
Removal of trial.
Order by court to which removed, Rule 2-505.
Striking order of removal.
Circuit courts, Rule 2-505.
Scheduling conferences.
Circuit courts, Rule 2-504.1.
Scheduling orders.
Circuit courts, Rule 2-504.
Voluntary dismissal.
Circuit courts, Rule 2-506.
District Court, Rule 3-506.
Prejudice.
Removal.
Grounds.
Circuit courts, Rule 2-505.
Pretrial conference.
Generally.
Circuit courts, Rules 2-504, 2-504.2.
District Court, Rule 3-504.
Matters to be considered, Rules 2-504, 2-504.2.
District Court, Rule 3-504.
Order.
Pretrial order.
Circuit courts, Rules 2-504, 2-504.2.
District Court, Rule 3-504.
Scheduling conference. Rule 2-504.1.
Pretrial release.
Criminal cases, Rule 4-216.
Privileges.
Continuances.
Legislative privileges.
Circuit courts, Rule 2-508.
District Court, Rule 3-508.
Prosecution.
Dismissal for lack of prosecution or jurisdiction.
Circuit courts, Rule 2-507.
District Court, Rule 3-507.
Recusal of judge.
District Court, Rule 3-505.

TRIAL —Cont'd
Rulings of court.
Objections.
Circuit courts, Rule 2-517.
District Court, Rule 3-517.
Scheduling conference, Rule 2-504.1.
Scheduling conferences.
Circuit courts, Rule 2-504.1.
Scheduling orders.
Circuit courts, Rule 2-504.
Separate trials.
Circuit courts, Rule 2-503.
District Court, Rule 3-503.
Separation of questions for decision by court.
Circuit courts, Rule 2-502.
Small claim actions.
Conduct of trial.
District Court, Rule 3-701.
Date and time.
District Court, Rule 3-701.
Stipulations.
Voluntary dismissal.
Circuit courts, Rule 2-506.
District Court, Rule 3-506.
Subpoenas.
Attachment.
Circuit courts, Rule 2-510.
District Court, Rule 3-510.
Depositions.
Objection to subpoena for deposition.
Circuit courts, Rule 2-510.
District Court, Rule 3-510.
Form.
Circuit courts, Rule 2-510.
District Court, Rule 3-510.
Hospital records.
Circuit courts, Rule 2-510.
District Court, Rule 3-510.
Issuance.
Circuit courts, Rule 2-510.
District Court, Rule 3-510.
Objection to subpoena for court proceedings.
Circuit courts, Rule 2-510.
District Court, Rule 3-510.
Preparation by clerk.
Criminal rules, Rule 4-265.
Preparation by parties.
Criminal rules, Rule 4-265.
Service.
Circuit courts, Rule 2-510.
District Court, Rule 3-510.
Use.
Circuit courts, Rule 2-510.
District Court, Rule 3-510.
Summary judgment.
Motion for summary judgment.
Circuit courts, Rule 2-501.
Third parties.
Voluntary dismissal.
Circuit courts, Rule 2-506.
District Court, Rule 3-506.

TRIAL —Cont'd
Time.
District Court, Rule 3-102.
Transmittal of record.
Removal of trial.
Circuit courts, Rule 2-505.
Verdicts.
Consolidation of trial.
Circuit courts, Rule 2-503.
Court verdicts.
Criminal rules, Rule 4-328.
Jury trial.
See VERDICT.
View by jury.
Attendance at view.
Circuit courts, Rule 2-515.
Other actions.
Circuit courts, Rule 2-515.
Voluntary dismissal.
Circuit courts, Rule 2-506.
District Court, Rule 3-506.
Witnesses.
Continuances.
Absent witnesses.
Circuit courts, Rule 2-508.
District Court, Rule 3-508.

TRUSTS AND TRUSTEES.
Assignees or trustees for creditors, Rules 13-101 to 13-703.
See RECEIVERS.
Attorneys at law.
Trust accounts, Rules 16-601 to 16-612.
See ATTORNEYS AT LAW.
Credit.
Receivers and assignees or trustees for creditors, Rules 13-101 to 13-703.
See RECEIVERS.
Fiduciaries generally.
See FIDUCIARIES.
Ground rent.
Accounting, Rule 12-501.
Conveyances.
Appointment of trustee, Rule 12-501.
Judicial sales.
Appointment by court, Rule 14-302.
Bond, surety, Rule 14-303.
Parties.
Real party in interest.
Circuit courts, Rule 2-201.
Receivers and assignees or trustees for creditors, Rules 13-101 to 13-703.
See RECEIVERS.

U

UNINCORPORATED ASSOCIATIONS.
Service of process.
Persons to be served.
Circuit courts, Rule 2-124.

UNINSURED MOTORISTS.
Automobile insurance fund.
See AUTOMOBILE INSURANCE FUND.

UNITED STATES.
Intervention.
Permissive intervention.
District Court, Rule 3-214.
Service of process.
Persons to be served.
Circuit courts, Rule 2-124.
District Court, Rule 3-124.

UNITED STATES COURTS.
Appeals.
Certification of questions of law from federal courts, Rule 8-305.

V

VENUE.
Actions.
Improper venue.
Transfer of action.
Circuit courts, Rule 2-327.
Automobile insurance fund.
Actions against fund, Rule 15-804.
Burial grounds.
Sale for other use, Rule 14-401.
Change of name, Rule 15-901.
Construction and interpretation.
Rules not to affect, Rule 1-201.
Detinue, Rule 12-602.
Divorce, Rule 9-201.
Eminent domain, Rule 12-202.
Executors and administrators.
Settlement of decedent's estate.
Probate.
Administrative or judicial probate, Rule 6-111.
Rules of construction, Rule 6-104.
Expungement of records.
Applications.
No charges filed, Rule 4-503.
Petitions.
Charges filed, Rule 4-504.
Fiduciaries.
Absent or unknown persons, Rule 10-601.
Foreclosures.
Commencement of actions, Rule 14-203.
Ground rent, Rule 12-501.
Guardian and ward.
Petition for appointment of guardian, Rule 10-201.
Standby guardians, Rules 10-402, 10-403.
Petition for appointment of guardian for property, Rule 10-301.
Petition to resign or appoint substitute or successor guardian, Rule 10-207.
Termination of guardianship, Rule 10-209.
Mechanics' liens, Rule 12-302.
Motions.
Preliminary motions.
Mandatory motions.
Circuit courts, Rule 2-322.

682

VENUE —Cont'd
Pleadings.
Improper venue.
Dismissal or transfer of action.
District Court, Rule 3-326.
Post conviction procedures, Rule 4-401.
Transfer of action.
Circuit courts, Rule 2-327.

VERDICT.
Court verdicts.
Criminal rules, Rule 4-328.
Criminal rules.
Court verdict, Rule 4-328.
Defined, Rule 4-102.
Jury trial, Rule 4-327.
Definitions, Rule 4-102.
Detinue, Rule 12-602.
District Court, Rule 12-602.
Directed verdicts.
Motions for judgment.
Circuit courts, Rule 2-519.
Eminent domain, Rule 12-208.
Judges.
Disability of judge.
After verdict or acceptance of plea.
Criminal rules, Rule 4-361.
Judgment notwithstanding the verdict.
See JUDGMENT NOTWITHSTANDING
THE VERDICT.
Jury trial.
Advisory verdicts disallowed.
Circuit courts, Rule 2-511.
Generally.
Circuit courts, Rule 2-522.
Poll of jury.
Criminal rules, Rule 4-327.
Return.
Criminal rules, Rule 4-327.
Sealed verdict.
Criminal rules, Rule 4-327.
Special verdict.
Circuit courts, Rule 2-522.
Two or more counts.
Criminal rules, Rule 4-327.
Two or more defendants, Rule 4-327.
New trial.
Motion for new trial.
Within ten days of verdict.
Criminal rules, Rule 4-331.
Pleas.
Guilty verdict.
Pleas to other offenses before sentencing,
Rule 4-244.
Replevin, Rule 12-601.
Returns.
Jury trial.
Criminal rules, Rule 4-327.
Special verdict.
Circuit courts, Rule 2-522.
Trial.
Consolidation of trial.
Circuit courts, Rule 2-503.

VERDICT —Cont'd
Trial —Cont'd
Court verdicts.
Criminal rules, Rule 4-328.
VETERANS.
Guardianship of person.
Beneficiary of United States Department of
Veterans Affairs.
Certificates in lieu of physicians'
certificates, Rule 10-202.
No hearing, objection not made, Rule
10-205.

VICTIMS.
Assault.
Spousal privilege.
Record of assertion, Rule 4-632.
Character of victim.
Admissibility to prove conduct, Rule 5-404.
Restitution by parents, Rule 4-342.
Sexual offense cases.
Rape shield, Rule 5-412.

VIDEOTAPE.
Depositions.
Expert witnesses.
Use of depositions.
Circuit courts, Rule 2-419.
Generally.
Circuit courts, Rule 2-416.
Notice.
Circuit courts, Rule 2-412.

VIDEOTAPE RECORDING.
Administration of courts.
Circuit court proceedings, Rule 16-405.
Appeals.
Record on appeal, Rule 8-415.
Circuit court proceedings, Rule 16-405.
Access to videotape recordings, Rule 16-406.

VIEW BY JURY.
Circuit courts, Rule 2-515.

VIEWS.
Eminent domain.
Board of property review, Rule 12-213.

VISITATION.
Educational seminars, Rule 9-204.1.
Family division and support services,
Rule 16-204.
**Mediation of child custody and visitation
disputes,** Rule 9-205.

VITAL STATISTICS.
Hearsay exceptions, Rule 5-803.

VOICE IDENTIFICATION, Rule 5-901.

VOLUNTARY DISMISSAL.
Circuit courts, Rule 2-506.
District Court, Rule 3-506.

W

WAIVER.
Attorneys at law.
Criminal rules, Rule 4-215.

INDEX

WAIVER —Cont'd
Executors and administrators.
Opening estates.
Personal representative.
Bond of personal representative, Rule 6-312.
Settlement of decedents' estates.
Waiver of notice.
Generally, Rule 6-126.
Expungement of records.
General waiver and release, Title 4, Form 4-503.2.
Disposition of expunged records, Rule 4-512.
Fees.
Filing.
Prepayment of filing fees, Rule 1-325.
Filing.
Fees.
Prepayment of filing fees, Rule 1-325.
Forms.
Executors and administrators.
Settlement of decedents' estates.
Waiver of notice, Rule 6-126.
Jurisdiction.
Juvenile courts.
Procedure upon waiver, Rule 4-222.
Jury trial.
Circuit courts, Rule 2-325.
Criminal rules, Rule 4-246.
Demand for jury trial.
Circuit courts, Rule 2-325.
Criminal rules, Rule 4-301.
District Court, Rule 3-325.
District Court, Rule 3-325.
Juvenile causes.
Emergency detention or shelter care.
Continued detention or shelter care, Rule 11-112.
Jurisdiction, Rule 11-113.
Order for waiver of jurisdiction.
Forms, Form 913-O/W.
Petition for waiver of juvenile jurisdiction.
Forms, Form 913-P/W.
Pretrial release hearing, Rule 4-222.
Probable cause determination, Rule 4-222.
Review by court, Rule 4-222.
Waiver petition.
Defined, Rule 11-101.
Motions.
Certain defenses not waived.
Circuit courts, Rule 2-324.
Pleadings.
Certain defenses not waived.
Circuit courts, Rule 2-324.
Demand for jury trial.
District Court, Rule 3-325.
Preliminary hearings.
District Court, Rule 4-221.
Presence of defendants, Rule 4-231.

WARRANTS.
Criminal rules.
Defined, Rule 4-102.
Execution.
Defendant not in custody, Rule 4-212.
Issuance, Rule 4-212.
Circuit courts, Rule 4-212.
District Court, Rule 4-212.
Procedure when defendant in custody.
Other offenses, Rule 4-212.
Search warrants, Rule 4-601.
Service.
Return of service, Rule 4-212.
Definitions, Rule 4-102.
Ejectment.
Warrant of resurvey, Rule 12-101.
Execution, Rule 1-361.
Inspection by public of files and records pertaining to, Rule 4-212.
Public inspection of files and records, Rule 4-212.
Searches and seizures, Rule 4-601.

WILLS.
Decedents' estates.
Settlement of decedents' estate.
Filing a will, Rule 6-151.
Proof of execution of will.
Form, Rule 6-152.
Forms.
Decedents' estates.
Settlement of decedents' estate.
Proof of execution of will, Rule 6-152.
Settlement of decedents' estate.
Proof of execution of will, Rule 6-152.
Petition for probate.
Form, Rule 6-122.
Registers of wills.
Decedents' estates.
Settlement of decedents' estate.
Filing a will, Rule 6-151.

WITNESSES.
Actions.
Convenience of parties and witnesses.
Transfer of action.
Circuit courts, Rule 2-327.
Affirmation, Rule 5-603.
Attorneys at law.
Discipline and inactive status.
Inquiry panel.
Complaints and investigations, Rule 16-706.
Rules of professional conduct.
Lawyers as witnesses, Prof. Cond. R. 3.7.
Auditors.
Hearings.
Circuit courts, Rule 2-543.
Authentication.
Subscribing witness, Rule 5-903.
Bias.
Impeachment, Rule 5-616.
Body attachment of material witness.
Application for continued detention.
Content, Rule 4-267.

684

MARYLAND DISTRICT RULES

Rescinded or transferred.

Editor's note. — The Court of Appeals, by Order dated April 6, 1984, rescinded Chapters 1 through 700 and Subtitles F, G, H, BT, and EX of Chapter 1100 of the Maryland Rules of Procedure and the Maryland District Rules, Rules U12 and U18, Subtitles BF and BK, Rule BQ50, and Subtitle BU of Chapter 1100 of the Maryland Rules of Procedure, and Forms 1 through 21, 611, the Bail Bond Forms, and the Forms for Expungement of Records in the Appendix of Forms, and substituted for the rescinded rules and forms Titles 1 through 4 of the Maryland Rules and related forms, effective July 1, 1984. The Order also approved and adopted, effective July 1, 1984, amendments to certain rules in Chapters 800 through 1300 of the Maryland Rules of Procedure and the Appendix of Forms and in Chapters 1100 and 1200 of the Maryland District Rules, submitted by the Court's Standing Committee on Rules of Practice and Procedure in its Eighty-second, Eighty-seventh and Eighty-eighth Reports and the Supplement to the Eighty-second Report, together with amendments made thereto by the Court. The Order provides that the new rules and forms shall "apply to all actions commenced on and after July 1, 1984, and insofar as practicable, to all actions then pending."

A table of comparable rules, relating those rules rescinded effective July 1, 1984, to the revised rules in Title 1 through Title 4, may be found in this volume as an appendix following the Maryland Rules.

The Court of Appeals, by Order dated June 5, 1996, effective January 1, 1997, rescinded Subtitles A, D, E, J, P, Q, R, T, U, V, W, Y, Z, BB, BD, BE, BG, BH, BJ, BL, BP, BQ, BR, BS, BW, and BY of Chapter 1100 of the Maryland Rules of Procedure, rescinded Subtitles P, BB, BQ, and BW of the Maryland District Rules, and rescinded Forms 22a, 23, 24, 25, and 26. The Order substituted for certain of the rules and forms rescinded new Title 9, Chapter 100, Title 10, Title 12, Title 13, Title 14, and Title 15 of the Maryland Rules of Procedure. Furthermore, the Order transferred, without readoption, Chapter 900, Chapter 1200, and Subtitles S, BU, and BV of Chapter 1100 of the Maryland Rules of Procedure and Chapter 1200 of the Maryland District Rules to be Title 9, Chapter 200, Title 11, and Title 16 of the Maryland Rules of Procedure. The Order provides that the new rules shall "apply to all actions commenced on or after January 1, 1997, and insofar as practicable, to all actions then pending."

A table of comparable rules, relating those rules rescinded effective January 1, 1997, to the revised rules in Title 9 through Title 16 may be found in this volume as an appendix following the Maryland Rules.

RULES GOVERNING ADMISSION TO THE BAR OF MARYLAND

This Court's Standing Committee on Rules of Practice and Procedure having submitted its Ninety-ninth Report to the Court recommending rescission of the current Rules Governing Admission to the Bar of the Maryland Rules of Procedure, the adoption of certain Proposed Rules in substitution therefor, and the adoption of conforming amendments to Rules BV2 and 1228, all as set forth in that Report published in the *Maryland Register,* Vol. 15, Issue 6, Pages 722-734 (March 11, 1988); and

The Rules Committee having submitted a Supplement to the Ninety-ninth Report, recommending adoption of proposed new Bar Admission Rules 11, 17, and 22 and certain amendments to proposed revised Bar Admission Rule 13, Rule BV2, and Rule 1228, all as set forth in that Supplement published in the *Maryland Register,* Vol. 17, Issue 10, Pages 1210-1216 (May 18, 1990); and

This Court having considered at open meetings, notice of which was posted as prescribed by law, all those proposed rules changes, together with the comments received and certain further amendments subsequently submitted by the Rules Committee, and having on its own motion amended certain of the proposed rules, it is this 28th day of June, 1990

ORDERED, by the Court of Appeals of Maryland, that the Rules Governing Admission to the Bar of Maryland adopted March 30, 1970, and all subsequent amendments thereto be, and they are hereby, rescinded effective August 1, 1990; and it is further

ORDERED, that proposed new Bar Admission Rule 17, Legal Assistance by Law Graduates, as set forth in the Supplement to the Ninety-ninth Report, be, and it is hereby, rejected; and it is further

ORDERED, that in substitution for the rules hereby rescinded, the Maryland Rules annexed to this Order be, and they are hereby, adopted in the form annexed hereto; and it is further

ORDERED, that the Rules amendments hereby adopted by this Court shall take effect August 1, 1990, and it is further

ORDERED, that a copy of this Order be published in the next issue of the *Maryland Register.*

> ROBERT C. MURPHY
> JOHN C. ELDRIDGE
> HARRY A. COLE
> LAWRENCE F. RODOWSKY
> JOHN F. McAULIFFE
> WILLIAM H. ADKINS II
> HOWARD S. CHASANOW

This Court having considered a proposed amendment to Bar Admission Rule 11 (Required Course on Professionalism) of the Maryland Rules of Procedure at an open meeting, notice of which was posted as prescribed by law, and finding that an emergency does in fact exist with reference to the proposed rules change, it is this 18th day of August, 1994

689

ORDERED, by the Court of Appeals of Maryland, that Bar Admission Rule 11 (Required Course on Professionalism) be, and it is hereby, amended and adopted in the form attached hereto, and it is further

ORDERED, that the rules change hereby adopted by this Court shall govern all courts of this State and all parties and their attorneys in all actions and proceedings; and shall take effect and apply to all actions commenced on and after August 18, 1994 and insofar as practicable to all actions then pending; and it is further

ORDERED, that a copy of this Order be published in the next issue of the *Maryland Register*.

ROBERT C. MURPHY
JOHN C. ELDRIDGE
LAWRENCE F. RODOWSKY
*
ROBERT L. KARWACKI
ROBERT M. BELL
IRMA S. RAKER
*Judge Chasanow declined to sign the Order.

The Court, by a Rules Order dated July 14, 1995, having extended the operation of Rule 11 of the Rules Governing Admission to the Bar of Maryland until December 31, 1995 pending a decision by the Court to extend, make permanent or rescind Rule 11, and

The Professionalism Course Evaluation Committee having been appointed by the Court to study the Professionalism Course as mandated by Rule 11 and to make recommendations to the Court concerning the continuation of the requirements of Rule 11 and the Committee having filed its report recommending that the requirements of Rule 11 be extended for a period of five years with provision for an additional evaluation by the Court at the end of that time, and

This Court having considered, at an open meeting, notice of which was posted as prescribed by law, the report and recommendation of the Professionalism Course Evaluation Committee, it is this 21st day of November 1995

ORDERED, by the Court of Appeals of Maryland, that Rule 11 (Required Course on Professionalism) be, and it is hereby, amended and adopted in the form attached hereto and it is further

ORDERED, that the rule change hereby adopted by this Court shall govern all courts of this State and all parties and their attorneys in all actions and proceedings; and shall take effect and apply to all actions commenced on and after January 1, 1996 and insofar as practicable to all actions then pending; and it is further

ORDERED, that a copy of this Order be published in the next issue of the *Maryland Register*.

ROBERT C. MURPHY
*
LAWRENCE F. RODOWSKY
*
ROBERT L. KARWACKI
ROBERT M. BELL
IRMA S. RAKER
*For reasons set forth in the attached dissenting opinion Judge Eldridge and Judge Chasanow declined to approve the adoption of the amendment to Rule 11(c).

Chasanow, J., dissents:

Although I believe that the professionalism course is an excellent and meaningful program, I dissent from Rule 11 because I believe that the course should be mandatory for all members of the bar, rather than just new admittees. The course was instituted because there is a perceived lack of professionalism among some members of the bar. To correct the problem, the course should be given to all lawyers, including those who are responsible for this perceived problem. Moreover, new graduates fresh from their professional responsibility courses in law school probably have less need for a professionalism course than older attorneys, many of whom were not required to take an ethics course in law school. New graduates are also likely to have acquired some sensitivity to minority and gender concerns, which constitute a significant part of the course. Senior members of the bar who began practicing law in a different era may need more guidance in these areas. Any experienced trial judge knows that as a general rule the new, eager, young lawyers, in their first year of practice tend to be respectful, diligent and conscientious practitioners. It is at least a year or so before any potential lack of professionalism begins to emerge.

The course is mandated at a time when the new graduates may be less than receptive; it is taken during the hectic, numbing period following successful completion of the bar examination, but before admission to the bar. It might be more meaningful after the new admittees have had some exposure to the practice of law. The lack of professionalism among some lawyers that the course is designed to address most likely developed during the practice of law, rather than before admission to the bar. Requiring the course for new graduates creates a false sense of security if the Court assumes it has solved the problem of lack of professionalism.

When Rule 11 was first adopted, many people anticipated that the course requirement would eventually be expanded to include all members of the bar. To date, this has not occurred. A proposed amendment to make the course a requirement for all lawyers has been rejected by the Court of Appeals by a five-to-two vote. The professionalism course is an admirable undertaking by the Maryland State Bar Association, but it is expensive. Costs of the course, over and above the fees paid by attendees, continue to grow every year and are currently in excess of thirty-thousand dollars per year. If the course were mandatory for all lawyers, these excess costs might be reduced since senior attorneys could afford to pay a higher fee. Further, any expenditures by the Bar Association would have a far greater impact on the profession. We senior members of the bar ought not impose a requirement on new admittees that we are unwilling to impose on ourselves. I respectfully dissent from the adoption of Rule 11, although the professionalism course is an excellent idea, it targets the least needy audience.

Judge Eldridge authorizes me to state that he joins in the views expressed in this dissenting opinion.

FOR FURTHER INFORMATION ADDRESS

Bedford T. Bentley, Jr., Secretary

State Board of Law Examiners

People's Resource Center

Room 1210

100 Community Place

Crownsville, Maryland 21032-2026

Telephone: (410) 514-7044

ADOPTED BY
THE COURT OF APPEALS
OF
MARYLAND

June 28, 1990, effective August 1, 1990, with amendments through November 15, 1997

State Board of Law Examiners

State of Maryland

Jonathan A. Azrael

Chairman

John F. Mudd
Robert H. Reinhart
Christopher B. Kehoe
Robert L. Bloom
Maurene Epps Webb
Katherine D. Savage

Forms for admission to the Bar are supplied by the State Board of Law Examiners, upon request.

Rule 1. Definitions.

In these Rules, the following definitions apply, except as expressly otherwise provided or as necessary implication requires:

(a) *Board*. "Board" means the Board of Law Examiners of the State of Maryland.

(b) *Court.* "Court" means the Court of Appeals of Maryland.

(c) *Code, Reference to.* Reference to an article and section of the Code means the article and section of the Annotated Code of Public General Laws of Maryland as from time to time amended.

(d) *Filed.* "Filed" means received in the office of the Secretary of the Board during normal business hours.

(e) *MBE.* "MBE" means the Multi-state Bar Examination published by the National Conference of Bar Examiners.

(f) *Oath.* "Oath" means a declaration or affirmation made under the penalties of perjury that a certain statement or fact is true.

(g) *State.* "State" means (1) a state, possession, territory, or commonwealth of the United States or (2) the District of Columbia.

Source. — This Rule is derived from former Rule 1.

Rule 2. Application for admission and preliminary determination of eligibility.

(a) *By application.* A person who meets the requirements of Rules 3 and 4 may apply for admission to the Bar of this State by filing an application for admission, accompanied by the prescribed fee, with the Board.

Committee note. — The application is the first step in the admission process. These steps include application for admission, proof of character, proof of graduation from an approved law school, application to take a particular bar examination, and passing of that examination.

(b) *Form of application.* The application shall be on a form prescribed by the Board and shall be under oath. The form shall elicit the information the Board considers appropriate concerning the applicant's character, education, and eligibility to become a candidate for admission. The application shall include an authorization for release of confidential information pertaining to character and fitness for the practice of law to a Character Committee, the Board, and the Court.

(c) *Time for filing.* (1) Without intent to take particular examination. At any time after the completion of pre-legal studies, a person may file an application for the purpose of determining whether there are any existing impediments to the applicant's qualifications for admission.

Committee note. — Subsection (c)(1) of this Rule is particularly intended to encourage persons whose eligibility may be in question for reasons pertaining to character and sufficiency of pre-legal education to seek early review by the Character Committee and Board.

(2) With intent to take particular examination. An applicant who intends to take the examination in July shall file the application no later than the preceding January 16 or, upon payment of the required late fee, no later than the preceding May 20. An applicant who intends to take the examination in February shall file the application no later than the preceding September 15

or, upon payment of the required late fee, no later than the preceding December 20.

(3) *Acceptance of late application.* Upon written request of the applicant and for good cause shown, the Board may accept an application filed after the applicable deadline for a late filing prescribed in subsection (c)(2) of this Rule. If the Board rejects the application, the applicant may file an exception with the Court within five days after notice of the rejection.

(d) *Preliminary determination of eligibility.* On receipt of an application, the Board shall determine whether the applicant has met the pre-legal education requirements set forth in Rule 3 and in Code, Business Occupations and Professions Article, § 10-207. If the Board concludes that the requirements have been met, it shall forward the character questionnaire portion of the application to a Character Commitee. If the Board concludes that the requirements have not been met, it shall promptly notify the applicant in writing.

(e) *Withdrawal of application.* At any time, an applicant may withdraw as a candidate for admission by filing written notice of withdrawal with the Board. No fees will be refunded.

(f) *Subsequent application.* A person who reapplies for admission after an earlier application has been withdrawn or rejected pursuant to Rule 5 must retake and pass the bar examination even if the person passed the examination when the earlier application was pending. If the person failed the examination when the earlier application was pending, the failure will be counted under Rule 9.

Source. — This Rule is derived as follows: Section *(a)* is in part derived from the first sentence of former Rule 2 b and in part new. Section *(b)* is new. Section *(c)* is derived from former Rule 2 a, 2 b, and f.

Section *(d)* is in part derived from former Rule 2 g and in part new. Section *(e)* is derived from former Rule 2 h. Section *(f)* is new.

Application for admission denied. In re Charles M., 313 Md. 168, 545 A.2d 7 (1988).

Stated in In re Hyland, 339 Md. 521, 663 A.2d 1309 (1995).

Rule 3. Pre-legal education.

An applicant for admission must have completed the pre-legal education necessary to meet the minimum requirements for admission to an American Bar Association approved law school.

Source. — This Rule is new.

Rule 4. Eligibility to take bar examination.

(a) *Legal education.* (1) In order to take the bar examination of this State a person either shall have graduated or shall be unqualifiedly eligible for graduation from a law school.

(2) The law school shall be located in a state and shall be approved by the American Bar Association.

(b) *Waiver.* The Board shall have discretion to waive the requirements of subsection (a)(2) of this Rule and of Rule 3 for any person who (1) has passed the bar examination of another state and is a member in good standing of the Bar of that state and (2) in the Board's opinion is qualified by reason of education, experience, or both to take the bar examination.

(c) *Minors.* If otherwise qualified a person who is under 18 years of age is eligible to take the bar examination but shall not be admitted to the Bar until 18 years of age.

Source. — This Rule is derived as follows: *Section (b)* is derived from former Rule 5 c.
Section (a) is derived from former Rule 5 b.   *Section (c)* is derived from former Rule 5 d.

Rule 5. Character review.

(a) *Burden of proof.* The applicant bears the burden of proving to the Character Committee, the Board, and the Court the applicant's good moral character and fitness for the practice of law. Failure or refusal to answer fully and candidly any question set forth in the application or any relevant question asked by a member of the Character Commitee, the Board, or the Court is sufficient cause for a finding that the applicant has not met this burden.

(b) *Investigation and report of character committee.* (1) On receipt of a character questionnaire forwarded by the Board pursuant to Rule 2 (d), the Character Committee shall (A) through one of its members, personally interview the applicant, (B) verify the facts stated in the questionnaire, contact the applicant's references, and make any further investigation it finds necessary or desirable, (C) evaluate the applicant's character and fitness for the practice of law, and (D) transmit to the Board a report of its investigation and a recommendation as to the approval or denial of the application for admission.

(2) If the Committee concludes that there may be grounds for recommending denial of the application, it shall notify the applicant and schedule a hearing. The hearing shall be conducted on the record and the applicant shall have the right to testify, to present witnesses, and to be represented by counsel. A transcript of the hearing shall be transmitted by the Committee to the Board along with the Committee's report. The Committee's report shall set forth findings of fact on which the recommendation is based and a statement supporting the conclusion. The Committee shall mail a copy of its report to the applicant, and a copy of the hearing transcript shall be furnished to the applicant upon payment of reasonable charges.

(c) *Hearing by board.* If the Board concludes after review of the Committee's report and the transcript that there may be grounds for recommending denial of the application, it shall promptly afford the applicant the opportunity for a hearing on the record made before the Committee. The Board shall mail a copy of its report and recommendation to the applicant and the Committee. If the Board decides to recommend denial of the application in its report to the Court, the Board shall first give the applicant an opportunity to withdraw the application. If the applicant withdraws the application, the Board shall retain the records. Otherwise, it shall transmit to the Court a report of its proceedings and a recommendation as to the approval or denial of the application together with all papers relating to the matter.

(d) *Review by court.* (1) If the applicant elects not to withdraw the application, after the Board submits its report and adverse recommendation the Court shall require the applicant to show cause why the application should not be denied.

(2) If the Board recommends approval of the application contrary to an adverse recommendation by the Committee, within 30 days after the filing of the Board's report the Committee may file with the Court exceptions to the Board's recommendation. The Committee shall mail copies of its exceptions to the applicant and the Board.

(3) Proceedings in the Court under this section shall be on the records made before the Character Committee and the Board. If the Court denies the application, the Board shall retain the records.

(e) *Continuing review.* All applicants remain subject to further Committee review and report until admitted to the Bar.

Source. — This Rule is derived as follows:
Section (a) is in part derived from the first sentence of former Rule 2 d and in part new.
Section (b) is in part derived from former Rule 4 b and in part new.
Section (c) is in part derived from former Rule 4 c and in part new.
Section (d) is in part derived from former Rule 4 c and in part new.
Section (e) is in part derived from former Rule 4 d.

Role of Court of Appeals. — The conclusion of the State Board of Law Examiners that an applicant does not possess the requisite moral character is entitled to great weight; to properly exercise its responsibility in regulating the conduct of attorneys, however, the Court of Appeals must independently evaluate the applicant's present moral character based upon the records made by the Character Committee and the Board. In re Hyland, 339 Md. 521, 663 A.2d 1309 (1995).

Evidence sufficient to find applicant failed to satisfy requirements. — Applicant was deemed to have failed to satisfy his burden that he possessed those qualities that comprise good moral character necessary for the practice of law where the applicant did not appreciate the fiduciary responsibility incumbent upon an attorney when entrusted with the monies of another person, where he did not appreciate the analogy between tax obligations and client trust account responsibilities, and where, in addition to his lack of candor and contradictory testimony on critical issues, the applicant displayed an inability to recognize his dereliction of a moral duty inherent in his past behaviors. In re Hyland, 339 Md. 521, 663 A.2d 1309 (1995).

Cited in In re Worthington, 336 Md. 555, 649 A.2d 599 (1994).

Rule 6. Petition to take a scheduled examination.

(a) *Filing.* An applicant may file a petition to take a scheduled bar examination if the applicant (1) is eligible under Rule 4 to take the bar examination and (2) has applied for admission pursuant to Rule 2 and the application has not been withdrawn or rejected pursuant to Rule 5. The petition shall be under oath and shall be filed on the form prescribed by the Board.

(b) *Certification by law school.* The petition shall include a certification, on a form prescribed by the Board, signed by the dean or other authorized official of the law school attended by the petitioner, showing (1) that the law school meets the requirements of Rule 4 (a) unless the requirements have been waived by the Board pursuant to Rule 4 (b); (2) that the petitioner either graduated on a stated date or is unqualifiedly eligible for graduation at the next commencement exercise, naming the date; and (3) that the petitioner, so far as is known to that official, has not been guilty of any criminal or dishonest conduct other than minor traffic offenses, except as noted on the certification, and is of good moral character.

(c) *Time for filing.* The petition shall be filed at least 20 days before the scheduled examination. Upon written request of a petitioner and for good cause shown, the Board may accept a petition filed after that deadline. If the Board rejects the petition, the petitioner may file an exception with the Court within five days after notice of the rejection.

(d) *Refunds.* If a petitioner withdraws the petition or fails to attend and take the examination, the examination fee will not be refunded except for good cause shown. The examination fee may not be applied to a subsequent examination unless the petitioner is permitted by the Board to defer taking the examination.

Source. — This Rule is derived from former Rule 5 a with the exception of section (d), which is new.

Rule 7. Bar examination.

(a) *Scheduling.* The Board shall administer a written examination twice annually, once in February and once in July. The examination shall be held on two successive days. The total duration of the examination shall be not more than 12 hours nor less than nine hours. The Board shall publish at least 30 days before an examination notice of the dates, times, and place or places of the examination.

(b) *Purpose of examination.* It is the policy of the Court that no quota of successful examiners be set, but that each examinee be judged for fitness to be a member of the Bar as demonstrated by the examination answers. To this end, the examination shall be designed to test the examinee's knowledge of legal principles in the subjects on which examined and the examinee's ability to recognize, analyze, and intelligibly discuss legal problems and to apply that knowledge in reasoning their solution. The examination will not be designed primarily to test information, memory, or experience.

(c) *Format and scope of examination.* The Board shall prepare and grade the examination. The Board may adopt the MBE as part of its examination. Essay answers shall be required on all parts of the examination except the MBE part. The Board shall define by rule the subject matter of the essay examination. An examination shall include at least one question dealing in whole or in part with professional conduct.

(d) *Grading.* (1) The Board shall grade the examination and shall by rule establish passing grades for the examination. If the examination includes the MBE, the Board may provide by rule that an examinee who fails one part (the MBE or the essay test) but passes the other may carry over the passing score to the next examination only. The Board may also provide by rule that an examinee may satisfy the MBE part of the Maryland examination requirement by applying a grade on an MBE taken in another jurisdiction at the same or the immediately preceding examination.

(2) At any time before it notifies examinees of the results, the Board, in its discretion and in the interest of fairness, may lower, but not raise, the passing grades it has established for any particular examination.

Source. — This Rule is derived as follows: *Section (a)* is derived from former Rule 7 a, and b. *Section (b)* is derived from former Rule 7 c. *Section (c)* is derived from former Rule 7 d and e. *Section (d)* is derived from former Rule 7 e.

Rule 8. Notice of grades and review procedure.

(a) *Notice of grades; alteration.* Notice of examination results shall be sent to each examinee by regular mail, postage prepaid. Successful examinees shall be notified only that they have passed. Unsuccessful examinees shall be given their grades in the detail the Board considers appropriate. Thereafter, the Board may not alter any examinee's grades except when necessary to correct a clerical error.

(b) *Review procedure.* On written request filed with the Board within 60 days after the mailing date of examination results, unsuccessful examinees may (1) in accordance with the procedures prescribed by the Board, review their examination books and the Board's analysis for the essay test and (2) upon payment of the required costs, obtain confirmation of their MBE scores. No further review of the MBE will be permitted.

Source. — This Rule is derived as follows: *Section (a)* is derived in part from former Rule 7 f and in part new. *Section (b)* is derived from former Rule 8 b.

Rule 9. Re-examination after failure.

(a) *Petition for re-examination.* An unsuccessful examinee may file a petition to take another scheduled examination. The petition shall be on the form prescribed by the Board and shall be accompanied by the required examination fee.

(b) *Time for filing.* The petition shall be filed at least 20 days before the scheduled examination. Upon written request of a petitioner and for good cause shown, the Board may accept a petition filed after that deadline. If the Board rejects the petition, the petitioner may file an exception with the Court within five days after notice of the rejection.

(c) *Deferment of re-examination.* To meet scheduling needs at either the July or the February examination, the Board may require a petitioner to defer re-examination for one setting.

(d) *Three or more failures — Re-examination conditional.* If a person fails three or more examinations, the Board may condition retaking of the examination on the successful completion of specified additional study.

(e) *No refunds.* If a petitioner withdraws the petition or fails to attend and take the examination, the examination fee will not be refunded and may not be applied to a subsequent examination unless the petitioner is required by the Board to defer retaking the examination or establishes good cause for the withdrawal or failure to attend.

697

Source. — This Rule is derived as follows: *Sections (a) and (b)* are derived from former Rule 8 a.

Sections (c) and (d) are derived from former Rule 8 c.

Rule 10. Report to court — Order.

(a) *Report and recommendations as to candidates.* As soon as practicable after each examination, the Board shall file with the Court a report of the names of the successful candidates and the Board's recommendation for admission. If proceedings as to the character of a candidate are pending, the Board's recommendation of that candidate shall be conditioned on the outcome of the proceedings.

(b) *Order of ratification.* On receipt of the Board's report, the Court shall enter an order fixing a date at least 30 days after the filing of the report for ratification of the Board's recommendations. The order shall include the names and addresses of all persons who are recommended for admission, including those who are conditionally recommended. The order shall state generally that all recommendations are conditioned on character approval, but shall not identify those persons as to whom proceedings are still pending. The order shall be published in the Maryland Register at least once before ratification of the Board's recommendations.

(c) *Exceptions.* Before ratification of the Board's report, any person may file with the Court exceptions relating to any relevant matter. For good cause shown the Court may permit the filing of exceptions after ratification of the Board's report and before the candidate's admission to the Bar. The Court shall give notice of the filing of exceptions to the candidate, the Board, and the Character Committee that passed on the candidate's application. A hearing on the exceptions shall be held to allow the exceptant and candidate to present evidence in support of or in opposition to the exceptions and the Board and Character Committee to be heard. The Court may hold the hearing or may refer the exceptions to the Board, the Character Committee, or an examiner for hearing. The Board, Character Committee, or examiner hearing the exceptions shall file with the Court, as soon as practicable after the hearing, a report of the proceedings. The Court may decide the exceptions without further hearing.

(d) *Ratification of board's report.* On expiration of the time fixed in the order entered pursuant to section (b) of this Rule, the Board's report and recommendations shall be ratified subject to the conditions stated in the recommendations and to any exceptions noted under section (c) of this Rule.

Source. — This Rule is derived as follows: *Section (a)* is derived from former Rule 11. *Section (b)* is derived from former Rule 12 a.

Section (c) is derived from former Rule 12 b. *Section (d)* is derived from former Rule 12 c.

Rule 11. Required course on professionalism.

(a) *Duty to complete course.* Before admission to the Bar, a person recommended for admission pursuant to Rule 10 shall complete a course on legal professionalism. For good cause shown, the Court of Appeals may admit a person who has not completed the course provided that the person represents to the Court that he or she will complete the next regularly scheduled course.

(b) *Course and faculty; costs.* The course and faculty shall be proposed by the Maryland State Bar Association and approved by the Court of Appeals. The Association shall give the course at least twice annually during the period between the announcement of examination results and the scheduled admission ceremony. The Association may charge a reasonable fee to defray the expenses of giving the course.

(c) *Duration of requirement; evaluation.* The requirement set forth in section (a) shall remain in force for a period of five years beginning January 1, 1996 and ending December 31, 2000. During that period the Court of Appeals shall evaluate the results of the course requirement to determine whether to extend the requirement. The Chief Judge of the Court of Appeals may appoint a committee consisting of one or more judges, lawyers, legal educators, bar association representatives, and other interested and knowledgeable persons to assist the Court in the evaluation. (Amended effective Aug. 18, 1994; July 14, 1995; Nov. 21, 1995, effective Jan. 1, 1996.)

Source. — This Rule is new.

Effect of amendments. — The 1994 amendment substituted "five" for "three" in the first sentence of (c).

The first 1995 amendment substituted "until December 31, 1995" for "for a period of five years from the effective date of this Rule" in the first sentence of (c).

The second 1995 amendment substituted "for a period of five years beginning January 1, 1996 and ending December 31, 2000" for "until December 31, 1995" in the first sentence of (c).

Applied in Attorney Grievance Comm'n v. Reamer, 328 Md. 32, 612 A.2d 895 (1992); In re Wyatt, 342 Md. 117, 673 A.2d 1356 (1996).

Cited in In re Kahn, 328 Md. 698, 616 A.2d 882 (1992); In re McManus, 335 Md. 19, 641 A.2d 870 (1994); In re Reinstatement of Clinton, 338 Md. 481, 659 A.2d 875 (1995).

Rule 12. Final order of admission.

When the Court has determined that a candidate is qualified to practice law and is of good moral character, it shall enter an order directing that the candidate be admitted to the Bar on taking the oath required by law. (Amended June 5, 1996, effective Jan. 1, 1997.)

Cross references. — See Code, Business and Professions Article, § 10-212, for form of oath. See also Maryland Rule 16-811 f (Clients' Security Fund—Payments to Fund) and Maryland Rule 16-702 (Attorney Grievance Commission—Disciplinary Fund), which require persons admitted to the Maryland Bar, as a condition precedent to the practice of law in this State, to pay an annual assessment to the Clients' Security Trust Fund and the Attorney Grievance Commission Disciplinary Fund.

Source. — This Rule is derived from former Rule 13.

Effect of amendments. — The 1996 amendment, in the Cross reference note, substituted "Rule 16-811 f" for "Rule 1228 f" and substituted "Rule 16-702" for "Rule BV2."

Rule 13. Out-of-state attorneys.

(a) *Eligibility for admission by attorney examination — Generally.* A person is eligible for admission to the Bar of this State under this Rule if the person

(1) is a member of the Bar of a state;

(2) has passed a written bar examination in a state;

(3) has the professional experience required by this Rule;

(4) successfully completes the attorney examination prescribed by this Rule; and

(5) possesses the good moral character and fitness necessary for the practice of law.

(b) *Required professional experience.* The professional experience required for admission under this Rule shall be on a full time basis as (1) a practitioner of law as provided in section (c) of this Rule; (2) a teacher of law at a law school approved by the American Bar Association; (3) a judge of a court of record in a state; or (4) a combination thereof.

(c) *Practitioner of law.* (1) Subject to paragraphs (2), (3), and (4) of this section, a practitioner of law is a person who has regularly engaged in the authorized practice of law

(A) in a state;

(B) as the principal means of earning a livelihood; and

(C) whose professional experience and responsibilities have been sufficient to satisfy the Board that the petitioner should be admitted under this Rule.

(2) As evidence of the requisite professional experience, for purposes of subsection (c) (1) (C) of this Rule, the Board may consider, among other things:

(A) the extent of the petitioner's experience in general practice;

(B) the petitioner's professional duties and responsibilities, the extent of contacts with and responsibility to clients or other beneficiaries of the petitioner's professional skills, the extent of professional contacts with practicing lawyers and judges, and the petitioner's professional reputation among those lawyers and judges; and

(C) if the petitioner is or has been a specialist, the extent of the petitioner's experience and reputation for competence in such specialty, and any professional articles or treatises that the petitioner has written.

(3) The Board may consider as the equivalent of practice of law in a state practice outside the United States if the Board concludes that the nature of the practice makes it the functional equivalent of practice within a state.

(d) *Duration of professional experience.* (1) A person shall have the professional experience required by section (b) of this Rule for (A) a total of ten years, or (B) at least five of the ten years immediately preceding the filing of a petition pursuant to this Rule.

(e) *Exceptional cases.* In exceptional cases, the Board may treat a petitioner's actual experience, although not meeting the literal requirements of subsections (c) (1) or (d) of this Rule, as the equivalent of the professional experience otherwise required by this Rule.

(f) *Petition.* (1) The petitioner shall file with the Board a petition under oath on a form prescribed by the Board, accompanied by the fees required by the Board and the costs assessed for the character and fitness investigation and report by the National Conference of Bar Examiners.

(2) The petitioner shall state (A) each jurisdiction in which the petitioner has been admitted to the Bar and whether each admission was by examination, by diploma privilege or on motion; and (B) the additional facts showing that the petitioner meets the requirements of section (a) of this Rule or should be qualified under section (e) of this Rule.

(3) The petitioner shall file with the petition the supporting data required by the Board as to the petitioner's professional experience, character, and fitness to practice law.

(4) The petitioner shall be under a continuing obligation to report to the Board any material change in information previously furnished.

(g) *Refunds.* If the Board determines on the face of the petition that the applicant is not qualified to sit for the attorney's examination and the petitioner elects to withdraw the petition without further proceedings, all fees shall be refunded. If in other circumstances a petitioner withdraws the petition or fails to attend and take the examination without permission from the Board, no fees will be refunded and the examination fee may not be applied to a subsequent examination unless the petitioner establishes good cause for the withdrawal or failure to attend.

(h) *Time for filing.* The petition shall be filed at least 60 days before the scheduled attorney examination that the petitioner wishes to take. On written request of the petitioner and for good cause shown, the Board may accept a petition filed after the deadline. If the Board rejects the petition, the petitioner may file an exception with the Court within five days after notice of the rejection.

(i) *Standard for admission and burden of proof.* (1) The petitioner bears the burden of proving to the Board and the Court that the petitioner is qualified on the basis of professional experience and possesses the good moral character and fitness necessary to practice law in this State.

(2) The Board shall recommend rejection of a petition if it is not satisfied that the petitioner possesses good moral character and fitness and that the contents of the petition are true and correct. Failure or refusal to answer fully and candidly any relevant questions asked by the Board, either orally or in writing, is sufficient cause for rejection of the petition.

(j) *Action by board on petition.* The Board shall investigate the matters set forth in the petition. (1) If the Board decides that the petition should be accepted, it shall mail notice of its decision to recommend acceptance of the petition to the petitioner. (2) If the Board concludes that there may be grounds for rejecting the petition, the Board shall notify the petitioner and shall afford the petitioner an opportunity for a hearing. The hearing will not be held until after the National Conference of Bar Examiners completes its investigation of the petitioner's character and fitness to practice law and reports to the Board. The petitioner may be represented by an attorney at the hearing. Promptly after the Board makes its final decision to recommend acceptance or rejection of the petition, the Board shall mail notice of its decision to the petitioner. (3) If the Board decides to recommend rejection of the petition, it shall file with the Court a report of its decision and all papers relating to the matter.

(k) *Exceptions.* Within 30 days after the Board mails notice of its adverse decision to the petitioner, the petitioner may file with the Court exceptions to the Board's decision. The petitioner shall mail or deliver to the Board a copy of the exceptions. The Court may hear the exceptions or may appoint an examiner to hear the evidence and shall afford the Board an opportunity to be heard on the exceptions.

(l) *Attorney examination.* The petitioner must pass an attorney examination prescribed by the Board. The Board shall define, by rule, the subject matter of the examination, prepare the examination, and establish the passing grade. The Board shall administer the attorney examination on a date and at a time during the administration of the regular examination pursuant to Rule 7 and shall publish at least 30 days in advance notice of the date and time of the examination. The Board shall grade the examination and shall send notice of examination results to each examinee by regular mail, postage prepaid. Successful examinees shall be notified only that they have passed. Unsuccessful examinees shall be given their grades in the detail the Board considers appropriate. Review by unsuccessful examinees shall be in accordance with the provisions of Rule 8 (b).

(m) *Re-examination.* In the event of failure on the first examination, a petitioner may file a petition to retake the examination, but a petitioner may not be admitted under this Rule after failing four examinations. A petition for re-examination shall be accompanied by the required fees. Failure to pass the attorney examination shall not preclude any person from taking the regular examination.

(n) *Report to court — Order.* The Board shall file a report and recommendations pursuant to Rule 10. Proceedings on the report, including the disposition of any exceptions filed, shall be as prescribed in that Rule. If the Court determines that the petitioner has met all the requirements of this Rule, it shall enter an order directing that the petitioner be admitted to the Bar of Maryland on taking the oath required by law.

(o) *Required course on professionalism.* A petitioner recommended for admission pursuant to section (n) of this Rule shall comply with Rule 11. (Amended June 5, 1996, effective Jan. 1, 1997.)

Cross references. — See Code, Business Occupations and Professions Article, § 10-212 for form of oath. See also Maryland Rule 16-811 f (Clients' Security Fund—Payments to Fund) and Maryland Rule 16-702 (Attorney Grievance Commission—Disciplinary Fund) which require persons admitted to the Maryland Bar, as a condition precedent to the practice of law in this State, to pay an annual assessment to the Clients' Security Trust Fund and the Attorney Grievance Commission Disciplinary Fund.

Source. — This Rule is derived in part from former Rule 14 and is in part new.

Effect of amendments. — The 1996 amendment, in the Cross reference note, substituted "Rule 16-811 f" for "Rule 1228 f" and substituted "Rule 16-702" for "Rule BV2."

Maryland Law Review. — For article, "Survey of Developments in Maryland Law, 1984-85," see 45 Md. L. Rev. 473 (1986).

"Practice of law" is a term of art connoting much more than merely working with legally related matters. In re Mark W., 303 Md. 1, 491 A.2d 576 (1985).

Employment as a hearing examiner for the Maryland Department of Employment and Training does not constitute practice of law so as to permit an individual to become a member of the Maryland Bar without taking the usual bar examination. In re Mark W., 303 Md. 1, 491 A.2d 576 (1985).

Purpose of the Rule is to require only enough "practice" (practical experience) to demonstrate no need to take a "full" bar examination. In re R.G.S., 312 Md. 626, 541 A.2d 977 (1988).

Applicant for admission was practicing law, within the meaning of Rule, and period of practice, added to his full-time professorship, added up to the requisite number of years within the required time span prior to the date applicant submitted petition for admission. In re R.G.S., 312 Md. 626, 541 A.2d 977 (1988).

"Practice of law" as used in the unauthorized practice statutes need not be read as synonymous with "practice of law" as used in this Rule. In re R.G.S., 312 Md. 626, 541 A.2d 977 (1988).

Work of attorney was actual practice within the meaning of this Rule, but was not unauthorized practice within the meaning of former Art. 10, § 1. In re R.G.S., 312 Md. 626, 541 A.2d 977 (1988).

Disclosure of material facts required. — This Rule is designed to afford a benefit to lawyers who have practiced lawfully for at least a minimum period of time. The reason for this privilege rests on the assumption that a lawyer who has regularly engaged in the practice of law has sufficient legal knowledge to demonstrate at least minimum competence; it is, therefore, of basic importance that the Board of Law Examiners have before it information from which it can determine whether an applicant has engaged in practice to the extent required by the Rule and it is important that an applicant disclose to the Board all facts bearing on this subject. Attorney Grievance Comm'n v. Keehan, 311 Md. 161, 533 A.2d 278 (1987).

Material, deliberate omission. — Attorney's failure to disclose in his application for admission to the Maryland Bar that, although he had a Pennsylvania license and a Pennsylvania office, he worked full-time for a Baltimore corporation and only worked at his legal practice 10-15 hours per week was material, deliberate omission for which disbarment was the appropriate sanction. Attorney Grievance Comm'n v. Keehan, 311 Md. 161, 533 A.2d 278 (1987).

Rule 14. Special admission of out-of-state attorneys.

(a) *Motion for special admission.* A member of the Bar of this State who is an attorney of record in an action pending in any court of this State or before an administrative agency of this State or any of its political subdivisions, may move, in writing, that an attorney who is a member in good standing of the Bar of another state be admitted to practice in this State for the limited purpose of appearing and participating in the action as co-counsel with the movant. If the action is pending in a court, the motion shall be filed in that court. If the action is pending before an administrative agency, the motion shall be filed in the circuit court for the county in which the principal office of the agency is located or in any other circuit to which the action may be appealed and shall include the movant's signed certification that copies of the motion have been furnished to the agency and to all parties of record.

(b) *Certification by out-of-state attorney.* The attorney whose special admission is moved shall certify in writing the number of times the attorney has been specially admitted during the twelve months immediately preceding the filing of the motion. The certification may be filed as a separate paper or may be included in the motion under an appropriate heading.

(c) *Order.* The court by order may admit specially or deny the special admission of an attorney. In either case, the clerk shall forward a copy of the order to the State Court Administrator, who shall maintain a docket of all attorneys granted or denied special admission. When the order grants or denies the special admission of an attorney in an action pending before an administrative agency, the clerk also shall forward a copy of the order to the agency.

(d) *Limitations on out-of-state attorney's practice.* An attorney specially admitted may act only as co-counsel for a party represented by an attorney of record in the action who is admitted to practice in this State. The specially admitted attorney may participate in the court or administrative proceedings only when accompanied by the Maryland attorney, unless the latter's presence is waived by the judge or administrative hearing officer presiding over the action. Any out-of-state attorney so admitted is subjected to the Maryland Rules of Professional Conduct.

Cross references. — See Code, Business Occupations and Professions Article, § 10-215.

Committee note. — The Committee has not recommended a numerical limitation on the number of appearances pro hac vice to be allowed any attorney. Specialized expertise of out-of-state attorneys or other special circumstances may be important factors to be considered by judges in assessing whether Maryland litigants have access to effective representation. This Rule is not intended, however, to permit extensive or systematic practice by attorneys not licensed in Maryland. The Committee is primarily concerned with assuring professional responsibility of attorneys in Maryland by avoiding circumvention of Rule 13 (Out-of-State Attorneys) or *Kemp Pontiac Cadillac, Inc. et al vs. S & M Construction Co., Inc.*, 33 Md. App. 516 (1976). The Committee also noted that payment to the Clients' Security Trust Fund of the Bar of Maryland by an attorney admitted specially for the purposes of an action is not required by existing statute or rule of court.

Source. — This Rule is derived from former Rule 20.

Editor's note. — For forms for motion and order for special admission of out-of-state attorneys, see Forms RGAB 20/M and RGAB 20/O in Appendix: Forms following the Maryland Rules in this volume.

Petition for readmission. — Four principal criteria have to be evaluated in a petition for readmission to the Maryland bar: (1) the nature and circumstances of petitioner's original misconduct; (2) petitioner's subsequent conduct and reformation; (3) petitioner's present character; and (4) petitioner's present qualifications and competence to practice law. In re Keehan, 342 Md. 121, 674 A.2d 510 (1996).

Applied in Attorney Grievance Comm'n v. Ray, 343 Md. 254, 680 A.2d 1101 (1996).

Cited in Attorney Grievance Comm'n v. James, 340 Md. 318, 666 A.2d 1246 (1995); Turkey Point Property Owners' Ass'n v. Anderson, 106 Md. App. 710, 666 A.2d 904 (1995).

Rule 15. Special authorization for out-of-state attorneys to practice in this state.

(a) *Eligibility.* Subject to the provisions of this Rule, a member of the Bar of another state who is employed by or associated with an organized legal services program that is sponsored or approved by Legal Aid Bureau, Inc. may practice in this State pursuant to that organized legal services program, if (1) the individual is a graduate of a law school meeting the requirements of Rule 4 (a) (2), (2) the legal services program provides legal assistance to indigents in this State, and (3) the individual will practice under the superivision of a member of the Bar of this State.

(b) *Proof of eligibility.* To obtain authorization to practice under this Rule the out-of-state attorney shall file with the Clerk of the Court of Appeals a written request accompanied by (1) evidence of graduation from a law school as defined in Rule 4 (a) (2), (2) a certificate of the highest court of another state certifying that the attorney is a member in good standing of the Bar of that state, and (3) a statement signed by the Executive Director of Legal Aid Bureau, Inc., that the attorney is currently employed by or associated with an approved organized legal services program.

(c) *Certificate of authorization to practice.* Upon the filing of the proof of eligibility required by this Rule, the Clerk of the Court of Appeals shall issue a certificate under the seal of the Court certifying that the attorney is authorized to practice under this Rule. The certificate shall contain the effective date and expiration date of the special authorization to practice. The expiration date shall be no later than two years after the effective date.

(d) *Automatic termination before expiration.* Authorization to practice under this Rule is automatically terminated before its expiration date if the attorney ceases to be employed by or associated with an approved organized legal services program in this State. Within five days after cessation of the attorney's employment or association, the Executive Director of Legal Aid Bureau, Inc. shall file with the Clerk of the Court of Appeals notice of the termination of authorization.

(e) *Revocation or suspension.* At any time, the Court, in its discretion, may revoke or suspend authorization to practice under this Rule either by written notice to the attorney or by amendment or deletion of this Rule.

(f) *Special authorization not admission.* Out-of-state attorneys authorized to practice under this Rule are not, and shall not represent themselves to be members of the Bar of this State, except in connection with practice that is authorized under this Rule. They shall be required to make payments to the Clients' Security Trust Fund and the Disciplinary Fund.

Source. — This Rule is derived from former Rule 19.

Rule 16. Legal assistance by law students.

(a) *Definitions.* As used in this Rule, the following terms have the following meanings:

(1) Law school. "Law school" means a law school meeting the requirements of Rule 4 (a) (2).

(2) Clinical program. "Clinical program" means a law school program for credit, in which a student obtains experience in the operation of the legal system by engaging in the practice of law, that is (A) under the direction of a faculty member of the school and (B) has been approved by the Section Council of the Section of Legal Education and Admissions to the Bar of the Maryland State Bar Association, Inc.

(3) Supervising attorney. "Supervising attorney" means an attorney who is a member in good standing of the Bar of this State and whose service as a supervising attorney for the clinical program is approved by the dean of the law school in which the law student is enrolled or by the dean's designee.

(b) *Eligibility.* A law student enrolled in a clinical program is eligible to engage in the practice of law as provided in this Rule if the student:

(1) is enrolled in a law school;

(2) has read and is familiar with the Maryland Rules of Professional Conduct and the relevant Maryland Rules of Procedure; and

(3) has been certified in accordance with section (c) of this Rule.

(c) *Certification.* (1) Contents and filing. The dean of the law school shall file the certification of a student with the Clerk of the Court of Appeals. It shall state that the student is in good academic standing and has successfully completed legal studies in the law school amounting to the equivalent of at least one-third of the total credit hours required to complete the law school program. It shall also state its effective date and expiration date, which shall be no later than one year after the effective date.

(2) Withdrawal or suspension. The dean may withdraw the certificate at any time by mailing a notice to that effect to the Clerk of the Court of Appeals. It shall automatically be suspended upon the issuance of an unfavorable report of the Character Committee made in connection with the student's application for registration as a candidate for admission to the Bar. Upon reversal of the Character Committee, the certification shall be reinstated.

(d) *Practice.* In connection with a clinical program, a law student for whom a certificate is in effect may appear in any trial court or the Court of Special Appeals or otherwise engage in the practice of law in Maryland provided that the supervising attorney (1) is satisfied that the student is competent to perform the duties assigned, (2) assumes responsibility for the quality of the student's work, (3) directs and assists the student to the extent necessary, in the supervising attorney's professional judgment, to ensure that the student's participation is effective on behalf of the client the student represents, and (4) accompanies the student when the student appears in court or before an administrative agency. The law student shall neither ask for nor receive personal compensation of any kind for service rendered under this Rule.

Source. — This Rule is derived from former Rule 18.

Maryland Law Review. — For article, "Missed Manners in Courtroom Decorum," see 50 Md. L. Rev. 945 (1991).

Rule 17. Character committees.

The Court shall appoint a Character Committee for each of the eight judicial circuits of the State. Each Character Committee shall consist of not less than five members whose terms shall be for five years each and which shall be staggered. The Court shall designate the chair of each Committee, and may provide compensation to the members. Each Committee shall elect a secretary.

Source. — This Rule is derived from former Rule 4 a and e.

Cited in In re Hyland, 339 Md. 521, 663 A.2d 1309 (1995).

Rule 18. Fees.

The Board shall prescribe the fees, subject to approval by the Court, to be paid by applicants under Rules 2 and 7 and by petitioners under Rule 13.

Cross references. — See Code, Business Occupations and Professions Article, § 10-208 (b) for maximum examination fee allowed by law.

Source. — This Rule is new and replaces former Rules 2 e, 6, 8 a, and 14 c.

Rule 19. Confidentiality.

(a) *Proceedings before committee or board; general policy.* Except as provided in sections (b) and (c) of this Rule, proceedings before a Character Committee or the Board and the papers, evidence, and information relating to those proceedings are confidential and shall not be open to public inspection or subject to court process or compulsory disclosure.

(b) *Right of applicant.* (1) Except as provided in paragraph (2) of this section, an applicant has the right to attend all hearings before a Character Committee or the Board pertaining to his or her application and be informed of and inspect all papers, evidence, and information received or considered by the Committee or the Board pertaining to the applicant.

(2) This section does not apply to (A) papers or evidence received or considered by a Character Committee of the Board if the Committee or Board, without a hearing, recommends the applicant's admission; (B) personal memoranda, notes, and work papers of members or staff of a Character Committee or the Board; (C) correspondence between or among members or staff of a Character Committee or the Board; or (D) an applicant's bar examination grades and answers, except as authorized in Rule 8 and Rule 13.

(c) *When disclosure authorized.* The Board may disclose:

(1) statistical information that does not reveal the identity of any individual applicant;

(2) the fact that an applicant has passed the bar examination and the date of the examination;

(3) any material pertaining to an applicant that the applicant would be entitled to inspect under section (b) of this Rule, if the applicant has consented in writing to the disclosure;

(4) any material pertaining to an applicant requested by a court of this State, another state, or the United States for use in (A) a disciplinary proceeding pending in that court against the applicant as an attorney or judge; (B) a proceeding pending in that court for reinstatement of the applicant as an attorney after disbarment; or (C) a proceeding pending in that court for original admission of the applicant to the Bar;

(5) any material pertaining to an applicant requested by a judicial nominating commission or the Governor of this State, a committee of the Senate of Maryland, or a committee of the United States Senate in connection with an application by or nomination of the applicant for judicial office;

(6) to a law school, the names of persons who graduated from that law school who took a bar examination and whether they passed or failed the examination; and

(7) to the National Conference of Bar Examiners, identifying information (including name, Social Security Number, birthdate, date of application, and date of examination) of persons who have filed applications for admission pursuant to Rule 2 or petitions to take the attorney's examination pursuant to Rule 13.

Unless information disclosed pursuant to paragraphs (4) and (5) of this section is disclosed with the written consent of the applicant, an applicant shall receive a copy of the information and may rebut, in writing, any matter contained in it. Upon receipt of a written rebuttal, the Board shall forward a copy to the person or entity to whom the information was disclosed.

(d) *Proceedings in the court of appeals.* Unless the Court otherwise orders in a particular case, proceedings in the Court of Appeals shall be open.

Source. — This Rule is new.

Rule 20. The Board.

(a) *Authority to adopt rules.* The Board may adopt rules to carry out the requirements of these Rules and to facilitate the conduct of examinations. The Rules of the Board shall be published in the Code, Maryland Rules, following these Rules.

(b) *Amendment of Board rules. — Publication.* Any amendment of the Board's rules shall be published at least once in a daily newspaper of general circulation in this State. The amendment shall be published at least 45 days before the examination at which it is to become effective, except that an amendment that substantially increases the area of subject-matter knowledge required for any examination shall be published at least one year before the examination.

(c) *Assistants.* The Board may appoint the assistants necessary for the proper conduct of its business. Each assistant shall be an attorney admitted by the Court of Appeals and shall serve at the pleasure of the Board.

(d) *Compensation of Board members and assistants.* The members of the Board and assistants shall receive the compensation fixed from time to time by the Court.

(e) *Secretary to the Board.* The Court may appoint a secretary to the Board, to hold office during the pleasure of the Court. The secretary shall have the administrative powers and duties that the Board may prescribe.

Source. — This Rule is derived as follows: *Section (a)* is derived from former Rule 7 h and 9 a.
Section (b) is derived from former Rule 7 h and i.
Section (c) is derived from former Rule 9 c.
Section (d) is derived from former Rule 16.
Section (e) is derived from former Rule 17.

Rule 21. Suspension or revocation of license of attorney ineligible for admission.

If an attorney admitted to the Bar of this State is discovered to have been ineligible for admission under circumstances that do not warrant disbarment or other disciplinary proceedings, the Court of Appeals may, upon a recommendation by the Board and after notice and opportunity to be heard, suspend or revoke the attorney's license. In the case of a suspension the Court shall specify in its order the duration of the suspension and the conditions upon which the suspension may be lifted.

Source. — This Rule is new.

Rule 22. Subpoena power of board and character committees.

(a) *Subpoena.* In any proceeding before the Board or a Character Committee pursuant to Bar Admission Rule 5 or Bar Admission Rule 13, the Board or Committee, on its own motion or the motion of an applicant, may cause a subpoena to be issued by a clerk pursuant to Rule 2-510. The subpoena shall issue from the Circuit Court for Anne Arundel County if incident to Board proceedings or from the circuit court in the county in which Character Committee proceedings are pending, and the proceedings may not be docketed in court. The subpoena shall not divulge the name of the applicant, except to the extent this requirement is impracticable. The sheriff's return shall be made as directed in the subpoena. The Character Committee or the Board, as applicable, shall maintain dockets and files of all papers filed in the proceedings.

(b) *Sanctions.* If a person is subpoenaed to appear and give testimony or to produce books, documents, or other tangible things and fails to do so, the party who requested the subpoena, by motion that does not divulge the name of the applicant (except to the extent that this requirement is impracticable), may request the court to issue an attachment pursuant to Rule 2-510 (h), or to cite the person for contempt pursuant to Title 15, Chapter 200 of the Maryland Rules, or both.

(c) *Court rules.* All court costs in proceedings under this Rule shall be assessable to and paid by the State. (Added June 7, 1994, effective Oct. 1, 1994; amended June 5, 1996, effective Jan. 1, 1997.)

Source. — This Rule is new.

———————

Effect of amendments. — The 1996 amendment substituted "Title 15, Chapter 200" for "Subtitle P, Chapter 1100" in (b).

RULES OF THE BOARD.

Pursuant to Rule 20 of the Court of Appeals' Rules Governing Admission to the Bar of Maryland, the State Board of Law Examiners adopted the following Rules of the Board on October 8, 1990 to be effective immediately and superseding all previous Rules of the Board:

Board Rule 1. Application fees.

a. *General Bar examination.* 1. An Application filed pursuant to the Court's Bar Admission Rule 2 shall be accompanied by a check or money order payable to the State Board of Law Examiners in the amount of:

(i) $125 if timely filed, or

(ii) $175 if filed late.

2. A petition to take a scheduled bar examination pursuant to the Court's Bar Admission Rule 6 shall be accompanied by a check or money order in the amount of $90.

b. *Out-of-state attorney examination.* 1. A petition filed pursuant to the Court's Bar Admission Rule 13 shall be accompanied by a check or money order payable to the State Board of Law Examiners in the amount of $400 and a separate check, money order, or credit card authorization for the National Conference of Bar Examiners in such amount as required to cover the cost of the character and fitness investigation and report.

2. A petition for re-examination filed pursuant to the Court's Bar Admission Rule 13 shall be accompanied by a check or money order payable to the State Board of Law Examiners in the amount of $90.

Board Rule 2. Filing late for good cause.

An applicant's written request for acceptance of an application or petition filed late for good cause pursuant to the Court's Bar Admission Rule 2 c (3), Rule 6 or Rule 13 h shall include a statement indicating:

(a) whether the applicant's failure to timely file was due to facts and circumstances beyond the applicant's control and stating those facts and circumstances,

(b) whether the applicant presently has a bar application pending with any other jurisdiction,

(c) whether the applicant presently is a member of the Bar of any other jurisdiction, and

(d) the specific nature of the hardship which would result if the applicant's request is denied.

Board Rule 3. Examination — Subject matter.

Pursuant to section c of Rule 7 (Bar Examination), Rules Governing Admission to the Bar of Maryland, the subject matter of the Maryland Bar Examination is defined as follows:

AGENCY

The law of agency will be included on the examination only to the extent provided in the definitions of Business Associations, Contracts and Torts.

BUSINESS ASSOCIATIONS

The legal principles pertaining to doing business in such forms as stock corporation including close corporation, sole proprietorship, joint venture, partnership, limited partnership, including rights, obligations and liabilities of partners, powers and liabilities of directors and officers, the rights and powers of shareholders, shareholders' suits and the issuance of shares and dividends distribution; related principles of agency.

COMMERCIAL TRANSACTIONS

The law governing commercial transactions including negotiable instruments, sales and sales financing, secured transactions, rights and remedies of buyers and sellers with emphasis on the Uniform Commercial Code as the prevailing commercial legislation.

CONSTITUTIONAL LAW

The interpretation of the Constitution of the United States and its amendments, division of powers between the states and national government, powers of the President, the Congress, and the Supreme Court, limitations on the powers of the state and national government.

CONTRACTS

The consideration of agreements enforceable at law. The subject includes: (a) formation of contracts — offer and acceptance, mistake, fraud, misrepresentation or duress, contractual capacity, effect of illegality, consideration; informal contracts; (b) third-party beneficiary contracts; (c) assignment of contracts; (d) statute of frauds; (e) parol evidence rule, interpretation of contracts; (f) performance-conditions, failure of consideration, aleatory promises, rights of defaulting plaintiff, substantial performance, specific performance, (g) breach of contract and remedies therefor, including measure of damages; (h) impossibility of performance, frustration of purpose; and (i) discharge of contracts. This subject may also include law dealing with an agent's ability to bind a principal to a contract, and the agent's personal liability on a contract made for a principal.

CRIMINAL LAW AND PROCEDURE

The law of crimes against the person; crimes against public peace and morals; property crimes; crimes involving the breach of public trust or civic duty, obstruction of justice; criminal responsibility, causation, justification and other defenses; constitutional limitations and protections.

EVIDENCE

The law governing the proof of issues of fact in civil and criminal trials including functions of the court and jury; competence of witnesses; examination, cross-examination and impeachment of witnesses; presumptions, burden of producing evidence and burden of persuasion; privileges against disclosure of information; relevancy; demonstrative, experimental and scientific evidence; opinion evidence; admissibility of writings; parol evidence rule; hearsay rule; judicial notice. The Board's Test will cover only the Maryland substantive Law of Evidence, common law and statutory.

FAMILY LAW

The principles of Maryland law regarding creation of (or the existence of) the marriage relationship; termination of the marriage; alimony and support of the marriage partner; support and custody of children; marital property issues; and prenuptial agreements. Includes both statutory and common law principles of Maryland law and procedure except for matters of adoption, paternity, and juvenile law.

(Adopted Apr. 8, 1992, effective beginning with the July 1993 bar examination.)

MARYLAND CIVIL PROCEDURE

The various procedural steps and matters involved in an action at law or in equity, from commencement of the action to final disposition on appeal. The subject includes: (a) jurisdiction of courts; (b) venue; (c) parties and process; (d) forms of pleading; (e) motions and other means of raising procedural objections or defenses, including affirmative defenses and counter-claims; (f) discovery and other pre-trial procedures; (g) trial practice; (h) entry, effect and enforcement of judgments; (i) methods of taking appeal or otherwise securing appellate review; and (j) appellate practice and procedure. The subject embraces civil procedure and practice in the State courts. Federal Rules of practice and procedure are not covered on the examination.

PROFESSIONAL CONDUCT

The Rules of Professional Conduct as adopted by Maryland Rule 16-812. These are contained in Maryland Rules Volume 2, Appendix.

PROPERTY

The fundamentals of real property law including concepts of possession; concurrent and consecutive future estates in land (and their counterparts in testamentary and *inter vivos* trusts); leaseholds and landlord-tenant relationships; fixtures and the distinction between real and personal property; covenants enforceable in equity; easements, profits and licenses; rights of user and exploitation in land (including rights to lateral and subjacent support); contracts of sale of real estate; the statute of limitations on real actions (adverse possession) and prescription; conveyancing priorities and recording (including marketable title); remedies. Problems of rules against perpetuities will appear only on the MBE test (Board Rule 4).

TORTS

The law of civil wrongs. The subject includes, but is not limited to: (a) negligent torts including causation, standard of care, primary negligence, comparative and contributory negligence, assumption of risk, limitations on liability, contribution and indemnity; impact of insurance; (b) intentional torts; (c) strict liability, products liability; (d) nuisance; (e) invasion of privacy; (f) defamation; (g) vicarious liability; and (h) defenses, immunity and privilege, and damages in connection with any of these areas.

Effect of amendments. — The 1992 amendment, effective beginning with the July 1993 bar examination, adds Family Law to the list of essay examination subjects.

Board Rule 4. Multistate bar examination — Board test.

a. *Authorization.* Pursuant to section c of Rule 7 (Bar Examination), Rules Governing Admission to the Bar of Maryland, the State Board of Law Examiners adopts the Multistate Bar Examination as part of the Maryland Bar Examination.

b. *Board's test.* One part of the examination (the Board's test) will be prepared and graded by the Board and will consist entirely of questions requiring essay answers. The Board's test will not contain subject-matter labels. Single problems may involve two or more subjects. The weight and time estimated to answer each problem or group of problems will be noted on the problem sheet.

c. *MBE test.* The other part of the examination (the MBE test) will consist entirely of multiple-choice questions prepared and graded by or under the direction of the National Conference of Bar Examiners. The MBE test will not contain subject-matter labels.

d. *Requirements for passing.* To pass, a candidate must attain either:

(i) a score of at least 70% on the Board test and a scaled score of at least 120 on the MBE test; or

(ii) a combined score of at least 70%, giving the two scores equal weight.

e. *Carry over of scores.* 1. The Board will recognize, as part of its examination, the scaled score of any candidate on an MBE test taken in another jurisdiction at the same or the immediately preceding administration of the Multistate Bar Examination, provided, however, that a scaled score carried forward from the preceding administration may not be less than 140.

2. A candidate who takes both parts of the Maryland Bar Examination and who fails to pass, but who attains a score of at least 70% on the Board's test, or a scaled score of at least 140 on the MBE test, may elect, in a Petition for Retake, to carry over the score so attained to the next succeeding examination only. An applicant may not retake that part of the examination for which the applicant elects, under this section, to carry over a score.

f. *Adjustment of requirements.* For any particular examination the Board may, in the interest of fairness, lower (but not raise) any or all of the foregoing requirements at any time before notice of the results.

Board Rule 5. Out-of-state attorney examination.

a. *Subject matter.* The out-of-state attorney examination will be prepared and graded by the Board and will consist entirely of questions requiring essay answers. It will relate to:

(i) Maryland Rules of Procedure governing practice and procedure in civil and criminal cases in all the Courts of the State of Maryland, including the Appendix of forms (*Maryland Rules,* Volumes 1 and 2),

(ii) the Rules of Professional Conduct, as adopted by Maryland Rule 16-812 (*Maryland Rules,* Volume 2),

(iii) and the provisions of the *Courts and Judicial Proceedings Article* of the Annotated Code of Maryland.

b. *Time — Duration.* The attorney examination shall be conducted during a part of the essay day of each regularly scheduled bar examination and will have a total of three hours writing time for the entire test. The point score allotted for each question will be noted on the examination sheet.

c. *Requirement for passing.* In order to pass the examination, a petitioner shall attain a score of at least 70% of the total point score allotted to the entire test. (Amended effective Dec. 14, 1994.)

Effect of amendments. — The 1994 amendment rewrote a.

Index to Rules Governing Admission to the Bar of Maryland

INTERNAL OPERATING RULES
OF THE COURT OF APPEALS
OF MARYLAND

I. PREAMBLE.

A recent amendment to the Open Meetings Act, State Government Article, Section 10-507 (b), provides: "[a] public body shall adopt and enforce reasonable rules regarding the conduct of persons attending its meetings and the videotaping, televising, photographing, broadcasting, or recording of its meetings." In accordance with this provision, the following rules have been adopted by the Court of Appeals of Maryland effective January 1, 1992.

II. CONDUCT OF PROCEEDINGS.

Rule 1. Open meeting.
The Court shall conduct all proceedings involving the exercise of its authority under Md. Constitution, Art. IV, Section 18 (a) to adopt or modify Rules of Practice and Procedure at a meeting open to the public. The meeting may be in the Courtroom, in the Court's conference room, or at any other suitable place designated by the Court. Advance notice of the meeting shall be given in the manner designated by the Court.

Rule 2. Opportunity for comment.
(a) *Written comment.* If the proposed changes have been included in a Report from the Court's Standing Committee on Rules of Practice and Procedure that has been published in the Md. Register, written comments may be filed within the time and in the manner specified in the Notice published in the Md. Register. If the proposed changes have not been published in the Md. Register, written comments may be filed within the time and in the manner specified by the Court. Comments not filed in accordance with this section will ordinarily not be considered by the Court.

(b) *Oral comment.* (1) The Court may conduct a public hearing with respect to proposed changes in the Md. Rules. Persons desiring to be heard must notify the Clerk of Court at least two days before the hearing of their desire to be heard and of the amount of time needed to address the Court. The Court may prescribe a shorter period for oral presentation and may pose questions to the person addressing the Court.

(2) If the Court does not conduct a public hearing, persons attending the open meeting may not address the Court unless requested by the Court.

Rule 3. Record of proceedings.

The Clerk of the Court of Appeals shall serve as recording secretary at all public hearings and open meetings. The Clerk shall monitor an audio recording of the proceedings which the Clerk shall retain as a permanent record and make available upon request. Tape recording or videotaping by persons in attendance is prohibited.

Rule 4. Doors.

In order to furnish the public easy access to rules proceedings, doors to the court or conference room shall remain open at all times during all public hearings and open meetings.

Rule 5. Personal conduct.

Persons attending rules proceedings are prohibited from smoking, eating, or drinking during the proceedings. Anyone who violates this rule may be removed from the vicinity.

Rule 6. Disruptive behavior.

If the Chief Judge determines that the behavior of a person is disrupting a rules proceeding, the Chief Judge may have the person removed.

III. EXTENDED COVERAGE.

Rule 7. Nature and extent.

Extended coverage, as defined in Maryland Rule 16-109a1, shall be permitted during rules proceedings unless prohibited or limited in accordance with these rules.

Rule 8. Coverage at public hearing.

Ordinarily, extended coverage will be permitted at a public hearing provided a request for coverage is made to the Clerk of Court at least five days before the proceeding to be covered. For good cause shown the Court may honor a request which does not comply with the requirements of this subsection.

Rule 9. Coverage at open meeting.

Absent exceptional circumstances, extended coverage shall not be permitted during open meetings. If coverage is sought, a request must be made in writing at least five days before the meeting and shall set forth the exceptional circumstances warranting extended coverage. A decision by the Court denying coverage is not intended to restrict the right of the media to report the proceedings.

Rule 10. Standards of conduct and technology.

Anyone who is permitted to conduct extended coverage of a rules proceeding must adhere to the standards of conduct and technology set forth in Maryland Rule 16-109 f.

Index to the Internal Operating Rules of the Court of Appeals of Maryland

FEDERAL RULES OF APPELLATE PROCEDURE FOR UNITED STATES COURTS OF APPEALS; LOCAL RULES AND INTERNAL OPERATING PROCEDURES OF THE FOURTH CIRCUIT

As amended through December 1, 1998

723

NOTICE: Automated Voice Information System Fourth Circuit Opinion Release Line. — Opinions released each day by the U.S. Court of Appeals for the Fourth Circuit are announced on an Automated Voice Information System line. Opinions are announced at 3:30 p.m. each day by case number, case name, and disposition. You may reach the Opinion line at the following numbers: 1-804-771-2084 and 1-800-362-7992.

NOTICE: Proposed Amendments to Local Rules and Internal Operating Procedures. — Please take notice that the Court intends to amend its Local Rules and Internal Operating Procedures to conform to the December 1, 1998 amendments to the Federal Rules of Appellate Procedure. For ease of reference, the proposed amendments to the Local Rules and Internal Operating Procedures and commentary on the local amendments are set out with the text of the December 1, 1998 amendments to the Federal Rules of Appellate Procedure.

The December 1, 1998 amendments to the Federal Rules of Appellate Procedure make stylistic revisions and, in addition, make significant substantive changes to: Rule 26.1 governing corporate disclosure statements; Rule 27 governing motions; Rule 29 governing amicus curiae briefs; Rule 32 governing the form of briefs; Rule 35 governing petitions for rehearing en banc; and Rule 41 governing the mandate.

The proposed amendments to the Local Rules and Internal Operating Procedures are made to conform the Court's rules and procedures to the new federal rules. In addition to these conforming amendments, the Court makes the following changes to its rules and operating procedures:

Local Rule 12(c) governing transmission of the record in expedited appeals is amended to conform to Local Rule 10(a).

I.O.P. 12.1 describing what docket numbers are assigned to particular case types is deleted.

Local Rule 27(b) is amended to substitute the word "procedural" for "formal" in describing motions which may be acted on by the clerk.

Local Rule 28(b) regarding attachments to briefs is amended to conform to Local Rule 32(c).

Local Rule 34(d) is amended to make explicit that the Court may shorten the time allotted for oral argument when extended argument is unnecessary.

Local Rule 34(e) is amended to clarify the time within which motions to submit on the briefs must be filed.

Local Rule 45 is amended to eliminate the requirement that the clerk notify appellant personally of counsel's default before dismissing an appeal for want of prosecution. As amended, the local rule requires the clerk to notify counsel if appellant is represented by counsel, and to notify appellant personally if appellant is proceeding pro se.

The proposed amendments to the Local Rules and Internal Operating Procedures will take effect December 1, 1998, subject to amendment in light of comments received.

TITLE I. APPLICABILITY OF RULES.

Rule 1. Scope of rules and title.

(a) *Scope of rules.* (1) These rules govern procedure in the United States courts of appeals.

(2) When these rules provide for filing a motion or other document in the district court, the procedure must comply with the practice of the district court.

(b) *Rules do not affect jurisdiction.* These rules do not extend or limit the jurisdiction of the courts of appeals.

(c) *Title.* These rules are to be known as the Federal Rules of Appellate Procedure. (Amended by order adopted April 30, 1979, effective August 1, 1979; by order adopted April 25, 1989, corrected May 1, 1989, effective December 1, 1989; by order adopted April 29, 1994, effective December 1, 1994; and by order adopted April 24, 1998, effective December 1, 1998.)

Editor's note. — Subdivision (c) of this rule was formerly codified as FRAP 48.

Rule 2. Suspension of rules.

On its own or a party's motion, a court of appeals may — to expedite its decision or for other good cause — suspend any provision of these rules in a particular case and order proceedings as it directs, except as otherwise provided in Rule 26(b). (Amended by order adopted April 24, 1998, effective December 1, 1998.)

Court may not waive jurisdictional requirements if they are not met. — Although a court may construe the rules liberally in determining whether they have been complied with, it may not waive the jurisdictional requirements of FRAP Rules 3 and 4, even for "good cause shown" under this rule, if it finds that they have not been met. Torres v. Oakland Scavenger Co., 487 U.S. 312, 108 S. Ct. 2405, 101 L. Ed. 2d 285 (1988).

TITLE II. APPEALS FROM JUDGMENTS AND ORDERS OF DISTRICT COURTS.

Rule 3. Appeal as of right — How taken.

(a) *Filing the notice of appeal.* (1) An appeal permitted by law as of right from a district court to a court of appeals may be taken only by filing a notice of appeal with the district clerk within the time allowed by Rule 4. At the time of filing, the appellant must furnish the clerk with enough copies of the notice to enable the clerk to comply with Rule 3(d).

(2) An appellant's failure to take any step other than the timely filing of a notice of appeal does not affect the validity of the appeal, but is ground only for the court of appeals to act as it considers appropriate, including dismissing the appeal.

(3) An appeal from a judgment by a magistrate judge in a civil case is taken in the same way as an appeal from any other district court judgment.

(4) An appeal by permission under 28 U.S.C. § 1292(b) or an appeal in a bankruptcy case may be taken only in the manner prescribed by Rules 5 and 6, respectively.

(b) *Joint or consolidated appeals.* (1) When two or more parties are entitled to appeal from a district-court judgment or order, and their interests make joinder practicable, they may file a joint notice of appeal. They may then proceed on appeal as a single appellant.

(2) When the parties have filed separate timely notices of appeal, the appeals may be joined or consolidated by the court of appeals.

(c) *Content of the notice of appeal.* (1) The notice of appeal must:

(A) specify the party or parties taking the appeal by naming each one in the caption or body of the notice, but an attorney representing more than one party may describe those parties with such terms as "all plaintiffs," "the defendants," "the plaintiffs A, B, et al.," or "all defendants except X";

(B) designate the judgment, order, or part thereof being appealed; and

(C) name the court to which the appeal is taken.

(2) A pro se notice of appeal is considered filed on behalf of the signer and the signer's spouse and minor children (if they are parties), unless the notice clearly indicates otherwise.

(3) In a class action, whether or not the class has been certified, the notice of appeal is sufficient if it names one person qualified to bring the appeal as representative of the class.

(4) An appeal must not be dismissed for informality of form or title of the notice of appeal, or for failure to name a party whose intent to appeal is otherwise clear from the notice.

(5) Form 1 in the Appendix of Forms is a suggested form of a notice of appeal.

(d) *Serving the notice of appeal.* (1) The district clerk must serve notice of the filing of a notice of appeal by mailing a copy to each party's counsel of record — excluding the appellant's — or, if a party is proceeding pro se, to the party's last known address. When a defendant in a criminal case appeals, the clerk must also serve a copy of the notice of appeal on the defendant, either by personal service or by mail addressed to the defendant. The clerk must promptly send a copy of the notice of appeal and of the docket entries — and any later docket entries — to the clerk of the court of appeals named in the notice. The district clerk must note, on each copy, the date when the notice of appeal was filed.

(2) If an inmate confined in an institution files a notice of appeal in the manner provided by Rule 4(c), the district clerk must also note the date when the clerk docketed the notice.

(3) The district clerk's failure to serve notice does not affect the validity of the appeal. The clerk must note on the docket the names of the parties to whom the clerk mails copies, with the date of mailing. Service is sufficient despite the death of a party or the party's counsel.

(e) *Payment of fees.* Upon filing a notice of appeal, the appellant must pay the district clerk all required fees. The district clerk receives the appellate docket fee on behalf of the court of appeals. (Amended by order adopted April 30, 1979, effective August 1, 1979; by order adopted March 10, 1986, effective July 1, 1986; by order adopted April 25, 1989, effective December 1,1989; by order adopted April 22, 1993, effective December 1, 1993; by order adopted April 29, 1994, effective December 1, 1994; and by order adopted April 24, 1998, effective December 1, 1998.)

Court may not waive jurisdictional requirements if they are not met. — Although a court may construe the rules liberally in determining whether they have been complied with, it may not waive the jurisdictional requirements of this rule and FRAP Rule 4, even for "good cause shown" under FRAP Rule 2, if it finds that they have not been met. Torres v. Oakland Scavenger Co., 487 U.S. 312, 108 S. Ct. 2405, 101 L. Ed. 2d 285 (1988).

Committee view that requirements were jurisdictional was of weight in rule construction. — Supreme Court's conclusion that the Advisory Committee viewed the requirements of this rule as jurisdictional in nature, although not determinative, was "of weight" in the Supreme Court's construction of the rule. Torres v. Oakland Scavenger Co., 487 U.S. 312, 108 S. Ct. 2405, 101 L. Ed. 2d 285 (1988).

Litigant has complied with rule if action functional equivalent. — If a litigant files papers in a fashion that is technically at variance with the letter of a procedural rule, a court may nonetheless find that the litigant has complied with the rule if the litigant's action is the functional equivalent of what the rule requires. Torres v. Oakland Scavenger Co., 487 U.S. 312, 108 S. Ct. 2405, 101 L. Ed. 2d 285 (1988).

The specificity requirement of this rule is met only by some designation that gives fair notice of the specific individual or entity seeking to appeal. Torres v. Oakland Scavenger Co., 487 U.S. 312, 108 S. Ct. 2405, 101 L. Ed. 2d 285 (1988).

Use of "et al." was not sufficient to indicate intention to appeal. — Where notice of appeal omitted petitioner's name, the use of "et al." in the notice of appeal was not sufficient to indicate his intention to appeal; the purpose of the specificity requirement of this rule is to provide notice both to the opposition and to the court of the identity of the appellant or appellants; and the use of the phrase "et al.," which literally means "and others," utterly failed to provide such notice to either intended recipient. Torres v. Oakland Scavenger Co., 487 U.S. 312, 108 S. Ct. 2405, 101 L. Ed. 2d 285 (1988).

Court had no jurisdiction over party omitted in notice of appeal. — Where notice of appeal omitted petitioner's name, petitioner failed to comply with the specificity requirement of this rule, even liberally construed; petitioner did not file the functional equivalent of a notice of appeal, he was never named or otherwise designated, however inartfully, in the notice of appeal filed by the fifteen other intervenors, and Nor did petitioner seek leave to amend the notice of appeal within the time limits set by FRAP Rule 4, thus, the Supreme Court was correct that it never had jurisdiction over petitioner's appeal. Torres v. Oakland Scavenger Co., 487 U.S. 312, 108 S. Ct. 2405, 101 L. Ed. 2d 285 (1988).

"Harmless error" analysis not applicable to notice of appeal defects. — Where petitioner argued that courts of appeals should have applied "harmless error" analysis to defects in a notice of appeal, this argument misunderstood the nature of a jurisdictional

requirement: litigant's failure to clear a jurisdictional hurdle can never be "harmless" or
waived by a court. Torres v. Oakland Scavenger Co., 487 U.S. 312, 108 S. Ct. 2405, 101 L.
Ed. 2d 285 (1988).

Local Rule 3(a). Filing and docket fees.

Upon filing a notice of appeal appellant shall pay the clerk of the district court a fee of $105.00, which includes a $5.00 filing fee for the notice of appeal, and a $100.00 fee for docketing the appeal in this Court.

Local Rule 3(b). Docketing statement.

To assist counsel in giving prompt attention to the substance of an appeal, to help reduce the ordering of unnecessary transcripts, to provide the Clerk of the Court of Appeals at the commencement of an appeal with the information needed for effective case management, and to provide necessary information for any mediation conference conducted under Local Rule 33, counsel filing a notice of appeal for any direct or cross-appeal must complete and file a docketing statement, using the form provided by the clerk of the district court. The Clerk of the Court of Appeals will provide a similar form for petitions for review, applications for enforcement, and Tax Court appeals.

Two copies of the docketing statement and attachments must be received and filed in the Court of Appeals within 14 days of filing the notice of appeal, with a copy served on the opposing party or parties. Docketing statements for petitions for review, applications for enforcement, and Tax Court appeals must be received and filed with the Clerk of the Court of Appeals within 14 days of docketing of the petition, application, or tax appeal. A copy of the docketing statement must be served on the opposing party or parties.

Each copy of the docketing statement served or filed shall have attached to it copies of:
(a) the notice of appeal, application for enforcement, or petition for review;
(b) the docket sheet of the court or agency from which the appeal is taken;
(c) the judgment or order sought to be reviewed and any opinion or findings;
(d) any opinion, findings, or recommendation of a magistrate judge, an administrative law judge, a Social Security Appeals Council, or a bankruptcy court underlying the order at issue; and
(e) any transcript order.

Although a party will not be precluded from raising additional issues, counsel will make every effort to include in the docketing statement all of the issues that will be presented to the Court. Failure to file the docketing statement within the time set forth above will cause the Court to initiate the process for dismissing a case under Local Rule 45.

If an opposing party concludes that the docketing statement is in any way inaccurate, incomplete, or misleading, the Clerk's Office should be informed in writing of any errors and any proposed additions or corrections within 7 days of service of the docketing statement, with copies to all other parties. (Amended by order effective September 28, 1994; and by order effective December 1, 1995.)

COMMENT

Proposed Local Rule 3(b) changes the "each party" requirement of existing I.O.P. 3.2 to "counsel" to reflect this Court's practice of not requiring docketing statements from parties proceedings pro se.

Rule 3.1. Appeal from a judgment of a magistrate judge in a civil case.

[Abrogated by order adopted April 24, 1998, effective December 1, 1998.]

Editor's note. — Rule 3.1, which was adopted effective July 1, 1986; and amended by order adopted April 22, 1993, effective December 1, 1993, was abrogated by order adopted April 24, 1998, effective December 1, 1998.

I.O.P. 3.1. Transmission of district court order.

The clerk of the district court shall transmit to the Clerk of the Court of Appeals a copy of the order appealed from, along with copies of the materials required by FRAP 3(d)(1). (Amended effective December 1, 1998.)

Rule 4. Appeal as of right — When taken.

(a) *Appeal in a civil case.* (1) Time for filing a notice of appeal. (A) In a civil case, except as provided in Rules 4(a)(1)(B), 4(a)(4), and 4(c), the notice of appeal required by Rule 3 must be filed with the district clerk within 30 days after the judgment or order appealed from is entered.

(B) When the United States or its officer or agency is a party, the notice of appeal may be filed by any party within 60 days after the judgment or order appealed from is entered.

(2) Filing before entry of judgment. A notice of appeal filed after the court announces a decision or order — but before the entry of the judgment or order — is treated as filed on the date of and after the entry.

(3) Multiple appeals. If one party timely files a notice of appeal, any other party may file a notice of appeal within 14 days after the date when the first notice was filed, or within the time otherwise prescribed by this Rule 4(a), whichever period ends later.

(4) Effect of a motion on a notice of appeal. (A) If a party timely files in the district court any of the following motions under the Federal Rules of Civil Procedure, the time to file an appeal runs for all parties from the entry of the order disposing of the last such remaining motion:

(i) for judgment under Rule 50(b);

(ii) to amend or make additional factual findings under Rule 52(b), whether or not granting the motion would alter the judgment;

(iii) for attorney's fees under Rule 54 if the district court extends the time to appeal under Rule 58;

(iv) to alter or amend the judgment under Rule 59;

(v) for a new trial under Rule 59; or

(vi) for relief under Rule 60 if the motion is filed no later than 10 days (computed using Federal Rule of Civil Procedure 6(a)) after the judgment is entered.

(B)(i) If a party files a notice of appeal after the court announces or enters a judgment — but before it disposes of any motion listed in Rule 4(a)(4)(A) —

the notice becomes effective to appeal a judgment or order, in whole or in part, when the order disposing of the last such remaining motion is entered.

(ii) A party intending to challenge an order disposing of any motion listed in Rule 4(a)(4)(A), or a judgment altered or amended upon such a motion, must file a notice of appeal, or an amended notice of appeal — in compliance with Rule 3(c) — within the time prescribed by this Rule measured from the entry of the order disposing of the last such remaining motion.

(iii) No additional fee is required to file an amended notice.

(5) Motion for extension of time. (A) The district court may extend the time to file a notice of appeal if:

(i) a party so moves no later than 30 days after the time prescribed by this Rule 4(a) expires; and

(ii) that party shows excusable neglect or good cause.

(B) A motion filed before the expiration of the time prescribed in Rule 4(a)(1) or (3) may be *ex parte* unless the court requires otherwise. If the motion is filed after the expiration of the prescribed time, notice must be given to the other parties in accordance with local rules.

(C) No extension under this Rule 4(a)(5) may exceed 30 days after the prescribed time or 10 days after the date when the order granting the motion is entered, whichever is later.

(6) Reopening the time to file an appeal. The district court may reopen the time to file an appeal for a period of 14 days after the date when its order to reopen is entered, but only if all the following conditions are satisfied:

(A) the motion is filed within 180 days after the judgment or order is entered or within 7 days after the moving party receives notice of the entry, whichever is earlier;

(B) the court finds that the moving party was entitled to notice of the entry of the judgment or order sought to be appealed but did not receive the notice from the district court or any party within 21 days after entry; and

(C) the court finds that no party would be prejudiced.

(7) Entry defined. A judgment or order is entered for purposes of this Rule 4(a) when it is entered in compliance with Rules 58 and 79(a) of the Federal Rules of Civil Procedure.

(b) *Appeal in a criminal case.* (1) Time for filing a notice of appeal. (A) In a criminal case, a defendant's notice of appeal must be filed in the district court within 10 days after the later of:

(i) the entry of either the judgment or the order being appealed; or

(ii) the filing of the government's notice of appeal.

(B) When the government is entitled to appeal, its notice of appeal must be filed in the district court within 30 days after the later of:

(i) the entry of the judgment or order being appealed; or

(ii) the filing of a notice of appeal by any defendant.

(2) Filing before entry of judgment. A notice of appeal filed after the court announces a decision, sentence, or order — but before the entry of the judgment or order — is treated as filed on the date of and after the entry.

(3) Effect of a motion on a notice of appeal. (A) If a defendant timely makes any of the following motions under the Federal Rules of Criminal Procedure,

the notice of appeal from a judgment of conviction must be filed within 10 days after the entry of the order disposing of the last such remaining motion, or within 10 days after the entry of the judgment of conviction, whichever period ends later. This provision applies to a timely motion:

(i) for judgment of acquittal under Rule 29;

(ii) for a new trial under Rule 33, but if based on newly discovered evidence, only if the motion is made no later than 10 days after the entry of the judgment; or

(iii) for arrest of judgment under Rule 34.

(B) A notice of appeal filed after the court announces a decision, sentence, or order — but before it disposes of any of the motions referred to in Rule 4(b)(3)(A) — becomes effective upon the later of the following:

(i) the entry of the order disposing of the last such remaining motion; or

(ii) the entry of the judgment of conviction.

(C) A valid notice of appeal is effective — without amendment — to appeal from an order disposing of any of the motions referred to in Rule 4(b)(3)(A).

(4) Motion for extension of time. Upon a finding of excusable neglect or good cause, the district court may — before or after the time has expired, with or without motion and notice — extend the time to file a notice of appeal for a period not to exceed 30 days from the expiration of the time otherwise prescribed by this Rule 4(b).

(5) Jurisdiction. The filing of a notice of appeal under this Rule 4(b) does not divest a district court of jurisdiction to correct a sentence under Federal Rule of Criminal Procedure 35(c), nor does the filing of a motion under 35(c) affect the validity of a notice of appeal filed before the entry of the order disposing of the motion.

(6) Entry defined. A judgment or order is entered for purposes of this Rule 4(b) when it is entered on the criminal docket.

(c) *Appeal by an inmate confined in an institution.* (1) If an inmate confined in an institution files a notice of appeal in either a civil or a criminal case, the notice is timely if it is deposited in the institution's internal mail system on or before the last day for filing. If an institution has a system designed for legal mail, the inmate must use that system to receive the benefit of this rule. Timely filing may be shown by a declaration in compliance with 28 U.S.C. § 1746 or by a notarized statement, either of which must set forth the date of deposit and state that first-class postage has been prepaid.

(2) If an inmate files the first notice of appeal in a civil case under this Rule 4(c), the 14-day period provided in Rule 4(a)(3) for another party to file a notice of appeal runs from the date when the district court dockets the first notice.

(3) When a defendant in a criminal case files a notice of appeal under this Rule 4(c), the 30-day period for the government to file its notice of appeal runs from the entry of the judgment or order appealed from or from the district court's docketing of the defendant's notice of appeal, whichever is later.

(d) *Mistaken filing in the court of appeals.* If a notice of appeal in either a civil or a criminal case is mistakenly filed in the court of appeals, the clerk of that court must note on the notice the date when it was received and send it to the district clerk. The notice is then considered filed in the district court on the date so noted. (Amended by order adopted April 30, 1979, effective August 1, 1979; by P.L. 100-690, § 7111, signed November 18, 1988; by order adopted April 30, 1991, effective December 1, 1991; by order adopted April 22, 1993, effective December1, 1993; by order adopted April 27, 1995, effective December 1, 1995; and by order adopted April 24, 1998, effective December 1, 1998.)

Broad construction favored. — In general, courts have construed Rule 4(a)(1) broadly. Buonocore v. Harris, 65 F.3d 347 (4th Cir. 1995).

Subdivision (b) considered mandatory and jurisdictional. — In the absence of extraordinary circumstances, subdivision (b) of this rule is considered mandatory and jurisdictional. Morin v. United States, 522 F.2d 8 (4th Cir. 1975).

Compliance with subdivision (b) is mandatory and jurisdictional. United States v. Schuchardt, 685 F.2d 901 (4th Cir. 1982).

Notice of appeal in a civil suit must be filed within thirty days of the entry of judgment. This limitation is mandatory and jurisdictional. Thompson v. E.I. DuPont de Nemours & Co., 76 F.3d 530 (4th Cir. 1996).

Court may not waive jurisdictional requirements if they are not met. — Although a court may construe the rules liberally in determining whether they have been complied with, it may not waive the jurisdictional requirements of FRAP Rule 3 and this rule, even for "good cause shown" under FRAP Rule 2, if it finds that they have not been met. Torres v. Oakland Scavenger Co., 487 U.S. 312, 108 S. Ct. 2405, 101 L. Ed. 2d 285 (1988).

Where the United States is a "party," the 60-day period in which to appeal applies to all parties to the case, not just the United States. Buonocore v. Harris, 65 F.3d 347 (4th Cir. 1995).

Order granting motion to quash subpoenas was criminal proceeding. — In an appeal where the district court granted movant's motion to quash subpoenas issued by two grand juries with respect to certain papers in its possession, and where the effect of the district court's order was that movant's subsidiary had to turn over all of the papers in its possession to the grand jury, proceeding was criminal rather than civil so that subdivision (b) applied to the proceeding rather than subdivision (a). United States v. Under Seal, 902 F.2d 244 (4th Cir. 1990).

Entry of judgment for purposes of notice of appeal. — A notice of appeal must be filed within thirty days of entry of judgment. Entry of judgment consists of two steps: Creation of a document setting out the judgment and a notation of the document on the docket sheet. The thirty-day period does not begin to run until after the document is entered on the docket sheet. Wilson v. Murray, 806 F.2d 1232

(4th Cir. 1986), cert. denied, 484 U.S. 870, 108 S. Ct. 197, 98 L. Ed. 2d 149 (1987).

Pro se prisoners' notices of appeal are deemed filed with the district court when delivered to prison authorities for forwarding and filing. Wilder v. Chairman of Cent. Classification Bd., 926 F.2d 367 (4th Cir.), cert. denied, 926 U.S. 367, 112 S. Ct. 109, 116 L. Ed. 2d 78 (1991).

A bare notice of appeal cannot be construed as a motion for extension of time under subdivision (a)(5). Wilder v. Chairman of Cent. Classification Bd., 926 F.2d 367 (4th Cir.), cert. denied, 926 U.S. 367, 112 S. Ct. 109, 116 L. Ed. 2d 78 (1991).

Extension of filing period under subdivisions (a) and (b) compared. — Unlike subdivision (a), the language of subdivision (b) empowers the district court to extend the filing period with or without motion. United States v. Reyes, 759 F.2d 351 (4th Cir.), cert. denied, 474 U.S. 857, 106 S. Ct. 164, 88 L. Ed. 2d 136 (1985).

Opportunity to show excusable neglect for late filing. — A criminal defendant who has filed his notice of appeal beyond the time specified in subdivision (b), but within the thirty-day permissible extension period, should have the opportunity to seek relief by showing excusable neglect. United States v. Reyes, 759 F.2d 351 (4th Cir.), cert. denied, 474 U.S. 857, 106 S. Ct. 164, 88 L. Ed. 2d 136 (1985).

Move to vacate temporary restraining order qualifies as motion "to alter or amend judgment." — The plaintiff's contention that the notice of appeal, filed February 14, 1975, was filed more than thirty days after entry of the temporary restraining order (TRO) on December 31, 1974, overlooked the fact that defendants moved to vacate the TRO on January 6, 1975, which qualifies as a motion "to alter or amend judgment" within the meaning of Rule 59, Federal Rules of Civil Procedure. By the terms of Rule 4(a), Federal Rules of Appellate Procedure, the "full time for appeal (thirty days) ... commences to run and is to be computed from the entry of (the) ... (order) granting or denying a motion under Rule 59 to alter or amend the judgment ...." January 20, 1975, was thus the date that the appeal period of thirty days began to run, and February 14, 1975, was within the period. Virginia v. Tenneco, Inc., 538 F.2d 1026 (4th Cir. 1976).

Court of appeals lacks jurisdiction where notice not given in time. — By virtue of subdivision (b) a court of appeals does not have jurisdiction to treat the issues sought to be raised on appeal where notice of appeal was not given within ten days after entry of the judgment, the time was not otherwise extended by order of the district court, and the subsequent motion for a new trial based on newly discovered evidence was not made before or within ten days after entry of the judgment. United States v. Williams, 415 F.2d 232 (4th Cir. 1969).

But belated appeal may be allowed where defendant is prevented from complying. — The original ten-day appeal period prescribed by the federal rules of court as to filing the notice of appeal in criminal cases is jurisdictional. But if a defendant attempted to exercise his right to appeal within the ten-day period specified by the rules and, without fault on his part, was prevented from effective communication with the clerk or the district judge, the defendant may be allowed a belated appeal. United States v. Meyers, 406 F.2d 1015 (4th Cir. 1969) (construing former Fed. R. Crim. P. 37(a)).

And court may extend ten-day period on showing of "excusable neglect." — Subdivision (b) permits a district court upon a showing of "excusable neglect" before or after the expiration of the ten-day appeal time to extend the time for filing a notice of appeal for an additional thirty days. United States v. Meyers, 406 F.2d 1015 (4th Cir. 1969).

A non-prisoner litigant who entrusts his filing with the postal processes, without taking further steps to ensure that the notice of appeal is timely filed with the district court, cannot establish excusable neglect. Thompson v. E.I. DuPont de Nemours & Co., 76 F.3d 530 (4th Cir. 1996).

The good cause standard is only applicable to motions for enlargement of time filed within thirty days of entry of judgment. Thompson v. E.I. DuPont de Nemours & Co., 76 F.3d 530 (4th Cir. 1996).

Notice to pro se litigant of right to extension. — When a pro se litigant files a notice of appeal that is untimely but within the period during which an extension of time might be granted pursuant to this rule, the litigant must be informed of the rule and provided an opportunity to establish excusable neglect. Shah v. Hutto, 704 F.2d 717 (4th Cir. 1983), cert. denied, 466 U.S. 975, 104 S. Ct. 2354, 80 L. Ed. 2d 827 (1984).

District court has no jurisdiction to reconsider and vacate an order of that court which has become final in a criminal case because of the expiration of the time to appeal. United States v. Breit, 754 F.2d 526 (4th Cir. 1985).

Correction of error as to matter not dealt with below. — Without filing a cross-appeal, an appellee may not attack the decree with a view either to enlarging his own rights thereunder or of lessening the rights of his adversary, where what he seeks is to correct an error or to supplement the decree with respect to a matter not dealt with below. Thurston v. United States, 810 F.2d 438 (4th Cir. 1987).

Applied in United States v. Bodden, 736 F.2d 142 (4th Cir. 1984).

Rule 5. Appeal by permission.

(a) *Petition for permission to appeal.* (1) To request permission to appeal when an appeal is within the court of appeals' discretion, a party must file a petition for permission to appeal. The petition must be filed with the circuit clerk with proof of service on all other parties to the district-court action.

(2) The petition must be filed within the time specified by the statute or rule authorizing the appeal or, if no such time is specified, within the time provided by Rule 4(a) for filing a notice of appeal.

(3) If a party cannot petition for appeal unless the district court first enters an order granting permission to do so or stating that the necessary conditions are met, the district court may amend its order, either on its own or in response to a party's motion, to include the required permission or statement. In that event, the time to petition runs from entry of the amended order.

(b) *Contents of the petition; answer or cross-petition; oral argument.* (1) The petition must include the following:

(A) the facts necessary to understand the question presented;

(B) the question itself;

(C) the relief sought;

(D) the reasons why the appeal should be allowed and is authorized by a statute or rule; and

(E) an attached copy of:

(i) the order, decree, or judgment complained of and any related opinion or memorandum, and

(E)(ii) any order stating the district court's permission to appeal or finding that the necessary conditions are met.

(2) A party may file an answer in opposition or a cross-petition within 7 days after the petition is served.

(3) The petition and answer will be submitted without oral argument unless the court of appeals orders otherwise.

(c) *Form of papers; number of copies.* All papers must conform to Rule 32(a)(1). An original and 3 copies must be filed unless the court requires a different number by local rule or by order in a particular case.

(d) *Grant of permission; fees; cost bond; filing the record.* (1) Within 10 days after the entry of an order granting permission to appeal, the appellant must:

(A) pay the district clerk all required fees; and

(B) file a cost bond if required under Rule 7.

(2) A notice of appeal need not be filed. The date when the order granting permission to appeal is entered serves as the date of the notice of appeal for calculating time under these rules.

(3) The district clerk must notify the circuit clerk once the petitioner has paid the fees. Upon receiving this notice, the circuit clerk must enter the appeal on the docket. The record must be forwarded and filed in accordance with Rules 11 and 12(c). (Amended by order adopted April 30, 1979, effective August 1, 1979; by order adopted April 29, 1994, effective December 1, 1994; and by order adopted April 24, 1998, effective December 1, 1998.)

Applied in Peanut Corp. of Am. v. Hollywood Brands, Inc., 696 F.2d 311 (4th Cir. 1982); City of Va. Beach v. Roanoke River Basin Ass'n, 776 F.2d 484 (4th Cir. 1985).

Local Rule 5. Interlocutory orders.

The Court of Appeals will initially enter a petition for permission to appeal upon the miscellaneous docket; a docket fee shall not be required unless the petition is granted. A Disclosure of Corporate Affiliations and Other Entities with a Direct Financial Interest in Litigation statement must be filed with the petition and answer. See FRAP 26.1, Local Rule 26.1 and Form A. Upon granting the petition, the Court of Appeals will notify the district court by copy of the order and transfer the case to the regular docket.

Rule 5.1. Appeal by leave under 28 U.S.C. § 636(c)(5).

[Abrogated.]

Editor's note. — Rule 5.1 which was adopted March 10, 1986, effective July 1, 1986; amended by order adopted April 22, 1993, effective December 1, 1993; and by order adopted April 29, 1994, effective December 1, 1994 was abrogated by order adopted April 24, 1998, effective December 1, 1998.

Rule 6. Appeal in a bankruptcy case from a final judgment, order, or decree of a district court or of a bankruptcy appellate panel.

(a) *Appeal from a judgment, order or decree of a district court exercising original jurisdiction in a bankruptcy case.* An appeal to a court of appeals from a final judgment, order or decree of a district court exercising jurisdiction under 28 U.S.C. § 1334 is taken as any other civil appeal under these rules.

(b) *Appeal from a judgment, order or decree of a district court or bankruptcy appellate panel exercising appellate jurisdiction in a bankruptcy case.* (1) Applicability of other rules. These rules apply to an appeal to a court of appeals under 28 U.S.C. § 158(d) from a final judgment, order or decree of a district court or bankruptcy appellate panel exercising appellate jurisdiction under 28 U.S.C. § 158(a) or (b). But there are 3 exceptions:

(A) Rules 4(a)(4), 4(b), 9, 10, 11, 12(b), 13-20, 22-23, and 24(b) do not apply;

(B) the reference in Rule 3(c) to "Form 1 in the Appendix of Forms" must be read as a reference to Form 5; and

(C) when the appeal is from a bankruptcy appellate panel, the term "district court" as used in any applicable rule means "appellate panel".

(2) Additional rules. In addition to the rules made applicable by Rule 6(b)(1), the following rules apply:

(A) Motion for rehearing. (i) If a timely motion for rehearing under Bankruptcy Rule 8015 is filed, the time to appeal for all parties runs from the entry of the order disposing of the motion. A notice of appeal filed after the district court or bankruptcy appellate panel announces or enters a judgment, order, or decree — but before disposition of the motion for rehearing — becomes effective when the order disposing of the motion for rehearing is entered.

(ii) Appellate review of the order disposing of the motion requires the party, in compliance with Rules 3(c) and 6(b)(1)(B), to amend a previously filed notice of appeal. A party intending to challenge an altered or amended judgment, order, or decree must file a notice of appeal or amended notice of appeal within the time prescribed by Rule 4 — excluding Rules 4(a)(4) and 4(b) — measured from the entry of the order disposing of the motion.

(iii) No additional fee is required to file an amended notice.

(B) The record on appeal. (i) Within 10 days after filing the notice of appeal, the appellant must file with the clerk possessing the record assembled in accordance with Bankruptcy Rule 8006 — and serve on the appellee — a statement of the issues to be presented on appeal and a designation of the record to be certified and sent to the circuit clerk.

(ii) An appellee who believes that other parts of the record are necessary must, within 10 days after being served with the appellant's designation, file with the clerk and serve on the appellant a designation of additional parts to be included.

(iii) The record on appeal consists of:

• the redesignated record as provided above;

• the proceedings in the district court or bankruptcy appellate panel; and

• a certified copy of the docket entries prepared by the clerk under Rule 3(d).

(C) Forwarding the record. (i) When the record is complete, the district clerk or bankruptcy appellate panel clerk must number the documents constituting the record and send them promptly to the circuit clerk together with a list of the documents correspondingly numbered and reasonably identified. Unless directed to do so by a party or the circuit clerk, the clerk will not send to the court of appeals documents of unusual bulk or weight, physical exhibits other than documents, or other parts of the record designated for omission by local rule of the court of appeals. If the exhibits are unusually bulky or heavy, a party must arrange with the clerks in advance for their transportation and receipt.

(ii) All parties must do whatever else is necessary to enable the clerk to assemble and forward the record. The court of appeals may provided by rule or order that a certified copy of the docket entries be sent in place of the redesignated record, but any party may request at any time during the pendency of the appeal that the redesignated record be sent.

(D) Filing the record. (D) Upon receiving the record — or a certified copy of the docket entries sent in place of the redesignated record — the circuit clerk must file it and immediately notify all parties of the filing date. (Amended by order adopted April 30, 1979, effective August 1, 1979; by order adopted April 25, 1989, effective December 1, 1989; by order adopted April 30, 1991, effective December 1,1991; by order adopted April 22, 1993, effective December 1, 1993; and by order adopted April 24, 1998, effective December 1 1998.)

I.O.P. 6.1. Bankruptcy appeals.

The Fourth Circuit has not established panels of three bankruptcy judges to hear appeals from bankruptcy courts pursuant to 28 U.S.C. § 158.

Rule 7. Bond for costs on appeal in a civil case.

In a civil case, the district court may require an appellant to file a bond or provide other security in any form and amount necessary to ensure payment of costs on appeal. Rule 8(b) appiles to a surety on a bond given under this rule. (Amended by order adopted April 30, 1979, effective August 1, 1979; and by order adopted April 24, 1998, effective December 1, 1998.)

Rule 8. Stay or injunction pending appeal.

(a) *Motion for stay.* (1) Initial motion in the district court. A party must ordinarily move first in the district court for the following relief:

(A) a stay of the judgment or order of a district court pending appeal;

(B) approval of a supersedeas bond; or

(C) an order suspending, modifying, restoring, or granting an injunction while an appeal is pending.

(2) Motion in the Court of Appeals; conditions on relief. A motion for the relief mentioned in Rule 8(a)(1) may be made to the court of appeals or to one of its judges.

(A) The motion must:

(i) show that moving first in the district court would be impracticable; or

(ii) state that, a motion having been made, the district court denied the motion or failed to afford the relief requested and state any reasons given by the district court for its action.

(B) The motion must also include:

(i) the reasons for granting the relief requested and the facts relied on;

(ii) originals or copies of affidavits or other sworn statements supporting facts subject to dispute; and

(iii) relevant parts of the record.

(C) The moving party must give reasonable notice of the motion to all parties.

(D) A motion under this Rule 8(a)(2) must be filed with the circuit clerk and normally will be considered by a panel of the court. But in an exceptional case in which time requirements make that procedure impracticable, the motion may be made to and considered by a single judge.

(E) The court may condition relief on a party's filing a bond or other appropriate security in the district court.

(b) *Proceeding against a surety.* If a party gives security in the form of a bond or stipulation or other undertaking with one or more sureties, each surety submits to the jurisdiction of the district court and irrevocably appoints the district clerk as the surety's agent on whom any papers affecting the surety's liability on the bond or undertaking may be served. On motion, a surety's liability may be enforced in the district court without the necessity of an independent action. The motion and any notice that the district court prescribes may be served on the district clerk, who must promptly mail a copy to each surety whose address is known.

(c) *Stay in a criminal case.* Rule 38 of the Federal Rules of Criminal Procedure governs a stay in a criminal case. (Amended by order adopted March 10, 1986, effective July 1, 1986; by order adopted April 27, 1995, effective December 1, 1995; and by order adopted April 24, 1998, effective December 1, 1998.)

Applied in City of Alexandria v. Helms, 719 F.2d 699 (4th Cir. 1983); Morris v. City of Danville, 744 F.2d 1041 (4th Cir. 1984); Kennedy v. Block, 784 F.2d 1220 (4th Cir. 1986).

Local Rule 8. Stay or injunction pending appeal.

Filing a notice of appeal does not automatically stay the operation of the judgment, order or decision for which review is sought. If an application to the district court for temporary relief pending appeal is not practicable, counsel must make a specific showing of the reasons the application was not made to the district court in the first instance. Any motion to the Court of Appeals should include copies of all previous applications for relief and their outcome. A Disclosure of Corporate Affiliations and Other Entities with a Direct Financial Interest in Litigation statement must accompany the motion and any response unless the parties have previously filed disclosure statements with the Court in the case. See FRAP 26.1, Local Rule 26.1, and Form A. If any party deems that parts of the record or other materials are essential to a fair presentation of the issues regarding a motion, copies of these papers must be attached to each copy of the motion. The motion will usually be considered by a panel of the Court. If time is of the essence, a single judge who should ordinarily be resident in the state of the trial court proceeding may determine the motion or grant temporary relief until the matter can be considered by the Court. The selection of motion panels is similar to the process set forth in I.O.P. 34.1 for hearing panels. An order granting a stay or injunction pending appeal remains in effect until issuance of the mandate or further order of the Court and may be conditioned upon the filing of a supersedeas bond in the district court.

Rule 9. Release in a criminal case.

(a) *Release before judgment of conviction.* (1) The district court must state in writing, or orally on the record, the reasons for an order regarding release or detention of a defendant in a criminal case. A party appealing from the order must file with the court of appeals a copy of the district court's order and the court's statement of reasons as soon as practicable after filing the notice of appeal. An appellant who questions the factual basis for the district court's order must file a transcript of the release proceedings or an explanation of why a transcript was not obtained.

(2) After reasonable notice to the appellee, the court of appeals must promptly determine the appeal on the basis of the papers, affidavits, and parts of the record that the parties present or the court requires. Unless the court so orders, briefs need not be filed.

(3) The court of appeals or one of its judges may order the defendant's release pending the disposition of the appeal.

(b) *Release after judgment of conviction.* A party entitled to do so may obtain review of a district-court order regarding release after a judgment of conviction by filing a notice of appeal from that order in the district court, or by filing a motion in the court of appeals if the party has already filed a notice of appeal from the judgment of conviction. Both the order and the review are subject to Rule 9(a). The papers filed by the party seeking review must include a copy of the judgment of conviction.

(c) *Criteria for release.* The court release must make its decision regarding release in accordance with the applicable provisions of 18 U.S.C. §§ 3142, 3143, and 3145(c). (Amended by order adopted April 24, 1972, effective October 1, 1972; by order effective October 12, 1984; by order adopted April 29, 1994, effective December 1, 1994; and by order adopted April 24, 1998, effective December 1, 1998.)

Local Rule 9(a). Release prior to judgment of conviction.

A criminal defendant may be released in accordance with the conditions set by the district court prior to judgment of conviction. If the district court refuses to release the prisoner, or sets conditions for release that cannot be met, the order is appealable as a matter of right and will be given prompt consideration by the Court of Appeals. Counsel should submit memoranda in support of their position on appeal and, in cases involving corporate defendants, Disclosure of Corporate Affiliations and Other Entities with a Direct Financial Interest in Litigation statements required by FRAP 26.1 and Local Rule 26.1 and Form A. The appeal is usually decided without oral argument upon the materials presented by the parties. A motion for release pending determination of the appeal may be filed. The motion may be acted upon by a single judge, but the appeal itself must be submitted to a three-judge panel for decision.

Local Rule 9(b). Release after conviction and notice of appeal.

After the district court has ruled on a motion for bail or reduction of bail pending appeal, the appellant may renew the motion for release, or for a modification of the conditions of release, before the Court of Appeals without noting an additional appeal. A copy of the district court statement of reasons should accompany the motion. The motion will be submitted to a three-judge panel for decision.

Local Rule 9(c). Recalcitrant witnesses.

When an appeal arises from the incarceration of a witness who refuses to testify or produce evidence in any court or grand jury proceeding, the Court of Appeals is required by statute, 28 U.S.C. § 1826, to decide the appeal within 30 days of the filing of the notice of appeal. Therefore, counsel should immediately contact the Clerk's Office regarding all such witness contempt matters so that the appeal may be expedited for resolution within the statutory guidelines.

Rule 10. The record on appeal.

(a) *Composition of the record on appeal.* The following items constitute the record on appeal:

(1) the original papers and exhibits filed in the district court;

(2) the transcript of proceedings, if any; and

(3) a certified copy of the docket entries prepared by the district clerk.

(b) *The transcript of proceedings.* (1) Appellant's duty to order. (1) Within 10 days after filing the notice of appeal or entry of an order disposing of the last timely remaining motion of a type specified in Rule 4(a)(4)(A), whichever is later, the appellant must do either of the following:

(A) order from the reporter a transcript of such parts of the proceedings not already on file as the appellant considers necessary, subject to a local rule of the court of appeals and with the following qualifications:

(A)(i) the order must be in writing;

(ii) if the cost of the transcript is to be paid by the United States under the Criminal Justice Act, the order must so state; and

(iii) the appellant must, within the same period, file a copy of the order with the district clerk; or

(B) file a certificate stating that no transcript will be ordered.

(2) Unsupported finding or conclusion. If the appellant intends to urge on appeal that a finding or conclusion is unsupported by the evidence or is contrary to the evidence, the appellant must include in the record a transcript of all evidence relevant to that finding or conclusion.

(3) Partial transcript. Unless the entire transcript is ordered:

(A) the appellant must — within the 10 days provided in Rule 10(b)(1) — file a statement of the issues that the appellant intends to present on the appeal and must serve on the appellee a copy of both the order or certificate and the statement;

(B) if the appellee considers it necessary to have a transcript of other parts of the proceedings, the appellee must, within 10 days after the service of the order or certificate and the statement of the issues, file and serve on the appellant a designation of additional parts to be ordered; and

(3) unless within 10 days after service of that designation the appellant has ordered all such parts, and has so notified the appellee, the appellee may within the following 10 days either order the parts or move in the district court for an order requiring the appellant to do so.

(4) *Payment.* At the time of ordering, a party must make satisfactory arrangements with the reporter for paying the cost of the transcript.

(c) *Statement of the evidence when the proceedings were not recorded or when a transcript is unavailable.* If the transcript of a hearing or trial is unavailable, the appellant may prepare a statement of the evidence or proceedings from the best available means, including the appellant's recollection. The statement must be served on the appellee, who may serve objections or proposed amendments within 10 days after being served. The statement and any objections or proposed amendments must then be submitted to the district court for settlement and approval. As settled and approved, the statement must be included by the district clerk in the record on appeal.

(d) *Agreed statement as the record on appeal.* In place of the record on appeal as defined in Rule 10(a), the parties may prepare, sign, and submit to the district court a statement of the case showing how the issues presented by the appeal arose and were decided in the district court. The statement must set forth only those facts averred and proved or sought to be proved that are essential to the court's resolution of the issues. If the statement is truthful, it —together with any additions that the district court may consider necessary to a full presentation of the issues on appeal — must be approved by the district court and must then be certified to the court of appeals as the record on appeal. The district clerk must then send it to the circuit clerk within the time provided by Rule 11. A copy of the agreed statement may be filed in place of the appendix required by Rule 30.

(e) *Correction or modification of the record.* (1) If any difference arises about whether the record truly discloses what occurred in the district court, the difference shall be submitted to and settled by that court and the record conformed accordingly.

(2) If anything material to either party is omitted from or misstated in the record by error or accident, the omission or misstatement may be corrected and a supplemental record may be certified and forwarded:

(A) on stipulation of the parties;

(B) by the district court before or after the record has been forwarded; or

(C) by the court of appeals.

(3) All other questions as to the form and content of the record must be presented to the court of appeals. (Amended by order adopted April 30, 1979, effective August 1, 1979; by order adopted March 10, 1986, effective July 1, 1986; by order adopted April 30, 1991, effective December 1, 1991; by order adopted April 22, 1993, effective December 1, 1993; by order adopted April 27, 1995, effective December 1, 1995; and by order adopted April 24, 1998, effective December 1, 1998.)

Subdivision (e) of this rule vests authority in the district court to conform the record to what occurred in the district court either by supplying what has been omitted or correcting what has been erroneously transcribed. This power exists before or after the record is transmitted to the court of appeals, and the court of appeals on its own initiative may direct, inter alia, that any omission from the record be supplied. United States v. Greenwell, 418 F.2d 845 (4th Cir. 1969).

District judge directed to certify statement regarding security measures used at criminal trial. — See United States v. Greenwell, 418 F.2d 845 (4th Cir. 1969).

Applied in Mullins Coal Co. v. Clark, 759 F.2d 1142 (4th Cir. 1985).

Local Rule 10(a). Retention of the record on appeal in the district court.

In cases in which all parties are represented by counsel on appeal, the district court clerk will transmit a certificate to the Clerk of the Court of Appeals as soon as the record on appeal is complete. The certificate will state that the record is complete and available to the Court of Appeals upon request. Receipt of the district court clerk's certificate will have the same effect as the receipt of the record on appeal. The district court will then retain the record on appeal until and unless a judge of this Court asks the Clerk of this Court to obtain it. Upon receipt of a request from the Clerk of the Court of Appeals, the clerk of the district court will assemble and transmit the record on appeal within 24 hours.

Local Rule 10(b). Records on appeal.

The preparation and transmittal of the record on appeal is the obligation of the clerk of the lower court, board or agency, and any questions concerning form or content should be addressed to the trial forum in the first instance. A record on appeal consists of a specific number of volumes of pleadings, transcripts, and exhibits. Parties should check with the clerk of the lower court, board or agency to determine whether everything relevant to the issues on appeal will be included initially in the record on appeal in order to obviate motions to supplement the record. The record is transmitted to the appellate court as soon as it is complete, except as provided in Local Rule 10(a). Local Rule 10(a) does not apply to records in cases in which one or more parties are proceeding without counsel on appeal.

Local Rule 10(c). Transcripts.

(1) *Responsibilities and designation.* The appellant has the duty of ordering transcript of all parts of the proceedings material to the issues to be raised on appeal whether favorable or unfavorable to appellant's position. Transcript Order forms are provided to appellant by the clerk of the district court at the time the notice of appeal is filed. Appellant should complete the form and distribute the appropriate parts of the form to the Clerk of the Court of Appeals, the court reporter, the clerk of the district court, and the appellee.

Before the transcript order is mailed, appellant must make appropriate financial arrangements with the court reporter for either immediate payment in full or in other form acceptable to the court reporter, payment pursuant to the Criminal Justice Act, or at government expense pursuant to 28 U.S.C. § 753(f).

In cross-appeals each party must order those parts of the transcript pertinent to the issues of such appeals. The parties are encouraged to agree upon those parts of the transcript jointly needed and to apportion the cost, with additional portions being ordered and paid for by the party considering them essential to that party's appeal.

If the entire transcript of proceedings is not to be prepared, the appellant's docketing statement filed pursuant to Local Rule 3(b) may constitute the statement of issues required by FRAP 10(b)(3)(A).

(2) *Monitoring and receipt by clerk.* Failure to order timely a transcript, failure to make satisfactory financial arrangements with the court reporter, or failure to specify in adequate detail those proceedings to be transcribed will subject the appeal to dismissal by the clerk for want of prosecution pursuant to Local Rule 45. The Clerk's Office is charged with monitoring the status of transcripts pending with court reporters.

(3) *Statement in lieu of transcript.* The parties may prepare and sign a statement of the case in lieu of the transcript or the entire record on appeal. The use of a statement in lieu of a transcript of a hearing substantially accelerates the appellate process. The statement should contain a description of the essential facts averred and proved or sought to be proved and a summary of pertinent testimony.

(4) *Guidelines for preparation of appellate transcripts in the Fourth Circuit.* An appendix to these rules contains the guidelines adopted by the Fourth Circuit Judicial Council to define the obligations of appellants, appellees, clerks of the district court, court reporters and the Clerk of the Court of Appeals in the ordering, preparation, and filing of transcripts completed pursuant to these rules.

Local Rule 10(d). Sealed records.

The Court of Appeals expects that motions to seal all or any part of the record will be presented to, and resolved by, the lower court or agency — in accordance with applicable law — during the course of trial, hearing, or other proceedings below. In the rare event that a change of circumstances occurs during the pendency of an appeal that warrants reconsideration of a sealing issue decided below, or initial consideration of the need to seal all or part of the record on appeal, an appropriate motion may be filed with the Clerk of the Court of Appeals. Such motions will be referred by the clerk to a panel of the Court.

Material contained in the record subject to a protective order remains subject to that order on appeal unless modified or amended by the Court of Appeals. Material subject to a protective order shall be available to counsel only if permitted by that order.

In any case involving sealed materials, at the time of filing a brief or appendix counsel shall file a separate certification as to whether a copy of, or excerpt from, any sealed document is included in the appendix, or argument relating to any sealed document is included in the brief. If the certification is affirmative, the appendix or brief will be sealed by order of this Court. Every effort shall be made by counsel to include such sealed material, and argument related thereto, in a supplement to the brief or appendix which can be sealed, thereby avoiding the need to seal the remainder of the brief or appendix.

Local Rule 10(e). Supplemental records, modification or correction.

Disputes concerning the accuracy or composition of the record on appeal should be resolved in the trial court in the first instance, although the Court of Appeals has the power, either on motion or of its own accord, to require that the record be corrected or supplemented. It is unnecessary to seek permission of the Court of Appeals to supplement the record and the record may be supplemented by the parties by stipulation or by order of the district court at any time during the appellate process.

Rule 11. Forwarding the record.

(a) *Appellant's duty.* An appellant filing a notice of appeal must comply with Rule 10(b) and must do whatever else is necessary to enable the clerk to assemble and forward the record. If there are multiple appeals from a judgment or order, the clerk must forward a single record.

(b) *Duties of reporter and district clerk.* (1) Reporter's duty to prepare and file a transcript. The reporter must prepare and file a transcript as follows:

(A) Upon receiving an order for a transcript, the reporter must enter at the foot of the order the date of its receipt and the expected completion date and send a copy, so endorsed, to the circuit clerk.

(B) If the transcript cannot be completed within 30 days of the reporter's receipt of the order, the reporter may request the circuit clerk to grant additional time to complete it. The clerk must note on the docket the action taken and notify the parties.

(C) When a transcript is complete, the reporter must file it with the district clerk and notify the circuit clerk of the filing.

(D) If the reporter fails to file the transcript on time, the circuit clerk must notify the district judge and do whatever else the court of appeals directs.

(2) District clerk's duty to forward. When the record is complete, the district clerk must number the documents constituting the record and send them promptly to the circuit clerk together with a list of the documents correspondingly numbered and reasonably identified. Unless directed to do so by a party or the circuit clerk, the district clerk will not send to the court of appeals documents of unusual bulk or weight, physical exhibits other than documents, or other parts of the record designated for omission by local rule of the court of appeals. If the exhibits are unusually bulky or heavy, a party must arrange with the clerks in advance for their transportation and receipt.

(c) *Retaining the record temporarily in the district court for use in preparing the appeal.* The parties may stipulate, or the district court on motion may order, that the district clerk retain the record temporarily for the parties to use in preparing the papers on appeal. In that event the district clerk must certify to the circuit clerk that the record on appeal is complete. Upon receipt of the appellee's brief, or earlier if the court orders or the parties agree, the appellant must request the district clerk to forward the record.

(d) [Abrogated by order adopted April 24, 1998, effective December 1, 1998.]

(e) *Retaining the record by court order.* (1) The court of appeals may, by order or local rule, provide that a certified copy of the docket entries be forwarded instead of the entire record. But a party may at any time during the appeal request that designated parts of the record be forwarded.

(2) The district court may order the record or some part of it retained if the court needs it while the appeal is pending, subject, however, to call by the court of appeals.

(3) If part or all of the record is ordered retained, the district clerk must send to the court of appeals a copy of the order and the docket entries together with the parts of the original record allowed by the district court and copies of any parts of the record designated by the parties.

(f) *Retaining parts of the record in the district court by stipulation of the parties.* The parties may agree by written stipulation filed in the district court that designated parts of the record be retained in the district court subject to call by the court of appeals or request by a party. The parts of the record so designated remain a part of the record on appeal.

(g) *Record for a preliminary motion in the court of appeals.* If, before the record is forwarded, a party makes any of the following motions in the court of appeals:

- for dismissal;
- for release;
- for a stay pending appeal;
- for additional security on the bond on appeal or on a supersedeas bond; or
- for any other intermediate order —

the district clerk must send the court of appeals any parts of the record designated by any party. (Amended by order adopted April 30, 1979, effective August 1, 1979; by order adopted March 10, 1986, effective July 1, 1986; and by order adopted April 24, 1998, effective December 1, 1998.)

Local Rule 11(a). Transcript acknowledgments.

Upon receipt of an order for a transcript, the Clerk of the Court of Appeals will prepare for the reporter a transcript order acknowledgment which will set forth the date the transcript order was received in the Clerk's Office and the transcript due date, computed from the order receipt date in accordance with the time limits set forth in the applicable district court reporter management plan. If the transcript order is correct in all respects, except for an order date error in the reporter's favor, no response will be required from the reporter. If the reporter believes that there is a problem with the transcript order, he or she must complete a copy of the acknowledgment form noting the problem and return it to the Court of Appeals within 7 days of receipt of the form by the reporter, or within such further time as the Court of Appeals allows. The time for completion of the transcript will automatically cease to run until the problem has been remedied. The Clerk of the Court of Appeals will send a new transcript order acknowledgment setting forth new transcript order and filing dates taking into account the delay caused by resolving the problem with the original transcript order.

Local Rule 11(b). Time limits for filing transcripts.

Although FRAP 11(b)(1)(B) requires that transcripts be completed within 30 days from the purchase order date, this Court routinely uses instead the time limits set forth in the district court reporter management plans. All of the plans establish a 60-day period for preparation of transcripts, with the following exceptions:

(1) Special provisions adopted by the Fourth Circuit Judicial Council for appeals by incarcerated criminal defendants.

(a) transcripts of 1000 pages or less shall be filed within 30 days of transcript order and completion of satisfactory financial arrangements.

(b) transcripts of more than 1000 pages shall be filed within the time ordered by the Clerk of the Court of Appeals.

(2) Special circumstances, such as

(a) bail appeals,

(b) death penalty cases, or

(c) other expedited procedures in which the transcript shall be filed within the time ordered by the Clerk of the Court of Appeals.

Local Rule 11(c). Exhibits.

Counsel should be aware that certain portions of the record will not be transmitted to the Court of Appeals as part of the record. If bulky documents and physical exhibits are required by a party for oral argument, the party must make advance arrangements with the clerks of both courts for their transportation and receipt. Such arrangements are best made after the completion of the briefing schedule on appeal and receipt of notice of oral argument.

Local Rule 11(d). Access of counsel to original record.

Counsel desiring to use the record on appeal in preparing their case should make arrangements with the clerk of the district court for access to the record. Under Local Rule 10(a), records in cases in which all parties are represented by counsel are retained by the district court clerk during appeal unless a judge of the Court of Appeals requests that they be obtained. If the record is transmitted to the Court of Appeals, the record may be withdrawn upon proper application and returned to the trial court or the nearest district court clerk's office for counsel's review. Law professors representing indigents by Court appointment may request that the record be sent to the law school for their review.

I.O.P. 11.1. Sanctions for court reporter's failure to file a timely transcript.

The Fourth Circuit Judicial Council has implemented a resolution of the Judicial Conference of the United States which mandates sanctions for the late delivery of transcripts. For transcripts not delivered within 60 days of the date ordered and payment received therefor, the reporter may charge only 90 percent of the prescribed fee; for a transcript not delivered within 90 days the reporter may charge only 80 percent of the prescribed fee with the following exception. For transcripts not delivered within the time limits set forth in Local Rule 11(b), the reporter may charge only 90 percent of the prescribed fee; for a transcript not delivered within 30 days after that time the reporter may charge only 80 percent of the prescribed fee. The time period in criminal proceedings for the preparation of transcripts that are ordered before sentencing shall not begin to run until after entry of the judgment and commitment order.

COMMENT

New I.O.P. 11.1 incorporates proposed language which would, in combination with proposed changes to the Fourth Circuit Guidelines for Preparation of Appellate Transcripts, permit preparation of transcript to begin after conviction but before sentencing upon certification by counsel that the defendant intends to appeal. If transcript is ordered prior to sentencing, the court reporter's time limits for filing the transcript would not begin to run until after entry of the judgment and commitment order.

Rule 12. Docketing the appeal; filing a representation statement; filing the record.

(a) *Docketing the appeal.* Upon receiving the copy of the notice of appeal and the docket entries from the district clerk under Rule 3(d), the circuit clerk must docket the appeal under the title of the district-court action and must identify the appellant, adding the appellant's name if necessary.

(b) *Filing a representation statement.* Unless the court of appeals designates another time, the attorney who filed the notice of appeal must, within 10 days after filing the notice, file a statement with the circuit clerk naming the parties that the attorney represents on appeal.

(c) *Filing the record, partial record, or certificate.* Upon receiving the record, partial record, or district clerk's certificate as provided in Rule 11, the circuit clerk must file it and immediately notify all parties of the filing date. (Amended by order adopted April 30, 1979, effective August 1, 1979; by order adopted March 10, 1986, effective July 1, 1986; by order adopted April 22, 1993, effective December 1, 1993; and by order adopted April 24, 1998, effective December 1, 1998.)

Local Rule 12(a). Appeals by aggrieved non-parties in the lower court.

If the appellant was not a party to the lower court proceeding, the appeal shall be styled "In re _____, Appellant," and the title of the action in the district court shall also be given.

Local Rule 12(b). Joint appeals/cross-appeals and consolidations.

For the purpose of identifying consolidated appeals and cross-appeals, the earliest docketed appeal will be designated the lead case and identified by an "L" following its docket number. The parties should designate lead counsel for each side and communicate lead counsel's identity in writing to the clerk within 10 days of the consolidation order. Although most consolidations will be on the Court's own motion, a party is not precluded from filing a request.

Local Rule 12(c). Expedition of appeals.

The Court on its own motion or on motion of the parties may expedite an appeal for briefing and oral argument. Any motion to expedite should state clearly the reasons supporting expedition, the ability of the parties to present the appeal on the existing record, and the need for oral argument. (Amended by order effective December 1, 1998.)

COMMENT

The last sentence of Local Rule 12(c) has been deleted because Local Rule 10(a) does not require that the record be transmitted to the Court of Appeals.

Local Rule 12(d). Abeyance.

In the interest of docket control the Court may, either on its own motion or upon request, place a case in abeyance pending disposition of matters before this Court or other courts which may affect the ultimate resolution of an appeal. During the period of time a case is held in abeyance the appeal remains on the docket but nothing is done to advance the case to maturity and resolution. If a case is held in abeyance for cases other than a Fourth Circuit case, the parties will be required to make periodic status reports.

Local Rule 12(e). Intervention.

A party who appeared as an intervenor in a lower court proceeding shall be considered a party to the appeal upon filing a notice of appearance. Otherwise, a motion for leave to intervene must be filed with the Court of Appeals. Any notice of appearance or motion to intervene should indicate the side upon which the movant proposes to intervene. The provisions of FRAP 15(d) govern intervention in appeals from administrative agencies. Intervenors are required to join in the brief for the side which they support unless leave to file a separate brief is granted by the Court.

I.O.P. 12.1. Organization of the Court's docket.

[Deleted effective December 1, 1998.]

COMMENT

I.O.P. 12.1 has been deleted. The court has, in the past, made several adjustments to docket assignments to reflect changes in the court's caseload. Since the docket assignment information in the I.O.P. is not of significant import to persons practicing before the court, the proposed draft would delete the I.O.P. rather than continue the practice of modifying it.

TITLE III. REVIEW OF DECISIONS OF THE UNITED STATES TAX COURT.

Rule 13. Review of a decision of the Tax Court.

(a) *How obtained; time for filing notice of appeal.* (1) Review of a decision of the United States Tax Court is commenced by filing a notice of appeal with the Tax Court clerk within 90 days after the entry of the Tax Court's decision. At the time of filing, the appellant must furnish the clerk with enough copies of the notice to enable the clerk to comply with Rule 3(d). If one party files a timely notice of appeal, any other party may file a notice of appeal within 120 days after the Tax Court's decision is entered.

(2) If, under Tax Court rules, a party makes a timely motion to vacate or revise the Tax Court's decision, the time to file a notice of appeal runs from the entry of the order disposing of the motion or from the entry of a new decision, whichever is later.

(b) *Notice of appeal; how filed.* The notice of appeal may be filed either at the Tax Court clerk's office in the District of Columbia or by mail addressed to the clerk. If sent by mail the notice is considered filed on the postmark date, subject to § 7502 of the Internal Revenue Code, as amended, and the applicable regulations.

(c) *Contents of the notice of appeal; service; effect of filing and service.* Rule 3 prescribes the contents of a notice of appeal, the manner of service, and the effect of its filing and service. Form 2 in the Appendix of Forms is a suggested form of a notice of appeal.

(d) *The record on appeal; forwarding; filing.* (1) An appeal from the Tax Court is governed by the parts of Rules 10, 11, and 12 regarding the record on appeal from a district court, the time and manner of forwarding and filing, and the docketing in the court of appeals. References in those rules and in Rule 3 to the district court and district clerk are to be read as referring to the Tax Court and its clerk.

(2) If an appeal from a Tax Court decision is taken to more than one court of appeals, the original record must be sent to the court named in the first notice of appeal filed. In an appeal to any other court of appeals, the appellant must apply to that other court to make provision for the record. (Amended by order adopted April 30, 1979, effective August 1, 1979; by order adopted April 29, 1994, effective December 1, 1994; and by order adopted April 24, 1998, effective December 1, 1998.)

Rule 14. Applicability of other rules to the review of a Tax Court decision.

All provisions of these rules, except Rules 4-9, 15-20, and 22-23, apply to the review of a Tax Court decision. (Amended by order adopted April 24, 1998, effective December 1, 1998.)

TITLE IV. REVIEW AND ENFORCEMENT OF ORDERS OF ADMINISTRATIVE AGENCIES, BOARDS, COMMISSIONS AND OFFICERS.

Rule 15. Review or enforcement of an agency order — How obtained; intervention.

(a) *Petition for review; joint petition.* (1) Review of an agency order is commenced by filing, within the time prescribed by law, a petition for review with the clerk of a court of appeals authorized to review the agency order. If their interests make joinder practicable, two or more persons may join in a petition to the same court to review the same order.

(2) The petition must:

(A) name each party seeking review either in the caption or the body of the petition — using such terms as "et al.," "petitioners," or "respondents" does not effectively name the parties;

(B) name the agency as a respondent (even though not named in the petition, the United States is a respondent if required by statute); and

(C) specify the order or part thereof to be reviewed.

(3) Form 3 in the Appendix of Forms is a suggested form of a petition for review.

(4) In this rule "agency" includes an agency, board, commission, or officer; "petition for review" includes a petition to enjoin, suspend, modify, or otherwise review, or a notice of appeal, whichever form is indicated by the applicable statute.

(b) *Application or cross-application to enforce an order; answer; default.* (1) An application to enforce an agency order must be filed with the clerk of a court of appeals authorized to enforce the order. If a petition is filed to review an agency order that the court may enforce, a party opposing the petition may file a cross-application for enforcement.

(2) Within 20 days after the application for enforcement is filed, the respondent must serve on the applicant an answer to the application and file it with the clerk. If the respondent fails to answer in time, the court will enter judgment for the relief requested.

(3) The application must contain a concise statement of the proceedings in which the order was entered, the facts upon which venue is based, and the relief requested.

(c) *Service of petition or application.* The circuit clerk must serve a copy of the petition for review, or an application or cross-application to enforce an agency order, on each respondent as prescribed by Rule 3(d), unless a different manner of service is prescribed by statute. At the time of filing, the petitioner must:

(1) serve, or have served, a copy on each party admitted to participate in the agency proceedings, except for the respondents;

(2) file with the clerk a list of those so served; and

(3) give the clerk enough copies of the petition or application to serve each respondent.

(d) *Intervention.* Unless a statute provides another method, a person who wants to intervene in a proceeding under this rule must file a motion for leave to intervene with the circuit clerk and serve a copy on all parties. The motion — or other notice of intervention authorized by statute — must be filed within 30 days after the petition for review is filed and must contain a concise statement of the interest of the moving party and the grounds for intervention.

(e) *Payment of fees.* When filing any separate or joint petition for review in a court of appeals, the petitioner must pay the circuit clerk all required fees. (Amended by order adopted April 22, 1993, effective December 1, 1993; and by order adopted April 24, 1998, effective December 1, 1998.)

Local Rule 15(a). Docketing fee.

Upon filing a petition for review of an agency order, petitioner shall pay the prescribed docketing fee of $100, payable to the Clerk, U.S. Court of Appeals, or submit a properly executed application for leave to proceed in forma pauperis. (Added by order effective September 28, 1994; and by order effective December 4, 1996.)

Local Rule 15(b). Petitions for review.

Whenever filing a petition for review or an application or cross-application for enforcement, the party shall attach to the petition, application or cross-application a copy of the agency order for which review or enforcement is sought. The petition, application or cross-application shall also be accompanied by a list of respondents specifically identifying the respondents' names and the addresses where respondents may be served with copies of the petition, application or cross-application. (Adopted by order effective December 4, 1996.)

Rule 15.1. Briefs and oral argument in National Labor Relations Board proceedings.

In either an enforcement or a review proceeding, a party adverse to the National Labor Relations Board proceeds first on briefing and at oral argument, unless the court orders otherwise. (Adopted by order adopted March 10, 1986, effective July 1, 1986; and amended by order adopted April 24, 1998, effective December 1, 1998.)

Rule 16. The record on review or enforcement.

(a) *Composition of the record.* The record on review or enforcement of an agency order consists of:

(1) the order involved;

(2) any findings or report on which it is based; and

(3) the pleadings, evidence, and other parts of the proceedings before the agency.

(b) *Omissions from or misstatements in the record.* The parties may at any time, by stipulation, supply any omission from the record or correct a misstatement, or the court may so direct. If necessary, the court may direct that a supplemental record be prepared and filed. (Amended by order adopted April 24, 1998, effective December 1, 1998.)

Rule 17. Filing of the record.

(a) *Agency to file; time for filing; notice of filing.* The agency must file the record with the circuit clerk within 40 days after being served with a petition for review, unless the statute authorizing review provides otherwise, or within 40 days after it files an application for enforcement unless the respondent fails to answer or the court orders otherwise. The court may shorten or extend the time to file the record. The clerk must notify all parties of the date when the record is filed.

(b) *Filing; what constitutes.* (1) The agency must file:

(A) the original or a certified copy of the entire record or parts designated by the parties; or

(B) a certified list adequately describing all documents, transcripts of testimony, exhibits, and other material constituting the record, or describing those parts designated by the parties.

(2) The parties may stipulate in writing that no record or certified list be filed. The date when the stipulation is filed with the circuit clerk is treated as the date when the record is filed.

(3) The agency must retain any portion of the record not filed with the clerk. All parts of the record retained by the agency are a part of the record on review for all purposes and, if the court or a party so requests, must be sent to the court regardless of any prior stipulation. (Amended by order adopted April 24, 1998, effective December 1, 1998.)

Rule 18. Stay pending review.

(a) *Motion for a stay*. (1) Initial motion before the agency. A petitioner must ordinarily move first before the agency for a stay pending review of its decision or order.

(2) Motion in the court of appeals. A motion for a stay may be made to the court of appeals or one of its judges.

(A) The motion must:

(i) show that moving first before the agency would be impracticable; or

(ii) state that, a motion having been made, the agency denied the motion or failed to afford the relief requested and state any reasons given by the agency for its action.

(B) The motion must also include:

(i) the reasons for granting the relief requested and the facts relied on;

(ii) originals or copies of affidavits or other sworn statements supporting facts subject to dispute; and

(iii) relevant parts of the record.

(C) The moving party must give reasonable notice of the motion to all parties.

(D) The motion must be filed with the circuit clerk and normally will be considered by a panel of the court. But in an exceptional case in which time requirements make that procedure impracticable, the motion may be made to and considered by a single judge.

(b) *Bond*. The court may condition relief on the filing of a bond or other appropriate security. (Amended by order adopted April 24, 1998, effective December 1, 1998.)

Local Rule 18. Procedures.

This Court's local rules accompanying FRAP 8 and 27 apply also to applications for stays under FRAP 18.

COMMENT

The proposed Local Rule simply revises the language of existing I.O.P. 18 which cross-references the procedures found in FRAP 8 and 27.

Rule 19. Settlement of a judgment enforcing an agency order in part.

When the court files an opinion directing entry of judgment enforcing the agency's order in part, the agency must within 14 days file with the clerk and serve on each other party a proposed judgment conforming to the opinion. A party who disagrees with the agency's proposed judgment must within 7 days file with the clerk and serve the agency with a proposed judgment that the party believes conforms to the opinion. The court will settle the judgment and direct entry without further hearing or argument. (Amended by order adopted March 10, 1986, effective July 1, 1986; and by order adopted April 24, 1998, effective December 1, 1998.)

Rule 20. Applicability of rules to the review or enforcement of an agency order.

All provisions of these rules, except Rules 3-14 and 22-23, apply to the review or enforcement of an agency order. In these rules, "appellant" includes a petitioner or applicant, and "appellee" includes a respondent. (Amended by order adopted April 24, 1998, effective December 1, 1998.)

TITLE V. EXTRAORDINARY WRITS.

Rule 21. Writs of mandamus and prohibition, and other extraordinary writs.

(a) *Mandamus or prohibition to a court: petition, filing, service, and docketing.* (1) A party petitioning for a writ of mandamus or prohibition directed to a court must file a petition with the circuit clerk with proof of service on all parties to the proceeding in the trial court. The party must also provide a copy to the trial-court judge. All parties to the proceeding in the trial court other than the petitioner are respondents for all purposes.

(2) (A) The petition must be titled "In re [name of petitioner]."

(B) The petition must state:

(i) the relief sought;

(ii) the issues presented;

(iii) the facts necessary to understand the issue presented by the petition; and

(iv) the reasons why the writ should issue.

(C) The petition must include a copy of any order or opinion or parts of the record that may be essential to understand the matters set forth in the petition.

(3) Upon receiving the prescribed docket fee, the clerk must docket the petition and submit it to the court.

(b) *Denial; order directing answer; briefs; precedence.* (1) The court may deny the petition without an answer. Otherwise, it must order the respondent, if any, to answer within a fixed time.

(2) The clerk must serve the order to respond on all persons directed to respond.

(3) Two or more respondents may answer jointly.

(4) The court of appeals may invite or order the trial-court judge to address the petition or may invite an amicus curiae to do so. The trial-court judge may request permission to address the petition but may not do so unless invited or ordered to do so by the court of appeals.

(5) If briefing or oral argument is required, the clerk must advise the parties, and when appropriate, the trial-court judge or amicus curiae.

(6) The proceeding must be given preference over ordinary civil cases.

(7) The circuit clerk must send a copy of the final disposition to the trial-court judge.

(c) *Other extraordinary writs.* An application for an extraordinary writ other than one provided for in Rule 21(a) must be made by filing a petition with the circuit clerk with proof of service on the respondents. Proceedings on the application must conform, so far as is practicable, to the procedures prescribed in Rule 21(a) and (b).

(d) *Form of papers; number of copies.* All papers must conform to Rule 32(a)(1). An original and 3 copies must be filed unless the court requires the filing of a different number by local rule or by order in a particular case. (Amended by order adopted April 29, 1994, effective December 1, 1994; by order adopted April 23, 1996, effective December 1, 1996; and by order adopted April 24, 1998, effective December 1, 1998.)

Mandamus is preferred method of review for orders restricting press activity related to criminal proceedings, but an appeal would be treated as a petition for mandamus if the party seeking review has standing and has substantially complied with the requirements of subdivision (a) of this rule concerning mandamus. Washington Post Co. v. United States, 807 F.2d 383 (4th Cir. 1986).

Local Rule 21(a). Case captions for extraordinary writs.

A petition for a writ of mandamus or writ of prohibition shall not bear the name of the district judge, but shall be entitled simply "In re _____, Petitioner." To the extent that relief is requested of a particular judge, unless otherwise ordered, the judge shall be represented pro forma by counsel for the party opposing the relief, who shall appear in the name of the party and not that of the judge.

Local Rule 21(b). Petitions for mandamus or prohibition.

Strict compliance with the requirements of FRAP 21 is required of all petitioners, even pro se litigants. Petitioner must pay the prescribed docket fee of $100, payable to the Clerk, U.S. Court of Appeals; submit the forms required by Local Rule 21(c)(1) for cases subject to that Local Rule; or submit a properly executed application for leave to proceed in forma pauperis. The parties are required to submit Disclosure of Corporate Affiliations and Other Entities with a Direct Financial Interest in Litigation statements with the petition and answer. See FRAP 26.1, Local Rule 26.1, and Form A.

After docketing, the clerk shall submit the application to a three-judge panel. If time is of the essence, application may be made to a single circuit judge, who ordinarily should be resident in the state of the trial court proceeding, seeking temporary relief under 28 U.S.C. § 1651 until the matter can be considered by a three-judge panel.

If the Court believes the writ should not be granted, it will deny the petition without requesting an answer. Otherwise the Court will direct the clerk to obtain an answer. After an answer has been filed, the Court ordinarily will decide the merits of the petition on the materials submitted without oral argument. Occasionally, however, briefs may be requested and the matter set for oral argument. (Amended by order effective September 25, 1996.)

Local Rule 21(c). Fees and costs for prisoner petitions for mandamus, prohibition, or other extraordinary relief.

(1) *Proceedings arising out of civil matters.* A prisoner filing a petition for writ of mandamus, prohibition, or other extraordinary relief in a matter arising out of a civil case must pay the full $100 docket fee. A prisoner who is unable to prepay this fee may apply to pay the fee in installments by filing with the Court of Appeals (1) an application to proceed without prepayment of fees; (2) a certified copy of the prisoner's trust fund account statement for the six-month period immediately preceding the filing of the notice of appeal, obtained from the appropriate official of each prison at which the prisoner is or was confined; and (3) a form consenting to the collection of fees from the prisoner's trust account.

The Court of Appeals will assess an initial partial filing fee of 20% of the greater of:

(a) the average monthly deposits to the prisoner's account for the six-month period immediately preceding the filing of the petition; or

(b) the average monthly balance in the prisoner's account for the six-month period immediately preceding the filing of the petition.

The Court will direct the agency having custody of the prisoner to collect this initial partial fee from the prisoner's trust account, and to collect the remainder of the $100 fee, as well as any other fees, costs, or sanctions imposed by the Court, in monthly installments of 20% of the preceding month's deposits credited to the prisoner's account. The agency having custody of the prisoner shall forward payments from the prisoner's account to the Clerk, U.S. Court of Appeals, each time the amount in the account exceeds $10 until all fees, costs, and sanctions are paid for the petition.

If a prisoner proceeding under this rule fails to file the forms or make the payments required by the Court, the appeal will be dismissed pursuant to Local Rule 45.

(2) *Effect of prior actions and appeals on proceedings arising out of civil matters.* A prisoner who has, on three or more prior occasions, while incarcerated or detained in any facility, brought an action or appeal in a court of the United States that was dismissed on the grounds that it was frivolous, malicious, or failed to state a claim upon which relief could be granted, may not proceed in a matter arising out of a civil case without prepayment of fees unless the prisoner is under imminent danger of serious physical injury.

(3) *Proceedings arising out of criminal matters.* A prisoner who is unable to prepay the full $100 docket fee for a petition for writ of mandamus, prohibition, or other extraordinary relief arising out of a criminal case may apply to proceed without the prepayment of fees by filing an application for leave to proceed in forma pauperis. (Adopted by order effective September 25, 1996.)

TITLE VI. HABEAS CORPUS; PROCEEDINGS IN FORMA PAUPERIS.

Rule 22. Habeas corpus and section 2255 proceedings.

(a) *Application for the original writ.* An application for a writ of habeas corpus must be made to the appropriate district court. If made to a circuit judge, the application must be transferred to the appropriate district court. If a district court denies an application made or transferred to it, renewal of the application before a circuit judge is not permitted. The applicant may, under 28 U.S.C. § 2253, appeal to the court of appeals from the district court's order denying the application.

(b) *Certificate of appealability.* (1) In a habeas corpus proceeding in which the detention complained of arises from process issued by a state court, or in a 28 U.S.C. § 2255 proceeding, the applicant cannot take an appeal unless a circuit justice or a circuit or district judge issues a certificate of appealability under 28 U.S.C. § 2253(c). If an applicant files a notice of appeal, the district judge who rendered the judgment must either issue a certificate of appealability or state why a certificate should not issue. The district clerk must send the certificate or statement to the court of appeals with the notice of appeal and the file of the district-court proceedings. If the district judge has denied the certificate, the applicant may request a circuit judge to issue the certificate.

(2) A request addressed to the court of appeals may be considered by a circuit judge or judges, as the court prescribes. If no express request for a certificate is filed, the notice of appeal constitutes a request addressed to the judges of the court of appeals.

(3) A certificate of appealability is not required when a state or its representative or the United States or its representative appeals. (Amended by order adopted April 24, 1998, effective December 1, 1998.)

Local Rule 22(a). Certificates of appealability.

All applications for certificates of appealability shall either be in the form of a motion under FRAP 27(a) or be accompanied by informal briefs pursuant to Local Rule 34(b), regardless of whether the petitioner is represented by counsel. An application for a certificate of appealability may be referred to a panel of three judges. If all the judges on the panel conclude that the certificate should not issue, the certificate will be denied; but if any judge of such panel is of the opinion that the applicant has made a substantial showing of the denial of a constitutional right, the certificate will issue. The certificate shall indicate which specific issue or issues satisfy the required showing. If the Court grants a certificate of appealability, it may thereafter affirm, reverse or remand without further briefing or direct full briefing and oral argument. (Amended by order effective December 1, 1995; amended by order effective June 5, 1996; and amended by order effective December 1, 1998.)

COMMENT

Local Rule 22(a) has been amended to delete reference to an accompanying memorandum of law because FRAP 27(a)(2)(c)(i) bars memoranda in support of motions.

Local Rule 22(b). Death penalty cases and motions for stay of execution.

(1) *Statement certifying existence of sentence of death.* Whenever a petition for writ of habeas corpus or motion to vacate a federal sentence in which a sentence of death is involved is filed in the district court or the Court of Appeals, the petitioner shall file with the petition a statement certifying the existence of a sentence of death and the emergency nature of the proceedings and listing any proposed date of execution, any previous cases filed by petitioner in federal court and any cases filed by petitioner pending in any other court. The clerk of the district court shall immediately forward to the Court of Appeals a copy of any such statement filed, and shall immediately notify by telephone the Court of Appeals upon issuance of a final order in that case. If a notice of appeal is filed, the clerk of the district court shall transmit the available record forthwith. The clerk of the Court of Appeals will maintain a special docket for such cases and these cases shall be presented to the Court of Appeals on an expedited basis.

(2) *Lodging of documents.* In cases in which an execution date has been set, counsel shall lodge with the clerk of the Court of Appeals all district court documents as they are filed and any pertinent state court materials. If an execution date is imminent, counsel may also lodge proposed appellate papers in anticipation of having to seek emergency appellate relief.

(3) *Motion for stay of execution.* Any motion for stay of execution shall be considered initially in conjunction with any pending application for a certificate of appealability. Should a party file a motion to stay execution or a motion to vacate an order granting a stay of execution, the following documents shall accompany such motion:

(a) The habeas petition or motion to vacate filed in the district court;

(b) Each brief or memorandum of authorities filed by either party in the district court;

(c) Any available transcript of proceedings before the district court;

(d) The memorandum opinion giving the reasons advanced by the district court for denying relief;

(e) The district court judgment denying relief;

(f) The application to the district court for stay;

(g) Any certificate of appealability or order denying a certificate of appealability;

(h) The district court order granting or denying a stay and a statement of reasons for its action; and

(i) A copy of the docket entries of the district court. (Amended by order effective December 1, 1995; and effective June 5, 1996.)

COMMENT

Local Rule 22(b) has been modified to include within its procedures federal death penalty cases filed pursuant to 28 U.S.C. § 2255.

Local Rule 22(c). Petitions for rehearing in death penalty cases.

(1) *All death penalty cases.* Once the Court's mandate has issued in a death penalty case, any petition for rehearing (with or without a suggestion for rehearing en banc) should be accompanied by motion to recall the mandate and a motion to stay the execution.

Counsel should be aware that the process for distributing materials by the Clerk's Office ordinarily requires a minimum of three days for all members of the Court to receive a petition. Generally, the Court will not enter a stay of execution solely to allow for additional time for counsel to prepare, or for the Court to consider, a petition for rehearing, with or without a suggestion for rehearing en banc. Consequently, counsel should take all possible steps to assure that any such petition is filed sufficiently in advance of the scheduled execution date to allow it to be considered by the Court. Counsel should notify the Clerk's Office promptly of their intention to file a petition for rehearing so that arrangements can be made in advance for the most expeditious consideration of the matter by the Court.

(2) *Emergency petitions.* In extraordinary circumstances, when the petition cannot be filed earlier than three days before a scheduled execution date, the Clerk's Office will endeavor to inform the members of the panel that issued the Court's decision of the filing of a petition for rehearing (with or without a suggestion for rehearing en banc) within a shorter period of time. At the direction of a panel member, similar efforts will be made to inform the full Court of the matter. The Clerk's Office will give notice to counsel by telephone of the Court's decision on such petitions. (Amended by order effective December 1, 1995; and by order effective December 1, 1998.)

Local Rule 22(d). Motions for authorization.

Any individual seeking to file in the district court a second or successive application for relief pursuant to 28 U.S.C. § 2254 or § 2255 shall first file a motion with the Court of Appeals for authorization as required by 28 U.S.C. § 2244, on the form provided by the clerk for such motions. The motion shall be entitled "In re _____, Movant." The motion must be accompanied by copies of the § 2254 or § 2255 application which movant seeks authorization to file in the district court, as well as all prior § 2254 or § 2255 applications challenging the same conviction and sentence, all court opinions and orders disposing of those applications, and all magistrate judge's reports and recommendations issued on those applications. The movant shall serve a copy of the motion with attachments on the respondent named in the proposed application and shall file an original and three copies of the motion with attachments in the Court of Appeals. Failure to provide the requisite information and attachments may result in denial of the motion for authorization.

If the Court requires a response to the motion, it will direct that the response be received by the clerk for filing within no more than seven days. The Court will enter an order granting or denying authorization within 30 days of receipt of the motion by the clerk for filing, and the clerk will certify a copy of the order to the district court. If authorization is granted, a copy of the application will be attached to the certified order for filing in the district court. No motion or request for reconsideration, petition for rehearing, or any other paper seeking review of the granting or denial of authorization will be allowed. (Adopted by order effective June 5, 1996.)

I.O.P. 22.1. Death penalty cases.

Once a notice of appeal has been filed in a case involving a sentence of death where an execution date has been set, a panel of three judges will be promptly identified for consideration of all matters related to the case. At least one member of the panel selected will be from the state where petitioner's conviction arose, unless such judge or judges are unavailable. The position of coordinator of case information in death penalty cases has been established in the Clerk's Office of the Court of Appeals for the purpose of establishing personal liaison with district court personnel and counsel to aid in the expeditious treatment of appeals involving a sentence of death. An expedited briefing schedule will be established when necessary to allow the Court the opportunity to review all issues presented.

Rule 23. Custody or release of a prisoner in a habeas corpus proceeding.

(a) *Transfer of custody pending review.* Pending review of a decision in a habeas corpus proceeding commenced before a court, justice, or judge of the United States for the release of a prisoner, the person having custody of the prisoner must not transfer custody to another unless a transfer is directed in accordance with this rule. When, upon application, a custodian shows the need for a transfer, the court, justice, or judge rendering the decision under review may authorize the transfer and substitute the successor custodian as a party.

(b) *Detention or release pending review of decision not to release.* While a decision not to release a prisoner is under review, the court or judge rendering the decision, or the court of appeals, or the Supreme Court, or a judge or justice of either court, may order that the prisoner be:

(1) detained in the custody from which release is sought;

(2) detained in other appropriate custody; or

(3) released on personal recognizance, with or without surety.

(c) *Release pending review of decision ordering release.* While a decision ordering the release of a prisoner is under review, the prisoner must — unless the court or judge rendering the decision, or the court of appeals, or the Supreme Court, or a judge or justice of either court orders otherwise — be released on personal recognizance, with or without surety.

(d) *Modification of the initial order on custody.* An initial order governing the prisoner's custody or release, including any recognizance or surety, continues in effect pending review unless for special reasons shown to the court of appeals or the Supreme Court, or to a judge or justice of either court, the order is modified or an independent order regarding custody, release, or surety is issued. (Amended by order adopted March 10, 1986, effective July 1, 1986, and by order adopted April 29, 1994, effective December 1, 1994, and by order adopted April 23, 1996, effective December 1, 1996 and by order adopted April 24, 1998, effective December 1, 1998.)

Rule 24. Proceeding in forma pauperis.

(a) *Leave to proceed in forma pauperis.* (1) Motion in the district court. Except as stated in Rule 24(a)(3), a party to a district-court action who desires to appeal in forma pauperis must file a motion in the district court. The party must attach an affidavit that:

(A) shows in the detail prescribed by Form 4 of the Appendix of Forms, the party's inability to pay or to give security for fees and costs;

(B) claims an entitlement to redress; and

(C) states the issues that the party intends to present on appeal.

(2) Action on the motion. If the district court grants the motion, the party may proceed on appeal without prepaying or giving security for fees and costs. If the district court denies the motion, it must state its reasons in writing.

(3) Prior approval. A party who was permitted to proceed in forma pauperis in the district-court action, or who was determined to be financially unable to obtain an adequate defense in a criminal case, may proceed on appeal in forma pauperis without further authorization, unless the district court — before or after the notice of appeal is filed — certifies that the appeal is not taken in good faith or finds that the party is not otherwise entitled to proceed in forma pauperis. In that event, the district court must state in writing its reasons for the certification or finding.

(4) Notice of district court's denial. The district clerk must immediately notify the parties and the court of appeals when the district court does any of the following:

(A) denies a motion to proceed on appeal in forma pauperis;

(B) certifies that the appeal is not taken in good faith; or

(C) finds that the party is not otherwise entitled to proceed in forma pauperis.

(5) Motion in the court of appeals. A party may file a motion to proceed on appeal in forma pauperis in the court of appeals within 30 days after service of the notice prescribed in Rule 24(a)(4). The motion must include a copy of the affidavit filed in the district court and the district court's statement of reasons for its action. If no affidavit was filed in the district court, the party must include the affidavit prescribed by Rule 24(a)(1).

(b) *Leave to proceed in forma pauperis on appeal or review of an adminis-trative-agency proceeding.* When an appeal or review of a proceeding before an administrative agency, board, commission, or officer (including for the purpose of this rule the United States Tax Court) proceeds directly in a court of appeals, a party may file in the court of appeals a motion for leave to proceed on appeal in forma pauperis with an affidavit prescribed by Rule 24(a)(1).

(c) *Leave to use original record.* A party allowed to proceed on appeal in forma pauperis may request that the appeal be heard on the original record without reproducing any part. (Amended by order adopted April 30, 1979, effective August 1, 1979; by order adopted March 10, 1986, effective July 1, 1986; and by order adopted April 24, 1998, effective December 1, 1998.)

Local Rule 24. Prisoner appeals.

(a) *Payment of fees and costs required.* A prisoner appealing a judgment in a civil action must pay in full the $105 fee required for commencement of the appeal. A prisoner who is unable to prepay this fee may apply to pay the fee in installments by filing with the Court of Appeals (1) an application to proceed without prepayment of fees; (2) a certified copy of the prisoner's trust fund account statement or institutional equivalent for the six-month period immediately preceding the filing of the notice of appeal, obtained from the appropriate official of each prison at which the prisoner is or was confined; and (3) a form consenting to the collection of fees from the prisoner's trust account.

The Court of Appeals will assess an initial partial filing fee of 20% of the greater of:

(1) the average monthly deposits to the prisoner's account for the six-month period immediately preceding the filing of the notice of appeal; or

(2) the average monthly balance in the prisoner's account for the six-month period immediately preceding the filing of the notice of appeal.

Based upon the prisoner's consent, the Court will direct the agency having custody of the prisoner to collect this initial partial fee from the prisoner's trust account, and to collect the remainder of the $105 filing fee, as well as any other fees, costs, or sanctions imposed by the Court of Appeals, in monthly installments of 20% of the preceding month's deposits credited to the prisoner's account. The agency having custody of the prisoner shall forward payments from the prisoner's account to the clerk of the district court each time the amount in the account exceeds $10 until all fees, costs, and sanctions are paid for the appeal.

If a prisoner proceeding under this rule fails to file the forms or make the payments required by the Court, the appeal will be dismissed pursuant to Local Rule 45.

(b) *Effect of prior actions and appeals.* A prisoner who has, on three or more prior occasions, while incarcerated or detained in any facility, brought an action or appeal in a court of the United States that was dismissed on the grounds that it was frivolous, malicious, or failed to state a claim upon which relief could be granted, may not proceed on appeal without prepayment of fees unless the prisoner is under imminent danger of serious physical injury. (Adopted by order effective June 5, 1996.)

TITLE VII. GENERAL PROVISIONS.

Rule 25. Filing and service.

(a) *Filing.* (1) Filing with the clerk. A paper required or permitted to be filed in a court of appeals must be filed with the clerk.

(2) Filing: Method and timeliness. (A) In general. Filing may be accomplished by mail addressed to the clerk, but filing is not timely unless the clerk receives the papers within the time fixed for filing.

(B) A brief or appendix. A brief or appendix is timely filed, however, if on or before the last day for filing, it is:

(i) mailed to the clerk by First-Class Mail, or other class of mail that is at least as expeditious, postage prepaid; or

(ii) dispatched to a third-party commercial carrier for delivery to the clerk within 3 calendar days.

(C) Inmate filing. A paper filed by an inmate confined in an institution is timely if deposited in the institution's internal mailing system on or before the last day for filing. If an institution has a system designed for legal mail, the inmate must use that system to receive the benefit of this rule. Timely filing may be shown by a declaration in compliance with 28 U.S.C. § 1746 or by a notarized statement, either of which must set forth the date of deposit and state that first-class postage has been prepaid.

(D) Electronic filing. A court of appeals may by local rule permit papers to be filed, signed, or verified by electronic means that are consistent with technical standards, if any, that the Judicial Conference of the United States establishes. A paper filed by electronic means in compliance with a local rule constitutes a written paper for the purpose of applying these rules.

(3) Filing a motion with a judge. If a motion requests relief that may be granted by a single judge, the judge may permit the motion to be filed with the judge; the judge must note the filing date on the motion and give it to the clerk.

(4) Clerk's refusal of documents. The clerk must not refuse to accept for filing any paper presented for that purpose solely because it is not presented in proper form as required by these rules or by any local rule or practice.

(b) *Service of all papers required.* Unless a rule requires service by the clerk, a party must, at or before the time of filing a paper, serve a copy on the other parties to the appeal or review. Service on a party represented by counsel must be made on the party's counsel.

(c) *Manner of service.* Service may be personal, by mail, or by third-party commercial carrier for delivery within 3 calendar days. When reasonably considering such factors as the immediacy of the relief sought, distance, and cost, service on a party must be by a manner at least as expeditious as the manner used to file the paper with the court. Personal service includes delivery of the copy to a responsible person at the office of counsel. Service by mail or by commercial carrier is complete on mailing or delivery to the carrier.

(d) *Proof of service.* (1) A paper presented for filing must contain either of the following:

(A) an acknowledgment of service by the person served; or

(B) proof of service consisting of a statement by the person who made service certifying:

(i) the date and manner of service;

(ii) the names of the persons served; and

(iii) their mailing addresses or the addresses of the places of delivery.

(2) When a brief or appendix is filed by mailing or dispatch in accordance with Rule 25(a)(2)(B), the proof of service must also state the date and manner by which the document was mailed or dispatched to the clerk.

(3) Proof of service may appear on or be affixed to the papers filed.

(e) *Number of copies.* When these rules require the filing or furnishing of a number of copies, a court may require a different number by local rule or by order in a particular case. (Amended by order effective July 1, 1986, by order adopted April 30, 1991, effective December 1, 1991, by order adopted April 22, 1993, effective December 1, 1993, by order adopted April 29, 1994, effective December 1, 1994, and by order adopted April 23, 1996, effective December 1, 1996, and by order adopted April 24, 1998, effective December 1, 1998.)

Local Rule 25(a). Paper size, number of copies, attachments.

(1) *Paper size.* The Judicial Conference of the United States has adopted 8½ x 11 inch letter-size paper as the standard for use throughout the federal judiciary. All documents and other papers submitted to this Court must conform to this standard.

(2) *Number of copies, attachments.* Unless otherwise provided by rule, all papers except briefs and appendices submitted to the Fourth Circuit for filing and for consideration by the Court must be in the form of an original paper and three copies. Any attachments to motions which are necessary to an understanding of the matters set forth in the motion must be submitted with three copies and conform to the standard paper size unless advance permission is sought to submit oversized materials. (Amended by order effective December 1, 1995; and by order effective December 1, 1998.)

COMMENT

Local Rule 25(a) has been amended to delete the reference to typeset briefs because FRAP 32(a) no longer provides for typeset briefs.

Local Rule 25(b). Filing papers, service, certificate of service.

(1) *Filing papers.* Papers except briefs and appendices are not timely filed unless actually received by the Clerk's Office within the time fixed for filing. Papers are deemed filed upon receipt by the Clerk's Office and papers may be presented either in person or by mail.

Papers may be transmitted for filing by use of telephonic facsimile transmission equipment. In such cases, the original document signed by counsel need not be filed. Although the Clerk's Office has a fax machine, material may be transmitted directly to the Clerk's Office only when an emergency situation exists and advance permission has been obtained to use the Clerk's Office machine. Several printing services in Richmond will accept papers by fax for filing with the Court. Their telephone numbers may be obtained from the Clerk's Office.

(2) *Service.* Service on a party represented by counsel must be on all counsel of record.

(3) *Certificate of service.* All papers must be accompanied by a valid certificate of service. The certificate of service of a brief should be bound with the brief as the last, unnumbered page. A certificate of service can be prepared in advance of actual mailing or hand delivery of the paper served. If service is not actually accomplished in the manner and on the date stated in the certificate, an amended certificate of service is required. (Amended by order effective December 1, 1995; and order effective December 1, 1998.)

COMMENT

The first sentence of the last paragraph of Rule 25(b)(1) has been moved to Local Rule 27(d) because it refers to the filing of responses to motions. The final sentence of Local Rule 25(b)(1) has been deleted because it duplicates the information in the first sentence of Local Rule 27(d)(1).

Rule 26. Computing and extending time.

(a) *Computation of time.* The following rules apply in computing any period of time specified in these rules or in any local rule, court order, or applicable statute:

(1) Exclude the day of the act, event, or default that begins the period.

(2) Exclude intermediate Saturdays, Sundays, and legal holidays when the period is less than 7 days, unless stated in calendar days.

(3) Include the last day of the period unless it is a Saturday, Sunday, legal holiday, or — if the act to be done is filing a paper in court — a day on which the weather or other conditions make the clerk's office inaccessible.

(4) As used in this rule, "legal holiday" means New Year's Day, Martin Luther King, Jr.'s Birthday, Presidents' Day, Memorial Day, Independence Day, Labor Day, Columbus Day, Veterans' Day, Thanksgiving Day, Christmas Day, and any other day declared a holiday by the President, Congress, or the state in which is located either the district court that rendered the challenged judgment or order, or the circuit clerk's principal office.

(b) *Extending time.* For good cause, the court may extend the time prescribed by these rules or by its order to perform any act, or may permit an act to be done after that time expires. But the court may not extend the time to file:

(1) a notice of appeal (except as authorized in Rule 4) or a petition for permission to appeal; or

(2) a notice of appeal from or a petition to enjoin, set aside, suspend, modify, enforce, or otherwise review an order of an administrative agency, board, commission, or officer of the United States, unless specifically authorized by law.

(c) *Additional time after service.* When a party is required or permitted to act within a prescribed period after a paper is served on that party, 3 calendar days are added to the prescribed period unless the paper is delivered on the date of service stated in the proof of service. (Amended by order adopted March 1, 1971, effective July 1, 1971, by order effective July 1, 1986, by order adopted April 25, 1989, effective December 1, 1989, by order adopted April 30, 1991, effective December 1, 1991, and by order adopted April 23, 1996, effective December 1, 1996; and by order adopted April 24, 1998, effective December 1, 1998.)

Extension granted merely to prevent unduly harsh result for failure to comply with Rule 41 FRAP. — See Caperton v. Beatrice Pocahontas Coal Co., 585 F.2d 683 (4th Cir. 1978).

Applied in United States v. Breit, 754 F.2d 526 (4th Cir. 1985).

Local Rule 26. State holidays and inclement weather.

Whenever a party in computing a filing or service date relies upon an extension of time due to the inaccessibility of the Clerk's Office because of inclement weather or other conditions, or due to a state holiday, counsel must certify such reliance in the certificate of service or by separate written declaration.

Rule 26.1. Corporate disclosure statement.

(a) *Who must file.* Any nongovernmental corporate party to a proceeding in a court of appeals must file a statement identifying all its parent corporations and listing any publicly held company that owns 10% or more of the party's stock.

(b) *Time for filing.* A party must file the statement with the principal brief or upon filing a motion, response, petition, or answer in the court of appeals, whichever occurs first, unless a local rule requires earlier filing. Even if the statement has already been filed, the party's principal brief must include the statement before the table of contents.

(c) *Number of copies.* If the statement is filed before the principal brief, the party must file an original and 3 copies unless the court requires a different number by local rule or by order in a particular case. (Adopted by order April 25, 1989, effective December 1, 1989, amended by order adopted April 30, 1991, effective December 1, 1991, and by order adopted April 29, 1994, effective December 1, 1994; and by order adopted April 24, 1998, effective December 1, 1998.)

Local Rule 26.1. Disclosure of corporate affiliations and other entities with a direct financial interest in litigation.

(a) All parties to a civil or bankruptcy case, and all corporate defendants in a criminal case, whether or not they are covered by the terms of FRAP 26.1, shall file a corporate affiliate/financial interest disclosure statement. This rule does not apply to the United States, to state and local governments in cases in which the opposing party is proceeding without counsel, or to parties proceeding in forma pauperis.

(b) The statement shall set forth the information required by FRAP 26.1 and the following:

(1) A trade association shall identify in the disclosure statement all members of the association, their parent corporations, and any publicly held companies that own 10% or more of a member's stock.

(2) All parties shall identify any publicly held corporation, whether or not a party to the present litigation, that has a direct financial interest in the outcome of the litigation by reason of a franchise, lease, other profit sharing agreement, insurance, or indemnity agreement.

(3) Whenever required by FRAP 26.1 or this rule to disclose information about a corporation that has issued shares to the public, a party shall also disclose information about similarly situated master limited partnerships, real estate investment trusts, or other legal entities whose shares are publicly held or traded.

(c) The disclosure statement shall be on a form provided by the Clerk. A negative statement is required if a party has no disclosures to make.

(d) The disclosure statement shall be filed within 10 days of receipt of the notice of docketing and the disclosure form, unless earlier pleadings are submitted for the Court's consideration, in which case the disclosure statement shall be filed at that time. The parties are required to amend their disclosure statements when necessary to maintain their current accuracy.

Local Rule 26.1(b)(1) has been changed to conform the disclosure requirements for trade associations to the general amendments in FRAP 26.1.

Rule 27. Motions.

(a) *In general.* (1) Application for relief. An application for an order or other relief is made by motion unless these rules prescribe another form. A motion must be in writing unless the court permits otherwise.

(2) Contents of a motion. (A) Grounds and relief sought. A motion must state with particularity the grounds for the motion, the relief sought, and the legal argument necessary to support it.

(B) Accompanying documents. (i) Any affidavit or other paper necessary to support a motion must be served and filed with the motion.

(ii) An affidavit must contain only factual information, not legal argument.

(iii) A motion seeking substantive relief must include a copy of the trial court's opinion or agency's decision as a separate exhibit.

(C) Documents barred or not required. (i) A separate brief supporting or responding to a motion must not be filed.

(ii) A notice of motion is not required.

(iii) A proposed order is not required.

(3) Response. (A) Time to file. Any party may file a response to a motion; Rule 27(a)(2) governs its contents. The response must be filed within 10 days after service of the motion unless the court shortens or extends the time. A motion authorized by Rules 8, 9, 18, or 41 may be granted before the 10-day period runs only if the court gives reasonable notice to the parties that it intends to act sooner.

(B) Request for affirmative relief. A response may include a motion for affirmative relief. The time to respond to the new motion, and to reply to that response, are governed by Rule 27(a)(3)(A) and (a)(4). The title of the response must alert the court to the request for relief.

(4) Reply to response. Any reply to a response must be filed within 7 days after service of the response. A reply must not present matters that do not relate to the response.

(b) *Disposition of a motion for a procedural order.* The court may act on a motion for a procedural order — including a motion under Rule 26(b) — at any time without awaiting a response, and may, by rule or by order in a particular case, authorize its clerk to act on specified types of procedural motions. A party adversely affected by the court's, or the clerk's, action may file a motion to reconsider, vacate, or modify that action. Timely opposition filed after the motion is granted in whole or in part does not constitute a request to reconsider, vacate, or modify the disposition; a motion requesting that relief must be filed.

(c) *Power of a single judge to entertain a motion.* A circuit judge may act alone on any motion, but may not dismiss or otherwise determine an appeal or other proceeding. A court of appeals may provide by rule or by order in a particular case that only the court may act on any motion or class of motions. The court may review the action of a single judge.

(d) *Form of papers; page limits; and number of copies.* (1) Format. (A) Reproduction. A motion, response, or reply may be reproduced by any process that yields a clear black image on light paper. The paper must be opaque and unglazed. Only one side of the paper may be used.

(B) Cover. A cover is not required but there must be a caption that includes the case number, the name of the court, the title of the case, and a brief descriptive title indicating the purpose of the motion and identifying the party or parties for whom it is filed.

(C) Binding. The document must be bound in any manner that is secure, does not obscure the text, and permits the document to lie reasonably flat when open.

(D) Paper size, line spacing, and margins. The document must be on 8½ by 11 inch paper. The text must be double-spaced, but quotations more than two lines long may be indented and single-spaced. Headings and footnotes may be single-spaced. Margins must be at least one inch on all four sides. Page numbers may be placed in the margins, but no text may appear there.

(2) Page limits. A motion or a response to a motion must not exceed 20 pages, exclusive of the corporate disclosure statement and accompanying documents authorized by Rule 27(a)(2)(B), unless the court permits or directs otherwise. A reply to a response must not exceed 10 pages.

(3) Number of copies. An original and 3 copies must be filed unless the court requires a different number by local rule or by order in a particular case.

(e) *Oral argument.* A motion will be decided without oral argument unless the court orders otherwise. (Amended by order adopted April 30, 1979, effective August 1, 1979; by order adopted April 25, 1989, effective December 1, 1989; by order adopted April 29, 1994, effective December 1, 1994 and by order adopted April 24, 1998, effective December 1, 1998.)

Local Rule 27(a). Content of motions, notification and consent.

In cases where all parties are represented by counsel, all motions shall contain a statement by counsel that counsel for the other parties to the appeal have been informed of the intended filing of the motion. The statement shall indicate whether the other parties consent to the granting of the motion, or intend to file responses in opposition. (Redesignated and amended by order effective December 1, 1998.)

COMMENT

Former Local Rule 27(a) has been deleted as unnecessary because the provision has been incorporated into FRAP 27(e).

Local Rule 27(b). Procedural orders acted on by clerk; reconsideration thereof.

Motions and applications for orders if consented to, or if unopposed after due notice to all interested parties has been given or waived, or if the orders sought are procedural or relate to the preparation or printing of the appendix and briefs on appeal, or are such as are ordinarily granted as of course and without notice or hearing, need not be submitted to the Court, or to a judge thereof.

Such orders may be entered for the Court by the clerk, who shall forthwith send copies thereof to the parties.

Any party adversely affected by an order entered by the clerk pursuant to this rule shall be entitled to request reconsideration of the clerk's action by the Court, if within 14 days after entry of the order, such party shall file with the clerk and serve upon the parties to the proceedings a request, in writing, for reconsideration, vacation or modification of the order, stating the grounds for such request. The clerk shall thereupon submit to the Court the request for reconsideration, vacation or modification, the motion or application upon which the order was entered, and any responses by other parties which may have been filed in support or opposition to the request. The Court may thereafter take such action as may be proper.

COMMENT

Local Rule 27(c) has been designated as 27(b), and the title has been changed from "Non-Controversial orders granted by the clerk" to "Procedural orders acted on by the clerk." The change better characterizes the clerk's delegation of authority.

Local Rule 27(c). Form of papers; number of copies.

All motions should be filed with the clerk and comply with FRAP 27(d). Three copies must be filed with the original. A Disclosure of Corporate Affiliations and Other Entities with a Direct Financial Interest in Litigation statement must accompany the motion unless previously filed with the Court. See FRAP 26.1, Local Rule 26.1, and Form A. Counsel should always review carefully the specific rule which authorizes relief to ascertain the requirements and any motion should contain or be accompanied by any supporting documents required by a specific rule. If a motion is supported by attachments, these materials should also be served and filed with each copy of the motion. The parties should not make requests for procedural and substantive relief in a single motion, but should make each request in a separate motion. (Redesignated and amended by order effective December 1, 1998.)

Local Rule 27(d). Responses; replies.

(1) *Responses.* Although any party may file a response to a motion, a party need not respond to a motion until requested to do so by the Court. The three-day mailing period permitted by FRAP 26(c) does not apply to responses requested by the Court or clerk by letter wherein a response date is set forth in the request. A Disclosure of Corporate Affiliations and Other Financial Entities with a Direct Financial Interest in Litigation statement must accompany any response to a motion unless previously filed with the Court. See FRAP 26.1, Local Rule 26.1, and Form A. If the Court acts upon a motion without a response, any party adversely affected by such action may by application to the Court request reconsideration, vacation or modification of the Court's action.

(2) *Replies.* The Court will not ordinarily await the filing of a reply before reviewing a motion and response. If movant intends to file a reply and does not want the Court to actively consider the motion and response until a reply is filed, movant shall notify the clerk in writing of the intended filing of the reply

and request that this Court not act on the motion until the reply is received. (Amended by order effective December 1, 1995; and redesignated and amended by order effective December 1, 1998.)

COMMENT

Local Rule 27(e) has been redesignated Local Rule 27(d) and the seven-day period for filing a response has been deleted from the local rule because FRAP 27(a)(3)(A) now affords ten days for a response. Reference in the local rule to the absence of a standard time period for filing a reply is deleted because FRAP 27(a)(4) now provides a seven-day reply period. The local rule retains, however, the statement that the court will ordinarily not await the filing of a reply before reviewing the motion or response. Replies are not routinely filed and waiting an additonal seven days before actively considering a matter simply delays the disposition of motions by the court. The local rule is amended to provide that when a movant intends to file a reply, the movant shall inform the clerk that a reply is forthcoming and specifically request that the motion not be considered until a reply is received. Subsection 3 of the local rule has been deleted because the statement is now contained in FRAP 27(a)(2)(C)(iii).

Local Rule 27(e). Single judges and emergency motions.

A single judge of the Fourth Circuit may entertain and decide motions, except a single judge may not dismiss or otherwise ultimately determine an appeal. Presentation of certain emergency motions can be made by application to a single judge at the judge's resident chambers, but it is a matter of an individual judge's discretion as to whether he or she will entertain an emergency motion as a single judge. Applications to a single judge should ordinarily be made to a circuit judge who is resident in the state where the application originated. If time permits, counsel are urged to follow the preferred procedure of presenting all motions to the clerk for presentation to the Court. Counsel should contact the Clerk's Office before making application to a single judge and copies of all papers presented to the judge should also be presented to the clerk for filing. The action of a single judge may be reviewed by the Court or a panel thereof.

Motions filed with the clerk may be submitted and decided by a single judge or by a two- or three-judge panel of the Court. When deemed advisable, motions may be submitted to the full Court for decision. (Redesignated by order effective December 1, 1998.)

Local Rule 27(f). Motions for summary disposition.

Motions for summary affirmance, reversal or dismissal are reserved for extraordinary cases only and should not be filed routinely. Counsel contemplating filing a motion to dispose summarily of an appeal should carefully consider whether the issues raised on appeal are in fact manifestly unsubstantial and appropriate for disposition by motion. Motions for summary affirmance or reversal are seldom granted.

Motions for summary disposition should be made only after briefs are filed. If such motions are submitted before the completion of the briefing schedule, the Court will defer action on the motion until the case is mature for full consideration.

Motions to dismiss based upon the ground that the appeal is not within the jurisdiction of the Court or for other procedural grounds may be filed at anytime. The Court may also sua sponte summarily dispose of any appeal at any time. (Redesignated by order effective December 1, 1998.)

Rule 28. Briefs.

(a) *Appellant's brief.* The appellant's brief must contain, under appropriate headings and in the order indicated:

(1) a corporate disclosure statement if required by Rule 26.1;

(2) a table of contents, with page references;

(3) a table of authorities — cases (alphabetically arranged), statutes, and other authorities — with references to the pages of the brief where they are cited;

(4) a jurisdictional statement, including:

(A) the basis for the district court's or agency's subject-matter jurisdiction, with citations to applicable statutory provisions and stating relevant facts establishing jurisdiction;

(B) the basis for the court of appeals' jurisdiction, with citations to applicable statutory provisions and stating relevant facts establishing jurisdiction;

(C) the filing dates establishing the timeliness of the appeal or petition for review; and

(D) an assertion that the appeal is from a final order or judgment that disposes of all parties' claims, or information establishing the court of appeals' jurisdiction on some other basis;

(5) a statement of the issues presented for review;

(6) a statement of the case briefly indicating the nature of the case, the course of proceedings, and the disposition below;

(7) a statement of facts relevant to the issues submitted for review with appropriate references to the record (see Rule 28(e));

(8) a summary of the argument, which must contain a succinct, clear, and accurate statement of the arguments made in the body of the brief, and which must not merely repeat the argument headings;

(9) the argument, which must contain:

(A) appellant's contentions and the reasons for them, with citations to the authorities and parts of the record on which the appellant relies; and

(B) for each issue, a concise statement of the applicable standard of review (which may appear in the discussion of the issue or under a separate heading placed before the discussion of issues);

(10) a short conclusion stating the precise relief sought; and

(11) the certificate of compliance, if required by Rule 32(a)(7).

(b) *Appellee's brief.* The appellee's brief must conform to the requirements of Rule 28(a)(1)-(9) and (11), except that none of the following need appear unless the appellee is dissatisfied with the appellant's statement:

(1) the jurisdictional statement;

(2) the statement of the issues;

(3) the statement of the case;

(4) the statement of the facts; and

(5) the statement of the standard of review.

(c) *Reply brief.* The appellant may file a brief in reply to the appellee's brief. An appellee who has cross-appealed may file a brief in reply to the appellant's response to the issues presented by the cross-appeal. Unless the court permits, no further briefs may be filed. A reply brief must contain a table of contents, with page references, and a table of authorities — cases (alphabetically arranged), statutes, and other authorities — with references to the pages of the reply brief where they are cited.

(d) *References in briefs to parties.* In briefs and at oral argument, counsel should minimize use of the terms "appellant " and "appellee." To make briefs clear, counsel should use the parties' actual names or the designations used in the lower court or agency proceeding, or such descriptive terms as "the employee," "the injured person," "the taxpayer," "the ship," "the stevedore."

(e) *References to the record.* References to the parts of the record contained in the appendix filed with the appellant's brief must be to the pages of the appendix. If the appendix is prepared after the briefs are filed, a party referring to the record must follow one of the methods detailed in Rule 30(c). If the original record is used under Rule 30(f) and is not consecutively paginated, or if the brief refers to an unreproduced part of the record, any reference must be to the page of the original document. For example:

- Answer p. 7;
- Motion for Judgment p. 2;
- Transcript p. 231.

Only clear abbreviations may be used. A party referring to evidence whose admissibility is in controversy must cite the pages of the appendix or of the transcript at which the evidence was identified, offered, and received or rejected.

(f) *Reproduction of statutes, rules, regulations, etc.* If the court's determination of the issues presented requires the study of statutes, rules, regulations, etc., the relevant parts must be set out in the brief or in an addendum at the end, or may be supplied to the court in pamphlet form.

(g) [Reserved]

(h) *Briefs in a case involving a cross-appeal.* If a cross-appeal is filed, the party who files a notice of appeal first is the appellant for the purposes of this rule and Rules 30, 31, and 34. If notices are filed on the same day, the plaintiff in the proceeding below is the appellant. These designations may be modified by agreement of the parties or by court order. With respect to appellee's cross-appeal and response to appellant's brief, appellee's brief must conform to the requirements of Rule 28(a)(1)-(11). But an appellee who is satisfied with appellant's statement need not include a statement of the case or of the facts.

(i) *Briefs in a case involving multiple appellants or appellees.* In a case involving more than one appellant or appellee, including consolidated cases, any number of appellants or appellees may join in a brief, and any party may adopt by reference a part of another's brief. Parties may also join in briefs.

(j) *Citation of supplemental authorities.* If pertinent and significant authorities come to a party's attention after the party's brief has been filed — or after oral argument but before decision — a party may promptly advise the circuit clerk by letter, with a copy to all other parties, setting forth the citations. The letter must state without argument the reasons for the supplemental citations, referring either to the page of the brief or to a point argued orally. Any response must be made promptly and must be similarly limited. (Amended by order adopted April 30, 1979, effective August 1, 1979; by order adopted June 30, 1979, effective August 1, 1979; by order adopted March 10, 1986, effective July 1, 1986; by order adopted April 25, 1989, corrected May 1, 1989, effective December 1, 1989; by order adopted April 30, 1991, effective December 1, 1991; by order adopted April 22, 1993, effective December 1, 1993; by order adopted April 29, 1994, effective December 1, 1994; and by order adopted April 24, 1998, effective December 1, 1998.)

Court will not search through record to find material which parties failed to provide. — United States Court of Appeals will not sift through the record to piece together support for computer corporation's contentions that a computer program developed by one of its competitors, infringed upon the copyrights it held in its "Claims Express" and "EDI Link" computer programs where it had not identified any evidence demonstrating that district court clearly erred in finding that the program developed by competitor was not substantially similar to either Claims Express or EDI Link. Comprehensive Technologies Int'l, Inc. v. Software Artisans, Inc., 3 F.3d 730 (4th Cir. 1993).

Failure to include contentions constitute abandonment of claims. — Where none of the briefs filed by either party contains "contentions" about the application of the Virginia Constitution's Declaration of Rights or the Virginia Act for Religious Freedom to the instant case, or citations to authorities that might illuminate the special rights that state charter and religious-freedom statute are said to guarantee, the parties failed to appeal the district court's grant of summary judgment with respect to these state-law theories of recovery; failure of this nature constitutes abandonment of the claims, and precludes appellate court from considering them further herein. Rosenberger v. Rector & Visitors of Univ. of Va., 18 F.3d 269 (4th Cir. 1994).

Applied in Columbus-America Discovery Group v. Atlantic Mut. Ins. Co., 56 F.3d 556 (4th Cir. 1995); Winfield v. Bass, 67 F.3d 529 (4th Cir. 1995).

Local Rule 28(a). Consolidated cases and briefs.

Related appeals or petitions for review will be consolidated in the Office of the Clerk, with notice to all parties, at the time a briefing schedule is established. One brief shall be permitted per side, including parties permitted to intervene, in all cases consolidated by Court order, unless leave to the contrary is granted upon good cause shown. In consolidated cases lead counsel shall be selected by the attorneys on each side and that person's identity made known in writing to the clerk within 7 days of the date of the order of consolidation. In the absence of an agreement by counsel, the clerk shall designate lead counsel. The individual so designated shall be responsible for the coordination, preparation and filing of the briefs and appendix.

Local Rule 28(b). Attachments to briefs.

Each party shall include, in the body of the brief or in an addendum thereto, the verbatim text of the relevant portion of any constitutional provision, treaty, statute, ordinance, rule or regulation cited in the brief, if its construction is sought, there is controversy among the parties concerning its proper application to the case, or it is otherwise pertinent to the substantive issues on appeal. Each party shall also include in the addendum any unpublished opinion cited pursuant to Local Rule 36(c). Should a party wish to supplement the brief with matters other than those enumerated above, the additional material shall be presented to the Court under separate cover, accompanied by a motion for leave to file that specifically identifies the proposed material, indicates whether it is a matter of record, and sets forth good cause for deviating from the general prohibition of attachments to briefs. (Amended by order effective December 1, 1998.)

COMMENT

The last sentence of Local Rule 28(b) has been deleted because the clerk's current practice is to hold a non-conforming brief and require its correction rather than return the brief for resubmission in proper form.

Local Rule 28(c). Responsibilities of counsel listed on a brief.

The Court will interpret the listing of an attorney on a brief as a representation that he or she is capable of arguing the appeal if lead counsel is unavailable.

Editor's note. — Effective September 28, 1994, former Local Rule (c), relating to statements of standards of review for a case on appeal, was eliminated due to conflict with FRAP 28(a)(5) concerning placement of the standard of review.

Local Rule 28(d). Joint appeals and consolidations.

Where multiple parties are directed to file a consolidated brief, counsel on the same side of the case should confer and agree upon a means for assuring that the positions of all parties are addressed within the length limits allowed and that each counsel will have an opportunity to review and approve the consolidated brief before it is filed.

Motions to file separate briefs are not favored by the Court and are granted only upon a particularized showing of good cause, such as, but not limited to, cases in which the interests of the parties are adverse. Generally unacceptable grounds for requests to file separate briefs include representations that the issues presented require a brief in excess of the length limitations established by FRAP 32(a)(7) (appropriately addressed by a motion to exceed length limit), that counsel cannot coordinate their efforts due to different geographical locations, or that the participation of separate counsel in the proceedings below entitles each party to separate briefs on appeal.

If a motion to file separate briefs is granted, the length of such briefs may be limited by the Court. The parties shall continue to share the time allowed for oral argument. (Amended by order effective December 1, 1995; redesignated and amended by order effective December 1, 1998.)

COMMENT

Proposed Local Rule 28(e) adds language to existing I.O.P. 28.2 to cross-reference the 40-page proportional type requirement contained in proposed Local Rule 28(d) (existing I.O.P. 28.1).

[Former] Local Rule 28(d) has been moved to Local Rule 32(b) and amended to conform to FRAP 32(a)(7).

Local Rule 28(e). Citation of additional authorities.

Counsel may, without leave of Court, present a letter drawing the Court's attention to supplemental authorities under Rule 28(j). An original and three copies of the letter should be filed with the clerk and a copy of the letter should be mailed to all counsel of record. No argument should be made in the letter.

The Court may grant leave for or direct the filing of additional memoranda, which may include additional argument, before, during or after oral argument. (Redesignated by order effective December 1,1998.)

Local Rule 28(f). Statement of facts.

Every opening brief filed by appellants in this court shall include a separate section, the title which is STATEMENT OF FACTS. In this section the attorneys will prepare a narrative statement of all of the facts necessary for the Court to reach the conclusion which the brief desires. The said STATEMENT OF FACTS will include exhibit, record, transcript, or appendix references showing the source of the facts stated. An appellee's brief shall also include a STATEMENT OF FACTS so prepared unless appellee is satisfied with appellant's statement of facts. (Adopted by order effective June 5, 1996; amended by order effective December 4, 1996; and redesignated and amended by order effective December 1, 1998.)

COMMENT

Local Rule 28(g), which has been redesignated as 28(f), has been amended to conform to FRAP 28(a)(7) (listing the statement of facts as a separate section) and FRAP 28(b) (providing that appellee is not required to include a statement of facts unless appellee is dissatisfied with appellant's statement).

Rule 29. Brief of an amicus curiae.

(a) *When permitted.* The United States or its officer or agency, or a State, Territory, Commonwealth, or the District of Columbia may file an amicus-curiae brief without the consent of the parties or leave of court. Any other amicus curiae may file a brief only by leave of court or if the brief states that all parties have consented to its filing.

(b) *Motion for leave to file.* The motion must be accompanied by the proposed brief and state:

(1) the movant's interest; and

(2) the reason why an amicus brief is desirable and why the matters asserted are relevant to the disposition of the case.

(c) *Contents and form.* An amicus brief must comply with Rule 32. In addition to the requirements of Rule 32, the cover must identify the party or parties supported and indicate whether the brief supports affirmance or reversal. If an amicus curiae is a corporation, the brief must include a disclosure statement like that required of parties by Rule 26.1. An amicus brief need not comply with Rule 28, but must include the following:

(1) a table of contents, with page references;

(2) a table of authorities — cases (alphabetically arranged), statutes and other authorities — with references to the pages of the brief where they are cited;

(3) a concise statement of the identity of the amicus curiae, its interest in the case, and the source of its authority to file;

(4) an argument, which may be preceded by a summary and which need not include a statement of the applicable standard of review; and

(5) a certificate of compliance, if required by Rule 32(a)(7).

(d) *Length*. Except by the court's permission, an amicus brief may be no more than one-half the maximum length authorized by these rules for a party's principal brief. If the court grants a party permission to file a longer brief, that extension does not affect the length of an amicus brief.

(e) *Time for filing*. An amicus curiae must file its brief, accompanied by a motion for filing when necessary, no later than 7 days after the principal brief of the party being supported is filed. An amicus curiae that does not support either party must file its brief no later than 7 days after the appellant's or petitioner's principal brief is filed. A court may grant leave for later filing, specifying the time within which an opposing party may answer.

(f) *Reply brief*. Except by the court's permission, an amicus curiae may not file a reply brief.

(g) *Oral argument*. An amicus curiae may participate in oral argument only with the court's permission. (Amended by order adopted April 24, 1998, effective December 1, 1998.)

Local Rule 29. Motion for leave to file brief as amicus curiae.
[Deleted.]

COMMENT

Local Rule 29 has been deleted because the federal rule now details the filing requirements for amicus curiae briefs.

Rule 30. Appendix to the briefs.

(a) *Appellant's responsibility*. (1) Contents of the appendix. The appellant must prepare and file an appendix to the briefs containing:

(A) the relevant docket entries in the proceeding below;

(B) the relevant portions of the pleadings, charge, findings, or opinion;

(C) the judgment, order, or decision in quesstion; and

(D) other parts of the record to which the parties wish to direct the court's attention.

(2) Excluded material. Memoranda of law in the district court should not be included in the appendix unless they have independent relevance. Parts of the record may be relied on by the court or the parties even though not included in the appendix.

(3) Time to file; Number of copies. Unless filing is deferred under Rule 30(c), the appellant must file 10 copies of the appendix with the brief and must serve one copy on counsel for each party separately represented. An unrepresented party proceeding in forma pauperis must file 4 legible copies with the clerk, and one copy must be served on counsel for each separately represented party. The court may by local rule or by order in a particular case require the filing or service of a different number.

(b) *All parties' responsibilities*. (1) Determining the contents of the appendix. The parties are encouraged to agree on the contents of the appendix. In the absence of an agreement, the appellant must, within 10 days after the record is filed, serve on the appellee a designation of the parts of the record the appellant intends to include in the appendix and a statement of the issues the appellant intends to present for review. The appellee may, within 10 days after receiving the designation, serve on the appellant a designation of additional parts to which it wishes to direct the court's attention. The appellant must include the designated parts in the appendix. The parties must not engage in unnecessary designation of parts of the record, because the entire record is available to the court. This paragraph applies also to a cross-appellant and a cross-appellee.

(2) Costs of appendix. Unless the parties agree otherwise, the appellant must pay the cost of the appendix. If the appellant considers parts of the record designated by the appellee to be unnecessary, the appellant may advise the appellee, who must then advance the cost of including those parts. The cost of the appendix is a taxable cost. But if any party causes unnecessary parts of the record to be included in the appendix, the court may impose the cost of those parts on that party. Each circuit must, by local rule, provide for sanctions against attorneys who unreasonably and vexatiously increase litigation costs by including unnecessary material in the appendix.

(c) *Deferred appendix.* (1) Deferral until after briefs are filed. The court may provide by rule for classes of cases or by order in a particular case that preparation of the appendix may be deferred until after the briefs have been filed and that the appendix may be filed 21 days after the appellee's brief is served. Even though the filing of the appendix may be deferred, Rule 30(b) applies; except that a party must designate the parts of the record it wants included in the appendix when it serves its brief, and need not include a statement of the issues presented.

(2) References to the record. (A) If the deferred appendix is used, the parties may cite in their briefs the pertinent pages of the record. When the appendix is prepared, the record pages cited in the briefs must be indicated by inserting record page numbers, in brackets, at places in the appendix where those pages of the record appear.

(B) A party who wants to refer directly to pages of the apppendix may serve and file copies of the brief within the time required by Rule 31(a), containing appropriate references to pertinent pages of the record. In that event, within 14 days after the appendix is filed, the party must serve and file copies of the brief, containing references to the pages of the appendix in place of or in addition to the references to the pertinent pages of the record. Except for the correction of typographical errors, no other changes may be made to the brief.

(d) *Format of the appendix.* The appendix must begin with a table of contents identifying the page at which each part begins. The relevant docket entries must follow the table of contents. Other parts of the record must follow chronologically. When pages from the transcript of proceedings are placed in the appendix, the transcript page numbers must be shown in brackets immediately before the included pages. Omissions in the text of papers or of the transcript must be indicated by asterisks. Immaterial formal matters (captions, subscriptions, acknowledgments, etc.) should be omitted.

(e) *Reproduction of exhibits.* Exhibits designated for inclusion in the appendix may be reproduced in a separate volume, or volumes, suitably indexed. Four copies must be filed with the appendix and one copy shall be served on counsel for each separately represented party. If a transcript of a proceeding before an administrative agency, board, commission, or officer used in an action in the district court action and has been designated for inclusion in the appendix, the transcript must be places in the appendix as an exhibit.

(f) *Appeal on the original record without an appendix.* The court may, either by rule for all cases or classes of cases or by order in a particular case, dispense with the appendix and permit an appeal to proceed on the original record with any copies of the record, or relevant parts, that the court may order the parties to file. (Amended by order adopted March 30, 1970, effective July 1, 1970; by order adopted March 10, 1986, effective July 1, 1986; by order adopted April 30, 1991, effective December 1,1991; by order adopted April 29, 1994, effective December 1, 1994; and by order adopted April 24, 1998, effective December 1, 1998.)

The obligation to file an appendix is clearly that of the appellant. United States v. Seaboard Coast Line R.R., 517 F.2d 881 (4th Cir. 1975).

Appeal dismissed where appendix failed to meet minimum requirements. — The government's appeal from an order dismissing a complaint in an action under the Carmack amendment was dismissed, where the brief filed by the government purported to include an appendix, but the appendix failed to meet the minimum requirements of subdivision (a), where the appendix to the government's brief consisted of two pages reproducing only two bills of lading and where the government neither sought nor obtained an order under subdivision (c) which authorizes the filing of a deferred appendix, nor did it seek or obtain an order under subdivision (f) authorizing an appeal to be heard on the original record. United States v. Seaboard Coast Line R.R., 517 F.2d 881 (4th Cir. 1975).

Applied in Sivertsen v. Guardian Life Ins. Co., 423 F.2d 443 (4th Cir. 1970); Webb v. Hutto, 720 F.2d 375 (4th Cir. 1983).

Local Rule 30(a). Attorney sanctions for unnecessary appendix designations.

The Court, on its own motion or on motion of any party, may impose sanctions against attorneys who unreasonably and vexatiously increase the costs of litigation through the inclusion of unnecessary material in the appendix. Attorneys shall receive reasonable notice and opportunity to respond before the imposition of any sanction. A party's motion for the imposition of sanctions will be entertained only if filed within 14 days after entry of judgment and only if counsel for the moving party previously objected to the designation of the allegedly unnecessary material in writing to opposing counsel within 10 days of the material's designation.

Local Rule 30(b). Appendix contents; number of copies.

Although there is no limit on the length of the appendix except as provided in Local Rule 32(a), it is unnecessary to include everything in the appendix. The appendix should contain only those parts of the record vital to the understanding of the basic issues on appeal. The use of a selectively abridged record allows the judges to refer easily to relevant parts of the record and saves the parties the considerable expense of reproducing the entire record.

In all criminal appeals seeking review of the application of the sentencing guidelines, appellant shall include the sentencing hearing transcript and presentence report in the appendix.

Pursuant to the authority granted by FRAP 30(a)(3), the Court requires that only six copies of the appendix must be filed with appellant's opening brief and a copy served on counsel for each party separately represented. Appointed counsel may file five copies and any party proceeding in forma pauperis who is not represented by court-appointed counsel may file four copies. If the Court allows a deferred appendix the parties routinely file four page-proof copies of the brief in lieu of the requisite number of copies. After the deferred appendix is filed, the parties must replace their page-proof copies with the requisite number of copies of their final brief, which must contain proper references to the appendix. (Amended by order effective December 1, 1995; and order effective December 1, 1998.)

Editor's note. — Local Rule 30(b) cross-references the 250-page limitation on appendices in court-appointed criminal cases as provided in Local Rule 32(a).

COMMENT

Proposed Local Rule 30(b) adds language to existing I.O.P. 30.1 by cross-referencing the 250-page limitation on appendices in court-appointed criminal cases as provided in proposed Local Rule 32(b) (existing I.O.P. 32.1).

Local Rule 30(c). Responsibility of parties.

Notwithstanding that FRAP 30 provides that the appellant shall prepare and file the appendix, the Court considers the coordination of preparing the appendix to be the responsibility of both sides. The failure of a side to designate does not absolve the other side from the responsibility.

Except under the most extraordinary circumstances, supplementary appendices will not be accepted. If the appellant omits from the appendix the portions designated by the appellee, the appellant will be required to file a corrected appendix incorporating such material, and to bear the cost regardless of the outcome of the appeal.

If a party files a motion for leave to file a supplemental appendix, the motion must specifically identify the contents of the supplemental appendix, state that the items are matters of record, and set forth good cause why the original appendix should not be returned for insertion of the additional materials.

Local Rule 30(d). Dispensing with appendix.

Motions to proceed on the original record pursuant to FRAP 30(f) are carefully reviewed in the Fourth Circuit and are not usually granted unless the appellant is proceeding in forma pauperis, the record is short, or the appeal is expedited. Even if the motion is granted, counsel must include an abbreviated appendix consisting of:

   i. pertinent district court docket entries,

   ii. indictment or complaint,

   iii. judgment or order being appealed,

   iv. notice of appeal,

   v. any crucial portions of the transcript of proceedings referred to in appellant's brief,

   vi. a copy of the order granting leave to proceed on the original record.

The requisite number of copies of the abbreviated appendix as set forth in Local Rule 30(b) must be filed with the brief, but it may be included as part of the brief rather than being reproduced separately. (Amended by order effective December 1, 1995.)

Rule 31. Serving and filing briefs.

(a) *Time to serve and file a brief.* (1) The appellant must serve and file a brief within 40 days after the record is filed. The appellee must serve and file a brief within 30 days after the appellant's brief is served. The appellant may serve and file a reply brief within 14 days after service of the appellee's brief but a reply must be filed at least 3 days before argument, unless the court, for good cause, allows a later filing.

(2) A court of appeals that routinely considers cases on the merits promptly after the briefs are filed may shorten the time to serve and file briefs, either by local rule or by order in a particular case.

(b) *Number of copies.* Twenty-five copies of each brief must be filed with the clerk and 2 copies must be served on counsel for each separately represented party. An unrepresented party proceeding in forma pauperis must file 4 legible copies with the clerk, and one copy must be served on counsel for each separately represented party. The court may by local rule or by order in a particular case require the filing or service of a different number.

(c) *Consequence of failure to file.* If an appellant fails to file a brief within the time provided by this rule, or within an extended time, an appellee may move to dismiss the appeal. An appellee who fails to file a brief will not be heard at oral argument unless the court grants permission. (Amended by order adopted March 30, 1970, effective July 1, 1970; by order adopted March 10, 1986, effective July 1, 1986; by order adopted April 29, 1994, effective December 1, 1994; and by order adopted April 24, 1998, effective December 1, 1998.)

Local Rule 31(a). Shortened time for service and filing of briefs in criminal cases.

Pursuant to the authority conferred by FRAP 31(a)(2), the time for serving and filing briefs in criminal appeals is shortened as follows: the appellant shall serve and file appellant's brief and appendix within thirty-five days after the date on which the briefing order is filed; the appellee shall serve and file appellee's brief within twenty-one days after service of the brief of the appellant; the appellant may serve and file a reply brief within ten days after service of the brief of the appellee. (Amended by order effective December 1, 1998.)

Local Rule 31(b). Briefing orders.

A formal briefing schedule shall be sent to the parties upon receipt of the record, notification that the record is complete pursuant to Local Rule 10(a), or when the Clerk determines that no hearing was held for which a transcript is necessary — whichever occurs first. Thus, the time for designating the contents of the joint appendix and the filing of briefs is controlled by the briefing order and not the receipt of the record as provided in FRAP 31(a)(1).

(Amended by order effective December 4, 1991; by order effective December 1, 1995; and by order effective December 1, 1998.)

Editor's note. — Rule 31(b) reflects that the establishment of a briefing schedule trig- gers the time for designation of the joint ap- pendix.

Local Rule 31(c). Filing and service.

Briefs and appendices are deemed filed on the date of mailing if first class mail or other classes of mail at least as expeditious are used. If a courier service is used, the briefs and appendices are deemed timely filed if the briefs and appendices are given to the courier service on or before the due date to be dispatched to the Clerk's Office for delivery within three calendar days. Filing must be within the time allowed by the briefing order. A brief must be accompanied by a valid certificate of service, which should be bound with the brief as the last, unnumbered page. A certificate of service can be prepared in advance of actual mailing or hand delivery of the paper served. If service is not actually accomplished in the manner and on the date stated in the certificate, an amended certificate of service is required.

Extensions will be granted only when extraordinary circumstances exist. A motion for an extension of time to file a brief must be filed well in advance of the date the brief is due and must set forth the additional time requested and the reasons for the request. The Court discourages these motions and may deny the motion entirely or grant a lesser period of time than the time requested. (Amended effective December 4, 1996.)

Local Rule 31(d). Number of copies.

Each party must file eight copies of the brief with the clerk and serve two copies on counsel for each party separately represented. Appointed counsel may file six copies and serve one copy on counsel for each party separately represented. Any party proceeding in forma pauperis who is not represented by Court-appointed counsel may file four copies, with service of one copy on counsel for each party separately represented. If an en banc hearing or rehearing en banc is scheduled, additional copies of briefs may be requested. (Amended by order effective December 4, 1991; and by order effective December 1, 1998.)

Rule 32. Form of briefs, appendices and other papers.

(a) *Form of a brief.* (1) Reproduction. (A) A brief may be reproduced by any process that yields a clear black image on light paper. The paper must be opaque and unglazed. Only one side of the paper may be used.

(B) Text must be reproduced with a clarity that equals or exceeds the output of a laser printer.

(C) Photographs, illustrations, and tables may be reproduced by any method that results in a good copy of the original; a glossy finish is acceptable if the original is glossy.

(2) Cover. Except for filings by unrepresented parties, the cover of the appellant's brief must be blue; the appellee's, red; an intervenor's or amicus curiae's, green; and any reply brief, gray. The front cover of a brief must contain:

(A) the number of the case centered at the top;

(B) the name of the court;

(C) the title of the case (see Rule 12(a));

(D) the nature of the proceeding (e.g., Appeal, Petition for Review) and the name of the court, agency, or board below;

(E) the title of the brief, identifying the party or parties for whom the brief is filed; and

(F) the name, office address, and telephone number of counsel representing the party for whom the brief is filed.

(3) Binding. The brief must be bound in any manner that is secure, does not obscure the text, and permits the brief to lie reasonably flat when open.

(4) Paper size, line spacing, and margins. The brief must be on 8 ½ by 11 inch paper. The text must be double-spaced, but quotations more than two lines long may be indented and single-spaced. Headings and footnotes may be single-spaced. Margins must be at least one inch on all four sides. Page numbers may be placed in the margins, but no text may appear there.

(5) Typeface. Either a proportionally spaced or a monospaced face may be used.

(A) A proportionally spaced face must include serifs, but sans-serif type may be used in headings and captions. A proportionally spaced face must be 14-point or larger.

(B) A monospaced face may not contain more than 10 ½ characters per inch.

(6) Type styles. A brief must be set in a plain, roman style, although italics or boldface may be used for emphasis. Case names must be italicized or underlined.

(7) Length. (A) Page limitation. A principal brief may not exceed 30 pages, or a reply brief 15 pages, unless it complies with Rule 32(a)(7)(B) and (C).

(B) Type-volume limitation. (i) A principal brief is acceptable if:

• it contains no more than 14,000 words; or

• it uses a monospaced face and contains no more than 1,300 lines of text.

(ii) A reply brief is acceptable if it contains no more than half of the type volume specified in Rule 32(a)(7)(B)(i).

(iii) Headings, footnotes, and quotations count toward the word and line limitations. The corporate disclosure statement, table of contents, table of citations, statement with respect to oral argument, any addendum containing statutes, rules or regulations, and any certificates of counsel do not count toward the limitation.

(C) Certificate of compliance. A brief submitted under Rule 32(a)(7)(B) must include a certificate by the attorney, or an unrepresented party, that the brief complies with the type-volume limitation. The person preparing the certificate may rely on the word or line count of the word-processing system used to prepare the brief. The certificate must state either:

(i) the number of words in the brief; or

(ii) the number of lines of monospaced type in the brief.

(b) *Form of an appendix.* An appendix must comply with Rule 32(a)(1), (2), (3), and (4), with the following exceptions:

(1) The cover of a separately bound appendix must be white.

(2) An appendix may include a legible photocopy of any document found in the record or of a printed judicial or agency decision.

(3) When necessary to facilitate inclusion of odd-sized documents such as technical drawings, an appendix may be a size other than 8 ½ by 11 inches, and need not lie reasonably flat when opened.

(c) *Form of other papers.* (1) Motion. The form of a motion is governed by Rule 27(d).

(2) Other papers. Any other paper, including a petition for rehearing and a petition for rehearing en banc, and any response to such a petition, must be reproduced in the manner prescribed by Rule 32(a), with the following exceptions:

(A) a cover is not necessary if the caption and signature page of the paper together contain the information required by Rule 32(a)(2); and

(B) Rule 32(a)(7) does not apply.

(d) *Local variation.* Every court of appeals must accept documents that comply with the form requirements of this rule. By local rule or order in a particular case a court of appeals may accept documents that do not meet all of the form requirements of this rule. (Amended by order adopted April 24, 1998, effective December 1, 1998.)

Local Rule 32(a). Reproduction of briefs and appendices.

Double-sided copying of briefs is permitted but not preferred. Double-sided copying of appendices is preferred in all cases. If an appendix is prepared by a commercial printer in a court-appointed case, the materials contained in the appendix should be reproduced on both sides of a sheet because reimbursement for copying expenses will be limited to 35 cents per double-sided sheet of the joint appendix. No joint appendix in a court-appointed case should exceed 250 sheets without advance permission from the Court; unless such permission is granted, reimbursement of copy expenses will be limited to 250 sheets. (Amended by order effective December 1, 1998.)

Local Rule 32(b). Length of briefs.

The Fourth Circuit encourages short, concise briefs. Under no circumstances may a brief exceed the limits set forth in FRAP 32(a)(7) without the Court's advance permission.

A motion for permission to submit a longer brief must be made to the Court of Appeals at least 10 days prior to the due date of the brief and must be supported by a statement of reasons. These motions are not favored and will be granted only for exceptional reasons. (Amended by order effective December 1, 1998.)

Local Rule 32(c). Correction of briefs and appendices.

If briefs, appendices, or other papers are illegible or are not in the form required by the federal rules or by this Court's local rules or standards when filed, counsel will be required to file corrected copies of the document. If the corrected copies are not submitted within the time allowed by the clerk, they must be accompanied by a motion to file out of time. (Amended by order effective December 1, 1998.)

COMMENT

Proposed Local Rule 32(d) changes the procedure set forth in existing I.O.P. 32.4 to reflect that the clerk no longer returns briefs for correction, but instead requires the submission of a corrected brief. Counsel may contact the clerk to make arrangements for the return of the original briefs at counsel's expense rather than filing an entirely new set.

Former Local Rule 32(a) has been deleted in its entirety as superseded by FRAP 32(a)(7).

Former Local Rule 32(b) has been redesignated Local Rule 32(a). Consistent with the FRAP amendments, it deletes reference to typeset briefs. It recasts as a preference the court's former requirement that materials in the joint appendix be reproduced on both sides of a sheet in court-appointed cases. FRAP 32(d) requires the court to accept any document in conformity with the requirements of FRAP but permits the court by local rule or order in a particular case to accept documents that do not meet all the FRAP form requirements. FRAP 32(a)(1) and 32(b) provide that briefs and appendices should be copied on only one side of the paper. Several years ago, the Court adopted a double-sided copying require-

ment and limited the size of the appendix to control excessive reproduction costs in Criminal Justice Act cases. The provision has proved an effective cost reduction mechanism which should be retained if possible. The amended local rule does this by stating that reimbursement will be limited to $.35 per double-sided sheet if the appendix is reproduced by a commercial printer, and that reimbursement will be limited to 250 sheets (500 pages) unless counsel obtained leave to file a longer appendix.

Local Rule 32(b) contains some of the information previously found in old Local Rule 28(d), but deletes the second sentence of old Local Rule 28(d), which was superseded by limits set forth in FRAP 32(a)(7). The last sentence of former Local Rule 28(d) has also been deleted from Local Rule 32(b) because footnotes and narrow margins can no longer be used to circumvent the size limitations for briefs established by the new rules.

Former Local Rule 32(c) has been deleted because FRAP 32(a)(2)(F) requires counsel's phone number.

Rule 33. Appeal conferences.

The court may direct the attorneys — and, when appropriate, the parties — to participate in one or more conferences to address any matter that may aid in disposing of the proceedings, including simplifying the issues and discussing settlement. A judge or other person designated by the court may preside over the conference, which may be conducted in person or by telephone. Before a settlement conference, the attorneys must consult with their clients and obtain as much authority as feasible to settle the case. The court may, as a result of the conference, enter an order controlling the course of proceedings or implementing any settlement agreement. (Amended by order adopted April 29, 1994, effective December 1, 1994; and by order adopted April 24, 1998, effective December 1, 1998.)

Local Rule 33. Circuit mediation conferences.

All civil and agency cases in which all parties are represented by counsel on appeal will be reviewed by a circuit mediator after the filing of the docketing statements required by Local Rule 3(b). The circuit mediator will determine whether a mediation conference may assist either the Court or the parties. Counsel for a party may also request a conference if counsel believes it will be of assistance to the Court or the parties. Counsel's participation is required at any scheduled conference. Mediation conferences will generally be conducted by telephone but may be conducted in person in the discretion of a circuit mediator. Mediation conferences may be adjourned from time to time by a circuit mediator. Purposes of the mediation conference include:

(a) Jurisdictional review;

(b) Simplification, clarification, and reduction of issues;

(c) Discussion of settlement; and

(d) Consideration of any other matter relating to the efficient management and disposition of the appeal.

Although the time allowed for filing of briefs is not automatically tolled by proceedings under this local rule, if the parties wish to pursue, or are engaged in, settlement discussions, counsel for any party may move to extend the briefing schedule. The mediator, through the Clerk of the Court, may enter orders which control the course of proceedings and, upon agreement of the parties, dispose of the case.

Statements and comments made during all mediation conferences, and papers or electronic information generated during the process, are not included in Court files except to the extent disclosed by orders entered under this local rule. Information disclosed in the mediation process shall be kept confidential and shall not be disclosed by a circuit mediator, counsel, or parties to the judges deciding the appeal or to any other person outside the mediation program participants.

COMMENT

Local Rule 33 has been amended to reflect the Court conference attorneys' preference for granting a definite extension rather than an indefinite suspension of a briefing schedule during settlement discussions.

Rule 34. Oral argument.

(a) *In general.* (1) Party's statement. Any party may file, or a court may require by local rule, a statement explaining why oral argument should, or need not, be permitted.

(2) Standards. Oral argument must be allowed in every case unless a panel of three judges who have examined the briefs and record unanimously agrees that oral argument is unnecessary for any of the following reasons:

. (A) the appeal is frivolous;

(B) the dispositive issue or issues have been authoritatively decided; or

(C) the facts and legal arguments are adequately presented in the briefs and record, and the decisional process would not be significantly aided by oral argument.

(b) *Notice of argument; postponement.* The clerk must advise all parties whether oral argument will be scheduled, and, if so, the date, time, and place for it, and the time allowed for each side. A motion to postpone the argument or to allow longer argument must be filed reasonably in advance of the hearing date.

(c) *Order and content of argument.* The appellant opens and concludes the argument. Counsel must not read at length from briefs, records, or authorities.

(d) *Cross-appeals and separate appeals.* If there is a cross-appeal, Rule 28(h) determines which party is the appellant and which is the appellee for purposes of oral argument. Unless the court directs otherwise, a cross-appeal or separate appeal must be argued when the initial appeal is argued. Separate parties should avoid duplicative argument.

(e) *Nonappearance of a party.* If the appellee fails to appear for argument, the court must hear appellant's argument. If the appellant fails to appear for argument, the court may hear the appellee's argument. If neither party appears, the case will be decided on the briefs, unless the court orders otherwise.

(f) *Submission on briefs.* The parties may agree to submit a case for decision on the briefs, but the court may direct that the case be argued.

(g) *Use of physical exhibits at argument; removal.* Counsel intending to use physical exhibits other than documents at the argument must arrange to place them in the courtroom on the day of the argument before the court convenes. After the argument, counsel must remove the exhibits from the courtroom, unless the court directs otherwise. The clerk may destroy or dispose of the exhibits if counsel does not reclaim them within a reasonable time after the clerk gives notice to remove them. (Amended by order adopted April 30, 1979, effective August 1, 1979, by order effective July 1, 1986, by order adopted April 30, 1991, effective December 1, 1991, and by order adopted April 22, 1993, effective December 1, 1993; and by order adopted April 24, 1998, effective December 1, 1998.)

Local Rule 34(a). Oral argument; pre-argument review and summary disposition of appeals; statement regarding the need for oral argument.

In the interest of docket control and to expedite the final disposition of pending cases, the chief judge may designate a panel or panels to review any pending case at any time before argument for disposition under this rule.

In reviewing pending cases before argument, the panel will utilize the minimum standards set forth in FRAP 34(a)(2). If all of the judges of the panel to which a pending appeal has been referred conclude that oral argument is not to be allowed, they may make any appropriate disposition without oral argument including, but not limited to, affirmance or reversal.

Because any case may be decided without oral argument, all major arguments should be fully developed in the briefs. In furtherance of the disposition of pending cases under this rule, parties may include in their briefs at the conclusion of the argument a statement setting forth the reasons why, in their opinion, oral argument should be heard. (Amended by order effective December 1, 1998.)

Local Rule 34(b). Informal briefs.

Whenever an application for a certificate of appealability from the denial of a writ of habeas corpus or a motion under 28 U.S.C. § 2255 is filed, or whenever any pro se appeal is filed, the clerk shall notify the appellant that appellant shall file, within twenty-one days after receipt of such notice, an informal brief, listing the specific issues and supporting facts and arguments raised on appeal. Appellant's informal brief and any informal brief filed by appellee shall be considered, together with the record and other relevant papers, by the panel to which the proceeding has been referred. The Court will limit its review to the issues raised in the informal brief.

The informal brief may be submitted on a form provided by the clerk and shall provide the specific information required by the form. The parties need not limit their briefs solely to the form. An additional supporting memorandum may be attached if a party deems it necessary in order to address adequately the issues raised, but the briefs with any attachments shall not exceed the length limitations established by FRAP 32(a)(7). It is not necessary to cite cases in an informal brief. Two copies of the brief and attachments, if any, must be filed with the Court and a copy mailed to opposing counsel.

Once an informal briefing schedule has been established the parties may file a formal brief only with the permission of the Court. The Court initially reviews cases that are informally briefed under its procedures set forth in Local Rule 34(a) pertaining to pre-argument review.

If the panel reviewing an informal brief submitted by an indigent pro se litigant determines that further briefing and possible oral argument would be of assistance, counsel will be appointed and directed to file additional formal briefs. In any appeal that has been informally briefed, the Court may direct that additional briefs be filed prior to oral argument. (Amended by order effective December 1, 1998.)

COMMENT

Local Rule 34(b) has been amended to delete the requirement of the Clerk sending the pro se party a copy of the local rule. Instead, the Clerk's office sends instructions on how to complete the informal briefing form.

Local Rule 34(c). Court sessions and notification to counsel.

The Court sits in Richmond, Virginia, for five consecutive days in October, November, December, February, March, April, May and June for its regular court terms. Court sessions are usually the first full week of each month, but adjustments are made because of holidays and elections, and special sessions may be scheduled at any time, anywhere in the circuit. Panels of the Court also regularly sit in the first full week of a scheduled month in Baltimore, Maryland, usually at least three times per year. On specified days during the summer months, panels sit in various cities throughout the circuit.

The Court initially hears and decides cases in panels consisting of three judges with the Chief Judge or most senior active judge presiding. Each panel regularly hears oral argument in four cases each day during court week; additional cases are added as required.

Attorneys appearing for oral argument must register with the Clerk's Office on the morning of argument to learn of courtroom assignment, order of appearance, and allocation of oral argument time. Counsel not already a member of the Fourth Circuit bar will be admitted to practice before the Court at that time upon compliance with the provisions of Local Rule 46(b). Registration commences at 8:00 a.m. and must be completed by 8:30 a.m., with the exception of Friday when registration commences at 7:15 a.m. and must be completed by 7:45 a.m.

The Court convenes at 9:30 a.m., with the exception of Friday, when it convenes at 8:30 a.m.

Preparation for the argument calendar begins in the Clerk's Office approximately two months prior to argument. Immediately upon receiving notice that a case has been tentatively assigned to an argument session, counsel must inform the clerk of any conflict or other matter that would affect scheduling of the case for that session. Once a case has been scheduled for argument, it will be removed from the argument calendar only for extreme unforeseeable problems. Excusal from an established oral argument date is not granted because of a prior professional commitment. Although a case will not be removed from the calendar because of a scheduling conflict by counsel after the notification of oral argument has been issued, the Court may direct another lawyer from the same firm to argue the appeal if counsel of record cannot be present.

COMMENT

Local Rule 34(c) deletes reference to the January session of Court because Court is no longer held in January. The rule also adds that counsel will be admitted to the bar of the Court only when counsel complies with the provisions of Local Rule 46(b). Proposed Local Rule 34(c) also changes existing I.O.P. 34.1 to reflect that the registration and oral argument for cases on Fridays is 45 minutes earlier than on other days of the Court session. Proposed Local Rule 34(c) also reflects the preference of the Court, as a matter of practice, to receive notice of any scheduling conflict when counsel receives notice of the tentative calendaring of a case for oral argument.

Local Rule 34(d). Argument time.

Briefs for the cases assigned to a hearing panel are distributed by the clerk to the judges on a hearing panel at the time the hearing panel assignments are made. The members of the Court hearing oral argument will have read the briefs before the hearing and therefore will be familiar with the case. In oral argument, counsel should emphasize the dispositive issues.

Since the appellant is allowed to open and close the argument, counsel for appellant should indicate at registration before oral argument how much time counsel wants to reserve for rebuttal. It is recommended that no more than two attorneys argue per side. Each side is normally allowed 30 minutes, even in consolidated cases, but counsel may not need the full time allotted or the Court may shorten the time allotted. In social security disability cases, black lung cases, and labor cases where the primary issue is whether the agency's decision is supported by substantial evidence and in criminal cases where the primary issue involves the application of the sentencing guidelines, each side is limited to 15 minutes. In black lung cases in which the Director, Office of Workers' Compensation Programs, has been granted leave to file a separate brief, the Director will share argument time with whichever side the Director's brief supports.

If counsel believes that more time is needed for oral argument, a written motion for additional time must be submitted well in advance of the hearing date. Such motions are discouraged by the Court and are seldom granted. The Court may sua sponte extend the allotted time during the argument or it may terminate the argument whenever in its judgment further argument is unnecessary. (Amended by order effective December 1, 1998.)

COMMENT

Proposed Local Rule 34(d) reflects the Court's current practice regarding the sharing of time for oral argument with the Director, Office of Workers' Compensation Programs, in black lung appeals.

Local Rule 34(d) was amended to provide that the court may reduce argument time from 30 minutes when extended argument is unnecessary.

Local Rule 34(e). Motion to submit on briefs.

As soon as possible upon completion of the briefing schedule or within 10 days of tentative notification of oral argument, whichever is earlier, any party may file a motion to submit the case on the briefs without the necessity of oral argument. Such motions are not granted as a matter of course. A motion to submit on briefs should not be used to alleviate a scheduling conflict after the notification of oral argument has been issued. (Amended by order effective December 1, 1998.)

COMMENT

Local Rule 34(e) has been amended to conform to the court's practice of requiring that motions to submit on the briefs be filed within ten days of notification to counsel that a case is tentatively calendared. This notification may occur before briefing is completed.

I.O.P. 34.1. Calendar assignments and panel composition.

The Clerk of Court maintains a list of mature cases available for oral argument and on a monthly basis merges those cases with a list of three-judge panels provided by a computer program designed to achieve total random selection.

The composition of each panel usually changes each day during court week except on those occasions where only one panel is sitting in a given geographical location. Every effort is made to assign cases for oral argument to judges who have had previous involvement with the case on appeal by way of a preargument motion or a previous decision concerning the matter, but there is no guarantee that any of the judges who have previously been involved with an appeal will be assigned to a hearing panel. The varied assignment of judges to panels and the independent assignment of varied cases to panels is designed, insofar as practicable, to assure the opportunity for each judge to sit with all other judges an equal number of times, and to assure that both the appearance and the fact of presentation of particular types of cases to particular judges is avoided.

I.O.P. 34.2. Disposition without oral argument.

A decision against oral argument must be unanimous, and if a case is decided without oral argument the decision on the merits must be unanimous also. Whenever at least one member of the review panel determines that oral argument would be of assistance, the panel notifies the clerk who places the case on the oral argument calendar.

Rule 35. En banc determination.

(a) *When hearing or rehearing en banc may be ordered.* A majority of the circuit judges who are in regular active service may order that an appeal or other proceeding be heard or reheard by the court of appeals en banc. An en banc hearing or rehearing is not favored and ordinarily will not be ordered unless:

(1) en banc consideration is necessary to secure or maintain uniformity of the court's decisions; or

(2) the proceeding involves a question of exceptional importance.

(b) *Petition for hearing or rehearing en banc.* A party may petition for a hearing or rehearing en banc.

(1) The petition must begin with a statement that either:

(A) the panel decision conflicts with a decision of the United States Supreme Court or of the court to which the petition is addressed (with citation to the conflicting case or cases) and consideration by the full court is therefore necessary to secure and maintain uniformity of the court's decisions; or

(B) the proceeding involves one or more questions of exceptional importance, each of which must be concisely stated; for example, a petition may assert that a proceeding presents a question of exceptional importance if it involves an issue on which the panel decision conflicts with the authoritative decisions of other United States Courts of Appeals that have addressed the issue.

(2) Except by the court's permission, a petition for an en banc hearing or rehearing must not exceed 15 pages, excluding material not counted under Rule 32.

(3) For purposes of the page limit in Rule 35(b)(2), if a party files both a petition for panel rehearing and a petition for rehearing en banc, they are considered a single document even if they are filed separately, unless separate filing is required by local rule.

(c) *Time for petition for hearing or rehearing en banc.* A petition that an appeal be heard initially en banc must be filed by the date when the appellee's brief is due. A petition for a rehearing en banc must be filed within the time prescribed by Rule 40 for filing a petition for rehearing.

(d) *Number of copies.* The number of copies to be filed must be prescribed by local rule and may be altered by order in a particular case.

(e) *Response.* No response may be filed to a petition for an en banc consideration unless the court orders a response.

(f) *Call for a vote.* A vote need not be taken to determine whether the case will be heard or reheard en banc unless a judge calls for a vote. (Amended by order adopted April 30, 1979, effective August 1, 1979, and by order adopted April 29, 1994, effective December 1, 1994 and by order adopted April 24, 1998, effective December 1, 1998.)

Local Rule 35. En banc proceedings.

(a) *Petition for rehearing en banc.* A petition for rehearing en banc must be made at the same time, and in the same document, as a petition for rehearing. The request for en banc consideration shall be stated plainly in the title of the petition. Petitions for rehearing en banc will be distributed to all active and senior judges of the Court, and to any visiting judge who may have heard and decided the appeal.

(b) *Decision to hear or rehear a case en banc.* A majority of the circuit judges who are in regular active service may grant a hearing or rehearing en banc. For purposes of determining a majority under this rule, the term majority means of all judges of the Court in regular active service who are presently serving, without regard to whether a judge is disqualified. Unless a judge requests that a poll be taken on the petition, none will be taken. If no poll is requested, the panel's order on a petition for rehearing will bear the notation that no member of the Court requested a poll. If a poll is requested and hearing or rehearing en banc is denied, the order will reflect the vote of each participating judge. A judge who joins the Court after a petition has been submitted to the Court, and before an order has been entered, will be eligible to vote on the decision to hear or rehear a case en banc.

(c) *Decision of cases heard or reheard en banc.* An en banc hearing will be before all eligible, active and participating judges of the Court. An en banc rehearing will be before all eligible and participating active judges, and any senior judge of the Court who sat on the panel that decided the case originally. An active judge who takes senior status after a case is heard or reheard by an en banc Court will be eligible to participate in the en banc decision. A judge who joins the Court after argument of a case to an en banc Court will not be eligible to participate in the decision of the case. A judge who joins the Court after submission of a case to an en banc Court without oral argument will participate in the decision of the case. Granting of rehearing en banc vacates the previous panel judgment and opinion; the rehearing is a review of the judgment or decision from which review is sought and not a review of the judgment of the panel. (The circuit takes the position that the change of wording in 28 U.S.C. § 46(c) referring to participation in en banc decisions does not alter the long-standing rule that the en banc court reviews the decision from which review is sought in this Court, not the decision of a panel.)

(d) *Additional copies of briefs and appendix for en banc hearing or rehearing.* The Court's order granting hearing or rehearing en banc may require the parties to file additional copies of the briefs and appendix. Each party will bear the initial cost of additional copies of its own briefs. The party that requested the hearing or rehearing en banc will bear the initial cost of filing additional copies of the appendix. In the event that cross petitions for hearing or rehearing en banc are granted, the parties will share equally the initial cost of preparing additional copies of the appendix. (Amended effective December 4, 1996; and effective December 1, 1998.)

Rule 36. Entry of judgment; notice.

(a) *Entry.* A judgment is entered when it is noted on the docket. The clerk must prepare, sign, and enter the judgment:

(1) after receiving the court's opinion — but if settlement of the judgment's form is required, after final settlement; or

(2) if a judgment is rendered without an opinion, as the court instructs.

(b) *Notice.* On the date when judgment is entered, the clerk must mail to all parties a copy of the opinion — or the judgment, if no opinion was written — and a notice of the date when the judgment was entered. (Amended by order adopted April 24, 1998, effective December 1, 1998.)

Local Rule 36(a). Publication of decisions.

Opinions delivered by the Court will be published only if the opinion satisfies one or more of the standards for publication:

i. It establishes, alters, modifies, clarifies, or explains a rule of law within this Circuit; or

ii. It involves a legal issue of continuing public interest; or

iii. It criticizes existing law; or

iv. It contains a historical review of a legal rule that is not duplicative; or

v. It resolves a conflict between panels of this Court, or creates a conflict with a decision in another circuit.

The Court will publish opinions only in cases that have been fully briefed and presented at oral argument. Opinions in such cases will be published if the author or a majority of the joining judges believes the opinion satisfies one or more of the standards for publication, and all members of the Court have acknowledged in writing their receipt of the proposed opinion. A judge may file a published opinion without obtaining all acknowledgments only if the opinion has been in circulation for ten days.

Local Rule 36(b). Unpublished dispositions.

Unpublished opinions give counsel, the parties, and the lower court or agency a statement of the reasons for the decision. They may not recite all of the facts or background of the case and may simply adopt the reasoning of the lower court. They are sent only to the trial court or agency in which the case originated, to counsel for all parties in the case, and to litigants in the case not represented by counsel. Any individual or institution may receive copies of all published and certain unpublished opinions of the Court by paying an annual subscription fee for this service. In addition, copies of such opinions are sent to all circuit judges, district judges, bankruptcy judges, magistrate judges, clerks of district court, United States Attorneys, and Federal Public Defenders upon request. All opinions are available on ABBS, the Appellate Bulletin Board System, for a minimum of six months after issuance. The Federal Reporter periodically lists the result in all cases involving unpublished opinions. Copies of any unpublished opinion are retained in the file of the case in the Clerk's Office and a copy may be obtained from the Clerk's Office for $2.00.

Counsel may move for publication of an unpublished opinion, citing reasons. If such motion is granted, the unpublished opinion will be published without change in result.

COMMENT

Proposed Local Rule 36(b) changes EDOS to ABBS to reflect the new name of the Appellate Bulletin Board System. All opinions issued on or after January 1, 1995 will be maintained on the ABBS for a minimum of six months.

Local Rule 36(c). Citation of unpublished dispositions.

In the absence of unusual circumstances, this Court will not cite an unpublished disposition in any of its published opinions or unpublished dispositions. Citation of this Court's unpublished dispositions in briefs and oral arguments in this Court and in the district courts within this Circuit is disfavored, except for the purpose of establishing res judicata, estoppel, or the law of the case.

If counsel believes, nevertheless, that an unpublished disposition of any court has precedential value in relation to a material issue in a case and that there is no published opinion that would serve as well, such disposition may be cited if counsel serves a copy thereof on all other parties in the case and on the Court. Such service may be accomplished by including a copy of the disposition in an attachment or addendum to the brief pursuant to the procedures set forth in Local Rule 28(b).

I.O.P. 36.1. Opinion preparation assignments.

The custom of the Fourth Circuit is to reserve judgment at the conclusion of oral argument. A conference of the panel is held promptly after oral argument, usually immediately after the presentation of the case. Although a tentative decision may be reached at this conference, additional conferences are sometimes necessary. Opinion assignments are made by the Chief Judge on the basis of recommendations from the presiding judge of each panel on which the Chief Judge did not sit.

I.O.P. 36.2. Circulation of opinions in argued cases and announcement of decision.

Although one judge writes the opinion, every panel member is equally involved in the process of decision. An appeal may be heard and decided by two of the three judges assigned to a panel, when one judge becomes unavailable. If a panel is reduced to two and the two cannot agree, however, the case will be reargued before a new three-judge panel which may or may not include prior panel members.

When a proposed opinion in an argued case is prepared and submitted to other panel members copies are provided to the non-sitting judges including the senior judges and their comments are solicited. The opinion is then finalized. The Clerk's Office never receives advance notice of when a decision will be rendered, so counsel should not call for such information.

It is the policy of the Fourth Circuit to mail a copy of the opinion to counsel on the day judgment is entered. Upon written request, counsel will be called on that day and informed of the disposition of the case; the text of the opinion will not be read over the telephone.

COMMENT

I.O.P. 36.2 has been amended to reflect that the Court no longer prints all opinions.

I.O.P. 36.3. Summary opinions.

If all judges on a panel of the Court agree following oral argument that an opinion in a case would have no precedential value, and that summary disposition is otherwise appropriate, the Court may decide the appeal by summary opinion. A summary opinion identifies the decision appealed from, sets forth the Court's decision and the reason or reasons therefor, and resolves any outstanding motions in the case. It does not discuss the facts or elaborate on the Court's reasoning.

Rule 37. Interest on judgments.

(a) *When the court affirms.* Unless the law provides otherwise, if a money judgment in a civil case is affirmed, whatever interest is allowed by law is payable from the date when the district court's judgment was entered.

(b) *When the court reverses.* If the court modifies or reverses a judgment with a direction that a money judgment be entered in the district court, the mandate must contain instructions about the allowance of interest. (Amended by order adopted April 24, 1998, effective December 1, 1998.)

Rule 38. Frivolous appeal — Damages and costs.

If a court of appeals determines that an appeal is frivolous, it may, after a separately filed motion or notice from the court and reasonable opportunity to respond, award just damages and single or double costs to the appellee. (Amended by order adopted April 29, 1994, effective December 1, 1994; and by order adopted April 24, 1998, effective December 1, 1998.)

Applied in Gaiters v. Lynn, 831 F.2d 51 (4th Cir. 1987); Bast v. Cohen, Dunn & Sinclair, 59 F.3d 492 (4th Cir. 1995).

Rule 39. Costs.

(a) *Against whom assessed.* The following rules apply unless the law provides or the court orders otherwise:

(1) if an appeal is dismissed, costs are taxed against the appellant, unless the parties agree otherwise;

(2) if a judgment is affirmed, costs are taxed against the appellant;

(3) if a judgment is reversed, costs are taxed against the appellee;

(4) if a judgment is affirmed in part, reversed in part, modified, or vacated, costs are taxed only as the court orders.

(b) *Costs for and against the United States.* Costs for or against the United States, its agency, or officer will be assessed under Rule 39 (a) only if authorized by law.

(c) *Costs of copies.* Each court of appeals must, by local rule, fix the maximum rate for taxing the cost of producing necessary copies of a brief or appendix, or copies of records authorized by Rule 30(f). The rate must not exceed that generally charged for such work in the area where the clerk's office is located and should encourage economical methods of copying.

(d) *Bill of costs; objections; insertion in mandate.* (1) A party who wants costs taxed must — within 14 days after entry of judgment — file with the circuit clerk, with proof of service, an itemized and verified bill of costs.

(2) Objections must be filed within 10 days after service of the bill of costs, unless the court extends the time.

(3) The clerk must prepare and certify an itemized statement of costs for insertion in the mandate, but issuance of the mandate must not be delayed for taxing costs. If the mandate issues before costs are finally determined, the district clerk must — upon the circuit clerk's request — add the statement of costs, or any amendment of it, to the mandate.

(e) *Costs on appeal taxable in the district court.* The following costs on appeal are taxable in the district court for the benefit of the party entitled to costs under this rule:

(1) the preparation and transmission of the record;

(2) the reporter's transcript, if needed to determine the appeal;

(3) premiums paid for a supersedeas bond or other bond to preserve rights pending appeal; and

(4) the fee for filing the notice of appeal. (Amended by order adopted April 30, 1979, effective August 1, 1979, and by order effective July 1, 1986; and by order adopted April 24, 1998, effective December 1, 1998.)

Discretion of court. — Under this Rule, an appellate court has wide discretion in the taxation of costs. Square Constr. Co. v. Washington Metro. Area Transit Auth., 800 F.2d 1256 (4th Cir. 1986).

Local Rule 39(a). Printing costs.

The cost of printing or otherwise producing necessary copies of briefs and appendices shall be taxable as costs at a rate equal to actual cost, but not higher than $4.00 per page of photographic reproduction of typed material. (Amended effective December 1, 1998.)

COMMENT

Local Rule 39(a) has been amended to delete reference to printing costs for typeset briefs.

Local Rule 39(b). Bill of costs.

The verified bill of costs may be that of a party or counsel, and should be accompanied by the printer's itemized statement of charges. When costs are sought for or against the United States, counsel should cite the statutory authority relied upon. Taxation of costs will not be delayed by the filing of a petition for rehearing or other postjudgment motion. A late affidavit for costs must be accompanied by a motion for leave to file. The clerk rules on all bills of costs and objections in the first instance.

Local Rule 39(c). Recovery of costs in the district court.

The only costs generally taxable in the Court of Appeals are: (1) the docketing fee if the case is reversed; and (2) the cost of printing or reproducing briefs and appendices, including exhibits.

Although some costs are "taxable" in the Court of Appeals, all costs are recoverable in the district court after issuance of the mandate. If the matter of costs has not been settled before issuance of the mandate, the clerk will send a supplemental "Bill of Costs" to the district court for inclusion in the mandate at a later date.

Various costs incidental to an appeal must be settled at the district court level. Among such items are: (1) the cost of the reporter's transcript; (2) the fee for filing the notice of appeal; (3) the fee for preparing and transmitting the record; and (4) the premiums paid for any required appeal bond. Application for recovery of these expenses by the successful party on appeal must be made in the district court, and should be made only after issuance of the mandate by the Court of Appeals. These costs, if erroneously applied for in the Court of Appeals, will be disallowed without prejudice to the right to reapply for them in the district court.

COMMENT

Existing I.O.P. 39 has been reorganized into proposed Local Rules 39(b) and (c), with redundancies eliminated.

Rule 40. Petition for panel rehearing.

(a) *Time to file; contents; answer; action by the court if granted.* (1) Time. Unless the time is shortened or extended by order or local rule, a petition for panel rehearing may be filed within 14 days after entry of judgment. But in a civil case, if the United States or its officer or agency is a party, the time within which any party may seek rehearing is 45 days after entry of judgment, unless an order shortens or extends the time.

(2) Contents. The petition must state with particularity each point of law or fact that the petitioner believes the court has overlooked or misapprehended and must argue in support of the petition. Oral argument is not permitted.

(3) Answer. Unless the court requests, no answer to a petition for panel rehearing is permitted. But ordinarily rehearing will not be granted in the absence of such a request.

(4) Action by the court. If a petition for panel rehearing is granted, the court may do any of the following:

(A) make a final disposition of the case without reargument;

(B) restore the case to the calendar for reargument or resubmission; or

(C) issue any other appropriate order.

(b) *Form of petition; length.* The petition must comply in form with Rule 32. Copies must be served and filed as Rule 31 prescribes. Unless the court permits or a local rule provides otherwise, a petition for panel rehearing must not exceed 15 pages. (Amended by order adopted April 30, 1979, effective August 1, 1979, and by order adopted April 29, 1994, effective December 1, 1994; and by order adopted April 24, 1998, effective December 1, 1998.)

Local Rule 40(a). Filing of petition.

Although petitions for rehearing are filed in a great many cases, few are granted. Filing a petition solely for purposes of delay or in order merely to reargue the case is an abuse of privilege.

Whenever a request for rehearing en banc is contained in a petition, such fact must be stated plainly on the cover of and in the title of the document.

The Court requires 4 copies of the petition. If the petition contains a request for rehearing en banc, the Court requires 20 copies. In either case, a pro se party who is indigent need file only the original. (Amended effective December 1, 1998.)

Local Rule 40(b). Statement of purpose.

A petition for rehearing must contain an introduction stating that, in counsel's judgment, one or more of the following situations exist:

i. A material factual or legal matter was overlooked in the decision.

ii. A change in the law occurred after the case was submitted and was overlooked by the panel.

iii. The opinion is in conflict with a decision of the United States Supreme Court, this Court, or another court of appeals and the conflict is not addressed in the opinion.

iv. The proceeding involves one or more questions of exceptional importance.

A petition should only be made to direct the Court's attention to one or more of the above situations. The points to be raised should be succinctly listed in counsel's statement of purpose. (Amended effective December 1, 1998.)

COMMENT

Local Rule 40(b) has been amended to add a fourth ground for filing a petition for rehearing. The local rule now incorporates the standard contained in FRAP 35(b)(1). Because the statement of purpose section of a petition for rehearing is not a requirement of FRAP, the provision in Local Rule 40(b) regarding rejection of a petition which fails to contain such a statement has been deleted.

Local Rule 40(c). Time limits for filing petitions.

The Court strictly enforces the time limits for filing petitions for rehearing and petitions for rehearing en banc. The Clerk's Office will deny as untimely any petition received in the Clerk's Office later than 45 days after entry of judgment in any civil case where the United States, or an agency or officer thereof is a party, or 14 days after the entry of judgment in any other case. The only grounds for an extension of time to file a petition, or to accept an untimely petition, are as follows:

i. the death or serious illness of counsel, or of a member of counsel's immediate family (or in the case of a party proceeding without counsel, the death or serious illness of the party or a member of the party's immediate family); or

ii. an extraordinary circumstance wholly beyond the control of counsel or of a party proceeding without counsel.

Petitions for rehearing and petitions for en banc rehearing from incarcerated persons proceeding without the assistance of counsel are deemed filed when they are delivered to prison or jail officials. All other such petitions are deemed filed only when received in the Clerk's Office. (Amended effective December 1, 1998.)

Local Rule 40(d). Papers filed after denial of a petition for rehearing.

Except for timely petitions for rehearing en banc, cost and attorney fee matters, and other matters ancillary to the filing of an application for writ of certiorari with the Supreme Court, the Office of the Clerk shall not receive motions or other papers requesting further relief in a case after the Court has denied a petition for rehearing or the time for filing a petition for rehearing has expired. (Amended effective December 1, 1998.)

I.O.P. 40.1. Submission of petitions for rehearing to the court.

The Clerk's Office will hold any petition for rehearing or petition for rehearing en banc, until the time for filing all such petitions, or any extension thereof granted in the particular case, has run. Thereafter, all petitions for rehearing in the same case will be distributed to the Court simultaneously. (Amended effective December 1, 1998.)

I.O.P. 40.2. Panel rehearing.

The panel of judges who heard and decided the appeal will rule on the petition for rehearing. Such panel may include a senior circuit judge or a visiting judge sitting in the Fourth Circuit by designation.

If a petition for rehearing is granted, the original judgment and opinion of the Court are vacated and the case will be reheard before the original panel. The Court may direct the filing of additional briefs, or the parties may seek leave of Court to file additional briefs.

COMMENT

Proposed I.O.P. 40.2 changes the reference to visiting judges in existing I.O.P. 40.5 to delete reference to district or federal appellate judges because visiting judges with this Court have included judges from the Court of International Trade pursuant to designation under 28 U.S.C. § 293. The I.O.P. also deletes the requirement of setting forth the vote of the panel on a petition for rehearing because the Court does not now disclose that information in its routine orders.

Rule 41. Mandate, contents, issuance and effective date; stay.

(a) *Contents.* Unless the court directs that a formal mandate issue, the mandate consists of a certified copy of the judgment, a copy of the court's opinion, if any, and any direction about costs.

(b) *When issued.* The court's mandate must issue 7 days after the time to file a petition for rehearing expires, or 7 days after entry of an order denying a timely petition for panel rehearing, rehearing en banc, or motion for stay of mandate, whichever is later. The court may shorten or extend the time.

(c) *Effective date.* The mandate is effective when issued.

(d) *Staying the mandate.* (1) On petition for rehearing or motion. The timely filing of a petition for panel rehearing, petition for rehearing en banc, or motion for stay of mandate, stays the mandate until disposition of the petition or motion, unless the court orders otherwise.

(2) Pending petition for certiorari. (A) A party may move to stay the mandate pending the filing of a petition for a writ of certiorari in the Supreme Court. The motion must be served on all parties and must show that the certiorari petition would present a substantial question and that there is good cause for a stay.

(B) The stay must not exceed 90 days, unless the period is extended for good cause or unless the party who obtained the stay files a petition for the writ and so notifies the circuit clerk in writing within the period of the stay. In that case, the stay continues until the Supreme Court's final disposition.

(C) The court may require a bond or other security as a condition to granting or continuing a stay of the mandate.

(D) The court of appeals must issue the mandate immediately when a copy of a Supreme Court order denying the petition for writ of certiorari is filed. (Amended by order adopted April 29, 1994, effective December 1, 1994; and by order adopted April 24, 1998, effective December 1, 1998.)

Local Rule 41. Motion for stay of the mandate.

A motion for stay of the issuance of the mandate shall not be granted simply upon request. Ordinarily the motion shall be denied unless there is a specific showing that it is not frivolous or filed merely for delay. The motion must present a substantial question or set forth good or probable cause for a stay. Stay requests are normally acted upon without a request for a response.

COMMENT

Proposed Local Rule 41 deletes the requirement in existing I.O.P. 41.2 that only one copy of a motion for stay of mandate need be filed. The preferred practice is that counsel file an original and three copies, like other pleading.

I.O.P. 41.1. Issuance of the mandate.

On the date of issuance of the mandate, the Clerk of the Court will issue written notice to the parties and the clerk of the lower court that the judgment of the Court of Appeals takes effect that day. The trial court record will be returned to the clerk of that court once the mandate has issued.

COMMENT

I.O.P. 41.1 has been changed to reflect the actual practice that records often go back to the lower court under separate cover within a few days of issuance of the mandate. This is especially true if the Clerk's office must get the records back from chambers or the Office of Staff Counsel.

I.O.P. 41.2. Petitions for writs of certiorari.

A petition for a writ of certiorari must be filed with the Supreme Court within 90 days of the entry of judgment in a criminal case or a civil case. The time for the petition does not run from the issuance of the mandate, but from the date of judgment which is also the opinion date. If a petition for rehearing or a petition for rehearing en banc is timely filed, the time runs from the date of denial of that petition. Counsel should consult the Rules of the Supreme Court for details on how to proceed with the petition.

The Rules of the Supreme Court do not require that the record accompany a petition for certiorari and the record will not be forwarded unless specifically requested by the petitioner or counsel. Requests to certify and transmit the record to the Supreme Court prior to action on the petition for a writ of certiorari are disfavored by the Supreme Court. The Clerk of the Supreme Court will request the record from the Court of Appeals when review of the record is desired by the Supreme Court prior to action on a petition for writ of certiorari or upon granting certiorari if the record has not been transmitted earlier. The same procedures are followed for Supreme Court review by certification pursuant to 28 U.S.C. § 1254(2).

If a case is remanded to the Court of Appeals from the Supreme Court, the case shall be reopened under the original docket number and the Court of Appeals may require additional briefs and oral argument, summarily dispose of the case or take any other action consistent with the Supreme Court's opinion. (Amended effective December 1, 1998.)

COMMENT

I.O.P. 41.2 is amended to clarify, consistent with amendments to FRAP 35, that a timely petition for rehearing en banc will now stay the time to petition for certiorari.

Rule 42. Voluntary dismissal.

(a) *Dismissal in the district court.* Before an appeal has been docketed by the circuit clerk, the district court may dismiss the appeal on the filing of a stipulation signed by all parties or on the appellant's motion with notice to all parties.

(b) *Dismissal in the court of appeals.* The circuit clerk may dismiss a docketed appeal if the parties file a signed dismissal agreement specifying how costs are to be paid and pay any fees that are due. But no mandate or other process may issue without a court order. An appeal may be dismissed on the appellant's motion on terms agreed to by the parties or fixed by the court. (Amended by order adopted April 24, 1998, effective December 1, 1998.)

Local Rule 42. Voluntary dismissals.

In civil cases, the stipulation of dismissal or motion for voluntary dismissal may be signed by counsel. In criminal cases, however, the agreement or motion must be signed or consented to by the individual party appellant personally or counsel must file a statement setting forth the basis for counsel's understanding that the appellant wishes to dismiss the appeal and the efforts made to obtain the appellant's written consent. Counsel must serve a copy of this statement on appellant.

COMMENT

Proposed Local Rule 42 adds language to existing I.O.P. 42.1 to reflect the Court's current practice regarding the additional steps necessary in a criminal case for counsel to obtain a voluntary dismissal.

Rule 43. Substitution of parties.

(a) *Death of a party.* (1) If a party dies after a notice of appeal has been filed or while a proceeding is pending in the court of appeals, the decedent's personal representative may be substituted as a party on motion filed with the circuit clerk by the representative or by any party. A party's motion must be served on the representative in accordance with Rule 25. If the decedent has no representative, any party may suggest the death on the record, and the court of appeals may then direct appropriate proceedings.

(2) If a party entitled to appeal dies before filing a notice of appeal, the decedent's personal representative — or, if there is no personal representative, the decedent's attorney of record — may file a notice of appeal within the time prescribed by these rules. After the notice of appeal is filed, substitution must be in accordance with Rule 43(a)(1).

(3) If a party against whom an appeal may be taken dies after entry of a judgment or order in the district court, but before a notice of appeal is filed, an appellant may proceed as if the death had not occurred. After the notice of appeal is filed, substitution must be in accordance with Rule 43(a)(1).

(b) *Substitution for a reason other than death.* If a party needs to be substituted for any reason other than death, the procedure prescribed in Rule 43(a) applies.

(c) *Public officer: identification; substitution.* (1) Identification of party. A public officer who is a party to an appeal or other proceeding in an official capacity may be described as a party by the public officer's official title rather than by name. But the court may require the public officer's name to be added.

(2) Automatic stubstitution of officeholder. When a public officer who is a party to an appeal or other proceeding in an official capacity dies, resigns, or otherwise ceases to hold office, the action does not abate. The public officer's successor is automatically substituted as a party. Proceedings following the substitution are to be in the name of the substituted party, but any misnomer that does not affect the substantial rights of the parties may be disregarded. An order of substitution may be entered at any time, but failure to enter an order does not affect the substitution. (Amended by order effective July 1, 1986; and by order adopted April 24, 1998, effective December 1, 1998.)

Rule 44. Case involving a constitutional question when the United States is not a party.

If a party questions the constitutionality of an Act of Congress in a proceeding in which the United States or its agency, officer, or employee is not a party in an official capacity, the questioning party must give written notice to the circuit clerk immediately upon the filing of the record or as soon as the question is raised in the court of appeals. The clerk must then certify that fact to the Attorney General. (Amended by order adopted April 24, 1998, effective December 1, 1998.)

Rule 45. Clerk's duties.

(a) *General provisions.* (1) Qualifications. The circuit clerk must take the oath and post any bond required by law. Neither the clerk nor any deputy clerk may practice as an attorney or counselor in any court while in office.

(2) When court is open. The court of appeals is always open for filing any paper, issuing and returning process, making a motion, and entering an order. The clerk's office with the clerk or a deputy in attendance must be open during business hours on all days except Saturdays, Sundays, and legal holidays. A court may provide by local rule or by order that the clerk's office be open for specified hours on Saturdays or on legal holidays other than New Year's Day, Martin Luther King, Jr.'s Birthday, Presidents' Day, Memorial Day, Independence Day, Labor Day, Columbus Day, Veterans' Day, Thanksgiving Day, and Christmas Day.

(b) *Records.* (1) The docket. The circuit clerk must maintain a docket and an index of all docketed cases in the manner prescribed by the Director of the Administrative Office of the United States Courts. The clerk must record all papers filed with the clerk and all process, orders, and judgments.

(2) Calendar. Under the court's direction, the clerk must prepare a calendar of cases awaiting argument. In placing cases on the calendar for argument, the clerk must give preference to appeals in criminal cases and to other proceedings and appeals entitled to preference by law.

(3) Other records. The clerk must keep other books and records required by the Director of the Administrative Office of the United States Courts, with the approval of the Judicial Conference of the United States, or by the court.

(c) *Notice of an order or judgment.* Upon the entry of an order or judgment, the circuit clerk must immediately serve by mail a notice of entry on each party to the proceeding, with a copy of any opinion, and must note the mailing on the docket. Service on a party represented by counsel must be made on counsel.

(d) *Custody of records and papers.* The circuit clerk has custody of the court's records and papers. Unless the court orders or instructs otherwise, the clerk must not permit an original record or paper to be taken from the clerk's office. Upon disposition of the case, original papers constituting the record on appeal or review must be returned to the court or agency from which they were received. The clerk must preserve a copy of any brief, appendix, or other paper that has been filed. (Amended by order adopted March 1, 1971, effective July 1, 1971, and by order effective July 1, 1986; and by order adopted April 24, 1998, effective December 1, 1998.)

Local Rule 45. Dismissals for failure to prosecute.

When an appellant in either a docketed or non-docketed appeal fails to comply with the Federal Rules of Appellate Procedure or the rules or directives of this Court, the clerk shall notify the appellant or, if appellant is represented by counsel, appellant's counsel that upon the expiration of 15 days from the date thereof the appeal will be dismissed for want of prosecution, unless prior to that date appellant remedies the default. Should the appellant fail to comply within said 15-day period, the clerk shall then enter an order dismissing said appeal for want of prosecution, and shall issue a certified copy thereof to the clerk of the district court as and for the mandate. In no case shall the appellant be entitled to reinstate the case and remedy the default after the same shall have been dismissed under this rule, unless by order of this Court for good cause shown. The dismissal of an appeal shall not limit the authority of this Court, in an appropriate case, to take disciplinary action against defaulting counsel. (Amended effective December 1, 1998.)

COMMENT

Local Rule 45 eliminates the requirement that the clerk notify appellant personally of counsel's default before dismissing an appeal for failure to prosecute.

I.O.P. 45.1. Clerk's Office.

The Clerk's Office is located on the fifth floor of the United States Courthouse Annex in Richmond, Virginia, and is open from 8:30 a.m. to 5:00 p.m. every weekday, except federal holidays. All correspondence concerning cases pending before the Court should be addressed to:

Clerk, United States Court of Appeals
for the Fourth Circuit
1100 East Main Street, Suite 501
Richmond, Virginia 23219
Telephone 804/771-2213

I.O.P. 45.2. Public information.

Information concerning the status of appeals and the operation of rules and procedures may be obtained from the Clerk's Office by telephone inquiry. Matters of public record may be reviewed upon request at the Clerk's Office and case documents may be transmitted to the district court for review by counsel upon proper application to the Clerk's Office.

COMMENT

Existing I.O.P. 45.3 was deleted as being redundant of Local Rule 45, after minor additions were made to the local rule.

Local Rule 45 eliminates the requirement that the clerk notify appellant personally of counsel's default before dismissing an appeal for failure to prosecute.

Rule 46. Attorneys.

(a) *Admission to the bar.* (1) Eligibility. An attorney is eligible for admission to the bar of a court of appeals if that attorney is of good moral and professional character and is admitted to practice before the Supreme Court of the United States, the highest court of a state, another United States court of appeals, or a United States district court (including the district courts for Guam, the Northern Mariana Islands, and the Virgin Islands).

(2) Application. An applicant must file an application for admission, on a form approved by the court that contains the applicant's personal statement showing eligibility for membership. The applicant must subscribe to the following oath or affirmation:

"I, _____, do solemnly swear [or affirm] that I will conduct myself as an attorney and counselor of this court, uprightly and according to law; and that I will support the Constitution of the United States."

(3) Admission procedures. On written or oral motion of a member of the court's bar, the court will act on the application. An applicant may be admitted by oral motion in open court. But, unless the court orders otherwise, an applicant need not appear before the court to be admitted. Upon admission, an applicant must pay the clerk the fee prescribed by local rule or court order.

(b) *Suspension or disbarment.* (1) Standard. A member of the court's bar is subject to suspension or disbarment by the court if the member:

(A) has been suspended or disbarred from practice in any other court; or

(B) is guilty of conduct unbecoming a member of the court's bar.

(2) Procedure. The member must be given an opportunity to show good cause, within the time prescribed by the court, why the member should not be suspended or disbarred.

(3) Order. The court must enter an appropriate order after the member responds and a hearing is held, if requested, or after the time prescribed for a response expires, if no response is made.

(c) *Discipline.* A court of appeals may discipline an attorney who practices before it for conduct unbecoming a member of the bar or for failure to comply with any court rule. First, however, the court must afford the attorney reasonable notice, an opportunity to show cause to the contrary, and, if requested, a hearing. (Amended by order effective July 1, 1986; and by order adopted April 24, 1998, effective December 1, 1998.)

Local Rule 46(a). Legal assistance to indigents by law students.

An eligible law student with the written consent of an indigent and the attorney of record may appear in this Court on behalf of that indigent in any case. An eligible law student with the written consent of the United States Attorney or authorized representative may also appear in this Court on behalf of the United States in any case. An eligible law student with the written consent of the State Attorney General or authorized representative may also appear in this Court on behalf of that state in any case. In each case, the written consent shall be filed with the clerk.

An eligible law student may assist in the preparation of briefs and other documents to be filed in this Court, but such briefs or documents must be signed by the attorney of record. The student may also participate in oral argument with leave of the Court, but only in the presence of the attorney of record. The attorney of record shall assume personal professional responsibility for the law student's work and for supervising the quality of that work. The attorney should be familiar with the case and prepared to supplement or correct any written or oral statement made by the student.

In order to make an appearance pursuant to this rule, the law student must:

1. Be duly enrolled in a law school approved by the American Bar Association;

2. Have completed legal studies amounting to at least four (4) semesters, or the equivalent if the school is on some basis other than a semester basis;

3. Be certified by the dean of the student's law school as being of good character and competent legal ability which certification shall be filed with the clerk. This certification may be withdrawn by the dean at any time by mailing notice to the clerk or by termination by this Court without notice of hearing and without any showing of cause;

4. Be introduced to the Court by an attorney admitted to practice before this Court;

5. Neither ask for nor receive any compensation or remuneration of any kind from the person on whose behalf the student renders services, but this shall not prevent an attorney, legal aid bureau, law school, public defender agency, a State, or the United States from paying compensation to the eligible law student, nor shall it prevent any agency from making such charges for its services as it may otherwise properly require;

6. Certify in writing that he or she has read and is familiar with the Code of Professional Responsibility or Rules of Professional Conduct in force in the state in which the student's law school is located.

Local Rule 46(b). Admission to practice.

Only attorneys admitted to the bar of this Court may practice before the Court. An attorney may be named on a brief filed in this Court without being admitted to the bar of the Fourth Circuit, provided that at least one lawyer admitted to practice in this Court also appears on the brief. Any other document submitted by an attorney who is not a member of the bar of the Fourth Circuit will be accepted for filing conditioned on his or her qualifying for membership within a reasonable time.

Each applicant for admission to the bar of this Court shall file with the clerk an application on the form approved by the Court and furnished by the clerk. Thereafter, upon written or oral motion of a member of the bar of the Court, the Court will act upon the application. A qualified attorney may be admitted upon personal appearance in open court. It is not necessary that an applicant appear in open court for the purpose of being admitted unless the Court shall otherwise order.

The requisite $40.00 fee must accompany the application, but attorneys appointed by the Court to represent a party in forma pauperis, counsel for the United States and any agency thereof who has a case pending before this Court, and law clerks to the judges of the Court and to the district judges, magistrate judges, and bankruptcy judges within this Circuit shall be admitted to the bar of this Court without the payment of an admission fee.

Fees collected by the clerk from applicants for admission shall be deposited in a bank designated by the Court and shall be used for the benefit of the bench and bar in the administration of justice. A certificate indicating that an attorney has been admitted to practice before the Fourth Circuit will be sent to counsel by mail after admission.

Local Rule 46(c). Appearance of counsel; withdrawal; substitutions.

Each attorney of record must file a written appearance with the clerk within 10 days after the appeal is docketed or after being retained or appointed. At the time of docketing, the clerk will send to each counsel or party in the trial court a "designation of counsel" form. This form should be filled out and returned to the Clerk of the Fourth Circuit within 10 days. Thereafter, the Court will send correspondence, notices of oral argument, and copies of final decisions only to those attorneys who have filed their appearance forms. More than one attorney of the same firm may sign the same form. This form does not affect the credit line listed on printed opinions, as that information is furnished to publishing firms from those names listed on the briefs.

Once an appearance in an appeal has been filed, an attorney may not withdraw from representation without notice to the party he or she is representing and consent of the Court. A motion to withdraw should state fully the reason for the request. Substitution of counsel of record can be accomplished by submitting a counsel of record form or written appearance for new counsel along with existing counsel's motion to withdraw or strike appearance.

Local Rule 46(d). Appointment of counsel.

In direct criminal appeals of indigents, appointment of counsel is made upon the docketing of the appeal without prior notice to the attorney who represented the indigent in the case below. The Court will pay a maximum of $2,500 plus reasonable expenses in direct criminal appeals. The duty of counsel appointed under the CJA extends through advising an unsuccessful appellant in writing of the right to seek review in the Supreme Court. If the appellant requests in writing that a petition for a writ of certiorari be filed and in counsel's considered judgment there are grounds for seeking Supreme Court review, counsel shall file such a petition. If appellant requests that a petition for a writ of certiorari be filed but counsel believes that such a petition would be frivolous, counsel may file a motion to withdraw with the Court of Appeals. The motion must reflect that a copy was served on the client and that the client was informed of the right to file a response to the motion within seven days. The Clerk will hold the motion after filing for fifteen days before submitting it to the Court to allow time for appellant's response, if any, to be received.

Assignment of counsel is discretionary in other indigent cases. Therefore, such cases receive a preliminary review before a decision is made regarding appointment of counsel. In assigning counsel, the Court may direct counsel to brief a particular issue, but counsel is free to address any additional issues which appear to be meritorious.

Unless compensation for legal services becomes available to assigned counsel by statute, the Court will pay the attorney a maximum fee of $750 plus expenses.

To receive payment from the Court, court-appointed or court-assigned counsel in all cases must submit to the Clerk's Office an itemized statement of expenses, with receipts, within sixty days of final disposition of the case. Depending upon the course of the case, this may be sixty days from (1) the date of judgment, (2) dismissal of the appeal, or (3) denial of a petition for rehearing. Before the expiration of the sixty-day time period the Court, for good cause shown, may grant counsel an extension of time to file the application for compensation and reimbursement. If court-appointed counsel files a petition for writ of certiorari with the Supreme Court, the 60-day period for applying for compensation and reimbursement runs from the date of filing the petition for writ of certiorari.

COMMENT

Proposed Local Rule 46(d) extends the time period for filing a CJA voucher until 60 days after filing of a petition for writ of certiorari. This is the preferred procedure over having court-appointed counsel file a supplemental voucher after filing of certiorari as set forth in existing I.O.P. 46.3. Proposed Local Rule 46(d) also adds the requirement that court-appointed counsel inform the client of the right to file a response to a motion to withdraw and reflects that the Clerk will hold the motion to withdraw for fifteen days before submitting it to the Court to allow time for the client's response.

Local Rule 46(e). Attorney's fees and expenses.

The Court may award attorney's fees and expenses whenever authorized by statute. Any application for an award must include a reference to the statutory basis for the request and a detailed itemization of the amounts requested. Court-appointed counsel may apply for an award of fees and expenses, but any award by the Court is in lieu of the regular appointment fees provided by the Court. In certain agency cases, counsel may submit the standard government form for fees and expenses provided by the agency for approval by the Court.

Local Rule 46(f). Proceeding pro se.

An individual may proceed without the aid of counsel, but should so inform the Court at the earliest possible time. In any pro se appeal, the clerk shall notify the parties that they shall file informal briefs as provided by Local Rule 34(b). The Court will limit its review to the issues raised in the informal briefs and will consider the need for the appointment of counsel when reviewing the appeal under Local Rule 334(a). Cases involving pro se litigants are ordinarily not scheduled for oral argument.

Local Rule 46(g). Rules of disciplinary enforcement.

(1) A member of the bar of this Court may be disciplined by this Court as a result of

(a) Conviction in any court of the United States, the District of Columbia, or any state, territory or commonwealth of the United States, of any felony or of any lesser crime involving false swearing, misrepresentation, fraud, willful failure to file income tax returns, deceit, bribery, extortion, misappropriation, or theft;

(b) Imposition of discipline by any other court of whose bar the attorney is a member, or an attorney's disbarment by consent or resignation from the bar of such court while an investigation into allegations of misconduct is pending;

(c) Conduct with respect to this Court which violates the rules of professional conduct or responsibility in effect in the state or other jurisdiction in which the attorney maintains his or her principal office, the Federal Rules of Appellate Procedure, the local rules of this Court, or orders or other instructions of this Court; or

(d) Any other conduct unbecoming a member of the bar of this Court.

(2) Discipline may consist of disbarment, suspension from practice before this Court, monetary sanction, removal from the roster of attorneys eligible for appointment as Court-appointed counsel, reprimand, or any other sanction that the Court may deem appropriate. Disbarment is the presumed discipline for conviction of a crime specified in paragraph (1)(a) above. The identical discipline imposed by another court is presumed appropriate for discipline taken as a result of that other court's action pursuant to paragraph (1)(b). A monetary sanction imposed on disciplinary grounds is the personal responsibility of the attorney disciplined, and may not be reimbursed by a client.

(3) The clerk reviews reports received from other courts concerning discipline imposed on members of the bar of this Court. He refers to the Court all disbarments, suspensions, resignations during the pendency of misconduct investigations, and other actions sufficient to cast doubt upon the member's continuing qualification to practice before this Court.

(4) The clerk issues a notice to show cause why a member of the bar shall not be disciplined by this Court upon receipt of official notification of an attorney's conviction of a crime specified in paragraph (1)(a) or of the imposition of discipline by another court referred to this Court pursuant to paragraph (3) above, or upon the Court's determination that cause may exist for discipline pursuant to paragraphs (1)(c) or (1)(d). Such notice is sent by certified mail, directs that a response be filed within 30 days of the date of the notice, and directs that the attorney complete and return to the clerk within that time a declaration of the names and addresses of other bars to which he or she is admitted, using the form supplied by the clerk, whether or not the attorney chooses otherwise to respond to the notice. The clerk also appends a copy of Local Rule 46(g).

(5) Upon receiving official notification that a member of the bar has been convicted of a crime specified in paragraph (1)(a), the clerk automatically will issue an order suspending the attorney's privilege to practice before this Court pending the Court's determination of appropriate discipline.

(6) An attorney to whom a notice to show cause has been sent may consent to disbarment, by filing with the clerk an affidavit stating that the attorney desires to consent to disbarment and that:

(a) The attorney's consent is freely and voluntarily rendered; the attorney is not being subjected to coercion or duress; the attorney is fully aware of the implications of so consenting;

(b) The attorney is aware that there is a presently pending proceeding involving allegations that there exist grounds for the attorney's discipline, the nature of which the attorney shall specifically set forth;

(c) The attorney acknowledges that the material facts so alleged are true; and

(d) The attorney so consents because the attorney knows that he or she cannot successfully defend himself or herself.

The order disbarring the attorney on consent is a matter of public record. However, the affidavit will not be publicly disclosed or made available for use in any other proceeding except upon order of this Court.

(7) If the attorney fails to respond to the notice within 30 days, or such other time as the court shall allow, the clerk enters an order imposing the presump-

tive discipline. If no presumptive discipline is specified for the conduct, the clerk notifies the Court of the attorney's non-response and the Court takes such action as it deems appropriate.

(8) All matters pertaining to discipline of attorneys are submitted to the Court's Standing Panel on Attorney Discipline, which consists of three active circuit judges, each of whom is appointed by the Chief Judge to serve on the Panel for a three-year term. The initial members of the Standing Panel are appointed for terms of one, two, and three years so that the Panel members' terms are staggered for continuity of decision making. If any member of the Standing Panel is unable to hear a particular matter, the clerk randomly designates another active circuit judge to the Panel for the purpose of disposing of that matter.

(9) The Standing Panel considers all materials submitted by an attorney to whom notice to show cause has issued. The Panel may request further information from a court that has previously imposed discipline on the attorney, or from its disciplinary agency. A copy of any such information is made available to the attorney or to his or her counsel. Should an attorney request a hearing on the matter it will be heard by the Standing Panel at a time and place of its choosing.

(10) The Court may at any time appoint counsel to investigate or prosecute a disciplinary matter, or to represent an indigent attorney instructed to show cause. The Court prefers to appoint as prosecuting counsel the disciplinary agency of the highest court of the state in which the attorney maintains his or her principal office. However, if the state disciplinary agency declines appointment, or the Court deems other counsel more appropriate, it may appoint any other member of the bar as prosecuting counsel. Counsel appointed either for prosecution or defense will be compensated for his or her services according to the Court's plan for appointment of counsel in criminal cases, from the attorney admission fund.

(11) The Court's order imposing discipline will set forth the nature of the discipline imposed; if disbarment or suspension from practice before the Court, the terms upon which reinstatement will occur or be considered by the Court; and any instructions to the clerk concerning the notification of the Court's action to be given to other courts or official bodies.

(12) The clerk is responsible for

(a) Automatically initiating show cause proceedings when official notice of an attorney's conviction of a crime specified in paragraph (1)(a) or discipline by another court pursuant to paragraph (3) is brought to his or her attention;

(b) Bringing to the attention of the Standing Panel instances of violations by members of the bar of this Court of the Federal Rules of Appellate Procedure, this Court's local rules or this Court's orders or other instructions that may warrant discipline;

(c) Obtaining declarations of the names and addresses of other bars of which an attorney possibly subject to discipline by this Court may be a member; and

(d) Unless directed otherwise by the Court, within 10 days of the imposition of discipline upon a member of the bar of this Court, notifying all other courts of those bars the attorney reports that he or she is a member, and the American

Bar Association's National Disciplinary Data Bank, of the Court's action, enclosing a certified copy of the Court's order.

COMMENT

Proposed Local Rule 46(g) deletes the reference in existing I.O.P. 46.6 to violation of internal operating procedures as grounds for discipline because there are no more directives in the remaining internal operating procedures.

Rule 47. Rules of a court of appeals.

(a) *Local rules.* (1) Each court of appeals acting by a majority of its judges in regular active service may, after giving appropriate public notice and opportunity for comment, make and amend rules governing its practice. A generally applicable direction to parties or lawyers regarding practice before a court must be in a local rule rather than an internal operating procedure or standing order. A local rule must be consistent with — but not duplicative of — Acts of Congress and rules adopted under 28 U.S.C. § 2072 and must conform to any uniform numbering system prescribed by the Judicial Conference of the United States. Each circuit clerk must send the Administrative Office of the United States Courts a copy of each local rule and internal operating procedure when it is promulgated or amended.

(2) A local rule imposing a requirement of form must not be enforced in a manner that causes a party to lose rights because of a nonwillful failure to comply with the requirement.

(b) *Procedure when there is no controlling law.* A court of appeals may regulate practice in a particular case in any manner consistent with federal law, these rules, and local rules of the circuit. No sanction or other disadvantage may be imposed for noncompliance with any requirement not in federal law, federal rules, or the local circuit rules unless the alleged violator has been furnished in the particular case with actual notice of the requirement. (Amended by order adopted April 27, 1995, effective December 1, 1995; and by order adopted April 24, 1998, effective December 1, 1998.)

Local Rule 47(a). Procedures for adoption of local rules and internal operating procedures.

Following tentative approval of an amendment to its local rules or internal operating procedures, and consultation with its Advisory Committee on Rules and Procedures, the Court of Appeals will provide public notice of the proposed amendment and an opportunity for comment.

The Court will set a period for comment for each proposed amendment, based upon the urgency of the matter involved. If the Court determines that there is an immediate need for a rule, the Court may provide that an amendment take immediate effect, and promptly thereafter afford notice and opportunity for comment.

Notice of a proposed amendment will be provided by distribution of the proposed change to all district judges, bankruptcy judges, magistrate judges, district and bankruptcy clerks, United States Attorneys, and state bar associations within the Circuit. Notice will also be sent to all legal newspapers and bar journals within the Circuit. Such notice shall include the text of a proposed amendment, unless it is lengthy. If the amendment is lengthy, the notice will describe the purpose and effect of the proposed amendment, and advise interested parties to obtain copies of the text of the proposed amendment from the clerk. Any person or organization requesting routine notice of proposed amendments to the Court's rules and internal operating procedures may, by letter to the clerk, be placed on the mailing list for such proposed changes.

All comments will be addressed to the Clerk of the Court of Appeals. If comments are received, they will be circulated to all members of the Court prior to the effective date of the proposed amendment, unless the amendment was given immediate effect.

Local Rule 47(b). Advisory committee on rules and procedures.

The Court's Advisory Committee on Rules and Procedures shall consist of five attorneys, one from each of the states constituting the Fourth Circuit.

The members shall be appointed by the Chief Judge of the Circuit for three-year terms. The terms shall be staggered, so that no more than two members' terms expire in any year. No person may serve more than two full three-year terms.

The Chief Judge of the Circuit shall designate one of the members to serve as chair of the Committee. The clerk shall serve as the Court's principal liaison with the Committee.

The Committee shall study the Court's local rules and internal operating procedures, make recommendations concerning them, and advise the Court concerning all proposed changes to them.

I.O.P. 47.1. Judicial conference.

(a) There shall be held each year a conference of all the circuit and district judges, all bankruptcy judges and all full-time magistrate judges of the Circuit for the purpose of considering the business of the courts, advising means of improving the administration of justice within such Circuit, and discussion of ideas with respect to the administration of justice. It shall be the duty of every judge of the Circuit in active service and every full-time magistrate judge to attend such conference.

(b) The first day of the conference shall be devoted to a session for the judges alone, in which there shall be discussed matters affecting the state of the dockets and the administration of justice in their respective districts.

(c) Members of the bar to be chosen, as hereafter set forth, shall be members of the conference and shall participate in its discussions and deliberations on the second and third days.

(d) Members of the conference from the bar shall be as provided in I.O.P. 47.2 as approved by the active circuit judges sitting from time to time in administrative session.

(e) The Circuit Executive of this Court shall be the secretary of the conference, and shall make and preserve an accurate record of its proceedings.

(f) Each member of the bar chosen to be a member of the conference shall pay an annual membership fee in an amount fixed by the Court of Appeals, to be applied to the payment of the expenses of the conference as approved by the

Chief Judge of the Circuit. The payment of the annual membership fee by members of the bar is a condition to retention of conference membership. The Chief Judge may excuse the payment of the fee in individual cases.

I.O.P. 47.2. Bar membership in the judicial conference of the circuit.

Commencing with the 1997 annual conference, the members of the conference of the bar are as follows:

A. Ex officio members.

1. The Attorney General of the United States, or designee.

2. The presidents of the state bar associations of the states of the Circuit. When two bar associations in the same state are both recognized under this rule, the president of each shall be entitled to attend, and the maximum number of members of the conference from the bar, from any state, under this provision, shall be limited to two. As long as there is only one state bar association in Maryland, the Bar Association of Baltimore City may be treated as a state bar association under this provision.

3. All United States Attorneys in the Circuit.

4. All Federal Public Defenders in the Circuit.

5. All Chief Justices of the courts of last resort of the states comprising this Circuit.

6. All Attorneys General of the states comprising this Circuit.

7. The Chief Judge of the United States Court of Appeals for the Armed Forces.

8. The Chief Judge of the United States Tax Court.

9. One representative of each accredited law school within the Circuit.

B. Members designated by judges.

1. Each active and senior circuit judge and each active and senior district judge may annually designate two lawyers to be invited by the Chief Judge as guests of the conference.

2. By attending three conferences as guests invited under (1) above, a lawyer retains permanent membership in the conference. Permanent membership entitles the member to attend all conferences.

Rule 48. Masters.

(a) *Appointment; powers.* A court of appeals may appoint a special master to hold hearings, if necessary, and to recommend factual findings and disposition in matters ancillary to proceedings in the court. Unless the order referring a matter to a master specifies or limits the master's powers, those powers include, but are not limited to, the following:

(1) regulating all aspects of a hearing;

(2) taking all appropriate action for the effcient performance of the master's duties under the order;

(3) requiring the production of evidence on all matters embraced in the reference; and

(4) administering oaths and examining witnesses and parties.

(b) *Compensation.* If the master is not a judge or court employee, the court must determine the master's compensation and whether the cost is to be charged to any party. (Added by order adopted April 29, 1994, effective December 1, 1994; and by order adopted April 24, 1998, effective December 1, 1998.)

Editor's note. — The provisions of this rule are new. Former FRAP 48 is now codified as subdivision (c) of FRAP 1.

APPENDIX OF FORMS.

Form 1. Notice of appeal to a Court of Appeals from a judgment or order of a District Court.

United States District Court for the _____

District of _____

File Number _____

A. B., Plaintiff	)	
	)	
v.	)	Notice of Appeal
	)	
C. D., Defendant	)	

Notice is hereby given that _____ (here name all parties taking the appeal) _____ (plaintiffs) (defendants) in the above named case,* hereby appeal to the United States Court of Appeals for the _____ Circuit (from the final judgment) (from the order (describing it)) entered in this action on the _____ day of _____, 19____.

(s)_____

_____

(Address)

Attorney for _____

Address: _____

Form 2. Notice of appeal to a Court of Appeals from a decision of the Tax Court**.

United States Tax Court
Washington, D.C.

A.B., Petitioner	)	
v.	)	Docket No. _____
Commissioner of Internal Revenue,	)	
Respondent	)	

Notice of Appeal

Notice is hereby given that _____ here name all parties taking the appeal* _____, hereby appeal to the United States Court of Appeals for the _____ Circuit from [that part of] the decision of this court entered in the above captioned proceeding on the ____ day of _____, 19____ [relating to _____].

---

* See Rule 3(c) for permissible ways of identifying appellants.

** The name of the Tax Court of the United States has been changed to United States Tax Court by Pub. L. 91-172, § 951, Dec. 30, 1969, 83 Stat. 730 (26 U.S.C. § 7441).

(s)_____

Counsel for _____

(Address) _____

Form 3. Petition for review of order of an agency, board, commission or officer.

United States Court of Appeals for the _____ Circuit

A.B., Petitioner	)	
	)	
v.	)	*Petition for Review*
	)	
XYZ Commission, Respondent	)	

_____ (here name all parties bringing the petition) _____hereby petition the court for review of the Order of the XYZ Commission (describe the order) entered on _____, 19____.

_____

Attorney for Petitioner.

Address: _____

Form 4. Affidavit to accompany motion for leave to appeal in forma pauperis.

United States District Court for the _____

District of _____

United States of America	)	
	)	
v.	)	No. _____
	)	
A. B.	)	

Affidavit in Support of Motion to Proceed on Appeal in Forma Pauperis

I, _____, being first duly sworn, depose and say that I am the _____, in the above-entitled case; that in support of my motion to proceed on appeal without being required to prepay fees, costs or give security therefor, I state that because of my poverty I am unable to pay the costs of said proceeding or to give security therefor; that I believe I am entitled to redress; and that the issues which I desire to present on appeal are the following:

I further swear that the responses which I have made to the questions and instructions below relating to my ability to pay the cost of prosecuting the appeal are true.

1. Are you presently employed?
   a. If the answer is yes, state the amount of your salary or wages per month and give the name and address of your employer.
   b. If the answer is no, state the date of your last employment and the amount of the salary and wages per month which you received.

2. Have you received within the past twelve months any income from a business, profession or other form of self-employment, or in the form of rent payments, interest dividends, or other source?

   a. If the answer is yes, describe each source of income, and state the amount received from each during the past twelve months.

3. Do you own any cash or checking or savings account?

   a. If the answer is yes, state the total value of the items owned.

4. Do you own any real estate, stocks, bonds, notes, automobiles, or other valuable property (excluding ordinary household furnishings and clothing)?

   a. If the answer is yes, describe the property and state its approximate value.

5. List the persons who are dependent upon you for support and state your relationship to those persons.

I understand that a false statement or answer to any questions in this affidavit will subject me to penalties for perjury.

_____

SUBSCRIBED AND SWORN TO before me
this _____ day of _____, 19____.

Let the applicant proceed without prepayment of costs or fees or the necessity of giving security therefor.

_____
District Judge

Form 5. Notice of appeal to a Court of Appeals from a judgment or order of a District Court or a bankruptcy appellate panel.

United States District Court for the _____
District of _____

In re	)	
_____,	)	
Debtor	)	
A.B., Plaintiff	)	
	)	
	)	File No. _____
v.	)	
	)	
C.D., Defendant	)	

Notice of Appeal to United States Court of Appeals
for the _____ Circuit

_____, the plaintiff [or defendant or other party] appeals to the United States Court of Appeals for the _____ Circuit from the final

815

judgment [or order or decree] of the district court for the district of
_____ [or bankruptcy appellate panel of the _____ circuit],
entered in this case on _____, 19____ [here describe the judgment, order,
or decree] _____

    The parties to the judgment [or order or decree] appealed from and the
names and addresses of their respective attorneys are as follows:

Dated _____

Signed _____

Attorney for Appellant

Address: _____

_____

Form A. Disclosure of corporate affiliations and other entities with a direct financial interest in litigation.

NOTE: ONLY ONE FORM NEED BE COMPLETED FOR A PARTY EVEN IF
THIS PARTY IS REPRESENTED BY MORE THAN ONE ATTOR-
NEY. DISCLOSURES MUST BE FILED ON BEHALF OF INDIVID-
UALS AS WELL AS CORPORATIONS AND OTHER LEGAL ENTI-
TIES. DISCLOSE PUBLICLY OWNED CORPORATIONS AND
ENTITIES ONLY EXCLUDE WHOLLY OWNED SUBSIDIARIES.
COUNSEL HAS A CONTINUING DUTY TO UPDATE THIS INFOR-
MATION.

Pursuant to FRAP 26.1 and Local Rule 26.1, _____

(name of party)

who is _____,

(appellant/appellee)

makes the following disclosure:

1.   Is the party a publicly held corporation or other publicly held entity?
(check one)   ( ) YES   ( ) NO

2.   Is the party a parent, subsidiary, or affiliate of, or a trade association
representing, a publicly held corporation, or other publicly held entity
(see Local Rule 26.1(b))?
(check one)   ( ) YES   ( ) NO

    If the answer is YES, state the name of the entity and its relationship to
the party:

3.   Is there any other publicly held corporation, or other publicly held
entity, that has a direct financial interest in the outcome of the litigation
(see Local Rule 26.1(b)(3))?
(check one)   ( ) YES   ( ) NO

    If the answer is YES, state the name of the entity and the nature of its
financial interest:

816

_____   _____
                (Signature of counsel)   (date)

(Amended June 25, 1993.)

Form B. Appearance of counsel.
No. _____

THE CLERK WILL ENTER MY APPEARANCE AS COUNSEL ON BEHALF
OF:

_____ as the
                                    (party name)

[ ] appellant(s)   [ ] appellee(s)   [ ] amicus curiae
[ ] petitioner(s)   [ ] respondent(s)   [ ] intervenor(s)

_____
                (signature)

Area Code & Phone No.: _____

[ ] IF YOU WILL NOT BE PARTICIPATING IN THIS CASE, PLEASE
    CHECK HERE AND RETURN, AND GIVE US THE NAME AND
    ADDRESS OF ANOTHER ATTORNEY, IF ANY, WHO WILL PROVIDE
    APPELLATE REPRESENTATION.

NOTE: Must be signed by an Attorney admitted to practice before the United
States Court of Appeals for the Fourth Circuit pursuant to Internal Operating
Procedure 46.1. Individual and not firm names must be signed.

If your name has changed since you were admitted to the Fourth Circuit Bar
PLEASE show the name under which you were admitted.

Form C. Certificate of death penalty case — Fourth Circuit Local Rule 22(b).

UNITED STATES DISTRICT COURT		
DISTRICT	LOCATION	DOCKET NUMBER
CASE CAPTION		DATE FILED
PETITIONER V. RESPONDENT		FEE STATUS ☐ PAID ☐ IFP ☐ IFP PENDING
COUNSEL FOR PETITIONER (name, address, and telephone number)	COUNSEL FOR RESPONDENT (name, address, and telephone number)	
INSTITUTION OF INCARCERATION		EXECUTION DATE

EXPLANATION OF EMERGENCY NATURE OF PROCEEDINGS (attach another page if necessary)

HAS PETITIONER PREVIOUSLY FILED CASES IN FEDERAL COURT?

☐ NO   ☐ YES (give caption, number, filing date, disposition and disposition date)

DOES PETITIONER HAVE CASES PENDING IN OTHER COURTS?

☐ NO   ☐ YES (give court, caption, number, filing date and status)

I HEREBY CERTIFY UNDER PENALTY OF PERJURY THAT THE PETITIONER IS PRESENTLY UNDER A SENTENCE OF DEATH AND THAT THE INFORMATION PROVIDED ON THIS FORM IS CURRENTLY ACCURATE AND CORRECT.

SIGNATURE	DATE

NOTE: The Court of Appeals periodically will request case status reports. Petitioner is under a continuing affirmative obligation to immediately notify the Fourth Circuit of any changes or additions to the information contained on this form.

APPENDIX A. RESOLUTION RESPECTING BAR MEMBERSHIP IN THE JUDICIAL CONFERENCE OF THE CIRCUIT.

Transferred.

Editor's note. — By order dated April 30, 1992, former Appendix A was transferred to be I.O.P. 47.2, effective June 30, 1992.

APPENDIX B. GUIDELINES FOR PREPARATION OF APPELLATE TRANSCRIPTS IN THE FOURTH CIRCUIT.

Revision effective December 4, 1996.

I. INTRODUCTION

A. *Purpose.* These guidelines set forth in detail the following:

1. Duties of the district court clerk's office, appellant and appellee in ordering the transcript;

2. Responsibilities of the court reporter for preparing and timely filing the transcript;

3. Duties of the court of appeals for acknowledging transcript orders and monitoring the timeliness of the filing of transcripts;

4. Procedures for court reporters to follow in requesting extensions of time and waivers of fee sanctions;

5. Criteria to be used by the court of appeals in acting on requests for extensions and waivers;

6. Common problems that have been encountered by court reporters and the court of appeals in the ordering, preparation and filing of transcripts; and

7. Provisions for supplementation of these Guidelines by local procedures adopted by a district court.

B. *Relation to Federal Rules of Appellate Procedure.* Although Rule 11(b), Federal Rules of Appellate Procedure, requires transcripts to be filed within thirty days of the purchase order date, the court of appeals will use the time limits set forth in the district court reporter management plans governing the application of fee sanctions as the time periods within which transcripts will be due. All of the plans establish a 60-day period for preparation of transcripts without financial penalty. Exceptions are:

1. Special provisions adopted by the Fourth Circuit Judicial Council for appeals by incarcerated criminal defendants;

2. Special circumstances, such as

(a) bail appeals,

(b) death penalty cases,

(c) expedited sentencing appeals,

(d) recalcitrant witness appeals, or

(e) other expedited procedures.

The Table on the next page sets forth the time requirements in detail.

TABLE OF TRANSCRIPT DUE DATES AND APPLICABLE SANCTIONS

NATURE OF CASE	LENGTH OF TRANSCRIPT	TRANSCRIPT DUE	10% FEE SANCTION	20% FEE SANCTION
Direct criminal appeals, appellant incarcerated	1000 pages or less	within 30 days of transcript order or judgment and commitment order, whichever is later	if filed after 30th day	if filed after 60th day
	more than 1000 pages	as ordered by clerk following consultation with reporter and parties	if due date missed	if due date missed by more than 30 days
All other cases, in other than exceptional circumstances	any length	within 60 days of transcript order or judgment and commitment order, whichever is later	if filed after 60th day	if filed after 90th day
Exceptional circumstances (e.g., bail appeals, death penalty cases, expedited sentencing appeals, etc.)	any length	as ordered by clerk following consultation with reporter and parties	*	*

---

*Twenty percent fee sanction automatically imposed if due date missed. Letter to chief district judge, after consultation with chief circuit judge requiring immediate preparation of the transcript.

C. *Effective date.* These guidelines will take effect on June 1, 1986, and will apply to all Fourth Circuit cases subject to F.R.A.P. 11(b) in which the transcript is ordered after that date.

D. *Definitions.* For purposes of these Guidelines, references to appellant-appellee will refer to counsel for appellant-appellee unless appellant-appellee is proceeding pro se, in which case all duties and responsibilities are those of appellant-appellee individually.

II. ORDERING AND ACKNOWLEDGING TRANSCRIPTS

A. *Duties of district court clerk's office.* 1. When a notice of appeal is filed, the district court clerk's office will furnish appellant with a copy of the Transcript Order form.

2. Upon entry of an order authorizing preparation of a transcript at government expense pursuant to the Criminal Justice Act or 28 U.S.C. § 753(f), the district court reporter coordinator or appeals deputy will notify the court of appeals of the date on which the order was entered.

3. When substitute reporters or contract reporters are used, the district court reporter coordinator or district court appeals deputy will furnish them

with copies of these guidelines and explain the procedures to be followed in preparing appellate transcripts.

4. When the transcript is filed, the district court clerk's office will see that the court reporter or the court reporter coordinator mails a copy of the reporter's certification to the court of appeals.

B. *Duties of appellant.* 1. Within ten days after filing the notice of appeal, the appellant is required by F.R.A.P. 10(b)(1) to order from the court reporter such transcript of the proceedings as the appellant deems necessary.

2. By service of a copy of the Docketing Statement, appellant will notify appellee(s) that (a) a transcript is not needed for the appeal, (b) a transcript is already on file in the district court, or (c) less than the complete transcript will be ordered. The statement of issues in the Docketing Statement will satisfy the requirement of F.R.A.P. 10(b)(3).

3. Before a transcript can be ordered, the appellant must obtain from the court reporter an estimate of the length of the transcript and make appropriate financial arrangements with the reporter (1) by immediate payment in full or by another payment arrangement acceptable to the reporter, (2) payment pursuant to the Criminal Justice Act, or (3) payment at government expense pursuant to 28 U.S.C. § 753(f). [Local Rule 10(c)(1)]. Payment or acknowledgment of financial arrangements satisfactory to the reporter must accompany the court reporter's copy of the Transcript Order. [F.R.A.P. 10(b)(4)].

4. In criminal cases, counsel may seek authorization from the district court to order transcript after entry of verdict but prior to sentencing. The district court may authorize the early ordering of transcript if it determines that defense counsel has informed the defendant of the right to appeal and the defendant has instructed counsel to appeal regardless of the nature or length of the sentence imposed. The time requirements for the preparation of transcripts that are ordered before sentencing shall not begin to run until after entry of the judgment and commitment order.

5. To order a transcript, the appellant completes the Transcript Order form furnished by the district court clerk's office and distributes the copies as follows:

court reporter — mail original to court reporter within 10 days of filing notice of appeal

district court — file copy in district court clerk's office within 10 days of filing notice of appeal

court of appeals — attach copies to both copies of Docketing Statement filed in court of appeals clerk's office within 14 days of filing notice of appeal

opposing counsel — attach copies to Docketing Statement served on opposing counsel within 14 days of filing notice of appeal

A separate Transcript Order must be prepared for each court reporter from whom a transcript is requested.

6. Failure by the appellant to timely order a transcript, failure to make satisfactory financial arrangements with the court reporter, or failure to specify in adequate detail those proceedings to be transcribed will subject the appeal to dismissal by the clerk of the court of appeals for want of prosecution pursuant to Local Rule 45.

7. When supplemental transcripts are requested, appellant must complete another Transcript Order form, make satisfactory financial arrangements with the reporter, and distribute copies to the same persons to whom the original Transcript Order was sent.

8. If payment is waived by the reporter at the time of ordering the transcript, the appellant must make full payment upon receipt of the reporter's invoice. If payment is not made within a reasonable period of time, the appeal will be subject to dismissal by the clerk of the court of appeals pursuant to Local Rule 45.

9. Transcripts ordered under the Criminal Justice Act do not include opening and closing statements, voir dire, or jury instructions unless prior special authorization has been received by appellant. CJA Form 24 forms should be obtained from the district court and submitted to the district court judge for approval. In multi-defendant cases involving CJA defendants, only original transcripts should be purchased from the court reporter(s). Requests for copies will be arranged by the district court using commercial printers. Contact the district court reporter coordinator or district court clerk's office for further instructions.

10. When an appellant has ordered a transcript, he or she is obligated to pay the reporter for it. If the appeal is dismissed voluntarily, the appellant is nonetheless responsible to the reporter for the cost of transcript prepared prior to the reporter's receipt of notification from the appellant of the appeal's dismissal.

C. *Duties of appellee.* 1. If the appellee deems a transcript of other parts of the proceedings to be necessary, he or she is required by F.R.A.P. 10(b)(3), within ten days after service of the Docketing Statement by the appellant, to file and serve on the appellant a designation of additional parts to be included. Unless within ten days after service of such designation the appellant has ordered such parts, and has so notified the appellee, the appellee may within the following ten days either order the parts or move the district court for an order requiring the appellant to do so.

2. If the appellee wishes to obtain a copy of the transcript which has been ordered by the appellant, he or she may do so by ordering the copy directly from the court reporter. Satisfactory financial arrangements must be completed with the reporter before obtaining the copy. It is not appellant's responsibility to order and pay for a copy of the transcript for appellee.

D. *Duties of the court reporter.* 1. Upon receipt of the Transcript Order form and completion of satisfactory financial arrangements, the reporter must prepare the required transcript within the time set forth in the applicable district court reporter management plan.

2. The appellant attaches copies of the transcript order to the two copies of the Docketing Statement filed with the court of appeals. Upon receiving the transcript order, the court of appeals will complete and send to the reporter, and to the court reporter coordinator and the district court, a Transcript Order Acknowledgment form to verify the transcript order. A copy of the Acknowledgment form will be sent to the reporter along with a photocopy of the

Transcript Order. The Acknowledgment will contain the order date and the date by which the transcript must be filed to avoid sanctions. The order date set out in the Transcript Order Acknowledgment form will be the date the Transcript Order form was received by the court of appeals. The due date is computed from this date by the court of appeals in accordance with the time specified in the district court reporter management plans. If the Transcript Order form is complete and accurate and satisfactory financial arrangements have been completed, NO RESPONSE IS REQUIRED FROM THE COURT REPORTER TO THE TRANSCRIPT ORDER FORM OR THE TRANSCRIPT ACKNOWLEDGMENT FORM.

3. If there is a problem with the order date (*e.g.,* the court reporter had not received the Transcript Order by the date it was received in the court of appeals), with financial arrangements with the appellant, with identification of the transcript ordered, with proper designation of the court reporters involved in the case, or with any other aspect of the Transcript Order, the court reporter must complete and mail a copy of the Acknowledgment form to the court of appeals within seven days of receipt by the reporter (time may be extended for vacation, serious illness or other unusual circumstances). A copy should also be sent to the court reporter coordinator. The court reporter need not inform the court of appeals if he or she in fact received the Transcript Order before the order date shown on the Acknowledgment. The court reporter may use any additional time so created for preparation of the transcript without fear of incurring a sanction for late filing. The court of appeals' Acknowledgment constitutes an implied fee sanction waiver to the due date set forth on the form.

4. The time for completion of the transcript will stop running automatically upon the reporter's mailing of the Acknowledgment form, indicating a problem with the terms of the order, for whatever reasonable period of time is required for the reporter or district court reporter coordinator to resolve the problem with the appellant. The court of appeals transcript coordinator will be in touch with the reporter or district court reporter coordinator upon receipt of the Acknowledgment form to offer assistance, such as notification to the appellant that the appeal will be dismissed if the problem is not remedied promptly.

5. When the problem has been remedied, the court of appeals will send a revised Transcript Order Acknowledgment setting forth a new transcript filing date reflecting the delay caused by the problem with the original Transcript Order.

6. Unless the court of appeals is notified of a problem with the Transcript Order, or of some other reason why the information on the Transcript Order Acknowledgment form prepared by the court of appeals is incorrect, the reporter will be held to the schedule set forth therein absent the granting of an extension of time. It is the court reporter's responsibility to notify the court of appeals of any problem.

7. If the transcript is estimated to be more than 1000 pages and is ordered in a criminal appeal in which the appellant is incarcerated, the reporter will receive an acknowledgment form with the order date and a due date which will be established by the court of appeals.

8. When the transcript has been completed and the court copy filed in the district court, a copy of the reporter's certification setting forth the date the transcript was filed in the district court must be sent to the court of appeals by the court reporter, or by the court reporter coordinator, to notify the court of appeals that the transcript has been filed and to provide a means for the court of appeals to verify that the proper fee reduction was taken by the reporter if the transcript was not timely filed.

9. Unless a written motion is filed by the appellant with the court of appeals, and an extension granted by the clerk of the court of appeals, requests by an appellant that a reporter suspend or delay preparation of a transcript that has been ordered will have no effect on the date the transcript is due, or on the appellant's obligation to pay for it when it is prepared. The only exception is when a motion for voluntary dismissal of the appeal has been granted; in that instance the appellant is responsible for paying only for that portion of the transcript completed prior to the reporter's receipt of notification from the appellant of the appeal's dismissal.

E. *Duties of Court of Appeals.* 1. F.R.A.P. 10(b)(1) requires the appellant to order the transcript within ten days after filing the notice of appeal. If the completed form is not received by the court of appeals within that time, making reasonable allowance for delivery by mail, the court of appeals will notify the appellant that no order has been received and that failure to comply with F.R.A.P. 10(b)(1) will subject the appeal to dismissal by the clerk for want of prosecution pursuant to Local Rule 45.

2. When the court of appeals receives the Transcript Order form, it will be reviewed for any obvious defects (e.g., multiple reporters on one form, or incompleteness as far as nature of proceedings requested or certification of satisfaction of financial requirements). If it appears to be in order, the court of appeals will prepare for the reporter a Transcript Order Acknowledgment showing the date the Transcript Order was received in the court of appeals and the due date, computed in accordance with the time limits set forth in the applicable district court reporter management plan. The court of appeals clerk's office will work together with reporters and parties to remedy any deficiencies in the Transcript Order that are brought to its attention by the reporter. (See Sections D. 3 - 8 for full description of procedures.)

III. REPORTS

Reports on outstanding transcripts will be generated monthly and will be distributed to the court reporters involved, as well as to the district court clerks or their court reporter coordinators. If the report shows a transcript outstanding when it has actually been filed, the reporter or district court reporter coordinator should call the court of appeals and report the date of filing. If everything in the report is correct and none of the transcripts are overdue, no response is required from the reporter.

IV. TIME LIMITS FOR FILING TRANSCRIPTS— FEE REDUCTION SANCTIONS

A. *Requests for extensions of time.* As set forth in the district court reporter management plans, all requests for extensions of time for the filing of appellate transcripts (F.R.A.P. 11(b) transcripts) are submitted to the clerk of the court of appeals. They should be in writing, on the designated form. A request for an extension of time will automatically constitute a corresponding request for a waiver of any applicable fee reduction sanction. Requests for extensions must be mailed ten days in advance of the deadline from which relief is sought, unless unforeseen circumstances make later requests necessary, in which case the reasons will be set out by the reporter in the request. When requesting an extension, the information furnished should be very specific. Failure to submit complete information will delay action on the request and lead to additional paperwork for the reporter. After reviewing the request for extension, the court of appeals will issue an order granting, granting in part, or denying the request, which will set forth the resulting timeframes for purposes of fee sanction imposition. Counsel, the district court reporter coordinator, and the district court clerk will also receive copies of this order.

B. *Grounds for extensions of time.* 1. Excessive burden of transcript, considering length and complexity of the proceedings ordered within a short period of time. District court reporter coordinators are expected to make court reporter assignments within a district so as to anticipate and to avoid to the extent possible the imposition of excessive transcript loads on individual reporters. When these efforts are unsuccessful, reporters may apply for relief from applicable fee sanctions and have the court of appeals assign the relative priority to be given to competing appellate transcript orders. The fact that a reporter has accumulated orders for more than 3000 pages within three months will be presumed to establish the existence of an "excessive burden." The existence of outstanding overdue transcripts may or may not be grounds for extending the time for subsequently ordered transcripts. In computing the amount of transcript for purposes of demonstrating excessive burden, the reporter can include all transcripts ordered within ninety days of the request for extension. The reporter may include transcript obligations for the district court as well as those ordered for appellate purposes. However, the orders must be "firm orders". A "firm order" for an appellate transcript is one for which the court of appeals has received a Transcript Order from the appellant. For a district court transcript it is an order communicated by a judge or a party; it cannot be a reporter's speculation that an order will be forthcoming.

2. Vacation. A reporter can plan to take reasonable vacations, as authorized by the district court, and obtain extensions of deadlines that would fall within those periods or become impossible to meet in light of them.

3. Unavoidable, excessive time required for attendance in court. It is the responsibility of the district court reporter coordinator to adjust reporter assignments to ensure that the needs of the trial and appellate courts can be met. Occasions may arise, nonetheless, when a court reporter's courtroom obligations, including official travel required to reach the courtroom, prevent

his or her meeting transcript obligations. Reasonable extensions of time will be given in such instances.

4. Incapacitation or serious illness. A reporter may certify to the clerk of the court of appeals that he or she has become temporarily incapacitated or seriously ill, and obtain reasonable relief from pending deadlines. This ground does not include common colds or other ailments that would not prevent attendance in court.

5. Unforeseen emergencies. Reporters may seek extensions for any other good cause which makes the completion of a transcript within the allotted time impossible.

V. SANCTIONS

A. *Fee reduction sanctions.* An official court reporter will be required to deduct from his or her charges for a completed transcript not timely filed with the district court the amount of any fee reduction sanction applicable by the terms of a district court reporter management plan.

B. *Removal from courtroom and request for substitute reporter.* The chief judge of the court of appeals, following consultation with the chief judge of the district court, may order a reporter to remain out of the courtroom, and pay the costs of a satisfactory substitute reporter, if a transcript is ninety days overdue.

VI. MONITORING OF TRANSCRIPT FILING

The clerk of the court of appeals will monitor the filing of all appellate transcripts and the fees charged by reporters when a transcript is filed untimely. The fee sanction mechanism exists by virtue of the district court reporter management plans which require reporters to take fee reductions if a transcript is not filed on time. Therefore, the court of appeals will not issue a sanction order. It is the reporter's duty to abide by the provisions of his or her district court reporter management plan and to take a fee reduction if one is applicable.

The court of appeals will take no action if the transcript is filed on time or, if not filed on time, the appropriate fee reduction has been taken as shown by the copy of the certification that the reporter submitted to the court of appeals when the transcript was filed. If a fee reduction was applicable and was not taken by the reporter, the court of appeals will send a letter to the reporter setting forth the fee reduction that should have been taken. Copies of this letter will be sent to counsel, the district court reporter coordinator (if any) and the judge to whom the reporter reports or the chief district judge. If the certification is not submitted within a reasonable period after the filing of the transcript, the reporter will be requested to submit a copy of his or her invoice.

The court of appeals will also send a letter to the chief district judge when a transcript is sixty days overdue. The letter will identify the particular transcript involved and the date of the order. Copies of the letter will be sent to the judge (if any) to whom the reporter reports, the district court reporter coordinator, the district court clerk, and the reporter. The letter will alert the chief judge of the district court to the possibility that the reporter may be required to remain out of the courtroom, paying for a substitute reporter, until the transcript is completed, if the transcript becomes ninety days overdue.

VII. COMMON PROBLEMS

A. *Transcripts prepared at government expense.* 1. Criminal Justice Act [18 U.S.C. § 3006A(6)]. When the reporter receives the approved CJA form, preparation of the transcript should begin immediately. The date of receipt of the approved CJA form will begin the running of the time for delivery of the transcript and the imposition of sanctions, except when the transcript is ordered before sentencing as set forth in II.B.4 above.

Pursuant to the provisions of the September 1987 amendment to the Guidelines for the Administration of the Criminal Justice Act, in multi-defendant cases involving CJA defendants, no more than one original transcript should be purchased from the court reporter on behalf of CJA defendants. One of the appointed counsel or the district court should arrange for the duplication, at commercially competitive rates, of enough copies of the transcript(s) for each of the CJA defendants for whom a transcript has been approved.

2. In forma pauperis litigants [28 U.S.C. § 753(f)]. When an order is entered directing preparation of a transcript at government expense pursuant to 28 U.S.C. § 753(f), the transcript order date is the date the reporter receives the court's order authorizing preparation of the transcript. The order date is not postponed until receipt of a completed AO Form 19, since the government is under an obligation to pay for the transcript once it is ordered by the court.

B. *Supplemental transcripts.* Supplemental transcripts are usually ordered after the original transcript has been filed and a briefing schedule established by the court of appeals. Therefore, these transcripts should be expedited. Counsel is under an obligation to notify the court of appeals that a supplemental transcript has been ordered. The court of appeals will then send the Transcript Order Acknowledgment form to the reporter with the request that the reporter prepare these transcripts as quickly as possible.

C. *Expedited proceedings.* When a transcript is requested for an expedited proceeding, the due date for filing the transcript is established by the court of appeals. If an expedited transcript is requested and prepared within seven days after receipt or notification of the order, the court reporter may charge the higher rates for expedited transcripts.

Transcripts for appeals arising from a criminal sentence imposed under 18 U.S.C. § 3742 will only be expedited if a motion for expedited review of criminal sentence is granted by the court of appeals. Only those portions of the transcript pertinent to the appeal must be prepared on an expedited basis. The court reporter will be notified by the court of appeals when a motion to expedite has been granted.

In bail appeals, only the portion of the transcript dealing with the bail issue should be ordered on a rush basis. Even though there may be other portions of the transcript that the appellant has ordered, the portion dealing with the bail issue should be prepared first.

In expedited proceedings, a twenty percent fee sanction from the regular transcript rate will be imposed if the due date is missed. At the same time, a letter will be sent to the chief judge of the district court, advising of the delinquency and warning that the chief judge of the court of appeals may order the reporter to remain out of the courtroom, and pay the costs of a satisfactory substitute reporter, if the transcript is not filed immediately. IF THE COURT REPORTER ANTICIPATES A PROBLEM WITH PROMPT PREPARATION OF AN EXPEDITED TRANSCRIPT, THE DISTRICT COURT REPORTER COORDINATOR AND THE COURT OF APPEALS SHOULD BE NOTIFIED IMMEDIATELY.

D. *Payment for transcript.* The court of appeals approves of reporters' demanding a substantial deposit or full payment in advance for preparation of a transcript. In those instances where a reporter does not demand full payment in advance, and upon transcript completion has not been paid fully by the appellant, the following procedures should be followed:

1. Timely file the court copy of the transcript with the district court clerk's office.

2. Contact the court of appeals immediately and a letter will be sent to the appellant stating that if full payment is not made to the court reporter within fifteen days of the date of the letter, the appeal will be dismissed for failure to prosecute.

Fee reduction sanctions will be applicable if the court copy of the transcript is not timely filed. Problems with payment for the transcript after its completion will have no effect on the established due date.

E. *Substitute reporters.* When an official court reporter hires a substitute, the official reporter still retains responsibility for the timely filing of the transcript. All provisions applicable to an official court reporter will be applicable to the substitute. If there is a problem with the filing of a transcript, the official court reporter will be notified as well as the substitute reporter. All correspondence and orders by the court of appeals will be sent to both reporters. The substitute can request extensions of time and waivers of applicable fee sanctions from the court of appeals. However, all guidelines applicable to the official reporter will be applicable to the substitute reporter and the proper procedures for requesting extensions must be followed.

F. *Contract reporters.* Contractual reporting services in district courts are provided as supplements to the services of official staff. Contractual services are used after the district court reporter coordinator has determined that no official court reporter is available. Contract reporters must follow the procedures set out below.

1. All contractors are subject to the provisions of the Terms and Conditions of AO Form 355, Contracts for Court Reporting Services, governing time of filing (30 days from date of order) and fee sanctions for late delivery of transcripts (2% for each day or fraction of a day the transcript is late, but not less than 10% and not more than 50% of the price of the transcript).

2. All contractors — whether or not the written standard contract is signed — must meet the Terms and Conditions of AO Form 355 as set forth above.

3. Extensions of time for filing transcripts for F.R.A.P. 11(b) cases may be requested in writing following the procedures set forth in these Guidelines. However, the court of appeals cannot waive the fee sanctions set out in AO Form 355. A waiver of applicable fee reduction sanctions may be requested, in writing, from the contracting officer. A copy of the letter requesting a waiver of fee sanctions should be sent to the court of appeals.

G. *Filing of transcripts with the district court.* When the proceedings that are transcribed have been taken in another division of the district court, the reporter may file the court copy of the transcript in the district in which his or her office is located. That division will file stamp the copy and forward it to the appropriate division for inclusion in the record to be transmitted to the court of appeals.

VIII. ADDITIONAL LOCAL PROCEDURES

Following prior consultation with the clerk of the court of appeals, a district court may institute supplemental local procedures designed to adapt these Guidelines to the structure of court reporting services in place in that district.

UNITED STATES COURT OF APPEALS
FOR THE FOURTH CIRCUIT

TRANSCRIPT ORDER

READ INSTRUCTIONS ON BACK PAGE BEFORE COMPLETING

Case Style _____
Dist. Ct. No. _____ District of _____
Date Notice of Appeal filed _____ Ct. of Appeals No. _____
Name of Court Reporter/Electronic Rec. _____
Address of Reporter _____

TO BE COMPLETED BY PARTY ORDERING TRANSCRIPT—DO NOT SUBMIT FORM UNTIL FINANCIAL ARRANGEMENTS HAVE BEEN MADE WITH THE REPORTER. IF THIS COMPLETED FORM IS NOT MAILED TO THE COURT REPORTER AND A COPY FILED WITH THE DISTRICT COURT CLERK WITHIN TEN (10) DAYS AFTER FILING NOTICE OF APPEAL, THE APPEAL WILL BE SUBJECT TO DISMISSAL PURSUANT TO FOURTH CIRCUIT LOCAL RULE 45. ADDITIONAL COPIES OF THIS FORM MUST BE FILED WITH TWO COPIES OF APPELLANT'S DOCKETING STATEMENT WITH THE CLERK OF THE COURT OF APPEALS WITHIN FOURTEEN DAYS OF FILING THE NOTICE OF APPEAL. A SEPARATE TRANSCRIPT ORDER MUST BE COMPLETED FOR EACH REPORTER FROM WHOM A TRANSCRIPT IS REQUESTED.

A. This constitutes an order of the transcript of the following proceedings [check appropriate box(es) and indicate total number of pages].

PROCEEDING	HEARING DATE(S)
☐ Voir Dire	_____
☐ Opening Statement (Plaintiff)	_____
☐ Opening Statement (Defendant)	_____
☐ Closing Argument (Plaintiff)	_____
☐ Closing Argument (Defendant)	_____
☐ Opinion of Court	_____
☐ Jury Instructions	_____
☐ Sentencing	_____
☐ Bail Hearing	_____
☐ Pre-Trial Proceedings (specify)	_____
	_____
☐ Testimony (specify) _____	_____
_____	_____
_____	_____
☐ Other (specify) _____	_____
_____	_____

TOTAL ESTIMATED PAGES _____

NOTE: *FAILURE TO SPECIFY IN ADEQUATE DETAIL THOSE PRO-CEEDINGS TO BE TRANSCRIBED IS GROUNDS FOR DISMISSAL OF AN APPEAL.*

B. I certify that I have contacted the court reporter (or coordinator if electronic recording from the District of Maryland) and satisfactory financial arrangements for payment of the transcript have been made.

☐ Private funds. (Deposit of $_____ enclosed with court reporter's copy. Check No. _____.)

☐ Criminal Justice Act. A CJA Form 24 has been submitted to the district judge. (Attach a photocopy of the CJA 24 to the court of appeals' and reporter's copies.

☐ Government expense (civil case). IFP has been granted and a motion for transcript at government expense has been submitted to the district judge.

☐ Advance payment waived by court reporter.

Signature _____ Typed Name _____

Address _____

Telephone No. _____ Date Mailed to Reporter _____

INSTRUCTIONS FOR COURT REPORTER

It is the appellant's responsibility to contact the reporter and make satisfactory financial arrangements before completing the Transcript Order form. Appellant must mail the form to the reporter and all other parties within ten days after filing the notice of appeal. When the court of appeals receives its copy of the Transcript Order form from appellant, it will send the reporter and the district court reporter coordinator, if any, a Transcript Order Acknowledgement form setting forth the date the transcript was ordered (date the court of appeals received its copy of the Transcript Order form) and the due date (computed in accordance with the district court reporter management plan). UNLESS THERE IS A PROBLEM WITH THE TRANSCRIPT ORDER, NO RESPONSE IS NECESSARY FROM THE REPORTER TO EITHER FORM. If there is a problem with the Transcript Order, a copy of the Transcript Order Acknowledgement form must be completed within seven days of receipt by the reporter (time may be extended for vacation, serious illness or other unusual circumstance), one copy mailed to the court of appeals, and a copy forwarded to the district court reporter coordinator. The time for completion of the transcript will stop automatically upon the reporter's mailing of the Acknowledgement form, indicating a problem with the terms of the Transcript Order, for whatever reasonable period of time is required for the reporter to resolve the problem with the appellant. When the problem has been remedied, the court of appeals will send a revised Transcript Order Acknowledgement setting forth a new transcript filing date reflecting the delay caused by the problem with the original Transcript Order.

Written requests for extension of time and waiver of applicable fee reduction sanctions must be addressed to the clerk of the court of appeals for any transcript which cannot be completed within the time set forth on the Acknowledgement form. Information furnished in support of the request must be very specific and follow the procedures set forth in the Guidelines for Preparation of Appellate Transcripts in the Fourth Circuit (copies of these Guidelines are available in the district court clerk's office). THE CLERK OF THE COURT OF APPEALS WILL GRANT WAIVERS SPARINGLY AND ONLY WHEN THERE ARE EXTENUATING CIRCUMSTANCES.

Unless a written motion is filed by the appellant with the court of appeals and an extension or waiver granted by the clerk of the court of appeals, requests by an appellant that a reporter suspend or delay preparation of a transcript that has been ordered will have no effect on the date the transcript is due, or on the appellant's obligation to pay for it when it is prepared.

TO INSURE THAT ALL COPIES ARE LEGIBLE, THIS FORM SHOULD BE TYPED. IF IT IS IMPOSSIBLE TO TYPE, USE A BALLPOINT PEN, PRESS FIRMLY, AND CHECK ALL COPIES AFTER COMPLETION.

INSTRUCTIONS TO APPELLANT FOR ORDERING TRANSCRIPT

You have ten days after filing your notice of appeal to order transcript from the court reporter and file a copy of this form with the clerk of the district court. Within fourteen days of filing the notice of appeal, additional copies of this form must be filed with two copies of the Docketing Statement with the clerk of the court of appeals and served with the Docketing Statement on opposing counsel.

DO NOT SUBMIT THIS FORM UNTIL YOU HAVE MADE SATISFACTORY FINANCIAL ARRANGEMENTS WITH THE COURT REPORTER.

1. Contact each court reporter involved in reporting the proceedings, obtain an estimate of total pages, and make arrangements for payment. If you are unsure of the reporter(s) involved, contact the district court clerk's office for

that information. A SEPARATE TRANSCRIPT ORDER MUST BE PRE-PARED FOR EACH COURT REPORTER FROM WHOM A TRANSCRIPT IS REQUESTED. MAKE COPIES OF BLANK FORM AS NECESSARY.

2. If payment is waived by the reporter until completion of the transcript, the appellant must remit full payment within a reasonable period of time upon receipt of the reporter's invoice.

3. If this was an electronic recording from the District of Maryland, contact the district court reporter coordinator for further instructions.

4. Transcripts ordered under the Criminal Justice Act do not include opening and closing statements, voir dire, or jury instructions unless prior special authorization has been received by the appellant. Request CJA Form 24 from the district court and submit the form(s) to the district court judge for approval. A separate CJA Form 24 must be completed for each court reporter. In multi-defendant cases involving CJA defendants, only original transcripts should be purchased from the court reporter(s). Requests for copies will be arranged by the district court using commercial printers. Contact the district court reporter coordinator or district court clerk's office for further instructions.

5. Complete the Transcript Order in its entirety.

6. Distribute the Transcript Order as follows:

court reporter — mail original to court reporter within 10 days of filing notice of appeal

district court — file copy in district court clerk's office within 10 days of filing notice of appeal

court of appeals — attach copies to both copies of Docketing Statement filed in court of appeals clerk's office within 14 days of filing notice of appeal

opposing counsel — attach copy to Docketing Statement served on opposing counsel within 14 days of filing notice of appeal

If the transcript order is not filed within the time periods set forth above, procedures will be initiated to dismiss the appeal for failure to prosecute.

If you have further questions, contact the Clerk's Office, U.S. Court of Appeals (804/771-2213).

UNITED STATES COURT OF APPEALS FOR THE
FOURTH CIRCUIT

Transcript Order Acknowledgment

TO:

No. _____, _____ v. _____ (C/A or Crim. _____)

A Transcript Order for this case was received by the court of appeals on _____.

By the terms of the district court reporter management plan for your district, the transcript will be due on _____. If it is filed after that date, financial sanctions will be applicable.

DO NOT return this form if the Transcript Order is clear, you are the proper person from whom a transcript should be ordered, satisfactory financial arrangements have been made, the date of the order appears correct and the order is otherwise clear and correct. If there are problems with the Transcript Order, check the appropriate box below and return one copy to the court of appeals and the other copy to the district court reporter coordinator. This transcript will be deemed ordered and due on the above date if a response is not mailed within seven (7) days of receipt of this Acknowledgment by the reporter.

_____ Criminal Justice Act funds have not been approved (C.J.A. 24)

_____ Motion for transcript at government expense has not been granted [28 U.S.C. § 753(f)]

_____ Satisfactory financial arrangements have not been made. Reason: _____ Deposit not received; _____ Other (specify) _____

_____ Transcript Order is unclear — proceedings requested should be more specific or dates of proceedings are incorrect

_____ Transcript Order has not been received by reporter, or _____ was received by court of appeals

_____ Other (specify) _____

_____

_____

UNITED STATES COURT OF APPEALS FOR THE
FOURTH CIRCUIT

Court of Appeals No. _____ Dist. Ct. No. _____

Style of Case _____

REQUEST FOR EXTENSION OF TIME AND WAIVER OF
APPLICABLE FEE REDUCTION SANCTION

I request that an extension of time and waiver of applicable fee reduction sanctions be given until _____ for the filing of the transcript which is due on _____. As of this date, approximately _____ pages have been completed and _____ pages are yet to be transcribed. JUSTIFICATION THEREFOR IS AS FOLLOWS:

A. Outstanding district court and/or appellate transcripts (include court of appeals or district court docket number for each case listed) filed within 90 days of this request:

Case Name & Docket Number   *Date Ordered*   *Date Due*   *Pages*

_____

_____

_____

_____

_____

B. In-court time (give total days or hours by month):

_____

C. Travel (give hours spent traveling to and from court by month):

_____

D. Vacation (list dates): _____

E. Incapacitation or serious illness (specify): _____

_____

F. Unforeseen emergencies (be specific): _____

_____   _____

    Date   Court Reporter

USE ADDITIONAL SHEETS TO PROVIDE DETAIL

CERTIFICATION OF FILING OF TRANSCRIPT

Case Style _____

District Court Number _____

Court of Appeals Number _____

  The transcript was filed in the United States District Court on _____

_____

I certify that (check one):

_____ The transcript was timely filed; *or*

_____ A fee reduction sanction of _____ percent of the total cost of the
transcript was taken.

                                     _____

                                            Court Reporter

APPENDIX C. PLAN OF THE UNITED STATES COURT OF APPEALS FOR THE FOURTH CIRCUIT IN IMPLEMENTATION OF THE CRIMINAL JUSTICE ACT.

Effective March 30, 1995.

As amended through February 26, 1996.

The Judicial Council of the Fourth Circuit adopts the following plan, in implementation of the Criminal Justice Act.

I. RIGHT TO COUNSEL

1. *Direct appeals.* In every direct appeal involving a person

(a) who is charged with a felony or misdemeanor (other than a petty offense), or with juvenile delinquency by the commission of an act which, if committed by an adult, would be such a felony or misdemeanor, or with a violation of probation, or who is held in custody as a material witness, or who appeals from parole proceedings conducted pursuant to 18 U.S.C. § 4106A, or,

(b) for whom the Sixth Amendment to the Constitution requires the appointment of counsel or for whom, in a case in which he faces the loss of liberty, any federal law requires the appointment of counsel,

whether the appeal be by a defendant from a judgment of conviction or from an order revoking probation, or by the United States from a judgment of acquittal or dismissal, a defendant shall be entitled to be represented by counsel as a matter of right.

If the appeal involves a petty offense for which confinement is authorized, the court may appoint counsel for a financially eligible person upon a determination that the interests of justice so require.

In these cases, unless an application for the appointment of counsel has already been received, or notice of appearance has been filed by retained counsel, the clerk of this court shall promptly notify the defendant of his right to counsel and shall inform him that counsel will be appointed if he is financially unable to obtain adequate representation. Where an attorney had previously been appointed to represent the defendant in district court, that attorney shall be reappointed, without prior notice, upon the docketing of the appeal in this court. If there is no such reappointment, either because defendant appeared pro se or was represented by retained counsel in the district court, the clerk shall appoint the attorney of record in the district court, where appropriate, or select an appointee from a panel of approved attorneys.

In pro se cases in which the appellant exercises his right to represent himself as suggested by *Faretta v. California,* 422 U.S. 806 (1975); 28 U.S.C. § 1654, the court may find it appropriate to appoint standby counsel for the appellant to assist in the appeal to protect the integrity and ensure the continuity of the judicial proceedings. (*McKaskle v. Wiggins,* 465 U.S. 168 (1984); *Faretta, supra).* Accordingly, if a pro se appellant is represented, at least in part, by standby counsel, compensation may be provided under the CJA.

2. *Collateral proceedings.* In an appeal in a collateral proceeding brought by the petitioner from an order denying the relief requested pursuant to 28 U.S.C. §§ 2241, 2254, or 2255, a petitioner shall not be entitled to be represented by counsel as a matter of right. In these cases, counsel will be appointed only after the court has decided to hear the case on the merits, as in the granting of leave to appeal or the issuance of a certificate of probable cause. However, in an appeal brought by the United States or a state from an order granting the relief requested, a petitioner shall be entitled to representation as a matter of right.

Similarly, in an appeal under 18 U.S.C. § 4245, a defendant shall not be entitled to be represented by appointed counsel, unless the appeal is taken by the United States.

In any case brought pursuant to 28 U.S.C. §§ 2241, 2254, or 2255, the court may, on motion of the petitioner or on its own motion, appoint counsel where the court determines that (a) petitioner is financially unable to obtain adequate representation and (b) the interests of justice require legal representation, as when petitioner needs the assistance of counsel to go forward with an apparently meritorious petition. The clerk shall thereupon appoint the attorney of record in the district court, where appropriate, or select an appointee from a panel of approved attorneys. This process also applies to cases involving an appeal under 18 U.S.C. § 4245.

Where a petitioner is under sentence of death, the clerk shall appoint counsel upon receipt of the notice of appeal.

II. APPOINTMENT OF COUNSEL

1. *Court order.* Every appointment of counsel pursuant to the Criminal Justice Act and this Plan shall be made by an order of this court. A prerequisite to appointment shall be an affirmative finding by the court that a defendant is financially unable to employ counsel. However, where counsel was appointed in the lower court, this court will presume, until reason to the contrary appears, that the defendant remains financially unable to retain counsel, and no such finding shall be required.

The selection of counsel under the Criminal Justice Act shall be the exclusive responsibility of the court, and no person entitled to court-appointed counsel shall be permitted to select counsel to represent him.

2. *Retroactivity.* An appointment may be made retroactive to include any representation furnished to an indigent by an attorney prior to appointment pursuant to this Plan.

3. *Scope.* A person for whom counsel is appointed shall be represented at every stage of the proceedings, through appeal, including ancillary matters appropriate to the proceedings and a petition for writ of certiorari to the Supreme Court.

4. *Substitution of counsel.* The court may, in the interests of justice, substitute one appointed counsel for another at any stage of the proceedings.

The total compensation to be paid both attorneys shall not exceed the statutory maximum for one appointment, unless the case involves extended or complex representation.

5. *One attorney for multiple defendants.* In appeals involving multiple defendants, separate counsel will normally be appointed for each defendant, unless there has been a waiver on the record by the defendants or good cause is shown. If one attorney is appointed to represent more than one defendant, a separate order of appointment shall be entered for each defendant. The attorney may be compensated for his services up to the maximum for each defendant represented; however, time spent in common on one or more defendants must be prorated.

6. *Multiple appointments for one defendant.* In capital cases, and in other cases of extreme difficulty where the interests of justice so require, the court may appoint an additional attorney to represent a defendant. Each attorney so appointed shall be eligible to receive the maximum compensation allowed under the Criminal Justice Act.

7. *Defendant's objection to appointed attorney.* The court shall give consideration to a defendant's expression of dissatisfaction with his counsel only if specific grounds for dissatisfaction are stated. Appointed counsel shall be relieved only when the court, in its discretion, determines that the interests of justice so require.

8. *Attorney's motion to withdraw.* An attorney appointed to represent a defendant in the lower court is generally obliged to continue that representation upon appeal. An attorney who does not desire to continue the representation must file a motion to withdraw with the clerk of this court promptly after filing the notice of appeal. The motion must set forth specific grounds for granting withdrawal; defendant's dissatisfaction with counsel is not sufficient grounds. Also, should counsel, during the course of an appeal, encounter a specific reason which suggests the inappropriateness of further representation of the defendant, counsel should promptly file a motion to withdraw. In any event, counsel has a duty to continue to represent the defendant until a motion to withdraw is granted.

III. DEFENDANT'S FINANCIAL STATUS

1. *Filing application.* A defendant who, in the district court, was represented by employed counsel, or was unrepresented, or was represented by appointed counsel but has nonetheless been requested to file a new application in this court, may apply to this court for the appointment of counsel. Such application shall be accompanied by an affidavit disclosing the applicant's financial status and any resources available to him to compensate counsel.

2. *Re-examination by court.* The court, at any time, may re-examine a defendant's financial status as it bears upon the appointment of counsel and, thereupon, (a) appoint counsel to represent the defendant, if the defendant is not already represented or is unable to pay previously retained counsel, (b) terminate the appointment of counsel, or (c) require a partial payment of counsel fees by the defendant. The defendant shall furnish such financial and

related information as may be requested during the re-examination, unless he desires to proceed without counsel.

3. *Insufficiency of funds; partial payment.* If a defendant's net financial resources and anticipated income are in excess of the amount needed to provide him and his dependents with the necessities of life and to provide for his release on bond, but are insufficient to pay fully for retained counsel, this court will find the defendant eligible for the appointment of counsel but will direct him to pay the available excess funds to the clerk at the time of appointment. The court may increase or decrease the amount of such payments and impose appropriate conditions, where applicable. All such payments by the defendant shall be received pursuant to the prescriptions of subsection (f) of the Criminal Justice Act.

4. *Family resources.* Funds and property standing in the name of, or held by, members of a defendant's family will be considered available for the payment of the fees of retained counsel if there is a finding, upon a reasonable basis of fact, that the family has indicated a willingness and a financial ability to pay all or part of the costs of representation. The initial determination of a defendant's eligibility for the appointment of counsel should be made without regard to family resources unless the family plans and is financially able to retain counsel promptly.

5. *Attorney's information.* If at any time after appointment, counsel obtains information that a client is financially able to make payment, in whole or in part, for legal services in connection with his representation, and the source of the attorney's information is not protected as a privileged communication, counsel shall so advise this court.

IV. PANEL OF ATTORNEYS

1. *Composition.* The clerk, subject to this court's approval, shall prepare a list of attorneys from which appointments shall be made. Attorneys, to be eligible for appointment, must be admitted to practice before this court under Rule 46 of the Federal Rules of Appellate Procedure, and must be competent to provide adequate representation to those persons entitled to counsel under the Criminal Justice Act. In preparing a list, the clerk may review and consider the panels approved for use in the several District Courts in the Fourth Circuit, the recommendations of Bar Associations, Legal Aid Agencies, and Defender Organizations, if any, and the court's own experience with attorneys.

2. *Periodic revision.* The panel shall be revised periodically to ensure an adequate number of competent attorneys to provide effective representation to all persons entitled to appointed counsel.

3. *Appointments.* Appointments shall be made by the clerk on a rotational basis, subject to this court's discretion. Consideration will be given to the nature of the case, the place of the trial, the residence of the indigent person if on bail, the place of confinement, and other relevant matters. In death penalty cases at least one attorney appointed must have been admitted to practice in the Fourth Circuit Court of Appeals for not less than five years, and must have had not less than three years experience in the handling of appeals in the

Fourth Circuit in felony cases. For good cause however, the court may appoint another attorney whose background, knowledge, or experience would otherwise enable him or her to properly represent the petitioner, with due consideration to the seriousness of the possible penalty and to the unique and complex nature of the litigation. The Court will look to the factors articulated in the American Bar Association's guidelines for selection of appellate counsel in capital cases including the length of bar membership, general experience in criminal defense litigation, and specific experience in death penalty appeals and appeals of murder, aggravated murder or other serious felonies. The Court will also consider whether counsel has attended and successfully completed a recent training or educational program on criminal advocacy which focused on the appeal of cases in which a sentence of death was imposed. Finally, the Court will review the availability of ongoing consultation support to appointed counsel from experienced counsel.

When the court determines that the appointment of an attorney, who is not a member of the CJA panel, is appropriate in the interest of justice, judicial economy, or some other compelling circumstance warranting his or her appointment, the attorney may be admitted to the CJA panel pro hac vice and appointed to represent the appellant. These appointments should be made only in exceptional circumstances, such as the appointment in a death penalty case of an attorney furnished by a state or local public defender organization or legal aid agency where the attorney had represented the appellant during prior state court proceedings. Further, the attorney should possess such qualities as would qualify him or her for admission to the CJA panel in the ordinary course of panel selection.

4. *Removal from the panel.* An attorney may be removed from the panel by the clerk for twice refusing to accept an appointment or by the court for any good reason.

V. ATTORNEY'S DUTY TO CONTINUE REPRESENTATION

1. *Trial counsel.* Every attorney, including retained counsel, who represented a defendant in the district court shall continue to represent the client after termination of those proceedings, unless relieved of further responsibility by this court. Where counsel has not been relieved:

If there is a judgment of conviction or an order revoking probation, counsel shall inform the defendant of his right to appeal and of his right to have counsel appointed on appeal. If so requested by the defendant, counsel shall file a timely notice of appeal. Thereafter, unless the defendant otherwise so instructs, counsel shall take appropriate and timely steps to perfect and present the appeal, including, where appropriate, the ordering of such part of the transcript as may be necessary for consideration on appeal.

Similarly, if there is an appeal by the United States from an order or judgment adverse to it, counsel shall continue to represent the client.

In any case brought pursuant to 28 U.S.C. §§ 2241, 2254, or 2255 which results in an order by the district court denying the relief requested, counsel shall inform the petitioner of his right to appeal and of the court's authority to appoint appellate counsel in its discretion. If so requested by the petitioner, counsel shall file a timely notice of appeal and a motion for appointment of appellate counsel, and counsel's duty is thereby ended. On the other hand, if petitioner is granted the relief requested, counsel shall continue to represent the petitioner in the event the respondent appeals the judgment.

2. *Appellate counsel.* Every attorney, including retained counsel, who represents a defendant in this court shall continue to represent his client after termination of the appeal unless relieved of further responsibility by this court or the Supreme Court. Where counsel has not been relieved:

If the judgment of this court is adverse to the defendant, counsel shall inform the defendant, in writing, of his right to petition the Supreme Court for a writ of certiorari. If the defendant, in writing, so requests and in counsel's considered judgment there are grounds for seeking Supreme Court review, counsel shall prepare and file a timely petition for such a writ and transmit a copy to the defendant. Thereafter, unless otherwise instructed by the Supreme Court or its clerk, or unless any applicable rule, order or plan of the Supreme Court shall otherwise provide, counsel shall take whatever further steps are necessary to protect the rights of the defendant, until the petition is granted or denied.

If the appellant requests that a petition for writ of certiorari be filed but counsel believes that such a petition would be frivolous, counsel may file a motion to withdraw with this court wherein counsel requests to be relieved of the responsibility of filing a petition for writ of certiorari. The motion must reflect that a copy was served on the client.

If the United States seeks a writ of certiorari to review a judgement of this court, counsel shall take all necessary steps to oppose the United States' petition.

Similarly, in any proceeding brought pursuant to 28 U.S.C. §§ 2241, 2254, or 2255 which results in an order by this court, appointed counsel shall take those steps necessary, as set forth above, to protect the rights of the defendant in the Supreme Court.

(Amended by order effective March 30, 1995.)

VI. COMPENSATION AND REIMBURSEMENT OF EXPENSES

1. *Voucher.* Upon the completion of service in this court, appointed counsel shall submit a voucher for compensation and reimbursement on the Criminal Justice Act form currently approved by the Administrative Office of the United States Courts. Vouchers shall be submitted no later than 60 days after the final disposition of the case, unless good cause is shown. The clerk will determine the amount of compensation and reimbursement to be paid. The approved voucher will then be reviewed by the Circuit Executive, signed by the Chief Judge, and forwarded to the Administrative Office for payment or further handling.

2. *Hourly rates.* For work done before January 1, 1996, counsel may be compensated at rates not exceeding $60.00 per hour for time expended in court and $40.00 per hour for time reasonably expended out of court. For work done

on or after January 1, 1996, counsel may be compensated at rates not exceeding $65.00 per hour for in court time and $45.00 per hour for out of court time unless the Judicial Conference determines that a higher rate is justified. In death penalty cases these maximum rates do not apply. Counsel in these cases may be compensated at such rates as the Court determines to be reasonably necessary, within the $75 — $125 per hour range. Time spent awaiting oral argument is considered to be time expended out of court.

3. *Maximum compensation allowable.* In any direct appeal, except in death penalty cases and in appeals from probation revocation proceedings, the total compensation, exclusive of expenses, shall not exceed $2,500.00 for an attorney's services rendered in this court. In death penalty cases compensation is in such amounts as the court determines to be reasonably necessary.

In any collateral proceeding, or in any case where a post-trial motion has been made after the entry of judgment, or in appeals from probation revocation proceedings, the total compensation, exclusive of expenses, shall not exceed $750.00 for an attorney's services rendered in this court.

In all cases where there has been a substitution of counsel, or where multiple defendants have been represented by one attorney or multiple appointments have been made for one defendant, total compensation shall be determined pursuant to Section II, Paragraphs 4, 5, and 6.

Payment in excess of the prescribed limitations may be made to provide fair compensation in a case involving extended or complex representation, upon approval by the Chief Judge of this court or other active circuit judge designated by him. Counsel claiming in excess of the statutory maximum must submit with his voucher a detailed memorandum supporting and justifying counsel's claim that the representation given was in a complex or extended case, and that the excess payment is necessary to provide fair compensation. If the legal or factual issues in a case are unusual, thus requiring the expenditure of more time, skill and effort by the lawyer than would normally be required in an average case, the case is "complex". If more time is reasonably required for total processing than would normally be required in the average case, the case is "extended". Attorneys seeking compensation have the burden of providing sufficient details to support their claim that the case is more complex or time consuming than the average case. This burden also exists with regard to the reasonableness of hours claimed for representation.

4. *Reimbursable expenses.* Counsel shall be entitled to reimbursement for reasonably incurred out-of-pocket expenditures. Travel by privately owned automobile should be claimed at the mileage rate currently applicable to federal employee travel, plus parking fees and tolls. Transportation other than by privately owned automobile should be claimed on an actual expense basis. Necessary airline travel will be reimbursed only at coach class rates. Expenditures for meals and lodging, as well as for telephone toll calls, telegrams, and copying are reimbursable. The cost of photocopying or similar copying services is reimbursable, while the cost of printing is not. Where photocopying services are performed in counsel's office, the reimbursement shall be limited to out-of-pocket expenses, not to exceed 15 cents per copy. For photocopying and other services in preparation of briefs and appendices by commercial printers,

reimbursement shall not exceed 35 cents per copy. All materials contained in appendices prepared by commercial printers in court-appointed cases will be reproduced on both sides of a sheet. No joint appendix in a court-appointed case shall exceed 250 sheets without advance permission from the Court. Compensation paid to law students for legal research is reimbursable, but expenses incurred by the law student in assisting counsel are not. When necessary for adequate representation in death penalty cases, reasonable employment and compensation of public and private organizations which provide consulting services to counsel are reimbursable to assist in such areas as records completion, identification of potential issues, exhaustion of state remedies, and review of draft pleadings and briefs. Detailed receipts are required for all travel and lodging expenses, non-office copying services, and any other expense in excess of $50.00. Failure to provide detailed receipts may result in the expense being denied. Any expense in excess of $50.00 must be itemized in a manner which will permit a review of the amount expended.

5. *Representation to the Supreme Court.* Counsel's time and expenses involved in the preparation of a petition for a writ of certiorari to the Supreme Court, and in the protection of the defendant's rights up until the time that Court disposes of a petition, should be included in the voucher for services performed in this court.

6. *Number of copies.* Appointed counsel is required to file six copies of the brief and five copies of the appendix with the clerk of the court, with service of one copy on counsel for each party separately represented. Appointed counsel shall be entitled to reimbursement for the cost of photocopying required copies.

7. *Non-reimbursable expenses.* General office overhead, personal items and non-legal personal services for the person represented, filing fees, services of process, and printing are non-reimbursable. (A person represented under the Criminal Justice Act is not required to pay filing fees or costs, or give security therefore, nor must he file the 28 U.S.C. § 1915(a) affidavit, for an appeal.)

8. *Authorized transcripts.* Authorized transcripts should not be claimed in the voucher by an attorney. The Administrative Office will pay the appropriate court reporter directly.

9. *Interim payment of expenses.* This court, in rare cases, will entertain requests for interim reimbursement of extraordinary and substantial expenses.

10. *Direct payment from person represented.* No appointed counsel shall accept a payment or a promise of payment from a defendant for representation in this court without prior authorization from the court on an appropriate Criminal Justice Act form.

11. *Public defender.* Where a defendant is represented by a federal public defender, the defender shall be compensated solely by his federal salary and shall not submit a Criminal Justice Act form for compensation.

12. *Non-appointed co-counsel.* Non-appointed attorneys may not be compensated, but an appointed attorney may claim compensation for services furnished by a partner, associate, or co-counsel, within the maximum compensation allowed to the appointed attorney.

(Amended by order effective March 31, 1993, by order effective March 30, 1995, and by order effective February 26, 1996.)

VII. RULES, REGULATIONS, FORMS

1. *Rules and regulations.* This Plan shall be subject to and held to have been amended pro tanto by any rule or regulation adopted by the Judicial Conference of the United States concerning the operation of plans under the Criminal Justice Act.

The Judicial Council or this court may adopt rules or regulations concerning the operation of this Plan, which, when promulgated, shall have the same force as provisions of this Plan.

2. *Forms.* Forms approved by the Administrative Office of the United States Courts for use in the administration of the Criminal Justice Act shall be used whenever appropriate. Where there are no approved forms, this court may approve and require the use of designated forms or other instruments.

VIII. ADMINISTRATION

Generally; clerk's office. Any act to be done by the court may be done by any judge of the court, by the clerk, or by a deputy clerk pursuant to delegated authority.

IX. DEFINITIONS

1. *Supreme Court.* Supreme Court of the United States.
2. *Administrative Office.* Administrative Office of the United States Courts.
3. *This Court; the Court.* The United States Court of Appeals for the Fourth Circuit.
4. *Criminal Justice Act.* Criminal Justice Act of 1964, 18 U.S.C. § 3006A, as amended by Public Law 91-447, approved October 14, 1970; Public Law 93-412, approved September 3, 1974; Public Law 97-164, approved April 2, 1982; Public Law 98-473, approved October 12, 1984; and Public Law 99-651, approved November 14, 1986.
5. *Defendant; defendants.* Where appropriate in this Plan, the word "defendant" or "defendants" shall be construed to include petitioner or petitioners in a collateral proceeding.
6. *Judicial Council.* Judicial Council of the Fourth Judicial Circuit of the United States.

X. AMENDMENTS

This Plan may be amended at any time by the Judicial Council effective when a copy of the amendatory resolution is filed with the Administrative Office or at such later date as may be specified in the resolution.

XI. EFFECTIVE DATE

This amended plan is effective February 26, 1996.

(Amended by order effective March 30, 1995, and by order effective February 26, 1996.)

APPENDIX D. DOCKETING STATEMENT INSTRUCTIONS.

1. Counsel for appellant must file two copies of a docketing statement with all attachments within fourteen days of filing the notice of appeal for every case appealed or cross-appealed to the court of appeals. The docketing statement must be received by the court of appeals clerk's office within the fourteen days allowed to be deemed timely filed. Copies must be served on the opposing party or parties.

2. The attorney filing the notice of appeal is responsible for filing the docketing statement, even if different counsel will handle the appeal. In the case of multiple appellants represented by separate counsel, the parties must confer and decide who will file the docketing statement. Appellants proceeding pro se may file a docketing statement, but are not required to do so.

3. The docketing statement is not a brief but will be used by the circuit mediator for pre-briefing review of civil cases in which all parties are represented by counsel, and in mediation conducted in such cases under Fourth Circuit Local Rule 33. The nature of proceedings and relief sought should be stated succinctly. The issues should be framed with reference to the specific facts and circumstances of the case. Conclusory statements such as "the judgment of the trial court is not supported by the law or facts" are unacceptable. Although a party will not be precluded from raising additional issues in the brief, counsel should make every effort to include in the docketing statement all of the issues that will be presented to the Court. The docketing statement should not contain motions or other requests for interim relief. If counsel in a civil case believes a mediation conference would be beneficial, counsel may make a confidential request for mediation by contacting the Office of the Circuit Mediator directly at (919) 541-7848.

4. Counsel's failure to file the docketing statement within the time set forth will cause the Court to initiate the process for dismissal of the appeal under Fourth Circuit Local Rule 45.

5. If an opposing party concludes that the docketing statement is in any way inaccurate, incomplete, or misleading, that party should file two copies of any additions or corrections to the docketing statement with the clerk's office within seven days of service of the docketing statement, with copies to all other parties.

6. You must attach to this docketing statement:
   a.) ADDITIONAL PAGES CONTAINING EXTENDED ANSWERS TO QUESTIONS ON THIS FORM.
   b.) THE NOTICE OF APPEAL.
   c.) THE DISTRICT COURT DOCKET SHEET.
   d.) A COPY OF THE ORDER OR JUDGMENT FROM WHICH THE APPEAL IS TAKEN.
   e.) ANY OPINION OR FINDINGS.
   f.) ANY OPINION, FINDINGS, OR RECOMMENDATION OF A UNITED STATES MAGISTRATE JUDGE, AN ADMINISTRATIVE LAW JUDGE, A SOCIAL SECURITY APPEALS COUNCIL, OR A BANKRUPTCY COURT.

g.) A COPY OF THE TRANSCRIPT ORDER, IF ANY.

h.) A CERTIFICATE OF SERVICE FOR THIS DOCKETING STATE-MENT.

DOCKETING STATEMENT

Caption of Case   4CCA Docket No.

                                   Type of Action

                                   ____ Civil

v.   ____ Criminal/Prisoner

                                   ____ Cross Appeal

District _____ Judge _____

District Court Docket Number _____

Statute or other authority establishing jurisdiction in the:

District Court _____

Court of Appeals _____

A. Timeliness of Appeal

    1. Date of entry of judgment or order appealed from _____

    2. Date this notice of appeal filed _____

        If cross appeal, date first notice of appeal filed _____

    3. Filing date of any post-judgment motion filed by any party which tolls time under FRAP 4(a)(4) or 4(b) _____

    4. Date of entry of order deciding above post-judgment motion _____

    5. Filing date of any motion to extend time under FRAP 4(a)(5), 4(a)(6) or 4(b) _____

        Time extended to _____

B. Finality of Order or Judgment

    1. Is the order or judgment appealed from a final decision on the merits? Yes ( ) No ( )

    2. If no,

        a.) Did the district court order entry of judgment as to fewer than all claims or all parties pursuant to FRCP 54(b)? Yes ( ) No ( )

        b.) Is the order appealed from a collateral or interlocutory order reviewable under any exception to the finality rule? Yes ( ) No ( )

If yes, explain _____

(Criminal only)

    3. Has the defendant been convicted? Yes ( ) No ( )

    4. Has a sentence been imposed? Yes ( ) No ( )

        Term _____

    5. Is the defendant incarcerated? Yes ( ) No ( )

C. Has this case previously been appealed? Yes ( ) No ( )

If yes, give the case name, docket number and disposition of each prior appeal on a separate page.

D. Based on your present knowledge:

Will this appeal involve a question of first impression? Yes ( ) No ( )

If yes, please explain briefly on a separate page.

E. Are any related cases or cases raising related issues pending in this court, any district court of this circuit, or the Supreme Court?   Yes ( ) No ( )
    If yes, cite the case and the manner in which it is related on a separate page. If abeyance, consolidation, or in seriation argument is warranted, counsel must file a separate motion seeking such relief.
    If related case is pending in this Court, has it been accepted for mediation by the Office of the Circuit Mediator?   Yes ( ) No ( )

F. State the nature of the suit, the relief sought, and the outcome below. Attach additional page if necessary.

G. Issues to be raised on appeal. Attach additional page if necessary.

H. Is settlement being discussed?   Yes ( ) No ( )

I. Is disposition on motions, memoranda, or abbreviated briefing schedule appropriate?   Yes ( ) No ( )
    If yes, you must file an appropriate motion.
    Is oral argument necessary?   Yes ( ) No ( )

J. Were there any in-court proceedings below?   Yes ( ) No ( )
    Is a transcript necessary for this appeal?   Yes ( ) No ( )
    If yes, is transcript already on file with district court?   Yes ( ) No ( )
    If transcript is not already on file, attach copy of transcript order.

K. List each adverse party to the appeal. If no attorney, give address and telephone number of the adverse party. Attach additional page if necessary.

    1. Adverse party _____
        Attorney _____
        Address _____
        _____
        Telephone _____

    2. Adverse party _____
        Attorney _____
        Address _____
        _____
        Telephone _____

L. If this case arises out of a bankruptcy proceeding, attach a copy of the caption of the case in the bankruptcy court showing the parties' status as debtor, creditor, trustee, plaintiff, defendant, etc.

M. List name(s) and address(es) of appellant(s) who filed this notice of appeal and appellant's counsel. Attach additional page if necessary.
    Appellant(s) Name _____
    Address _____
    _____
    _____
    Telephone _____
    Attorney's Name _____
    Firm _____
    Address _____

Telephone _____

Will you be handling the appeal? (In criminal cases counsel below will handle the appeal unless relieved by this court.)   Yes ( ) No ( )

FRAP 12(b) provides that each attorney who files a notice of appeal must file with the clerk of the court of appeals a statement naming each party represented on appeal by that attorney. Any counsel, other than the attorney filing this form, who filed a notice of appeal must provide the requisite statement to be attached to this form.

Signature _____

Date _____

ATTACH:

1. ADDITIONAL PAGES CONTAINING EXTENDED ANSWERS TO QUESTIONS ON THIS FORM.
2. THE NOTICE OF APPEAL.
3. THE DISTRICT COURT DOCKET SHEET.
4. A COPY OF THE ORDER OR JUDGMENT FROM WHICH THE APPEAL IS TAKEN.
5. ANY OPINION OR FINDINGS.
6. ANY OPINION, FINDINGS, OR RECOMMENDATION OF A UNITED STATES MAGISTRATE JUDGE, AN ADMINISTRATIVE LAW JUDGE, A SOCIAL SECURITY APPEALS COUNCIL, OR A BANKRUPTCY COURT.
7. A COPY OF THE TRANSCRIPT ORDER, IF ANY.
8. A CERTIFICATE OF SERVICE FOR THIS DOCKETING STATEMENT.

APPENDIX E. DOCKETING STATEMENT — AGENCY INSTRUCTIONS.

1. Counsel for the petitioner or applicant must file two copies of a docketing statement for any petition for review, cross petition, application for enforcement, or cross application within fourteen days of docketing of the petition or application. The docketing statement must be received by the clerk's office within the fourteen days allowed to be deemed timely filed. Copies must be served on the opposing party or parties. Petitioners proceeding pro se may file a docketing statement but are not required to do so.

2. Only one docketing statement shall be filed for each petition or application. If there are multiple petitioners or applicants, the parties should confer and decide who will file the docketing statement. A list of all names and addresses of parties, their attorneys and attorneys' names and addresses, and a certification that all parties have conferred and concurred in the filing must be attached to the docketing statement.

3. The docketing statement is not a brief and should not contain argument or motions. The nature of proceedings and relief sought should be stated succinctly. The issues should be expressed in terms and circumstances of the case but without unnecessary detail. Conclusory statements such as "the findings of the administrative law judge are not supported by the law or facts" are unacceptable. Although a party will not be precluded from raising additional issues, counsel should make every effort to include in the docketing statement all of the issues that will be presented to the Court. The docketing statement will be used in any mediation conducted under Fourth Circuit Local Rule 33. If counsel in a case in which all parties are represented by counsel believes a mediation conference would be beneficial, counsel may make a confidential request for mediation by contacting the Office of the Circuit Mediator directly at (919)541-7848.

4. Counsel's failure to file the docketing statement within the time set forth above will cause the Court to initiate the process for dismissal under Fourth Circuit Local Rule 45.

5. If an opposing party concludes that the docketing statement is in any way inaccurate, incomplete, or misleading, that party should file two copies of any additions or corrections to the docketing statement with the clerk's office within seven (7) days of service of the docketing statement, with copies to all other parties.

DOCKETING STATEMENT—AGENCY

Re:

Type of Action
____ Application for Enforcement
____ Petition for Review
____ Cross Petition

Name of Agency _____
Administrative Law Judge _____
Agency Number _____
Statute or other authority establishing jurisdiction in the Court of
Appeals _____

A. Timeliness
    1. Date of entry of order _____
    2. Time allowed for review or enforcement _____
       Authority _____

B. Finality
    1. Tribunal or board issuing order or regulation _____
    2. Is the order or judgment appealed from a final decision on the merits?   yes ( ) no ( )
    3. If no, is the order appealed from a collateral or interlocutory order reviewable under any exception to the finality rule?   yes ( ) no ( ) If yes, explain _____

C. If INS case, is petitioner an aggravated felon?   yes ( ) no ( )
    If yes, do you intend to file a motion to stay deportation?   yes ( ) no ( )

D. Has this case been before the court previously?   yes ( ) no ( )
    If yes, give case name, docket number, and disposition of each prior appeal on a separate sheet.

E. Is there any case now pending or about to be brought before this court, any other court or administrative agency, or the Supreme Court which either arises from the same case or controversy or involves substantially related issues?   yes ( ) no ( )
    If yes, cite the case and manner in which it is related on a separate sheet. If abeyance, consolidation, or in seriation argument is warranted, counsel must file a separate motion seeking such relief.
    If related case is pending in this Court, has it been accepted for mediation by the Court's Pre-argument Conference Program?   yes ( ) no ( )

F. State the nature of the proceeding, the relief sought, and the outcome below. Attach additional page if necessary.

G. Issues to be raised on petition or application. Attach additional page if necessary.

H. Is settlement being discussed?   yes ( ) no ( )

I. Is disposition on motions, memoranda, or abbreviated briefing schedule appropriate?   yes ( ) no ( )
    If yes, you must file an appropriate motion. Is oral argument necessary?   yes ( ) no ( )

J. List each adverse party to this action. Attach additional sheets if necessary. If no attorney, give address and telephone number of the adverse party.

      Adverse party _____

      Attorney _____

      Address _____

      Telephone _____

K. Petitioner's or Applicant's Name _____

    Address _____

    _____

    Telephone _____

L. Attorney or pro se litigant filing this docketing statement.
    Will you be handling the appeal?   yes ( ) no ( )

    Name _____

    Attorney ( )   Pro Se ( )

    Firm _____

    Address _____

    Telephone _____

If this is a joint statement by multiple petitioners or applicants, add the names and addresses of other petitioners or applicants and their counsel on an additional sheet, accompanied by a certification that all petitioners or applicants concur in this filing.

              Signature _____

              Date _____

EACH COPY OF THIS DOCKETING STATEMENT SERVED OR FILED SHALL HAVE ATTACHED TO IT COPIES OF:

(1) THE APPLICATION FOR ENFORCEMENT, OR PETITION FOR REVIEW;

(2) THE DOCKET SHEET OF THE AGENCY FROM WHICH THE APPEAL IS TAKEN;

(3) THE JUDGMENT OR ORDER SOUGHT TO BE REVIEWED AND ANY OPINION OR FINDING;

(4) ANY OPINION, FINDINGS, OR RECOMMENDATION OF AN ADMINISTRATIVE LAW JUDGE UNDERLYING THE ORDER AT ISSUE;

(5) ANY TRANSCRIPT ORDER; AND

(6) A CERTIFICATE OF SERVICE FOR THIS DOCKETING STATEMENT.

APPENDIX F. DOCKETING STATEMENT
— TAX COURT.

1. Counsel for appellant must file two copies of a docketing statement with all attachments for every case appealed or cross-appealed to the court of appeals within fourteen days of the docketing of the appeal. The docketing statement must be received by the clerk's office within the fourteen days allowed to be deemed timely filed. Copies must be served on the opposing party or parties.

2. The attorney filing the notice of appeal is responsible for filing the docketing statement, even if different counsel will handle the appeal. In the case of multiple appellants represented by separate counsel, the parties must confer and decide who will file the docketing statement. Appellants proceeding pro se may file a docketing statement, but are not required to do so.

3. The docketing statement is not a brief and should not contain argument or motions. The nature of proceedings and relief sought should be stated succinctly. The issues should be expressed in terms and circumstances of the case but without unnecessary detail. Conclusory statements such as "the judgment of the tax court is not supported by the law or facts" are unacceptable. Although a party will not be precluded from raising additional issues, counsel should make every effort to include in the docketing statement all of the issues that will be presented to the Court. The docketing statement will be used in any mediation conducted under Fourth Circuit Local Rule 33. If counsel in a case in which all parties are represented by counsel believes a mediation conference would be beneficial, counsel may make a confidential request for mediation by contacting the Office of the Circuit Mediator directly at (919)541-7848.

4. Counsel's failure to file the docketing statement within the time set forth above will cause the Court to initiate the process for dismissal of the appeal under Fourth Circuit Local Rule 45.

5. If an opposing party concludes that the docketing statement is in any way inaccurate, incomplete, or misleading, that party should file two copies of any additions or corrections to the docketing statement with the clerk's office within seven (7) days of service of the docketing statement, with copies to all other parties.

DOCKETING STATEMENT—TAX COURT

Re:
Tax Court Docket Number _____
Judge _____
Statute or other authority establishing jurisdiction in the:
    Tax Court _____
    Court of Appeals _____
A. Timeliness of Appeal
    1. Date of entry of judgment or order appealed from _____.

   2.   Date this notice of appeal filed _____.
       If cross appeal, date first notice of appeal filed _____.
B. Finality of Order or Judgment
   1.   Is the order or judgment appealed from a final decision on the merits? yes ( ) no ( )
   2.   If no, is the order appealed from a collateral or interlocutory order reviewable under any exception to the finality rule? yes ( ) no ( )
       If yes, explain

C. Has this case previously been appealed? yes ( ) no ( )
   If yes, give the case name, docket number, and disposition of each prior appeal on a separate sheet.
D. Are any related cases or cases raising related issues pending in this court, the Tax Court or the Supreme Court? yes ( ) no ( )
   If yes, cite the case and the manner in which it is related on a separate sheet. If abeyance, consolidation, or in seriation argument is warranted, counsel must file a separate motion seeking such relief.
   If related case is pending in this court, has it been accepted for mediation by the court's Pre-argument Conference Program? yes ( ) no ( )
E. State the nature of the suit, the relief sought and the outcome below. Attach additional page if necessary.
F. Issues to be raised on appeal. Attach additional page if necessary.
G. Is settlement being discussed? yes ( ) no ( )
H. Is disposition on motions, memoranda, or an abbreviated briefing schedule appropriate? yes ( ) no ( )
   If yes, you must file an appropriate motion.
   Is oral argument necessary? yes ( ) no ( )
I. List each adverse party to the appeal. Attach additional sheets if necessary. If no attorney, give address and telephone number of the adverse party.
   1.   Adverse party _____
       Attorney _____
       Address _____

       Telephone _____
J. List name(s) and address(es) of appellant(s) who filed this notice of appeal and appellant's counsel. Attach additional page if necessary.
   Appellant(s) Name _____
   Address _____
   Telephone _____
   Attorney's Name _____
   Firm _____
   Address _____
   Telephone _____
   Will you be handling the appeal? yes ( ) no ( )
   FRAP 12 (b) provides that each attorney who files a notice of appeal must file with the clerk of the court of appeals a statement naming each party

represented on appeal by that attorney. Any counsel, other than the attorney filing this form, who filed a notice of appeal must provide the requisite statement to be attached to this form.

Signature _____

Date _____

ATTACH:
1. ADDITIONAL PAGES, IF ANY, CONTAINING EXTENDED AN-SWERS TO QUESTIONS ON THIS FORM.
2. THE NOTICE OF APPEAL.
3. A COPY OF THE ORDER OR JUDGMENT FROM WHICH THE APPEAL IS TAKEN.
4. ANY OPINION OR FINDINGS.
5. A CERTIFICATE OF SERVICE.

APPENDIX G. DEATH PENALTY REPRESENTATION IN THE FOURTH CIRCUIT.

UNITED STATES COURT OF APPEALS

FOR THE FOURTH CIRCUIT

JUDICIAL COUNCIL

In the Matter of Death Penalty Representation   *

                                                                        No. 113

In the Fourth Circuit   *

ORDER

The Report of the Death Penalty Committee, which is attached to and made a part of this Order, is hereby adopted by the Fourth Circuit Judicial Council. The official policy of the Fourth Circuit shall be:

(1) Federal Public Defenders may be appointed to represent individuals charged with federal capital crimes and collateral attacks on federal capital convictions and sentences.

(2) Federal Public Defenders shall not be appointed to represent criminal defendants petitioning pursuant to 28 U.S.C.A. Section 2254 for relief from a state death sentence.

(3) The limitations on time for decision set forth in 28 U.S.C.A. Section 2266 shall apply at the district and circuit court levels and the Circuit Executive is authorized to inquire into the reasons for any noncompliance with the limitations.

and it is so ORDERED.

FOR THE COUNCIL:

/s/ J. Harvie Wilkinson III

_____

Chief Judge

Date: October 3, 1996

I. STATUTORY PROVISIONS PRESENTLY APPLICABLE
TO APPOINTMENT OF ATTORNEYS FOR
CAPITAL REPRESENTATION

A. APPOINTMENT OF COUNSEL FOR INDIGENT CAPITAL DEFENDANTS IS STATUTORILY GUARANTEED FOR FEDERAL TRIALS, DIRECT APPEAL FROM FEDERAL CONVICTIONS, § 2255 PROCEEDINGS, AND § 2254 PROCEEDINGS.

Congress has enacted special provisions guaranteeing that "in every criminal action in which a defendant is charged with a crime which may be punishable by death" and in "any post conviction proceeding under section 2254 or 2255 of Title 28, seeking to vacate or set aside a death sentence, any defendant who is or becomes financially unable to obtain adequate representation ... shall be entitled to the appointment of one or more attorneys." 21 U.S.C.A. § 848(q)(4) (West Supp. 1996). Any defendant indicted for a federal capital crime is entitled to have two attorneys appointed. 18 U.S.C.A. § 3005 (West Supp. 1996).

B. THE MINIMUM QUALIFICATIONS OF APPOINTED COUNSEL ARE STATUTORILY DEFINED.

The lead attorney appointed to represent one indicted on an offense punishable by death "must have been admitted to practice in the court in which the prosecution is to be tried for not less than five years, and must have had not less than three years experience in the actual trial of felony prosecutions in that court." 21 U.S.C.A. § 848(q)(5). And, at least one of the attorneys appointed to represent a defendant indicted with a federal capital crime must "be learned in the law applicable to capital cases." 18 U.S.C.A. § 3005.

A lead attorney appointed after conviction to represent a capital defendant on direct appeal, or during § 2255 proceedings, "must have been admitted to practice in the court of appeals for not less than five years, and must have had not less than three years experience in the handling of appeals in that court in felony cases." 21 U.S.C.A. § 848(q)(6).

A court may, for good cause shown, appoint another attorney who does not meet the requirements set forth in § 848(q)(5)-(6), but whose experience otherwise enables him or her to adequately represent the defendant. 21 U.S.C.A. § 848(q)(7).

Attorneys that have been appointed typically continue the representation on appeal. *See* 21 U.S.C.A. § 848(q)(8) (providing that once appointed attorneys continue representation throughout subsequent proceedings); 18 U.S.C.A. § 3006A(c) (West 1985).

C. COMPENSATION FOR FEES IS PRESENTLY LIMITED ONLY TO A "REASONABLE FEE" IN THE VIEW OF THE DISTRICT COURT.

Attorneys appointed pursuant to § 848(q) may be compensated at the statutory ceiling of $125 per hour for both in-court and out-of-court time. 21 U.S.C.A. § 848(q)(10)(A). Counsel is also bound by the limitation of $7,500 for investigative, expert, and other reasonably necessary expenses unless a higher fee is approved by the court. 21 U.S.C.A. § 848(q)(10)(B).

II. RECOMMENDATIONS

A. SOLICIT QUALIFIED AND INTERESTED COUNSEL AND MAIN-
TAIN LISTS OF ATTORNEYS QUALIFYING FOR APPOINTMENT AS
LEAD COUNSEL AND SECOND-CHAIR COUNSEL.

District Court

** **It is recommended that a plan be adopted under which the district court would contact the bar and solicit applications for a panel of attorneys qualified to represent capital defendants.**

Some districts have experienced difficulty in locating qualified and inter-ested counsel to undertake capital representation. But, it is believed that there are many attorneys who would seek the opportunity for appointment if they were made aware of that opportunity. Accordingly, it is recommended that on a district-by-district basis, a program of solicitation of the bar should be implemented in order to increase the number of attorneys seeking appoint-ment.

** **It is recommended that the district courts maintain lists of those attorneys qualified to represent capital defendants as lead coun-sel and as second-chair counsel and that these attorneys' exper-tise in trial, appellate, and habeas representation be identified.**

Because the statutory requirements for lead counsel are more stringent than those for second-chair counsel, courts should maintain separate lists of those attorneys who are qualified for each type of appointment. In addition to the statutory qualifications, specialized skills and experience are necessary to represent capital defendants in trial, appellate, and habeas proceedings. Courts may find separate lists of attorneys with trial, appellate, and/or habeas experience useful. Alternatively, courts may conclude that some other method of identifying various types and levels of expertise is preferable.

In ascertaining which attorneys of those expressing an interest in capital representation and seeking appointment are qualified to be placed on lists of those available for appointment as lead and second-chair counsel, the court may wish to consider appointment of an oversight committee composed of district judges, magistrate judges, district court clerks, and the Federal Public Defender, *see* 18 U.S.C.A. § 3005.

It is envisioned that over time attorneys chosen for appointment from the second-chair counsel list will develop the qualifications to be placed on the lead counsel list, and that appointment of second-chair attorneys is desirable in order to develop a wider range of expertise available for lead counsel appoint-ment. In addition, special consideration should be given to appointment of the attorney who represented a § 2254 petitioner during state collateral proceed-ings, if interested in appointment and qualified for it. *See* 21 U.S.C.A. § 848(q)(7).

Circuit Court

** **It is recommended that the circuit court solicit the bar for applications, maintain lists of those attorneys qualified to repre-**

sent capital defendants as lead counsel and as second-chair counsel, and identify attorneys' expertise in appellate and habeas representation.

Although attorneys that have been appointed at the district court level typically continue their representation on appeal, from time to time it is necessary to appoint attorneys pursuant to § 848(q) during appellate proceedings. Consequently, it is recommended that a plan to solicit the bar for applications for appointment to capital representation be adopted and that lists of those attorneys qualified and interested in capital representation as lead and second-chair counsel be maintained.

B. USE FEDERAL PUBLIC DEFENDERS FOR REPRESENTATION OF FEDERAL CAPITAL CHARGES AND COLLATERAL ATTACKS ON FEDERAL CAPITAL CONVICTIONS AND SENTENCES; DO NOT UTILIZE FEDERAL PUBLIC DEFENDERS FOR PROSECUTION OF HABEAS PROCEEDINGS FILED BY STATE PRISONERS.

** **It is recommended that federal public defenders be utilized for representation of individuals charged with federal capital crimes and collateral attacks on federal capital convictions.**

Providing representation for defendants charged with federal crimes punishable by the death penalty is within the statutory responsibility of the Federal Public Defender (FPD) to provide representation for all indigents charged with federal crimes. It is contemplated that FPDs will be placed in the pool of attorneys available to represent capital defendants in federal capital trials, on direct appeal, and in § 2255 proceedings. For some period of time, until FPDs develop the qualifications and experience, their appointments may be limited to second-chair positions. *See* 21 U.S.C.A. § 848(q)(7). However, such appointments should be encouraged whenever possible in order to permit FPDs to attain expertise in this area.

** **It is recommended that FPDs not be appointed to represent criminal defendants petitioning pursuant to 28 U.S.C.A. § 2254 for relief from a state death sentence.**

The consensus of opinion among FPDs in the circuit is that FPD representation in § 2254 proceedings challenging a state sentence of death is undesirable for a number of reasons. First, the prospect of a federal agency opposing the validity of state convictions creates the appearance of an unacceptable conflict between separate and independent sovereigns. Second, although the FPD is authorized to represent defendants seeking a writ of habeas corpus, encouraging such representation is problematic because litigation of collateral state-court proceedings and issues may be necessary, raising the question of the appropriateness of FPDs appearing in state court and presenting issues outside their traditional area of expertise. Finally, appointing FPDs to represent § 2254 petitioners could be viewed as an attempt to circumvent the will of Congress, given its recent decision to withdraw funding from death penalty resource centers.

859

C. IMPOSE RESTRAINTS ON TIME FOR DECISION.

** **It is recommended that the limitations on time for decision set forth in 28 U.S.C.A. § 2266 be adopted at the district and circuit court levels and that the circuit executive be authorized to inquire into the reasons for any noncompliance with the limitations.**

Under 28 U.S.C.A. § 2266 (enacted by the Antiterrorism and Effective Death Penalty Act of 1996), proceedings brought pursuant to § 2254 that are governed by Chapter 154 of Title 28 and proceedings brought pursuant to § 2255 in which the defendant was sentenced to death must be decided by the district court and the circuit court within specified time limits. The district court is required to render a decision and enter a final judgment (including a resolution of any motion to alter or amend the judgment) within 180 days of the date on which the petition is filed, subject to an extension of up to 30 days if the district court determines that the ends of justice would best be served by the delay. See 28 U.S.C.A. § 2266(a)-(b). The court of appeals is required to render a decision within 120 days of the date on which the reply brief is filed and to rule on any petition for rehearing or suggestion for rehearing en banc within 30 days of the date the petition/suggestion is filed or the date a response thereto is filed, whichever is later. See 28 U.S.C.A. § 2266(c). Furthermore, if the petition/suggestion is granted, any hearing must be conducted and a final decision rendered within 120 days of the entry of the order granting rehearing. Id. And, following a remand by the court of appeals en banc or the Supreme Court for further proceedings, the period for decision runs from the date the remand is ordered. Id.

The time limitations imposed by § 2266 are applicable only in those § 2254 proceedings governed by Chapter 154, (i.e., those challenging a state death sentence where the state has adopted specified procedures for appointment of counsel to represent the defendant in state post-conviction proceedings) and in § 2255 proceedings in which the defendant was sentenced to death. As such, the limitations presently will not apply to the majority of § 2254 petitions challenging a death sentence because of the relatively recent adoption of those mechanisms. See Bennett v. Angelone, No. 95-4004, 1996 WL 469705, at *4 (4th Cir. Aug. 20, 1996) (stating that question of whether Virginia's mechanism for appointment of counsel satisfied requirements for application of Chapter 154 was irrelevant because Chapter 154 would not apply when the mechanism was not in place during the petitioner's state collateral proceedings). Time constraints, however, are sorely needed at present. See, e.g., Correll v. Thompson, 63 F.3d 1279, 1285 n.4 (4th Cir. 1995), cert. denied, 116 S. Ct. 688 (1996) (noting that § 2254 petition was pending in district court for in excess of three years prior to final decision). Consequently, it is recommended that the time limitations for decision imposed by § 2266 be adopted and implemented by rule immediately. It is contemplated that the limitations would apply to cases pending when the rule became effective, but that the limitations would apply prospectively. (For example, an appeal in a § 2255 proceeding challenging a death sentence that had been argued to this court and was pending decision would have to be decided within 120 days of the date the rule becomes effective.)

Additionally, it is recommended that a mechanism be established to track cases to which the time limitations apply, and in the event that cases remain pending after the date on which they were due to be decided, the Circuit Executive be authorized to make appropriate inquiry on behalf of the Judicial Council to seek an explanation of the reasons why the judge or panel of judges faile to comply with the time limitation.

Index to Rules and Internal Operating Procedures for the Fourth Circuit Court of Appeals

A

FORMS —Cont'd
Death penalty cases.
Certificate of death penalty case, Fed. App. (4th Cir.) Form C.
In forma pauperis.
Affidavit to accompany motion for leave to appeal, Fed. App. (4th Cir.) Form 4.
Notice of appeal.
Decision of United States tax court, Fed. App. (4th Cir.) Form 2.
Judgment or order of bankruptcy appellate panel, Fed. App. (4th Cir.) Form 5.
Judgment or order of district court, Fed. App. (4th Cir.) Forms 1, 5.
Officer.
Petition for review of order of officer, Fed. App. (4th Cir.) Form 3.
Transcript order, Appx. B.

H

HABEAS CORPUS.
Death penalty cases, Fed. App. (4th Cir.) Rule 22(b).
Motions for authorization, Fed. App. (4th Cir.) Rule 22(d).

I

INDIGENT PERSONS.
In forma pauperis.
Affidavit to accompany motion for leave to appeal, Fed. App. (4th Cir.) Form 4.
Law students.
Legal assistance to indigents by law students, Fed. App. (4th Cir.) Rule 46.

IN FORMA PAUPERIS.
Forms.
Affidavit to accompany motion for leave to appeal, Fed. App. (4th Cir.) Form 4.

INJUNCTIONS.
Stay or injunction pending appeal, Fed. App. (4th Cir.) Rule 8.

INTERLOCUTORY ORDERS, Fed. App. (4th Cir.) Rule 5.

INTERNAL OPERATING PROCEDURES.
Advisory committee, Fed. App. (4th Cir.) Rule 47(b).
Procedure for adoption, Fed. App. (4th Cir.) Rule 47(a).

INTERVENTION.
Motion to intervene, Fed. App. (4th Cir.) Rule 12(e).
Notice of appearance, Fed. App. (4th Cir.) Rule 12(e).

J

JOINT APPEALS.
Briefs, Fed. App. (4th Cir.) Rule 28 (d).

JUDGES.
Single judges.
Applications to a single judge, Fed. App. (4th Cir.) Rule 27(e).
Motions before single judge, Fed. App. (4th Cir.) Rule 27(e).
Three judge panels.
Argument time, Fed. App. (4th Cir.) Rule 34(d).
Composition of panel, I.O.P. 34.1.

JUDGMENT OF CONVICTION.
Release prior to judgment of conviction, Fed. App. (4th Cir.) Rule 9(a).

JUDICIAL CONFERENCE, I.O.P. 47.1.
Bar membership resolution, I.O.P. 47.2.

L

LAW STUDENTS.
Indigent persons.
Legal assistance to indigents by law students, Fed. App. (4th Cir.) Rule 46.

LEAD COUNSEL.
Unavailability.
Counsel listed on brief.
Deemed capable of arguing appeal in lead counsel's absence, Fed. App. (4th Cir.) Rule 28(d).

LEGAL ASSISTANCE TO INDIGENTS BY LAW STUDENTS, Fed. App. (4th Cir.) Rule 46.

LOCAL RULES.
Advisory committee, Fed. App. (4th Cir.) Rule 47(b).
Procedure for adoption, Fed. App. (4th Cir.) Rule 47(a).

M

MANDAMUS.
Case captions, Fed. App. (4th Cir.) Rule 21(a).
Petitions for special writs, Fed. App. (4th Cir.) Rule 21(b).
Fees and costs for prisoner petitions, Fed. App. (4th Cir.) Rule 21(c).

MANDATE.
Motion for stay of the mandate, Fed. App. (4th Cir.) Rule 41.
What constitutes the mandate, I.O.P. 41.1.

MOTIONS.
Attachments to motions, Fed. App. (4th Cir.) Rule 25(a).
Authorization, Fed. App. (4th Cir.) Rule 22(d).
Briefs.
Submitting the case on the brief, Fed. App. (4th Cir.) Rule 34(e).

RULES OF THE JUDICIAL COUNCIL OF THE FOURTH CIRCUIT GOVERNING COMPLAINTS OF JUDICIAL MISCONDUCT AND DISABILITY

(Includes amendments received as of November 1, 1997)

Editor's note. — This set of rules, effective September 1, 1991, supersedes the former Fourth Circuit Judicial Council Rules for Handling Complaints of Judicial Misconduct or Disability.

Notice to persons considering filing a complaint of judicial misconduct or disability.

Most complaints of judicial misconduct or disability filed pursuant to 28 U.S.C. § 372(c) in the United States Court of Appeals for the Fourth Circuit in recent years have been dismissed because they did not allege conduct falling within the reach of the statute. The time and effort of complainants, and of the Court, are wasted by complaints concerning matters that do not come within the coverage of the statute. This notice is issued to draw attention to those portions of the statute, and the Fourth Circuit Judicial Council's Rules Governing Complaints of Judicial Misconduct and Disability, that describe the sorts of conduct that are, and are not, properly raised in a judicial complaint.

The law authorizes complaints about judges who have "engaged in conduct prejudicial to the effective and expeditious administration of the courts." This term includes such things as the use of a judge's office to obtain special treatment for friends and relatives, acceptance of bribes, improperly engaging in discussions with lawyers or parties to cases in the absence of representatives of opposing parties, and other abuses of judicial office. It could include habitual failure to decide matters in a timely fashion, or bias against persons of a particular class as demonstrated by actions in a series of cases over a substantial period of time.

This term does not include a judge's making wrong decisions — even very wrong decisions — in particular cases. A complaint that a judge has exhibited bias toward a particular person, made an improper ruling or series of procedural rulings in a case, treated a person or party unfairly, or wrongly decided a case, is not a ground for relief under the judicial complaint and disability statute. Such matters can, and should, be raised in an appeal of the judge's decision to the United States Court of Appeals for the Fourth Circuit, following the Federal Rules of Appellate Procedure.

The statute also authorizes complaints about judges who are "unable to discharge all the duties of office by reason of mental or physical disability." A judge is mentally or physically disabled if he or she is unable to comprehend the nature of the proceedings over which he or she presides, to understand the principles of law involved, or to remember testimony and argument sufficiently well to render fair judgments in the matters coming before him or her for decision. The statute is designed to cover both temporary and permanent disability. The statute does not attempt to define the conditions that could produce such disability, but they could include a mental disease or defect, senility, or drug or alcohol dependency.

These subjects are covered in further detail in Rule 1 of the Fourth Circuit Rules Governing Complaints of Judicial Misconduct or Disability and in §§ 1 and 3(B) of 28 U.S.C. § 372(c).

Clerk

CHAPTER I. FILING A COMPLAINT.

Rule 1. When to use the complaint procedure.

(a) *Purpose of the procedure.* The purpose of the complaint procedure is to improve the administration of justice in the federal courts by taking action when judges have engaged in conduct that does not meet the standards expected of federal judicial officers or are physically or mentally unable to perform their duties. The law's purpose is essentially forward-looking and not punitive. The emphasis is on conditions that interfere with the proper administration of justice in the courts.

(b) *What may be complained about.* The law authorizes complaints about United States circuit judges, district judges, bankruptcy judges or magistrate judges who have "engaged in conduct prejudicial to the effective and expeditious administration of the business of the courts" or who are "unable to discharge all the duties of office by reason of mental or physical disability."

"Conduct prejudicial to the effective and expeditious administration of the business of the courts" is not a precise term. It includes such things as use of the judge's office to obtain special treatment for friends and relatives, acceptance of bribes, improperly engaging in discussions with lawyers or parties to cases in the absence of representatives of opposing parties, and other abuses of judicial office. It does not include making wrong decisions — even very wrong decisions — in cases. The law provides that a complaint may be dismissed if it is "directly related to the merits of a decision or procedural ruling."

"Mental or physical disability" may include temporary conditions as well as permanent disability.

(c) *Who may be complained about.* The complaint procedure applies to judges of the United States court of appeals, judges of United States district courts, judges of United States bankruptcy courts, and United States magistrate judges. These rules apply, in particular, only to judges of the United States Court of Appeals for the Fourth Circuit and to district judges, bankruptcy judges, and magistrate judges of federal courts within the Fourth Circuit. The circuit includes the federal courts in the states of Maryland, North Carolina, South Carolina, Virginia and West Virginia.

Complaints about other officials of federal courts should be made to their supervisors in the various courts. If such a complaint cannot be resolved satisfactorily at lower levels, it may be referred to the chief judge of the court in which the official is employed. The circuit executive, whose address is 1100 East Main Street, Suite 617, Richmond, Virginia 23219-3538, is sometimes able to provide assistance in resolving such complaints.

(d) *Time for filing complaints.* A complaint may be filed at any time. However, complaints should be filed promptly. A complaint may be dismissed if it is filed so long after the events in question that the delay will make fair consideration of the matter impossible. A complaint may also be dismissed if it does not indicate the existence of a current problem with the administration of the business of the courts.

(e) *Limitations on use of the procedure.* The complaint procedure is not intended to provide a means of obtaining review of a judge's decision or ruling in a case. The judicial council of the circuit, the body that takes action under the complaint procedure, does not have the power to change a decision or ruling. Only a court can do that.

The complaint procedure may not be used to have a judge disqualified from sitting on a particular case. A motion for disqualification should be made in the case.

Also, the complaint procedure may not be used to force a ruling on a particular motion or other matter that has been before the judge too long. A petition for mandamus can sometimes be used for that purpose.

Rule 2. How to file a complaint.

(a) *Form.* Complaints should be filed on the official form for filing complaints, which is reproduced in the appendix to these rules. Forms may be obtained by writing or telephoning the Clerk of the Court of Appeals, 1100 East Main Street, Richmond, Virginia 23219, 804-771-2213. Forms may be picked up in person at the office of the Clerk of the Court of Appeals or any district court or bankruptcy court within the circuit.

(b) *Statement of facts.* A statement should be attached to the complaint form, setting forth with particularity the facts on which the claim of misconduct or disability is based. The statement should not be longer than five pages (five sides), and the paper size should not be larger than the paper the form is printed on. Normally, a statement of facts will include —

(1) A statement of what occurred;

(2) The time and place of the occurrence or occurrences;

(3) Any other information that would assist an investigator in checking the facts, such as the presence of a court reporter or other witness and their names and addresses.

(c) *Legibility.* Complaints should be typewritten if possible. If not typewritten, they must be legible.

(d) *Submission of documents.* Documents such as excerpts from transcripts may be submitted as evidence of the behavior complained about; if they are, the statement of facts should refer to the specific pages in the documents on which relevant material appears.

(e) *Number of copies.* Only an original is required.

(f) *Signature and oath.* The form must be signed and the truth of the statements verified in writing under oath. As an alternative to taking an oath, the complainant may declare under penalty of perjury that the statements are true. The complainant's address must also be provided.

(g) *Anonymous complaints.* Anonymous complaints are not handled under these rules. However, anonymous complaints received by the clerk will be forwarded to the chief judge of the circuit for such action as the chief judge considers appropriate. See Rule 20.

(h) *Where to file.* Complaints should be sent to

Clerk, United States Court of Appeals
   for the Fourth Circuit
1100 East Main Street, Room 501
Richmond, Virginia 23219

The envelope should be marked "Complaint of Misconduct" or "Complaint of Disability." The name of the judge complained about should *not* appear on the envelope.

(i) *No fee required.* There is no filing fee for complaints of misconduct or disability.

(j) *Chief judge's authority to initiate complaint.* In the interest of effective and expeditious administration of the business of the courts and on the basis of information available to the chief judge of the circuit, the chief judge may, by written order stating reasons therefor, identify a complaint as authorized by 28 U.S.C. § 372(c)(1) and thereby dispense with the filing of a written complaint.

A chief judge who has identified a complaint under this rule will not be considered a complainant and, subject to the second sentence of Rule 18(a), will perform all functions assigned to the chief judge under these rules for the determination of complaints filed by a complainant.

Editor's note. — This rule was reissued with technical amendments on March 31, 1993.

Rule 3. Action by clerk of court of appeals upon receipt of a complaint.

(a) *Receipt of complaint in proper form.* (1) Upon receipt of a complaint against a judge filed in proper form under these rules, the Clerk of the Court of Appeals will open a file, assign a docket number, and acknowledge receipt of the complaint. The clerk will promptly send copies of the complaint to the chief judge of the circuit (or the judge authorized to act as chief judge under Rule 18(f)), to the circuit executive, and to each judge whose conduct is the subject of the complaint. The original of the complaint will be retained by the clerk.

Upon the issuance of an order by the chief judge identifying a complaint under Rule 2(j), the clerk will thereafter expeditiously process such complaint as otherwise provided by these rules.

(2) If a district judge or magistrate judge is complained about, the clerk will also send a copy of the complaint to the chief judge of the district court in which the judge or magistrate judge holds his or her appointment. If a bankruptcy judge is complained about, the clerk will send copies to the chief judges of the district court and the bankruptcy court. However, if a chief judge of a district court or bankruptcy court is a subject of the complaint, the chief judge's copy will be sent to the judge of such court in regular active service who is most senior in date of commission among those who are not subjects of the complaint.

(b) *Receipt of complaint about official other than a judge of the Fourth Circuit.* If the clerk receives a complaint about an official other than a judge of the Fourth Circuit, the clerk will not accept the complaint for filing and will advise the complainant in writing of the procedure for processing such complaints.

(c) *Receipt of complaint about a judge of the Fourth Circuit and another official.* If a complaint is received about a judge of the Fourth Circuit and another official, the clerk will accept the complaint for filing only with regard to the judge and will advise the complainant accordingly.

(d) *Receipt of complaint not in proper form.* If the clerk receives a complaint against a judge of this circuit that does not comply with the requirements of Rule 2, the clerk will accept the complaint for filing, advise the complainant in writing of the defects in the submission, require that they be remedied within fifteen days of the date of the clerk's letter, and dismiss the complaint without prejudice if the complainant does not remedy them. The clerk will notify the chief judge and the circuit executive of each such dismissal. The chief judge may direct the reinstatement of any such complaint.

CHAPTER II. REVIEW OF A COMPLAINT BY THE CHIEF JUDGE.

Rule 4. Review by the chief judge.

(a) *Purpose of chief judge's review.* When a complaint in proper form is sent to the chief judge by the clerk's office, the chief judge will review the complaint to determine whether it should be (1) dismissed, (2) concluded on the ground that corrective action has been taken, (3) concluded because intervening events have made action on the complaint no longer necessary, or (4) referred to a special committee.

(b) *Inquiry by chief judge.* In determining what action to take, the chief judge may conduct a limited inquiry for the purpose of determining (1) whether appropriate corrective action has been or can be taken without the necessity of a formal investigation, (2) whether intervening events have made action on the complaint unnecessary, and (3) whether the facts stated in the complaint are either plainly untrue or are incapable of being established through investigation. For this purpose, the chief judge may, individually or through the circuit executive, request the judge whose conduct is complained of to file a written response to the complaint. The chief judge may also, individually or through the circuit executive, communicate orally or in writing with the complainant, the judge whose conduct is complained of, and other people who may have knowledge of the matter, and may review any transcripts or other relevant documents. The chief judge will not undertake to make findings of fact about any matter that is reasonably in dispute.

(c) *Dismissal.* A complaint will be dismissed if the chief judge concludes —

(1) that the claimed conduct, even if the claim is true, is not "conduct prejudicial to the effective and expeditious administration of the business of the courts" and does not indicate a mental or physical disability resulting in inability to discharge the duties of office;

(2) that the complaint is directly related to the merits of a decision or procedural ruling;

(3) that the complaint is frivolous, a term that includes making charges that are wholly unsupported;

(4) that, under the statute, the complaint is otherwise not appropriate for consideration.

(d) *Corrective action.* The complaint proceeding will be concluded if the chief judge determines that appropriate action has been taken to remedy the problem raised by the complaint or that action on the complaint is no longer necessary because of intervening events.

(e) *Appointment of special committee.* If the complaint is not dismissed or concluded, the chief judge will promptly appoint a special committee, constituted as provided in Rule 9, to investigate the complaint and make recommendations to the judicial council. However, ordinarily a special committee will not be appointed until the judge complained about has been invited to respond to the complaint and has been allowed a reasonable time to do so. In the discretion of the chief judge, separate complaints may be joined and assigned to a single special committee; similarly, a single complaint about more than one judge may be severed and more than one special committee appointed.

(f) *Notice of chief judge's action.* (1) If the complaint is dismissed or the proceeding concluded on the basis of corrective action taken or because intervening events have made action on the complaint unnecessary, the chief judge will prepare a supporting memorandum that sets forth the allegations of the complaint and the reasons for the disposition. The memorandum will not include the name of the complainant or the judge whose conduct was complained of. The order and the supporting memorandum will be provided to the complainant, the judge, and any judge entitled to receive a copy of the complaint pursuant to Rule 3(a)(2). The complainant will be notified of the right to petition the judicial council for review of the decision and of the deadline for filing a petition.

(2) If a special committee is appointed, the clerk will notify the complainant, the judge whose conduct is complained of, and any judge entitled to receive a copy of the complaint pursuant to Rule 3(a)(2) that the matter has been referred and will inform them of the membership of the committee.

(g) *Public availability of chief judge's decision.* Materials related to the chief judge's decision will be made public at the time and in the manner set forth in Rule 17.

(h) *Report to judicial council.* The clerk will report annually to the judicial council of the circuit on actions taken under this rule.

CHAPTER III. REVIEW OF CHIEF JUDGE'S DISPOSITION OF A COMPLAINT.

Rule 5. Petition for review of chief judge's disposition.

If the chief judge dismisses a complaint or concludes the proceeding on the ground that corrective action has been taken or that intervening events have made action unnecessary, a petition for review may be addressed to the judicial council of the circuit. The judicial council may affirm the order of the chief judge, return the matter to the chief judge for further action, or, in exceptional cases, take other appropriate action.

Rule 6. How to petition for review of a disposition by the chief judge.

(a) *Time.* A petition for review must be received in the office of the Clerk of the Court of Appeals within 30 days of the date of the clerk's letter to the complainant transmitting the chief judge's order.

(b) *Form.* A petition should be in the form of a letter, addressed to the Clerk of the Court of Appeals, beginning "I hereby petition the judicial council for review of the chief judge's order. . . ." There is no need to enclose a copy of the original complaint.

(c) *Legibility.* Petitions should be typewritten if possible. If not typewritten, they must be legible.

(d) *Number of copies.* Only an original is required.

(e) *Statement of grounds for petition.* The letter should set forth a *brief* statement of the reasons why the petitioner believes that the chief judge should not have dismissed the complaint or concluded the proceeding. It should not repeat the complaint; the complaint will be available to members of the circuit council considering the petition.

(f) *Signature.* The letter must be signed.

(g) *Where to file.* Petition letters should be sent to

Clerk, United States Court of Appeals

   for the Fourth Circuit

1100 East Main Street, Room 501

Richmond, Virginia 23219

The envelope should be marked "Misconduct Petition" or "Disability Petition." The name of the judge complained of should *not* appear on the envelope.

(h) *No fee required.* There is no fee for filing a petition under this procedure.

Editor's note. — This rule was reissued with technical amendments on March 31, 1993.

Rule 7. Action by clerk of court of appeals upon receipt of a petition for review.

(a) *Receipt of timely petition in proper form.* Upon receipt of a petition for review filed within the time allowed and in proper form under these rules, the Clerk of the Court of Appeals will acknowledge receipt of the petition. The clerk will promptly send to the circuit executive copies of (1) the complaint form and statement of facts, (2) any response filed by the judge, (3) any record of information received by the chief judge in connection with the chief judge's consideration of the complaint, (4) the chief judge's order disposing of the complaint, (5) any memorandum in support of the chief judge's order, (6) the petition for review, (7) any other documents in the files of the clerk that appear to be relevant and material to the petition, and (8) a list of any documents in the clerk's files that are not being sent because they are not considered relevant and material. Upon receipt of these materials the circuit executive will promptly send copies to each member of the judicial council except for any member disqualified under Rule 18. The clerk will also send the same materials to the chief judge of the circuit, and each judge whose conduct is at issue, except that materials previously sent to a person may be omitted.

(b) *Receipt of untimely petition.* The clerk will dismiss a petition that is received after the deadline set forth in Rule 6(a).

(c) *Receipt of timely petition not in proper form.* Upon receipt of a petition filed within the time allowed but not in proper form under these rules (including a document that is ambiguous about whether a petition for review is intended), the clerk will acknowledge receipt of the petition, call the petitioner's attention to the deficiencies, and give the petitioner the opportunity to correct the deficiencies within 15 days of the date of the clerk's letter or within the original deadline for filing the petition, whichever is later. If the deficiencies are corrected within the time allowed, the clerk will proceed in accordance with paragraph (a) of this rule. If the deficiencies are not corrected, the clerk will dismiss the petition.

Rule 8. Review by the judicial council of a chief judge's order.

(a) *Mail ballot.* Each member of the judicial council to whom a ballot was sent will return a signed ballot, or otherwise communicate the member's vote, to the circuit executive. The ballot form will provide opportunities to vote to (1) affirm the chief judge's disposition, or (2) place the petition on the agenda of a meeting of the judicial council. The form will also provide an opportunity for members to indicate that they have disqualified themselves from participating in consideration of the petition.

Votes will be tabulated when all members of the judicial council to whom ballots were sent have either voted or indicated that they are disqualified. Members who have disqualified themselves will be treated for this purpose as if ballots had not been sent to them.

If all of the votes cast should be for affirmance, the chief judge's order will be affirmed, and the circuit executive will prepare an appropriate order to that effect. If any of the members vote to place the petition on the agenda of a council meeting, that will be done.

(b) *Availability of documents.* Upon request, the clerk will make available to any member of the judicial council or to the judge complained about any document from the files that was not sent to the council members pursuant to Rule 7(a).

(c) *Vote at meeting of judicial council.* If a petition is placed on the agenda of a meeting of the judicial council, council action may be taken by a majority of the members present and voting.

(d) *Rights of judge complained about.* (1) At any time after the filing of a petition for review by a complainant, the judge complained about may file a written response with the Clerk of the Court of Appeals and shall do so if requested by the judicial council. The clerk will promptly distribute copies of the response to each member of the judicial council who is not disqualified, to the chief judge, and to the complainant. The judge may not otherwise communicate with council members about the matter, either orally or in writing.

(2) The judge complained about will be provided by the clerk with copies of any communications that may be addressed to the members of the judicial council by the complainant.

(e) *Notice of council decision.* (1) The circuit executive will transmit the council's order, any accompanying memorandum in support of the order, and any ballots returned, to the Clerk of the Court of Appeals for inclusion in the official file.

(2) The order of the judicial council, together with any accompanying memorandum in support of the order, will be provided by the clerk to the complainant, the judge, and any judge entitled to receive a copy of the complaint pursuant to Rule 3(a)(2).

(3) If the decision is unfavorable to the complainant, the complainant will be notified by the clerk that the law provides for no further review of the decision.

(4) A memorandum supporting a council order will not include the name of the complainant or the judge whose conduct was complained of. If the order of the council affirms the chief judge's disposition, a supporting memorandum

will be prepared only if the judicial council concludes that there is a need to supplement the chief judge's explanation.

(f) *Public availability of council decision.* Materials related to the council's decision will be made public at the time and in the manner set forth in Rule 17.

CHAPTER IV. INVESTIGATION AND RECOMMENDATION BY SPECIAL COMMITTEE.

Rule 9. Appointment of special committee.

(a) *Membership.* A special committee appointed pursuant to Rule 4(e) will consist of the chief judge of the circuit and equal numbers of circuit and district judges. If a complaint is about a district judge, bankruptcy judge, or magistrate judge, the district judge members of the committee will be from districts other than the district of the judge complained about.

(b) *Presiding officer.* At the time of appointing the committee, the chief judge will designate one of its members (who may be the chief judge) as the presiding officer. When designating another member of the committee as the presiding officer, the chief judge may also delegate to such member the authority to direct the Clerk of the Court of Appeals to issue subpoenas related to proceedings of the committee.

(c) *Bankruptcy judge or magistrate judge as adviser.* If the judicial officer complained about is a bankruptcy judge or magistrate judge, the chief judge may designate a bankruptcy judge or magistrate judge, as the case may be, to serve as an adviser to the committee. The chief judge will designate such an adviser if, within two days of notification of the appointment of the committee, the bankruptcy judge, or magistrate judge complained about requests that an adviser be designated. The adviser will be from a district other than the district of the bankruptcy judge or magistrate judge complained about. The adviser will not vote but will have the other privileges of a member of the committee.

(d) *Provision of documents.* The clerk will send to each member of the committee and to the adviser, if any, copies of (1) the complaint form and statement of facts, and (2) any other documents on file pertaining to the complaint (or to that portion of the complaint referred to the special committee).

(e) *Continuing qualification of committee members.* A member of a special committee who was qualified at the time of appointment may continue to serve on the committee even though the member relinquishes the position of chief judge, active circuit judge, or active district judge, as the case may be, but only if the member continues to hold office under Article III, Section 1, of the Constitution of the United States.

(f) *Inability of committee member to complete service.* In the event that a member of a special committee can no longer serve because of death, disability, disqualification, resignation, retirement from office, or other reason, the chief judge of the circuit will determine whether to appoint a replacement member, either a circuit or district judge as the case may be. However, no special committee appointed under these rules will function with only a single member, and the quorum and voting requirements for a two-member committee will be applied as if the committee had three members.

Rule 10. Conduct of an investigation.

(a) *Extent and methods to be determined by committee.* Each special committee will determine the extent of the investigation and the methods of conducting it that are appropriate in light of the allegations of the complaint. If, in the course of the investigation, the committee develops reason to believe that the judge may have engaged in misconduct that is beyond the scope of the complaint, the committee may, with written notice to the judge, expand the scope of the investigation to encompass such misconduct.

(b) *Criminal matters.* In the event that the complaint alleges criminal conduct on the part of a judge, or in the event that the committee becomes aware of possible criminal conduct, the committee will consult with the appropriate prosecuting authorities to the extent permitted by 28 U.S.C. § 372(c)(14) in an effort to avoid compromising any criminal investigation. However, the committee will make its own determination about the timing of its activities, having in mind the importance of ensuring the proper administration of the business of the courts.

(c) *Staff.* The committee may arrange for staff assistance in the conduct of the investigation. It may use existing staff of the circuit executive or may arrange, through the Administrative Office of the United States Courts, for the hiring of special staff to assist in the investigation.

(d) *Delegation.* The committee may delegate duties in its discretion to sub-committees, to staff members, to individual committee members, or to an adviser designated under Rule 9(c). The authority to exercise the committee's subpoena powers may be delegated only to the presiding officer. In the case of failure to comply with such subpoena, the judicial council or special committee may institute a contempt proceeding consistent with 28 U.S.C. § 332(d).

(e) *Report.* The committee will file with the clerk for transmission through the circuit executive to the judicial council a comprehensive report of its investigation, including findings of the investigation and the committee's recommendations for council action. Any findings adverse to the judge will be based on evidence in the record. The report will be accompanied by a statement of the vote by which it was adopted, any separate or dissenting statements of committee members, and the record of any hearings held pursuant to Rule 11.

(f) *Voting.* All actions of the committee will be by vote of a majority of all of the members of the committee.

Rule 11. Conduct of hearings by special committee.

(a) *Purpose of hearings.* The committee may hold hearings to take testimony and receive other evidence, to hear argument, or both. If the committee is investigating allegations against more than one judge it may, in its discretion, hold joint hearings or separate hearings.

(b) *Notice to judge complained about.* The judge complained about will be given adequate notice in writing of any hearing held, its purposes, the names of any witnesses whom the committee intends to call, and the text of any statements that have been taken from such witnesses. The judge may at any time suggest additional witnesses to the committee.

(c) *Committee witnesses.* All persons who are believed to have substantial information to offer will be called as committee witnesses. Such witnesses may include the complainant and the judge complained about. The witnesses will be questioned by committee members, staff, or both. The judge will be afforded the opportunity to cross-examine committee witnesses, personally or through counsel.

(d) *Witnesses called by the judge.* The judge complained about may also call witnesses and may examine them personally or through counsel. Such witnesses may also be examined by committee members, staff, or both.

(e) *Witness fees.* Witness fees will be paid as provided in 28 U.S.C. § 1821.

(f) *Rules of evidence; oath.* The Federal Rules of Evidence will apply to any evidentiary hearing except to the extent that departures from the adversarial format of a trial make them inappropriate. All testimony taken at such a hearing will be given under oath or affirmation.

(g) *Record and transcript.* A record and transcript will be made of any hearing held.

(h) *Supporting personnel.* The Clerk of the Court of Appeals will arrange for the attendance at such hearings of deputy clerks, court reporters, and other necessary staff, from the staff of the court of appeals or the staff of a district court proximate to the location of the hearing.

Rule 12. Rights of judge in investigation.

(a) *Notice.* The judge complained about is entitled to written notice of the investigation (Rule 4(f)), to written notice of expansion of the scope of an investigation (Rule 10(a)), and to written notice of any hearing (Rule 11(b)).

(b) *Presentation of evidence.* The judge is entitled to a hearing, and has the right to present evidence and to compel the attendance of witnesses and the production of documents at the hearing. Upon request of the judge, the chief judge or his designee will direct the Clerk of the Court of Appeals to issue a subpoena in accordance with 28 U.S.C. § 332(d)(1).

(c) *Presentation of argument.* The judge may, at any time, submit to the clerk written argument for consideration by the special committee, and will be given a reasonable opportunity to present oral argument at an appropriate stage of the investigation.

(d) *Attendance at hearings.* The judge will have the right to attend any hearing held by the special committee and to receive copies of the transcript and any documents introduced, as well as to receive copies of any written arguments submitted by the complainant to the committee.

(e) *Receipt of committee's report.* The judge will have the right to receive the report of the special committee at the time it is filed with the judicial council.

(f) *Representation by counsel.* The judge may be represented by counsel in the exercise of any of the rights enumerated in this rule. The costs of such representation may be borne by the United States as provided in Rule 14(h).

Rule 13. Rights of complainant in investigation.

(a) *Notice.* The complainant is entitled to written notice of the investigation as provided in Rule 4(f). Upon the filing of the special committee's report to the judicial council, the complainant will be notified by the clerk that the report has been filed and is before the council for decision. Although the complainant is not entitled to a copy of the report of the special committee, the judicial council may, in its discretion, release a copy of the report of the special committee to the complainant.

(b) *Opportunity to provide evidence.* The complainant is entitled to be interviewed by a representative of the committee. If it is believed that the complainant has substantial information to offer, the complainant will be called as a witness at a hearing.

(c) *Presentation of argument.* The complainant may at any time submit to the clerk written argument for consideration by the special committee. In the discretion of the special committee, the complainant may be permitted to offer oral argument.

(d) *Representation by counsel.* A complainant may submit written argument through counsel and, if permitted to offer oral argument, may do so through counsel.

CHAPTER V. JUDICIAL COUNCIL CONSIDERATION OF RECOMMENDATIONS OF SPECIAL COMMITTEE.

Rule 14. Action by judicial council.

(a) *Purpose of judicial council consideration.* After receipt of a report of a special committee, the judicial council will determine whether to dismiss the complaint, conclude the proceeding on the ground that corrective action has been taken or that intervening events make action unnecessary, refer the complaint to the Judicial Conference of the United States, or order corrective action.

(b) *Basis of council action.* Subject to the rights of the judge to submit argument to the council as provided in Rule 15(a), the council may take action on the basis of the report of the special committee and the record of any hearings held. If the council finds that the report and record provide an inadequate basis for decision, it may (1) order further investigation and a further report by the special committee or (2) conduct such additional investigation as it deems appropriate.

(c) *Dismissal.* The council will dismiss a complaint if it concludes —

(1) That the claimed conduct, even if the claim is true, is not "conduct prejudicial to the effective and expeditious administration of the business of the courts" and does not indicate a mental or physical disability resulting in inability to discharge the duties of office;

(2) That the complaint is directly related to the merits of a decision or procedural ruling;

(3) That the facts on which the complaint is based have not been demonstrated; or

(4) That, under the statute, the complaint is otherwise not appropriate for consideration.

(d) *Conclusion of the proceeding on the basis of corrective action taken.* The council will conclude the complaint proceeding if it determines that appropriate action has already been taken to remedy the problem identified in the complaint or that intervening events make such action unnecessary.

(e) *Referral to judicial conference of the United States.* The judicial council may, in its discretion, refer a complaint to the Judicial Conference of the United States with the council's recommendations for action. It is required to refer such a complaint to the Judicial Conference of the United States if the council determines that a circuit judge or district judge may have engaged in conduct —

(1) That might constitute ground for impeachment; or

(2) That, in the interest of justice, is not amenable to resolution by the judicial council.

(f) *Order of corrective action.* If the complaint is not disposed of under paragraphs (c) through (e) of this rule, the judicial council will take other action to assure the effective and expeditious administration of the business of the courts. Such action may include, among other measures —

(1) Censuring or reprimanding the judge, either by private communication or by public announcement;

(2) Ordering that, for a fixed temporary period, no new cases be assigned to the judge;

(3) In the case of a magistrate judge, ordering the chief judge of the district court to take action specified by the council, including the initiation of removal proceedings pursuant to 28 U.S.C. § 631(i);

(4) In the case of a bankruptcy judge, removing the judge from office pursuant to 28 U.S.C. § 152;

(5) In the case of a circuit or district judge, requesting the judge to retire voluntarily with the provision (if necessary) that ordinary length-of-service requirements will be waived;

(6) In the case of a circuit or district judge who is eligible to retire but does not do so, certifying the disability of the judge under 28 U.S.C. § 372(b) so that an additional judge may be appointed.

(g) *Combination of actions.* Referral of a complaint to the Judicial Conference of the United States under paragraph (e) or to a district court under paragraph (f)(3) of this rule will not preclude the council from simultaneously taking such other action under paragraph (f) as is within its power.

(h) *Recommendation about fees.* Upon the request of a judge whose conduct is the subject of a complaint, the judicial council may, if the complaint has been finally dismissed, recommend that the Director of the Administrative Office of the United States Courts award reimbursement, from funds appropriated to the judiciary, for those reasonable expenses, including attorneys' fees, incurred by that judge during the investigation, which would not have been incurred but for the requirements of 28 U.S.C. § 372(c) and these rules.

(i) *Notice of action of judicial council.* Council action will be by written order. Unless the council finds that, for extraordinary reasons, it would be contrary to the interests of justice, the order will be accompanied by a memorandum setting forth the factual determinations on which it is based and the reasons for the council action. The memorandum will not include the name of the complainant or of the judge whose conduct was complained about. The order and the supporting memorandum will be provided by the clerk to the complainant, the judge, and any judge entitled to receive a copy of the complaint pursuant to Rule 3(a)(2). However, if the complaint has been referred to the Judicial Conference of the United States pursuant to paragraph (e) of this rule and the council determines that disclosure would be contrary to the interests of justice, such disclosure need not be made. The complainant and the judge will be notified by the clerk of any right to seek review of the judicial council's decision by the Judicial Conference of the United States and of the procedure for filing a petition for review.

(j) *Public availability of council action.* Materials related to the council's action will be made public at the time and in the manner set forth in Rule 17.

Rule 15. Procedures for judicial council consideration of a special committee's report.

(a) *Rights of judge complained about.* Within 15 days after the receipt of the report of a special committee, the judge complained about may file a written response with the Clerk of the Court of Appeals, who will forward it to all members of the judicial council and to the circuit executive. The judge will also be given an opportunity to present oral argument to the council, personally or through counsel. The judge may not otherwise communicate with council members about the matter, either orally or in writing.

(b) *Conduct of additional investigation by the council.* If the judicial council decides to conduct additional investigation, the judge complained about will be given adequate prior notice in writing of that decision and of the general scope and purpose of the additional investigation. The conduct of the investigation will be generally in accordance with the procedures set forth in Rules 10 through 13 for the conduct of an investigation by a special committee. However, if hearings are held, the council may limit testimony to avoid unnecessary repetition of testimony presented before the special committee.

(c) *Voting.* Council action will be taken by a majority of those members of the council who are not disqualified, except that a decision to remove a bankruptcy judge from office requires a majority of all the members of the council.

CHAPTER VI. MISCELLANEOUS RULES.

Rule 16. Confidentiality.

(a) *General rule.* Consideration of a complaint by the chief judge, a special committee, or the judicial council will be treated as confidential business, and information about such consideration will not be disclosed by any judge, or employee of the judicial branch or any person who records or transcribes testimony except in accordance with these rules.

(b) *Files.* All files related to complaints of misconduct or disability, whether maintained by the clerk, the circuit executive, the chief judge, members of a special committee, members of the judicial council, or staff, will be maintained separate and apart from all other files and records, with appropriate security precautions to ensure confidentiality.

(c) *Disclosure in memoranda of reasons.* Memoranda supporting orders of the chief judge or the judicial council, and dissenting opinions or separate statements of members of the council, may contain such information and exhibits as the authors deem appropriate, and such information and exhibits may be made public pursuant to Rule 17.

(d) *Availability to judicial conference.* In the event that a complaint is referred under Rule 14(e) to the Judicial Conference of the United States, the clerk will provide the Judicial Conference with copies of the report of the special committee and any other documents and records that were before the judicial council at the time of its determination. Upon request of the Judicial Conference or its Committee to Review Circuit Council Conduct and Disability Orders, in connection with their consideration of a referred complaint or a petition under 28 U.S.C. § 372(c)(10) for review of a council order, the clerk will furnish any other records related to the investigation.

(e) *Availability to district court.* In the event that the judicial council directs the initiation of proceedings for removal of a magistrate judge under Rule 14(f)(3), the clerk will provide to the chief judge of the district court copies of the report of the special committee and any other documents and records that were before the judicial council at the time of its determination. Upon request of the chief judge of the district court, the judicial council may authorize release of any other records relating to the investigation.

(f) *Impeachment proceedings.* The judicial council may release to the legislative branch any materials that are believed necessary to an impeachment investigation of a judge or a trial on articles of impeachment.

(g) *Consent of judge complained about.* Any materials from the files may be disclosed to any person upon the written consent of both the judge complained about and the chief judge of the circuit. The chief judge may require that the identity of the complainant be shielded in any materials disclosed.

(h) *Disclosure by judicial council in special circumstances.* The judicial council may authorize disclosure of information about the consideration of a complaint, including the papers, documents, and transcripts relating to the investigation, to the extent that the council concludes that such disclosure is justified by special circumstances and is not prohibited by 28 U.S.C. § 372(c)(14).

(i) *Disclosure of identity by judge complained about.* Nothing in this rule will preclude the judge complained about from acknowledging that he or she is the judge referred to in documents made public pursuant to Rule 17.

Rule 17. Public availability of decisions.

(a) *General rule.* A docket-sheet record of orders of the chief judge and the judicial council and the texts of any memoranda supporting such orders and any dissenting opinions or separate statements by members of the judicial council will be made public when final action on the complaint has been taken and is no longer subject to review.

(1) If the complaint is finally disposed of without appointment of a special committee, or if it is disposed of by council order dismissing the complaint for reasons other than mootness or because intervening events have made action

on the complaint unnecessary, the publicly available materials will not disclose the name of the judge complained about without his or her consent.

(2) If the complaint is finally disposed of by censure or reprimand by means of private communication, the publicly available materials will not disclose either the name of the judge complained about or the text of the reprimand.

(3) If the complaint is finally disposed of by any other action taken pursuant to Rule 14(d) or (f) except dismissal because intervening events have made action on the complaint unnecessary, the text of the dispositive order will be included in the materials made public, and the name of the judge will be disclosed.

(4) If the complaint is dismissed as moot, or because intervening events have made action on the complaint unnecessary, at any time after the appointment of a special committee, the judicial council will determine whether the name of the judge is to be disclosed.

The name of the complainant will not be disclosed in materials made public under this rule unless the chief judge orders such disclosure.

(b) *Manner of making public.* The records referred to in paragraph (a) will be made public by placing them in a publicly accessible file in the office of the Clerk of the Court of Appeals at 1100 East Main Street, Room 501, Richmond, Virginia 23219. The clerk will send copies of the publicly available materials to the Federal Judicial Center, Thurgood Marshall Federal Judicary Building, Washington, DC 20002-8003, where such materials will also be available for public inspection. In cases in which memoranda appear to have precedential value, the chief judge may cause them to be published.

(c) *Decision of Judicial Conference standing committee.* To the extent consistent with the policy of the Judicial Conference Committee to Review Circuit Council Conduct and Disability Orders, opinions of that committee about complaints arising from this circuit will also be made available to the public in the office of the Clerk of the Court of Appeals.

(d) *Special rule for decisions of judicial council.* When the judicial council has taken final action on the basis of a report of a special committee, and no petition for review has been filed with the Judicial Conference within 30 days of the council's action, the materials referred to in paragraph (a) will be made public in accordance with this rule as if there were no further right of review.

(e) *Complaints referred to the Judicial Conference of the United States.* If a complaint is referred to the Judicial Conference of the United States pursuant to Rule 14(e), materials relating to the complaint will be made public only as may be ordered by the Judicial Conference.

Editor's note. — This rule was reissued with technical amendments on March 31, 1993.

Rule 18. Disqualification.

(a) *Complainant.* If the complaint is filed by a judge, that judge will be disqualified from participation in any consideration of the complaint except to the extent that these rules provide for participation by a complainant. A chief judge who has identified a complaint under Rule 2(j) will not be automatically disqualified from participating in the consideration of the complaint but may consider in his or her discretion whether the circumstances warrant disqualification.

(b) *Judge complained about.* A judge whose conduct is the subject of a complaint will be disqualified from participating in any consideration of the complaint except to the extent that these rules provide for participation by a judge who is complained about.

(c) *Disqualification of chief judge on consideration of a petition for review of a chief judge's order.* If a petition for review of a chief judge's order dismissing a complaint or concluding a proceeding is filed with the judicial council pursuant to Rule 5, the chief judge will not participate in the council's consideration of the petition. In such a case, the chief judge may file a written communication with the clerk for transmission to all of the members of the judicial council and the circuit executive, with copies provided to the complainant and to the judge complained about. The chief judge may not otherwise communicate with council members about the matter, either orally or in writing.

(d) *Member of special committee not disqualified.* A member of the judicial council who is appointed to a special committee will not be disqualified from participating in council consideration of the committee's report.

(e) *Judge under investigation.* Upon appointment of a special committee, the judge complained about will automatically be disqualified from serving on (1) any special committee appointed under Rule 4(e), (2) the judicial council of the circuit, (3) the Judicial Conference of the United States, and (4) the Committee to Review Circuit Council Conduct and Disability Orders of the Judicial Conference of the United States. The disqualification will continue until all proceedings regarding the complaint are finally terminated, with no further right of review. The proceedings will be deemed terminated 30 days after the final action of the judicial council if no petition for review has at that time been filed with the Judicial Conference.

(f) *Substitute for disqualified chief judge.* If the chief judge of the circuit is disqualified from participating in consideration of the complaint, the duties and responsibilities of the chief judge under these rules will be assigned to the circuit judge in regular active service who is the most senior in date of commission of those who are not disqualified. If all circuit judges in regular active service are disqualified, the judicial council may determine whether to refer the complaint to a circuit judge from another circuit pursuant to 28 U.S.C. § 291 (a), or whether it is necessary, appropriate, and in the interest of sound judicial administration to permit the chief judge to dispose of the complaint on the merits. Members of the judicial council who are named in the complaint may participate in this determination if necessary to obtain a quorum of the judicial council.

(g) *Judicial council action where multiple judges are disqualified.* Notwithstanding any other provision in these rules to the contrary, a member of the judicial council who is a subject of the complaint may participate in the disposition thereof if (a) participation by members who are subjects of the complaint is necessary to obtain a quorum of the judicial council, and (b) the judicial council votes that it is necessary, appropriate, and in the interest of sound judicial administration that such complained-against members be eligible to act. Members of the judicial council who are subjects of the complaint may participate in this determination if necessary to obtain a quorum of the judicial council. Under no circumstances, however, shall the judge who acted as chief judge of the circuit in ruling on the complaint under Rule 4 be permitted to participate in this determination.

Rule 19. Withdrawal of complaints and petitions for review.

(a) *Complaint pending before chief judge.* A complaint that is before the chief judge for a decision under Rule 4 may be withdrawn by the complainant with the consent of the chief judge.

(b) *Complaint pending before special committee or judicial council.* After a complaint has been referred to a special committee for investigation, the complaint may be withdrawn by the complainant only with the consent of both (1) the judge complained about and (2) the special committee (before its report has been filed) or the judicial council.

(c) *Petition for review of chief judge's disposition.* A petition to the judicial council for review of the chief judge's disposition of a complaint may be withdrawn by the petitioner at any time before the judicial council acts on the petition.

Rule 20. Availability of other procedures.

The availability of the complaint procedure under these rules and 28 U.S.C. § 372(c) will not preclude the chief judge of the circuit or the judicial council of the circuit from considering any information that may come to their attention suggesting that a judge has engaged in conduct prejudicial to the effective and expeditious administration of the business of the courts or is unable to discharge all the duties of office by reason of disability.

Rule 21. Availability of rules and forms.

These rules and copies of the complaint form prescribed by Rule 2 will be available without charge in the office of the Clerk of the Court of Appeals, 1100 East Main Street, Room 501, Richmond, Virginia 23219, and in each office of the clerk of a district court or bankruptcy court within this circuit.

Editor's note. — This rule was reissued with technical amendments on March 31, 1993.

Rule 22. Effective date.

These rules apply to complaints filed on or after September 1, 1991 and to all complaints pending as of that date that were filed on or after March 1, 1991. The handling of complaints filed before that date will be governed by the rules previously in effect.

Rule 23. Advisory committee.

The advisory committee appointed by the Court of Appeals for the Fourth Circuit for the study of rules of practice and internal operating procedures under Fourth Circuit Local Rule 47(b) shall also constitute the advisory committee for the study of these rules, as provided by 28 U.S.C. § 2077(b), and shall make any appropriate recommendations to the circuit judicial council concerning these rules.

FORMS.

UNITED STATES COURT OF APPEALS
FOR THE FOURTH CIRCUIT

COMPLAINT OF JUDICIAL MISCONDUCT OR DISABILITY

MAIL THIS FORM TO THE CLERK, UNITED STATES COURT OF AP-
PEALS, 1100 EAST MAIN STREET, ROOM 501, RICHMOND, VIRGINIA
23219. MARK THE ENVELOPE "JUDICIAL MISCONDUCT COMPLAINT"
OR "JUDICIAL DISABILITY COMPLAINT." DO NOT PUT THE NAME OF
THE JUDGE ON THE ENVELOPE.

1. Complainant's name: _____
   Address: _____

   _____

   Daytime telephone: _____
2. Judge complained about:
   Name: _____
   Court: _____
3. Does this complaint concern the behavior of the judge in a particular
   lawsuit or lawsuits?

         [ ] Yes   [ ] No

   If "yes," give the following information about each lawsuit (use the reverse
   side if there is more than one):
   Court:
   Docket number:
   Are (were) you a party or lawyer in the lawsuit?

         [ ] Party   [ ] Lawyer   [ ] Neither

   If a party, give the name, address, and telephone number of your lawyer:
   Docket numbers of any appeals to the Fourth Circuit:
4. Have you filed any lawsuits against the judge?

         [ ] Yes   [ ] No

   If "yes," give the following information about each lawsuit (use the reverse
   side if there is more than one):
   Court:
   Docket number:
   Present status of suit:
   Name, address, and telephone number of your lawyer:
   Court to which any appeal has been taken:
   Docket number of the appeal:
   Present status of the appeal:
5. On separate sheets of paper, not larger than the paper on which this form
   is printed, describe the conduct or the evidence of disability that is the
   subject of this complaint. See Rule 2(b) and 2(d). Do not use more than 5
   pages (5 sides). Most complaints do not require that much.
6. You should either

       (1) check the first box below and sign this form in the presence of a
   notary public; or

(2) check the second box and sign the form. You do not need a notary public if you check the second box.

[ ] I swear (affirm) that —

[ ] I declare under penalty of perjury that —

(1) I have read Rules 1 and 2 of the Rules of the Judicial Council of the Fourth Circuit Governing Complaints of Judicial Misconduct or Disability, and

(2) The statements made in this complaint are true and correct to the best of my knowledge.

_____
(Signature)

Executed on _____
(Date)

Sworn and subscribed to
before me _____
(Date)

_____
(Notary Public)

My commission expires:

Editor's note. — This form was reissued with technical amendments effective March 31, 1993.

Index to Rules of the Judicial Council of the Fourth Circuit Governing Complaints of Judicial Misconduct and Disability

893

RULES OF THE UNITED STATES DISTRICT COURT FOR THE DISTRICT OF MARYLAND

With amendments received through July 1, 1997

Editor's note. — These Rules supplement the Federal Rules of Civil Procedure, the Federal Rules of Criminal Procedure, the Supplemental Rules for Certain Admiralty and Maritime Claims, Rules of Procedure for the Trial of Misdemeanors before United States Magistrates and the Bankruptcy Rules.

CROSS REFERENCE TO UNIFORM NUMBERING SYSTEM

I. Scope of Rules

UNIFORM NO.
LRCiv.

II. Commencement of Action; Process; Service and Filing of Pleadings and Other Papers

I. CIVIL.

Rule 101. Counsel.

1. *Who may appear as counsel; who may appear pro se.* a. Generally. Except as otherwise provided in this Rule and in LR 112.3, only members of the Bar of this Court may appear as counsel in civil cases. Only individuals may represent themselves. Individuals representing themselves are responsible for performing all duties imposed upon counsel by these Rules and all other applicable federal rules of procedure.

b. Pro hac vice. The Court may permit any attorney (except a member of the Maryland Bar) who is a member in good standing of the Bar of any other United States Court or of the highest court of any state to appear and participate as counsel in a particular civil case. Such permission shall not constitute formal admission to the Bar of this Court. However, an attorney admitted *pro hac vice* is subject to the disciplinary jurisdiction of this Court. Any party represented by an attorney who has been admitted *pro hac vice* must also be represented by an attorney who has been formally admitted to the Bar of this Court.

c. Appearance for obtaining deposition subpoenas. It shall not be necessary for counsel to be admitted to the Bar of this Court in order to obtain a subpoena for depositions to be taken in this District for cases pending in other Districts. However, an attorney seeking such a subpoena is subjected to the disciplinary jurisdiction of this Court.

2. *Withdrawal of appearance.* a. Individuals. In the case of an individual, appearance of counsel may be withdrawn only with leave of Court and if (1) appearance of other counsel has been entered, or (2) withdrawing counsel files

a certificate stating (a) the name and last known address of the client, and (b) that a written notice has been mailed to or otherwise served upon the client at least five days previously advising the client of counsel's proposed withdrawal and notifying the client either to have new counsel enter an appearance or to advise the Clerk that the client will be proceeding without counsel. If the withdrawal of counsel's appearance is permitted, the Clerk shall notify the party that the party will be deemed to be proceeding *pro se* unless and until new counsel enters an appearance on behalf of the party.

b. Parties other than individuals. In the case of any party other than an individual, including corporations, partnerships, unincorporated associations and government entities, appearance of counsel may be withdrawn only with leave of Court and if (1) appearance of other counsel has been entered, or (2) withdrawing counsel files a certificate stating (a) the name and last known address of the client, and (b) that the written notice has been mailed to or otherwise served upon the client at least five days previously advising the client of counsel's proposed withdrawal and notifying it that it must have new counsel enter an appearance or be subject to the dismissal of its claims and/or default judgment on claims against it. In the event that within thirty days of the filing of the motion to withdraw, new counsel has not entered an appearance, the Court may take such action, if any, that it deems appropriate, including granting the motion to withdraw and dismissing any affirmative claim for relief asserted by the party and/or directing the party to show cause why a default should not be entered on claims asserted against it.

Rule 102. General filing and service requirements.

1. *Signatures, identifying information and proof of service.* a. Signatures. i. When party represented by counsel. When a party is represented by counsel, the Clerk shall accept for filing only papers signed by a member of the Bar of this Court whose appearance is entered on behalf of that party.

ii. When party appears *pro se*. When a party is appearing *pro se,* the Clerk will accept for filing only papers signed by that party. Any attorney who has prepared any paper which is submitted for filing by a *pro se* litigant shall likewise sign the paper.

b. Identifying information. i. Required on all court papers. At the bottom of all Court papers counsel and *pro se* litigants shall state their name, address and telephone number. Counsel shall also state their bar numbers.

ii. Duty to keep current address on file. Counsel and *pro se* litigants must file with the Clerk in every case which they have pending a statement of their current address. If a *pro se* plaintiff resides outside of the District the party shall keep on file with the Clerk an address within the District where notices can be served. These obligations are continuing, and if any *pro se* litigant or counsel fails to comply with them, the Court may enter an order dismissing any affirmative claims for relief filed by the party or on behalf of the client and may enter a default judgment on any claims asserted against the party or on behalf of the client.

c. Proof of service. All Court papers other than the original complaint must bear a certificate signed by counsel stating that the service required by Fed. R. Civ. P. 5(a) has been made.

d. Electronic transmission. Unless otherwise ordered by the Court, no paper may be transmitted to the Court by electronic transmission. If agreed upon by counsel, service of a paper may be made upon opposing counsel by electronic transmission.

2. *Format of court papers.* a. Caption. The case caption on all Court papers shall contain only a short title, consisting of the names of the first plaintiff and the first defendant only, and the civil action number. This rule shall not apply to the original complaint (which shall contain the names and addresses of all parties and the county of residence of any Maryland party) or any pleading seeking to add a new party (which shall contain the short caption and the name and address of the parties sought to be added and the county of residence of any Maryland party sought to be added). If the parties have consented to proceeding before a Magistrate Judge, the caption shall contain the name of the Magistrate Judge in parentheses after the civil action number.

b. Margins, spacing and numbering and 2-hole punched. All papers filed with the Court shall be on paper not to exceed 8 ½" x 11", with a top margin of at least 1 ½" and left-hand margin of 1" and a right-hand margin of ½". Lines of text shall be double spaced except for quotations and footnotes. Pages shall be numbered at the bottom of every page after the first page. Typed, printed or written material shall appear only on the front side of any page. All papers shall be two-hole punched on the top of each page.

c. Legibility. No paper shall be accepted for filing unless it is legible.

3. *Issuance of subpoenas in pro se, in forma pauperis cases.* The Clerk shall not issue any subpoena under Fed. R. Civ. P. 45(a)(3) to any *pro se* litigant proceeding *in forma pauperis* without first obtaining an order from the Court authorizing the issuance of the subpoena. Before entering any such order the Court may require the litigant to state the reasons why the subpoena should be issued, and the Court may refuse to authorize issuance of the subpoena if it concludes that the subpoena imposes undue burden or expense on the person subject to the subpoena or upon the U.S. Marshal or other court officer who would be required to serve it under 28 U.S.C. § 1915.

4. *Interdivisional filing.* Unless otherwise ordered by the Court, if a case designated to one division under the Court's standing order is assigned to a judge in the other division, any pleadings, motions, memoranda or other papers may be filed in the designated division and, if such filing is made within any applicable deadline, shall be deemed to be timely.

Rule 103. Institution of suit and pleadings.

1. *Civil cover sheet/extra copies of complaint/designation of related cases.* a. Civil cover sheet and extra copies of complaint. When filing a complaint, counsel shall submit to the Clerk a complete civil cover sheet and two copies of the Complaint.

b. Related cases. i. Designation by plaintiff. If counsel for a plaintiff in a civil action believes that the action being filed and one or more other civil actions or proceedings previously decided or pending in this Court (1) arise from the same or identical transactions, happenings, or events; (2) involve the identical parties or property; (3) involve the same patent or trademark; or (4) for any other reason would entail substantial duplication of labor if heard by different judges, counsel shall indicate that fact by designating the case as a "related case" on the civil cover sheet. A copy of the cover sheet shall be served on all parties.

ii. Designation by defendant. If counsel for a defendant believes that a case is related to a prior case and that fact has not been noted on the civil cover sheet by plaintiff, counsel for the defendant shall bring that information to the attention of all parties and the Clerk, and the Clerk shall note it on the cover sheet and inform the judge to whom the new case has been assigned.

iii. Resolution of disputes. Any disputes regarding the designation of a case as being related to another case shall be presented by motion to the judge to whom the new or latter case has been assigned.

2. *Process.* a. Number of copies. Counsel shall submit to the Clerk the following number of copies when process is to be served: (a) two copies of any summons for each party to be served; (b) four copies of a warrant for arrest or summons with process of maritime attachment and garnishment for tangible property or two copies of such papers for intangible property; and (c) two copies of all writs, including writs of possession, replevin, execution, garnishment and attachment before a judgment.

b. When served by Marshal. Unless otherwise ordered by the Court, the United States Marshal shall not serve any process or subpoenas except the following: (a) all process for a party proceeding *in forma pauperis* without counsel, (b) warrants of arrests *in rem* or process of maritime attachment and garnishment, (c) writs of attachment before judgment, execution, possession and replevin, (d) process served under 28 U.S.C. Section 2361, and (e) when requested by the plaintiff, process in suits where the plaintiff is authorized to proceed as a seaman under 28 U.S.C. § 1916. Unless otherwise ordered by the Court and except for a party who is proceeding *in forma pauperis* or as a seaman under 28 U.S.C. Section 1916, the Marshal may require a party to pay or secure the fees and expenses before serving any process which this Rule requires that the Marshal serve.

c. Waiver procedure. Whenever the waiver procedure under Fed. R. Civ. P. 4(d) is invoked, counsel shall submit to the Clerk a written notice identifying the defendant(s) to whom the notice and request to waive service of summons is being sent. The notice shall be filed upon the filing of the complaint or such later date that counsel decides to invoke the waiver procedure.

3. *Disclosure of affiliations and financial interest.* When filing an initial pleading or promptly after learning of the information to be disclosed, counsel shall submit to the Clerk two copies of a written statement (separate from any pleading) containing the following information:

a. Corporate affiliation. The identity of any parent or other affiliate of a corporate party and the description of the relationship between the party and such affiliates.

b. Financial interests in the outcome of the litigation. The identity of any corporation, unincorporated association, partnership or other business entity, not a party to the case, which may have any financial interest whatsoever in the outcome of litigation and the nature of its financial interest. The term "financial interest in the outcome of the litigation" includes a potential obligation of an insurance company or other person to represent or to indemnify any party to the case. Any notice given to the Clerk under this Rule shall not be considered as an admission by the insurance company or other person that it does in fact have an obligation to defend the litigation or to indemnify a party or as a waiver of any rights that it might have in connection with the subject matter of the litigation.

4. *Security for costs.* Any party against whom affirmative relief (other than a compulsory counterclaim) is filed may file a motion requesting that the party seeking the affirmative relief give security for costs if that party is not a resident of this district. Upon the filing of the motion, the Court shall issue a show cause order to the party seeking affirmative relief. A party who does not show cause why such security should not be required shall deposit with the Clerk on the date that the show cause response is due or on such later date as may be set by the Court the sum of $150 or such higher amount as the Court determines is appropriate. The Court may dismiss the claim of a party who fails to deposit the required security. This Rule shall not apply to any party proceeding *in forma pauperis* or as a seaman under 28 U.S.C. Section 1916.

5. *Removal.* a. Certification of filing of State court papers. Any party effecting removal shall file with the notice true and legible copies of all process, pleadings, papers and orders which have been served upon that party. Within 30 days thereafter the party shall file true and legible copies of all other papers then on file in the State Court, together with a certification from counsel that all filings in the State Court action have been filed in the United States District Court.

b. Filing memoranda re pending motions. If a motion is pending at the time of removal as to which a legal memorandum has not been submitted, the moving party shall file a supporting memorandum within fourteen days of the date of removal. If at the time of removal a motion is pending as to which a legal memorandum has been submitted, the party opposing the motion shall file an opposition memorandum on the date that the opposition memorandum was due in the State court or within fourteen days of the date of removal, whichever is earlier.

6. *Amendments of pleadings.* a. Original of proposed amendment to accompany motion. Whenever a party files a motion requesting leave to file an amended pleading, the original of the proposed amended pleading shall accompany the motion. If the motion is granted, an additional copy of the amended pleading need not be filed. The amended pleading shall be deemed to have been served, for the purpose of determining the time for response under Fed. R. Civ. P. 15(a), on the date that the Court grants leave for its filing.

b. Exhibits to amended pleadings. Unless otherwise ordered by the Court, only newly added exhibits are to be attached to an amended pleading. However, if the amended pleading adds a new party, counsel shall serve all exhibits referred to in the amended pleading upon the new party.

c. Highlighting of amendments. Unless otherwise ordered by the Court, the party filing an amended pleading shall provide to all counsel and to the Clerk, (1) a clean copy of the amended pleading, and (2) a copy of the amended pleading in which stricken material has been lined through or enclosed in brackets and new material has been underlined or set forth in bold-faced type.

d. Requested consent of other counsel. Before filing a motion requesting leave to file an amended pleading, counsel shall attempt to obtain the consent of other counsel. Counsel shall state in the motion whether or not the consent of other counsel has been obtained.

7. *Third-party complaints.* a. A third-party plaintiff shall file with the Clerk only the third-party complaint itself and not all the prior pleadings attached thereto.

b. Unless otherwise ordered by the Court, a third party plaintiff shall serve upon a third party defendant copies of all papers (other than notices of previously held depositions) which the parties have previously served upon one another and shall make all previously-conducted discovery materials available for review by the third party defendant.

8. *Dismissal for want of prosecution.* a. Failure to effect service. If a party demanding affirmative relief has not effected service of process within 120 days of filing the pleading seeking the affirmative relief, the Court may enter an order asking the party to show cause why the claim should not be dismissed. If the party fails to show good cause within fourteen days of the entry of the order or such other time as may be set by the Court, the claim shall be dismissed without prejudice.

b. Dormancy of action for nine months. If no paper has been filed in Court in any action for more than nine months, the Court may enter an order asking the parties to show cause why all affirmative claims for relief asserted in the action should not be dismissed. If good cause is not shown within ten days of the entry of the show cause order or such other time as may be set by the Court, such claims shall be dismissed without prejudice.

9. *Scheduling orders.* a. Categories of actions generally exempted from Fed. R. Civ. P. 16(b). All categories of actions in which ordinarily discovery is not conducted and additional parties are not added are exempted from Fed. R. Civ. P. 16(b). These categories of actions include petitions filed under 28 U.S.C. § 2254, motions filed under 28 U.S.C. § 2255, Social Security appeals, bankruptcy appeals, appeals on the record from administrative agencies, motions to enforce arbitration awards, forfeiture actions, actions seeking enforcement of judgments and mortgage or deed of trust foreclosures. In all actions in which a scheduling order is not entered under Fed. R. Civ. P. 16(b), the presiding judge will enter such orders as are necessary to assure the prompt and expeditious resolution of the litigation.

b. Actions exempted from the consultation requirement of Fed. R. Civ. P. 16(b). All actions except ones which the presiding judge notifies the parties that he or she designates to be complex, e.g., antitrust, mass tort, patent infringement, RICO and securities fraud actions in which all parties are represented by counsel, are exempted from the requirement of Fed. R. Civ. P. 16(b) that the court consult with counsel (or unrepresented parties) or await a report from the parties under Fed. R. Civ. P. 26(f) before entering a scheduling order. All scheduling orders, however, shall provide that any party who believes that any deadline set in the scheduling order is unreasonable may request in writing a modification of the order or that a conference be held for the purpose of seeking a modification of the order.

Rule 104. Discovery.

1. *Limitation on number of requests for production and requests for admission.* Unless otherwise ordered by the Court or agreed upon by the parties, no party shall serve upon any other party, at one time or cumulatively, more than 30 requests for production or more than 30 requests for admission (other than requests propounded for the purpose of establishing the authenticity of documents or the fact that documents constitute business records), including all parts and sub-parts.

2. *Timely written discovery requests required.* Interrogatories, requests for production, and written deposition questions, must be made at a sufficiently early time to assure that they are answered before the expiration of the discovery deadline set by the Court. Unless otherwise ordered by the Court, no discovery deadline will be extended because written discovery requests remain unanswered at its expiration.

3. *Discovery to proceed despite existence of disputes.* Unless otherwise ordered by the Court, the existence of a discovery dispute as to one matter does not justify delay in taking any other discovery.

4. *Commencement of discovery.* a. Actions in which Fed. R. Civ. P. 26(a)(1) applies. In actions in which Fed. R. Civ. P. 26(a)(1) applies, the initial disclosures required by that Rule shall be made on or before the date set in the scheduling order entered by the presiding judge for the making of such disclosures. Unless otherwise ordered by the Court or agreed upon by the parties, discovery shall be stayed until the initial disclosures are made.

b. Actions in which Fed. R. Civ. P. 26(a)(1) does not apply. In actions in which Fed. R. Civ. P. 26(a)(1) does not apply, discovery shall not commence until a scheduling order has been entered unless otherwise ordered by the Court or agreed upon by the parties.

c. Discovery stayed pending resolution of 12(b)(1) or 12(b)(2) motions. Unless otherwise ordered by the Court, the filing of any motion under Fed. R. Civ. P. 12(b)(1) or 12(b)(2) will stay discovery except as to facts relating to the issues raised by a 12(b)(1) or 12(b)(2) motion.

5. *Discovery materials not to be filed with court.* Unless otherwise ordered by the Court, written discovery requests, responses thereto depositions and disclosures under Fed. R. Civ. P. 26(a) shall not be filed with the Court. Unless otherwise ordered by the Court in a particular case, it is not necessary that the party propounding discovery file any notice concerning the discovery being taken, provided that any party filing a motion to compel shall state in the motion the date on which and the party to whom the discovery in question was propounded. The party propounding written discovery or taking a deposition shall be responsible for retaining the original copies of the discovery materials (including the certificates of service) and shall make them available for inspection by any other party.

6. *Format of responses to interrogatories and requests for production.* Responses to interrogatories and requests for production shall set forth each interrogatory or request followed by the answer and/or a brief statement of the grounds for objection, including a citation of the main applicable authorities (if any).

7. *Conference of counsel required.* Counsel shall confer with one another concerning a discovery dispute and make sincere attempts to resolve the differences between them. The Court will not consider any discovery motion unless the moving party has filed a certificate reciting (a) the date, time and place of discovery conference, the names of all persons participating therein and any issues remaining to be resolved, or (b) counsel's attempts to hold such a conference without success.

8. *Procedure re motions to compel.* The following procedure shall be followed in litigating motions to compel answers to interrogatories and requests for production or entry upon land as to which a response has been served. This procedure shall not govern motions to compel (a) answers to interrogatories or to requests for production or entry upon land where no responses at all have been served, (b) answers to deposition questions or (c) responses to discovery requests directed to a non-party. Such latter motions shall be filed with the Court and treated as any non-discovery motion, except that, as to disputes concerning discovery directed to a non-party, unless otherwise directed by the Court, the Court will not consider the motion until a conference has been held under LR 104.8.b. and a certificate has been filed under LR 104.8.c.

a. Service of motions papers. If a party who has propounded interrogatories or requests for production is dissatisfied with the response to them, that party shall serve a motion to compel within twenty days of the party's receipt of the response. The memorandum in support of the motion shall set forth, as to each response to which the motion is directed, the discovery request, the response thereto and the asserted basis for the insufficiency of the response. The opposing party shall serve a memorandum in opposition to the motion within fourteen days thereafter. The moving party shall serve any reply memorandum within eleven days thereafter. The parties shall file with the Court notices of service of the motion and memoranda but not the motion and memoranda themselves. Extensions of time given by the parties to one another to serve any paper hereunder need not be approved by the Court, provided, however, that no extension of time limits set in any scheduling order entered by the Court shall be made without the Court's prior approval.

b. Conference of counsel. Counsel are encouraged to confer with one another before or immediately after a motion to compel is filed. If they are unable to resolve their disputes, counsel must hold the conference required by L.R. 104.7 after serving upon one another all of the papers relating to the motion to compel.

c. Filing of certificate of conference and motion papers. If counsel fail to resolve their differences during their conference, the parties seeking the motion to compel shall file (i) the certificate required by L.R. 104.7, and (ii) the original and two copies of its motion and memorandum concerning the motion to compel and three copies of all other memoranda concerning the motion.

9. *Smoking during depositions prohibited.* Unless all persons present otherwise agree, smoking is prohibited in the room in which a deposition is being taken.

10. *Actions and witnesses exempted from provisions of Fed. R. Civ. P. 26(a)(1), (2)(B), (d) and (f).* a. Fed. R. Civ. P. 26(a)(1). Unless otherwise ordered

by the Court, FELA actions, Jones Act actions, actions involving claims for physical injuries arising out of the alleged commission of common law torts (excluding product liability actions and medical malpractice actions) and actions involving constitutional claims for the alleged use of excessive force (except prisoner cases, other cases in which one of the parties is appearing *pro se* and any *Monell*—type claims included in such actions) are subject to the provisions of Fed. R. Civ. P. 26(a)(1). All other actions are exempted from that rule.

b. Fed. R. Civ. P. 26(a)(2)(B). Unless otherwise ordered by the Court, a party must provide the disclosures required by Fed. R. Civ. P. 26(a)(2)(B) only as to experts retained or specially employed by a party to provide expert testimony. The disclosures need not be provided as to hybrid fact/expert witnesses such as treating physicians. The party must disclose the existence of any hybrid fact/expert witness pursuant to Fed. R. Civ. P. 26(a)(2)(A), and an adverse party may obtain the opinions of such witnesses (to the extent appropriate) through interrogatories, document production requests and depositions.

c. Fed. R. Civ. P. 26(d) and 26(f). Unless otherwise ordered by the Court, all actions are exempted from the first sentence of Fed. R. Civ. P. 26(d) and Fed. R. Civ. P. 26(f) except those which the presiding judge notifies the parties that he or she designates to be complex.

11. *Fees and costs.* a. Interpretation of Fed. R. Civ. P. 26(b)(4)(c). Unless otherwise ordered by the Court, any reasonable fee charged by an expert for the time spent in a discovery deposition and in traveling to and from the deposition shall be paid by the party taking the deposition. The fee charged by the expert for time spent preparing for the deposition shall be paid by the party designating the expert. The expert may not charge an opposing party for a discovery deposition a fee at any hourly rate higher than the rate that he or she charges for the preparation of his or her report.

b. Limitation on the amount of fees of treating physician. Unless otherwise ordered by the Court, a treating physician shall not charge a fee higher than the hourly fee that he or she customarily charges for in-office patient consultation or $200 per hour, whichever is lower, for any work that he or she performs in connection with any discovery matter or for the taking of a *de bene esse* deposition. Any party noticing a deposition of a treating physician shall (after conferring with opposing counsel) advise the physician of the number of hours that will be required for the deposition (both on direct and cross examination). The treating physician may not charge for any hours exceeding this estimate, provided that the deposition is completed within the estimate, and may terminate the deposition when the estimated time has elapsed.

c. Limitation on cost of photocopying. Unless otherwise ordered by the Court, the maximum amount that a party may charge as a photocopying expense when producing documents in response to a discovery request or subpoena is 15 cents per page.

12. *Familiarity with Discovery Guidelines.* Counsel should be familiar with the Discovery Guidelines that are an appendix to these Rules.

13. *Proposed confidentiality orders.* Any proposed confidentiality order shall include (a) a definition of confidentiality consistent with Fed. R. Civ. P. 26(c)(7);

(b) a method for challenging particular designations of confidentiality with the burden remaining on the party seeking confidentiality to justify it under Rule 26(c); (c) a provision that whenever materials subject to the confidentiality order (or any pleading, motion or memorandum referring to them) are proposed to be filed in the court record under seal, the party making such filing must simultaneously submit a motion and accompanying order pursuant to L.R. 105.11; and (d) a provision permitting the Clerk to return to counsel or destroy any sealed material at the end of the litigation.

Rule 105. Motions, briefs and memoranda.

1. *Memoranda required; number of copies.* Any motion and opposition to a motion shall be filed with the Clerk and be accompanied by a memorandum setting forth the reasoning and authorities in support of it. The original and two copies of all motions and memoranda shall be filed provided, however that if counsel considers it to be impractical to file two copies of voluminous exhibits appended to a motion or memorandum, they may contact the judge to whom the case is assigned to ask permission not to file such copies.

2. *Filing schedule.* a. General. All motions must be filed within deadlines set by the Court. Unless otherwise ordered by the Court, all memoranda in opposition to a motion shall be filed within fourteen days of the service of the motion and any reply memoranda within eleven days after service of the opposition memoranda. Unless otherwise ordered by the Court, surreply memoranda are not permitted to be filed. Where service is made by mail, the provisions of Fed. R. Civ. P. 6(e) apply.

b. Last-minute filing prohibited. In no event, unless otherwise ordered by the Court, is any memorandum to be filed after 5:00 on the afternoon before the last business day preceding the day on which the proceeding to which the memorandum relates is to be held. For example, a memorandum relating to a proceeding to be held on a Monday must be filed by 5:00 p.m. the previous Thursday.

c. Where more than one party plans to file summary judgment motion. In a two-party case, if both parties intend to file summary judgment motions, counsel are to agree among themselves which party is to file the initial motion. After that motion has been filed, the other party shall file a cross-motion accompanied by a single memorandum (both opposing the first party's motion and in support of its own cross-motion), the first party shall then file an opposition/reply and the second party may then file a reply. If more than two parties intend to file motions in a multi-party case, counsel shall submit a proposed briefing schedule when submitting their status report.

3. *Limitations on length.* Unless otherwise ordered by the Court, memoranda in support of a motion or in opposition thereto and trial briefs shall not exceed fifty pages, and reply memoranda shall not exceed twenty-five pages, exclusive of (a) affidavits and exhibits, (b) tables of contents and citations and (c) addenda containing statutes, rules, regulations and similar material.

4. *When table of contents and citations required.* A table of contents shall be included in any memorandum or brief exceeding twenty-five pages in length.

5. *Appendices.* a. Appendix of cases not generally reported. Every memorandum or brief shall be accompanied by an appendix containing any opinions

cited therein which are not reported in WESTLAW or in West's Federal or regional reports. A copy of the appendix shall be served upon other counsel.

b. *Appendix of exhibits.* If any motion, memorandum or brief is accompanied by more than five exhibits, the exhibits shall be tabbed and indexed.

6. *Hearings.* Counsel may (but need not) file a request for hearing. Unless otherwise ordered by the Court, however, all motions shall be decided on the memoranda without a hearing.

7. *Trial briefs.* Unless otherwise ordered by the Court, counsel may (but need not) submit trial briefs.

8. *Motions for sanctions.* a. Not to be filed as a matter of course. The Court expects that motions for sanctions will not be filed as a matter of course. The Court will consider in appropriate cases imposing sanctions upon parties who file unjustified sanctions motions.

b. Responses required only upon court order. Unless otherwise ordered by the Court, a party need not respond to any motion filed under Fed. R. Civ. P. 11 or 28 U.S.C. § 1927. The Court shall not grant any motion without requesting a response.

9. *Motions for extension of time.* a. Requested consent of, and notice to, other counsel. Before filing a motion to postpone any proceeding or to extend the time for the filing of any paper or the taking of any other required action counsel shall attempt to obtain the consent of other counsel and shall give notice of the motion to other counsel a reasonable time before presentation of the motion to the Court. Counsel shall state in the motion whether or not the consent of other counsel has been obtained.

b. Responsibility to serve order. The Clerk shall send a copy of any order postponing any proceeding or extending the time for filing any paper or the taking of any other required action to counsel for the moving party. If any such postponement or extension is approved pursuant to a stipulation of the parties, the Clerk shall send a copy of the order approving the stipulation to counsel for the plaintiff. Counsel to whom the order is sent shall notify all other counsel of the postponement or extension.

10. *Motions to reconsider.* Except as otherwise provided in Fed. R. Civ. P. 60, any motion to reconsider any order issued by the Court shall be filed with the Clerk not later than 10 days after entry of the order.

11. *Sealing.* Any motion seeking the sealing of pleadings, motions, exhibits or other papers to be filed in the court record shall include (a) proposed reasons supported by specific factual representations to justify the sealing and (b) an explanation why alternatives to sealing would not provide sufficient protection. The Court will not rule upon the motion until at least 14 days after it is entered on the public docket to permit the filing of objections by interested parties. Materials that are the subject of the motion shall remain temporarily sealed pending a ruling by the Court. If the motion is denied, the party making the filing will be given an opportunity to withdraw the materials.

Cited in Koffman v. Osteoimplant Technology, Inc., 182 Bankr. 115 (D. Md. 1995).

Rule 106. Pretrial procedure.

1. *When pretrial order required.* A pretrial order must be submitted in all cases except the following: (a) prisoner habeas corpus petitions; (b) prisoner civil rights cases; (c) collection cases brought by the United States; (d) land condemnation cases; (e) *in rem* forfeiture actions brought by the United States; (f) administrative appeals brought against the Secretary of the Department of Health and Human Services; (g) foreclosure actions; (h) petitions brought by the United States to enforce a summons of the Internal Revenue Service; (i) appeals from rulings of the Bankruptcy Court; (j) appeals from judgments of United States Magistrate Judges; and (k) suits to enforce or quash subpoenas.

2. *Contents of pretrial order.* A proposed pretrial order shall contain the following:

a. A brief statement of facts that each plaintiff proposes to prove in support of that plaintiff's claims, together with a listing of the separate legal theories relied upon in support of each claim.

b. A brief statement of facts that each defendant proposes to prove or rely upon as a defense thereto, together with a listing of the separate legal theories relied upon in support of each affirmative defense.

c. Similar statements as to any counterclaim, crossclaim, or third-party claim.

d. Any amendments required of the pleadings.

e. Any issue in the pleadings that is to be abandoned.

f. Stipulations of fact or, if the parties are unable to agree, requested stipulations of fact.

g. The details of the damages claimed or any other relief sought as of the date of the pretrial conference.

h. A listing of each document or other exhibit, including summaries of other evidence, other than those expected to be used solely for impeachment, separately identifying those which each party expects to offer and those which each party may offer if the need arises. The listing shall indicate which exhibits the parties agree may be offered in evidence without the usual authentication. This requirement may be met by attaching an exhibit list to the pretrial order.

i. A list for each party of the name, address and telephone number of each witness, other than those expected to be called solely for impeachment, separately identifying those whom the party expects to present and those whom the party may call if the need arises.

j. A list for each party of the name and specialties of experts the party proposes to call as witnesses.

k. A list of the pages and/or lines of any portion of a deposition to be offered in a party's case in chief or any counter-designations under Rule 32 (a) (4) Fed. R. Civ. P.

l. Any other pretrial relief, including a reference to pending motions, which is requested.

m. Any other matters added by the Court.

3. *Responsibility for preparing pretrial order.* The plaintiff shall prepare the first draft of the pretrial order covering all matters which the plaintiff proposes

to include in the pretrial order. Unless otherwise ordered by the Court or agreed upon by counsel, the plaintiff shall serve a copy of a draft upon opposing counsel fifteen days before the proposed pretrial order is due to be filed. Unless otherwise ordered by the Court or agreed upon by counsel, opposing counsel shall serve any proposed revisions and additions upon plaintiff's counsel at least five days before the order is due to be filed. If counsel are unable to agree upon any particular provision of the proposed order, counsel for each party shall submit to the Judge by the filing date a draft proposal on the provision in dispute.

4. *Submission of pretrial order.* a. Time. Unless otherwise ordered by the Court, the pretrial order shall be submitted to the Judge five days before the pretrial conference is to be held.

b. Number of copies. The original and one copy of the pretrial order shall be submitted.

c. Fed. R. Civ. P. 26(a)(3) disclosures. Submission of a pretrial order containing the information required by L.R. 106.2 within the time limits prescribed by L.R. 106.3 and L.R. 106.4 shall be deemed to constitute compliance with Fed. R. Civ. P. 26(a)(3).

5. *Approval and entry of pretrial order.* After approving the pretrial order the Judge shall sign it and transmit it to the Clerk for entry in the record.

6. *Pretrial conference.* The pretrial conference shall be attended by at least one of the attorneys for each of the parties who will actually participate in the trial. Attorneys attending the conference shall be familiar with all aspects of the case and shall confer with their clients before the conference to obtain authority from them to enter into stipulations. If the case involves numerous exhibits, counsel shall be prepared to discuss proposals for the orderly presentation of the exhibits at trial.

7. *Pretrial preparation of exhibits.* a. Pretrial numbering. Prior to trial counsel shall attach tags to all exhibits clearly identifying their proponent and number. Tags may be obtained from the Clerk. Counsel shall file with the Clerk and serve upon opposing counsel at least one business day prior to the scheduled trial date two copies of an exhibit list. Counsel shall retain the exhibits until they are presented at trial. This Rule does not apply to exhibits to be used solely for impeachment.

b. Pretrial review of exhibits. Prior to trial counsel shall meet for the purpose of reviewing and making available for copying one another's proposed exhibits. All exhibits which are proffered at trial shall be precisely the same in form and substance as the exhibits which were made available for review and copying prior to trial unless counsel otherwise indicates to opposing counsel.

8. *Jury instructions, voir dire questions and special verdict forms.* a. Submission procedure. The original and two copies of proposed instructions, voir dire questions and special verdict forms shall be submitted to the Judge and, unless otherwise ordered by the Court, simultaneously served upon other counsel at such time as is ordered by the Court.

b. Contents of proposed instructions. Proposed instructions shall be numbered and shall set forth in a separate paragraph or on a separate paper a citation to any authorities upon which they are based. Counsel may submit any proposed instructions which they deem appropriate but, unless otherwise ordered by the Court, counsel need not submit proposed instructions on general matters not particular to the case. Upon request the Court shall provide to counsel a copy of its customary general instructions prior to the instructions submission deadline.

Rule 107. Trial.

1. [Reserved for future use]

2. *Postponements — Client consent required.* No motion seeking the postponement of any trial shall be made by any counsel without the knowledge and consent of the client whom that counsel represents.

3. *Subpoenas — Timely service.* As provided in LR 103.2.b, unless ordered by the Court, the United States Marshal shall not serve trial subpoenas except for a party who is proceeding *in forma pauperis* without counsel.

4. *Imposition of jury costs for late settlement.* Except for good cause shown, whenever the settlement of an action tried by a jury causes a trial to be postponed, cancelled or terminated before a verdict, all juror costs shall be imposed upon the parties unless counsel has notified the Court and the Clerk's Office of the settlement at least one full business day prior to the day on which the trial is scheduled to begin. The costs shall be assessed equally against the parties and their counsel unless otherwise ordered by Court.

5. *Exhibits.* a. Pretrial numbering and exchange of exhibits. Counsel are to number exhibits prior to trial in accordance with LR 106.7.a. At trial counsel need not hand to other counsel for review any exhibit which prior to trial was made available for review and copying in accordance with LR 106.7.b.

b. Admission into evidence. Unless otherwise ordered by the Court or unless counsel requests that a particular exhibit be marked for identification only, whenever an exhibit number is first mentioned by counsel during the examination of a witness at trial, the exhibit shall be deemed to be admitted into evidence unless opposing counsel then asserts an objection to it.

c. Circulation to jury. The Court may permit counsel to circulate exhibits among the jurors at trial. However, if such permission is granted, counsel shall be expected to continue with questioning of the witness while the exhibit is being circulated unless the Court otherwise orders. Counsel shall not abuse this procedure by seeking to circulate exhibits at the conclusion of the examination.

d. Disposition. i. Pending appeal. From the conclusion of trial to the expiration of the time in which to file a notice of appeal or, in the event that an appeal is taken, until the transmission of the record to the Fourth Circuit, the Clerk shall retain all documentary exhibits except ones of unusual bulk or weight. Documents of unusual bulk or weight and all non-documentary exhibits shall remain in the custody of the attorney presenting them, who (a) shall permit inspection of them by counsel for any other party for the purpose of preparing the record on appeal, (b) shall be charged with the responsibility for their safekeeping and (c) if requested, shall transmit them to the appellate court.

ii. Upon final termination of action. Upon the final termination of an action, the Clerk shall send a notice to counsel advising them to remove from the record within thirty days of the notice all exhibits which they presented. If any counsel fails to do so, the Clerk shall destroy or otherwise dispose of the exhibits.

iii. Firearms, contraband and currency. In any action to which the United States is a party, the United States Attorney's Office shall maintain custody throughout the proceedings of any firearms, contraband or currency which have been presented as exhibits and shall be responsible for their safekeeping.

6. *Obligation to anticipate evidentiary objections.* Counsel are under an obligation to anticipate evidentiary objections and, whenever possible, to bring them to the attention of the Court before they are formally asserted so that they can be resolved when the jurors are not present.

7. *Exclusion of witness.* Witnesses need not be excluded unless a party invokes the exclusion of witness rule. "Exclusion of witness rule" means that only parties (or the designated representatives of parties, their counsel and expert witnesses approved by the Court) may be present in the courtroom during the course of trial and that no person may directly or indirectly advise a witness (other than a party or expert witness) of what the testimony of another witness has been. Subject to this constraint, counsel may prepare their witnesses for trial during the course of trial.

8. *Time limitations.* a. Presentations to jury. Unless otherwise ordered by the Court, no opening statement or closing argument (including rebuttal argument) shall exceed one hour.

b. Presentation of evidence. In cases which it deems exceptional, the Court may, after consultation with counsel and giving respect to their views, impose in advance reasonable time limitations on presentation of evidence.

9. *Courtroom etiquette.* a. Counsel to stand when addressing court. Unless otherwise permitted by the Court, counsel shall stand whenever addressing the Court except in stating brief evidentiary objections.

b. Movement in the courtroom. i. Generally. Unless otherwise ordered by the Court counsel may conduct their examination of witnesses from any reasonable location in the well of the court.

ii. Approaching witnesses. Unless otherwise ordered by the Court, counsel may approach a witness to show an exhibit without prior approval of the Court but may not do so for any other reason.

c. Persons to be referred to by surname. Unless otherwise ordered by the Court, counsel shall refer by surname to all parties, witnesses or other persons whose names may be mentioned during the course of trial (except persons under the age of 18).

10. *One attorney per witness.* Only one attorney for each party may conduct the examination of any witness. Only that attorney may object to questions asked by opposing counsel during the examination of that witness.

11. *Order of questioning and argument.* a. Unless otherwise ordered by the Court, co-parties represented by different counsel will examine witnesses and present argument in the order in which they are named in the complaint, and third-party defendants will examine witnesses after defendants have done so.

b. Limitation on redundant cross-examination. In cases involving parties who share common interest, the judge may order that counsel for those parties designate one of themselves as "lead counsel" for each witness. The counsel so designated shall be the only counsel authorized to conduct cross-examination concerning matters which relate to the common interests shared by the parties.

12. *No waiver of motion for judgment as a matter of law by introduction of evidence.* A party does not waive the right to move for a judgment as a matter of law (or, in a non-jury case, to move to dismiss) by introducing evidence during the course of the presentation of an opposing party's case.

13. *Witnesses excused at conclusion of testimony.* Unless counsel otherwise so indicate, a witness shall be excused at the conclusion of the witness' testimony.

14. *Speaking with witness on the stand.* Unless otherwise ordered by the Court, during all breaks and recesses counsel may speak with a witness while conducting a direct examination of the witness but (with the exceptions noted below) may not discuss testimony with the witness, including a party, while the witness is on cross, re-direct or re-cross examination. Notwithstanding the foregoing, unless otherwise ordered by the Court, counsel representing a defendant in a criminal case may confer with the defendant during breaks and recesses, and a non-party witness may confer with the witness' own counsel at any time.

15. *Mistrial and imposition of costs for unfair conduct.* If any witness volunteers unfairly prejudicial testimony not fairly responsive to the question asked or if counsel commits any prejudicial error during the course of trial (including failing to advise a witness of evidence which the Court has ruled is inadmissible with the result that the witness refers to such evidence), the Court may order a mistrial and impose upon the responsible person all jury costs thus far incurred.

16. *Interviews of jurors prohibited.* Unless otherwise ordered by the Court, no attorney or party shall directly or through an agent interview or question any juror, alternate juror or prospective juror with respect to that juror's jury service.

Rule 108. Judgments.

1. *Judgment by confession.* a. Complaint, related papers and attachments. A complaint requesting the entry of judgment by confession shall be filed by the plaintiff accompanied by the written instrument authorizing the confession of judgment and entitling the plaintiff to a claim for liquidated damages and supported by an affidavit made by the plaintiff or someone on that party's behalf stating the specific circumstances of the defendant's execution of said instrument, and including, where known, the age and education of the defendant, and further including the amount due thereunder, and the post office address (including street address if needed to effect mail delivery) of the defendant.

b. Review by court re: entry of judgment. Upon review of the aforesaid papers, the court may direct the entry of judgment upon a finding that the aforesaid papers prima facie establish (1) a voluntary, knowing, and intelligent waiver by the defendant of the right to notice and a prejudgment hearing on the merits of the claim of the plaintiff for liquidated damages and (2) a meritorious claim of the plaintiff for liquidated damages against the defendant.

c. Notice to defendants. Immediately upon the entry of a judgment pursuant to paragraph b. above, the Clerk shall issue a notice for the defendant notifying said party of the entry of the judgment and requiring defendant to appear in the cause wherein it is entered within thirty (30) days or such other time as may be required by statute or rule after the service of the notice and show, if such be the case, that said party did not voluntarily, knowingly, and intelligently waive the right to notice and a prejudgment hearing on the merits of the claim or otherwise show cause why the judgment should be vacated, opened or modified.

d. Application to vacate judgment. Application to vacate, open or modify the judgment must be made by motion within thirty (30) days after service of the notice; or such other time as may be required by statute or rule. The motion shall be made on the ground that the defendant has a meritorious defense to the cause of action. It shall set forth fully the facts relied on for such defense. A copy of the motion shall be served on the plaintiff or his attorney. If no application is made within the time allowed, the judgment shall be final.

e. Determination of motion. The motion shall be considered and determined as promptly as possible by the Court. If the evidence presented establishes that there are substantial and sufficient grounds for an actual controversy as to the merits of the case, the Court shall order the judgment by confession vacated, opened or modified with leave to the defendant to file a pleading and the case shall stand for trial. If the evidence does not establish that there are substantial and sufficient grounds for actual controversy as to the merits of the case, the judgment shall stand to the same extent as a final judgment.

f. Failure to effect service. If the notice issued under section c. is not served despite reasonable efforts to effect service, the Court, upon petition of the plaintiff setting forth an account of the efforts made to effect service, shall provide for notice to the defendant in the manner provided by statute or rule.

g. Address of defendant unknown. Where the affidavit indicates that the address of the defendant is unknown, a judgment shall not be entered except upon order of court, and the Court shall provide notice to the defendant pursuant to statute or rule.

h. Entry of judgment by confession. Except as authorized by this rule, judgment by confession shall be entered only upon order of court, after such notice and upon such terms as the Court may direct.

i. Sale on execution upon judgment by confession. Unless otherwise ordered by the court, a sale on execution upon a judgment by confession shall not be made until after judgment has become final under sections c., d. and e. of this rule.

Rule 109. Post-trial proceedings.

1. *Bill of costs.* a. Time for filing. Unless otherwise ordered by the Court, a bill of costs shall be filed within twenty days of the entry of judgment, of the entry of an order denying a motion, filed under Fed. R. Civ. P. 50(b), 52(b) or 59,

or an order remanding to state court any removed action. A bill for costs incurred on appeal taxable in this Court should be filed within twenty days of the issuance of the mandate by the Court of Appeals or, in the event of review by the Supreme Court, within twenty days of the entry of judgment by the Supreme Court. Non-compliance with these time limits shall be deemed a waiver of costs.

b. Contents. In any case where any costs other than the fee for filing the action are being requested, the bill of costs shall be supported by affidavit and accompanied by a memorandum setting forth the grounds and authorities supporting the request. Any vouchers or bills supporting the cost being requested shall be attached as exhibits.

c. Objections. A party objecting to any requested costs shall submit a memorandum in opposition to the request within the time permitted by L.R. 105.2. If no such memorandum is filed within the required time, the Clerk may without notice or hearing tax all of the requested costs.

2. *Motions requesting attorney's fees.* a. Time for filing. Unless otherwise provided by statute, LR 109.2.c., an order remanding to state court any removed action, or otherwise ordered by the Court, any motion (including motions filed under Fed. R. Civ. P. 11) requesting the award of attorney's fees must be filed within fourteen days of the entry of judgment for all services performed prior thereto. The motion may be supplemented to request fees for any work done thereafter in connection with any post-trial motion. A motion seeking fees for services performed on appeal shall be filed within fourteen days of the issuance of the mandate by the Court of Appeals or, in the event of review by the Supreme Court, within fourteen days of the entry of judgment by the Supreme Court. Non-compliance with these time limits shall be deemed to be a waiver of any claim for attorney's fees.

b. Contents. Any motion requesting the award of attorney's fees must set forth the nature of the case, the claims as to which the party prevailed, the claims as to which the party did not prevail, a detailed description of the work performed broken down by hours or fractions thereof expended on each task, the attorney's customary fee for such like work, the customary fee for like work prevailing in the attorney's community, a listing of any expenditures for which reimbursement is sought, any additional factors which are required by the case law, and any additional factors that the attorney wishes to bring to the Court's attention. Any motion for attorney's fees in civil rights and discrimination cases shall be prepared in accordance with the Rules and Guidelines for Determining Lodestar Attorneys' Fees in Civil Rights and Discrimination Cases that are an appendix to these Rules.

c. Social Security cases. The provisions of Rules 109.2.a and 109.2.b shall apply to motions requesting an award of attorney's fees under 42 U.S.C. Section 406(b) with the following exception and additions: (i) the motion must be filed within thirty days of the entry of judgment; (ii) a copy of the certificate of award of benefits or the issuance of the certificate of award of benefits by the Department of Health and Human Services, whichever last occurs must be attached to the motion; and (iii) the motion may not seek any award of fees for representation of the claimant in administrative proceedings.

Rule 110. Appeal.

1. *Bonds.* a. Amount. Unless otherwise ordered by the Court, the amount of any supersedeas bond filed to stay execution of a money judgment pending appeal shall be 120% of the amount of the judgment plus an additional $500 to cover costs on appeal.

b. Waiver for state and municipal agencies. Unless otherwise ordered by the Court, the State of Maryland, any of its political subdivisions and any agents thereof shall not be required to post a supersedeas or appeal bond.

Rule 111. Settlement.

1. *Settlement orders.* When the Court has been notified by counsel that a case has been settled, the Court may enter an order dismissing the case and providing for the payment of costs. Such an order of dismissal shall be without prejudice to the right of a party to move for good cause to reopen the case within a time set by the Court if the settlement is not consummated. Alternatively, the Court, upon being notified by counsel that a case has been settled, may require counsel to submit within sixty (60) days a proposed order providing for settlement, in default of which the Court may enter such judgment or other order as may be deemed appropriate.

An order entered pursuant to this Rule means that the entire case, including all claims, counter-claims, cross-claims, third-party claims and claims for attorney's fees and costs has been settled, unless otherwise stated in the order.

2. *Settlement conference.* A settlement conference shall be attended by trial counsel and such parties and representatives of parties as the Court may require.

Rule 112. Special proceedings.

1. *Habeas corpus and section 2255 motions.* a. Applicability of general rules. Petitions for habeas corpus filed pursuant to 28 U.S.C. Section 2254 and motions filed pursuant to 28 U.S.C. Section 2255 shall be governed, respectively, by the Rules Governing Section 2255 Cases In The United States District Courts and the Rules Governing Section 2255 Proceedings In The United States District Courts.

b. Return of insufficient petitions. The Clerk of the Court shall return petitions that do not comply with Rules 2 and 3 of the above Rules but shall retain a copy of them as required by said Rules.

c. Form. Petitions shall be filed on forms as they are approved from time to time by order of the Court.

d. Filing fee for Section 2254 actions. A filing fee of $5.00 shall be required for Section 2254 actions unless the Court authorizes the petitioner to proceed *in forma pauperis*. The Court generally will not authorize a petitioner who has $25.00 or more available after payment of the fee to proceed *in forma pauperis*.

e. No responses to § 2255 motions required without court order. The Government need not respond to a motion filed under § 2255 unless requested by the Court.

2. *Prisoners' civil rights actions.* a. Forms. All *pro se* civil rights actions brought by inmates of penal institutions shall be filed on forms approved from

time to time by order of the Court. Petitions to proceed *in forma pauperis* shall likewise be filed on forms approved from time to time by the Court. The Court may authorize penal institutions to produce, stock or distribute such approved forms.

b. Filing and service. All communications shall be directed to and filed with the Clerk and a copy of them served upon the opposing party or counsel in accordance with Fed. R. Civ. P. 5.

3. *Multi-district litigation.* a. Numbering and docketing. A group of actions transferred to this district under 28 U.S.C. Section 1407 shall be given the composite number previously assigned by the Multi-District Panel. Individual actions within the group shall be given specific civil action numbers. The Clerk shall maintain a multi-district litigation sheet for the group of actions compositely numbered. All papers submitted for filing shall be docketed only on this sheet.

b. Counsel need not be member of the Bar of this Court. Counsel representing a party in a transferred action need not be a member of the Bar of this Court, and such a party need not have resident counsel.

c. Notification of address. Upon receipt of an order of transfer, all counsel in the transferred action shall notify the Clerk of their names, addresses and telephone numbers. No party may list more than one attorney as its representative for purpose of service.

4. *Condemnation cases — Request for immediate possession.* A plaintiff in a condemnation case seeking immediate possession of land shall submit a statement reciting (a) whether or not the land is improved and, if so, a specific description of the improvements, (b) whether or not the land is occupied and, if so, the name and address of the occupant and (c) whether the owner and the occupant consent to plaintiff's taking immediate possession.

5. *Review of jeopardy assessments.* All actions arising under 26 U.S.C. Section 7429 shall bear the designation "Review of Jeopardy Assessment" on the complaint next to the style of the case. A proposed show cause order shall be submitted with the complaint, and the Clerk shall immediately bring the action to the attention of the Court. Failure to comply with this Rule may result in dismissal of the action.

Rule 113. Disposition of exhibits.

1. *Pending appeal.* [existing L.R. 107.5.c.i]

2. *Upon final termination of action.* Upon the final termination of an action, the Clerk shall send a notice to counsel advising them to remove from the record within thirty days of the notice all trial and hearing exhibits and all sealed materials which they presented at any time during the pendency of the action. If any counsel fails to do so, the Clerk may return the materials to the parties, destroy same or otherwise dispose of them.

3. *Firearms, contraband and currency.* [existing L.R. 107.5.d.iii]

II. CRIMINAL.

Rule 201. Counsel.

1. *Who may appear as counsel.* Any attorney who meets the qualifications for admission to the bar of this Court may represent a defendant in a criminal case.

2. *Appointment of counsel.* Counsel for indigent defendants shall be appointed in accordance with the procedures established by the plan as adopted and amended by the Court from time to time pursuant to 18 U.S.C. Section 3006A. The plan is available for public inspection in the Clerk's Office.

3. *Withdrawal of appearance.* Counsel for a defendant may withdraw their appearance only with leave of Court.

Rule 202. General filing and service requirements.

The provisions of LR 102 (other than the requirement of LR 102.1.a.1. that where a party is represented by Counsel, all papers filed with the Clerk must be signed by a member of the Bar of this Court) apply to criminal proceedings.

Rule 203. Speedy trial plan.

The order establishing time limits and procedures to assure the prompt disposition of criminal cases and certain juvenile proceedings as adopted and amended from time to time by Court order is available for public inspection in the Clerk's Office.

Rule 204. Release of information by attorneys.

1. *Generally.* An attorney shall not directly or indirectly release or authorize the public release of any information or opinion concerning any imminent or pending criminal litigation if there is a reasonable likelihood that the release of the information or opinion will interfere with a fair trial or otherwise prejudice the due administration of justice.

2. *Investigations.* Any attorney participating in any grand jury or other investigation shall not make any extra-judicial public statement which goes beyond the public record or which is not necessary to inform the public that the investigation is underway, to describe the general scope of the investigation, to obtain assistance in the apprehension of a suspect, to warn the public of any danger, or otherwise to aid in the progress of the investigation.

3. *Pretrial.* From the time of arrest, issuance of an arrest warrant or the filing of a complaint, information, or indictment in any criminal matter until the commencement of trial or disposition without trial, a lawyer associated with the prosecution or defense shall not release or authorize the release, for dissemination by any means of public communication, of any extra-judicial statement concerning:

(a) The prior criminal record (including arrests, indictments, or other charges of crime), or the character or reputation of the accused, except that the lawyer may make a factual statement of the accused's name, age, residence, occupation, and family status, and if the accused has not been apprehended, a lawyer associated with the prosecution may release any information necessary to aid in the apprehension or to warn the public of any dangers that person may present;

(b) The existence or contents of any confession, admission, or statement given by the accused, or the refusal or failure of the accused to make any statement;

(c) The performance of any examinations or tests or the accused's refusal or failure to submit to an examination or test;

(d) The identity, testimony, or credibility of prospective witnesses, except that the lawyer may announce the identity of the victim if the announcement is not otherwise prohibited by law;

(e) The possibility of a plea of guilty to the offense charged or a lesser offense;

(f) Any opinion as to the accused's guilt or innocence or as to the merits of the case or the evidence in the case.

The foregoing shall not be construed to preclude the lawyer, in the proper discharge of official or professional obligations, from announcing the fact and circumstances of arrest (including time and place of arrest, resistance, pursuit, and use of weapons), the identity of the investigating and arresting officer or agency, and the length of the investigation; from making an announcement, at the time of seizure of any physical evidence other than a confession, admission or statement, which is limited to a description of the evidence seized; from disclosing the nature, substance, or text of the charge, including a brief description of the offense charged; from quoting or referring without comment to public court records in the case; from announcing the scheduling or result of any stage in the judicial process; from requesting assistance in obtaining evidence; or from announcing without further comment that the accused denies the charges which have been made.

4. *Trial.* During a jury trial, including the period of selection of the jury, no lawyer associated with the prosecution or defense shall give or authorize any extra-judicial statement or interview, relating to the trial or the parties or issues in the trial, for dissemination by any means of public communication, except that the lawyer may quote from or refer without comment to public court records in the case.

5. *Scope of rule.* Nothing in this Rule is intended to preclude the formulation or application of more restrictive rules relating to the release of information about juvenile or other offenders, to preclude the holding of hearings or the lawful issuance of reports by legislative, administrative, or investigative bodies, or to preclude any lawyer from replying to any public charges of misconduct that are made.

6. *Penalty.* Any violation of this Rule may be treated as a contempt of Court and may subject the violator to the disciplinary action of the Court.

Rule 205. Release of information by Court personnel.

No person associated with the Court, including any member of the Clerk's Office, of the U.S. Marshal's Office, the staff of any Judge or Magistrate Judge, and any court reporter shall directly or indirectly disclose to any person, without prior authorization by the Court, any information relating to a pending investigation or case which is not part of the public court records. By way of illustration and not by way of limitation, no Court personnel shall divulge any information concerning arguments and hearings held in chambers or otherwise outside the presence of the public.

Rule 206. Bail.

1. *Grounds for insufficiency.* a. Property otherwise pledged. Unless otherwise ordered by the Court, property serving as security for bail pledged in any other Court shall not be accepted as security for bail ordered in this Court.

b. Person acting under power of attorney. Bail shall not be taken from a person under a power of attorney or other written instrument, save in cases of corporate surety, where the power of attorney or written instrument has first been filed with and approved by the Clerk.

2. *Traffic offenses.* If any person taken into custody for violation of any traffic law or regulation triable before a United States Magistrate Judge is a member of a travel club, automobile association or other organization providing its members with guaranteed appearance bond service and if the terms and conditions of such service are set forth on the defendant's membership card, the membership card may be accepted, in accordance with its terms and conditions and subject to its monetary limits, in lieu of cash or corporate undertaking. The card shall be retained by the judicial officer setting bail and shall be transmitted forthwith to the organization issuing it, according to its established procedures, in exchange for other security to be furnished to the Court.

3. *Forfeiture procedure.* a. General. When a bail is forfeited by order of the Court, the Clerk shall send to the defendant; defense counsel and to the surety a copy of the forfeiture order by regular mail. Within ten days of the date of the order, the surety shall either produce the defendant in Court or shall deposit in the registry of the Court the sum forfeited. A surety who fails to comply with this requirement within the ten-day period shall be prohibited from writing any other bails in this Court until compliance has been accomplished. In the case of a corporate surety, this provision shall apply both to the bondsman and the corporate surety.

b. Judgment by default. Judgment by default upon any forfeiture shall be entered in accordance with the provisions of Fed. R. Crim. P. 46 (e) (3).

4. *Prepayment of fees.* The Marshal may require any party (other than one whom the Court has found to be indigent) to pay or secure fees and expenses before serving any writ.

Rule 207. Motions.

The provisions of LR 105 (except LR 105.8) apply to criminal proceedings.

Rule 208. Arrest to arraignment.

[Reserved for future use]

Rule 209. Discovery.

[Reserved for future use]

Rule 210. Pretrial procedure.

The provisions of LR 106.7 (to the extent that under otherwise applicable law exhibits must be disclosed prior to trial) and LR 106.8 apply to criminal proceedings.

Rule 211. Trial.

The provisions of LR 107.2, 107.5(a), and 107.5(b) (to the extent that under otherwise applicable law exhibits must be disclosed prior to trial), 107.5(c), 107.6, 107.7, 107.8, 107.9, 107.10, 107.11, 107.12, 107.13, 107.14, and 107.16 apply to criminal proceedings.

Rule 212. Post-trial motions.

[Reserved for future use]

Rule 213. Sentencing.

1. *Confidentiality of presentence and probation records.* a. Generally. Unless the Court orders that a presentence report or portion thereof be placed in the public record, a presentence report is a confidential internal Court document to which the public has no right of access. Except as otherwise authorized by Fed. R. Crim. P. 32(c), by this Rule or otherwise by law, the probation department shall not, unless otherwise ordered by the Court, disclose to any person any presentence or probation supervision record.

b. Procedure upon demand by judicial process. When the production of a presentence or probation record or the testimony of a probation officer concerning information learned during the performance of official duty is commanded by subpoena or other judicial process, the probation officer shall seek instruction from the Court and request that the Court issue an appropriate order. Except in the most unusual circumstances, the Court shall order that the probation officer be excused from honoring the subpoena or other judicial process and that the requested disclosure not be made.

c. Limited disclosure by direction of the Chief Probation Officer. The Chief Probation Officer may authorize the disclosure of a presentence or probation supervision record to law enforcement agencies, rehabilitation agencies and bona fide research agencies for use in the normal course of their duties. If authorizing such a disclosure, the Chief U.S. Probation Officer shall promulgate written guidelines to assure the security and confidentiality of the disclosed information.

d. Disclosure under 18 U.S.C. Section 4208(b). In any case governed by 18 U.S.C. Section 4208 (repealed by Pub. L. 98-473), a copy of a presentence report may be furnished by the Probation Office to the United States Parole Commission or to the Bureau of Prisons for the sole purpose of performing their official duties relating to parole. The copy shall be deemed to have been lent to the Parole Commission and the Bureau of Prisons and to remain under the continuing control of the Court during the time that it is in the temporary custody of those agencies. Any copy lent to the Parole Commission and the Bureau of Prisons shall contain a legend, in a form prescribed by the Chief Probation Officer, restricting the use of the report.

e. *Non-disclosure of probation officer's recommendations.* Unless otherwise ordered in a particular case by the Court, the probation officer's recommendation on the sentence is not to be disclosed to the defendant, the defendant's counsel, or the attorney for the Government.

2. *Entry of scheduling order.* In any case governed by the Sentencing Guidelines promulgated by the United States Sentencing Commission, the Court shall enter an order relating to the sentencing process, in a form prescribed by the Court *en banc,* at the time of entry of a plea of *nolo contendere* or guilty or after a verdict of guilty after trial. The form of order is available for public inspection in the Clerk's Office.

3. *Misdemeanor cases.* Pursuant to Section 6A1.2(d) of the Sentencing Guidelines and Policy Statements of the United States Sentencing Commission, in any case for which there has been no conviction above the level of a Class A misdemeanor, (which includes all misdemeanors and infractions), the judicial officer may permit the parties to make oral statements at or before sentencing of the sentencing factors to be relied upon at sentencing in lieu of a written statement.

Pursuant to Section 6B1.4(c) of the Sentencing Guidelines and Policy Statements of the United States Sentencing Commission, a judicial officer taking a plea of guilty or *nolo contendere* pursuant to a plea agreement, for any offense or offenses not above the level of a Class A misdemeanor (which includes all misdemeanors and infractions), may permit the parties to make any required stipulation of facts relative to sentencing orally, on the record, at the time the plea agreement is offered, in lieu of a written stipulation.

Rule 214. Disposition of exhibits.
The provisions of LR 113 apply to criminal proceedings.

III. UNITED STATES MAGISTRATE JUDGES.

Rule 301. Authority of United States Magistrate Judges.
1. *Geographical jurisdiction.* All Magistrate Judges have jurisdiction to try, hear and determine cases within their original and referred jurisdiction throughout the entire District of Maryland and in such cases arising in adjoining districts pursuant to separate authorizations.

2. *Recording.* All court proceedings before Magistrate Judges shall be recorded either electronically or by a court reporter.

3. *Criminal cases.* All Magistrate Judges are specially designated to conduct criminal cases with the consent of the defendant, including trial, judgment, sentence, and revocation of probation or supervised release, in conformity with and subject to the limitations of 18 U.S.C. § 3401, Fed. R. Crim. P. 58, and any other applicable law of the United States. All full-time Magistrate Judges may conduct a jury trial in any misdemeanor case when the defendant so requests and is entitled to trial by jury under the Constitution and laws of the United States.

4. *Civil cases.* Pursuant to 28 U.S.C. § 636(c), with the consent of the parties, a District Judge may designate a full-time Magistrate Judge to conduct any or all proceedings, including trial, in a jury or nonjury civil matter, and to order the entry of final judgment in the case. Cases referred to a Magistrate Judge shall be randomly assigned.

Upon the filing of any civil case, the Clerk of Court shall notify the parties of their right to proceed by consent before a Magistrate Judge. The form and content of the notice shall be as provided in Fed. R. Civ. P. forms 33 and 34. If all parties consent, the plaintiff shall be responsible for filing executed consent forms with the Clerk of Court.

Nothing contained herein shall preclude any District Judge or Magistrate Judge from inquiring about or suggesting to the parties a reference of any case to a Magistrate Judge, without persuasion or inducement. Every effort shall be made by court personnel to protect the voluntariness of the parties' consent.

Any judgment entered by a Magistrate Judge in a case referred pursuant to this Rule shall be the final judgment of the District Court, unless reversed, modified, or remanded on appeal. Pursuant to Fed. R. Civ. P. 73(c) and (d), any appeal shall lie to the Court of Appeals as it would from any other judgment of the District Court, unless the parties consent to appeal on the record to a District Judge and thereafter by petition only to the Court of Appeals.

5. *Authority under 28 U.S.C. § 636(b).* a. Nondispositive matters. Pursuant to 28 U.S.C. § 636(b), a District Judge may designate a full-time Magistrate Judge to hear and determine (including the passage of final orders as to all or any part of) any pretrial matter pending before the Court except those listed in Section 5.b. below. Nondispositive pretrial matters include, but are not limited to, discovery disputes and pretrial orders under Fed. R. Civ. P. 16.

Any objections to a Magistrate Judge's order must be served and filed within ten days of the entry of the order, pursuant to Fed. R. Civ. P. 72(a). A District Judge may reconsider, modify, or set aside any portion of the Magistrate Judge's order found to be clearly erroneous or contrary to law.

b. Dispositive matters. Pursuant to 28 U.S.C. § 636(b), a District Judge may designate a full-time Magistrate Judge to conduct hearings, if necessary, including evidentiary hearings, and to submit to the District Judge proposed findings of fact and recommendations for action to be taken by the District Judge as to any of the following:

(i) a motion for injunctive relief;

(ii) a motion for judgment on the pleadings;

(iii) a motion for summary judgment;

(iv) a motion by a defendant to dismiss or quash an indictment or information;

(v) a motion to suppress evidence in a criminal case;

(vi) a motion to dismiss or permit maintenance of a class action;

(vii) a motion to dismiss for failure to state a claim upon which relief can be granted;

(viii) a motion to involuntarily dismiss an action;

(ix) a motion to review an administrative determination as to Social Security or related benefits, pursuant to 42 U.S.C. § 405(g);

(x) prisoner petitions challenging conditions of confinement; and

(xi) applications for post-trial relief under 28 U.S.C. § 2254 and § 2255 made by individuals convicted of criminal offenses.

Any objections must be served and filed within ten days after a copy of the proposed findings and recommendations is served on the party wishing to object, pursuant to Fed. R. Civ. P. 72(b). When the proceedings before the Magistrate Judge have been electronically recorded, transcription of the record shall not be necessary unless otherwise directed by the Court.

The District Judge shall make a *de novo* determination as to those portions of the proposed findings and recommendations to which specific objections are made. The District Judge may accept, reject, or modify the recommended decision, may receive further evidence, or may recommit the matter to the Magistrate Judge with instructions.

c. Designation as special master. A District Judge may designate a Magistrate Judge to serve as a special master pursuant to and in accordance with Fed. R. Civ. P. 53. With consent of the parties, such designation may be made without regard to the limitations of Fed. R. Civ. P. 53(b). Appeals from the decision of a Magistrate Judge designated as a special master pursuant to this Rule shall be taken in accordance with Fed. R. Civ. P. 53(e).

6. *Other duties.* All Magistrate Judges are specially designated to exercise all powers heretofore held by United States Commissioners, to exercise all other powers authorized by 28 U.S.C. § 636(a) and (g), or any other applicable law, and to perform such additional duties as are not inconsistent with the Constitution and laws of the United States. These powers and duties include, but are not limited to, the following:

a. Consideration of criminal complaints and affidavits and issuance of arrest warrants or summonses pursuant to Fed. R. Crim. P. 3, 4, and 9.

b. Conduct of initial appearance proceedings for defendants pursuant to Fed. R. Crim. P. 5.

c. Conduct of preliminary examinations pursuant to Fed. R. Crim. P. 5.1 and 18 U.S.C. § 3060.

d. Receipt of grand jury returns pursuant to Fed. R. Crim. P. 6(f) and issuance of bench warrants on indictments pursuant to Fed. R. Crim. P. 9.

e. Acceptance of waivers of indictment pursuant to Fed. R. Crim. P. 7(b).

f. Conduct of preliminary hearings in probation or supervised release revocation proceedings pursuant to Fed. R. Crim. P. 32.1.

g. Conduct of initial proceedings pursuant to Fed. R. Crim. P. 40 for defendants charged in other districts.

h. Issuance of search and seizure warrants pursuant to Fed. R. Crim. P. 41.

i. Appointment of attorneys pursuant to 18 U.S.C. § 3006A and Fed. R. Crim. P. 44.

j. Issuance of orders concerning release or detention of defendants and material witnesses and forfeiture or exoneration of bond pursuant to 18 U.S.C. § 3141 *et seq.*, and Fed. R. Crim. P. 32.1, 40 and 46.

k. Direction of the payment of basic transportation and subsistence expenses for released persons financially unable to bear such costs, pursuant to 18 U.S.C. §§ 4282 and 4285.

l. Issuance of orders permitting dismissals, on the government's motion, of violation notices, complaints, informations, and indictments in criminal cases pursuant to Fed. R. Crim. P. 48(a).

m. Handling of arraignments in criminal cases pursuant to Fed. R. Crim. P. 10, including acceptance of not guilty pleas, scheduling of motions, scheduling of pretrial conferences and trials, and issuance of bench warrants for the arrest of a defendant who fails to appear for arraignment before the Magistrate Judge.

n. Conduct of initial proceedings upon the appearance of an individual accused of an act of juvenile delinquency pursuant to 18 U.S.C. § 5034.

o. Appointment of interpreters pursuant to 28 U.S.C. §§ 1827 and 1828 in cases initiated by the United States.

p. Under appropriate conditions and when an order is required, issuance of orders for lineups, photographs, fingerprinting, palmprinting, voice identification, mental or physical examination, the taking of blood, urine, fingernail, hair, or bodily secretion samples (with appropriate medical safeguards required by due process considerations), and handwriting exemplars.

q. Upon the request of the United States Attorney, (1) authorization of the installation of pen registers and trap and trace devices, and execution of orders directing the telephone company to assist the Government in such installation; (2) authorization of the installation of beeper devices ("transponders") or other tracking devices; and (3) authorization of the installation of devices ("clone beepers") which duplicate signals received on a contact beeper or similar device, and execution of orders directing the company or other person furnishing the contact beeper to assist the Government in such installation.

r. Issuance of orders (1) under the provisions of Sec. 356 of the Tax Equity and Fiscal Responsibility Act of 1982 (P.L. 97-248) authorizing, pursuant to 26 U.S.C. § 6103 (as amended by P.L. 97-248), the disclosure of tax returns and return information for use in criminal proceedings, and (2) directing banks not to notify their customers of the issuance of subpoenas for financial records pursuant to 12 U.S.C. 3409 or 12 U.S.C. 3413(i).

s. Issuance of writs of habeas corpus *ad testificandum* and *ad prosequendum*.

t. Upon request of the United States Attorney, a Magistrate Judge shall have the authority to consider and approve an agreement between the Government and a defendant to defer prosecution in any petty offense or misdemeanor case for a period not to exceed one year from the date said agreement is approved by the Magistrate Judge.

u. Use of the services of the United States Probation Office for preparation of presentence investigations and other reports and recommendations.

v. Conduct of international extradition proceedings pursuant to 18 U.S.C. § 3184.

w. Appointment of counsel and performance of the verification functions set forth in 18 U.S.C. §§ 4107, 4108, and 4109 relating to proceedings for the transfer of offenders between the United States and foreign countries.

x. Issuance of warrants or orders permitting entry into and inspection of premises and/or seizure of property, as authorized by law, when properly requested by a government agency.

y. Issuance of show cause orders to enforce administrative summons or subpoenas.

z. Issuance of attachments, conduct of hearings, including evidentiary hearings, and submission to the District Judge of proposed findings of fact and recommendations with respect to the disposition of a petition to enforce compliance with a summons issued by the Internal Revenue Service.

aa. Consideration and granting or denial of motions of litigants to proceed *in forma pauperis*, with appeal to a District Judge.

ab. Appointment of counsel for indigent litigants pursuant to 28 U.S.C. § 1915(d) and other statutes.

ac. Making special appointments to serve process pursuant to Fed. R. Civ. P. 4(c).

ad. Organization of petit and grand juries.

ae. Conduct of voir dire and receipt of jury verdicts in civil and criminal cases being tried by a District Judge, on consent of the parties.

af. Supervision of proceedings on requests for letters rogatory in civil and criminal cases pursuant to 28 U.S.C. § 1782.

ag. Execution of exemplifications of court records.

ah. Issuance of orders in mortgage foreclosure proceedings prior to ratification of sale.

ai. Ordering and conducting prejudgment remedy proceedings in accordance with 28 U.S.C. §§ 3101-3105.

aj. Ordering and conducting supplementary proceedings in accordance with Md. R. Proc. 2-633, upon the filing of an appropriate affidavit.

ak. Review and issuance of orders concerning confessed judgments pursuant to Local Rule 108.b *supra*.

al. Review of default judgments and recommendations concerning damages.

am. Review of matters and issuance of orders under Local Admiralty Rule (LAR)(e)(4).

an. Issuance of orders for the deposit and withdrawal of registry funds in conjunction with matters over which Magistrate Judges exercise jurisdiction.

ao. Conduct of naturalization ceremonies.

ap. Admission of attorneys to the Bar of this Court.

aq. Any full-time Magistrate Judge is authorized to conduct proceedings for initial commitment of narcotics addicts under Title III of the Narcotics Addicts Rehabilitation Act. The Magistrate Judge, after conducting such proceedings, shall recommend to the District Judge the commitment of the addict or shall state his reasons for recommending against commitment. In a case where the Magistrate Judge recommends against commitment, the addict shall have a right to a hearing *de novo* before a District Judge.

The Magistrate Judge's recommendation shall be transmitted forthwith to the Chambers Judge for appropriate action.

ar. All Magistrate Judges for the District of Maryland are specially designated to commit persons to St. Elizabeth's Hospital, Washington, D.C., in accordance with the provisions of the District of Columbia Code, Section 21-902.

7. *Part-time magistrate judges.* Nothing in these Local Rules shall be deemed an assignment to part-time Magistrate Judges of additional duties

under 28 U.S.C. § 636(b) other than those permitted by Rule 7 of the Conflict of Interest Rules for Part-Time Magistrate Judges adopted by the Judicial Conference pursuant to 28 U.S.C. § 632(b).

Rule 302. Appeals from decisions by Magistrate Judges.

1. *Criminal cases.* Appeals in criminal cases shall be made to the District Court within ten days from entry of the decision, order, judgment of conviction or sentence in accordance with Fed. R. Crim. P. 58(g)(2) and other applicable statutes and rules.

Within 30 days of the docketing of the appeal, the appellant shall file with the Clerk of Court and serve on the appellee a memorandum stating the exact points of law, facts, and authorities on which the appeal is based. The appellee shall file an answering memorandum within 30 days thereafter. The Court may extend these times upon a showing of good cause. If an appellant fails to file a memorandum within the time provided, the Court may dismiss the appeal. All appeals shall be decided on the record and the parties' memoranda, unless the Court, in its discretion, orders oral argument.

2. *Civil cases.* Appeals in civil cases referred by consent pursuant to Local Rule 301.4 and in which the parties have elected an appeal to a Judge of the District Court shall be governed by Fed. R. Civ. P. 74-76. Briefs shall not exceed 20 typewritten pages, without leave of court. The appeal will be decided on the briefs and the record, unless the court, in its discretion, orders oral argument.

Rule 303. Designation of Chief Magistrate Judge.

The Chief District Judge shall have the authority to designate one of the full-time Magistrate Judges as Chief United States Magistrate Judge for the District of Maryland. The Chief Magistrate Judge shall perform such duties in connection with the administration of the Magistrate Judges' system within this district as the Chief District Judge may, from time to time, assign.

Rule 304. Forfeiture of collateral.

1. *General provisions.* a. The provisions of this Rule do not create or otherwise define an offense. This Rule applies to petty offenses which have otherwise been created and/or defined by federal statutes, regulations, or applicable state statutes lawfully assimilated by virtue of the Assimilative Crimes Act (18 U.S.C. 13) which petty offenses are committed within the jurisdiction of the United States District Court for the District of Maryland.

b. When an asterisk (*) is inserted next to a listed violation, *no* forfeiture of collateral will be permitted. Forfeiture of collateral will not be permitted unless same is specifically authorized by the collateral schedule hereinafter provided, except as authorized by Paragraph (d) below. For any offense not specifically listed, a mandatory appearance will be required except as may be authorized by Paragraph (d) below.

c. In the event any non-mandatory offense is one of a number of multiple offenses, and any one of such multiple offenses is a mandatory appearance offense, the arresting officer or officer issuing a violation notice *shall* treat *all* offenses which otherwise would have been non-mandatory as a mandatory appearance offense. In the event any non-mandatory offense is deemed by the arresting officer or officer issuing a violation notice to be of an aggravated nature, the officer may treat the offense as a mandatory appearance offense. The arresting officer or officer issuing a violation notice may, within his discretion, always treat *any* offense as a mandatory appearance offense notwithstanding the fact that forfeiture of collateral may otherwise be permitted pursuant to this Rule.

d. Notwithstanding any other provision contained in this Rule, at the request or recommendation of, or with the consent of the prosecuting authority, the United States Magistrate Judge may set or authorize the setting of collateral for *any* petty offense. Notwithstanding *any* other provision contained in this Rule, at the request or recommendation of, or with the consent of the prosecuting authority, the United States Magistrate Judge may increase or decrease *any* collateral which may otherwise be authorized or set pursuant to this Rule. The United States Magistrate Judge may require a mandatory appearance for *any* petty offense so long as any collateral which may have been previously authorized and set pursuant to this Rule has not been received prior to the Magistrate Judge's issuance of a notice of mandatory appearance.

e. At no time may collateral be set in an amount greater than the maximum fine authorized for the offense charged, nor may collateral be less than any mandatory minimum fine which may be required as a penalty for the offense charged. Should any collateral erroneously be set higher than the authorized maximum fine then the collateral shall automatically be reduced to said authorized maximum fine. Should any collateral erroneously be set in an amount less than a required mandatory minimum fine, the amount of collateral shall automatically be increased to said mandatory minimum.

f. A collateral offense shall be processed by giving an alleged offender a violation notice or citation with mail-in envelope (comparable to DD Form 1805 in use on military installations or in such other form as may otherwise be approved by the Court) the notice or citation setting forth the offense, the date and location thereof, name of the issuing officer, the full name, address, date of birth, and any other identifying data, which may include Social Security Number, concerning the offender and the amount of collateral which can be forfeited. It shall further contain instructions to pay the collateral to the Clerk of the Court, or if the offender wishes to contest the charge, to indicate the option to appear before a United States Magistrate Judge for trial or other appropriate proceedings, in either event by mailing the form to the Clerk of the Court within seven (7) days of receipt of the violation notice or citation. The violation notice or citation shall also set forth the date and time upon which the matter will be heard before a United States Magistrate Judge or otherwise indicate that the defendant will be notified when to appear in the future.

g. The Clerk shall establish a Central Violations Bureau for the processing of violation notices, citations and collateral. The address of the Central Violations Bureau shall be Central Violations Bureau, Clerk, United States District Court, United States Courthouse, Baltimore, Maryland 21201 or such other address as may be subsequently approved by the Court. All violation notices and citations issued to alleged offenders shall show the appropriate address for the receipt of collateral or notice that a defendant desires a hearing before the United States Magistrate Judge.

h. For any petty offense in which collateral is *not* set, the defendant shall be issued a violation notice or citation containing the information required in Paragraphs (f) and (g) above, except that in the space provided for the amount of collateral there shall be inserted the letters "M.A." which letters shall indicate mandatory appearance required, directing the defendant to appear before a United States Magistrate Judge at a specified date and time or otherwise indicating that the defendant will be notified when to appear in the future. However, if the arresting officer has reason to believe that the person charged with an offense may not appear as required, the officer may take the alleged offender before a United States Magistrate Judge or other judicial officer as set forth in 18 U.S.C. 3041 without unnecessary delay for the purpose of setting appropriate conditions of release in accordance with the provisions of 18 U.S.C. 3146.

i. Except in exceptional circumstances, a violation notice or citation shall charge only one offense. If an alleged offender is deemed to have committed more than one offense, each offense shall be charged on a separate violation notice or citation. Nothing contained in this Rule shall be deemed to prohibit the prosecution of a petty offense by means of a criminal complaint, criminal information, or indictment.

j. The payment of collateral for any offense in which collateral is *set* as authorized by this Rule, shall cause said collateral to be forfeited to the United States and payment and forfeiture of said collateral shall signify that the defendant does not contest the charge nor requires a hearing before a United States Magistrate Judge. If collateral is paid and forfeited, such action shall be tantamount to a finding of guilty, and the defendant shall be deemed convicted of any offense for which collateral is paid and forfeited. Upon conviction, the Clerk or United States Magistrate Judge shall certify the record of any conviction of a traffic violation, but not to include parking offenses, to the appropriate State Motor Vehicle Administration.

k. Whenever a check is returned to the Clerk as uncollectible for any reason within the control of the payor, the offense for which the collateral was posted shall be referred promptly to the appropriate United States Magistrate Judge for the scheduling of a mandatory appearance or such other action as may be deemed appropriate by the United States Magistrate Judge.

l. When any alleged offender fails to pay any collateral set pursuant to this Rule and fails to appear in response to a Notice to Appear or Summons, the United States Magistrate Judge may consider and treat the offense as a mandatory appearance offense, and thereafter refuse any tender of the payment of collateral and set the case for hearing, or in the Magistrate Judge's discretion, increase the amount of collateral. A United States Magistrate Judge may also issue a warrant for the arrest of the alleged offender as authorized by Fed. R. Crim. P. 58(d)(3) and/or set the case for hearing.

m. For offenses designated as "Hunting and Fishing," "Wildlife," or "Migratory Bird Treaty Act," in the case of an aggravated offense, multiple offenses, an offense involving a defendant who has previously been convicted of an

936

offense in the above categories, or for any other reason deemed appropriate by
the Office of the United States Attorney for the District of Maryland or any
other attorney acting under the authority of the United States Attorney to
represent the Government in proceedings before United States Magistrate
Judges, the arresting officer or officer issuing a violation notice shall have the
discretion to set collateral within the minimum and maximum limits hereinafter specified, subject to prior authorization from the Office of the United
States Attorney for the District of Maryland or any other attorney acting under
the authority of the United States Attorney for the District of Maryland.
Otherwise, the collateral shall be the minimum amount provided for in the
collateral schedule.

n. In the event the payment is received by the Clerk before the Violation
Notice is forwarded to a Magistrate Judge for collection, the Clerk shall retain
and process it. Should it be necessary for the Court or United States
Magistrate Judge to issue an arrest warrant as a result of any alleged
violator's failure to appear, the amount of collateral shall automatically triple
from the amount originally set on the violation notice or citation. For good
cause shown, the Court and/or United State [States] Magistrate Judge may
reduce the collateral. Nothing contained herein shall prevent the United
States Magistrate Judge from requiring a mandatory appearance.

o. In any mandatory appearance case or in the event that any authorized
collateral is not forfeited, should any alleged violator fail to appear in response
to a Notice to Appear or Summons, the United States Magistrate Judge, Clerk
of the Court, Central Violations Bureau and/or the United States Marshal may,
in coordination with the Maryland Department of Transportation Motor
Vehicle Administration, utilize the Motor Vehicle Administration violation and
flagging procedures so as to prohibit an alleged violator who fails to appear in
connection with any parking or traffic offense from obtaining a current motor
vehicle registration from the State of Maryland until such time as any
outstanding offenses are disposed of according to law. The Clerk or United
States Magistrate Judge shall not authorize the release of any flag upon the
vehicle registration of an alleged violator until such time as all collateral is
paid by cash, certified check or money order, and forfeited, except that in the
event a trial is requested, no hearing or trial shall be held until such time as
the total collateral is deposited with the Clerk or United States Magistrate
Judge. Upon the deposit of said collateral, any flag upon the vehicle registration of the alleged violator shall be released. For good cause shown, in the
interest of justice or in otherwise exceptional circumstances, the United States
Magistrate Judge may reduce the amount of collateral to be paid and forfeited
or deposited under this paragraph and authorize the release of any flag upon
the vehicle registration of the alleged violator upon the payment or deposit of
such reduced amount, unless it is determined by the United States Magistrate
[Judge] that no payment or deposit shall be required.

p. The provisions of this Rule shall apply to petty offenses alleged to have
been committed by a juvenile prior to the filing of the Attorney General's
certification referred to in 18 U.S.C. 5032 and 18 U.S.C. 3401(g). After the
filing of such certification, the provisions of this Rule shall apply only in the

event that the juvenile, with the advice of counsel, files a written request to be prosecuted as an adult.

q. Nothing contained in this Rule shall prevent the issuance of a warrant of arrest in accordance with Fed. R. Crim. P. 58(d)(3) or any other lawful authority.

2. *Schedule of monetary collateral and mandatory appearance offenses.* The Court shall approve a schedule of monetary collateral and mandatory appearance offenses, which schedule shall be filed with the Clerk as a public document. The Court may amend the schedule from time to time.

IV. BANKRUPTCY PROCEEDINGS.

Rule 401. Rules in Bankruptcy Court proceedings.
Proceedings in the Bankruptcy Court shall be governed by Local Bankruptcy Rules as adopted from time to time by order of the Court.

Rule 402. Referral of bankruptcy cases and proceedings.
Pursuant to 28 U.S.C. Section 157(a), all cases under Title 11 of the United States Code and proceedings arising under Title 11 or arising in or related to cases under Title 11 shall be deemed to be referred to the Bankruptcy Judges of this District.

Cited in In re Lewis, 170 Bankr. 861 (Bankr. D. Md. 1994); Koffman v. Osteoimplant Technology, Inc., 182 Bankr. 115 (D. Md. 1995).

Rule 403. Appeals to the District Court.
1. *Manner of appeal.* a. Generally. Appeals to the District Court from the Bankruptcy Court shall be taken in the manner prescribed in Part VIII of the Bankruptcy Rules, Rules 8001 et seq.

b. Bankruptcy Court opinion as appendix. Appellant shall append to appellant's opening brief a copy of the opinion of the Bankruptcy Court that is being appealed from.

2. *Dismissal for non-compliance with Bankruptcy Rule 8006.* Whenever the appellant fails to designate the contents of the record on appeal or to file a statement of the issues to be presented on appeal within the time required by Bankruptcy Rule 8006, the Bankruptcy Clerk shall forward forthwith to the Clerk of the District Court a partial record consisting of a copy of the order or judgment appealed from, the notice of appeal, a copy of the docket entries and such other papers as the Bankruptcy Clerk deems relevant to the appeal. (The District Court may thereafter order the Bankruptcy Clerk to transmit any other relevant papers to the Clerk of the District Court). When the partial record has been filed in the District Court, the Court may, upon motion of the appellee (which is to be filed in the District Court) or upon its own initiative, dismiss the appeal for non-compliance with Bankruptcy Rule 8006 after giving the appellant an opportunity to explain the non-compliance and upon considering whether the non-compliance had prejudicial effect on the other parties.

3. *Dismissal for non-compliance with Bankruptcy Rule 8009.* Whenever the appellant fails to serve and file a brief within the time required by Bankruptcy

Rule 8009, the District Court may, upon motion of the appellee (to be filed in the District Court) or upon its own initiative, dismiss the appeal after giving the appellant an opportunity to explain the non-compliance and upon considering whether the non-compliance had prejudicial effect on the other parties.

4. *Procedure re motion to stay pending appeal.* An appellant seeking a stay pending appeal by the District Court of an order entered by the Bankruptcy Court shall file with the Clerk of the District Court a motion to stay and copies of all papers in the record of the Bankruptcy Court relevant to the appeal. Upon the filing of these papers the Clerk of the District Court shall immediately open a civil file and the District Court shall give immediate consideration to the motion to stay. If the underlying appeal is ultimately perfected, it will be assigned the same civil action number as was assigned to the motion to stay.

5. *Bankruptcy court certification re interlocutory appeal.* Whenever there has been filed in the District Court an application for leave to appeal an interlocutory order of the Bankruptcy Court, the Bankruptcy Court shall, upon request of the District Court, submit to the District Court a written certification stating whether, in its opinion, the interlocutory order involves a controlling question of law as to which there is substantial ground for difference of opinion and whether an immediate appeal of it may materially advance the ultimate termination of the case. The District Court shall thereafter determine whether to grant or deny the application for leave to appeal.

Rule 404. Rules of procedure under 28 U.S.C. Section 1334.

A. *Filing of pleadings and papers.* (1) General rule. When a case or proceeding has been referred by this Court to the Bankruptcy Court, all papers and pleadings in or related to such case or proceeding shall be filed with the Clerk in the Bankruptcy Court pursuant to Local Bankruptcy Rules 1 and 2.

(2) Withdrawal of reference of certain bankruptcy proceedings. (a) Filing of motion for withdrawal of reference with bankruptcy clerk. A motion pursuant to 28 U.S.C. § 157(d) to withdraw the reference of any bankruptcy case, contested matter or adversary proceeding referred to the Bankruptcy Court pursuant to 28 U.S.C. § 157(a) shall be filed with the Clerk in the Bankruptcy Court.

(b) Withdrawal of reference of bankruptcy cases. A motion to withdraw the reference of a case to the Bankruptcy Court must be timely filed, and in any event, before the case is closed.

(c) Withdrawal of reference of adversary proceeding or contested matter. A motion to withdraw an adversary proceeding or a contested matter which has been referred to the Bankruptcy Court must be filed by the earlier of eleven (11) days before the date scheduled for the first hearing on the merits and;

(i) in the case of an adversary proceeding, within twenty (20) days after the last pleading is permitted to be filed pursuant to Bankruptcy Rule 7012; or

(ii) in the case of a contested matter, within twenty (20) days after the last memorandum is permitted to be filed pursuant to Local Bankruptcy Rule 30(b)(4).

(3) Filing of pleadings in transferred cases. (a) If an entire case has been transferred from the Bankruptcy Court, all pleadings and papers in or related to such case shall be filed with the Clerk in the District Court.

(b) Where only a portion of an entire case has been transferred, pleadings and papers with respect to the case (including any parts thereof that have been withdrawn, transferred, or removed) shall continue to be filed with the Clerk in the Bankruptcy Court. The Clerk in the Bankruptcy Court shall keep a docket sheet of all pleadings and papers filed in bankruptcy-related matters which are to be transferred to the District Court. All such pleadings and papers shall be formally transferred to the Clerk in the District Court promptly following the entry of the pleading or paper upon the docket sheet of the Bankruptcy Court.

(4) Upon withdrawal, transfer or removal of any complaint to the District Court, plaintiff shall forward to defendant a notice and request to waive service of summons or the Clerk shall issue a District Court summons pursuant to Fed. R. Civ. P. 4(d), unless either of the aforementioned has already occurred pursuant to the Bankruptcy Rules.

(5) This subsection (5) governs proceedings in personal injury tort and wrongful death actions which must be tried in the District Court pursuant to 28 U.S.C. § 157(b)(5). Except for the procedures contained within this subsection, these personal injury tort and wrongful death actions shall be instituted and all pleadings and papers filed in the same manner as all other cases under 28 U.S.C. § 1334. However, beneath the bankruptcy number, the pleading or other paper shall designate the pleading or paper as a "SECTION 157(b)(5) MATTER." When filing a complaint a completed civil cover sheet (A.O. Form JS-44c) should be submitted beneath the cover sheet required by Local Bankruptcy Rule 2(e). No summons shall be issued until the case is transferred to the District Court. However, upon filing the complaint, the Clerk in the Bankruptcy Court shall immediately transfer the case to the District Court and plaintiff shall forward to defendant(s) a notice and request to waive service of summons or the Clerk of the District Court shall issue a summons pursuant to Fed. R. Civ. P. 4(d).

B. *Motions concerning venue in bankruptcy cases and proceedings.* All motions concerning venue in cases arising under Title 11 or arising in or related to cases under Title 11 shall be determined by the Bankruptcy Court, except in those cases to be tried in the District Court pursuant to 28 U.S.C. § 157(b)(5).

Rule 405. Jury trial.

1. *Demand.* In any bankruptcy proceeding any party may demand a trial by jury of any issue triable of right by a jury by (1) serving upon the other parties a demand therefore in writing at any time after the commencement of the action and not later than 10 days after the service of the last pleading directed to such issue, and (2) filing the demand as required by Bankruptcy Rule 7005. Such demand may be indorsed upon a pleading of the party. If the adversary proceeding is one that has been removed from another court, any demand previously made under the rules of that court, shall constitute a demand for trial by a jury under this rule.

2. *Specification of issues.* In the demand a party may specify the issues which the party wishes so tried; otherwise the party shall be deemed to have

demanded trial by jury for all the issues so triable. If the party as demanded trial by jury for only some of the issues, any other party within 10 days after service of the demand or such lesser time as the court may order, may serve a demand for trial by jury of any other or all of the issues of fact in the action.

3. *Waiver.* The failure of a party to serve and file a demand as required by this rule constitutes a waiver by the party of trial by jury. A demand for trial by jury made as herein provided may not be withdrawn without the consent of the parties.

V. COURT ADMINISTRATION AND SECURITY.

Rule 501. Assignment of cases.

All cases will be assigned to one of the Judges of the Court. With the exception of asbestos cases and cases referred to Magistrate Judges, all proceedings in a particular case will usually be held before the Judge to whom that case is assigned.

Rule 502. Jury selection plan.

The Jury Selection Plan as adopted and amended from time to time by Court order shall be available for public inspection in the Clerk's Office.

Rule 503. No attorneys or court personnel as sureties.

No member of the Bar, of the Clerk's Office, of the U.S. Marshal's Office or of the staff of any Judge or Magistrate Judge shall act as surety on any bond or undertaking in any action or proceeding in the Court.

Rule 504. Hours of Clerk's Office.

1. *Hours of actual operation.* The Clerk's Office shall be open from 9:00 a.m. to 5:00 p.m. on all days except Saturdays, Sundays, the legal holidays specified in Fed. R. Civ. P. 77(c) and the day after Thanksgiving.

2. *"Night box".* A "night box" will be open on the first floor of the courthouse in Baltimore in which filings can be made up to 11:00 p.m., Monday through Friday. Counsel who deposit a paper in the night box should so notify the Clerk's Office the following day.

Rule 505. Courthouse security.

1. *Inspection of entering persons.* All persons entering any federal court facility in this District and all items carried by them shall be subject to appropriate screening and checking by any United States Marshal or any security officer or any law enforcement officer on duty. Any person who refuses fully to cooperate in such screening or checking may be denied entrance to the courthouse.

2. *Confiscation of weapons and contraband.* Any weapons (unless carried by law enforcement officers on their official duties) shall be impounded by the person conducting inspection. Property thus impounded may be retained for use as evidence and may be forfeited, destroyed or otherwise disposed of in

accordance with law. Any person unlawfully carrying such property is subject to criminal prosecution.

Rule 506. Photographing and recording court proceedings and courthouse spaces.

1. *Photographing, recording and transmitting court proceedings.* Unless otherwise ordered by the Chief Judge, no court proceeding may be photographed, video recorded, audio recorded, broadcast, televised or otherwise transmitted except as follows:

a. Persons presiding over naturalization proceedings may authorize the use of cameras or video recorders during the proceedings.

b. Judges presiding over ceremonial proceedings may authorize the use of cameras and video recorders during the proceedings.

c. Official court reporters and official electronic recorders employed by the Clerk's Office shall record court proceedings, provided, however, that no court reporter or electronic recorder shall use or permit to be used any official recording of a court proceeding in connection with any radio or television broadcast.

d. Any judge may authorize a court reporter privately retained by one or more parties to record a court proceeding if any official court reporter or official electronic recorder is unavailable or unable to perform the necessary recording.

2. *Photographing, video recording and televising courthouse spaces.*
a. Courtrooms and other public spaces. Unless otherwise ordered by the Chief Judge, no courtroom or other public space in the courthouse may be photographed, video recorded or televised except as follows:

(i). On the day of naturalization proceedings, persons being naturalized and their families and friends may use cameras in the public spaces on the first floor;

(ii). On the day of receptions or other social events, persons attending the event may us cameras in the space where the event is being held; and

(iii). Employees of the General Services Administration and GSA architects and contractors may use cameras in the courtrooms and other public spaces when court is not in session.

b. Office spaces. Cameras may not be used in any office within the courthouse except with the approval of the person in charge of the office.

3. *Penalties.* Any camera, recording device or other equipment used in violation of this Rule may be impounded. Any violation of this Rule may be treated as a contempt of Court and any violator who is a member of the Bar may be subject to the disciplinary action of the Court.

Rule 507. Copying and removal of court papers.

1. *Copying.* Upon the request of any person and the prepayment of any fees set by the schedule adopted from time to time by Court order, the Clerk may deliver to the requesting person a copy of any court paper appearing on the public record.

2. *Removal of original papers prohibited.* Unless otherwise ordered by the Court, no court paper or any paper connected with the business of the Clerk

shall be taken out of the Clerk's Office, provided, however, that authorized Court personnel may remove such papers for the purpose of carrying them to a courtroom or the chambers of a Judge or Magistrate Judge.

Rule 508. Investment of registry funds.

The Court shall by standing order set the amount of funds deposited in the Court Registry which shall be invested at interest. These funds shall be placed in an interest bearing account or such other investment as is ordered by the Court. Funds in any one case will be divided as necessary to assure full F.D.I.C. coverage of principal and interest. All funds invested at interest will be assessed a charge pursuant to the fee schedule set by the Judicial Conference of the United States.

In the event the Clerk is not present for service of the order required by Fed. R. Civ. P. 67, such service shall be made upon the Chief Deputy Clerk or the Finance Clerk, only.

Rule 509. Records disposition.

1. *Actions involving title to realty.* The official file in any case involving title to realty shall be deemed to be a permanent record of the Court and shall not be destroyed.

2. *Actions involving monetary judgments.* The file in any action in which a judgment for damages and/or costs has been entered shall be retained by the Clerk as long as the judgment remains in full force and effect.

Rule 510. Unclaimed funds in the registry.

Funds in the registry unclaimed for more than two years shall be transferred, with the approval of the Court, to the Treasury. They may be withdrawn from the Treasury by the claimant pursuant to the procedure set forth in 28 U.S.C. Section 2042.

Rule 511. Request for financial disclosure reports.

1. *Form.* Any request for a financial disclosure report filed with the Clerk shall be submitted on the form prescribed by the Clerk. The Clerk shall make copies of such forms available to the public.

2. *Penalty for misuse of report.* Any person who obtains or uses the report for any unlawful purpose, for any commercial purpose (other than the dissemination of information to the general public), for determining or establishing the credit rating of any individual or for use, directly or indirectly, in the solicitation of money for any political, charitable, or other purpose may be held in contempt of court.

Rule 512. Lapse in appropriations.

This Rules [Rule] shall become effective only when Congress fails to enact legislation to fund operations of the United States Courts. The Anti-Deficiency Act, 31 U.S.C. § 655 limits permissible government activities in the event of such a failure to those otherwise "authorized by law" or those needed to meet "cases of emergency involving the safety of human life or the protection of property."

This Court is directly involved in the judicial process, and under the Constitution and laws of the United States, it is always open to exercise the judicial power of the United States. Thus, the Court must continue, even in the absence of funding by Congress, to receive new cases, and hear and dispose of pending cases. Activities will, however, be limited as nearly as practical to those functions necessary and essential to continue the resolution of pending cases. The Court shall advise the United States Marshal and the General Services Administration of the level of building and security services necessary to maintain such court operations.

The Court finds that Judges' staff [staffs,] Magistrates Judges' staffs, the Clerk's Office, the Probation Department Office, the Federal Public Defender's Office, the Pretrial Services Office, Criminal Justice Act attorneys, Official Court Reporters, and Jurors are all essential to the continuation of court operations. Work of all personnel shall be limited to those essential functions set forth above. In the event any personnel are not engaged in those services, they shall be furloughed for the period of lapsed appropriations.

The Court will recognize that the United States Attorney, as an officer of the Department of Justice, may have to restrict the role of the staff of the United States Attorney's Office to cases "essential to protect life and property."

VI. MISCELLANEOUS.

Rule 601. Definitions.

1. *"The court" and "The judge"*. Except in the Supplemental Admiralty and Maritime Rules (see LAR(a)(3)), the terms "The Court" and "The Judge" mean "United States Magistrate Judge" as to all proceedings pending before a United States Magistrate Judge.

2. *Statutory references*. All references in these Local Rules to specific statutes or rules of procedure shall be deemed to apply to any amended or renumbered versions of such statutes or rules as may be promulgated in the future.

Rule 602. Fines.

Any attorney who fails to appear at or who is late for a proceeding scheduled by the Court or who shall fail to submit a timely status report to the Court may be fined by the Court up to $250.00. The Clerk shall maintain a record of fines imposed under this Rule and shall refer to the Disciplinary Committee of the Court for appropriate action the name of any attorney against whom more than two fines have been imposed within five years. Nothing contained in this Rule shall be construed as limiting the power of a Judge of this Court, in addition to imposing a fine hereunder, to assess costs against an attorney for a non-appearance or lateness, or to punish any such offending attorney in any other way for contempt of court.

Rule 603. Special orders in widely publicized and sensational cases.

In a widely publicized or sensational criminal or civil case, the Court, on motion of either party or on its own motion, in the exercise of its general powers, may issue a special order governing such matters as extrajudicial statements by parties and witnesses likely to interfere with the rights of the accused to a fair trial by an impartial jury, the seating and conduct in the courtroom of spectators and news media representatives, the management and sequestration of jurors and witnesses, and any other matters which the Court may deem appropriate for inclusion in such an order.

Rule 604. Suspension of rules.

For good cause shown, the Court may in a particular case suspend the provisions of any of these Rules upon application of a party or upon its own motion and may order proceedings in accordance with its direction.

Cited in Koffman v. Osteoimplant Technology, Inc., 182 Bankr. 115 (D. Md. 1995).

Rule 605. Amendment of rules.

1. *Regular procedure.* The Court shall annually consider proposed amendments to these Rules. Any person may submit proposed amendments to the Chief Judge on or before November 30th. Any such proposals will be reviewed by the Rules Committee of the Court which will recommend to the Court as a whole any amendments which it believes should be adopted. On or before April 1st the Court will cause to be published in The Daily Record notice of the substance of any amendment (subject to public notice and comment) which a majority of the members of the Court have agreed should be adopted. The Clerk shall maintain for public inspection at least five copies of any proposed amendments. Any member of the public may submit comments on a proposed amendment to the Chief Judge within thirty days of the first public notice of the proposed amendment or such later date as may be set by the Court. The Court will take final action upon the proposed amendments after giving consideration to any such comments which have been submitted. Unless otherwise ordered by the Court, the effective date of any amendment shall be July 1st of the year in which it is adopted.

2. *Emergency procedure.* The Court may adopt a rule necessary to meet any condition of emergency without complying with the procedure set forth in LR 605.1. If such an emergency rule is adopted, public notice of it shall be given promptly after its adoption and it shall be submitted for public consideration in accordance with LR 605.1 during the next regular amendment cycle.

VII. ATTORNEY ADMISSION, ASSISTANCE AND DISCIPLINE.

Rule 701. Admission.

1. *Qualifications.* a. General. Except as provided in subsection b of this rule, an attorney is qualified for admission to the bar of this district if the attorney is a member in good standing of the highest court of any State (or the District of Columbia) in which the attorney maintains his or her principal law office, or of the Court of Appeals of Maryland, is of good private and professional character, is familiar with the Code of Professional Responsibility, the Federal Rules of Civil and Criminal Procedure, the Federal Rules of Evidence, the Federal Rules of Appellate Procedure and these Local Rules and is willing, available and competent to accept appointments by the court to represent indigent parties in criminal or civil cases in this district unless the acceptance of such appointments is inconsistent with an attorney's professional employment obligations as, for example, a government attorney.

b. Reciprocity with other jurisdictions. No attorney, other than a member of the Maryland bar, who maintains his or her principal law office outside the District of Maryland may be a member of the bar of this district if the United States District Court for the district in which the attorney maintains his or her principal law office has a local rule that denies membership in its bar to any attorney who (1) is a member of the Maryland bar maintaining his or her principal law office in Maryland, and (2) meets other qualifications set by that district parallelling those set forth in subsection a of this rule.

2. *Procedure.* a. Original applications. Each applicant for admission to the bar shall file an application, accompanied by a motion filed by the applicant's sponsor. The application and motion shall be on forms prescribed by the Court and shall be made available by the Clerk to applicants upon request. The applicant's sponsor must be a member of the bar of this Court and must have known the applicant for at least one year. The latter requirement may be waived if the sponsor sets forth sufficient grounds in the motion for admission to satisfy the Court that the sponsor has reason to know that the applicant is qualified for admission. Each applicant for admission shall also pay any original admission fee set by the Court.

b. Renewal applications. Each member of the bar of this Court shall submit an application to renew her or his membership every three years from the date of her or his original admission. The application shall be on a form prescribed by the Court and shall be sent by the Clerk to each member of the bar of the Court at least 30 days prior to the date on which the application is due. The applicant for renewal shall also pay any renewal fee set by the Court. A timely renewal application shall be granted if the applicant meets all of the qualifications for admission to the bar of this Court and if she or he pays the renewal fee. Failure to submit a timely renewal application or to pay the renewal fee will cause the attorney's membership in the bar of this Court to be stricken.

Rule 702. Student practice.

1. *Eligibility.* Any eligible law student in a law school accredited by the American Bar Association may, under the conditions stated below, interview, advise, negotiate with or on behalf of a party, and appear before any magistrate judge or district court judge in this district.

2. *Requirements.* For a student to be eligible to practice, the following requirements must be met:

a. The conduct of the case must be under the supervision of a member of the bar of this district and that supervisor must be present with and prepared to assist the student at any court appearances, assume full professional responsibility for the student's work, and read, approve and co-sign all papers filed with the court.

b. The student must be in his or her final two years of law school.

c. The student must be enrolled for credit in a law school clinical program.

d. The program must maintain professional liability insurance for its activities and those of its supervisors and participating students.

e. The student may not accept personal compensation from a client or other source, although the supervisor or the law school clinical program may accept compensation.

3. *Petition to practice.* Before a student shall be eligible under this Rule, the dean of the student's law school shall file with the clerk of this court a petition listing: the names of the enrolled students, the names of the supervisors and the address of an office in this district to which the court may send all notices in connection with this Rule. The petition shall include a certification that, in the opinion of the dean and the faculty, the students have adequate knowledge of the procedural rules and substantive law, and that the activities of the students will be adequately supervised as required by this Rule. Upon written approval by the chief judge, or a designated judge, of this district, to be filed with the clerk of this court, the listed students shall be authorized to practice pursuant to this Rule and subject to the further order of this court. The written approval of the said judge as to both students and supervisors shall remain in effect for twelve months from the date of approval, unless withdrawn or unless, by further petition by the dean, the said judge shall extend the privilege.

Rule 703. Attorneys subject to discipline.

Any attorney practicing before this Court or who has practiced before this Court in any way shall be deemed thereby to have conferred disciplinary jurisdiction upon the Court for any alleged misconduct of that attorney. To the extent appropriate, all Rules set forth herein as applicable to attorneys admitted to practice before the Court shall also be deemed applicable to and enforceable against any attorney participating in any manner in any proceeding in this Court, whether or not admitted to practice before the Court.

Rule 704. Rules of Professional Conduct.

This Court shall apply the Rules of Professional Conduct as they have been adopted by the Maryland Court of Appeals.

Rule 705. Disciplinary proceedings.

1. *Allegations of misconduct.* a. Referral for investigation. When allegations of misconduct which, if substantiated, would warrant discipline of an attorney shall come to the attention of a Judge of this Court, the Judge shall refer the matter to the Court's Disciplinary Committee. If the Disciplinary Committee determines that further investigation is necessary, it may refer the matter to Maryland Bar Counsel to conduct an investigation. Alternatively, the Court, upon the recommendation of the Disciplinary Committee, may appoint one or more members of the bar of the Court as counsel to conduct the investigation. Notice of any such appointment shall be given to the respondent-attorney, and the respondent-attorney may move to disqualify counsel so appointed within fifteen days after service of the notice.

b. Recommendation by counsel. After the conclusion of the investigation, counsel shall submit to the Disciplinary Committee a recommendation that a formal hearing be held or that the matter be disposed of by dismissal, admonition, deferral or otherwise. The Disciplinary Committee shall take such action as it deems appropriate.

c. Initiation of formal proceedings. If formal disciplinary proceedings are to be initiated, the Court shall issue an order requiring the respondent-attorney to show cause within thirty days after service of the order why the attorney should not be disciplined.

d. Hearing. If the respondent-attorney's answer to the show cause order raises any issue of fact or if the respondent-attorney wishes to be heard in mitigation, a hearing shall be held before one or more Judges of the Court, provided however that if the disciplinary proceeding is predicated upon the complaint of a Judge of this Court the hearing shall be conducted before a panel of three other Judges of this Court appointed by the Chief Judge or, if there are less than three Judges eligible to serve or the Chief Judge is the complainant, the panel shall be appointed by the Chief Judge of the Fourth Circuit Court of Appeals.

e. Confidentiality. Proceedings under this section shall be confidential except that any opinion and order entered by the Court disbarring, suspending, or imposing other discipline upon an attorney shall be placed on the public record.

f. Disbarment by consent while under disciplinary investigation or prosecution. i. Any respondent-attorney may consent to disbarment while a disciplinary investigation or proceeding is pending against that attorney, but only by delivering to the Court an affidavit stating that the attorney desires to consent to disbarment and that: (1) the attorney's consent is freely and voluntarily rendered; (2) the attorney is not being subjected to coercion or duress; (3) the attorney is fully aware of the implications of so consenting; (4) the attorney is aware that there is a presently pending investigation or proceeding involving allegations that there exist grounds for the attorney's discipline the nature of which the attorney shall specifically set forth; (5) the attorney acknowledges that the material facts so alleged are true, unless such acknowledgment would involve the admission of a crime; and (6) the attorney so consents because the attorney knows that if charges were predicated upon the matters under investigation, or if the proceeding were prosecuted, the attorney could not successfully defend himself.

ii. Upon receipt of the required affidavit, the Court shall enter an order disbarring the attorney.

iii. The order disbarring the attorney on consent shall be a matter of public record. However, the affidavit required under the provisions of this Rule shall not be publicly disclosed or made available for use in any other proceeding except upon order of the Court.

2. *Criminal convictions.* a. Serious crimes. i. Definition. For purposes of this Rule the term "serious crime" shall include any felony and any lesser crime a necessary element of which, as determined by the statutory or common law definition of such crime in the jurisdiction where the judgment was entered, involved false swearing, misrepresentation, fraud, willful failure to file income tax returns, deceit, bribery, extortion, misappropriation, theft, or an attempt or a conspiracy or solicitation of another to commit any of the above.

ii. Suspension. Upon the filing with the Court of a certified copy of a judgment of conviction demonstrating that any attorney admitted to practice before the Court has been convicted in any Court of the United States, or the District of Columbia, or of any state, territory, commonwealth or possession of the United States of a serious crime, the Court shall enter an order immediately suspending that attorney, whether the conviction resulted from a plea of guilty or *nolo contendere* or from a verdict after trial or otherwise, and regardless of the pendency of any appeal. Such order shall continue until final disposition of a disciplinary proceeding to be commenced upon the conviction. A copy of such order shall immediately be served upon the attorney. Upon good cause shown, the Court may set aside such order when it appears in the interest of justice to do so.

iii. Referral for investigation. The Disciplinary Committee may, pursuant to LR 705.1, refer the matter to counsel for investigation and initiation of disciplinary proceedings.

iv. Lifting of suspension. An attorney who has been suspended under the provisions of this Rule will be reinstated immediately upon the filing of a certificate demonstrating that the underlying conviction has been reversed, but the reinstatement will not terminate any disciplinary proceeding then pending against the attorney, the disposition of which shall be determined by the Court on the basis of all available evidence pertaining to both guilt and the extent of discipline to be imposed.

b. Other crimes. The Disciplinary Committee may, pursuant to LR 705.1, refer to counsel for investigation and initiation of disciplinary proceedings any attorney who has been convicted of any crime other than a serious crime.

3. *Discipline imposed by other courts.* a. Attorney's duty to disclose. Any attorney admitted to practice before this Court shall, upon being subjected to public discipline by any other Court of the United States or the District of Columbia, or by a court of any state, territory, commonwealth or possession of the United States, promptly inform the Clerk of this Court of such action.

b. Notification to attorney. Upon the filing of a certified or exemplified copy of a judgment or order demonstrating that an attorney admitted to practice before this Court has been disciplined by another Court, this Court shall forthwith issue a notice directed to the attorney containing:

(i) a copy of the judgment or order from the other court;

(ii) an order immediately suspending the attorney, in the event the discipline imposed by the other Court consists of suspension or disbarment; and

(iii) an order directing the attorney to show cause within 30 days after service of the order why the imposition of identical discipline by this Court would be unwarranted.

c. Stay. In the event the discipline imposed in the other jurisdiction has been stayed there, any reciprocal discipline imposed in this Court shall be deferred until such stay expires.

d. Imposition of identical discipline. This Court shall impose the identical discipline imposed by the other Court unless the respondent-attorney demonstrates, or this Court finds, that upon the face of the record upon which the discipline in another jurisdiction is predicated it clearly appears:

(i) that the procedure was so lacking in notice or opportunity to be heard as to constitute a deprivation of due process; or

(ii) that there was such an infirmity of proof establishing the misconduct as to give rise to the clear conviction that this Court could not, consistent with its duty, accept as final the conclusion of the other Court on that subject; or

(iii) that the imposition of the same discipline by this Court would result in grave injustice; or

(iv) that the misconduct established is deemed by this Court to warrant substantially different discipline.

Where this Court determines that any of said elements exist, it shall enter such other order as it deems appropriate.

4. *Reinstatement.* a. When court order required. An attorney suspended for three months or less shall be automatically reinstated at the end of the period of suspension upon the filing with the Court of an affidavit of compliance with the provisions of the order. An attorney suspended for more than three months or disbarred may not resume practice until reinstated by order of this Court.

b. Time of application following disbarment. A person who has been disbarred after hearing or by consent may not apply for reinstatement until the expiration of at least five years from the effective date of the disbarment.

c. Hearing on application. Petitions for reinstatement by a disbarred or suspended attorney shall be filed with the Chief Judge of this Court. Upon receipt of the petition, the Chief Judge may promptly refer the petition to counsel and shall assign the matter for prompt hearing before one or more Judges of this Court, provided however that if the disciplinary proceeding was predicated upon the complaint of a Judge of this Court the hearing shall be conducted before a panel of three other Judges of this Court appointed by the Chief Judge, or, if there are less than three Judges eligible to serve or the Chief Judge was the complainant, by a panel appointed by the Chief Judge of the Court of Appeals of the Fourth Circuit. The Judge or Judges assigned to the matter shall, within 30 days after referral, schedule a hearing at which the petitioner shall have the burden of demonstrating by clear and convincing evidence that he has the moral qualifications, competency and learning in the law required for admission to practice law before this Court and that his resumption of the practice of law will not be detrimental to the integrity and standing of the Bar or to the administration of justice, or subversive of the public interest.

d. Appointment of counsel. The Court may, pursuant to LR 105.1, appoint counsel to investigate whether the petition for reinstatement should be granted and to participate in the reinstatement hearing.

e. Conditions of reinstatement. If the petitioner is found unfit to resume the practice of law, the petition shall be dismissed. If the petitioner is found fit to resume the practice of law, the Court may enter an order of reinstatement, provided that the order may make reinstatement conditional upon the payment of all or part of the costs of the proceedings, and upon the making of partial or complete restitution to parties harmed by the petitioner whose conduct led to the suspension or disbarment. Provided further, that if the petitioner has been suspended or disbarred for five years or more, reinstatement may be conditioned upon the furnishing of proof of competency and learning in the law, which proof may include certification by the bar examiners of a state or other jurisdiction of the attorney's successful completion of an examination for admission to practice subsequent to the date of suspension or disbarment.

f. Successive petitions. No petition for reinstatement shall be filed within one year following an adverse judgment upon a petition for reinstatement filed by or on behalf of the same person.

5. *Dissemination of information.* a. To other courts. Whenever it appears that any person convicted of any crime or disbarred or suspended or censured or disbarred on consent by this Court is admitted to practice law in any other jurisdiction or before any other court, the Clerk of this Court shall, within ten days of the conviction, disbarment, suspension, censure, or disbarment on consent, transmit to the disciplinary authority in such other jurisdiction, or for such other court, a certificate of the conviction or a certified or exemplified copy of the judgment or order of disbarment, suspension, censure or disbarment on consent, as well as the last known office and residence addresses of the defendant or respondent.

b. To the American Bar Association. The Clerk shall promptly notify the National Discipline Data Bank operated by the American Bar Association of any order imposing public discipline upon any attorney admitted to practice before this Court.

VIII. SUPPLEMENTAL ADMIRALTY AND MARITIME RULES.

Local Admiralty Rule (a). Scope, citation and definitions.

Local Admiralty Rule (a)(1). Scope.

These local admiralty rules apply only to civil actions that are governed by the Supplemental Rules for Certain Admiralty and Maritime Claims (Supplemental Rule or Rules). All other local rules are applicable in these cases, but to the extent that another local rule is inconsistent with the applicable local admiralty rules, the local admiralty rules shall govern.

Local Admiralty Rule (a)(2). Citation.

The local admiralty rules may be cited by the letters "LAR" and the lower case letters and numbers in parentheses that appear at the beginning of each section. The lower case letter is intended to associate the local admiralty rule with the Supplemental Rule that bears the same capital letter.

Local Admiralty Rule (a)(3). Definitions.

As used in the local admiralty rules, "Court" means a United States District Judge; "judicial officer" means a United States District Judge or a United States Magistrate Judge; "clerk of court" means the Clerk of the District Court and includes deputy clerks of court; and "Marshal" means the United States Marshal and includes deputy marshals.

Local Admiralty Rule (b). Maritime attachment and garnishment.

Local Admiralty Rule (b)(1). Affidavit that defendant is not found within the district.

The affidavit required by Supplemental Rule B(1) to accompany the complaint shall list the efforts made by and on behalf of plaintiff to find and serve the defendant within the district.

Local Admiralty Rule (b)(2). Use of state procedure.

When the plaintiff invokes a state procedure in order to attach or garnish under Fed. R. Civ. P. 4(e), the process of attachment or garnishment shall so state.

Local Admiralty Rule (c). Actions in rem: Special provisions.

Local Admiralty Rule (c)(1). Intangible property.

The summons issued pursuant to Supplemental Rule C(3) shall direct the person having control of intangible property to show cause no later than 10 days after service why the intangible property should not be delivered to the Court to abide further order of the Court. A judicial officer for good cause shown may lengthen or shorten the time. Service of the summons shall have the effect of an arrest of the intangible property and bring it within the control of the Court. Upon order of the Court, the person who is served may deliver or pay over to the Clerk of Court the intangible property proceeded against to the extent sufficient to satisfy the plaintiff's claim. If such delivery or payment is made, the person served is excused from the duty to show cause.

Local Admiralty Rule (c)(2). Publication of notice of action and arrest.

The notice required by Supplemental Rule C(4) shall be published by the Marshal at the request of the plaintiff once in a newspaper of general circulation in the city or county where the property has been seized. If the arrest or seizure occurs in Baltimore City, publication shall be made once in both The Sun and the Baltimore Afro-American newspapers. If either of these newspapers fails to publish the notice on the date or dates requested, the publication of the notice in the other newspaper shall be deemed to be sufficient compliance with this Rule, subject to the requirement of Rule C(4) of the Supplemental Rules for Certain Admiralty and Maritime Claims that public notice "be given in a newspaper of general circulation in the district." The notice shall contain:

(a) The court, title, and number of the action;

(b) The date of the arrest;

(c) The identity of the property arrested;

(d) The name, address, telephone number, and bar number of the attorney for plaintiff;

(e) A statement that the claim of a person who is entitled to possession or who claims an interest pursuant to Supplemental Rule C(6) must be filed with the Clerk and served on the attorney for plaintiff within 10 days after publication;

(f) A statement that an answer to the complaint must be filed and served within 20 days after the claim is filed, and that otherwise, default may be entered and condemnation ordered;

(g) A statement that motions to intervene under Fed. R. Civ. P. 24 by persons claiming maritime liens or other interests and claims for expenses of administration under LAR (e)(10)(d) shall be filed within a time fixed by the Court; and

(h) The name, address, and telephone number of the Marshal.

Local Admiralty Rule (c)(3). Notice requirements.

(a) *Default judgments.* A party seeking a default judgment in an action *in rem* must satisfy the judge that due notice of the action and arrest of the property has been given (1) by publication as required in LAR (c)(2), and (2) by service of the complaint and warrant of arrest upon the master or other person having custody of the property. (3) If the defendant property is a vessel documented under the laws of the United States, plaintiff must attempt to notify all persons identified as having an interest in the vessel in the United States Coast Guard Certificate of Ownership, (4) If the defendant property is a vessel numbered as provided in the Federal Boat Safety Act, plaintiff must attempt to notify the owner as named in the records of the issuing authority.

(b) *Ship Mortgage Act.* For purposes of the Ship Mortgage Act, 46 U.S.C.A. Sec. 951, notice to the Master of a vessel, or the person having physical custody thereof, by service of the Warrant of Arrest and Complaint shall be deemed in compliance with the notice requirements of such Act, as to all persons, except as to those who have recorded a notice of claim of lien.

(c) The notification requirement is satisfied by mailing copies of the warrant of arrest and complaint to the person's address using any form of mail requiring a return receipt.

Local Admiralty Rule (c)(4). Entry of default and default judgment.

After the time for filing a claim or answer has expired, the plaintiff may move for entry of default under Fed. R. Civ. P. 55(a). Default will be entered upon showing by affidavit or certificate of counsel that:

(a) Notice has been given as required by LAR (c)(3)(a) (1 and 2) and

(b) Notice has been attempted as required by LAR (c)(3)(a) (3 and 4), where appropriate, and

(c) The time for filing a claim or answer has expired, and

(d) No one has appeared to claim the property.

The plaintiff may move for judgment under Fed. R. Civ. P. 55(b) at any time after default has been entered.

Local Admiralty Rule (d). Possessory, petitory, and partition actions.

Local Admiralty Rule (d). Return date.

In an action under Supplemental Rule D, a judicial officer may order that the claim and answer be filed on a date earlier than 20 days after arrest. The order may also set a date for expedited hearing of the action.

Local Admiralty Rule (e). Actions *in rem* and *quasi in rem:* General Provisions.

Local Admiralty Rule (e)(1). Itemized demand for judgment.

The demand for judgment in every complaint filed under Supplemental Rule B or C shall allege the dollar amount of the debt or damages for which the action was commenced. The demand for judgment shall also allege the nature of other items of damage.

Local Admiralty Rule (e)(2). Salvage action complaints.

In an action for a salvage award, the complaint shall allege the dollar value of the vessel, cargo, freight, and other property salved, and the dollar amount of the award claimed.

Local Admiralty Rule (e)(3). Verification of pleadings.

Every complaint in Supplemental Rule B, C, and D actions shall be verified upon oath or solemn affirmation, or in the form provided by 28 U.S.C. Sec. 1746, by a party or by an authorized officer of a corporate party. If no party or authorized corporate officer is readily available, verification of a complaint may be made by an agent, attorney in fact, or attorney of record, who shall state the sources of the knowledge, information and belief contained in the complaint; declare that the document verified is true to the best of that knowledge, information, and belief; state why verification is not made by the party or an authorized corporate officer; and state that the affiant is authorized so to verify. A verification not made by a party or authorized corporate officer will be deemed to have been made by the party as if verified personally. If the verification was not made by a party or authorized corporate officer, any interested party may move, with or without requesting a stay, for the personal oath of a party or an authorized corporate officer, which shall be procured by commission or as otherwise ordered.

Local Admiralty Rule (e)(4). Review by judicial officer.

Unless otherwise required by the judicial officer, the review of complaints and papers called for by Supplemental Rules B(1) and C(3) does not require the affiant party or attorney to be present. Any complaint presented to a judicial officer for review shall be accompanied by a form of order to the Clerk which, upon signature by the judicial officer, shall direct the arrest, attachment, or garnishment sought by the applicant.

Local Admiralty Rule (e)(5). Instructions to the marshal.

The party who requests a warrant of arrest or process of attachment or garnishment shall provide instructions to the Marshal.

Local Admiralty Rule (e)(6). Property in possession of United States officer.

When the property to be attached or arrested is in the custody of an employee or officer of the United States, the Marshal will deliver a copy of the complaint and warrant of arrest or summons and process of attachment or garnishment to that officer or employee if present, and otherwise to the custodian of the property. The Marshal will instruct the officer or employee or custodian to retain custody of the property until ordered to do otherwise by a judicial officer.

Local Admiralty Rule (e)(7). Adversary hearing.

An adversary hearing following arrest or attachment or garnishment under Supplemental Rule E(4)(f) shall be conducted by the Court within three court days after a request for such hearing, unless otherwise ordered.

Local Admiralty Rule (e)(8). Security deposit for seizure of vessels.

The party(ies) who seeks arrest or attachment of a vessel or property aboard a vessel shall deposit with the Marshal $3,000 for vessels more than 65 feet in length overall or $500 for vessels 65 feet in length overall or less. These deposits shall be used to cover the expenses of the Marshal including, but not limited to, dockage, keepers, maintenance, and insurance. The party(ies) shall advance additional sums from time to time as requested by the Marshal to cover the estimated expenses until the property is released or disposed of as provided in Supplemental Rule E.

Local Admiralty Rule (e)(9). Intervenors' claims and sharing of Marshal's fees and expenses.

(a) *Intervention before sale.* When a vessel or other property has been arrested, attached, or garnished, and is in the hands of the Marshal or custodian substituted therefor, anyone having a claim against the vessel or property is required to present the claim by filing an intervening complaint under Fed. R. Civ. P. 24, and not by filing an original complaint, unless otherwise ordered by a judicial officer. An order permitting intervention may be signed *ex parte* at the time of filing the motion, subject to the right of any party to object to such intervention within 15 days after receipt of a copy of the motion and proposed pleading. Such motions shall not be subject to the provisions of Local Rule No. 105. Upon the signing of an order permitting intervention the Clerk shall forthwith deliver a conformed copy of the intervening complaint to the Marshal, who shall deliver the copy to the vessel or custodian of the property. Intervenors shall thereafter be subject to the rights and obligations of parties, and the vessel or property shall stand arrested, attached, or garnished by the intervenor. An intervenor shall not be required to advance a security deposit to the Marshal for seizure of a vessel as required by LAR (e)(8). Release of property arrested, attached, or garnished by an intervenor shall be done in accordance with Supplemental Rule E.

(b) *Sharing Marshal's fees and expenses before sale.* Upon motion by any party, security deposits may be ordered to be paid or shared by any party who has arrested, attached, or garnished a vessel or property aboard a vessel in amount or proportions to be determined by a judicial officer.

(c) *Intervention after sale.* After ratification of sale and payment of the purchase price, any person having a claim against the vessel or property that arose before ratification must present the same by intervening complaint, pursuant to LAR (e)(9)(a), against the proceeds of the sale and may not proceed against the vessel unless the Court shall otherwise order for good cause shown. Where an intervening complaint prays service of process *in rem,* the filing of such intervening complaint with the Clerk shall be deemed to be a claim against such proceeds without the issuance of an *in rem* process, unless the Court shall otherwise order for good cause shown. The Court shall allow a period of at least thirty (30) days after due ratification of the sale for the submission of such claims.

Local Admiralty Rule (e)(10). Custody of property.

(a) *Safekeeping of property.* When a vessel or other property is brought into the Marshal's custody by arrest or attachment, the Marshal shall arrange for adequate safekeeping, which may include the placing of keepers on or near the vessel. A substitute custodian in place of the Marshal may be appointed by order of the Court.

(b) *Employment of vessel's officers and crew by marshal.* All officers and members of the crew employed on a vessel of 750 gross tons or more shall be deemed employees of the Marshal for the period of 120 hours after the attachment or arrest of the vessel unless the Marshal, pursuant to a court order, has notified the officers and members of the crew that they are not so employed or unless the vessel is released from attachment or arrest. If the vessel is not released within 120 hours, the Marshal shall, on request of the seizing party, immediately thereafter designate which, if any, officers and members of the crew he is continuing to employ to preserve the vessel and shall promptly notify the remaining officers and members of the crew that they are no longer in his employ and are no longer in the service of the vessel and are free to depart from the vessel. The notice required by the preceding sentence shall be by written notice posted in a prominent place in each of the mess rooms or dining salons used by the officers and unlicensed personnel aboard the vessel.

(c) *Normal vessel operations and movement of the vessel.* Following arrest, attachment, or garnishment of a vessel or property aboard a vessel, normal vessel operations shall be permitted to commence or continue unless otherwise ordered by the Court. No movement of the vessel shall take place unless authorized by order of a judicial officer.

(d) *Procedure for filing claims by suppliers for payment of charges.* A person who furnishes supplies or services to a vessel, cargo, or other property in custody of the Court who has not been paid and claims the right to payment as an expense of administration shall submit an invoice to the Clerk in the form of a verified claim within the time period set by the Court for intervention after sale pursuant to LAR (e)(9)(c). The supplier must serve copies of the claim on the Marshal, substitute custodian if one has been appointed, and all parties of record. The Court may consider the claims individually or schedule a single hearing for all claims.

Local Admiralty Rule (e)(11). Sale of property.

(a) *Notice.* Notice of sale of property in an action *in rem* shall be published under such terms and conditions as set by the Court.

(b) *Payment of bid.* These provisions apply unless otherwise ordered in the order of sale: The person whose bid is accepted shall immediately pay the Marshal the full purchase price if the bid is $1,000 or less. If the bid exceeds $1,000, the bidder shall immediately pay a deposit of at least $1,000 or 10% of the bid, whichever is greater, and shall pay the balance within three days after the day on which the bid was accepted. If an objection to the sale is filed within that three-day period, the bidder is excused from paying the balance of the purchase price until three court days after the sale is confirmed. Payment shall be made in cash, by certified check, or by cashier's check.

(c) *Default.* If the successful bidder does not pay the balance of the purchase price within the time allowed, the bidder is deemed to be in default. In such a case, the judicial officer may accept the second highest bid or arrange a new sale. The defaulting bidder's deposit shall be forfeited and applied to any additional costs incurred by the Marshal because of the default, the balance being retained in the registry of the Court awaiting its order.

(d) *Report of sale by marshal.* At the conclusion of the sale, the Marshal shall forthwith file a written report with the Court of the fact of sale, the date, the price obtained, the name and address of the successful bidder, and any other pertinent information.

(e) *Time and procedure for objection to sale.* An interested person may object to the sale by filing a written objection with the Clerk within three court days following the sale, serving the objection on all parties of record, the successful bidder, and the Marshal, and depositing such sum with the Marshal as determined by him to be sufficient to pay the expense of keeping the property for at least seven days. Payment to the Marshal shall be in cash, certified check, or cashier's check.

(f) *Confirmation of sale.* A sale shall be confirmed by order of the Court within five court days, but no sooner than three court days, after the sale. If an objection to the sale has been filed, the Court shall hold a hearing on the confirmation of the sale. The Marshal shall transfer title to the purchaser upon the order of the Court.

(g) *Disposition of deposits.* (1) Objection Sustained. If an objection is sustained, sums deposited by the successful bidder will be returned to the bidder forthwith. The sum deposited by the objector will be applied to pay the fees and expenses incurred by the Marshal in keeping the property until it is resold, and any balance remaining shall be returned to the objector. The objector will be reimbursed for the expense of keeping the property from the proceeds of a subsequent sale.

(2) Objection Overruled. If the objection is overruled, the sum deposited by the objector will be applied to pay the expense of keeping the property from the day the objection was filed until the day the sale is confirmed, and any balance remaining will be returned to the objector forthwith.

Local Admiralty Rule (e)(12). Discharge of stipulations for value and other security.

When an order is entered in any cause marking the case "Dismissed" or "Agreed and Settled," or "Agreed, Settled and Satisfied," the entry shall operate as a cancellation of all stipulations for value or other security provided to release the property seized that were filed in the case, unless otherwise provided in the order or by the Court.

Local Admiralty Rule (f). Limitation of liability.

Local Admiralty Rule (f). Security for costs.

The amount of security for costs under Supplemental Rule F(1) shall be $1,000, and it may be combined with the security for value and interest, unless otherwise ordered.

APPENDIX A
DISCOVERY GUIDELINES OF THE UNITED STATES DISTRICT COURT FOR THE DISTRICT OF MARYLAND.

Adopted September 11, 1995

Guideline 1. Conduct of discovery.

a) The purpose of these Guidelines is to facilitate the just, speedy, and inexpensive conduct of discovery in all civil cases before the Court, and these Guidelines will be construed and administered accordingly with respect to all attorneys, parties, and non-parties involved in discovery of civil cases before this Court.

b) Compliance with these Guidelines will be considered by the Court in resolving discovery disputes including whether sanctions should be awarded pursuant to Fed. R. Civ. P. 37.

c) Attorneys are expected to behave professionally and with courtesy towards all involved in the discovery process, including but not limited to opposing counsel, parties and non-parties.

d) Whenever possible attorneys are expected to communicate with each other in good faith throughout the discovery process to resolve disputes without the need for intervention by the Court. In the event that such good faith efforts are unsuccessful, they should be promptly referred to the Court for resolution.

e) To the extent that any part of these Guidelines is considered by the Court to conflict with any Federal Rule of Civil Procedure, Local Rule of this Court, or order of this Court in a particular case, then the conflicting rule or order should be considered to be governing.

Guideline 2. Stipulations setting discovery deadlines.

a) Subject to approval by the Court, attorneys are encouraged to enter into written discovery stipulations to supplement the Court's scheduling order.

Guideline 3. Expert witness fees.

a) Unless counsel agree that each party will pay its own experts, the party taking an expert witness's deposition ordinarily pays the expert's fee for the time spent in deposition and related travel. *See* Local Rule 104.11.a. Accordingly, counsel for the party that designated the expert witness should try to assure that the fee charged by the expert to the party taking the deposition is fair and reasonable. In the event a dispute arises as to the reasonableness or other aspects of an expert's fee, counsel should promptly confer and attempt in good faith to resolve the dispute without the involvement of the Court. If counsel are unsuccessful, the expert's deposition shall proceed on the date noted, unless the Court orders otherwise, and the dispute respecting payment shall be brought to the Court's attention promptly. The factors that may be considered in determining whether a fee is reasonable include, but are not limited to: (1) the expert's area of expertise; (2) the expert's education and training; (3) the fee being charged to the party who designated the expert; and (4) the fees ordinarily charged by the expert for non-litigation services, such as office consultations with patients or clients.

b) Recognizing that a treating physician may be considered both a fact witness and an expert, the Court has chosen to impose a specific limitation on the fee a treating physician may charge to either party. It is implicit in Rule 104.11.b, which requries counsel to estimate the hours of deposition time required, that the physician may charge a fee for the entire time he or she reserved in accordance with the estimate, even if counsel conclude the deposition early. Further, unless the physician received notice at least two business days in advance of a cancellation, the physician is entitled to be paid for any time reserved that cannot reasonably be filled. Every effort should be made to schedule depositions at a time convenient for the witness, and to use videotaped *de bene esse* depositions rather than requiring the physician's presence at trial. Note that the Rule does not limit the reasonable fee a treating physician may charge if required to testify in court.

Guideline 4. Guidelines in scheduling depositions.

a) Attorneys are expected to make a good faith effort to coordinate deposition dates with opposing counsel, parties, and non-party deponents, prior to noting a deposition.

b) Before agreeing to a deposition date, an attorney is expected to attempt to clear the date with his/her client if the client is a deponent, or wishes to attend the deposition, and with any witnesses the attorney agrees to attempt to produce at the deposition without the need to have the witness served with a subpoena.

c) An agreed upon deposition date is presumptive binding. An attorney seeking to change an agreed upon date has a duty to coordinate a new date before changing the agreed date.

Guideline 5. Deposition questioning, objections and procedure.

a) An attorney should not intentionally ask a witness a question that misstates or mischaracterizes the witness' previous answer.

b) During the taking of a deposition it is presumptively improper for an attorney to make objections which are not consistent with Fed. R. Civ. P. 30(d)(1). Objections should be stated as simply, concisely and non-argumentatively as possible to avoid coaching or making suggestions to the deponent, and to minimize interruptions in the questioning of the deponent (for example: "objection, leading"; "objection, asked and answered"; "objection, compound question"; "objection, form"). If an attorney desires to make an objection for the record during the taking of a deposition that reasonably could have the effect of coaching or suggesting to the deponent how to answer, then the deponent, at the request of any of the attorneys present, or, at the request of a party if unrepresented by an attorney, shall be excused from the deposition during the making of the objection.

c) An attorney should not repeatedly ask the same or substantially identical question of a deponent if the question already has been asked and fully and responsively answered by the deponent. Upon objection by counsel for the deponent, or by the deponent if unrepresented, it is presumptively improper for an attorney to continue to ask the same or substantially identical question of a witness unless the previous answer was evasive or incomplete.

d) It is presumptively improper to instruct a witness not to answer a question during the taking of a deposition unless under the circumstances permitted by Fed. R. Civ. P. 30(d)(1). However, it is also presumptively improper to ask questions clearly beyond the scope of discovery permitted by Fed. R. Civ. P. 26(b)(1), particularly of a personal nature, and continuing to do so after objection shall be evidence that the deposition is being conducted in bad faith or in such a manner as unreasonably to annoy, embarrass or oppress the deponent or party, which is prohibited by Fed. R. Civ. P. 30(d)(3).

e) If requested to supply an explanation as to the basis for an objection, the objecting attorney should do so, consistent with Guideline 5(b) above.

f) While the interrogation of the deponent is in progress neither an attorney nor the deponent should initiate a private conversation except for the purpose of determining whether a privilege should be asserted. To do so otherwise is presumptively improper.

g) During breaks in the taking of a deposition no one should discuss with the deponent the substance of the prior testimony given by the deponent during the deposition. Counsel for the deponent may discuss with the deponent at such time whether a privilege should be asserted or otherwise engage in discussion not regarding the substance of the witness's prior testimony.

h) Unless otherwise ordered by the Court, the following persons may, without advance notice, attend a deposition: individual parties; a representative of non-individual parties; and expert witnesses of parties. Except for the persons identified above, counsel shall notify other parties not later than five (5) business days before the taking of a deposition if counsel desires to have a non-party present during a deposition. If the parties are unable to agree to the attendance of this person, then the person shall not be entitled to attend the deposition unless the party desiring to have the person attend obtains a Court order permitting him/her to do so. Unless ordered by the Court, however, a dispute regarding who may attend a deposition shall not be grounds for delaying the deposition. All persons present during the taking of a deposition should be identified on the record before the deposition begins.

i) Except for the person recording the deposition in accordance with Fed. R. Civ. P. 30(b), during the taking of a deposition no one may record the testimony without the consent of the deponent and all parties in attendance, unless otherwise ordered by the Court.

Intent of section (c). — Section (c) of this guideline was intended to strike a balance between an attorney's right to continue an inquiry where a deponent's response is evasive or incomplete with the defending attorney's legitimate desire to prevent the deposing attorney from employing the abusive tactic of repeatedly asking the same, or substantially the same, question, despite having received a complete and nonevasive answer. Boyd v. University of Md. Med. Sys., 173 F.R.D. 143 (D. Md. 1997).

Guideline 6. Assertions of privilege at depositions.

a) When a claim of privilege is asserted during a deposition, and information is not provided on the basis of such assertion:

i) In accordance with Fed. R. Civ. P. 26(b)(5) the person asserting the privilege shall identify during the deposition the nature of the privilege (including work product) that is being claimed.

ii) After a claim of privilege has been asserted, the person seeking disclosure shall have reasonable latitude during the deposition to question the witness to establish other relevant information concerning the assertion of privilege, including: (i) the applicability of the particular privilege being asserted; (ii) any circumstances which may constitute an exception to the assertion of the privilege; (iii) any circumstances which may result in the privilege having been waived; and (iv) any circumstances that may overcome a claim of qualified privilege. In accordance with Fed. R. Civ. P. 26(b)(5) the party asserting the privilege, in providing the foregoing information, shall not be required to reveal the information which is itself privileged or protected from disclosure.

Guideline 7. Making a record of improper conduct during a deposition.

Upon request of any attorney, party unrepresented by an attorney, or the deponent if unrepresented by an attorney, the person recording the deposition in accordance with Fed. R. Civ. P. 30(b) shall enter on the record a description by the requesting person of conduct of any attorney, party, or person attending the deposition which violates these guidelines, the Federal Rule of Civil Procedure, or the Local Rules of this Court.

Guideline 8. Delay in responding to discovery requests.

a) *Interrogatories, requests for production of documents and requests for admission of facts and genuineness of documents.* The Federal Rules of Civil Procedure designate the time prescribed for responding to interrogatories, requests for production of documents, and requests for admission of facts and genuineness of documents. Nothing contained in these guidelines modifies the time limits prescribed by the Federal Rules of Civil Procedure. Attorneys shall make good faith efforts to respond to discovery requests within the time prescribed by those rules.

Absent exigent circumstances, attorneys seeking additional time to respond to discovery requests shall contact opposing counsel as soon as practical after receipt of the discovery request, but not later than three days before the response is due. In multiple party cases, the attorney wanting additional time shall contact the attorney for the party propounding the discovery.

A request for additional time which does not conflict with a scheduling deadline imposed by the Federal Rules of Civil Procedure, the Local Rules of this Court or a Court order should not be unreasonably refused. If a request for additional time is granted, the requesting party shall promptly prepare a writing which memorializes the agreement which shall be served on all parties but need not be submitted to the Court for approval.

Unless otherwise provided by the Local Rules of this Court, no stipulation which modifies a Court-imposed deadline shall be deemed effective unless and until the Court approves the stipulation.

b) *Depositions.* Unless otherwise ordered by the Court or agreed upon by the parties, eleven days notice shall be deemed to be "reasonable notice" within the meaning of Fed. R. Civ. P. 30(b)(1), for the noting of depositions.

Guideline 9. Guidelines concerning interrogatories, requests for production of documents, answers to interrogatories and written responses to document requests.

a) A party may object to an interrogatory, document request, or part thereof, while simultaneously providing partial or incomplete answers to the request. If a partial or incomplete answer is provided, the answering party shall state that the answer is partial or incomplete.

b) No part of an interrogatory or document request should be left unanswered merely because an objection is interposed to another part of the interrogatory or document request.

c) In accordance with Fed. R. Civ. P. 26(b)(5), where a claim of privilege is asserted in objecting to any interrogatory, document request, or part thereof, and information is not provided on the basis of such assertion:

i) The party asserting the privilege shall, in the objection to the interrogatory, document request, or part thereof, identify with specificity the nature of the privilege (including work product) that is being claimed;

ii) The following information should be provided in the objection, if known or reasonably available, unless divulging such information would cause disclosure of the allegedly privileged information;

(a) For oral communications:

(i) the name of the person making the communication and the names of persons present while the communication was made, and where not apparent, the relationship of the persons present to the person making the communication;

(ii) the date and place of the communication; and

(iii) the general subject matter of the communication.

(b) For documents:

(i) the type of document;

(ii) the general subject matter of the document;

(iii) the date of the document; and

(iv) such other information as is sufficient to identify the document, including, where appropriate, the author, addressee, custodian, and any other recipient of the document, and where not apparent, the relationship of the author, addressee, custodian, and any other recipient to each other.

iii) Within twenty days after the receipt of the information contained in paragraph (ii), the party seeking disclosure of the information withheld may serve a motion to compel in accordance with the Local Rule 104.8.

d) In addition to paper copies, parties are encouraged, but not required, to exchange discovery requests and responses on computer disk in an ASCII or other commonly-accepted format if requested in order to reduce the clerical effort required to prepare responses and motions.

APPENDIX B
RULES AND GUIDELINES FOR DETERMINING
LODESTAR ATTORNEYS' FEES IN CIVIL
RIGHTS AND DISCRIMINATION CASES.[1]

1. *Mandatory rules regarding billing format, time recordation, and submission of quarterly statements.* a. Time shall be recorded by specific task and lawyer or other professional performing the task as set forth more fully in Local Rule 109.2.b.

b. Fee application, accompanied by time records, shall be submitted in the following format organized by litigation phase.[2]

Case development, background investigation and case administration (Includes initial investigations, file setup, preparation of budgets, and routine communications with client, co-counsel, opposing counsel, and the court)

Pleadings

Interrogatories, document production and other discovery

Depositions (Includes time spent preparing for depositions)

Motions practice

Attending court hearings

Trial preparation and post-trial motions

Attending trial

ADR

Fee petition preparation

c. Counsel for a party intending to seek fees if the party prevails shall submit to opposing counsel quarterly statements showing the amount of time spent on the case and the total value of that time. These statements need not be in the "litigation phase" format provided in Guideline 1.02 or otherwise reflect how time has been spent. The first such statement is due at the end of the first quarter in which the action is filed.

d. Upon request by the judicial officer (or private mediator agreed upon by the parties) presiding over a settlement conference, counsel for all parties (with the exception of public lawyers who do not ordinarily keep time records)

---

1. These rules and guidelines apply to cases in which a prevailing party would be entitled to reasonable attorneys' fees under 42 U.S.C. section 1988(b) and to cases brought under Title VII of the Civil Rights Act of 1964, the Age Discrimination in Employment Act, the Equal Pay Act, the Americans With Disabilities Act, the Rehabilitation Act, the Individuals With Disabilities Education Act, the Family and Medical Leave Act and equivalent statutes. They do not apply to Social Security Cases.

2. In general, preparation time and travel time should be reported under the category to which they relate. For example, time spent preparing for and traveling to and from a court hearing should be recorded under the category "Court hearings." Factual investigation should also be listed under the specific category to which it relates. For example, time spent with a witness to obtain an affidavit for a summary judgment motion or opposition should be included under the category "Motions practice." Similarly, a telephone conversation or a meeting with a client held for the purpose of preparing interrogatory answers should be included under the category "Interrogatories, document production and other written discovery." Of course, each of these tasks must be separately recorded in the back-up documentation in accordance with Guideline 1.01.

shall turn over to that officer (or mediator) statements of time and the value of that time in the "litigation phase" format provided in Guideline 1.02.

e. If during the course of a fee award dispute a judicial officer orders that the billing records of counsel for the party opposing fees must be turned over to the party requesting fees, those billing records shall be submitted in the "litigation phase" format.

2. *Guidelines re compensable and non-compensable time.* a. Where plaintiffs with both common and conflicting interests are represented by different lawyers, there shall be a lead attorney for each task (e.g., preparing for and speaking at depositions on issues of common interest and preparing pleadings, motions, and memorandum), and other lawyers shall be compensated only to the extent that they provide input into the activity directly related to their own client's interests.

b. Only one lawyer for each separately represented party shall be compensated for attending depositions.[3]

c. Only one lawyer for each party shall be compensated for client and third party conferences.

d. Only one lawyer for each party shall be compensated for attending hearings.[4]

e. Generally, only one lawyer is to be compensated for intra-office conferences. If during such a conference one lawyer is seeking the advice of another lawyer, the time may be charged at the rate of the more senior lawyer. Compensation may be paid for the attendance of more than one lawyer at periodic conferences of defined duration held for the purpose of work organization and delegation of tasks in cases where such conferences are reasonably necessary for the proper management of the litigation.

f. Travel. i. Whenever possible time spent in traveling should be devoted to doing substantive work for a client and should be billed (at the usual rate) to that client. If the travel time is devoted to work for a client other than the matter for which fees are sought, then the travel time should not be included in any fee request. If the travel time is devoted to substantive work for the

---

3. Departure from this guideline would be appropriate upon a showing of a valid reason for sending two attorneys to the deposition, e.g. that the less senior attorney's presence is necessary because he organized numerous documents important to the deposition but the deposition is of a critical witness whom the more senior attorney should properly depose. Departure from the guideline also would be appropriate upon a showing that more than one retained attorney representing the defendant attended the deposition and charged the time for her attendance. (If two lawyers from a public law office representing a defendant attend a deposition, the court should consider this fact and the role played by the second lawyer, i.e., whether she provided assistance, including representation of a separate public agency or individual defendant, or was present for merely educational purposes, in determining whether plaintiff should also be compensated for having a second lawyer attend.)

4. The same considerations discussed in footnote 3 concerning attendance by more than one lawyer at a deposition also apply to attendance by more than one lawyer at a hearing. There is no guideline as to whether more than one lawyer for each party is to be compensated for attending trial. This must depend upon the complexity of the case and the role that each lawyer is playing. For example, if a junior lawyer is present at trial primarily for for the purpose of organizing documents but takes a minor witness for educational purposes, consideration should be given to billing her time at a paralegal's rate.

client whose representation is the subject of the fee request, then the time should be billed for the substantive work, not travel time.

ii. Up to 2 hours of travel time (each way and each day) to and from a court appearance, deposition, witness interview, or similar proceeding that cannot be devoted to substantive work may be charged at the lawyer's usual rate.

iii. Time spent in long-distance travel above the 2 hours limit each way that cannot be devoted to substantive work, may be charged at one-half of the lawyer's usual rate.

3. *Guidelines re hourly rates.*[5]. a. Lawyers admitted to the bar for less than eight years: $ 135-170.

b. Lawyers admitted to the bar for more than eight years: $ 190-225.

c. Paralegals and law clerks: $ 65.

4. *Reimbursable expenses.* a. Generally, reasonable out-of-pocket expenses (including long-distance telephone calls, express and overnight delivery services, computerized on-line research and faxes) are compensable at actual cost.

b. Mileage is compensable at 0.30 per mile.

c. In-house copying is compensable at 0.15 per page; commercial copying is compensable at actual cost.

---

5. These rates are intended solely to provide practical guidance to lawyers and judges when requesting, challenging and awarding fees. The factors established by case law obviously govern over them. However, the guidelines may serve to make the fee petition less onerous by narrowing the debate over the range of a reasonable hourly rate in many cases. The guidelines were derived by informally surveying members of the bar concerning hourly rates paid on the defense side in employment discrimination and civil rights cases and adding an upward adjustment to account for the risk of nonpayment faced by a plaintiff's lawyer in the event that her client does not prevail. The guideline rates also are generally comparable to those applied by the court in several recent cases involving the award of fees to plaintiffs' counsel after considering affidavits submitted in support of such rates. They do not apply to cases governed by the Prison Litigation Reform Act, which sets an hourly rate by statute.

APPENDIX C
REGULATIONS GOVERNING THE REIMBURSEMENT
OF EXPENSES IN PRO BONO CASES IN THE
UNITED STATES DISTRICT COURT FOR
THE DISTRICT OF MARYLAND.

I. *Eligibility for Reimbursement.* When an attorney has been appointed to represent an indigent party in a civil matter before this Court, that attorney shall be allowed to petition the Court for reimbursement of out-of-pocket expenses, hereinafter defined, incurred in the preparation and presentation of said matter, subject to these regulations. The limit applicable to such expenses, as contained in this Court's Admissions' Fund Plan, is Five Hundred ($500.00) dollars.

II. *Restrictions on Eligibility.* A. Any costs that are either waived or recoverable under the provisions of Title 18, U.S. Code or Title 28, U.S. Code or which have been recovered under any other plan of reimbursement shall not be reimbursed from the Admissions Fund.

B. In no case shall an appointed attorney for a party who has been awarded costs and/or fees pursuant to a judgment in a suit before this Court be eligible for reimbursement of costs and/or fees from the Admissions Fund.

C. Only those costs associated with the preparation or presentation of a civil action in the United States District Court for the District of Maryland shall be approved for reimbursement. No costs associated with the preparation or presentation of an appeal to the U.S. Court of Appeals or the U.S. Supreme Court shall be reimbursed from the Admissions Fund.

III. *Procedures for Petitioning for Reimbursement.* A. Within thirty (30) days of the entry of a judgment in a case in which an attorney is appointed and the attorney is not otherwise ineligible under these regulations, the appointed attorney shall file with the presiding Judicial Officer a request for reimbursement of costs incurred in the preparation of the case on a form approved by the Court and available from the Clerk. Where it is considered necessary and appropriate, the presiding Judicial Officer may approve an interim reimbursement of extraordinary and substantial expenses incurred in the appointed case.

B. In cases in which an appointed attorney has withdrawn or has been dismissed prior to the entry of a judgment, that attorney shall file a request for reimbursement within thirty (30) days of such withdrawal or dismissal. Any work product obtained with expenditures from the Admissions Fund shall subsequently be provided to the newly-appointed counsel or, where no new counsel is appointed, to the party for whom counsel was appointed.

C. In cases where interim reimbursements are approved and paid and appointed counsel subsequently recovers previously reimbursed expenses, counsel shall, with [within] thirty (30) days from said recovery, return to the Admissions Fund an amount up to the amount previously reimbursed, depending on the amount of the recovery.

IV. *Reimbursable Expenses.* The following out-of-pocket expenses may be reimbursed upon approval by the presiding Judicial Officer:

1. Depositions and Transcripts. The costs of transcripts or depositions shall not exceed the regular copy rate as established by the Judicial Conference of the United States and in effect at the time any transcript or deposition was taken, unless some rate was previously provided for by order of court. Except as otherwise ordered by the Court, only the cost of the original of any transcript shall be allowed. In a deposition noted by appointed counsel only the cost of an original will be allowed. In a deposition noted by one of the other parties, only the cost of one copy will be allowed. In the interest of efficiency and recognizing the use of audio tapes, counsel are encouraged to use audio tape for depositions. If audio tape depositions are used and transcription of those tapes is performed by counsel's office staff, the Court may reimburse counsel at a rate not to exceed one-half the regular copy rate per page as established by the Judicial Conference of the United States and in effect at the time the deposition [is] taken.

2. Investigative, Expert or Other Services. A. Counsel may request (in an *ex parte* application) investigative, expert or other services necessary for the adequate preparation of a matter. The Court, upon finding after appropriate *ex parte* inquiry that the services are necessary, may authorize them.

B. Without prior request, counsel may obtain, subject to later review, investigative, expert or other services necessary for the adequate preparation of the case. Counsel should note that approval of this type of expenditure is not automatic and should be prepared to defend his or her reasons for not requesting prior approval.

C. The maximum total compensation to be paid to a person for investigative, expert or other services shall not exceed the sum of Five Hundred ($500.00) Dollars.

3. Travel Expenses. Travel by privately owned car, for trips in excess of 50 miles (each way), may be claimed at the then current rate prescribed for federal judiciary employees who use a private car for official business, plus parking fees, tolls and similar expenses.

4. Service of Papers/Witness Fees. Fees for service of papers and the appearance of witnesses that are not otherwise avoided, waived or recoverable may be reimbursed from the Admissions Fund.

5. Interpreter Services. Costs of interpreter services not otherwise avoided, waived or recoverable may be reimbursed from the Admissions Fund.

6. Photocopies, Photographs, Telephone Toll Calls, etc. Actual out-of-pocket expenses incurred for items such as photocopying, photographs, toll calls and telegrams necessary for the preparation of the case may be reimbursed from the Admissions Fund.

7. Other Expenses. Expenses other than those in sections one through six, above, may be approved by the presiding Judicial Officer. No single expense under this section exceeding $100.00 shall be reimbursed unless approval was obtained from the presiding Judicial Officer (*ex parte*) prior to the expenditure. When requesting reimbursement under this section, a detailed description of the expenses should be attached to the petition filed with the Judicial Officer.

V. *Restrictions on Reimbursement.* A. General office expenses, including personnel costs, rent, telephone services, secretarial help (see exception in section IV., 1) office photocopying equipment, and any other general expenses that would normally be reflected in a fee charged to a client are not reimburseable from the Admissions Fund.

B. The presiding Judicial Officer may disallow reimbursement for any expense based upon the absence of documentation.

C. The presiding Judicial Officer may disallow reimbursement of expenses if he or she determines that appointed counsel did not pursue reasonable courses of recovery of expenses, including seeking statutorily permitted costs and fees, prior to application for reimbursement from the Admissions Fund.

D. Under no circumstances shall Admissions Fund funds be authorized to pay for costs or fees taxed against a party or appointed counsel, as a result of a Court ruling or as part of a judgment obtained by an adverse party in a civil action before this Court.

E. The maximum amount that may be reimbursed from the Admissions Fund is Five Hundred ($500.00) Dollars.

VI. *Miscellaneous.* It is the policy of this Court to require and encourage members of its Bar to represent parties who cannot afford counsel. In furtherance of this policy and in addition to the CLE and other educational programs listed in this Court's Admissions Fund Plan, the Advisory Committee may in its discretion authorize the use of funds as a reward and/or inducement to members of the Bar of this Court who accept appointments to represent indigent parties.

Approved by the Judges at the Bench Meeting of January 20, 1985. Amendments to change Judge to Judicial Officer in Sections III, A., IV, 1 & 2 and V, B & C approved at the Bench Meeting of February 12, 1985. Amendment to change level of payment from $300.00 to $500.00 approved by the Advisory Committee and the Bench on November 4, 1987.

Index to Rules of the U.S. District Court for the District of Maryland

973

CIVIL PRACTICE —Cont'd
Interrogatories —Cont'd
Responses.
Format, Rule 104.
Judgments.
Instructions.
Pretrial procedure.
Submission, Rule 106.
Judgment by confession, Rule 108.
Magistrate judges.
Authority of generally, Rule 301.
Motions, Rule 105.
Attorneys' fees.
Motions requesting, Rule 109.
Discovery.
Motions to compel, Rule 104.
Judgment by confession, Rule 108.
Multi-district litigation.
Special proceedings, Rule 112.
Notice.
Judgment by confession.
Notice to defendants, Rule 108.
Orders.
Pretrial order, Rule 106.
Scheduling orders, Rule 103.
Settlement orders, Rule 111.
Pleadings, Rule 103.
Amendment of pleadings, Rule 103.
Pretrial proceedings, Rule 106.
Prisoners.
Civil rights actions.
Attorneys' fees guidelines, Appx. B.
Special proceedings, Rule 112.
Production of documents and things.
Discovery guidelines, Appx. A.
Requests for production.
Limitation, Rule 104.
Responses.
Format, Rule 104.
Removal of cases, Rule 103.
Scheduling orders, Rule 103.
Service of process, Rule 102.
Judgment by confession.
Notice to defendants, Rule 108.
Prisoners' civil rights actions, Rule 112.
Proof of service, Rule 102.
Waiver procedure.
Notice to clerk, Rule 103.
When served by marshal, Rule 103.
Settlements, Rule 111.
Signatures.
Papers, Rule 102.
Special proceedings, Rule 112.
Subpoenas.
Depositions.
Attorneys at law.
Appearance for obtaining, Rule 101.
Issuance in pro se, in forma pauperis cases, Rule 102.
Service of trial subpoenas, Rule 107.
Time.
Attorneys' fees.
Motions requesting.
Filing, Rule 109.

CIVIL PRACTICE —Cont'd
Time —Cont'd
Bill of costs.
Filing, Rule 109.
Extension of time.
Motions, Rule 105.
Trial.
Limitations of time, Rule 107.
Trial, Rule 107.
Verdict.
Directed verdict.
Waiver of motion.
No waiver by introduction of evidence, Rule 107.
Witnesses.
Examination of witnesses, Rule 107.
One attorney per witness, Rule 107.
Exclusion of witnesses, Rule 107.
CIVIL RIGHTS CASES.
Attorney fee guidelines, Appx. B.
Prisoners' civil rights actions, Rule 112.
CLERKS OF COURT.
Office of clerk.
Hours of operation, Rule 504.
"Night box," Rule 504.
COLLATERAL.
Forfeiture.
Magistrate judges, Rule 304.
CONDEMNATION.
Civil practice.
Special proceedings, Rule 112.
CONDUCT IN COURTROOM.
Civil practice.
Trial etiquette, Rule 107.
CONFERENCES.
Pretrial conferences.
Exemptions, Rule 103.
CONFIDENTIALITY.
Attorney disciplinary proceedings, Rule 705.
Criminal practice.
Sentencing.
Presentence and probation records, Rule 213.
Discovery.
Proposed confidentiality orders, Rule 104.
CONTEMPT.
Attorneys at law.
Failure to appear.
Fines.
Power to punish for contempt not limited, Rule 602.
Cameras and recording devices.
Violation of prohibition, Rule 506.
Financial disclosure report.
Request for.
Misuse of report, Rule 511.
COPIES.
Complaints.
Submission to clerk, Rule 103.
Court papers, Rule 507.

MAGISTRATE JUDGES —Cont'd
Infractions.
Authority, Rule 301.
Jurisdiction, Rule 301.
Masters.
Designation as special master, Rule 301.
Petty offenses.
Collateral.
Forfeiture, Rule 304.

MARITIME.
Supplemental admiralty and maritime rules.
See ADMIRALTY AND MARITIME RULES.

MARSHALS.
Admiralty and maritime rules.
Actions in rem and quasi in rem.
Instructions to marshals, LAR (e)(5).

MASS TORT ACTIONS.
Discovery, Rule 104.

MASTERS.
Magistrate judges.
Designation as special master, Rule 301.

MISDEMEANORS.
Criminal practice.
Sentencing in misdemeanor cases, Rule 213.

MOTIONS.
Attorneys' fees.
Civil practice.
Motions requesting, Rule 109.
Bankruptcy.
Venue.
Rules of procedure under 28 U.S.C. Section 1334.
Motions concerning venue, Rule 404.
Withdrawal of reference of certain bankruptcy proceedings.
Rules of procedure under 28 U.S.C. Section 1334, Rule 404.
Civil practice, Rule 105.
Attorneys' fees.
Motions requesting, Rule 109.
Discovery.
Motions to compel, Rule 104.
Judgment by confession, Rule 108.
Criminal practice, Rule 207.

N

NOTICE.
Admiralty and maritime rules.
Actions in rem.
Publication of notice of action and arrest, LAR (c)(2).
Requirements, LAR (c)(3).
Amendment of rules, Rule 605.
Civil practice.
Judgment by confession.
Notice to defendants, Rule 108.

O

ORDERS.
Civil practice.
Pretrial order, Rule 106.
Scheduling orders, Rule 103.
Settlement orders, Rule 111.
Widely publicized and sensational cases.
Special orders, Rule 603.

P

PARTITION ACTIONS.
Admiralty and maritime rules.
Return date, LAR (d).

PATENT INFRINGEMENT ACTIONS.
Discovery, Rule 104.

PETITIONS.
Attorneys at law.
Admission of attorneys, Rule 701.
Student practice, Rule 702.

PETTY OFFENSES.
Magistrate judges.
Collateral.
Forfeiture, Rule 304.

PHOTOGRAPHING COURT PROCEEDINGS, Rule 506.

PHYSICIANS.
Discovery fees, Appx. A. Rule 104.

PLEADINGS.
Admiralty and maritime rules.
Actions in rem and quasi in rem.
Verification of pleadings, LAR (e)(3).
Bankruptcy.
Filing of pleadings.
Rules of procedure under 28 U.S.C. Section 1334, Rule 404.
Civil practice, Rule 103.
Amendment of pleadings, Rule 103.

PRETRIAL CONFERENCES.
Exemptions, Rule 103.

PRETRIAL PROCEEDINGS.
Civil practice, Rule 106.
Criminal practice, Rule 210.
Release of information by attorneys, Rule 204.

PRISONERS.
Civil practice.
Civil rights actions.
Attorney fee guidelines, Appx. B.
Special proceedings, Rule 112.

PRIVILEGED COMMUNICATIONS.
Assertion of privilege at deposition, Appx. A.

PROBATION.
Criminal practice.
Confidentiality of probation records, Rule 213.

UNITED STATES BANKRUPTCY COURT FOR THE DISTRICT OF MARYLAND LOCAL BANKRUPTCY RULES

LOCAL BANKRUPTCY RULES

Effective May 1, 1997, with amendments received through November 1, 1997.

IN THE UNITED STATES BANKRUPTCY COURT FOR THE DISTRICT OF MARYLAND

LOCAL BANKRUPTCY RULES

PART I.

Rule 1002-1. Petition — General.

(a) *Rejection of certain deficient petitions.* The Clerk may not accept a petition and must reject it if:

(1) the petition is not signed with an original signature;

(2) the party filing the petition neither pays the prescribed filing fee with the petition nor files with the petition an application to pay the required fee in installments, if eligible to do so;

(3) the debtor does not file the master mailing matrix with the petition, unless the debtor files completed Schedules E and F with the petition;

(4) a Chapter 11 debtor does not file the list of twenty (20) largest unsecured creditors with the petition; or

(5) the petition is submitted by a debtor who is not an individual and is not represented by an attorney who is a member of the bar of the District Court.

(6) the petition is submitted by a person who, under either 11 U.S.C. § 109(g) or an order of court, may not be a debtor at the time of the submission of the petition.

(b) *Other deficient petitions and papers — Notice of deficient filing.* The Clerk can issue a notice:

(1) specifying deficiencies — except those described in Subsection (a) — in the petition, schedules, and associated papers; and

(2) stating that the petition, schedule or associated papers may be stricken or the case dismissed if the deficiencies are not corrected within five (5) business days after the date of issuance of the deficiency notice.

(c) *Verification of authority to file — Corporations.* There must be filed with a corporate debtor's voluntary petition a certified copy of the resolution authorizing the filing of the bankruptcy petition. The resolution must show approval by the corporate body empowered by applicable law to authorize filing a bankruptcy petition.

Rule 1004-1. Voluntary petition — Partnership.

Individuals who sign a voluntary petition for a partnership debtor must file with the petition a signed statement that all general partners join in or consent to the filing of the petition. Not later than two (2) business days after filing the petition, the person or persons who sign the petition must mail a copy of the petition to all general partners and file a certificate of compliance with this requirement.

Rule 1006-1. Filing fees — Installment payments.

(a) *Tender of payment.* The filing fee may be paid in cash or by cashier's check, certified check or negotiable money order made payable to "Clerk, United States Bankruptcy Court." Payment by an attorney's check will be accepted only if the check is drawn on the account of the attorney for the debtor or on the account of a law firm of which the attorney for the debtor is a member, partner, associate or of counsel. The Clerk shall maintain a list of attorneys and law firms whose checks have been dishonored and may refuse to accept the checks of such attorneys or firms.

(b) *Payment of fees in installments.* The Clerk may approve for the Court an application by an individual to pay the filing and administrative fees in installments that proposes a payment plan no less than in accordance with the following schedule:

	At Filing	1 Month After Filing	2 Months After Filing	3 Months After Filing
Chapter 7	25%	25%	25%	25%
Chapter 11	50%	50%	—	—
Chapter 12	25%	25%	25%	25%
Chapter 13	25%	25%	25%	25%

Rule 1007-1. Lists, schedules & statements.

(a) *Chapter 7, 12 and 13 cases.* In a Chapter 7, 12 or 13 case, the debtor must file an original and three (3) copies of the petition, lists, schedules and statements required by Bankruptcy Rule 1007.

(b) *Chapter 9 and 11 cases.* In a Chapter 9 or 11 case, the debtor must file and original and six (6) copies of the petition, lists, schedules and statements required by Bankruptcy Rule 1007.

(c) *Chapter 13 plans.* See Local Rule 3015-1.

Rule 1007-2. Mailing list or matrix.

(a) *Matrix contents.* A debtor must file with the voluntary petition a master mailing matrix containing the names and addresses of all creditors, the United States Trustee, the Maryland Comptroller of the Treasury and, if a creditor, the Internal Revenue Service. In a case under Chapter 11, the debtor must include in the matrix the taxing authority for each county in which the debtor holds an interest in real estate.

(b) *Matrix form.* The master mailing matrix must be submitted in the form required by the Clerk.

(c) *Supplemental matrix.* The debtor must file a supplemental mailing matrix with any schedule or amended schedule that contains changes in address of an entity entitled to notice or adds the names of entities not listed on the original matrix. The supplemental matrix must conform to the form required by the Clerk.

(d) *Verification.* The master mailing matrix and any supplemental mailing matrix must be dated and verified. The verification must state that to the best of the affiant's knowledge, information and belief the documents are accurate and correct.

Rule 1009-1. Amendments to lists and schedules.

When filing amended schedules that add previously unscheduled creditors, a debtor must follow the following procedures:

(a) Notice to United States Trustee. The debtor must send a copy of the amendment to the office of the United States Trustee and to any trustee appointed in the case.

(b) Notice to creditors. The debtor must send to each creditor added or whose status is changed by the schedule amendment:

(1) a copy of the amendment;

(2) a copy of the original Order for Meeting of Creditors; and

(3) a copy of each order that establishes or extends a bar date for claims or for complaints to determine the dischargeability of debts.

(c) Certificate of compliance. The debtor must file a certificate of compliance with this Rule, together with a dated and clearly titled supplemental mailing matrix that includes the names and correct mailing addresses of all newly scheduled creditors.

Rule 1015-1. Joint administration/consolidation.

The estates of spouses filing a joint petition will be deemed consolidated under § 302(b) of the Bankruptcy Code unless otherwise ordered on the motion of a party in interest made within thirty (30) days after conclusion of the meeting of creditors held under § 341 of the Bankruptcy Code.

Rule 1017-1. Dismissal or suspension of case or proceeding.

The Court may dismiss any case on its own motion for failure of the debtor to file timely a required document, such as the Statement of Financial Affairs, a Schedule, the Statement of Intention under Bankruptcy Code § 521, a matrix or a Chapter 13 Plan. The dismissal may be entered after ten (10) days' notice to the debtor, counsel to the debtor and the United States Trustee and an opportunity for hearing.

Rule 1020-1. Chapter 11 small business cases — General.

(a) *Election to be considered a small business under § 1121(e) of the Bankruptcy Code.* A debtor that is a qualifying small business may elect to be considered a small business under Bankruptcy Code § 1121(e) by filing a written statement of election no later than sixty (60) days after the date of the order for relief or by a later date fixed by the Court, for cause.

(b) *Approval of disclosure statement.* See Local Rule 3017-1.

PART II.

Rule 2002-1. Notice to creditors & other interested parties.

(a) *Measuring period.* A debtor, creditor, official committee, and any other party in interest sending a notice of proposed action to other parties in interest must give recipients no less than twenty (20) days from the date of completion of service to file an objection to the action described in the notice, unless the Bankruptcy Rules specifically require a different time or unless otherwise ordered by the Court or these rules.

(b) *Content.* In addition to the information required by specific notices, notices must contain sufficient information to enable a party in interest to make a reasonably well-informed decision whether to object to the action proposed in the notice. The notice must state (1) by when the objection must be filed and upon whom objections must be served; (2) that the action may be authorized without further order or notice if no timely objection is filed; (3) that the Court, in its discretion, may conduct a hearing or determine the matter without a hearing regardless of whether an objection is filed; (4) that an objection must state the facts and legal grounds on which the objection is based; and (5) the name of the party giving notice or its attorney, together with the address and the telephone number of the party to be contacted if parties in interest have questions regarding the subject of the notice. A notice may not state that an objecting party must attend a court hearing in support of any objection made.

(c) *Certificate of service.* A party must file a certificate of service of a notice given under these Rules or the Bankruptcy Rules within five (5) days after completion of service.

(d) *Content of objections.* An objecting party must state the authority for the objection either in its filed objection or in an accompanying memorandum of fact and law. An objecting party must certify that copies of the objection and of any supporting memorandum have been sent to the opposing party or parties and their counsel.

(e) *Sale notices.* See Local Rule 6004-1.

(f) *Technical requirements for notices.* A party sending a notice must show the date of completion of service conspicuously on the face of the notice.

(g) *Limitation of notice — Chapter 7.* Notices to creditors in cases under Chapter 7 required by Bankruptcy Rule 2002(a) may be limited as provided under Bankruptcy Rule 2002(h) to (1) creditors that hold claims for which proofs of claim have been filed and (2) such other creditors who may file timely claims.

(h) *Limitation of notice — Chapter 11.* In Chapter 11 cases, where official committees are appointed and the number of creditors exceeds thirty (30), the following notices can be limited to the debtor, the United States Trustee, the members of all official committees or committee counsel, if appointed, and to those creditors and equity security holders who file and serve on counsel for the debtor a written request for notices:

(1) the proposed use, sale or lease of property of the estate other than in the ordinary course of business;

(2) the hearing on the approval of a compromise or settlement of a controversy — other than the approval of an agreement pursuant to Bankruptcy Rule 4001(d);

(3) a hearing on an application for compensation or reimbursement of expenses; and

(4) such other notices as the Court orders.

(i) *Voluntary dismissal — Chapter 7 or 11.* Notices of a motion by debtor to dismiss a voluntary case under Chapter 7 or 11 must be sent to all parties in interest.

(j) *Continued meetings and hearings.* If a hearing or meeting is continued or rescheduled at the request of a party, or for reason of the failure of a party to appear or comply with applicable law or rules, that party must send notice of the continued or rescheduled hearing or meeting to all creditors and other entities entitled to notice and file a certificate of that notice.

Rule 2007-1. Trustees — Chapter 11.

(a) *Motion to appoint trustee or examiner.* In a case under Chapter 11 a party filing a motion for an order to appoint a trustee or an examiner under Bankruptcy Code § 1104(a) or § 1104(c) must comply with Rule 9014.

(b) *Election of trustee.* (1) Request for an election. A party filing a request to convene a meeting of creditors for the purpose of electing a trustee in a Chapter 11 reorganization case must send a copy of the request to the United States Trustee in accordance with Bankruptcy Rule 5005 within the time prescribed by Bankruptcy Code § 1104(b). Any person appointed by the United States Trustee under Bankruptcy Code § 1104(d) and approved in accordance with subdivision (c) of this Rule will serve as trustee, pending court approval of the person elected.

(2) Manner of election and notice. An election of a trustee under Bankruptcy Code § 1104(b) must be conducted in accordance with Bankruptcy Rules 2003(b)(3) and 2006. Notice of the Bankruptcy Code § 1104(b) meeting of creditors must be given in accordance with Bankruptcy Rule 2002. The United States Trustee will preside at the meeting. A proxy for the purpose of voting in the election can be solicited. Only a committee of creditors appointed under Bankruptcy Code § 1102, or any other party entitled to solicit a voting proxy pursuant to Bankruptcy Rule 1006 can solicit a trustee election voting proxy.

(3) Report of election and resolution of disputes. (A) Report of undisputed election. If the trustee election is not disputed, the United States Trustee must promptly file a report of the election, stating the name and address of the person elected and a statement that the election is undisputed. The United States Trustee must file with the report an application for approval of the appointment in accordance with subdivision (c) of this Rule. The report constitutes appointment of the elected person to serve as trustee, subject to Court approval, as of the date of entry of the order approving the appointment.

(B) Disputed election. If the election is disputed, the United States Trustee must promptly file a report stating that the election is disputed, informing the Court of the nature of the dispute, and listing the name and address of any candidate elected under any alternative presented by the dispute. A verified statement by each candidate elected under such alternative presented by the dispute, stating the candidate's connections with the debtor, creditors, any other party in interest, their respective attorneys and accountants, the United States Trustee, and any person employed in the office of the United States Trustee must accompany the report. Not later than the date on which the report of the disputed election is filed, the United States Trustee must mail a copy of the report and each verified statement to any party in interest that has made a request to convene a meeting under Bankruptcy Code § 1104(b) or to receive a copy of the report, and to any committee appointed under Bankruptcy Code § 1102. Unless a motion for the resolution of the dispute is filed not later than ten (10) days after the United States Trustee files the report, any person appointed by the United States Trustee under Bankruptcy Code § 1104(d) and approved in accordance with subdivision (c) of this Rule shall serve as trustee. If a motion for the resolution of the dispute is timely filed, and the Court determines the result of the election and approves the person elected, the report will constitute appointment of the elected person as of the date of entry of the order approving the appointment.

(c) *Approval of appointment.* An order approving the appointment of a trustee elected under Bankruptcy Code § 1104(b) or appointed under Bankruptcy Code § 1104(d), or the appointment of an examiner under Bankruptcy Code § 1104(d), will be made on application of the United States Trustee. The United States Trustee must state in the application the name of the person appointed and, to the best of the applicant's knowledge, all the person's connections with the debtor, creditors, any other parties in interest, their respective attorneys and accountants, the United States Trustee, and persons employed in the office of the United States Trustee. Unless the person has been elected under Bankruptcy Code § 1104(b), the application must state the names of the parties in interest with whom the United States Trustee consulted regarding the appointment. The application must be accompanied by a verified statement of the person appointed stating the person's connections with the debtor, creditors, any other party in interest, their respective attorneys and accountants, the United States Trustee, and any person employed in the office of the United States Trustee.

Rule 2015-1. Compensation by debtor in Chapter 11.

(a) The rate of compensation paid by debtor in possession to its officers, directors or partners shall not exceed the rate of compensation paid to those persons ninety (90) days prior to the filing of the petition, unless otherwise ordered by the Court.

(b) The debtor shall file a statement containing the following information within twenty (20) days after filing a petition in a Chapter 11 case:

(1) a statement specifying the duties and positions of the following:

(A) the debtor, if an individual;

(B) the members of the partnership;

(C) the officers and directors of the corporation, and any other insiders;

(2) the rate of compensation paid to each ninety (90) days prior to and at the time of the filing of the petition; and

(3) the rate of compensation of each as of the time the statement is filed.

Rule 2016-1. Compensation of professionals.

(a) *Applications for compensation by professionals.* Unless the Court orders otherwise, all professionals seeking compensation pursuant to Bankruptcy Code §§ 327, 328, 330, and 331, including attorneys, accountants, examiners, investment bankers and real estate advisors, must prepare and submit their applications for compensation in accordance with the Guidelines attached as Appendix D to these Rules. This Rule applies to cases filed after April 30, 1994.

(b) *Disclosure of compensation.* The attorney for the debtor must file a Bankruptcy Rule 2016(b) disclosure statement with the petition. If the debtor's attorney's appearance is entered after the filing of the petition, the attorney must file the Bankruptcy Rule 2016(b) disclosure statement at the time of entry of appearance.

Rule 2070-1. Administrative expenses.

Motions for the allowance or payment of administrative expenses must be served upon the trustee, any committee elected under § 705 or appointed under § 1102 of the Bankruptcy Code or its authorized agent, or in a Chapter 11 case, if no committee of unsecured creditors has been appointed, to those creditors on the list filed pursuant to Bankruptcy Rule 1007(d), the United States Trustee, and to those parties in interest who have filed written requests for notice.

Rule 2072-1. Notice to other courts with pending actions.

The debtor or other party filing a bankruptcy case must promptly send notice of the bankruptcy filing to the following persons:

(a) the clerk of any court where the debtor is a party to a pending civil action and all other parties of record; and

(b) any judge specially assigned to a pending civil action in which the debtor is a party.

The notice must be substantially in accordance with the form entitled "Notice of Filing of Case In Bankruptcy Court," attached as Appendix E to these Rules.

Rule 2081-1. Chapter 11 — Scheduled claims.

The debtor in a Chapter 11 case must serve on each creditor whose claim is listed on a schedule as disputed, contingent, or unliquidated, notice of that listing within fifteen (15) days after filing the schedule or within fifteen (15) days after adding a disputed creditor to a previously filed schedule. The notice must state that such creditor has the right to file a proof of claim and the failure to do so may prevent the creditor from voting on the plan or participating in any distribution. The debtor must file a certificate of service of the notice within five (5) days of service.

Rule 2081-2. Chapter 11 accelerated cases — Chapter 11(a).

(a) *Designation of Chapter 11(a) cases.* In a case other than one commenced as a small business case or a single-asset real estate case, the Court, for cause shown, can at any time, with or without motion or notice, designate a Chapter 11 case for accelerated treatment. A Chapter 11 case designated for accelerated treatment is referred to in these rules as a "Chapter 11(a) case."

(b) *Reconsideration.* A party in interest can, at any time, request that the Court reconsider a Chapter 11(a) designation; and the Court, for cause shown, can at any time, with or without motion or notice, rescind a Chapter 11(a) designation.

PART III.

Rule 3007-1. Claims — Objections.

(a) *Objection.* In addition to the service required by Bankruptcy Rules 9014 and 7004(b), an objecting party must serve a copy of the objection and any supporting memorandum and affidavit on the claimant at the address (and in care of the individual) shown on the proof of claim and must certify that service to the Court. The objection must conspicuously state that:

(1) within thirty (30) days after the date on the certificate of service of the objection, the claimant may file and serve a memorandum in opposition, together with any documents and other evidence the claimant wishes to attach in support of its claim, unless the claimant wishes to rely solely upon the proof of claim; and

(2) an interested party may request a hearing that will be held in the Court's discretion.

(b) *Adversary proceeding.* This Rule does not apply where an objection to a claim is joined with a request for relief of a kind specified in Bankruptcy Rule 7001 and thereby becomes an adversary proceeding.

(c) *Chapter 12 and 13 cases.* In Chapter 12 and 13 cases, an objecting party must attach a copy of the proof of claim to the objection, together with a copy of all attachments thereto.

Rule 3014-1. Bankruptcy Code § 1111(b) election in Chapter 11(a) reorganization cases.

A Bankruptcy Code § 1111(b) election in a Chapter 11(a) case can be made at any time prior to the conclusion of the confirmation hearing.

Rule 3015-1. Chapter 13 plans — Copies, service.

(a) If a debtor files a plan with the petition, the debtor must file: one (1) original plan signed by the debtor or by each debtor in a joint case; one (1) copy for each creditor listed in Schedules D, E, and F; one (1) copy for the Internal Revenue Service if it is a scheduled creditor; one (1) for the Maryland Comptroller of the Treasury; and two (2) additional copies.

(b) If a debtor files an original or an amended plan after the filing of the petition, the debtor must mail a copy of the plan to each creditor, the Internal Revenue Service if it is a scheduled creditor, the Maryland Comptroller of the Treasury, the Chapter 13 trustee, and the United States Trustee; and the debtor must promptly certify the mailing to the Court.

Rule 3015-2. Chapter 13 — Confirmation.

Debtors and their counsel must attend all scheduled confirmation hearings unless excused by the Chapter 13 trustee or the Court.

Rule 3016-1. Chapter 11(a) accelerated case plan.

(a) *Time for filing plan in Chapter 11(a) accelerated case.* The Court will set a time by which the Chapter 11(a) debtor must file a plan, no earlier than sixty (60) days after the entry of the order designating the case for accelerated treatment.

(b) *Extension of time.* The Court can, with or without motion or notice, extend the time set under section (a) of this Rule for filing a plan.

(c) *Failure to file plan.* The failure of a debtor to file a plan within a time set by the Court under section (a) or (b) of this Rule will constitute cause for dismissing the case or converting the case to a case under Chapter 7 pursuant to Bankruptcy Code § 1112(b)(4).

Rule 3016-2. Chapter 11(a) accelerated case disclosure statement.

(a) *Time for filing.* The Court will set a time by which a Chapter 11(a) debtor must file a disclosure statement, no earlier than sixty (60) days after the entry of the order designating the case for accelerated treatment.

(b) *Extension of time.* The Court can, with or without motion or notice, extend any time set under section (a) of this Rule for filing a disclosure statement.

(c) *Failure to file disclosure statement.* The failure of a debtor to file a disclosure statement within a time set by the Court under section (a) or (b) of this Rule will constitute cause for dismissing the case or converting the case to a case under Chapter 7 pursuant to Bankruptcy Code § 1112(b)(3).

(d) *Content.* The disclosure statement for a Chapter 11(a) plan must include a liquidation analysis and a projected budget that contains plan payments.

Rule 3017-1. Disclosure statement — Small business cases.

(a) *Conditional approval.* If a qualifying debtor has made a timely election to be considered a small business under § 1121(e) of the Bankruptcy Code, the Court may, on application of the plan proponent, conditionally approve a disclosure statement filed under Bankruptcy Rule 3016. On or before conditional approval of the disclosure statement, the Court will:

(1) fix a time by which the holders of claims and interests can accept or reject the plan;

(2) fix a time for filing objections to the disclosure statement;

(3) set a date for a final approval hearing of the disclosure statement if a timely objection is filed; and

(4) set a date for the confirmation hearing.

(b) *Application of Bankruptcy Rule 3017.* If a disclosure statement is conditionally approved, Bankruptcy Rules 3017(a), (b), (c), and (e) do not apply. Conditional approval of a disclosure statement is considered approval of the disclosure statement under Bankruptcy Rule 3017(d).

(c) *Objections and final approval hearing.* Notice of the time set for filing objections and of the disclosure statement final approval hearing must be sent under Bankruptcy Rule 2002. The notice can be combined with notice of the plan confirmation hearing. Objections to the disclosure statement must be filed by such date fixed by the Court, or if no date is fixed, objections must be filed before final approval of the disclosure statement. Objections must be sent to the United States Trustee and served on the debtor, the plan proponent, any committee appointed under the Bankruptcy Code and any other entity designated by the Court. If a timely objection to the disclosure statement is filed, the Court can hold a hearing to consider final approval before or combined with the hearing on confirmation of the plan.

(d) *Content.* The disclosure statement for a small business case plan must include a liquidation analysis and a projected budget that contains plan payments.

Rule 3017-2. Conditional approval of disclosure statement, objections, and hearing in Chapter 11(a) accelerated case.

(a) *Conditional approval.* The Court can conditionally approve a disclosure statement filed by a Chapter 11(a) debtor prior to giving notice of a hearing on the disclosure statement.

(b) *Application of Bankruptcy Rule 3017.* A disclosure statement conditionally approved by the Court can be sent to creditors and equity security holders under Bankruptcy Code § 1125(c) and Bankruptcy Rule 3017(d)(2) and can be used to solicit acceptances or rejections of a plan under Bankruptcy Code § 1125(b).

(c) *Objections.* Objections to Chapter 11(a) disclosure statements must be filed and served on the debtor, the plan proponent, any committee appointed under the Bankruptcy Code and any other entity designated by the Court, at least two (2) days before final approval of the disclosure statement, or by an earlier date set by the Court.

(d) *Disclosure statement final approval.* If no objection to or request to modify the Chapter 11(a) disclosure statement is timely filed, the conditional approval of the disclosure statement becomes final at the plan confirmation hearing.

(e) *Disclosure statement objections hearing.* An objection to or request to modify the Chapter 11(a) disclosure statement will be considered at the confirmation hearing held under Bankruptcy Code § 1128(a) and Bankruptcy Rule 3020(b).

(f) *Disclosure statement amendment.* If the Court determines that a disclosure statement should not be approved in its current form, the debtor can amend the disclosure statement and the Court can conditionally approve the amended disclosure statement which the debtor will then send to creditors. In that event, the Court may continue the confirmation hearing and set new dates for filing objections to confirmation and for filing plan acceptances or rejections.

Rule 3018-1. Ballots — Voting on plans.

(a) *Tally.* The tally of ballots in Chapter 11 cases must be filed with the Clerk no later than the third business day prior to the confirmation hearing. The tally must substantially conform to the form prescribed by the Court and available from the Clerk.

(b) *Disputed claims.* A creditor will have the right, if demanded in a timely response to an objection to its claim, to a hearing on temporary allowance of its claim for the purpose of accepting or rejecting a plan.

Rule 3022-1. Completion of the administration of confirmed Chapter 11 plans.

(a) *Fully administered plan.* A Chapter 11 plan will be deemed fully administered under Bankruptcy Rule 3022:

(1) after the completion of the following:

(A) six (6) months have elapsed after the entry of a final order of confirmation that has become nonappealable;

(B) the deposits required by the plan have been distributed;

(C) the property proposed by the plan to be transferred has been transferred;

(D) the debtor or the successor of the debtor under the plan has assumed the business or the management of the property dealt with by the plan;

(E) payments under the plan have commenced; and

(F) all motions, contested matters, and adversary proceedings have been finally resolved; or

(2) at another time specifically defined by the plan.

(b) *Certification.* A proponent of a confirmed plan that is fully administered must file forthwith a certification of full administration. The certification must include a final summary report of the disbursements, distributions, and transfers that have been made pursuant to the plan, together with a description of other acts taken to consummate the plan. The certificate must also describe any matters involving consummation of the confirmed plan that have not been fully resolved.

(c) *Final order.* The plan proponent must file with the Court and serve on the U.S. Trustee an application for a final order closing the case with the certificate of full administration.

(d) *Progress reports.* The plan proponent shall file and serve on the U.S. Trustee reports of progress towards full administration of the plan until the proponent files a final certification and report. The first report must be filed six (6) months after the order of confirmation. Subsequent reports must be filed every six (6) months thereafter.

Rule 3070-1. Chapter 13 — Special procedures.

(a) *Payments to secured creditors.* After the filing of a petition in a case under Chapter 13, and regardless of any provision in a proposed plan, the debtor must continue to make the regular payments as and when due on debts secured by property to be retained by the debtor. The Court can modify this requirement on motion.

(b) *Modification of secured claims.* In plans providing for modification of secured claims by the payment of the value of the collateral under a plan, the trustee will credit debtor for the amount paid under subparagraph (a) above. After confirmation of the plan, the debtor shall document the postpetition payments made. The secured claim will be reduced by the amount of the payments made.

(c) *Trustee expenses and Clerk's fees.* Upon dismissal or conversion of a Chapter 13 case, any funds that the trustee holds in a case will be charged for the trustee's allowed expenses and any outstanding Clerk's fees.

PART IV.

Rule 4001-1. Automatic stay — Relief from.

(a) *Order directing course of proceeding.* Upon the filing of a motion for relief from stay pursuant to § 362(d) of the Bankruptcy Code, the Court will issue an Order Directing Course of Proceeding that will set the time of hearing on the motion.

(1) The moving party must serve the Order upon the persons entitled to notice of the hearing under Bankruptcy Rules 4001(a), 7004, and 9014 within five (5) business days after the date of the Order Directing Course of Proceeding.

(2) The moving party must file a certification of service of the Order within five (5) days after completion of service.

(b) *Responses to motions for relief from automatic stay.* (1) Time for filing response. A response must be filed within seventeen (17) days after the date of the Order Directing Course of Proceeding. If a timely response is not filed, the Court may grant the relief requested by default.

(2) Form. The response must include detailed responses to each paragraph of the motion in conformity with Federal Rules of Civil Procedure 8(b) and (d) and state all defenses to the motion.

(3) Responses by standing Chapter 12 and 13 trustees. Standing Chapter 12 and Chapter 13 trustees are not required to respond to motions for relief from stay.

Rule 4002-1. Current address and telephone number of debtor.

(a) *Address of debtor.* All debtors must maintain a statement of current address with the Clerk. This obligation continues until the case is closed.

(b) *Debtor's telephone number.* Debtors proceeding in proper person must maintain a statement of the debtor's current telephone number with the Clerk. This obligation continues until the case is closed.

Rule 4003-1. Objection to claim of exemptions.

Required notice to debtor. An objection to the list of property claimed as exempt must contain conspicuous notice that:

(a) any opposition to the objection must be filed and served within thirty (30) days after the date of the certificate of service of the objection; and

(b) a hearing will be held on the objection at the discretion of the Court.

Rule 4003-2. Motions to avoid liens.

(a) *Issuance of Order Directing Course of Proceeding.* Upon the filing of a motion to avoid a lien under Bankruptcy Code § 522(f), the Court will issue an Order Directing Course of Proceeding.

(b) *Service of Order Directing Course of Proceeding.* Within five (5) business days after the date of the Order Directing Course of Proceeding, the moving party or counsel must serve a copy of the Order, together with the motion, on the respondent(s), counsel for respondent(s), and any trustee. Service shall be in accordance with Bankruptcy Rule 7004.

(c) *Certificate of service.* Within five (5) days after completion of service of the order and motion, the moving party or counsel for the moving party must file a certificate of service.

(d) *Responses to motion to avoid lien — Time for filing.* Any responsive pleading or objection to a Bankruptcy Code § 522(f) motion must be filed within thirty (30) days after the date of the Order Directing Course of Proceeding.

(e) *Resolution of motion to avoid lien*. The Court can grant or deny the relief sought in a motion without a hearing.

Rule 4007-1. Dischargeability complaints under 11 U.S.C. § 523(a)(15).

In an adversary proceeding where a claim is made under § 523(a)(15), plaintiff shall file with the complaint (1) copies of the order, agreement, or any other document relied upon as the source of the obligation, and (2) a financial statement in the form annexed as Appendix F to these Rules. Defendant shall file with the answer to the complaint a copy of the financial statement using the same form. The parties have a continuing obligation to update the financial statements during the pendency of the adversary proceeding.

PART V.

Rule 5001-1. Court administration — Lapse in appropriations.

This Rule will become effective only when Congress fails to enact legislation to fund operations of the United States Courts. The Anti-Deficiency Act, 31 U.S.C. § 1515, limits permissible government activities in the event of such a failure to those otherwise "authorized by law" or those needed to meet "cases of emergency involving the safety of human life or the protection of property."

This Court is directly involved in the judicial process and under the Constitution and laws of the United States, it is always open to exercise the judicial power of the United States as a unit of the District Court. Thus, the Court must continue, even in the absence of funding by Congress, to receive new cases, and to hear and dispose of pending cases. Activities will, however, be limited as nearly as practical to those functions necessary and essential to continue the resolution of pending cases. The Court will advise the United States Marshal and the General Services Administration of the level of building and security services necessary to maintain such Court operations.

The Court finds that Judges' staffs and the Clerk and the Clerk's staff are persons essential to the continuation of court operations. Work of all personnel shall be limited to those essential functions set forth above.

Rule 5001-2. Clerk — Office location/hours.

(a) *Office hours*. The office hours of the Clerk in the Greenbelt and Baltimore divisions shall be from 8:00 a.m. to 4:00 p.m. on all days, except Saturdays, Sundays, and holidays observed by the United States District Court for the District of Maryland.

(b) *"Night box"*. A "night box" is located in the lobby of each of the United States Courthouses in Baltimore and in Greenbelt. Bankruptcy petitions, pleadings and other papers may be placed in the night box for filing after regular office hours and until the Courthouse is closed. The night box is intended as an after-hours convenience, and it is not intended as an alternative for filing papers during regular office hours. Petitions, pleadings and other papers deposited in the night box will be "date stamped" as of the business day prior to the earliest retrieval each day. When a Courthouse is closed, arrangements may be made for emergency filings by contacting a designated court representative. The names of the designated court representative are posted on each night box and on notice boards in the divisional offices.

(c) *Division of business.* The division of business for the United States Bankruptcy Court for the District of Maryland is as follows:

(1) Cases originating in Allegany, Calvert, Charles, Frederick, Garrett, Montgomery, Prince George's, St. Mary's, and Washington Counties are assigned to the Greenbelt Divisional Office, 300 U.S. Courthouse, 6500 Cherrywood Lane, Greenbelt, Maryland, 20770.

(2) Cases originating in Baltimore City and Baltimore, Anne Arundel, Caroline, Carroll, Cecil, Dorchester, Harford, Howard, Kent, Queen Anne's, Somerset, Talbot, Wicomico, and Worcester Counties are assigned to the Baltimore Divisional Office, 8515 U.S. Courthouse, 101 West Lombard Street, Baltimore, Maryland, 21201.

Rule 5003-1. Court papers — Removal of.

(a) *Removal, copies.* Except as provided in this Rule, no Court record or paper filed in or connected with a case can be taken out of the Clerk's office without a Court order. The Clerk will arrange for the duplication of any unrestricted Court paper on the request of any person and prepayment of the cost thereof.

(b) *Claims.* With prior consent of the Clerk, trustees can remove that portion of a file containing proofs of claim from the Clerk's office.

(c) *Chapter 12 and 13.* In Chapter 12 and 13 cases, the Clerk may designate the trustee to maintain the claims record and to hold the original proofs of claim for the Clerk. The trustee must return forthwith the proofs of claim upon closing, conversion or dismissal of the case.

Rule 5005-1. Filing papers — Size of papers.

Pleadings, exhibits to pleadings where practicable, and other papers must be legible and must be on 8½ × 11 inch paper. All papers (other than the mailing matrix) must be punctured by a standard two-hole punch centered along the top margin.

Rule 5011-1. Abstention.

(a) *Adversary proceeding.* In an adversary proceeding, a motion for abstention pursuant to 28 U.S.C. § 1334(c), must be filed within the time prescribed for filing an answer under Bankruptcy Rule 7012(a).

(b) *Contested matter.* In a contested matter, a motion for abstention pursuant to 28 U.S.C. § 1334(c) must be filed within thirty (30) days from the date indicated on the certificate of service on the pleading initiating the contested matter.

Rule 5071-1. Motions for postponement/continuances.

(a) *Court order required.* A Court order is required for any postponement of a hearing, pretrial conference, or trial.

(b) *Notice to client and other parties.* A motion for a postponement of a hearing, pretrial conference, or trial may not be made without the knowledge of the client of counsel moving for the postponement. Notice of such motion, together with the reasons therefor, must be given to all other parties or their counsel before filing unless such notice is waived.

(c) *Conflicting engagement.* A motion for a postponement of a hearing or trial on the grounds of a conflicting engagement must be filed within ten (10) days after the date such conflict became apparent. There shall be attached to the motion written evidence of the conflicting engagement.

(d) *Meeting of creditors.* A request for postponement of the meeting of creditors held under Bankruptcy Code § 341 shall be handled as follows:

(1) in Chapter 12 and 13 cases requests shall be made to the standing trustee assigned to the case;

(2) in Chapter 7 cases requests shall be made to the interim trustee;

(3) in Chapter 11 cases requests shall be made to the Assistant U.S. Trustee assigned to the division of Court where the case is pending.

Rule 5073-1. Photography, recording devices and broadcasting.

(a) *General prohibition.* Unless otherwise ordered by the Court, no court proceeding can be photographed, videotaped, televised, recorded, reproduced, or broadcast in any way except by an official court reporter.

(b) *Impounding of recording equipment.* Except for (1) portable dictating equipment to be used by members of the Bar when inspecting official records, and (2) equipment to be used by official court reporters or official electronic sound recorders, no cameras, recording equipment, or broadcasting equipment may be brought into a courtroom unless otherwise ordered by the Court. Such equipment is subject to being impounded.

(c) *Court reporters.* A court reporter, electronic sound recorder, or other person must not use or permit to be used any recording of a Court proceeding on or in connection with any radio or television broadcast.

(d) *Penalty.* A violation of this Rule may be treated as a contempt of Court. A violator who is a member of the Bar may be subjected to disciplinary action.

PART VI.

Rule 6004-1. Sale of estate property.

(a) *Sale notices.* Notices of private sale of estate property by the trustee must include the following:

(1) if an appraisal has been performed,

(A) the appraised value of the asset being sold;

(B) the date of the appraisal; and

(C) the name and address of the appraiser;

(2) if no appraisal has been performed, the scheduled value of the asset being sold;

(3) the purchaser's identity;

(4) a full description of any relationship between the purchaser and any party in interest; and

(5) a statement of all consideration paid and to be paid by the purchaser and the payment terms.

(b) *Disclosure of sale charges.* Unless included in the notice of sale, the following charges cannot be paid from a bankruptcy estate in connection with the sale of estate property:

(1) points, loan origination fees, loan enabling fees or other buyer financing charges for the purchase of property of the estate; and

(2) documentary stamps, transfer taxes, or recording fees.

(c) *Sale without objection.* If no timely written objection is filed, the sale shall be deemed authorized upon expiration of the notice period. This paragraph does not apply to sales free and clear of liens or of interests of persons other than the debtor.

(d) *Clerk's certificate.* A party in interest may request a Clerk's certificate that no objection to the notice has been filed. The Clerk will charge a certification fee.

Rule 6006-1. Executory contracts — Unexpired leases.

(a) *Notice required.* Parties seeking the assumption, rejection, or assignment of an executory contract or unexpired lease must give notice of the proposed action to the other party to the executory contract or unexpired lease, any official committee, or in the absence of a committee, to the holders of the ten (10) largest unsecured claims taken from debtor's list filed pursuant to Bankruptcy Rule 1007(d) or Schedule F, the trustee, the United States Trustee, and parties requesting notice. The notice must state that the Court may rule upon the request without a hearing if there is no timely request for a hearing.

(b) *Motion to reject a collective bargaining agreement.* A party moving to reject a collective bargaining agreement must file the following with the motion:

(1) an affidavit demonstrating compliance with Bankruptcy Code § 1113(b); and

(2) a certificate of service that the moving party has served the motion and affidavit on the authorized representative of the employees covered by the collective bargaining agreement.

Rule 6070-1. Tax returns and tax refunds.

The provisions of this Rule are limited to the Internal Revenue Service and the Maryland Comptroller of the Treasury, Income Tax Division, herein referred to as the "Tax Authorities."

(a) Authority to make refunds. Unless otherwise directed by the trustee or the Court, after sixty (60) days have elapsed from the date of the filing of the petition, the Tax Authorities are authorized to make an income tax refund in the ordinary course of business.

(b) Notice to trustee and court. It is the duty of the debtor, within five (5) days of receipt of a tax refund or notice of tax assessment or deficiency, to file with the Court and in Chapter 7 cases to send to the trustee a copy of the refund check and transmittal letter, the tax assessment or deficiency notice, and other relevant documents.

(c) Offset; assessment; automatic stay. (1) The Tax Authorities can offset any refund or overpayment due a debtor against any taxes due the United

States or the State of Maryland, provided that the Tax Authority has filed a proof of claim that is not disputed.

(2) The Tax Authorities can assess any tax liability that can be satisfied by offsetting an overpayment when that tax liability has not previously been assessed. The Tax Authorities will send notice of assessment and offset to the debtor prior to or substantially concurrent with the assessment and offset.

PART VII.

Rule 7001-1. Trustees' filing fees.

Payment of the filing fee for an adversary proceeding filed by a trustee may be deferred pending acquisition of sufficient funds by the trustee to pay such fees in full or pro rata with other expenses of administration.

Rule 7003-1. Adversary cover sheet.

A party filing an adversary proceeding complaint must file with the Clerk a completed adversary proceeding cover sheet. A party filing a complaint under 28 U.S.C. § 157(b)(5) must file both an adversary proceeding cover sheet and a district court cover sheet.

Rule 7005-1. Filing of discovery materials.

Unless otherwise ordered by the Court, a party may not file with the Court either written discovery requests, responses to discovery or depositions (other than as exhibits to motions). A party propounding written discovery or taking a deposition or providing a discovery response must file a notice stating: (a) the type of discovery or response served; (b) the date and type of service; and (c) the person(s) served. Parties must retain the original copies of the discovery materials and make them available for inspection by any other party.

Rule 7012-1. Core or non-core matters.

(a) Prior to trial a party may move for a ruling that an adversary proceeding is core or non-core. The Court will ordinarily allow adverse parties fourteen (14) days from the service of the motion to file responses. A motion does not postpone any time periods unless ordered by the Court.

(b) At any time before the conclusion of a matter on the merits, a party to a proceeding may file a consent to the entry of a final order by the Bankruptcy Court under 28 U.S.C. § 157(c)(2).

Rule 7016-1. Pretrial procedures.

(a) *General.* The Court can, in any adversary proceeding or contested matter, direct the attorney for a party or a party appearing *pro se* to appear before it or the Clerk for a preliminary scheduling or pretrial conference pursuant to Bankruptcy Rule 7016.

(b) *Notice.* The Court will determine the form and manner of notice of a scheduling or pretrial conference. The notice will be sent only to counsel admitted to practice before the District Court, counsel admitted *pro hac vice* or to parties proceeding *pro se.*

(c) *Pretrial statement.* Pursuant to an order or notice that the Court has directed to all parties to the proceeding or matter, each party will file a pretrial statement with the Court at least three (3) business days prior to the scheduled pretrial conference, with copies sent to all other attorneys of record or parties proceeding *pro se.* Each party must state the following in its pretrial statement:

(1) a brief statement of facts that the party proposes to prove in support of a claim or defense, together with a list of separate legal theories relied upon in support of each claim or defense;

(2) any required pleading amendments;

(3) any pleaded, but abandoned issue;

(4) stipulations of fact, or, if unable to agree, a statement of matters on which the party requests an admission;

(5) the details of the damage claimed or any other relief sought as of the pretrial conference date;

(6) a listing of the documents and records to be offered in evidence by the party at the trial other than those expected to be used solely for impeachment, indicating which documents the party expects to introduce in evidence without the usual authentication;

(7) a listing of the names and specialties of experts that the party proposes to call as witnesses;

(8) a statement of a counsel of record that he or she has explored and discussed all reasonable avenues of settlement prior to the pretrial conference; and

(9) any other pretrial relief which the party will request or the Court shall direct.

(d) *Pretrial order.* In an order issued at the conclusion of the final pretrial conference, the Court can incorporate one or more of the parties' pretrial statements.

(e) *Required pre-filing of exhibits.* (1) Adversary proceedings and Chapter 11 lift stays. In all adversary proceedings and in motions seeking relief from stay in Chapter 11 cases, each party must pre-file all exhibits which that party intends to introduce into evidence, except for exhibits to be offered solely for rebuttal. Each party must include in the pre-filed exhibits any report by an expert whom the party may call as a witness, or if no report has been prepared, an affidavit by such expert as to the expert's direct testimony. The exhibits must be filed within the time limits set in the scheduling order, or order directing course of proceeding. In adversary proceedings, if opposing parties do not file written objections to pre-filed exhibits by the time specified in the scheduling order, the exhibits will be admitted into evidence.

(2) Method of pre-filing of exhibits. All pre-filed exhibits must be filed within the time limits set in the scheduling order or order directing course of proceeding by submission of an original and two (2) copies. Each set of exhibits must be bound or affixed together and must have at the beginning an exhibit list identifying each exhibit by number. Each exhibit must be tabbed by exhibit number. An additional copy must be furnished to each other party in the matter.

(3) Size. To the extent possible, all exhibits must be reduced to 8-1/2 by 11 inches.

(4) Failure to pre-file exhibits. Exhibits that are not pre-filed as required by this Rule can be excluded from evidence.

(f) *Proof of amount of claim or debt.* (1) Required verified statement. In all adversary proceedings and all contested matters, any party seeking to prove the amount of any claim or debt must introduce into evidence an affidavit setting forth the amount of the alleged claim or debt, itemized by component, unless the information is contained in a previously filed pleading in the matter and verified pursuant to 28 U.S.C. § 1746.

(2) Exclusive method of proof. Direct testimony as to the amount of the debt or claim will be only by introduction of the affidavit, or a verified pleading, unless an objection to the admission into evidence of the affidavit or verified pleading is made. The declarant must be present in the courtroom for cross-examination, or a hearsay objection to the admission into evidence of the affidavit or verified pleading can be granted.

(3) Pre-filing requirement. In adversary proceedings and Chapter 11 motions for relief from stay, the required affidavit or verified pleading must be pre-filed as an exhibit, in accordance with subsections (f)(1) and (2) of this Rule.

Rule 7026-1. Discovery — General.

(a) *Discovery request limits.* A party may not serve on any other party in a contested matter or an adversary proceeding more than thirty (30) interrogatories, more than thirty (30) requests for production, and thirty (30) requests for admissions, including all parts and sub-parts.

(b) *Timely written discovery requests required.* All discovery requests must be made at a sufficiently early date to assure that the time for response expires before any discovery deadlines set by the Court.

(c) *Discovery to proceed despite existence of disputes.* Unless otherwise ordered by the Court, a discovery dispute as to one matter does not justify delay in taking or responding to any other discovery.

(d) *Discovery stayed pending resolution of Bankruptcy Rule 7012(b)(2) motion.* The filing of a motion pursuant to Bankruptcy Rule 7012(b)(2) stays discovery unless the movant presents matters outside the pleading.

(e) *Format of responses.* Responses to discovery must restate each request followed by the answer or a brief statement of the grounds for objection.

(f) *Conference of counsel required.* Counsel must confer concerning a discovery dispute and make good faith attempts to resolve their differences. The Court will not entertain to resolve a discovery dispute unless the moving party has filed a certificate stating:

(1) the date, time, and place of the discovery conference; the names of all persons participating and any unresolved issues remaining; or

(2) the moving party's attempts to hold such a conference without success.

(g) *Smoking during depositions prohibited.* Unless all persons present agree, no one can smoke in a room where a deposition is being taken.

(h) *Depositions of experts.* The party taking the deposition of an expert shall pay a reasonable fee for the time spent in deposition and traveling to and from the deposition. The party designating the expert will pay any fee charged by the expert for time spent in preparing for the deposition.

(i) *Discovery Guidelines.* Discovery Guidelines adopted by the Court and set forth in Appendix B govern the conduct of discovery.

(j) *Required initial disclosures.* (1) Bankruptcy Rules 7026(a)(1)(A), (B) and (C), 7026(d), and 7026(f) do not apply to (A) adversary proceedings to revoke an Order of Confirmation of a Chapter 11, Chapter 12, or Chapter 13 plan or to revoke a discharge, and (B) contested matters.

(2) Bankruptcy Rule 7026(d) is applicable only in those matters where a meeting of the parties is required.

Rule 7054-1. Allowance of costs.

No costs will be allowed in adversary proceedings in excess of filing fees unless the entitled party files a Bill of Costs within twenty (20) days after the entry of the judgment or order.

Rule 7054-2. Attorneys' fees.

Unless a longer period is fixed by statute or by the Court, motions by a prevailing party for an award of attorneys' fees must be filed within twenty (20) days after the entry of judgment or order.

Rule 7055-1. Default — Failure to prosecute.

(a) *Clerk's notice.* If, upon the expiration of six (6) months after the filing of the last pleading, it appears to the Clerk that no significant activity has since occurred in an adversary proceeding or contested matter in which there is no schedule hearing, the Clerk will send written notice to all parties to the adversary proceeding or contested matter that the proceeding or matter will be denied or dismissed without prejudice unless, within thirty (30) days after the date of the notice, the plaintiff or movant presents good and sufficient cause in writing why the dismissal or denial should not be ordered.

(b) *Court action.* If the Court finds the cause sufficient, the Clerk will note the same on the motion or adversary docket and provide notice thereof to the parties. An order of denial or dismissal without prejudice can be entered in any case when there is no response to the Clerk's notice.

PART VIII.

Rule 8001-1. Appeals.

See Local District Court Rule 83.19.1.

PART IX.

Rule 9001-1. Definitions and rules of construction.

(a) *Definitions in Bankruptcy Rules.* The definitions of words and phrases in Bankruptcy Rule 9001 and the definitions adopted by reference therein apply in these Local Rules.

(b) *Rules of construction.* The rules of construction contained in Bankruptcy Code § 102 apply to these Local Rules.

(c) *Bankruptcy Code.* In these Local Rules, reference to the Bankruptcy Code means title 11 of the United States Code.

(d) *Bankruptcy Rules.* In these Local Rules, reference to a Bankruptcy Rule or Rules means the Federal Rules of Bankruptcy Procedure.

(e) *District Court.* In these Local Rules, reference to the District Court means the United States District Court for the District of Maryland.

(f) *File.* Where the word "file" appears in these Local Rules, such filing is to be made with the appropriate divisional office of the Clerk of the United States Bankruptcy Court for the District of Maryland.

Rule 9010-1. Pro se parties.

(a) *Who may appear pro se.* Only individuals may represent themselves.

(b) *Responsibilities of parties appearing pro se.* Individuals representing themselves are responsible for performing all duties imposed on counsel by the Bankruptcy Code, the Bankruptcy Rules, these Rules, and applicable federal or state law.

Rule 9010-2. Current information.

(a) *Duty to keep current information on file.* Counsel and parties appearing *pro se* must file and maintain a statement of current address and telephone number in every case in which such person appears. This obligation is continuing until the case is closed.

(b) *Excusable neglect.* Should any person fail to maintain a current address with the Clerk and as a result, either for lack of response or lack of an appearance, the Court enters an order dismissing any affirmative claim for relief or enters a judgment by default or otherwise against such person or such person's client, the failure to maintain a current address shall not be considered excusable neglect.

Rule 9010-3. Attorneys — Who may appear as counsel.

(a) *Generally.* Except as otherwise provided in this Rule only members of the Bar of the District Court may appear as counsel. Only individuals may represent themselves.

(b) *Admission pro hac vice.* (1) The Court can permit any attorney (except a member of the Maryland Bar) who is a member in good standing of the Bar of any other United States Court or of the highest court of any state to appear and participate as counsel in a particular bankruptcy case. Such permission will not constitute formal admission to the Bar of the District Court. An attorney admitted *pro hac vice* is subject to the disciplinary jurisdiction of the District Court.

(2) A party represented by an attorney who has been admitted *pro hac vice* must also be represented by an attorney who is a member of the Bar of the District Court.

(3) The application for admission *pro hac vice* shall be made in the form of Appendix G to these Rules.

(c) *Certain actions not requiring admission.* An attorney need not be admitted to the Bar of the District Court in order to file a proof of claim for a client or to file a fee application as principal of a professional group.

(d) *Appearance for obtaining deposition subpoenas.* It is not be necessary for counsel to be admitted to the Bar of the District Court in order to obtain a subpoena for depositions to be taken in this district for cases pending in other districts. However, an attorney seeking such a subpoena is subject to the disciplinary jurisdiction of the District Court.

Rule 9010-4. Withdrawal of appearance of an attorney.

(a) *When individuals are clients.* If the client is an individual, appearance of counsel may be withdrawn only with leave of Court and if: (1) appearance of other counsel has been entered or (2) withdrawing counsel files a certificate stating: (A) the name and last known address of the client, and (B) that a written notice has been mailed to or otherwise served upon the client at least five (5) days previously advising the client of counsel's proposed withdrawal and notifying the client either to have new counsel enter an appearance or to advise the Clerk that the client will be proceeding without counsel.

(b) *When clients are other than individuals.* If the client is other than an individual, including corporations, partnerships, unincorporated associations and government entities, appearance of counsel may be withdrawn only with leave of Court and if: (1) appearance of other counsel has been entered or (2) withdrawing counsel files a certificate stating: (A) the name and last known address of the client and (B) that a written notice has been mailed to or otherwise served upon the client at least five (5) days previously advising the client of counsel's proposed withdrawal and notifying the client that it must have new counsel enter an appearance or be subject to dismissal of its case, dismissal of its claims and/or judgment by default on claims against it. If after twenty (20) days of the filing of the motion to withdraw, new counsel has not entered an appearance, and the Court has granted the motion to withdraw, the Court will take appropriate action, including dismissing any affirmative claim for relief asserted by the party or entering a default against the unrepresented party.

Rule 9010-5. Attorneys for debtors — Duties.

(a) An attorney who files a petition in bankruptcy on behalf of a debtor, or who subsequently enters an appearance on behalf of a debtor other than as special counsel approved under Bankruptcy Code § 327(e), will be counsel of record in all matters arising during the administration of the case, such as adversary matters and motions for relief from stay, except as set forth below;

(b) In an individual case commenced under or converted to Chapter 7, representation will continue through discharge and continue as to any matter pending at the time of the discharge. However, an attorney representing an individual debtor may exclude adversary proceedings provided that debtor's written acknowledgement of this limitation is filed with counsel's Bankruptcy Rule 2016(b) statement;

(c) In a case under Chapter 11, representation of a debtor will continue until the case is closed or dismissed;

(d) In a case under Chapter 12 or 13, representation will continue for the earlier of ten (10) days after the entry of an order of dismissal of the case or ninety (90) days after the entry of an order confirming the debtor's plan;

(e) If a case is converted to a case under another chapter, the Rule under the latter chapter governs; and

(f) This Rule supersedes all retainer agreements unless otherwise ordered by the Court for cause.

Rule 9011-1. Signatures, federal bar number.

This Rule augments Bankruptcy Rule 9011. An individual signing pleadings must state the signer's printed name, post office and business address and telephone number. If the signer is an attorney admitted to practice before the United States District Court for the District of Maryland, the attorney shall include his or her federal bar number as listed on the Attorney Admission List.

Rule 9013-1. Motions practice.

(a) *Requirement of written motion.* All motions must be in writing and filed with the Court, unless made during a hearing or trial.

(b) *Procedure for motions other than motions for relief from stay and to avoid liens.* (1) All motions must state with particularity the grounds therefor and the relief or order sought. Supplementing Local Rule 9013-3 as to moving parties, responding parties must file with the Court, at the time of filing a response, a proposed order stating the requested disposition.

(2) Parties can file with or append to their motion and memorandum, or to their responsive pleading and opposing memorandum, supporting affidavits or documents establishing the elements of entitlement to the relief sought or any defense.

(3) Any responsive pleading and memorandum in opposition to a motion must be filed within fourteen (14) days from the date of service of said motion.

(4) Except as otherwise provided in the Bankruptcy Code, the Bankruptcy Rules, these Rules or by the Court, a motion can be decided on the pleadings and memoranda filed.

Rule 9013-2. Briefs and memoranda of law.

A party must file with each motion a brief memorandum of fact and law entitling the movant to the relief claimed or a statement that no memorandum will be filed and that the movant will rely solely upon the motion.

Rule 9013-3. Orders — Proposed.

All requests for relief, except motions to dismiss or convert, and pleadings initiating adversary proceedings under Bankruptcy Rule 7001 must be accompanied by proposed order. The proposed order must contain a specific title describing the nature and effect of the order. The names and addresses of all counsel or other parties in interest who should receive copies of the order shall be set forth in the lower left-hand corner of the final page of the proposed order or carried over to another page. The chapter of the case shall be stated in the caption.

Rule 9013-4. Certificate of service.

(a) Any required certificate of service for a pleading, notice, objection or other paper must be in compliance with Federal Rule of Civil Procedure 5 and applicable provisions of the Bankruptcy Rules.

(b) The certificate shall be placed at the end of the item served and endorsed by an attorney of record, the party's authorized agent or by a party if not represented by an attorney.

(c) The certificate must state:

(1) the date and method of service;

(2) the names and addresses of the persons served; and

(3) if persons are served in a representative capacity, the parties whom they represent.

(d) It is the obligation of an attorney or party that files a pleading to determine every party with a cognizable interest in the pleading that should receive a copy and the current address of each. A certificate of service by an attorney, the attorney's authorized agent, or party constitutes a representation to the court by the attorney and party that all such parties have been served properly. A violation of this paragraph (d) shall be subject to an appropriate sanction.

Rule 9014-1. Discovery.

Local Rule 7026-1 applies in contested matters.

Rule 9014-2. Default and dismissal for non-prosecution.

Local Rule 7055-1 applies in contested matters.

Rule 9015-1. Jury trials.

(a) *Jury trials.* Federal Rules of Civil Procedure 38, 39, 47-51 and 81(c) — insofar as they apply to jury trials — apply in cases and adversary proceedings except that a demand under Federal Rule of Civil Procedure 38(b) must be filed in accordance with Bankruptcy Rule 5005. Rule 405 (83.21) of the Rules of the District Court also applies in cases and adversary proceedings.

(b) *Consent to have trial conducted by bankruptcy judge.* A party demanding a jury trial must state whether the party consents to have the trials conducted by a bankruptcy judge. Within fourteen (14) days after the filing of a jury demand, each other party must file a statement as to that party's consent to trial by the bankruptcy judge.

Rule 9019-1. Settlements and agreed orders.

(a) *Order.* Subject to the requirements of Bankruptcy Rule 2002(a)(3), 4001(d), and 9019, when the Court is advised by the moving party that an adversary proceeding or contested matter has been settled, the Court can enter an order dismissing the adversary proceeding or contested matter and providing for the payment of costs. An order of dismissal will be without prejudice to the right of a party to move for good cause to reopen the proceeding or matter within a reasonable time after settlement should have occurred if the settlement is not consummated. Alternatively, the Court, upon notification by counsel that a proceeding or matter has been settled, can require counsel to submit, with ten (10) days, a proposed order providing for the settlement, in default of which the Court can enter judgment or other appropriate order.

(b) *Complete disposition.* An order entered pursuant to this Rule has the effect of noting the settlement of the entire adversary proceeding or contested matter, including all claims, counterclaims, third-party claims, and cross-claims, unless otherwise stated.

Rule 9029-1. Local Rules — General.

Any judge of this Court can suspend or modify a requirement or provision of any of these Rules in a particular case, adversary proceeding or contested matter on the Court's own motion or on motion of a party.

Rule 9033-1. Proposed findings of fact and conclusions of law in non-core proceeding.

When a party has objected to proposed findings or conclusions pursuant to Bankruptcy Rule 9033(b), for the purpose of preparing the record and identifying the issues for the District Court, the parties will follow the procedures set forth in Bankruptcy Rule 8006 by treating the objection(s) as an appeal. The bankruptcy judge may order the designated extract supplemented.

Rule 9036-1. Notice by electronic transmission.

In addition to methods of notice available under the Bankruptcy Rules, notice may be given by hand-delivery or facsimile transmission, except that the Clerk shall not accept for filing any facsimile transmission. All notices given by facsimile transmission shall be followed by hard copy notice mailed by the next business day.

Rule 9070-1. Exhibits.

(a) *Pending appeal.* From the conclusion of a hearing or trial to the expiration of the time within which to file a notice of appeal or, in the event that an appeal is taken, until the transmission of the record to the District Court, the Clerk will retain all documentary exhibits except ones of unusual bulk or weight. Documents of unusual bulk or weight and all non-documentary exhibits will remain in the custody of the attorney presenting them, who (1) will permit inspection of them by counsel for another party for the purpose of preparing the record on appeal, (2) will be responsibile for their safekeeping, and (3) if requested, will send them to the appellate court.

(b) *Upon final termination of action.* Upon the closing of a contested matter or adversary proceeding, the Clerk will send a notice to all counsel advising counsel to remove, within thirty (30) days, all trial and hearing exhibits and all sealed materials that counsel presented at any time during the pendency of the contested matter or adversary proceeding. If a party fails to remove exhibits, the Clerk may return the exhibits and materials to a party, destroy them, or otherwise dispose of them, in the Clerk's discretion.

APPENDIX A. RULES OF U.S. DISTRICT COURT (MD).

IV. BANKRUPTCY PROCEEDINGS.

Rule 401. Rules in Bankruptcy Court proceedings.

Proceedings in the Bankruptcy Court shall be governed by Local Bankruptcy Rules as adopted from time to time by order of the Court.

Rule 402. Referral of bankruptcy cases and proceedings.

Pursuant to 28 U.S.C. Section 157(a), all cases under Title 11 of the United States Code and proceedings arising under Title 11 or arising in or related to cases under Title 11 shall be deemed to be referred to the Bankruptcy Judges of this District.

Rule 403. Appeal to the District Court.

1. *Manner of appeal.* a. Generally. Appeals to the District Court from the Bankruptcy Court shall be taken in the manner prescribed in Part VIII of the Bankruptcy Rules, Rules 8001, et seq.

b. Bankruptcy Court opinion as Appendix. Appellant shall append to appellant's opening brief a copy of the opinion of the Bankruptcy Court that it is being appealed from.

2. *Dismissal for non-compliance with Bankruptcy Rule 8006.* Whenever the appellant fails to designate the contents of the record on appeal or to file a statement of the issues to be presented on appeal within the time required by Bankruptcy Rule 8006, the Bankruptcy Clerk shall forward forthwith to the Clerk of the District Court a partial record consisting of a copy of the docket entries and such other papers as the Bankruptcy Clerk deems relevant to the appeal. (The District Court may thereafter order the Bankruptcy Clerk to transmit any other relevant papers to the Clerk of the District Court). When the partial record has been filed in the District Court, the Court may, upon motion of the appellee (which is to be filed in the District Court) or upon its own initiative, dismiss the appeal for non-compliance with Bankruptcy Rule 8006 after giving the appellant an opportunity to explain the non-compliance and upon considering whether the non-compliance had prejudicial effect on the other parties.

3. *Dismissal for non-compliance with Bankruptcy Rule 8009.* Whenever the appellant fails to serve and file a brief within the time required by Bankruptcy Rule 8009, the District Court may, upon motion of the appellee (to be filed in the District Court) or upon its own initiative, dismiss the appeal after giving the appellant an opportunity to explain the non-compliance and upon considering whether the non-compliance had prejudicial effect on the other parties.

4. *Procedure re motion to stay pending appeal.* An appellant seeking a stay pending appeal by the District Court of an order entered by the Bankruptcy Court shall file with the Clerk of the District Court a motion to stay and copies of all papers in the record of the Bankruptcy Court relevant to the appeal. Upon the filing of these papers the Clerk of the District Court shall immediately open a civil file and the District Court shall give immediate consideration

to the motion to stay. If the underlying appeal is ultimately perfected, it will be assigned the same civil action number as was assigned to the motion to stay.

5. *Bankruptcy Court certification re interlocutory appeal.* Whenever there has been filed in the District Court an application for leave to appeal an interlocutory order of the Bankruptcy Court, the Bankruptcy Court shall, upon request of the District Court, submit to the District Court a written certification stating whether, in its opinion, the interlocutory order involves a controlling question of law as to which there is substantial ground for difference of opinion and whether an immediate appeal of it may materially advance the ultimate termination of the case. The District Court shall thereafter determine whether to grant or deny the application for leave to appeal.

Rule 404. Rules of procedure under 28 U.S.C. Section 1334.

A. *Filing of pleadings and papers.* (1) General rule. When a case or proceeding has been referred by this Court to the Bankruptcy Court, all papers and pleadings in or related to such case or proceeding shall be filed with the Clerk in the Bankruptcy Court pursuant to Local Bankruptcy Rules 1 and 2.

(2) Withdrawal of reference of certain bankruptcy proceedings. (a) Filing of motion for withdrawal of reference with bankruptcy clerk. A motion pursuant to 28 U.S.C. § 157(d) to withdraw the reference of any bankruptcy case, contested matter or adversary proceeding referred to the Bankruptcy Court pursuant to 28 U.S.C. § 157(a) shall be filed with the Clerk in the Bankruptcy Court.

(b) Withdrawal of reference of bankruptcy cases. A motion to withdraw the reference of a case to the Bankruptcy Court must be timely filed, and in any event, before the case is closed.

(c) Withdrawal of reference of adversary proceeding or contested matter. A motion to withdraw an adversary proceeding or a contested matter which has been referred to the Bankruptcy Court must be filed by the earlier of eleven (11) days before the date scheduled for the first hearing on the merits and;

(i) in the case of an adversary proceeding, within twenty (20) days after the last pleading is permitted to be filed pursuant to Bankruptcy Rule 7012; or

(ii) in the case of a contested matter, within twenty (20) days after the last memorandum is permitted to be filed pursuant to Local Bankruptcy Rule 30(b)(4).

(3) Filing of pleadings in transferred cases. (a) If an entire case has been transferred from the Bankruptcy Court, all pleadings and papers in or related to such case shall be filed with the Clerk in the District Court.

(b) Where only a portion of an entire case has been transferred, pleadings and papers with respect to the case (including any parts thereof that have been withdrawn, transferred, or removed) shall continue to be filed with the Clerk in the Bankruptcy Court. The Clerk in the Bankruptcy Court shall keep a docket sheet of all pleadings and papers filed in bankruptcy-related matters which are to be transferred to the District Court. All such pleadings and papers shall be formally transferred to the Clerk in the District Court promptly following the entry of the pleading or paper upon the docket sheet of the Bankruptcy Court.

(4) Upon withdrawal, transfer or removal of any complaint to the District Court, plaintiff shall forward to defendant a notice and request to waive service of summons or the Clerk shall issue a District Court summons pursuant to Fed. R. Civ. P. 4(d), unless either of the aforementioned has already occurred pursuant to the Bankruptcy Rules.

(5) This subsection (5) governs proceedings in personal injury tort and wrongful death actions which must be tried in the District Court pursuant to 28 U.S.C. § 157(b)(5). Except for the procedures contained within this subsection, these personal injury tort and wrongful death actions shall be instituted and all pleadings and papers filed in the same manner as all other cases under 28 U.S.C. § 1334. However, beneath the bankruptcy number, the pleading or other paper shall designate the pleading or paper as a "SECTION 157(b)(5) MATTER." When filing a complaint a completed civil cover sheet (A.O. Form JS-44c) should be submitted beneath the cover sheet required by Local Bankruptcy Rule 2(e). No summons shall be issued until the case is transferred to the District Court. However, upon filing the complaint, the Clerk in the Bankruptcy Court shall forward to the defendant(s) a notice and request to waive service of summons or the Clerk of the District Court shall issue a summons pursuant to Fed. R. Civ. P. 4(d).

B. *Motions concerning venue in bankruptcy cases and proceedings.* All motions concerning venue in cases arising under Title 11 or arising in or related to cases under Title 11 shall be determined by the Bankruptcy Court, except in those cases to be tried in the District Court pursuant to 28 U.S.C. § 157(b)(5).

Rule 405. Jury trial.

1. *Demand.* In any bankruptcy proceeding any party may demand a trial by jury of any issue triable of right by jury by (1) serving upon the other parties a demand therefor in writing at any time after the commencement of the action and not later than 10 days after the service of the last pleading directed to such issue, and (2) filing the demand as required by Bankruptcy Rule 7005. Such demand may be endorsed upon a pleading of the party. If the adversary proceeding is one that has been removed from another court, any demand previously made under the rules of that court shall constitute a demand for trial by jury under this rule.

2. *Specification of issues.* In the demand a party may specify the issues which the party wishes so tried; otherwise the party shall be deemed to have demanded trial by jury for all the issues so triable. If the party has demanded trial by jury for only some of the issues, any other party within 10 days after service of the demand or such lesser time as the court may order, may serve a demand for trial by jury of any other or all of the issues of fact in the action.

3. *Waiver.* The failure of a party to serve and file a demand as required by this Rule constitutes a waiver by the party of trial by jury. A demand for trial by jury made as herein provided may not be withdrawn without the consent of the parties.

APPENDIX B. DISCOVERY GUIDELINES OF THE UNITED STATES BANKRUPTCY COURT FOR THE DISTRICT OF MARYLAND.

The Discovery Guidelines of the Maryland State Bar Association were approved in 1986 by the Board of Governors of the Maryland Bar Association and by the conference of Circuit Court Judges. Although they are not officially part of the Maryland Rules and have not been adopted or approved by the Court of Appeals, the following Guidelines may be of significant value in interpreting and applying Title 2, Chapter 400 of the Maryland Rules and are designed to eliminate unnecessary discovery disputes:

Guideline 1: Conduct of discovery.

(a) The purpose of these Guidelines is to facilitate the just, speedy, and inexpensive conduct of discovery in all adversary proceedings and contested matters before the Court, and these Guidelines will be construed and administered accordingly with respect to all attorneys, parties, and non-parties involved in discovery before this Court.

(b) Compliance with these Guidelines will be considered by the Court in resolving discovery disputes including whether sanctions should be awarded pursuant to Bankruptcy Rule 7037 and Fed. R. Civ. P. 37.

(c) Attorneys are expected to behave professionally and with courtesy towards all involved in the discovery process, including but not limited to opposing counsel, parties and non-parties.

(d) Whenever possible, attorneys are expected to communicate with each other in good faith throughout the discovery process to resolve disputes without the need for intervention by the Court. In the event that such good faith efforts are unsuccessful, they should be promptly referred to the Court for resolution.

(e) To the extent that any part of these Guidelines is considered by the Court to conflict with any Bankruptcy Rule, applicable Federal Rule of Civil Procedure, Local Bankruptcy Rule, or order of this Court in a particular proceeding or matter, then the conflicting rule or order should be considered to be governing.

Guideline 2: Stipulations setting discovery deadlines.

Subject to approval by the Court, attorneys are encouraged to enter into written discovery stipulations to supplement the Court's scheduling order.

Guideline 3: Expert witness fees.

Unless counsel agree that each party will pay its own experts, the party taking an expert witness' deposition ordinarily pays the expert's fee for the time spent in deposition and related travel. *See* Local Bankr. Rule 7026-1(h). Accordingly, counsel for the party that designated the expert witness should try to assure that the fee charged by the expert to the party taking the deposition is fair and reasonable. In the event a dispute arises as to the reasonableness of the fee, counsel should promptly confer and attempt in good faith to resolve the dispute without the involvement of the Court. If counsel are unsuccessful, the expert's deposition shall proceed on the date noted, unless the Court orders otherwise, and the dispute respecting payment shall be brought to the Court's attention promptly. The factors that may be considered in determining whether a fee is reasonable include, but are not limited to: (1) the expert's area of expertise; (2) the expert's education and training; (3) the fee being charged to the party who designated the expert; and (4) the fees ordinarily charged by the expert for non-litigation services, such as office consultations with patients or clients.

Guideline 4: Guidelines in scheduling depositions.

(a) Attorneys are expected to make a good faith effort to coordinate deposition dates with opposing counsel, parties, and non-party deponents, prior to noting a deposition.

(b) Before agreeing to a deposition date, an attorney is expected to attempt to clear the date with his/her client if the client is a deponent, or wishes to attend the deposition, and with any witnesses the attorney agrees to attempt to produce at the deposition without the need to have the witness served with a subpoena.

(c) An agreed upon deposition date is presumptively binding. An attorney seeking to change an agreed upon date has a duty to coordinate a new date before changing the agreed date.

Guideline 5: Deposition questioning, objections and procedure.

(a) An attorney should not intentionally ask a witness a question that misstates or mischaracterizes the witness' previous answer.

(b) During the taking of a deposition it is presumptively improper for an attorney to make objections or give instructions to the deponent that coach or suggest to the deponent the substance of how a question should be answered or to make objections which are not consistent with Fed. R. Civ. P. 30(d)(1), made applicable by Bankr. Rule 7030. Objections should be stated as simply, concisely and non-argumentatively as possible to avoid coaching or making suggestions to the deponent, and to minimize interruptions in the questioning of the deponent (for example: "objection, leading"; "objection, form"). If an attorney desires to make an objection for the record during the taking of a deposition that reasonably could have the effect of coaching or suggesting to the deponent how to answer, then the deponent, at the request of any of the attorneys present, or, at the request of a party if unrepresented by an attorney, shall be excused from the deposition during the making of an objection.

(c) An attorney should not repeatedly ask the same or substantially identical question of a deponent if the question already has been asked and fully and responsively answered by the deponent. Upon objection by counsel for the deponent, or by the deponent if unrepresented, it is presumptively improper for an attorney to continue to ask the same or substantially identical question of a witness unless the previous answer was evasive or incomplete.

(d) It is presumptively improper to instruct a witness not to answer a question during the taking of a deposition unless under the circumstances permitted by Fed. R. Civ. P. 30(d)(1), Bankr. R. 7030. However, it is also presumptively improper to ask questions clearly beyond the scope of discovery permitted by Fed. R. Civ. P. 26(b)(1), Bankr. R. 7026, particularly of a personal nature, and continuing to do so after objection shall be evidence that the deposition is being conducted in bad faith or in such a manner as unreasonably to annoy, embarrass or oppress the deponent or party, which is prohibited by Fed. R. Civ. P. 30(d)(3).

(e) If requested to supply an explanation as to the basis for an objection, the objecting attorney should do so, consistent with Guideline 5(b) above.

(f) While the interrogation of the deponent is in progress, neither an attorney nor the deponent should initiate a private conversation except for the purpose of determining whether a privilege should be asserted. To do so otherwise is presumptively improper.

(g) During breaks in the taking of a deposition no one should discuss with the deponent the substance of the prior testimony given by the deponent during the deposition. Counsel for the deponent may discuss with the deponent at such time whether a privilege should be asserted or otherwise engage in discussion not regarding the substance of the witness' prior testimony.

(h) Unless otherwise ordered by the Court, the following persons may, without advance notice, attend a deposition: individual parties; a representative of non-individual parties; and expert witnesses of parties. Except for the persons identified above, counsel shall notify other parties not later than five (5) business days before the taking of a deposition if counsel desires to have a non-party present during a deposition. If the parties are unable to agree to the attendance of this person, then the person shall not be entitled to attend the deposition unless the party desiring to have the person attend obtains a Court order permitting him/her to do so. Unless ordered by the Court, however, a dispute regarding who may attend a deposition shall not be grounds for delaying the deposition. All persons present during the taking of a deposition should be identified on the record before the deposition begins.

(i) Except for the person recording the deposition in accordance with Fed. R. Civ. P. 30(b), Bankr. R. 7030, during the taking of a deposition no one may record the testimony without the consent of the deponent and all parties in attendance, unless otherwise ordered by the Court.

Guideline 6: Assertions of privilege at depositions.

(a) When a claim of privilege is asserted during a deposition, and information is not provided on the basis of such assertion:

(i) In accordance with Fed. R. Civ. P. 26(b)(5), Bankr. R. 7026, the person asserting the privilege shall identify during the deposition the nature of the privilege (including work product) that is being claimed.

(ii) After a claim of privilege has been asserted, the person seeking disclosure shall have reasonable latitude during the deposition to question the witness to establish other relevant information concerning the assertion of the privilege, including: (i) the applicability of this particular privilege being asserted; (ii) any circumstances which may constitute an exception to the assertion of the privilege; (iii) any circumstances which may result in the privilege having been waived; and (iv) any circumstances that may overcome a claim of qualified privilege. In accordance with Fed. R. Civ. P. 26(b)(5), Bankr. R. 7026, the party asserting the privilege, in providing the foregoing information, shall not be required to reveal the information which is itself privileged or protected from disclosure.

Guideline 7: Making a record of improper conduct during a deposition.

Upon request of any attorney, party unrepresented by an attorney, or the deponent if unrepresented by an attorney, the person recording the deposition in accordance with Fed. R. Civ. P. 30(b), Bankr. R. 7030, shall enter on the record a description by the requesting person of conduct of any attorney, party, or person attending the deposition which violates these Guidelines, the Bankruptcy Rules, applicable Federal Rules of Civil Procedure, or the Local Rules of this Court.

Guideline 8: Delay in responding to discovery requests.

(a) *Interrogatories, Requests for Production of Documents and Requests for Admission of Facts and Genuineness of Documents.* The Bankruptcy Rules and applicable Federal Rules of Civil Procedure designate the time prescribed for responding to interrogatories, requests for production of documents, and requests for admission of facts and genuineness of documents. Nothing contained in the Guidelines modifies the time limits prescribed by the Bankruptcy Rules or applicable Federal Rules of Civil Procedure. Attorneys shall make good faith efforts to respond to discovery requests within the time prescribed by those rules.

Absent exigent circumstances, attorneys seeking additional time to respond to discovery request shall contact opposing counsel as soon as practical after receipt of the discovery request, but not later than three days before the response is due. In multiple party cases, the attorney wanting additional time shall contact the attorney for the party propounding the discovery.

A request for additional time which does not conflict with the scheduling deadline imposed by the Bankruptcy Rules, applicable Federal Rules of Civil Procedure, the Local Rules of this Court or a Court order should not be unreasonably refused. If a request for additional time is granted, the requesting party shall promptly prepare a writing which memorializes the agreement which shall be served on all parties but need not be submitted to the Court for approval.

Unless otherwise provided by the Local Rules of this Court, no stipulation which modifies a Court-imposed deadline shall be deemed effective unless and until the Court approves the stipulation.

(b) *Depositions.* Unless otherwise ordered by the Court or agreed upon by the parties eleven days notice shall be deemed a "reasonable notice" within the meaning of Fed. R. Civ. P. 30(b)(10), Bankr. R. 7030 for the noting of depositions.

Guideline 9: Guidelines concerning interrogatories, requests for production of documents, answers to interrogatories and written responses to document requests.

(a) A party may object to an interrogatory, document request, or part thereof, while simultaneously providing partial or incomplete answers to the request. If a partial or incomplete answer is provided, the answering party shall state that the answer is partial or incomplete.

(b) No part of an interrogatory or document request should be left unanswered merely because an objection is interposed to another part of the interrogatory or document request.

(c) In accordance with Fed. R. Civ. P. 26(b)(5), Bankr. R. 7026, where a claim of privilege is asserted in objecting to any interrogatory, document request, or part thereof, and information is not provided on the basis of such assertion:

(i) The party asserting the privilege shall, in the objection to the interrogatory, document request, or part thereof, identify with specificity the nature of the privilege (including work product) that is being claimed;

(ii) The following information should be provided in the objection, if known or reasonably available, unless divulging such information would cause disclosure of the allegedly privileged information:

(A) For oral communications:

(i) the name of the person making the communication and the names of persons present while the communication was made, and where not apparent, the relationship of the persons present to the person making the communication;

(ii) the date and place of the communication; and

(iii) the general subject matter of the communication.

(B) For documents:

(i) the type of document;

(ii) the general subject matter of the document;

(iii) the date of the document; and

(iv) such other information as is sufficient to identify the document, including, where appropriate, the author, addressee, custodian, and any other recipient of the document, and where not apparent, the relationship of the author, addressee, custodian, and any other recipient to each other.

(iii) Within twenty days after the receipt of the information contained in paragraph (ii), the party seeking disclosure of the information withheld may serve a motion to compel in accordance with the Local Bankr. Rule 7026-1.

(d) In addition to paper copies, parties are encouraged, but not required, to exchange discovery requests and responses on computer disk in an ASCII or other commonly-accepted format if requested in order to reduce the clerical effort required to prepare responses and motions.

APPENDIX C. SUGGESTED SUMMARY OF REAFFIRMATION AGREEMENT.

The filing of the suggested Summary of Reaffirmation Agreement is sufficient to bring this matter before the court and satisfies the requirement of counsel under 11 U.S.C. § 524. It is also suggested that individuals filing in proper person follow this form to the extent possible. The form should be attached to the proposed reaffirmation agreement.

UNITED STATES BANKRUPTCY COURT
DISTRICT OF MARYLAND
ROCKVILLE DIVISION

SUMMARY OF REAFFIRMATION AGREEMENT

Name of Debtor(s)
_____

Case No.
_____

INSTRUCTIONS

1. Complete debtor's name and bankruptcy case number above.
2. PART A — Complete each item. Both the debtor(s) and creditor must sign.
3. PART B — Must be signed by the attorney who represents the debtor(s) in bankruptcy.
4. File the fully completed form by mailing or delivering it to: Clerk, United States Bankruptcy Court

PART A — AGREEMENT

Creditor's Name and Address	Terms of New Agreement
	a) Amount
	    Principal $ _____
	    Interest Rate (APR) _____
	    Monthly Payments $ _____

Reason for Entry into Agreement	b) Security (collateral)
	    Description: _____
	
	    Present Market Value $ _____

The parties understand that this agreement is purely voluntary and that the debtor(s) may rescind the agreement by giving notice of rescission to the creditor at any time prior to discharge or within sixty (60) days after such agreement is filed with the Clerk, whichever occurs later. This agreement was entered into before the date of discharge in the above case.

Date: _____   _____
                                   Creditor's Signature

                                   _____
                                   Debtor's Signature

                                   _____
                                   Joint Debtor's Signature, if applicable

PART B — ATTORNEY'S DECLARATION

_____

This agreement represents a fully informed and voluntary agreement by the
debtor(s) that does not impose an undue hardship on the debtor(s) or any
dependent of the debtor(s).

Date: _____   _____
                                   Signature of Debtor's Attorney

_____

APPENDIX D. COMPENSATION GUIDELINES FOR PROFESSIONALS IN THE UNITED STATES BANKRUPTCY COURT FOR THE DISTRICT OF MARYLAND.

The following guidelines apply to professional fee applications in all bankruptcy cases in the United States Bankruptcy Court for the District of Maryland. These guidelines shall apply to all professionals seeking compensation pursuant to 11 U.S.C. §§ 327, 328, 330 and 331, including attorneys, accountants, examiners, investment bankers and real estate advisors, unless the court, in the order employing such professional or other order, provides otherwise. These guidelines set forth information to be contained in both interim and final applications for the approval of fees and expenses.

Although conformity to these guidelines will ensure that certain necessary information is included to assist the court in its review of professional fee applications, it must be remembered that the following are guidelines only. Applications for compensation may vary from case to case, and each application must be reviewed on its own merits depending upon the facts and circumstances of the case. Familiarity with and adherence to the following guidelines will, it is hoped, promote the submission of more uniform professional fee applications containing adequate information, and facilitate a meaningful review process and more expeditious action by the court.

A. Format of fee applications. Bankruptcy Rule 2016(a) sets forth certain requirements with respect to professional fee applications. The application should set forth a detailed statement of (1) the services rendered, (2) the time expended, (3) the expenses incurred, (4) the amounts requested, (5) the rates charged for such services, (6) how the services rendered were necessary to the administration of, or beneficial at the time at which the services were rendered toward the completion of, the case, (7) information relevant to a determination that the services were performed within a reasonable amount of time commensurate with the complexity, importance and nature of the problem, issue or task addressed, and (8) an affirmation that the compensation requested is reasonable based upon the customary compensation and reimbursement of expenses charged by the applicant and comparably skilled professionals in nonbankruptcy matters. In addition, applications should include a statement as to what payments have been made or promised to the applicant, the source of the compensation paid or promised, whether there is any sharing arrangement and the particulars as to any such sharing arrangement. Applications should also set forth the date the order approving employment was entered and the dates of entry of any previous orders approving interim compensation to the applicant and the amounts of compensation previously approved. Finally, fee applications should include a "lodestar" analysis and discussion of the factors identified in *Johnson v. Georgia Highway Express, Inc.,* 488 F.2d 714 (5th Cir. 1974), and adopted by the Fourth Circuit in *Barber v. Kimbrell's, Inc.,* 577 F.2d 216 (4th Cir. 1978), *Anderson v. Booth,* 658 F.2d 246 (4th Cir. 1978) and *Harman v. Levin,* 772 F.2d 1150 (4th Cir. 1985).

B. Description of services rendered and time expended. Daily time sheets or a listing of daily time entries, in legible form, should be included in or attached to the application.[1] The time sheets or time entries should provide an itemized listing of all services performed by each professional and paraprofessional and the time spent on each matter indicated. The applicable billing rate for each professional and paraprofessional should be indicated.

Each professional and paraprofessional should record time in increments of tenths of an hour and keep contemporaneous time records. Time records should set forth in reasonable detail an appropriate narrative description of the services rendered. As a general rule, the description should include indications of the participants in and the length and nature of the activities undertaken. Examples of insufficient descriptions include "telephone call," "telephone call to X," "conference with client," "research," "review of documents," "review of pleadings," and "correspondence." Examples of satisfactory descriptions are set forth in footnote 3.

The broad "lumping" of services, or the grouping of different tasks within one block of time, should generally be avoided in favor of more specific descriptions.[2] In recording time for each day, each professional and paraprofessional may describe in one entry the nature of the services rendered on a given task during that day and the aggregate time expended that day on such task, provided, however, that if the professional or paraprofessional works more than one hour on a task on any given day, the time record for that day should include internally, within the description of services for that day, the amount of time spent on each particular activity. A hypothetical time record complying with the foregoing is included below.[3]

The description of services required to be set forth is not intended to require the disclosure of privileged or confidential information, provided, that if additional detail is required, the court may direct that such additional information be furnished subject to appropriate protective conditions. Information set forth in a fee application shall not operate as a waiver of any applicable privilege, including the attorney/client privilege or work product doctrine.

Charges for conferences between individuals in the same firm on the same case are not objectionable, if reasonable, necessary and limited. Similarly, more than one professional may charge for attending a meeting or hearing on behalf of the same client if such attendance is reasonable, necessary and limited. An explanation as to why more than one professional attended such meeting or hearing may in certain circumstances be required, particularly if

---

[1] Fee applications for matters handled on a contingent fee basis and applications required to be submitted pursuant to § 506(b) should also conform to the applicable format guidelines set forth herein.

[2] Notwithstanding the general prohibition of "lumping", time entries for periods of one hour or less on a given day may be grouped together provided that a reasonable description of the services rendered within such time entry is provided.

[3] A complying time entry would be:

"internal conference with X re cash collateral (.3); revise draft motion re cash collateral (.8); conf. call with Y and Z re cash collateral hearing (.5); review documents re cash collateral motion (1.1); legal research re cash collateral hearing (.5) ... Total Time 3.2"

such multiple professional attendance does not appear to be reasonable in a particular situation.[4]

Ordinarily, time entries should be organized by tasks and presented chronologically. An applicant should either organize the time sheets or present a time entry listing by discrete tasks where an application covers multiple tasks undertaken by the applicant during the time period covered by the application. Within each task identified, the time entries of all timekeepers working on such task should appear chronologically. In addition, the application should include a summary by timekeeper of the time spent on each task, the billing value for each timekeeper and a total billing amount for each task. Finally, the application should also include a brief narrative description as to why each task was undertaken, the current status thereof and the results or benefits achieved to date.

It is not the intent of these guidelines to set forth a definitive listing of what tasks should be separately identified in each case or each professional fee application. However, where a discrete activity can reasonably be expected to continue over a period of at least three months and can reasonably be expected to constitute 10-20% or more of the fees to be sought for an interim period, the professional should present a separate chronological listing of time entries for such matter to the extent reasonably practicable. Examples of categories which might comprise separate tasks in a particular case are set forth below.[5]

Subject to court approval, a trustee may employ himself or herself, or a firm with which the trustee is affiliated, as a professional. In such cases, applications for compensation should distinguish services rendered as trustee from those rendered by the professional seeking compensation.

Compensation sought for time spent traveling should indicate the mode and time of travel, the necessity for travel and whether any substantive work was performed while traveling (*e.g.*, preparing for hearing). If excessive or unreasonable, compensation for travel time may be reduced. If time is spent during

---

[4] In appropriate cases where there are multiple counsel from different firms representing the same party, such counsel may be required to submit their applications simultaneously.

[5] *Sample Task Listing for Attorneys*

Asset analysis and recovery.
Asset disposition/sales/leases/executory contracts.
Business operations.
Case administration.
Claims administration and objections.
Fee/employment applications and objections.
Financing/cash collateral.
Litigation [separately identify larger litigation matters as discrete tasks.]
Meetings of creditors.
Plan and disclosure statement.

Sample Task Listing for Accountants

Accounting/auditing.
Business analysis.
Corporate finance.
Data analysis.
Litigation consulting.
Tax issues.
Valuation/projections.

travel working on other matters, such travel time should not also be billed to the bankruptcy case.

Compensation for time spent preparing and defending fee applications is appropriate if reasonable. Compensation for the preparation of fee applications will be based on the level and skill reasonably required to prepare the application.

C. Reimbursement for disbursements and expenses. Disbursements and expenses for which reimbursement is sought should be summarized in the fee application by category and any unusual items explained. Excessive charges will not be reimbursed. The following are guidelines with respect to some (but not necessarily all) of the categories of reimburseable disbursements and expenses:

Photocopying. The applicable charge for photocopying should be the actual cost of such copying not to exceed 20¢ per page or, if an outside service is used, the actual cost of such copying.

Facsimile transmission. Charges for out-going facsimile transmissions to long-distance telephone numbers are reimburseable at the lower of (i) toll charges or (ii) if such amount is not readily determinable, $1.25 per page for domestic and $2.50 per page for international transmissions. Charges for incoming facsimile transmissions are not reimburseable.

Mileage. The applicable charge for automobile mileage should not exceed the government approved rate, plus actual parking charges incurred.

Travel. The actual expenses incurred for out-of-town travel are reimburseable. However, first-class airfare, luxury accommodations and deluxe meals are not reimburseable, nor are personal or incidental charges unless necessary as a result of unforeseen circumstances.

Computerized legal research. Reasonable expenses may be charged for computerized legal research, including Lexis and Westlaw, provided that there is a description of the legal research undertaken and the charges do not exceed the actual cost to the attorney.

Postage, telephone, courier and freight. The cost of postage, freight, overnight delivery, courier services and telephone toll charges may be reimburseable, if reasonably incurred. Only the long distance component of cellular telephone charges is reimbursible. Charges for services such as messengers and overnight mail should not be incurred indiscriminately. Charges for local telephone services are not reimburseable. If normal, routine first-class postage is not customarily charged to other clients, then such postage would not be reimburseable; however, special postage charges or bulk mailings would ordinarily be reimburseable.

Court costs. Court costs and disbursements are reimburseable.

Meals. Charges for meals are generally not reimburseable unless justified under appropriate circumstances or unless incurred as part of otherwise reimbursable out-of-town travel.

Overtime charges. Overtime for non-professional and paraprofessional staff is reimburseable only if specifically justified in the application as necessary under the circumstances. Overtime charges for professional staff is not reimburseable.

Word processing, proofreading, secretarial and other staff services. Daytime, ordinary business hour charges for word processing, proofreading, secretarial, library and other staff services (exclusive of paraprofessional services) are generally considered office overhead items and, therefore, not reimburseable unless specifically justified in exceptional circumstances.

With respect to all disbursements and expenses for which reimbursement is sought, it must be understood that they must be of a kind and at a rate customarily charged to and collected from other clients and subject to the test of reasonableness under the circumstances of each case.

Each professional fee application in which the applicant is seeking reimbursement for expenses should include a statement that, with respect to expenses for which reimbursement is sought, the applicant is familiar with and has submitted the application in conformity with the "Compensation Guidelines for Professionals in the United States Bankruptcy Court for the District of Maryland."

D. Lodestar analysis, Johnson factors and billing judgment. Each professional fee application should contain a "lodestar" analysis and discussion of the *Johnson v. Georgia Highway Express, Inc. (supra)* factors, as adopted by the Fourth Circuit in *Barber v. Kimbrell's, Inc. (supra),* including a statement as to the professional's application of billing judgment to the compensation sought by such professional.

The "lodestar" analysis should include a summary listing the name of each professional and paraprofessional for whom compensation is sought, the number of hours worked by each identified individual, that individual's hourly rate (which should not exceed such individual's standard hourly rate in other bankruptcy and non-bankruptcy matters), the total compensation sought for each such individual and a total of all compensation sought for the period in question, before and after applying billing judgment to the compensation requested. A similar detailed summary of disbursements and expenses by category should also be presented.

The fee application should discuss the application of the twelve *Johnson v. Georgia Highway Express, Inc.* factors, to the extent that they apply in each particular case. Those factors may be summarized as follows:

1. the time and labor expended;
2. the novelty and difficulty of the questions raised;
3. the skill required to properly perform the professional services rendered;
4. the professional's opportunity costs in pursuing the matter;
5. the customary fee for like work;
6. the professional's expectations as to compensation at the outset of the matter;
7. the time limitations imposed by the client or circumstances;
8. the amount in controversy and the results obtained;
9. the experience, reputation and ability of the professional;
10. the desirability or undesirability of the case within the professional community in which the case arose;
11. the nature and length of the professional relationship between the professional and client; and

12. professional fee awards in similar cases.

Not all of the foregoing twelve factors will be applicable to every fee application. However, they should be considered in the professional's exercise of billing judgment and discussed in the fee application. If a particular factor is not considered to be applicable, the application should so state. In addition, if the professional believes that other factors are relevant to the compensation requested, the foregoing list is not intended to be exhaustive. Professionals are encouraged to state all facts and circumstances that such professional believes to be relevant to the compensation requested.

In the final analysis, in making its determination with respect to a fee application and the amount of compensation to be awarded, the court will consider the nature, the extent, and the value of the services rendered.

APPENDIX E.
NOTICE OF FILING OF CASE IN BANKRUPTCY COURT.

IN THE CIRCUIT COURT FOR
_____ COUNTY, MARYLAND

IN RE: :

        vs.   :   Civil No. _____

                :

_____   :

NOTICE OF FILING OF CASE IN BANKRUPTCY COURT

You are hereby notified of the filing of a case in the _____ Division of the United States Bankruptcy Court for the District of Maryland for the following debtor(s): _____. The bankruptcy case No. is _____. It is a case under Chapter _____, filed on _____. The case is now pending.

Attorney for Debtor(s)   **OR**   Debtor(s), if Pro Se

Name: _____   Name: _____

Address: _____   Address: _____

Tel. No. _____   Tel. No. _____

OR

Attorney for Petitioning Creditor(s) _____
Address: _____
Tel. No. _____
Petitioning Creditor(s) _____

* * * * * *

I hereby certify that copies of the foregoing Notice of Filing of Case in Bankruptcy Court were mailed this _____ day of _____, 19____, to the Judge of this court assigned this case and to the following counsel of record:

_____
Signature of Affiant

APPENDIX F. FINANCIAL STATEMENT.

UNITED STATES BANKRUPTCY COURT FOR THE
DISTRICT OF MARYLAND

IN RE   :

_____ :

                                    Case No. _____

                                    Chapter _____

                                    Adversary Proceeding No. ___

FINANCIAL STATEMENT

Monthly Income		Monthly Expenses:	Party	Children	Expenses Now Paid by Spouse
Gross:	$ _____	Rent			_____
Less Deductions:		House			
Federal tax	_____	Payment			_____
State tax	_____	Utilities:			
FICA or	_____	Heat			
Retirement	_____	Gas &			
All other		Light			_____
deductions:	_____	Telephone			_____
	_____	Food			_____
	_____	Clothing			_____
		Medical,			
Net Income:	$ _____	Dental			_____
		Transportation			
Income from					_____
property	_____	Insurance:			
Income from any		Life			_____
other sources	_____	Health			_____
Tax Refund	_____	Auto			_____
Monies from		Other			_____
spouse	_____	Child Care			
		Expense			_____
		Recreation			_____
		Incidentals			_____
		Periodic Pymts.			
		(attach list)			_____
Total Monies		**Total**			
Received	$ _____	**Expenses**			_____

Assets: **Liabilities**

_____	$ _____	_____	$ _____
_____	_____	_____	_____
_____	_____	_____	_____
_____	_____	_____	_____
_____	_____	_____	_____

Total Assets: $ _____   **Total Liabilities:** $ _____

I HEARBY SWEAR OR AFFIRM UNDER THE PENAL-
TIES OF PERJURY THAT THE ABOVE FINANCIAL
STATEMENT IS TRUE AND CORRECT.

_____

            (Party)   (Date)

APPENDIX G. MOTION FOR ADMISSION PRO HAC VICE.

Note: Effective 7/1/95 — $50.00 Filing Fee (non-refundable) Required for Motion for Admission Pro hac Vice, Payable to Clerk, U.S. District Court

IN UNITED STATES BANKRUPTCY COURT
FOR THE DISTRICT OF MARYLAND

```
_____     *
                                  *     Bankruptcy Case No. _____
            Plaintiff(s),         *
v.                                *
                                  *
                                  *     Adversary No. _____
                                  *
_____     *
            Defendant(s).         *
****************************************************************************
```

MOTION FOR ADMISSION PRO HAC VICE

Pursuant to Local Rule 4 (a) (2) of this court, and Local Rule 101.1 (b) of the U.S. District Court for the District of Maryland, _____, Esquire, a member of the bar of this court, moves the admission of _____, Esquire, to appear *PRO HAC VICE* in the captioned preceding as counsel for _____ _____. Movant and the proposed admittee respectfully certify as follows:

1) The proposed admittee is not a member of the Bar of Maryland.

2) The proposed admittee is a member in good standing of the bar(s) of the state(s) of _____

_____ and/or the following United States

Court(s): _____

_____

_____

_____

_____

3) During the twelve (12) months immediately preceding the filing of this motion, the proposed admittee had been admitted *PRO HAC VICE* in this court in the following matters:

_____

_____

4) The proposed admittee has never been disbarred, suspended, or denied admission to practice, or has set forth all relevant facts, including disposition, as follows: _____

_____

_____

_____

5) The proposed admittee is familiar with the Federal Rules of Bankruptcy Procedure, the Local Rules of the United States Bankruptcy Court for the District of Maryland, and the Federal Rules of Evidence, and the Rules of Professional Conduct, and understands that he/she shall be subject to the disciplinary jurisdiction of this court.

6) Co-counsel for the proposed admittee in this proceeding will be the undersigned or _____, Esquire, who has been formally admitted to the bar of the U.S. District Court for the District of Maryland.

7) It is understood that admission *PRO HAC VICE* does not constitute formal admission to the bar of the U.S. District Court for the District of Maryland.

Respectfully submitted,

Movant: Proposed Admittee:

_____   _____
Signature   Signature

_____   _____
Address   Address

_____   _____

_____   _____
Office Phone Number   Office Phone Number

_____
Maryland U.S. District Court Number

ORDER

Motion _____ Granted

Motion _____ Granted subject to payment of $50.00 filing fee to Clerk of
    Court

Date _____   _____

                                      United States Bankruptcy Judge
                                      for the District of Maryland

Index to Rules of the U.S. Bankruptcy Court for the District of Maryland Local Bankruptcy Rules